CONTRACT LAW

CASES AND MATERIALS

Contract Law: Cases and Materials presents a selection of well-chosen cases and illuminating commentary ideal for introducing students to the study of contract law in Australia. Developed to accompany Stewart, Swain and Fairweather's *Contract Law: Principles and Context* ('*Principles* text'), this casebook maintains the accessibility of the *Principles* text while providing the depth and analysis of topics required to learn contract law.

Following the structure of the *Principles* text, this text explores areas not traditionally covered in other casebooks, such as resolving disputes, preparing to make a contract, preliminary agreements and interpreting contracts. Each chapter also briefly explores contracts in international contexts.

The hallmark features of this casebook are its:

- coverage and choice of cases, with succinct summaries and clear and concise extracts
- considered and relevant analysis and commentary
- coverage of international law
- extensive internal pedagogy including flowcharts and numerous review questions.

Contract Law: Cases and Materials takes a practical approach to student learning and integrates rich pedagogy to build critical thinking and analysis skills, making it an invaluable resource for contract law students.

Kenneth Yin is a lecturer at Edith Cowan University.

Simon Kozlina is a lecturer at Western Sydney University.

Kelly Green is a teaching scholar at Deakin University.

Luca Siliquini-Cinelli is a lecturer at the University of Dundee.

Emmanuel Laryea is Associate Professor at Monash University.

Lisa Spagnolo is a Senior Lecturer at Monash University.

CONTRACT LAW

CASES AND MATERIALS

Kenneth Yin
Simon Kozlina
Kelly Green
Luca Siliquini-Cinelli
Emmanuel Laryea
Lisa Spagnolo

CAMBRIDGE
UNIVERSITY PRESS

CAMBRIDGE
UNIVERSITY PRESS

University Printing House, Cambridge CB2 8BS, United Kingdom

One Liberty Plaza, 20th Floor, New York, NY 10006, USA

477 Williamstown Road, Port Melbourne, VIC 3207, Australia

314–321, 3rd Floor, Plot 3, Splendor Forum, Jasola District Centre, New Delhi – 110025, India

79 Anson Road, #06–04/06, Singapore 079906

Cambridge University Press is part of the University of Cambridge.

It furthers the University's mission by disseminating knowledge in the pursuit of education, learning and research at the highest international levels of excellence.

www.cambridge.org
Information on this title: www.cambridge.org/9781108435277

First published 2021

Cover designed by Anne-Marie Reeves
Typeset by SPi Global
Printed in China by C & C Offset Printing Co., Ltd, August 2020

A catalogue record for this publication is available from the British Library

A catalogue record for this book is available from the National Library of Australia

ISBN 978-1-108-43527-7 Paperback

Additional resources for this publication at www.cambridge.edu.au/academic/contractlaw

CONTENTS

TABLE OF CASES

TABLE OF STATUTES

Australia

NORTHERN TERRITORY

QUEENSLAND

SOUTH AUSTRALIA

TASMANIA

VICTORIA

WESTERN AUSTRALIA

Brazil

France

New Zealand

People's Republic of China

Switzerland

United Kingdom

United States of America

European Parliament

Hague Conference on Private International Law

International Instruments

ACKNOWLEDGMENTS

The authors and Cambridge University Press would like to thank the following for permission to reproduce material in this book.

Extracts from *UN Convention on Contracts for the International Sale of Goods* (United Nations publications, Sales No: E.10.V.14): © 2020 United Nations. Used with permission of the United Nations.

Extracts from International Institute for the Unification of Private Law (UNIDROIT), *Principles of International Commercial Contracts* (2016): reproduced by kind permission of the International Institute for the Unification of Private Law (UNIDROIT). Readers are reminded that the complete text of the UNIDROIT Principles of International Commercial Contracts 2016 is composed of both black-letter rules and accompanying Comments. The full text is available in book form directly from UNIDROIT and is also available on the UNIDROIT website at https://www.unidroit.org/instruments/commercial-contracts/unidroit-principles-2016. For select case law and bibliography relating to the Principles, see www.unilex.info.

Extract from R Fells and N Sheer, *Effective Negotiation: From Research to Results,* (Cambridge University Press, 4th ed, 2020): reproduced with permission from Cambridge University Press.

Extract from Janet O'Sullivan 'Rescission as a Self-Help Remedy: A Critical Analysis' (2000) 59(3) *Cambridge Law Journal* 509–543: reproduced with permission from Cambridge Law Journal.

Extract from Attorney-General's Department, *Improving Australia's Law and Justice Framework: A Discussion Paper to Explore the Scope for Reforming Australian Contract Law* (Attorney-General's Department, 2012): © Commonwealth of Australia 2012, licensed under CC BY 3.0 AU, https://creativecommons.org/licenses/by/3.0/au/.

Extract from M Giancaspro, 'Is a "Smart Contract" Really a Smart Idea? Insights from a Legal Perspective' (2017) 33 *Computer Law and Security Review* 825–835: reprinted with permission from Elsevier.

Extract from JN Adams and R Brownsword, 'The Ideologies of Contract' (1987) 7(2) *Legal Studies* 205–223: © The Society of Legal Scholars.

Extract from L Mulcahy, 'The Limitations of Love and Altruism—Feminist Perspectives on Contract Law' in Linda Mulcahy and Sally Wheeler (eds), *Feminist Perspectives on Contract Law* (Glasshouse Press, 2005) 1–19: © Taylor and Francis.

Extracts from RA Barnett, 'Contract is not Promise', in Gregory Klass, George Letsas and Prince Saprai (eds), *Philosophical Foundations of Contract Law* (Oxford University Press, 2014) 42–57; H Collins, *Regulating Contracts* (Oxford University Press, 1999); SA Smith, *Atiyah's Introduction to the Law of Contract* (Clarendon Press, 2005): reproduced with permission of the Oxford University Press through PLSclear.

Extract from P Vincent-Jones, 'Contractual Governance: Institutional and Organizational Analysis' (2000) 20(3) *Oxford Journal of Legal Studies* 317–351: © Oxford University Press and reproduced with permission under STM signatory guidelines.

Extracts from John Gava, 'Can Contract Law Be Justified on Economic Grounds' (2006) 25(1) *University of Queensland Law Journal* 253–269; L Siliquini-Cinelli, 'Taking (Legal) Traditions Seriously, or Why Australian Contract Law Should not be Codified: An Unconventional Inquiry' (2015) 34(1) *University of Queensland Law Journal* 99–122: reproduced with permission from *University of Queensland Law Journal.*

Extract from Q Zhou, 'What Can Contract Lawyers Learn from Law and Economics?' (2011) 30(1) *University of Tasmania Law Review* 157–173: reproduced with permission from *University of Tasmania Law Review.*

Extracts from the Australian Law Journal Reports (ALJR); Commonwealth Law Reports (CLR); Federal Court Reports (FCR); South Australian Law Reports (SALR): reproduced with permission of Thomson Reuters (Professional) Australia Limited, legal.thomsonreuters .com.au.

Extracts from Federal Court of Australia (FCA) cases; Federal Court of Australia Full Court (FCAFC) cases: © Federal Court of Australia and licensed under a Creative Commons Attribution 4.0 International licence (CC BY 4.0, https://creativecommons.org/licenses/by/4.0/).

Extracts from High Court of Australia (HCA) cases: reproduced with permission of the High Court of Australia.

Extracts from New South Wales Court of Appeal (NSWCA) cases; New South Wales Supreme Court (NSWSC) cases: © State of New South Wales (Department of Justice). For current information go to www.justice.nsw.gov.au. Reproduced under Creative Commons Attribution 4.0 license (CC BY 4.0, https://creativecommons.org/licenses/by/4.0/legalcode).

Extracts from New South Wales Law Reports (NSWLR) cases: © Council of Law Reporting for New South Wales.

Extracts from Queensland Supreme Court: Court of Appeal (QCA) cases: reproduced with permission of the Supreme Court Library Queensland and Queensland Courts.

Extract from Queensland Reports (Qd R) case: reproduced with permission of The Incorporated Council of Law Reporting for the State of Queensland.

Extracts from South Australian Supreme Court (SASC) cases: right to reproduce this material belongs to the Attorney-General for the State of South Australia and the South Australian Courts Administration Authority.

Extracts from Victorian Reports (VR) cases: reproduced with permission from the Supreme Court Council for Law Reporting, Victoria.

Extracts from Western Australia Supreme Court (WASC) cases; Western Australian Supreme Court: Court of Appeal (WASCA) cases: reproduced with permission from the Supreme Court of Western Australia.

Extracts from Law Reports, Appeal Cases (AC) cases; Law Reports, King's Bench (KB) cases; Law Reports, Queen's Bench Division (QB); Weekly Law Reports (WLR) cases: reproduced with permission of the Incorporated Council of Law Reporting for England and Wales.

Extract from *Semelhago v Paramadevan* [1996] 2 SCR 415: reproduced with the permission of the Supreme Court of Canada, 2019.

Extracts from Australian Commonwealth legislation: sourced from the Federal Register of Legislation and reproduced under Creative Commons Attribution 4.0 International (CC BY 4.0, https://creativecommons.org/licenses/by/4.0/). For the latest information on Australian Government law please go to https://www.legislation.gov.au.

Extracts from New South Wales legislation: © New South Wales Government.

Extracts from Northern Territory legislation: copyright in Northern Territory legislation is owned by the Northern Territory. The Attorney-General asserts copyright on behalf of the Northern Territory.

Extracts from Queensland legislation: © The State of Queensland and licensed under a Creative Commons Attribution 4.0 International licence (CC BY 4.0, https://creativecommons.org/licenses/by/4.0/).

Extract from South Australian legislation: © State of South Australia. Reproduced under Creative Commons Attribution 4.0 International (CC BY 4.0, https://creativecommons.org/licenses/by/4.0/). Sourced from the South Australian Legislation website on January 2019. For the latest information on South Australian Government legislation, please go to www.legislation.sa.gov.au/.

Extracts from Victorian legislation: © State of Victoria, Australia. Copyright in all legislation of the Parliament of the State of Victoria, Australia, is owned by the Crown in right of the State of Victoria, Australia. DISCLAIMER: This product or service contains an unofficial version of the legislation of the Parliament of State of Victoria. The State of Victoria accepts no responsibility for the accuracy and completeness of any legislation contained in this product or provided through this service.

Extracts from Western Australian legislation: sourced from the Western Australian Legislation website. For the latest information on Western Australian legislation, visit www.legislation.wa.gov.au. Reproduced under CC BY 4.0 license, https://creativecommons.org/licenses/by/4.0/.

Extract from *Contracts (Rights of Third Parties) Act 1999* (UK): © Crown and database right and licensed under the Open Government Licence 3.0.

Every effort has been made to trace and acknowledge copyright. The publisher apologises for any accidental infringement and welcomes information that would redress this situation.

PART 1

INTRODUCTION

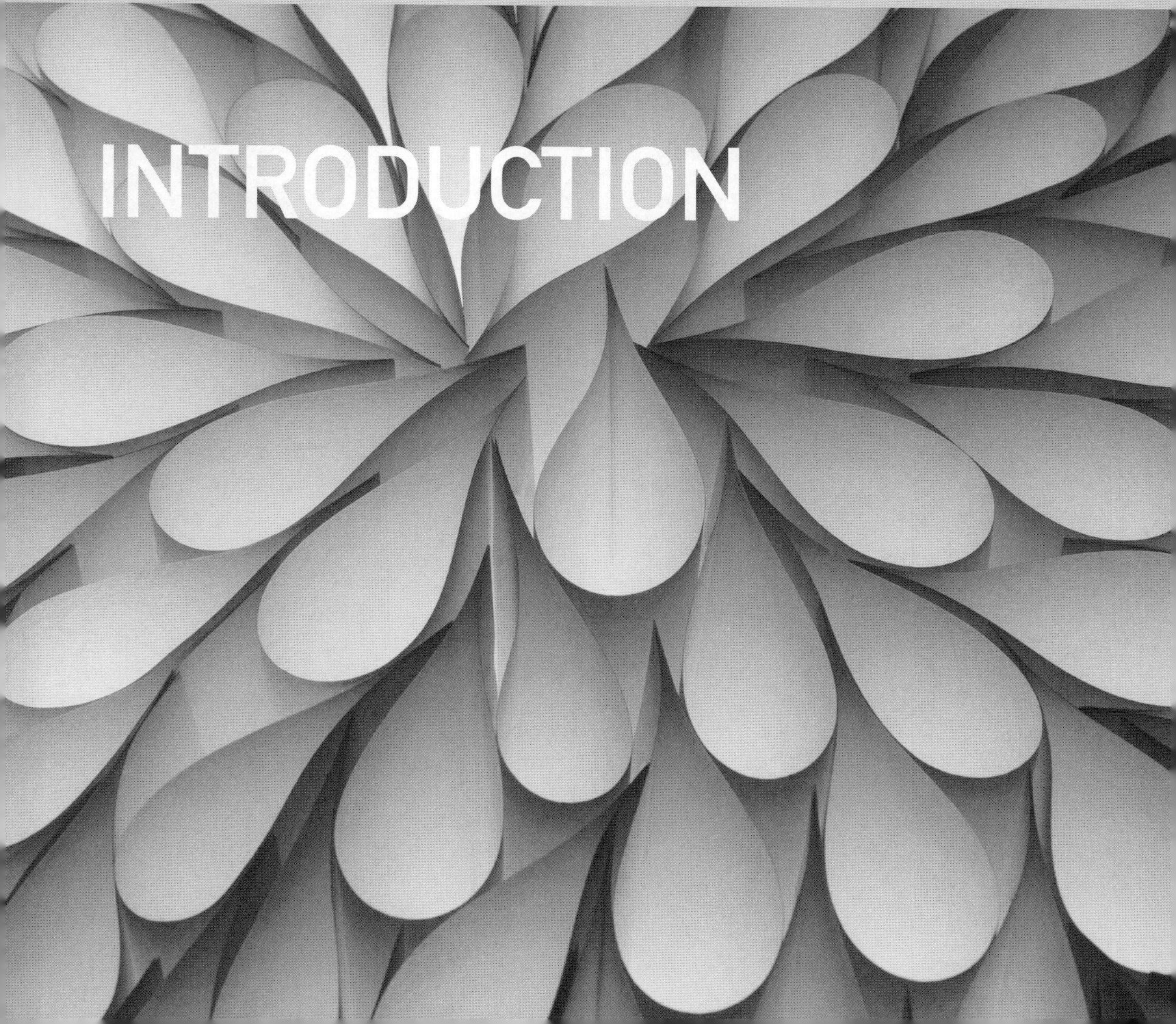

1

SOME BASIC QUESTIONS

1.1 Overview

This chapter deals with some basic questions which surround the contract law dimension. The concepts of 'contract' and 'contract law' are introduced. It will discuss why the law distinguishes between contracts and transactions that are not legally binding, and thus, unenforceable. In so doing, it will show why the notion of 'bargain' lies at the core of contractual arrangements. Furthermore, it will show why contracts underpin market societies and why the concept of contract is being increasingly fragmentised. Finally, attention is paid to the English origins of Australian contract law, as well as to its modern and contemporary sources.

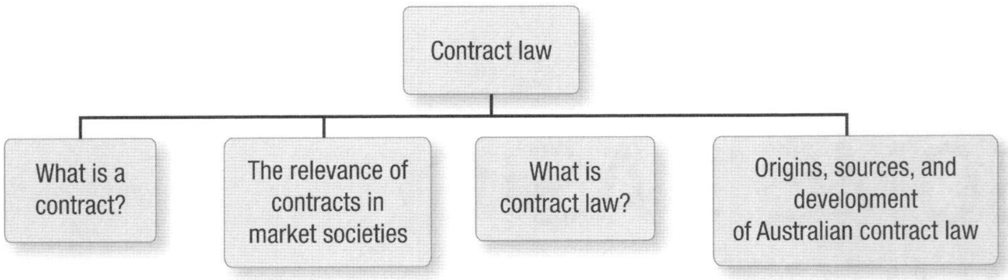

1.2 What is a contract?

Factor	Short explanation	Relevant authorities	*Principles* text*
Contract as promise	A contract is a legally enforceable promise	JW Carter, E Peden and GJ Tolhurst, *Contract Law in Australia* (LexisNexis Butterworths, 5th ed, 2007) B Coote, 'The Essence of Contract – Part I' (1988) 1(1) *Journal of Contract Law* 91 JW Carter, *Australian Contract Law* (Butterworths LexisNexis, 6th ed, 2013)	Chapter 1: 1.02

* Consult the corresponding section(s) of the *Principles* text for more detail.

Contracts are a class of obligations.[1] In Australia, a contract is an agreement between two or more parties, involving one or more promises that are given for something in return, and that the parties intend to be legally enforceable. The term 'party' refers to an individual or an artificial entity (such as a corporation or a state) that the law treats as if it were a person.

1 Andrew Burrows, *Understanding the Law of Obligations: Essays on Contract, Tort and Restitution*, (Hart Publishing, 1998); Keith Mason, John W Carter and Greg J Tolhurst, *Mason & Carter's Restitution Law in Australia* (Butterworths LexisNexis, 3rd ed, 2016).

Corporations or governments can enter into legally binding agreements, even though they necessarily have to act through the agency of human beings: see **4.1**, **8.2**.

Contracts are voluntary undertakings: *Australian Woollen Mills v Commonwealth* (1954) 92 CLR 424, 457. The parties are left free to decide whether or not to negotiate and/or bind themselves to each other: see **5.2** and **6.3**. From this, it follows that it is illegal to coerce a party into a contract by threats or undue pressure: see **19.2**. Yet, both freedom of contract and equality of bargaining power are 'assumptions'[2], which, in real-life situations, have to be adjusted. Further, in certain cases, such as when dealings are made with standard-form contracts or when one party is a consumer, these assumptions are reverted: see **4.4**, **9.2, 11.2**, **20.3**.

Australian contract law is informed by the view which understands contracts as bargains: the law compels the person who made the promise ('the promisor') to perform the promise or pay damages for non-performance only if something is given or promised in return by the other person ('the promisee'[3]). Hence, a promise is legally binding only if it is made under seal or supported by 'consideration': see **5.6**. The latter is a technical term which refers to that which is given or accepted in return for a promise ('*quid pro quo*'). Scholars tend to argue that the view that understands contracts as the law of bargains emerged in the nineteenth century to counter-balance the erosion of the classical will theory as brought about by the adoption of an objective model of contracting. Consideration, it is further maintained, is the product of this view. Yet it has been noted that the will theory was the dominant model of contract until the twentieth century, and the idea that contracts are based on exchange long predates the nineteenth century in the doctrine of consideration.[4] What matters for our purposes, however, is that the bargain theory established itself also against the promise, reasonable expectations, and reliance theories: see **2.3**.

Further requirements for an agreement to be legally binding are the parties' intention to create legal relations (a requirement which is directly related to the principle of free consent, mentioned above) and their capacity to bind themselves in a contractual relationship. Importantly, in some cases, the law also prescribes that the terms of a transaction are set out in a formal document. Hence, certain contracts may be required to be in writing or by deed, as well as evidenced in writing: see **5.9**. As only the promises that meet these requirements are contracts, it is of the essence to distinguish between contractual relationships and arrangements which the law does not categorise as such, and thus, cannot be enforced because they are not legally binding. The doctrine of estoppel plays a fundamental role in this respect as it allows a promisee to go to court and hold a promisor to their commitment, where the promisee has relied on the promise to their detriment: see **7.2**.

2 John W Carter, *Contract Law in Australia* (Butterworths LexisNexis, 6th ed, 2013) 8, extract below.

3 See John W Carter, Elisabeth Peden and Greg J Tolhurst, *Contract Law in Australia* (Butterworths LexisNexis, 5th ed, 2007) at 1-01, extract below.

4 David Ibbetson, *A Historical Introduction to the Law of Obligations* (Oxford University Press, 1999); Nick Seddon, Rick Bigwood and Manfred Ellinghaus *Chesire & Fifoot Law of Contract* (Butterworths LexisNexis, 10th Australian ed, 2012) 1263; Warren Swain, *The Law of Contract 1670–1870* (Cambridge University Press, 2015).

JW Carter, E Peden and GJ Tolhurst, *Contract Law in Australia* (LexisNexis Butterworths, 5th ed, 2007)

[1-01] A contract is a legally binding promise or agreement. The person (or persons) who makes a promise is termed the 'promisor'. The person (or persons) to whom the promise is made is termed the 'promisee'.

B Coote, 'The Essence of Contract – Part I' (1988) 1(1) *Journal of Contract Law* 91

[94] Almost invariably, common law textbooks have defined contracts in terms of promise or agreement or of a combination of the two. And, as we shall see, promise and agreement are linked respectively to what have been, historically, the two main contract theories.

A third element in some definitions has been a statement that contracts create rights *in personam* rather than rights *in rem*; that being [95] a distinction which descends from Roman law. For present purposes, its significance is twofold. It requires of a contract that, at its formation, at least some element should still need to be performed or fulfilled. It therefore excludes from the category of contracts transactions, such as conveyances, which have the effect of granting or transferring rights *in rem* by the very fact of being executed.

1 In terms of agreement

Of the leading modern English contract texts, both *Treitel* and *Cheshire and Fifoot* define contract in terms of agreement. Definitions in those terms go back to *Doctor and Student* in the sixteenth century and to such later works as *Blackstone* and the earlier editions of *Chitty.* The current edition of *Treitel* states that a contract is 'an agreement giving rise to obligations which are enforced or recognised by law'. Such definitions have the advantage of being centred on an incident of the vast majority of contracts whether under common law or under the systems which derive from Roman law. In that sense, they correspond with popular perceptions of what contracts are about. Their disadvantage is that if they are confined to agreements they necessarily exclude contracts which are not agreements. Such contracts can be made at common law by the use of a deed and they have their equivalents under the Scottish system, for example. For this reason, if no other, a number of writers who include agreements in their definitions refer also to promises in the alternative.

An alternative response would be to deny that arrangements made without agreement can be contracts at all. This is what *Cheshire and Fifoot* have done.

> [A party] is [by deed] bound, not because he has made a contract but because he has chosen to act within the limits of a prescribed formula. The idea of [96] bargain, fundamental to the English conception of contract is absent. An Englishman is liable, not because he has made a promise but because he has made a bargain.

By combining agreement with the notion of bargain in their definition of contract under English law, the learned authors have raised a second set of problems, to which reference will be made when the bargain theory comes to be considered.

2 In terms of promise

Of all English textbook definitions of contract, the most famous is probably that by Sir Frederick Pollock. A contract, he wrote, is 'a promise or set of promises which the law will enforce'. The definition contained in the American *Restatement of the Law of Contracts* is not dissimilar:

> A contract is a promise or set of promises for the breach of which the law gives a remedy or the performance of which the law in some way recognises as a duty.

Definitions in such terms have the advantage of being wide enough to cover contracts which are not the subject of agreements. Their disadvantage is that they may be too comprehensive. They are wide enough to include promises which the law enforces even though neither deed nor consideration is present. Amongst them would be those promises enforceable under the law of torts or by reason of estoppel which have, in recent times, raised questions about the limits of contract.

They are promises of a kind which led to the inclusion of s 90 in the *Restatement of the Law of Contracts*, and they may frequently form part of courses on the law of contract. But whether they should now be classed as being themselves contracts is, in effect, what the present inquiry is about. In classical common law contract theory, at least, it is clear that in the absence of either seal or consideration they could not be so considered.

Another supposed disadvantage of definitions in terms of promise has sometimes been thought to lie in the very nature of a promise. Some philosophers and others have assumed that promises must involve the [97] doing (or refraining from doing) of some act in the future. If promises were so limited, there could, prima facie, be no place in contract for a warranty, the essence of which is a statement of past or present fact rather than the promise of something to be done in the future. On this sort of reasoning, s 2(2) of the Restatement of Contracts provided that warranties were to be treated as promises or undertakings to be answerable for damage caused by the non-happening of the event or the non-existence of the fact warranted. The effect of that provision was to substitute the secondary for the primary obligation. The better view is that past or present fact can be the subject of a promise. To suppose otherwise, it will be suggested, is to misunderstand the distinguishing characteristic of a promise.

JW Carter, *Australian Contract Law* (Butterworths LexisNexis, 6th ed, 2013)

[8] [1-08] **Paradigm situation**. The modern law of contract assumes freedom of contract; that is, freedom to decide whether to contract and to negotiate contractual terms. It also assumes a paradigm situation of one-to-one negotiation of all the terms of an agreement by parties with equal bargaining strengths concerned to maximise their individual positions. It must be recognised that although it is without doubt 'an attribute of a free society ... that it is generally left to the parties themselves to make bargains' [quoting *Biotechnology Australia Pty Ltd v Pace* (1988) 15 NSWLR 130, 133 K(irby P)] these assumptions are frequently contradicted or qualified by events in the real world. In many situations adjustments must be made in the conception or application of principle based on these assumptions.

QUESTIONS

(1) What is a contract?

(2) In what terms can a contract be defined?

(3) Why do the notions of 'binding promise' and 'bargain' lie at the core of contractual arrangements?

1.3 The relevance of contracts in market societies

Factor	Short explanation	Relevant authorities	*Principles* text*
Contracts underpin modern economies	Market exchanges lie at the root of modern society Contract is the tool through which most exchanges are made	H Collins, *Regulating Contracts* (Oxford University Press, 1999) P Zumbansen, 'The Law of Society: Governance Through Contract' (2007) 14(2) *Indiana Journal of Global Legal Studies* 191 S Mouzas and M Furmston, 'A Proposed Taxonomy of Contracts' (2013) 30(1) *Journal of Contract Law* 1	Chapter 1: 1.01 Chapter 2: 2.04

* Consult the corresponding section(s) of the *Principles* text for more detail.

Humans' progression from ancient forms of aggregation to the modern form of polity would not have been possible without the intensification of trade and the evolution of exchange methods. In a classic work on the subject, which was written under the influence of the modern process of industrialisation, Sir Henry Maine contended that such progression reflected that from 'status to contract'.[5] This is certainly correct: market exchanges lie at the root of modern society and contract is the tool through which most exchanges are made.

Notwithstanding the above, it should be borne in mind that contracts' function depends on our conceptualisation of them, which in turn depends on which theory is used to operationalise them. By way of an example, the will theory and the bargain theory are two different expressions of an individualistic understanding of contractual relationships: the former gives priority to the parties' *subjective* intention, whereas the latter—upon which, as mentioned, Australian contract law is based—to their agreement as *objectively* expressed through the 'reciprocal conventional inducement' (see **2.3**)[6].

5 Henry Maine, *Ancient Law. Its Connection with the Early History of Society and Its Relations to Modern Ideas* (John Murry, 14th ed, 1981) ch 5.

6 Brian Coote, 'The Essence of Contract – Part I' (1988) 1(1) *Journal of Contract Law* 91–112, 101.

In short, it may be said that the notion of contract is a socio-legal one. The reason for this is two-fold: first, as a form of 'association', contracts are the 'law of society'[7]; second, the role that contractual agreements play in societal development depends on our conceptualisation of human relations as well as on the function that we assign to (contract) law in regulating them. Proof of this is given by what contracts are currently undergoing: the sophistication of trade and pluralisation of regulative phenomena at the global, transnational, and local levels has led to the need to develop new taxonomies which decode the functioning and effect of contracting in its various aspects.[8] For the very same reason, there is the tendency to divide between 'governance *by* contract' and 'governance *of* contract'.[9]

H Collins, *Regulating Contracts* (Oxford University Press, 1999)

[13] Before examining any regulation of contracts, we should devote some time to the idea of a contractual relation itself. This relation plainly differs from other types of human association, such as those found between friends, neighbours, members of a club, and between members of a family. Such an investigation of the social institution of contract presents a considerable problem, because the idea of contract possesses a confusing surplus of meanings.

We use the idea of contract in numerous contexts: from a commonplace purchase of goods from a shop, to abstract theories of the foundations of political obligations in modern societies, the Social Contract. Furthermore, each conception or use of the idea of contract can be examined from a variety of perspectives or discourses, including morality, politics, economics, and law. We can ask of both the shop purchase and the hypothetical Social Contract; is the bargain fair, just, efficient, or binding?

Even within a particular discourse such as law, we discover a rich variety of themes and emphases about contracts. The practising lawyer identifies the key function of contracts as the planning of an economic relation. The legal scholar views the rules of contract law as a particular source of private law obligations. The socio-legal scholar perhaps considers contract law as a tool for the regulation of economic and social transactions. Finally, the judge treats contracts as creating binding rules of law between the parties, breach of which provides a justification for the imposition of state sanctions.

This multiplicity of contexts and meanings signifies that the idea of contract is used not only to describe a key economic institution in a market economy, but also to express more generally a central form, of human association in modern society. [. . .]

How Contract Thinks About Association

A contract creates a relationship between people. It comprises a distinctive type of human association. What distinguishes a contractual relation from [14] other forms of association, such as links of status, kinship, friendship, and membership of a community or an organisation? Some caution is required in answering this question, because contract is such an abstract idea that many kinds of relationship such as marriage or an exchange of gifts between friends can be perceived, at the price

7 Hugh Collins, *Regulating Contracts* (Oxford University Press, 1999); Peer Zumbansen, 'The Law of Society: Governance Through Contract' (2007) 14(2) *Indiana Journal of Global Legal Studies* 191–233, extracts below.

8 Stefanos Mouzas and Michael Furmston, 'A Proposed Taxonomy of Contracts' (2013) 30(1) *Journal of Contract Law* 1–11, extract below.

9 Zumbansen (n 7), extract below.

of some distortion, as contractual. My contention is, however, that a paradigm meaning can be attributed to the idea of contract.

[. . .]

When we try to distance ourselves from the legal conception of the meaning of contractual relations, we can observe that contracts establish [15] a discrete communication system between the individuals. Whatever their prior relationship, a contractual agreement constitutes a distinct and isolated specification of particular undertakings. The contract may be made between friends, for example, who already have diffuse expectations of loyalty and support established through previous interactions including exchanges. [. . .] The contractual relation creates new, more specific expectations, but simultaneously it tends to exclude the surrounding normative context in the evaluation of whether those expectations have been fulfilled or disappointed.

Furthermore, unlike other social interactions which may create diffuse expectations for the future, such as the formation of a friendship or the making of a gift, a contractual relation empowers the parties to create their own distinct understanding of how this particular relationship should proceed.

[. . .]

The contract constructs an image of the human association that reduces its complexity to the elements and trajectories that have significance within the contractual framework. The contract thinks about events, for instance, by examining human actions and words within a narrow time-frame; the prior pattern of the social [16] relation between the parties and their sentiments of trust and loyalty are irrelevant to this construction of knowledge.

[. . .] Four characteristics of the meaning of contractual association stand out in this approach.

(1) The association marked by a contract consists of isolated or discrete commitments, which have an exclusionary force in practical reasoning, so that these commitments tend to displace other normative standards derived from the social context of the contractual relation, including other forms of association such as friendship and status. Contract therefore reduces the complexity of human association, rendering social relations susceptible to management and reconstruction.
(2) The commitments identified by a contract tend to be temporary and specific. Contract therefore reasons about associations in such a way that they can either be completed (the money is exchanged for the goods) or broken (no payment is made). Association is therefore understood by contract as finite in duration, and always susceptible to dissolution.
(3) Contract thinks about association as a personal bond between the parties to the agreement, so that it neither imposes obligations on others nor confers any rights on third parties. This personal bond is a private relationship between individuals rather than a social undertaking towards a community.
(4) Contract thinks about association as an artificial and almost infinitely malleable construction, the product of a voluntary choice by individuals.

The way in which the contract thinks about the relation is not the same as the way in which the law of contract thinks about the same events. Both [17] communication systems construct their own knowledge of the world within their own criteria of relevance. It is quite possible, for instance, for two people to believe that they have entered a contractual relation, and permit that framework to provide a normative guide to their behaviour, even though in law the events do not count as a contract at all. The differences between the two communication systems will be of great interest to us here, but for the time being we concentrate upon the contractual relation rather than legal reasoning.

P Zumbansen, 'The Law of Society: Governance Through Contract' (2007) 14(2) *Indiana Journal of Global Legal Studies* 191

[192]–[193] [. . .] [W]e are well advised to study contracts in their socio-economic, historical, and cultural context. A careful reading of scholars such as Henry Sumner Maine, Morris Cohen, Robert Hale, Karl Llewellyn, Stewart Macaulay, and Ian Macneil offers a deeper understanding of the institutional and normative dimensions of contractual governance. Their analysis is particularly helpful in assessing ongoing shifts away from a welfare state-based regulation (governance) of contractual relations. Such shifts are occurring on two levels. First, they take place against the backdrop of a neo-liberal critique of government interference into allegedly private relations. Second, the return to formalism in contract law, which privileges a functionalist, purportedly technical and autonomous, design and execution of contractual agreements over the view of regulated contracts, is linked to a particular concept of sovereignty.

[. . .]

[233] The perception of a contract's different rationalities has important repercussions for both governance *by* contract and governance *of* contract. While contractual governance describes a complex, multidimensional arrangement of societal exchanges (governance *by* contract), the latter describes a particularly challenging role for legal governance (adjudication, regulation, and enforcement of contracts).

In this vein, the current emphasis on 'governing contracts' reflects on the way that the law is intimately and irreversibly implicated in the evolution of particular societal discourses. Legal regulation of contract, in this reading, requires the law constantly to translate conflicting, overlapping, and diverging societal rationalities into its own legal language. As the reflexive law of contractual governance is engaged in this process of translation, it transforms its tension between form and substance into a dangerous, yet existential reflexive practice on the employed formal procedures and substantive assessments. Its oscillation with other societal rationalities is the death of this societal law. It is from this death that it will re-emerge as the law of society.

S Mouzas and M Furmston, 'A Proposed Taxonomy of Contracts' (2013) 30(1) *Journal of Contract Law* 1

[2] The idea of taxonomy derives from the Aristotelian concept of *taxis* which means order. The term taxis implies a system, a structure or a pattern in which multiple 'elements of various kind are related to each other'. As the life of the law has not been logic but experience, traditional efforts to create taxis (order) in contract law embrace classifications based on the subject matter of contracts, for example, sale of goods, sale of land, employment, or insurance.

Classifications based on the subject matter of contracts are useful but they do not reveal deeper underlying elements that are related to each other. Moving beyond the subject matter of contracts, extant contract taxonomies are severely limited to theoretical dichotomies, for example, contract *in personam* versus contract *in rem*, discrete versus relational contract. Our attempt to identify a 'taxis' in contracts is guided by two rather pragmatic questions. The first question is whether the law of contract is the same for all contracts; the second question is whether we can identify criteria that could help us distinguish between different contracts on the basis of their real-life usage.

Although we can identify with certainty some distinctive characteristics in particular types of contracts, the general principle in English law is that the same legal principles should apply to the law of contract as a whole. In other words, English law proceeds on the basis that there is a single law of contract applicable to all contracts, together with rules applicable to individual contracts. This is a distinctive feature of common law contract law. Books on criminal law discuss both general principles and specific crimes. Books on tort proceed similarly though there are probably tort courses in universities which cover only negligence and related topics. In other systems, books and courses on contract law consider in some detail the law relating to specific contracts.

Recognising that there are a number of different and overlapping ways of classifying contracts, we can identify at least seven ways of doing this:

(1) by the subject matter;
(2) by the way the contract is made;
(3) by the function of contracts;
(4) by the time-horizon;
(5) by the ability to renegotiate terms;
(6) by the involvement of consumers; and
(7) by the existence of mutual trust.

QUESTIONS

(1) What is the reason as to why contractual arrangements underpin market societies?
(2) What is meant by the statement that 'contracts are a form of association'?
(3) Why is there a need to develop new taxonomies to categorise contractual relationships?

1.4 The functions of contract law

Factor	Short explanation	Relevant authorities	*Principles* text*
Contract law as part of the 'law of obligations'	Contract law is that area of private law which regulates private arrangements		Chapter 1: 1.06 Chapter 7: 7.02
Justifications for contract law	Contract law has three functions: (1) it defines which agreements are enforceable; (2) it regulates the parties' obligations in terms of rights and duties; and (3) it sets out the remedies in case of breach	SA Smith, *Atiyah's Introduction to the Law of Contract* (Clarendon Press, 2005) JW Carter, *Contract Law in Australia* (Butterworths LexisNexis, 6th ed, 2013) L Siliquini-Cinelli and A Hutchison (eds), *The Constitutional Dimension of Contract Law: A Comparative Perspective* (Springer, 2017) vol 1	Chapter 1: 1.04–1.05 Chapter 5: 5.01 Chapter 20: 20.20

* Consult the corresponding section(s) of the *Principles* text for more detail.

Broadly defined, contract law is the body of law which (1) regulates those arrangements that are categorised as contractual, and (2) gives rise to enforceable promises under the doctrine of estoppel, mentioned earlier. Hence, in terms of taxonomy, contract law is part of the law of obligations—a fundamental branch of private law (as opposed to public law, under which fall, for instance, administrative and constitutional law). From this it follows that, as the law of society, contract law has a strict relationship with other branches of law, such as consumer regulation (see **20.4**), and the law of restitutions and torts (see **24.1**).[10]

Contract law lies at the core of the Western Legal Tradition, of which Australian law is a part. Historically, it was the Romans who developed the first types of contracts in a systematic and coherent manner. However, Roman law had a number of individual contracts, but not a 'general theory' of contract.[11] It was only in modern times, when market societies arose and the first processes of industrialisation took place, that 'the law of contract' as is understood and applied today originated and developed.

The foregoing begs the question as to what is, in practical terms, the justification for a general law of contract in a time in which, as discussed above, the concept of contract is highly fragmented. When engaging with this interrogative, scholars point to the need for consistency and certainty[12] and hold that contract law absolves three functions: (1) it defines which agreements are enforceable; (2) it regulates the parties' obligations in terms of rights and duties; (3) it sets out the remedies in case of breach.[13] Finally, scholars have more recently stressed the public (and in particular, constitutional) function that contract law has come to play in contemporary modes of transactions (see also **2.3**).[14]

SA Smith, *Atiyah's Introduction to the Law of Contract* (Clarendon Press, 2005)

The Justification for Contract Law

[3] [W]hat, if anything, is the justification for contract law? Assuming that contracts are voluntary undertakings, why should the law enforce such undertakings? Stated differently, on what basis is it legitimate for the state, acting through the courts, to sanction individuals for breaking contracts? Why lend the state's support to what is an essentially private complaint?

Virtually all societies have evolved laws for the enforcement of contracts, so it is no surprise that most commentators believe that, while certain aspects of the law may pose difficulties, in broad terms the law of contract is justifiable. More specifically, two kinds of justifications are typically given for the law of contract. The first, which is associated with 'economic' and other broadly 'utilitarian' approaches to law, justifies contract law on the basis that it facilitates mutually beneficial exchanges, and so promotes overall social welfare or social 'wealth' (broadly defined).

10 Burrows (n 1); Mason, Carter and Tolhurst (n 1).
11 Alan Watson, *Legal Transplants. An Approach to Comparative Law* (University of Georgia Press, 1993).
12 Carter (n 2), extract below.
13 Lindy Willmott, Sharon Christensen, Des Butler and Bill Dixon, *Contract Law* (Oxford University Press, 4th ed, 2013) 4.
14 Luca Siliquini-Cinelli and Andrew Hutchison (eds), *The Constitutional Dimension of Contract Law: A Comparative Perspective* (Springer, 2017–2018) vol 1 and 2, extract below.

The underlying idea is that where two parties freely agree on a contract involving, say, a simple exchange of money for goods, the seller does so because he thinks he will be better off with the money than with the goods, and the buyer does so because she prefers the goods to the money. Both parties thus emerge from the exchange better off (in one sense) than they were before, and since society's wealth is made up of the total wealth of its members, even a simple exchange of this kind can improve social wealth. In short, contract law (and the officials needed to enforce the law) is a justified use of the state's resources because it helps everyone to become better off. [. . .]

[4] [. . .] From an economic perspective, the primary reason a law of contract is needed is that most exchanges of any complexity cannot be performed simultaneously. One or both parties will have to perform in the future, which means that the other party has to have confidence that she will perform. Suppose that I want a special machine made to order for my factory. A manufacturer could make the machine, and then sell the finished product to me in a simultaneous exchange of machine for cash. But the manufacturer is likely to be worried that I might change my mind at the last minute, leaving him with a machine that is difficult to sell. I might also worry that the manufacturer will change his mind, and decide not to make the machine. Admittedly, there are many reasons aside from the law that each of us might keep to our agreement, such as our interests in our reputation or simply our sense of morality. Nonetheless, it is clear that the risk of non-performance will sometimes dissuade people from entering otherwise beneficial deferred exchanges. It is because of this risk that a law of contract is needed. The fundamental role of contract law, in the economic theory now being considered, is to facilitate the making and performing of deferred exchanges. The law fulfils this role in many ways, but the most fundamental is by providing remedies for breaches of contract, either in the form of orders that breaching parties perform or orders that they pay damages.

Thus interpreted, contract law's essential purpose is to secure cooperation in human behaviour, and particularly in exchange. In sophisticated modern societies this cooperation has led to a massive and elaborate system of credit—and 'credit' is simply another word for 'trust' or 'reliance'. In the simplest sort of case, where businesses provide goods or services on credit to consumers, they trust or rely on the consumer to pay and in the meantime they allow the consumers to have the goods. Generally, the consumers will ultimately pay, but if they fail to do so some sanction is needed: the law of contract provides that sanction.

So contract law ultimately provides the backing needed to support the whole institution of credit. A moment's reflection is enough to show to what extent this is true not only in commercial matters, but in all walks of life. The value of consumers' bank accounts, their right to occupy their houses if rented or mortgaged, their employment, their insurance, their shareholdings, and many other matters of vital importance to them, all depend on the fact that the law of contract will enable them to [5] realise their rights. In the striking phrase of Roscoe Pound, 'Wealth, in a commercial age, is made up largely of promises.'

The second general justification that is commonly given for the law of contract can be described more quickly. The individualist or 'moral' justification focuses not on the social benefits of contracting, but on the rights and duties of individual contracting parties.

According to this view, when courts order that contracts be performed, the reason is that the defendants have duties, owed to the claimants (not society), to do what they contracted to do.

The economic and moral justifications each provide a plausible justification for the general institution of contract law and, as we shall see in later chapters, for many specific contract law rules. It seems plausible to suppose, therefore, that the best overall justification for the law of contract combines each of these accounts. The idea that contract law is justified on two grounds—an economic ground and a moral ground—is indeed a common conclusion. And as a matter of history, it is clear that lawmakers have been influenced by both grounds (and many others as well). But it is worth noting that many contract scholars are uncomfortable defending a 'mixed' justification of this kind. The reason is straightforward: the two justifications have opposite starting points. The economic view supposes that society's interests take precedence over those of the individual, while the moral view supposes the opposite. A justification for contract law that simultaneously adopts both justifications thus might be thought to raise as many questions as it answers.

JW Carter, *Contract Law in Australia* (Butterworths LexisNexis, 6th ed, 2013)

[6] [1-06] Awareness of a 'general law of contract' is a phenomenon of the late 19th century. Previously such legal subjects as, for example, sales and insurance were recognised, but there was not a body of general principles linking them all. Under the synthesising influence of textbooks and law school curricula, the general principles have been derived. It would be easy, though wrong, to assume that such special contracts are the offshoots of the trunk of general principle rather than vice versa.

Therefore, whatever may have been the position at various times in the past, for 100 years the courts have been seeking to find, elucidate and apply general principles. It is simply too late to turn back the clock even if it was ever desirable to do so. Since the usual approach today is to look for guidance in general principles, specific types of contracts are regarded as governed by those principles unless there are good reasons for applying special rules.

[...]

[13] The Role of Contract Law

[1-14] **Consistency and Certainty**. Consistency and certainty in the law are not merely an indulgence for the benefit of lawyers and law students: they are essential to confident planning for the future by all. But what must be acknowledged is something which the lawyer, steeped in doctrine, has not always been prepared to recognise, namely, that doctrine is formed not in a vacuum but in response to particular problems in time and space.

Similarly, the future violability of legal doctrine depends on considerations extrinsic to the system of doctrine itself, in general its capacity to provide just and efficient solutions to contemporary problems.

[1-15] **Dispute resolution**. The study of contract law is principally a study of legal decisions. Yet, the role of contract law in determining the resolution of contractual disputes can be overestimated. The cost and delay involved in litigation are considerable, notwithstanding persistent attempts to reduce both. Arbitration, as an alternative, has often proved to be even more expensive and time consuming. Both also involve considerable indirect and non-financial costs; for example, expenditure of the parties' [14] own time and energy in preparing for trial, and the worry and mental strain imposed on the litigants and their witnesses.

These problems would not disappear if the adversory system of litigation were to be abandoned in favour of an inquisitional model. But the law now encourages (by institutional means) the conciliation process as part of 'alternative' dispute resolution processes. These conspire or should conspire to make resort to the courts and to arbitration a last resort. Yet it is the ordinary courts (and, to a lesser extent, arbitration) that give life, power and practical significance to the general principles of contract law in society.

As well as reducing the role played by the general principles of contract law by its incursions into the substantive law, parliament has established various tribunals, commissions, boards and committees with jurisdiction to hear and determine particular classes of contractual or contract-related disputes. Examples are industrial tribunals in relation to employment disputes, and consumer tribunals in relation to disputes arising out of the supply of goods or services (particularly credit) by traders to consumers. A number of reasons for this development can be cited. These include:

- that a solution is more likely to emanate from persons having specialist expertise and experience than those expert in abstract legal principles;
- that the amount at stake does not warrant the exhaustive factual and legal exploration to which adversaries before the ordinary courts are entitled; and
- that there is a public interest in the ascertainment of the truth and the resolution of certain classes of contractual or contract-related disputes which is inhibited by the ordinary courts' application of the technical rules of evidence and procedure.

It should be noted that many of the recent attempts to devise procedures to avoid the need to resort to litigation themselves involve contracts. Thus, where parties to a contractual dispute agree to use a mediator to assist the resolution, the procedure is itself a contractual one.

L Siliquini-Cinelli and A Hutchison (eds), *The Constitutional Dimension of Contract Law: A Comparative Perspective* (Springer, 2017) vol 1

[vii] One of the hallmarks of the present era is the discourse surrounding Fundamental rights and the necessity that the law takes cognisance of these. Various national and supranational Human rights instruments have been developed and implemented in order to transition society away from atrocity and callousness toward a more just and inclusive future. In some countries, this is done through the mechanism of a supreme Constitution, while in others international conventions or ordinary legislation holds sway. Contract law has increasingly been playing a pivotal role in this phenomenon. According to many, this has been done especially through the much debated 'civilising mission' of contract, a notion that itself constitutes the canon of the Western liberal principle of 'civilised economy'. The movement away from the belief in the absolute freedom of contract, which reached its zenith in the nineteenth century, to the principles of fairness and justice that underpin contract law today, is often deemed to be a testament to this civilising influence.

[. . .]

[ix] In jurisdictions with a history of Human rights abuses, such as Germany, Italy or South Africa, the necessity for a Constitution to entrench Human rights and transform society is of great importance, and will have a deep impact on the implementation of the Constitution in question. In other countries, such as Australia, where a Bill of Rights is lacking and the Constitution, in Gaudron

J's words, 'until 1967 ... was blatantly discriminatory', the spread of fundamental values and policies within the private law dimension takes place differently in such a way as to fill the void of weak equal treatment provisions at the federal level.

In the context of Contract law in particular, there is a potential for a Human rights- and constitutional-values-based revision of the law to have an impact on core concepts such as freedom of contract, possibly through a greater emphasis on policies and mechanisms protecting weaker parties. There may also be a distinction here between strictly Commercial law, in which business-to-business contracting operates subject to only minimal regulation and judicial interference, and specific statutory regimes designed to address an inequality of bargaining power, such as those dealing with consumers, tenants and employees.

QUESTIONS

(1) What are the three main functions of contract law?

(2) Given that contracts are voluntary undertakings, what are the moral and economic justifications for having a branch of law regulating them?

(3) What is the role of contract law, and particularly of legal decisions, in resolving contractual disputes?

(4) Why is it important to speak of a 'constitutional dimension' of contract law?

1.5 The origins, development, and sources of Australian contract law

Factor	Short explanation	Relevant authorities	*Principles* text*
Australian contract law is rooted in its English counterpart Australian contract law has been developing its own peculiar elements		*Cullen v Trappell* (1980) 146 CLR 1 *Paciocco v Australia and New Zealand Banking Group Ltd* (2016) 258 CLR 525 *Commonwealth Bank of Australia v Barker* (2014) 253 CLR 169 *Minister of State for Immigration and Ethnic Affairs v Teoh* (1995) 183 CLR 273 MP Ellinghaus, 'An Australian Contract Law?'(1989) 2(1) *Journal of Contract Law* 13	Chapter 3: 3.21–3.23

* Consult the corresponding section(s) of the *Principles* text for more detail.

Australian contract law originated from its English counterpart: when the British colonists arrived in Australia at the end of the eighteenth century, they brought with them the English common law and any legislation (such as the *Statute of Frauds 1677*) that was not of its nature concerned only with British circumstances. Australian contract law is, therefore, the result of what may be defined as a transplanting process.[15] The term 'common law' has different meanings: for the purposes of this book, we refer to it as the judge-made body of rules formulated and developed by judges from the twelfth century. In this sense, it should be borne in mind that the terms 'Common law' (capital 'C') refers instead to the branch of the Western Legal Tradition of which Australian law is part.

Once the colonies had been established, each of them could pass legislation of their own, and their courts could, in theory, develop their own version of the common law. However, it was only towards the end of the twentieth century that the High Court showed the intention to play an active role in the realisation of an autonomous law of contract (*Cullen v Trappell*, extract below; but see also *Parker v The Queen* (1963) 111 CLR 610). While Australian contract law is developing along an increasingly independent path, particularly with regard to the protection of reasonable expectations, its key features remain in line with the essence of British law of contract. In *Paciocco v Australia and New Zealand Banking Group Ltd* (2016) 258 CLR 525, at 539–40 below, French J reflected on the impact that the contemporary, increasingly autonomous development of the Australian law of contract has on the essence of the Common law tradition as a whole.

At the time of writing, the primary sources of the law of contract in Australia are the common law and equity. However, increasingly statutes are supplementing the judge-made law of contract, particularly in relation to consumer protection. Further, a reference must also be made to the *United Nations Convention on the International Sale of Goods 1980* (also known as the '*CISG*' or 'Vienna Convention'). The *CISG*'s horizon of application is limited to international sale contracts and has been considered as a pivotal achievement towards a uniform regime centred around the notions of certainty and fairness. In addition, attention must also be paid to a whole series of rules and principles that do not have direct legal effect, but which, as outlined in the textbook, are nonetheless intended to influence contractual behaviour (usually labelled 'soft law').

A few things should be noted. First, the relationship between equity and common law. The term 'equity' refers to a subset of the common law that has its roots in the decisions of the English Court of Chancery. Such decisions were the expression of equitable principles in circumstances where the common law principles applied in other courts would unfairly deny relief. As the Court of Chancery was abolished by the *Supreme Court of Judicature Acts* of 1873 and 1875, equity was then applied by the same courts which would apply the common law. While the Australian colonies (and later States) did not have an equivalent to the Court of Chancery, their Supreme Courts did—to varying degrees—have separate procedures or divisions for equitable matters. The separate administration of common law and equity persisted until recently. Still today, the New South Wales Supreme Court has an Equity Division, with a separate Chief Judge. The importance of comprehending the working logic of equitable principles and doctrines is due to the role that they play in contract law theory and practice.[16]

15 Watson (n 11).
16 RP Meagher, JD Heydon and MJ Leeming, *Meagher, Gummow & Lehane's Equity: Doctrines & Remedies* (Butterworths LexisNexis, 5th ed, 2014).

Examples are the doctrines of promissory estoppel (see **7.2**), relief against forfeiture (see **16.7**) and unconscionable bargains (see **20.2**), the equitable remedies of rectification and rescission (see **3.2** and **18.6**), specific performance and injunction (see **22.2**).

With respect to the role of legislation, it will suffice to note that while Australian contract law is strongly moulded by its Common law (and thus, judge-made) roots, it nevertheless displays significant statutory developments which both formally and substantially embellish the law of contract. While there is no statute codifying contract law, there are several pieces of legislation which regulate particular types of transactions. The Australian Consumer Law (ACL), for instance, is a statutory regime which was enacted as Schedule 2 of the *Competition and Consumer Act 2010* (Cth). Currently under review (cf CAANZ 2016), the ACL deals, among other things, with unconscionable undertakings (see **20.4**) Importantly, the ACL applies as a federal, State or Territory law. The distinction is relevant from a formal/procedural point of view as it is only the Australian Competition and Consumer Commission ('ACCC') that has the authority to commence certain proceedings under the federal version; and it is the Federal Court or Federal Circuit Court that must hear those proceedings, rather than a State court. In some cases, the enactment of statutory norms introduced a regime similar to that in the United Kingdom (as is the case with the transfer of property regimes, which have been moulded around the *Sale of Goods Act 1893* (UK)—but the same may also be said in regard to the statutes regulating bills of exchange, marine insurance contracts, partnership and commercial sale of goods contracts). Yet, in others cases, the Australian legislator has instead taken the opportunity to reform the area of law in question by introducing significant innovations (as is the case with the *Insurance Contracts Act 1984* (Cth)).

Finally, the study of the development of Australian contract law has also been shaped by the ratification of the *CISG*, mentioned earlier. While the importance of having adopted an *international* regulatory framework for the sale of goods cannot be overestimated, it should be borne in mind that the *CISG* only applies to the rights and obligations of the parties under that contract (cf. Article 4). As such, the *CISG* is a source of law for those international sales of goods: 'between parties whose places of business are in different States; (a) when the States are Contracting States; or (b) when the rules of private international law lead to the application of the law of a Contracting State' (cf. Article 1(1)). The *CISG* does not, however, apply automatically: in Australia, the ratification of a treaty by the federal government may create obligations under international law unless or until the instrument concerned is expressly given such effect by legislation (see *Minister of State for Immigration and Ethnic Affairs v Teoh* (1995) at 286–8, extract below). Should an international instrument be ratified, it is still open to an Australian court to refer to it in resolving a question of statutory interpretation, or indeed in refining or developing the common law. In regard to the so-called 'transnational' law of commerce: see **3.1**.

Cullen v Trappell (1980) 146 CLR 1

Facts and issues

The plaintiff, aged 32, stopped on a highway while travelling from Sydney to Perth to assist another motorist whose car had broken down. He was injured when a semi-trailer struck that car. The issues arose as to whether the diminished earning capacity should be quantified by reference to the victim's gross earnings or net of tax, and secondly, as to how the interest on the awarded damages has to be calculated.

Decision

In assessing damages for personal injuries which have resulted in loss or diminution of the plaintiff's earning capacity, a court should take into account the income tax which the plaintiff would have had to pay on the earnings of which his injuries had deprived him.

Per Barwick CJ at 5:

> I feel I ought at the outset to state explicitly the approach which, in my opinion, this court ought now to make to the decision of principles of the common law applicable in Australia. Long since, the court decided that it was not bound by the decisions of the Court of Appeal or of the House of Lords. For a considerable time, thinking uniformity of decision in matters of common law within the British Commonwealth (or at least as between the courts of the United Kingdom and this court) desirable, the court made a considerable endeavour to maintain that uniformity even to the point of deferring to a decision of the English Court of Appeal rather than maintain one of its own: see *Waghorn v Waghorn* (1942) 65 CLR 289 at 292. But the maintenance of that uniformity could scarce survive the decision of the Privy Council in *Australian Consolidated Press Ltd v Uren* [1969] 1 AC 590; [1968] ALR 3; (1967) 117 CLR 221.
>
> [6] Now, however, with the passage of the *Privy Council (Limitation of Appeals) Act 1968–1973 (Cth)*, and the subsequent *Privy Council (Appeals from the High Court) Act, 1975* (Cth), the court has ceased to be bound by decisions of the Privy Council. This court has become the final court of appeal, not merely in matters of federal jurisdiction but as to the principles of the common law applicable throughout Australia. The court has expressed itself in this sense in *Viro v R* (1978) 18 ALR 257.
>
> It is, of course, proper to acknowledge the tremendous advantage Australia has had by its inheritance of the common law. The capacity of the judiciary to declare the common law is a notable feature of the common law system itself. It is for the final court of appeal in each juristic unit administering the common law ultimately to declare what is the common law. This, in any case, is a very heavy responsibility, but even more so in the case of this court which has become such a final court of appeal, long after the final court of appeal in the juristic unit of the United Kingdom has had an opportunity to declare the common law.
>
> Whilst the courts have the responsibility of declaring what the common law is, that law exists apart from any such declaration. Thus, in the hands of a final court of appeal there remains a question whether any prior declaration of the common law has correctly expressed and declared that law. Where a decision binds in point of precedent no such question arises: but where there is no binding precedent, the question must, if a prior decision be challenged, be answered by the final court of appeal itself.
>
> In *Mutual Life & Citizens' Assurance Co Ltd v Evatt* (1968) 122 CLR 556 at 563; [1969] ALR 3 at 6, I had occasion to advert to the situation where, when this court was asked to declare the common law, there was no relevant binding precedent. The situation now is that, when the court is asked, particularly for the first time, to declare the common law, there are no precedents binding on this court. Thus, what I then wrote has now a wider area of application.
>
> What ought the approach of this court to be when, for the first time, it is asked to declare the principles of the common law in some particular area of human activity? It seems to me the court cannot act as if it were bound by declarations of the common law not made in its own juristic system. It must, in my opinion, itself closely examine the principles of the common law and determine for itself whether or not such prior declarations correctly declare the common law. If, of course, the court itself concludes that the common law is in accordance with such

> declarations, then the court should for itself make a like declaration for the purposes of the Australian people: the court cannot alter the common law which it is satisfied has been correctly declared. Any such change must be left to the appropriate legislature. If, however, the court is convinced on its examination of principle that the declaration already made is erroneous, then it seems to me the court is bound to declare the common law for Australia in that sense which the court thinks is correct.

Paciocco v Australia and New Zealand Banking Group Ltd (2016) 258 CLR 525

Facts and issues

Mr Paciocco (first appellant) controlled Speedy Development Group Pty Ltd (second appellant). Mr Paciocco held consumer credit card and deposit accounts with the respondent, Australia and New Zealand Banking Group Limited (ANZ). Speedy Development Group Pty Ltd held a business deposit account with Australia and New Zealand Banking Group Limited. Importantly, all of the accounts were charged various fees by ANZ. The consumer and business deposit accounts were charged honour fees, dishonour fees and non-payment fees. The consumer credit card accounts held by Mr Paciocco were charged over-limit fees and late payment fees.

There were several issues to be solved in this case. First, whether both appellants were applicants in representative proceedings against ANZ under Part IVA of the *Federal Court of Australia Act 1976* (Cth). Second, whether the provisions for the various fees were unenforceable as penalties. Finally, whether the inclusion of such fees was in contravention of various statutory provisions relating to unconscionable conduct and, with respect to Mr Paciocco only, unjust and unfair contract terms.

Decision

The trial judge found that only some of the fees were penalties. Mr Paciocco and ANZ appealed to the Federal Court of Australia (Full Court). ANZ succeeded in its appeal. Mr Paciocco and Speedy Development Group Pty Ltd appealed then to the High Court. The High Court eventually dismissed both appeals.

Per French CJ at 539:

> It is more than half a century since Dixon CJ said that this Court would no longer adhere to the policy that it ought to follow the decisions of the House of Lords at the expense of its own opinions. That change of direction was occasioned by the judgment of the House of Lords in *Director of Public Prosecutions v Smith*, which the Chief Justice considered laid down propositions which were 'misconceived and wrong'. Twenty-five years later that evolutionary change was well entrenched. Mason CJ observed extra-judicially that the value of English judgments, like those of Canada, New Zealand and the United States, 'depend[ed] on the persuasive force of their reasoning.' [quoting Mason, 'Future Directions in Australian Law', (1987) 13 *Monash University Law Review* 149–63, 154]. So too, no doubt, for the courts of the United Kingdom as they consider the decisions of courts of other common law jurisdictions.
>
> The common law in Australia is the common law of Australia. So much was affirmed in the unanimous judgment of this Court in *Lange v Australian Broadcasting Corporation* and in cases

that followed it. Following the enactment of the Australia Acts and the abolition of the last remaining avenue of appeal to the Privy Council from the Supreme Courts of the States, s 80 of the *Judiciary Act* was [540] amended by substituting the term 'common law in Australia' for the term 'common law of England' [quoting *Law and Justice Legislation Amendment Act* 1988 (Cth) s 41(1)]. The common law of England was a source of law for legal development in Australia, but not the only source. Moreover, as the alternative claims in the present case demonstrate, there are few areas of the common law which are untouched by statutory regimes reflecting public policy settings which may differ from one jurisdiction to another

Differences have emerged from time to time between the common law of Australia and that of the United Kingdom in a number of areas. Those differences have not heralded the coming of winters of mutual exceptionalism. All of the common law jurisdictions are rich sources of comparative law whose traditions are worthy of the highest respect, particularly those of the United Kingdom as the first source. No doubt in a global economy convergence, particularly in commercial law, is preferable to divergence even if harmonisation is beyond reach. The common law process will not always be the best way of achieving convergence between common law jurisdictions. The penalty rule in the United Kingdom, a product of that process, was described by Lord Neuberger and Lord Sumption in their joint judgment in *Cavendish* as 'an ancient, haphazardly constructed edifice which has not weathered well'. More than one account of its construction and more than one view of whether it should be abrogated or extended or subsumed by legislative reform is reasonably open. There has been much activity in this area within national jurisdictions and in the development of internationally applicable model rules and principles which were discussed in *Cavendish* in the judgments of Lord Mance and Lord Hodge. It may be that in this country statutory law reform offers more promise than debates about the true reading of English legal history.

Commonwealth Bank of Australia v Barker (2014) 253 CLR 169

Facts and issues

Stephen Barker's employment was terminated by the Commonwealth Bank of Australia (CBA) in April 2009. Prior to that, Mr Barker was informed that his position was to be made redundant. He was also informed that CBA's preference was for him to be redeployed within CBA itself, but if that was not the case, then his employment would be terminated approximately four weeks thereafter. Mr Barker was subsequently denied access to his CBA email account and voicemail which resulted in Mr Barker not being informed that an alternative position within CBA was available until 26 March. He did not receive any information about the recruitment process from the recruitment consultant, nor was the option of retraining him for the role discussed with him. The issue is whether the conduct of CBA amounted to a breach of an implied term of mutual trust and confidence which resulted in Mr Barker being denied the opportunity of redeployment within CBA.

Decision

The primary judge held there was a term of mutual trust and confidence implied in the agreement between Mr Barker and CBA. It was held further that CBA's breach of its own redeployment policy amounted to a breach of that implied term. The Full Court, by majority, agreed with the primary judge that a term of mutual trust and confidence was implied by law into the agreement but disagreed with the primary judge in the second part of its ruling, that is, in treating the term as co-extensive with an obligation to observe the redeployment policy. It was held that the term required CBA to take active steps to consult with Mr Barker regarding possible redeployment opportunities within CBA and to give him an opportunity to apply for such positions. It was further held that the primary judge viewed CBA's failure to make contact with Mr Barker for a period as unreasonable and therefore found that the term had been breached.

CBA appealed to the High Court. The issue on appeal was whether employment contracts contain a term implied by law of mutual trust and confidence. In allowing the appeal, the Court held that such a term was not necessary in employment contracts and therefore there was no justification for implying by law such a term into all employment contracts.

Per French CJ, Bell and Keane JJ at 185:

> Judicial decisions about employment contracts in other common law jurisdictions, including the United Kingdom, attract the cautionary observation that Australian judges must 'subject [foreign rules] to inspection at the border to determine their adaptability to native soil' [quoting Paul Finn, 'Statutes and the Common Law' (1992) 22 *University of Western Australia Law Review* 7, 13; quoting Roger J Traynor, 'Statutes Revolving in Common-Law Orbits' (1968) 17 *Catholic University Law Review* 401, 409]. That is not an injunction to legal protectionism. It is simply a statement about the sensible use of comparative law.
>
> **The implication of terms**
>
> The common law in Australia must evolve within the limits of judicial power and not trespass into the province of legislative action. This Court and, to a lesser extent, intermediate appeal courts have a law-making function. That function can only be exercised as an incident of the adjudication of particular disputes. The first point of reference in its exercise is 'the web of established legal principle' [quoting M McHugh, 'The Judicial Method' (1999) 73 *Australian Law Journal* 37, 48]. As Brennan J said in *Dietrich v The Queen*: There must be constraints on the exercise of the power, else the courts would cross 'the Rubicon that divides the judicial and the legislative powers'.

Minister of State for Immigration and Ethnic Affairs v Teoh (1995) 183 CLR 273

Facts and issues

Mr Teoh, a Malaysian citizen, has a conviction for importing and possessing heroin. On the basis of that conviction, the Immigration Minister of Australia ordered that Mr Teoh be deported from Australia, leaving behind his family and children in Australia. Australia has ratified the *Convention on the Rights of the Child* ('*CRC*') but has not incorporated that into its national law. The issue is therefore to what extent is the *CRC* applicable in Australia?

Decision

On appeal from Mr Teoh, the deportation order was overturned by the Federal Court of Australia. In subsequently reviewing the matter, the High Court of Australia held that the ratification created an expectation that in matters concerning children, the best interests of the child would be the paramount consideration.

Per Mason CJ, Bell and Deane J at 286:

The status of the Convention in Australian law

It is well established that the provisions of an international treaty to which Australia is a party do not form part of Australian law unless [287] those provisions have been validly incorporated into our municipal law by statute. This principle has its foundation in the proposition that in our constitutional system the making and ratification of treaties fall within the province of the Executive in the exercise of its prerogative power whereas the making and the alteration of the law fall within the province of Parliament, not the Executive. So, a treaty which has not been incorporated into our municipal law cannot operate as a direct source of individual rights and obligations under that law. In this case, it is common ground that the provisions of the Convention have not been incorporated in this way. It is not suggested that the declaration made pursuant to s 47(1) of the *Human Rights and Equal Opportunity Commission Act* has this effect.

But the fact that the Convention has not been incorporated into Australian law does not mean that its ratification holds no significance for Australian law. Where a statute or subordinate legislation is ambiguous, the courts should favour that construction which accords with Australia's obligations under a treaty or international convention to which Australia is a party, at least in those cases in which the legislation is enacted after, or in contemplation of, entry into, or ratification of, the relevant international instrument. That is because Parliament, prima facie, intends to give effect to Australia's obligations under international law.

It is accepted that a statute is to be interpreted and applied, as far as its language permits, so that it is in conformity and not in conflict with the established rules of international law. The form in which this principle has been expressed might be thought to lend support to the view that the proposition enunciated in the preceding paragraph should be stated so as to require the courts to favour a construction, as far as the language of the legislation permits, that is in conformity and not in conflict with Australia's international obligations. That indeed is how we would regard the proposition as stated in the preceding paragraph.

In this context, there are strong reasons for rejecting a narrow conception of ambiguity. If the language of the legislation is susceptible of a construction which is consistent with the terms of the international instrument and the obligations which it imposes on Australia, then that construction should prevail. So expressed, the principle is no more than a canon of construction and does not import the [288] terms of the treaty or convention into our municipal law as a source of individual rights and obligations.

Apart from influencing the construction of a statute or subordinate legislation, an international convention may play a part in the development by the courts of the common law. The provisions of an international convention to which Australia is a party, especially one which declares universal fundamental rights, may be used by the courts as a legitimate guide in developing the common law. But the courts should act in this fashion with due circumspection when the Parliament itself has not seen fit to incorporate the provisions of a convention into our domestic law. Judicial development of the common law must not be seen as a backdoor means of importing an unincorporated convention into Australian law. A cautious approach to the development of the common law by reference to international conventions would be consistent with the approach which the courts have hitherto adopted to the development of the common law by reference to statutory policy and statutory materials. Much will depend upon the nature of the relevant provision, the extent to which it has been accepted by the international community, the purpose which it is intended to serve and its relationship to the existing principles of our domestic law.

MP Ellinghaus, 'An Australian Contract Law?' (1989) 2(1) *Journal of Contract Law* 13

[28] New Perspectives

Diminution of English influence

What is at stake is not, of course, the development of a law of contract branded with specifically Australian virtues and loaded with local colour, or isolated from outside influence, but simply one that cleaves to our own social condition. Although some similarities between English and Australian society continue to exist, rooted as they are in language [29] and modern history, and reinforced by the continuing import of English immigrants, entertainments and ideas, it is nevertheless true that there are fundamental differences between the two countries. For example, Australians inhabit a continent of 7,682,000 square kilometres with a population density of 2.1 per square kilometre; the English inhabit an island of 244,000 square kilometres at a density of 231.3 per square kilometre.

In 1986 3.4 million of a total population of 16 million, or one in five, Australians were foreign-born; of these, 2.2 million, or one in seven Australians, were from other than the United Kingdom, Ireland and North America, in other words, from legal systems presumably not derived from the English model. In the United Kingdom 3.3 million of a total population of 56 million, or one in seventeen, was foreign born. Moreover, Australia is situated in proximity to Asia and Oceania, where its trading partners are increasingly to be found, and which supply an increasing percentage of its immigrants. The United Kingdom is an island adjunct of Europe, on the opposite side of the globe, and is now a member of the European Economic Community. Increasing divergencies in the law of contract are a certain result of their respective situations.

Such points of comparison may vary in the degree to which they manifestly bear on issues of legal order, and specifically on the issue whether the contract law of the one place should be hitched to that of the other. Nevertheless they are structurally significant for the functioning of their respective societies. Given 'the profoundly indigenous sources of social being', the differences which they reflect must have enough impact on transactions to make it unwise to apply to the contracts of one the law devised in the other. Despite this, the combined efforts of Australian judges, practitioners, and scholars have created a situation in which, notwithstanding its formal independence, much of Australian contract law continues to be made in London. We have continued to [30] accept 'ready-made solutions from the United Kingdom instead of evolving answers for ourselves'.

Affirmative action is needed to accelerate the rate of change in this situation. All ex-colonial cultures must endure this irritating phase of 'self-conscious attempt to turn one's back on the parent tradition and to create a new one rooted in the native soil', before reaching a stage 'where self-consciousness has largely disappeared'.

The routine citation of English cases should therefore be dropped.

This is so particularly of the 'classic decisions'. 'The classic decisions — usually English — should not be omitted merely because of their age or origin', say the authors of the most recent of our casebooks on contract.

The revealing phrase in this otherwise unexceptionable proposition is that between hyphens: 'usually English'. Whose classics are we talking about? Would it not seem odd now in, say, literature, painting or history, to number Wordsworth, Constable, or Gibbon among ours? It is not enough, moreover, merely to stipulate that if there is relevant Australian authority it should be cited in preference to English authority'.

Contingencies which have not yet been considered by Australian courts are contingencies for which there is as yet no specific Australian rule, and for which the leeways of choice are open.

The argument in such a case should be about what principle is best applied in Australia, not about the degree of persuasiveness of an English decision in point.

Above all, Australian contract lawyers need a much more vigorous and comprehensive exposure to their own case-law. The space taken up in Australian reports, case-books and texts by the discussion of English precedent is not vacant space, but could be filled many times over with Australian material. Only the full exposure of that material, and its scrutiny without the constant bifurcation of attention to English doctrine, will enable such questions to be answered as: What elements of contract law have been found to be most important for transactions in and with Australia, situated in its particular global, continental and social geography? What are the most articulate opinions, the best passages, the classic dicta, of Australian judges and commentators?

Precisely to what doctrine are we committed by Australian decision, and what remains in the realm, at best, of the persuasive? In law above all, with its constant tendency to ossify, it is important that Australian lawyers realise fully the extent of their leeways of choice; without this [31] realisation the will and capacity to devise their own solutions must remain stunted.

QUESTIONS

(1) Why has Australia been developing an autonomous contract law independent of its English counterpart?

(2) What are the benefits and perils of a distinctively Australian approach to contracts?

(3) What is the rule that *Minister of State for Immigration and Ethnic Affairs v Teoh* (1995) 183 CLR 273 has established in regard to the application of international instruments?

1.6 International perspectives

With the rapid rise of globalised trade since the 1970s, it became apparent that differing contractual regimes within various countries could pose problems for contracting parties wishing to contract across national borders. Thus, the UN Trade Law Branch (UNCITRAL) developed the *CISG* in 1980, which was adopted by Australia in 1988: see **Chapter 25**, fn 25. Therefore, the Australian law of contract in relation to international commercial sales is the *CISG*, unless contracting parties opt out by including a clause within their contract: **25.4.1.1**. The *CISG* creates a uniform law for international contracts that applies in 91 countries to increase predictability of rules for parties contracting internationally. As a uniform law, the *CISG* continues to develop autonomously, separately from the rest of Australian contract law, and sources of jurisprudence for the *CISG* include court decisions from other jurisdictions which have adopted the *CISG*, scholarship, as well as the legislative history within the diplomatic conferences and Working Groups at UN Trade Law Branch, from which the *CISG* originated. For more discussion on the applicability and interpretation of the *CISG*, see **Chapter 25**.

Other soft rules may sometimes apply to international contracts. Of particular note is the UNIDROIT Principles of International Commercial Contracts, which provides extensive rules concerning international contracts, but will not apply unless contracting parties opt in: **25.4.3**. See **Chapter 25** for more details.

1.7 Review

- The law distinguishes between contracts and transactions that are not legally binding, and thus, unenforceable
- The notion of 'bargain' lies at the core of contractual arrangements
- Contracts underpin market societies
- The concept of 'contract' is being increasingly fragmentised
- Australian contract law derives from its English counterpart but has been developing its own peculiar elements.

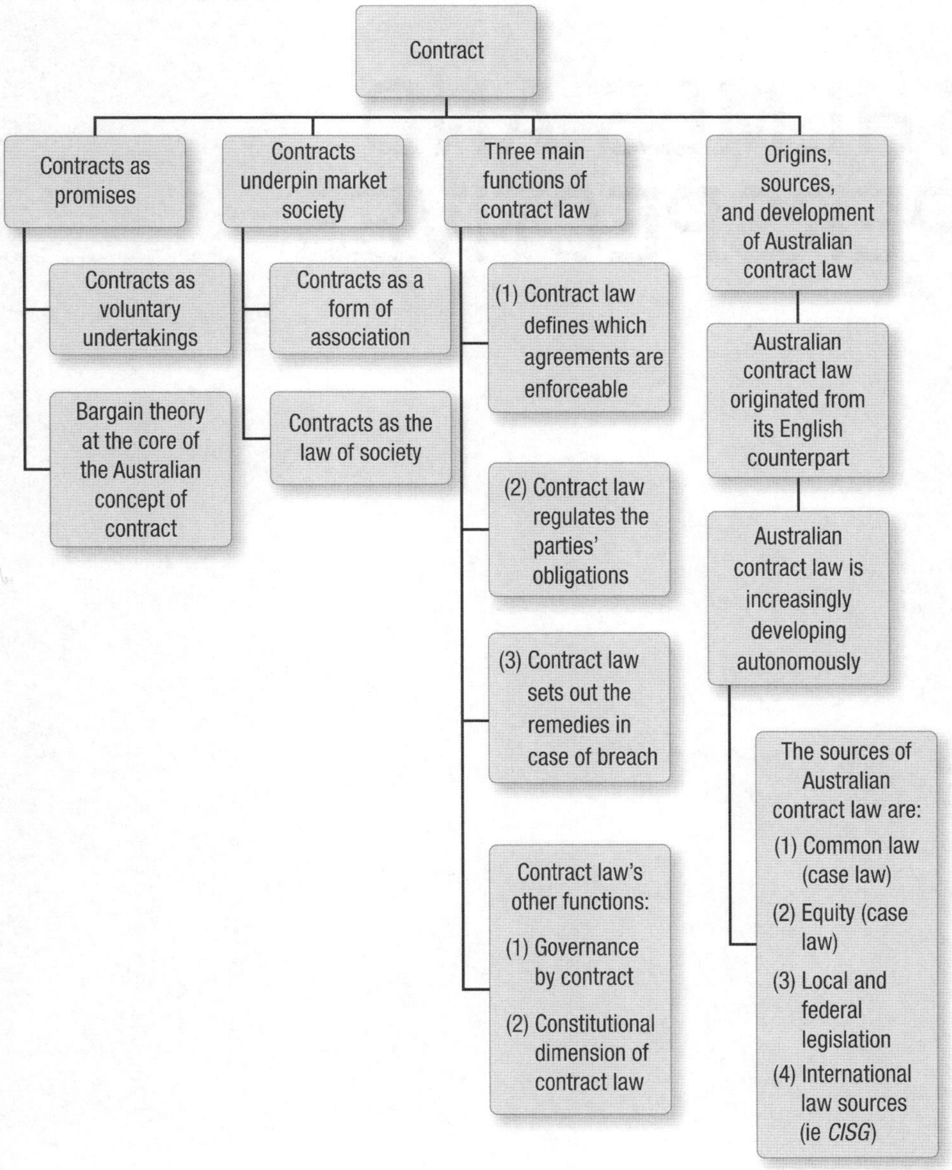

2

THEMES AND PERSPECTIVES

2.1 Overview

Having set out what contracts and contract law are for in the previous chapter, the following pages outline some of the most important developments in the Common law tradition and in Australian contract law more specifically. Contrary to what might be said about other branches of the law of obligations—such as tort law—contract law is rather static. However, a few major changes have occurred since the end of the so-called 'classical period' of contract (the nineteenth century), at both the theoretical and practical level. As the literature on the subject is seemingly endless, it would be impossible to cover all the themes and related aspects here. Thus, attention is paid to some of the main ones only.

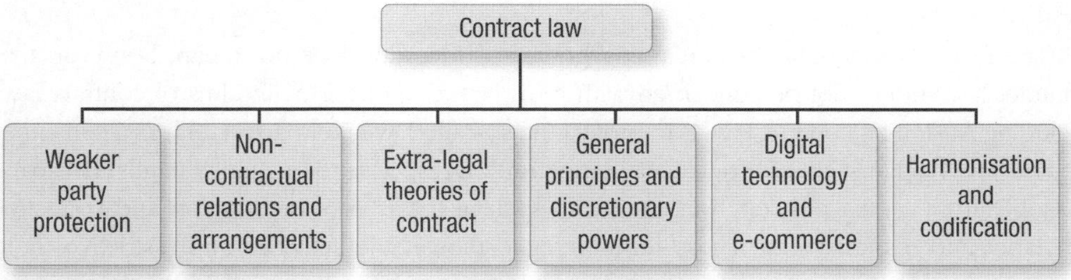

2.2 Contract in practice: inequality of bargaining powers and the (ir)relevance of contract law

Factor	Short explanation	Relevant authorities	*Principles* text*
Power imbalances in contractual dealings Irrelevance of contract law?	Inequality of bargaining powers is a fact. One of the main aims of contract law, also in Australia, is to protect the so-called 'weaker party' (such a consumer or a business) against abusive practices Empirical research shows that most transactions occur outside the purview of the law of contract	S Macaulay, 'Non-contractual Relations in Business: A Preliminary Study' (1963) 28(1) *American Sociological Review* 55 John Gava, 'Can Contract Law Be Justified on Economic Grounds?' (2006) 25(1) *University of Queensland Law Journal* 253 *Competition and Consumer Act 2010* (Cth) Pt IV ss 45, 45DB	Chapter 2: 2.02–2.03 Chapter 2: 2.04

* Consult the corresponding section(s) of the *Principles* text for more detail.

While a contract is a voluntary undertaking and has at its core the notions of agreement, intention to create legal relations and bargain, in practice most contracts are entered into without any prior negotiation. A classic example is represented by those transactions that take place through the so-called 'standard form contracts'; ie contracts whose terms are drafted by one party only: see **4.2**. Further, many (mostly standardised) contracts involve interactions with an automated system (such as a ticket machine or an online booking tool) whose engineering or programming does not permit any form of negotiation. It would be impossible to fully understand this aspect of contract formation practices without realising that, more often than not, there is a profound imbalance of power relations between (future) contracting parties. This is not only the case in most consumer transactions, but also in business ones. Lack of alternatives (actual or perceived) for one party; lack of bargaining skill (especially in a non-haggling society); and informational asymmetries are some of the main reasons for this.

The fact that inequality of bargaining powers is a reality does not mean, however, that contract law should not be concerned with it. In fact, one of the main aims of contract law, including Australian contract law, is to protect the so-called 'weaker party' (such as a consumer or a business) against abusive practices. Importantly, a response to inequality might also arrive not only from media publicity but also from societal forms of shared action and collective solidarity and responsibility. These terms refer to those civic activities and restrictive trade practices carried out by trade unions, trade associations, consumer associations, etc in respect to Part IV of the *Competition and Consumer Act 2010* (extract below).

Since Stewart Macaulay's pioneering study regarding contract law's limited impact on business transaction practices[1], a great deal of commentators have stressed the increasing role played by non-contractual relations and arrangements in the pre-contractual, contractual, and post-contractual phases. These include all those situations where a contract is entered into with little planning or modified through informal adjustments, as well as those where disputes are settled without regard to legal rights.[2] To this trend, one must add the so-called 'hybridisation of contract'.[3]

S Macaulay, 'Non-contractual Relations in Business: A Preliminary Study' (1963) 28(1) *American Sociological Review* 55

[56] *The creation of exchange relationships*

1 Stewart Macaulay, 'Non-contractual Relations in Business: A Preliminary Study' (1963) 28(1) *American Sociological Review* 55–67, extract below.

2 See Hugh Beale and Tony Dugdale, 'Contracts Between Businessmen: Planning and the Use of Contractual Remedies' (1975) 2(1) *British Journal of Law and Society* 45–60; Lisa Bernstein, 'Opting out of the Legal System: Extralegal Contractual Relations in the Diamond Industry' (1992) 21(1) *Journal of Legal Studies* 115–157; John Gava, 'Can Contract Law be Justified on Economic Grounds' (2006) 25(2) *University of Queensland Law Journal* 253–269, extract below; Hugh Collins, *Regulating Contracts* (Oxford University Press, 1999) ch 6;

John Gava, 'How Should Judges Decide Commercial Contract Cases?' (2013) 30(1) *Journal of Contract Law* 133–155; Frank Carrigan, 'The Trivial Nature of Strict Legalism' (2013) 13(1) *Oxford University Commonwealth Law Journal* 1–7.

3 Gunther Teubner, 'In the Blind Spot: The Hybridization of Contracting' (2006) 8(1) *Theoretical Inquiries in Law* 51–71.

[. . .]

[60] (1) [M]any business exchanges reflect a high degree of planning about the four categories—description, contingencies, defective performances and legal sanction—but (2) many, if not most, exchanges reflect no planning, or only a minimal amount of it, especially concerning legal sanctions and the effect of defective performances. As a result, the opportunity for good faith disputes during the life of the exchange relationship often is present.

The adjustment of exchange relationships and the settling of disputes.

While a [61] significant amount of creating business exchanges is done on a fairly non-contractual basis, the creation of exchanges usually is far more contractual than the adjustment of such relationships and the settlement of disputes. Exchanges are adjusted when the obligations of one or both parties are modified by agreement during the life of the relationship. For example, the buyer may be allowed to cancel all or part of the goods he has ordered because he no longer needs them; the seller may be paid more than the contract price by the buyer because of unusual changed circumstances. Dispute settlement involves determining whether or not a party has performed as agreed and, if he has not, doing something about it. For example, a court may have to interpret the meaning of a contract, determine what the alleged defaulting party has done and determine what, if any, remedy the aggrieved party is entitled to. Or one party may assert that the other is in default, refuse to proceed with performing the contract and refuse to deal ever again with the alleged defaulter. If the alleged defaulter, who in fact may not be in default, takes no action, the dispute is then 'settled'.

[. . .]

Why are relatively non-contractual practices so common? In most situations contract is not needed. Often its functions are served by other devices. Most problems are avoided without resort to detailed planning or legal sanctions because usually there is little room for honest misunderstandings or good faith differences of opinion about the nature and quality of a seller's performance. Although the parties fail to cover all foreseeable contingencies, they will exercise care to see that both understand the primary obligation on each side. Either products are standardized with an accepted description or specifications are written calling for production to certain tolerances or results. Those who write and read specifications are experienced professionals who will know the customs of their industry and those of the industries with [63] which they deal. Consequently, these customs can fill gaps in the express agreements of the parties. Finally, most products can be tested to see if they are what was ordered; typically in manufacturing industry we are not dealing with questions of taste or judgment where people can differ in good faith.

When defaults occur they are not likely to be disastrous because of techniques of risk avoidance or risk spreading. One can deal with firms of good reputation or he may be able to get some form of security to guarantee performance. One can insure against many breaches of contract where the risks justify the costs. Sellers set up reserves for bad debts on their books and can sell some of their accounts receivable. Buyers can place orders with two or more suppliers of the same item so that a default by one will not stop the buyer's assembly lines.

Moreover, contract and contract law are often thought unnecessary because there are many effective non-legal sanctions. Two norms are widely accepted. (1) Commitments are to be honored in almost all situations; one does not welsh on a deal. (2) One ought to produce a good product and stand behind it.

J Gava, 'Can Contract Law Be Justified on Economic Grounds?' (2006) 25(1) *University of Queensland Law Journal* 253

[264] [. . .] contract law is of little direct use to business people. As a form of insurance or as a last resort mechanism when preferred tools are not available, law is attractive only because of its formalist nature, not because of the specific nature or usefulness of particular doctrines. And [. . .] it is the process associated with formalism and not the particular rules of classical contract, which is attractive to business. If this is true it is unlikely that the common law of contract evolved in response to business needs. Rather, it is more likely that, since the royal courts were being asked to settle contract disputes, the judges had to fashion some system of rules to do this. But the particular regime that they created, which has come down to us as the law of contract, was the creation of professional judges who tried to create a system of rules which expressed their legalistic notion of fairness and which developed according to the institutional pressures of a professional judiciary and bar. It is extremely unlikely that the rules gave effect to the day-to-day expectations and desires of the market. But, because of its formalist nature, market players used it when it suited their purposes.

Competition and Consumer Act 2010 (Cth) Pt IV s 45

Contracts, arrangements or understandings that restrict dealings or affect competition

(1) A corporation must not:

- **(a)** make a contract or arrangement, or arrive at an understanding, if a provision of the proposed contract, arrangement or understanding has the purpose, or would have or be likely to have the effect, of substantially lessening competition; or
- **(b)** give effect to a provision of a contract, arrangement or understanding, if that provision has the purpose, or has or is likely to have the effect, of substantially lessening competition; or
- **(c)** engage with one or more persons in a concerted practice that has the purpose, or has or is likely to have the effect, of substantially lessening competition.

(2) Paragraph (1)(b) applies in relation to contracts or arrangements made, or understandings arrived at, before or after the commencement of this section.

[. . .]

Competition and Consumer Act 2010 (Cth) Pt IV s 45DB

Boycotts affecting trade or commerce

(1) A person must not, in concert with another person, engage in conduct for the purpose, and having or likely to have the effect, of preventing or substantially hindering a third person (who is not an employer of the first person) from engaging in trade or commerce involving the movement of goods between Australia and places outside Australia.

Note 1: Conduct that would otherwise contravene this section can be authorised under section 88.

Note 2: This section also has effect subject to section 45DD, which deals with permitted boycotts.

(2) A person is taken to engage in conduct for a purpose mentioned in subsection (1) if the person engages in the conduct for purposes that include that purpose.

QUESTIONS

(1) Why, according to Stewart Macaulay, does contract law play a limited role in business transactions?

(2) What is John Gava's argument regarding contract law and business people?

(3) Elaborate on the legal and extra-legal responses to power imbalances in contractual dealings.

2.3 Post-classical and contemporary developments in (Australian) contract law

Factor	Short explanation	Relevant authorities	*Principles text**
From individualism to welfarism From doctrine to discretion From paper to smart contracts Codification and harmonisation New theoretical and critical approaches	Contract law is rather static However, a few major changes have occurred since the 'classical period' of contract law, in the nineteenth century	JN Adams and R Brownsword, 'The Ideologies of Contract' (1987) 7(2) *Legal Studies* 205 P Vincent-Jones, 'Contractual Governance: Institutional and Organizational Analysis' (2000) 20(3) *Oxford Journal of Legal Studies* 317 M Giancaspro, 'Is a "Smart Contract" Really a Smart Idea? Insights from a Legal Perspective' (2017) 33 *Computer Law and Security Review* 825 Attorney-General's Department, *Improving Australia's Law and Justice Framework: A Discussion Paper to Explore the Scope for Reforming Australian Contract Law* (Attorney-General's Department, 2012)	Chapter 2: 2.05–2.06 Chapter 2: 2.07–2.09 Chapter 2: 2.10 Chapter 2: 2.11–2.13 Chapter 2: 2.14–2.17 Chapter 1: 1.10–1.11

(cont.)

Factor	Short explanation	Relevant authorities	*Principles* text*
		W Swain, 'Contract Codification in Australia: Is it Necessary, Desirable and Possible?' (2014) 36(1) *Sydney Law Review* 131 L Siliquini-Cinelli, 'Taking (Legal) Traditions Seriously, or Why Australian Contract Law Should Not Be Codified: An Unconventional Inquiry' (2015) 34(1) *University of Queensland Law Journal* 99 C Fried, *Contract as Promise: A Theory of Contractual Obligation* (Harvard University Press, 1981) L Mulcahy, 'The Limitations of Love and Altruism – Feminist Perspectives on Contract Law' in Linda Mulcahy and Sally Wheeler (eds), *Feminist Perspectives on Contract Law* (Glasshouse Press, 2005) 1 P Drahos and S Parker, 'Critical Contract Law in Australia' (1990) 3(1) *Journal of Contract Law* 30 AW Katz, 'Economic Foundations of Contract Law', in Gregory Klass, George Letsas and Prince Saprai (eds), *Philosophical Foundations of Contract Law* (Oxford University Press, 2014) 171 Q Zhou, 'What Can Contract Lawyers Learn from Law and Economics?' (2011) 30(1) *University of Tasmania Law Review* 157 RE Barnett, 'Contract Is Not Promise; Contract Is Consent', in Gregory Klass, George Letsas and Prince Saprai (eds), *Philosophical Foundations of Contract Law* (Oxford University Press, 2014) 42	

* Consult the corresponding section(s) of the *Principles* text for more detail.

Some very important changes have occurred both in the theory and practice of the law of contract since the end of nineteenth century—an age known as the 'classical period' of contract.[4] While such classical notions as freedom to contract and intention to create legal relations remain two cornerstones of the law of contract in Australia and other Common law jurisdictions, today's legal and doctrinal frameworks have certainly moved away from the individualist and voluntarist assumptions which characterised contract law theory and practice in the nineteenth century.[5]

One of the main purposes of classical principles was to promote certainty: see Lord Mansfield's statement in *Vallejo v Wheeler* (1774) 1 Cowp 143, 98 ER 1012, [1017]: 'In all mercantile transactions the great object should be certainty: and therefore, it is of more consequence that a rule should be certain, than whether the rule is established one way or the other'. This was done in at least two ways: through formal rules that purported to leave judges little discretion in their application; and an emphasis on freedom of contract, discouraging any search for distributive justice (eg rules on adequacy of consideration). Post-classical and contemporary ideas and doctrines are instead aimed at pursuing different objectives such as, among others, social protection. The rise of statutory regulation aimed at protecting the weaker party as well as fast-evolving doctrinal debates concerning the relationship between marketisation, welfarism, and regulation are among the many examples one might give in this sense.[6] However, some protective regimes have been challenged in turn by the rise of neoliberalism and privatisation dynamics. The new quasi-public functions played by contracts are increasingly delegated to the private sector and spread among multiple orderings of society through contracts.[7]

In particular, a few major changes need to be mentioned:

- The legislative and judicial responses to the increasing demand for social protection in the face of marketisation, particularly in consumer transactions: see **20.4**.[8]
- The shift away from hard and fast rules that help promote certainty in the law, towards generalised principles (such as those of good faith, co-operation and fair dealing), equitable doctrines, and discretionary powers that aim to achieve 'just' outcomes in particular circumstances, as in consumer transactions: see **1.3**; **12.3**; **20.4**.[9]

4 Patrick S Atiyah, *The Rise and Fall of Freedom of Contract* (Clarendon Press, 1979).

5 Nick Seddon, Rick Bigwood and Manfred Ellinghaus, *Cheshire & Fifoot Law of Contract* (Butterworths LexisNexis, 10th Australian ed, 2012) ch 28; Stephen A Smith, *Contract Theory* (Oxford University Press, 2004).

6 Ian Ayres and John Braithwaite, *Responsive Regulation* (Oxford University Press, 1992); Gunther Teubner, *Law as an Autopoietic System* (Blackwell, 1993); Liam Murphy, 'The Practice of Promise and Contract' in Gregory Klass, George Letsas and Prince Saprai (eds), *Philosophical Foundations of Contract Law* (Oxford University Press, 2014) 151–170; Roger Brownsword, Rob AJ van Gestel and Hans-W Micklitz (eds), *Contract and Regulation: A Handbook on New Methods of Law Making in Private Law* (Edward Elgar Publishing, 2017).

7 TC Daintith, 'Regulation by Contract: the New Prerogative' (1979) 32 *Current Legal Problems* 41–64; P Vincent-Jones, 'Contractual Governance: Institutional and Organizational Analysis' (2000) 20(3) *Oxford Journal of Legal Studies* 317–351, extract below.

8 See also John N Adams and Roger Brownsword, 'The Ideologies of Contract' (1987) 7(2) *Legal Studies* 205–223, extract below; Brownsword et al (n 6).

9 See also Brownsword et al (n 6); critically, see Jonathan Morgan, *Contract Law Minimalism: A Formalist Restatement of Commercial Contract Law* (Cambridge University Press, 2013) 89.

- The growing use of information technologies not just to facilitate communications between parties or the recording of concluded agreements, but to structure transactions or indeed whole markets: see **5.3; 9.2** (see *Electronic Transactions Act 1999* (Cth); *Electronic Transactions Act 2000* (NSW); *Electronic Transactions (Victoria) Act 2000* (Vic); *Electronic Transactions (Queensland) Act 2001* (Qld); *Electronic Transactions Act 2011* (WA); *Electronic Transactions Act 2000* (SA); *Electronic Transactions Act 2000* (Tas); *Electronic Transactions Act 2001* (ACT); *Electronic Transactions (Northern Territory) Act 2000* (NT)).[10]
- The shift towards the codification of rules about contracts and/or the harmonisation of the laws that apply in different jurisdictions.[11]
- The emergence and spread of extra-legal (ie moral, relational, feminist, economic, critical, etc) approaches to contract.[12]

---

10 See also Eliza Karolina Mik, '"Updating" the Electronic Transactions Act? Australia's Accession to the UN Convention on the Use of Electronic Communications in International Contracts 2005' (2010) 26(2) *Journal of Contract Law* 184–207; OECD Digital Economy Outlook 2017 (OECD Publishing, 2017); M Giancaspro, 'Is a "Smart Contract" Really a Smart Idea? Insights from a Legal Perspective' (2017) 33 *Computer Law and Security Review* 825–835, extract below; Brownsword et al (n 6) 4–6.

11 MP Ellinghaus, EW Wright and M Karras, *Models of Contract Law: An Empirical Evaluation of Their Utility* (Themis Press, 2005); Ted Wright, M Ellinghaus and D Kelly, 'A Draft Australian Law of Contract' (2014) <https://papers.ssrn.com/sol3/Papers.cfm?abstract_id=2403603>; Attorney-General's Department, *Improving Australia's Law and Justice Framework: A Discussion Paper to Explore the Scope for Reforming Australian Contract Law* (Attorney-General's Department, 2012); Andrew Stewart, 'What's Wrong with the Australian Law of Contract?' (2012) 29(1) *Journal of Contract Law* 74–90; Warren Swain, 'Contract Codification in Australia: Is it Necessary, Desirable and Possible?' (2014) 36(1) *Sydney Law Review* 131–149, extract below; Luca Siliquini-Cinelli, 'Taking (Legal) Traditions Seriously, or Why Australian Contract Law Should Not Be Codified: An Unconventional Inquiry' (2015) 34(1) *University of Queensland Law Journal* 99–122, extract below.

12 Ian R Macneil, 'Contracts: Adjustment of Long-Term Economic Relations under Classical, Neoclassical, and Relational Contract Law' (1978) 72 *Northwestern University Law Review* 854–905; Ian R Macneil, 'Relational Contract Theory as Sociology: A Reply to Professors Lindenberg and de Vos' (1987) 143(2) *Journal of Institutional and Theoretical Economics* 272–290; Ian R Macneil, 'Reflections on Relational Contract Theory after a Neo-classical Seminar' in David Campbell, Hugh Collins and John Wightman (eds), *Implicit Dimensions of Contract: Discrete, Relational and Network Contracts* (Hart Publishing, 2003) 207–217; David Campbell and Hugh Collins, 'Discovering the Implicit Dimensions of Contracts', in David Campbell, Hugh Collins and John Wightman (eds), *Implicit Dimensions of Contract: Discrete, Relational and Network Contracts* (Hart Publishing, 2003) 25–49, extract below; Anthony T Kronman and Richard A Posner (eds), *The Economics of Contract Law* (Little, Brown & Co, 1979); Charles Fried, *Contract as Promise: A Theory of Contractual Obligation* (Harvard University Press, 1981), extract below; Mary Joe Frug, 'Re-Reading Contracts: A Feminist Analysis of a Contracts Casebook' (1985) 34 *American University Law Review* 1065–1140; Randy E Barnett, 'A Consent Theory of Contract' (1986) 86 *Columbia Law Review* 269–321; CJ Goetz and RE Scott, 'Enforcing Promises: An Examination of the Basis of Contract' (1990) 89 *Yale Law Journal* 1261–1322; Peter Drahos and Stephen Parker, 'Critical Contract Law in Australia' (1990) 3(1) *Journal of Contract Law* 30–49, extract below; Vivien Goldwasser and Toni Ciro, 'Standards of Behaviour in Commercial Contracting' (2002) 30 *Australian Business Law Review* 369–394; Linda Mulcahy, 'The Limitations of Love and Altruism – Feminist Perspectives on Contract Law' in Linda Mulcahy and Sally Wheeler (eds), *Feminist Perspectives on Contract Law* (*Glasshouse Press*, 2005) 1–19, extract below; Richard Austen-Baker, 'Comprehensive Contract Theory: A Four-Norm Model of Contract Relations' (2009) 25(3) *Journal of Contract Law* 216–243; Qi Zhou, 'What Can Contract Lawyers Learn from Law and Economics?' (2011) 30(1) *University of Tasmania Law Review* 157–173, extract below; Mitja Kovač, *Comparative Contract Law and Economics* (Edward Elgar Publishing, 2011); Martin Hogg, *Promises and Contract Law: Comparative Perspectives*, (Cambridge University Press, 2011); Catherine Mitchell, *Contract Law and Contract Practice: Bridging the Gap between Legal Reasoning and Commercial Expectation* (Hart Publishing, 2013); Randy E Barnett, 'Contract Is Not Promise; Contract Is Consent' in Gregory Klass, George Letsas and Prince Saprai (eds), *Philosophical*

JN Adams and Roger Brownsword, 'The Ideologies of Contract' (1987) 7(2) *Legal Studies* 205

[206] 1. Market-Individualism

The ideology of Market-Individualism has both market and individualistic strands. The strands are mutually supportive, but it aids exposition to separate them. We can look first at the market side of this ideology and then at its individualistic aspect.

(1) The market ideology

According to Market-Individualism, the market place is a site for competitive exchange. The function of contract is not simply to facilitate exchange, it is to facilitate competitive exchange. Contract establishes the [207] ground rules within which competitive commerce can be conducted.

Thus, subject to fraud, mistake, coercion and the like, bargains made in the market must be kept. In many ways, the line drawn between (actionable) misrepresentation and mere non-disclosure, epitomises this view.

There are minimal restraints on contractors: the law of the market is not the law of the jungle, and this rules out misrepresentations. However, non-disclosure of some informational advantage is simply prudent bargaining – contractors are involved in a competitive situation and cannot be expected to disclose their hands.' In line with these assumptions, the market-individualist philosophy attaches importance to the following considerations.

First, security of transactions is to be promoted. This means that where a party, having entered the market, reasonably assumes that he has concluded a bargain, then that assumption should be protected.

This interest in security of contract receives doctrinal recognition in the objective approach to contractual intention, the traditional caution with respect to subjective mistake, and the protection of third party purchasers. Ideally, of course, security of transactions means that a party gets the performance he has bargained for, but, as the market reveals an increasing number of transactions where performance is delayed, the opportunities for non-performance increase. To protect the innocent party, contract espouses the expectation measure of damages (it is the next best thing to actual performance), and in the principle of sanctity of contract (which we will consider under the individualistic side of Market-Individualism) it takes a hard line against excuses for non-performance.

Secondly, it is important for those who enter into the market to know where they stand. This means that the ground rules of contract should be clear. Hence, the restrictions on contracting must not only be minimal (in line with the competitive nature of the market), but also must be clearly defined (in line with the market demand for predictability, calculability etc). The postal acceptance rule is a model for Market-Individualism in the sense that it is clear, simple, and not hedged around with qualifications which leave contractors constantly unsure of their position. Similarly, the

Foundations of Contract Law (Oxford University Press, 2014) 42–57, extract below; Murphy (n 6); Avery W Katz, 'Economic Foundations of Contract Law' in Gregory Klass, George Letsas and Prince Saprai (eds), *Philosophical Foundations of Contract Law* (Oxford University Press, 2014) 171–192, extract below; generally, see Seddon et al (n 5) ch 28; Smith (n 5).

traditional classification approach to withdrawal encapsulates all the virtues of certainty, which are dear to Market-Individualism.

Thirdly, since contract is concerned essentially with the facilitation of market operations, the law should accommodate commercial practice, [208] rather than the other way round. Deference to commercial practice is evident in the market-individualist doctrine of incorporation of terms by reasonable notice, as it is in the *Hillas v Arcos* approach to certainty of terms and the re-alignment of the law in *The Eugymedon*. Also, we should not overlook the import of the commonplace that many of the rules concerning formation (eg the rules determining whether a display of goods is an offer or an invitation to treat) simply hinge on convenience.

This may well be a statement of the obvious, but the obvious should never be neglected. Contract's concern to avoid market inconvenience is a measure of its commitment to the market-individualist policy of facilitating market dealing.

(2) The Individualistic Ideology

A persistent theme in Market-Individualism is that judges should play a non-interventionist role with respect to contracts. This distinctive non-interventionism derives from the individualistic side of the ideology. The essential idea is that parties should enter the market, choose their fellow-contractors, set their own terms, strike their bargains and stick to them. The linchpins of this individualistic philosophy are the doctrines of 'freedom of contract' and 'sanctity of contract'.

The emphasis of freedom of contract is on the parties' freedom of choice.

First, the parties should be free to choose one another as contractual partners (ie partner-freedom). Like the tango, contract takes two. And, ideally the two should consensually choose one another. Secondly, the parties should be free to choose their own terms (ie term-freedom).

Contract is competitive, but the exchange should be consensual. Contract is about unforced choice.

[. . .]

[210] 2. Consumer-Welfarism

The consumer-welfarist ideology stands for a policy of consumer protection, and for principles of fairness and reasonableness in contract.

It does not start with the market-individualist premise that all contracts should be minimally regulated. Rather, it presupposes that consumer contracts are to be closely regulated, and that commercial contracts, although still ordinarily to be viewed as competitive transactions, are to be subject to rather more regulation than Market-Individualism would allow. The difficulties with Consumer-Welfarism appear as soon as one attempts to identify its particular guiding principles (ie its operative principles and conceptions of fairness and reasonableness).

Without attempting to draw up an exhaustive list of the particular principles of Consumer-Welfarism, we suggest that the following number amongst its leading ideas:

(1) The principle of constancy: parties should not 'blow hot and cold' in their dealings with one another, even in the absence of a bargain. A person should not encourage another to act in a particular way or to form a particular expectation (or acquiesce in another's so acting or forming an expectation) only then to act inconsistently with that encouragement (or acquiescence). This

principle is relevant to the protection of unilateral contract offerees. Most importantly, however, it is this principle which underpins High Trees and equitable estoppel, and which creates the opening in English law for the protection of reasonable reliance.

(2) The principle of proportionality: an innocent party's remedies for breach should be proportionate to the seriousness of the consequences of the breach. This straightforwardly underwrites the 'Hong Kong' approach to withdrawal. We can also see this principle at work in regulating contractual provisions dealing with the amount of damages.

Thus, penalty clauses are to be rejected because they bear no relationship to the innocent party's real loss (they are disproportionately [211] excessive) and exemption clauses are unreasonable because they err in the opposite direction.

(3) The principle of bad faith: a party who cites a good legal principle in bad faith should not be allowed to rely on that principle. Hence, for example, in *The Hansa Nord*, the buyer was not allowed to rely (in bad faith) on the breach as a legitimate ground for withdrawal; and, in *Nicolene Lid v Simmonds*, the seller was not allowed to rely (in bad faith) on the alleged uncertainty of the contract. In both cases, we can sense that the courts were aware of the danger of one party planting traps in the contract, in order to facilitate release if so desired.

(4) The principle that no man should profit from his own wrong: this was a principle of which Lord Atkin was certainly conscious in *Bell v Lever Bros Ltd*, even though it yielded to his market-individualist thinking.

However, the so-called equitable doctrine of common mistake draws unequivocal support from this principle.

(5) The principle of unjust enrichment: no party, even though innocent, should be allowed unfairly to enrich himself at the expense of another. Accordingly, it is unreasonable for an innocent party to use another's breach as an opportunity for unfair enrichment: hence, again, the prohibition on penalty clauses, the anxiety about the use made of cost of performance damages, and perhaps the argument in *White & Carter* which (unsuccessfully) pleaded the unreasonableness of continued performance. Equally, frustration should not entail unfair financial advantage.

(6) The better loss-bearer principle: where a loss has to be allocated to one of two innocent parties, it is reasonable to allocate it to the party who is better able to carry the loss. As a rule of thumb, commercial parties are deemed to be better loss-bearers than consumers. The decisions in *Ingram v Little*, and *Oscar Chess Ltd v Williams* exemplify this principle.

(7) The principle of exploitation: a stronger party should not be allowed to exploit the weakness of another's bargaining situation; but parties of equal bargaining strength should be assumed to have a non-exploitative relationship. The first part of this principle, its positive interventionist aspect, pushes for a general principle of unconscionability, and justifies the policy of consumer-protection. The latter (qualifying) aspect of the [212] principle, however, is equally important, for it invites a non-interventionist approach to commercial contracts

(8) The principle of a fair deal for consumers: consumers should be afforded protection against sharp advertising practice, against misleading statements, against false representations, and against restrictions on their ordinary rights. Moreover, consumer disappointment should be properly compensated.

(9) The principle of informational advantage: representors who have special informational advantage must stand by their representations; but representees who have equal informational

opportunity present no special case for protection. The positive aspect of the principle of informational advantage is protective, but its negative aspect offers no succour to representees who are judged able to check out statements for themselves.

(10) The principle of responsibility for fault: contractors who are at fault should not be able to avoid responsibility for their fault. This principle threatens both exemption clauses which deal with negligence; and indemnity clauses which purport to pass on the risk of negligence liability.

(11) The paternalistic principle: contractors who enter into imprudent agreements may be relieved from their bargains where justice so requires. The case for paternalistic relief is at its most compelling where the party is weak or naive. Although the Consumer-Welfarist line on common mistake and frustration suggests a general concern to cushion the effects of harsh bargains, it is an open question to what extent Consumer-Welfarism would push the paternalistic principle for the benefit of commercial contractors.

As we have seen, some of these ideas can generate novel doctrines such as equitable estoppel and unconscionability. However, Consumer-Welfarism also attempts to feed reasonableness into such existing contractual categories as implied terms, mistake, and frustration (thereby opening the door to the employment of the particular principles of the [213] ideology). Whilst Lord Denning's attempts to make such a move in respect of implied terms and frustration have failed, the equitable doctrine of common mistake continues to enjoy support. The most spectacular doctrinal success, however, has been with exemption clauses which are, of course, generally regulated now under a regime of reasonableness by [the *Unfair Contract Terms Act 1977*].

Consumer-Welfarism suffers from its pluralistic scheme of principles. Where a dispute clearly falls under just one of its principles, there is no difficulty; but, as soon as more than one principle is relevant, there is potentially a conflict. Without a rigid hierarchy of principles, the outcome of such conflicts will be unpredictable, as different judges will attach different weights to particular principles. It follows that Consumer-Welfarism is unlikely ever to attain the unity and consistency of its market-individualist rival.

P Vincent-Jones, 'Contractual Governance: Institutional and Organizational Analysis' (2000) 20(3) *Oxford Journal of Legal Studies* 317

[319] At the *institutional* level, contractual relationships are regulated through legal doctrine, legislative rules and various non-legal norms, and through 'policy-driven' regulatory regimes governing the provision of particular public services and relations between citizens and the state. At the *organizational* level, the role of contract depends on divisions between the firm and the market and between public and private sectors, and on how these boundaries are drawn (or are influenced) by government economic and competition policy. The trends in the recent period towards outsourcing by private firms and privatization of public services have had significant implications for contract. The role of contract as an instrument of authority working within hierarchies through the contract of

employment is giving way increasingly to contract as an instrument of market and quasi-market exchange.

[. . .]

[350] The norms generated by and surrounding contractual relations provide a medium through which regulatory objectives might be achieved through legal and policy initiatives. Government policy generally, together with more specific interventions aimed at reducing the size of the public sector or increasing efficiency within public bodies by subjecting them to market forces, work through and impact upon the contract mechanism. The power of contract needs to be harnessed to publicly accountable goals, whatever the organizational form through which these goals are to be pursued. In the private sector generally the problem is how to use the productive potential of markets and competition in a manner leading to outcomes that are welfare-enhancing.

[. . .]

[351] The quest for responsive regulation needs to respect the 'paramount values' of democracy, participation, and citizenship, associated with the five underlying key values. The overall conclusion is that governance arrangements in both economic and social spheres should be decided through careful consideration of the various interests and conditions obtaining in different settings, following full public and local debate about policy goals and the best means to their achievement. The fundamental issue then becomes one not just of effectiveness, but of legitimacy: for what purposes and under what circumstances should contractual arrangements be imposed and powers conferred? The government should aim to increase the level of public participation in decisions concerning the organizational and institutional frameworks, so that citizen and consumer interests may adequately be represented in determining optimal forms of governance.

M Giancaspro, 'Is a "Smart Contract" Really a Smart Idea? Insights from a Legal Perspective' (2017) 33 *Computer Law and Security Review* 825

[827] There are obvious advantages to using smart contracts. For one, they offer the promise of increased efficiency. Transactions facilitated through smart contracts operating on a blockchain are not validated by a trusted intermediary but by consensus of the network's users. Rather than a bank, credit provider, insurance company or the like enabling the digital transfer of property on the terms of the agreement, the coding of the smart contract does all of the work autonomously (once the transaction has been verified through the completion of cryptographic protocols). The miners on the blockchain—the contract parties—need only decide upon the content of their agreement and the contract effectively executes itself. This process of disintermediation improves efficiency by allowing the blockchain to address all critical aspects of the transaction from record-keeping to auditing, monitoring and enforcement. Subsequently, settlements can take place in far quicker time given that there is no significant period of delay during which a traditional intermediary would authorise and process the transaction. Transfers occurring on the blockchain are instant. With further refinement of distributed ledger technology and smart programming, instantaneous

settlement for even the most complex of transactions becomes a very real prospect. Moreover, automating a number of key processes during the life of a contract translates to reduced human involvement; if 'fewer hands' are required to create and fulfil a contract, efficiency is likely to be improved.

Smart contracts may also result in reduced transaction and legal costs. The absence of any central authority or trusted intermediary in a blockchain, and the manner in which blocks of transactions are openly verified and added to the chain by its miners, means that many of the numerous transaction and legal costs that would normally be incurred through intermediated transactions are removed. Such fees are typically in the nature of service or administration fees, or legal costs associated with the preparation, supervision and execution of written contracts. A common example is a contract formed via credit card purchase: a consumer purchases an item from a merchant and pays via credit card; the merchant then applies a surcharge (said to represent the cost to the merchant of accepting payment by credit card); the credit card company similarly applies its fees. All of these costs are entirely avoidable through the use of a blockchain. The potential cost savings from utilising smart contracts are not limited to the transactions themselves; given their relative simplicity, they are likely to significantly reduce infrastructure costs. Proverbially 'cutting out the middle man' through the use of smart contracts is therefore a means for businesses, governments and consumers to potentially dramatically reduce operational and commercial expenses. A consequential advantage of this reduction in overheads is that the bar of entry for users is lowered.

A final opportunity presented by smart contracts is greater transparency and anonymity. With the decentralisation of data through distributed ledgers such as blockchains comes greater transparency. The lack of a central authority or trusted intermediary validating and collating all transactions, and the transparent nature of the blockchain, means commercial arrangements conducted through smart contracts within a public (unpermissioned) ledger are visible to all miners.

Attorney-General's Department, *Improving Australia's Law and Justice Framework: A Discussion Paper to Explore the Scope for Reforming Australian Contract Law* (Attorney-General's Department, 2012)

[5] Harmonisation

2.10 Harmonisation of the law across States and Territories could facilitate trade between parties in different jurisdictions. Differences in contract law between different jurisdictions increase the risks and costs involved in cross-border transactions. Currently, Australian contract law differs between Australian jurisdictions in several areas due to the existence of non-uniform State and Territory statutes, imposing additional costs and lessening predictability. Examples of difference include variations between the general Property Acts, the Sale of Goods Acts, and laws governing the legal capacity of minors to contract, the consequences of discharging a contract by frustration, and the ability of third party beneficiaries to enforce contracts.

[19] Restatement

6.4 Broadly speaking, a restatement would seek to express the existing law in a single text without attempting to change the substance of the law except, perhaps, to resolve inconsistencies or a lack of clarity. A restatement could take the form of a non-binding US style restatement or a binding codification. Such an approach would make sense if accessibility is prioritised as the major driver for reform. One issue to consider would be the extent to which a restatement or codification should seek to go into detail (lessening its accessibility) or should confine itself to high-level principles (which might undermine predictability).

W Swain, 'Contract Codification in Australia: Is It Necessary, Desirable and Possible?' (2014) 36(1) *Sydney Law Review* 131

[148] A Contract Code for Australia?

The creation of a contract code would not be impossible. All the evidence across the last 200 years shows that ambitious projects can succeed. Rather than full-scale codification, there is a certain amount of support for the idea of a restatement of Australian contract law. Restatements can be extremely valuable. They derive authority from the standing of those involved in the process. A restatement can do more than restate. There is some disagreement on the extent to which the various American restatements have introduced progressive reform. One leading American legal historian has argued that the restatements were 'reforms that did not reform'. At a basic level, the fact that a restatement may be forced to make a choice between conflicting rules involves a reform for somebody. The case for a restatement in Australia is rather less compelling than in the United States. There are many fewer jurisdictions and a unified common law. There is no equivalent body to the American Law Institute, which could carry out the task of producing a restatement. The law of contract is also fairly stable. Some of the function of stating the law can be done just as well by the writers of legal treatise, albeit that these works only carry the authority of the individual authors rather than a larger body.

Even within common law legal systems there is strong judicial support for a more radical option. Lord Scarman, Kirby J and Arden LJ have all put the case for codes. It is probably no coincidence that at one point all three had headed either the English or Australian Law Reform Commissions. Codes tend to be supported by those who favour going further than a restatement of the existing law, and who actually want to change the law more radically. This makes it particularly glib to [149] suggest that the objections to codification are 'misguided and exaggerated'. In fact, much of the evidence points in the other direction. Many of the arguments made in favour of codification are built on untested idealism. The harmonisation argument does carry some weight. Nevertheless, these results could be achieved more easily in other ways. It is perfectly possible to favour substantive reform and be sceptical about the merits of codifying contract law. The evidence of the last 30 or so years does not suggest that Australian judges are incapable of reforming contract doctrine, although it can be argued that the pace of innovation in the High Court may have slowed in recent years.

There are considerable obstacles in the way of a successful code. A few have been highlighted. Lessons can certainly be learnt from other jurisdictions.

What may seem attractive in the context of an academic seminar may be a rather different proposition in practice. There is no guarantee that the outcome of such deliberations will be satisfactory. There was some heavyweight criticism of codification from the Chief Justice of New South Wales, Bathurst CJ. Some of the other experienced practitioners and academics who responded to the consultation were also sceptical about the project. If, as has been suggested, the whole exercise is likely to be driven by bureaucrats, politicians and 'stakeholders', rather than the [Australian Law Reform Commission] in consultation with experts, there are further grounds to fear the worse. It is only necessary to look across the Tasman Sea. The New Zealand contract statutes, which share some of the features of a code, are not usually regarded as an unqualified success. It would be going too far to describe the idea of a contract code for Australia as a 'calamity', but it is something that should be approached with the upmost caution. To go into the process without recognising the pitfalls involved will produce an outcome that is not only unsatisfactory, but may leave us with a body of contract doctrine which may be little better or even worse than that it is intended to replace.

L Siliquini-Cinelli, 'Taking (Legal) Traditions Seriously, or Why Australian Contract Law Should Not Be Codified: An Unconventional Inquiry' (2015) 34(1) *University of Queensland Law Journal* 99

[99] In a compelling passage of his *Law, Legislation and Liberty*, Friedrich Hayek vehemently claimed that 'however careful we may think out beforehand every single act of law-making, we are never free to redesign completely the legal system as a whole [because] [l]aw-making is necessarily a continuous process in which every step produces hitherto unforeseen consequences for what we can or must do next'. [. . .] I consider the issue of the necessity of and opportunity for Australian contract law to be codified as a typical example of this.

[. . .]

[104] I would suggest that the promoters of codification are (sometimes unconsciously) influenced by what Hayek has persuasively defined as the fallacy of 'constructivist rationalism'. In particular, while inquiring into the relationship among freedom, reason, and tradition, Hayek has, I think successfully, demonstrated that Western culture is rooted in two different anthropological and biopolitical conceptions of the theory of liberty: 'one empirical and unsystematic, the other speculative and rationalistic – the first based on an interpretation of traditions and institutions which has spontaneously grown up and were but imperfectly understood, the second aiming at the construction of a utopia, which has often been tried but never successfully'.

The first, 'evolutionary' tradition is that of the English experience, while the second, 'rationalistic' one is that of France. As a consequence, English common law (and, thus, Australian common law) is rooted in the former. For present purposes, it is also worth mentioning that this dichotomy reflects a primary antithesis that historians usually describe in terms of 'artificial/natural' modes of socio-political and legal thinking. [. . .] [105] As comparative law teaches us, codification is the most powerful expression of the rationalistic and constructivist conception of social development. The rationalist attitude towards social phenomena is indeed sadly affected by what Hayek has persuasively defined as the 'constructivist fallacy', that is, the belief that 'everything to which man owes his achievements is a product of his reasoning [and that] [i]nstitutions and practices which have not been designed in this matter can be beneficial only by accident'. In particular, according to Hayek, such a fallacy has profoundly affected legal reasoning in Civil law countries, making it seem that 'law' is anything but synonymous with 'legislation'. While arguing this, Hayek spent much effort in explaining that this distortive approach to legal phenomena *(i)* is rooted in anthropomorphic modes of thinking, *(ii)* received the most complete expression in Descartes, and *(iii)* was finally spread throughout the Western legal tradition by the French Revolution and the modern, 'intentional' (that is, artificial and mechanical) dimension of the Civil legal tradition that it created. [. . .]

[113] According to the then-Attorney General of Australia, some of the historical foundations of Australian contract law represent a risk to the 'autonomy and the true intentions of the parties [involved]'. Putting aside the unsatisfactory essence of this claim, it should be noted that its trajectory lines up with Western attempts to standardise ways of living and obscure local sensibilities. In these ways, the global order project, and the universalisation of liberal thought which lies behind it, neutralises distinctions between traditions in anthropological and biopolitical terms.

From the legal perspective, this approach sees the historical 'cohabitation' of different legal rules from within, and of national legal systems from without, as key obstacles to overcome. The global 'spatial turn' that sociopolitical theory is undergoing, which is overturning the classic idea of 'space' as a 'representative surface', is testament to this.

Yet although this (subversive) phenomenon of obfuscation of (legal) traditions is not 'new' or particularly powerful, much sociopolitical, geopolitical, anthropological, and biopolitical data suggest that the distinction within the Western legal tradition between the Common and Civil law traditions has not fully disappeared yet.

C Fried, *Contract as Promise: A Theory of Contractual Obligation* (Harvard University Press, 1981)

[1] The promise principle, which in this book I argue is the moral basis of contract law, is that principle by which persons may impose on themselves obligations where none existed before. [. . .]

[8] By promising we put in another man's hands a new power to accomplish his will, though only a moral power: what he sought to do alone he may now expect to do with our promised help, and to give him this new facility was our very purpose in promising. By promising we transform a choice that was morally neutral into one that is morally compelled. Morality, which must be permanent and beyond our particular will if the grounds for our willing are to be secure, is itself invoked, molded to allow us better to work that particular will. [. . .]

L Mulcahy, 'The Limitations of Love and Altruism—Feminist Perspectives on Contract Law' in Linda Mulcahy and Sally Wheeler (eds), *Feminist Perspectives on Contract Law* (Glasshouse Press, 2005) 1

[1] The law of contract is an area which is ripe for feminist analysis. Of the 'core' common law subjects, it is the one most obviously imbued with values associated with the marginalisation of women and the feminine. The emphasis placed on self-regarding, autonomous and competitive

contractors by classical and neo-classical scholars has led to calls that the law of contract is phallocentric and centrally located in a suppression of the feminist voice and feminist values [. . .]. Indeed, the identification of a correlation between the characteristics of masculinity and the ethos and philosophy of classical legal doctrine has been central to feminist engagements with the law. Nothing better embodies masculine abstracted relations with each other rather than the model of the discrete contractual transaction with which the majority of scholarship in the field remains concerned.

[. . .]

The task of introducing a feminist perspective on contract law is a difficult one. It has been argued that traditional legal doctrine has, for the last 200 years, systematically neglected alternative ways of thinking [. . .]. The law's cognition of women has taken place through the eyes of male legislators and male judges. The fact that the majority of writers in the field are male and that authorship of the mainstream texts has tended to pass through a male line is apparent from a review of current publishers' catalogues. When we teach our students about the philosophical underpinnings of contract, we talk of such writers as Smith, Bentham, Atiyah, Fried and Gilmore, and Llewelyn. [. . .] Our students are challenged when asked to name leading cases involving women. Even when remembered, those that do exist, including the disappointed newlywed in *Curtis v Chemical Cleaning and Dyeing Co Ltd*, the bargaining sillies in undue influence cases like *Barclays Bank v O'Brien*, the [2] scheming wife in *D and C Builders*, do much more to reinforce prevailing stereotypes of women in the contractual sphere than they do to challenge them.

Introducing an alternative vision of contractual relationships is made even more difficult by the common law's predisposition to look to the past. Critical and socio-legal approaches to the study of law are more popular than even before, but student textbooks and scholarship in the field continue to focus on analysing legal problems by reference to the test of tradition. [. . .] The very rules, which rely for their legitimacy on tradition, have helped to structure gendered relations in the law and recreated particular notions of voluntary relations. This can only be a barrier to feminist scholarship, which demands that the gendered structures underpinning modern doctrine are revisited and the notion of obligation reconfigured.

P Drahos and S Parker, 'Critical Contract Law in Australia' (1990) 3(1) *Journal of Contract Law* 30

[32] The Crisis in Australian Contract Law and the Demise of Legal Formalism

Claims to the effect that Australian contract law is entering a period of crisis, in the literal sense of a turning point or time when a decision is called for, are increasingly being made. To Finn, for example, Australian common law as a whole is in a watershed period and by way of illustration he suggests that consideration is under seige and privity has taken a mortal blow.

The decision of the High Court in *Waltons Stores* in 1988 usually features prominently in any catalogue of recent upheavals. It was held there that words and conduct during negotiations gave rise to liability even though no contract eventuated and no tort was established (s 52 of the Trade Practices Act 1974 apparently going untested). The liability was found in promissory estoppel.

By using it as a sword not a shield the primary convention whereby Anglo-Australian law had kept promissory estoppel and contract apart was abrogated and the future role of consideration as the primary sign of liability has been thrown into doubt. Of course, *Waltons Stores* is not the only aspect or illustration of the supposed turning point but it is certainly a highly visible one and we hear that it has caused concern amongst senior commercial practitioners about how they can now predict when morality, the market and the law will be brought together.

It is tempting to attribute this supposed watershed in Australian contract law wholly to changing social and judicial attitudes about business practice. But there may also be a broader backcloth in the development of Australian law and legal reasoning generally. The divergence of Australian and English law has recently become a theme of the Chief Justice, Sir Anthony Mason, and he has noted examples in tort and equity which he suggests illustrates an emerging Australian common law. He has predicted that the 'independence of Australian contract law will become more pronounced as Australian judges shape the common law of contract to accord with Australian circumstances, needs and values'.

The Chief Justice has also been remarking on legal reasoning. This might be due to the need to explain how divergence and the system of precedent can coexist. Sir Anthony, and other judges dealing with this theme, tend to [33] characterise recent years as the demise of formalism. Formalism, as we will see, is variously defined but a fair definition of the kind they refer to embodies claims about a gapless system of general rules from which can logically be deduced the outcome of a particular dispute without resort to justifications external to the system or consideration of the consequences of a decision. Formalism, therefore is rule-oriented and non-consequentialist. It may be contrasted with substantive models of legal reasoning which openly invite consideration of moral, social and economic factors in legal decision-making.

One is naturally led to speculate about a relationship between this divergence of Australian and English contract law and the acknowledgment that formalistic reasoning has declined. Hugh Collins has argued that the classical law of contract 'represents one of the acmes of legal formalist scholarship by virtue of its clear rules and their clusters of logical derivatives'. Could it be that what were previously regarded as clear rules and logical derivatives in contract law are no longer seen that way because the standards of acceptable legal reasoning have increasingly permitted the entry of external considerations? If so, then these external considerations are likely to be indigenous ones rather than imports from the United Kingdom and will lead to different outcomes from those produced by the courts in the Strand.

So much is plausible. To be persuaded that fundamental change is under way, however, one would surely need more. What is the nature of these external considerations? How do they differ from the considerations previously underlying the rules? How do they enter the system? How are they processed once they are there? More central still, what is involved in the activity of theory construction about an area of law which allows us to know that things are different now? These are difficult questions which lawyers have tended to shy away from. In a similar vein, Collins has noted: Normally, like planets circling a star, political philosophy and the law of contracts affect each other's path without their orbits ever coinciding.

Waltons Stores v Maher is a good case to try and bring them together because, as Ramsay tells us, arguments concerning the scope of promissory estoppel or pre-contractual reliance are inherently ethical and political in nature. Critical legal studies, given its preoccupations with liberal philosophy, the market order, legal reasoning and contract, seems an obvious body of theory that could develop further these hypotheses and help us know what is going on in Australian contract law.

AW Katz, 'Economic Foundations of Contract Law' in Gregory Klass, George Letsas and Prince Saprai (eds), *Philosophical Foundations of Contract Law* (Oxford University Press, 2014) 171

[171] Since at least the time of Lord Mansfield, it has been commonplace to view the law of contracts as an important tool for facilitating and regulating economic activity. But in order fully to understand this basic function, it is not possible to treat the law as an autonomous system. Rather, one must understand the substance of the human activity that contract law aims to govern, and the meaning of the communications that arise out of that activity. The economic approach to contract proposes to use the tools and methods of economics as the means toward such understanding.

Q Zhou, 'What Can Contract Lawyers Learn from Law and Economics?' (2011) 30(1) *University of Tasmania Law Review* 157

[159] III Illustrations

Evaluating the Effectiveness of Law

[. . .]

[162] Compared with the UK regulatory design, the Australian approach to the regulation of fraudulent misrepresentation deserves special praise. [. . .] Unlike UK law, *Australian Consumer Law* focuses more on private legal [163] enforcement, offering a wide of [sic] ranges of legal remedies for victims of misrepresentation. Along with traditional rules at common law, misrepresentations were largely regulated by s 52 of the *Trade Practices Act 1974* (Cth), which is now replaced by s 18 of the newly enacted *Australian Consumer Law*. It provides that a person must not, in trade or commerce, engage in conduct that is misleading or deceptive, or is likely to mislead or to deceive. Contravention of s 18 is subject to the remedies of injunction, damages and compensatory orders, as set out in Chapter 5 of the *Australian Consumer Law*. Under the *Australian Consumer Law*, both the regulator and the affected persons can seek the remedy of an injunction to stop a business from engaging in conduct in breach of s 18. Furthermore, the affected persons may apply to a court for damages to compensate actual losses or apply for compensatory orders to compensate potential losses which they are likely to suffer as a result of the contravention of s 18.

This is a smart strategy. The conventional view is that the imperfect legal enforcement of private law sanctions should be addressed by public law mechanisms. Rather than relying entirely on public enforcement agencies, the *Australian Consumer Law* is largely enforced by private parties. This regulatory design significantly enhances legal deterrence. Unlike the remedy of rescission which can only be exercised by the contracting party, the *Australian Consumer Law* allows both regulators and affected persons to seek injunctions and claim damages. The affected persons include the contracting party and other persons adversely affected by the misleading or deceptive behaviour of a business. This rule indeed encourages more private parties to enforce the law. In particular, it creates a strong incentive for competitors of the fraudulent firm to bring the action by alleging that the firm uses misleading or deceptive practices. In addition, as it is private law litigation which is brought by individuals or firms, the claimants partly bear the cost of legal enforcement. Compared with the situation where the law is entirely enforced by a regulatory body, the Australian regulatory design is less costly to the government.

Moreover, it is easier for the claimant to sue in the action of damages for contravention of s 18, rather than in the action of fraudulent misrepresentation at common law. To establish a claim for damages under s 18, the claimant does not need to prove the representor's fraudulent intention as required at common law. This also makes it easier [164] for the claimant to establish the claim, and accordingly enhance the legal deterrence.

Nonetheless, it should also be noted that contract law, from a conventional perspective, is not designed to pursue legal deterrence. This is reflected in many rules and doctrines in contract law, such as that both punitive damages and penalty clauses are strictly prohibited. The default remedy for breach of contract is expectation damages, which is aimed at putting the parties back to the position where they would have been, had the contract been perfectly performed. The purpose of contract law remedy is compensation, not deterrence. But even though contract law is not aimed at pursuing legal deterrence, it is by no means correct to say that contract law remedies have no deterrence effect in reality. As discussed above, a rational contracting party sees legal remedies as a cost for his breach of the contract and will take it into account when assessing the payoff derived from his breach. Inevitably, the remedies will affect his decision to breach the contract. This consequential effect must be considered in any serious legal analysis. The impact of the law on people's behaviour should not be ignored, just because the law may not be designed to have such impact.

Although the above analysis is very simplistic, it is surely a useful exercise. One of the main differences between the economic analysis and the conventional legal study is that the former focuses on *ex ante* questions and the latter on *ex post* ones. Undoubtedly, both analyses are important for contract lawyers. Insufficient consideration of *ex ante* questions will hamper the understanding of contract law. As a consequence, there is a tendency to see contract law more as a remedy to solve disputes, but rarely consider it as a mechanism to avoid problems beforehand. Obviously, the economic analysis can help us achieve a more balanced view.

RE Barnett, 'Contract is Not Promise; Contract Is Consent' in Gregory Klass, George Letsas and Prince Saprai (eds), *Philosophical Foundations of Contract Law* (Oxford University Press, 2014) 42

[48] [The criterion of contractual enforceability that I have elaborated] is explicitly acknowledged in English law [. . .]: courts should presumptively enforce private commitments when there exists a

manifested intention to create a legal relation. Another formulation of this approach is that, to determine the prima facie case of contract, we should determine whether there was a manifested intention to be legally bound. I refer to this criterion, in short, as consent.

This special sense of 'consent' is to be distinguished from promise. To promise is to commit to do or refrain from doing something. To consent to contract is to commit to be legally responsible for nonperformance of a promise. So consent is a commitment in addition to whatever moral commitment inheres in a promise.

[49] Moreover, contractual consent is to be distinguished from subjective assent. Consent is the voluntary communication by one person to another person of a particular message: that one intends to alter an already existing legal relation between the parties to create a new one. [...]

A 'consent theory' of contractual enforcement provides a general criterion of contractual enforceability that strikes a reasonable and workable balance among the party-based, substance-based, and process principles that comprise the core concerns of contract. Requiring a manifested intention to be legally bound facilitates the will or private autonomy of the parties, because one's manifested intention is highly likely to reflect an underlying subjective assent. The existence of a manifested intention to be legally bound also helps distinguish those commitments that merit legal protection, upon which reliance is justified, from those that do not. [...]

Adherence to a criterion of consent would tend to limit enforceability to value-enhancing or efficient commitments (whether gratuitous or as part of an exchange) in which, *ex ante*, the parties view enforceability to be worth more to them than its costs. [...]

Finally, the criterion of consent helps place the bargain principle in proper perspective. The existence of a bargain in a commercial context is very likely to indicate the existence of an intention to be legally bound. The absence of bargain in non-commercial settings is apt to reflect the absence of such consent.

QUESTIONS

(1) What it is meant by extra-legal developments in contract law?

(2) What are the reasons in favour of or against the codification of Australian contract law?

(3) When did the economic analysis of law emerge and what are its main differences from the conventional approach to law (briefly)?

2.4 International perspectives

Many of the themes discussed above intersect with international perspectives. Indeed, the Australian e-commerce laws (discussed at **2.3** above) are implementations of the 2005 UN *Convention on the Use of Electronic Communications in International Contracts*. Likewise, the Discussion Paper of the Attorney-General's Department, which considered potential codification of Australia's contract law, also floated the possibility of harmonising and modernising it. Modernisation was discussed in terms of the global trend to reform domestic contract laws to reflect certain international instruments, namely the *CISG* and UNIDROIT Principles, which are discussed in **Chapter 25**. There are now dozens of domestic contract laws which have already, to varying degrees, been reformed to reflect global contract rules found in these instruments, including Germany, China, many Eastern European countries, France, Netherlands, and many African states.

Another topic raised in this chapter is the need to protect weaker parties in the post-classical period. This is a concern of most jurisdictions, and has been the province of many domestic rules which address potential disadvantages faced by consumers. However, for international transactions, a global solution is yet to be found. Online international consumer contracts are increasingly gaining ground, but in many cases, protection for consumers such as the ACL may apply to the contract. In international commercial contracts, some would argue that similar needs for protection still arises where bargaining power is unequal, despite the fact the parties are commercial businesses. The *CISG* contains no express provisions providing for protection, but its provisions are subject to interpretation to promote good faith (Article 7(1)), and thus a particular interpretation of an obligation within the *CISG* might, in some instances, promote fairness: see **25.5.4**. It is noteworthy, however, that mandatory domestic laws designed to regulate conduct of commercial entities still regulate certain aspects of fairness in relation to contracts governed by the *CISG*. Thus s 18 ACL would still apply. The UNIDROIT Principles contain provisions which are overtly designed to address unfair outcomes within contracts where one party has taken advantage of special disadvantages of the other: **19.4.3**.

2.5 Review

A few major changes have occurred since the end of the so-called 'classical period' of contract (the nineteenth century):

- (Ir)relevance of contract law
- Protection of the weaker party
- Legislative and judicial responses to the increasing demand for social protection in the face of marketisation, particularly in consumer transactions
- The shift away from hard and fast rules that help promote certainty in the law towards generalised principles (such as those of good faith, co-operation and fair dealing), equitable doctrines, and discretionary powers that aim to achieve 'just' outcomes in particular circumstances, as in consumer transactions
- Growing use of information technology, not just to facilitate communications between parties or the recording of concluded agreements but to structure transactions or indeed whole markets
- Shift towards the codification of rules about contracts and/or the harmonisation of the laws that apply in different jurisdictions
- Emergence and spread of extra-legal (ie moral, relational, feminist, economic, critical etc) approaches to contracting

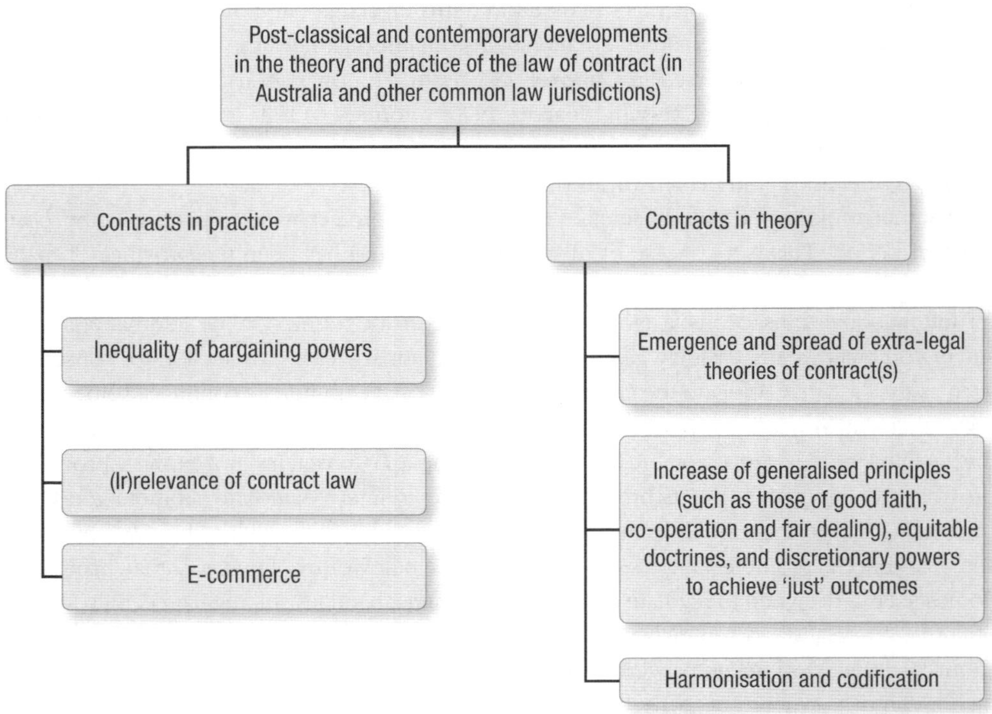

TIPS FOR APPLYING THE LAW IN PRACTICE

The first step is to recognise that inequality of bargaining powers is a social fact. Legal measures are taken to ensure that the stronger party does not take an unfair advantage of their position. A response to inequality might also arrive not only from media publicity but also from societal forms of shared action and collective solidarity and responsibility. It is also important to remember that contrary to other private law branches, contract law is rather static. Nonetheless, over the past few decades there have been some important developments within the contract law dimension. These include the legislative and judicial responses to the increasing demand for social protection in the face of marketisation, particularly in consumer transactions; the shift away from hard and fast rules that help promote certainty in the law towards generalised principles (such as those of good faith, co-operation and fair dealing), equitable doctrines, and discretionary powers that aim to achieve 'just' outcomes in particular circumstances, as in consumer transactions; the growing use of information technologies not just to facilitate communications between parties or the recording of concluded agreements, but to structure transactions or indeed whole markets; the shift towards the codification of rules about contracts and/or the harmonisation of the laws that apply in different jurisdictions; and the emergence and spread of extra-legal (ie moral, relational, feminist, economic, critical etc) approaches to contract.

RESEARCH QUESTION

Briefly outline the movement from individualist to welfarist assumptions in contract law.

3

RESOLVING CONTRACTUAL DISPUTES

3.1 Overview

This chapter provides an introductory overview of the methods by which the parties to a contract can solve disputes over the meaning, effect, and performance of the contract. It is seen that several options are available, depending on what occurred and what remedies are being sought. These remedies are discussed in greater detail throughout the book.

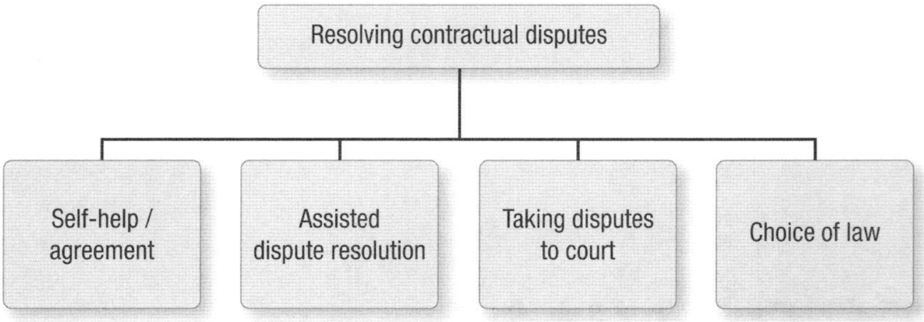

3.2 Self-help/agreement

Factor	Short explanation	Relevant authorities	*Principles* text*
Most matters do not need external assistance	Parties might avoid or solve their dispute by: (a) withholding performance; (b) elaborating specific payment schemes involving deposits and part payments; (c) allowing the other party to terminate the contract. Another similar remedy is that of rescission of the contract Formal and informal negotiated resolution techniques are increasingly being used	Janet O'Sullivan, 'Rescission as a Self-Help Remedy: A Critical Analysis' (2000) 59(3) *Cambridge Law Journal* 509	Chapter 2: 2.04 Chapter 3: 3.03, 3.05–3.06 Chapter 4: 4.02 Chapter 12: 12.07 Chapter 13: 13.09 Chapter 16: 16.01–16.04 Chapter 17: 17.05–17.06 Chapter 18: 18.12

* Consult the corresponding section(s) of the *Principles* text for more detail.

A party that is not satisfied with how the contract has (not) been performed by the other party—ie a consumer who is concerned about the quality of the goods or the services provided; a contractor who has not been paid for earlier work, etc—may withhold performance of some or all of their obligations: see **12.3** This resistance has the important effect of putting the onus on the other party to object and, eventually, take the matter to court to either compel the relevant performance or seek compensation. A party considering these self-help options should also consider the financial consequences which their decision might lead to if the other party successfully litigates.

Parties may also agree on specific payment schemes to, for instance, ensure the other party's ongoing co-operation or commitment to the project. The usual way of doing this is by requiring the payment of a deposit, either when the contract is signed or, at least, before work commences: see **17.3**. A contract may also specifically allow a party to *terminate* it in particular circumstances: see **16.1**. This ought not be confused with the *rescission* of a contract, a term which refers to a form of termination which operates retrospectively from when the contract had been entered into (ab initio). The remedy of rescission is available in cases of misrepresentation, duress, undue influence, or unconscionability—ie in all those cases where the very source of the contractual relationship, agreement and voluntary consent, have been affected. Whether rescission is a self-help or a court-ordered remedy is a debated matter (*Alati v Kruger* [1955] HCA 64; ALR 1047; JD Heydon, MJ Leeming and PG Turner, *Meagher, Gummow & Lehane's Equity: Doctrines & Remedies*[1]; Janet O'Sullivan, 'Rescission as a Self-Help Remedy: A Critical Analysis'[2], extract below).

Formal (ie through a lawyer or other representative) and informal negotiated resolution techniques are increasingly being used: see **3.3**. A settlement agreement can also be reached if proceedings have commenced: see **3.4**. Importantly, while through the negotiated settlement the parties can also modify some of the terms of the original contract, it is unclear what the legal effects of this change are: see **13.2**. Particularly in the case of formal settlements, the parties may choose to record their agreement in writing: see **4.2** for a discussion as to whether the settlement is binding also before it has been put in writing.

Janet O'Sullivan, 'Rescission as a Self-Help Remedy: A Critical Analysis' (2000) 59(3) *Cambridge Law Journal* 509

[509] [. . .] Until relatively recently, the term rescission was used whenever a contract was brought to an end otherwise than by performance, such as, for example, termination of a contract by [510] failure of a condition precedent. In particular, the term was used at common law in the nineteenth century to describe the termination of a contract by one party on acceptance of the other's repudiatory breach. Today, it is recognised that this process does not involve avoidance ab initio, but merely prospective termination of outstanding executory obligations and that 'rescission' is a misleading and inappropriate label for this significantly different concept.

Thus far, it would seem that rescission is simple enough to define. However, any investigation of rescission runs almost immediately into two features that cause problems throughout the English law of obligations and property. These are, first, the terminological and analytical confusion which can be traced to the jurisdictional divide between law and equity [. . .]. Secondly, the reliance on metaphor – it is difficult to describe precisely what is meant by rescission without recourse to language, more suited to haberdashery, of unravelling and cutting away, sometimes at the expense of precise analysis. [. . .]

[528] [. . .] [T]he difficulties inherent in the self-help analysis of rescission stem from the restitutionary implications of rescinding an executed contract or other disposition.

1 (LexisNexis Butterworths, 5th ed, 2015) [25.095]–[25.110].
2 (2000) 59(3) *Cambridge Law Journal* 509–543.

Rescission of a purely executory contract is a relatively simple process and it does not much matter whether the rescission is treated as being effected by the plaintiffs own election or by subsequent judicial order. Where the matter is not disputed by the other party, a court order will in practice be unnecessary, but this does not detract from the premise that rescission properly so called should be regarded as a judicial remedy only. Where one party intimates his intention to 'rescind' a purely executory contract and the other party concurs, the resulting abandonment of the contract is not the result of rescission but of a contractual compromise.

There is of course no need to insist on a decree of rescission in such a case, but equally no need to regard it as an example of rescission as a self-help remedy. In much the same way, a 'letter before action' demanding financial compensation following a breach of contract, which is not disputed but which is met in full by the party in breach, is not regarded as a self-help exercise of the remedy of damages.

[529] Turning then to executed transactions [. . .] the self-help analysis of rescission has two related aspects. The first is that the plaintiff can rescind by his own act of election, generally by giving notice to the other party. In other words, there is no theoretical legal requirement to obtain a court order, even though in practice this will frequently be necessary (if for example the other party disputes the plaintiffs entitlement to rescind). The second is that, where judicial rescission is obtained, it is nonetheless still the plaintiff's election which is regarded as the operative rescinding event, so the judicial relief is in some way 'backdated' to the date of the plaintiff's election.

QUESTION

What are the disadvantages identified by Janet O'Sullivan regarding the qualification of rescission as a self-help remedy (pages 529ff)?

3.3 Assisted dispute resolution

Factor	Short explanation	Relevant authorities	*Principles* text*
No post-contractual agreement has been reached	There are various ways of seeking assistance from third parties	*TCL Air Conditioner (Zhongshan) Co Ltd v Judges of the Federal Court of Australia* (2013) 251 CLR 533 *Commercial Arbitration Act 2011* (Vic) ss 34–36	Chapter 3: 3.07–3.09

* Consult the corresponding section(s) of the *Principles* text for more detail.

There are various types of *ombudsman* that assist consumers and/or small businesses to resolve complaints about their dealings with certain types of supplier. These include the Telecommunications Industry Ombudsman, the Australian Financial Complaints Authority and the Australian Small Business and Family Enterprise Ombudsman. Legislation on these bodies' prerogatives and power is extensive: *Telecommunications (Consumer Protection and Service Standards) Act 1999* (Cth) Pt 6; *Treasury Laws Amendment (Putting Consumers First – Establishment of the Australian Financial Complaints Authority) Act 2018* (Cth); *Australian Small Business and Family Enterprise Ombudsman Act 2015* (Cth); see also www.tio.com.au, www.afca.org.au and www.asbfeo.gov.au).

Alternatively, the parties may opt for an alternative dispute resolution mechanism, such as mediation, conciliation, appraisal, expert determination, or arbitration. These can operate either within or outside the court or tribunal in question (Tania Sourdin, *Alternative Dispute Resolution*[3]; *Federal Court Rules* (Cth) Pt 28; *TCL Air Conditioner (Zhongshan) Co Ltd v Judges of the Federal Court of Australia* (2013) 251 CLR 533, extract below). Here too legislation is extensive, as each State and Territory has statutes dealing with claims by contractors for progress payments in relation to building work (*Building and Construction Industry Security of Payment Act 1999* (NSW); *Construction Contracts Act 2004* (WA); see also Jeremy Coggins, Tom Davie, Tony Earls and Phil Evans, *Understanding Construction Law*;[4] *Shoalhaven City Council v Firedam Civil Engineering Pty Ltd* (2011) 244 CLR 305; *Mickovski v Financial Ombudsman Service Ltd* (2012) 36 VR 456; *Australian Vintage Ltd v Belvino Investments No 2 Pty Ltd* (2015) 90 NSWLR 367; *Probuild Constructions (Australia) Pty Ltd v Shade Systems Pty Ltd* (2018) 264 CLR 1).

Each Australian jurisdiction has legislation that gives effect to agreements for the arbitration of commercial disputes (*Commercial Arbitration Act 2010* (NSW); *Commercial Arbitration Act 2011* (Vic); *Commercial Arbitration Act 2013* (Qld); *Commercial Arbitration Act 2012* (WA); *Commercial Arbitration Act 2011* (SA); *Commercial Arbitration Act 2011 (Tas); Commercial Arbitration Act 2017* (ACT); *Commercial Arbitration (National Uniform Legislation) Act 2011* (NT). These are based on UNCITRAL's Model Law on International Commercial Arbitration 1985, as amended in 2006. Importantly, while the term 'commercial' is not defined, it has been established that it does not to cover employment contracts: *Chief Executive Officer of the Australian Sports Anti-Doping Authority v 34 Players* [2014] VSC 635. At the federal level, Part III of the *International Arbitration Act 1974* (Cth) applies to arbitration agreements made in relation to international trade and commerce. Part II also provides for the recognition and enforcement of arbitral awards made outside Australia, in accordance with the UNCITRAL *Convention on the Recognition and Enforcement of Foreign Arbitral Awards 1958*. Below is an extract from the *Commercial Arbitration Act 2011* (Vic) on how an award can be challenged in court.

TCL Air Conditioner (Zhongshan) Co Ltd v Judges of the Federal Court of Australia (2013) 251 CLR 533

Facts and issues

In 2008, the Chinese company TLC Air Conditioner (TLC) and Castel Electronics Pty Ltd (Castel) entered into a contract for the distribution of TLC's products in Australia by Castel. According to the contract, which also had arbitral provisions, Castel had the exclusive distribution rights for such products. Issues arose when TLC started selling non-TLC products in Australia. The parties tried to resolve the matter through the agreed arbitration provisions. However, TLC did not pay and argued that, because the awards had been granted in Australia, the arbitral tribunal's decision had not complied with the notion of 'foreign award' of the *International Arbitration Act 1974* (Cth). Further, TLC applied for an order restraining the Federal Court of Australia from enforcing the awards. The application was made on the grounds of Articles 35 and 36 of the Model Law, which gave authority to the Court to enforce foreign awards but did not specify which Court had jurisdiction for enforcing 'non-foreign' awards (like the awards in this case).

3 (Lawbook Co, 5th ed, 2016) ch 8.
4 (LexisNexis Butterworths, 2016) 50–70.

Decision

The appeal was rejected. Per French CJ and Gageler J at 566:

Judicial power and arbitration

The exercise of judicial power is an assertion of the sovereign, public authority of a polity. Whilst it is 'both right and important to observe that the determination of rights and liabilities lies at the heart of the judicial function', parties are free to agree to submit their differences or disputes as to their legal rights and liabilities for decision by an ascertained or ascertainable third party, whether a person or a body. As will be explained, where parties do so agree, 'the decision maker does not exercise judicial power, but a power of private arbitration'.

An agreement to submit disputes to arbitration does not, apart from statute, take from a party the power to invoke the jurisdiction of the courts to enforce that party's rights by instituting an action to determine a dispute of a kind that the parties have agreed should be [576] arbitrated. The jurisdiction of the courts is not and cannot be ousted by a private agreement.

However, if parties do go to arbitration and the arbitrator makes an award, the making of the award has legal significance in respect of the parties' dispute and their rights and liabilities. As the plurality in *Dobbs* said: 'if, before the institution of an action, an award was made, *it* [the award] governed the rights of the parties and precluded them from asserting in the Courts the claims which the award determined' (emphasis added). In such a case, the arbitrator's award governs the rights of the parties because '[b]y submitting the claims to arbitration, the parties confer upon the arbitrator an authority conclusively to determine them'.

This gives rise to the general rule that an award made by an arbitrator pursuant to such authority is final and conclusive. Further, the arbitrator's making of an award in exercise of such authority both extinguishes the original cause of action and imposes new obligations on the parties in substitution for the rights and liabilities which were the subject of the dispute referred to arbitration. The former rights of the parties are discharged by an accord and satisfaction. The accord is the agreement to submit disputes to arbitration; the satisfaction is the making of an award in fulfilment of the agreement to arbitrate.

It follows that when an arbitral award is enforced by curial process, the obligations sought to be enforced are those which are created by the award in substitution for the rights and liabilities which were the subject of the dispute referred to arbitration. A party may sue on an award as a cause of action or, in some cases, as in this case, seek enforcement of the award pursuant to the IA Act [*International Arbitration Act 1974*].

The proposition identified as underpinning TCL's submissions assumes, wrongly, that the rights and liabilities which are in dispute in an arbitration continue despite the making of an award. That is, it assumes, wrongly, that the courts will not give effect to the discharge of those pre-existing rights and liabilities by the accord and satisfaction which is effected by a reference to arbitration and the making of an award.

Commercial Arbitration Act 2011 (Vic) ss 34–36

Part 7—Recourse against award

34 Application for setting aside as exclusive recourse against arbitral award (cf Model Law Art 34)

(1) Recourse to the Court against an arbitral award may be made only by an application for setting aside in accordance with subsections (2) and (3) or by an appeal under section 34A.

Note: The Model Law does not provide for appeals under section 34A.

(2) An arbitral award may be set aside by the Court only if—

(a) the party making the application furnishes proof that–

(i) a party to the arbitration agreement referred to in section 7 was under some incapacity; or the arbitration agreement is not valid under the law to which the parties have subjected it or, failing any indication in it, under the law of this State; or

(ii) the party making the application was not given proper notice of the appointment of an arbitral tribunal or of the arbitral proceedings or was otherwise unable to present the party's case; or

(iii) the award deals with a dispute not contemplated by or not falling within the terms of the submission to arbitration, or contains decisions on matters beyond the scope of the submission to arbitration, provided that, if the decisions on matters submitted to arbitration can be separated from those not so submitted, only that part of the award which contains decisions on matters not submitted to arbitration may be set aside; or

(iv) the composition of the arbitral tribunal or the arbitral procedure was not in accordance with the agreement of the parties, unless such agreement was in conflict with a provision of this Act from which the parties cannot derogate, or, failing such agreement, was not in accordance with this Act; or

(b) the Court finds that—

(i) the subject-matter of the dispute is not capable of settlement by arbitration under the law of this State; or

(ii) the award is in conflict with the public policy of this State.

(3) An application for setting aside may not be made after 3 months have elapsed from the date on which the party making that application had received the award or, if a request had been made under section 33, from the date on which that request had been disposed of by the arbitral tribunal.

(4) The Court, when asked to set aside an award, may, where appropriate and so requested by a party, suspend the setting aside of proceedings for a period of time determined by it in order to give the arbitral tribunal an opportunity to resume the arbitral proceedings or to take such other action as in the arbitral tribunal's opinion will eliminate the grounds for setting aside.

34A Appeals against awards

(1) An appeal lies to the Court on a question of law arising out of an award if—

(a) the parties agree, before the end of the appeal period referred to in subsection (6), that an appeal may be made under this section; and

(b) the Court grants leave.

(2) An appeal under this section may be brought by any of the parties to an arbitration agreement.

(3) The Court must not grant leave unless it is satisfied—

(a) that the determination of the question will substantially affect the rights of one or more parties; and

(b) that the question is one which the arbitral tribunal was asked to determine; and

(c) that, on the basis of the findings of fact in the award—

(i) the decision of the tribunal on the question is obviously wrong; or

(ii) the question is one of general public importance and the decision of the tribunal is at least open to serious doubt; and

(d) that, despite the agreement of the parties to resolve the matter by arbitration, it is just and proper in all the circumstances for the Court to determine the question.

(4) An application for leave to appeal must identify the question of law to be determined and state the grounds on which it is alleged that leave to appeal should be granted.

(5) The Court is to determine an application for leave to appeal without a hearing unless it appears to the Court that a hearing is required.

(6) An appeal may not be made under this section after 3 months have elapsed from the date on which the party making the appeal received the award or, if a request had been made under section 33, from the date on which that request had been disposed of by the arbitral tribunal (in this section referred to as the appeal period).

(7) On the determination of an appeal under this section the Court may by order—

(a) confirm the award; or

(b) vary the award; or

(c) remit the award, together with the Court's opinion on the question of law which was the subject of the appeal, to the arbitrator for reconsideration or, where a new arbitrator has been appointed, to that arbitrator for consideration; or

(d) set aside the award in whole or in part.

(8) The Court must not exercise its power to set aside an award, in whole or in part, unless it is satisfied that it would be inappropriate to remit the matters in question to the arbitral tribunal for reconsideration.

(9) Where the award is remitted under subsection (7)(c) the arbitrator must, unless the order otherwise directs, make the award within 3 months after the date of the order.

(10) The Court may make any leave which it grants under subsection (3)(c) subject to the applicant complying with any conditions it considers appropriate.

(11) Where the award of an arbitrator is varied on an appeal under this section, the award as varied has effect (except for the purposes of this section) as if it were the award of the arbitrator.

Part 8 – Recognition and enforcement of awards

35 Recognition and enforcement (cf Model Law Art 35)

(1) An arbitral award, irrespective of the State or Territory in which it was made, is to be recognised in this State as binding and, on application in writing to the Court, is to be enforced subject to the provisions of this section and section 36.

(2) The party relying on an award or applying for its enforcement must supply the original award or a copy of the original award.

(3) If the award is not made in English, the Court may request the party to supply a translation of it into English.

Note: So much of Art 35(2) of the Model Law as provides for the translation of an award that is not in the official language of the enforcing State has been modified.

36 Grounds for refusing recognition or enforcement (cf Model Law Art 36)

(1) Recognition or enforcement of an arbitral award, irrespective of the State or Territory in which it was made, may be refused only–

(a) at the request of the party against whom it is invoked, if that party furnishes to the Court proof that–

(i) a party to the arbitration agreement was under some incapacity, or the arbitration agreement is not valid under the law to which the parties have subjected it or, failing any indication in it, under the law of the State or Territory where the award was made; or

(ii) the party against whom the award is invoked was not given proper notice of the appointment of an arbitrator or of the arbitral proceedings or was otherwise unable to present the party's case; or

(iii) the award deals with a dispute not contemplated by or not falling within the terms of the submission to arbitration, or it contains decisions on matters beyond the scope of the submission to arbitration, provided that, if the decisions on matters submitted to arbitration can be separated from those not so submitted, that part of the award which contains decisions on matters submitted to arbitration may be recognised and enforced; or

(iv) the composition of the arbitral tribunal or the arbitral procedure was not in accordance with the agreement of the parties or, failing such agreement, was not in accordance with the law of the State or Territory where the arbitration took place; or

(v) the award has not yet become binding on the parties or has been set aside or suspended by a court of the State or Territory in which, or under the law of which, that award was made; or

(b) if the Court finds that–

(i) the subject-matter of the dispute is not capable of settlement by arbitration under the law of this State; or

(ii) the recognition or enforcement of the award would be contrary to the public policy of this State.

(2) If an application for setting aside or suspension of an award has been made to a court referred to in subsection (1)(a)(v), the Court may, if it considers it proper, adjourn its decision and may also, on the application of the party claiming recognition or enforcement of the award, order the party to provide appropriate security.

QUESTION

On what grounds did the High Court reject TLC's appeal in *TCL Air Conditioner (Zhongshan) Co Ltd v Judges of the Federal Court of Australia* (2013) 251 CLR 533?

3.4 Taking disputes to court

Factor	Short explanation	Relevant authorities	*Principles* text*
There are many judicial remedies	Judicial remedies can be classified in various ways and serve different purposes There are different legislative and judicial sources at both the Federal and local levels	*Warman International Ltd v Dwyer* (1995) 182 CLR 544 *Australian Building and Construction Commissioner v Construction, Forestry, Mining and Energy Union* (2018) 262 CLR 157 Australian Consumer Law ss 229, 230, 232(6), 236, 237, 243(b), (d), 247, 260 *Federal Court of Australia Act 1976* (Cth) s 21	Chapter 3: 3.11–3.20 Chapter 9: 9.42 Chapter 18: 18.02, 18.05, 18.15–18.17, 18.31–18.32 Chapter 20: 20.20

(cont.)

Factor	Short explanation	Relevant authorities	*Principles* text*
		Supreme Court Act 1935 (SA) s 17 *Limitation Act* 1969 (NSW) s 14(1)(a)	

* Consult the corresponding section(s) of the *Principles* text for more detail.

There are many different orders or remedies that a court may grant to resolve a contractual dispute. These can either be common law (ie damages) or equitable remedies (ie injunction, specific performance). There are different legislative and judicial sources at both the federal and local levels. Most of these remedies and sources are explored in more detail later in the book, especially in **Part VII**. For a detailed discussion, see also Chapter 3 of the *Principles* text. Below are extracts of some of the provisions and cases mentioned in the latter.

Warman International Ltd v Dwyer (1995) 182 CLR 544

Facts and issues

This case concerns Warman International Ltd (Warman) and its general manager, Brian Dwyer. Warman's business included an agency for the distribution of gearboxes manufactured in Italy by Bonfiglioli. In 1986, Mr Dwyer informed Warman that Bonfiglioli were considering manufacturing the gearboxes directly in Australia and were interested in entering into a join arrangement with them. Warman declined. However, Mr Dwyer informed Bonfiglioli that he was soon to leave Warman and set up his own business. Thereafter, the Bonfiglioli Transmission (Aust) Pty Ltd (BTA) and Engineering Transmission Agencies Pty Ltd (ETA) were incorporated with negotiations continuing between February and April 1988. In June 1988, Bonfiglioli terminated the agency contract with Warman and Dwyer resigned as general manager. BTA's shares were equally distributed between the parties in August 1988 (whereas ETA remained owned and controlled by Mr Dwyer only). In September 1988, FinBonfiglioli SpA (a company within the Bonfiglioli group) and BTA entered into a venture agreement with Mr Dwyer and his wife for the assembly and distribution of Bonfiglioli gearboxes in Australia for 20 years. In October 1988, Warman brought proceedings against Mr Dwyer for breach of the fiduciary relationship he had with Warman. The trial judge found for Warman and allowed them to recover equitable damages. While the Court of Appeal upheld the trial judge's decision, the majority held that Warman was only entitled to recover its loss flowing from the breaches of fiduciary duty. The Court dissented with the trial judge on the account of profits, which, it was held, should not have been ordered. Warman appealed.

Decision

The appeal was allowed. Per Mason CJ, Brennan J, Dean J, Dawson J and Gaudron J at 565:

> **The basis for an account of profits**
>
> In determining the proper basis for an account of profits, it is of first importance in this, as in other cases, to ascertain precisely what it was that was acquired in consequence of the fiduciary's breach of duty. And, in some situations, it may also be relevant to ascertain what was lost by the

plaintiff. The starting point in the present case is that Warman's Bonfiglioli agency business rested on the contract by which Bonfiglioli appointed Warman its exclusive Australian distributor of gearboxes and other components. The contract was terminable by Bonfiglioli on three months' notice to Warman. The local goodwill associated with the Bonfiglioli products distributed by Warman — the local product goodwill — was the property of Bonfiglioli just as the local product goodwill in Australia in Hospital Products was that of the United States principal. That, of course, is not to deny the existence in Warman of a goodwill associated with its distribution of Bonfiglioli products. It does not appear that any distinction was drawn at trial between the goodwill of Bonfiglioli and that of Warman or that any attempt was made to identify and value each of them.

But, in light of the fact that the contract was terminable on three months' notice and that Bonfiglioli was dissatisfied with the Australian arrangements and wished to engage in local assembly, it is reasonable to conclude that, in all likelihood, the Warman distributorship would not have endured for much longer in any event. That seems to have been the view of the trial judge from the findings he made. No doubt Dwyer's disloyal machinations played a part in Bonfiglioli's disenchantment with Warman. At the same time, it seems fairly clear that the relationship between Warman and Bonfiglioli was not mutually enthusiastic and that the association was destined to end.

Precisely when it would have ended were it not for Dwyer's breach of fiduciary obligation is unclear. Earlier in these reasons we set out the findings of the trial judge as they bear on that issue. It seems to us that his Honour, when his findings are properly understood, valued the Bonfiglioli distributorship business in the [566] hands of Warman by reference to one year's profits on the basis that, taking account of the various contingencies including the remote possibility that the agency might have continued indefinitely, the distributorship, in all likelihood, would have remained on foot for a further year but no more. That view about what would have happened in the absence of Dwyer's breach of fiduciary obligation was certainly open to his Honour. It should be accepted as correct.

That means that the immediate detriment sustained by Warman by reason of Dwyer's breach of fiduciary obligation, was the loss of an agency (i.e., the Bonfiglioli agency) which, on the probabilities, would otherwise have survived for, but only for, a further year. The advantage gained by BTA (and, indirectly, by Dwyer as a shareholder in BTA) from Dwyer's breach of fiduciary duty was not, however, confined to profits or other financial benefits directly attributable to the carrying on of the Bonfiglioli agency during the year following the termination of Warman's distribution agreement. Dwyer's breach of fiduciary duty included, to the knowledge of BTA, the persuasion of employees of Warman to leave Warman and join BTA. It was on the basis of the acquisition of the Bonfiglioli agency that the entitlement to assemble the Bonfiglioli products locally was acquired and exploited by BTA. In so far as ETA is concerned, the associated distributorship business of that company was likewise established upon the basis of BTA's acquisition of the Bonfiglioli agency.

If all of the issued shares in BTA were owned by Dwyer, it might be difficult to reach any conclusion other than that the whole of BTA's assembly and distributorship business had been built upon Dwyer's breach of fiduciary duty. On balance, however, it seems to us that the fact that BTA was half owned by the Bonfiglioli interests precludes that conclusion in the circumstances of this case. As has been mentioned, the local goodwill associated with the Bonfiglioli products had always remained the property of Bonfiglioli. Warman was entitled to exploit that local goodwill only during the period of its distributorship. Warman's agency had not extended at all to the local assembly of the Bonfiglioli products. Realistically, the main basis of BTA's business was what Bonfiglioli had always retained and been entitled to exploit, namely, the local goodwill of the Bonfiglioli products after the termination of Warman's agency and the right to assemble those products locally. Nonetheless, the fact remains that BTA knowingly benefited from Dwyer's breach of fiduciary duty in the manner and to the extent which has been indicated above. In these circumstances, the appropriate approach is to see BTA's business as built, to the extent of that benefit, upon Dwyer's breach of fiduciary duty but [567] otherwise upon Bonfiglioli's ownership of local goodwill and local assembly rights. Similarly, ETA's business, being complementary to BTA's business, can properly be seen as indirectly and correspondingly based upon those foundations.

Once that is accepted, as in our opinion it must be, it seems to us that the appropriate order for an account is an order which is restricted to requiring an account of the profits of BTA's and ETA's business for a limited initial period. The critical question is what is the appropriate duration of that limited initial period. The starting point must be the finding that, were it not for Dwyer's breach of fiduciary duty, Warman's Bonfiglioli distributorship would probably have continued for, but only for, a further period of one year. Clearly, any order against BTA for an account of profits must encompass an account on an appropriate basis for any profits earned by it from the exploitation of the Bonfiglioli agency during that period. Such an order must, however, take account of other advantages knowingly gained by BTA by reason of Dwyer's breach of fiduciary obligation. As has been said, the entitlement to assemble the Bonfiglioli products locally was based upon the Bonfiglioli agency. More important, the acquisition of the services of former Warman employees through Dwyer's breach of fiduciary obligation enabled BTA effectively to take over the limited goodwill of Warman's agency business (as distinct from the local goodwill of the Bonfiglioli products) and to derive benefits from the experience, contacts and know-how of those employees. Those benefits would, at least to some extent, have endured beyond the initial one year period.

As has been indicated, the basis upon which an account of profits should be taken is often extremely difficult to determine in practice. It is so in the present case. Indeed, what is required in the present case is essentially what Lord Wilberforce described as a 'judicial estimation of the available indications'. However, even after making full allowance for the limits of judicial discretion, it appears to us that the learned trial judge's order requiring accounts of four years' profits plus payment of a purchase price for goodwill at the end of that period went beyond what is fair and equitable in the circumstances. It seems to us that, in all the circumstances and in the context of what is said in the following two paragraphs, the adequate and appropriate period in respect of which an account of BTA's profits should be ordered is a total period of two years. An [568] account of profits in respect of that period would, in our view, clearly cover the whole of the benefits acquired by BTA through Dwyer's breach of fiduciary duty. It follows from what has been said above that the period of two years is also the appropriate period in respect of which an account of profits should be ordered against ETA.

In deciding which of the two approaches discussed by Upjohn J in In re Jarvis (decd) should be applied, it is relevant to ascertain the relationship of the distributorship business as it was carried on by Warman and as it was later carried on by BTA and ETA. The local assembly aspect of the business of Bonfiglioli was new but it was relatively small in comparison with the whole, employing only one man full-time and a couple of part-time helpers. There were differences in the complementary agencies and there was a substantial increase in the level of stock maintained by the respondents compared with the level maintained by Warman. Despite these differences, the distributorship business conducted by Warman — importation of Bonfiglioli components — became the core business of BTA. The question whether a particular business acquired by a defendant as a result of misuse of his position is sufficiently the same as that formerly conducted by the plaintiff is essentially a question of fact. In the present case, Dwyer was asked in cross-examination:

> Would it be fair to say that the business operated by BTA and ETA has been carved out of the business that was operated by the Queensland branch of the engineering agency division of Warman?

He replied:

> Generally, yes.

That answer accords with the evidence as a whole.

In these circumstances, the respondents should be ordered to account on the basis of the approach less favourable to them; they must account for the entirety of the net profits of the businesses before tax less an appropriate allowance for expenses, skill, expertise, effort and resources contributed by them. There is insufficient material before this Court to determine what that allowance should be. Nor is it possible to adopt the trial judge's approach that the appropriate order is for an account of one-half of the profits of the relevant years since that approach was based, to some extent, on his Honour's conclusion that the account should be [569] only in respect of 'the proportion of the defendants' business which flowed to them by reason of the breach'.

[...]

Conclusion

In the result and subject to what is said in the preceding paragraph, we would allow the appeal and set aside the orders made by the Court of Appeal. In lieu thereof, we would allow the appeal to that Court, set aside the orders made by the trial judge other than the orders for costs and order that the matter be remitted to enable accounts to be taken of the profits made by the businesses conducted by BTA and ETA in their first two years of operation, which appear to be the two years commencing on 12 September 1988, that being the date on which the joint venture agreement between Bonfiglioli, BTA and the Dwyers was executed. It will be for the trial judge to determine the amount of interest accruing on the amount due, after making due allowance for the expenses, skill, expertise, efforts, capital and resources contributed by the respondents. That part of the amount found due on the taking of the account which relates to BTA's profits (together with interest thereon) should be secured by an equitable charge over the assets of BTA and that part of that amount which relates to ETA's profits (together with interest thereon) should be secured by an equitable charge over the assets of that company. The respondents should be ordered to pay the costs of the appellants in this Court. The orders for costs made in the courts below should remain undisturbed. The costs of the taking of the accounts should be in the discretion of the Supreme Court.

Australian Building and Construction Commissioner v Construction, Forestry, Mining and Energy Union (2018) 262 CLR 157

Facts and issues

This case concerned section 348 of the *Fair Work Act 2009* (Cth) (FWA), according to which 'A person must not organise or take, or threaten to organise or take, any action against another person with intent to coerce the other person, or a third person, to engage in industrial activity.' In 2013, Mr Myles, an officer of the Construction, Forestry, Mining and Energy Union (CFMEU) blocked a pour at a construction site demanding that there be a CFMEU delegate on the site. The primary judge found against Mr Myles and the CFMEU, who admitted to contravening section 348 FWA. The primary judge also made a non-indemnification order under section 545(1) FWA, stating that the CFMEU 'must not directly or indirectly indemnify' Mr Myles against penalty 'in whole or in part, whether by agreement, or by making a payment to the Commonwealth, or by making any other payment or reimbursement, or howsoever otherwise'. The Full Court held that the primary judge had no power under s 545(1) to make that latter order.

Decision

The appeal was allowed. The High Court agreed with the Full Court and further held that under s 546, the Full Court had the implied power to give Mr Myle an order barring him from seeking or accepting an indemnity from CFMEU. Per Keane, Nettle and Gordon JJ at 190:

> **The correct construction of s 545(1)**
>
> ***(i) Preventative, remedial and compensatory orders***
>
> As Jessup J observed in the Full Court, it assists in the construction of s 545(1) to have regard to its legislative history. But the starting point of the process must be the text of s 545(1) read in the context of the *Fair Work Act* as a whole and, in particular, in light of s 546. So approached, the first and most immediate point of [191] significance is the breadth of the terms in which s 545(1) empowers the court to make any order the court considers appropriate. What is 'appropriate' for the purpose of s 545(1) falls to be determined in light of the purpose of the section and is not to be artificially limited. As the ABCC submitted, such broad terms of empowerment are constrained only by limitations that are strictly required by the language and purpose of the section. To adopt and adapt the language of Flick J in *Transport Workers' Union of Australia, NSW Branch v No Fuss Liquid Waste Pty Ltd*, the object and purpose of the power under s 545(1) is quite separate and distinct from that of the power under s 546 to order that a contravener pay a pecuniary penalty.
>
> The second point of significance is contextual, and it points the other way. It will be observed that all of the example orders listed in s 545(2) are directed to preventing the occurrence of an apprehended contravention, remedying the effects of a committed contravention or compensating victims of a contravention for the consequences of the contravention. None of the example orders is penal. That suggests that the types of orders that may be regarded as 'appropriate' within the meaning of s 545(1) are limited to preventative, remedial or compensatory orders, or at least do not include penal orders.
>
> The third point dovetails with the second. As was earlier set out, the chapeau to s 545(2) expressly provides that the sub-section does not limit s 545(1). Standing alone, that could be taken to mean that s 545(2) does not in any way limit the scope of s 545(1). If so, it would permit of the possibility that s 545(1) extends to 'appropriate' penal orders, notwithstanding that the example orders in s 545(2) are not penal. But, read in the context of s 545 as a whole, and particularly in light of the absence from s 545 of any explicit or apparently implicit suggestion of a penal purpose, the stipulation that s 545(2) does not limit s 545(1) presents as more likely to mean that the preventative, remedial and compensatory orders instanced in s 545(2) do not limit [192] the range of preventative, remedial and compensatory orders open to be made under s 545(1).
>
> The fourth point is also contextual and it augments the third. Critically, the only form of penal order to which the *Fair Work Act* specifically refers is a pecuniary penalty order; and s 546 is the only provision of the *Fair Work Act* that expressly provides for the imposition of pecuniary penalty orders. That strongly implies that s 546 is the sole repository of the power to make penal orders and, in turn, that provides powerful support for the conclusion that orders appropriately made under s 545(1) are limited to preventative, remedial and compensatory orders.
>
> The fifth point draws on the historical context to which Jessup J referred. As his Honour observed, given the legislative antecedents of s 545(1), it is less than likely that the expression 'any order the court considers appropriate' was designed radically to alter the preventative, remedial and compensatory nature of the power for which the legislative antecedents of s 545(1) had long provided by introducing a power to make penal orders. And as Jessup J also observed, it is significant that there is no mention in the extrinsic materials of any such intention. Seen, therefore, against the background of the provision's legislative history, it presents as more probable that the purpose of conferring a free-standing power to make any

order considered to be 'appropriate' was to delimit the scope of preventative, remedial and compensatory orders open to be made under that provision. That observation also provides support for the conclusion that s 546 is the sole repository of the power to make penal orders.

The sixth point concerns the stipulation in s 546(5) that, to avoid doubt, a court may make a pecuniary penalty order in addition to one or more orders made under s 545. Ex facie that stipulation is equivocal. But, contrary to the ABCC's submissions, on closer examination it does not suggest that s 545(1) enables the making of penal orders. As authority shows, the purpose and effect of s 546(5) is to make clear that a court may impose a pecuniary penalty under s 546 [193] notwithstanding that it may also have made, or proposes to make, preventative, remedial and compensatory orders under s 545.

The final consideration is s 564 of the *Fair Work Act*. Section 23 of the *Federal Court of Australia Act* empowers the Federal Court to make such orders as it considers 'appropriate' to be made in the exercise of its jurisdiction and powers, as an incident of the general grant to it as a superior court of law and equity of the jurisdiction to deal with such matters. The power conferred by s 23 extends to making orders necessary to ensure the effective exercise of the determination of a matter and orders reasonably required or legally ancillary to ensuring that the court's order is effective according to its tenor. But the power conferred by s 23 does not extend to making penal orders. Consequently, the fact that s 564 provides that nothing in the *Fair Work Act* limits the orders that may be made under s 23 of the *Federal Court of Australia Act* does not suggest that the power conferred by s 545(1) extends to making penal orders. Rather, s 564 serves to make clear that the range of preventative, remedial and compensatory orders which may be made under s 545 does not, by implication, restrict the range of non-penal orders open to be made under s 23.

In the result, despite the breadth of the power conferred by s 545(1), it should be concluded that it is limited to making appropriate preventative, remedial and compensatory orders and as such does not include a power to make penal orders.

(ii) Nature of a non-indemnification order

The question then is whether a non-indemnification order of the kind in issue is a preventative, remedial or compensatory order within the ambit of s 545(1) or whether it is to be conceived of as penal and thus beyond the ambit of the power conferred by that provision.

As the ABCC submitted, the non-indemnification order did not increase the penalty imposed on Myles. It was and remains a penalty of $18,000. Nor did it increase the penalty imposed on the CFMEU, which was and remains a penalty of $60,000. And, although the non-indemnification order was calculated to deter Myles and, through him, the CFMEU from committing further contraventions of the civil remedy provisions of the *Fair Work Act*, the fact that an order is designed to deter future contraventions does not necessarily make it a [194] penal order. For example, an order that an employer submit its employment records to regular auditing might be calculated to deter the employer from committing contraventions of civil remedy provisions prohibiting the underpayment of employee entitlements. But it could not be regarded as a penal order. Likewise, the fact that an order 'touches upon' a pecuniary penalty does not necessarily mean that it is a penal order. For example, an asset preservation order may be designed to ensure that funds are available to meet a pecuniary penalty order but it could not itself be regarded as a penal order.

By contrast, however, a non-indemnification order of the kind in issue not only is directly connected to the pecuniary penalty order in respect of which it is made, but also serves to maintain the sting or burden of the pecuniary penalty order by prohibiting a pass-through of liability. In those respects, it is as much a penal order as an order that a pecuniary penalty be paid on terms, or that a pecuniary penalty be suspended pending compliance with an undertaking to desist from further contravention, or that a pecuniary penalty be payable only in the event of a failure to comply with an undertaking, or that a pecuniary penalty shall become payable only upon the happening of an identified event.

There are a number of cases in the Federal Court and the Federal Circuit Court (and in the latter's predecessor) in which orders as to the terms and conditions on which pecuniary penalties are payable, or which had the effect of suspending the operation of pecuniary penalty orders, were purportedly made under s 545(1). As will be explained, those orders are better conceived of as sustained by power implicit in s 546 to do what is reasonably required for, or legally ancillary to, the accomplishment of the specific remedy of pecuniary penalties for which s 546 provides. Since s 545 is confined to preventative, remedial and compensatory orders, it does not support the making of a non-indemnification order in respect of a pecuniary penalty because such an order is properly understood as a penal order. Likewise, despite the breadth of s 23 of the *Federal Court of Australia Act*, given that s 23 does not extend to making penal orders, it will not support the making of a non-indemnification order in respect of a pecuniary penalty.

[...]

[196] Certainly, the power expressly conferred by s 546 is limited to making an order that a person 'pay a pecuniary penalty'. But, as has been observed, the express grant of power carries with it implied power to do everything necessary for the effective exercise of the power to impose a pecuniary penalty; and thus implied power to make such further orders as are reasonably required for, or legally ancillary to, the accomplishment of the deterrent effect that the penalty is calculated to achieve. Thus, for example, as counsel for Myles and the CFMEU rightly conceded, where a contravener is subjected to a pecuniary penalty, s 546 imports an implied power to accomplish the effect which the penalty is calculated to achieve by ordering, say, that the penalty be paid on terms; or paid conditionally upon a specified occurrence; or paid in default of compliance with an identified requirement.

Parity of reasoning dictates that s 546 also imports implied power to achieve the effect which a pecuniary penalty is calculated to achieve by ordering that a contravener pay the penalty personally; or where, as here, joint contraveners are ordered to pay pecuniary penalties in respect of certain contraventions — each according to his, her or its relative share of responsibility for the contravention — implied power to achieve the relative degrees of sting or burden determined by the judge by ordering that neither contravener seek or accept indemnity or [197] contribution from the other. The implied power to make a personal payment order is closely analogous to the court's power to order a contemnor to pay a fine personally, and an order that joint contraveners not indemnify each other in respect of the penalties imposed on each of them is essentially similar.

Given that s 546 expressly empowers the court to order a specific person to pay a pecuniary penalty, it is no stretch to accept that there is power in s 546 to make orders designed to ensure that the person against whom the order is made cannot avoid the incidence of the penalty. It is to take too narrow a view of the purpose of s 546 to regard the provision as being concerned with no more than that an amount of money be paid by someone in discharge of a debt created by order of the court. Section 546 is not about the creation and collection of debts; it is about penalising a contravention of the law. It is to take too narrow a view of the extent of the power conferred by s 546 to deny that it extends to the making of orders designed to ensure that a particular person cannot defeat the purpose of an order that the person pay the penalty imposed on him or her.

Myles and the CFMEU contended that it could not be reasoned by analogy with the court's power to punish for contempt that the court has implied power under s 546 to make a personal payment order prohibiting a contravener from seeking or accepting indemnity in respect of a pecuniary penalty. Counsel for Myles and the CFMEU invoked an observation of Jessup J in the Full Court, in relation to s 545(1), that the power to punish for contempt is different because in the case of contempt the court is:

> exercising its jurisdiction, as a superior court of record, to punish for contempt, and to do so effectively. It [is] not concerned with the extent of the power given by a specific statutory provision, as we are here.

That argument should be rejected. In *Australian Building Construction Employees' and Builders Labourers' Federation v Minister of State for Industrial Relations*, the power to punish for contempt was the statutory power accorded to the Federal Court by s 31 of the *Federal Court of Australia Act*: a power analogous to that possessed by the High Court to make an order that is just. The [198] trial judge in that case (Keely J) determined that the punishment that was just in relation to the Federation was a fine of $15,000. To make the punishment effective, his Honour further ordered that the Federation pay the fine personally or by an agent properly authorised in writing. On appeal to the Full Court, Evatt and Deane JJ saw no reason to interfere with the further order and observed that it could well serve as a model in the future. The considerations that apply in this case, although different, are logically comparable. The power to impose a pecuniary penalty under s 546 is a statutory power to impose such penalty as is considered to be just. The penalty that the primary judge considered to be just in Myles' case was a pecuniary penalty of $18,000. As has been explained, s 546 imports an implied power to make such further orders as are reasonably required for, or legally ancillary to, the accomplishment of the effect that the pecuniary penalty is calculated to achieve. In this case, the primary judge considered that, in order to accomplish the deterrent effect which the penalty of $18,000 was calculated to achieve, it was necessary to order that Myles not be indemnified by the CFMEU in respect of that penalty. Accordingly, although it was not the course her Honour took, it would have been open to the primary judge in exercise of the power conferred by s 546 to make a personal payment order prohibiting Myles from seeking or receiving indemnity from the CFMEU.

Australian Consumer Law ss 229, 230, 232(6), 236, 237, 243(b), (d), 247, 260

229 Indemnification of officers

(1) A body corporate (the *first body*), or a body corporate related to the first body, commits an offence if it indemnifies a person (whether by agreement or by making a payment and whether directly or through an interposed entity) against either of the following liabilities incurred as an officer (within the meaning of the *Corporations Act 2001*) of the first body:

(a) a liability to pay a pecuniary penalty under section 224;

(b) legal costs incurred in defending or resisting proceedings in which the person is found to have such a liability.

Penalty: $2,750.

(2) For the purposes of subsection (1), the outcome of proceedings is the outcome of the proceedings and any appeal in relation to the proceedings.

230 Certain indemnities not authorised and certain documents void

(1) Section 229 does not authorise anything that would otherwise be unlawful.

(2) Anything that purports to indemnify a person against a liability is void to the extent that it contravenes section 229.

[...]

Division 2 — Injunctions

232 Injunctions

[...]

(6) Without limiting subsection (1), the court may grant an injunction under that subsection requiring a person to do any of the following:

(a) refund money;

(b) transfer property;

(c) honour a promise;

(d) destroy or dispose of goods.

[. . .]

Division 3 — Damages

236 Actions for damages

(1) If:

(a) a person (the *claimant*) suffers loss or damage because of the conduct of another person; and

(b) the conduct contravened a provision of Chapter 2 or 3;

the claimant may recover the amount of the loss or damage by action against that other person, or against any person involved in the contravention.

(2) An action under subsection (1) may be commenced at any time within 6 years after the day on which the cause of action that relates to the conduct accrued.

Division 4 — Compensation orders etc. for injured persons and orders for non-party consumers

Subdivision A — Compensation orders etc. for injured persons

237 Compensation orders etc. on application by an injured person or the regulator

(1) A court may:

(a) on application of a person (the *injured person*) who has suffered, or is likely to suffer, loss or damage because of the conduct of another person that:

(i) was engaged in a contravention of a provision of Chapter 2, 3 or 4; or

(ii) constitutes applying or relying on, or purporting to apply or rely on, a term of a contract that has been declared under section 250 to be an unfair term; or

(b) on the application of the regulator made on behalf of one or more such injured persons;

make such order or orders as the court thinks appropriate against the person who engaged in the conduct, or a person involved in that conduct.

Note 1: For applications for an order or orders under this subsection, see section 242.

Note 2: The orders that the court may make include all or any of the orders set out in section 243.

(2) The order must be an order that the court considers will:

(a) compensate the injured person, or any such injured persons, in whole or in part for the loss or damage; or

(b) prevent or reduce the loss or damage suffered, or likely to be suffered, by the injured person or any such injured persons.

(3) An application under subsection (1) may be made at any time within 6 years after the day on which:

(a) if subsection (1)(a)(i) applies—the cause of action that relates to the conduct referred to in that subsection accrued; or

(b) if subsection (1)(a)(ii) applies—the declaration referred to in that subsection is made.

[. . .]

Subdivision C — Miscellaneous

243 Kinds of orders that may be made

Without limiting section 237(1), 238(1) or 239(1), the orders that a court may make under any of those sections against a person (the *respondent*) include all or any of the following:

[. . .]

(b) an order:

(i) varying such a contract or arrangement in such manner as is specified in the order; and

(ii) if the court thinks fit–declaring the contract or arrangement to have had effect as so varied on and after such date as is specified in the order (which may be a date that is before the date on which the order is made);

[. . .]

(d) an order directing the respondent to refund money or return property to the injured person;

[. . .]

247 Adverse publicity orders

(1) A court may, on application of the regulator, make an adverse publicity order in relation to a person who:

(a) has contravened a provision of Part 2-2 or Chapter 3; or

(b) has committed an offence against Chapter 4.

(2) An *adverse publicity order* in relation to a person is an order that requires the person:

(a) to disclose, in the way and to the persons specified in the order, such information as is so specified, being information that the person has possession of or access to; and

(b) to publish, at the person's expense and in the way specified in the order, an advertisement in the terms specified in, or determined in accordance with, the order.

(3) This section does not limit a court's powers under any other provision of this Schedule.

[. . .]

Part 5-4 — Remedies relating to guarantees

Division 1 — Action against suppliers

Subdivision A — Action against suppliers of goods

[. . .]

260 When a failure to comply with a guarantee is a major failure

A failure to comply with a guarantee referred to in section 259(1)(b) that applies to a supply of goods is a *major failure* if:

(a) the goods would not have been acquired by a reasonable consumer fully acquainted with the nature and extent of the failure; or

(b) the goods depart in one or more significant respects:

(i) if they were supplied by description–from that description; or

(ii) if they were supplied by reference to a sample or demonstration model–from that sample or demonstration model; or

(c) the goods are substantially unfit for a purpose for which goods of the same kind are commonly supplied and they cannot, easily and within a reasonable time, be remedied to make them fit for such a purpose; or

(d) the goods are unfit for a disclosed purpose that was made known to:
  (i) the supplier of the goods; or
  (ii) a person by whom any prior negotiations or arrangements in relation to the acquisition of the goods were conducted or made;
  and they cannot, easily and within a reasonable time, be remedied to make them fit for such a purpose; or

(e) the goods are not of acceptable quality because they are unsafe.

Federal Court of Australia Act 1976 (Cth) s 21

Declarations of right

(1) The Court may, in civil proceedings in relation to a matter in which it has original jurisdiction, make binding declarations of right, whether or not any consequential relief is or could be claimed.

(2) A suit is not open to objection on the ground that a declaratory order only is sought.

Supreme Court Act 1935 (SA) s 17

Part 2 — Jurisdiction and powers of the court
Division 1 — Jurisdiction
17 — General jurisdiction

(1) The court shall be a court of law and equity.

(2) There shall be vested in the court—
  (a) the like jurisdiction, in and for the State, as was formerly vested in, or capable of being exercised by, all or any of the courts in England, following: [...]

Limitation Act 1969 (NSW) s 14(1)(a)

14 General

(1) An action on any of the following causes of action is not maintainable if brought after the expiration of a limitation period of six years running from the date on which the cause of action first accrues to the plaintiff or to a person through whom the plaintiff claims:
  (a) a cause of action founded on contract (including quasi contract) not being a cause of action founded on a deed, [...]

QUESTION

Why, in *Australian Building and Construction Commissioner v Construction, Forestry, Mining and Energy Union* (2018) 262 CLR 157, did the High Court hold that, under s 546, the Full Court had the implied power to give Mr Myles an order barring him from seeking or accepting an indemnity from the CFMEU?

3.5 Choice of law

Factor	Short explanation	Relevant authorities	*Principles* text*
By 'choice of law' it is meant both the proper law of the contract and which court(s) has (have) jurisdiction over the dispute	The parties have a considerable degree of freedom in determining the law of contract and jurisdiction, but there also are mandatory provisions	*Oceanic Sun Line Special Shipping Co Inc v Fay* (1988) 165 CLR 197 *Service and Execution of Process Act 1992* (Cth) ss 15, 20	Chapter 3: 3.22

* Consult the corresponding section(s) of the *Principles* text for more detail.

For a detailed discussion of the topic, see Chapter 3 of the *Principles* text. Below are extracts of some of the provisions and cases mentioned in the latter.

Oceanic Sun Line Special Shipping Co Inc v Fay (1988) 165 CLR 197

Facts and issues

Dr Fay brought proceedings in the New South Wales Supreme Court against Oceanic for the injuries he incurred during a cruise in Greece. The issue arose as to whether the Supreme Court had jurisdiction over the dispute as while the ticket had been purchased in New South Wales, according to the clauses printed on it, any action against Oceanic had to be brought in Athens. Dr Fay was not given a copy of the terms and conditions prior to entering into the contract. Dr Fay was only given the opportunity to either inspect the ticket at a Oceanic office or get one once in Athens. A reference to the ticket's clauses was only made in the brochure Dr Faye had been shown by the travel agent. However, Dr Faye did not read it, nor did the agent have a sample ticket to show.

Decision

The case represented an opportunity to determine whether the English doctrine of *forum non conveniens* applies, as summarised by Lord Goff in *Spiliada Maritime Corporation v Cansulex Ltd*

[1986] 3 WLR 972, 983. According to the doctrine, a court does not have jurisdiction if there is a more appropriate forum for the parties. The High Court's majority, including Deane J, held that the 'clearly inappropriate' forum test applies instead. The appeal was dismissed.

Per Deane J at 252:

> There are three main reference points to which regard should be paid in deciding whether the United Kingdom doctrine [of forum *non conveniens*] should be accepted as the law of this country. They are legal principle, decided authority and policy.
>
> [. . .]
>
> [253]. When one turns to policy, the position seems to me to be not clear. Obviously, there is considerable force in the approach that if the tribunals of another country provide a more appropriate forum for the determination of a claim, it should not be brought in this country in the absence of some good and sufficient reason (cf. per Lord Denning M.R., *MacShannon v. Rockware Glass Ltd.* (1977) 1 WLR 376, at p 380; 2 All ER 449, at pp 451–452). The factors of public interest convenience, to which the United States (but not the United Kingdom) courts would seem to be giving increasing weight, are likewise of some cogency. The costs of the administration of justice are high and judicial resources are limited. In this country, as in the United States, court lists in many jurisdictions are congested, most judges are overworked and justice is far too often delayed. There is much to be said for the view that the courts (including jurors) should not be troubled by actions which would more appropriately be brought in some foreign tribunal. The consideration of the overall balance of private convenience to the actual parties prima facie favours a rule that a plaintiff should be required to litigate in the most appropriate forum. Finally, international comity supports the approach that the courts of this country should refrain from hearing actions in circumstances corresponding to those in which courts of other countries would refrain from entertaining them on the ground that they should more appropriately be brought in Australia.
>
> [254] Some of the above policy considerations (e.g. the workload of judges) are not, however, of the kind which are usually taken into account by Australian courts in formulating principles of law. More important, policy considerations do not all point in the one direction. The desirability of a plaintiff bringing an action in the most appropriate court does not obliterate the undesirability of further expanding the scope of a discretion to refuse to exercise competent jurisdiction. Apart from considerations of principle, any further expansion of that discretion is likely to lead to increased uncertainty for litigants and more litigation about where to litigate. The force of the argument based on public interest convenience is difficult to assess in circumstances where there is nothing before the court to suggest that there would be more than a small number of actions brought in this country which would survive the traditional test but which would nevertheless have been more appropriately brought in some foreign tribunal. The strength of the appeal to judicial comity is also difficult to assess in circumstances where some leading western countries, particularly in relation to actions by their own residents, decline to observe even the judicial restraint shown by common law courts under traditional doctrine (see, e.g., Professor Friedrich Juenger, 'Judicial Jurisdiction in the United States and in the European Communities: A Comparison', Michigan Law Review, vol.82 (1984), 1195, esp. at pp.1204–1205). Moreover, if one turns from what is praised as judicial comity to what is condemned as judicial chauvinism, it seems that the broader forum non conveniens discretion is liable to bring with it the notion that '(c)itizens or residents deserve somewhat more deference than foreign plaintiffs' (see Piper Aircraft, at p 256, n.23). The effect of the adoption of that approach in Piper Aircraft was concisely identified (at p 262) by Stevens J. (with the concurrence of Brennan J.) in dissent as being that 'Pennsylvania was not a convenient forum in which to litigate a claim

against a Pennsylvania company that a plane was defectively designed and manufactured in Pennsylvania'. At least, any judicial chauvinism which might, in earlier times, have been implicit in traditional principle was well intentioned towards the foreign plaintiff.

The conclusion to which I have come in relation to the arguments based on policy is that they are persuasive but not compelling. In my [255] view, they are not sufficiently strong to warrant a decision by this Court to depart from existing principle and authority at least at this stage of the development of the law. If the law of this country is to be changed in that regard, it seems to me to be preferable that it be done by legislation enacted after full inquiry and informed assessment of international as well as domestic considerations of a kind which this Court is not equipped to make of its own initiative (cf. per Black J., dissenting, *Gulf Oil Corp. v. Gilbert*, at p 517). Such legislation could lay down comprehensive rules and guidelines and could avoid the judicial discretion to stay or dismiss proceedings on inappropriate forum grounds being undesirably unconfined. Accordingly, I would not alter established principle in favour of a judicial adoption of the broader forum non conveniens doctrine.

Service and Execution of Process Act 1992 (Cth) ss 15, 20

Part 2 — Service of process in civil and criminal proceedings
Division 1 — Initiating process in civil proceedings

[...]

Section 15 Initiating process may be served in any part of Australia

(1) An initiating process issued in a State may be served in another State.

(2) Service on an individual must be effected in the same way as service of such an initiating process in the place of issue.

(3) Service on a company or a registered body must be effected in accordance with section 9.

(4) Service on any other body corporate must be effected in accordance with section 10.

(5) Service on a body politic (for example, the Commonwealth or a State) must be effected in the same way in which process of the Supreme Court of the State in which service is to be effected may be served on the body politic.

[...]

Section 20 Stay of proceedings

(1) This section does not apply in relation to a proceeding in which the Supreme Court of a State is the court of issue.

(2) The person served may apply to the court of issue for an order staying the proceeding.

(3) The court may order that the proceeding be stayed if it is satisfied that a court of another State that has jurisdiction to determine all the matters in issue between the parties is the appropriate court to determine those matters.

(4) The matters that the court is to take into account in determining whether that court of another State is the appropriate court for the proceeding include:

   (a) the places of residence of the parties and of the witnesses likely to be called in the proceeding; and

   (b) the place where the subject matter of the proceeding is situated; and

(c) the financial circumstances of the parties, so far as the court is aware of them; and
(d) any agreement between the parties about the court or place in which the proceeding should be instituted; and
(e) the law that would be most appropriate to apply in the proceeding; and
(f) whether a related or similar proceeding has been commenced against the person served or another person;

but do not include the fact that the proceeding was commenced in the place of issue.

(5) The court's order may be made subject to such conditions as the court considers just and appropriate in order to facilitate determination of the matter in issue without delay or undue expense.

(6) The court may determine the application for an order without a hearing unless the applicant or a party objects.

(7) For the purposes of determining the application, the court may hold a hearing by audio link or audiovisual link.

(8) A person who is entitled to practise as a barrister, solicitor or both before a court in:
(a) the place of issue; or
(b) another State in which a person is participating in the hearing by audio link or audiovisual link;

has a right of audience before the court at the hearing.

(9) This section does not affect the court's power to stay a proceeding on a ground other than the ground mentioned in subsection (3).

(10) This section does not affect the operation of:
(a) the *Jurisdiction of Courts (Cross-vesting) Act 1987*; or
(b) a corresponding law of a State.

QUESTION

What it is meant by proper law of contract and what was held in *Oceanic Sun Line Special Shipping Co Inc v Fay* (1988) 165 CLR 197?

3.6 International perspectives

Australian arbitration law is largely modelled on the 1985 UNCITRAL Model Law on International Commercial Arbitration (amended 2006), as mentioned above. This means that Australian law in relation to both domestic and international commercial arbitrations is essentially internationalised. Choice of law is discussed above. It should be noted that, in relation to cross-border commercial sales contracts, art 1(1)(a) of the *CISG* will apply if both parties are from *CISG* Member States. Furthermore, art 1(1)(b) of the *CISG* will apply if the conflict of laws rule of the forum (eg an Australian court) lead to the law of a country which is a CISG Member State. This will mean that, in most situations, the *CISG* will apply by default. However, parties still enjoy autonomy to opt out, which they can do by agreement to exclude application of the *CISG*, usually by way of a clause to that effect: art 6 *CISG* (see **25.4.1.1**).

3.7 Review

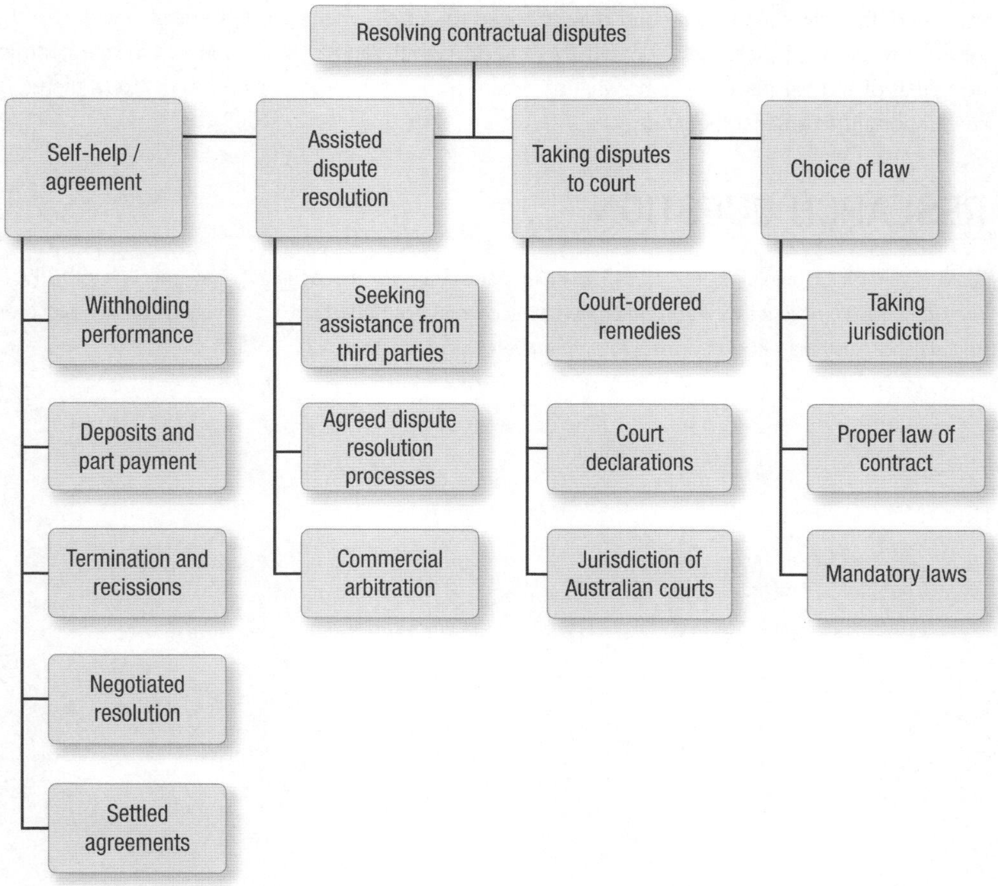

- There are various methods by which the parties to a contract can solve disputes over the meaning, effect, and performance of the contract.
- Several options are available, depending on what occurred and what remedies are being sought.
- If the parties wish to take their dispute to court, they need to take into account different legislative and judicial sources at both the Federal and local levels.
- Under the freedom to contract doctrine, the parties have a considerable degree of freedom in determining the law of contract and jurisdiction, but there also are mandatory provisions.

TIPS FOR APPLYING THE LAW IN PRACTICE

Resolving contractual disputes is no easy task. Several factors ought to be considered alongside the parties' intention at the time the contract was entered into and when the dispute arose. First, it requires a careful interpretation (that is, construction) of the contractual terms. Second, a solid understanding of local and federal provisions is also required. Both tasks require time and experience. A good example is the procedure regarding the identification of the proper law of the contract. Identifying such law through contractual interpretation (ie by interpreting the contract's express and implied terms) is not the end of the matter. A forum court may still need to decide whether a statute that operates in the forum is to be regarded as having mandatory effect, notwithstanding the proper law of the contract being that of another place. Knowing what has been ruled in past decisions on this matter is therefore very important to an effective strategy.

RESEARCH QUESTION

Read James McLachlan, 'Forum Non Conveniens and Stays of Proceedings in Australia' (1990) 49(1) *The Cambridge Law Journal* 37 and outline what, according to McLachlan, is the real difference between English and Australian courts on the *forum non conveniens* doctrine.

PART II

MAKING A CONTRACT

4

PREPARING TO MAKE A CONTRACT

4.1 Overview

This chapter explores the steps leading to a contractual agreement. The main purpose of the chapter is to show that there are many ways in which a contract can or should be negotiated. In the same context, attention is also paid to the authority of agents to contract on behalf of the corporation or government they represent, to the widespread use of the so-called 'standard form contracts', and to some of the conventional drafting styles, particularly in regard to commercial contracts. Finally, the chapter considers the obligations that the (future) parties to a contract are required to fulfil while negotiating.

4.2 Preparing and settling the terms

Factor	Short explanation	Relevant authorities	*Principles* text*
There are many ways to enter into a contract	A contract may be concluded orally or in writing, as well as in person or through the activity of agents Negotiations may be extensive or short, formal or informal, precise or imprecise or not even take place at all (as in the case of standard form contracts) The drafting styles vary considerably in light of the nature of the transaction as well as of the parties' intentions and interests	R Fells and N Sheer, *Effective Negotiation: From Research to Results* (Cambridge University Press, 4th ed, 2020) A Robertson, 'The Limits of Voluntariness in Contract' (2005) 29(1) *Melbourne University Law Review* 177 J Morgan, *Contract Minimalism: A Formalist Restatement of Commercial Contract Law* (Cambridge University Press, 2013) *Petersen v Moloney* (1951) 84 CLR 91 *Venuti and Venuti v Toop Real Estate Group Pty Ltd* [2004] SASC 23 *Franklins Pty Ltd v Metcash Trading Ltd* (2009) 76 NSWLR 603 *Alstom Ltd v Yokogawa Australia Pty Ltd (No 7)* [2012] SASC 49	Chapter 2: 2.02 Chapter 3: 3.07–3.09 Chapter 6: 6.03 Chapter 13: 13.01

* Consult the corresponding section(s) of the *Principles* text for more detail.

As discussed, contracts are a particular class of voluntary undertakings. At the core of this categorisation lies the doctrine of freedom of contract as epitomised by the notion of 'agreement', which is itself underpinned by those of 'enforceable promise' and 'bargain' (or 'exchange'): see **1.4**. From this, it follows that the way through which the parties to a future contract reach their agreement plays a fundamental role in determining whether or not a contract exists, and if so, their respective rights and obligations. By way of an example, the general rule is that a party will be bound by the terms of the contractual document she has signed even though she has not read its content: *L'Estrange v F Graucob Ltd* [1934] 2 KB 394. Yet exceptions apply, as in the cases of misrepresentation, fraud, or mistake: see **18.2** and **18.5**.

The first requirement to form a valid contract is an agreement. Given that agreement involves consensus and that contractual intent must be determined objectively, the rule is that agreement is reached when the offer is accepted: see **5.3**. Yet, as the estoppel doctrine makes it clear, it would be misleading to think that no obligations generate during the bargaining period: see **7.2**. An analysis of the negotiation phase serves to address the problems that arise in the pre-contractual process, as well as to contextualise the instruments available to the parties to efficiently solve them. This not only requires a discussion of the parties' bargaining strategies, but also the negotiation techniques, judicial limitations, and statutory requirements.[1] Importantly, while in the majority of cases the commercial nature of the arrangement makes it clear that the parties did intend to enter into a contractual relationship, there are situations in which this is less clear. In these cases, the court would have to take corollary events and surrounding circumstances into consideration to determine whether or not a contract exists (*Al Azhari v 27 Scott Street Pty Ltd* [2017] VSC 600, [26]).

As a general rule, a contract may be concluded orally or in writing. Certain contracts must, however, be made in writing: see **5.9**. Contracts may also be concluded in person or through the activity of agents: see **8.4**. An agent is a person who has been granted authority by the principal to act on their behalf. Corporations and governments necessarily have to make contracts through the agency of individuals. Agents may play different roles depending on the agreement they have with the principal and other requirements (*Petersen v Moloney* (1951) 84 CLR 91, extract below; *Venuti and Venuti v Toop Real Estate Group Pty Ltd* [2004] SASC 23, extract below; *Pavlovic v Universal Music Australia Pty Ltd* (2015) 90 NSWLR 605; *Malouf v Constantinou* [2017] NSWSC 923).

Negotiations may be extensive or short, formal or informal, precise or imprecise. Importantly, they may not take place at all as in the case of standard form contracts—a term which refers to those arrangements whose terms are standardised. Important examples in this category include consumer contracts, agreements for the sale of land prepared by real estate institutes or law societies, or the various building contracts prepared by Standards Australia Ltd, and the more or less standardised 'precedent banks' maintained by law firms. Given the spread and pitfalls of such mode of contracting, both the courts and the legislator have established important requirements that have to be met for a contract to be valid and have even negated the possibility to insert particular terms in the contract. Classic examples are the duty imposed

1 See Roger Fisher and William Ury, *Getting to Say Yes: Negotiating Agreement Without Giving In* (Houghton Mifflin, 1981); Chris Provis, 'Interests vs Positions: A Critique of the Distinction' (1996) 12(4) *Negotiation Journal* 305–323; Tania Sourdin, *Alternative Dispute Resolution* (Lawbook Co, 5th ed, 2016) ch 2.

on businesses to ensure their customers are given reasonable notice of the existence and content of such terms, or the unfair contract terms regulation for consumer and small business transactions: see **9.7**, **11.4**, **20.4**; see also *Insurance Contracts Act 1984* (Cth) s 35.[2]

A corollary of the doctrine of freedom of contract is that the parties are free to decide the terms of their own agreement, subject to the law prescribing otherwise. Hence, in the case of written contracts, drafting styles vary considerably; not only in light of the parties' intention and interests, but also of the overall transaction: see **5.9**, **6.2**, **9.4**, **10.2**, **11.3**, **13.2**, **14.2**, **15.1**, **16.1**, **21.1**.[3] This explains why, as set out by Morgan[4], research on individually drafted contracts is not as statistically valid as that on individually drafted contracts.

A contract will generally start by identifying the parties to the agreement. Some contracts will then go on to 'recite' the nature, origins or purposes of the transaction. Recitals of this sort may, within certain limits, be used as an aid to interpreting the operative provisions of the contract: see *Franklins v Metcash* [2009] NSWCA 407, [379]–[390], below; *Malouf v Constantinou* [2017] NSWSC 923, [90]–[93], [108]. The principal obligations of the parties will then be detailed. There may also be ancillary obligations; for example, to 'warrant' (promise) that certain things have been done or that certain assumptions may be made, or to take out insurance against specified risks. While some terms are essential to contracts of a particular kind (see: **5.9**, **16.2**), others are inserted as a matter of practice and replicate the position that the parties would obtain anyway under the general law. These include:

- *entire agreement* clauses, stipulating that the written terms operate to the exclusion of any separate documents or verbal assurances (see **9.2**);
- stipulations that *variations* may only be agreed in writing (see **13.2**);
- requirements as to the giving of *notices* by one party to the other; for example to address specified problems, or to terminate the contract;
- permission for one party to assign its rights or obligations under the contract to another party (see **Chapter 14**);
- clauses purporting to make any invalid provision *severable* from the rest of the contract (see **5.5**, **11.2**, **21.2**);
- procedures for the *resolution of disputes* arising under the contract (see **3.3**); and
- *choice of law* provisions, indicating which jurisdiction's rules are to govern the contract, and/or whose courts are to have jurisdiction if any litigation is commenced (see **3.5** and **25.2**).

2 See Australian Competition and Consumer Commission, *Unfair Contract Terms: Industry Review Outcomes* (ACCC, 2013); Australian Competition and Consumer Commission, *Unfair Terms in Small Business Contracts: A Review of Selected Industries* (ACCC, 2016).

3 See also Andrew Robertson, 'The Limits of Voluntariness in Contract' (2005) 29(1) *Melbourne University Law Review* 177–217, extract below; Julie-Anne Tarr, Anthony Tarr and Malcolm Clarke, *Insurance: The Laws of Australia* (Law Book Co, 2009) 102–104; Michael Asprey, *Plain Language for Lawyers* (Federation Press, 4th ed, 2010); Peter Butt, *Modern Legal Drafting: A Guide to Using Clearer Language* (Cambridge University Press, 3rd ed, 2013).

4 Jonathan Morgan, *Contract Minimalism: A Formalist Restatement of Commercial Contract Law* (Cambridge University Press, 2013) 213–215, extract below.

R Fells and N Sheer, *Effective Negotiation: From Research to Results*, (Cambridge University Press, 4th ed, 2020)

[3] What is negotiation?

... First, negotiation is a process — a sequence of activities or tasks that need to be worked through, tasks that will be outlined later ... Negotiation is a 'mixed-motive' interaction (Schelling 1960, p. 89); competitiveness exists because each negotiator is standing in the way of the other achieving their goal; at the same time, cooperation is needed because without the other's help neither party will achieve anything at all. Managing this mix of competitiveness and cooperativeness can be a challenge. Because negotiation is a process, negotiators constantly have to make choices about what moves to make next. These choices affect how the negotiations unfold and what the outcome will be. A good negotiator will have a preferred path — a script or storyline — that they would like the negotiation to follow. We will introduce the idea of developing a negotiation image as one way to manage this process effectively.

[4] Second, two parties are needed for a negotiation — so while a negotiator has to make choices about how they would like the negotiations to proceed, the other party is making choices too. What actually happens is the result of these choices — action and reaction — on both sides of the negotiating table. Often negotiators forget the fundamental and obvious point that negotiation is two-sided. Yet ignoring the other party is a mistake made even by effective negotiators (Sebenius 2001). As an example of the two-sidedness of negotiation and the fact that the other party has choices too, Wang, Northcraft and van Kleef (2012) found that anger expressed by a negotiator led to the other negotiator making concessions — the desired result. However, concessions were not inevitable and, as well as making a concession, negotiators often chose to retaliate. We think the other party will do what we want them to do and are surprised when they don't; this is one reason why negotiation is messy and needs managing carefully. So we must always consider the choices the other party has when deciding our own strategy and tactics. In fact, we should be 'other-directed' as soon as we start to prepare for a negotiation; this does not mean agreeing with the other party, but rather working hard to understand exactly where they are coming from on the issues under negotiation.

[...]

[6] The DNA of negotiation

What makes a negotiation work? There are several elements that might be regarded as the DNA of negotiation — elements that are hard-wired into the process of reaching an agreement and hold the negotiation together. They are integral to the strategies that negotiators can employ, and so need to be understood in order to manage the process more effectively. If any one of them is ignored, then it is likely that the negotiation will not go well. And we should be aware that they can be used but can also be abused.

Describing negotiation in terms of DNA creates an image that helps our understanding of the process. The DNA helix represents two parties who seem to be jostling for position, yet are inextricably linked — an indication of both the competitiveness and cooperation inherent in any negotiation. The twists reflect the fact [7] that negotiation is not straightforward. The links between the two strands of the DNA can be viewed as the key elements that give life and structure to a negotiation — reciprocity, trust, power, and information exchange. [...] Here we present a brief overview.

Reciprocity is a feature of many social interactions, including negotiation. What one party does tends to be matched or reciprocated by the other. This does not happen all the time, but it does occur often enough to influence the pattern and progress of the negotiation. It is an aspect of the process that can be managed.

Trust is an expectation that the other party will act in a beneficial rather than exploitative way. A lot of emphasis is placed on building trust — particularly when trying to create a cooperative negotiation — but trust is easily over-estimated, and is fragile. Thinking about trust also leads to thinking about the behavioural ethics involved in negotiation.

Information — or more often, the lack of it — is central in reaching an agreement, and so forms another link in the negotiation DNA. No matter how much negotiators prepare, there are always things that they do not know (but wish they did). Many strategies and tactics are designed to improve the negotiators' understanding of what is and is not possible as an outcome and a well-established principle is that more information leads to better outcomes (Thompson 1991). Because of this, negotiation can be viewed as a process of information exchange — particularly information about possible solutions on the one hand and walk-away alternatives on the other.

Another important feature of a negotiation is power. Paradoxically, this has a great deal to do with the potential consequence if the parties were not negotiating. The power that negotiators have relates to the alternatives open to them — ways other than negotiation to achieve their desired objectives. Negotiation can be viewed as a process whereby the alternatives that negotiators think they have are changed.

The lack of power, reflected in concern about having only a poor alternative, brings negotiators to the negotiating table and keeps them there. The level of trust between the parties determines the quality of the agreement they will then achieve. To a large extent, this trust is built through reciprocity. The basic mechanism to get to understand all this in a negotiation is information exchange.

None of these elements — reciprocity, trust, power and information — are clear-cut; nor are they mechanistic or precise. This is why negotiation is complex, relatively difficult and unpredictable. To be a good negotiator means having a practical understanding of a negotiation's DNA, which helps a negotiator to manage the process while recognising that all the uncertainty and difficulties can never be eliminated.

DNA imagery has its limitations: the two strands never meet, perhaps signifying that the parties never reach agreement. That said, having an image or script that resonates with the key aspects of the negotiation creates a mental framework to help a negotiator guide the process to an agreement.

A Robertson, 'The Limits of Voluntariness in Contract' (2005) 29(1) *Melbourne University Law Review* 177

[187] A Standard Form Contract

The first question is the extent to which standard form contracting undermines the voluntariness claim. This depends on the extent to which standard forms are used and whether the contractual obligations and curtailments of rights arising from standard forms can properly be seen as voluntary. A number of issues need to be considered. First, how widespread is the use of standard forms in contracting? Second, how often are standard forms read by the non-drafting party? Third, can voluntary obligations arise from unread terms? Fourth, to what extent is it possible to avoid known, undesirable terms of standard form contracts? Fifth, how far does the law go towards ensuring that that the obligations that arise from standard form terms are voluntary? In particular, to what extent does the law ensure that parties are not bound by terms that they have not read, terms whose implications they could not understand, or terms that are difficult or impossible to avoid in practice?

1 The Use of Standard Forms

In 1971, W David Slawson estimated that 99 per cent of all contracts were made on terms presented by one party to the other in a standard form. This estimate has since been widely accepted as an accurate assessment of the percentage of written contracts made on standard form terms. While it would be difficult for any researcher to generate meaningful data comparing the use of standard forms with the use of [188] fully negotiated contracts, personal and professional experience leads scholars who write on this topic to accept that standard forms dominate all forms of contracting, other than agreements that are wholly oral (including routine retail purchases), and non-routine commercial contracts.

2 The Failure to Read

(a) The Empirical Evidence

It is well accepted that standard form contracts are rarely read by the non-drafting party, and rarely understood on the odd occasions when they are read. Some say they are not meant to be read. The failure of consumers to read standard form contracts has been recognised by the courts in the US, the United Kingdom, Canada and Australia. Empirical evidence suggests that even businesspeople commonly fail to read standard forms.

J Morgan, *Contract Minimalism: A Formalist Restatement of Commercial Contract Law* (Cambridge University Press, 2013)

Contract terms

[213] [. . .] [A]n important source of commercial norms is the standard forms that govern various trades, as laid down by trade associations. There is of course an overlap between such standard forms and the terms of individually drafted contracts. In theory, the latter provide direct evidence of what particular parties want, or at least what their legal advisers decide is in their best interests. But there are clear drawbacks with such research. Unlike a standard form that is used in countless transactions in a given trade (or by one major corporation), an individual contract has no statistical significance and is not hallowed by usage. It may now be possible to carry out statistically rigorous studies using such resources as the archive of the University of Missouri's Contracting and Organizations Research Institute, founded in 2000 and now containing over 690,000 contracts (primarily corporate contracts filed with the US Securities and Exchange Commission). Geis suggests that automated search technology may permit such information to be analysed — so slaking the unsatisfied thirst for empirical data about contracts. Furthermore, the storage of all decided cases in electronic databases gives another promising archive of contract provisions and the courts' treatment of them. But the selection of cases to litigate to trial is an obvious source for unrepresentative sampling. Geis allows that his argument may be overoptimistic.

The dangers of *unsystematic* research are well demonstrated in the literature. A cursory examination of arguments for and against formalism reveals quite inconsistent claims about the preferred techniques of contract drafters. Prominent advocates of a formalist approach claim this is reflected in contract drafting. Scott states that: 'Sellers of complex products, for example, universally disclaim the [Uniform Commercial Code]'s merchantability standard in favour of making an [214] express warranty that precisely describes important aspects of the seller's performance obligation.' Force majeure clauses list precisely the excusing events in place of the vague frustration doctrine, and so on. Schwartz criticizes the prevalence of standards rather than rules in modern contract doctrine on the basis that parties could easily include such standards in their contracts if they wanted them – but (he claims) they do not. Similar assumptions pervade Schwartz and Scott's seminal joint article. Addressing 'contract design' directly, Eggleston, Posner and Zeckhauser claim that, contrary to the complex recommendations of economic analysis, most contracts are simple and easy to understand. Even well-resourced and professionally advised parties opt for simple contracts, they claim, exploding the standard 'transaction cost barrier' explanation for simple contracts. Other explanations are suggested: that proposing simple contracts maximizes the contract surplus (less is dissipated in haggling over the detailed terms); signals trustworthiness (whereas complexity may create fears of obfuscation or outright 'sharp practice'); or minimizes enforcement cost (limiting obligations to those that are easily verifiable). Some apparently empirical research is cited. Subsequent studies provide further support – for example, that business-to-business 'boilerplate' contracts are much shorter than those in consumer contracts (the suggested explanation being a reduced need to contract around (pro-consumer) default rules). In fairness to Eggleston *et al.*, they do accept that their suggested explanations need to be empirically tested. But one does not have to seek far to find quite opposite claims about contract drafting. Triantis claims (*pace* Scott) that 'vague terms' are 'ubiquitous' in the contracts of sophisticated commercial parties, with 'expressions such as "reasonableness," "good faith" and "best efforts"' being 'very common'. Bowers seems to view standards like 'reasonable time' or 'good faith' as unavoidably present in commercial contracts when the alternative is 'no provision at all or else an elaborate, expensive contract clause precisely fit to an improbable future context'. Kraus and Walt argue [215] that commercial parties expect contracts to be interpreted 'in light of commercial practice' because 'the material terms of most commercial contracts are vague or ambiguous'. The authors at least admit that this claim about contract drafting is 'speculation'. But it would be better for all sides of the debate to avoid speculating how 'typical' parties draft contracts in the absence of sound empirical evidence.

Petersen v Moloney (1951) 84 CLR 91

Facts and issues

The defendant, Moloney, alleged that he purchased the plaintiff's house and its contents through a duly authorised agent of the plaintiff, Pulbrook. Further, Moloney alleged that on 28th March 1949 he paid the sum claimed to Pulbrook as the agent of the plaintiff and for and on account of the plaintiff. The agent, however, went bankrupt and did not transfer the money to the plaintiff. Petersen sued both Moloney for the price of the house and Pulbrook for the sum he had received from Moloney. The issue arose as to whether Petersen's agent had the authority to receive payment and transfer the relative sum to him. It emerged that authority to Pulbrook was given orally and was an authority to sell Petersen's house and contents for £700 and to apply that sum towards the purchase by Petersen of another property from a Mrs Tucker, for whom Pulbrook also acted as agent. At court, Pulbrook admitted that he received the £700 from Moloney as agent for Petersen, and alleged that he had, with the authority and at the direction of the plaintiff, paid that sum to Mrs Tucker.

Decision

The appeal was allowed. Per Dixon, Fullagar and Kitto JJ at 94:

> [94] In connection with sales and purchases of property the word 'agent' is apt to be used in a misleading way. The legal conception of agency is expressed in the maxim '*Qui facit per alium facit per se*', and an 'agent' is a person who is able, by virtue of authority conferred upon him, to create or affect legal rights and duties as between another person, who is called his principal, and third parties. When a person is employed to find a buyer of property, he is commonly said to be employed as an agent, and the term 'estate agent' is a common description of a class of persons whose business is to find buyers for owners who wish to sell property. But the mere employment of such a person under the designation of agent does not, apart from the general rule that the employer will be responsible for misrepresentations made by him, necessarily create any authority to do anything which will affect the legal position of his employer. He may, of course, be given any express authority which the employer thinks fit to give him, and estoppels may arise, but the law does not imply from the mere fact of employment to find a purchaser a general authority to do on behalf of the employer anything which may be incidental to the effecting of a sale. In the present case it is clear that the plaintiff employed Pulbrook to find a purchaser for her house and its contents. But it must, we think, be regarded as settled law that an agent employed to find a purchaser has no implied authority to receive the purchase money in the sense that a receipt by him is a receipt by his principal and will therefore discharge the purchaser: see *Mynn v. Joliffe* [1834] EngR 545; (1834) 1 M & Rob 326 (174 ER 112); *Drakeford v. Piercy* (1866) 7 B & S 515; 14 LT 403; *Egan v. Ross* (1928) 29 SR (NSW) 382, at p 388; 46 WN 90, at p 93 (per Harvey C.J. in Eq.) and *Butwick v. Grant* (1924) 2 KB 483, at pp 487, 488, in which Horridge J. considers certain dicta which might have been regarded as supporting the contrary view. On the other hand, the act of the agent in receiving the purchase money may, if he has purported to receive it on behalf of the vendor, though without authority, be subsequently ratified by the vendor. Here it is to be observed that the pleadings raise only the issue of actual authority in Pulbrook to receive the money on behalf of the plaintiff. There is no plea of ratification, or of anything said or done subsequent to payment which could have the effect of substituting Pulbrook for Moloney as the person liable to the plaintiff, and there is no plea of estoppel. It is also to be observed that the prior authority pleaded is not in terms an authority to receive money but an authority to sell property and apply the proceeds in a particular way. Such an authority obviously involves or implies an authority to receive the proceeds, but the actual terms of the authority pleaded are not without importance.
>
> [95] If we put on one side for the moment a conflict of evidence as to certain matters which were put as bearing on Pulbrook's authority, we find that, although the witnesses were not agreed on many matters of detail, the nature and course of the two transactions relevant to this case emerge fairly clearly. The documentary evidence is, of course, of great importance.

Venuti and Venuti v Toop Real Estate Pty Ltd [2004] SASC 23

Facts and issues

The Venutis, prior to an auction which had been scheduled for Sunday 1 December 1996, instructed the respondent that the reserve price for the property was $235,000. Mr Anthony Toop, an experienced auctioneer, was appointed as the auctioneer. Mr Turner put forward the first bid for $270,000, well above the reserve price. Mr Toop, when the bid was made, queried the bidder as to whether it was his intention to bid that amount. In the same context, Mr Toop gave the bidder an opportunity to revise his bid. Mr Turner said he actually meant $170,000 and not $270,000. The auction then proceeded but there was no bid in excess of the reserve price. Hence the auction failed. Mr Turner made no further bids. However, prior to the auction two formal offers had been made. There had also been six open inspections and the property had been advertised with a price guide of $200,000 plus. The property sold eventually some weeks after the auction for $215,000 to a person who was not at the auction.

What had to be determined in this case were the extent and content of Mr Toop's authority. In particular, it had to be determined whether Mr Toop was required to ask Mr Turner to clarify that he had in fact intended to purchase the property for $270,000. The Venutis argued that Mr Toop should have consulted them at the stage the bid was made, rather than asking Mr Turner about his bid. In court, it emerged that Mr Turner was known to Mr Toop. The Venutis also alleged that Mr Toop was attempting to conceal that friendship and that therefore these factors should be used against him in assessing his credibility.

Decision

The appeal was dismissed. Per Anderson J at [17]:

> In the end, it seems to me that there was ample evidence available to the learned Magistrate to enable him to make the finding that Mr Turner's bid for $270,000 was a mistake. The learned Magistrate said:
>
>> In querying the bid Mr Toop was satisfying the duty he owed the plaintiffs to ensure Mr Turner knew in the clearest terms that the bid was $270,000. His knowledge of the prevailing property market and the property's history was such as to alert him to the fact, which turned out to be the case, that the bid was mistaken.
>
> [18] I think the learned Magistrate was right in coming to that conclusion. In all of this I cannot see how Mr Toop acted negligently in questioning or clarifying the bid. There was no breach of any contractual duty to the appellants.
>
> [19] It is clear from Mr Turner's evidence that he would never have purchased the property for $270,000. He in fact made no further bids after his first bid was corrected. He said that he made the bid to get the auction going and if Mr Toop had not clarified the bid, he would have realised his mistake and withdrawn the bid. He was not challenged on this statement in cross-examination. The appellants were in a position where they were unable to prove that Mr Turner would have signed an enforceable contract. His evidence was to the contrary and accepted by the learned Magistrate. I agree that there was abundant evidence to show that Mr Turner was never going to buy the property for anything near the amount of his mistaken bid.
>
> [20] In my view there are no consequences that would flow in any event from any alleged breach. The learned Magistrate rightly assessed any loss of a chance as zero.
>
> [21] When Mr Turner made his bid in terms of contract law he was making an offer. As such, the offer could be withdrawn before acceptance; the acceptance in this case would have been on the fall of the hammer.
>
> [22] The bid was not accepted by the auctioneer because as has already been discussed he believed it was a mistake. If the bid had been accepted, the offer from Mr Turner would have converted into an oral contract only.
>
> [23] Such a contract is not enforceable as a contract relating to the sale of land until there is a signed note or memorandum of the contract – see *Law of Property Act 1936* s 26(1).

[24] Also see generally for the discussion above *Halsbury's Law of Australia* at [30-120], and the authorities referred to therein.

[25] In my opinion therefore this appeal should be dismissed with an order that the appellants pay the respondent's costs.

Franklins Pty Ltd v Metcash Trading Ltd (2009) 76 NSWLR 603

Facts and issues

Franklins, a supermarket retailer with no experience in the Australian grocery industry, and Metcash, an established supplier, entered into a written contract for the supply of products to be sold in Franklins' supermarkets. During the negotiation phase, the parties agreed that Franklins would pay a 'wholesale price'— a term which referred to an amount 'less all allowances and discounts [such as]'. A few examples were subsequently listed. The issue arose as to what allowances and discounts had been included into the contract. The dispute centred around the definition of 'wholesale price' in the supply agreement, with Metcash claiming that only certain allowances and discounts were to be deducted.

Decision

The appeal was allowed. Per Campbell JA at 695:

> **Use of Recitals — Principles**
>
> There is a common and long-standing practice of including in a deed or agreement certain introductory words, traditionally called recitals, that are written in the document before words such as 'Now this deed witnesses...' or 'It is agreed...' that state the operative content of the deed. Recitals can be of various kinds — including statements of the factual background to the transaction, statements of the intention or object of the parties in entering the transaction, or statements that the parties (or one or other of them) have agreed to do or will do certain acts.
>
> Because of this variety of recitals, and because the task of the court is to interpret the particular document that is in dispute, statements in cases to the effect that recitals should always be treated in some particular way in construction of an agreement should be treated with caution, and as subject to the context in which they were uttered. In particular, relevant types of context could be the type of recital that was being considered in the particular case, the type of operative provision the recital is sought to be used as an aid to construction of, and whether other assistance can be derived from other operative provisions of the document in construing the provision that is in question. Subject to that caveat, there are some principles that emerge from the case law, which might at least constitute guidelines as to how recitals can be used in construction of an operative provision.
>
> (1) The recitals are a part of the agreement, and can be used as an aid to construction of an operative provision in an agreement: *Lee v Alexander* (1883) 8 App Cas 853 at 870; *Orr v Mitchell* [1893] AC 238 at 252-3, 254; *Inland Revenue Commissioners v Raphael* [1935] AC 96 at 143.
>
> (2) Nevertheless, there is a distinction between the operative terms of a contract and the recitals. Although the recitals can assist in the construction of a contract, they are not themselves operative terms: *Bath and Mountague's Case* (1693) 3 Chan Cas 55 at 101; [1685] EngR 4120; 22 ER 963 at 991; *Young v Smith* (1865) LR 1 Eq 180 at 183; *IRC v Raphael* at 135, 144.
>
> (3) There is a great deal of authority from the 19th and early 20th Century to the effect that the manner in which the recital can be used depends upon whether either the recital or the operative provision is 'ambiguous': eg, *Ex parte Dawes, In re Moon* (1886) 17 QBD 275 at 286; *In re*

Michell's Trusts (1878) 9 Ch D 5 at 9; *Young v Smith* at 183-4; *Orr v Mitchell* at 254; Morrison & Goolden, *Norton on Deeds*, 2nd ed (1928) Sweet & Maxwell, at p 197 ff. These authorities take the view that recitals can be used to determine the meaning of an ambiguous operative [696] provision, but cannot cut down operative words that are clear and unambiguous, even if the recital is also clear and unambiguous and is contrary to the operative provision: *Ex parte Dawes, In re Moon* at 286; see also *Walsh v Trevanion* (1850) 15 QB 733 at 751; 117 ER 636 at 642 and *Mackenzie v Duke of Devonshire* [1896] AC 400 at 405–6, 407, 408. These authorities have been applied by intermediate courts of appeal in Australia: *O'Loughlin v Mount* (1998) 71 SASR 206 at 217–19; *Chacmol Holdings Pty Ltd v Handberg* [2005] FCAFC 40; (2005) 215 ALR 748 at [38]–[50], [105]; *Harpur v Levy* [2007] VSCA 128; (2007) 16 VR 587 at 601 [63]; *Ellis v Dariush-Far* [2007] QCA 398; (2007) 242 ALR 635 at [18], and by Isaacs J in dissent in *Bebarfald & Co Ltd v Macintosh* [1911] HCA 8; (1911) 12 CLR 139 at 161–3.

(4) There are also more recent authorities which state that recitals can provide a means of proving background facts that are themselves legitimate aids to construction: *Rutter (Inspector of Taxes) v Charles Sharpe & Co Ltd* [1979] 1 WLR 1429 at 1433D; *Peppers Hotel Management Pty Ltd v Hotel Capital Partners Ltd* [2004] NSWCA 114; (2004) 12 BPR 22,879 at [77]–[78]; *Square Mile Partnership Limited v Fitzmaurice McCall Limited* [2006] EWCA Civ 1690; [2007] 2 BCLC 23 at [52], see also section 53(2)(a) *Conveyancing Act 1919*. They can be at the least an admission by the party to the deed of the truth of the matter stated, under the general law concerning evidence. In some circumstances they could give rise to an estoppel by deed, or an estoppel by convention, that prevented a party to the document asserting the contrary of the fact stated in the recital: *Greer v Kettle* [1938] AC 156 at 170-1; *Cousens v Grayridge Pty Ltd* [2000] VSCA 96 at [57]; *Caboche v Ramsay* [1993] FCA 611; (1993) 119 ALR 215 at 236–7; [1993] FCA 611; 27 ATR 479 at 499 (FCAFC); *Eslea Holdings Ltd v Butts* (1986) 6 NSWLR 175 at 188.

(5) Recitals which state that parties, or one or other of them, will carry out a particular action can be used to support an implied term in the agreement: *Ansett Transport Industries (Operations) Pty Ltd v Commonwealth* [1977] HCA 71; (1977) 139 CLR 54 at 72; *Aspdin v Austin* (1844) 5 QB 671 at 683–5; [1844] EngR 231; 114 ER 1402 at 1407–8, but not recitals which merely set out the objects of the parties: *Ansett Transport Industries (Operations) Pty Ltd v Commonwealth* at 62–3, 73, 85–6. There is no occasion to make the implication if the document contains an express covenant relating to the same subject matter: *Dawes v Tredwell* (1881) 18 Ch D 354 at 359 cited in *O'Loughlin v Mount* at 217.

An illustration of how their status might merely be that of guidelines is found in *Tom Elvin Pty Ltd v Knell* [2003] ACTSC 36 at [19], where Crispin J said:

> Despite the apparently unequivocal statements in some of the authorities cited that case I am not persuaded that operative parts of a deed, even if otherwise apparently clear and unambiguous, could never be read down by reference to the recitals. I am inclined to think that there may be cases in which the recitals may so clearly spell out the scope of the intended transaction that it would be an affront to common sense not to treat them as providing a context within which operative provisions in the deed should be construed.

[697] I also note the leaving open of the question by Maxwell P in his dissenting judgment in *Harpur v Levy* at 592 [17].

Although much of the older English authority on the subject of recitals seems to insist upon a preliminary finding of 'ambiguity' in the operative provisions of a contract before the recitals can be used as an aid to interpretation, it appears that this was simply part of the wider requirement insisted upon at the time that unambiguous words be interpreted without any extrinsic aids. This seems evident from the explanation of 'ambiguity' in the speech of [. . .].

It seems likely from this passage that the requirement of ambiguity did not exist as a special rule relevant to the use of recitals, but rather as part of the general rule relating to context. However, Lord Macnaghten clearly contemplates, in the final sentence, that recitals can be used to interpret the operative provisions of a contract.

The way in which a perceived need to find ambiguity before one could go outside the operative provisions of a document for assistance in construing that document was the nineteenth century view also appears in the statement in *Lee v Alexander* at 869-70 of when recitals could be an aid to construction. Lord Blackburn (in construing a dispositive clause in a deed of conveyance) explained how recitals (narrative) could be used:

> I take the canon of construction to be that where the description of the premises assigned is clear and unambiguous, effect must be given to it by the Court, even though convinced from other parts of the deed that it was not what the parties meant to say. But general words following a specific description rarely, if ever, clearly and unambiguously express that everything which may come within that general description is to pass. They may, and more commonly do, mean that if there is anything which virtually and in substance is part of the thing described, though it may be not perfectly described, that shall pass; and consequently I think it is legitimate to look at the narrative in the deed, and still more at the dispositive words used, in order to see whether there appears on the face of the conveyance a sufficient indication that it was intended to restrict those general words, secundum subjectam materiem.

(As to the last phrase, see *further Leaway Pty Ltd v Newcastle City Council (No 2)* at 773–5.)

Similarly, in *IRC v Raphael* at 142-3, Lord Wright (with whom Lord Thankerton agreed), before commencing to examine the authorities relating to the use of recitals, said:

> It must be remembered at the outset that the Court, while it seeks to give effect to the intention of the parties, must give effect to that intention as [698] expressed, that is, it must ascertain the meaning of the words actually used. ... The words actually used must no doubt be construed with reference to the facts known to the parties and in contemplation of which the parties must be deemed to have used them: such facts may be proved by extrinsic evidence or appear in recitals ...

However, after examining the authorities, his Lordship felt constrained by the earlier authority of *Mackenzie v Duke of Devonshire*, particularly the forceful words of Lord Halsbury LC at 406.

This reasoning, which proceeds on the basis that it is possible to interpret an operative provision in a contract in an acontextual manner, cannot stand with the High Court's statements that interpretation necessarily involves a consideration of the words of the contract in their context: *Maggbury* at 188 [11], *Pacific Carriers* at 462 [22], *Toll v Alphapharm* at 179 [40], *IATA v Ansett* at 160 [8], 174 [53]. The criticisms of Lord Hoffmann in *Charter Reinsurance v Fagan and Mannai*, and the triumph of the 'common sense principles by which any serious utterance would be interpreted in ordinary life' over 'the old intellectual baggage of "legal" interpretation' which occurred in Investors Compensation means that, insofar as these earlier decisions require a finding of 'ambiguity', and proceed on the basis that it is possible to read the operative provisions without the aid of context, those decisions should not be followed. It would follow then that the recitals in a deed can be looked at as part of the surrounding circumstances of the contract without a need to find ambiguity in the operative provisions of the contract.

However, it should be emphasised that (at least for recitals not saying that one or other party will carry out a particular action) the recital is merely a means by which the surrounding circumstances and purpose of the transaction can be ascertained. Where recitals purport to record the surrounding circumstances and purpose of a transaction, it is those surrounding circumstances or purposes 'as can be got from the language of the recital in the deed itself' that are used to construe the contract (*Rutter v Charles* Sharpe at 1433D; see also *Peppers Hotel Management v Hotel Capital Partners* at [77]–[78] (per McColl JA); *Square Mile Partnership* at [52]; Lewison, *The Interpretation of Contracts*, at [10.11], p 396–7). As Lord Wright put it in *IRC v Raphael* at 144: 'The nature of recitals as statements of facts which are in the contemplation of the parties, is illustrated by the Scotch term "narrative".'

That a recital can be looked at as part of the surrounding circumstances of the contract still leaves room for the rule (accepted by intermediate courts of appeal in Australia and by Isaacs J in *Bebarfald & Co Ltd v Macintosh*) that where the recital is in conflict with the true interpretation of an operative provision (according to the modern standards of interpretation), the operative provision prevails. Strictly speaking, that is not so much a rule of construction as a reflection of the fact that recitals are not operative provisions in a contract.

Alstom Ltd v Yokogawa Australia Pty Ltd (No 7) [2012] SASC 49

Facts and issues

Flinders Power Partnership owned a power station in South Australia. They entered into a contract for its refurbishment with Alstom Power as head contractor. Alstom subcontracted the works associated with the refurbishment project to a joint venture (YMRL) comprising Yokogawa Australia (EC&I contract). Because of delays and completion issues, Flinders Power Partnership withheld a sum of the contract price on account of liquidated damages. A settlement agreement was negotiated between the parties, under which Alstom paid a certain sum to Flinders Power Partnership. Alstom subsequently proceeded with claims against Yokogawa arising out of delay to completion and other alleged breaches, including for the recovery of the amounts paid to Flinders Power Partnership. For their own part, Yokogawa alleged various breaches of contract and contractual entitlements against Alstom. The issue arose as to what were Alstom and Yokohama's rights and whether any obligations had been breached.

Decision

The decision covers many issues. For the purposes of our analysis, Bleby J held that Alstom could only recover what they had claimed based on the express clauses of the contract they had entered into with Yokogawa. Per Bleby J:

3.3 A drafting disaster

[89] The EC&I contract is in a deceptively simple form. Including the one Attachment and one Schedule, it covers a mere 40 pages described as 'Special Conditions of Contract'. Those Special Conditions of Contract were the key to the EC&I contract. They set out the changes which were to be applied to the terms of the head contract to reflect the agreed terms of the EC&I contract. They provided for the incorporation into the EC&I contract of the whole of the head contract subject to a number of specified alterations, omissions and additions.

[90] That is not necessarily a poor drafting technique if done competently, in appropriate circumstances and with care. However, in a contract of this complexity I began my journey into the EC&I contract with a certain sense of trepidation — 'I looked on, I thought, I reflected, I admired, in a state of stupefaction not altogether unmingled with fear!' My first fears were more than justified. As will be seen from the extent of these reasons necessarily devoted to the interpretation of the EC&I contract, the clumsiness, in this case, of the superimposing technique has created a drafting disaster.

[91] A cursory analysis of the EC&I contract reveals how poorly drafted it was. The superimposition of terms results in numerous ambiguities, inconsistencies, lacunae and, in some cases,

grammatical nonsense. As this litigation shows, it has provided fertile ground for dispute as to the contract's real meaning and effect. The parties were even unable to agree on the complete text of the EC&I contract.

[92] This was a contract between three large multi-national corporations for a contract sum of almost $34 million. Breaches of it had ramifications for the performance of another contract worth $148.5 million inclusive of GST. It is almost inconceivable that such parties would allow themselves, without competent legal advice, to enter into a contract for a project of the size and complexity of this one where the contract was so poorly drafted and so obviously defective. It stands as an appalling indictment against those responsible for its drafting. It also stands with what Alstom acknowledges on its part was defective project control, poor project management, senior management revoking project manager decisions, inexperienced and changing personnel and what I consider to be incompetent programming and a blind determination by Alstom to lay the blame for failure on anyone but itself, together with some instances within YDRML of poor personnel management, internal insubordination and an absence of clear reporting. These features, but particularly the contract, have resulted in protracted litigation at an additional cost which must now equal or exceed the amounts in dispute, to say nothing of the ongoing cost of executive time in preparing for and managing the litigation.

QUESTIONS

(1) Contextualise the freedom of contract doctrine from the perspective of the negotiation phase.

(2) What is a standard form contract?

(3) What is meant by the term 'recitals' and what role do they play in contracts?

(4) What should be done to avoid ending up with a 'drafting disaster' in particularly complex contracts such as that which Justice Bleby discussed in *Alstom Ltd v Yokogawa Pty Ltd (No7)* [2012] SASC 49?

4.3 Pre-contractual obligations to disclose information

Factor	Short explanation	Relevant authorities	*Principles* text*
As a general rule, there are no obligations to disclose information during the negotiations phase Common law as well as statutory exceptions and prohibitions apply	As the parties to a contract have conflicting interests, they are not required to disclose the information they posses Exceptions have, however, been created for certain situations—such as in the case of fiduciary relationships or insurance contracts	JW Carter, *Contract Law in Australia* (LexisNexis, 6th ed, 2012) *Taylor v Johnson* (1983) 151 CLR 422	Chapter 4: 4.07–4.09 Chapter 6: 6.02 Chapter 11: 11.13 Chapter 12: 12.16 Chapter 18: 18.10, 18.39 Chapter 20: 20.04

* Consult the corresponding section(s) of the *Principles* text for more detail.

In 1597, Sir Francis Bacon famously stated that 'knowledge itself is power'. This view underpins the contract law dimension as well. As a general rule under Australian contract law, a party contemplating or negotiating a contract is not obliged to disclose information, no matter how relevant or important: see Gleeson CJ's statement in *Lam v Ausintel* (1989) at 475:

> Where parties are dealing at arm's length in a commercial situation in which they have conflicting interests it will often be the case that one party will be aware of information which, if known to the other, would or might cause that other party to take a different negotiating stance. This does not in itself impose any obligation on the first party to bring the information to the attention of the other party, and failure to do so would not, without more, ordinarily be regarded as dishonesty or even sharp practice...'.

See also *W Scott Fell and Co Ltd v Lloyd* (1906) 4 CLR 572; *Wood v Balfour* [2011] NSWCA 382. This is due to the working logic of contractual arrangements, which the parties enter into because of their contrasting legal and economic interests. Such a self-interested understanding of contracting is clearly evidenced by the functioning of the consideration doctrine which as discussed, views contracts as bargains.

Common law and statutory exceptions as well as prohibitions apply to this general rule.[5] Classic examples of common law exceptions are the misrepresentation regime (which also applies where a statement is literally true, but in context implies something else that is false, or where a party fails to correct a statement that was originally true, but has since become false); the estoppel and unconscionable bargains doctrines; the obligations which have to be fulfilled in a fiduciary relationship: see **4.3**, **6.2**, **7.2**, **11.2**, **12.4**, **18.4**, **19.2**, **20.2**; *Taylor v Johnson* (1983) 151 CLR 422, extract below; *Commercial Bank of Australia Ltd v Amadio* (1983) 151 CLR 447; *Commonwealth Bank of Australia v Smith* (1991) 42 FCR 390; *Westpac Banking Corporation Ltd v Robinson* (1993) 30 NSWLR 668; *Antov v Bokan* [2018] NSWSC 1474. Further, the duty to act with utmost good faith is required for insurance contracts—as Gleeson CJ and Crennan J noted in *CGU Insurance v AMP Financial Planning* (2007) 235 CLR 1 at [15]: 'the classic example of an insured's obligation of utmost good faith is a requirement of full disclosure to an insurer'.[6]

The most common ways in which liability for pre-contractual conduct may arise at common law are:

- An assurance given by one of the parties becomes *incorporated* into a resulting contract, so that there is liability for breach of contract if the assurance is not met (see **9.3)**;
- One party intentionally or recklessly deceives the other, exposing them to an award of damages for the tort of *deceit* (see **18.2**);
- A party is liable in the tort of *negligence* for careless conduct, for example in relation to the provision of information (see **18.2**); or
- A party's statements or conduct provide the basis for some form of *estoppel* (see **7.2**).

5 For an introduction, see Paul D Finn, 'Good Faith and Nondisclosure' in PD Finn (ed), *Essays on Torts* (Law Book Co, 1989) 150–182.

6 For a law and economics contextualisation, see Anthony Duggan, Michael Bryan and Frances Hanks, *Contractual Non-Disclosure: An Applied Study in Modern Contract Theory* (Longman Professional, 1994); Mitja Kovač, *Comparative Contract Law and Economics* (Edward Elgar Publishing, 2011).

With respect to the statutory requirements, common examples are the obligation to disclose information under ss 13 and 21–22 of the *Insurance Contracts Act 1984* (Cth); s 674 of the *Corporations Act 2001* (Cth) (below), which requires listed companies to disclose information that might affect the price of certain types of security; and ss 4 and 18 ACL on misleading representations and deceptive conduct (below; see **18.4** and also *Henjo Investments Pty Ltd v Collins Marrickville Pty Ltd* (1988) 39 FCR 546). The rationale and application of s 18 ACL have attracted much discussion as the norm has replaced the much-debated s 52 of the *Trade Practices Act 1974* (Cth). The courts have particularly focused on the notion of 'reasonable expectation' (see *Demagogue Pty Ltd v Ramensky* (1992) 39 FCR 31; *Miller & Associates Insurance Broking Pty Ltd v BMW Australia Finance Ltd* (2010) 241 CLR 357; *Clifford v Vegas Enterprises Pty Ltd* [2011] FCAFC 135; *Traderight (NSW) Pty Ltd v Bank of Queensland Ltd* [2015] NSWCA 94; *Fitzgerald v Deloitte Services Pty Ltd* [2017] NSWCA 139). Further examples are the *Sale of Land Act 1962* (Vic) Pt II Div 2; *National Credit Code* s 16, below; *National Consumer Credit Protection Regulations 2010* regs 72–74; *Retail and Commercial Leases Act 1995* (SA) s 12, below; and *Competition and Consumer (Industry Codes—Franchising) Regulation 2014* Sch 1 cll 8–11, Annexures 1–2).

The interrogative as to whether there is an implied duty to act in good faith under Australian contract law has been keeping the courts and scholars busy since the early 1990s. In the famous case of *Walford v Miles* [1992] 2 AC 128, 138, Lord Ackner stated 'the concept of a duty to carry on negotiations in good faith is inherently repugnant to the adversarial position of the parties when involved in negotiations'.[7] Further, as Carter and Furmston have noted: 'in the application of doctrine, English and Australian courts have promoted good faith and achieved results which are, for the most part, consistent with the operation of a general concept of that kind. Rule formulation is today less emphatic than in the 19th century, and rule application is more pragmatic'.[8]

And indeed, some commentators have argued that Australian contract law is slowly moving[9] towards the conceptualisation of such implied duty in the form of an organising principle (see also *North East Solutions Pty Ltd v Masters Home Improvement Australia Pty Ltd* [2016] VSC 1; *Paciocco v Australia and New Zealand Banking Group Ltd* (2015) 236 FCR 199; *Mineralogy Pty Ltd v Sino Iron Pty Ltd (No 6)* [2015] FCA 825; *Commonwealth Bank of Australia v Barker* [2014] HCA 32; *United Group Rail Services Ltd v Rail Corporation of New South Wales* [2009] NSWCA 177, 58; *Renard Constructions (ME) Pty Ltd v Minister for Public Works* (1992) 26 NSWLR 234, 258).

---

7 But see David Campbell, 'Adam Smith and the Social Foundation of Agreement: Walford v Miles as a Relational Contract' (2017) 21(3) *Edinburgh Law Review* 376–404.

8 JW Carter and MP Furmston, 'Good Faith and Fairness in the Negotiation of Contracts Part I' (1994) 8 *Journal of Contract Law* 1, 5.

9 Howard Munro, 'The "Good Faith" Controversy in Australian Commercial Law: A Survey of the Spectrum of Academic Legal Opinion' (2008) 28(1) *University of Queensland Law Journal* 167–179; John W Carter, *Contract Law in Australia* (LexisNexis, 6th ed, 2012), extract below; John W Carter and Wayne Courtney, 'Good Faith in Contracts: Is There an Implied Promise to Act Honestly?' (2017) 75(3) *Cambridge Law Journal* 608–619; Luca Siliquini-Cinelli and Andrew Hutchison, 'Constitutionalism, Good Faith and the Doctrine of Specific Performance: Rights, Duties and Equitable Discretion' (2016) 133(1) *South African Law Journal* 73–101.

JW Carter, *Contract Law in Australia* (LexisNexis, 6th ed, 2012)

[22] Some General Points

[2-02] **Introduction**. Australian Contract law is rapidly moving towards three propositions:

(1) In most contracts (perhaps all contracts) a requirement of good faith must be implied, at least in connection with termination pursuant to an express term of the contract, but perhaps more generally.
(2) Where it is present, the source of the implied requirement of good faith is an implied term of the contract.
(3) The implied requirement of good faith is satisfied by a party who has acted honestly and reasonably.

Judicial support for these three propositions is found mainly in cases purporting to apply the decision of the New South Wales Court of Appeal in *Renard Constructions (ME) Pty Ltd v Minister for Public Works*. In *Renard* it was held that the ability of the principal under a building contract to rely on a show cause procedure was subject to requirements of reasonableness.

Priestley JA said:

> The contract can in my opinion only be effective as a workable business document under which the promises of each party to the other may be fulfilled, if the sub-clause is read in the way I have indicated, that is, as subject to requirements of reasonableness.

It is because this requirement of reasonableness has in the subsequent cases been rationalised by reference to good faith that Australian courts have come to regard reasonableness as a key ingredient of good faith.

There is also considerable support for a requirement of good faith (although not necessarily the element of reasonable conduct) in academic writings.

Taylor v Johnson (1983) 151 CLR 422

Facts and issues

This case concerns a unilateral mistake about the value of two lots of land which Johnson, the defendant, gave Taylor, the plaintiff, an option to purchase. In particular, the sale concerned five acres of land for $15,000. Johnson refused the pay Taylor, claiming that she was under the mistaken belief that the agreements provided for $15,000 per acre. Taylor claimed specific performance, while Johnson sought to set the contract aside for lack of agreement and intention to create legal relations.

Decision

The appeal was dismissed. Per Mason ACJ, Murphy J and Deane J at 428:

> [428] The judgments of Blackburn and Hannen JJ. in *Smith v. Hughes* (1871) LR 6 QB 597, at pp 607, 609 provide support for the proposition that a contract is void if one party to the contract enters into it under a serious mistake as to the content or existence of a fundamental term and the other party has knowledge of that mistake. That approach accorded with what has been called the 'subjective theory' of the nature of the assent necessary to constitute a valid contract (but cf. Holland, *Elements of Jurisprudence*, 12th ed. (1916), pp. 264–265). The

'subjective theory', it will be recalled, was advanced by, among others, Mr. T. Cyprian Williams in his *Vendor and Purchaser*, 4th ed. (1936), p. 748, n. (m), and is that the true consent of the parties is essential to a valid contract. The contrary view, namely that described as the 'objective theory', was asserted by, among others, Holmes J. in *The Common Law* (1881), Lecture IX, and is that the law is concerned, not with the real intentions of the parties, but with the outward manifestations of those intentions. In practice, as between the contracting parties, there is little difference in the result of the application of the two competing theories since allied with any assertion of the 'subjective theory' is acceptance of one manifestation of the doctrine of estoppel which would ordinarily operate to preclude one who had so conducted himself that a reasonable man would believe that he was assenting to the terms of a proposed contract, from leading evidence as to what his real intentions were.

As a matter of legal technique there is a significant difference between the two theories. This is best illustrated by setting out the [429] consequences which flow from the application of each theory to a case in which a contract is successfully impeached on the ground of unilateral mistake. According to the subjective theory, there is no binding contract either at common law or in equity, equity following the common law in this respect. Of course in deciding whether the contract is void ab initio for the unilateral mistake, regard will be had to the doctrine of estoppel in order to determine whether effect should be given to the claim that there has been unilateral mistake. On the other hand, according to the objective theory, there is a contract which, in conformity which the common law, continues to be binding, unless and until it is avoided in accordance with equitable principles which take as their foundation a contract valid at common law but transform it so that it becomes voidable. The important distinction between the two approaches is that, according to the subjective theory, the contract is void ab initio, whereas according to the objective theory, it is voidable only.

While the sounds of conflict have not been completely stilled, the clear trend in decided cases and academic writings has been to leave the objective theory in command of the field. It is unnecessary to examine the reasons for this. A convenient statement of them can be found in *Williston on Contracts*, 3rd ed. (1970), vol. 13, s. 1537. In the United Kingdom, the decisive turning point leading to the near eclipse of the subjective theory was probably the speech of Lord Atkin in *Bell v. Lever Brothers Ltd.* [1931] UKHL 2; (1932) AC 161, at pp 217–227. In due course, Denning L.J., basing himself on Lord Atkin's speech, formulated a more general proposition than Lord Atkin's comments would, on analysis, warrant (see Lord Atkin's example of a case where 'unilateral mistake by the seller of goods will prevent a contract from arising' (1932) AC, at pp 217–218. In *Solle v. Butcher* (1950) 1 KB 671, at p 691, Denning L.J. said:

> . . . once a contract has been made, that is to say, once the parties, whatever their inmost states of mind, have to all outward appearances agreed with sufficient certainty in the same terms on the same subject matter, then the contract is good unless and until it is set aside for failure of some condition on which the existence of the contract depends, or for fraud, or on some equitable ground.

His Lordship then went on to say:

> Neither party can rely on his own mistake to say it was a nullity from the beginning, no matter that it was a mistake which to his mind was fundamental, and no matter that the other party knew that he was under a mistake.

While the mistake in *Solle v. Butcher* was a mistake of fact which [430] affected the operation of a formal written contract, it is plain that the above remarks of Denning L.J. were intended to extend to a mistake as to the existence or content of an actual term of such a contract.

In *McRae v. Commonwealth Disposals Commission* [1951] HCA 79; (1951) 84 CLR 377, at pp 407–408 and in *Svanosio v. McNamara* [1956] HCA 55; (1956) 96 CLR 186, at pp 195–196, which were cases involving formal written contracts, Dixon C.J. and Fullagar J. referred with approval to the remarks of Denning L.J. In Svanosio, their Honours quoted those remarks and continued (1956) 96 CLR, at p 196:

> 'Mistake' might, of course, afford a ground on which equity would refuse specific performance of a contract, and there may be cases of 'mistake' in which it would be so inequitable that a party should be held to his contract that equity would set it aside. No rule can be laid down a priori as to such cases: see an article by Professor R. A. Blackburn in *Res Judicatae* (1955), vol. 7, p. 43. But we would agree with Professor Shatwell (1955) 33 Can BR, at pp 186, 187 that it is difficult to conceive any circumstances in which equity could properly give relief by setting aside the contract unless there has been fraud or misrepresentation or a condition can be found expressed or implied in the contract.

Denning L.J., in *Solle v. Butcher*, had likewise expressed the view that, in the absence of fraud or misrepresentation, resort must be had to equity to escape from the terms of the contract on the ground of unilateral mistake.

McRae and Svanosio, like *Solle v. Butcher*, were not cases involving a mistake as to the existence or content of an actual term of the written contract. There is, however, nothing in the joint judgments of Dixon C.J. and Fullagar J. which would exclude such a case from their acceptance of the general proposition that neither party to a contract 'can rely on his own mistake to say it was a nullity from the beginning, no matter that it was a mistake which to his mind was fundamental, and no matter that the other party knew that he was under a mistake' (1950) 1 KB 671, at p 691. Whether that proposition should properly be accepted as applying in the case of an informal contract or in the case where there is a mistake as to the identity of the other party are questions which can be left to another day. It would seem that it does not apply in a case where the mistake is as to the nature of the contract. For the present, but not without hesitation (see, e.g., *Robert A. Munro & Co. v. Meyer* (1930) 2 KB 312, at pp 333–334; *Chitty on Contracts*, 24th ed. (1977) vol. 1, par. 337; *Joscelyne v Nissen*) [431], we are prepared to accept it as applicable to a case, such as the present, where the mistake is as to the existence or content of an actual term in a formal written contract. It therefore becomes necessary to consider the scope of the basis upon which relief in equity is available from the contractual consequences of unilateral mistake. Dixon C.J. and Fullagar J. referred, in the above passage from their judgment in Svanosio, to a difficulty in conceiving circumstances in which equity could properly give relief by setting aside the contract unless there had been fraud or misrepresentation or a condition could be found expressed or implied in the contract. Presumably, their Honours were referring to 'fraud' in the wide equitable sense which includes unconscionable dealing. If they were not, we do not share the difficulty to which they referred. To the contrary, it seems to us that the reported cases, including Solle v. Butcher itself, readily provide concrete examples of such circumstances.

In *Torrance v. Bolton* (1872) LR 8 Ch App 118, at p 124, James L.J. (with whom Mellish L.J. agreed) explained the basis upon which a contract for sale was set aside in a case of unilateral mistake as being the ordinary jurisdiction of equity 'to deal with' any instrument or other transaction 'in which the Court is of opinion that it is unconscientious for a person to avail himself of the legal advantage which he has obtained'. Special circumstances will ordinarily need to be shown before it would be unconscientious for one party to a written contract to enforce it against another party who was under a mistake as to its terms or its subject matter.

In *Solle v. Butcher* (1950) 1 KB, at p 692 Denning L.J. gave, as examples of such special circumstances, the case where the mistake of the one party has been induced by a material misrepresentation of the other and the case where 'one party, knowing that the other is mistaken about the terms of an offer, or the identity of the person by whom it is made, lets him remain under his delusion and concludes a contract on the mistaken terms instead of pointing out the mistake'. In *Riverlate Properties Ltd. v. Paul* (1975) Ch 133, at p 145, the English Court of Appeal accepted that a conveyance which included a building, due to a mistake on the part of one party which was known to the other party, could be rescinded, though rectification in that situation appeared to be a preferable remedy. (See also, as to rectification for unilateral mistake, *Thomas Bates & Son Ltd. v. Wyndham's (Lingerie) Ltd.*

[. . .]

[432] The particular proposition of law which we see as appropriate and adequate for disposing of the present appeal may be narrowly stated. It is that a party who has entered into a written contract under a serious mistake about its contents in relation to a fundamental term will be entitled in equity to an order rescinding the contract if the other party is aware that circumstances exist which indicate that the first party is entering the contract under some serious mistake or misapprehension about either the content or subject matter of that term and deliberately sets out to ensure that the first party does not become aware of the existence of his mistake or misapprehension. What we have said is sufficient to demonstrate the broad basis of support which the authorities provide for that proposition. Moreover, and perhaps more importantly, it is a principle which is best calculated to do justice between the parties to a contract in the situation which it contemplates. In such a [433] situation it is unfair that the mistaken party should be held to the written contract by the other party whose lack of precise knowledge of the first party's actual mistake proceeds from wilful ignorance because, knowing or having reason to know that there is some mistake or misapprehension, he engages deliberately in a course of conduct which is designed to inhibit discovery of it. Our comment can, for present purposes, be limited in its application to the case where the second party has not materially altered his position and the rights of strangers have not intervened.

Applying the above-mentioned principle to the present case, it is apparent that the appeal must fail. It is now common ground between the parties that, at the time she signed both option and contract, Mrs. Johnson mistakenly believed that the relevant document stipulated that the purchase price was $15,000 per acre whereas the stipulated purchase price was $15,000 in total. The stipulation as to price was plainly a fundamental term of the contract (see *Webster v. Cecil*; *Garrard v. Frankel*; *Hartog v. Colin & Shields*. As we have already indicated, we are of the view that the proper inference to be drawn from the evidence is that, both at the time when Mrs. Johnson executed the option and at the time when she executed the contract, Mr. Taylor believed that she was under some serious mistake or misapprehension about either the terms (the price) or the subject matter (its value) of the relevant transaction. The avoidance of mention of the purchase price after the 'idle curiosity' conversation and the circumstances in which Mr. Taylor procured the execution of the option, including his wrong statement that he did not have a copy of the option which he could make available to Mrs. Johnson, lead, in our view, plainly to the inference that he deliberately set out to ensure that Mrs. Johnson did not become aware that she was being induced to grant the option and, subsequently, to enter into the contract by some material mistake or misapprehension as to its terms or subject matter.

QUESTIONS

(1) What are the six bodies of law which Finn describes as imposing a duty to disclose information while negotiating, and why does Finn believe such matters are ultimately matters of social policy?

(2) Elaborate on the High Court's reflections in *Taylor v Johnson* (1983) 151 CLR 422, at 428–33, on the difference between the 'subject' and 'objective' theories of the nature of the assent necessary to constitute a valid contract, and contextualise them in relation to the Court's judgment.

(3) Explain why, in *Demagogue Pty Ltd v Ramensky* (1992) 39 FCR 31, the Full Court stressed the importance of opting for a contextualised approach to the notion of 'mere silence' in relation to the pre-contractual duty to disclose information.

4.4 Anticipated contracts that fail to materialise

Factor	Short explanation	Relevant theories and requirements	*Principles* text*
What are the consequences when a party decides not to conclude a contract?	As a general rule, parties are left free not to finalise their contractual arrangement	*Sabemo Pty Ltd v North Sydney Municipal Council* [1977] 2 NSWLR 880 *Leading Edge Events Australia Pty Ltd v Kiri Te Kanawa* [2007] NSWSC 228 *E K Nominees Pty Ltd v Woolworths Ltd* [2006] NSWSC 1172 *British Steel Corporation v Cleveland Bridge and Engineering Co Ltd* [1984] 1 All ER 504	Chapter 4: 4.12 Chapter 24: 24.10

* Consult the corresponding section(s) of the *Principles* text for more detail.

The fact that contracts are voluntary undertakings (freedom of contract) also means that, as a general rule, a party is left free to decide not to finalise the arrangement until the contract is concluded. In these cases, the issue arises as to what the other party is entitled to. In particular, the question to be answered is what are the other party's rights in relation to her expectation that the contract would be concluded, as well as to the expenses she might have incurred?[10]

10 For a comparative analysis, see Martin Hogg, *Promises and Contract Law: Comparative Perspective* (Cambridge University Press, 2011) 179–203.

As a logical progression, the first thing to ascertain is whether the party which has refused to go ahead with the contract has acted misleadingly or deceptively (see s 18 ACL; *Leading Edge Events Australia Pty Ltd v Kiri Te Kanawa* [2007] NSWSC 228, extract below; *E K Nominees Pty Ltd v Woolworths Ltd* [2006] NSWSC 1172). The doctrine of estoppel may also apply, provided that its requirements are met: see **7.2**. Further, there is the possibility for the injured party to seek restitution for any benefits they had conferred on the other party: see **24.1**. In addition, a performing party may be entitled to reasonable remuneration (the so-called *quantum meruit*; see *British Steel Corporation v Cleveland Bridge and Engineering Co Ltd* [1984] 1 All ER 504; extract below).

Where a payment is made by one party to the other in anticipation of this being required under a contract, it can be recovered on the basis that there is a 'total failure of consideration' for the payment (see **24.2**; *Nu Line Construction Group Pty Ltd v Fowler* [2014] NSWCA 51). However, no such claim can be made where a party incurs expense tendering or preparing for a contract that they know they may not be awarded:

> In considering this application I must endeavour to reconcile two important principles. First, although the costs to be awarded to the plaintiffs may not indemnify them for their actual costs incurred, they are entitled to all costs in accordance with the scale which are necessary and proper for the attainment of justice [...]. This objective is not achieved by denying them the reasonable costs of preparation and trial. Nor is it achieved by assuming that they are entitled to representation at an inadequate level of experience and competence. Second, the second defendant ought not be required to bear a greater burden than the rules and the practice of the court customarily impose on unsuccessful litigants. (*Brenner v First Artists' Management Pty Ltd* [1993] VicRp 71; [1993] 2 VR 221, at 259.

Finally, in *Sabemo Pty Ltd v North Sydney Municipal Council* [1977] 2 NSWLR 880, 901, extract below, Sheppard J stressed the importance of the reason(s) why a contract is not entered into. In this case, the defendant council had decided, for its own reasons, not to go ahead with a proposed land development. The plaintiff, which had spent a lot of money preparing various schemes for the council to consider, was held to be entitled to recover reasonable remuneration for that work. The decision is generally considered to be a controversial application of the principle of *unjust enrichment*; see **24.1**. Were the facts to recur today, the case might well be argued and decided on the basis of promissory estoppel instead. Nevertheless, it has been followed in at least some subsequent cases: see eg *Leading Edge Events v Te Kanawa* [2007] NSWSC 228, extract below.

Sabemo Pty Ltd v North Sydney Municipal Council [1977] 2 NSWLR 880

Facts and issues

North Sydney Council invited proposals for the redevelopment of a land it owned. It was then announced that Sabemo was the successful tenderer. After that, Sabemo commenced working for North Sydney Council. However, no contract was entered into and North Sydney Council decided not to proceed with the proposal. The issue arose as to whether the refusal was legitimate.

Decision

Sabemo was awarded a *quantum meruit* as North Sydney Council deliberatively decided not to continue with the project after the parties failed to reach an agreement.

Per Sheppard J at 901:

> [. . .] To my mind the defendant's decision to drop the proposal is the determining factor. If the transaction had gone off because the parties were unable to agree, then I think it would be correct, harking back to the expressions used by the judges in the Jennings and Chapman case, and in the Brewer Street case, to say that each party had taken a risk, in incurring the expenditure which it did, that the transaction might go off because of a bona fide failure to reach agreement on some point of substance in such a complex transaction. But I do not think it right to say that that risk should be so borne, when one party has taken it upon itself to change its mind about the entirety of the proposal.
>
> As I have said, substantial and continuing work had been done over a period of three years or more. It seems to me to be unthinkable that the plaintiff would have been prepared to do what it did, if it had thought that the defendant might change its mind about proceeding with the proposal. It is true that the defendant is a council the members of which are elected from time to time, and that, therefore, it might not be expected necessarily to be as consistent in its approach to problems as a different sort of undertaking. But for more than three years its consistent policy had been to proceed with a scheme which would give it adequate accommodation for its various activities free from any obligation to pay rent therefor, and with the knowledge that, in due course of time when the lease expired, all would revert to it. It seems to me that, in those circumstances, the defendant is not entitled to have this problem considered differently than would be the case if it were an undertaking, public or private, the identity of whose members was not likely to undergo the same degree of change.
>
> Much reliance was placed by counsel for the defendant upon the areas of disagreement which had emerged in the negotiations between the solicitors and to which I have earlier referred. It was not of course for him to demonstrate that the transaction would have gone off because of failure to agree upon one or more of those matters. As he rightly submitted, it was for the plaintiff to establish that, notwithstanding the areas of disagreement which there were, the transaction would have proceeded, but for the defendant's decision to drop it. I have given that submission much thought, but have reached the conclusion that I should be satisfied that the probabilities were that agreement would have been reached notwithstanding statements by the defendant's solicitors that indicate in respect of at least some of them an apparently uncompromising stand. I am led to take the view that I have by the oral evidence which was led, particularly that of Dr. Fitzpatrick. He had no doubt that agreement would have been reached. No evidence to suggest any different situation was called for the defendant.

Leading Edge Events Australia Pty Ltd v Kiri Te Kanawa [2007] NSWSC 228

Facts and issues

Leading Edge Events Australia, a company that promotes events in the entertainment industry, alleged that it entered into a contract with Mittane Limited, a company incorporated in Switzerland, to provide the services of Kiri Te Kanawa (Dame Kiri), a renowned opera singer, to perform at concerts with John Farnham (Mr Farnham), a renowned Australian popular singer, in Sydney on

5 February 2005 and in Melbourne on 12 and 13 February 2005. Leading Edge made a number of claims. First, that in breach of that agreement, Mittane Limited refused to provide the services of Dame Kiri to perform at the concerts. Second, that Dame Kiri warranted that she would perform at the concerts, and in breach of that warranty failed to perform. Leading Edge also sought to recover what they had spent on a *quantum meruit* basis. In addition, Leading Edge put forward a number of claims against Dame Kiri for breach of s 42 of the *Fair Trading Act 1987* (NSW) (FTA), and against NGM and Mittane for breach of s 52 of the *Trade Practices Act 1974* (Cth) (TPA) in relation to alleged representations that Dame Kiri would perform at the concerts. Finally, there were claims against Dame Kiri and Mr Grace that within the meaning of s 75B of the TPA they were knowingly involved respectively in Mittane's and NGM's breaches of s 52 of the TPA. The main issue here was whether, and if so, when, the contract was entered into. This had to be determined via a detailed analysis of the communications, both oral and written, between the parties and others during the period June 2003 to April 2004. The majority of that analysis is in any event necessary for the determination of Leading Edge's other claims in estoppel and for misleading or deceptive conduct. In these circumstances, it is appropriate to describe the parties and others who were part of or party to those communications and events over that period.

Decision

The court dismissed Leading Edge's claims against Mittane for breach of contract; against Dame Kiri for breach of collateral warranty; against Dame Kiri for breach of s 42 of the *Fair Trading Act;* against NGM and Mittane for breaches of s 52 *TPA*; and against Dame Kiri and Mr Grace for accessorial liability under s 75B *TPA*. Leading Edge, however, succeeded in establishing an entitlement to recover from Mittane its reasonable costs in the amount of $128,063.21.

Per Bergin J at [284]:

> **Misleading or deceptive conduct**
>
> The plaintiff made a number of claims of misleading or deceptive conduct. It claimed that Dame Kiri had breached s 42 of the FTA; that NGM and Mittane breached s 52 of the TPA; and that Mr Grace and Dame Kiri were accessorily liable under s 75B of the TPA in respect of the alleged breaches of s 52 of the TPA by NGM and Mittane.
>
> [285] The Commercial List Statement does not enable the ascertainment with any precision of the true basis upon which it is claimed the representation alleged to have been made by Dame Kiri arose or was made. The Commercial List Statement alleges that Dame Kiri represented to the plaintiff that 'she would perform at the Concerts'. The particulars to that claim by reference to earlier parts of the 'pleading' rely upon the broad claims of telephone calls, emails and/or letters over an eight month period without any particular detail. The schedule (Ex Z) was equally unhelpful. It is apparent that the plaintiff claims that from the quagmire of emails, letters and conversations, one could extract the representation that Dame Kiri 'would perform at the Concerts'. Even in final address, counsel for the plaintiff did not point to any particular document or conversation that amounts to such a representation. Certainly there were emails and conversations in which the parties discussed the venues, the fee, the launch, the accommodation and the various arrangement for air tickets and helicopter trips but the claim that Dame Kiri 'would perform', if made, was always subject to the finalisation of the contract between Mittane and the plaintiff.
>
> [286] The plaintiff also claimed that Dame Kiri was under a duty to inform it that she would not be performing at the Concerts and that her silence until after the Auckland meeting was misleading or deceptive. In this regard, the plaintiff relied upon an email from Mr Gleeson to Mr Grace on 19 February 2004 referred to earlier in this judgment which included the statement,

'For your ears only — Kiri is still making negative sounds about the concerts with Farnham'. The plaintiff claims that as at 19 February 2004, Dame Kiri had obviously been having discussions with Mr Gleeson in which she had expressed a negative attitude to performing at the Concerts and that she had a duty to advise the plaintiff that she was not going to perform at the Concerts.

[287] Dame Kiri was far from silent about her concerns with Mr Farnham's style. As I have already said she raised them directly with Mr Williams on 9 December 2003 when she telephoned him in Mr Grace's presence. Mr Williams knew from that date, if not earlier, that Dame Kiri wanted to meet with Mr Farnham and establish whether a rapport was possible and to plan the musical programme. It is obvious that two highly successful performing artists would need careful management so that their respective needs were met. Mr Williams knew that there was a possibility that Dame Kiri and Mr Farnham may not have the necessary rapport to assuage Dame Kiri's concerns.

[288] The plaintiff relied upon the same conduct referred to in relation to the claim for expenses to allege that Dame Kiri breached s 42 of the FTA. It is important to distinguish this claim from the claim that it was reasonable to assume that a contract would be entered into. A major problem for the plaintiff, even if the representation had been made, is that I am not satisfied that it can establish the requisite reliance upon such a representation for the purposes of the breach of s 42 of the FTA. The plaintiff requested that Mittane and/or Mr Grace/NGM have Dame Kiri confirm that she would be bound to perform at the Concerts by signing the agreement between Mittane and the plaintiff. When the plaintiff was advised that Mittane would not allow Dame Kiri to sign the agreement, it then requested that Dame Kiri sign a 'side letter'. Far from relying upon any alleged representation it seems to me that the plaintiff was concerned that it did not have a promise that Dame Kiri would perform at the Concerts.

[289] I am not satisfied that the plaintiff has established that Dame Kiri has breached s 42 of the FTA.

[290] The claim against Mittane for misleading or deceptive conduct seems to me to be quite hopeless. The claim as pleaded is that by sending the Contract (the Mittane Letter) on 16 December 2003 Mittane represented that it 'could, and would, procure' that Dame Kiri 'would perform at the Concerts'. As I have already said, this was a draft contract that was subject to further negotiations. The mere sending of the document to the plaintiff did not amount to such a representation.

[291] There is also a claim against Mittane that it had a duty to inform the plaintiff if Dame Kiri 'was not to perform at the Concerts'. It is alleged that its 'silence' following the representation was misleading or deceptive. Even if the representation had been made, by sending the draft contract, Mittane did not remain silent. When it was instructed that Dame Kiri did not wish to perform at the Concerts it ceased negotiations. It is true that Mittane did not expressly state that Dame Kiri did not want to perform at the Concerts, however the cessation of negotiations meant that she would not do so. The plaintiff's claims that Mittane was in breach of s 52 of the TPA fails. It follows that the plaintiff's claim against Dame Kiri for accessorial liability must also fail.

[292] The plaintiff claims that NGM breached s 52 of the TPA by representing to the plaintiff that Dame Kiri 'would perform at the Concerts'. Mr Cobden submitted that if there is a representation at all to be extracted from the 'great morass' of emails and conversations as pleaded over the eight month period, then it could only be along the lines of a representation that 'if agreement on all other issues is reached, these are suitable dates, and a suitable fee, for Dame Kiri to perform'. It was submitted that such a representation was never made untrue until the withdrawal from negotiations. I agree with these submissions.

[293] The plaintiff claimed that NGM had a duty to advise the plaintiff that Dame Kiri was making 'negative sounds' about the Concerts and that NGM's silence in this regard was misleading or deceptive. Mr Grace was cross-examined about the email from Mr Gleeson and agreed that he had not disclosed to the plaintiff that Dame Kiri had apparently discussed her negativity about the Concerts with Mr Gleeson. He gave the following evidence in cross-examination (tr 402):

Q. Was that because it was for your ears only that you didn't inform?

A. I think it is because as Kiri's manager I had heard her concerns because I was with her in Norwich and I was one thousand miles away and Paul Gleeson obviously was hearing the same concerns and I felt it was best that as Kiri was my, I didn't want to discuss things with Kiri over the phone so I thought I would wait and talk to her about her concerns when I got to New Zealand.

[294] Even if NGM had a duty to inform the plaintiff that Dame Kiri would not perform at the Concerts, that point had not been reached at the time that Mr Gleeson informed Mr Grace of Dame Kiri's 'negative sounds'. It must be remembered that this was only six days after Dame Kiri had penned her fax to Mr Grace requesting information about the launch. It is clear that some of her 'concerns' had probably been caused by the lack of communication with Mr Grace in the first two weeks of February. The plaintiff has not established that Dame Kiri had decided not to perform at the Concerts prior to 23 March 2004.

[295] The plaintiff relied upon NGM/Mr Grace's approval of the artwork for the launch as conduct amounting to a representation that Dame Kiri 'would perform' at the Concerts. The plaintiff assumed that a contract would be entered into with Mittane and I have found that this assumption was reasonable. That finding does not amount to a finding that NGM/Mr Grace represented that Dame Kiri 'would perform' at the Concerts. There is a distinction between those two positions. Even if the approval of the artwork were to amount to such a representation the plaintiff has the difficulty that it did not rely upon this representation, rather it wanted the side letter so that it did have representation or promise that Dame Kiri would perform at the Concerts.

[296] The plaintiff's claim against NGM in respect of a breach of s 52 of the TPA fails. Accordingly the plaintiffs' case against Mr Grace for accessorial liability pursuant to s 75B of the TPA fails.

Conclusion

[297] The plaintiff has failed to establish: (1) the claim against Mittane for breach of contract; (2) the claim against Dame Kiri for breach of collateral warranty; (3) the claim against Dame Kiri for breach of s 42 of the *Fair Trading Act*; (4) the claims against NGM and Mittane for breaches of s 52 of the *Trade Practices Act*; and (5) the claims against Dame Kiri and Mr Grace for accessorial liability under s 75B of the *Trade Practices Act.* All of those claims will be dismissed. The plaintiff has succeeded in establishing an entitlement to recover from Mittane its reasonable costs in the amount of $128,063.21. Before entering judgment in the plaintiff's favour in respect of that claim I will hear submissions on the award of interest.

[298] The parties are to bring in short minutes of order together with an agreed order for costs. If the parties are unable to agree on a costs order I will hear argument when the matter is fixed for the filing of short minutes and submissions on interest. The parties should make contact with my Associate to re-list the proceedings for finalising these aspects of the matter. Such contact should be made by no later than 20 April 2007.

E K Nominees Pty Ltd v Woolworths Ltd [2006] NSWSC 1172

Facts and issues

Woolworths and E K Nominees commenced negotiations regarding the construction of a supermarket in Auburn. After Woolworths confirmed their interest in the project, E K Nominees commenced preparing the land on the site while Woolworths made a formal offer to take a lease of a supermarket to be constructed on it. While the offer was approved by Woolworth's board, the approval itself was subject to entry into an agreement for lease and lease. However, Woolworths was aware that E K Nominees commenced working on the site and asked to expedite the construction works. In January 2002, Woolworths was approached by a third party regarding the construction of another supermarket at another site, made a formal expression of interest, and engaged in negotiations without informing E K Nominees. E K Nominees were only informed later on by a contractor, who told them that Woolworths decided to proceed with the new site rather than the Auburn one. Once approached by E K Nominees, Woolworths responded 'there is no decision made whether we go on your site, the Queen Street site, or both'. However, Woolworths decided to proceed with the development proposal at the new site and not with the agreement for lease of the Auburn Road site.

Decision

The Court held that E K Nominees was entitled to wasted expenditure less any retained benefit. Per White J at [131]:

> **Representation that Likelihood of Woolworths Entering Into Agreement for Lease had Not Materially Changed**
>
> E K Nominees alleged that by not disclosing to E K Nominees until about 7 May 2002 to E K Nominees that it had entered into negotiations for the grant of a lease at the Queen Street site, Woolworths represented to E K Nominees from early January 2002 until about 7 May 2002 that there had been no material change to the likelihood of entry by Woolworths into a lease of part of the Auburn Road site for the operation of a supermarket. This was a representation conveyed by conduct and silence. It was alleged to be misleading.
>
> [132] Woolworths denied that such a representation was conveyed. It submitted that it is not reasonable to expect in a negotiation between commercial parties that one party would inform the other party to the negotiations if an alternative opportunity presented itself which might have some ultimate impact upon the likelihood of a deal being consummated. It submitted that it was not misleading to fail to disclose the discussions in relation to the Queen Street site as E K Nominees was not entitled to believe that if an opportunity for Woolworths to take a lease of that property arose, that would be a matter which would be communicated to it.
>
> [133] In *Lam v Ausintel Investments Australia Pty Ltd & Ors* (1989) 97 FLR 458 at 475; [1990] ATPR 40-990 at 50,880, Gleeson CJ said:
>
>> Where parties are dealing at arm's length in a commercial situation in which they have conflicting interests it will often be the case that one party will be aware of information which, if known to the other, would or might cause that other party to take a different negotiating stance. This does not in itself impose any obligation on the first party to bring the information to the attention of the other party, and failure to do so would not, without more, ordinarily be regarded as dishonesty or even sharp practice. It would normally only be if there were an obligation of full disclosure that a different result would follow. That could occur, for example, by reason of some feature of the relationship between the parties, or because previous communications between them gave rise to a duty to add to or correct earlier information.
>
> [134] The present case involves more than the parties negotiating upon the terms of an agreement for lease. If that were all that were involved, I would readily accept the submission for Woolworths that there were no circumstances which gave rise to a reasonable expectation by E K Nominees that, if an alternative opportunity presented itself to Woolworths which affected the likelihood of the negotiations with E K Nominees being consummated, that fact would be disclosed.

[135] This is not merely a case in which the parties were negotiating with a view to entering into an agreement for lease. E K Nominees had spent, and was continuing to spend, substantial sums of money in order to satisfy the deferred commencement conditions of the development consent and otherwise to move the development forward as quickly as possible, with a view to expediting the date on which Woolworths could open its supermarket. It was doing so with Woolworths' knowledge and encouragement.

[136] That was not merely a matter of choice for E K Nominees. The effect of Woolworths' letter of 5 December 2000 was that if E K Nominees did not demonstrate its commitment to the project and to Woolworths' development program, then Woolworths could make a claim on it for its costs and loss of profit. By the same letter, Woolworths had held out that Woolworths' approval would be 'operative' for a period of twelve months from the time it was granted, thereby implying that provided the conditions of Woolworths' board's approval were met, and provided the parties could agree upon the matters to be included in the agreement for lease, Woolworths would not resile from its intention to enter into an agreement for lease. That was reinforced by the further provision in Woolworths' letter of 5 December 2000 that Woolworths could elect to terminate what it described as 'the agreement' without being liable for any claim if legal documentation were not executed, apparently within the period of twelve months following notification of Woolworths' board's approval, if E K Nominees could not satisfy it on the progress of the development. That letter is to be read in the context of the earlier correspondence in which E K Nominees had sought and obtained an assurance that Woolworths was genuinely pursuing the Auburn Road site as a location for the Woolworths supermarket. The parties knew that there was a superior site in which Woolworths was interested.

[137] In that context, E K Nominees could reasonably have expected that if a new proposal arose in relation to the Queen Street site, it would be told about it, or at least, it would be told that Woolworths may have to reconsider whether to proceed with the Auburn Road site.

[138] The negotiations for the agreement for lease were not carried on with any haste. In contrast, the architects and consultants retained by E K Nominees worked hard to satisfy the deferred commencement conditions of the development consent and to expedite the development. They had Woolworths' encouragement and co-operation in doing so. Against the background summarised above, Woolworths' conduct in encouraging that work, whilst at the same time evincing no need for haste in the negotiations for the agreement for lease, impliedly represented that there was no material change in the likelihood of Woolworths entering into the agreement for lease. Nothing was said to indicate that anything had changed which would affect the likelihood of its doing so.

[139] Accordingly, I consider that both of the representations alleged by E K Nominees were impliedly made by Woolworths.

Misleading and Deceptive Conduct by Non-Disclosure

[140] It is Woolworths' failure to disclose its response to the approach from Mr Markham in relation to the Queen Street site, or to disclose the alleged change in its intention to take up a lease of the Auburn Road site, or in the likelihood of its proceeding to enter into an agreement for lease of part of the Auburn Road site, which is claimed to make its conduct misleading.

[...]

[143] Woolworths submitted that at all times until 7 May 2002 it did intend to enter into an agreement for lease or lease if the terms were finally settled between the parties. It submitted that the relevant organ of Woolworths whose intention was to be considered was the Woolworths Property Committee. The committee did not make a decision to proceed with the Queen Street site until 7 May 2002, and did not decide not to proceed with the Auburn Road site until 4 June 2002. Accordingly, Woolworths did not cease to hold the intention of entering

into an agreement for lease with E K Nominees prior to 4 June 2002. If Mr Hunt was the relevant person whose intentions were to be attributed to Woolworths, Woolworths submitted that Mr Hunt continued to hold the intention that Woolworths would enter into an agreement for lease with E K Nominees during the relevant period.

[144] The question whether Woolworths ceased to hold the intention of entering into an agreement for lease with E K Nominees prior to 6 May 2002 requires identification of the individuals within Woolworths whose state of mind should be imputed to Woolworths. Woolworths submitted that it was only the members of its Property Committee whose intentions could be attributed to it. The Property Committee was exercising delegated authority from the board of directors. It was only the state of mind of the individuals comprising that committee which represented the state of mind of the company (*Tesco Supermarkets Ltd v Nattrass* [1971] UKHL 1; [1972] AC 153 at 170–171; *El Ajou v Dollar Land Holdings plc* [1993] EWCA Civ 4; [1994] 2 All ER 685 at 695–696, 705).

[145] If the position were unaffected by statute, I would accept this submission. I also accept that there is no evidence that members of the Woolworths Property Committee changed their intentions in relation to Woolworths entering into a lease of the Auburn Road site at any time before the Property Committee meeting on 7 May 2002. However, s 84(1) and (5) of the *Trade Practices Act* must be considered.

[. . .]

Change to Likelihood of Woolworths' Proceeding with Auburn Road

[150] I therefore turn to the second way in which E K Nominees put its case, namely, by reference to the implied representation that there had been no material change in the likelihood of Woolworths entering into a lease of the Auburn Road site.

[151] Counsel for Woolworths submitted that an implied representation to that effect could only be misleading or deceptive if either Woolworths did not believe the matter impliedly conveyed, or if there were no reasonable grounds for it to have a belief in the truth of that representation. Counsel submitted that there was no basis to find that the Woolworths Property Committee did not genuinely believe during the relevant period that the likelihood of Woolworths entering a lease at Auburn Road was unchanged because it did not meet to consider the issue until 7 May 2002. So much may be accepted. It was then submitted that Mr Hunt's evidence in his affidavit, that he did not have any belief that there had been any adverse impact on the prospects of Woolworths' proceeding with the establishment of a supermarket at the Auburn Road site, should be accepted.

[152] It was submitted that there were reasonable grounds for the belief to which Mr Hunt deposed because:

(a) of Woolworths' long and unsuccessful history in dealing with the Queen Street site, the chief problem being that the shape and size of the site was such that neither Woolworths' architects, nor RAAD's architects, could create a design for a Big W store that satisfied the requirements of the Big W division;
(b) Holdmark held no more than an option to purchase;
(c) Holdmark was contacting other potential major tenants;
(d) the Woolworths Property Committee had given an operative approval for a supermarket at the Auburn Road site and had not given consideration to the establishment of a new Woolworths supermarket at the Queen Street site. To this can be added Mr Hunt's evidence that he was aware of no case in which a development did not proceed once it had been approved by the Woolworths Property Committee;
(e) the process of putting a submission to the Property Committee involved obtaining external demographic data and performing internal financial modelling which would take at least three weeks after receipt of the information from the demographers;

(f) even after the Property Committee gave approval to proceed with the supermarket at the Queen Street site on 7 May 2002, there was still a real chance that Woolworths would operate two supermarkets in the Auburn area; and

(g) well after January 2002, Woolworths proceeded with its work on a design for a supermarket at Auburn Road and negotiated the terms of the draft agreement for lease and lease.

[153] In my view, notwithstanding these considerations, once Woolworths indicated its willingness to treat with Holdmark, there was a materially reduced likelihood of Woolworths proceeding to take a lease of the Auburn Road site. I also conclude that Mr Hunt was of the same view, notwithstanding his evidence to the contrary. It is true that in previous years, neither Woolworths' architects, nor RAAD's architects, had been able to create a design for the site which satisfied the requirements of the Big W division. However, matters had moved on. RAAD was no longer the owner of the site. New architects were engaged by Holdmark who were well known to Woolworths in this area and were well reputed. The 2001 decision to proceed with the Auburn Road site was made in the context of RAAD having sold the site to a purely residential developer. The prospects of a retail development involving Woolworths then appeared to be remote. In 2002, a new developer, Holdmark, had taken an option over the site.

[154] The fact that as at January 2002, Holdmark only had an option, and had not purchased the site, was neither here nor there. The purpose of a developer's taking an option to buy the site was to investigate the possibility of acquiring the site if arrangements could be made for an appropriate development. Mr Isaac said that, in his experience 'ninety-nine out of one hundred sites I have ever known have been by way of option. I have only exercised the option if the supermarket or whatever it was, committed to the site.' The Queen Street site was plainly superior to the Auburn Road site. Notwithstanding his evidence to the contrary, I consider that Mr Hunt believed that if the requirements of the Big W division could be satisfied, the Queen Street site would be the preferred option for Woolworths , and in that event, it would be in Woolworths' best interest not to proceed with the Auburn Road site. His submission to the Woolworths Property Committee of 30 April 2002 proceeded on that basis. Enough demographic assessment had already been made of the two sites for Mr Hunt to know that the Queen Street site was the preferred site. The fact that there was still a chance that Woolworths would operate two supermarkets in Auburn did not detract from the fact that by Woolworths' taking up the invitation of Markham Corporation to treat in relation to the Queen Street site, there was a material diminution in the likelihood of Woolworths' proceeding with the Auburn Road site.

[155] It was submitted for Woolworths that E K Nominees could not reasonably have expected that Woolworths would disclose confidential discussions with another property developer. The correspondence from Markham Corporation was addressed as being 'in confidence'. However, I do not accept that Woolworths was required to yield to Markham Corporation's request that its communications be kept confidential. In any event, Woolworths was not entitled to keep its dealings with Markham Corporation confidential at the expense of misleading E K Nominees, which continued to carry out work on the project ignorant of the changed circumstances. If Woolworths felt compelled to respect Markham Corporation's confidence, it could still have advised E K Nominees that it might have to reconsider its decision to enter into an agreement for lease with E K Nominees.

[156] There was a material change to the likelihood of Woolworths entering into an agreement for lease with E K Nominees from the time that Woolworths decided that the approach from Markham Corporation was one which was worth pursuing. That date was no later than 29 January 2002. On that day, Mr Hunt prepared a letter formally expressing interest in working with Mr Markham to secure a suitable retail opportunity for Big W and the supermarkets division. Woolworths' failure to disclose its changed position, whilst continuing to encourage E K Nominees to carry out work on the project, and continuing to negotiate terms of the

agreement for lease, was conduct, in trade or commerce, which was misleading or deceptive, or likely to mislead or deceive.

[. . .]

Conclusion

[291] E K Nominees is entitled to equitable compensation in a sum of $1,126,316, plus interest pursuant to s 100 of the *Civil Procedure Act*. Again, I presume no claim is made for GST paid on the expenditures. If there is an issue about that matter, I will hear argument when short minutes are brought in. There will need to be a calculation of interest based on the times at which E K Nominees paid Simhilt. I direct the plaintiff's counsel to bring in a calculation of interest and a minute of judgment to be entered.

[292] The short minutes should provide for the defendant to pay the plaintiff's costs.

British Steel Corporation v Cleveland Bridge and Engineering Co Ltd [1984] 1 All ER 504

Facts and issues

Cleveland Bridge and Engineering required steel nodes to construct a steel framework for a bank in Saudi Arabia. They asked British Steel Corp to deliver them, which they did while negotiations were still underway. Almost all nodes were delivered behind schedule, but the last one was delivered late. British Steel sued for payment and Cleveland Bridge and Engineering claimed damages for late delivery. The issue arose as to what were the parties' rights given the lack of a contract.

Decision

The Court held that since no contract had been entered into, the parties could only count on default remedies. As a result, British Steel was entitled to recover a reasonable price for the work done, whereas no remedies were available to Cleveland Bridge and Engineering for late delivery.

Per Goff J at 509:

> Now the question whether in a case such as the present any contract has come into existence must depend on a true construction of the relevant communications which have passed between the parties and the effect (if any) of their actions pursuant to those communications. There can be no hard and fast answer to the question whether a letter of intent will give rise to a binding agreement: everything must depend on the circumstances of the particular case. In most cases, where work is done pursuant to a request contained in a letter of intent, it will not matter whether a contract did or did not come into existence, because, if the party who has acted on the request is simply claiming payment, his claim will usually be based on a *quantum meruit*, and it will make no difference whether that claim is contractual or quasi-contractual. Of course, a *quantum meruit* claim (like the old actions for money had and received and for money paid) straddles the boundaries of what we now call contract and restitution, so the mere framing of a claim as a *quantum meruit* claim, or a claim for a reasonable sum, does not assist in classifying the claim as contractual or quasi contractual. But where, as here, one party is seeking to claim damages for breach of contract, the question whether any contract came into existence is of crucial importance.
>
> As a matter of analysis the contract (if any) which may come into existence following a letter of intent may take one of two forms: either there may be an ordinary executory contract, under

which each party assumes reciprocal obligations to the other; or there [510] may be what is sometimes called an 'if' contract, ie a contract under which A requests B to carry out a certain performance and promises B that, if he does so, he will receive a certain performance in return, usually remuneration for his performance. The latter transaction is really no more than a standing offer which, if acted on before it lapses or is lawfully withdrawn, will result in a binding contract.

The former type of contract was held to exist by Mr Edgar Fay QC, the offical Referee, in *Turriff Construction Ltd v Regalia Knitting Mills Ltd* (1971) 202 EG 169; and it is the type of contract for which counsel for CBE contended in the present case. Of course, as I have already said, everything must depend on the facts of the particular case; but certainly, on the facts of the present case (and, as I imagine, on the facts of most cases), this must be a very difficult submission to maintain. It is only necessary to look at the terms of CBE's letter of intent in the present case to appreciate the difficulties. In that letter, the request to BSC to proceed immediately with the work was stated to be 'pending the preparation and issuing to you of the official form of sub-contract', being a sub-contract which was plainly in a state of negotiation, not least on the issues of price, delivery dates, and the applicable terms and conditions. In these circumstances, it is very difficult to see how BSC, by starting work, bound themselves to any contractual performance. No doubt it was envisaged by CBE at the time they sent the letter that negotiations had reached an advanced stage, and that a formal contract would soon be signed; but, since the parties were still in a state of negotiation, it is impossible to say with any degree of certainty what the material terms of that contract would be. I find myself quite unable to conclude that, by starting work in these circumstances, BSC bound themselves to complete the work. In the course of argument, I put to counsel for CBE the question whether BSC were free at any time, after starting work, to cease work. His submission was that they were not free to do so, even if negotiations on the terms of the formal contract broke down completely. I find this submission to be so repugnant to common sense and the commercial realities that I am unable to accept it. It is perhaps revealing that, on 4 April 1979, BSC did indeed state that they were not prepared to proceed with the contract until they had an agreed specification, a reaction which, in my judgment, reflected not only the commercial, but also the legal, realities of the situation.

I therefore reject CBE's submission that a binding executory contract came into existence in this case. There remains the question whether, by reason of BSC carrying out work pursuant to the request contained in CBE's letter of intent, there came into existence a contract by virtue of which BSC were entitled to claim reasonable remuneration; ie whether there was an 'if' contract of the kind I have described. In the course of argument, I was attracted by this alternative (really on the basis that, not only was it analytically possible, but also that it could provide a vehicle for certain contractual obligations of BSC concerning their performance, eg implied terms as to the quality of goods supplied by them). But the more I have considered the case, the less attractive I have found this alternative. The real difficulty is to be found in the factual matrix of the transaction, and in particular the fact that the work was being done pending a formal subcontract the terms of which were still in a state of negotiation. It is, of course, a notorious fact that, when a contract is made for the supply of goods on a scale and in circumstances such as the present, it will in all probability be subject to standard terms, usually the standard terms of the supplier. Such standard terms will frequently legislate, not only for the liability of the seller for defects, but also for the damages (if any) for which the seller will be liable in the event not only of defects in the goods but also of late delivery. It is a commonplace that a seller of goods may exclude liability for consequential loss, and may agree liquidated damages for delay. In the present case, an unresolved dispute broke out between the parties on the question whether CBE's or BSC's standard terms were to apply, the former providing no limit to the seller's liability for delay and the latter excluding such liability altogether. Accordingly, when, in a case such as the present, the parties are still in a state of negotiation, it is impossible to predicate what liability (if any) will be assumed by the seller for, eg, defective goods or late delivery, if a formal contract should be entered into. In these circumstances, if the buyer asks the seller to commence work 'pending' the parties entering into a formal contract, it is difficult to [511] infer from the buyer acting on that request that he is assuming any responsibility for his a performance, except such responsibility as will rest on him under the terms of the contract which both parties confidently anticipate they will shortly enter into. It would be an extraordinary result if, by acting on such a request in such circumstances, the buyer were to assume an unlimited liability for his contractual performance, when he would never assume such liability under any contract which he entered into.

For these reasons, I reject the solution of the 'if' contract. In my judgment, the true analysis of the situation is simply this. Both parties confidently expected a formal contract to eventuate. In these circumstances, to expedite performance under that anticipated contract, one requested the other to commence the contract work, and the other complied with that request. If thereafter, as anticipated, a contract was entered into, the work done as requested will be treated as having been performed under that contract; if, contrary to their expectation, no contract was entered into, then the performance of the work is not referable to any contract the terms of which can be ascertained, and the law simply imposes an obligation on the party who made the request to pay a reasonable sum for such work as has been done pursuant to that request, such an obligation sounding in quasi contract or, as we now say, in restitution. Consistently with that solution, the party making the request may find himself liable to pay for work which he would not have had to pay for as such if the anticipated contract had come into existence, eg preparatory work which will, if the contract is made, be allowed for in the price of the finished work (cf *William Lacey (Hounslow) Ltd v Davis* (1957) 2 All ER 712, (1957) 1 WLR 932). This solution moreover accords with authority: see the decision in *Lacey v Davis*, the decision of the Court of Appeal in *Sanders & Forster Ltd v A Monk & Co Ltd* [1980] CA Transcript 35, though that decision rested in part on a concession, and the crisp dictum of Parker J in *OTM Ltd v Hydranautics* [1981] 2 Lloyd's Rep 211 at 214, when he said of a letter of intent that 'its only effect would be to enable the defendants to recover on a quantum meruit for work done pursuant to the direction' contained in the letter. I only wish to add to this part of my judgment the footnote that, even if I had concluded that in the circumstances of the present case there was a contract between the parties and that that contract was of the kind I have described as an 'if' contract, then I would still have concluded that there was no obligation under that contract on the part of BSC to continue with or complete the contract work, and therefore no obligation on their part to complete the work within a reasonable time. However, my conclusion in the present case is that the parties never entered into any contract at all.

QUESTIONS

(1) Discuss why, in *Leading Edge Events Australia Pty Ltd v Kiri Te Kanawa* [2007] NSWSC 228, it was held that should a party's words or conduct suggest that they are prepared to enter into a contract, but they ultimately decide not to go ahead, that will not of itself be misleading or deceptive.

(2) Elaborate on the view that Sheppard J set out in *Sabemo Pty Ltd v North Sydney Municipal Council* [1977] 2 NSWLR 880 regarding the importance of the reason(s) why a contract is not entered into.

(3) Discuss why, in *British Steel Corporation v Cleveland Bridge and Engineering Co Ltd* [1984] 1 All ER 504, Goff J rejected CBE's submission that a binding executory contract came into existence.

4.5 International perspectives

Where the contract is an international sale between commercial parties to which the *CISG* applies (see **25.4.1** regarding applicability), some of the issues discussed above are covered by the *CISG*'s provisions, whilst others are not. The effect of entire agreement clauses and no oral modification clauses will be determined under its rules, as discussed at **25.5.6**. Whether or not standard terms are incorporated into the contract is a question determined by the *CISG* as a matter of formation of contract: see **25.7.3**. Arguably, whether 'surprising terms' contained within standard terms are incorporated is also a matter determined by those rules. However, the validity of standard terms is an issue outside the *CISG*'s scope, and will fall for determination under the applicable domestic law: art 4(a) *CISG*. Likewise, domestic rules will apply in respect of the following issues where *CISG* otherwise governs the contract: agency mistake affecting validity, and actions where the contract fails to materialise. Parties to contracts governed by the *CISG* remain subject to the ACL s 18 on misleading conduct where the ACL applies.

The UNIDROIT Principles capture a broader range of issues, but are much more rarely applicable in practice (see **25.4.3** on applicability). In particular, in relation to agency, the UNIDROIT Principles arts 2.2.1–2.2.10 contain detailed rules outlining the effect of agency in contract. Moreover, the UNIDROIT Principles purport to create a form of pre-contractual liability where contractual negotiations break down in circumstances of bad faith in art 2.1.15: see further **25.8.7**. The extensive nature of good faith obligations within the UNIDROIT Principles means that parties might in some instances be liable for pre-contractual failures to disclose. Like the *CISG*, the UNIDROIT Principles in arts 2.1.17 and 2.1.18 deal with entire agreement clauses and no oral modification clauses, and at arts 2.1.19–2.1.22 with standard form contracts; but, contrary to the *CISG*, the UNIDROIT Principles arts 3.1.1–3.3.2 contain rules concerning validity, including for mistake at arts 3.2.1–3.2.2: **25.7.10**, and provide for restitution if contracts are avoided for such issues: art 3.2.15. If applicable, ACL s 18 continues to apply to contracts governed by the UNIDROIT Principles.

4.6 Review

- There are many ways in which a contract can or should be negotiated
- Most transactions occur via standard form contracts
- Drafting styles differ considerably
- The (future) parties to a contract are required to fulfil certain obligations during the negotiation phase

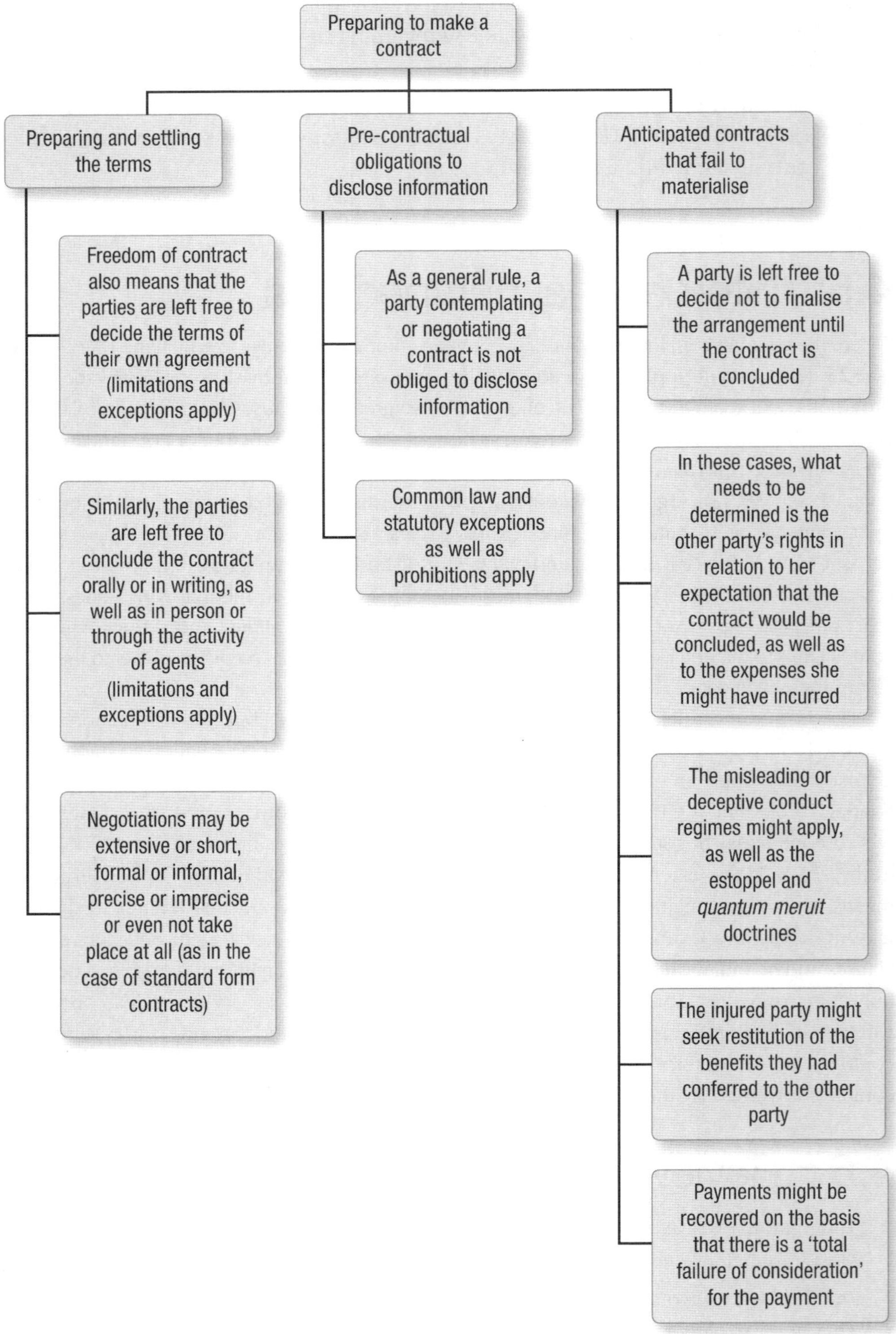
Preparing to make a contract
Preparing and settling the terms
Freedom of contract also means that the parties are left free to decide the terms of their own agreement (limitations and exceptions apply)
Similarly, the parties are left free to conclude the contract orally or in writing, as well as in person or through the activity of agents (limitations and exceptions apply)
Negotiations may be extensive or short, formal or informal, precise or imprecise or even not take place at all (as in the case of standard form contracts)
Pre-contractual obligations to disclose information
As a general rule, a party contemplating or negotiating a contract is not obliged to disclose information
Common law and statutory exceptions as well as prohibitions apply
Anticipated contracts that fail to materialise
A party is left free to decide not to finalise the arrangement until the contract is concluded
In these cases, what needs to be determined is the other party's rights in relation to her expectation that the contract would be concluded, as well as to the expenses she might have incurred
The misleading or deceptive conduct regimes might apply, as well as the estoppel and *quantum meruit* doctrines
The injured party might seek restitution of the benefits they had conferred to the other party
Payments might be recovered on the basis that there is a 'total failure of consideration' for the payment

TIPS FOR APPLYING THE LAW IN PRACTICE

First, it is fundamental to gain a detailed understanding of your party's intention(s)—ie why they want to enter into a contract. This is of the essence if you are to find an efficient way to protect their rights and interests. Second, what needs to be determined is whether the law allows the party to do what she intends to achieve with the contract, and if so, how this has to be done for the arrangement to be deemed legally valid, and thus enforceable in case of dispute. Amongst the many elements that must be considered, a pivotal one is whether the contract needs to comply with any formalities. A familiarity with the various bargaining techniques and drafting styles discussed in this chapter is therefore very important. Of equal significance is being aware that the rule permitting pre-contractual silence is by no means absolute: there are clear pre-contractual obligations to disclose information and a party's failure to comply might be treated as a misrepresentation. This would render the contract voidable.

PROBLEM QUESTIONS

In March 2017, John and Alison decided to build a granny flat at the rear of their home so that John's parents could sell their home interstate and move in with them. John was a carpenter by trade and did all the carpentry work himself, after he had the foundation professionally laid. However, he needed a certified electrician to do the electrical work to complete the job. John hired Matthew, a certified electrician, on the recommendation of one of John's mates. John and Matthew discussed the work that needed to be done and the fact that it had to be completed by 1 July 2017, because his in-laws were flying up that day to move in. John and Matthew jointly figured that the work would take three days to complete. However, Matthew told John that, while he was interested in carrying out the work, he would give him confirmation in due course. Matthew also told John that he (John) would have to pay $500 in advance and a further $3,500 on completion of the work. Further, Matthew told John that it would be good if he (John) could purchase some of the materials himself so that there would be no delays once he commenced carrying out the work.

John, who was under the impression that Matthew would in fact do the job, made a transfer of $500 in his favour and purchased all the materials Matthew had mentioned for a total expenditure of $4,500. In early April, John called Matthew to touch base and see when he would commence the electrical work. Matthew replied saying, 'I am sorry mate, but something else has come up. It's a hectic period and I won't be able to finish your flat. Call my good friend Andrew, he might be able to do it.' Irritated, John said 'Ok bye', hung up the phone and immediately called Andrew, who did in fact commence the electrical work for the flat. However, after working on the job for two days in mid-May, he had to leave the job for several days to do other work he had previously arranged. He promised John he would be back in time to complete the work by 1 July . However, Andrew never returned to complete the job. John seeks now advice as to whether he has any course of action against Matthew, as he believes that had Matthew had done the work like he made John believe, none of this would have happened.

RESEARCH QUESTIONS

(1) Does Australian contract law have an implied duty to act in good faith?

(2) Elaborate on the spread of standardised forms of contracting from the perspective of the contract law requirements of 'agreement' and 'intention to create legal relations'.

5

FORMATION

5.1 Overview

There are a number of elements needed for a contract to be formed. These are: intention to create legal relations, agreement, consideration, capacity, and compliance with any applicable formalities. This chapter will discuss all of these elements, considering in particular:

- the role of presumptions in determining intention to create legal relations;
- how it is determined whether or not an agreement has been reached;
- the nature of and requirements for consideration;
- the importance of certainty and completeness in the formation of contracts;
- parties who may lack the capacity to enter into a contract; and
- the formalities that are required in relation to specific types of contracts (eg contracts for the sale and purchase of land) to be binding.

It will also briefly discuss the nature and effect of conditional contracts.[1]

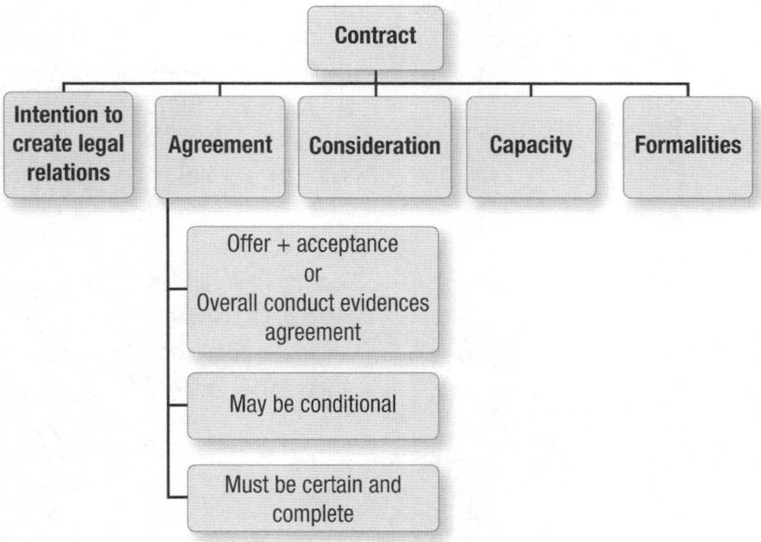

5.2 Intention to create legal relations

In order for it to be said that a valid contract has been formed, the parties must have intended to create legal relations. What this means is that the parties must have intended to create a *legal* relationship with *legal* consequences in the event of breach and the ability to seek a remedy through the court process. The question of the parties' intention in entering into the agreement is determined objectively, with reference to the reasonable person's view of the words and conduct of those parties. This objective approach is discussed in the following case extracts.

1 Noting that the issues surrounding preliminary agreements are covered at length in **Chapter 6**.

Concept	Short explanation	Relevant authorities	*Principles* text*
Intention to create legal relations must be present for an agreement to be binding	In making an agreement, the parties must intend to become legally bound in the sense that legal consequences will arise if the agreement is breached. This intention is determined objectively	*Air Great Lakes Pty Ltd v K S Easter (Holdings) Pty Ltd* (1985) 2 NSWLR 309	Chapter 5: 5.02–5.04
All surrounding circumstances are relevant to determining intention	The conduct of the parties, the nature of the relationship between the parties and the nature of the agreement are all relevant factors when assessing whether or not an intention to create legal relations exists	*Ermogenous v Greek Orthodox Community of SA Inc* (2002) 209 CLR 95 *Rose & Frank Co v J R Crompton & Bros Ltd* [1923] 2 KB 261 *Administration of the Territory of Papua New Guinea v Leahy* (1961) 105 CLR 6 *Balfour v Balfour* [1919] 2 KB 571 *Evans v Secretary, Department of Families, Housing, Community Services and Indigenous Affairs* (2012) 289 ALR 237	Chapter 5: 5.05–5.09

* Consult the corresponding section(s) of the *Principles* text for more detail.

Air Great Lakes Pty Ltd v K S Easter (Holdings) Pty Ltd (1985) 2 NSWLR 309

Facts and issues

The parties entered into an agreement pursuant to which K S Easter (Holdings) Pty Ltd ('K S Easter') agreed to purchase from Air Great Lakes Pty Ltd ('Air Great Lakes') the former's commuter airline service. In response to Air Great Lakes alleging that it had abandoned the contract, K S Easter argued that the parties did not intend to be legally bound by the document in question, despite it being signed. This argument succeeded at first instance and Air Great Lakes appealed. An issue to be determined by the Court of Appeal, therefore, was whether the parties had intended to create legal relations.

Decision

Per Mahoney JA at 330:

> It is generally accepted that, in determining whether what the parties have done results in a binding contract, their intention is significant. And there is reference in the cases and the textbooks to the question whether, for there to be a binding contract, it is necessary that the parties have an actual or subjective intention to contract . . . But questions in that form are, I think, apt to mislead: it is, in my opinion, of more assistance to ask whether actual or subjective intention to contract plays a part in determining whether there is a binding contract, and (if it does) what part it plays.
>
> The proper view is, in my opinion, that the existence of a contract is a consequence which the law imposes upon, or sees as a result of, what the parties have said and done. Actual subjective intention to contract is a factor which the law takes into account in determining whether a contract exists but it is not, or not always, the determining factor.
>
> The matter may be tested by an example: A says, 'I promise to sell Black Acre to B for $100'; and B says, 'I promise to buy Black Acre from A for that price', the promises being made orally. In such a case, a binding contract will be held to exist. And this will be so even though neither A nor B subjectively adverted to (and therefore had no actual subjective intention as to) whether, by the exchange of those promises, a binding contract would be made. The law will hold a binding contract to have been made even though neither had any actual subjective intention that there be a contract, in the sense that neither party gave any thought to the matter.
>
> The law looks, in this regard, to what the parties have done, viz, to their exchange of promises to buy and sell; and it treats the fact of that exchange as prima facie sufficient for imposing on them the legal relationship of contract. It will determine whether, according to what they said and did, they exchanged congruent promises: if they did, a contract will prima facie result.
>
> But this does not mean that actual subjective intention qua contract may not be relevant. Thus, if A, notwithstanding what he said, had the actual subjective intention that no contract should result, a binding contract may not be held to exist. If the terms of A's promise were such that B, as a reasonable man, would take it to involve a legal commitment and B did not know that A did not intend that there be a binding contract, then a binding [331] contract would result. A would not be permitted to set up, against such a meaning of what he had said, a contrary subjective intention.
>
> But the result would not, I think, be the same if B knew of A's actual subjective intention. The law would not, I think, impose the relationship of contract where, eg, A thought he was play-acting and B knew of that fact. A's actual subjective intention would be effective to prevent the contract arising. A fortiori, if both A and B had the intention that no contract should result, and each knew of it, then none would be imposed. And, I think, this notwithstanding that a reasonable bystander would take from what they said and did that there was an exchange of congruent promises and a mutual purpose to contract. I put aside for this purpose special cases, of estoppel, third party rights, and the like.
>
> The result is therefore that intention to contract, in the subjective sense, is relevant to but not determinative of the existence of a binding contract. It acts, in a sense, as a limiting factor, that is, as a reason for not giving to what on the face of it is an exchange of congruent promises, the legal consequences which would otherwise be given to it. And on this basis, it is, in principle, relevant to know what was the actual subjective intention of each party, in the example that I have given, in order to determine whether the legal relationship of contract is to be held to exist. More correctly, it is relevant to know the intention of the one party where it is the intention of or known to the other.

5.2.1 Determining intention

The onus is on the party alleging the existence of a binding contract to establish an intention to create legal relations. The traditional approach to determining intention was to characterise the nature of the relationship and, from this characterisation, apply a presumption to determine whether intention existed. Thus domestic, family or social agreements were presumed not to carry with them an intention to create a legally binding agreement. On the other hand, commercial agreements were presumed to carry with them the necessary intention to create a legally binding agreement. The use of these presumptions was questioned by the High Court in *Ermogenous v Greek Orthodox Community*,[2] extracted below.

Ermogenous v Greek Orthodox Community of SA Inc (2002) 209 CLR 95

Facts and issues

Ermogenous was appointed by the Greek Orthodox Community of SA Inc ('the Community') as the Archbishop of the Greek Orthodox Church in Australia. Ermogenous acted in this role for over 23 years, receiving a regular stipend from the Community who in turn dictated his duties in this role. Once Ermogenous resigned from his position he brought a claim under the *Industrial and Employee Relations Act 1994* (SA) for long service leave and annual leave. The claim was made on the basis that there was a contract of employment between the parties, rendering Ermogenous an 'employee' and therefore entitling him to such benefits. An Industrial Magistrate upheld Ermogenous' claim and, when the Community appealed to the Industrial Relations Court of South Australia, both a single judge and the Full Court upheld this decision. The Full Court of the Supreme Court of South Australia, however, upheld the Community's appeal and dismissed Ermogenous' claim, finding that no contract of employment existed between the parties. Ermogenous appealed to the High Court.

A key issue to be determined was whether the Full Court of the Supreme Court was wrong to hold that the parties did not intend to enter into a legally binding relationship.

Decision

Per Gaudron, McHugh, Hayne and Callinan JJ at 105:

> 'It is of the essence of contract, regarded as a class of obligations, that there is a voluntary assumption of a legally enforceable duty.' (*Australian Woollen Mills Pty Ltd v The Commonwealth* (1954) 92 CLR 424 at 457, per Dixon CJ, Williams, Webb, Fullagar and Kitto JJ) To be a legally enforceable duty there must, of course, be identifiable parties to the arrangement, the terms of the arrangement must be certain, and, unless recorded as a deed, there must generally be real consideration for the agreement. Yet '[t]he circumstances may show that [the parties] did not intend, or cannot be regarded as having intended, to subject their

2 (2002) 209 CLR 95 ('*Ermogenous*').

agreement to the adjudication of the courts' (*South Australia v The Commonwealth* (1962) 108 CLR 130 at 154 per Windeyer J).

Because the inquiry about this last aspect may take account of the subject matter of the agreement, the status of the parties to it, their relationship to one another, and other surrounding circumstances, not only is there obvious difficulty in formulating rules intended to prescribe the kinds of cases in which an intention to create contractual relations should, or should not, be found to exist, it would be wrong to do so. Because the search for the 'intention to create contractual relations' requires an objective assessment of the state of affairs between the parties (as distinct from the identification of any uncommunicated subjective reservation or intention that either may harbour) the circumstances which might properly be taken into account in deciding whether there was the relevant intention are so varied as to preclude the formation of any prescriptive rules. Although the word 'intention' is used in this context, it is used in the same sense as it is used in other contractual contexts. It describes what it is that would objectively be conveyed by what was said or done, having regard to [106] the circumstances in which those statements and actions happened. It is not a search for the uncommunicated subjective motives or intentions of the parties.

In this context of intention to create legal relations there is frequent reference to 'presumptions'. It is said that it may be presumed that there are some 'family arrangements' which are not intended to give rise to legal obligations and it was said in this case that it should not be presumed that there was an intention to create legal relations because it was a matter concerning the engagement of a minister of religion. For our part, we doubt the utility of using the language of presumptions in this context. At best, the use of that language does no more than invite attention to identifying the party who bears the onus of proof. In this case, where issue was joined about the existence of a legally binding contract between the parties, there could be no doubt that it was for the appellant to demonstrate that there was such a contract. Reference to presumptions may serve only to distract attention from that more basic and important proposition.

More importantly, the use of the language of presumptions may lead, as it did in this case, to treating one proposition (that an intention to create legal relations is not to be presumed) as equivalent to another, different proposition (that generally, or usually, or it is to be presumed that, an arrangement about remuneration of a minister of religion will not give rise to legally enforceable obligations).

In upholding the findings of the Industrial Magistrate in relation to the question of intention, their Honours found that he had in fact:

[112] ... examined, with care, all of the objective circumstances which bore on whether the parties intended to make a contract, as distinct from an arrangement binding only in honour.

The Industrial Magistrate did not make the error which the majority in the Full Court of the Supreme Court attributed to him. Even if the Industrial Magistrate did make that error, the inference which the Full Court drew about the absence of an intention to create legal relations was an inference that was not open on the facts that had been found at trial.

Kirby J came to the same conclusion, albeit in a separate judgment. The appeal was allowed.

Consequently, when approaching the issue of intention, the question is to be determined by conducting an objective assessment of the circumstances surrounding the agreement which would include, but would not be limited to, a consideration of the nature of the relationship between the parties and the character of the agreement itself.

Rose & Frank Co v J R Crompton & Bros Ltd [1923] 2 KB 261

Facts and issues

Rose & Frank Co ('Rose & Frank') and J R Crompton & Brothers ('J R Crompton') entered into an agreement relating to the supply of tissue paper. The agreement provided, in part: '[t]his arrangement is not entered into ... as a formal or legal agreement, and shall not be subject to legal jurisdiction in the law courts'. Rose & Frank sued for breach of contract following what it alleged to be wrongful repudiation of the agreement by J R Crompton. At issue was whether or not the parties intended to be legally bound by the agreement. It was found at first instance that the agreement was binding. J R Crompton appealed this decision.

Decision

Per Atkin LJ at 293:

> To create a contract there must be a common intention of the parties to enter into legal obligations, mutually communicated expressly or impliedly. Such an intention ordinarily will be inferred when parties enter into an agreement which in other respects conforms to the rules of law as to the formation of contracts. It may be negatived impliedly by the nature of the agreed promise or promises, as in the case of offer and acceptance of hospitality, or of some agreements made in the course of family life between members of a family as in *Balfour* v. *Balfour.* If the intention may be negatived impliedly it may be negatived expressly. In this document, construed as a whole, I find myself driven to the conclusion that the clause in question expresses in clear terms the mutual intention of the parties not to enter into legal obligations in respect to the matters upon which they are recording their agreement. I have never seen such a clause before, but I see nothing necessarily absurd in business men seeking to regulate their business relations by mutual promises which fall short of legal obligations, and rest on obligations of either honour or self-interest, or perhaps both.

The appeal was allowed.

Administration of the Territory of Papua and New Guinea v Leahy (1961) 105 CLR 6

Facts and issues

Leahy kept cattle on land leased from the Administration of the Territory of Papua and New Guinea ('the Administration'). The Administration agreed to carry out tick eradication works on the property which did not succeed in eliminating the infestation. Leahy brought an action against the Administration for breach of contract in relation to which he was successful at first instance. At issue on appeal was whether the agreement was contractual in nature.

Decision

Per Dixon CJ at 10:

> In my opinion this appeal must be allowed on the simple ground that the facts in no way support the conclusion that the defendant, the Administration of the Territory, entered into any such

> contractual relation with the plaintiff as his pleading alleges or as has been found in his favour. I am clearly of opinion that the Administration of the Territory, by its officers, did not contract with the plaintiff; there was no intention on their part to enter into any contract, to undertake contractual obligations or to do or undertake more than was considered naturally and properly incident to carrying out their governmental or departmental function in the conditions prevailing. They were merely pursuing the policy adopted for the eradication of tick.

McTiernan J (at 11) agreed:

> It was not an express or implied term of the arrangement that the respondent should make any payment for the treatment of the cattle. I cannot agree that the Administration through its officers intended to enter into legal relations when, at the request of the respondent, it undertook the organization of the tick eradication campaign with respect to his cattle. The conduct of the parties constituted an administrative arrangement by which the Administration in pursuance of its agricultural policy, gave assistance to an owner of stock to prevent that stock contracting a disease which was prevalent in the Territory. The work done by the Administration was analagous to a social service which generally does not have as its basis a legal relationship of a contractual nature and from which no right of action would arise in favour of the citizen who is receiving the services if the Government acts inefficiently in performing them.

The same conclusion was reached by Kitto J at 20:

> From first to last the Department showed itself to be doing no more than giving effect to a general policy of dispensing aid to individual cattle owners as a means of coping with a recognized menace to an important part of the Territory's economy. And the respondent's [21] attitude throughout was that of a private person appealing for government assistance on the ground that the Department, by doing for him what it insisted ought to be done on his property, would be performing a function of government in accordance with its settled policy. The whole atmosphere of the correspondence and discussions that took place was different from that which exists between contracting parties.

Balfour v Balfour [1919] 2 KB 571

Facts and issues

Mr Balfour worked and lived in Ceylon, Sri Lanka. While Mrs Balfour had originally accompanied him to Ceylon, she was unable to return with him after a trip back to England due to her poor health. Before leaving for Ceylon, Mr Balfour agreed to pay Mrs Balfour £30 per month while she remained in England on the basis that she would support herself and not call on him for any further assistance. At the time the agreement was made, the parties were on good terms. However, their marriage subsequently broke down—Mrs Balfour never returned to Ceylon and Mr Balfour ultimately stopped making the monthly payments. Mrs Balfour obtained an order for alimony, but also brought proceedings to recover these monthly payments which had not been paid. She succeeded at first instance and Mr Balfour appealed. The issue before the Court of Appeal was whether the agreement was enforceable; that is, had the parties intended this agreement, made between a husband and a wife, to be legally binding?

Decision

Per Atkin LJ at 578:

> It is quite common, and it is the natural and inevitable result of the relationship of husband and wife, that the two spouses should make arrangements between themselves — agreements such as are in dispute in this action ... To my mind those agreements, or many of them, do not result in contracts at all, and they do not result in contracts even though there may be what as between other parties would constitute consideration for the agreement ... [579] Nevertheless they are not contracts, and they are not contracts because the parties did not intend that they should be attended by legal consequences. To my mind it would be of the worst possible example to hold that agreements such as this resulted in legal obligations which could be enforced in the Courts ... [These agreements] are not sued upon, not because the parties are reluctant to enforce their legal rights when the agreement is broken, but because the parties, in the inception of the arrangement, never intended that they should be sued upon. Agreements such as these are outside the realm of contracts altogether ... [I]t appears to me to be plainly established that the promise here was [580] not intended by either party to be attended by legal consequences. I think the onus was upon the plaintiff, and the plaintiff has not established any contract.

The appeal was allowed.

Evans v Secretary, Department of Families, Housing, Community Services and Indigenous Affairs (2012) 289 ALR 237

Facts and issues

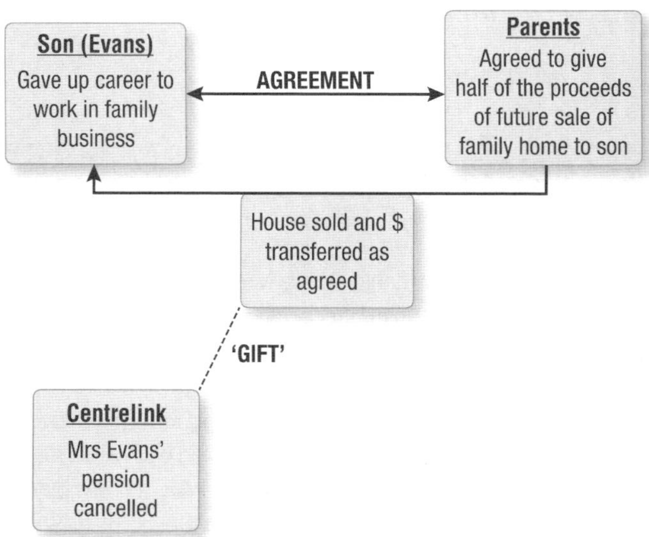

Evans agreed with his parents to give up his own career and instead work for the family business as managing director. In return, his parents agreed to give him half of the proceeds from the sale of the family home, whenever this sale occurred in the future. The house was ultimately sold and half the proceeds were duly transferred by Mrs Evans to her son, Mr Evans having predeceased the sale. As a result of this transaction Mrs Evans' aged pension was cancelled, with Centrelink viewing the transfer of funds as a gift. This decision was unsuccessfully challenged in both the Social Security Appeals Tribunal and the Administrative Appeals Tribunal on the basis that the transfer was made pursuant to a legally binding contract. On appeal in the Federal Court, Evans was again unsuccessful and appealed to the Full Court. Ultimately, the issue to be determined was whether a presumption remained (following *Ermogenous*) that arrangements between an adult child and his parents were not intended to create contractual relations.

Decision

Per Rares, Buchanan and Griffiths JJ at 240:

> The tribunal observed there was 'a rebuttable presumption of fact that close relatives such as parent and child do not intend their arrangements to create legal relations' and cited *Jones v Padavatton* [1969] 1 WLR 328; [1969] 2 All ER 616 in support of this proposition. The primary judge rejected the appellant's argument that this presumption was not now the law in Australia. The appellant had relied below on what Gaudron, McHugh, Hayne and Callinan JJ had said in *Ermogenous* 209 CLR at 105–107 [24]–[28] where they doubted the utility of using the language of presumptions in the context of discerning whether parties intended to create legal relationships. The primary judge concluded, after reviewing *Jones* [1969] 1 WLR 328 and a number of subsequent Australian cases, that their Honours' observations in *Ermogenous* did 'no more than provide a salutary warning that the presumption is not necessarily determinative nor that its application is mandatory, and that it could be erroneous to afford it undue weight'. He concluded that *Ermogenous* did not indicate that the presumption applied by the tribunal was no longer good law ...
>
> [241] In our opinion, *Ermogenous* 209 CLR at 105–107 [24]–[28] rejected the use of presumptions as a basis for ascertaining whether parties intended to enter into contractual relations. Their Honours explained that the question in every case was whether an objective assessment of the state of affairs between the parties, in the context in which they were dealing evinced an intention to create contractual relations. That enquiry can take account of the subject matter of the agreement, the status of the parties to it, their relationship to one another and other surrounding circumstances.
>
> [...]
>
> [242] The fundamental question, whatever the circumstances of the parties, is whether in the situation in which they were, did their words and conduct objectively assessed, evince an intention that they intended to assume legally binding contractual obligations to each other? The family or other relationship is one circumstance that is relevant.
>
> Where a parent asks a child to change his or her life, such as by giving up a job or career to look after a family business or to nurse or care for the parent in old age, on the holding out of a reward, the circumstances may warrant the inference that a legally binding contract was intended ...
>
> Much depends on an evaluation of the actual circumstances. There will, of course, be situations in which language or conduct that is capable of being viewed as contractual if it were between strangers, could be viewed differently if it occurred between family members or friends. Although the characterisation of promises made between persons in family, domestic and social relationships is not be governed by a presumption that they are not contractual, nonetheless courts must be careful not to convert informal situations that frequently arise in circumstances that involve love, friendship and concomitant human emotional feelings of duty or responsibility, into the stuff of daily commercial life. Hence, the importance of considering, objectively, all the circumstances in arriving at a conclusion in respect of whether the parties intended to enter into

> contractual relations, free from suggested presumptions. The surest and safest way to proceed is, as the plurality held in *Ermogenous* 209 CLR at 106 [26]–[27], by examining objectively the actual circumstances and context of the parties' dealings to ascertain whether what they said and did evinced an intention to contract as opposed to expressing a sincere, but legally insufficient, promise or commitment that reflected the trust or love shared between them.
>
> All that said, there was no error in the finding of the primary judge that the tribunal ultimately made an unappellable finding of fact that it had not been established that Mr Evans and his parents had intended to make a legally enforceable contract. Although the tribunal referred to a rebuttable presumption of fact that close relatives such as parent and child do not intend their arrangements to create legal relations, it is clear that the tribunal's finding would have been no different if the reference had not been made . . .

The appeal was dismissed with the Court making reference to a complete lack of evidence being produced by Evans or Mrs Evans (prior to her passing) as to the nature of the agreement. The Court thereby concluded that the Tribunal was entitled to find it was not satisfied that a legally binding agreement was intended.

QUESTIONS

(1) Is a subjective or an objective approach used by the courts in Australia to determine the intention of the parties in entering into an agreement? When might a party's subjective intention be relevant?

(2) What is the traditional presumptive position regarding intention for: (a) commercial arrangements; and (b) personal/domestic arrangements? Does this presumptive approach still hold?

5.3 Establishing agreement

To determine whether an agreement has been reached between the parties, the approach commonly adopted is to look at whether there has been an offer made by one party to another party which is then accepted by that second party. It must be kept in mind, however, that this is an analytic tool to assist in determining whether an agreement has been reached and that the overriding question is whether the parties' conduct evidences an agreement showing an intention to be legally bound.

5.3.1 Offer

Concept	Short explanation	Relevant authorities	*Principles* text*
An offer is a promise to do or not to do something	It is made on the basis that the offeree behaves in a certain way in response It can be made to a particular person, a group of people or to the world at large	*Carlill v Carbolic Smoke Ball Company* [1893] 1 QB 256	Chapter 5: 5.11

Concept	Short explanation	Relevant authorities	*Principles* text*
An offer is different to an invitation to deal	An invitation to deal is essentially a statement which opens negotiations. There is no intention that this invitation be accepted to form a binding contract Examples: display of goods in self-service shops, auctions, requests for tenders	*Pharmaceutical Society of Great Britain v Boots Cash Chemists (Southern) Ltd* [1953] 1 QB 401 *AGC (Advances) Ltd v McWhirter* (1977) 1 BPR 9454 *Blackpool and Fylde Aero Club v Blackpool Borough Council* [1990] 1 WLR 1195	Chapter 5: 5.12–5.15
An offer can be terminated prior to acceptance	Termination of an offer can occur due to: • revocation • rejection (including by way of counter-offer) • the offeree failing to accept during a stipulated time • death of the offeror • failure of a condition (which the offer was made subject to)	*Byrne & Co v Van Tienhoven & Co* (1880) LR 5 CPD 344 *Dickinson v Dodds* (1876) 2 Ch D 463	Chapter 5: 5.16

* Consult the corresponding section(s) of the *Principles* text for more detail.

Carlill v Carbolic Smoke Ball Company [1893] 1 QB 256

Facts and issues

Carbolic Smoke Ball Company ('Carbolic') produced a medical preparation which it called 'The Carbolic Smoke Ball'. Carbolic placed an advertisement in a number of newspapers offering a £100 reward to 'any person who contracts the increasing epidemic influenza, colds, or any disease caused by taking cold, after having used the ball three times daily for two weeks according to the printed directions supplied with each ball'. Mrs Carlill, having seen the advertisement, purchased a Smoke Ball, used it as directed and nevertheless contracted influenza. Consequently, she claimed an entitlement to the £100 reward offered in the advertisement placed by Carbolic. At first instance, it was held that she was entitled to recover this reward. Carbolic appealed this decision. The key issue was whether there was a valid offer which could therefore be said to have been accepted by Mrs Carlill to form a binding contract.

Decision

Per Bowen LJ at 268:

> It was also said that the contract is made with all the world — that is, with everybody; and that you cannot contract with everybody. It is not a contract made with all the world. There is the fallacy of the argument. It is an offer made to all the world; and why should not an offer be made to all the world which is to ripen into a contract with anybody who comes forward and performs the condition? It is an offer to become liable to any one who, before it is retracted, performs the condition, and, although the offer is made to the world, the contract is made with that limited portion of the public who come forward and perform the condition on the faith of the advertisement. It is not like cases in which you offer to negotiate, or you issue advertisements that you have got a stock of books to sell, or houses to let, in which case there is no offer to be bound by any contract. Such advertisements are offers to negotiate – offers to receive offers – offers to chaffer, as, I think, some learned judge in one of the cases has said. If this is an offer to be bound, then it is a contract the moment the person fulfils the condition. [269] That seems to me to be sense . . .

An offer requires intention to be bound and therefore needs to be distinguished from an invitation to deal.

Pharmaceutical Society of Great Britain v Boots Cash Chemists (Southern) Ltd [1953] 1 QB 401

Facts and issues

Boots Cash Chemists (Southern) Ltd ('Boots') was the owner and operator of a chemist which included a pharmacy. The store was set up in a manner which allowed customers to essentially serve themselves by selecting items from the shelves, placing them in supplied baskets and then proceeding to the register. A qualified pharmacist supervised the sale of all drugs. However, the Pharmaceutical Society of Great Britain ('the Society') brought an action against Boots alleging it had infringed the *Pharmacy and Poisons Act 1933* ('the Act') regarding the supervision of all sales of poisons listed therein. In the course of this action, it was necessary for the Court to determine the issue of whether the self-service system amounted to an offer by Boots to sell the drugs, thereby infringing the Act. At first instance, no infringement was said to have occurred. This decision was appealed by the Society.

Decision

Per Somervell LJ at 405:

> The point taken by the plaintiffs is this: it is said that the purchase is complete if and when a customer going round the shelves takes an article and puts it in the receptacle which he or she is carrying, and that therefore, if that is right, when the customer comes to the pay desk, having completed the tour of the premises, the registered pharmacist, if so minded, has no power to say: 'This drug ought not to be sold to this customer.' Whether and in what circumstances he would have that power we need not inquire, but one can, of course, see that there is a difference if supervision can only be exercised at a time when the contract is completed.
>
> . . . Whether the view contended for by the plaintiffs is the right view depends on what are the legal implications of this layout — the invitation to the customer. Is a contract to be regarded as

being completed when the article is put into the receptacle, or is this to be regarded as a more organized way of doing what is done already in many types of shops — and a bookseller is perhaps the best example — namely, enabling customers to have free access to what is in the shop, to look at the different articles, and then, ultimately, having got the ones which they wish to buy, to come up to the assistant saying 'I want this'? The assistant in 999 times out of 1,000 says 'That is all right,' and the money passes and [406] the transaction is completed. I agree with what the Lord Chief Justice has said, and with the reasons which he has given for his conclusion, that in the case of an ordinary shop, although goods are displayed and it is intended that customers should go and choose what they want, the contract is not completed until, the customer having indicated the articles which he needs, the shopkeeper, or someone on his behalf, accepts that offer. Then the contract is completed. I can see no reason at all, that being clearly the normal position, for drawing any different implication as a result of this layout.

The Lord Chief Justice, I think, expressed one of the most formidable difficulties in the way of the plaintiffs' contention when he pointed out that, if the plaintiffs are right, once an article has been placed in the receptacle the customer himself is bound and would have no right, without paying for the first article, to substitute an article which he saw later of a similar kind and which he perhaps preferred. I can see no reason for implying from this self-service arrangement any implication other than that which the Lord Chief Justice found in it, namely, that it is a convenient method of enabling customers to see what there is and choose, and possibly put back and substitute, articles which they wish to have, and then to go up to the cashier and offer to buy what they have so far chosen. On that conclusion the case fails, because it is admitted that there was supervision in the sense required by the Act and at the appropriate moment of time.

The appeal was dismissed.

AGC (Advances) Ltd v McWhirter (1977) 1 BPR 9454

Facts and issues

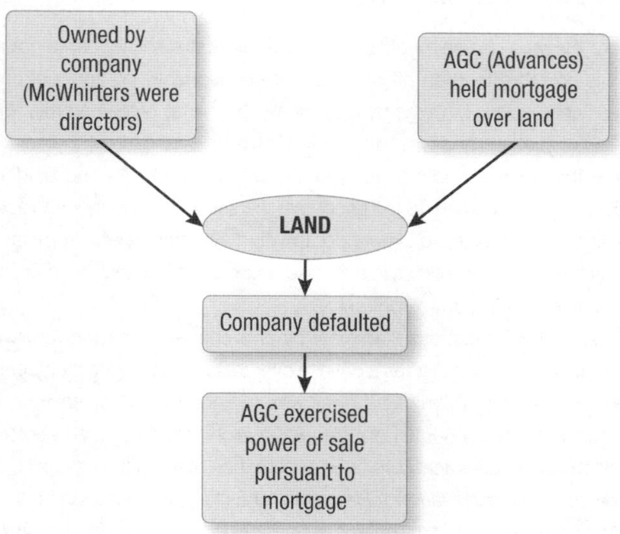

The McWhirters were the directors of a company which owned land subject to a mortgage held by AGC (Advances) Ltd ('AGC'). Upon default under the mortgage, AGC exercised its power of sale. At auction, the highest bid received was below the reserve price leading AGC to instruct its agent to remove the reserve. Subsequently, the McWhirters outbid the previous highest bidder (by $500) to become the highest bidders. However, AGC did not accept their offer and instead sold the property to an earlier bidder at a price below that offered by the McWhirters. The McWhirters lodged a caveat over the land on the basis that a contract had been formed at auction. AGC brought proceedings for removal of the caveat. The issue for determination by the Court was whether a contract had been formed between the McWhirters and AGC.

Decision

Per Holland J at [9456]:

> The basis of the defendant's assertion that a contract had come into existence was that, once the reserve price was withdrawn and it was announced at the auction that the property was 'on the market', the plaintiff became an offerer for sale to the highest bidder and Mr McWhirter's bid, being the highest, constituted acceptance of the offer, thereby making a contract irrespective of whether the auctioneer actually knocked the property down to him. The theory of this submission was that a vendor who puts a property up for sale by auction without reserve to the highest bidder undertakes to sell to the highest bidder and that each bidder is a conditional purchaser, the condition being that no-one bids a higher price. This theory of such an auction was rejected by the King's Bench Division of the Courts in England nearly 200 years ago in *Payne v Cave* (1789) 3 TR 148; 100 ER 502 ... The trial judge, Lord Kenyon, non-suited the plaintiff and the King's Bench Division upheld the non-suit. The court said (at TR 149; ER 503);
>
> > The auctioneer is the agent of the vendor, and the assent of both parties is necessary to make the contract binding; that is signified on the part of the seller by knocking down the hammer, which was not done here till the defendant had retracted. An auction is not unaptly called *locus poenitentiae*. Every bidding is no [9457] more than an offer on one side, which is not binding on the other side till it is assented to. But according to what is now contended for, one party would be bound by the offer, and the other not, which can never be allowed.
>
> It is clear that the *ratio decidendi* of *Payne v Cave*, was that the bidder is not a conditional purchaser but is no more than an offeror and that consequently no contract can come into existence unless and until his bid is accepted, usually, by the fall of the hammer. In my opinion, this is still the law of auctions and was not affected in the present case by the announcement at the auction that the highest bidder should be the purchaser and that no bidding should be retracted or by the announcement to the effect that the sale was no longer subject to a reserve price. This means that it is open to the vendor to withdraw the property from sale at any time before a bid has been accepted or, as in this case, to decline to accept a bid from a party with whom the vendor does not wish to contract.
>
> The question whether an express statement by or on behalf of the vendor that the auction sale will be 'without reserve' constitutes a definite offer to sell to the highest bidder has been the subject of debate. The proposition that it does was rejected by a Scottish court in *Fenwick v McDonald Frazer & Co* (1904) 6 F (Ct of Sess) 850 which held that no agreement was made unless and until the auctioneer acknowledged acceptance of the bid by the fall of his hammer; however, some obiter dicta in *Warlow v Harrison* ... has kept the question open ...
>
> [9458] ... An auction remains, in my opinion, an invitation to treat. If the fact that there is a reserve price is notified, it indicates to the bidders that an offer below the reserve price will or may not be

considered. If the sale is advertised as being without reserve or to the highest bidder, it means that the highest bid is an offer that is liable to be accepted and, if accepted, will make a contract but the vendor remains free to withdraw the property from sale or decline to accept any bid . . .

Blackpool and Fylde Aero Club Ltd v Blackpool Borough Council [1990] 1 WLR 1195

Facts and issues

Blackpool Borough Council ('the Council') invited tenders for a concession to operate pleasure flights from the airport it owned and managed. Blackpool and Fylde Aero Club ('the Club') submitted a tender on time as required but, as a result of an error by the Council, its tender was deemed late and was not considered. The Club claimed breach of contract by the Council on the basis that the latter had warranted that if tenders were received on time they would be considered. The Council appealed a first instance decision that it was in breach of contract. At issue was whether the invitation to treat, via tender, could create a legally binding obligation on the Council to consider all tenders which conformed with the conditions of the tender request.

Decision

Per Bingham LJ at 1200:

> Firstly, it was submitted that an invitation to tender in this form was well established to be no more than a proclamation of willingness to receive offers. Even without the first sentence of the council's invitation to tender in this case, the council would not have been bound to accept the highest or any tender. An invitation to tender in this form was an invitation to treat, and no contract of any kind would come into existence unless or until, if ever, the council chose to accept any tender or other offer . . .
>
> Secondly, counsel submitted that on a reasonable reading of this invitation to tender the council could not be understood to be undertaking to consider all timely tenders submitted. The statement that late tenders would not be considered did not mean that timely tenders would. If the council had meant that it could have said it . . .
>
> [1201] I found great force in the submissions made on behalf of the council and agree with much of what was said. Indeed, for much of the hearing I was of opinion that the judge's decision, although fully in accord with the merits as I see them, could not be sustained in principle. But I am in the end persuaded that the argument proves too much. During the hearing the following questions were raised: what if, in a situation such as the present, the council had opened and thereupon accepted the first tender received, even though the deadline had not expired and other invitees had not yet responded? Or if the council had considered and accepted a tender admittedly received well after the deadline? Counsel answered that although by so acting the council might breach its own standing orders, and might fairly be accused of discreditable conduct, it would not be in breach of any legal obligation because at that stage there would be none to breach. This is a conclusion I cannot accept, and if it were accepted there would in my view be an unacceptable discrepancy between the law of contract and the confident assumptions of commercial parties, both tenderers . . . and invitors . . .
>
> A tendering procedure of this kind is, in many respects, heavily weighted in favour of the invitor. He can invite tenders from as many or as few parties as he chooses. He need not tell any

of them who else, or how many others, he has invited. The invitee may often, although not here, be put to considerable labour and expense in preparing a tender, ordinarily without recompense if he is unsuccessful. The invitation to tender may itself, in a complex case, although again not here, involve time and expense to prepare, but the invitor does not commit himself to proceed with the project, whatever it is; he need not accept the highest tender; he need not accept any tender; he need not give reasons to justify his acceptance or rejection of any tender received. The risk to which the tenderer is exposed does not end with the risk that his tender may not be the highest (or, as the case may be, lowest). But where, as here, tenders are solicited from selected parties all of them known to the invitor, and where a local authority's invitation prescribes a clear, orderly and familiar procedure (draft contract conditions available for inspection and plainly not open to negotiation, a prescribed common form of tender, the supply of envelopes designed to preserve the absolute anonymity of tenderers and clearly to identify the tender in question and an absolute deadline) the invitee is in my judgment protected at least to this extent: if he submits a conforming tender before the deadline he is entitled, not as a matter of mere expectation but of contractual right, to be sure that his tender will after the deadline be opened and considered in conjunction with all other conforming tenders or at least that his tender will be considered if others are . . .

[1202] . . . In all the circumstances of this case (and I say nothing about any other) I have no doubt that the parties did intend to create contractual relations to the limited extent contended for . . . I think it plain that the council's invitation to tender was, to this limited extent, an offer, and the club's submission of a timely and conforming tender an acceptance.

The appeal was dismissed.

If it is clear that an offer has been made, it must not have been terminated prior to acceptance by the offeree. Termination of an offer can occur in a number of ways, including by way of revocation or rejection. The principles surrounding revocation of offers are discussed in the following case extracts.

Byrne & Co v Van Tienhoven & Co (1880) LR 5 CPD 344

Facts and issues

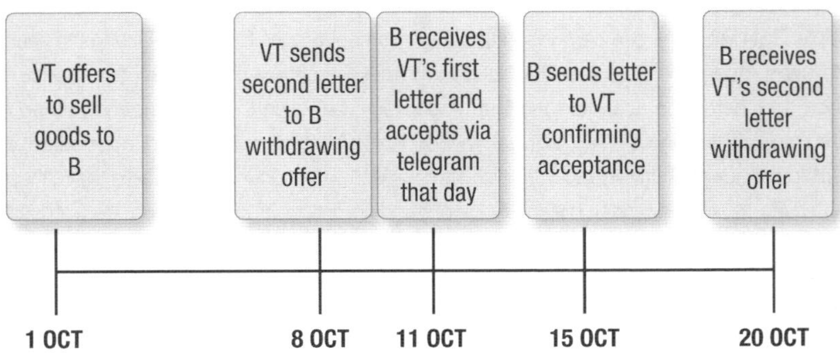

Van Tienhoven & Co ('Van Tienhoven') sent a letter to Byrne & Co ('Byrne') on 1 October offering to sell goods to Byrne. The letter was received by Byrne on 11 October and the offer accepted by it via telegram on the same day. Byrne also sent a letter indicating its acceptance on 15 October. However, on 8 October, Van Tienhoven sent a letter to Byrne withdrawing its offer—the letter was only received by Byrne on 20 October. By this time, Byrne had already resold the goods but Van Tienhoven subsequently refused to supply the goods. Byrne therefore brought an action for damages. The issue here was whether the offer had been revoked prior to acceptance.

Decision

Per Lindley J at 347:

> There is no doubt that an offer can be withdrawn before it is accepted, and it is immaterial whether the offer is expressed to be open for acceptance for a given time or not: *Routledge v Grant*. (1) For the decision of the present case, however, it is necessary to consider two other questions, viz.: 1. Whether a withdrawal of an offer has any effect until it is communicated to the person to whom the offer has been sent? 2. Whether posting a letter of withdrawal is a communication to the person to whom the letter is sent?
>
> It is curious that neither of these questions appears to have been actually decided in this country. As regards the first question. I am aware that Pothier and some other writers of celebrity are of opinion that there can be no contract if an offer is withdrawn before it is accepted, although the withdrawal is not communicated to the person to whom the offer has been made. The reason for this opinion is that there is not in fact any such consent by both parties as is essential to constitute a contract between them. Against this view, however, it has been urged that a state of mind not notified cannot be regarded in dealings between man and man; and that an uncommunicated revocation is for all practical purposes and in point of law no revocation at all. This is the view taken in the United States: see *Tayloe v Merchants Fire Insurance Co.* (2) ... This view, moreover, appears to me much more in accordance with the general principles of English law than the view maintained by Pothier. I pass, therefore, to the next question, [348] viz., whether posting the letter of revocation was a sufficient communication of it to the plaintiff. The offer was posted on the 1st of October, the withdrawal was posted on the 8th, and did not reach the plaintiff until after he had posted his letter of the 11th, accepting the offer. It may be taken as now settled that where an offer is made and accepted by letters sent through the post, the contract is completed the moment the letter accepting the offer is posted: *Harris' Case* (1); *Dunlop v Higgins* (2), even although it never reaches its destination. When, however, these authorities are looked at, it will be seen that they are based upon the principle that the writer of the offer has expressly or impliedly assented to treat an answer to him by a letter duly posted as a sufficient acceptance and notification to himself, or, in other words, he has made the post office his agent to receive the acceptance and notification of it. But this principle appears to me to be inapplicable to the case of the withdrawal of an offer ... In my opinion the withdrawal by the defendants on the 8th of October of their offer of the 1st was inoperative; and a complete contract binding on both parties was entered into on the 11th of October, when the plaintiffs accepted the offer of the 1st, which they had no reason to suppose had been withdrawn. Before leaving this part of the case it may be as well to point out the extreme injustice and inconvenience which any other conclusion would produce. If the defendants' contention were to prevail no person who had received an offer by post and had accepted it would know his position until he had waited such a time as to be quite sure that a letter

> withdrawing the offer had not been posted before his acceptance of it. It appears to me that both legal [349] principles, and practical convenience require that a person who has accepted an offer not known to him to have been revoked, shall be in a position safely to act upon the footing that the offer and acceptance constitute a contract binding on both parties.

Dickinson v Dodds (1876) 2 Ch D 463

Facts and issues

Dodds signed and delivered a document to Dickinson on 10 June by which he agreed to sell his property to Dickinson. However, the document also provided that the offer was to be left open until 12 June. Dickinson accepted the offer but did not immediately communicate this acceptance to Dodds as he believed he had until 12 June to respond. On 11 June, however, he heard from a third party that Dodds had been offering or agreeing to sell the property to someone else. Consequently, Dickinson left formal notice of his acceptance at Dodds' residence on 11 June and had his agent give a copy of this acceptance to Dodds the next morning. Dodds informed the agent that it was too late as he had sold the property, which he had in fact done on 11 June. Dickinson brought proceedings for specific performance and succeeded at first instance. Dodds appealed. The issue before the Court was whether the offer was revoked prior to acceptance by Dickinson.

Decision

Per James LJ at 471:

> The document, though beginning 'I hereby agree to sell,' was nothing but an offer, and was only intended to be an offer, for the Plaintiff himself tells us that he required time to consider whether he would enter into an agreement or not. Unless both parties had then agreed there was no concluded agreement then made; it was [472] in effect and substance only an offer to sell . . . There was no consideration given for the undertaking or promise, to whatever extent it may be considered binding, to keep the property unsold until 9 o'clock on Friday morning; but apparently *Dickinson* was of opinion, and probably *Dodds* was of the same opinion, that he

(*Dodds*) was bound by that promise, and could not in any way withdraw from it, or retract it, until 9 o'clock on Friday morning . . . But it is clear settled law, on one of the clearest principles of law, that this promise, being a mere *nudum pactum*, was not binding, and that at any moment before a complete acceptance by *Dickinson* of the offer, *Dodds* was as free as *Dickinson* himself. Well, that being the state of things, it is said that the only mode in which *Dodds* could assert that freedom was by actually and distinctly saying to *Dickinson*, 'Now I withdraw my offer.' It appears to me that there is neither principle nor authority for the proposition that there must be an express and actual withdrawal of the offer, or what is called a retractation (sic). It must, to constitute a contract, appear that the two minds were at one, at the same moment of time, that is, that there was an offer continuing up to the time of the acceptance. If there was not such a continuing offer, then the acceptance comes to nothing. Of course it may well be that the one man is bound in some way or other to let the other man know that his mind with regard to the offer has been changed; but in this case, beyond all question, the Plaintiff knew that *Dodds* was no longer minded to sell the property to him as plainly and clearly as if *Dodds* had told him in so many words, 'I withdraw the offer.' This is evident from the Plaintiff's own statements . . .

[473] It is to my mind quite clear that before there was any attempt at acceptance by the Plaintiff, he was perfectly well aware that *Dodds* had changed his mind, and that he had in fact agreed to sell the property to [the third party]. It is impossible, therefore, to say there was ever that existence of the same mind between the two parties which is essential in point of law to the making of an agreement. I am of opinion, therefore, that the Plaintiff has failed to prove that there was any binding contract between *Dodds* and himself.

Per Mellish LJ at 473:

I am of the same opinion . . . [475] It is admitted law that, if a man who makes an offer dies, the offer cannot be accepted after he is dead, and parting with the property has very much the same effect as the death of the owner, for it makes the performance of the offer impossible. I am clearly of opinion that, just as when a man who has made an offer dies before it is accepted it is impossible that it can then be accepted, so when once the person to whom the offer was made knows that the property has been sold to some one else, it is too late for him to accept the offer, and on that ground I am clearly of opinion that there was no binding contract for the sale of this property by *Dodds* to *Dickinson* . . .

The appeal was allowed.

QUESTIONS

(1) What is the difference between an offer and an invitation to deal? Why is this difference significant?

(2) What is required for an offer to be revoked?

(3) Are vendors who sell their property by way of auction bound to accept the highest bid? How is an auction where no reserve is specified classified —as an offer by the vendor, or merely as an invitation to deal?

5.4 Acceptance

Concept	Short explanation	Relevant authorities	*Principles* text*
Acceptance must occur for a contract to be formed	Acceptance is a clear statement by the offeree agreeing to the offer made by the offeror Acceptance can be communicated orally, in writing or through the offeree's conduct	*Empirnall Holdings Pty Ltd v Machon Paull Partners Pty Ltd* (1988) 14 NSWLR 523	Chapter 5: 5.17–5.18
Acceptance must be *in response to* the offer	There must be a link between the offeree's statement or conduct and the offer. That is, either must have been *as a result of* the offer, rather than occurring independently or without knowledge of the offer	*R v Clarke* (1927) 40 CLR 227	Chapter 5: 5.19
Acceptance must *correspond to* the offer	The offeree's words or conduct, in order to be said to amount to an acceptance of an offer, must be consistent with that offer. If not, it may be that the offeree is seen as actually making a counter-offer	*Butler Machine Tool Co Ltd v Ex-Cell-O Corporation (England) Ltd* [1979] 1 WLR 401	Chapter 5: 5.23
Generally speaking, acceptance must be communicated to the offeror	The general rule is that acceptance is not effective until it is communicated to the offeror. (The exception to this are unilateral contracts where meeting the requirements stipulated in the offer is generally enough. See eg *Carlill v Carbolic Smoke Ball Company* discussed at **5.3.1** above) Acceptance occurs *when* it is received by the offeror except in cases where the postal exception rule applies Acceptance is generally said to occur *where* it was received by the offeror	*Bressan v Squires* [1974] 2 NSWLR 460 *Brinkibon Ltd v Stahag Stahl und Stahl-Warendhandelsgesellschaft mbH* [1983] 2 AC 34 *Electronic Transactions Act 1999* (Cth) ss 5, 14, 14A, 14B	Chapter 5: 5.19–5.21

* Consult the corresponding section(s) of the *Principles* text for more detail.

To form an agreement, an offer must be accepted by the offeree. This acceptance can be indicated orally, in writing or by conduct but it must be an undeniable agreement by the offeree to the offer. That is, the actions of the offeree must be attributable, at least in part, to the offer. The question of whether or not acceptance has occurred is approached objectively on the basis of whether a reasonable person would consider the conduct of the offeree to indicate to the offeror that the offer has been accepted. Generally speaking, the law considers an offer to have been accepted at the point at which that acceptance is received by the offeror. However, the postal acceptance rule does modify this position. Silence alone does not constitute acceptance of an offer, but it may be the case in such circumstances that the offeree's conduct will amount to acceptance of the offer in the sense that he or she has taken the benefit of the offer. These principles, and those surrounding if and when acceptance has occurred, are discussed in the following case extracts.

Empirnall Holdings Pty Ltd v Machon Paull Partners Pty Ltd (1988) 14 NSWLR 523

Facts and issues

Empirnall Holdings Pty Ltd ('Empirnall') (a property development company) engaged Machon Paull Partners Pty Ltd ('Machon Paull') (an architectural and project management company) in relation to a particular development project. Machon Paull, in the midst of undertaking work for Empirnall, prepared and delivered a contract to Empirnall for signing. The contract was never signed. However, Empirnall paid Machon Paull, in accordance with the terms contained in the unsigned contract, for the work it continued to undertake on the development project. Subsequently, Empirnall began experiencing financial difficulty resulting in large amounts of money it owed to Machon Paull remaining outstanding. The issue was whether there was a contract between Empirnall and Machon Paull in accordance with the terms of the printed (but unsigned) contract. Significantly, there was a clause in the contract which provided for Machon Paull to obtain a charge over the relevant land in circumstances of outstanding debt. As Empirnall was potentially heading for liquidation, this was significant as it would place Machon Paull in a preferred position to other creditors. At first instance, the issue was answered in the affirmative and Empirnall appealed.

Decision

Per McHugh JA at 534:

> Under the common law theory of contract, the silent acceptance of an offer is generally insufficient to create any contract: *Brogden v Metropolitan Railway Co* (1877) 2 App Cas 666 at 692 and *Robophone Facilities Ltd v Blank* [1966] 1 WLR 1428 at 1432; [1966] 3 All ER 128 at 131-132. The objective theory of contract requires an external manifestation of assent to an offer. Convenience, and especially commercial convenience, has given rise to the rule that the acceptance of the offer should be communicated to the offeror. After a reasonable period has elapsed, silence is seen as a rejection and not a acceptance of the offer. Nevertheless, communication of acceptance is not always necessary. The offeror will be bound if he dispenses with the need to communicate the acceptance of his offer: *Carlill v Carbolic Smoke Ball Co* [1893] 1 QB 256 at 269. However, an offeror cannot erect a contract between himself and the offeree by the device of stating that unless he hears from the offeree he will consider the

offeree bound. He cannot assert that he will regard silence as acceptance: *Felthouse v Bindley* (1862) 11 CB (NS) 869 at 875; 142 ER 1037 at 1040 and *Fairline Shipping Corporation v Adamson* [1975] QB 180 at 189. The common law's concern with the protection of freedom is opposed to the notion that a person must take action to reject an uninvited offer or be bound by contractual obligations.

Nevertheless, the silence of an offeree in conjunction with the other circumstances of the case may indicate that he has accepted the offer: *Rust v Abbey Life Assurance Co Ltd* [1979] 2 Lloyd's Rep 334 at 340. The offeree may be under a duty to communicate his rejection of an offer. If he fails to do so, his silence will generally be regarded as an acceptance of the offer sufficient to form a contract. Many cases decided in United States jurisdictions have held that the custom of the trade, the course of dealing, or the previous relationship between the parties imposed a duty on the offeree to reject the offer or be bound: *CMI Clothesmakers Inc v ASK Knits Inc* 380 NYS 2d 447 (1975); *Brooks Towers Corporation v Hunkin-Conkey* [535] *Construction Co* 454 F 2d 1203 (1972); *Alliance Manufacturing Co Inc v Foti* 146 So 2d 464 (1962). But more often than not the offeree will be bound because, knowing of the terms of the offer and the offeror's intention to enter into a contract, he has exercised a choice and taken the benefit of the offer. In *Laurel Race Course Inc v Regal Construction Co Inc* 333 A 2d 319 (1975) a contractor proposed that it would do additional work upon the basis that, if the work was the result of its defective workmanship under the original contract, there would be no charge. Otherwise the work would be charged on a 'cost-plus' basis. The building owner made no reply to this offer. The contractor commenced work on the job to the knowledge of the building owner who was held bound by the terms of the offer. Speaking for the Court of Appeals for Maryland, Judge Levine said (at 329):

> Where the offeree with reasonable opportunity to reject offered services takes the benefit of them under circumstances which would indicate to a reasonable person that they were offered with the expectation of compensation, he assents to the terms proposed and thus accepts the offer.

This formulation states acceptance in terms of a rule of law. However, the question is one of fact. A more accurate statement is that where an offeree with a reasonable opportunity to reject the offer of goods or services takes the benefit of them under circumstances which indicate that they were to be paid for in accordance with the offer, it is open to the tribunal of fact to hold D that the offer was accepted according to its terms. . .

The ultimate issue is whether a reasonable bystander would regard the conduct of the offeree, including his silence, as signalling to the offeror that his offer has been accepted . . .

On or about 14 September 1983, Empirnall through its agent became aware that Machon wished to undertake the work on the basis that their relationship would be governed by the terms of a written contract. The letter of 3 October 1983 made it clear that Machon expected that their relationship would be governed by the standard form of contract BCP1. But the letter of 19 October 1983 went further. It made it clear that the work which Machon would perform was offered on the terms and conditions contained in the documents sent on 3 October 1983. From that point on Empirnall took the benefit of the work with knowledge of the terms on which it was offered. It is not an acceptable conclusion that Machon offered to perform the work on some basis other than that contained in the written document. Machon had made it plain that it was not prepared to do work under an oral, open contract. Nor is it possible to regard the work as offered on the basis that Empirnall would pay reasonable remuneration for its performance. The work went on for a considerable period. Progress claims were submitted and paid. One of the items costed was the price of the standard form of the written contract.

In these circumstances Empirnall's acceptance of the work, when [536] considered objectively, should be taken as an acceptance of the work on the terms and conditions offered by Machon. The case is not so much one of acceptance by silence as one of taking the benefit of

> an offer with knowledge of its terms and knowledge of the offeror's reliance on payment being made in return for his work . . .
>
> Since Empirnall has taken the benefit of the work with knowledge of the terms on which it was offered, an objective bystander would conclude that Empirnall had accepted the offer on those terms and conditions.

R v Clarke (1927) 40 CLR 227

Facts and issues

In response to the murder of two police officers, the Government of Western Australia offered a reward for information which led to the arrest and conviction of those responsible. Clarke, who had seen this reward offer, subsequently provided information which resulted in the arrest of one person, and the arrest and conviction of another, in relation to the murder of one of the police officers. He then claimed the reward. However, the Government refused to pay him the reward—at the time he provided the relevant information, he himself had been charged in relation to the murder of one of the police officers. Clarke's proceedings to recover the reward amount succeeded on his appeal to the Supreme Court of Western Australia. The Crown appealed. At issue was whether Clarke's conduct in providing the information amounted to an acceptance of the reward offer.

Decision

Per Isaacs ACJ at 231:

> The facts of this case, including inferences, are not, as I understand, in dispute. They amount to this: The information for which Clarke claims the reward was given by him when he was under arrest . . . on a charge of murder, and was given by him in circumstances which show that in giving the information he was not acting on or in pursuance of or in reliance upon or in return for the consideration contained in the proclamation, but exclusively in order to clear himself from a false charge of murder. In other words, he was acting with reference to a specific criminal charge against himself, and not with reference to a general request by the community for information against other persons . . . He has, in my opinion, neither a legal nor a moral claim to the reward. The learned Chief Justice held that [232] Clarke never accepted or intended to accept the offer in the proclamation, and, unless the mere giving of the information without such intention amounted in law to an acceptance of the offer . . . there was [no] 'acceptance' . . . and therefore there was no contract. I do not understand either of the learned Judges who formed the majority to controvert this. But they held that *Williams* v. *Carwardine* (1) has stood so long that it should be regarded as accurate, and that, so regarded, it entitled the respondent to judgment. As reported in the four places where it is found (2), it is a difficult case to follow . . . But two circumstances are important. One is the pregnant question of *Denman* C.J. as to the plaintiff's knowledge of the handbill . . . The other circumstance is the stress placed on motive. The Lord Chief Justice clearly attached importance to the answer given to his question. He, doubtless, finally drew the inference that, having knowledge of the request in the handbill, the plaintiff at last determined to accede, and did accede, to that request, and so acted in response to it, although moved thereto by the incentive supplied by her stings of conscience . . . [233] If the decision in *Williams* v. *Carwardine* (1) went no further than I have said, it is in line with the acknowledged and settled theories of contract . . . It is unquestionable–putting aside what are called formal contracts or quasi-contracts–that to create a contractual obligation there must be

both offer and acceptance. It is the union of these which constitutes the binding tie, the *obligatio.* The present type of case is no exception. It is not true to say that since such an offer calls for information of a certain description, then, provided only information of that description is in fact given, the informant is entitled to the reward. That is not true unless the word 'given' is interpreted as 'given in exchange for the offer' – in other words, given in performance of the bargain which is contemplated by the offer and of which the offer is intended to form part. Performance in that case is the implied method of acceptance, and it simultaneously effects the double purpose of acceptance and performance. But acceptance is essential to contractual obligation, because without it there is no agreement, and in the absence of agreement, actual or imputed, there can be no contract . . .

[234] The controlling principle, then, is that to establish the *consensus* without which no true contract can exist, acceptance is as essential as offer, even in a case of the present class where the same act is at once sufficient for both acceptance and performance. But acceptance and performance of condition, as shown by the judicial [235] reasoning quoted, involve that the person accepting and performing must act on the offer . . . Instances easily suggest themselves where precisely the same act done with reference to an offer would be performance of the condition, but done with reference to a totally distinct object would not be such a performance. An offer of £100 to any person who should swim a hundred yards in the harbour on the first day of the year, would be met by voluntarily performing the feat with reference to the offer, but would not in my opinion be satisfied by a person who was accidentally or maliciously thrown overboard on that date and swam the distance simply to save his life, without any thought of the offer. The offeror might or might not feel morally impelled to give the sum in such a case, but would be under no contractual obligation to do so. [236] . . . On the question of fact whether Clarke in making his statement of 10th June acted upon the offer in the proclamation, the learned [237] Chief Justice, who saw and heard him give his testimony, answered that question in the negative. . . The appeal . . . should, in my opinion, for the reasons stated, be allowed, and the judgment of *McMillan* C.J. restored.

The appeal was allowed.

Butler Machine Tool Co Ltd v Ex-Cell-O Corporation (England) Ltd [1979] 1 WLR 401

Facts and issues

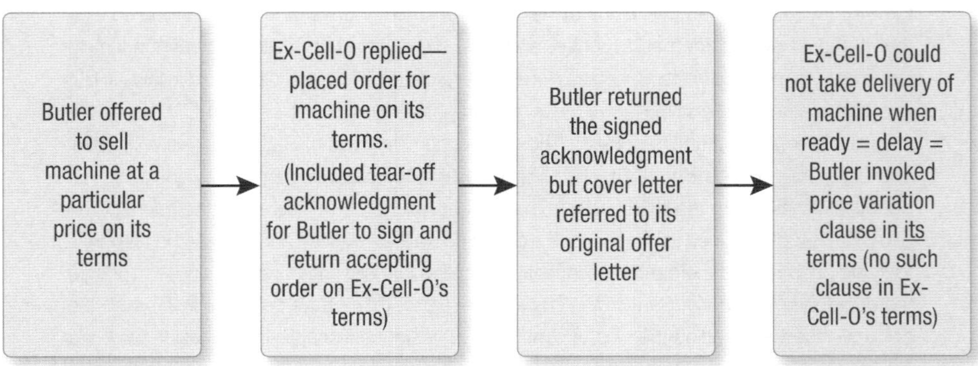

Butler Machine Tool Co Ltd ('Butler') offered to sell a particular machine to Ex-Cell-O Corporation (England) Ltd ('Ex-Cell-O') at a specified price and pursuant to various terms and conditions contained in its quotation document. By way of reply, Ex-Cell-O placed an order with Butler for the machine but indicated that the supply was to be made on the terms and conditions contained in Ex-Cell-O's order. An acknowledgment tear-off slip was included, which Butler signed and returned, although referring to its original quotation in the cover letter. There were a number of differences between these terms and conditions and those contained in Butler's quotation. Most notably, Butler's quotation included a price variation clause which allowed the price charged for the machine to be varied, depending on the ultimate delivery date. This was not provided for in the terms contained in Ex-Cell-O's order. There was a delay in Ex-Cell-O accepting delivery of the machine and Butler sought a higher purchase price in reliance on the price variation clause found in the terms and conditions of its quotation. Butler succeeded at first instance and Ex-Cell-O appealed. The issues to be decided were at what point acceptance had occurred and on what terms the contract had ultimately been concluded.

Decision

Per Lord Denning MR at 403:

> No doubt a contract was ... concluded. But on what terms? The sellers [Butler] rely on their general conditions and on their last letter which said [404] 'in accordance with our revised quotation of May 23' (which had on the back the price variation clause). The buyers rely on the acknowledgment signed by the sellers which accepted the buyer's order 'on the terms and conditions stated thereon' (which did not include a price variation clause).
>
> If those documents are analysed in our traditional method, the result would seem to me to be this: the quotation of May 23, 1969, was an offer by the sellers to the buyers containing the terms and conditions on the back. The order of May 27, 1969, purported to be an acceptance of that offer in that it was for the same machine at the same price, but it contained such additions as to cost of installation, date of delivery and so forth that it was in law a rejection of the offer and constituted a counter-offer. That is clear from *Hyde v. Wrench* (1840) 3 Beav. 334. As Megaw J. said in *Trollope & Colls Ltd.* v. *Atomic Power Constructions Ltd.* [1963] 1 W.L.R. 333, 337: '... the counter-offer kills the original offer.' The letter of the sellers of June 5, 1969, was an acceptance of that counter-offer, as is shown by the acknowledgment which the sellers signed and returned to the buyers. The reference to the quotation of May 23 referred only to the price and identity of the machine.
>
> To go on with the facts of the case. The important thing is that the sellers did not keep the contractual date of delivery which was March/April 1970. The machine was ready about September 1970 but by that time the buyers' production schedule had to be re-arranged as they could not accept delivery until November 1970. Meanwhile the sellers had invoked the price increase clause. They sought to charge the buyers an increase due to the rise in costs between May 27, 1969 (when the order was given), and April 1, 1970 (when the machine ought to have been delivered). It came to £2,892. The buyers rejected the claim. The judge held that the sellers were entitled to the sum of £2,892 under the price variation clause. He did not apply the traditional method of analysis by way of offer and counter-offer. He said that in the quotation of May 23, 1969, 'one finds the price variation clause appearing under a most emphatic heading stating that it is a term or condition that is to prevail.' So he held that it did prevail.
>
> I have much sympathy with the judge's approach to this case. In many of these cases our traditional analysis of offer, counter-offer, rejection, acceptance and so forth is out of date. This was observed by Lord Wilberforce in *New Zealand Shipping Co. Ltd.* v. *A. M. Satterthwaite & Co. Ltd.* [1975] A.C. 154, 167. The better way is to look at all the documents passing between the parties — and glean from them, or from the conduct of the parties, whether they have

reached agreement on all material points — even though there may be differences between the forms and conditions printed on the back of them. As Lord Cairns said in *Brogden* v. *Metropolitan Railway Co.* (1877) 2 App.Cas. 666, 672:

> ... there may be a *consensus* between the parties far short of a complete mode of expressing it, and that *consensus* may be discovered from letters or from other documents of an imperfect and incomplete description; ...

Applying this guide, it will be found that in most cases when there is a 'battle of forms,' there is a contract as soon as the last of the forms is sent and received without objection being taken to it. That is well observed in *Benjamin's Sale of Goods*, 9th ed. (1974), p. 84. The difficulty is to decide which form, or which part of which form, is a term or condition of the contract. In some cases the battle is won by the man who fires the last shot. [405] He is the man who puts forward the latest terms and conditions: and, if they are not objected to by the other party, he may be taken to have agreed to them. Such was *British Road Services Ltd.* v. *Arthur V. Crutchley & Co. Ltd.* [1968] 1 Lloyd's Rep. 271, 281–282, *per* Lord Pearson; and the illustration given by Professor Guest in *Anson's Law of Contract*, 24th ed., pp. 37, 38 when he says that 'the terms of the contract consist of the terms of the offer subject to the modifications contained in the acceptance.' In some cases the battle is won by the man who gets the blow in first. If he offers to sell at a named price on the terms and conditions stated on the back: and the buyer orders the goods purporting to accept the offer — on an order form with his own different terms and conditions on the back — then if the difference is so material that it would affect the price, the buyer ought not to be allowed to take advantage of the difference unless he draws it specifically to the attention of the seller. There are yet other cases where the battle depends on the shots fired on both sides. There is a concluded contract but the forms vary. The terms and conditions of both parties are to be construed together. If they can be reconciled so as to give a harmonious result, all well and good. If differences are irreconcilable — so that they are mutually contradictory — then the conflicting terms may have to be scrapped and replaced by a reasonable implication.

In the present case the judge thought that the sellers in their original quotation got their blow in first: especially by the provision that 'these terms and conditions shall prevail over any terms and conditions in the buyer's order.' It was so emphatic that the price variation clause continued through all the subsequent dealings and that the buyers must be taken to have agreed to it. I can understand that point of view. But I think that the documents have to be considered as a whole. And, as a matter of construction, I think the acknowledgment of June 5, 1969, is the decisive document. It makes it clear that the contract was on the buyers' terms and not on the sellers' terms: and the buyers' terms did not include a price variation clause.

I would therefore allow the appeal and enter judgment for the defendants.

The appeal was allowed.

Bressan v Squires [1974] 2 NSWLR 460

Facts and issues

Bressan brought an action for specific performance in relation to an option to purchase property given to him by Squires. The option contained a clause which provided that the option could be exercised by Bressan 'by notice in writing addressed to [Squires] at any time on or before 20th December, 1972'. Bressan claimed that this option had been validly exercised when he posted a letter notifying Squires of such on 18 December 1972. However, Squires refused to sell the property, claiming that the option had not been validly exercised as she had received the letter from Bressan on 21 December 1972. The issue to be decided by the court was whether the option had been properly exercised so that a contract had been formed.

Decision

Per Bowen CJ at 461:

> The general rule is, of course, that a contract is not concluded until acceptance of an offer is actually communicated to the offeror. To this rule there is an exception in the case of acceptance by post.
>
> There have been various formulations of the exception and various reasons assigned for its existence. Many of these reasons have later been said to be unsound. The exception, it seems, is really based upon notions of expediency and convenience, as these are envisaged by the courts from time to time. It is an important exception, since it may determine not only whether or when a contract has been made but also where it has been made.
>
> A formulation of the exception, which is often quoted, is that of Lord Herschell in *Henthorn v. Fraser* (1). His Lordship said: 'Where the circumstances are such that it must have been within the contemplation of the parties that, according to the ordinary usages of mankind, the post might be used as a means of communicating the acceptance of an offer, the acceptance is complete as soon as it is posted.'
>
> According to this formulation, all that needs to be in contemplation of the parties is the post as a mode, indeed as a possible or permitted mode, [462] for the law to impose the consequence that the contract is concluded by the action of posting. It is not required that it should be within the contemplation of the parties that the action of posting should have the consequence of concluding the contract; this, of course, would apply in relatively fewer cases, and would narrow the application of the exception. At first reading, it might be thought that the formulation by Dixon C.J. and Fullagar J. in *Tallerman & Co. Pty. Ltd. v. Nathan's Merchandise (Victoria) Pty. Ltd.* (2) constituted an adoption of this narrower basis. Their Honours said: 'The general rule is that a contract is not completed until acceptance of an offer is actually communicated to the offeror, and a finding that a contract is completed by the posting of a letter of acceptance cannot be justified unless it is to be inferred that the offeror contemplated and intended that his offer might be accepted by the doing of that act: see *Henthorn v. Fraser* (3), per Kay, L.J.'
>
> The reference made by their Honours to the judgment of Kay L.J. in *Henthorn v. Fraser*, however, suggests to my mind they were not intending to narrow the exception.
>
> In the present case the parties must, in my view, have contemplated that the option might be exercised by means of a notice sent through the post.
>
> Accordingly the exception applies and there is here a concluded contract, unless there is some other ground for holding this result does not follow.

Bressan's case ultimately failed as his Honour concluded that, as a matter of construction, the option here required actual notice to Squires on or before 20 December 1972 and that, since this had not occurred, the option had not been validly exercised.

Brinkibon Ltd v Stahag Stahl und Stahl-Warendhandelsgesellschaft mbH [1983] 2 AC 34

Facts and issues

Brinkibon Ltd ('Brinkibon') sought to bring an action against Stahag Stahl und Stahl-Warendhandelsgesellschaft mbH ('Stahag Stahl')—it alleged that the latter had breached a contract between the two relating to the purchase and sale (respectively) of steel bars. Acceptance of Stahag Stahl's offer had occurred by way of a telex sent by Brinkibon in England to Stahag Stahl in Austria. As part of a question regarding jurisdiction, it needed to be determined at what point the acceptance became effective so as to form a binding contract—when it was sent or when it was received? Although Brinkibon succeeded at first instance, the Court of Appeal overturned this original finding. Brinkibon appealed this decision to the House of Lords.

Decision

Per Lord Wilberforce at 41, summarising the issue in the case as:

> . . . whether an acceptance by telex sent from London but received in Vienna causes a contract to be made in London, or in Vienna. If the acceptance had been sent by post, or by telegram, then, on existing authorities, it would have been complete when put into the hands of the post office — in London. If on the other hand it had been telephoned, it would have been complete when heard by the offeror — in Vienna. So in which category is a telex communication to be placed? Existing authority of the Court of Appeal decides in favour of the latter category, i.e. a telex is to be assimilated to other methods of instantaneous communication: see *Entores Ltd. v. Miles Far East Corporation* [1955] 2 Q.B. 327. The appellants ask that this case, which has stood for 30 years, should now be reviewed.
>
> Now such review as is necessary must be made against the background of the law as to the making of contracts. The general rule, it is hardly necessary to state, is that a contract is formed *when* acceptance of an offer is communicated by the offeree to the offeror. And if it is necessary to determine *where* a contract is formed (as to which I have already commented) it appears logical that this should be at the place where acceptance is communicated to the offeror. In the common case of contracts, whether oral or in writing inter praesentes, there is no difficulty; and again logic demands that even where there is not mutual presence at the same place and at the same time, if communication is instantaneous, for example by telephone or radio communication, the same result should follow.
>
> Then there is the case — very common — of communication at a distance, to meet which the so called 'postal rule' has developed. . . The rationale for it. . . has since been well explained. Mellish L.J. in *In re Imperial Land Co. of Marseilles (Harris' Case)* (1872) L.R. 7 Ch.App. 587, 594 ascribed it to the extraordinary and mischievous consequences which would follow if it were held that an offer might be revoked at any time until the letter accepting it had been actually received . . . In these cases too it seems logical to say that the place, as well as the time, of acceptance should be *where* (as *when*) the acceptance is put into the charge of the post office.
>
> In this situation, with a general rule covering instantaneous communication inter praesentes, or at a distance, with an exception applying to [42] non-instantaneous communication at a distance, how should communications by telex be categorised? In *Entores Ltd.* v. *Miles Far East Corporation* [1955] 2 Q.B. 327 the Court of Appeal classified them with instantaneous communications. Their ruling, which has passed into the textbooks . . . appears not to have caused either adverse comment, or any difficulty to business men. I would accept it as a general

rule. Where the condition of simultaneity is met, and where it appears to be within the mutual intention of the parties that contractual exchanges should take place in this way, I think it a sound rule, but not necessarily a universal rule.

Since 1955 the use of telex communication has been greatly expanded, and there are many variants on it. The senders and recipients may not be the principals to the contemplated contract. They may be servants or agents with limited authority. The message may not reach, or be intended to reach, the designated recipient immediately: messages may be sent out of office hours, or at night, with the intention, or upon the assumption, that they will be read at a later time. There may be some error or default at the recipient's end which prevents receipt at the time contemplated and believed in by the sender. The message may have been sent and/or received through machines operated by third persons. And many other variations may occur. No universal rule can cover all such cases: they must be resolved by reference to the intentions of the parties, by sound business practice and in some cases by a judgment where the risks should lie: see *Household Fire and Carriage Accident Insurance Co. Ltd.* v. *Grant*, 4 Ex.D. 216, 227 *per* Baggallay L.J. and *Henthorn* v. *Fraser* [1892] 2 Ch. 27 *per* Lord Herschell.

The present case is, as *Entores Ltd. v. Miles Far East Corporation* [1955] 2 Q.B. 327 itself, the simple case of instantaneous communication between principals, and, in accordance with the general rule, involves that the contract (if any) was made when and where the acceptance was received. This was on May 4, 1979, in Vienna.

The appeal was dismissed.

Electronic Transactions Act 1999 (Cth) ss 5, 14, 14A, 14B

Section 5 Definitions

(1) In this Act, unless the contrary intention appears:

[...]

addressee of an electronic communication means a person who is intended by the originator to receive the electronic communication, but does not include a person acting as an intermediary with respect to the electronic communication.

automated message system means a computer program or an electronic or other automated means used to initiate an action or respond to data messages in whole or in part, without review or intervention by a natural person each time an action is initiated or a response is generated by the system ...

consent includes consent that can reasonably be inferred from the conduct of the person concerned ...

electronic communication means:

(a) a communication of information in the form of data, text or images by means of guided and/or unguided electromagnetic energy; or

(b) a communication of information in the form of speech by means of guided and/or unguided electromagnetic energy, where the speech is processed at its destination by an automated voice recognition system ...

originator of an electronic communication means a person by whom, or on whose behalf, the electronic communication has been sent or generated before storage, if any, but does not include a person acting as an intermediary with respect to the electronic communication ...

place of business means:

(a) in relation to a person, other than an entity referred to in paragraph (b)—a place where the person maintains a non-transitory establishment to pursue an economic activity other than the temporary provision of goods or services out of a specific location; or

(b) in relation to a government, an authority of a government or a non-profit body—a place where any operations or activities are carried out by that government, authority or body.

transaction includes:

(a) any transaction in the nature of a contract, agreement or other arrangement; and

(b) any statement, declaration, demand, notice or request, including an offer and the acceptance of an offer, that the parties are required to make or choose to make in connection with the formation or performance of a contract, agreement or other arrangement; and

(c) any transaction of a non-commercial nature . . .

Section 14 Time of dispatch

(1) For the purposes of a law of the Commonwealth, unless otherwise agreed between the originator and the addressee of an electronic communication, the time of dispatch of the electronic communication is:

(a) the time when the electronic communication leaves an information system under the control of the originator or of the party who sent it on behalf of the originator; or

(b) if the electronic communication has not left an information system under the control of the originator or of the party who sent it on behalf of the originator—the time when the electronic communication is received by the addressee.

Note: Paragraph (b) would apply to a case where the parties exchange electronic communications through the same information system.

[. . .]

Section 14A Time of receipt

(1) For the purposes of a law of the Commonwealth, unless otherwise agreed between the originator and the addressee of an electronic communication:

(a) the time of receipt of the electronic communication is the time when the electronic communication becomes capable of being retrieved by the addressee at an electronic address designated by the addressee; or

(b) the time of receipt of the electronic communication at another electronic address of the addressee is the time when both:

(i) the electronic communication has become capable of being retrieved by the addressee at that address; and

(ii) the addressee has become aware that the electronic communication has been sent to that address.

[. . .]

Section 14B Place of dispatch and place of receipt

(1) For the purposes of a law of the Commonwealth, unless otherwise agreed between the originator and the addressee of an electronic communication:

(a) the electronic communication is taken to have been dispatched at the place where the originator has its place of business; and

(b) the electronic communication is taken to have been received at the place where the addressee has its place of business.

(2) For the purposes of the application of subsection (1) to an electronic communication:

(a) a party's place of business is assumed to be the location indicated by that party, unless another party demonstrates that the party making the indication does not have a place of business at that location; and

(b) if a party has not indicated a place of business and has only one place of business, it is to be assumed that that place is the party's place of business; and

(c) if a party has not indicated a place of business and has more than one place of business, the place of business is that which has the closest relationship to the underlying transaction, having regard to the circumstances known to or contemplated by the parties at any time before or at the conclusion of the transaction; and

(d) if a party has not indicated a place of business and has more than one place of business, but paragraph (c) does not apply—it is to be assumed that the party's principal place of business is the party's only place of business; and

(e) if a party is a natural person and does not have a place of business—it is to be assumed that the party's place of business is the place of the party's habitual residence.

[...]

Essentially, pursuant to the *Electronic Transactions Act 1999* (Cth), where the parties have envisaged the use of email as a means of acceptance, acceptance is said to occur when the email is sent. If email was not actually contemplated as a means of acceptance, such acceptance is said to occur when it comes to the attention of the person receiving it. Additionally, the place at which the contract is said to have been made is the recipient's place of business, even if they retrieve the email from a different location. This is an important point in terms of determining jurisdiction.

QUESTIONS

(1) What is the test for acceptance by conduct, as identified by the Court in *Empirnall Holdings Pty Ltd v Machon Paull Partners Pty Ltd* (1988) 14 NSWLR 523?

(2) In what circumstances can silence amount to acceptance?

(3) It is well established that acceptance must occur in response to the offer. What if the offeree has dual motives (one being to accept the offer) —is this sufficient?

5.5 Conditional contracts

Where parties enter into a contract, but do not want to be bound immediately by the obligations contained therein, they may choose to make the agreement conditional. In other words, the obligations of one or both parties to the contract are suspended or provisional until a condition is or is not met; that is, something happens or does not happen. Common examples include contracts containing 'subject to contract' clauses and those containing 'subject to finance' clauses.

Agreements to agree are discussed at length at **6.3**.[3] The principles surrounding 'subject to finance' clauses are discussed in the following case extract.

Concept	Short explanation	Relevant authorities	*Principles* text*
A contract may be conditional	A conditional contract is one in which obligations are put on hold until or made provisional on the fulfilment or non-fulfilment of a condition; eg 'subject to contract' clauses and 'subject to finance' clauses	*Meehan v Jones* (1982) 149 CLR 571	Chapter 5: 5.24–5.26. See also: • Chapter 6, where the concept of preliminary agreements is discussed at length • Chapter 16, where termination of a contract on the basis of non-fulfilment of a condition is discussed

* Consult the corresponding section(s) of the *Principles* text for more detail.

Meehan v Jones (1982) 149 CLR 571

Facts and issues

The Jones' agreed to sell Meehan land which they owned in Queensland upon which an oil refinery was built. Special condition 1(b) of the contract provided that the agreement was subject to 'The Purchaser ... receiving approval for finance on satisfactory terms and conditions in an amount sufficient to complete the purchase ...' by 31 July 1979. By letter dated 13 July 1979, the Jones' advised that they were rescinding the contract primarily on the ground that it was void for uncertainty. The Jones' then sold the land to a third party. On 30 July 1979, Meehan notified the Jones' that he had obtained finance as required to enable the purchase to be completed. He brought an action against the Jones' for specific performance, which was dismissed both at first instance and upon appeal to the Supreme Court of Queensland. Meehan subsequently appealed to the High Court. There were a number of issues to be determined in this case, including, relevantly:

- whether there was a binding contract;
- whether the word 'satisfactory' in special condition 1(b) should be determined objectively or subjectively;
- whether a subject to finance clause constitutes a condition precedent or a condition subsequent; and
- what the parties' obligations are in relation to such 'subject to finance' clauses.

Decision

Per Gibbs CJ at 578:

3 See particularly the discussion of *Masters v Cameron* (1954) 91 CLR 353.

Of course it is obvious enough that every such case must depend on the particular words of the contract in question, and that it is not profitable to compare with each other cases decided on different contractual provisions. However, it may be possible to state principles which will provide some guidance through the thicket of decisions.

When the words of a condition state that a contract is subject to finance, or to suitable finance, or to satisfactory finance, the question immediately arises whether the test which is required to be applied is a subjective or an objective one. On the one hand, the contract may be conditional upon the purchaser obtaining finance which he finds sufficient or satisfactory — such finance as he honestly thinks he needs to complete the purchase. On the other hand, the condition may be fulfilled if finance is available which the purchaser ought to find sufficient, or which ought reasonably to satisfy him, even though he honestly, but unreasonably, regards it as insufficient or unsatisfactory. The fact that opinions may differ as to which of these two meanings is given to the words of the clause does not mean that the clause is uncertain. If the Court, in construing the contract, can decide which of the two possible meanings is that which the parties intended, there will be no uncertainty . . .

It is only if the court is unable to put any definite meaning on the contract that it can be said to be uncertain.

If the words of the condition are understood to import a subjective test – if the condition is fulfilled if the purchaser honestly thinks that the finance is satisfactory – it is impossible in my opinion to regard the condition as uncertain. The question whether the purchaser does think the finance satisfactory is a simple question of fact. In most cases it will be a question easily answered; if the purchaser thinks the finance satisfactory, he will normally seek to complete the contract, whereas if he does not think it satisfactory, usually he will not attempt to complete. In any case, whether the purchaser is satisfied is simply a question of fact, because, to use the well known words of Bowen L.J., 'the state of a man's mind is as [579] much a fact as the state of his digestion' *(Edgington v. Fitzmaurice* (43)). However if the test is purely subjective, the question will arise whether any binding agreement has been made at all. That is a question which I shall later discuss.

On the other hand, if the test is an objective one, and the question is whether the finance ought reasonably to be regarded as satisfactory, I should not have thought that the clause is too indefinite for the courts to be able to attribute any particular contractual intention to the parties. It is true that the condition may, as Holland J. said in *Grime v. Bartholomew* (44), be 'silent as to amount, term of the loan, rate of interest, conditions of repayment, class of lender, secured or unsecured or form of security'. Nevertheless, a court which had evidence of the financial position of the purchaser, the amount required the complete the contract and the prevailing rates and conditions on which loans are made by various classes of lenders should not find it unduly difficult to decide what finance a reasonable man, in the position of the purchaser, would regard as satisfactory . . .

[580]. . .It seems to me that unless a clause of this kind makes a clear indication to the contrary, its natural effect is to leave it to the purchaser to determine whether or not the available finance is suitable to his needs. A clause such as special condition 1 (b), which speaks of 'satisfactory terms and conditions', in its natural meaning requires that the purchaser be satisfied. A cautious purchaser might be satisfied only with finance which was repayable over a long term and at comparatively low rates of interest, whereas a more adventurous purchaser might wish to proceed with the sale even though the term of the loan was short and the rate of interest high. It would be strange if an adventurous purchaser, having obtained finance on terms which were satisfactory to him, but at which a reasonable man might cavil, could be told by the vendor that the sale would not proceed, although the vendor was to be paid out in full and

> would have no interest in the purchaser's financial situation thereafter. Equally it would hardly seem likely that the parties would intend that a purchaser should be bound to complete if he honestly regarded the terms and conditions on which finance was available as unsatisfactory, notwithstanding that a court might take a different view. The intention of such a clause in my opinion is to leave it to the purchaser himself to decide whether the terms and conditions on which finance is available are satisfactory. The [581] condition prevents a purchaser from being obliged to go through with a sale when he does not believe that he can raise the necessary funds. Such a condition is generally entirely for the protection of the purchaser, and it is the satisfaction of the purchaser, not that of some hypothetical reasonable man, that will satisfy the condition. No doubt it may be implied that the purchaser will act honestly in deciding whether or not he is satisfied. However, it does not seem to me necessary, in order to give business efficacy to a contract, that a condition should be implied that the purchaser will make reasonable efforts to obtain finance. The parties may expect that he will, but he does not contract to so do.
>
> Although there is nothing uncertain about a clause which speaks of terms and conditions which satisfy the purchaser, the question nevertheless arises, when a contract is made conditional on such a clause, whether the contract is illusory ... The submission on behalf of the respondents in the present case was that the condition left a discretion or option to the purchaser to decide whether he would carry out the contract and that the purported contract was therefore illusory. In my opinion that principle does not apply where the discretion or option of the contracting party relates, not to the performance of the contractual obligations themselves, but only to the fulfilment of a condition upon which the contract depends ... [In relation to conditional agreements] ... [t]he fact that the condition is one whose performance [582] lies wholly or partly within the power of one of the parties to the contract does not mean that there is no binding contract once the condition is fulfilled. There is a concluded agreement as to the terms of the contract which, if the condition is satisfied, leaves no discretion in either party as to whether he shall carry them out. Once the condition is fulfilled, within the time allowed by the contract for its fulfilment, the contract becomes completely binding.
>
> It is clear that the condition in special condition 1 (b) is not a condition precedent to contract. Certain obligations under the contract attached immediately the contract was signed although the condition had not been fulfilled. For example, the provisions with regard to the deposit, and with regard to the giving and answering of requisitions on title, became immediately effective. Whether the contract is described as a condition precedent to completion, or as a condition subsequent, seems largely a matter of words ...
>
> For these reasons, special condition 1 (b) effectively and certainly described a condition on whose fulfilment the obligation to complete the contract depended. The possibility that the satisfaction might be that of the nominee did not introduce an element of uncertainty, for on no view was the satisfaction of the vendors necessary. Once approval was given by any lender for the making of a loan on terms and conditions regarded as satisfactory by the purchaser or his nominee the condition was fulfilled. Thereafter both the vendors and the purchaser were bound to complete.

Agreeing that 'subject to finance' clauses are capable of being enforced, Mason J added at 588:

> Primarily the object of such a clause is to benefit or protect the purchaser *(Zieme v. Gregory* (64); *Barber v. Crickett* (65); *Beauchamp v. Beauchamp* (66)), by ensuring that he is not under a binding obligation to complete if he is unable to obtain finance. Here there is nothing in the contract or other materials to suggest that the object of the clause was not to protect the purchaser, though there is the question whether the condition is exclusively for his benefit, a

matter to be discussed later. The primary object of the condition being the protection of the purchaser, it is sensible to treat it as stipulating for finance that is satisfactory to the purchaser or his nominee, subject to an implied obligation that he will act honestly, or honestly and reasonably, in endeavouring to obtain finance and in deciding whether to accept or reject proposals for finance.

In general this is the view which has been taken in New Zealand *(Barber v. Crickett* (67) – where the contract was made conditional on the purchaser 'arranging the necessary mortgage finance to purchase the property'; *Scott v. Rania* (68); *Gardner v. Gould* (69)); in Victoria *(Zieme v. Gregory* (70); cf. *Jubal v. McHenry* (71)); in Queensland *(Gagliardi v. lAmont* (72); *Bradford v. Zahra* (73); cf. *Hines v. Good* (74)). In New South Wales a contrary view has been taken . . .

[589] . . . To say that a 'subject to finance' or 'subject to finance on satisfactory terms and conditions' clause denotes finance which is satisfactory to the purchaser is not to say that he has an absolute or unfettered right to decide what is satisfactory. To concede such a right would certainly serve the object of the clause in protecting him. But it would do so at the expense of the legitimate expectations of the vendor by enabling the purchaser to escape from the contract on a mere declaration that he could not obtain suitable finance. With some justification the vendor can claim that the agreement made by the parties is not an option but a binding contract which relieves the purchaser from performance only in the event that, acting honestly, or honestly and reasonably, he is unable to obtain suitable finance.

There is in this formulation no element of uncertainty – the courts are quite capable of deciding whether the purchaser is acting honestly and reasonably. The limitation that the purchaser must act honestly, or honestly and reasonably, takes the case out of the principle that: ' . . . where words which by themselves constitute a promise are accompanied by words which show that the promisor is [590] to have a discretion or option as to whether he will carry out that which purports to be the promise, the result is that there is no contract on which an action can be brought.' See *Thorby v. Goldberg* (79), citing *Loftus v. Roberts* (80), *Placer Development Ltd. v. The Commonwealth* (81), cited by Gibbs 1. in *Godecke v. Kirwan* (82). The judgment of the purchaser as to what constitutes finance on satisfactory terms is not an unfettered discretion – it must be reached honestly, or honestly and reasonably . . .

In this case it is not necessary to decide whether the purchaser, in [591] deciding whether finance is on satisfactory terms, is bound to act honestly or whether he is also bound to act reasonably. The cases already mentioned appear to support the first rather than the second alternative. And there is some ground for thinking that the parties contemplated that the question was to be left to the honest judgment of the purchaser rather than to the judgment of a court as to whether the purchaser acted reasonably in the circumstances.

On the other hand, it has been said that a condition of this type imports an obligation or promise on the part of the purchaser to act honestly and reasonably . . . The reasoning which underlies the decisions of this Court upholding the implication of an obligation on the part of a party to a contract to do all that was reasonable on his part to obtain a statutory consent applies with equal force here. In *Butts v. O'Dwyer* (98), Dixon C.J., Williams, Webb and Kitto JJ. said:

> It has been held in cases too numerous to mention both before and after the classic statement of Bowen LJ. in the case of *The Moorcock* (99) that the law raises an implication from the presumed intention of the parties where it is necessary to do so in order to give to the transaction such efficacy as both parties must have intended that it should have.

Here the expressed intention of the parties was that the purchaser would obtain finance; his obtaining of finance on satisfactory terms was necessary to give the transaction its intended efficacy. The consequence would be that he had an obligation to do all that was reasonable on his part to obtain that finance. It would make for greater consistency to say that, if the purchaser is bound to act reasonably in seeking to obtain finance, he is bound to act reasonably as well as honestly in deciding whether the finance was satisfactory. So understood the special condition would preserve an even balance between the vendors and the purchaser. However, I have no need to decide the question. Here it makes no difference whether the purchaser was under an obligation to act honestly or honestly and reasonably in deciding whether the terms of an offer of finance were satisfactory.

Although the binding words of the special condition suggest that [592] its effect is to make the existence of the contract conditional, it is more sensible to regard the provision as one which provides for the determination of a valid and binding contract in the event that the purchaser or his nominee is unable to obtain approval for satisfactory finance on or before the appointed date. In accordance with the principle established in *New Zealand Shipping Co. v. Societe des Ateliers et Chantiers de France* (1) and extended in *Suttor v. Gundowda Pty. Ltd.* (2), each party has the right to avoid the contract on the non-performance of the condition, notwithstanding that non-performance may occur without default on the part of the purchaser, i.e. he may fail to procure finance despite every endeavour on his part. I say 'each party' because it seems to me that, although the primary object of the condition is to protect the purchaser, it is perhaps difficult to assert that the clause is for his benefit exclusively when it states that the result of non-performance is that the contract shall be null and void, rather than null and void at the option of the purchaser. I see no justification for implying a right of avoidance on the part of the purchaser alone. In other circumstances to make this implication would be to reach a one-sided interpretation, allowing the purchaser to keep the contract on foot, despite non-performance of the condition, but denying the vendor the right to avoid. Here the vendors were protected by the fixing of the date for completion and the making of time of the essence. Even so, there is no adequate basis for concluding that the special condition authorized the purchaser alone to terminate.

Whether the condition is to be described as precedent or subsequent is an artificial and theoretical question. In one sense performance of the condition or non-avoidance for breach of it is precedent to the right of a party to call for the performance of a contract. In another sense there is a valid and binding contract which may be determined for non-performance of the condition, and in this sense the condition is subsequent, not precedent.

For the reasons I have given special condition 1(b) is valid.

QUESTIONS

(1) Why might parties enter into a conditional contract, such as an agreement to agree?

(2) In what real-life legal setting are 'subject to finance' clauses often utilised?

(3) Is a purchaser bound by a 'subject to finance' clause to look for finance? If so, do they need to seek finance on any particular terms?

5.6 Consideration

Concept	Short explanation	Relevant authorities	*Principles* text*
A contract must be supported by consideration	Consideration is the 'price' specified by the promisor for the promise given Thus, there is an element of 'exchange'—i.e. consideration is given *for* the promise	*Australian Woollen Mills Pty Ltd v Commonwealth* (1954) 92 CLR 424 *Beaton v McDivitt* (1987) 13 NSWLR 162	Chapter 5: 5.27–5.28
Past consideration cannot be good consideration	The promisor cannot specify as consideration something which has already occurred or has already been provided Exceptions to this general rule include where the consideration was originally provided at the promisor's request	*Roscorla v Thomas* (1842) 3 QB 234 *Pao On v Lau Yiu Long* [1980] AC 614	Chapter 5: 5.29
There is no requirement that the consideration go to the promisor	Consideration must be provided *by the promisee*—it does not necessarily need to be provided *to the promisor*	*Coulls v Bagot's Executor and Trustee Co Ltd* (1967) 119 CLR 460	Chapter 5: 5.30
Consideration can be anything the promisor specifies	It does not have to be seen objectively as having a 'value' The court does not inquire into the adequacy of consideration Consideration can include, for example, the compromise or settlement of a claim	*Chappell & Co Ltd v Nestle Co Ltd* [1960] AC 87 *Woolworths Ltd v Kelly* (1991) 22 NSWLR 189 *Wigan v Edwards* (1973) 47 ALJR 586	Chapter 5: 5.31, 5.33
Generally, the performance of a pre-existing obligation or duty cannot be good consideration	Where a party is performing a contractual obligation or a public duty they are already bound to perform, the general rule is that this does not amount to good consideration. There are a number of exceptions to this, including where a party goes further than that already required of them	*Musumeci v Winadell Pty Ltd* (1994) 34 NSWLR 723 (see **13.3.3** for extract) *Pao On v Lau Yiu Long* [1980] AC 614 *Glasbrook Brothers Ltd v Glamorgan County Council* [1935] AC 270 *Popiw v Popiw* [1959] VR 197	Chapter 5: 5.32, 5.34
Consideration must not be illusory	Consideration must be real in the sense of imposing an obligation upon the promisor	*Biotechnology Australia Pty Ltd v Pace* (1988) 15 NSWLR 130	Chapter 5: 5.35

* Consult the corresponding section(s) of the *Principles* text for more detail.

In order to form a binding agreement, consideration must be present. Consideration is the 'cost' which the promisor stipulates as being owed by the promisee in return for the promise which the promisor is making. It must, generally speaking, be provided in response to the promise. That said, there is no requirement that the consideration actually flow from the promisee to the promisor himself/herself/itself. Although consideration is often thought of in monetary terms, it can be anything the promisor specifies including, for example, the settlement of a dispute. However, where a party is already bound to do something because of a duty or an existing contractual obligation, performance of this duty or obligation will not normally amount to good consideration unless it can be said, for example, that the party has done something extra to that required pursuant to this duty or obligation. As a general requirement, it is important that an obligation actually be imposed otherwise the consideration will be considered illusory.

The following case extracts discuss the concept of and principles relating to consideration.

Australian Woollen Mills Pty Ltd v Commonwealth (1954) 92 CLR 424

Facts and issues

The Commonwealth Government established a subsidy scheme whereby it would pay a subsidy to manufacturers who purchased wool and used it for local manufacture. Australian Woollen Mills Pty Ltd ('Australian Woollen Mills') purchased large amounts of wool and, in return, received substantial amounts by way of subsidy prior to the Commonwealth Government ceasing the subsidy scheme. A dispute subsequently arose between the parties, with each alleging that the other owed it money. Australian Woollen Mills brought proceedings against the Commonwealth on the basis that the scheme had resulted in a contract between them, and that the Commonwealth owed it certain amounts pursuant to this contract. One of the issues to be decided was whether consideration was present.

Decision

The Court held at 456:

> The contract put forward by the plaintiff is thus seen to be of that type which is commonly said to be constituted by an offer of a promise for an act, the offer being accepted by the doing of the act. Such contracts are sometimes described as 'unilateral' contracts, but the term is open to criticism on the ground that it is unscientific and misleading. There must of necessity be two parties to a contractual obligation. The position in such cases is simply that the consideration on the part of the offeree is completely executed by the doing of the very thing which constitutes acceptance of the offer. A well-known example in which a contract was held to have been made is to be found in *Carlill v. Carbolic Smokeball Co.* (1), which has been recently referred to as 'that immortal case on unilateral contract' (*J. C. Smith*, *Law Quarterly Review*, vol. 69, p. 107). Other well-known examples are the cases in which a reward is offered for the giving of information or for the finding and returning of lost property (e.g. *Williams v. Carwardine* (2) and *England v. Davidson* (3)), and the cases in which there is forbearance by a creditor in return for the debtor's promise to give security (e.g. *Alliance Bank (Ltd.) v. Broom* (4)).
>
> In cases of this class it is necessary, in order that a contract may be established, that it should be made to appear that the statement or announcement which is relied on as a promise was

really offered as consideration for the doing of the act, and that the act was really done in consideration of a potential promise inherent in the statement or announcement. Between the statement or announcement, which is put forward as an offer capable of acceptance by the doing of an act, and the act which is put forward as the executed consideration for the alleged promise, there must subsist, so to speak, [457] the relation of a *quid pro quo*. One simple example will suffice to illustrate this. A, in Sydney, says to B in Melbourne: 'I will pay you £1,000 on your arrival in Sydney'. The next day B goes to Sydney. If these facts alone are proved, it is perfectly clear that no contract binding A to pay £1,000 to B is established. For all that appears there may be no relation whatever between A's statement and B's act. It is quite consistent with the facts proved that B intended to go to Sydney anyhow, and that A is merely announcing that, if and when B arrives in Sydney, he will make a gift to him. The necessary relation is not shown to exist between the announcement and the act. Proof of further facts, however, might suffice to establish a contract. For example, it might be proved that A, on the day before the £1,000 was mentioned, had told B that it was a matter of vital importance to him (A) that B should come to Sydney forthwith, and that B objected that to go to Sydney at the moment might involve him in financial loss. These further facts throw a different light on the statement on which B relies as an offer accepted by his going to Sydney. They are not necessarily conclusive but it is now possible to infer (a) that the statement that £1,000 would be paid to B on arrival in Sydney was intended as an offer of a promise, (b) that the promise was offered as the consideration for the doing of an act by B, and (c) that the doing of the act was at once the acceptance of an offer and the providing of an executed consideration for a promise. The necessary connection or relation between the announcement and the act is provided if the inference is drawn that A has requested B to go to Sydney.

... [460] Coming to the present case, it is impossible, in our opinion, to hold that any contract was constituted at any stage binding the Commonwealth to pay a subsidy to the plaintiff, or to any manufacturer, in consideration of a purchase of wool for local manufacture ...

[461] ... No relation of *quid pro quo* between a promise and an act can be inferred. If we ask whether there is an implied request or invitation to purchase wool, we cannot say that there is. If we ask whether the announcement that a subsidy would be paid was made in order to induce purchases of wool, no such intention can be inferred.

Judgment was made in favour of the Commonwealth Government.

Beaton v McDivitt (1987) 13 NSWLR 162

Facts and issues

McDivitt, worried about a potential increase in council rates in relation to a large property he owned, agreed to allow Beaton to move onto a portion of the property if Beaton agreed to undertake a form of cultivation known as 'permaculture' on the block. In return, McDivitt agreed to transfer that part of the land to Beaton in the future if the property was rezoned as he expected. Beaton moved onto the property and cultivated it as requested, also building a house. The relationship between the parties subsequently broke down and McDivitt blocked Beaton's access to the property. The issue to be determined was whether there was a contract between the parties. At first instance, a binding contract was found to exist but it was said to have been frustrated as the anticipated rezoning of the property had not occurred. Beaton appealed, seeking specific performance of the contract.

Decision

On the question of consideration, per Kirby P at 168:

> By our law, consideration is an essential requirement for an enforceable contract. Without consideration, a promise is unenforceable at law. The modern theory of consideration has arisen from the notion that a contract is a bargain struck between the parties by an exchange. By that modern theory, consideration must be satisfied in the form of a price in return for the promisor's promise or a quid pro quo. The price can be in the form of an act, forbearance or promise. In *Pollock on Contracts*, 13th ed, (1950) at 133 Sir Frederick Pollock, in words adopted by Lord Dunedin in *Dunlop Pneumatic Tyre Co Ltd v Selfridge and Co Ltd* [1915] AC 847 at 855, expressed the idea of consideration as the 'price in return' in the following way:
>
>> An act or forbearance of one party, or the promise thereof, is the price for which the promise of the other is bought, and the promise thus given for value is enforceable.
>
> The triumph of the bargain theory of consideration necessary for a contract amounts to a rejection of the theory of contractual obligation based upon reliance ... Whatever the origins and explanations for this shift ... it was necessary, thereafter, to have resort to courts of equity for the enforcement of claims based on relationships. For in the courts of law, duties arising from bargains entered between free parties were to be enforced, not duties deriving from suggested moral obligations such as those deriving from relationships.
>
> The High Court of Australia has accepted this 'modern' or bargain doctrine of consideration ... [i]n *Australian Woollen Mills Pty Ltd v The Commonwealth* (1954) 92 CLR 424 at 456-457 ...
>
> Young J (rightly in my opinion) was unable to find consideration in this sense in the facts of the present case. It is just not possible, however indulgently one approaches those facts with sympathy to the appellant, to classify the promises he made as a quid pro quo for the suggested promise of the respondent, in certain circumstances, to transfer title in the land to him ...

Per McHugh JA at 181:

> The ratio decidendi of *Australian Woollen Mills Pty Ltd v The Commonwealth* is that the expenditure of money in reliance on an announcement by the Government that it would pay a subsidy to a manufacturer on wool purchased and used for local manufacture is not itself sufficient to create a contract to pay the subsidy ...
>
> The reasoning of the High Court may not amount to an adoption of the extremes of the bargain theory of contract as understood in the United States. But the reasoning of the High Court in insisting on the necessity for a quid pro quo accepts the basic element of the bargain theory of consideration and amounts to a rejection of a reliance based theory of consideration ...
>
> [183] ... In the present case, I think that the promise made by Mr McDivitt was an offer which was intended to give rise to an obligation on the part of himself and his wife upon the plaintiff coming and working on the land. Mr McDivitt was concerned that the land would be rezoned, that the rates would go up, and that he would not be able to pay them when he went on the pension. Accordingly, he decided to subdivide the land. Upon the transfer of three of the blocks after subdivision, he would obtain a benefit because his rates would be reduced. This motivated him to offer the block in return for a person coming and working the block by means of organic farming. Thus the consideration for the transfer of the block was the act of the plaintiff in coming and working the block by means of organic farming at the request of the McDivitts ...

> [184] ... By entering onto lot B and performing work, the plaintiff has suffered sufficient detriment to constitute consideration even though he was obliged to work the land until the time of subdivision before he was entitled to the transfer of lot B ...

The appeal was, however, ultimately dismissed with Mahoney JA holding that, although a contract had been formed (agreeing with McHugh JA), it had been frustrated.

Past consideration, being something that has already been given or has already occurred, is generally not good consideration. This concept, as well as the exceptions to this general rule, are discussed in the below cases.

Roscorla v Thomas (1842) 3 QB 234

Facts and issues

Roscorla purchased a horse from Thomas. After the agreement was entered into, Thomas promised that the horse was sound and had no vices. Unfortunately for Roscorla, this turned out not to be the case. Consequently, Roscorla brought proceedings against Thomas alleging a breach of contract. Roscorla succeeded at first instance but Thomas appealed. At issue was whether consideration had been provided in relation to the promise that the horse was sound and had no vices.

Decision

Lord Denman CJ (on behalf of the Court) at 236:

> It may be taken as a general rule, subject to [237] exceptions not applicable to this case, that the promise must be coextensive with the consideration. In the present case, the only promise that would result from the consideration, as stated, and be coextensive with it, would be to deliver the horse upon request. The precedent sale, without a warranty, though at the request of the defendant, imposes no other duty or obligation upon him. It is clear, therefore, that the consideration stated would not raise an implied promise by the defendant that the horse was sound or free from vice.

The appeal was dismissed on the basis that the argued 'consideration' also did not provide support for an express promise, which the promise in this case was said to be.

Pao On v Lau Yiu Long [1980] AC 614

Facts and issues

Pao On held shares in Shing On Co. In return for shares in Shing On Co., Lau Yiu Long, majority shareholder of Fu Chip Co., offered to transfer shares in Fu Chip Co. to Pao On. An agreement to this effect was reached with the requirement that Pao On retain 60 per cent of the transferred shares until a specified time so as not to adversely impact the market in relation to Fu Chip Co. Originally, Lau Yiu Long agreed to indemnify Pao On if the value of the shares dropped during this period.

Pao On, subsequently realising that a loss would also occur if the shares increased in value during the period within which they could not be sold, extracted a new promise from Lau Yiu Long pursuant to which the latter agreed to indemnify the former if the value of the Fu Chip Co. shares dropped below a certain value during this period of time. The shares did drop in value and Pao On sought to rely on the indemnity. Lau Yiu Long, however, refused to indemnify Pao On and the latter succeeded in a claim at first instance. This decision was reversed by the High Court (of Hong Kong). Consequently, Pao On appealed to the Privy Council. One of the issues to be determined was whether there was consideration for the contract of indemnity.

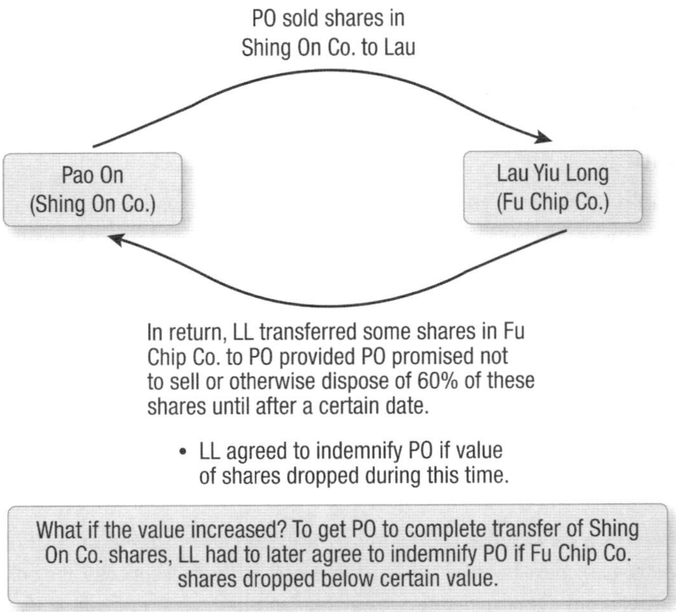

Decision

Regarding the question of past consideration, per Lord Scarman at 629:

> The Board agrees ... that the consideration expressly stated in the written guarantee is sufficient in law to support the defendants' promise of indemnity. An act done before the giving of a promise to make a payment or to confer some other benefit can sometimes be consideration for the promise. The act must have been done at the promisors' request: the parties must have understood that the act was to be remunerated either by a payment or the conferment of some other benefit: and payment, or the conferment of a benefit, must have been legally enforceable had it been promised in advance. All three features are present in this case. The promise given to Fu Chip under the main agreement not to sell the shares for a year was at the first defendant's request. The parties understood at the time of the main agreement that the restriction on selling must be compensated for by the benefit of a guarantee against a drop in price: and such a guarantee would be legally enforceable.

As to the matter of performance of a contractual duty amounting to consideration, per Lord Scarman at 632:

Their Lordships do not doubt that a promise to perform, or the performance of, a pre-existing contractual obligation to a third party can be valid consideration . . .

Unless, therefore, the guarantee was void as having been made for an illegal consideration or voidable on the ground of economic duress, the extrinsic evidence establishes that it was supported by valid consideration.

Mr. Leggatt for the defendants submits that the consideration is illegal as being against public policy. He submits that to secure a party's promise by a threat of repudiation of a pre-existing contractual obligation owed to another can be, and in the circumstances of this case was, an abuse of a dominant bargaining position and so contrary to public policy. This, he submits, is so even though economic duress cannot be proved. This submission found favour with the majority in the Court of Appeal. Their Lordships, however, consider it misconceived . . .

[633] . . . [W]here the pre-existing obligation is a contractual duty owed to a third party, some other ground of public policy must be relied on to invalidate the consideration (if otherwise legal); the defendants submit that the ground can be extortion by the abuse of a dominant bargaining position to threaten the repudiation of a contractual obligation. It is this application of public policy which Mr. Leggatt submits has been developed in the American cases. Beginning with the general rule that 'neither the performance of duty nor the promise to render a performance already required by duty is a sufficient consideration' the courts have (according to *Corbin on Contracts*, vol. 1, s. 171) advanced to the view:

> that the moral and economic elements in any case that involves the rule should be weighed by the court, and that the fact of pre-existing legal duty should not be in itself decisive.

[634] The American Law Institute in its *Restatement of the Law, Contracts*, Chapter 3, section 84 (d), has declared that performance (or promise of performance) of a contractual duty owed to a third person is sufficient consideration. This view (which accords with the statement of our law in *New Zealand Shipping Co. Ltd. v. A. M. Satterthwaite & Co. Ltd.* [1975] A.C. 154) appears to be generally accepted but only in cases where there is no suggestion of unfair economic pressure exerted to induce the making of what *Corbin on Contracts* calls 'the return promise.'. . .

[The] question . . . is whether, in a case where duress is not established, public policy may nevertheless invalidate the consideration if there has been a threat to repudiate a pre-existing contractual obligation or an unfair use of a dominating bargaining position. Their Lordships' conclusion is that where businessmen are negotiating at arm's length it is unnecessary for the achievement of justice, and unhelpful in the development of the law, to invoke such a rule of public policy. It would also create unacceptable anomaly. It is unnecessary because justice requires that men, who have negotiated at arm's length, be held to their bargains unless it can be shown that their consent was vitiated by fraud, mistake or duress. If a promise is induced by coercion of a man's will, the doctrine of duress suffices to do justice. The party coerced, if he chooses and acts in time, can avoid the contract. If there is no coercion, there can be no reason for avoiding the contract where there is shown to be a real consideration which is otherwise legal.

Such a rule of public policy as is now being considered would be unhelpful because it would render the law uncertain. It would become a question of fact and degree to determine in each case whether there had been, short of duress, an unfair use of a strong bargaining position. It would create anomaly because, if public policy invalidates the consideration, the effect is to make the contract void. But unless the facts are such as to support a plea of '*non est factum*,' which is not suggested in this case, duress does no more than confer upon the victim the

> opportunity, if taken in time, to avoid the contract. It would be strange if conduct less than duress could render a contract void, whereas duress does no more than render a contract voidable . . .
>
> [635] . . . Accordingly, the submission that the additional consideration established by the extrinsic evidence is invalid on the ground of public policy is rejected . . .

The appeal was allowed.

Although consideration must flow from the promisee, there is no corresponding requirement that this consideration must be provided to the promisor.

Coulls v Bagot's Executor and Trustee Co Ltd (1967) 119 CLR 460

Facts and issues

Mr Coulls entered into an agreement allowing O'Neil Construction Pty Ltd ('the company') to quarry and remove stone from land owned by him in return for £5 and the company agreeing to pay royalties at rates which were set out in the agreement. The agreement also gave the company authority to pay these royalties to his wife and himself as joint tenants. The agreement was signed by Mr Coulls, his wife and the company. Following the death of Mr Coulls, the executor of his Estate (Bagot's) applied to the court for a determination in relation to the issue of whether the company was entitled or bound to pay the royalties accruing pursuant to the agreement to Mrs Coulls or to the Estate. The majority of the High Court (consisting of McTiernan, Taylor and Owen JJ) found that the royalties were payable to the Estate and not to Mrs Coulls as the contract was concluded between Mr Coulls and the company. However, on the question of whether consideration must be paid to the promisor, Windeyer, Taylor and Owen JJ agreed with Barwick CJ as below (albeit in individual judgments).

Decision

Per Barwick CJ at 478:

> But as I construe this writing, we have here not a promise by A with B for consideration supplied by B to pay C. It was, in my opinion, a promise by A made to B and C for consideration to pay B and C. In such a case it cannot lie in the mouth of A, in my [479] opinion, to question whether the consideration which he received for his promise moved from both B and C or, as between themselves, only from one of them. His promise is not a gratuitous promise as between himself and the promisees as on the view I take of the agreement it was a promise in respect of which there was privity between A on the one hand and B and C on the other. Such a promise, in my opinion, is clearly enforceable in the joint lifetime of B and C: But it is only enforceable if both B and C are parties to the action to enforce it. B, though he only supplied the consideration, could not sue alone. If C were unwilling to join in the action as plaintiff, B no doubt, after suitable tender of costs, could join C as a defendant. And A's promise could be enforced. But the judgment would be for payment to B and C. If B would not join in an action to enforce A's promise, I see no reason why C should not sue joining B as a defendant. Again, in my opinion, A's promise would be enforced and a judgment in favour of B and C would result. In neither of

these cases could A successfully deny either privity or consideration. I find nothing in *Dunlop Pneumatic Tyre Co. Ltd.* v. *Selfridge & Co. Ltd.* to suggest that he could.

Upon the death of one of the joint promisees the promise remains on foot and remains enforceable but it is still the same promise given to B and C though, because of the death of one and the right of survivorship, the promise is now to pay the survivor. C, it seems to me, being the survivor, may enforce the promise by an action to which both B's estate and C are parties. However, C could not, in any event, in my opinion, be the sole plaintiff against A because A's promise was not made with C alone. Consequently, B's personal representative would need to be either a co-plaintiff or joined as a defendant, though in this case the judgment would be for C alone, the promise with B and C being to pay the survivor of them: see *Attwood* v. *Rattenbury*.

As exemplified by the following cases, consideration can be anything specified by the promisor.

Chappell & Co Ltd v Nestle Co Ltd [1960] AC 87

Facts and issues

In the context of a copyright dispute, the issue of what can constitute consideration arose. Nestle Co Ltd offered a gramophone record to customers who sent to it three wrappers from its chocolate bars along with a specified sum. From a consideration point of view, the question was whether these chocolate bar wrappers constituted 'consideration' for the sale of the record.

Decision

Per Lord Somervell of Harrow at 114:

> The question, then, is whether the three wrappers were part of the consideration or, as Jenkins L.J. held, a condition of making the purchase, like a ticket entitling a member to buy at a co-operative store.
>
> I think they are part of the consideration. They are so described in the offer. 'They,' the wrappers, 'will help you to get smash hit recordings.' They are so described in the record itself — 'all you have to do to get such new record is to send three wrappers from Nestlé's 6*d.* milk chocolate bars, together with postal order for 1*s.* 6*d.*' This is not conclusive but, however described, they are, in my view, in law part of the consideration. It is said that when received the wrappers are of no value to Nestlé's. This I would have thought irrelevant. A contracting party can stipulate for what consideration he chooses. A peppercorn does not cease to be good consideration if it is established that the promisee does not like pepper and will throw away the corn. As the whole object of selling the [115] record, if it was a sale, was to increase the sales of chocolate, it seems to me wrong not to treat the stipulated evidence of such sales as part of the consideration. For these reasons I would allow the appeal.

Consequently, a court will not conduct an inquiry into the adequacy of the consideration which has been specified by the promisor. The reasons why such an examination is not undertaken were summarised by Kirby P in the below case.

Woolworths Ltd v Kelly (1991) 22 NSWLR 189

Decision

Per Kirby P at 193:

> There are a number of reasons why the common law has declined to weigh the adequacy of consideration in judging whether a particular bargain amounts to a legally enforceable contract:
>
> (1) In the marketplace, in the myriad of situations which lead to contracts, different participants will put different values upon the bargain they are getting. The subject of a bargain may be specially important to a party. It may be valued for idiosyncratic, sentimental, ethical and other reasons as well as economic reasons. That is why it has been said so often that it is impossible for the law to indulge in an evaluation of the equivalence of the promises exchanged by parties to a contract: see, eg, *American University v Todd* 1 A 2d 595 (1938) at 598;
>
> (2) Judges deciding disputed contract cases are lawyers. Parties whose disputes come to law are advised by lawyers. Lawyers enjoy a special training. But that training may not prepare them to evaluate the multitude of economic and other decisions daily made by people of different, and even like, backgrounds in entering into bargains. The disinclination of the courts to become involved in economic evaluation derives, in part, from a realisation of the limited expertise of lawyers. That expertise does not necessarily qualify the lawyer to substitute his or her opinion about the wisdom of the bargain achieved for that of the parties, so long as some consideration for the bargain can be demonstrated;
>
> (3) If courts were to entertain disputes concerning the adequacy, or inadequacy, of consideration for a bargain, and if such issues were justiciable, they would lead to litigation prone to open up a vast territory of evidence. Courts would have to try the adequacy of consideration upon testimony. Different decision-makers would reach different conclusions upon the same evidence;
>
> (4) The prospect of such disputes would produce a great deal of uncertainty in an area of the law where certainty has great economic importance to society. In contract law it is highly desirable that uncertainty about whether a bargain is legally enforceable be minimised . . . ;
>
> (5) The law provides means, in particular cases, to challenge the adequacy of a bargain where some wrong or moral fault can be shown to justify the challenge. Thus, if there was no intention to enter into contractual relations at all, the bargain will not be enforced. Equitable relief will also sometimes be available to prevent enforcement of a contract contrary to conscience. [194] Statutory and other relief has been provided by law to meet cases of unconscionable or unjust contracts. Federal and State statutes have been enacted to provide expressly for such relief . . .
>
> Relief may be granted for mistake. Contracts may be rectified. Restitution may be ordered. But at law, the rule against inquiring into the adequacy or inadequacy of considerations stands firm. It should not, in my view, be changed . . . ;
>
> (6) The restraint of the common law in this regard is also an attribute of economic liberty. That liberty extracts a price in social terms. However, respecting the right of parties at law to reach their own bargains, untroubled by the paternalistic superintendence of the courts as to the adequacy of their bargains is the approach which the common law has adopted. It is an approach protective of economic freedom.

Consideration may take the form of the giving up of a claim or the compromise or settling of a legal dispute.

Wigan v Edwards (1973) 47 ALJR 586

Facts and issues

The Edwards purchased a house from Wigan which Wigan had constructed himself. Although Mr and Mrs Edwards inspected the house prior to construction being completed, there was no clause in the agreement warranting that the house had been constructed correctly or was sound. Despite this, the Edwards refused to settle on the purchase until certain remedial work had been carried out on the property in relation to a number of identified minor defects. In response, Wigan agreed in writing to undertake the work and also provided a guarantee that '[a]ny major faults in construction five years from purchase date I will repair'. Settlement proceeded but Wigan did not remedy the minor defects as promised and, additionally, a major defect relating to the concrete slab was discovered. Consequently, the Edwards instituted proceedings for breach of contract and were successful both at first instance and on appeal. Wigan subsequently appealed to the High Court. One of the issues to be determined by the High Court was whether or not consideration had been provided for the promises by Wigan to rectify both the minor defects and any subsequent major defects.

Decision

Per Mason J at 594:

> The general rule is that a promise to perform an existing duty is no consideration, at least when the promise is made by a party to a pre-existing contract, when it is made to the promisee under that contract, and it is to do no more than the promisor is bound to do under that contract. The rule expresses the concept that the new promise, indistinguishable from the old, is an illusory consideration. And it gives no comfort to a party who by merely threatening a breach of contract seeks to secure an additional contractual benefit from the other party on the footing that the first party's new promise of performance will provide sufficient consideration for that benefit.
>
> An important qualification to the general principle is that a promise do precisely what the promisor [595] is already bound to do is a sufficient consideration, when it is given by way of a bona fide compromise of a disputed claim, the promisor having asserted that he is not bound to perform the obligation under the pre-existing contract or that he has a cause of action under that contract. The qualification recognizes that for the Court itself to examine and determine the correctness of the promisor's claim would be a pointless exercise when the new bargain indicates that the promisee regarded the fresh promise as a benefit, presumably viewing the promise of performance as more advantageous than the remedies available to him for breach of contract. But the law, by insisting that the claim in dispute is one which was honestly or bona fide made, prevents the qualification from assisting the party who would seek to gain an unfair advantage by threatening unscrupulously to withhold performance under a contract.
>
> It is no objection to the existence of a bona fide compromise of a dispute that the Court considers that the claim made by the promisor that he was not bound under the former contract would not have succeeded had the issue been litigated (*Callisher v Bischoffsheim* (1870) LR 2 QB 449; *Miles v New Zealand Alford Estate Co* (1886) 32 Ch D 266). But it is perhaps open to question whether a bona fide compromise of a dispute is sufficiently established by showing that the promisor honestly believed that his claim was well founded. It has been said that it must also be shown that the claim was not vexatious or frivolous. In *Miles v New Zealand Alford Estate Co* (32 Ch D, at 291–2) Bowen LJ expressed himself in favour of the second formulation, whereas in the same case Cotton LJ (at 283–4) and Fry LJ (at 297–8) expressed themselves more obliquely. However, as I understand their observations, they are not inconsistent with what Bowen LJ had to say. In many courts in the United States a similar test to that adopted by Bowen LJ has been

adopted. *Williston on Contracts* 3rd ed, s 135 b, states: 'In many jurisdictions the tendency is to make the test the honesty of the claimant, provided the invalidity of the claim in law or in fact is not entirely obvious.' Even so, according to the author, the forbearance is insufficient consideration 'if the claim forborne is so lacking in any foundation as to make its assertion incompatible with both honesty and a reasonable degree of intelligence'.

The different expressions of the principle do not reflect an important conceptual difference. There will be few cases involving an honest or bona fide belief in a claim which is vexatious or frivolous. In this case it is unnecessary to choose between the competing formulations, for in my view the more stringent test, that favoured by Bowen LJ in *Miles' Case* is satisfied.

The judge found that the respondents honestly believed that, having regard to the defective condition of the house, they were not bound to complete. In my opinion his Honour was correct in so finding. Although it is my view that the majority of the defects on which the respondent relied would not have justified a refusal to complete the contract, there were many defects. In addition, the water had not been connected and the fence had not been erected. In these circumstances the respondents' claim that they would not complete cannot be described as a frivolous or vexatious claim.

The respondents merely asserted that they would not complete until the matters of which they complained were set right. They did not threaten to bring an action or to defend a suit for specific performance. However, a threat to bring an action or enter a defence is not an essential element of a bona fide compromise; it is enough if there is a claim (of the kind already discussed) that the contracting party is not bound to perform the contract. Clearly the respondents' claim was of this kind. Accordingly, in my view there was valuable consideration to support the agreement . . .

Generally, where a party is purporting to provide consideration in the form of the performance of an existing duty or obligation, this will not be sufficient. This principle, as well as the circumstances in which an exception might arise, are discussed in the following case extracts. Reference should also be made to the case of *Pao On v Lau Yiu Long*[4] as well as to *Musumeci v Winadell Pty Ltd*[5].

Glasbrook Brothers Ltd v Glamorgan County Council [1925] AC 270

Facts and issues

Glasbrook Brothers Ltd ('Glasbrook Bros'), the owners of a number of coal mines, sought additional protection from the local police on the occasion of a coal strike. While Glamorgan County Council ('the Council') (through the superintendent of the local police force) believed adequate protection would be provided by way of police posted at key watch points and a mobile force ready to attend as required, Glasbrook Bros disagreed. It insisted on having police billeted at its mine. The Council agreed to provide 70 men for this 'special duty' on the proviso that Glasbrook Bros pay for the associated costs. Although Glasbrook Bros agreed to this, once the strike ended, the police officers having been so billeted, it refused to pay. The Council brought an action to enforce the agreement and was successful both at first instance and when Glasbrook Bros appealed to the Court of

4 [1980] AC 614 (extracted above).
5 (1994) 34 NSWLR 723, discussed at **13.3**.

Appeal. Nevertheless, the latter decision was also appealed by Glasbrook Bros. At issue was whether there had been any consideration provided for Glasbrook Bros' promise to pay the costs. It was Glasbrook Bros' argument that the Council was duty-bound to provide police protection without payment and that therefore consideration was absent.

Decision

Per Viscount Cave LC at 277:

> No doubt there is an absolute and unconditional obligation binding the police authorities to take all steps which appear to them to be necessary for keeping the peace, for preventing crime, or for protecting property from criminal injury; and the public, who pay for this protection through the rates and taxes, cannot lawfully be called upon to make a further payment for that which is their right. This was laid down by Pickford L.J. in the case of *Glamorganshire Coal Co. v. Glamorganshire Standing Joint Committee* (1) in the following terms: 'If one party to a dispute is threatened with violence by the other party he is entitled to protection from such violence whether his contention in the dispute be right or wrong, and to allow the police authority to deny him protection from that violence unless he pays all the expense [278] in addition to the contribution which with other ratepayers he makes to the support of the police is only one degree less dangerous than to allow that authority to decide which party is right in the dispute and grant or withhold protection accordingly. There is a moral duty on each party to the dispute to do nothing to aggravate it and to take reasonable means of self-protection, but the discharge of this duty by them is not a condition precedent to the discharge by the police authority of their own duty.' With this statement of the law I entirely agree, and I think that any attempt by a police authority to extract payment for services which fall within the plain obligations of the police force, should be firmly discountenanced by the Courts. But it has always been recognized that, where individuals desire that services of a special kind which, though not within the obligations of a police authority, can most effectively be rendered by them, should be performed by members of the police force, the police authorities may (to use an expression which is found in the Police Pensions Act, 1890) 'lend' the services of constables for that purpose in consideration of payment. Instances are the lending of constables on the occasions of large gatherings in and outside private premises, as on the occasions of weddings, athletic or boxing contests or race meetings, and the provision of constables at large railway stations . . .
>
> [281] . . . If in the judgment of the police authorities, formed reasonably and in good faith, the garrison was necessary for the protection of life and property, then they were not entitled to make a charge for it, for that would be to exact a payment for the performance of a duty which they clearly owed to the appellants and their servants; but if they thought the garrison a superfluity and only acceded to Mr. James' request with a view to meeting his wishes, then in my opinion they were entitled to treat the garrison duty as special duty and to charge for it.

The appeal was dismissed.

Popiw v Popiw [1959] VR 197

Facts and issues

A few days after Mrs Popiw left him, Mr Popiw promised that if she returned to live with him he would put the title to their home in their joint names. Mrs Popiw returned but left again shortly thereafter following a series of disagreements with Mr Popiw. She then brought proceedings seeking a determination as to what, if any, legal interest she had in the home, as well as an order that the property be sold and the proceeds divided between herself and Mr Popiw. In support of her claim to the property, Mrs Popiw argued, among other things, that the agreement relating to the transfer of the property into joint names was a binding contract. One of the (multiple) issues arising from this argument was whether consideration had been provided for Mr Popiw's promise to complete this transfer.

Decision

Per Hudson J at 198:

> The objection that the act of the applicant in returning to cohabitation did not amount to a valid consideration for the respondent's promise was founded on the view that the applicant was already under a duty as the wife of the respondent to return to cohabitation and this being so it could not be said that by the act of the applicant she suffered any detriment or that the respondent gained any advantage in [199] exchange for his promise. It is stated in Pollock on Contracts (13th ed.), at p. 146 that 'neither the promise to do a thing nor the actual doing of it will be a good consideration if it is a thing which the party is already bound to do either by the general law or by a subsisting contract with the other party.'
>
> The learned editor is not alone among text book writers in expressing this view of the law and authority is not lacking for his proposition. But this view of the law was clearly rejected by the Court of Appeal in the case of *Ward v Byham*, [1956] 2 All ER 318, a case which does not appear to have found its way into the authorized reports. There it was held that the mother of an illegitimate child, already under a statutory duty to support that child, could enforce a promise by the father to pay her a weekly sum given inconsideration for her promise to look after the child. No question of compromise of affiliation proceedings was involved and Lord Denning, at p.319, said: 'I approach the case, therefore, on the footing that the mother, in looking after the child, is only doing what she is legally bound to do. Even so, I think there is sufficient consideration to support the promise. I have always thought that a promise to perform an existing duty, or the performance of it, should be regarded as good consideration, because it is a benefit to the person to whom it is given. Take this very case. It is as much a benefit for the father to have the child looked after by the mother as by a neighbour. If he gets the benefit for which he stipulated, he ought to honour his promise; and he ought not to avoid it by saying that the mother was herself under a duty to maintain the child.' In the face of this decision the respondent's contention in the present case appears to be untenable. I might say, however, that even if the rule were as stated in Pollock on Contracts, I should think it would have no application to the facts of the present case. Although it may be true to state that the applicant was under a duty to cohabit with the respondent there was no remedy open to the respondent to compel the performance of that duty. Furthermore there was evidence which I am prepared to accept that the respondent had assaulted and beaten the applicant, and though these assaults on the evidence before me fell far short of what would be necessary to constitute constructive desertion they might well have given the applicant just cause for leaving and remaining away from the matrimonial home.
>
> From a practical point of view therefore what the respondent was to get in exchange for his promise was something which must be regarded as far more advantageous to him than the right of cohabiting with his wife which he had no means of enforcing and the applicant in returning was submitting to a detriment in placing herself in a position which she could not have been compelled to occupy. On any view therefore I think there was good consideration for the respondent's promise.

Consideration must not be illusory; that is, it must impose a real obligation rather than a discretion. For example, a promise by Party A to purchase Party B's business for $3 million if Party A *chooses* to pay this amount is an example of illusory consideration. The following case extract provides another example of illusory consideration.

Biotechnology Australia Pty Ltd v Pace (1988) 15 NSWLR 130

Facts and issues

Biotechnology Australia Pty Ltd ('Biotechnology') employed Pace as a research scientist. It was a term of the agreement that Pace would have 'the option to participate in [Biotechnology's] senior staff equity sharing scheme'. However, both at the time the agreement was entered into and at the time Pace's employment was terminated, Biotechnology had not established such a scheme. Pace brought an action for breach of contract, alleging that a promise had been made (and broken) by Biotechnology in relation to its failure to establish this equity sharing scheme. Pace succeeded at first instance and Biotechnology appealed. One of the issues was whether the consideration provided was illusory.

Decision

McHugh JA made the following comments in relation to the issue of illusory consideration at 150:

> A contract made for a consideration which is illusory is unenforceable: *Placer Development Ltd v The Commonwealth* (1969) 121 CLR 353 at 356, [151] 360-361 and *Meehan v Jones* (1982) 149 CLR 571 at 581. A consideration is illusory if its payment or fulfilment depends upon an unfettered discretion vested in the promisor. Thus a promise by the Commonwealth that it will pay a subsidy 'of an amount or at a rate determined by the Commonwealth from time to time' is an illusory consideration: *Placer Development Ltd v The Commonwealth*. So is a promise that any services rendered by a person would 'be taken into consideration, and such remuneration be made as should be deemed right': *Taylor v Brewer* (1813) 1 M & S 290; 105 ER 108. Likewise the consideration is illusory where an employer promises to pay 'such sum of money as I may deem right as compensation for labour done': *Roberts v Smith* (1859) 4 H & N 315; 157 ER 861. The decision of the Privy Council in *Kofi-Sunkersette Obu v A Strauss & Co Ltd* [1951] AC 243 is also an illustration of an illusory consideration. The agreement between the parties provided that a 'commission is also to be paid to me by the company which I have agreed to leave to the discretion of the company'. The Judicial Committee said (at 250) that the court could not determine the basis and rate of the commission. 'To do so would involve not only making a new agreement for the parties but varying the existing agreement by transferring to the court the exercise of the discretion vested' in the company.
>
> In all these cases, there was an express or implied statement that the consideration was payable only if the promisor elected to do so. However, in the case of a commercial or employment agreement under which the promisee provides services, the proper conclusion ordinarily to be drawn is that the services or consideration were not intended to be performed gratuitously: cf *Way v Latillar* [1937] 3 All ER 759 at 763. In the absence of express words or necessary implication, it will be proper to conclude that the services were to be paid for by reference to some standard of measurement. The usual standard is that of reasonable remuneration based on market or industry criteria. Where there is a firm promise to pay or remunerate the promisee in return for his services, a conclusion that the consideration was illusory will

> only be drawn where no standard exists by which the promise can be valued. But even when no objective criterion of measurement is available, it may still be possible to infer a promise to act honestly and/or reasonably. Moreover, notwithstanding that the promisor retains a discretion, the consideration will not be illusory if the discretion must be exercised within specified parameters. In *Lewandowski v Mead Carney-BCA* F *Pty Ltd* [1973] 2 NSWLR 640, this Court held that a promise to pay 'a salary within a range of $7,000-$9,000 per annum' was not illusory. The promise imported an obligation to pay a minimum salary of $7,000 per annum. In *Thorby v Goldberg* (1964) 112 CLR 597, the High Court held that a contract was made although one party was given 'considerable discretion' as to how it carried out its obligations. Kitto J said (at 605) that 'an agreement is not void for uncertainty because it leaves one party or group of parties a latitude of choice as to the manner in which agreed stipulations shall be carried into effect, nor does it for that reason fall short of being a concluded contract'.

On the facts, McHugh JA concluded that the consideration was illusory as it was at Biotechnology's discretion whether or not it established the scheme.

QUESTIONS

(1) What is not good consideration? Provide an example.

(2) What is the reason for the general rule that performance of a contractual duty already owed by the promisor to the promisee is not good consideration?

(3) Why does the court not inquire into the adequacy of the consideration provided in return for a promise?

5.7 Certainty and completeness

Concept	Short explanation	Relevant authorities	*Principles text**
An agreement must be certain and complete. Vague or ambiguous, illusory or incomplete agreements will be unenforceable	If an agreement is either uncertain (because it is vague or ambiguous or illusory) or incomplete then it will be unenforceable *Vague/ambiguous*: court cannot give a definite meaning to the words used *Incomplete agreement*: all essential terms are not dealt with in the agreement *Illusory agreement*: performance of promise is discretionary	*Upper Hunter County District Council v Australian Chilling and Freezing Co Ltd* (1968) 118 CLR 429 *Whitlock v Brew* (1968) 118 CLR 445 *Godecke v Kirwan* (1973) 129 CLR 629 *Biotechnology Australia Pty Ltd v Pace* (1988) 15 NSWLR 130 *Placer Development v Commonwealth* (1969) 121 CLR 353	Chapter 5: 5.36 Chapter 5: 5.37 Chapter 5: 5.38 Chapter 5: 5.39

Concept	Short explanation	Relevant authorities	*Principles* text*
Agreements to agree and agreements to negotiate in good faith are generally not enforceable	See **Chapter 6**	See **Chapter 6**	Chapter 6

* Consult the corresponding section(s) of the *Principles* text for more detail.

In order to be enforceable, a contract must be both certain and complete. An agreement may be uncertain because a definite meaning cannot be attributed to the words used—in other words, because the wording used is so vague and ambiguous that it is not clear what the parties intended. How the courts approach such agreements is outlined in the below case extract.

Upper Hunter County District Council v Australian Chilling and Freezing Co Ltd (1968) 118 CLR 429

Facts and issues

Australian Chilling and Freezing Co Ltd ('ACF') entered into an agreement with the Upper Hunter County District Council ('the Council') for the purchase and supply of electricity. In clause 5 of the agreement, it was stated that 'if the Supplier's costs shall vary in other respects than has been hereinbefore provided the Supplier shall have the right to vary the maximum charge and energy charge. . .'. In accordance with this clause, the Council (the 'Supplier' under the agreement) subsequently notified ACF of an increase in the charges. ACF argued that the Council did not have the right to vary its charges on the basis that clause 5 was void for uncertainty. ACF succeeded at first instance and the Council appealed to the High Court on this issue.

Decision

Per Barwick CJ at 436:

> But a contract of which there can be more than one possible meaning or which when construed can produce in its application more than one result is not therefore void for uncertainty. As long as it is capable of a meaning, it will ultimately bear that meaning which the courts, or in an appropriate case, an arbitrator, decides is its proper construction: and the court or arbitrator [437] will decide its application. The question becomes one of construction, of ascertaining the intention of the parties, and of applying it. Lord Tomlin's words in this connexion in *Hillas* & *Co. Ltd.* v. *Arcos Ltd.* (1) ought to be kept in mind. So long as the language employed by the parties, to use Lord Wright's words in *Scammell (G.)* & *Nephew Ltd.* v. *Ouston* (2) is not 'so obscure and so incapable of any definite or precise meaning that the Court is unable to attribute to the parties any particular contractual intention', the contract cannot be held to be void or uncertain or meaningless. In the search for that intention, no narrow or pedantic approach is warranted, particularly in the case of commercial arrangements. Thus will uncertainty of meaning, as distinct from absence of meaning or of intention, be resolved.

> I do not think there is any uncertainty or for that matter ambiguity in the expression 'supplier's costs' in cl. 5, however wide may be the area of possible disagreement as to its denotation in a particular case. A contract to build a bridge at cost could not, in my opinion, be held void for uncertainty: it could not properly, in my opinion, be said to be meaningless: nor is it, in my opinion, ambiguous. Endless might be the arguments pro and con as to whether or not in marginal cases some item of expenditure is as claimed a cost, or as to how much of an expenditure is a cost, of the particular activity. But to my mind, generally speaking, the concept of a cost of doing something is certain in the sense that it provides a criterion by reference to which the rights of the parties may ultimately and logically be worked out, if not by the parties then by the courts. There are no elements in the circumstances of this contract to deprive the concept of that certainty.

The appeal was allowed.

An agreement will also generally be unenforceable where it does not deal with all of the essential terms relating to the particular subject matter and is therefore incomplete.

Whitlock v Brew (1968) 118 CLR 445

Facts and issues

Brew entered into an agreement to purchase land from Whitlock. A special condition of the contract, clause 5, provided that Brew would immediately grant a lease to a petrol service station company 'upon such reasonable terms as commonly govern such a lease'. The contract was subsequently rescinded by Whitlock, and Brew brought action to recover the deposit he had paid on the basis that the contract was void for uncertainty. Brew was unsuccessful at first instance but successful on appeal to the Full Court of the Supreme Court of Victoria. Whitlock subsequently appealed to the High Court. The key issues in the case were whether clause 5 was void for uncertainty and, if it was, whether it could be severed, allowing the rest of the agreement to remain enforceable.

Decision

Per Kitto J at 456:

> The main problem in this case arises not from any uncertainty of language in the document headed 'contract of sale' but from the omission of the parties to reach a concluded agreement upon the matter to which special condition 5 is addressed ... [Apart from the portion of land and term of the lease] upon no other topic does the document indicate what the provisions of the lease are to be. It does say that the lease is to be granted 'upon such reasonable terms as commonly govern such a lease', and that would have been enough if evidence had established that for such a lease an ascertainable set of reasonable terms are in common use. But this has not been established, and the result is that the document does not record a consensus ad idem as to the duration of the term, the rent, or anything else except the commencing date and the premises intended to be let. Provision is indeed made for arbitration in the event of any dispute between the parties 'as to the interpretation or operation of this clause' ... [b]ut it clearly would not authorize an arbitrator to force upon the purchaser such terms [457] commonly to govern such a lease, for to do so would be to alter the contract.

The problem to which I have referred as the main problem is whether the fact that special condition 5 is, for this reason, of no contractual effect carries the consequence that the whole document is in like case, or whether, on the other hand, the provisions of the document apart from special condition 5 constitute by themselves a concluded contract from which that condition is properly to be considered a separate and severable provision. The document contains a provision specifically entitling the purchaser to vacant possession of the property sold upon acceptance of title and upon payment of £56,000. That sum was by a later provision made payable within forty-five days from the date of the document, the purchaser's liability to pay the balance of the purchase price, £109,000, being deferred for twenty years. Special condition 5, so far as it goes, is a direct qualification of the provision as to vacant possession, for what it sets itself to do is to saddle the purchaser's taking of possession with an immediate obligation to grant a lease to the Shell Co. It is therefore clear on the face of the document that the parties had no intention of agreeing upon a sale which would entitle the purchaser to receive vacant possession without having to grant any lease to the Shell Co.; and it follows that to treat the" contract" as binding though shorn of special condition 5 would be to turn the sale into a different sort of sale from that which the parties contemplated. Courts are of course anxious to hold parties to what they have agreed upon, but there can be no justification for holding them to something they have not agreed upon. In my opinion the decision of the Full Court of the Supreme Court that no concluded contract of sale was made between the parties is correct; and as it is agreed that if that be so the purchaser is entitled to recover the moneys he paid to the vendor under the supposed contract the Full Court's order that judgment be entered for the purchaser on his claim should be affirmed . . .

Per Taylor, Menzies and Owen JJ at 460:

The first question to be considered is whether the contention that special condition 5 is uncertain should be upheld . . . We are firmly of opinion that the expression 'upon such reasonable terms as govern such a lease' is not, in the context in which it appears, apt to refer to either the period for which, the contemplated lease is to subsist or to the rent to be payable thereunder. Nor do we think that the further expression 'as to the interpretation or operation' of this clause covers a dispute as to either of those matters. We, therefore, are of opinion that the clause is uncertain in that it neither specifies [461] nor provides a means for the determination as between the parties of the period for which the contemplated lease shall be granted or the rent which shall be payable thereunder.

It, therefore, becomes necessary to determine whether the condition is severable from the rest of the provisions of the contract or whether the whole contract falls . . . [The] general principle is stated by Knox C.J. in [*Life Insurance Co. of Australia Ltd v Phillips* (1925) 36 CLR 60]:

> When a contract contains a number of stipulations one of which is void for uncertainty, the question whether the whole contract is void depends on the intention of the parties to be gathered from the instrument as a whole. If the contract be divisible, the part which is void may be separated from the rest and does not affect its validity.

Observations in the same case make it clear that in seeking to ascertain the intention of the parties to a written contract extrinsic evidence may not be resorted to except where such evidence may be called in aid in the interpretation of the written instrument. Clearly enough, it seems to us, it is not to the point to make an independent examination of extrinsic facts, even if they were within the knowledge of both parties, and upon such evidence to conclude that a particular provision was or was not of importance to them or to either of them; the question for determination is the intention of the parties as disclosed by the contract into which they have

> entered ... Of course, cases may arise where a vague, uncertain or meaningless clause in a contract may simply be ignored ... But special condition 5 does not fall into any such category; nor can it be said to be a clause inserted solely for the benefit of one of the parties and capable of being waived by him. It is, in a sense, [462] definitive of the ultimate rights which it is contemplated the purchaser is to get under his contract. The clause provides that the respondent will *immediately upon taking possession* grant a lease the effect of which will be to deprive him of possession of part of the land in return for a promise to pay rent ... The case more closely resembles *Duggan* v. *Barnes* (3), where A agreed to sell land to B for a stated price and B undertook to grant a lease to any person who should purchase A's business. There the court had no difficulty in holding that B's undertaking was a material and inseverable part of the consideration for A's promises. In our view the same conclusion must be reached in this case and the fact that here it is the purchaser, and not the vendor, who is asserting the invalidity of the contract is of no consequence. In our opinion the appellant's appeal should be dismissed ...

The appeal was dismissed.

Godecke v Kirwan (1973) 129 CLR 629

Facts and issues

Godecke entered into an agreement to purchase land belonging to Kirwan. The agreement included a clause which provided, in part, that Godecke would, if required by Kirwan, 'execute a further agreement to be prepared at my costs by [Kirwan's] solicitors containing ... such other covenants and conditions as [Kirwan's solicitors] may reasonably require'. Godecke paid the deposit but Kirwan subsequently refused to proceed with the sale. To protect his purported interest in the land, Godecke lodged a caveat and Kirwan brought proceedings for the removal of this caveat. At first instance it was determined that the agreement was not binding as it contemplated the entering into of a formal contract (see the extract at **6.3**). Godecke appealed to the High Court. At issue was whether the agreement was incomplete and therefore unenforceable.

Decision

Per Walsh J at 642:

> It is clearly established that a binding agreement may be made which leaves some important matter, e.g. the price, to be settled by the decision of a third party. I agree with respect with the view of Bray C.J. that, subject to the qualifications to which he refers [in *Powell v Jones* [1968] SASR 394, 398], there is no reason in principle for holding that there cannot be any binding contract if some matter is left to be determined by one of the contracting parties.
>
> In the present case the parties set out all the principal terms which were to govern the sale and purchase of the land and these included provisions which imposed by implication an obligation to execute a formal contract. There was also a promise by the purchaser to execute, if required to do so, a further agreement in accordance with cl. 6. In my opinion, that clause should be construed as limited to permitting the insertion of covenants and conditions not inconsistent with those contained in the offer. It was limited also by the reference to the reasonableness of requiring the inclusion of the covenants and conditions. In my opinion, this does not mean that anything may be required which in the opinion of the solicitors is

reasonable. It means that what is required must be reasonable in an objective sense, and in case of [643] dispute this is a matter which the court can decide. Clause 6 does not mean that the purchaser is making an agreement to agree later upon additional provisions to govern the bargain. It means that he is agreeing presently to accept as part of the bargain such additional provisions, if any, as are required, provided that they satisfy the requirements of consistency with the other terms and of reasonableness to which I have referred . . .

For the foregoing reasons I am unable to agree with the view of the learned primary judge that this was a case in which all the terms of the contract had not been settled and which for that reason fell within the third class of the cases discussed in *Masters* v. *Cameron* (2). I am of opinion that a binding agreement was made.

The appeal was allowed.

Uncertainty will also arise where the agreement is illusory in nature because performance of the promise is discretionary.

Biotechnology Australia Pty Ltd v Pace (1988) 15 NSWLR 130

Facts and issues

The facts of this case are set out at **5.6** (p 169) above.

Decision

Per Kirby P at 134:

> The case law on ambiguous, uncertain and illusory contracts is enormous. Some of it is difficult to reconcile because of the different ways in which judges have classified disputed terms, for example, as so illusory as to deny a contract at all or so ambiguous or uncertain as to deny enforcement of the contract, although clearly one was intended. Some commentators urge that it is essential to maintain a 'sharp distinction' between terms which are vague, uncertain or ambiguous and those which are illusory: see, eg, H K Lücke, 'Illusory, Vague and Uncertain Contractual Terms' (1977) 6 Adel L Rev 1 at 2. Others suggest that the concepts are interchangeable or at least merge into each other along a spectrum which begins with the vague, passes through the ambiguous, reaches the uncertain and finally disappears into the illusory.
>
> [135] In the High Court of Australia, Taylor and Owen JJ sought to explain the distinction between terms which are illusory and those which are real but uncertain. They do so in their joint judgment in *Placer Development Ltd v The Commonwealth* (1969) 121 CLR 353 at 359–360:
>
> > . . . a promise to pay an unspecified amount of money is not enforceable where it expressly appears that the amount to be paid is to rest in the discretion of the promisor and the deficiency is not remedied by a subsequent provision that the promisor will, in this discretion, fix the amount of the payment. Promises of this character are treated by Pollock (*Principles of Contract*, 12th ed (1946) pp 38, 39) not as vague and uncertain promises — for their meaning is only too clear — but as illusory promises.
> >
> > [. . .]
>
> Accepting, therefore, the distinction (but acknowledging that, at the margins, there will be legitimate differences of view about the legal classification to be applied in the particular case),

the following general observations may be made about the task of classification required in cases of this sort:

(1) The determination of every case depends upon its own facts. The meaning of the agreement between the parties must be discovered objectively. Where there is suggested ambiguity or vagueness or where it is urged that a term is illusory, it may sometimes be both necessary and appropriate to have regard to extrinsic evidence in order to give meaning to that to which the parties have agreed: see, eg, *Kell v Harris* (1915) 15 SR (NSW) 473 at 479; 32 WN (NSW) 133 at 136 and *Raffles v Wichelhaus* (1864) 2 H & C 906; 159 ER 375.
(2) The court will endeavour to uphold the validity of the agreement between the parties: see *Hillas & Co Ltd v Arcos Ltd*. The court will attempt to avoid frustrating the wishes of the contracting parties so far as those wishes may be ascertained from the agreement between them: see *Meehan* (at 589); see also Barwick CJ in *Upper Hunter County District Council v Australian Chilling and Freezing Co Ltd* (1968) 118 CLR 429 at 437 where his Honour said that: '... In the search for that intention, no narrow or pedantic approach is warranted, particularly in the case of commercial arrangements.'
(3) But the court will not do so, where, in effect, it is asked to spell out, to an unacceptable extent, that to which the parties have themselves failed to agree. Nor will the court clarify that which is irremediably obscure. Most particularly, the court will not accept for itself a discretion which the parties have, by their agreement, reserved to one or other of them. To do so would not be to effect the contract but to change it: *Kofi-Sunkersette Obu v A Strauss & Co Ltd* [1951] AC 243 at 250 (PC).
(4) Views will differ about the classification of the challenged provision and whether the court can or cannot give effect to it. Usually, there is no objectively right decision in these cases. That fact is illustrated by the frequency with which there are strongly expressed differences of judicial opinion concerning whether the case falls on one side of the line or the other. So it was in *Placer Development* where Kitto, Taylor and Owen JJ found that a clause in an agreement with the Commonwealth relating to a conditional entitlement to a subsidy was unenforceable ... [136]
(5) Nevertheless, the differences of result are not simply the result of differing judicial opinion based on nothing more than personal predilection. True, it is possible that behind the willingness of courts to fashion with precision a term which the parties have failed or neglected to clarify could be analysed in terms of differing fundamental attitudes concerning the role of courts in disturbing the economic relations of contracting parties. I say no more of that. Alternatively, it has been suggested that the willingness of courts to give content to the expression 'subject to finance' in land title conveyancing transactions derives from the special nature of such transactions. In them, judges, familiar with the incidents of such contracts, feel confident that they can fill the gaps which the parties have left. In other cases, less familiar, they do not: see, eg, the comment by Professor K C T Sutton, 'Certainty of Contract' (1977) 7 Qld Law Soc J 5 at 11. However that may be, the court will pay regard to features of the agreement, of the relationship between the parties and of relevant external reference points in order to determine whether the term which is challenged can or can not be sustained.
(6) Matters which have been considered relevant in the determination of these cases include the following:
   (a) The provision in question, although an essential term, may be left in adequately clear terms to be settled by an identified third party who is given power to settle ambiguities and uncertainties: see, eg, *Foster v Wheeler* (1888) 38 Ch D 130 and *Axelsen v O'Brien* (1949) 80 CLR 219.
   (b) But even then, if the term is so vital that leaving it to one only of the parties unacceptably removes certainty in the arrangement, the court may or may not refuse to enforce it as

illusory or unacceptably uncertain: contrast, eg, *May and Butcher Ltd v The King* [1934] 2 KB 17(n) and the comment of Gibbs J in *Godecke v Kirwan* (1973) 129 CLR 629 at 646-647.

(c) Where there is a readily ascertainable external standard which is proved, the court will have regard to it in order to add flesh to the provision which, on its own, is unacceptably vague and uncertain or apparently illusory. This is what happened in *Sweet & Maxwell Ltd v Universal News Services Ltd* [1964] 2 QB 699: see also *Meehan v Jones* (at 589).

(d) Where a contract provides a term containing a specified range of possibilities, a court, rather than avoiding the contract will hold the party to providing at least the minimum provision in the range, that is to say the one which is the most favourable to it. This is what occurred in *Lewandowski v Mead Carney-BCA Pty Ltd* [1973] 2 NSWLR 640 at 643. The contract had provided for the payment of a salary in the range of $7,000 to $9,000 per annum. This Court (Jacobs P; Hardie and Bowen JJA concurring) held that the effect of the agreement between the parties was to prescribe the minimum of $7,000 so that the contract was not void for uncertainty.

With these principles in mind, I now turn back to the facts of the present case ...

[137] ... The problem for the Court is that the term is just too uncertain of content. It depends for fulfilment upon the decision of one party to the agreement only, namely the appellant. There is no external standard which can be appealed to in order to fix an 'appropriate' or 'reasonable' equity participation scheme, even assuming that to be what was intended or what the law would impute to the appellant ...

If, however, contrary to my view, the promise was not illusory for these reasons, it was nonetheless void for uncertainty because the challenged term contained within it too many elements which are uncertain. How many shares in Biotech were to be devoted to the participation scheme? What class of shares were to be held by the senior scientists such as the respondent? What were to be the terms of the options upon the shares would issue? In any differentiation between employees, where would the respondent stand? What rights would attach to the shares? Upon what terms were they to be acquired and subject to what terms disposed of by employees? ...

[138] ... I am of the opinion that the promise of the appellant did not, in the words of Kitto J in *Placer* (at 357), create any contractual obligation to the respondent which he may enforce in a court of law. It was rather, in his Honour's words in *Thorby v Goldberg* (1964) 112 CLR 597 at 603, a provision for 'future arrangements' not a contract concluded before the parties. Alternatively, if it was a term of the contract, it was irredeemably vague and uncertain and so unenforceable. I am therefore led to the conclusion that the course which Allen J took, although an understandable attempt to give effect to the presumed intention of the parties, cannot be sustained by reference to legal authority.

The appeal was allowed.

Placer Development Ltd v Commonwealth (1969) 121 CLR 353

Facts and issues

Placer Development Ltd ('Placer') entered into an agreement with the Commonwealth whereby it agreed to form a company ('the company') to produce timber products in Papua New Guinea and subsequently export these products to Australia. It was a term of this agreement (clause 14) that the Commonwealth would reimburse the company for any import duties paid on these products and not remitted but that this subsidy would be 'for an amount or at a rate determined by the Commonwealth from time to time' and would 'not exceed the amount of customs duty paid and not remitted'. For a number of years, the Commonwealth paid a subsidy which equated to the amount of the duty paid by the company. However, it subsequently ceased doing so and Placer consequently commenced proceedings. The parties requested that the High Court decide whether clause 14 obliged the Commonwealth to determine the amount or rate of subsidy and whether it was obliged to pay the subsidy to the company.

Decision

Per Kitto J at 355:

> [The question] is whether by virtue of cl. 14 the Commonwealth is obliged (again, to the plaintiff company) to pay to the timber company a subsidy which will recoup to the timber company all the customs duty paid by it on the importation of its plywood into Australia and not remitted. Again, the answer must be No. The Commonwealth has plainly retained a right to review and vary the amount or rate of subsidy, and such a reservation, as the Court observed in *Australian Woollen Mills Pty. Ltd.* v. *The Commonwealth* (1), 'cannot be reconciled with the conception that the Crown has promised to pay a subsidy of definite amount' . . .
>
> [356] . . . Cases in which a party's liability to make a payment is expressed as depending upon an exercise of discretion by that party have most often been cases of service agreements. The question there is usually whether the intention of the agreement is that the employer shall be entitled to decide whether any remuneration at all shall be paid and if so how much, or is that he shall be bound to pay at all events a reasonable remuneration. In other words, it is whether, on the one hand, the service is intended to be honorary unless the employer otherwise decides, or, on the other hand, a promise to pay a reasonable amount is to be implied. As may be seen from the case of *Bryant v. Flight* (1), in which Parke B. dissented from the decision of the Court, it is not always an easy question to decide; but the general principle is established which Vaughan Williams L.J. in *Loftus v. Roberts* (2), expressed in words that were subsequently adopted by Lord Wrenbury, as Buckley J., in *Broome* v. *Speak* (3). It is that wherever words which by themselves constitute a promise are accompanied by words showing that the promisor is to have a discretion or option as to whether he will carry out that which purports to be the promise, the result is that there is no contract on which an action can be brought at all. The succinct statement of the principle in *Leake on Contracts,* 3rd ed., p. 3: 'Promissory expressions reserving an option as to the performance do not create a contract' was approved by the Lord Justice, as it was later by Lord Wright in *Hillas and Co. Ltd.* v. *Arcos Ltd.* (4) . . .
>
> [357] . . . A promise of a governmental subsidy is meaningless in the absence of a specification of some amount or some basis of calculation. It carries no implication that at least a reasonable subsidy shall be paid, for there is no general standard of reasonableness with respect to the quantum of a subsidy. The expression in cl. 14 of the Agreement before us, 'a subsidy . . . of an amount or at a rate determined by the Commonwealth from time to time', indeed reflects the fact that a governmental or legislative determination of quantum is of the essence of a subsidy. The Commonwealth's promise is, in substance, a promise to pay such subsidy if any as may be decided upon from time to time by or under the authority of the appropriate repository of Commonwealth power, namely the Parliament. It therefore does not create any contractual obligation . . .

Taylor and Owen JJ agreed, stating at 361:

> Obviously there is a complete absence from the clause, and from the Agreement as a whole, of any indentifiable (sic) criteria by which it can be said the parties intended the amounts or rates to

be determined; this is left solely to the discretion of the Commonwealth. This being so the clause amounts to no more than a promise to pay what, in all the circumstances, the Commonwealth in its discretion thinks fit and, as such, is wholly unenforceable . . .

Menzies and Windeyer JJ dissented.

QUESTIONS

(1) In what circumstances will the courts conclude that an agreement is unenforceable on the basis that it is uncertain?

(2) When an agreement is vague or ambiguous, what attitude do the courts adopt toward it? Do courts readily find agreements unenforceable on the basis of uncertainty?

(3) For an agreement to be considered complete, is it necessary to have all matters included in great detail? Is it possible for a 'complete' agreement to leave certain matters to be determined in the future?

5.8 Capacity

Concept	Short explanation	Relevant authorities	*Principles* text*
A party must have capacity	Contractual capacity (the ability to enter into an enforceable agreement) is necessary to form a valid contract	–	Chapter 5: 5.41
Certain types of people may lack capacity	Capacity may be lacking in the case of minors or those who are mentally incapacitated, for example	*Goods Act 1958* (Vic) s 7 *Supreme Court Act 1986* (Vic) s 49 *Minors (Property and Contracts) Act 1970* (NSW) ss 19, 30–31 *Minors Contracts (Miscellaneous Provisions) Act 1979* (SA) ss 4–6 *Gibbons v Wright* (1954) 91 CLR 423	Chapter 5: 5.42–5.43

* Consult the corresponding section(s) of the *Principles* text for more detail.

Contractual capacity is the ability of a party to enter into a binding and enforceable agreement. Below are extracts which relate to two particular classes of people who may lack capacity: minors and those suffering from mental incapacity.

5.8.1 Minors

As a general rule, minors lack capacity to enter into contracts. Accordingly, both at common law and in legislation, the capacity of minors to enter into contracts is restricted. The below extracts illustrate this restriction on capacity, as well as providing examples of the kinds of contracts a minor can enter into (such as contracts for necessities).

Goods Act 1958 (Vic) s 7

Section 7

Capacity to buy and sell is regulated by the general law concerning capacity to contract and to transfer and acquire property: Provided that where necessaries are sold and delivered to a minor or to a person who by reason of mental incapacity or drunkenness is incompetent to contract he must pay a reasonable price therefor.

Necessaries in this section mean goods suitable to the condition in life of such minor or other person and to his actual requirements at the time of the sale and delivery.

[Refer also to *Sale of Goods Act 1896* (Qld) s 5; *Sale of Goods Act 1895* (WA) s 2; *Sale of Goods Act 1895* (SA) s 2; *Sale of Goods Act 1896* (Tas) s 7; *Sale of Goods Act 1954* (ACT) s 7; *Sale of Goods Act 1972* (NT) s 7.]

Supreme Court Act 1986 (Vic) s 49

Section 49

The following contracts entered into by a minor are void—

(a) contracts for the repayment of money lent or to be lent;

(b) contracts for payment for goods supplied or to be supplied, other than necessaries;

(c) accounts stated.

Minors (Property and Contracts) Act 1970 (NSW) ss 19, 30–31

Section 19

Where a minor participates in a civil act and his or her participation is for his or her benefit at the time of his or her participation, the civil act is presumptively binding on the minor.

[. . .]

Section 30

(1) Where a person participates in a civil act while the person is a minor, the civil act may be affirmed:

(a) while the person remains a minor, on the person's behalf by order of a court having jurisdiction under this section,

(b) after the person attains the age of eighteen years, by the person, or
(c) after the person's death, by the person's personal representative.

(2) The court may affirm a civil act on behalf of a minor participant in the civil act under paragraph (a) of subsection (1) on application by the minor participant or by any other person interested in the civil act.

(3) Subject to section 36, the court shall not affirm a civil act on behalf of a minor participant in the civil act under paragraph (a) of subsection (1) unless it appears to the court that the affirmation is for the benefit of the minor participant.

(4) Where a civil act is affirmed pursuant to this section by or on behalf of a minor participant in the civil act, or by the personal representative of a deceased minor participant in the civil act, the civil act is presumptively binding on the minor participant.

(5) An affirmation of a civil act under this section by a minor participant in the civil act or by the personal representative of a deceased minor participant in the civil act:
(a) may be by words, written or spoken, or by conduct, and
(b) need not be communicated to any person.

Section 31

(1) Where a minor has participated in a civil act, then, subject to sections 33 and 35 and subject to subsection (2), the minor participant may repudiate the civil act at any time during his or her minority or afterwards but before the minor attains the age of nineteen years.

(2) A repudiation of a civil act by a minor participant in the civil act does not have effect if it appears that, at the time of the repudiation, the civil act is for the benefit of the minor participant.

[See also s 35 ('Restriction on effect of repudiation') and s 37 ('Adjustment on repudiation').]

Minors Contracts (Miscellaneous Provisions) Act 1979 (SA) ss 4–6

Section 4

Where a person has entered into a contract that is, by reason of his minority at the time of entering into the contract, unenforceable against him, the contract shall remain unenforceable against him unless it is ratified by him, in writing, on or after the day on which he attains his majority.

Section 5

(1) When a person (other than a minor) guarantees the performance by a minor of his obligations under a contract, the guarantee shall be enforceable against the guarantor to the same extent as if the minor had, before entering into the contract to which the guarantee relates, attained his majority . . .

Section 6

(1) A contract with a minor shall have effect as if the minor had, before entering into the contract, attained his majority if, before the contract was entered into by the minor, its terms were approved by a court . . .

[See also s 7 ('Restitution of property to minor') and s 8 ('Appointment of agent to act on behalf of minor').]
[Note also: *Statute of Frauds (Amendment) Act 1828* (Imp); *Mercantile Law Act 1962* (ACT); *Minors Contracts Act 1988* (Tas).]

5.8.2 Mental incapacity

Where a party to an agreement was suffering from mental incapacity when it was entered into, in the sense of not being able to understand the nature of the contract being made, that agreement is voidable at their option if the other party knew or ought to have known of their disability. This issue is discussed in the following case extract.

Gibbons v Wright (1954) 91 CLR 423

Facts and issues

Gibbons owned two parcels of land jointly with her two sisters-in-law. The land was originally held as joint tenants but her sisters-in-law then severed the joint tenancy and converted ownership of the land into one of tenancy in common. Following the death of her sisters-in-law, Gibbons brought proceedings against the sisters' estates (through their executor, Wright) for a declaration that she was solely entitled to the land under the laws of survivorship. She based her assertion on the argument that the severance of the joint tenancy was not effective because the sisters-in-law did not have the requisite mental capacity needed to execute the relevant documents. Gibbons appealed to the High Court against the (adverse) decision of the Full Court in Tasmania. At issue was whether the sisters-in-law had possessed the required mental capacity when the joint tenancy was purportedly severed.

Decision

Per Dixon CJ, Kitto and Taylor JJ at 437:

> The learned Chief Justice was clearly right in treating the validity of the instruments in suit as depending upon the possession by Ethel Rose Gibbons and Olinda Gibbons of a degree of understanding relative to the nature of that which they were doing. The law does not prescribe any fixed standard of sanity as requisite for the validity of all transactions. It requires, in relation to each particular matter or piece of business transacted, that each party shall have such soundness of mind as to be capable of understanding the general nature of what he is doing by his participation. [438] ... The principle which the case supports ... appears to us to be that the mental capacity required by the law in respect of any instrument is relative to the particular transaction which is being effected by means of the instrument, and may be described as the capacity to understand the nature of that transaction when it is explained ...
>
> Ordinarily the nature of the transaction means in this connection the broad operation, the 'general purport' of the instrument; but in some cases it may mean the effect of a wider

> transaction which the instrument is a means of carrying out: *Manches v Trimborn [(1946) 174 L. T. 344, 345]*. In the present case, it was necessary, we think, that the two sisters should have been capable of understanding, if the matter had been explained to them, that by executing the mortgages and the memorandum of transfer they would be altering the character of their interests in the properties concerned, so that instead of the last survivor of the three joint tenants becoming entitled to the whole, each of them would be entitled to a one-third [439] share which would pass to her estate if she still owned it at her death. This is apparently not what the learned Chief Justice put to the jury . . . We shall therefore consider the case on the footing that the appellant has established that, at the respective dates of the mortgages and the memorandum of transfer, the sisters lacked that capacity to understand which was necessary for the complete validity of the instruments.
>
> But proof of this was not enough to entitle the appellant to succeed in the action if the result was that the instruments were merely voidable; for an instrument voidable by reason of the incapacity of a party, or by reason of any form of imposition upon a party, is valid unless and until it is avoided by that party or his representatives. It is clearly not open to other persons, such as one claiming adversely to the party, to elect against the validity of the instrument; and perhaps it was a realization of this which led the appellant to decline the opportunity she was given by the Full Court to amend the pleadings and have a new trial of the action. Neither Ethel Rose Gibbons nor Olinda Gibbons purported in her lifetime to avoid the instruments severing the joint tenancy, and the respondent as their executor has always affirmed their validity. Consequently the appellant must fail unless the law is that a deed disposing of property is absolutely void if at the time of its execution the disponor was incapable of understanding what he was doing, in the sense we have mentioned.

Their Honours conducted a review of the relevant authorities and concluded at 444:

> The point to be observed here is that proof of a conveyor's incapacity to understand the nature of the instrument is not proof that it is not his deed, and it therefore provides no logical ground for holding that the deed is void.

And at 449:

> Upon the authorities as they now stand, it appears to us that we ought to regard it as settled law that an instrument of conveyance executed by a person incapable of understanding its effect, in the sense of its general purport, is not on that account void, though in the circumstances it may be voidable by the conveyor or his representatives.

The appeal was dismissed.

QUESTIONS

(1) What is 'capacity'?

(2) Can a minor enter into a binding contract? If so, in what circumstances?

(3) If a party to a contract was suffering from mental incapacity at the time they entered into the agreement, will the agreement be void or voidable?

5.9 Formalities

Concept	Short explanation	Relevant authorities	*Principles* text*
Oral contracts can be binding, but certain contracts must be in writing	To be enforceable, contracts relating to land, contracts of guarantee and certain consumer contracts must be in writing	Contracts relating to land: *Instruments Act 1958* (Vic) s 126 *Property Law Act 1974* (Qld) s 59 Consumer contracts: *National Credit Code* ss 14, 18	Chapter 5: 5.44
Non-compliant contracts are unenforceable but not void	Consequently, non-contractual rights can vest in the parties despite formality requirements not being met. For example, remedies pursuant to restitution law, the equitable doctrine of part performance, and the right under property law to a constructive trust	*McBride v Sandland* (1918) 25 CLR 69 *Regent v Millett* (1976) 133 CLR 679 *Ogilvie v Ryan* [1976] 2 NSWLR 504	Chapter 5: 5.45

* Consult the corresponding section(s) of the *Principles* text for more detail.

Although it is possible for a verbal contract to be binding, in certain circumstances a written contract (signed by the parties) is required to establish a binding and enforceable agreement. These include contracts for the sale of land, contracts of guarantee, and certain consumer contracts.

5.9.1 Contracts relating to land

Instruments Act 1958 (Vic) s 126

Section 126

(1) An action must not be brought to charge a person ... upon a contract for the sale or other disposition of an interest in land unless the agreement on which the action is brought, or a memorandum or note of the agreement, is in writing signed by the person to be charged or by a person lawfully authorised in writing by that person to sign such an agreement, memorandum or note.

5.9.2 Contracts of guarantee

Property Law Act 1974 (Qld) s 59

Section 59

No action may be brought upon any contract for the sale or other disposition of land or any interest in land unless the contract upon which such action is brought, or some memorandum or note of the contract, is in writing, and signed by the party to be charged, or by some person by the party lawfully authorised.

5.9.3 Consumer contracts

National Credit Code ss 14, 18

Section 14

(1) A credit contract must be in the form of:

(a) a written contract document signed by the debtor and the credit provider; or

(b) a written contract document signed by the credit provider and constituting an offer to the debtor that is accepted by the debtor in accordance with the terms of the offer. . .

Section 18

The contract document must conform to the requirements of the regulations as to its form and the way it is expressed and, subject to any such requirements, may consist of one or more separate documents.

If the relevant formalities are not complied with, the agreement will not be enforceable. That said, other non-contractual rights may still arise. Some of these rights and the situations in which they might arise are discussed in the following cases.[6]

McBride v Sandland (1918) 25 CLR 69

Facts and issues

McBride and his daughter and son-in-law (the Sandlands) reached an oral agreement whereby McBride would purchase a group of properties and allow the Sandlands to lease one of these properties during his lifetime. Pursuant to this agreement, upon the death of McBride, the Sandlands were to have the property transferred to them. Mr Sandland died after many years of occupying the property with his wife. Subsequently, McBride entered into a written lease agreement with his daughter for a period of three years. When this lease came to an end, Mrs Sandland refused

6 See also the discussion of remedies pursuant to restitution law in **Chapter 24**, noting the case of *Pavey & Matthews Pty Ltd v Paul* (1987) 162 CLR 221.

to give up possession, claiming an interest on the basis of the original oral agreement between herself, her husband and McBride. Mrs Sandland succeeded at first instance and McBride appealed to the High Court. The issue was whether Mrs Sandland had an interest in the land pursuant to the oral agreement.

Decision

In the course of concluding that there was no contract as a result of the oral agreement and that part performance had not occurred, Isaacs and Rich JJ usefully summarised the elements of part performance (at 78):

> It will conduce to precision in dealing with the voluminous and complicated circumstances detailed in the evidence to state, so far as material to the present case, certain elements of part performance essential to raise the equity:—
>
> (1) The act relied on must be unequivocally and in its own nature referable to 'some such agreement as that alleged.' That is, it must be such as could be done with no other view than to perform such an agreement (*Maddison* v. *Alderson*; *Gunter* v. *Halsey*; *Ex parte Hooper*).
>
> (2) By 'some such agreement as that alleged' is meant some contract of the general nature of that alleged (*Maddison* v. *Alderson; Savage* v. *Carroll*; *Fry on Specific Performance,* 5th ed., at p. 292).
>
> (3) The proved circumstances in which the 'act' was done must be considered in order to judge whether it refers unequivocally to such an agreement as is alleged (*Savage* v. *Carroll*; *Hodson* v. *Heuland*). Expressions are found in some cases which, if literally read, are to the effect that mere possession by a stranger is sufficient to let in parol evidence of any contract alleged. Those cases were prior to *Maddison* v. *Alderson*, and the expressions if literally read appear to be too wide, because, so read, they would conflict with the requirement that the act must unequivocally refer to some such contract as is alleged, and because bare possession does not necessarily connote trespass or, alternatively, a contract at all; indeed, some contracts would not justify the act done. Possession may be the result or mere permission. But if the circumstances under which the possession was given are proved, then the Court may judge whether the act indicates permission or contract, and, if [79] contract, its general character. For instance, in *Frame* v. *Dawson* the expression 'some agreement' is used, we think, in contradistinction to the specific terms of the agreement, and not in the most general sense of any agreement whatever.
>
> (4) It must have been in fact done by the party relying on it on the faith of the agreement, and further the other party must have permitted it to be done on that footing. Otherwise there would not be 'fraud' in refusing to carry out the agreement, and fraud, that is moral turpitude, is the ground of jurisdiction (*Fry on Specific Performance,* 5th ed., par. 588; *McCormick* v. *Groqan*; *Whitbread* v. *Brockhurst*; *Phillips* v. *Alderton*).
>
> (5) It must be done by a party to the agreement (*Fry on Specific Performance,* par. 589).
>
> These requirements must be satisfied before the actual terms of the alleged agreement are allowed to be deposed to.
>
> Further, when those terms are established, it still remains to be shown:–
>
> (6) That there was a completed agreement (*Thynne* v. *Glengall*).
>
> (7) That the act was done under the terms of that agreement by force of that agreement (*Thynne* v. *Glengall*).

The appeal was allowed.

Regent v Millett (1976) 133 CLR 679

Facts and issues

The Regents bought a property and subsequently agreed with their daughter and her husband (the Milletts) that the latter could live in the property provided they agreed to pay off the mortgage. Once the mortgage was paid off, it was agreed that the property would be transferred to the Milletts. This agreement was oral and was not reduced to writing. The Milletts moved in to the property, began repaying the mortgage and also undertook substantial repairs on the house. When the Regents refused to transfer the house, the Milletts brought an action for specific performance of the oral agreement. The Regents pleaded, in defence, that the contract was not in writing as required and was therefore unenforceable. However, the Milletts were successful both at first instance and on appeal. Consequently, the Regents appealed to the High Court. The issue was whether sufficient part performance had occurred to render the oral agreement nevertheless enforceable.

Decision

Per Gibbs J at 682:

> In the action the appellants pleaded the *Statute of Frauds* (whose equivalent in New South Wales is s. 54A of the *Conveyancing Act,* 1919, as amended). There is no suggestion that the agreement is evidenced by any note or memorandum in writing and the sole question now raised in the case is whether there was part performance. The acts of part performance on which the respondents relied were (1) the taking of possession; (2) the effecting of repairs before December 1972; (3) the doing of the work on the renovations and additions in January 1973; (4) the making of the mortgage repayments.
>
> The learned trial judge held that these acts amounted to sufficient part performance and ordered specific performance of the agreement. His decision was affirmed by the Court of Appeal.
>
> The principle upon which the doctrine of part performance rests was stated by Lord Cranworth, Lord Chancellor in *Caton* v. *Caton* (9) in words which appear to have a direct application to the present case. He said:
>
>> . . . when one of two contracting parties has been induced, or allowed by the other, to alter his position on the faith of the contract, as for instance by taking possession of land, and expending money in building or other like acts, there it would be a fraud in the other party to set up the legal invalidity of the contract on the faith of which he induced, or allowed, the person contracting with him to act, and expend his money.
>
> The books are full of cases in which it has been held that the entry into possession alone, or the taking of possession coupled with the expenditure of money by one party on the improvement of property, with the cognizance of the other party to the contract, may amount to part performance (see the cases cited in *Halsbury's Laws of England,* 3rd ed., vol. 36, par. 416).
>
> The argument advanced on behalf of the appellants, when reduced to its essentials, depends upon two propositions. First, it was said that the acts relied on were not unequivocally referable to some such contract as that alleged by the respondents. Indeed, it was submitted that a narrower test should be adopted and that [683] it was necessary to establish 'such a performance as must necessarily imply the existence of the contract'–to use the words of Lord O'Hagan in *Maddison* v. *Alderson*. However, the test suggested by the Earl of Selborne L.C. in that case, that the acts relied upon as part performance 'must be unequivocally, and in their own nature, referable to some such agreement as that alleged', has been consistently accepted as a correct statement of the law. It is enough that the acts are unequivocally and in their own nature referable to some contract of the general nature of that alleged (see *McBride* v. *Sandland*).

> The second proposition submitted for the appellants was that the acts relied upon must have been done in part performance of the agreement alleged; in other words, the acts must have been done under the terms of that agreement and by force of that agreement. In support of this proposition particular reliance was placed on *Cooney* v. *Burns* and *McBride* v. *Sandland*.
>
> It may be said immediately that if the reasoning of their Lordships in the recent case of *Steadman* v. *Steadman* is accepted, the appellants' arguments must fail. However, it is unnecessary for the present decision to consider the questions that are raised by that case.
>
> In the present case the giving and taking of possession by itself was sufficient part performance of the contract and it is therefore unnecessary to consider whether the other acts relied upon would also, either alone or together, amount to part performance. The change of possession of land has been described as 'the act of part performance par excellence' — Williams: *The Statute of Frauds, Section IV,* p. 256. Of course, it may be proved that the taking of possession was referable to some other authority than the contract alleged. That was the situation in *McBride* v. *Sandland*. However, in the present case the circumstances under which possession was given indicate contract, to echo the words in *McBride* v. *Sandland* and the possession was unequivocally referable to some such contract as that alleged. The taking of possession was pursuant to the contract. It is true that the contract did not require the respondents to take possession, but if it were necessary that the acts of part performance should have been done in compliance with a requirement of the contract, the utility of the equitable doctrine would be reduced to vanishing point, and many cases which have proceeded on the [684] opposite view would have been wrongly decided. The Judicial Committee in *White* v. *Neaylon* indeed appears to have held that the effecting of improvements on property which were neither required nor permitted by the contract may be acts of part performance; but however that may be, it is clear that if a vendor permits a purchaser to take possession to which a contract of sale entitles him, the giving and taking of that possession will amount to part performance notwithstanding that under the contract the purchaser was entitled rather than bound to take possession.
>
> For these reasons the Court below was, in my opinion, right in holding that there were sufficient acts of part performance and the appeal should be dismissed.

The appeal was dismissed.

Ogilvie v Ryan [1976] 2 NSWLR 504

Facts and issues

Ryan and Ogilvie lived together for a number of years in a cottage owned by their employer. When their employer sold the cottage, Ogilvie proposed that he buy a house and that Ryan live in it with him. He stated that if Ryan agreed to look after him for the remainder of his life, the house would be hers for as long as she lived. Ryan agreed and Ogilvie purchased the house. Although Ryan cared for the defendant until his death, his Will made no mention of her. The executor of Ogilvie's estate commenced action to recover possession of the house on the basis that, among other things, the agreement was not recorded in writing pursuant to the requirements set out in the *Statute of Frauds*. The issue was whether Ryan had any interest in the property pursuant to the oral agreement with Ogilvie.

Decision

Per Holland J at 513:

> The question then is whether the law will give effect to the deceased's promise. The defendant relied firstly on a submission that, on the facts proved, a constructive trust arose; that is to say,

that the deceased in his lifetime, and his executor after his death, became bound in equity to hold the legal title to the subject property upon trust to permit the defendant during her life to occupy the same rent free for so long as she desired ...

[518] ... In my opinion, the most satisfactory explanation of equitable principles underlying the second category of cases is that an appropriate constructive trust will be declared in Equity to defeat a species of fraud, namely, that in which a defendant seeks to make an unconscionable use of his legal title by asserting it to defeat a beneficial interest in the property which he (or, as in this case, the testator for whom he is executor) has agreed to or promised; or which it was the common intention of the parties that the plaintiff should have, in return for benefits to be provided by, and in fact obtained from, the plaintiff in connection with their joint use or occupation of the property. The common ingredient of both categories is an unconscientious use of the legal title ...

In my opinion, the facts proved establish a constructive trust of the beneficial interest promised to the defendant, and the defendant is entitled to have this Court declare that trust in appropriate terms, and to rely upon it as a defence to the plaintiff's claim for possession based upon his legal title. It was [519] not contended that the plaintiff, as executor, would not be bound by such a trust, in the same way as the deceased was bound. It is well established that the declaration of a constructive trust is not inhibited by the *Statute of Frauds* or, more correctly for New South Wales, s. 54A of the *Conveyancing Act*, 1919 ...

Justice Holland then went on to discuss, in the alternative (although considering it unnecessary given the above conclusions regarding a constructive trust), Ryan's claim for specific performance on the basis of part performance.

QUESTIONS

(1) Does non-compliance with formalities mean there is/was no agreement? What is the effect of non-compliance with formalities?

(2) Do the parties have any rights pursuant to a contract which has not complied with applicable formalities?

(3) For what reason was the *Statute of Frauds 1677* (Imp) enacted?

5.10 International perspectives

Where a contract is an international commercial sale of goods, the *CISG* may apply: see **25.4.1** on applicability. If this is the case, then many of the above concepts are abolished. For example, the common law concept of consideration does not apply to contracts governed by the *CISG*, as it is sufficient that a binding agreement is formed: **25.7.4**. Formality requirements are abolished by arts 8(3) and 11 (unless parties have agreed otherwise, or a relevant country has made an art 96 reservation when ratifying the *CISG*, which is rarely the case): **25.6.1**. Thus contracts may be written, oral or a combination. However, note that the *CISG* does not apply to sales of land, guarantees or consumer contracts. The same observations hold for the less commonly applicable UNIDROIT Principles: see **25.7.10** and **25.6.1**.

Other issues are dealt with in a different manner to the Australian domestic contract law. Intent to create legal relations is not a separate element of formation, but instead is part of the elements which define offer and acceptance. Thus, there must be an intent to bind before an offer/acceptance can be said to exist: *CISG* **25.7.1** and **25.7.2**; UNIDROIT Principles: **25.7.7** and **25.7.8**. Similarly, certainty and completeness are matters subsumed into whether an offer is 'sufficiently definite': **25.7.1**. Notably, art 55 *CISG* will supply price according to that 'generally charged' price where parties have failed to agree on price: **25.7.1**. Revocation or withdrawal of offers are permissible (*CISG* **25.7.1**; UNIDROIT Principles **25.7.7**); however, where an offer appears to be 'firm', such as 'open until 12 June', it would be considered irrevocable: *CISG* **25.7.1**; UNIDROIT Principles **25.7.7** (contra *Dickinson v Dodds*). Like Australian domestic contract law, silence alone cannot be acceptance (*CISG* **25.7.2**, UNIDROIT Principles **25.7.8**), but silence combined with performance may indicate acceptance. Likewise, the receipt rule also prevails within the *CISG* concerning timing of acceptance, but the postal rule does not apply: *CISG* **25.7.2**; UNIDROIT Principles: **25.7.8**.

Other domestic rules remain relevant for contracts governed by the *CISG*. Capacity is an issue outside the scope of both *CISG* and UNIDROIT Principles, and is therefore determined under domestic law. It should be noted that the Australian law concerning electronic communications—ie the *Electronic Transactions Acts* legislation applicable in every State and Territory—adopts the 2005 *Convention on the Use of Electronic Communications in International Contracts* (e-CC).

5.11 Review

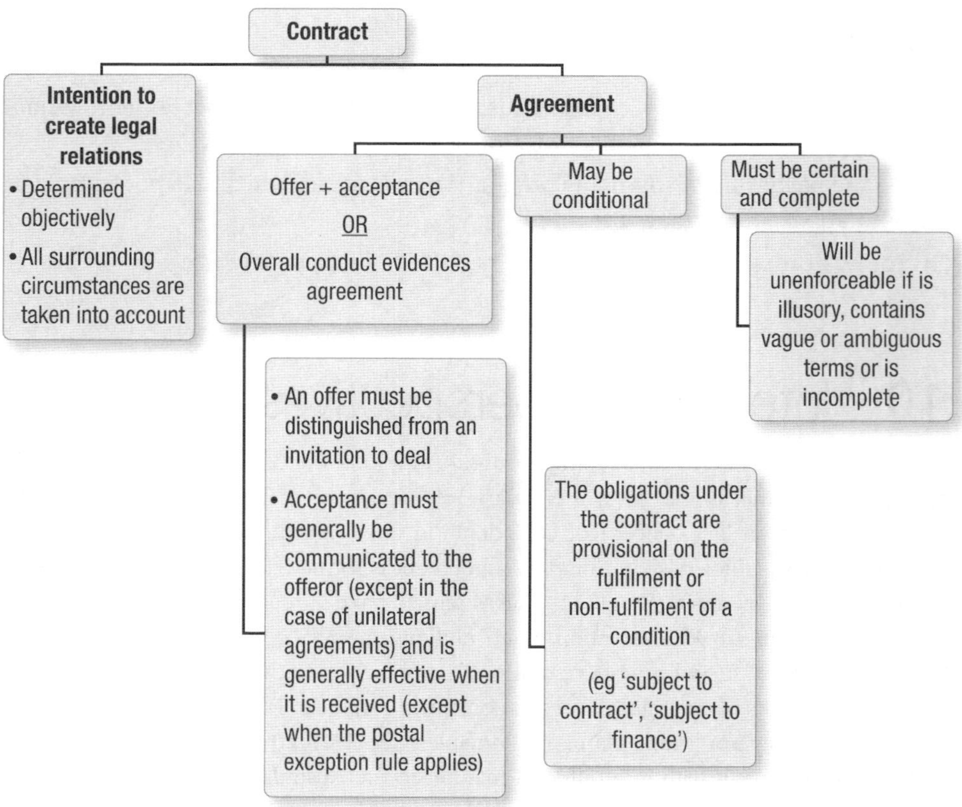

Contract (cont.)

Consideration

- A contract must be supported by consideration
- Consideration can be anything the promisor specifies and must move from the promisee
- Past consideration (except, for example, where provided at the promisor's request) is generally not good consideration
- Consideration must not be illusory—it must involve an obligation
- The performance of an existing obligation or duty will normally not amount to good consideration—exceptions include where the promisee does something over and above what is required

Capacity

- Capacity to enter into an enforceable agreement is required
- Certain types of people may lack capacity—these include minors and those suffering from mental incapacity

Formalities

- Oral agreements are enforceable
- But certain types of contracts must be in writing in order to be enforceable—these include: contracts relating to land, contracts of guarantee and consumer contracts
- If a contract does not comply with formalities, other non-contractual rights (eg restitutionary remedies) may be available to the parties

TIPS FOR APPLYING THE LAW IN PRACTICE

- Be wary of a presumptive approach when it comes to intention. While it is generally correct to say, for example, that parties to a commercial arrangement intend it to be legally binding, ultimately the court will consider all of the surrounding circumstances to determine whether intention to create legal relations was present. The relationship between the parties is only one factor in this determination.
- Remember that the offer and acceptance analysis is simply that, an analytic tool only—courts will look at the overall conduct of the parties to determine whether an agreement has been reached.
- Keep an eye out for situations where purported acceptance of an offer might actually constitute a counter-offer.
- When it comes to consideration, remember that it is an extremely broad and flexible concept so while it may not initially appear as if any 'traditional' form of consideration was provided in response to the promise (for example, money), make sure you look closely!
- The value of agreements to agree and agreements to negotiate in good faith should not be immediately dismissed. However, when preparing or analysing such agreements, as when preparing or analysing any agreement, it is important to assess whether the agreement is certain and complete. It should not be illusory, contain vague or ambiguous terms, or be silent on essential matters.

- Do not automatically assume that a minor or a person suffering from a mental illness lacks the capacity to enter into an enforceable agreement.
- Clients should be aware that if a contract is unenforceable because it did not comply with formalities then they may nevertheless have other non-contractual rights; for example, they may be able to obtain a remedy under the law of restitution.

PROBLEM QUESTIONS

(1) Robert wants to sell his car and becomes aware through a mutual friend (Tara) that Sally is looking for a new car. So Robert writes to Sally and offers to sell her his car for $8,000. Sally writes back stating that she wishes to purchase the car but that she can only afford to pay Robert $6,700. Robert needs at least $7,500 in order to pay off his new motorbike so writes back to Sally and says that he cannot accept less than $7,500 for the car. However, he also indicates in the letter, sent on 23 November, that he will give Sally until 28 November to think about what she wants to do. Sally receives Robert's letter on 25 November and, after much thought, decides that day that she will buy the car for $7,500; however, she does not get in touch with Robert (by writing or otherwise) to inform him of this as she is very busy at work. The next day, being 26 November, Sally happens to see Tara who mentions in passing that Robert has sold his car to Paul. Straight away Sally calls Robert and says that she will buy the car for $7,500, as per his last letter.

Is there a contract in existence between Sally and Robert in relation to the sale of the car?

(2) Gill has a bumper crop of apples. Unfortunately for Gill, so does the rest of Victoria's apple growing community. Colin indicates some slight interest in purchasing some apples and Gill states, 'I'm happy to sell you some apples, you just tell me how much you want to pay and that will be fine'.

Is the agreement for the supply of apples sufficiently certain to be enforceable?

(3) Samantha suffers from bipolar disorder which can impact her clarity of thinking at times. She is moving overseas and must sell her apartment in Toorak. Despite having multiple offers to choose from (there were many buyers interested in the property), she accepts Adam's offer which is $200,000 lower than another offer she received which was otherwise on exactly the same terms as Adam's offer (eg not subject to finance etc). Adam and Samantha's agreement is an oral one. Subsequently, it transpires that Samantha will no longer be relocating and she does not wish to proceed with the sale.

What arguments could Samantha advance in support of her claim that the contract is not enforceable?

RESEARCH QUESTION

What is the status of presumptions regarding intention to create legal relations following the decision of the High Court in *Ermogenous v Greek Orthodox Community of SA Inc* (2002) 209 CLR 95?

6

PRELIMINARY AGREEMENTS

6.1 Overview

Contractual disputes are most commonly concerned with the terms or performance (or lack thereof) of an agreement. However, disputes can arise as to whether or not there is in fact a contract in existence to begin with. This chapter examines the nature of preliminary agreements (including agreements to agree and agreements to negotiate in good faith) and the potential legal consequences that can flow from such agreements.

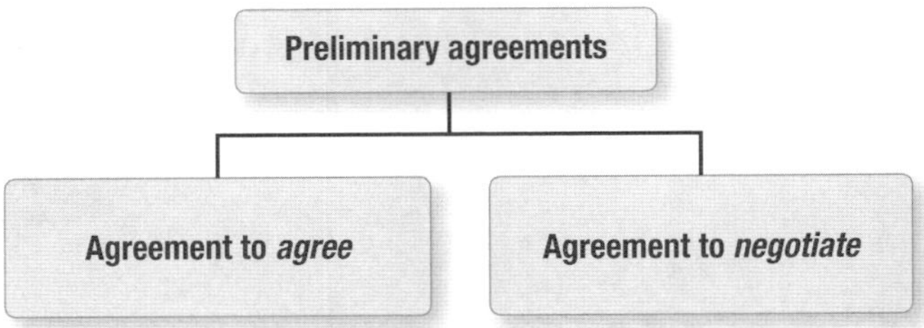

6.2 Intention and completeness of terms

Concept	Short explanation	Relevant authorities	*Principles* text*
Intention to be legally bound and completeness of terms are both key	Without the intention to create a legally binding agreement being present, as well as agreement regarding key terms having been reached, any arrangement will likely not amount to a binding contract	*Factory 5 Pty Ltd (in liq) v Victoria (No 2)* [2012] FCAFC 150	Chapter 6: 6.03–6.05.

* Consult the corresponding section(s) of the *Principles* text for more detail.

It is not uncommon for parties to wish to record their intention to reach an agreement at some point in the future, or their commitment to negotiate to reach an agreement. The question that arises in relation to such agreements is: are these legally binding? In answering this question, the intention of the parties is paramount and is determined objectively by the courts. As can be seen in the following case extract, whether or not the parties have reached agreement in relation to key terms is an important factor in ascertaining whether a binding contract was intended.

Factory 5 Pty Ltd (in liq) v Victoria (No 2) [2012] FCAFC 150

Facts and issues

Factory 5 entered into negotiations with Victoria to sell official merchandise at the 2006 Commonwealth Games in Melbourne. During the course of those negotiations, the parties signed a letter which appointed Factory 5 to this position but which also stated that this appointment was subject to the parties reaching agreement on terms in a long form contract. Negotiations ultimately broke down. At first instance, Factory 5's claim that the letter constituted a binding contract was dismissed on the basis that Factory 5 had abandoned the contract. Factory 5 appealed. One of the issues before the court was whether a binding contract had been entered into or whether the letter was simply an agreement to agree in the future.

Decision

Per Rares and Dodds-Streeton JJ at [64]:

> [The letter] expressly made the appointment of Factory 5 subject to three conditions:
>
> (1) the parties reaching agreement on a legally binding long form agreement;
> (2) that agreement being provided — drafted — by Melbourne 2006; and
> (3) the board of Melbourne 2006 approving the actual terms of the document to govern the parties' relationship.
>
> [65] None of those three conditions was ever satisfied. Before stating those conditions, the letter recorded that 'F[actory] 5 **is to be** appointed as Concessionaire subject to' them. (emphasis added) The words just emphasised indicated that the appointment would only occur in the future after satisfaction of the specified conditions. In addition, the letter noted that the parties would not make any public announcement until a long form agreement had been executed. That was another indicium that the terms of the letter were not intended by the parties, when considered objectively, to create a legally binding relationship in themselves: *Australian Broadcasting Corporation v XIVth Commonwealth Games Ltd* (1988) 18 NSWLR 540 at 548A-550D, 551B-D per Gleeson CJ with whom Hope and Mahoney JJA agreed. Here the 23 December 2004 letter amounted to an acceptable framework for the preparation of a long form agreement that required substantive further negotiation and agreement. As Gleeson CJ explained with his customary lucidity in *Geebung Investments Pty Ltd v Varga Group Investments Pty Ltd (No 8)* (1995) 7 BPR 14,551 at 14,552:
>
>> As the decision in the *Australian Broadcasting Corporation* case illustrates, the fact that parties to negotiations have agreed upon the major matter under discussion, confidently believing that the remaining matters to be decided will be sorted out later between them or their lawyers, without any difficulty, can sometimes create a misleading appearance of consensus. Such parties may well believe that they have a 'deal' or a 'bargain', and speak and act accordingly, whilst at the same time knowing and intending that further and more detailed agreement is necessary. For that reason, conduct such as shaking hands, or using the language of agreement, can be ambiguous. The resolution of the ambiguity may require more detailed factual and legal analysis.
>
> [66] The parties subsequently had difficulties, culminating in an impasse, in formulating a clause for the long form agreement to encapsulate when Factory 5 could exercise its right to manufacture or source its own supply of apparel. That provides a further indication that the 23 December 2004 letter did not amount to a concluded bargain: *Australian Broadcasting Corporation* 18 NSWLR at 550B-C. As the primary judge found, throughout the negotiation process for the long form agreement the parties were at issue about the appropriate wording for the concessionaire as manufacture clause. Melbourne 2006 had proposed using the expression 'reasonable commercial terms'. But, unsurprisingly Factory 5's lawyers considered that this lacked sufficient clarity. That demonstrated the absence of any earlier contractual consensus for which Factory 5 argued in the proceedings and the appeal. The argument must fail for the reasons, among others, Factory 5 had advanced in resisting the uncertain expression 'reasonable commercial terms' during the negotiations in 2005.

QUESTIONS

(1) How does the presence or absence of agreement in relation to key terms impact on an assessment of whether the parties intended to conclude a binding contract?

(2) Why was it that the court ultimately concluded in *Factory 5 Pty Ltd (in liq) v Victoria (No 2)* [2012] FCAFC 150 that the letter was merely 'an acceptable framework for the preparation of a long form agreement that required substantive further negotiation and agreement'?

(3) Can you think of an instance where the phrase 'reasonable commercial terms' might be sufficiently certain to enable a finding that a binding contract exists?

6.3 Agreements to agree

Concept	Short explanation	Relevant authorities	*Principles* text*
Parties can enter into an agreement to agree in the future	This 'agreement to agree' may be intended to be immediately binding, conditional upon the execution of a formal contract, or not binding	*Masters v Cameron* (1954) 91 CLR 353 *Stirnemann v Kaza Investments Pty Ltd* [2011] SASCFC 77 *Godecke v Kirwan* (1973) 129 CLR 629 *Baulkham Hills Private Hospital Pty Ltd v GR Securities Pty Ltd* (1986) 40 NSWLR 622	Chapter 6: 6.06, 6.08

* Consult the corresponding section(s) of the *Principles* text for more detail.

Where the parties have entered into an agreement to enter into an agreement in the future, this agreement can have a number of possible legal consequences, determined with reference to the intention of the parties.

In *Masters v Cameron*,[1] the High Court outlined three categories into which an agreement to agree may fall:

(1) The parties intend to be bound immediately regardless of whether a formal contract is executed, but propose that a subsequent restatement of terms be made.

(2) All terms have been agreed to and the agreement is binding but performance is conditional on the execution of a final contract.

(3) The parties have no intention to create a settled agreement unless and until a formal document is executed.

1 (1954) 91 CLR 353.

Masters v Cameron (1954) 91 CLR 353

Facts and issues

Masters agreed to purchase a farm from Cameron. To that end, both parties signed a document which contained a provision indicating that the agreement was 'subject to the preparation of a formal contract of sale' acceptable to Cameron's solicitors and the giving of possession on a specified date. Masters subsequently decided not to proceed with the purchase and sought to recover his deposit. The issue in this case was whether or not the signed document constituted a binding agreement for the sale and purchase of the property. Masters appealed from a decision at first instance that the document was a binding contract.

Decision

Per Dixon CJ, McTiernan and Kitto JJ at 360:

> The first question in the appeal is whether, as *Wolff* J. considered, this document on its true construction constitutes a binding contract between the respondent and the appellants, or only a record of terms upon which the signatories were agreed as a basis for the negotiation of a contract. Plainly enough they were agreed that there should be a sale and purchase, and the parties, the property, the price, and the date for possession were all clearly settled between them. All the essentials of a contract are there; but whether there is a contract depends entirely upon the meaning and effect of the final sentence in that portion of the document which the appellant signed.
>
> Where parties who have been in negotiation reach agreement upon terms of a contractual nature and also agree that the matter of their negotiation shall be dealt with by a formal contract, the case may belong to any of three cases. It may be one in which the parties have reached finality in arranging all the terms of their bargain and intend to be immediately bound to the performance of those terms, but at the same time propose to have the terms restated in a form which will be fuller or more precise but not different in effect. Or, secondly, it may be a case in which the parties have completely agreed upon all the terms of their bargain and intend no departure from or addition to that which their agreed terms express or imply, but nevertheless have made performance of one or more of the terms conditional upon the execution of a formal document. Or, thirdly, the case may be one in which the intention of the parties is not to make a concluded bargain at all, unless and until they execute a formal contract.
>
> In each of the first two cases there is a binding contract: in the first case a contract binding the parties at once to perform the agreed terms whether the contemplated formal document comes into existence or not, and to join (if they have so agreed) in settling and executing the formal document; and in the second case a contract binding the parties to join in bringing the formal contract into existence and then to carry it into execution. Of these two cases the first is the more common. Throughout the decisions on this branch of the law the proposition is insisted upon which Lord [361] *Blackburn* expressed in *Rossiter v. Miller* when he said that the mere fact that the parties have expressly stipulated that there shall afterwards be a formal agreement prepared, embodying the terms, which shall be signed by the parties does not, by itself, show that they continue merely in negotiation. His Lordship proceeded: ' . . . as soon as the fact is established of the final mutual assent of the parties so that those who draw up the formal agreement have not the power to vary the terms already settled, I think the contract is completed': see also *Sinclair, Scott & Co. Ltd. v. Naughton*. A case of the second class came before this Court in *Niesmann v. Collingridge* where all the essential terms of a contract had been agreed upon, and the only reference to the execution of a further document was in the term as to

price, which stipulated that payment should be made 'on the signing of the contract'. *Rich* and *Starke* JJ. observed that this did not make the signing of a contract a condition of agreement, but made it a condition of the obligation to pay, and carried a necessary implication that each party would sign a contract in accordance with the terms of agreement. Their Honours, agreeing with *Knox* C.J., held that there was no difficulty in decreeing specific performance of the agreement, 'and so compelling the performance of a stipulation of the agreement necessary to its carrying out and due completion': see also *O'Brien v. Dawson*.

Cases of the third class are fundamentally different. They are cases in which the terms of agreement are not intended to have, and therefore do not have, any binding effect of their own: *Governor &c. of the Poor of Kingston-upon-Hull v. Petch*. The parties may have so provided either because they have dealt only with major matters and contemplate that others will or may be regulated by provisions to be introduced into the formal document, as in *Summergreene v. Parker* or simply because they wish to reserve to themselves a right to withdraw at any time until the formal document is signed. These possibilities were both referred to in *Rossiter v. Miller*. Lord *O'Hagan* said: 'Undoubtedly, if any prospective contract, involving the possibility of new terms, or the modification of those already discussed, remains to be adopted, matters must be taken to be still in a train of negotiation, and a dissatisfied party may refuse to proceed. But when an agreement [362] embracing all the particulars essential for finality and completeness, even though it may be desired to reduce it to shape by a solicitor, is such that those particulars must remain unchanged, it is not, in my mind, less coercive because of the technical formality which remains to be made'. And Lord *Blackburn* said: 'parties often do enter into a negotiation meaning that, when they have (or think they have) come to one mind, the result shall be put into formal shape, and then (if on seeing the result in that shape they find they are agreed) signed and made binding; but that each party is to reserve to himself the right to retire from the contract, if, on looking at the formal contract, he finds that though it may represent what he said, it does not represent what he meant to say. Whenever, on the true construction of the evidence, this appears to be the intention, I think that the parties ought not to be held bound till they have executed the formal agreement'. So, as *Parker* J. said in *Von Hatzfeldt-Wildenburg v. Alexander* in such a case there is no enforceable contract, either because the condition is unfulfilled or because the law does not recognize a contract to enter into a contract.

The question depends upon the intention disclosed by the language the parties have employed, and no special form of words is essential to be used in order that there shall be no contract binding upon the parties before the execution of their agreement in its ultimate shape: *Farmer v. Honan*. Nor is any formula, such as 'subject to contract', so intractable as always and necessarily to produce that result: cf. *Filby v. Hounsell*. But the natural sense of such words was shown by the language of Lord *Westbury* when he said in *Chinnock v. Marchioness of Ely*: 'if to a proposal or offer an assent be given subject to a provision as to a contract, then the stipulation as to the contract is a term of the assent, and there is no agreement independent of that stipulation'. Again, Sir *George Jessel* M.R. said in *Crossley v. Maycock*: 'if the agreement is made subject to certain conditions then specified or to be specified by the party making it, or by his solicitor, then, until those conditions are accepted, there is no final agreement such as the Court will enforce'.

This being the natural meaning of 'subject to contract', 'subject to the preparation of a formal contract', and expressions [363] of similar import, it has been recognized throughout the cases on the topic that such words prima facie create an overriding condition, so that what has been agreed upon must be regarded as the intended basis for a future contract and not as constituting a contract . . .

[364] . . . In the present case the context provides no reason for holding that the case is outside the application of these authorities. The formal contract, it is true, is to be 'on the above

> terms and conditions', but it is to be acceptable to the vendor's solicitors, and the meaning is sufficiently evident that the contract shall contain, not only the stated terms and conditions expressed in a form satisfactory to the solicitors, but also whatever else the solicitors may fairly consider appropriate to the case. Accordingly the first of the four questions which went to trial should have been answered by saying that no binding contract for the sale and purchase of the property mentioned in the document dated 6th December 1951 was made between the defendant Cameron (the respondent) and the defendants Masters (the appellants) . . .

The appeal was allowed.

The following cases consider the types of agreements to agree which may nevertheless bind the parties.

Stirnemann v Kaza Investments Pty Ltd [2011] SASCFC 77

Facts and issues

Kaza Investments ('Kaza') entered into an agreement to purchase land from Stirnemann. The agreement was contained in a fax which made reference to 'further necessary paperwork to be prepared by a lawyer'. Stirnemann subsequently indicated that he did not wish to proceed with the sale. Kaza brought proceedings on the basis that a valid and binding agreement for the sale of the land had been reached and it succeeded at first instance. Stirnemann appealed. At issue was whether there was a binding agreement between the parties or whether, instead, the reference to 'further necessary paperwork' indicated that further steps needed to be taken before this could be said to be the case.

Decision

In dismissing the appeal, per Peek J at [15]:

> I consider that his Honour was plainly correct in his finding. The facsimile 'contract' included each of the fundamental elements of a valid contract for the sale of real property: the names of the vendor and purchaser, an adequate description of the land and the consideration. There was nothing in the words of the facsimile to suggest that the parties intended to re-negotiate any of these terms and nothing to suggest that the lawyer(s) drawing up the final contract would have the power to vary those essential terms. In the circumstances, the words 'I will arrange for further necessary paperwork to be prepared by a lawyer' meant no more than [Kaza] would arrange for a lawyer to provide such documents, *if any*, as were necessary to effect transfer and the formalities associated with settlement.

Godecke v Kirwan (1973) 129 CLR 629

Facts and issues

Refer to **5.7** (at p 174) for a discussion of the facts of this case. One of the issues which arose for determination was the impact of a statement in the document, which indicated that Godecke would 'execute a further agreement' if required by Kirwan for 'such other covenants and conditions as they may reasonably require', on the question of whether the parties had intended to enter into a binding contract.

Decision

Per Walsh J at 638:

> It has been held repeatedly that the question is one of construction in each case of the document or documents which are put forward as showing that a contract was made. But it is necessary to make some reference to the authorities. In *Von Hatzfeldt-Wildenburg* v. *Alexander* Parker J. used language which has been cited with approval in many later cases.
>
> He said:
>
>> It appears to be well settled by the authorities that if the documents or letters relied on as constituting a contract contemplate the execution of a further contract between the [639] parties, it is a question of construction 'whether the execution of the further contract is a condition or term of the bargain or whether it is a mere expression of the desire of the parties as to the manner in which the transaction already agreed to will in fact go through. In the former case there is no enforceable contract either because the condition is unfulfilled or because the law does not recognize a contract to enter into a contract. In the latter case there is a binding contract and the reference to the more formal document may be ignored.
>
> . . . The quoted passage cannot be accepted, in my opinion, without further explanation or elaboration, as a comprehensive statement of the tests by which in all cases it is to be determined as a matter of construction whether or not a binding contract has been made. It postulates a choice between two alternatives. It assumes that it must always be intended either that the execution of a further contract 'is a condition or term of the bargain' or 'a mere expression of the desire of the parties' as to the manner in which the transaction will go through. But there are cases in which a provision as to the execution of a further contract is not to be construed as a mere expression of desire or as a 'condition' of the bargain, if by that is meant a condition upon which is dependent the coming into existence of a binding agreement. It may be a term of a concluded agreement and may place upon the parties an obligation, capable of being specifically enforced by the court, to sign a further contract in accordance with the agreement which they have already made. The decision of this Court in *Niesmann* v. *Collingridge* is a direct authority for those propositions, which I have stated in a form based upon the language used in their judgment in that case by Rich and Starke JJ. In the same case Knox C.J. expressed the opinion that it was in the contemplation of the parties that a formal contract should be signed and that they meant that the acceptance of the offer should be followed by the execution of a contract by both parties. Thus the provision referring to a further contract was held not to be a mere expression of desire but to be one of the terms to which the parties had agreed. The exposition of the law on this subject which is contained in the judgment of this Court in *Masters* v. *Cameron* recognizes the [640] case of *Niesmann* v. *Collingridge* as a case belonging to the second of the three classes described, in which the execution of a formal contract is not a condition of the existence of a binding agreement, but is a condition of the performance of one or more of the terms of an agreement by which the parties are immediately bound.
>
> . . . I agree with the opinion of the learned primary judge that the parties intended that a further contract should be executed. The language used does not indicate a mere desire that this

> should be [641] done. But, in my opinion, they did not intend to make the execution of a formal contract a condition of the coming into existence of a binding agreement. They made an agreement of which one term was that possession was to be given and taken upon the signing and execution of a formal contract of sale within twenty-eight days and of which another term was that a further $32,000 should be paid at that time. From these provisions there should be implied a promise by each of the parties that he would sign a formal contract within the twenty-eight days and would do everything necessary to enable this to be done within that time. As in *Niesmann* v. *Collingridge* this was a term of the bargain that could be specifically enforced.

Per Gibbs J at 648:

> It is true that in *Masters* v. *Cameron* the Court described the class of case to which *Niesmann* v. *Collingridge* belongs as 'a case in which the parties have completely agreed upon all the terms of their bargain and intend no departure from or addition to that which their agreed terms express or imply, but nevertheless have made performance of one or more of the terms conditional upon the execution of a formal document'. In these remarks the Court was not, in my opinion, intending to exclude from the class a case in which the formal document, when executed, would include terms additional to those already expressed, provided that the additional terms did not depend on further agreement between the parties... the fact that the further agreement contemplated in the present case will contain additional covenants and conditions if the solicitors reasonably require them does not mean that the parties had not reached complete agreement, and the language of cl. 6 does not in any way suggest that the terms of the Offer and Acceptance were not intended to have binding force and to give rise to legal rights and duties.
>
> I hold, therefore, that the Offer and Acceptance constituted a valid and binding contract capable of being enforced by specific performance.
>
> I would allow the appeal.

Baulkham Hills Private Hospital Pty Ltd v GR Securities Pty Ltd (1986) 40 NSWLR 622

Facts and issues

Baulkham Hills Private Hospital agreed to purchase a hospital (and the land upon which it stood) from GR Securities. The agreement was contained in a number of letters and was expressed to be binding until a 'formal contract' was subsequently drawn up, to supersede the letters. The issue to be decided was whether the parties had entered into an immediately binding (informal) legal agreement in the form of the letters.

Decision

Per McLelland J at 627:

> There was a binding contract, if, and only if, by the exchange of letters the parties mutually communicated their respective assents to being legally bound by terms capable of having contractual effect: see the discussions in *Film Bars Pty Ltd v Pacific Film Laboratories Pty Ltd* (1979) 1 BPR 9251 at 9254ff and *Air Great Lakes Pty Ltd v K S Easter (Holdings) Pty Ltd* (1985) 2 NSWLR 309. In the last-mentioned case Mahoney JA (at 326) identified three questions which it is often useful to consider in such a context as the present, namely '... did the parties arrive at a consensus?; (if they did) was it such a consensus as was capable of forming a binding

contract?; and (if it was) did the parties intend that the consensus at which they arrived should constitute a binding contract?'

The answer to the first of these questions is obviously in the affirmative in the present case. The letters comprise offer, counter-offer, and acceptance, and manifest a clear consensus between the parties. The answers to the second and third questions are not so obvious. One element of the terms of the consensus is [628] important in relation to both these questions and may be conveniently dealt with separately.

'...legally binding agreement in principle...'

This phrase, occurring as it does in the letter of 21 March 1986, and tacitly adopted by the letter of 25 March 1986, was clearly part of the consensus. It was submitted on behalf of the defendants that it signified that although agreement had been reached on some terms, agreement had yet to be reached on others, from which it followed: (1) that regarded as an 'agreement to B agree' on those other terms, the consensus was incapable of forming a binding contract; and (2) that the parties could not have intended to be legally bound prior to agreement being reached on those other terms.

So far as the first of these matters is concerned, I do not accept that the words 'agreement in principle' in the present context import the idea that there must necessarily be agreement on further terms to be embodied in the 'formal contract' provided for in the consensus, as opposed to an expectation that there would or might be agreement on further terms to be so embodied. In other words, I do not consider that the phrase in question should be construed as an 'agreement to agree' on further terms, but rather as an indication, at the most, of an expectation of agreement on further terms.

So far as the second matter is concerned, I do not consider that any implication of an intention not to be legally bound which might otherwise be suggested by the words 'agreement in principle' can prevail over the clear import of the words 'legally binding'. The intention of the parties to be legally bound by their consensus is sufficiently clearly expressed to take the case out of the third class of cases referred to in *Masters v Cameron* (1954) 91 CLR 353 at 360–362, that is, '... cases in which the terms of agreement are not intended to have, and therefore do not have, any binding effect of their own' (at 361). There is in reality a fourth class of case additional to the three mentioned in *Masters v Cameron*, as recognised by Knox CJ, Rich J and Dixon J, in *Sinclair, Scott & Co v Naughton* (1929) 43 CLR 310 at 317, namely, '... one in which the parties were content to be bound immediately and exclusively by the terms which they had agreed upon whilst expecting to make a further contract in substitution for the first contract, containing, by consent, additional terms'. Their Honours refer to the speech of Lord Loreburn, in *Love & Stewart v S Instone & Co* (1917) 33 TLR 475 at 476, where his Lordship said that:

> It was quite lawful to make a bargain containing certain terms which one was content with, dealing with what one regarded as essentials, and at the same time to say that one would have a formal document drawn up with the full expectation that one would by consent insert in it a number of further terms. If that were the intention of the parties, then a bargain had been made, none the less that both parties felt quite sure that the formal document could comprise more than was contained in the preliminary bargain.

It seems to me that subject to the matters yet to be considered the present case falls into this fourth class as described in *Sinclair, Scott & Co v Naughton*.

Baulkham Hills Private Hospital was entitled to have the contract specifically performed.

QUESTIONS

(1) What are the circumstances (that is, the categories) outlined by the Court in *Masters v Cameron* (1954) 91 CLR 353 into which an agreement to agree might fall and therefore be binding and enforceable?

(2) Can an agreement to agree be binding, notwithstanding the fact that it contains a clause whereby the parties agree to enter into further agreements 'if necessary'?

(3) Do you believe that a fourth category, as proposed by the Court in *Baulkham Hills Private Hospital Pty Ltd v GR Securities Pty Ltd* (1986) 40 NSWLR 622, is necessary?

6.4 Agreements to negotiate

Concept	Short explanation	Relevant authorities	*Principles* text*
An agreement to negotiate/an agreement to negotiate in good faith can be entered into	The parties may enter into an agreement which sets out that they agree to enter into negotiations in the future	*Coal Cliff Collieries Pty Ltd v Sijehama Pty Ltd* (1991) 24 NSWLR 1 *United Group Rail Services Ltd v Rail Corporation New South Wales* (2009) 74 NSWLR 618	Chapter 6: 6.09

* Consult the corresponding section(s) of the *Principles* text for more detail.

Sometimes parties will enter into an agreement to negotiate the terms of a contract in the future. Of course, the question then becomes whether the parties can be forced to uphold that promise to negotiate. The following case extracts discuss the issues surrounding the enforcement of such agreements.

Coal Cliff Collieries Pty Ltd v Sijehama Pty Ltd (1991) 24 NSWLR 1

Facts and issues

Coal Cliff Collieries and Sijehama entered into an agreement regarding the joint development of coal mining rights pursuant to which they agreed to negotiate 'in good faith' (and execute) a joint venture agreement in the future. Negotiations broke down and no joint venture agreement was executed. At first instance, Sijehama succeeded in arguing that a breach of a legally binding agreement had occurred (the key issue in this case). Coal Cliff Collieries appealed this decision.

Decision

Per Kirby P at 22:

> I have already noted the basic law that courts will not enforce an agreement to agree. This is accepted by the High Court of Australia as part of the law of this country: see *Booker* (at 604).

> But that principle falls far short of resolving the issue presented by the present case upon which there is no clear binding authority of the High Court or of this Court.

His Honour concluded at 26:

> . . . I do not share the opinion of the English Court of Appeal that no promise to negotiate in good faith would ever be enforced by a court. I reject the notion that such a contract is unknown to the law, whatever its term. I agree with Lord Wright's speech in *Hillas* that, provided there was consideration for the promise, in some circumstance a promise to negotiate in good faith will be enforceable, depending upon its precise terms. Likewise I agree with Pain J in *Donwin* that, so long as the promise is clear and part of an undoubted agreement between the parties, the courts will not adopt a general principle that relief for the breach of such promise must be withheld. It follows that in this regard I agree with the conclusion of Clarke J on the principle presented by the first issue before him—and now before this Court.
>
> Nevertheless, alike with Goff LJ in *Mallozzi* and the substantial body of United States authority which has been cited in this case, I believe that the proper approach to be taken in each case depends upon the construction of the particular contract: see *Australia & New Zealand Banking Group Ltd v Frost Holdings Pty Ltd* [1989] VR 695; see note (1991) 65 ALJ 59. In many contracts it will be plain that the promise to negotiate is intended to be a binding legal obligation to which the parties should then be held. The clearest illustration of this class will be cases where an identified third party has been given the power to settle ambiguities and uncertainties: see *Foster v Wheeler* (1888) LR 38 Ch D 130; *Axelsen v O'Brien* (1949) 80 CLR 219 and *Biotechnology* (at 136). But even in such cases, the court may regard the failure to reach agreement on a particular term as such that the agreement should be classed as illusory or unacceptably uncertain: *Godecke v Kirwan* [27] (at 646f) and *Whitlock v Brew* (1968) 118 CLR 445 at 456. In that event, the court will not enforce the arrangement.
>
> In a small number of cases, by reference to a readily ascertainable external standard, the court may be able to add flesh to a provision which is otherwise unacceptably vague or uncertain or apparently illusory: see, eg, *Powell v Jones* [1968] SASR 394 at 399; *Sweet and Maxwell Ltd v Universal News Services Ltd* [1964] 2 QB 699; cf *Meehan v Jones* (1982) 149 CLR 571 at 589; *Jillcy Film Enterprises* (at 521); *Ridgeway Coal Co* (at 408).
>
> Finally, in many cases, the promise to negotiate in good faith will occur in the context of an 'arrangement' (to use a neutral term) which by its nature, purpose, context, other provisions or otherwise makes it clear that 'the promise is too illusory or too vague and uncertain to be enforceable': see McHugh JA in *Biotechnology* (at 156) and *Adaras Development Ltd v Marcona Corporation* [1975] 1 NZLR 324 at 331.
>
> In the present case, with every respect to Clarke J, I am of the opinion that this contract should be so classified. The review of the considerations which lead me to this conclusion has already been stated. This was not a case where an external arbitrator was nominated to resolve outstanding differences. There were many such differences at the time of the heads of agreement and a number remain even three years later when negotiations were finally broken off. A court would be extremely ill-equipped to fill the remaining blank spaces and to resolve questions which three years of painful negotiation between the solicitors for the parties had failed to remove. A court could not, in this case, appeal to objective standards or to its own experience — as it might in filling a blank space in a lease of domestic premises or a contract less complex and more familiar than one for a major mining development. At stake are commercial decisions involving adjustments which would contemplate binding the parties for years and deciding issues that lie well beyond the expertise of a court. How mining executives,

> attending to the interests of their corporation and its shareholders might act in negotiating such a complex transaction is quite unknowable. Therefore, although I agree with Clarke J that some contracts to negotiate in good faith may be enforced by our law, this was not such a contract. I repeat the caution which I have expressed elsewhere (as I did in *Biotechnology Australia Pty Ltd v Pace*) that courts should hold back from giving effect to arrangements which the parties have not concluded, at least in circumstances such as the present.

Ultimately, the agreement was held not to be binding as the overall arrangement was too illusory or vague and uncertain to be enforceable.

United Group Rail Services Ltd v Rail Corporation New South Wales (2009) 74 NSWLR 618

Facts and issues

United Group Rail Services Ltd entered into an agreement to design and build new rolling stock for Rail Corporation New South Wales. The agreement contained dispute resolution clauses which provided that, in the event of a dispute, the parties would meet and carry out 'genuine and good faith negotiations'. The issue was whether this agreement, which amounted to an agreement to negotiate in good faith, was enforceable. At first instance it was found that it was and United Group Rail Services Ltd appealed.

Decision

Per Allsop P at 637:

> The phrase 'genuine and good faith' in cl 35.11 is, as I have said, a composite phrase. It is a phrase concerning an obligation to behave in a particular way in the conduct of an essentially self-interested commercial activity: the negotiation of a resolution of a commercial dispute. Given that context, the content of the phrase involves the notions of honesty and genuineness. Whilst the activity is of a self-interested character, the parties [638] have not left its conduct unconstrained. They have promised to undertake negotiations in a genuine and good faith manner for a limited period (14 days). As a matter of language, the phrase 'genuine and good faith' in this context needs little explication: it connotes an honest and genuine approach to the task. This task, rooted as it is in the existing bargain, carries with it an honest and genuine commitment to the bargain (fidelity to the bargain) and to the process of negotiation for the designated purpose.
>
> ... The parties have mutually agreed to bring an approach of genuineness and good faith to that process of seeking resolution of any such disagreement. That agreement carried with it, in ordinary language, a requirement to bring an honestly held and genuine belief about their mutual rights and obligations and about the controversy to the negotiations, and to negotiate by reference to such beliefs.
>
> These are not empty obligations; nor do they represent empty rhetoric. An honest and genuine approach to settling a contractual dispute, giving fidelity to the existing bargain, does constrain a party. The constraint arises from the bargain the parties have willingly entered into. It requires the honest and genuine assessment of rights and obligations and it requires that a party negotiate by reference to such ...

> At [639]: With respect to those who assert to the contrary, a promise to negotiate (that is to treat and discuss) genuinely and in good faith with a view to resolving claims to entitlement by reference to a known body of rights and obligations, in a manner that respects the respective contractual rights of the parties, giving due allowance for honest and genuinely held views about those pre-existing rights is not vague, illusory or uncertain. It may be comprised of wide notions difficult to falsify. However, a business person, an arbitrator or a judge may well be able to identify some conduct (if it exists) which departs from the contractual norm that the parties have agreed, even if doubt may attend other conduct. If business people are prepared in the exercise of their commercial judgement to constrain themselves by reference to express words that are broad and general, but which have sensible and ascribable meaning, the task of the Court is to give effect to, and not to impede, such solemn express contractual provisions. It may well be that it will be difficult, in any given case, to conclude that a party has not undertaken an honest and genuine attempt to settle a dispute exhibiting a fidelity to the existing bargain. In other cases, however, such a conclusion might be blindingly obvious. Uncertainty of proof, however, does not mean that this is not a real obligation with real content.

Ipp JA and MacFarlan JA were in agreeance with Allsop J and the appeal was dismissed.

QUESTIONS

(1) In what circumstances can agreements to negotiate be binding?
(2) How does an agreement to negotiate differ from a mere 'contract to contract'?
(3) Do you agree that agreements to negotiate should be enforceable?

6.5 International perspectives

The issue concerning preliminary agreements is not a matter with which the *CISG* is directly concerned, as it governs transactions between commercial parties for the sale of goods. Where a preliminary agreement to negotiate is reached, the subject matter is not usually the goods, but the obligation to negotiate. However, framework agreements which envisage future sales of goods may interact with contracts of sale, since they will often set down the detailed terms of the anticipated future sales. It is generally considered that such framework agreements, unless agreed by parties, are not governed by the *CISG*. As discussed in **Chapter 25**, the *CISG* does not deal with pre-contractual liability. On the other hand, the UNIDROIT Principle purports to create extensive pre-contractual obligations which are likely to coincide and overlay preliminary agreements by parties to negotiate. This is because the UNIDROIT Principles contain extensive duties of good faith, obligations of confidentiality, and liability for parties that break negotiations in bad faith: **25.8.7**. For this reason, agreements to negotiate in good faith are theoretically more likely to be upheld under UNIDROIT Principles than the common law of Australian contract law. However, note that, as discussed at **25.8.7**, the UNIDROIT Principles would only apply where validly selected by parties within the preliminary agreement, and are rarely selected.

6.6 Review

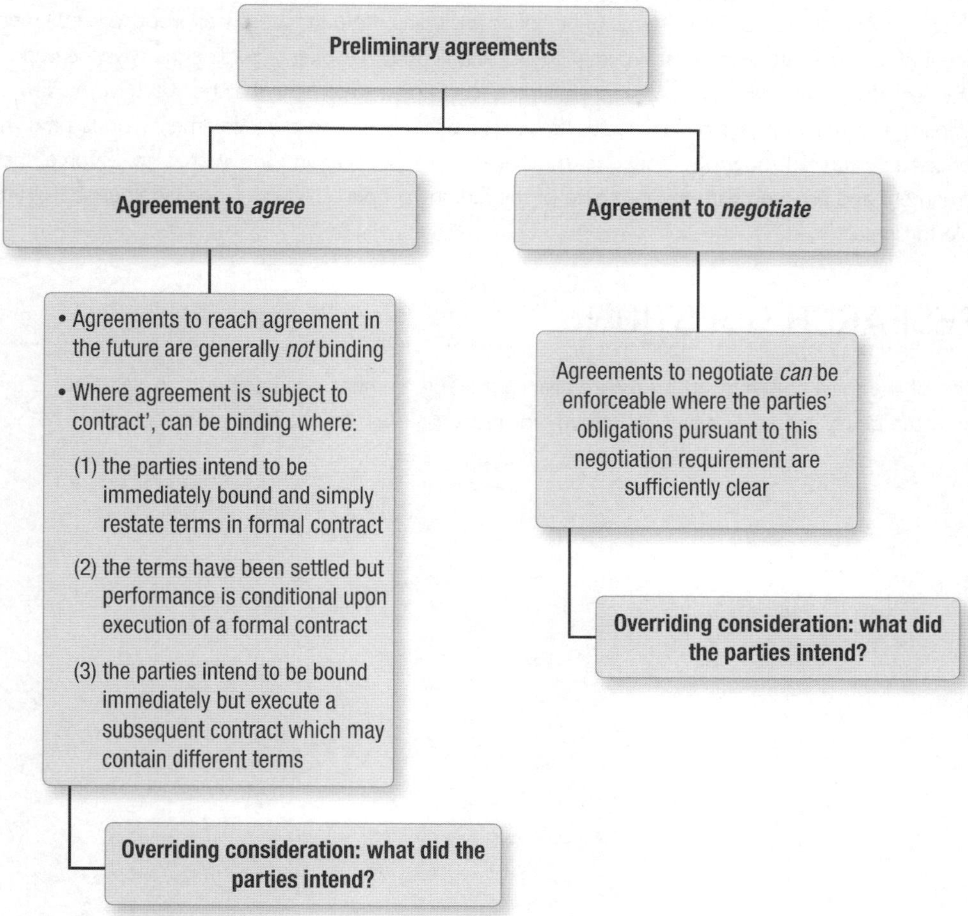

TIPS FOR APPLYING THE LAW IN PRACTICE

- Remember the general rule: agreements to enter into an agreement in the future are not binding. That said, it is important to identify the parties' intentions: what did they intend to occur when they entered into the agreement?
- Keep in mind that agreements which are expressed to be subject to the entering into of a 'formal contract' (or the like) can nevertheless be found to be binding where it can be said that they fall within one of the categories identified in *Masters v Cameron* (1954) 91 CLR 353 or *Baulkham Hills Private Hospital Pty Ltd v GR Securities Pty Ltd* (1986) 40 NSWLR 622.
- Clients should be made aware that, even if an agreement to negotiate is found to be enforceable, this does not equate to a requirement that the other party (or parties) will act reasonably in the course of any such negotiations, nor amount to a guarantee that a favourable outcome will be achieved via these negotiations.

PROBLEM QUESTION

Linda wants to purchase Brett's farming property in Victoria. On 17 November, she sends him an email which sets out all the necessary terms of her offer (including the purchase price, proposed settlement date and so on). Brett sends a return email to Linda, accepting her offer providing she pays the deposit by close of business the next day. His email also contains a statement that he will have his lawyer 'prepare a formal contract of sale for us to sign to officially record our agreement'. Linda pays the deposit as required; however, she does not hear from Brett again. She wishes to enforce their agreement and proceed with the purchase of the farming property. Advise Linda whether she will be able to do so.

RESEARCH QUESTION

One of the main arguments put forward against the enforcement of agreements to negotiate is that there can be no genuinely beneficial remedy for breach of such an obligation. Do you agree?

7

PROTECTING RELIANCE: THE DOCTRINE OF ESTOPPEL

7.1 Overview

This chapter discusses the concept of *estoppel* and its application to contractual relations, as well as some non-contractual relations. 'The object of estoppel is to preclude the unconscientious departure by a party from an assumption for which he or she bears some responsibility, and which has been adopted by another party as a basis of a course of conduct, an act or an omission which would operate to that other party's detriment if the assumption were not adhered to.'[1]

Estoppel may be used in many different ways. For instance, a person may plead an estoppel in order to:

- enforce a promise made for their benefit under a contract to which they are not a party, and which they may not be able to directly enforce due to the doctrine of privity (see **Chapter 8**);
- hold another party to a contract to an assurance made, but which is not formally a term of the contract (see **Chapters 9** and **18**);
- enforce a promise by one party to modify the obligations under a contract, though their variation is not supported by consideration, and therefore unenforceable at common law (see **Chapter 13**)
- prevent another party from terminating a contract in the face of an indication that they would not do that (see **16.1**);
- be availed of promise or interest that is otherwise not enforceable due to not having met writing requirements (see **9.2**);
- prevent another party from treating a contract as continuing when they appear to have terminated it (see **16.1**).
- enforce a gratuitous promise that could not be enforced at common law, due to lack of consideration (see **Chapter 5**);
- hold a person to an assurance that they will agree to a contract, despite the contract never actually being formed.

There are three main categories of *estoppel*:

- *estoppel by deed*, which precludes certain challenges to an assertion or allegation of fact that the estopped party has made in a deed;
- *estoppel by judgment* (or *by record*), which in its various forms (including cause of action estoppel, issue estoppel and *Anshun estoppel*) seeks to prevent the litigation of matters that either have already or could have been resolved in earlier proceedings; and
- *estoppel by conduct*, which can be used to prevent a party from acting inconsistently with an assumption they have either induced the other party to adopt, or which the two parties have jointly adopted as the basis for their dealings.

Estoppel by conduct is the category with which this chapter is mostly concerned. It encompasses *common law estoppel* (sometime referred to as *estoppel in pais*) and *equitable estoppel*.

1 Patrick Parkinson (ed), *The Principles of Equity* (Lawbook Company, 2nd ed, 2003) 211.

Common law estoppel is said to operate only upon assumptions or representations that relate to matters of *existing fact* (see *Principles* text at 7.02). As such, its role is limited to the establishment of facts based on which the parties' legal rights are decided. The parties' rights and obligations are determined on the basis that the represented facts exist. Equitable estoppel applies to representation as to future conduct. When established, its effect is to raise an equity in favour of the party seeking estoppel.

Equitable estoppel is the type that is raised in most, if not all, of the ways listed above. Hence, the focus of this chapter is on equitable estoppel. Historically, equitable estoppel is further divided into two species: *proprietary estoppel* and *promissory estoppel*. Proprietary estoppel allows a person who had been led to believe that they would be granted an interest in land to seek an order that it be conveyed to them, where they had either been encouraged or allowed to build on or otherwise improve that land. Promissory estoppel is more generic, and concerns promises as to the creation or enforcement of rights that may or may not concern interest in land.

In *Waltons Stores v Maher*[2], a majority of the High Court effectively brought together proprietary and promissory estoppel, in what is now often referred to as a unified doctrine of equitable estoppel. As they noted, the 'common thread' between the two species is the idea that where a party (A) has acted to their detriment on an assumption induced by another party (B), equity may intervene if B departs (or seeks to depart) from the induced assumption, if it would be unconscionable on B's part to do so. With the notion of a unified doctrine of equitable estoppel, both species share the same general requirements, operate as a cause of action and may apply even in the absence of any pre-existing legal relationship.

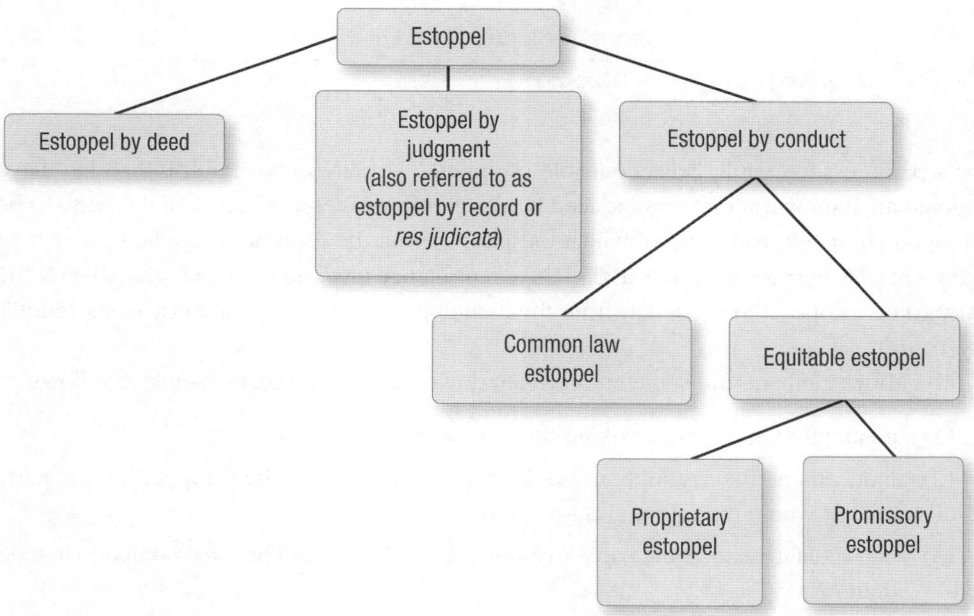

2 *Waltons Stores (Interstate) Ltd v Maher* (1988) 164 CLR 387.

The cases extracted in this chapter illustrate the nature and elements of equitable estoppel, situations in which equitable estoppel have been invoked, and remedies that may be granted when equitable estoppel is successfully invoked.

7.2 Elements of equitable estoppel

Concept	Short explanation	Relevant authorities	*Principles* text*
A party would be precluded from unconscientious departure from an assumption for which they bear responsibility, and which has been adopted by another party as a basis of a course of conduct, and which would operate to that other party's detriment if the assumption were not adhered to	While the party seeking to depart form the assumption may be entitled to do so at law, equity may intervene if allowing the departure would be unconscionable Thus, the party invoking estoppel must establish: (1) assumption induced by the party to be estopped; (2) detrimental reliance on the part of the party invoking estoppel; and (3) unjust or unconscientious result if departure is allowed	*Waltons Stores (Interstate) Ltd v Maher* (1988) 164 CLR 387 *Sidhu v Van Dyke* (2014) 251 CLR 505	Chapter 7: 7.06–7.11

* Consult the corresponding section(s) of the *Principles* text for more detail.

For a party to successfully raise equitable estoppel, that party must establish that they have adopted an assumption that was induced by the conduct or representation of the party to be estopped (*induced assumption*), which the party raising the estoppel has relied on to their detriment (*detrimental reliance*), and in the circumstance it would be unconscionable for the party to be estopped to be depart from the assumption they have created (*unconscionable departure*).

The above elements are sometimes broken down further, into six elements, as follows:

(1) assumption: the party invoking estoppel adopted an assumption

(2) inducement: the assumption was induced by the party to be estopped (ie the party against whom the estoppel is invoked)

(3) detrimental reliance: the party invoking estoppel has relied on the assumption to their detriment

(4) reasonableness: it was reasonable for the party invoking the estoppel to rely on the assumption in the manner they did

(5) departure: the party to be estopped has departed or has threatened to depart from the assumption they have created

(6) unconscionability: it will be unjust or unconscionable for the party to be estopped to be allowed to depart from the assumption they have created.

If these elements are present, the departing party may be estopped from resiling from the assumption, and some remedy may be given.

Waltons Stores (Interstate) Ltd v Maher (1988) 164 CLR 387

Facts and issue

Waltons Stores (Waltons) were negotiating to lease a store from Mr and Mrs Maher (Maher). There was a sense of urgency around the negotiations. Maher was to partially demolish an existing building on their land and rebuild to Waltons' specifications by 15 January 1984 (later extended to 5 February 1984). By early November 1983, the agreement was still not finalised, but Maher needed to commence work if they were to meet the deadline. On 7 November, Maher's solicitors contacted Waltons' solicitors to inform them that the agreement needed to be finalised in the next day or so to enable commencement of work to meet the January deadline, and that Maher did not want to commence demolition until the agreement was finalised. Later that day, Waltons' solicitors forwarded a lease for Maher to sign, adding 'you should note that we have not yet obtained our client's specific instructions to each amendment requested, but we believe that approval will be forthcoming. We shall let you know tomorrow if any amendments are not agreed to'. There was no further communication either way from Waltons' solicitor. Maher signed the lease on 11 November and forwarded it to Waltons' solicitors 'by way of exchange'. Waltons later had second thoughts about the lease and asked its solicitors to 'go slow' with completing the transaction. On 10 December, Waltons was made aware that demolition had commenced, but said nothing about their second thoughts. In early January 1984, Maher commenced the new building in accordance with the plans approved by Waltons. On 19 January, Waltons' solicitors wrote to Maher's solicitor advising that Waltons no longer wanted to proceed with the lease. By this stage, the building works were 40 per cent complete. Maher sought a declaration that there was in existence a valid and enforceable contract; or an order for specific performance; or damages.

The issues were whether there was an enforceable contract, though Waltons had yet to sign the lease and, if no, whether specific performance or damages would avail Maher on some other grounds.

Decision

The trial judge (Kearney J) awarded Maher damages on the ground that Waltons was estopped from denying the existence of a binding contract. Waltons' appeal to the NSW Court of Appeal was dismissed. Waltons appealed further to the High Court, which also dismissed the appeal on the basis of estoppel, though on differing reasoning.

Per Mason CJ and Wilson at 392:

> The issue in this appeal is whether, in the light of the facts, the appellant is estopped from denying the [393] existence of a binding contract that it would take a lease of the respondents'

premises at Nowra and, if so, whether the respondents can support the order made by the primary judge (Kearney J), affirmed by the New South Wales Court of Appeal, that the appellant pay to the respondent damages in lieu of specific performance of an agreement for a lease.

[. . .]

[395] As Dawson Waldron did not inform Morton & Harris on 8 November or immediately thereafter that the amendments discussed on 7 November were not acceptable to the appellant, Mr Elvy and the respondents were entitled to assume, in consequence of the statement in Dawson Waldron's letter of 7 November, that the appellant accepted the amendments and that exchange of contracts was a mere formality.

[. . .]

[397] The estoppel set up by the respondents and found by the primary judge was a common law estoppel in the form of a representation by the appellant constituted by its silence in circumstances where it should have spoken. Likewise, the Court of Appeal based the estoppel on common law principles as explained by Dixon J. in [398] *Thompson v. Palmer* (1933) 49 CLR 507, at p 547 and *Grundt v. Great Boulder Pty. Gold Mines Ltd.* (1937) 59 CLR 641, at pp 674–676:

[. . .]

Our conclusion that the respondents assumed that exchange of contracts would take place as a matter of course, not that exchange had in fact taken place, undermines the factual foundation for the common law estoppel by representation found by Kearney J. and the common law estoppel based on omission to correct a mistake favoured by the Court of Appeal. There is, as Mason and Deane JJ. pointed out in *Legione v. Hateley* (1983) 152 CLR 406, at p 432, a long line of authority to support the proposition that, to make out a case of common law estoppel by representation, the representation must be as to an existing fact, a promise or representation as to future conduct being insufficient.

[. . .]

[399] If there is any basis at all for holding that common law estoppel arises where there is a mistaken assumption as to future events, that basis must lie in reversing *Jorden v. Money* and in accepting the powerful dissent of Lord St. Leonards in that case. The repeated acceptance of *Jorden v. Money* over the years by courts of the highest authority makes this a formidable exercise.

[. . .]

This brings us to the doctrine of promissory estoppel on which the respondents relied in this Court to sustain the judgment in their favour. Promissory estoppel certainly extends to representations (or promises) as to future conduct: *Legione*, at p 432. So far the doctrine has been mainly confined to precluding departure from a representation by a person in a pre-existing contractual relationship that he will not enforce his contractual rights, whether they be pre-existing or rights to be acquired as a result of the representation.

[. . .]

In principle there is certainly no reason why the doctrine should not apply so as to preclude departure by a person from a representation that he will not enforce a non-contractual right.

[. . .]

[400] There has been for many years a reluctance to allow promissory estoppel to become the vehicle for the positive enforcement of a representation by a party that he would do

something in the future. Promissory estoppel, it has been said, is a defensive equity (*Hughes v. Metropolitan Railway Co*. (1877) 2 App Cas 439, at p 448; *Combe v. Combe* (1951) 2 KB 215, at pp 219–220 and the traditional notion has been that estoppel could only be relied upon defensively as a shield and not as a sword: *Perpetual Trustee Co. Ltd. v. Pacific Coal Co. Pty. Ltd*. (1953) 55 SR (NSW) 495, at pp 508, 518–519.

[. . .]

But the respondents ask us to drive promissory estoppel one step further by enforcing directly in the absence of a pre-existing relationship of any kind a non-contractual promise on which the representee has relied to his detriment. For the purposes of discussion, we shall assume that there was such a promise in the present case. The principal objection to the enforcement of such a promise is that it would outflank the principles of the law of contract. Holmes J. expressed his objection to the operation of promissory estoppel in this situation when he said 'It would cut up the doctrine of consideration by the roots, if a promisee could make a gratuitous promise binding by subsequently acting in reliance on it': *Commonwealth v. Scituate Savings Bank* (1884) 137 Mass. 301, at p 302. ... And Denning L.J. in *Combe v. Combe*, after noting that 'The doctrine of consideration is too firmly fixed to be overthrown by a side-wind', said (at p 220) that such a promise could only be enforced if it was supported by sufficient consideration.

[401] There is force in these objections and it may not be a sufficient answer to repeat the words of Lord Denning M.R. in *Crabb v. Arun District Council* (1976) Ch 179, at p 187, 'Equity comes in, true to form, to mitigate the rigours of strict law'. . . [403] *Crabb* [1976] Ch 179 was an instance of promissory estoppel. It lends assistance to the view that promissory estoppel may in some circumstances extend to the enforcement of a right not previously in existence where the defendant has encouraged in the plaintiff the belief that it will be granted and has acquiesced in action taken by the plaintiff in that belief.

[. . .]

[404] One may therefore discern in the cases a common thread which links them together, namely, the principle that equity will come to the relief of a plaintiff who has acted to his detriment on the basis of a basic assumption in relation to which the other party to the transaction has 'played such a part in the adoption of the assumption that it would be unfair or unjust if he were left free to ignore it'. . . Equity comes to the relief of such a plaintiff on the footing that it would be unconscionable conduct on the part of the other party to ignore the assumption.

[. . .]

[406] The foregoing review of the doctrine of promissory estoppel indicates that the doctrine extends to the enforcement of voluntary promises on the footing that a departure from the basic assumptions underlying the transaction between the parties must be unconscionable. As failure to fulfil a promise does not of itself amount to unconscionable conduct, mere reliance on an executory promise to do something, resulting in the promisee changing his position or suffering detriment, does not bring promissory estoppel into play. Something more would be required. *Humphreys Estate* suggests that this may be found, if at all, in the creation or encouragement by the party estopped in the other party of an assumption that a contract will come into existence or a promise will be performed and that the other party relied on that assumption to his detriment to the knowledge of the first party.

[. . .]

> But the crucial question remains: was [407] the appellant entitled to stand by in silence when it must have known that the respondents were proceeding on the assumption that they had an agreement and that completion of the exchange was a formality? The mere exercise of its legal right not to exchange contracts could not be said to amount to unconscionable conduct on the part of the appellant. But there were two other factors present in the situation which require to be taken into consideration. The first was the element of urgency that pervaded the negotiation of the terms of the proposed lease. As we have noted, the appellant was bound to give up possession of its existing commercial premises in Nowra in January 1984; the new building was to be available for fitting out by 15 January and completed by 5 February 1984. The respondents' solicitor had said to the appellant's solicitor on 7 November that it would be impossible for Maher to complete the building within the agreed time unless the agreement were concluded 'within the next day or two'. The outstanding details were agreed within a day or two thereafter, and the work of preparing the site commenced almost immediately.
>
> The second factor of importance is that the respondents executed the counterpart deed and it was forwarded to the appellant's solicitor on 11 November. The assumption on which the respondents acted thereafter was that completion of the necessary exchange was a formality. The next their solicitor heard from the appellant was a letter from its solicitors dated 19 January, informing him that the appellant did not intend to proceed with the matter. It had known, at least since 10 December, that costly work was proceeding on the site.
>
> It seems to us, in the light of these considerations, that the appellant was under an obligation to communicate with the respondents within a reasonable time after receiving the executed counterpart deed and certainly when it learnt on 10 December that demolition was proceeding. It had to choose whether to complete the contract or to warn the respondents that it had not yet decided upon the course it would take. It was not entitled simply to retain the counterpart deed executed by the respondents and do nothing.
>
> [...]
>
> The appellant's inaction, in all the circumstances, constituted clear encouragement or inducement to the respondents to continue to act on the basis of the assumption which they had made. It was unconscionable for it, knowing that the respondents were exposing themselves to detriment by acting on the basis of a false assumption, to adopt a course [408] of inaction which encouraged them in the course they had adopted. To express the point in the language of promissory estoppel the appellant is estopped in all the circumstances from retreating from its implied promise to complete the contract ...

Per Brennan J at 412:

> In the Courts below, the conclusion that Waltons was bound by an Agreement for Lease although it had abstained from executing and delivering the original Deed was put on somewhat different bases. Kearney J. found 'that (Mr and Mrs Maher) believed that they had an agreement. They were entitled, in my view, to assume that the exchange would be duly completed by (Waltons) and in those circumstances properly considered that they were bound to proceed with the greatest expedition with the building project for (Waltons).' His Honour further held 'that the circumstances do establish the requisite elements to create an

estoppel against (Waltons) denying that a concluded agreement by way of exchange did in fact exist between the parties.'

In the Court of Appeal, Priestley J.A. (with whom Glass and Samuels JJ.A. agreed) founded his judgment on another basis. His Honour stated his opinion to be 'that certainly by the time (Mr and Mrs Maher) began actual building in Berry Street at the [413] beginning of January (Waltons) had caused the respondents to assume that the fact was that notwithstanding they had never been notified of the exchange of agreements (and notwithstanding that no exchange of agreements had occurred) the deal that had been agreed between Mr Maher and Mr Elvy on the one hand and representatives of the appellant on the other was an agreement binding both the respondents and the appellant.'

In these three passages there are three distinct bases advanced for holding Waltons estopped from denying the existence of the contract sued upon. The first basis is an expectation by Mr Maher that Waltons would duly complete the exchange; the second basis is an assumption by Mr Maher that Waltons had duly completed the exchange; the third basis is an assumption by Mr Maher that there was a binding contract in existence whether or not an exchange had been completed. An expectation that Waltons would exchange contracts — the first basis — is radically different from an assumption that contracts had been exchanged — the second basis. The relevant assumption of fact which Mr Maher must have made if he expected that Waltons would exchange contracts is that contracts had not been exchanged. The first basis rests on an expectation as to what Waltons would do; it could be supported, if at all, only upon the principles of equitable estoppel. The second and third bases rest on assumptions as to an existing state of affairs; they could be supported, if at all, upon the principles of estoppel in pais. Estoppel in pais and equitable estoppel address different problems, though there are elements common to both.

The nature of an estoppel in pais is well established in this country. A party who induces another to make an assumption that a state of affairs exists, knowing or intending the other to act on that assumption, is estopped from asserting the existence of a different state of affairs as the foundation of their respective rights and liabilities if the other has acted in reliance on the assumption and would suffer detriment if the assumption were not adhered to.

[. . .]

[415] The scope of estoppel in pais does not extend to compel adherence to representations of intention. . . The limitation which *Jorden v. Money* (1854) 5 HLC 185 (10 ER 868) placed on the doctrine of estoppel in pais was that it 'does not apply to a case where the representation is not a representation of a fact, but a statement of something which the party intends or does not intend to do'.

[. . .]

[416] Equitable estoppel, on the other hand, does not operate by establishing an assumed state of affairs. Unlike an estoppel in pais, an equitable estoppel is a source of legal obligation. . . . An equitable estoppel is binding in conscience on the party estopped, and it is to be satisfied by that party doing or abstaining from doing something in order to prevent detriment to the party raising the estoppel, which that party would otherwise suffer by having acted or abstained from acting in reliance on the assumption or expectation which he has been induced to adopt. Perhaps equitable estoppel is more accurately described as an equity created by estoppel.

[. . .]

[418] When Mr Roth received the letter enclosing the executed counterpart Deed, he and his clients had two options: to retain it or to return it to Mr Elvy. It could be retained only on the terms on which it had been received, namely, by way of exchange. The continued retention of the executed counterpart Deed was justified only if Waltons intended and continued in its intention to execute and deliver the original Deed ... Mr Maher either assumed that a contract had been made or expected that, the matter having passed beyond the stage of negotiations, Waltons would execute and deliver the original Deed and was not free at that stage to withdraw. Kearney J. found that the Mahers 'believed that they had an agreement' because they had assumed 'that the exchange would be duly completed'. In reliance on that assumption or expectation Mr Maher proceeded to clear the site and build the store. Waltons discovered that Mr Maher was performing the work required under the proposed contract, and it must have known that Mr Maher would not have commenced that work if he had not assumed that a contract had been made or expected that Waltons was bound to enter into a contract. Waltons intended that he should act on that assumption or expectation by continuing to build the store in order that Waltons should enjoy the option of completing the exchange and proceeding to take the lease if it should appear expedient to do so. It was not disputed in this Court that the Mahers would suffer detriment if Mr Maher's expectation were to go unfulfilled.

Is this sufficient to create an equity in the Mahers ... 'an equity created by estoppel, or equitable estoppel, as it is sometimes called, by which the person who has made the expenditure is induced by the expectation of obtaining protection, and equity protects him so that an injustice may not be perpetrated'? The protection which equity extends is analogous to the protection given [419] by estoppel in pais to which Dixon J. referred in *Grundt v. Great Boulder*, that is, protection against the detriment which would flow from a party's change of position if the assumption (or expectation) that led to it were deserted ...

The element which both attracts the jurisdiction of a court of equity and shapes the remedy to be given is unconscionable conduct on the part of the person bound by the equity, and the remedy required to satisfy an equity varies according to the circumstances of the case. As Robert Goff J. said in *Amalgamated Property Co. v. Texas Bank* (1982) QB 84, at p 103: 'Of all doctrines, equitable estoppel is surely one of the most flexible.'

[...]

[420] Some indication of what constitutes unconscionable conduct can be gleaned from the instances in which an equity created by estoppel has been held to arise. If cases of equitable estoppel are in truth but particular instances of the operation of the general principles of equity, there is little purpose in dividing those cases into the categories of promissory and proprietary estoppel which are not necessarily exhaustive of the cases in which equity will intervene. Like Scarman L.J. in *Crabb v. Arun District Council*, at p 193, I do not find it generally helpful to divide into classes the cases in which an equity created by estoppel has been held to exist. However, the familiar categories serve to identify the characteristics of the circumstances which have been held to give rise to an equity in the party raising the estoppel. In cases of promissory estoppel, the equity binds the holder of a legal right who induces another to expect that that right will not be exercised against him... In cases of proprietary estoppel, the equity binds the owner of property who induces another to expect that an interest in the property will be conferred on him.

[...]

In all cases where an equity created by estoppel is raised, the party raising the equity has acted or abstained from acting on an assumption or expectation as to the legal relationship between himself and the party who induced him to adopt the assumption or expectation. The assumption or expectation does not relate to mere facts, whether existing or future. (An assumption as to a legal relationship may be an assumption that there is no legal relationship, as in the cases where A builds on B's land assuming it to be his own.)

[...]

[423] It is essential to the existence of an equity created by estoppel that the party who induces the adoption of the assumption or expectation knows or intends that the party who adopts it will act or abstain from acting in reliance on the assumption or expectation ... The unconscionable conduct which it is the object of equity to prevent is the failure of a party, who has induced the adoption of the assumption or expectation and who knew or intended that it would be relied on, to fulfil the assumption or expectation or otherwise to avoid the detriment which that failure would occasion. The object of the equity is not to compel the party bound to fulfil the assumption or expectation; it is to avoid the detriment which, if the assumption or expectation goes unfulfilled, will be suffered by the party who has been induced to act or to abstain from acting thereon.

If this object is kept steadily in mind, the concern that a general application of the principle of equitable estoppel would make non-contractual promises enforceable as contractual promises can be [424] allayed. A non-contractual promise can give rise to an equitable estoppel only when the promisor induces the promisee to assume or expect that the promise is intended to affect their legal relations and he knows or intends that the promisee will act or abstain from acting in reliance on the promise, and when the promisee does so act or abstain from acting and the promisee would suffer detriment by his action or inaction if the promisor were not to fulfil the promise. When these elements are present, equitable estoppel almost wears the appearance of contract, for the action or inaction of the promisee looks like consideration for the promise on which, as the promisor knew or intended, the promisee would act or abstain from acting.

[...]

[425] But there are differences between a contract and an equity created by estoppel. A contractual obligation is created by the agreement of the parties; an equity created by estoppel may be imposed irrespective of any agreement by the party bound. A contractual obligation must be supported by consideration; an equity created by estoppel need not be supported by what is, strictly speaking, consideration. The measure of a contractual obligation depends on the terms of the contract and the circumstances to which it applies; the measure of an equity created by estoppel varies according to what is necessary to prevent detriment resulting from unconscionable conduct.

[...]

[428] In my opinion, to establish an equitable estoppel, it is necessary for a plaintiff to prove that (1) the plaintiff assumed that a particular legal relationship then existed between the plaintiff and the defendant or expected that a particular legal relationship would exist between them and, in the latter case, that the defendant would not be free to withdraw from the expected legal relationship; (2) the [429] defendant has induced the plaintiff to adopt that assumption or expectation; (3) the plaintiff acts or abstains from acting in reliance on the assumption or expectation; (4) the defendant knew or intended him to do so; (5) the plaintiff's action or inaction will occasion detriment if the assumption or expectation is not fulfilled; and (6) the defendant has failed to act to avoid that detriment whether by fulfilling the assumption or expectation or otherwise.

> [. . .]
>
> This is such a case. . . [433]. . . The appeal should be dismissed.

Deane and Gaudron JJ took the view that Maher had acted on the assumption that Waltons had signed the lease (ie an assumption of fact) and were estopped from denying that fact (common law estoppel).

Sidhu v Van Dyke (2014) 251 CLR 505

Facts and issues

In 1996, Ms Van Dyke and her then husband moved into a house known as Oaks Cottage, which was located on a block of land known as the Homestead Block owned by Mr Sidhu and his wife. Towards the end of 1997, Sidhu and Van Dyke commenced a relationship, during which Sidhu promised Van Dyke that he would subdivide the land and transfer Oaks Cottage to her. Van Dyke continued in her relationship with Sidhu, performed unpaid work on the Homestead Block and Oaks Cottage and did not pursue gainful employment elsewhere. She also did not seek a property settlement from her husband when they divorced in 1998, after her husband discovered the relationship between Van Dyke and Sidhu. In 2006, the relationship between Sidhu and Van Dyke ended, and Sidhu refused to transfer Oaks Cottage to Van Dyke. Van Dyke commenced proceedings in the Supreme Court of New South Wales, claiming that Sidhu was estopped from departing from his promises, as she had acted in reliance on those representations to her detriment.

Decision

The trial judge was not satisfied that Van Dyke had acted to her detriment in reliance on Sidhu's assurances, and dismissed her claim.

The Court of Appeal allowed Van Dyke's appeal, holding that there was a presumption that Van Dyke acted to her detriment in reliance on Sidhu's representations, which Sidhu had failed to rebut. It concluded that Sidhu was estopped from departing from his assurances, and ordered him to pay Van Dyke equitable compensation in an amount to be assessed by reference to the market value of the Oaks Cottage.

The High Court unanimously dismissed Sidhu's appeal. It held that the Court of Appeal erred in presuming that Van Dyke had acted to her detriment in reliance on Sidhu's representations. Van Dyke bore the onus of proof in relation to detrimental reliance. However, Van Dyke's evidence at trial established that she had acted to her detriment in reliance on Sidhu's representations. On that basis, Van Dyke was entitled to equitable compensation in an amount to be assessed by reference to the value of the Oaks property.

Per French CJ, Kiefel, Bell and Keane JJ at 511:

> In *The Commonwealth v Verwayen*, Mason CJ described estoppel as 'a label which covers a complex array of rules spanning various categories'. His Honour went on to say of 'titles such as promissory estoppel, proprietary estoppel and estoppel by acquiescence' that they are all 'intended to serve the same fundamental purpose, namely "protection against the detriment

which would flow from a party's change of position if the assumption (or expectation) that led to it were deserted".'

[...]

[522] In point of principle, to speak of deploying a presumption of reliance in the context of equitable estoppel is to fail to recognise that it is the conduct of the representee induced by the representor which is the very foundation for equitable intervention. Reliance is a fact to be found; it is not to be imputed on the basis of evidence which falls short of proof of the fact. It is actual reliance by the promisee, and the state of affairs so created, which answers the concern that equitable estoppel not be allowed to outflank *Jorden v Money* by dispensing with the need [523] for consideration if a promise is to be enforceable as a contract. It is not the breach of promise, but the promisor's responsibility for the detrimental reliance by the promisee, which makes it unconscionable for the promisor to resile from his or her promise.

[...]

[525] Upon the breakdown of the respondent's marriage, she was confronted with difficult decisions relating to the course of her life and the care and maintenance of her child. The appellant's promises were objectively likely to have had a significant effect upon the decision-making of a person in the respondent's position. The appellant's assurances were integral to his proposal to the respondent to put their relationship on a firm long-term footing. It is unlikely that she would have thrown in her lot with the appellant and exerted herself as she did over a period of eight and a half years if he had not made the promises which he in fact made. To the contrary, it is likely that she would have sought to maximise her [526] own income for the benefit of herself and her infant son by seeking the most gainful form of employment.

[...]

[527] This category of equitable estoppel serves to vindicate the expectations of the representee against a party who seeks unconscionably to resile from an expectation he or she has created.

[...]

[528] In summary, on all the evidence, it should be found that the respondent was induced to remain at the property and to continue to work for the appellant and his wife by the assurances which he made. It is unconscionable for the appellant now to resile from his assurances.

QUESTIONS

(1) From the extracted judgments of *Waltons Stores (Interstate) Ltd v Maher*, what did Mason CJ and Wilson J (in their joint judgment), and Brennan J (in his separate judgment) see as the object of estoppel?

(2) In his judgment in *Waltons Stores (Interstate) Ltd v Maher*, Brennan J (at 420) stated that 'If cases of equitable estoppel are in truth but particular instances of the operation of the general principles of equity, there is little purpose in dividing those cases into the categories of promissory and proprietary estoppel which are not necessarily exhaustive of the cases in which equity will intervene.' He went on to unify the two categories of equitable estoppel. Do you agree with Brennan J?

(3) From your reading of the extracted judgments of *Waltons Stores (Interstate) Ltd v Maher*, is there still a distinction between equitable estoppel and estoppel *in pais* in Australian law? If your answer is yes, what is the difference?

7.3 Measure of relief

Concept	Short explanation	Relevant authorities	*Principles* text*
When equitable estoppel is held to apply, the courts grant relief (or remedy) to the party who raised the estoppel	The effect of establishing estoppel is to raise an equity in favour of the party who raised estoppel, which the courts endeavor to satisfy. In this context, the 'equity' is an entitlement to relief at the court's discretion. But there can be tension between the different possible reliefs that may be granted	*Giumelli v Giumelli* (1999) 196 CLR 101 *Sidhu v Van Dyke* (2014) 251 CLR 505	Chapter 7: 7.13

* Consult the corresponding section(s) of the *Principles* text for more detail.

When equitable estoppel is established, the courts grant relief (or remedy) to the party who raised the estoppel. The effect of establishing estoppel is to raise an equity in favour of the party who raised the estoppel, which the courts endeavor to satisfy. In this context, the 'equity' is an entitlement to relief at the court's discretion. But, the relief to be granted can raise issues. There may be a tension between granting the relying party the minimum equity to do justice (ie the minimum to prevent the injustice that would have resulted from the estopped party's departure from the assumption they have created) and granting what the relying party expected if the assumption had been fulfilled (expectation interest). These issues, and the courts' approaches, are discussed in the extracts from the cases below.

Giumelli v Giumelli (1999) 196 CLR 101

Facts and issues

Robert lived in a house he built on a property owned by his parents, from which they together ran an orchard business owned by his family. The parents promised that if he stayed to work the property they would subdivide it and transfer a portion including the house and orchard to Robert. On the faith of the promise, Robert stayed to work the property and gave up the opportunity to pursue a different career, including turning down an offer from his father-in-law. The relationship between Robert and his parents broke down when they disapproved of his new fiancé. The parents asked him to leave, and they refused to transfer the property to him. Robert's brother moved into the property and made improvements. Robert sued to compel the parents to transfer the property to him.

Decision

The trial judge held in favour of the parents. The Full Court of the Western Australian Supreme Court ordered that the property be transferred to Robert (ie the Court gave effect to Robert's expectation interest). The parents appealed to the High Court on the ground that the relief (transfer of property) granted by the Supreme Court went beyond the reversal of the detriment suffered by Robert (ie beyond the reliance interest). The High Court held that Robert was entitled to payment by the parents of a sum representing the present value of the promised lot, taking into account all considerations for which allowance should be made in calculating that sum so as to do equity between the parties to the action, as well as all relevant third parties.

Per Gleeson CJ, McHugh, Gummow and Callinan JJ at 111:

> This is an appeal from the Full Court of the Supreme Court of Western Australia. The Full Court (Rowland, Franklyn and Ipp JJ) allowed an appeal by the present respondent from a judgment entered by a judge of that Court (R D Nicholson J) and dismissed a cross-appeal by the present appellants. The Full Court granted a declaration that the appellants hold the whole of the land…'the Dwellingup property' upon trust and that, since May 1986, they have held the Dwellingup property upon trust to convey to the respondent what is presently an unsubdivided portion thereof, identified as 'the Promised Lot'. The appellants were ordered to do all things reasonably necessary to subdivide the Dwellingup property so as to create the Promised Lot, including the obtaining of State Planning Commission approval.
>
> […]
>
> [125] However, the appellants correctly challenge the Full Court order on other grounds. Before making an order designed to bring about a conveyance of the Promised Lot to the respondent, the Full Court was obliged to consider all the circumstances of the case. These circumstances included the still pending partnership action, the improvements to the Promised Lot by family members other than Robert, both before and after his residency there, the breakdown in family relationships and the continued residence on the Promised Lot of Steven [Robert's brother] and his family. It will be recalled that Steven is a party to the partnership action but not to the present action.
>
> When these matters are taken into account, it is apparent that the order made by the Full Court reflected what in *Verwayen* was described as the prima facie entitlement of Robert. However, qualification was necessary both to avoid injustice to others, particularly Steven and his family, and to avoid relief which went beyond what was required for conscientious conduct by Mr and Mrs Giumelli. The result points inexorably to relief expressed not in terms of acquisition of title to land but in a money sum…
>
> Whilst the holding of the Full Court with respect to the third promise should be upheld, the Full Court erred in the measure of relief which it granted in respect of the Promised Lot. This is a case for the fixing of a money sum to represent the value of the equitable claim of the respondent to the Promised Lot… The amount so ascertained, with interest, should be charged upon the whole of the Dwellingup property. There will be no requirement of a subdivision of the Promised Lot as part of the remedy.

Kirby J delivered a judgment in which he agreed with the plurality, 'that the equitable relief proper to all of the circumstances of the case was the provision to Mr Robert Giumelli of a money sum rather than the conveyance to him of the "Promised lot".'

Sidhu v Van Dyke (2014) 251 CLR 505

Facts and issue

In *Sidhu v Van Dyke,* above (**7.2** at p 220), Sidhu's second broad submission (in addition to his appeal on the ground of onus of proof of detrimental reliance) was that the Court of Appeal erred in ordering the payment of equitable compensation measured by reference to the value of the appellant's promises. Sidhu argued that his assurances were conditional upon the subdivision of the property and the consent of his wife, and contended that the Court of Appeal should have limited the relief granted to the respondent to what was necessary to compensate the respondent for the loss she suffered by relying on his promises. Extract of the High Court's decision on this issue is as below.

Decision

Per French CJ, Kiefel, Bell and Keane JJ at 528:

> **The measure of relief**
>
> In *Waltons Stores (Interstate) Ltd v Maher*, Brennan J said:
>
>> The protection which equity extends is analogous to the protection given by estoppel in pais to which Dixon J referred in *Grundt v Great Boulder*, ie, protection against the detriment which would flow from a party's change of position if the assumption (or expectation) that led to it were deserted.
>
> [529] In *The Commonwealth v Verwayen*, Deane J noted that:
>
>> There could be circumstances in which the potential damage to an allegedly estopped party was disproportionately greater than any detriment which would be sustained by the other party to an extent that good conscience could not reasonably be seen as precluding a departure from the assumed state of affairs if adequate compensation were made or offered by the allegedly estopped party for any detriment sustained by the other party.
>
> If the respondent had been induced to make a relatively small, readily quantifiable monetary outlay on the faith of the appellant's assurances, then it might not be unconscionable for the appellant to resile from his promises to the respondent on condition that he reimburse her for her outlay. But this case is one to which the observations of Nettle JA in *Donis v Donis* are apposite:[530]
>
>> [H]ere, the detriment suffered is of a kind and extent that involves life-changing decisions with irreversible consequences of a profoundly personal nature ... beyond the measure of money and such that the equity raised by the promisor's conduct can only be accounted for by substantial fulfilment of the assumption upon which the respondent's actions were based.
>
> ... There may be cases where '[i]t would be wholly inequitable and unjust to insist upon a disproportionate making good of the relevant assumption'; but in the circumstances of the present case, as in *Giumelli v Giumelli*, justice between the parties will not be done by a remedy the value of which falls short of holding the appellant to his promises. While it is true to say that 'the court, as a court of conscience, goes no further than is necessary to prevent unconscionable conduct', where the unconscionable conduct consists of resiling from a promise or

assurance which has induced conduct to the other party's detriment, the relief which is necessary in this sense is usually that which reflects the value of the promise.

In the circumstances of the present case, no reason has been identified by the appellant to conclude that good conscience does not require that the appellant be held to his promises. In particular, it is no answer for the appellant to say that the performance of his promises was conditional on the completion of the subdivision and the consent of his wife to the transfer to the respondent. His assurances to the respondent were expressed categorically so as to leave no room for doubt that he would ensure that the subdivision would proceed and that the consent of the appellant's wife would be forthcoming.

Conclusion and order

For the foregoing reasons, the decision of the Court of Appeal was correct.

The appeal should be dismissed with costs.

QUESTIONS

(1) According to the two cases extracted, what principles govern the measure of relief granted when equitable estoppel is established?

(2) Consider the reliefs granted by the High Court in *Giumelli v Giumelli* and *Sidhu v Van Dyke*. Are they consistent?

(3) Should the courts grant expectation interest in all situations where equitable estoppel is established?

7.4 International perspectives

7.4.1 *CISG*

The *CISG*, where applicable to international commercial sales (see **25.4.1**), does not provide remedies for situations where a contract has never been formed. However, a general principle underpinning the *CISG* is *venire contra factum proprium* (see **25.5.3**), which precludes inconsistent conduct by parties, especially where the mistaken party has relied upon their earlier conduct. This general principle is derived from provisions which demonstrate that the *CISG* aims to protect reliance interests, such as art 16(2)(b) which precludes revocation of an offer which has been reasonably relied upon by the offeree, and art 29(2) which precludes reliance on a 'no oral modification clause' where the party seeking to rely on the clause has acted inconsistently with it, such conduct having been relied upon by the other party. On these grounds, parties will be precluded from altering their position.

7.4.2 UNIDROIT Principles

Where applicable (see **25.4.3**), the UNIDROIT Principles go a step further, expressly stating the prohibition on inconsistent behavior in a separate provision:

UNIDROIT Principles art 1.8 (Inconsistent behaviour)

A party cannot act inconsistently with an understanding it has caused the other party to have and upon which that other party reasonably has acted in reliance to its detriment.

7.5 Review

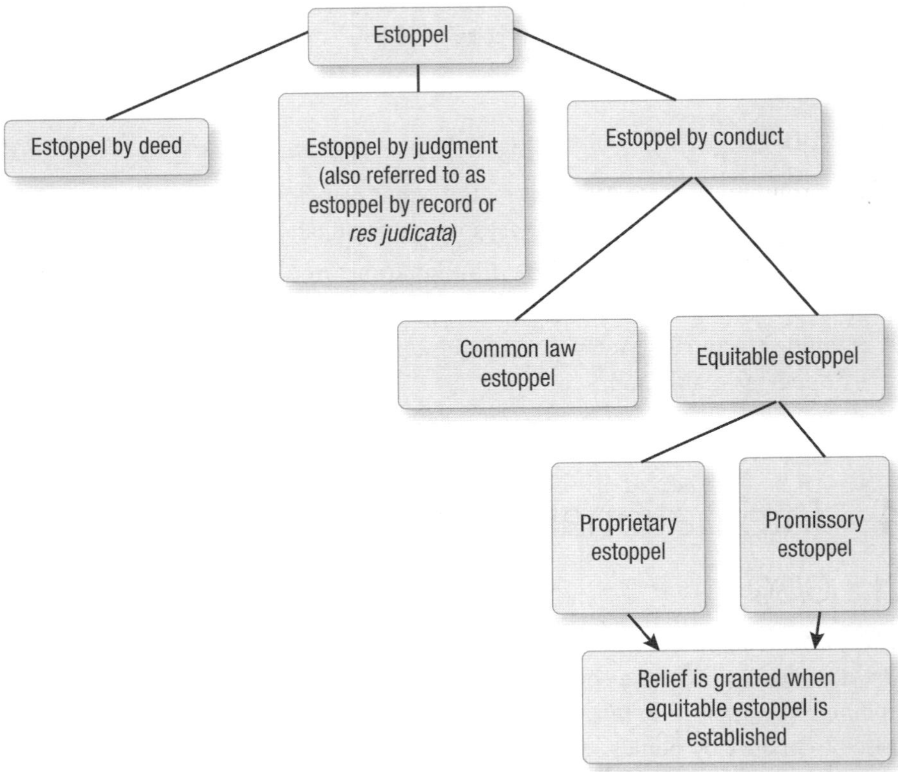

- Estoppel precludes unconscientious departure from an assumption a party has created.
- Estoppel may be used in many different ways. For instance, it can be used to:
  - circumvent the problems caused by the doctrine of privity (see **Chapter 8**)
  - enforce a promise not formally incorporated into a contract (see **Chapters 9** and **18**)
  - enforce variation of a contract not supported by consideration, and therefore unenforceable at common law (see **Chapter 13**)
  - prevent another party from terminating a contract they have indication they will not terminate (see **16.1**)
  - circumvent problems with writing requirements for certain contracts

  - prevent a party from treating a contract as continuing when they appear to have terminated it (see **16.1**)
  - enforce a gratuitous promise (see **Chapter 5**)
  - hold a person to an assurance that they will agree to a contract, despite the contract never actually being formed.
- Common law estoppel (sometime referred to as estoppel *in pais*) operates only upon assumptions or representations that relate to matters of existing fact (see *Principles* text at 7.02).
- Equitable estoppel (comprising proprietary estoppel and promissory estoppel) applies to representation as to future conduct. When established, its effect is to raise an equity in favour of the party seeking estoppel.
- In *Waltons Stores v Maher*, a majority of the High Court brought together proprietary and promissory estoppel, in what is now often referred to as a unified doctrine of equitable estoppel.
- When estoppel is established, the courts grant relief.

TIPS FOR APPLYING THE LAW IN PRACTICE

- Remember the object of estoppel, which is to preclude (estop) unconscientious departure by a party from an assumption created by that party.
- Note that a change of mind or renege on a promise does not necessarily trigger estoppel; it must be unconscionable in the circumstances for the party to renege.
- Keep in mind the importance of detriment (suffered or likely to be suffered) by the party seeking estoppel.

PROBLEM QUESTIONS

(1) Jim's wife, Susan, died. Jim and his mother-in-law (Joan) had discussions about Susan's burial.

Joan offered one of two adjoining plots she owns at Prestige Cemetery (with licences to bury two bodies in each plot) for the burial of her daughter. She promised to transfer the burial licence to Jim so that he could be buried with his wife when he died (and Joan, upon her death, was to be buried in the other plot with her late mother who was buried there, as her late husband had been cremated).

Susan was buried in the plot. A year after Susan was buried, Jim married Tanya.

Joan changed her mind and refused to transfer the burial licence to Jim.

Advise Jim as to whether estoppel will apply to preclude Joan from resiling from her promise to transfer the plot to him.

(Note: the facts are based on *Vosnakis v Arfaras* (2016) NSWCA 65)

(2) Phil has been admiring Daniel's car for some time. Daniel offers to sell the car to Phil for $15,000. Phil tells Daniel that he (Phil) will need to sell his own car to be able to buy Daniel's car, as he does not have $15,000 in savings. Phil asks Daniel to give him one week within which he would sell his car 'even if for dirt cheap' so he can top-up to by Daniel's car. Daniel tells Phil he will leave the offer open for one week. Phil advertises his car immediately, and tells Daniel. Two days later, Thomas sees Phil's advert, and calls Phil and arranges to inspect Phil's car. Thomas comes the following day to inspect Phil's car and buys it. Shortly after that, and before Phil could communicate his acceptance to Daniel, Phil receives a text message from Daniel that reads: 'Hi Phil, sorry to disappoint, but I have changed my mind about the car. I am no longer selling, so I have withdrawn my offer.'

Phil is devastated, as he has already sold his car to Thomas cheaply, and he now has no car. Will estoppel apply against Daniel?

(3) Superb Consult International Ltd (Superb) and Rutley International Ltd (Rutley) entered into an agreement under which Superb negotiated on behalf of, and assisted, Rutley to acquire the master franchise for Australia of Healthy Foods International, a popular international fast food chain known for serving healthy foods. Under the agreement, Rutley is to pay to Superb a commission on 'sales by Rutley International Ltd' of products to Healthy Foods International stores (clause 3). Clause 3 of the Letter of Agreement between Superb and Rutley provided:

> **(3)** One of the primary goals of negotiations with Healthy Foods International is to establish RUTLEY INTERNATIONAL LTD, or an associated entity, as a supplier of ingredients and other products to Healthy Foods International Master Franchisees or Healthy Foods International stores in Australia and in other countries. For all sales by RUTLEY INTERNATIONAL LTD to Healthy Foods International Master Franchisees and/or Healthy Foods International stores in Australia and in other countries, Superb Consult International Ltd shall receive a commission of 5% of the ex-factory price. The commission shall be calculated and paid, by RUTLEY INTERNATIONAL LTD, to Superb Consult International Ltd quarterly.

In the first three quarters after the deal, Rutley made the following payments to Superb in commissions: $150,000 (in Q1); $200,000 (in Q2); and $235,000 (in Q3).

The owners and directors of Rutley then incorporated another company, Smart Arc International Ltd (Smart Arc), and arranged for all supplies to Healthy Foods to be made by Smart Arc. Subsequently, Rutley payed made no commission payments to Superb, arguing that it no longer made any sales to Healthy Foods, and that commissions were only payable on sales by Rutley to Healthy Foods.

Would estoppel apply in this case?

RESEARCH QUESTIONS

(1) In *Saleh v Romanous* (2010) 79 NSWLR 453, Handley AJA held (at 462 [74]) that promissory estoppel is a 'restraint on the enforcement of rights, and thus, unlike a proprietary estoppel, must be negative in substance.'

What are the implications of this view? Is this view the correct position in Australia?

(2) Read the arguments, and the court's judgment, on estoppel in *Crown v Cosmopolitan Hotel* [2016] HCA 26. Do you think there was a case for estoppel in this case?

8

THE PARTIES TO A CONTRACT

8.1 Overview

A valid contract, once formed, confers rights and obligations on the *parties to the contract* (ie the persons (or organisations) who agree to be bound by the contract). At common law, only parties to a contract are able to enforce their rights under the contract or be burdened by (ie incur obligations under) the contract. A person who is not a party to a contract (ie a *third party*) cannot enforce a right purported to be conferred on them by a contract or be obligated to perform a burden purported to be imposed by a contract. Thus, in enforcing contracts, issues arise as to whether a person is a party (ie privy) to a contract. This chapter discusses the law regarding parties, particularly:

- identification of parties;
- issues that arise when benefits are conferred on third parties;
- avoidance of the privity rule through agency arrangements;
- circumvention of the privity rule through principles such as trust, unjust enrichment, estoppel, and claims in tort;
- statutory reform of the privity rule in various jurisdictions in Australia and overseas, and the situation under international contract laws.

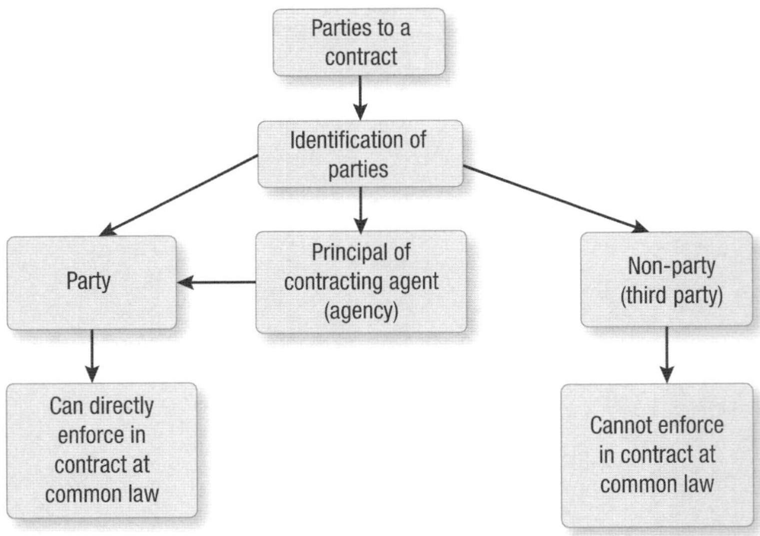

8.2 Identifying the parties

At common law, only parties to a contract can enforce rights under the contract or be burdened by (ie incur obligations under) the contract. A person who is not a party to a contract (ie a *third party*) cannot enforce benefits (rights) conferred on them by the contract or be obligated to perform a burden purported to be imposed by a contract. Consequently, sometimes the need arises to identify who the parties are. The High Court case of *Coulls v Bagot's Executor and Trustee* (1967) 119 CLR 460, extracted below, is a leading case on this issue in Australian law.

Concept	Short explanation	Relevant authorities	*Principles* text*
Due the privity rule, identification of parties to a contract becomes necessary	At common law, the privity rule specifies that only a party to a contract can enforce a right under the contract or be burdened by obligations under a contract. Consequently, it sometimes become necessary to identify the parties to a contract for the purposes of enforcement	*Coulls v Bagot's Executor and Trustee Co Ltd* (1967) 119 CLR 460	Chapter 8: 8.01, 8.05

* Consult the corresponding section(s) of the *Principles* text for more detail.

Coulls v Bagot's Executor and Trustee Co Ltd (1967) 119 CLR 460

Facts and issues

An agreement was signed in January 1959 granting to O'Neil Construction Pty Ltd (the company) a right to quarry and remove stone from a property owned by Arthur Coulls. Relevant terms of the agreement were as follows:

> **Agreement between Arthur Leopold Coulls and O'Neil Construction Proprietary Limited.**
>
> In consideration of the sum of 5 pounds, I Arthur Leopold Coulls, Anstey's Hill, Highbury East, give to O'Neil Construction Proprietary Ltd. the sole right to quarry and remove stone from an area of approximately 50 acres (fifty acres) situated around blue dolomite hill ... The approximate 50 acres is detailed in attached map ...
>
> O'Neil Construction Proprietary Ltd. agrees to pay at the rate of 3d. per ton for all stone quarried and sold, also a fixed minimum royalty of 12 pounds per week for a period of ten (10) years ...
>
> I authorise the above Company to pay all money connected with this agreement to my wife, Doris Sophia Coulls and myself, Arthur Leopold Coulls as joint tenants (or tenants-in-common?) (the one which goes to living partner).
>
> This agreement is effective from A. L. Coulls
> July 1st 1959 L. O'Neil
> D. S. Coulls.

The agreement was signed by Authur Coulls, Doris Coulls (Authur's wife) and L. O'Neil (on behalf of the company). Some years later, Mr Coulls died. The question arose as to whether Mrs Coulls or the deceased's estate was entitled to the royalties which accrued after Mr Coulls' death.

Decision

By a majority (Taylor and Owen JJ, and McTiernan J; Barwick CJ and Windeyer J, dissenting) the court held that Mrs Coulls was not a party to the contract.

Per McTiernan J at 482:

> Because Mrs. Coulls signed the document it is argued that she, as well as her husband, are parties to the agreement ... to pay the royalties to them jointly till one dies and then to pay them

to the survivor ... I am of opinion that this argument is contrary to the whole tenor of the document. The first part of it purports to be a transaction only between A. L. Coulls and the company. The words of the document including its heading 'Agreement between Arthur Leopold Coulls and O'Neil Construction Proprietary [483] Limited' countervail against the inference that Mrs. Coulls is a party, sought to be drawn from the fact that she signed it ...

I am of opinion that the correct view of the first part of the document is that it is a contract to which the only parties are A. L. Coulls and the company; and it is implied in the contract that the company is liable to pay to A. L. Coulls the royalties stipulated ... Accordingly, I hold that the provisions of the document do not impose on the company a contractual obligation to pay to Mrs. Coulls any royalty which accrues due from it after the death of the testator or at all.

Taylor and Owen JJ at 484:

We have said that the agreement was made between the testator and the company but there is a question whether the last named respondent was also a party ... [486] We observe first of all that there is nothing whatever in the contract apart from the last paragraph upon which a conclusion could be based that she was a party to the contract. On the contrary the contract purports expressly to be one made between Arthur Leopold Coulls and O'Neil Construction Pty. Ltd. It is the testator alone who engaged to give to the company the sole right to quarry and remove stone from the land described ... On its part the company agrees with the testator to pay royalties at the rates specified. But it is said that the only promise to pay royalties made by the company is that contained in the last paragraph and that this is a promise to pay 'all money connected with this agreement' [487] to the testator and his wife jointly during their lives and, after the death of one of them, to the survivor. In our view, however, this is not the effect of that paragraph; there was no express promise by the company to pay royalties to the wife nor is it possible to imply such a promise. One cannot doubt, of course, that the testator intended that the royalties should be paid to his wife after his death if she should survive him but it seems to us that the method which he chose to carry this intention into effect miscarried in spite of the fact that his wife's signature appears at the foot of the contract following those of the testator and L. O'Neil for the company. The evidence showed that the contract had been written out by the testator's wife at his request and it may have been thought that the effect of the last paragraph was to make her a party and that therefore her signature was necessary. But the mere fact that her signature appears does not make her a party; this is a question to be resolved upon a consideration of the written instrument itself. It seems to us that the terms of the last paragraph do not prescribe the persons who are to be entitled to demand and receive the royalties payable under the agreement and, therefore, do not negative the certain implication which would otherwise arise that it was the testator who was to be so entitled. On what other basis could the husband, alone, 'authorise' the survivor to receive them after the death of either himself or his wife? It is, of course, obvious that in the preparation of this informal agreement the persons concerned contemplated, and provided for, the contingency of the death of the testator or his wife during its currency and it is not without significance that, whereas the testator authorized his wife to receive the royalties payable after his death, there is no corresponding authorization by the wife in the event of her husband surviving her. We think it is clear that the only person entitled to demand royalties under the contract was the testator and that his wife was not a party to it ... We may say that we come to this conclusion with some regret since it operates to defeat what must, in the circumstances, be presumed to have been the manifest intention of the testator. In our opinion the appeal should be allowed ...

Per Windeyer J (dissenting) at 489:

When the document was executed the Watergully land belonged to the deceased. His wife had no proprietary interest in it ... [490] I think that the last clause must be read as part and parcel of a contract by which, in consideration of the grant by the deceased of the sole right to take stone

> from the land, the construction company promised to pay in the way provided. I think that the promise of the company was to pay for the stone at the rate stipulated, such payments to be made to the husband and wife jointly during their lives and thereafter to the survivor. Several factors lead me to that conclusion. The document was signed not only by the deceased and the representative of the construction company, but also by the wife. I can see no reason for her signature except upon the basis that she had an interest in the performance of the contract. It is not, I think, altogether incongruous that a contractual term as to the manner of payment should be introduced [491] by the words 'I authorise'. It was the deceased who could stipulate how his stone was to be paid for. His expression, 'I authorise', should I consider be read as equivalent to a requirement by him. It can hardly have been intended by him that an arrangement expressed to continue in favour of the survivor of himself and his wife should be destroyed if he died first. . . I therefore conclude that in the present case it was a term of the contract that, as from the death of Coulls (he having predeceased his wife), all moneys becoming due under the agreement should be payable to the respondent, Mrs. Coulls.

Barwick CJ delivered a separate, dissenting, judgment in which he held that there was privity between the company, on the one hand, and Mr and Mrs Coulls jointly on the other hand. Thus, upon the death of Mr Coulls, the promise remained on foot and enforceable by the survivor (Mrs Coulls).

QUESTIONS

(1) What were the reasons given by the majority of the Court in concluding that although Mrs Coulls signed the contract, she was not a party to the contract?

(2) What were the reasons given by the minority (dissenting judges) for their conclusion that Mrs Coulls was a party to the contract? (You may find it helpful reading Barwick CJ's judgment, which is not extracted in this casebook).

(3) All the justices based their decision on the content of the contract document, yet three justices (the majority) held that Mrs Coulls was not a party, while two justices (minority) concluded that she was a party to the contract. Which side do you find more convincing, and why?

8.3 Benefits conferred on third parties

Concept	Short explanation	Relevant authorities	*Principles* text*
The privity rule denies third-party beneficiaries under a contract the ability to directly enforce the contract	Although a contract may specifically confer benefits on a third-party (non-party) the third-party cannot enforce the contract to obtain the benefit. This is due to the common law privity rule, which specifies that only a party to contract can enforce the contract	*Trident General Insurance Co Ltd v McNiece Brothers Pty Ltd* (1988) 165 CLR 107	Chapter 8: 8.07–8.09

* Consult the corresponding section(s) of the *Principles* text for more detail.

Although a contract may confer benefits on a third party (ie non-party), the third party cannot directly enforce the contract to obtain the benefit, or a remedy, from the party who is to deliver the benefit if that party does not deliver. This is due to the common law privity rule, which holds that only a party to contract can enforce the contract. This may result in the clear intention of the parties being frustrated, sometimes leading to unjust outcomes, creating dilemma for the courts. The High Court case of *Trident General Insurance Co Ltd v McNiece Brothers Pty Ltd* (1988) 165 CLR 107, extracted below, illustrates this issue.

Trident General Insurance Co Ltd v McNiece Brothers Pty Ltd (1988) 165 CLR 107

Facts and issues

McNiece Brothers Pty Ltd ('McNiece') was a contractor for construction work being carried out at a site of Blue Circle Southern Cement Ltd ('Blue Circle'). Blue Circle had entered into a contract of insurance with Trident, in June 1977, covering the works. The insurance contract defined 'The Assured' as 'Blue Circle Southern Cement Limited, all its subsidiary, associated and related Companies, all Contractors and Sub-Contractors and/or Suppliers'. In 1979, a worker under the direction of McNiece's site engineer was seriously injured at the construction site. McNiece was found liable to pay damages to the worker. McNiece sought indemnity for the amount from Trident under the insurance policy contracted by Blue Circle. Trident denied liability on the ground that McNiece was not a party to the insurance contract. McNiece sued Trident.

The trial judge (Yeldham J) and, on appeal, the NSW Court of Appeal (McHugh JA, with whom Hope and Priestly JJA agreed) held in favour of McNiece. Trident appealed to the High Court.

Decision

The High Court held, by a majority (Mason CJ, Wilson, Toohey, Deane and Gaudron JJ; Brennan and Dawson JJ dissenting) in favour of McNiece, although for varying reasons.

Per Mason CJ and Wilson J at 110:

> This is an appeal from a unanimous decision of the New South Wales Court of Appeal (Hope, Priestley and McHugh JJ.A.) in which that court held that a third party, who was not a party to the insurance policy in question, but fell within the class of persons expressed to be insured by the policy, was indemnified in respect of an award of damages for negligence made against the third party: *Trident General Ins. v. McNiece Bros* (1987) 8 NSWLR 270. In so finding, the Court of Appeal [111] created an exception to the doctrine of privity of contract and to the requirement that consideration should move from the promisee ...
>
> [113] Trident's case in this Court is that the rules that only a party to a contract can sue on it and that consideration must move from the promisee are fundamental principles of the common law of contract ... [116] These 'fundamental' traditional rules, where they survive, have been under siege throughout the common law world. In the United Kingdom the Law Revision Committee ... recommended the abolition of the consideration rule and the privity rule ... The Committee stated that the English common law (an expression which, in the context of the Report in 1937, may be taken to include the Australian common law) was alone among modern systems of law in its insistence on the privity rule and observed that the United States had taken steps to mitigate the rigour of the rule ...

[117] Despite the criticisms and the proposals for reform, the traditional rules survive in the United Kingdom... Lord Diplock described the doctrine of privity as 'an anachronistic shortcoming that has for many years been regarded as a reproach to English private law'. And in this country, Windeyer J. reflected similar sentiments ... In Western Australia dissatisfaction with those rules has resulted in the enactment of s.11 of the *Property Law Act 1969* (WA), which confers in certain circumstances a right on a third party to sue on a contract for his benefit. In 1973 the Queensland Law Reform Commission recommended that the law be amended so as to allow that a contract conferring a benefit on a third party should be enforceable by him in his own name ... The recommendation was adopted and is expressed in s.55 of the *Property Law Act 1974* (Qld). And in New Zealand the *Contracts (Privity) Act 1982* (NZ), like the Queensland Act, allows the third party to enforce a contract made for his benefit by imposing an obligation on the promisor in favour of the third party where the parties intend that the third party should be able to enforce the provision for his benefit ...

[118] The Australian Law Reform Commission ... in its Report No. 20 on Insurance Contracts ... recommended that persons falling within the class of persons expressed by a policy to be entitled to indemnity should be able to sue on the policy... Section 48 of the *Insurance Contracts Act 1984* (Cth) gives effect to this recommendation ... [123] ... In the ultimate analysis the limited question we have to decide is whether the old rules apply to a policy of insurance. The injustice which would flow from such a result arises not only from its failure to give effect to the expressed intention of the person who takes out the insurance but also from the common intention of the parties and the circumstance that others, aware of the existence of the policy, will order their affairs accordingly... [124] ... This argument has even greater force when it is applied to an insurance against liabilities which is expressed to cover the insured and its sub-contractors. It stands to reason that many sub-contractors will assume that such an insurance is an effective indemnity in their favour and that they will refrain from making their own arrangements for insurance on that footing. That, it seems, is what happened in the present case ...

In the circumstances, notwithstanding the caution with which the Court ordinarily will review earlier authorities and the operation of long-established principle, we conclude that the principled development of the law requires that it be recognized that McNiece was entitled to succeed in the action.

Per Brennan J (dissenting) at 125:

The judgment in favour of McNiece was sustained solely on the basis that McNiece was entitled to sue on the policy in its own name and on its own behalf, the case being an exception to the doctrine of privity by which the common law limits to a promisee the right to sue to enforce a contractual promise. It was not suggested that agency, trust or estoppel availed McNiece. The facts excluded agency...The declaration by the Court of Appeal that policies of liability insurance are a common law exception to the doctrine of privity of contract and that the exception has existed for some time may come as a surprise to those who have seen no reference to such an exception in the books ...

[126] If policies of liability insurance are to be recognized as an exception to the doctrine, what are the features which might make them so? Excluding the principles of agency, trust and estoppel from consideration, what makes a 'non-party assured' who has furnished no consideration for a policy of loss insurance different from any other third party mentioned in a contract between promisor and promisee as a party who is to have the benefit of a promise? The difference suggested by McHugh J.A. was that commercial necessity, practice and widespread

> use, strengthened by analogy with modern statutes, established policies of loss insurance as exceptions to the doctrine of privity of contract. The fact that policies of loss insurance are frequently expressed to cover losses sustained by persons who are not parties to the contract and the fact that insurers ordinarily honour those contracts do not establish the kind of commercial practice that evokes the creation of a new principle of the common law . . . Nor is the argument for a judicially created exception advanced by considering modern statutory provisions. As Dawson J. points out, s.48 of the *Insurance Contracts Act 1984* (Cth) weakens rather than strengthens the proposition that a common law exception exists . . . [142] . . . In my opinion, the relief which the Court of Appeal granted to McNiece was misconceived and the appeal must be allowed.

Per Deane J at 144:

> What the Court of Appeal has held, and what McNiece has sought to maintain, is that, within the context of the general rule, a limited exception should be recognized in the field of liability insurance to enable a third party, who is specified or referred to (whether by name or otherwise) in the contract of insurance as a person to whom the insurance cover extends, to maintain a common law action against the insurer if 'the court is satisfied' that it was 'the intention of the parties' that the third party should have enforceable rights under the policy (see the judgment of Hope J.A., with which Priestley J.A. agreed, in the Court of Appeal (1987) 8 NSWLR 270, at pp.273–274) . . . Of its nature, the rule of privity operates within the confines of the law of contract. Within those confines, it neither operates to deny the validity of a promise to benefit a third party nor hinders proceedings by the promisee against the promisor for specific performance of such a contractual obligation . . .
>
> [145] If, within the confines of the law of contract, a third party who would be benefited by the performance of a contractual promise is left without redress, other principles of law operate (unhindered by the rule of privity) upon or within the context of contractual rights and obligations to avoid injustice in particular categories of case . . . If the insurer under such a policy induces, by his conduct, the third party to act to his detriment on the assumption that he is effectively indemnified under the policy, the insurer will, in an appropriate case, be estopped from denying the enforceability of such indemnity. . . . Again, if the insurer under such a policy has received the moneys payable for the promised indemnity but has then refused to indemnify the third party on the ground that the third party was not a party to the contract of insurance, the circumstances could conceivably be such as to give rise to a cause of action by the third party against the insurer founded upon principles [146] of unjust enrichment . . . It is, however, unnecessary in the present case to embark upon a detailed examination of questions of estoppel by conduct or to seek to identify what, if any, circumstances could found an action in unjust enrichment . . . The reason . . . is that it has not been suggested in the present case that Trident is estopped by its conduct from relying upon the rule of privity to deny liability to McNiece or that the circumstances are such as might arguably give rise to a right of action (in McNiece) founded on unjust enrichment.
>
> [. . .]
>
> [147] In the case of a policy of liability insurance under which the insurer agrees to indemnify both a party to the contract and others, there is no reason in principle or in common sense why the party to the contract should not hold the benefit of the insurer's promise to indemnify him on his own behalf and the benefit of the promise to indemnify others respectively upon trust for those others. Where the benefit of a contractual promise is held by the promisee as trustee for another, an action for enforcement of the promise or damages for its breach can be brought by the trustee. In such an action, the trustee can [148] recover, on behalf of the beneficiary, the

> damages sustained by the beneficiary by reason of breach. If the trustee of the promise declines to institute such proceedings, the beneficiary can bring proceedings against the promisor in his own name, joining the trustee as defendant . . .

His Honour concluded that trust would apply in this case, but noted that McNiece had not relied on trust at trial and, in the Court of Appeal, McNiece had been refused leave to amend its statement of claim to raise a claim based on trust. His Honour disagreed with the Court of Appeal on the refusal. He thought McNiece should have been allowed to raise a claim in trust and Trident given an opportunity to defend such a claim. He ultimately dismissed the appeal.

Dawson J, in dissenting, delivered a separate judgment in which he said the creation of the insurance contract exception results in the destruction of accepted principle (the privity rule). The court is neither a legislature nor a law reform agency. It would do more harm than good to attempt to reach a right result by the wrong means. He, therefore, allowed the appeal.

Toohey J, in a separate judgment, upheld the special exception to insurance contracts.

Gaudron J at 173:

> It is necessary to refer to the question of payment of premium because although I agree generally with the reasons for judgment of Mason C.J. and Wilson J., I differ from their Honours in two significant respects. It is as well to state them at the outset. In my view a promisor who has accepted an agreed consideration for a promise to benefit a third party comes under an obligation to the third party to fulfil that promise and the third party acquires a right to bring an action to secure the benefit of that promise. The right of the third party is not a right to sue on the contract: rather, it is a right independent of, but ordinarily corresponding in content and duration with, the obligation owed under the contract by the promisor to the promise . . .
>
> [174] Although the position of the third party is commonly expressed — and in my view accurately expressed — in terms of inability to sue on the contract, common understanding is that the consequence of the rules is that no obligation is owed by the promisor to the third party and no right is created in the third party to secure the benefit of the contract. For the sake of simplicity I leave out of account conduct by the promisor which may create some other recognizable obligation to the third party, or which may lead to an assumed state of affairs by reference to which their mutual rights and obligations will be determined.
>
> The source of the obligation to perform a contractual promise is the contract itself, but there is no reason in logic or in law why the existence of a contract should preclude the existence of another obligation ordinarily corresponding in content and duration with the contractual obligation, but having its source in law rather than in the contract . . . [175] . . . The obligation to make restitution and the concept of unjust enrichment are not limited to situations in which the parties stand in a contractual relationship, or would so stand but for some matter rendering the contract invalid or bringing the relationship to an end . . . [176] In my view it should now be recognized that a promisor who has accepted agreed consideration for a promise to benefit a third party is unjustly enriched at the expense of the third party to the extent that the promise is unfulfilled and the non-fulfilment does not attract proportional legal consequences . . . [177] On the basis that the appellant received the agreed consideration specified in the policy of insurance — a matter that has not been disputed — it came under an obligation to the respondent to fulfil its promise to indemnify it as provided in the policy. The respondent is entitled to maintain an action to enforce that obligation. Accordingly, the appeal should be dismissed.

QUESTIONS

(1) In their judgment (at 117), Mason CJ and Wilson J quoted Lord Diplock as having 'described the doctrine of privity as "an anachronistic shortcoming that has for many years been regarded as a reproach to English private law". And in this country [Australia], Windeyer J reflected similar sentiments.' Do you agree with these sentiments about the doctrine of privity?

(2) In the *Trident case*, who were the contracting parties and who was the third party intended to benefit from the contract of insurance? How did the privity rule present difficulties for the third party?

(3) In her judgment, Gaudron J stated (at 173), 'although I agree generally with the reasons for judgment of Mason C.J. and Wilson J., I differ from their Honours in two significant respects'. What is the difference between the reasons given by Mason CJ and Wilson J, on the one hand, and those of Gaudron J, on the other hand, in holding in favour of McNiece?

8.4 Avoiding privity through agency arrangements

Concept	Short explanation	Relevant authorities	*Principles* text*
Agency principles have been used to circumvent difficulties posed by the privity rule	An agent is a person who has power to enter into a contract on behalf of another person (the 'principal'). If an agent (A), acting on behalf of their principal (P), enters into a contract with another (B), then P is a party to the contract with B, and can enforce it	*Port Jackson Stevedoring Pty Ltd v Salmond & Spraggon (Australia) Pty Ltd (The 'New York Star')* (1978) 139 CLR 231	Chapter 8: 8.12

* Consult the corresponding section(s) of the *Principles* text for more detail.

An agent is a person who has power to enter into a contract on behalf of another person (the 'principal'). If an agent (A), acting on behalf of their principal (P), enters into a contract with another (B), then the parties to the contract are the P and B. The agent (A) may enter into the contract not only for their principal (P), but also on their own (A's) behalf too. In that case, (A), (B) and (P) would all be parties to the contract. As a party, (P) would avoid the issues with the privity rule. Thus, a person who appears to be third-party beneficiary under a contract, may be able to establish that they are a party (P) to the contract through the principle of agency, and therefore able to directly enforce the contract. But, (P) must establish that (A) was their agent, and this is where difficulties may arise. The case of *Port Jackson Stevedoring Pty Ltd v Salmond & Spraggon (Australia) Pty Ltd (The 'New York Star')* (1978) 139 CLR 231, which is extracted below, illustrates the issues.

Beyond agency, a third-party beneficiary under a contract may be able to procure the promised benefit through the use of legal principles other than contract, such as trust, unjust enrichment and estoppel.

Port Jackson Stevedoring Pty Ltd v Salmond & Spraggon (Australia) Pty Ltd (The 'New York Star') (1978) 139 CLR 231

Facts and issues

Schick Razor Company of Canada ('the consignor') shipped 37 cartons of razor blades valued at $14,684.98 from Canada to Sydney on the *New York Star*, a ship owned by Blue Star Line Ltd ('the carrier'). Blue Star Line Ltd issued a bill of lading to Schick. Schick, in turn, transmitted the bill of lading to Salmond & Spraggon (Australia) Pty Ltd ('the consignee'). The bill of lading contained contractual terms, including the following exemption and limitation clauses:

The Himalaya clause was as follows:

> (2) It is expressly agreed that no servant or agent of the Carrier (including every independent contractor from time to time employed by the Carrier) shall in any circumstances whatsoever be under any liability whatsoever to the Shipper, Consignee or Owner of the goods or to any holder of this Bill of Lading for any loss, damage or delay of whatsoever kind arising or resulting directly or indirectly from any act, neglect or default on his part while acting in the course of or in connection with his employment and, without prejudice to the generality of the foregoing provisions in this Clause, every exemption, limitation, condition and liberty herein contained and every right, exemption from liability, defence and immunity of whatsoever nature applicable to the Carrier or to which the Carrier is entitled hereunder shall also be available and shall extend to protect every such servant or agent of the Carrier acting as aforesaid and for the purpose of all the foregoing provisions of this Clause the Carrier is or shall be deemed to be acting as agent or trustee on behalf of and for the benefit of all persons who are or might be his servants or agents from time to time (including independent contractors as aforesaid) and all such persons shall to this extent be or be deemed to be parties to the contract in or evidenced by this Bill of Lading.

The time limitation clause was as follows:

> (17) In any event the Carrier and the ship shall be discharged from all liability in respect of loss or damage unless suit is brought within one year after the delivery of the goods or the date when the goods should have been delivered. Suit shall not be deemed brought until jurisdiction shall have been obtained over the Carrier and/or the ship by service.

In Sydney, the cargo was unloaded by Port Jackson Stevedoring ('PJS'), which was 49 per cent owned by the Blue Star Line. PJS commonly performed stevedoring work for Blue Star Line, and was aware of the terms of the bill of lading. PJS placed the cargo in a shed, where 33 out of 37 cartons were stolen (the four remaining cartons had been damaged in transit).

The consignee sued PJS in tort more than a year after the unloading. PJS relied on the exemption and Himalaya clauses. In the Supreme Court of New South Wales, Sheppard J held, among other things, that PJS had been negligent, but that it was entitled to the benefit of cl 17 of the bill of lading. Salmond & Spraggon appealed to the New South Wales Court of Appeal, which reversed the judgment, holding that PJS had given no consideration for the protections in the bill of lading and was therefore unable to rely on them. PJS appealed to the High Court of Australia.

In the High Court, the issues were: (1) whether PJS could rely on the limitation clause as a matter of contract ('privity' issue); and (2) whether the limitation clause covered the facts ('construction' issue).

Decision

On the privity issue, the High Court held, by a majority (Barwick CJ, Mason and Jacobs JJ) that PSJ could rely on the clauses on the basis of agency.

Per Barwick CJ at 240:

> Two questions have therefore to be dealt with: first, whether, whatever the scope of cll 2 and 17, the appellant had become a party to them and, secondly, whether the clauses included in their scope the activities of the carrier in removing consignments from the ship's tackles into store . . .
>
> Their Lordships in *The Eurymedon* adopted the dicta of Lord Reid in *Scruttons Ltd v Midland Silicones Ltd* [1962] AC 446 at 474. This adoption clearly lays down that the stevedore discharging the ship was entitled to the benefit of clauses such as cll 2 and 17 in the present bill of lading if, (1) the bill of lading made it clear that the carrier intended by its terms to protect the stevedore, (2) the carrier by the bill contracted for the stevedore's protection as well as for his own, (3) the authority of the carrier to act for the stevedore in this respect whether antecedently or by ratification was made out, and (4) that there was consideration moving from the stevedore . . .
>
> The terms of cl 2 make it abundantly clear that the carrier purported to contract with the consignor for independent contractors it might engage to handle the consignment . . .
>
> [243] As the authority of the carrier to make with the consignor an arrangement for the benefit of the appellant was made out, it cannot be doubted, in my opinion, that the carrier acted with the authority of the appellant as its agent to make an arrangement with the consignor for the protection of the appellant . . . To that arrangement there were two parties, the consignor and the appellant. By later accepting the bill the consignee became party to the arrangement with the consignor . . .
>
> [247] The relationship between the carrier and the stevedore was of long standing. The use of a bill of lading for consignments to Australia containing a Himalaya clause was well known between them. The ship's manifest would disclose to the stevedore the shipment in question and the identity of the consignor. The stevedore, in fact, removed from the ship's side into store, sorted and stacked the consignment. Charges for stacking and storing were presented to and paid by the consignee through the ship's agent. In the ordinary course, the goods would have been delivered to the consignee against presentation of the bill of lading. I would find it extremely difficult to fail to conclude in those circumstances that in stevedoring the shipment the stevedore was responding to the terms of the bill of lading, accepting both its obligations and seeking the benefit of its restrictions.

Per Mason and Jacobs JJ at 269:

> By accepting the bill of lading and asking for delivery of the goods, the consignee is entitled to the benefit of, and bound by, its stipulation as against the carrier . . . Moreover, in certain circumstances it has been held that the stevedore, notwithstanding that he is not a party to the

contract, will be entitled as against the consignee to the protection given to the carrier, its servants and agents (including independent contractors) by the bill of lading (*New Zealand Shipping Co Ltd v AM Satterhwaite & Co Ltd* (1978) 18 ALR 333 at 364; *(The Eurymedon)* [1975] AC 154) . . .

It is not now disputed that the first and second conditions mentioned by Lord Reid were satisfied in this case . . . [271] The issue as to the fourth condition is not disposed of quite so easily . . . It is necessary then to examine the question of consideration . . . In our view, the Court of Appeal in the present case could and should have drawn the inference that the appellant discharged the goods in reliance on the shipper's promise or offer of which it was aware. The contract here is indistinguishable from the contract upheld by the Judicial Committee in *The Eurymedon* . . . [274] . . . Accordingly, we are unable to share the Court of Appeal's view on this aspect of the case.

QUESTIONS

(1) According to Barwick CJ, what four elements must be satisfied by a person (a seemingly third party) who claims that a party had acted as their agent?

(2) In your opinion, would it be easy (or difficult) for a seemingly third-party beneficiary to avoid the privity rule through agency?

(3) Compare the *Trident* and the *New York Star* cases. Why did McNiece not use the agency principle to avoid problems with the privity rule?

8.5 Statutory reform of the privity rule

Due to perceived difficulties caused (to third-party beneficiaries of contracts) by the privity rule, there have been legislative reform in several jurisdictions, in Australia and overseas. Some of those legislative provisions are extracted below.

8.5.1 Australia

Insurance Contracts Act 1984 (Cth) s 48

Contracts of general insurance—entitlements of third party beneficiaries

(1) A third party beneficiary under a contract of general insurance has a right to recover from the insurer, in accordance with the contract, the amount of any loss suffered by the third party beneficiary even though the third party beneficiary is not a party to the contract.

(2) Subject to the contract, the third party beneficiary:

(a) has, in relation to the third party beneficiary's claim, the same obligations to the insurer as the third party beneficiary would have if the third party beneficiary were the insured; and

(b) may discharge the insured's obligations in relation to the loss.

(3) The insurer has the same defences to an action under this section as the insurer would have in an action by the insured, including, but not limited to, defences relating to the conduct of the insured (whether the conduct occurred before or after the contract was entered into).

Property Law Act 1969 (WA) s 11

Persons taking who are not parties

(1) A person may take an immediate or other interest in land or other property, or the benefit of any condition, right of entry, covenant or agreement over or respecting land or other property, although he is not named as a party to the conveyance or other instrument that relates to the land or property.

(2) Except in the case of a conveyance or other instrument to which subsection (1) applies, where a contract expressly in its terms purports to confer a benefit directly on a person who is not named as a party to the contract, the contract is, subject to subsection (3), enforceable by that person in his own name but —

(a) all defences that would have been available to the defendant in an action or proceeding in a court of competent jurisdiction to enforce the contract had the plaintiff in the action or proceeding been named as a party to the contract, shall be so available;

(b) each person named as a party to the contract shall be joined as a party to the action or proceeding; and

(c) such defendant in the action or proceeding shall be entitled to enforce as against such plaintiff, all the obligations that in the terms of the contract are imposed on the plaintiff for the benefit of the defendant.

(3) Unless the contract referred to in subsection (2) otherwise provides, the contract may be cancelled or modified by the mutual consent of the persons named as parties thereto at any time before the person referred to in that subsection has adopted it either expressly or by conduct.

Property Law Act 1974 (Qld) s 55

Contracts for the benefit of third parties

(1) A promisor who, for a valuable consideration moving from the promisee, promises to do or to refrain from doing an act or acts for the benefit of a beneficiary shall, upon acceptance by the beneficiary, be subject to a duty enforceable by the beneficiary to perform that promise.

(2) Prior to acceptance the promisor and promisee may, without the consent of the beneficiary, vary or discharge the terms of the promise and any duty arising from it.

(3) Upon acceptance—

(a) the beneficiary shall be entitled in the beneficiary's own name to such remedies and relief as may be just and convenient for the enforcement of the duty of the promisor, and relief by way of specific performance, injunction or otherwise shall not be refused solely on the ground that, as against the promisor, the beneficiary may be a volunteer; and

(b) the beneficiary shall be bound by the promise and subject to a duty enforceable against the beneficiary in the beneficiary's own name to do or refrain from doing such act or acts (if any) as may by the terms of the promise be required of the beneficiary; and

(c) the promisor shall be entitled to such remedies and relief as may be just and convenient for the enforcement of the duty of the beneficiary; and

(d) the terms of the promise and the duty of the promisor or the beneficiary may be varied or discharged with the consent of the promisor and the beneficiary.

(4) Subject to subsection (1), any matter which would in proceedings not brought in reliance on this section render a promise void, voidable or unenforceable, whether wholly or in part, or which in proceedings (not brought in reliance on this section) to enforce a promissory duty arising from a promise is available by way of defence shall, in like manner and to the like extent, render void, voidable or unenforceable or be available by way of defence in proceedings for the enforcement of a duty to which this section gives effect.

(5) In so far as a duty to which this section gives effect may be capable of creating and creates an interest in land, such interest shall, subject to section 12, be capable of being created and of subsisting in land under any Act but subject to that Act.

(6) In this section—

'acceptance' means an assent by words or conduct communicated by or on behalf of the beneficiary to the promisor, or to some person authorised on the promisor's behalf, in the manner (if any), and within the time, specified in the promise or, if no time is specified, within a reasonable time of the promise coming to the notice of the beneficiary.

'beneficiary' means a person other than the promisor or promisee, and includes a person who, at the time of acceptance is identified and in existence, although that person may not have been identified or in existence at the time when the promise was given.

'promise' means a promise—

(a) which is or appears to be intended to be legally binding; and

(b) which creates or appears to be intended to create a duty enforceable by a beneficiary;

and includes a promise whether made by deed, or in writing, or, subject to this Act, orally, or partly in writing and partly orally.

'promisee' means a person to whom a promise is made or given.

'promisor' means a person by whom a promise is made or given.

(7) Nothing in this section affects any right or remedy which exists or is available apart from this section.

(8) This section applies only to promises made after the commencement of this Act.

Law of Property Act 2000 (NT) s 56

Contracts for the benefit of third parties

(1) A promisor who, for valuable consideration moving from the promisee, promises to do or to refrain from doing an act or acts for the benefit of a beneficiary is, on acceptance by the beneficiary, subject to a duty enforceable by the beneficiary to perform that promise.

(2) Prior to acceptance by a beneficiary referred to in subsection (1), the promisor and promisee may, without the consent of the beneficiary, vary or discharge the terms of the promise and any duty arising from it.

(3) On acceptance by a beneficiary referred to in subsection (1):

(a) the beneficiary is entitled in the beneficiary's own name to the remedies and relief that are just and convenient for the enforcement of the duty of the promisor and relief by way of specific performance, injunction or otherwise is not to be refused only on the ground that, as against the promisor, the beneficiary may be a volunteer;

(b) the beneficiary is bound by the promise and subject to a duty enforceable against the beneficiary in the beneficiary's own name to do or refrain from doing any act that is required of the beneficiary by the terms of the promise;

(c) the promisor is entitled to the remedies and relief that are just and convenient for the enforcement of the duty of the beneficiary; and

(d) the terms of the promise and the duty of the promisor or the beneficiary may be varied or discharged with the consent of the promisor and the beneficiary.

(4) Subject to subsection (1), a matter that, in proceedings not brought in reliance on this section:

(a) would render a promise void, voidable or unenforceable, whether wholly or in part; or

(b) is available by way of defence to enforce a promissory duty arising from a promise,

renders the promise void, voidable or unenforceable or is available by way of defence to enforce the promissory duty in like manner and to the like extent as if in proceedings for the enforcement of a duty to which this section gives effect.

(5) To the extent that a duty to which this section gives effect may be capable of creating and creates an interest in land, the interest is, subject to section 11, capable of being created and of subsisting in land under an Act (but subject to that Act).

(6) In this section:

'acceptance' means an assent by words or conduct communicated by or on behalf of the beneficiary to the promisor, or to some person authorised on the promisor's behalf, in the manner (if any) and within the time specified in the promise or, if no time is specified, within a reasonable time of the promise coming to the notice of the beneficiary.

'beneficiary' means a person who is not the promisor or promisee and includes a person who, at the time of acceptance of a promise is identified and in existence although that person may not have been identified or in existence when the promise was made or given.

'promise' means a promise in writing that:

(a) is or appears to be intended to be legally binding; and

(b) creates or appears to be intended to create a duty enforceable by a beneficiary.

'promisee' means a person to whom a promise is made or given.

'promisor' means a person by whom a promise is made or given.

(7) Nothing in this section affects any right or remedy that exists or is available apart from this section.

(8) This section applies only to promises made after the commencement of this Act.

8.5.2 Overseas

Contracts (Rights of Third Parties) Act 1999 (UK) s 1

Right of third party to enforce contractual term.

(1) Subject to the provisions of this Act, a person who is not a party to a contract (a 'third party') may in his own right enforce a term of the contract if—

(a) the contract expressly provides that he may, or

(b) subject to subsection (2), the term purports to confer a benefit on him.

(2) Subsection (1)(b) does not apply if on a proper construction of the contract it appears that the parties did not intend the term to be enforceable by the third party.

(3) The third party must be expressly identified in the contract by name, as a member of a class or as answering a particular description but need not be in existence when the contract is entered into.

(4) This section does not confer a right on a third party to enforce a term of a contract otherwise than subject to and in accordance with any other relevant terms of the contract. For the purpose of exercising his right to enforce a term of the contract, there shall be available to the third party any remedy that would have been available to him in an action for breach of contract if he had been a party to the contract (and the rules relating to damages, injunctions, specific performance and other relief shall apply accordingly).

(5) Where a term of a contract excludes or limits liability in relation to any matter references in this Act to the third party enforcing the term shall be construed as references to his availing himself of the exclusion or limitation.

(6) In this Act, in relation to a term of a contract which is enforceable by a third party—

'the promisor' means the party to the contract against whom the term is enforceable by the third party, and

'the promisee' means the party to the contract by whom the term is enforceable against the promisor.

Contracts (Privity) Act 1982 (NZ) s 4

Deeds or contracts for the benefit of third parties

Where a promise contained in a deed or contract confers, or purports to confer, a benefit on a person, designated by name, description, or reference to a class, who is not a party to the deed or contract (whether or not the person is in existence at the time when the deed or contract is made), the promisor shall be under an obligation, enforceable at the suit of that person, to perform that promise:

provided that this section shall not apply to a promise which, on the proper construction of the deed or contract, is not intended to create, in respect of the benefit, an obligation enforceable at the suit of that person.

QUESTIONS

(1) Are the legislative reforms to the common law privity doctrine, in the jurisdictions where a reform has been implemented, necessary?

(2) Compare the various statutes in Australian jurisdictions reforming the common law privity doctrine. Are there differences and, or, similarities?

(3) In relation to the comparison exercise in question 2 above, if there are any differences, which provisions do you think are preferable, and why?

8.6 International perspectives

In the context of international commercial sales, the *CISG* does not contain an express provision concerning privity. However, rights and obligations within the *CISG* are expressed as belonging to 'the buyer' or 'the seller'. By contrast, for international commercial contracts governed by the UNIDROIT Principles, third-party rights are the subject of extensive provisions. Articles 5.2.1 to 5.2.5 of the UNIDROIT Principles set out the rights of third parties to enforce contracts.

8.6.1 UNIDROIT Principles

UNIDROIT Principles art 5.2.1 (Contracts in favour of third parties)

(1) The parties (the 'promisor' and the 'promisee') may confer by express or implied agreement a right on a third party (the 'beneficiary').

(2) The existence and content of the beneficiary's right against the promisor are determined by the agreement of the parties and are subject to any conditions or other limitations under the agreement.

This provision recognises third-party rights where they are expressly or implicitly conferred upon third parties by the contractual parties. However, the 'mere fact that a third party will benefit from the performance of the contract does not in itself' imply that the third party was implicitly conferred rights by the contract: UNIDROIT Principles, art 5.2.1, Comment. To enjoy these rights, the third party needs to be connected with the contract. It is not enough that a third party is the intended subsequent purchaser, donee or end user of goods or services: see UNIDROIT Principles, art 5.2.1, Comment (and examples therein).

8.7 Review

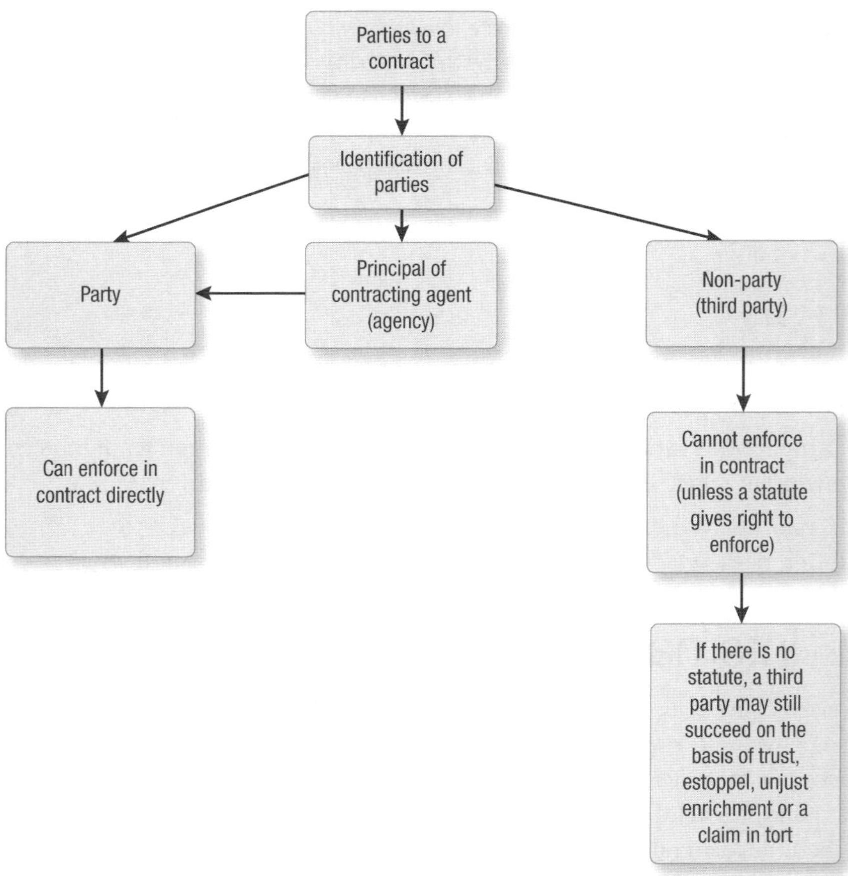

- The doctrine of privity holds that at common law only parties to a contract are able to enforce rights under the contract or be burdened by (ie incur obligations under) a contract.
- At common law, where a contract confers benefits on a third party, that third party cannot enforce the contract so as to procure the benefit or remedy if the party who is to deliver the benefit does not deliver. This is because the third party is not privy (ie is not a party) to the contract.
- A seemingly third party may be able to prove that they are a party to the contract through agency if they can establish someone (who may or may not themselves be a party to the contract) acted on their behalf as their agents.
- If agency cannot be established, a third party may still be able to enforce the contract through non-contract principles, such as trust, unjust enrichment and estoppel.
- Some jurisdictions have enacted legislation to override the common law doctrine of privity to enable third-party beneficiaries to directly enforce contracts in appropriate circumstances.

TIPS FOR APPLYING THE LAW IN PRACTICE

- Remember the effect of the doctrine of privity.
- Where a contract between two or more parties confer a benefit (or impose a burden) on a third party, consider the role of agency.
- Note that, beyond agency, third-party beneficiaries may be able to procure the benefits confered on them under a contract through non-contract principles, such as trust, unjust enrichment and estoppel.

PROBLEM QUESTIONS

(1) Son (S) pays Painter (P) $3,200 for P to paint the house of Son's Mother (M). P does not do the painting.

M seeks your advice as to whether she can directly enforce P's contractual obligation to paint. If M cannot enforce in contract, are there other principles by which the obligation may be enforced or remedy obtained against P?

For questions 2 and 3, consider the common facts below, and the further facts given under each of the questions. Advise Paul in respect of each of the scenarios below. Each scenario is independent of the other, and no scenario follows on from any other.

Common facts

Paul owns a building comprising eight apartments. Superb Appliances Ltd ('Superb') is a company that supplies and, if requested, installs appliances in homes. Wishing to refurbish some of his apartments, Paul approaches Superb to supply and install ovens and reverse-cycle air conditioners in five of the apartments. Superb agrees, and the two sign a contract. Clauses 10 and 11 of the contract provide:

> Clause 10: Superb Appliances Ltd uses the services of other tradespeople, contractors and subcontractors. Superb Appliances Ltd shall be deemed to be acting as agent of any tradesperson, contractor and subcontractor whose services Superb uses from time to time, and any such tradespersons whose services it uses in fulfilling this contract.

Clause 11: Neither Superb Appliances Ltd nor any tradesperson, contractor or subcontractor whose services Superb uses is liable for any damage caused by any appliance or equipment supplied and/or fitted or installed.

(2) Superb supplies the agreed ovens and air conditioners and procured the services of Sparky Ltd, the electrical company Superb regularly uses, to install the appliances. A week later, one of the ovens explodes due to a defect in electrical wiring during installation. The explosion damages existing walls, cabinets and other appliances in the kitchen area.

When Paul complains to Superb, he is referred to clauses 10 and 11 of the contract. Superb's representative, Dave, adds, 'We used the services of Sparky Ltd for the installation. The explosion was caused by defect in their work. We are not liable for that'.

When Paul approaches Sparky Ltd, they say they have no contract with Paul.

Paul wishes to know if he has a contractual relationship with Sparky Ltd.

(Note: Your discussion should be with regard to the privity doctrine only; ignore all other issues, including elements of contract formation.)

(3) Superb supplies the agreed ovens and air conditioners and procured the services of Sparky Ltd, the electrical company Superb regularly uses to install the appliances. A week later, one of the ovens explodes due to a defect in electrical wiring during installation. The explosion damages existing walls, cabinets and other appliances in the kitchen area.

Paul sues Sparky for the losses arising from the explosion.

Sparky is seeking to rely on Clause 11 of the contract between Paul and Superb Appliances Ltd to exempt themselves from liability.

Paul wishes to know whether Sparky can rely on the clause.

(Note: Your discussion should be with regard to the privity only; ignore all arguments that may affect Sparky Ltd's ability to rely on the clause, such as construction of exclusion clauses and the Australian Consumer Law.)

RESEARCH QUESTION

Should Australia adopt a uniform reform legislation on the doctrine of privity? If yes, why and how may that be achieved?

PART III

CONTRACTUAL OBLIGATIONS

9

TERMS AND OBLIGATIONS

9.1 Overview

Determining the enforceable promises of a contract is one of the key skills of a legal practitioner. Once questions of *formation* are resolved, the scope of the terms incorporated by the parties is key to the effective resolution of disputes. Terms are often characterised in different ways, depending on the context. In terms of incorporation, one relevant division is between *express terms* (promises explicitly considered by the parties) and *implied terms* (promises included in the contract but not expressly considered by the parties). Another division, within express terms, is whether terms are included through various methods of incorporation or via statements made before the contract is formed. Another method of classification is between *essential* and *non-essential terms*; although this issue, which flows into questions of *rights of termination*, is considered in more depth in **Chapter 16**. Another source of enforceable promises in some contracts is the *consumer guarantees* imposed by the Australian Consumer Law. This chapter examines each of these sources and classifications.

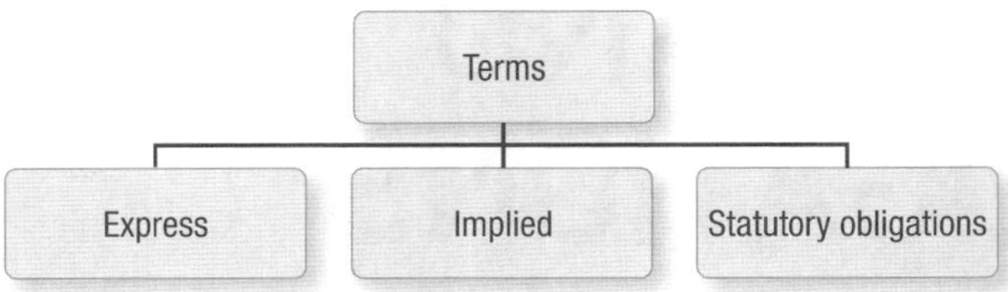

9.2 Incorporation of written terms

Concepts	Short explanation	Relevant authorities	*Principles* text*
Incorporation by signature	A signature on a written document incorporates all terms on the document in the contract, unless mitigated by fraud, misrepresentation or non est factum	*L'Estrange v F Graucob Ltd* [1934] 2 KB 394 *Toll (FGCT) v Alphapharm* (2004) 219 CLR 165 (see **10.2.1** for extract) *Curtis v Chemical Cleaning and Dyeing Co* [1951] 1 KB 805 *eBay International AG v Creative Festival Entertainment Pty Ltd* (2006) 170 FCR 450	Chapter 9: 9.04–9.05
Reasonable notice	A term is incorporated into a contract if reasonable notice is provided by the party proffering the term	*Parker v South Eastern Railway Co* (1877) 2 CPD 416 *Oceanic Sun Line Special Shipping Co Inc v Fay* (1988) 165 CLR 197 *Thornton v Shoe Lane Parking Ltd* [1971] 2 QB 163	Chapter 9: 9.06–9.07

Concepts	Short explanation	Relevant authorities	*Principles* text*
	Onerous or unusual terms may require additional steps to be taken	*Baltic Shipping Co v Dillon ('Mikhail Lermontov')* (1991) 22 NSWLR 1 *Interfoto Picture Library Ltd v Stiletto Visual Programmes Ltd* [1989] QB 433	
Other incorporation methods	A term may be incorporated into a contract through a prior course of dealing or by direct reference. Courts also retain a power to rectify contracts	*Henry Kendall & Sons v William Lillico & Sons Ltd* [1969] 2 AC 31	Chapter 9: 9.08–9.10 Chapter 18: 18.43–18.44

* Consult the corresponding section(s) of the *Principles* text for more detail.

9.2.1 Types of incorporation

In general, there are three forms of incorporation pursued by parties: signed acceptance, reasonable notice, and a prior course of dealing. Each of these forms is explained below.

9.2.2 Signed acceptance

A traditional form of incorporation is by signature, which is a compelling approach with a fairly high degree of certainty. The effect of a signature, and some early views on how to overcome that signature, was established in *L'Estrange v Graucob*. An application of this principle in a modern Australian context can be seen in *Toll v Alphapharm*. The limitations on incorporation of signature are examined in *Curtis v Chemical Cleaning and Dyeing*. All three cases are extracted below.

L'Estrange v F Graucob Ltd [1943] 2 KB 394

Facts and issues

L'Estrange, a café owner, intended to purchase an 'automatic cigarette slot machine' (a mechanical cigarette dispenser) for her business. Graucob, the manufacturer of the machine, presented L'Estrange with a brown-coloured form, which L'Estrange was asked to sign. The form, which was titled 'Sales Agreement', had several clauses printed on it, albeit in small writing, one of which was:

> This agreement contains all the terms and conditions under which I agree to purchase the machine specified above, and any express or implied condition, statement, or warranty, statutory or otherwise not stated herein is hereby excluded.

L'Estrange signed the form, although she did not read its contents. Payment was by way of a deposit then monthly payments for the next 18 months. The machine was duly delivered and installed but broke down regularly and was largely unreliable. L'Estrange sought to return the machine after two months of failed operation, terminate the contract, and reclaim some of the funds already paid. Graucob counter-sued for the balance of the purchase price.

The issue was whether the contract contained an implied warranty that the machine was fit for purpose or had such a warranty been excluded by the terms printed on the order form and incorporated into the contract by L'Estrange's signature.

At trial, both claims were upheld as L'Estrange was entitled to claim damages for breach of the implied warranty and Graucob was entitled to the remainder of the unpaid purchase price. Graucob appealed.

Decision

Appeal allowed: the incorporation of the printed terms by signature was effective.

Per Scrutton LJ at 402:

> The main question raised in the present case is whether that clause formed part of the contract. If it did, it clearly excluded any condition or warranty.
>
> In the course of the argument in the county court reference was made to the railway passenger and cloak-room ticket cases... The present case is not a ticket case, and it is distinguishable from the ticket cases. In *Parker v. South Eastern Ry. Co.* (1877) 2 CPD 416, Mellish L.J. laid down in a few sentences the law which is [403] applicable to this case. He there said: 'In an ordinary case, where an action is brought on a written agreement which is signed by the defendant, the agreement is proved by proving his signature, and, in the absence of fraud, it is wholly immaterial that he has not read the agreement and does not know its contents.' Having said that, he goes on to deal with the ticket cases, where there is no signature to the contractual document, the document being simply handed by the one party to the other: 'The parties may, however, reduce their agreement into writing, so that the writing constitutes the sole evidence of the agreement, without signing it; but in that case there must be evidence independently of the agreement itself to prove that the defendant has assented to it. In that case, also, if it is proved that the defendant has assented to the writing constituting the agreement between the parties, it is, in the absence of fraud, immaterial that the defendant had not read the agreement and did not know its contents.' In cases in which the contract is contained in a railway ticket or other unsigned document, it is necessary to prove that an alleged party was aware, or ought to have been aware, of its terms and conditions. These cases have no application when the document has been signed. When a document containing contractual terms is signed, then, in the absence of fraud, or, I will add, misrepresentation, the party signing it is bound, and it is wholly immaterial whether he has read the document or not.
>
> The plaintiff contended at the trial that she was induced by misrepresentation to sign the contract without knowing its terms, and that on that ground they are not binding upon her. The learned judge in his judgment makes no mention of that contention of the plaintiff, and he pronounces no finding as to the alleged misrepresentation. There is a further difficulty. Fraud is not mentioned in the pleadings, and I strongly object to deal with allegations of fraud where fraud is not expressly pleaded. I have read the evidence with care, and it contains no material upon which fraud [404] could be found. The plaintiff no doubt alleged that the defendants' agent represented to her that the document which was given her to be signed was an order

form, but according to the defendants' evidence no such statement was made to her by the agent. Moreover, whether the plaintiff was or was not told that the document was an order form, it was in fact an order form, and an order form is a contractual document. It may be either an acceptance or a proposal which may be accepted, but it always contains some contractual terms. There is no evidence that the plaintiff was induced to sign the contract by misrepresentation.

In this case the plaintiff has signed a document headed 'Sales Agreement,' which she admits had to do with an intended purchase, and which contained a clause excluding all conditions and warranties. That being so, the plaintiff, having put her signature to the document and not having been induced to do so by any fraud or misrepresentation, cannot be heard to say that she is not bound by the terms of the document because she has not read them.

... If the view which I have expressed as to the effect of a signed document is correct, the plaintiff has no ground of claim, and the judgment in her favour cannot stand. In my opinion, the judgment for [405] the plaintiff on the claim should be set aside and judgment entered for the defendants on the claim; and the judgment for the defendants on the counterclaim should stand.

Per Maugham LJ at 405:

I regret the decision to which I have come, but I am bound by legal rules and cannot decide the case on other considerations.

The material question is whether or not there was a contract in writing between the plaintiff and the defendants in the terms contained in the brown paper document. In the case of a formal contract between seller and buyer, such as a deed, there is a presumption which puts it beyond doubt that the parties intended that the document should contain the terms of their contract. The brown paper document is not a formal instrument of that character, yet, in my opinion, having been signed it may well constitute a contract in writing.

[...]

In the present case on February 7, 1933, an order form, for such I consider the brown paper document to be, was signed by the plaintiff. It was an elaborate form containing a number of clauses, and among them certain terms and conditions in regrettably small print but quite legible. The plaintiff having signed that document gave it to a canvasser of the defendants, who took it away. It had been filled up in ink by the canvasser before she signed it. Another document called an order confirmation dated February 9, 1933, was sent to her by the defendants. In my opinion the contract was concluded not when the brown order form was signed by the plaintiff but when the order confirmation was signed by the defendants. If the document signed by the plaintiff was a part of a contract in writing, it is impossible [406] to pick out certain clauses from it and ignore them as not binding on the plaintiff.

... I deal with this case on the footing that when the order confirmation was signed by the defendants confirming the order form which had been signed by the plaintiff, there was then a signed contract in writing between the parties. If that is so, then, subject to certain contingencies, there is no doubt that it was wholly immaterial whether the plaintiff read the small print or not. There can be no dispute as to the soundness in law of the statement of Mellish L.J. in *Parker v. South Eastern Ry. Co*, which has been read by my learned brother, to the effect that where a party has signed a written agreement it is immaterial to the question of his liability under it that he has not read it and does not know its contents. That is true in any case in which the agreement is held to be an agreement in writing ...

[407] In this case it is, in my view, an irrelevant circumstance that the plaintiff did not read, or hear of, the parts of the sales document which are in small print, and that document should

> have effect according to its terms. I may add, however, that I could wish that the contract had been in a simpler and more usual form. It is unfortunate that the important clause excluding conditions and warranties is in such small print. I also think that the order confirmation form should have contained an express statement to the effect that it was exclusive of all conditions and warranties.
>
> I agree that the appeal should be allowed.

Curtis v Chemical Cleaning and Dyeing Co [1951] 1 KB 805

Facts and issues

Curtis took her white satin wedding dress to Chemical Cleaning and Dyeing for cleaning. The shop assistant handed her a document titled 'Receipt' and asked Curtis to sign it. Curtis asked why her signature was required and the shop assistant replied that the document included a clause that limited liability for damage to beads and sequins, which were on the dress. The document actually contained a clause that stated, 'This or these articles is accepted on condition that the company is not liable for any damage howsoever arising, or delay'. Curtis signed the document and handed over her dress. When Curtis returned to collect the dress, there was a significant stain on the dress.

Curtis sued for damages on the basis of negligence by Chemical Cleaning and Dyeing, who attempted to rely on the exclusion clause on the document to avoid liability. At trial, Curtis succeeded. Chemical Cleaning and Dyeing appealed.

The issue was whether the exclusion clause could be relied on as it had been incorporated in the contract by signature or was there a misrepresentation that denied reliance on the exclusion clause?

Decision

Appeal dismissed: the innocent misrepresentation by the shop assistant vitiated the effect of the signature.

Per Somervell LJ at 808:

> . . . What was conveyed to the plaintiff, in my view, was that there were certain risks, in this case beads and sequins, which the defendants were not prepared to accept. She was asked to sign this document and she thought that its purpose was to exempt them from liability for beads and sequins, and that alone. That, I think, plainly is a misrepresentation. The words on the document purported to exempt them from all liability, howsoever arising. In those circumstances, I think, owing to that misrepresentation, this exception never became part of the contract between the parties. Mr. Lawrence [counsel for Chemical Cleaning and Dyeing] did comment on the fact that there was no finding in terms that the plaintiff was induced to sign by the misrepresentation, but I think that the note of her evidence makes it clear that she was so induced. On her evidence, which the county court judge clearly accepted, she asked why she had to sign the document. Obviously the answer which she received was what induced her to sign it.
>
> For these reasons I think that this appeal must be dismissed.

Per Denning LJ at 808:

> This case is of importance because of the many cases nowadays when people sign printed forms without reading them, only to find afterwards that they contain stringent clauses

exempting the other side from their common-law liabilities. In every such case it must be remembered that, if a person wishes to exempt himself from a liability which the common law imposes on him, he can only do it by an express stipulation brought home to the party affected, and assented to by him as part of the contract: ... If the party affected signs a written document, knowing it to be a contract which governs the relations between them, his signature is irrefragable evidence of his assent to the whole contract, including the exempting clauses, unless the signature is shown to be obtained by fraud or misrepresentation: *L'Estrange v. Graucob*. But what is a sufficient misrepresentation for this purpose? That is the point which Mr. Geoffrey Lawrence has raised in this appeal.

In my opinion any behaviour, by words or conduct, is sufficient to be a misrepresentation if it is such as to mislead the other party about the existence or extent of the exemption. If it conveys a false impression, that is enough. If the false impression [809] is created knowingly, it is a fraudulent misrepresentation; if it is created unwittingly, it is an innocent misrepresentation; but either is sufficient to disentitle the creator of it to the benefit of the exemption. In *Rex v. Kylsant (Lord)* [1932] 1 KB 442 it was held that a representation might be literally true but practically false, not because of what it said, but because of what it left unsaid; in short, because of what it implied. This is as true of an innocent misrepresentation as it is of a fraudulent misrepresentation. When one party puts forward a printed form for signature, failure by him to draw attention to the existence or extent of the exemption clause may in some circumstances convey the impression that there is no exemption at all, or at any rate not so wide an exemption as that which is in fact contained in the document. The present case is a good illustration. The customer said in evidence: 'When I was asked to sign the document I asked why? The assistant said I was to accept any responsibility for damage to beads and sequins. I did not read it all before I signed it'. In those circumstances, by failing to draw attention to the width of the exemption clause, the assistant created the false impression that the exemption only related to the beads and sequins, and that it did not extend to the material of which the dress was made. It was done perfectly innocently, but nevertheless a false impression was created. It was ... a sufficient misrepresentation to disentitle the cleaners from relying on the exemption, except in regard to beads and sequins.

In the present case the customer knew, from what the assistant said, that the document contained conditions. If nothing was said she might not have known it. In that case the document might reasonably be understood to be, like a boot repairer's receipt, only a voucher for the customer to produce when collecting the goods, and not understood to contain conditions exempting the cleaners from their common-law liability for negligence. In that case it would not protect the cleaners: see *Chapelton v. Barry Urban District Council* [1949] 1 KB 532. I say this because I do not wish it to be supposed that the cleaners would have been better off if the assistant had simply handed over the document to the customer without asking her to sign it; or if the customer were not so inquiring as the plaintiff, but were an unsuspecting person who signed whatever she was asked without question. In those circumstances the conduct of the cleaners might well be such that it conveyed the impression that the document contained no conditions, or, at any rate, no condition [810] exempting them from their common-law liability, in which case they could not rely on it.

The second point made by Mr. Geoffrey Lawrence was that, even if there was an innocent misrepresentation, the plaintiff cannot in point of law avoid the terms of the contract. He said that an innocent misrepresentation gives no right to damages but only to rescission; that rescission was not possible because the contract was executed; and that in any case rescission was of no use to the plaintiff because, once rescission has taken place, there would be no contract to sue upon. That is an attractive argument, but I do not think that it is right.

> One answer to it is that an executed contract can in a proper case be rescinded for innocent misrepresentation; and if this contract was rescinded the plaintiff could sue in tort for negligence, because the defendants, having entered upon the task of cleaning the dress, were under a duty to do it carefully. I do not pursue this, however, because I prefer to put it more simply. In my opinion when the signature to a condition, purporting to exempt a person from his common-law liabilities, is obtained by an innocent misrepresentation the party who has made that misrepresentation is disentitled to rely on the exemption. Whether you call that a rule of law or equity does not matter in these days. We have got too far beyond 1873 to trouble about distinctions of that kind. Scrutton and Maugham, L.JJ., in *L'Estrange v. Graucob* treated it as plain. I therefore agree that the appeal should be dismissed.

Singleton LJ agreed with the two other judgments. The appeal was dismissed.

9.2.3 Is electronic acceptance a signature?

Despite the ubiquity of electronic or online contracting, such as by purchasing items online, the legal significance of clicking 'I accept' is ambiguous. The issue is whether such a click is the functional and legal equivalent of a signature (such that any terms on the website or online form are incorporated into the contract) or whether other rules of incorporation may apply (such as in relation to reasonable notice). There have been surprisingly few cases on this issue but one such case is *eBay v Creative Festival Entertainment*, which examined several different scenarios.

eBay International AG v Creative Festival Entertainment Pty Ltd (2006) 170 FCR 450

Facts and issues

eBay, an online marketplace, provided a market for members to on-sell tickets originally sold by Creative Festival Entertainment to a music festival (the Big Day Out) organised by Creative Festival Entertainment. Tickets were sold by Creative Festival Entertainment by several means. As part of an anti-scalping strategy, Creative Festival Entertainment relied on a clause that 'prohibited' re-selling through online market sites (cl 6).

eBay argued that the clause was actually a misrepresentation (false statement of fact) that was actionable under the (now) Australian Consumer Law s 18 (then *Trade Practices Act 1974* (Cth) s 51A). The issue was whether the clause was a term of the contract or, if not, an actionable misrepresentation.

Decision

Claim upheld: the clause was not incorporated and was a misrepresentation.

Per Rares J at 456:

> **Principles for purchase of tickets without signature**
>
> Where a ticket or other document is intended by the issuer to contain terms of the contract such as an exemption clause or a foreign jurisdiction clause or other special condition, the issuer cannot rely on those terms unless, at the time of contract, it did all that was reasonably

necessary to bring the terms to the other party's attention: *Oceanic Sun Line Special Shipping Company Inc v Fay* (1988) 165 CLR 197 at 228-229 per Brennan J; *MacRobertson Miller Airline Services v Commissioner of State Taxation (WA)* (1975) 133 CLR 125 at 137 per Stephen J, 143 per Jacobs J; *Sydney Corporation v West* (1965) 114 CLR 481 at 485 per Barwick CJ and Taylor J; see too at 503 per Windeyer J.

In *Fay* 165 CLR at 228 Brennan J (with whom Gaudron J agreed on this contractual issue at 165 CLR at 261) considered arrangements which had been made for passengers to pay the fare in Australia for a cruise in Grecian waters. They received an exchange order in Australia that would be handed over in [457] Greece for the actual ticket. The exchange order was expressed in contractual language and reserved to the carrier the right to cancel any cruise. Brennan J considered that the contract was made when the fare was paid and that nothing in the wording of the ticket could affect the terms of the antecedent contract (165 CLR at 227). As he said, if no contract came into existence until the ticket was issued and accepted in Greece, there would be no consideration to support the carrier's right asserted in the exchange order to refuse to refund the passage money if the passenger cancelled. Brennan J referred to the consequence of forfeiture of the fare as a reason to find that (165 CLR at 228):

> The better analysis of the transaction is that the defendant was bound to issue a ticket in exchange for the exchange order in performance of a contract of carriage already made, but the defendant was given no right to introduce new conditions of carriage by printing them on the ticket. The payment of the fare may rightly be regarded as the price of an option to acquire a ticket, but the option was not to acquire a mere piece of paper. It was an option to acquire a voucher or certificate of entitlement to be carried on terms already agreed — not on terms which the parties had yet to agree on.
>
> It was too late after the original contract was made to add conditions which were not incorporated in it.

And Wilson and Toohey JJ (with whom Deane J agreed on this issue at 165 CLR at 256) said (165 CLR at 206):

> If a contract of carriage was not concluded before the respondent left Australia then it must follow that, notwithstanding that the entire passage money had been paid and that a particular cabin on a particular vessel had been allocated to him for a specified cruise and that although nothing remained for him to do except to present himself in Athens with the exchange order, the appellant came under no obligation to carry him until he did so. Such a construction of the circumstances flies in the face of common sense and cannot be accepted. When he left Australia the respondent had a contractual right to receive from the appellant on presentation of the exchange order in Athens a passage ticket which enabled him to board the vessel and occupy the specified cabin for the duration of the cruise subject only to such conditions as are found to form part of the contract.

Here, new condition 6 imposed, if it were contractual and enforceable, substantial limitations on the ability of an original purchaser or a holder of a ticket in dealing with it. Many online purchasers were given no notice of this; indeed all online purchasers of the Sydney and Gold Coast concerts knew nothing of it; and those purchasing from the Big Day Out website were informed only of old condition 6, but later received tickets with the new one. It is necessary to look at each of the 4 methods of sale to appreciate their potentially differing legal consequences . . .

Rares J then carefully detailed the procedures for buying and paying for tickets online via the 'Big Day Out' website.

[458] eBay contends that a contract in writing was made on the terms displayed on the Online Fulfilment website. eBay argues the contract was, in effect, signed electronically by the purchaser through his or her clicking on the relevant buttons agreeing to the terms and conditions, making payment and receiving the webpage and email confirmations of the order. On this analysis the contract was signed and completed after the payment and nominated purchaser details were accepted. The terms of the signed contract were those set out in the webpages detailing the terms and conditions in accordance with *Toll (FGCT) Pty Limited v Alphapharm Pty Limited* (2004) 219 CLR 165.

eBay argues that, objectively, a reasonable person in the position of the parties would have concluded that terms and conditions upon which the ticket was sold to the purchaser were those repeated five times throughout the process on the different webpages. These incorporated old condition 6. The ticket that was delivered in consequence of a transaction occurring online before 8 November 2006, however, contained new condition 6 which eBay says can have no contractual force or effect because it had been added without agreement after the contract was made. Thus, eBay says, in addition to the other inaccuracies it claims, the ticket in such cases is misleading because of its different terms and it conveys a false representation that new condition 6 is a part of the contract.

Creative contends that new condition 6 is merely a statement in different language to the same force and effect of old condition 6 and has no difference in substance.

I find that the contract for purchase of tickets made on the Big Day Out website before the wording of old condition 6 was changed, occurred on terms that included the old condition 6 and did not include new condition 6. Since all the tickets for the Sydney and Gold Coast concerts were sold prior to the change [459] in wording, it must follow that the 30,000 sold in this way from the Sydney concert and the 20,000 tickets sold for the Gold Coast concert contained terms which included old condition 6 and not new condition 6.

By sending a ticket with new condition 6, Creative represented that that was part of the contract under which the tickets were purchased and that the condition was effective as a condition of sale. That representation was in trade or commerce and was false. In particular, the ticket had the statement, which was false for online purchases from the Big Day Out website, that 'by purchasing this ticket you agree to' the inclusion of new condition 6. None of the tickets sold online by using the Big Day Out website prior to 8 November 2006 contained new condition 6. Creative was not entitled to represent to purchasers or to other persons into whose hands these tickets might come that new condition 6 had any contractual force or was at all relevant to the contract upon which the ticket had been acquired. Yet the very face of the ticket contradicted the contract which Creative had made on its website (or that of its agent, Online Fulfilment) with the purchaser.

Old condition 6 operated to confer upon Creative an election to avoid a ticket, if it were resold or transferred for profit or commercial gain. The ticket remained valid unless and until Creative acted by making its election: *Suttor v Gundowda Pty Ltd* (1950) 81 CLR 418. Moreover, old condition 6 indicated that the holder 'may be refused entry or rejected', again suggesting that Creative had first to exercise its election before that consequence would be asserted by it.

In contrast, new condition 6 is worded to operate upon the happening of an event, namely a resale for profit. On the occurrence of the event the ticket 'will be cancelled and the holder will be refused entry'. Creative says that the same contractual principles of construction apply and that the cancellation of the ticket, despite the imperative wording, is not a contractually automatic consequence of the occurrence of the event of resale for profit. That is because the purchaser is not entitled to rely upon his or her own default in adhering to the contractual requirements, but the innocent party, Creative, is entitled to elect whether to keep the contract alive and, if this is the true construction of the contract, it says that there is nothing misleading or deceptive about its use of words in new condition 6 to convey that meaning . . .

Rares J then carefully detailed the procedures for buying and paying for tickets online via the 'Ticketmaster' website.

> [463] It is common ground that during the whole of the process a purchaser from Ticketmaster online could not access any information which set out any conditions at all on the ticket or on the Big Day Out website. Thus, new condition 6 together with all the other provisions on the ticket were not communicated to the potential purchaser in the Ticketmaster online transaction. Nor was the potential purchaser given any opportunity to review or see those conditions. Nonetheless, the form of the transaction appeared to be one of a contract for purchase of the ticket which was recognised by the last two steps as having been 'just completed'. Tickets were not to be sent until late November, as the first page of the Ticketmaster online purchasing webpages stated. Thus, in the case of the Sydney concert which sold out on the day of its being first offered for sale on 13 October 2006, a purchaser would not even see the conditions sought to be imposed in the ticket itself until over six weeks after 'the transaction you have just completed' as noted on the final webpage in the series of purchase webpages. The question then arises as to whether anything on the ticket could, in those circumstances, constitute a term of the contract.
>
> [464] eBay said that the Ticketmaster online purchase was concluded when the final confirmation webpage came up, subject to the credit card and address details being valid. A purchaser could not replace or exchange the ticket or seek a refund after such a purchase. eBay's argument said that the only contract in this transaction was the one made using the online method of communication. Once that occurred, a purchaser was free to deal with the ticket as he or she saw fit. There was no notification to the purchaser that a sale by him or her in any circumstances was not permitted or would have a consequence of potential cancellation. There was no communication on Ticketmaster's website to draw to a purchaser's attention the existence of any condition such as new condition 6, nor was there any link provided for the purchaser to go to the Big Day Out webpage or any other source to find what conditions were sought to be imposed on the Big Day Out ticket that had been purchased in the transaction.
>
> Creative, on the other hand, argued that because the purchaser already had agreed to membership of Ticketmaster online and to the terms and conditions of use, the purchase policy bound the purchaser to the terms of Big Day Out's ticket. The purchase policy was said to be 'subject to, and incorporate[s] by this reference, the Terms of Use'. Thus, Creative argues that the purchaser was on notice that there will be terms on the ticket.
>
> Creative argued that there was in fact no contract formed until the ticket arrived and the purchaser had a reasonable opportunity to consider it. I am of opinion that that analysis ought not be accepted. The parties were contracting on Ticketmaster online in writing. They had to sign, albeit electronically, the terms of the purchase. They did so. The terms did not include any reference to, or ability to view, conditions now sought to be imposed on the ticket.
>
> The Ticketmaster online purchase was a contract in writing signed by the parties. By clicking on the relevant buttons and, by the computer bringing up all terms needed to purchase a ticket, on behalf of Ticketmaster as agent for Creative, the whole transaction was in writing, signed and agreed by the parties. A reasonable person in the position of the parties would have regarded the transaction completed on Ticketmasters' webpage as the contract: *Toll (FCGT) Pty Limited v Alphapharm Pty Limited* (2004) 219 CLR 165.
>
> When the purchaser received the ticket, the terms themselves precluded any opportunity to seek a refund (see condition of sale 3) because he or she was informed that tickets would not be exchanged or replaced, nor money refunded 'after purchase'. That is, the very transaction which had been confirmed by the series of webpages and the confirmation email generated by a Ticketmaster online transaction, could not be undone if the conditions of sale were part of the transaction. Creative's argument is similar to that rejected by Wilson, Toohey, Brennan and Gaudron JJ in *Fay* 165 CLR at 206, 228, 261. I reject it.

Because these conditions were not brought to the attention of the purchaser and were not available to the purchaser, perhaps for more than six weeks after the transaction was effected and the purchaser paid the price, I am of opinion that it is quite unrealistic to regard this ordinary consumer transaction as one in which the purchaser would have been free to return the ticket thereafter and receive a refund. The ordinary reasonable member of the public would be confronted with a representation on the reverse side of the ticket that the contract denied him or her the ability to return the ticket or get a refund on ascertaining that the conditions were unsatisfactory.

I am of opinion that condition of sale 3 is calculated to convey to a person [465] who bought online from Ticketmaster that the transaction was completed online at the time of the webpage transactions. It follows that it did not contain any terms on the ticket. The vague and general reference in Ticketmaster's purchaser policy to terms being on tickets, cannot substitute for the necessity to draw specifically to someone's attention unusual or significant terms affecting the proposed relationship, if it is sought to claim that the contract contains those terms. This is the more so when a term like new condition 6 is not otherwise available to a purchaser and their attention is not directed to it clearly or, as in this case, at all.

In *Thornton v Shoe Lane Parking Ltd* [1971] 2 QB 163 at 170D, Lord Denning MR gave his well known example of the need for a prominent prompt such as a red hand pointing to an exemption clause, which would draw a purchaser's attention to it. If the Ticketmaster online contract was entered into in writing on the webpages, it is impossible to incorporate the terms on the ticket by reference because the purchasers are told that the ticket would be sent to them some time later. Thus, in the case of the many thousands of people who purchased tickets through Ticketmaster online on 13 October 2006 for the Sydney concert, the tickets would only be sent to them over six weeks later in circumstances where there was no suggestion on Ticketmaster's webpages that there would be any contractual restriction on the capacity of a purchaser to sell the ticket.

Creative argued that the purchaser could somehow return the ticket if, when it was ultimately received, it contained terms that were not to the purchaser's satisfaction. I am of opinion that this is unrealistic. Creative for its own commercial purposes offered facilities to the public for instantaneous online ticket sales including through the Ticketmaster web facility. If Creative wanted to impose a condition of contract in the Ticketmaster online sales such as is in the old or new condition 6, it had to bring notice of such a condition to the attention of the purchaser online at the time of the purchase (*Fay* 165 CLR at 206, 228, 261).

Creative intends to sell over 220,000 tickets at $120 each, thereby generating revenue in the order of about $26 million. It is not unreasonable to expect it to get its contractual documents (including those online) right if it wants to rely on terms that have strict and perhaps drastic consequences for freedom of contract of purchasers from it. I am of opinion that a reasonable person considering the steps to purchase from Ticketmaster online would have considered them to amount to a contract between the purchaser and Creative, through the agency of Ticketmaster on the terms and conditions that were then and there available online. There was no incorporation by reference of provisions on the ticket.

Rares J then described the procedures for buying and paying for tickets 'over the counter' at a Ticketmaster office, which included noting 'There were some conditions posted on a notice on the back wall of Ticketmaster offices behind the counter which may have been too small to read.'

[466] Creative argued that when the purchaser was handed the ticket at the end of the over the counter sale he or she could review it and, if dissatisfied return it claiming a refund. The reality of the transaction is that the customer will have paid cash or had his or her credit card debited prior to the ticket being handed to him or her. The ticket itself contains a provision stating that no refunds would be made after purchase (condition of sale 3). And, there was nothing to draw particular attention to the operation of new condition 6 in the posited contractual relation created

by the transaction over the counter. Condition of sale 3 is calculated to convey a representation that if a contract has been entered into, unless the purchaser at the Ticketmaster counter has the astuteness of an experienced commercial lawyer dealing with ticket cases, and can recognise the ability to return the ticket and demand a refund, and then persuade Ticketmaster to give them a refund, the ordinary person would consider that the transaction was closed.

Again, whatever be the precise contractual analysis of the position, the very terms of the conditions of sale are calculated to convey to an ordinary reasonable person reading them that they cannot get out of the conditions. Ironically, it is Creative that has argued that the purchaser can eschew the conditions it wrote and imposed on the ticket telling the purchaser that they could not get a refund. This unattractive argument has no commercial morality about it. These are consumer transactions, mainly effected with young people who are not experienced in the commercial world. Creative used its own drafting of contractual terms and the representations they convey as to the efficacy of those contractual terms to assert that the purchaser cannot get a refund. It then had senior counsel argue that, applying classical contractual analysis, the purchaser could ignore its own ticket wording because the customer in fact had a right to a refund. The argument is less than meritorious. Creative's argument makes the very words condition of sale 3 commercial nonsense (*Zhu* 218 CLR at 559 [82]). I reject the argument.

9.2.4 Reasonable notice

The concept of reasonable notice as a method of incorporation emerges from a series of English cases often called the 'ticket cases', which allowed for terms to be incorporated by being printed on a ticket, if certain requirements were fulfilled. The classic statement of those requirements is found in the case of *Parker v South Eastern Railway Co*. The notion of reasonable notice evolved from those earlier ticket cases to have an application in any situation in which a contract may arise in the absence of signature. A recent Australian statement of the relevant principles of reasonable notice is the case of *Oceanic Sun Line v Fay*, although the traditional case on point is an earlier English decision of *Thornton v Shoe Lane Parking*, both of which are extracted below.

Parker v South Eastern Railway Co (1877) 2 CPD 416

Facts and issues

Parker handed over a bag to a clerk at a cloak room operated by the South Eastern Railway Company. Parker paid two shillings and, in return, the clerk handed Parker a piece of paper with writing on it. The piece of paper, or 'ticket', contained printing on the front that indicated the opening and closing times of the cloak room and the words 'See Back'. On the back of the ticket were words purporting to exclude liability for items worth more than 10 English pounds. The bag was subsequently lost or stolen. Parker sued South Eastern Railway. At trial, a jury found in favour of Parker.

The issue was whether the directions provided by the judge to the jury were correct. The directions asked the jury to determine if Parker had taken 'reasonable steps and proper caution' to inform himself of the conditions.

Decision

Appeal upheld: jury directions were incorrect as the relevant test was misstated.

Per Mellish LJ at [420]:

The question then is, whether the plaintiff was bound by the [421] conditions contained in the ticket. In an ordinary case, where an action is brought on a written agreement which is signed by the defendant, the agreement is proved by proving his signature, and, in the absence of fraud, it is wholly immaterial that he has not read the agreement and does not know its contents. The parties may, however, reduce their agreement into writing, so that the writing constitutes the sole evidence of the agreement, without signing it; but in that case there must be evidence independently of the agreement itself to prove that the defendant has assented to it. In that case, also, if it is proved that the defendant has assented to the writing constituting the agreement between the parties, it is, in the absence of fraud, immaterial that the defendant had not read the agreement and did not know its contents. Now if in the course of making a contract one party delivers to another a paper containing writing, and the party receiving the paper knows that the paper contains conditions which the party delivering it intends to constitute the contract, I have no doubt that the party receiving the paper does, by receiving and keeping it, assent to the conditions contained in it, although he does not read them, and does not know what they are ...

[422] Now the question we have to consider is whether the railway company were entitled to assume that a person depositing luggage, [423] and receiving a ticket in such a way that he could see that some writing was printed on it, would understand that the writing contained the conditions of contract, and this seems to me to depend upon whether people in general would in fact, and naturally, draw that inference. The railway company, as it seems to me, must be entitled to make some assumptions respecting the person who deposits luggage with them: I think they are entitled to assume that he can read, and that he understands the English language, and that he pays such attention to what he is about as may be reasonably expected from a person in such a transaction as that of depositing luggage in a cloak-room. The railway company must, however, take mankind as they find them, and if what they do is sufficient to inform people in general that the ticket contains conditions, I think that a particular plaintiff ought not to be in a better position than other persons on account of his exceptional ignorance or stupidity or carelessness. But if what the railway company do is not sufficient to convey to the minds of people in general that the ticket contains conditions, then they have received goods on deposit without obtaining the consent of the persons depositing them to the conditions limiting their liability. I am of opinion, therefore, that the proper direction to leave to the jury in these cases is, that if the person receiving the ticket did not see or know that there was any writing on the ticket, he is not bound by the conditions; that if he knew there was writing, and knew or believed that the writing contained conditions, then he is bound by the conditions; that if he knew there was writing on the ticket, but did not know or believe that the writing contained conditions, nevertheless he would be bound, if the delivering of the ticket to him in such a manner that he could see there was writing upon it, was, in the opinion of the jury, reasonable notice that the writing contained conditions.

I have lastly to consider whether the direction of the learned judge was correct, namely, 'Was the plaintiff, under the circumstances, under any obligation, in the exercise of reasonable and proper caution, to read or to make himself aware of the condition?' I think that this direction was not strictly accurate, and was calculated to mislead the jury. The plaintiff was certainly under no obligation to read the ticket, but was entitled to leave it unread if [424] he pleased, and the question does not appear to me to direct the attention of the jury to the real question, namely, whether the railway company did what was reasonably sufficient to give the plaintiff notice of the condition.

On the whole, I am of opinion that there ought to be a new trial.

Baggallay and Bramwell LJJ, in separate judgments, came to the same conclusion as Mellish LJ on the relevant law and direction to the jury, although Bramwell LJ believed the matter could be determined on appeal and decided the case in favour of South Eastern Railway, rather than order a retrial.

Oceanic Sun Line Special Shipping Co Inc v Fay (1988) 165 CLR 197

Facts and issues

Dr Fay and his wife, who both lived in Queensland, booked a cruise of the Greek islands (with the help of Dr Fay's mother in law, Mary Rossi—a travel agent) with Oceanic Sun Line, a Greek company, via JMA Tours, which was a New South Wales-based sales agent for Oceanic Sun Line. Before completing the booking, Dr Fay was provided with an Oceanic Sun Line brochure, which noted that the cruise was subject to terms and conditions printed on the ticket and also noted that a sample ticket was available for inspection at any Sun Line office. Dr Fay stated he did not read that part of the brochure, although it was found that no such ticket was actually available for inspection at JMA Tours' office. Before final payment, Dr Fay was provided with an 'exchange order' by JMA Tours, which would be handed over in exchange for the cruise tickets when in Greece. Once in Greece, the exchange order was exchanged for a ticket, on which was printed several terms including a limitation of liability to USD$5,000 (cl 12) and an exclusive foreign jurisdiction clause, which stated that any action must be brought in the courts of Athens, Greece (cl 13). During the cruise, Dr Fay was injured when a shot gun exploded while he was trap shooting on the ship. He commenced an action in negligence against Oceanic Sun Line in the Supreme Court of New South Wales. Oceanic Sun Line applied for a 'stay' of the New South Wales proceedings; however, the application was rejected by a single judge of the Supreme Court (Yeldham J) and the appeal by Oceanic Sun Line was dismissed by majority (Glass and McHugh JJA, Kirby P in dissent). Oceanic Sun Line appealed to the High Court.

An issue was whether the contract was formed in New South Wales such that the terms printed on the ticket received in Greece were not incorporated into the ticket. This was the minor of the two issues in the case; the majority of the Court's time and reasoning were spent on a different issue—the appropriate test in Australian law to determine where a case should be litigated—the *forum non conveniens* rule, on which point the decision was by majority in favour of Fay that New South Wales was an appropriate forum. For further discussion of this, see **3.5** at p 73 (Brennan, Deane and Gaudron JJ, Wilson and Toohey JJ in dissent).

Decision

Appeal dismissed: the contract was formed in New South Wales; the terms notified after the formation of the contract cannot be incorporated by notice.

Per Brennan J at 224:

> [W]hen a clause purporting to confer exclusive jurisdiction on the courts of a foreign country to determine claims arising under or out of the performance of a contract of carriage is found in a ticket issued to a passenger who, in this country, has paid his fare for carriage on a ship, aircraft, or vehicle operated by the defendant, a preliminary question must be decided: is the clause a term of the contract of carriage? To answer that question, it is necessary to decide when the contract of carriage is made and by reference to what system of law are its terms to be ascertained. The payment of the fare is not necessarily the making of the contract: it may be a pre-payment of the consideration payable under a contract of carriage yet to be made (that is the character which the defendant's submission would assign to the payment made on the plaintiffs behalf to J.M.A. Tours in Sydney) or it may be payment of the consideration payable under a contract of carriage thereupon made (the plaintiffs submission) or it may be the

payment of the price of an option to require the carrier to carry the passenger, perhaps subject to certain conditions. . . .

[225] The first step in determining whether the contract of carriage contains the exclusive foreign jurisdiction clause set out in cl. 13 of the ticket is to determine whether the contract of carriage was [226] entered into when Mary Rossi Travel (as agent for the plaintiff) paid the plaintiffs fare to J.M.A. Tours in Sydney (as agent for the defendant). If, as the defendant submits as one limb of its argument, no contract of carriage was made in Sydney, the contract of carriage must have been made in Greece at or after the time when the ticket was issued to Mrs. Rossi as the plaintiffs agent. The defendant's submission that no contract was made in Sydney is based on the indorsement on the exchange order which reserved to Sun Line the 'right to cancel any cruise'. The reservation of that right, it is said, makes any promise of carriage illusory and thus denies the existence of a contract of carriage. In *MacRobertson Miller Airline Services v. Commissioner of State Taxation (W.A.)*, the terms printed on an airline ticket, which had been issued on payment of the fare, reserved to the carrier the right to abandon any flight, to cancel any booking and to refuse to carry the passenger. It was held that the ticket was not liable to stamp duty as an agreement or memorandum of agreement. Barwick C.J. said:

> The exemption of the ticket in this case fully occupies the whole area of possible obligation, leaving no room for the existence of a contract of carriage.

Jacobs J. also regarded the exemption clause as showing that the carrier 'undertakes no executory obligation which creates rights in an obligee'. Stephen J. did not find it necessary to reach that conclusion. The defendant submits that the exemption clause in the exchange order is comparable with the clauses in the ticket in *MacRobertson Miller.* As the exemption clause in the exchange order is significantly different from the exemption clauses in the ticket in *MacRobertson Miller,* it is not necessary to analyse the construction which Barwick C.J. and Jacobs J. placed on those clauses in that case.

The exemption endorsed on the exchange order is not so wide as to preclude the existence of any contractual obligation on the part of the defendant when the exchange order was issued. To the contrary, the exchange order contains promises to refund the fare if the cruise is cancelled and to exchange the exchange order for a 'Sun Line ticket when boarding vessel' if the cruise is to proceed. So far as appears from the terms of the exchange order, if the cruise proceeds, the passenger is contractually entitled on presentation of the exchange order to a ticket entitling him to be carried. The defendant reserves no right to cancel any ticket or booking or to refuse to carry the passenger named in the [227] exchange order if the booked cruise proceeds. True it is that cl. 3 of the Sun Line ticket purports to reserve those rights but, if the contract is made when the fare is paid, the ticket cannot alter the parties' contractual rights and obligations. If it had been intended that no contract should come into existence before the issue of the ticket 'when boarding vessel', no consideration would have moved from the defendant to support the defendant's right (as asserted in the exchange order) to refuse to refund the passage money in the event of a passenger cancelling his passage. The proposition that no contract was made when the exchange order was issued in Sydney must be rejected. Next it is necessary to determine whether the contract then made was the contract of carriage and, if so, whether it contained the exclusive foreign jurisdiction clause.

The contract made when the exchange order was issued obliged the defendant to issue a ticket in exchange for the exchange order when the passenger was boarding the vessel. A ticket containing conditions of carriage is ordinarily treated as an offer by the carrier to carry on those conditions, no contract coming into existence until the offer is accepted by the passenger. This was a ground assigned by each of the judgments in *MacRobertson Miller* for holding the ticket not to be an agreement or a memorandum of agreement. Their Honours held that there was no contract of carriage until some time after the ticket had been issued – until the time when the passenger was provided with a seat (per Barwick C.J. (96)) or when the passenger had intimated his acceptance of the ticket and its conditions or after the passing of a reasonable time during which the passenger has had a reasonable opportunity of reading the ticket and its conditions (per Stephen J. (97)) or when the passenger presents the ticket and embarks on the carriage (per Jacobs J. (98)). As Stephen J. said (99):

> The conventional analysis of the formation of contracts for the carriage of passengers in those somewhat more leisurely transactions which involve the issue of a ticket in return for payment of a fare and the subsequent performance of the contract by the act of transportation, is to regard the ticket as the offer, the contract being made upon acceptance of that offer by the passenger.

But the conventional analysis cannot be applied to a ticket which the defendant is obliged to issue in exchange for an exchange order when a passenger is boarding a vessel. It can hardly have been the parties' intention at the time when the passenger pays his fare that the ticket to be given him on boarding should be a mere offer of [228] carriage. Much less could it have been their intention that the offer might contain exemption clauses which were unknown to the passenger when the original contract was made. The arrangements contemplated at the time of the issue of the exchange order for exchanging that document for a ticket cannot reasonably support the hypothesis that when issued the ticket might be a mere offer containing exemption clauses which should bind the plaintiff only upon subsequent acceptance. Apart from the insufficiency of opportunity for the passenger who is boarding a vessel to read the conditions printed on the ticket and to elect whether to accept them, the election could be made only after travelling to Greece and obtaining the ticket, and the terms of the exchange order would require a passenger who then elected to decline the offer to forfeit the fare already paid. The better analysis of the transaction is that the defendant was bound to issue a ticket in exchange for the exchange order in performance of a contract of carriage already made, but the defendant was given no right to introduce new conditions of carriage by printing them on the ticket. The payment of the fare may rightly be regarded as the price of an option to acquire a ticket, but the option was not to acquire a mere piece of paper. It was an option to acquire a voucher or certificate of entitlement to be carried on terms already agreed – not on terms which the parties had yet to agree on.

It was too late after the original contract was made to add conditions which were not incorporated in it. The inclusion of cl. 13 on the ticket could not alter the terms of a contract already made . . . A condition printed on a ticket is ineffective to alter a contract of carriage if the ticket is issued after the contract is made . . . Perhaps the defendant expected that the contract made when the exchange order was issued would contain all the terms and conditions which, according to the brochure given to Dr Fay, were printed on 'the Passenger Ticket Contract which may be inspected at any Sun Line office'. But, as we shall see, that expectation was not fulfilled, and not simply because no copy of the Passenger Ticket Contract was available at J.M.A. Tours in Sydney.

If a passenger signs and thereby binds himself to the terms of a contract of carriage containing a clause exempting the carrier from liability for loss arising out of the carriage, it is immaterial that the passenger did not trouble to discover the contents of the contract. But where an exemption clause is contained in a ticket or other [229] document intended by the carrier to contain the terms of carriage, yet the other party is not in fact aware when the contract is made that an exemption clause is intended to be a term of the contract, the carrier cannot rely on that clause unless, at the time of the contract, the carrier had done all that was reasonably necessary to bring the exemption clause to the passenger's notice: . . . *Thornton v. Shoe Lane*

> *Parking Ltd.* (5) per Lord Denning M.R., and (6) per Megaw L.J. In differing circumstances, different steps may be needed to bring an exemption clause to a passenger's notice, especially if the clause is an unusual one. In the present case, the only step which the defendant took to bring the exclusive foreign jurisdiction clause to the plaintiffs notice before the fare was paid was the note in the brochure that the conditions of carriage were printed in the (unavailable) Passenger Ticket Contract. In *Hollingworth v. Southern Ferries Ltd. (The 'Eagle')* [1977] 2 Lloyd's Rep. 70, it was held that a mere statement in a carrier's brochure that the carrier contracted on its conditions of carriage was not enough to make those conditions terms of a contract of carriage subsequently made with an intending passenger who had read the brochure. . . . As the contract of carriage was made when the exchange order was issued and as the exclusive jurisdiction clause contained in cl. 13 of the ticket was not then known to Dr Fay and as insufficient was done to bring such a clause to his attention, that clause was not incorporated into the contract of carriage and could not subsequently be incorporated by insertion in the ticket issued pursuant to the original contract.

Brennan J then went on to discuss the *forum non conveniens* rule and found New South Wales as an appropriate forum. Gaudron J agreed with the formation and incorporation analysis of Brennan J. Wilson and Toohey JJ came to a similar conclusion to Brennan J. Deane J did not address the incorporation issue.

Thornton v Shoe Lane Parking Ltd [1971] 2 QB 163

Facts and issues

Thornton attempted to drive his car into the 'automatic' Shoe Lane Parking station, which was novel in London at the time as it was amongst the first carparks that had an 'automatic' ticket machine to control entry rather than a human attendant. Next to the entrance to the carpark was a sign that stated, 'All Cars Parked At Owner's Risk'. To enter the carpark, Thornton approached a red traffic light which then turned green, at which point a machine issued a ticket. The ticket contained writing, which included the statement, 'This ticket is issued subject to the conditions of issue as displayed on the premises.' The 'conditions of issue' were displayed on a wall opposite the 'paying office', which was not directly visible from where the ticket was issued. The displayed conditions included the following clause:

> the company shall not be responsible or liable for any loss or misdelivery of or damage of whatever kind to the customer's motor vehicle, or any articles carried therein or thereon or of or to any accessories carried thereon or therein or injury to the customer or any other person occurring when the customer's motor vehicle is in the parking building howsoever that loss, misdelivery, damage or injury shall be caused.

Thornton took the ticket, entered the car park and left his car. Upon his return, Thornton was seriously injured when placing his luggage into the car. Thornton sued Shoe Lane Parking for damages.

At trial, Thornton was successful; however, damages were reduced as Mocatta J found that Thornton was 'half' responsible for his injuries. Shoe Lane Parking appealed.

The issue was whether the displayed clauses were part of the contract and thus excluded liability for Shoe Lane Parking.

Decision

Appeal dismissed: the clauses on the display were not incorporated into the contract.

Per Denning MR at 169:

> We have been referred to the ticket cases of former times from *Parker v. South Eastern Railway Co.* (1877) 2 C.P.D. 416 to *McCutcheon v. David MacBrayne Ltd.* [1964] 1 W.L.R. 125. They were concerned with railways, steamships and cloakrooms where booking clerks issued tickets to customers who took them away without reading them. In those cases the issue of the ticket was regarded as an offer by the company. If the customer took it and retained it without objection, his act was regarded as an acceptance of the offer: see *Watkins v. Rymill* (1833) 10 Q.B.D. 178, 188 and *Thompson v. London, Midland and Scottish Railway Co.* [1930] 1 K.B. 41, 47. These cases were based on the theory that the customer, on being handed the ticket, could refuse it and decline to enter into a contract on those terms. He could ask for his money back. That theory was, of course, a fiction. No customer in a thousand ever read the conditions. If he had stopped to do so, he would have missed the train or the boat.
>
> None of those cases has any application to a ticket which is issued by an automatic machine. The customer pays his money and gets a ticket. He cannot refuse it. He cannot get his money back. He may protest to the machine, even swear at it. But it will remain unmoved. He is committed beyond recall. He was committed at the very moment when he put his money into the machine. The contract was concluded at that time. It can be translated into offer and acceptance in this way: the offer is made when the proprietor of the machine holds it out as being ready to receive the money. The acceptance takes place when the customer puts his money into the slot. The terms of the offer are contained in the notice placed on or near the machine stating what is offered for the money. The customer is bound by those terms as long as they are sufficiently brought to his notice before-hand, but not otherwise. He is not bound by the terms printed on the ticket if they differ from the notice, because the ticket comes too late. The contract has already been made: see *Olley v. Marlborough Court Ltd.* [1949] 1 K.B. 532. The ticket is no more than a voucher or receipt for the money that has been paid (as in the deckchair case, *Chapelton v. Barry Urban District Council* [1940] 1 K.B. 532) on terms which have been offered and accepted before the ticket is issued.
>
> In the present case the offer was contained in the notice at the entrance giving the charges for garaging and saying 'at owner's risk', i.e., at the risk of the owner so far as damage to the car was concerned. The offer was accepted when Mr. Thornton drove up to the entrance and, by the movement of his car, turned the light from red to green, and the ticket was thrust at him. The contract was then concluded, and it could not be altered by any words printed on the ticket itself. In particular, it could not be altered so as to exempt the company from liability for personal injury due to their negligence.
>
> Assuming, however, that an automatic machine is a booking clerk in disguise — so that the old fashioned ticket cases still apply to it. We then have to go back to the three questions put by Mellish L.J. in *Parker v. South Eastern Railway Co.,* 2 C.P.D. 416, 423, subject to this qualification: Mellish L.J. used the word 'conditions' in the plural, whereas it would be more apt to use the word 'condition' in the singular, as indeed the [170] lord justice himself did on the next page. After all, the only condition that matters for this purpose is the exempting condition. It is no use telling the customer that the ticket is issued subject to some 'conditions' or other, without more: for he may reasonably regard 'conditions' in general as merely regulatory, and not as taking away his rights, unless the exempting condition is drawn specifically to his attention. (Alternatively, if the plural 'conditions' is used, it would be better prefaced with the word 'exempting', because the exempting conditions are the only conditions that matter for this

purpose.) Telescoping the three questions, they come to this: the customer is bound by the exempting condition if he knows that the ticket is issued subject to it; or, if the company did what was reasonably sufficient to give him notice of it.

Mr. Machin [counsel for Shoe Lane Parking] admitted here that the company did not do what was reasonably sufficient to give Mr. Thornton notice of the exempting condition. That admission was properly made. I do not pause to inquire whether the exempting condition is void for unreasonableness. All I say is that it is so wide and so destructive of rights that the court should not hold any man bound by it unless it is drawn to his attention in the most explicit way. It is an instance of what I had in mind in *J. Spurling Ltd. v. Bradshaw* [1956] 1 W.L.R. 461, 466. In order to give sufficient notice, it would need to be printed in red ink with a red hand pointing to it — or something equally startling. . . I do not think the garage company can escape liability by reason of the exemption condition. I would, therefore, dismiss the appeal.

At 170, Megaw LJ adopted the approach of the ticket cases and, having considered the first two questions outlined in *Hood v Anchor Line (Henderson Bros) Ltd* [1918] AC 837 and *Parker v South Eastern Railway*, he continued with the third question from that case.

. . . In the present case what has to be sought in answer to the third question is whether the defendant company did what was reasonable fairly to bring to the notice of the plaintiff, at or before the time when the contract was made, the existence of this particular condition. This condition is that part of the clause — a few words embedded in a lengthy clause — which Lord Denning M.R. has read, by which, in the midst of provisions as to damage to property, the defendants sought to exempt themselves from liability for any personal injury suffered by the customer while he was on their premises. Be it noted that such a condition is one which involves the abrogation of the right given to a person such as the plaintiff by statute, the *Occupiers Liability Act 1957*. True, it is open under that statute for the occupier of property by a contractual term to exclude that liability. In my view, however, before it can be said that a condition of that sort, restrictive of statutory rights, has been fairly brought to the notice of a party to a contract there must be some clear indication which would lead an ordinary sensible person to realise, at or before the time of making the contract, that a term of that sort, relating to personal injury, was sought to be included. I certainly would not accept that the position has been reached today in which it is to be assumed as a matter of general knowledge, custom, practice, or whatever is the phrase that is chosen to describe it, that when one is invited to go upon the property of another for such purposes as garaging a car, a contractual term is normally included that if one suffers any injury on those premises as a result of negligence on the part of the occupiers of the premises they shall not be liable.

Even if I were wrong in the view which I take that the third question has to be posed in relation to this particular term, it would still not avail the defendants here. In my view the judge was wholly right on the evidence in the conclusion which he reached that the defendants have not taken proper or adequate steps fairly to bring to the notice of the plaintiff at or before the time when the contract was made that any special conditions were sought to be imposed.

I think it is a highly relevant factor in considering whether proper steps were taken fairly to bring that matter to the notice of the plaintiff that the first attempt to bring to his notice the intended inclusion of those conditions was at a time when as a matter of hard reality it would have been practically impossible for him to withdraw from his intended entry upon the premises for the purpose of leaving his car there. It does not take much imagination to picture the indignation of the defendants if their potential customers, having taken their tickets and observed the reference therein to contractual conditions which, they said, could be seen in notices on the premises, were one after the other to get out of their cars, leaving the cars blocking the entrances to the garage, in order to search for, find and peruse the notices! Yet unless the defendants genuinely intended that potential customers should do just that, it would be fiction, if not farce, to treat those customers as persons who have been given a fair opportunity, [174] before the contracts are made, of discovering the conditions by which they are to be bound.

I agree that this appeal should be dismissed.

Per Sir Gordon Willmer at 174:

I have reached the same conclusion, and there is very little for me to add. It seems to me that the really distinguishing feature of this case is the fact that the ticket on which reliance is placed was issued out of an automatic machine. I think it is right to say — at any rate, it is the fact so far as the cases that have been called to our attention are concerned — that in all the previous so-called 'ticket cases' the ticket has been proffered by a human hand, and there has always been at least the notional opportunity for the customer to say — if he did not like the conditions – 'I do not like your conditions: I will not have this ticket.' But in the case of a ticket which is proffered by an automatic machine there is something quite irrevocable about the process. There can be no *locus poenitentiae*. I do not propose to say any more upon the difficult question which has been raised as to the precise moment when a contract was concluded in this case; but at least it seems to me that any attempt to introduce conditions after the irrevocable step has been taken of causing the machine to operate must be doomed to failure. It may be that those who operate garages of this nature, as well as those who install other types of automatic machines, should give their attention to this problem. But it seems to me that the judge below was on the right track when he said, towards the end of his judgment, that in this sort of case, if you do desire to impose upon your customers stringent conditions such as these, the least you can do is to post a prominent notice at the entrance to the premises, warning your customers that there are conditions which will apply. So far as the rest of the case is concerned, I agree with what has been said by my Lords and do not wish to add anything further.

9.2.5 Onerous or unusual terms

Terms in written documents that might be 'onerous' or 'unusual' may require additional warnings in order to demonstrate sufficient notice for incorporation. Although the specific requirements will change from case to case, the cases of *Oceanic Sun Line* (above), *Baltic Shipping v Dillon* (below) and *Interfoto* (below) are examples of where such additional steps were not taken. As emphasised in *Curtis* (above), this requirement does not apply to signed documents.

Baltic Shipping Co v Dillon ('Mikhail Lermontov') (1991) 22 NSWLR 1

Facts and issues

Dillon was injured while a passenger on the *Mikhail Lermontov*, a ship owned by Baltic Shipping Co and registered in then-Leningrad (now St Petersburg) in the then-Soviet Union (now Russia), when the boat foundered off the New Zealand coast and sank. Dillon suffered nervous shock, physical injuries and the loss of all her luggage, including precious mementoes of her recently-deceased husband.

Dillon had agreed to a 'deed of release' with Baltic Shipping in return for a payment of $4,786, which was much less than the damage she suffered. However, some time after signing the release, Dillon commenced litigation as part of a 'test case' claiming negligence and damages that included emotional stress and disappointment. Part way through the complicated litigation, Baltic Shipping Co admitted liability but disputed aspects of the damages claimed.

In addition to relying on the deed of release, Baltic Shipping also relied on clauses printed on the ticket issued by CTC Cruises (an agent for Baltic Shipping) to Dillon, one of which (clause 26) purported to limit recovery in respect of cabin luggage and baggage to '833 units of account per passenger per carriage' and which defined 'units of account' to be 'the special drawing right as defined by the International Monetary Fund'.

At trial, Carrruthers J found for Dillon and Baltic Shipping appealed.

The issue was whether clause 26 was incorporated into the agreement (a related issue was whether the release could be challenged by other statutes and whether the damages claimed were indeed recoverable).

Decision

Appeal dismissed: the terms on the form were not incorporated into the contract.

Per Gleeson CJ at 7:

> I see no justification for disregarding the stipulation in the booking form that the contract of carriage would be made only at the time of the issue of ticket to the respondent. That has two consequences. First, it renders inapplicable what has been called the "conventional analysis" exemplified by *Hood v Anchor Line (Henderson Bros), Ltd* [1918] AC 837. Upon that analysis the issue of the ticket is only an offer, and the contract is formed when the passenger, having had an opportunity to consider the terms of the offer, accepts it. That analysis would be contrary to the terms of the appellant's own document. Equally, however, the stipulation removes the possibility of a conclusion, similar to that arrived at in *Oceanic Sun Line Special Shipping Co Inc v Fay* (where there was no such stipulation), that the contract of carriage was made when the booking form issued or the balance of fare was paid.
>
> The fact that the contract was made when the ticket issued and not, for example, after the respondent received it and had been given an opportunity [8] to read and consider its terms, is significant. It is an important aspect of those ticket cases that yield to the conventional analysis that the corollary of the proposition that a contract of carriage comes into existence only when the passenger has received the ticket and been afforded an opportunity to consider its terms is that in such circumstances it is fair to treat the carrier as having done what was reasonably necessary to bring all the terms to the attention of the passenger and to treat the passenger as bound by those terms. The same does not apply, however, where it is the issue of the ticket by the carrier, rather than the passenger's uncomplaining acceptance of it after having had an opportunity to read it, that brings the contract into existence.
>
> ... It is to be noted that the documents relating to the transaction contemplated, as occurred, that the full fare would be paid by the respondent and that subsequently the appellant would perform the act of issuing a ticket to the respondent. That is the reverse of the conventional analysis. If the transaction must be described in terms of offer and acceptance it is the payment of the full fare by the intending passenger which makes (or completes) the offer and the appellant's act of issuing the ticket which constitutes the acceptance.

> This not being a case where the passenger signed and was thereby bound by the terms of the contract of carriage, there arises the question whether, prior to or at the time of making the contract, the carrier had done all that was reasonably necessary to bring the limitation clauses to the passenger's notice and give her an opportunity to decline to contract upon those terms. I would answer that question in the negative. The contract was made either when the ticket left the appellant's office or when it was received by the respondent. I would prefer the latter view: cf *Koon Wing Lan v Calwell* (1949) 80 CLR 533 at 574. Up to that time the only information the respondent had about conditions of carriage was that contained in the booking form. In view of the subject matter and content of the relevant limitation clauses I do not regard that as adequate to bring those particular clauses to the notice of the respondent. I refer particularly to what was said by Lord Denning MR in *Thornton v Shoe Lane Parking Ltd* [1971] 2 QB 163 at 170. It may well have been sufficient notice of many of the terms and conditions of carriage to have informed the respondent (in the booking form) that there were detailed terms and conditions and that if she were interested in what they were she could inspect a form of ticket at a CTC cruise office. However, I would not regard such a statement as adequate notice of the existence of clauses significantly limiting the appellants [9] common law liability in events such as those which occurred in the present case. In my view it is the fact, and extent, rather than the precise mechanics, of the limitation that are of primary importance.
>
> Accordingly, I do not regard the limitation clauses as forming part of the contract of carriage.

Per Kirby P at 22:

> Much time at the trial and before this Court was taken in examining the sequence of events which led to the issue of the passenger ticket with its terms and conditions. The appellant asserted that those terms and conditions were incorporated in the contract between it and the respondent by which she was carried on the cruise. It was not contested that the respondent had received such a passenger ticket. Her copy went down with the 'Mikhail Lermontov'. But there was no issue about the common form in which the terms and conditions appeared. The issue was whether those terms, including the provision for limitations on liability, had been accepted by the respondent so as to be incorporated in the contract between the parties . . .
>
> [23] The 'conventional analysis' for contracts of carriage such as the present was described in the House of Lords in a Scottish appeal, in *Hood v Anchor Line (Henderson Brothers), Ltd.* In that case, the question was asked rhetorically what more the shipowner could have done to give reasonable notice to the passenger of the conditions of the proposed contract limiting the shipowner's liability: see, eg, Lord Parmoor (at 848). In the facts of that case their Lordships concluded that 'the conditions printed on the face of [24] the ticket were part of the contractual relationship between the parties and, as such, binding on the appellant'.
>
> However, there has been much development of the law since 1918 in the analysis of contractual relations such as the present arising out of shipping and airline contracts. Brandon J (as Lord Brandon was then) in *Daly v General Steam Navigation Co Ltd ('Dragon')* [1979] 1 Lloyd's Rep 257 at 262, analysed the conclusion of the contract of carriage in that case between the owners of the '*Dragon*' and the injured plaintiffs. He held that the contract of carriage was concluded at the time the booking was made and confirmed. But at that time the shippers had taken no steps of any kind to bring to the notice of the passenger the conditions on which they later sought to rely. Accordingly, his Lordship held that the conditions contained in the printed form were not part of the contract. Thus, the shipowners could not subsequently, by issuing a ticket containing the conditions, introduce such conditions into the contract when it was not subject to them originally. Once the contract was entered, it was not possible, without novation and the agreement of the passenger, to add further terms. The decision in the *Dragon*

has been referred to, with apparent approval, in the High Court of Australia in *Oceanic Sun Line Special Shipping Co Inc v Fay* (at 208, 228, 229, 256).

In the present case I am inclined to take the appellant's own form (for I believe that the CTC Cruises form can be so described) and to analyse the entry into an agreement with the passenger in the terms clearly laid down by the appellant itself. This made it plain that the booking document was not the contract of carriage. Instead, that contract would arise 'only at the time of the issuing of tickets'. At that stage, unless the passenger took certain initiatives of her own, she would have had no knowledge of, or opportunity to influence, the conditions and regulations printed on the tickets. The fact that they were available to passengers at CTC Cruises offices scarcely amounted to a sufficient compliance with the appellant's responsibility to bring unusual conditions at least to the notice of passengers such as the respondent before they would be bound by them. There were a number of unusual conditions in the subject of terms and conditions. They included (by cl 26) reference to 'units of account' and 'special drawing rights' as defined by the International Monetary Fund. They also included (by cl 27) a duty of passengers to 'observe and obey all notices and by-laws of the Soviet Ministry of Merchant Marine displayed on board the ship'. They included the limitation of liability for damage expressed not in a dollar sum (which might have been understood) but in terms of the 'units of account' which would mean nothing to the ordinary passenger. Thus the liability in respect of death or personal injury was limited to the odd sum of 46,666 units of account. The liability in respect of loss or damage to luggage was limited to 833 units of account per passenger per carriage. There were other unusual terms and conditions. Yet these are the terms and conditions which, by the express language of the agent's booking form were purportedly fixed upon the passenger 'at the time of the issuing of tickets'. The passenger would have no knowledge of precisely when that time would come about. He or she would have no effective say in the terms then purportedly imposed. In answer to the rhetorical question of Lord Parmoor, I would say that there was more, before the time fixed, that the carrier could have done to bring [25] the unusual provisions at least to the notice of the passenger. At the very least it could have drawn to attention, on its booking form, the fact of the limitation of liability for personal injury and damage to luggage. By doing so it would alert passengers to the obligation to make their own, adequate arrangements. This was not done.

The result is that, applying what I take to be the approach sanctioned by the High Court in *Oceanic Sun Line Special Shipping Inc v Fay*, the contract of carriage here came into force at the time appointed and notified in the booking form. Yet at that time the respondent had not had a reasonable opportunity to see and agree to the terms and conditions which the appellant sought subsequently to impose upon her by the delivery of the passenger ticket. Once the contract was made, it was not open, without fresh agreement, for further terms and conditions to be imposed by the unilateral action of one contracting party. Thus the mere presentation by the appellant to the respondent of the passenger ticket with its terms and conditions would not fix the respondent with acceptance of those terms and conditions, simply because thereafter she began the cruise. She was entitled, in law, to take the view that she would be issued with a ticket which would contain no unusual provisions, specifically no provisions of which she was not on notice limiting the appellant's liability to her. She was entitled to regard the subsequent purported imposition of such conditions upon her by unilateral acts of the appellant as wholly ineffective. Almost certainly, the respondent gave no thought to these matters. It is probably only bored lawyers or travel executives who, in the solitude of a ship or airline cabin, actually read the fine print of terms and conditions such as those relied upon by the appellant here.

By the foregoing analysis, the respondent is not taken by law to have accepted the terms and conditions contained in the subsequently provided passenger ticket. In the claim in respect of

> luggage (the only one said to be relevant) she is therefore not limited to the sum specified by reference to 'units of account' in cl 3(b). Thus, her entitlement to damages generally may be calculated, as Carruthers J held, without limitation imposed by the contract of carriage.

On the other issues in the case, Kirby P found the deed of release to be unjust under the *Contracts Review Act 1980* (NSW) and was therefore of no effect. Kirby P also upheld the trial judge's findings in relation to Dillon claiming a range of damages, including for loss of enjoyment. Gleeson CJ agreed that the *Contracts Review Act 1980* (NSW) applied in this case. Mahoney JA, in dissent, found the contract was finally formed when the ticket was issued and the relevant clauses were incorporated but, if the contract was formed before this point, the terms of that contract included any terms included on the ticket when issued. Mahoney JA also rejected the claim under the *Contracts Review Act 1980* (NSW).

The decision was then appealed to the High Court of Australia—(1993) 176 CLR 344—the outcome of which was that Baltic Shipping's appeal was successful, but only in relation to restitution and the quantum of damages payable. The issue of incorporation was not challenged on appeal.

Interfoto Picture Library Ltd v Stiletto Visual Programmes Ltd [1989] QB 433

Facts and issues

Stiletto, an advertising agency, sought to use photos from Interfoto, a commercial photo library, in an advertising campaign. Following a phone call between employees of the two companies, 47 photographs were sent by Interfoto to Stiletto in a 'jiffy bag'. Also in the bag was a document containing printed clauses. One of those clauses ('No. 2') stated:

> All transparencies must be returned to us within 14 days from the date of posting/delivery/collection. A holding fee of £5 plus VAT per day will be charged for each transparency which is retained by you longer than the said period of 14 days save where a copyright licence is granted or we agree a longer period in writing with you.

Stiletto held onto the photographs for an extra two weeks before returning them to Interfoto (unused, as it turns out). Interfoto invoiced Stiletto for the holding fee in clause 'No. 2', which amounted to £3,783.50. Stiletto refused to pay and Interfoto sued Stiletto for the sum. At trial, the judge found in favour of Interfoto. Stiletto appealed.

The issue was whether the clauses printed on the document in the bag were incorporated into the agreement.

Decision

Appeal allowed: the terms were not incorporated as they were unusual and onerous and further steps had to be taken to bring them to the attention of Stiletto.

Per Dillon LJ at 436:

> The sum of £3,783.50 is calculated by the plaintiffs in strict accordance with condition 2 as the fee for the retention of 47 transparencies from 19 March to 2 April 1984. It is of course important to the plaintiffs to get their transparencies back reasonably quickly, if they are not wanted, since

if a transparency is out with one customer it cannot be offered to another customer, should occasion arise. It has to be said, however, that the holding fee charged by the plaintiffs by condition 2 is extremely high, and in my view exorbitant. The judge held that on a quantum meruit a reasonable charge would have been £3.50 per transparency per week, and not £5 per day, and he had evidence before him of the terms charged by some ten other photographic libraries, most of which charged less than £3.50 per week and only one of which charged more (£4 per transparency per week). It would seem therefore that the defendants would have had a strong case for saying that condition 2 was void and unenforceable as a penalty clause; but that point was not taken in the court below or in the notice of appeal.

The primary point taken in the court below was that condition 2 was not part of the contract between the parties because the delivery note was never supplied to the defendants at all. That the judge rejected on the facts; he found that the delivery note was supplied in the same jiffy bag with the transparencies, and that finding is not challenged in this court. He made no finding however that Mr. Beeching or any other representative of the defendants read condition 2 or any of the other printed conditions, and it is overwhelmingly probable that they did not.

An alternative argument for the defendants, in this court as below, was to the effect that any contract between the parties was made before the defendants knew of the existence of the delivery note viz. either in the course of the preliminary telephone conversation between Mr. Beeching and Miss Fraser, or when the jiffy bag containing the transparencies was received in the defendants' premises but before the bag was opened. I regard these submissions as unrealistic and unarguable. The original telephone call was merely a preliminary inquiry and did not give rise to any contract. But the contract came into existence when the plaintiffs sent the transparencies to the defendants and the defendants, after opening the bag, accepted them by Mr. Beeching's phone call to the plaintiffs at 3.10 on 5 March. The question is whether condition 2 was a term of that contract.

There was never any oral discussion of terms between the parties before the contract was made. In particular there was no discussion whatever of terms in the original telephone conversation when Mr. Beeching made his preliminary inquiry. The question is therefore whether condition 2 was sufficiently brought to the defendants' attention to make it a term of the contract which was only concluded after the defendants had received, and must have known that they had received the transparencies *and* the delivery note . . .

[438] Condition 2 of these plaintiffs' conditions is in my judgment a very onerous clause. The defendants could not conceivably have known, if their attention was not drawn to the clause, that the plaintiffs were proposing to charge a 'holding fee' for the retention of the transparencies at such a very high and exorbitant rate.

At the time of the ticket cases in the last century it was notorious that people hardly ever troubled to read printed conditions on a ticket or delivery note or similar document. That remains the case now. In the intervening years the printed conditions have tended to become more and more complicated and more and more one-sided in favour of the party who is imposing them, but the other parties, if they notice that there are printed conditions at all, generally still tend to assume that such conditions are only concerned with ancillary matters of form and are not of importance. In the ticket cases the courts held that the common law required that reasonable steps be taken to draw the other parties' attention to the printed conditions or they would not be part of the contract. It is, in my judgment, a logical development of the common law into modern conditions that it should be held, as it was in [439] *Thornton v. Shoe Lane Parking Ltd.* [1971] 2 Q.B. 163, that, if one condition in a set of printed conditions is particularly onerous or unusual, the party seeking to enforce it must show that that particular condition was fairly brought to the attention of the other party.

In the present case, nothing whatever was done by the plaintiffs to draw the defendants' attention particularly to condition 2; it was merely one of four columns' width of conditions printed across the foot of the delivery note. Consequently condition 2 never, in my judgment, became part of the contract between the parties.

I would therefore allow this appeal and reduce the amount of the judgment which the judge awarded against the defendants to the amount which he would have awarded on a quantum meruit on his alternative findings, i.e. the reasonable charge of £3.50 per transparency per week for the retention of the transparencies beyond a reasonable period, which he fixed at 14 days from the date of their receipt by the defendants.

Per Bingham LJ at 439:

In many civil law systems, and perhaps in most legal systems outside the common law world, the law of obligations recognises and enforces an overriding principle that in making and carrying out contracts parties should act in good faith. This does not simply mean that they should not deceive each other, a principle which any legal system must recognise; its effect is perhaps most aptly conveyed by such metaphorical colloquialisms as 'playing fair', 'coming clean' or 'putting one's cards face upwards on the table'. It is in essence a principle of fair and open dealing. In such a forum it might, I think, be held on the facts of this case that the plaintiffs were under a duty in all fairness to draw the defendants' attention specifically to the high price payable if the transparencies were not returned in time and, when the 14 days had expired, to point out to the defendants the high cost of continued failure to return them.

English law has, characteristically, committed itself to no such overriding principle but has developed piecemeal solutions in response to demonstrated problems of unfairness. Many examples could be given. Thus equity has intervened to strike down unconscionable bargains. Parliament has stepped in to regulate the imposition of exemption clauses and the form of certain hire-purchase agreements. The common law also has made its contribution, by holding that certain classes of contract require the utmost good faith, by treating as irrecoverable what purport to be agreed estimates of damage but are in truth a disguised penalty for breach, and in many other ways.

The well known cases on sufficiency of notice are in my view properly to be read in this context. At one level they are concerned with a question of pure contractual analysis, whether one party has done enough to give the other notice of the incorporation of a term in the contract. At another level they are concerned with a somewhat different question, whether it would in all the circumstances be fair (or reasonable) to hold a party bound by any conditions or by a particular condition of an unusual and stringent nature . . .

[445] The tendency of the English authorities has, I think, been to look at the nature of the transaction in question and the character of the parties to it; to consider what notice the party alleged to be bound was given of the particular condition said to bind him; and to resolve whether in all the circumstances it is fair to hold him bound by the condition in question. This may yield a result not very different from the civil law principle of good faith, at any rate so far as the formation of the contract is concerned.

Turning to the present case, I am satisfied for reasons which Dillon L.J. has given that no contract was made on the telephone when the defendants made their initial request. I am equally satisfied that no contract was made on delivery of the transparencies to the defendants before the opening of the jiffy bag in which they were contained. Once the jiffy bag was opened and the transparencies taken out with the delivery note, it is in my judgment an inescapable inference that the defendants would have recognised the delivery note as a document of a kind likely to contain contractual terms and would have seen that there were conditions printed in small but visible lettering on the face of the document. To the extent that the conditions so displayed were common form or usual terms regularly encountered in this business, I do not think the defendants could successfully contend that they were not incorporated into the contract.

The crucial question in the case is whether the plaintiffs can be said fairly and reasonably to have brought condition 2 to the notice of the defendants. The judge made no finding on the point, but I think that it is open to this court to draw an inference from the primary findings which he did make. In my opinion the plaintiffs did not do so. They delivered 47 transparencies, which was a number the defendants had not specifically asked for. Condition 2 contained a daily rate per transparency after the initial period of 14 days many times greater than was usual or (so far as the evidence shows) heard of. For these 47 transparencies there was to be a charge for each day of delay of £235 plus value added tax. The result would be that a venial period of delay, as here, would lead to an inordinate liability. The defendants are not to be relieved of that liability because they did not read the condition, although doubtless they did not; but in my judgment they are to be relieved because the plaintiffs did not do what was necessary to draw this unreasonable and extortionate clause fairly to their attention. I would accordingly allow the defendants' appeal and substitute for the judge's award the sum which he assessed upon the alternative basis of quantum meruit.

In reaching the conclusion I have expressed I would not wish to be taken as deciding that condition 2 was not challengeable as a disguised [446] penalty clause. This point was not argued before the judge nor raised in the notice of appeal. It was accordingly not argued before us. I have accordingly felt bound to assume, somewhat reluctantly, that condition 2 would be enforceable if fully and fairly brought to the defendants' attention.

There were only two judges sitting in this appeal from the County Court to the Court of Appeal.

9.2.6 Prior course of dealing

The third ground for incorporation is conceptually clear but operationally difficult. The concept is that written terms (which are not in a signed document and for which reasonable notice has not been provided) that have been used in a regular and consistent course of dealing may have been incorporated by the parties through a form of inferred acceptance. However, notable cases in this area tend to result in there being no incorporation because the documents in which the clauses were printed were not seen to be contractual in nature (see *DJ Hill v Walter H Wright* (1971) and *La Rosa v Nudrill* (2013), cited in the *Principles* text at 9.08). However, one successful example of incorporation through prior course of dealing involves the Suffolk Agricultural Poultry Producers' Association ('SAPPA'), also known as *Henry Kendall v William Lillico* (below).

Henry Kendall & Sons v William Lillico & Sons Ltd [1969] 2 AC 31

Facts and issues

Over quite some period of time, animal feed ('meal') for the chicks of pheasants and partridges was ordered by the Suffolk Agricultural Poultry Producers' Association ('SAPPA') from Grimsdale, a supplier of such feed. The order was arranged by a phone call from SAPPA to Grimsdale, after which Grimsdale would send SAPPA a 'contract note' that recorded details of the order. On the back of the contract note were printed terms, including one that excluded liability for latent defects. The feed supplied by Grimsdale contained defects, such that a toxin introduced into the meal during the production process resulted in the death or severe stunting of the chicks.

An issue was whether the terms printed on the back of the contract note were incorporated.

This report was a 'consolidated appeal' of two cases with similar legal issues, which is why the reported case name is *Henry Kendall & Sons v William Lillico & Sons*; the 'second' case in the consolidated appeal was *Grimsdale & Sons v Suffolk Agricultural Poultry Producers' Association (SAPPA),* which is the focus of this extract and was reported in earlier proceedings as *Hardwick Game Farm v Suffolk Agricultural Poultry Producers' Association*. The consolidated appeal litigated many issues, including issues of merchantable quality. Only the discussion in relation to incorporation is extracted below.

Decision

Appeals dismissed: the terms on the 'contract note' were incorporated into the agreement. Per Lord Pearce at 112:

> ... The only matter on this point which has given rise to real difficulty is [113] the question whether Grimsdale were protected by the latent defect clause in the conditions of sale printed on the contract note which they sent to SAPPA: 'The buyer under this contract takes the responsibility of any latent defects'. The trial judge held that these printed conditions did not apply to this oral sale of meal. In so doing he relied on a dictum of Lord Devlin in *McCutcheon's case* [1964] 1 W.L.R. 125. That case was, however, different from the present case. For there was no contractual document in that case. The carrier orally accepted goods for transport without importing written conditions. On some previous dealings with the plaintiff's agent the carrier had imported conditions by a written contract. On such occasions the carrier could have relied on the ticket cases and had the benefit of the conditions, although the consignor was not aware of their extent. But since he did not import any written terms on the particular occasion in question, he could not get the benefit of unknown conditions which were not imported into the transaction. The ordinary course of business was therefore no help to the carrier, since the transaction did not follow the ordinary course. And in that case the plaintiff's agent, acting in good faith, was unaware that the carrier was intending to import written conditions.
>
> In the present case. SAPPA had regularly received more than a hundred similar contract notes from Grimsdale in the course of dealing over three years. They knew of the existence of the conditions on the back of the contract note. They never raised any query or objection. The court's task is to decide what each party to an alleged contract would reasonably conclude from the utterances, writings or conduct of the other. The question, therefore, is not what SAPPA themselves thought or knew about the matter but what they should be taken as representing to Grimsdale about it or leading Grimsdale to believe. The only reasonable inference from the regular course of dealing over so long a period is that SAPPA were evincing an acceptance of, and a readiness to be bound by, the printed conditions of whose existence they were well aware although they had not troubled to read them. Thus the general conditions became part of the oral contract.

QUESTIONS

(1) What are the implications for employers/retailers if the statements of staff can have serious legal consequences such as those in *Curtis*? What strategies must they follow to make such contractual clauses effective?

(2) To what extent does *eBay International AG v Creative Festival Entertainment Pty Ltd* blur the differences between incorporation by signature and by notice in relation to online transactions? Does this decision support the notion that 'ticks' and 'clicks' are the online equivalent of signatures?

(3) Is it appropriate to consider the financial resources of the parties when determining what is reasonable?

(4) Carparks have indeed taken up the advice of Sir Gordon Willmer in *Thornton*; what is now found at the entrance to 'modern' carparks? In what ways do these measures resolve the issues identified in this case? Are the criticisms of Megaw LJ just as valid now as at the time of the case?

(5) In what ways does the reasoning in *Interfoto* still reflect the ideas inherent in the early 'ticket cases'? Has the law relating to notice substantially changed since this time?

9.3 Treating pre-contractual statements as express terms

Concepts	Short explanation	Relevant authorities	*Principles* text*
Pre-contractual statements may be terms of the contract	A pre-contractual statement may be a term rather than a representation if there is sufficient promissory intent, as seen in the words used, context to the statement, and status of those making and hearing the statement	*Oscar Chess Ltd v Williams* [1957] 1 WLR 370 *JJ Savage & Sons Pty Ltd v Blakney* (1970) 119 CLR 435 *Dick Bentley Productions Ltd v Harold Smith (Motors) Ltd* [1965] 1 WLR 623	Chapter 9: 9.11–9.12
The parol evidence rule	The parol evidence rule may restrict the evidence available to a court if there is a written document of the contract, unless the contract is partly written and partly oral, or there is a collateral contract	*Goss v Lord Nugent* (1833) 5 B & AD 58; 110 ER 713 *Equuscorp Pty Ltd v Glengallen Investments Pty Ltd* (2004) 218 CLR 471 *State Rail Authority of New South Wales v Heath Outdoor Pty Ltd* (1986) 7 NSWLR 170 *Hoyt's Pty Ltd v Spencer* (1919) 27 CLR 133	Chapter 9: 9.13–9.14

* Consult the corresponding section(s) of the *Principles* text for more detail.

9.3.1 Determining the status of pre-contractual statements

Two issues that need to be resolved when seeking to treat pre-contractual statements as express terms are: first, whether the statements are warranties or mere representations; and second, whether the pre-contractual statements are intended to have contractual effect. Both issues are discussed below.

9.3.2 Warranty or representation?

A fundamental question when the scope of a contract's terms could include pre-contractual statements is whether such statements are *warranties* (or, more precisely 'terms') of the contract or *representations* (ie statements about the contract but not enforceable promises). The difference between the two options relates to what remedies may be available if the statement is not fulfilled or true. Traditionally, the courts seek to find whether there is promissory intent present for which the courts will consider a range of factors, including the language and context of the statements, as well as the status and knowledge of the party making the statement. These factors are present in the 'classic' cases of *Oscar Chess*, *JJ Savage* and *Dick Bentley*, all of which are extracted below.

Oscar Chess Ltd v Williams [1957] 1 WLR 370

Facts and issues

Williams was interested in acquiring a new car from Oscar Chess, a car dealer, and Williams offered his mother's car as a trade-in to partly off-set the price of the new car. Both Williams and Oscar Chess believed the traded-in car to be a 1948 Morris, which was corroborated by the car's 'registration book'. However, the registration book had been fraudulently altered by a previous (unknown) owner and the car was actually from 1939. If known at the time of the trade in, Oscar Chess would have offered a far lower price for the traded-in car (£175 instead of £290). At trial, the judge found that the statements by Williams were terms.

The issue was whether the statement by Williams that the car was a 1948 Morris was a term or a representation.

Decision

Appeal allowed: the statement was not a term of the contract.

Per Denning MR at 373:

> I entirely agree with the judge that both parties assumed that the Morris was a 1948 model and that this assumption was fundamental to the contract. But this does not prove that the representation was a term of the contract. The assumption was based by both of them on the date given in the registration book as the date of first registration. They both believed it was a 1948 model whereas it was only a 1939 one. They were both mistaken and their mistake was of fundamental importance.
>
> The effect of such a mistake is this: It does not make the contract a nullity from the beginning, but it does in some circumstances enable the contract to be set aside in equity. If the buyer had come promptly, he might have succeeded in getting the whole transaction set aside in equity on the ground of this [374] mistake: see *Solle v. Butcher* [1950] 1 K.B. 671; but he did not do so

and it is now too late for him to do it: see *Leaf v. International Galleries* [1950] 2 K.B. 86. His only remedy is in damages, and to recover these he must prove a warranty.

In saying that he must prove a warranty, I use the word 'warranty' in its ordinary English meaning to denote a binding promise. Everyone knows what a man means when he says 'I guarantee it' or 'I warrant it' or 'I give you my word on it'. He means that he binds himself to it. That is the meaning it has borne in English law for 300 years from the leading case of *Chandelor v. Lopus* (1603) Cro.Jac. 4. onwards. During the last 50 years, however, some lawyers have come to use the word 'warranty' in another sense. They use it to denote a subsidiary term in a contract as distinct from a vital term which they call a 'condition'. In so doing they depart from the ordinary meaning, not only of the word 'warranty' but also of the word 'condition'. There is no harm in their doing this, so long as they confine this technical use to its proper sphere, namely to distinguish between a vital term, the breach of which gives the right to treat the contract as at an end, and a subsidiary term which does not. But the trouble comes when one person uses the word 'warranty' in its ordinary meaning and another uses it in its technical meaning. When Holt C.J., in *Crosse v. Gardner* (1689) Carth. 90 and *Medina v. Stoughton* (1699) 1 Salk. 210, made his famous ruling that an affirmation at the time of a sale is a warranty, provided it appears on evidence to be so intended, he used the word 'warranty' in its ordinary English meaning of a binding promise: and when Lord Haldane L.C. and Lord Moulton in 1913 in *Heilbut, Symons & Co. v. Buckleton* [1913] A.C. 30, adopted his ruling, they used it likewise in its ordinary meaning. These different uses of the word seem to have been the source of confusion in the present case. The judge did not ask himself, 'Was the representation (that it was a 1948 Morris) intended to be a warranty?' He asked himself, 'Was it fundamental to the contract?' He answered it by saying that it was fundamental; and therefore it was a condition and not a warranty. By concentrating on whether it was fundamental, he seems to me to have missed the crucial point in the case which is whether it was a term of the contract at all. The crucial question is: was it a binding promise or only an innocent misrepresentation? The technical distinction between a 'condition' and a 'warranty' is quite immaterial in this case, because it is far too late for the buyer to reject the car. He can at best only claim damages. The material distinction here is between a statement which is a term of the contract and a statement which is only an innocent misrepresentation. This distinction is best expressed by the [375] ruling of Lord Holt: Was it intended as a warranty or not? using the word warranty there in its ordinary English meaning: because it gives the exact shade of meaning that is required. It is something to which a man must be taken to bind himself.

In applying Lord Holt's test, however, some misunderstanding has arisen by the use of the word 'intended'. It is sometimes supposed that the tribunal must look into the minds of the parties to see what they themselves intended. That is a mistake. Lord Moulton made it quite clear that 'The intention of the parties can only be deduced from the totality of the evidence.' The question whether a warranty was intended depends on the conduct of the parties, on their words and behaviour, rather than on their thoughts. If an intelligent bystander would reasonably infer that a warranty was intended, that will suffice. And this, when the facts are not in dispute, is a question of law. That is shown by itself, where the House of Lords upset the finding by a jury of a warranty.

It is instructive to take some recent instances to show how the courts have approached this question. When the seller states a fact which is or should be within his own knowledge and of which the buyer is ignorant, intending that the buyer should act on it, and he does so, it is easy to infer a warranty: see *Couchman v. Hill* [1947] K.B. 554, where the farmer stated that the heifer was unserved, and *Harling v. Eddy* [1951] 2 K.B. 739, where he stated that there was nothing wrong with her. So also if he makes a promise about something which is or should be within his own control: see *Birch v. Paramount Estates Ltd*. (Unreported: Oct. 2, 1956 (C.A.)), decided on October 2, 1956, in this court, where the seller stated that the house would be as good as the show house. But if the seller, when he states a fact, makes it clear that he has no knowledge of his own but has got his information elsewhere, and is merely passing it on, it is not so easy to imply a warranty. Such a case was *Routledge v. McKay* [1954] 1 W.L.R. 615, where the seller 'stated that it was a 1942 model and pointed to the corroboration found in the book', and it was held that there was no warranty.

Turning now to the present case, much depends on the precise words that were used. If the seller says 'I believe it is a 1948 Morris. Here is the registration book to prove it', there is clearly no warranty. It is a statement of belief, not a contractual promise. But if the seller says 'I guarantee that it is a 1948 Morris. This is borne out by the registration book, but you need not rely solely on that. I give you my own guarantee that it is', there is clearly a warranty. The seller is making himself contractually responsible, even though the registration book is wrong.

[376] In this case much reliance was placed by the judge on the fact that the buyer looked up Glass's Guide and paid £290 on the footing that it was a 1948 model: but that fact seems to me to be neutral. Both sides believed the car to have been made in 1948 and in that belief the buyer paid £290. That belief can be just as firmly based on the buyer's own inspection of the log-book as on a contractual warranty by the seller.

Once that fact is put on one side I ask myself: What is the proper inference from the known facts? It must have been obvious to both that the seller had himself no personal knowledge of the year when the car was made. He only became owner after a great number of changes. He must have been relying on the registration book. It is unlikely that such a person would warrant the year of manufacture. The most he would do would be to state his belief, and then produce the registration book in verification of it. In these circumstances the intelligent bystander would, I suggest, say that the seller did not intend to bind himself so as to warrant that it was a 1948 model. If the seller was asked to pledge himself to it, he would at once have said 'I cannot do that. I have only the log-book to go by, the same as you.'...

[377] One final word: It seems to me clear that the motor-dealers who bought the car relied on the year stated in the log-book. If they had wished to make sure of it, they could have checked it then and there, by taking the engine number and chassis number and writing to the makers. They did not do so at the time, but only eight months later. They are experts, and, not having made that check at the time, I do not think they should now be allowed to recover against the innocent seller who produced to them all the evidence he had, namely, the registration book. I agree that it is hard on the dealers to have paid more than the car is worth: but it would be equally hard on the seller to make him pay the difference. He would never have bought the Hillman at all unless he had got the allowance of £290 for the Morris. The best course in all these cases would be to 'shunt' the difference down the train of innocent sellers until one reaches the rogue who perpetrated the fraud: but he can rarely be traced, or if he can, he rarely has the money to pay the damages. So one is left to decide between a number of innocent people who is to bear the loss. That can only be done by applying the law about representations and warranties as we know it: and that is what I have tried to do. If the rogue can be traced, he can be sued by whomsoever has suffered the loss: but if he cannot be traced, the loss must lie where it falls. It should not be inflicted on innocent sellers, who sold the car many months, perhaps many years before, and have forgotten all about it and have conducted their affairs on the basis that the transaction was concluded. Such a seller would not be able to recollect after all this length of time the exact words he used, such as whether he said 'I believe it is a 1948 model', or 'I warrant it is a 1948 model'. The right course is to let the buyer set aside the transaction if he finds out the mistake quickly and comes promptly before other interests have irretrievably intervened; otherwise the loss must lie where it falls: and that is, I think, the course prescribed by law. I would allow this appeal accordingly.

Hodson LJ came to the same conclusion as Denning MR, on the basis that the outcome in *Routledge v McKay* was determinative of this situation. Morris LJ, in dissent, quoted extensively from the trial judge's reasoning and found no basis for overturning the trial judge's finding that the statement was a term based on the evidence.

JJ Savage & Sons Pty Ltd v Blakney (1970) 119 CLR 435

Facts and issues

Blakney sought to buy a speed boat from JJ Savage. The engine and maximum speed of the boat was an important issue for Blakney, and Blakney sought the advice of JJ Savage on a range of possible options. A letter from JJ Savage indicated that a particular engine would achieve an 'estimated maximum speed of 15 miles per hour'; however, the actual order did not indicate a maximum speed for the engine ordered. When delivered, the boat failed to achieve this speed. Blakney sued for breach of contract. At trial, the judge found the statement in the letter was merely a representation, not a term. On appeal, the Full Court of the Victorian Supreme Court agreed but found the statement was a collateral warranty, for which damages could be sought. Blakney appealed to the High Court.

The issue was whether the statement in the pre-contractual report was a term of the contract or a mere representation.

Decision

Appeal upheld: the statement was not a term of the contract.

Per Barwick CJ, Kitto, Menzies, Owen and Walsh JJ at 441:

> . . . The trial judge was of opinion that the statement in the appellant's letter was an estimate only, expressed as an expectancy, and not an unequivocal promise of a future speed. The Full Court, after referring to a dictionary meaning of the word 'estimate', thought the expression 'estimated speed 15 m.p.h.' in the appellant's [442] letter should be construed as 'approximate speed 15 m.p.h.'.
>
> In our opinion, this was an unwarranted substitution which stripped the words of the letter of their most significant meaning. The actual words used by the appellant in the letter should be considered. So far from being a promissory expression, 'estimated speed 15 m.p.h.' indicates, in our opinion, an expression of opinion as the result 'of approximate calculation based on probability' to use the dictionary equivalent of 'estimate' referred to by the Full Court. There is no need to resort to cases decided upon different facts and circumstances in order to determine the significance in this case of the actual words used by the respondent. The words in themselves tend, in our opinion, against the inference of a promise that the boat would in fact achieve the nominated speed.
>
> The Full Court seems to have thought it sufficient in order to establish a collateral warranty that without the statement as to the estimated speed the contract of purchase would never have been made. But that circumstance is, in our opinion, in itself insufficient to support the conclusion that a warranty was given. So much can be said of an innocent representation inducing a contract. The question is whether there was a promise by the appellant that the boat would in fact attain the stated speed if powered by the stipulated engine, the entry into the contract to purchase the boat providing the consideration to make the promise effective.

The expression in *De Lassalle v. Guildford* [1901] 2 K.B. 215, 222 that without the statement the contract in that case would not have been made does not, in our opinion, provide an alternative and independent ground on which a collateral warranty can be established. Such a fact is but a step in some circumstances towards the only conclusion which will support a collateral warranty, namely, that the statement so relied on was promissory and not merely representational.

When the letter which we have quoted was written, the negotiations for the construction and delivery of the boat were incomplete. On receipt of the letter there were three courses open to the respondent. He could have required the attainment of the speed to be inserted in the specification as a condition of the contract; or he could have sought from the appellant a promise – however expressed, whether as an assurance, guarantee, promise or otherwise — that the boat would attain the speed as a prerequisite to his ordering the boat; or he could be content to form his own judgment as to the suitable power unit for the boat relying upon the opinion of the appellant of whose reputation and experience in the [443] relevant field he had, as the trial judge found, a high regard. Only the second course would give rise to a collateral warranty.

In our opinion, there is nothing in the evidence before the trial judge to support the view that the respondent took either the first or second of these courses: the only conclusion open upon that evidence was that the respondent took the third course; he accepted the appellant's estimate of what the boat would do under the power of the 4/53 G.M. diesel as sufficient to found his (the respondent's) own judgment as to the powering of the vessel. As he said 'I prefer upon your advice the G.M. 4/53'. That the statement actually made by the appellant was intended to have some commercial significance upon a matter of importance to the respondent can be conceded; that the respondent was intended to act upon it, and that he did act upon it, is clearly made out. But those facts do not warrant the conclusion that the statement was itself promissory.

In our opinion, so far from it being shown that the trial judge was wrong in refusing to draw the conclusion that the appellant made a promissory statement as to the attainable speed of the cruiser (which he did by deciding that there was no condition of the contract in the stated terms) we are satisfied that he took the only course permitted by the material before him. In our opinion, the appeal should be allowed.

Dick Bentley Productions Ltd v Harold Smith (Motors) Ltd [1965] 1 WLR 623

Facts and issues

Charles Walter ('Dick') Bentley intended to purchase a 'well vetted' Bentley motor vehicle and sought the assistance of Harold Smith, a car dealer. After some searching, Harold Smith informed Dick Bentley of a suitable one—a Park Ward drophead coupé Bentley motor vehicle—and said at two inspections by Bentley that the car had only been driven 20,000 miles since the engine and gearbox were replaced. In reality, the car had been driven closer to 100,000 miles. After the second inspection, Bentley purchased the car. The car performed poorly and required significant repairs. Bentley sued Harold Smith for damages to cover the repairs. At trial, the judge found in favour of Dick Bentley. Harold Smith appealed.

The issue was whether Harold Smith's statement that the car had only been driven for 20,000 miles since the engine and gearbox were replaced was a term of the contract or merely a representation.

Decision

Appeal dismissed: the pre-contractual statement was a term of the contract.

Per Lord Denning MR at 627:

> The first point is whether this representation, namely, that it had done 20,000 miles only since it had been fitted with a replacement engine and gearbox, was an innocent misrepresentation (which does not give rise to damages), or whether it was a warranty. It was said by Holt C.J., and repeated in *Heilbut, Symons & Co. v. Buckleton* [1913] A.C. 30, 49, that: 'An affirmation at the time of the sale is a warranty, provided it appear on evidence to be so intended.' But that word 'intended' has given rise to difficulties. I endeavoured to explain in *Oscar Chess Ltd. v. Williams* [1957] 1 W.L.R. 370, 375 that the question whether a warranty was intended depends on the conduct of the parties, on their words and behaviour, rather than on their thoughts. If an intelligent bystander would reasonably infer that a warranty was intended, that will suffice. What conduct, then? What words and behaviour lead to the inference of a warranty?
>
> . . . [T]he maker of the representation can rebut this inference if he can show that it really was an innocent misrepresentation, in that he was in fact innocent of fault in making it, and that it would not be reasonable in the [628] circumstances for him to be bound by it. In the *Oscar Chess case* the inference was rebutted. There a man had bought a second-hand car and received with it a log-book which stated the year of the car, 1948. He afterwards resold the car. When he resold it he simply repeated what was in the log-book and passed it on to the buyer. He honestly believed on reasonable grounds that it was true. He was completely innocent of any fault. There was no warranty by him, but only an innocent misrepresentation. Whereas in the present case it is very different. The inference is not rebutted. Here we have a dealer, Smith, who was in a position to know, or at least to find out, the history of the car. He could get it by writing to the makers. He did not do so. Indeed, it was done later. When the history of this car was examined, his statement turned out to be quite wrong. He ought to have known better. There was no reasonable foundation for it. . . .
>
> The judge found that the representations were not dishonest. Smith was not guilty of fraud. But he made the statement as to 20,000 miles without any foundation. And the judge was [629] well justified in finding that there was a warranty. The judge said:
>
>> I have no hesitation [in saying] that as a matter of law the statement was a warranty. Mr. Smith stated a fact that should be within his own knowledge. He had jumped to a conclusion and stated it as a fact. A fact that a buyer would act on.
>
> That is ample foundation for the inference of a warranty. [. . .]

Salmon LJ at 629:

> I agree. I have no doubt at all that the judge reached a correct conclusion when he decided that Smith gave a warranty to the plaintiff and that that warranty was broken. Was what Smith said intended and understood as a legally binding promise? If so, it was a warranty and as such may be part of the contract of sale or collateral to it. In effect, Smith said:
>
>> If you will enter into a contract to buy this motor car from me for £1,850, I undertake that you will be getting a motor car which has done no more than 20,000 miles since it was fitted with a new engine and a new gearbox.
>
> I have no doubt at all that what was said by Smith was so understood and was intended to be so understood by Bentley. . . . I accordingly agree that the appeal should be dismissed.

Danckwerts LJ agreed with Lord Denning MR.

9.3.3 The parol evidence rule

The strong preference of contract law to rely on written evidence for contractual promises over verbal statements is demonstrated in the sometimes 'circular' reasoning in the parol evidence rule. The strict application of the rule, which purports to exclude from court any evidence of pre-contractual statements where there exists a written document of the contract, has given way to a more general 'presumption' in favour of written evidence of contracts. This development is seen in the differences between a 'classic' statement of the rule in *Goss v Lord Nugent* and the more recent cases of *Equuscorp v Glengallen Investments* and *State Rail Authority v Heath Outdoor*, all of which are extracted below.

Goss v Lord Nugent (1833) 5 B & AD 58; 110 ER 713

Facts and issues

Thomas Goss sought to sell several plots of land to George Lord Nugent, the contract for which was recorded in a written document. However, after a deposit was paid, Goss was not able to show 'good title' (or full ownership) to one of the plots of land. Lord Nugent verbally agreed not to require good title for the questionable plot. Goss completed the transfers but Lord Nugent then refused to pay the rest of the purchase price because title had not been passed on that one plot of land. Goss sued Lord Nugent for the remainder of the purchase price. At trial, a jury found in favour of Goss. Lord Nugent 'appealed' (or more accurately, Lord Nugent brought a 'rule nisi', which is effectively a claim that a decision should not take effect).

The issue was whether Goss could introduce evidence of the oral statement by Lord Nugent that good title was not required.

Decision

The 'appeal' was 'upheld' (or more accurately, the 'rule nisi' was made 'absolute').

Per Denman CJ (on behalf of the Court) at 64:

> By the general rules of the common law, if there be a contract which has been reduced into writing, verbal evidence is not allowed to be given of what passed between the parties, either before the written instrument was made, or during the time that it was in a state of [65] preparation, so as to add to or subtract from, or in any manner to vary or qualify the written contract; but after the agreement has been reduced into writing, it is competent to the parties, at any time before breach of it, by a new contract not in writing, either altogether to waive, dissolve, or annul the former agreements, or in any manner to add to, or subtract from, or vary or qualify the terms of it, and thus to make a new contract; which is to be proved, partly by the written agreement, and partly by the subsequent verbal terms engrafted upon what will be thus left of the written agreement.
>
> And if the present contract was not subject to the controul [sic] of any Act of Parliament, we think that it would have been competent for the parties, by word of mouth, to dispense with requiring a good title to be made to the lot in question, and that the action might be maintained.
>
> But the *Statute of Frauds* has made certain regulations as to contracts for the sale of lands; and by the 29 Car. 2, c. 3, s. 4, it is enacted, that no action shall be brought whereby to charge any person upon any contract or sale of lands, tenements, or hereditaments, or any interest in or concerning the same, unless the agreement upon which such action shall be brought, or some memorandum or note thereof, shall be in writing, and signed by the party to be charged therewith, or some other person thereunto by him lawfully authorized.

... [66] [T]his is not a waiver and abandonment of the whole written agreement, but only a part of it; and the question is, what is the effect of that?

It may be said by the plaintiff, that this does not in any degree vary what is to be done by either party; that the same land is to be conveyed, there is to be the same extent of interest in the land, and it is to be conveyed at the same time, and the same price is to be paid, and that it is only an abandonment of a collateral point.

But we think the object of the Statute of Frauds was to exclude all oral evidence as to contracts for the sale of lands, and that any contract which is sought to be enforced must be proved by writing only.

But, in the present case, the written contract is not that which is sought to be enforced, it is a new contract which the parties have entered into, and that new contract is to be proved, partly by the former written agreement, and partly by the new verbal agreement; the present contract, therefore, is not a contract entirely in writing; and as to the title being collateral to the land, the title appears to us to be a most essential part of the contract; for, if there be not a good title, the land may, in some instances, better not be conveyed at all ; but our opinion is not formed upon the stipulation about the title being an essential part of the agreement, but upon [67] the general effect and meaning of the Statute of Frauds, and that the contract now brought forward by the plaintiff is not wholly a contract in writing.

Equuscorp Pty Ltd v Glengallen Investments Pty Ltd (2004) 218 CLR 471

Facts and issues

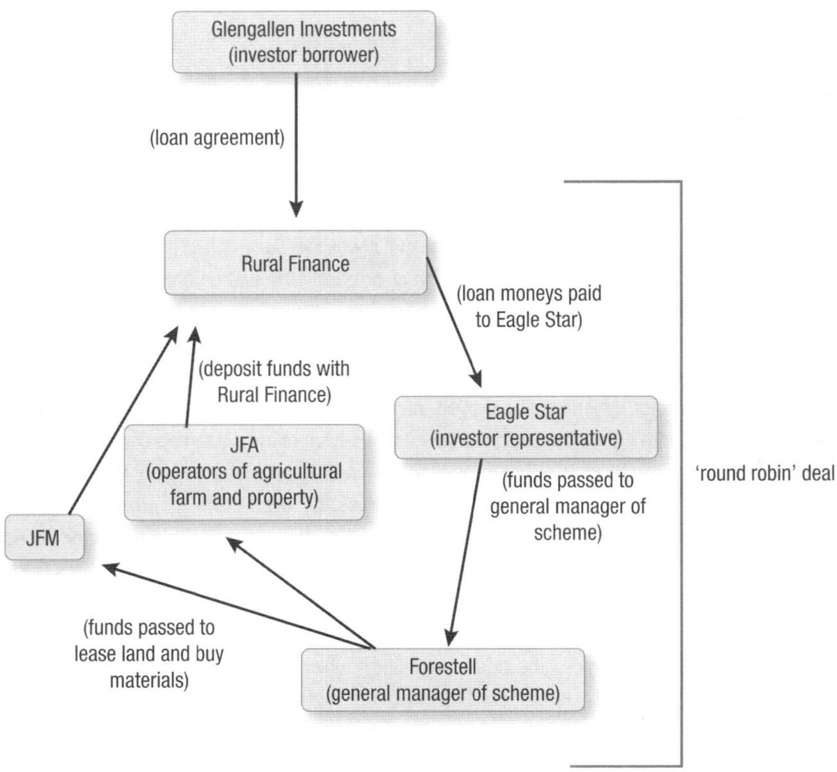

As part of a purported 'tax effective' investment scheme, potential investors in a speculative aquaculture project entered into a series of transactions, in which money was borrowed by each investor from Rural Finance, who then provided that money to Eagle Star (a representative of all the investors), who then passed that money to Forestell (general manager of the scheme), who then transferred those funds to John Farm Management ('JFM') (manager of the aquaculture project) and Farmer Johnson Aquaculture ('FJA') (owner of the land where the aquaculture project was based), both of whom then deposited the funds in an interest-bearing account with Rural Finance. In reality, no 'money' actually changed hands and the transactions only existed 'on paper', in what is sometimes called a 'round robin' arrangement.

Glengallen Investments, an investor in the scheme, entered into the scheme on 30 June 1989, the last day of the financial year, by signing and executing a written loan agreement with Rural Finance, although there had been extensive discussions with the arrangers of the scheme in the weeks preceding the signing of the agreement about what the investors may be liable for in the future. (The purported 'tax effectiveness' arose out of an apparent payment of $581 by the investor and in return the investor could claim a tax deduction of $5061 from the investor's taxable income in that financial year.)

Some time later, Rural Finance assigned its rights under the loan agreements to Equuscorp. Unsurprisingly, the aquaculture project was unsuccessful and the loans were never repaid. Rural Finance and Equuscorp sought to enforce the loans directly from the investors.

At trial, Helman J found there was no loan by Rural Finance to Glengallen and the other investors. An appeal by Equuscorp and Rural Finance was dismissed. Equuscorp and Rural Finance appealed to the High Court.

The issue was whether the written loan agreement entered into on 30 June 1989 was enforceable or was its operation limited by pre-contractual statements made by the parties.

Decision

Appeal upheld: the written loan agreement was validly executed and was not curtailed by the pre-contractual verbal statements.

Per Gleeson CJ, McHugh, Kirby, Hayne and Callinan JJ at 482:

> Debate in the courts below, about whether the loan agreements were wholly oral, as the respondents alleged, or wholly written, as Equuscorp and Rural Finance contended, proceeded upon the premise that the critical question was whether the primary judge should have acted on his acceptance of oral evidence given on the respondents' behalf of some conversations that were said to have occurred before the written loan agreements were signed. That, in turn, was seen as a question to be decided by reference to whether subsequent events (including those we have mentioned) made it more or less probable that during these conversations some consensus was reached that the loans were 'limited recourse'. But behind these arguments lies a more fundamental issue which the respondents' contentions did not address, whether in the courts below or on appeal to this Court.
>
> It is, and always has been, common ground that each of the respondents executed a written loan agreement on 30 June 1989. The respondents alleged that the 'operative agreement' was not contained in that writing. It was said that the relevant agreement was reached earlier and was wholly oral. Yet it was *not* said that the written agreement should be rectified. It was *not* said that a defence of *non est factum* was available. It was *not* said that the written agreement was executed by mistake, or that its execution

was procured by misrepresentation as to its contents or effect. (The misrepresentation alleged was as to what had been said in the conversations, not what the document was or provided.)

[483] The respondents each having executed a loan agreement, each is bound by it. Having executed the document, and not having been induced to do so by fraud, mistake, or misrepresentation, the respondents cannot now be heard to say that they are not bound by the agreement recorded in it (*L'Estrange v F Graucob Ltd* [1934] 2 KB 394). The parol evidence rule (*Hoyt's Pty Ltd v Spencer* (1919) 27 CLR 133), the limited operation of the defence of *non est factum* (*Petelin v Cullen* (1975) 132 CLR 355) and the development of the equitable remedy of rectification (*Taylor v Johnson* (1983) 151 CLR 422), all proceed from the premise that a party executing a written agreement is bound by it. Yet fundamental to the respondents' case that the operative agreements between the parties were wholly oral, and reached earlier than the execution of the written agreements, was the proposition that the written agreements subsequently executed not only *may* be ignored, they *must* be. That is not so. Having executed the agreement, each respondent is bound by it unless able to rely on a defence of *non est factum*, or able to have it rectified. The respondents attempted neither.

There are reasons why the law adopts this position. First, it accords with the 'general test of objectivity [that] is of pervasive influence in the law of contract' (*Australian Broadcasting Corporation v XIVth Commonwealth Games Ltd* (1988) 18 NSWLR 540 at 549, per Gleeson CJ). The legal rights and obligations of the parties turn upon what their words and conduct would be reasonably understood to convey, not upon actual beliefs or intentions (*Gissing v Gissing* [1971] AC 886 at 906, per Lord Diplock; *Ashington Piggeries Ltd v Christopher Hill Ltd* [1972] AC 441 at 502, per Lord Diplock).

Secondly, in the nature of things, oral agreements will sometimes be disputable. Resolving such disputation is commonly difficult, time-consuming, expensive and problematic. Where parties enter into a written agreement, the Court will generally hold them to the obligations which they have assumed by that agreement. At least, it will do so unless relief is afforded by the operation of statute or some other legal or equitable principle applicable to the case. Different questions may arise where the execution of the written agreement is contested; but that is not the case here. In a time of growing international trade with parties in legal systems having the same or even stronger deference to the obligations of written agreements (and frequently communicating in different languages and from the standpoint of different cultures) this is not a time to ignore the rules of the common law upholding obligations undertaken in written agreements. It is a time to maintain those rules. They are not unbending. They allow for exceptions. But the exceptions must be [484] proved according to established categories. The obligations of written agreements between parties cannot simply be ignored or brushed aside.

The conclusion that the respondents are bound by the written loan agreements may leave open the possibility that an earlier consensus reached by the parties was in each case a collateral agreement (made in consideration of the parties later executing the written agreement), but that has never been the respondents' case. In another case it may leave open the possibility that the contract is partly oral and partly in writing. But that cannot be so here. The oral limited recourse terms alleged by the respondents contradict the terms of the written loan agreement. If there was an earlier, oral, consensus, it was discharged and the parties' agreement recorded in the writing they executed. It is the written loan agreement which governed the relationship between Rural Finance and each respondent.

State Rail Authority of New South Wales v Heath Outdoor Pty Ltd (1986) 7 NSWLR 170

Facts and issues

State Rail Authority of New South Wales ('SRA') intended to rent out space along train lines owned by the New South Wales Government and operated by SRA for 'inter-station' advertising hoardings. After some negotiation, Heath Outdoor entered into a five-year contract with SRA to build and operate such hoardings, initially at one location (under the '1981 contract') and later at 138 locations (under the '1982 contract').

The written contract (both in 1981 and 1982) contained a right of termination clause:

> Condition 6. The Authority may terminate this contract at any time upon giving to the advertiser one (1) calendar month's notice in writing of its intention so to do, but such action shall not give rise to any claim for compensation whatsoever on the part of the advertiser.

However, Mr Low, on behalf of Heath Outdoor, alleged that Mr Giles, an employee of the SRA, made a number of statements before the 1981 contract was signed, including that 'it is very difficult for me to have that clause or any other clause altered' and 'the only time that that clause is ever invoked is for non-payment of rent or if somebody wants to advertise objectionable advertising content'.

After entering into the 1982 contract, Heath Outdoor entered into a five-year advertising contract with a cigarette manufacturer to put cigarette-related advertising on every inter-station hoarding. In March 1983, the NSW Government announced that cigarette-related advertising would be phased out from government transport vehicles and property. Despite negotiations with Heath Outdoor and the cigarette manufacturer, SRA terminated the contract in November 1983 after providing one month's notice.

Heath Outdoor sued SRA for breach of the contract. At trial, Holland J found for Heath Outdoor (who found the 1982 contract was varied in 1983 such that the right to terminate on one month's notice was removed). SRA appealed.

An issue was whether the contract was partly written and partly oral such that the exercise of Condition 6 was curtailed. (Other issues were whether Heath Outdoor could rely on an estoppel claim to enforce any pre-contractual statements.)

Decision

Appeal upheld: the written contract had not been varied by the pre-contractual statements and the contract was not partly written and partly oral.

Per Kirby P at 173:

> [Kirby P largely agreed with McHugh JA (extracted below) but made additional observations about Condition 6.]
>
> Condition 6 gave the SRA the right to terminate the contract at any time upon giving Heath Outdoor one calendar month's notice in writing of its intention to do so. I see no reason why this over-riding entitlement, reserved by the SRA, may not stand with the provision of the letter specifying a five year contract period. That period will apply, unless the right reserved by condition 6 is exercised, as it was here. The reservation of such a right, particularly in the case of a public authority, substantially dependent upon annual appropriations, is neither surprising nor unusual.

Secondly, I am prepared to assume that the oral evidence concerning the alleged 'assurances' given by the officer of the SRA, Mr Giles, to Mr Low of Heath Outdoor may be admitted to establish that the written contract did not constitute the whole of the agreement between the parties. However, even upon that assumption, I agree with McHugh JA that the repeated assertions by Mr Giles that he had no authority to change any condition of the written contract prevents either the variation of the written contract or the creation of a collateral and inconsistent contract based upon Mr Giles' statements. On the contrary, those statements reiterated the fact that condition 6 was impervious to removal or variation by anything Mr Giles could do. Any relief to Heath Outdoor must accordingly be found, not in the substance of the agreement between the parties (as varied or elaborated by Mr Giles) but in the law of estoppel.

[178] . . . The facts that Heath Outdoor, after signing the contract which contained condition 6, proceeded to expend funds erecting signs and also entered a contract with Rothmans of Pall Mall (Aust) Ltd which render Heath Outdoor liable in damages, are a commercial misfortune for Heath Outdoor. But in my view this is a misfortune which Heath Outdoor accepted when Mr Low accepted and signed the agreement containing the offensive condition 6. A conclusion to the contrary effectively writes condition 6 out of the contract on the ground that it cannot be enforced without an offence to conscience. There is a basic inconsistency between the conclusion that the contract was not varied or elaborated by the conversations with Mr Giles and the holding that it would be unconscionable to enforce the contract following Mr Giles 'assurances'. It is desirable that the law of contract should be as certain, consistent and as simple as the courts can make it. Especially is this true of commercial contracts such as the present.

Per McHugh JA at 191:

The next submission of the plaintiff was that the 1981 contract was partly oral and partly written. The plaintiff submitted that it is always open to a party to show that a written document is not the binding record of their contract: *Gordon v Macgregor* (1909) 8 CLR 316 at 323; *Hoyt's Pty Ltd v Spencer* (1919) 27 CLR 133 at 143-144; *J Evans & Son (Portsmouth) Ltd v Andrea Merzario Ltd* [1976] 1 WLR 1078; [1976] 2 All ER 930. It is then said that the statements by Mr Giles about condition 6 were part of the contractual terms between the parties.

A preliminary question which arises is whether the so called parol evidence rule prevents reliance on the oral assurances of Mr Giles. Under that rule parol evidence is not admissible to contradict or vary the terms of a written agreement. But it is a rule whose scope and rationale is often misunderstood. It has no operation until it is first determined that the terms of the agreement are wholly contained in writing. The tendering of oral evidence to prove a contractual term, therefore, cannot be excluded until it is determined that any terms in writing record the whole of the parties' agreement: *Corbin on Contracts* (1960) vol 3 at 385; *Air Great Lakes Pty Ltd v K S Easter (Holdings) Pty Ltd* (1985) 2 NSWLR 309 at 337.

When a person alleges that an agreement was partly oral and partly written, it is not always easy to determine whether the writing is the exclusive repository of the bargain. Williston claims that, when a document appears on its face to be a complete record of the parties' contract, it is conclusively presumed to be the contract: *Williston on Contracts*, 3rd ed (1961), s 633. However, Corbin takes a different view and says that the issue is whether the parties assented to a particular writing as the complete and accurate 'integration' of the contract: *Corbin on Contracts* (1960) vol 3 at 358-359. Support for Williston's approach is to be found in the judgment of Street CJ in *L G Thorne & Co Pty Ltd v Thomas Borthwick & Sons (A/asia) Ltd*

(1956) 56 SR (NSW) 81 at 88; 73 WN (NSW) 9 at 14. But in my opinion the correct rule is that the existence of writing which appears to represent a written contract between the parties is no more than an evidentiary foundation for a conclusion that their agreement is wholly in writing: *Gillespie Brothers & Co* [192] *v Cheney, Eggar & Co* [1896] 2 QB 59 at 62; *Turner v Forwood* [1951] 1 All ER 746 at 749; *J Evans & Son (Portsmouth) Ltd v Andrea Merzario Ltd* at 1083; 935. In my opinion the English Law Commission correctly stated the law when it said:

> ... the mere production of a contractual document, however complete it may look, cannot as a matter of law exclude evidence of oral terms if the other party asserts that such terms were agreed. If that assertion is proved, evidence of the oral terms cannot be excluded because the court will, by definition, have found that the contractual terms are partly to be found in what was agreed orally as well as the document in question. No parol evidence rule could apply. On the other hand, if that assertion is not proved, there can be no place for a parol evidence rule because the court will have found that all the terms of the contract were set out in the document in question and, by implication, will thereby have excluded evidence of terms being found elsewhere.

While I think that the plaintiff was entitled to rely on the oral assurances of Mr Giles in support of its claim that the advertising contract and/or letter of 12 October 1981 did not contain the whole terms of the parties' agreement, I am of opinion that on the evidence the submission that the contract was partly oral should be rejected. The proper conclusion to be drawn from the discussion between the parties is that, as a matter of contract, condition 6 was one of the contractual terms and that its literal effect was to give the defendant an unfettered right to terminate the contract. Mr Giles made it plain that he had no authority to change any condition of the contract. Mr Low accepted this. He said that it became apparent to him that Mr Giles was going to have difficulty getting the clauses changed if he had to take them away. Mr Giles also informed Mr Low that the document was a standard authority document which could not be changed. Whatever effect the discussion between Mr Low and Mr Giles had, it did not add to the terms of the contract.

Moreover, it is not possible to conclude that the assurances amounted to a collateral contract, since the terms of the assurances contradict the terms of condition 6: *Hoyt's Pty Ltd v Spencer*. The main contract can be the consideration for a collateral contract only when the terms of the collateral contract do not reduce or alter the rights created by the main contract: *Hoyt's Pty Ltd v Spencer* at 139; *Maybury v Atlantic Union Oil Co Ltd* (1953) 89 CLR 507 at 518.

Glass JA largely agreed with the analysis of McHugh JA.

9.3.4 Collateral contracts

One way to circumvent the parol evidence rule is for a pre-contractual statement to be found to be part of a collateral contract, which makes the pre-contractual statement a promise that is enforceable on its own terms. A collateral contract arises when one party makes a promise, and in return the other party enters into another or 'main' contract. The entering into the main contract is the consideration that makes the first party's promise binding. There are restrictions on the realisation of collateral contracts, including that the promises in the collateral contract cannot be inconsistent with the obligations in the main contract, as was examined in the case of *Hoyt's v Spencer* (extracted below).

Hoyt's Pty Ltd v Spencer (1919) 27 CLR 133

Facts and issues

Hoyt's, which operated movie theatres, negotiated and entered into a four-year sublease with Spencer for a property leased by Spencer from [twelve] co-owners or 'head lessors'. The written lease between Hoyt's and Spencer included a right ('proviso') of Spencer to terminate the agreement on four weeks' notice. Hoyt's alleged Spencer stated before the written lease was signed that Spencer would not exercise the right to terminate unless directed to do so by the head lessors. Some time later, Spencer gave Hoyt's four weeks' notice of the intention to terminate the sublease, even though he was not directed to do so by the head lessors.

Hoyt's vacated the premises, then sued Spencer for breach of contract. The Full Court of the Supreme Court effectively dismissed the action. Hoyt's sought a demurrer on Spencer's defence, which is a form of appeal that, even if the alleged facts are proved, those facts have no legal effect; the demurrer was dismissed. Hoyt's appealed to the High Court.

The issue was whether the pre-contractual statements by Spencer could be enforceable as a collateral contract or were excluded by the parol evidence rule.

Decision

Appeal dismissed: the pre-contractual statement is not enforceable as a collateral contract.

Per Knox CJ at 138:

> From the authorities referred to during the argument the following [139] propositions may be deduced, viz.:—
>
> (a) When parties negotiate an agreement by parol and subsequently reduce it to writing, the writing constitutes the contract, or at any rate is conclusive evidence of its terms, . . . subject, of course, to the right of either party to proceed for its rectification or rescission on sufficient grounds.
>
> (b) A distinct collateral agreement, . . . whether oral or in writing, and whether prior to or contemporaneous with the main agreement, is valid and enforceable even though the main agreement be in writing, provided the two may consistently stand together so that the provisions of the main agreement remain in full force and effect notwithstanding the collateral agreement. This proposition is illustrated by the decisions in *Lindley v. Lacey* (17 C.B. (N.S.), 578), *Erskine v. Adeane* (L.R. 8 Ch., 756), *De Lassalle* v. *Guildford* ((1901) 2 K.B., 215) and other cases.
>
> (c) There may be a contract the consideration for which is the making of some other contract *(Heilbut Symons & Co. v. Buckleton* ((1913) A.C., at p. 47)). This proposition, properly understood, in no way conflicts with the other propositions set out above. It does not say that any contract the alleged consideration for which is the making of another contract is necessarily valid and enforceable. Whether it is so or not depends, in my opinion, on the nature and contents of the two contracts. For instance, if the main contract was to buy a house for £1,000, payable as to 25 per cent in cash on signing the contract, and as to the balance by promissory notes of equal amounts at 12, 24 and 36 months, and the so-called collateral contract made by the vendor in consideration of the purchaser signing the main contract provided that, the vendor should not be entitled to receive any cash but the whole purchase money should be paid by promissory notes extending over a period of five years, it seems clear to me that the so-called collateral contract would not be valid or enforceable

> at law or in equity, though it might possibly afford ground for a suit in equity for rectification of the main contract or be set up as a defence to a suit by the vendor for specific performance of that contract. The reason for this conclusion is that the alleged consideration for the collateral contract is the assumption by the purchaser of the obligations specified [140] in the main contract, which obligations are immediately varied or abrogated by the collateral contract. The result is, in effect, as if one party said: 'I will sign a contract to pay you £1,000 for a house, £250 in cash and the balance by promissory notes at 12, 24 and 36 months, if in consideration of my signing that contract you will enter into an agreement with me that you will not seek to enforce payment of the £250 cash or delivery of the agreed promissory notes but will accept other promissory notes of different amounts and currency.' In such a case the consideration for the so-called collateral contract is the assumption of obligations which, *ex hypothesi,* the purchaser does not, and does not intend to, assume. In my opinion, the application of the propositions *(a)* and *(b),* set out above, to the question for decision in the present case leads to the conclusion that the decision of the majority in the Supreme Court was correct.

The contention for the plaintiff Company may be stated as follows: 'In consideration of obtaining a lease of premises for a term, we agreed *(inter alia)* to accept a lease giving the lessor an unqualified right to determine the lease on giving four weeks' notice, but we only consented to execute the lease in consideration of a promise by the lessor that his power to terminate the lease should be qualified by restricting its exercise to an occasion on which his lessors should request and require him to exercise it.' This is tantamount to saying that under the proviso of the lease the agreement is that the lessor may determine the lease by giving four weeks' notice whenever he chooses to do so, but under the agreement sued on the lessor is bound not to determine the lease by notice unless requested and required by his lessors so to do; or, in other words, that he has the right under the proviso to determine the lease, but is liable to an action for damages for breach of the collateral agreement if he does so.

In my opinion it is impossible to maintain that the agreement on which the present action is founded would not, if valid and enforceable, modify or vary the agreement contained in the lease executed by the parties in regard to a matter expressly dealt with by a provision of the lease, viz., the right to determine it during the currency of the term for which it was granted. If this be so, [141] it is clear that the two agreements – that on which the action is founded and that contained in the proviso in the memorandum of lease – are inconsistent, and so cannot stand together.

... Consequently the agreement on which this action is founded does not fulfil the requirement of proposition *(b)* set forth above, and the reasoning of *Blackburn* J. in *Angell* v. *Duke* (32 L.T., 320) applies. That being so, the agreement, though admittedly made in fact, cannot be used by either party as the foundation of proceedings against the other to enforce it or to recover damages for its breach.

For these reasons I am of opinion that the appeal should be dismissed.

Per Isaacs J at 143:

... [A]s the argument has occupied the attention of two Courts and concerns a topic of the law — collateral agreements — which touches every phase of contract — mercantile and otherwise — I think it desirable to state the way in which I view it.

When two parties are entering into contractual relations with respect to a given subject matter, they may (apart from special technical requirements) elect to conclude their bargain without writing, or they may elect to record it in writing, and, if in writing, they may further decide to have it under seal. But in whatever form they determine to leave their bargain, they may further agree to have one contract only, or to have separate and distinct contracts. All that is for the parties themselves to resolve upon. If they determine to make one contract only, then the terms they decide to include are the only terms that affect them contractually. It connotes that all else is abandoned. And that is the case whatever the form of the contract. If the matter is not committed to writing, though the principle is clear, the evidence is manifestly open to great dispute. But if the parties agree to commit their agreement to writing, then what is written is the conclusive record of the terms of their agreement, and, unless it can be shown that the document was not intended as the complete record of their bargain, no oral evidence can be admitted to alter or qualify it . . .

[145] The main contract here, when utilized to form the consideration for the collateral contract, must be taken exactly as it is. Its provisions do not change according as it is considered as an independent contract or as a consideration [146] for the collateral contract. A principle that must govern the bargain of a contractual promise made in consideration of entering into the main contract is that the parties shall have and be subject to *all* (not some only) of the respective benefits and burdens of the main contract. When the collateral promise is truly consistent with the main contract, that principle has full play. The main contract is not then interfered with. The collateral contract alters, as every contract must, the contractual relations of the parties; but it does not alter, and from the simple statement of the bargain is not intended to alter, the contractual relations which are established by the main contract. When both are worked out, it may be that in the final outcome the parties are in the same position as if those contractual relations had been varied. But the practical result cannot affect the independence and legal effect of each contract; and that is what we are here concerned with . . .

[147] The truth is that a collateral contract, which may be either antecedent or contemporaneous (per *Erle* C.J. and *Byles* J. in *Lindley v. Lacey* (17 C.B. (N.S.), at pp. 586, 587) and per *Cockburn* C.J. in *Angell v. Duke* (L.R. 10 Q.B., 174, at p.177)), being supplementary only to the main contract, cannot impinge on it, or alter its provisions or the *rights created by it*; consequently, where the main contract is relied on as the consideration in whole or part for the promise contained in the collateral contract, it is a wholly inconsistent and impossible contention that the other party is not to have the full benefit of the main contract as made; and the [148] appellant's first contention is therefore unsound. If in any case the Court finds two enforceable agreements executed in such circumstances that one is intended to affect the other, no doubt such effect will be given to them as the superimposing operation of the governing contract requires; but in that case it is not collateral, but dominant. (See the observations of *Fry* J. in *Gartside v. Silkstone and Dodworth Coal and Iron Co.* (21 Ch. D. 762, at pp.767–768).)

It only remains to consider whether the alleged promise does leave the contractual rights of the respondent under the main contract unimpaired. *Ex concessis* [trans. 'based on what has already been conceded'], it does not. The very argument on which the claim is founded is that but for the additional promise the respondent had the power by virtue of the proviso to do what he did. And the plaintiff's case is that that power was cut down by the further promise. There is at once a conflict between the two, with the result that the appellant, though in one breath conceding the full extent of the proviso as a consideration, yet, in the next, cuts it down almost to the point of rendering it nugatory.

In my opinion the judgment should be affirmed, and this appeal dismissed.

Rich J agreed with the other judgments.

QUESTIONS

(1) To what extent are *Oscar Chess* and *JJ Savage* examples of a judge inferring an objective intention from a series of subjective factors? Denning MR seems at pains to recognise that there is no 'fair' outcome here, but how compelling is his justification for where the loss should lie? What might the alternate approach be?

(2) Why does McHugh JA in *State Rail Authority v Heath Outdoor* refer to the 'so called parol evidence rule'? What is the status of the parol evidence rule if the reasoning in this judgment is followed? Is the rule really just an example of 'circular reasoning'?

(3) The outcome of *Equuscorp v Glengallen* underscores the importance placed on written agreements, and the Court provides several justifications for that position, including by reference to 'international trade', 'different languages' and 'different cultures'. How compelling are these justifications? How do they differ from the justifications of the rule in previous centuries?

(4) In what ways is a collateral contract an effective method to circumvent the parol evidence rule? What are the risks with this approach?

(5) To what extent is the concept of a collateral contract itself a 'circular argument'?

9.4 Terms implied in fact

Concepts	Short explanation	Relevant authorities	*Principles* text*
Terms implied in fact	Terms may be implied into a contract if, on the facts of the contract, the terms are necessary for business efficacy	*Byrne v Australian Airlines Ltd* (1995) 185 CLR 410 *Codelfa Construction Pty Ltd v State Rail Authority of New South Wales* (1982) 149 CLR 337	Chapter 9: 9.20–9.23

* Consult the corresponding section(s) of the *Principles* text for more detail.

9.4.1 The tests for implication in fact

A term implied in fact requires a court to conclude the parties to the specific contract being examined would have included such a term if they had turned their minds to it. The test, or rather 'overlapping tests', require five factors to be fulfilled: (1) such a term is reasonable and equitable; (2) the term must be necessary to give business efficacy to the contract; (3) the term is so obvious that it goes without saying; (4) the term must be capable of clear expression; and (5) the term must not contradict any express terms. The case of *Byrne v Australian Airlines* (1995) (extracted below) examined and modified the preceding English view on the tests established in *BP Refinery v Hastings Shire Council* (1977).

Byrne v Australian Airlines Ltd (1995) 185 CLR 410

Facts and issues

Byrne and a colleague (Frew) were employed for at least 20 years at Sydney Airport as baggage handlers by Australian Airlines (a now defunct domestic airline, subsumed by QANTAS in 1992). After allegations of pilfering (usually defined to mean the stealing of items of limited value), the employees were sacked. The employees claimed the sackings were harsh, unjust or unreasonable, which was a breach of the relevant industry award, Transport Workers (Airlines) Award 1988, which did not allow such dismissals. The trial judge found the terminations were not harsh, unjust or unreasonable; however, this finding was reversed on appeal by the Full Court of the Federal Court, although the Full Court also found no damages were claimable. The employees appealed to the High Court.

The issue was whether the prohibition against harsh, unjust or unreasonable dismissal was part of the employee's contract of employment. One argument was that the terms of the award could be implied into the contract of employment.

Decision

Appeal dismissed: the term could not be implied into the contract of employment.

Per Brennan CJ, Dawson and Toohey JJ at 422:

> **Implied term**
>
> The implication which the appellants seek to make is based upon the presumed or imputed intention of the parties. In that context, the remarks of the majority in the Privy Council in *BP Refinery (Westernport) Pty Ltd v Shire of Hastings* are frequently called in aid: '(1) [the implication] must be reasonable and equitable; (2) it must be necessary to give business efficacy to the contract, so that no term will be implied if the contract is effective without it; (3) it must be so obvious that "it goes without saying"; (4) it must be capable of clear expression; (5) it must not contradict any express term of the contract.' In laying down those criteria, it was recognised that there was a degree of overlap. Further, as Deane J has observed, the cases in which the criteria in *BP Refinery (Westernport) Pty Ltd v Shire of Hastings* have been applied in this Court are cases in which there was a formal contract, complete on its face. He pointed out that a rigid approach should be avoided in cases, such as the present, where there is no formal contract. In those cases the actual terms of the contract must first be inferred before any question of implication arises. That is to say, it is necessary to arrive at some conclusion as to the actual intention of the parties before considering any presumed or imputed intention. And the test to be then applied was in a later case formulated by Deane J in these terms:
>
>> The most that can be said consistently with the need for some degree of flexibility is that, in a case where it is apparent that the parties have not attempted to spell out the full terms of their contract, a court should imply a term by reference to the imputed intention of the parties if, but only if, it can be seen that the implication of the particular term is necessary for the reasonable or effective operation of a contract of that nature in the circumstances of the case. That general statement of principle is subject to the qualification that a term may be implied in a contract by established mercantile usage or professional practice or by a past course of dealing between the parties.

That is, we think, the appropriate test to apply in this case and the answer must be that it is not necessary to imply a term in the form of cl II(a) for the reasonable or effective operation of the contract of employment in all the circumstances. In the absence of any provision in the award and of any express provision in the contract of [423] employment the law would regard it as a legal incident of the contract that it should be terminable upon reasonable notice or summarily for serious breach. Clause 11(a) may alter that position, but there is no reason to presume that any alteration was intended by the parties to form a term of their contract, nor any reason to impute such an intention to them. Plainly, the fact that the inclusion of such a term would, if it were breached, support an action for damages by the employee is no ground for saying that the term is necessary for the reasonable or effective operation of the contract. The contract is capable of operating reasonably and effectively in the absence of such a term and in the presence of an award provision offering limited remedies in the event of breach. The argument that cl 11(a) constituted an implied term of the contract of employment should be rejected.

Per McHugh and Gummow JJ at 441:

Business efficacy

We turn now to consider the submission that cl 11(a) was implied as a term from the particular circumstances of the case and to give effect to some apparent underlying intention of the parties about providing business efficacy. Reliance here was placed upon the well-known statement of the Privy Council in *BP Refinery (Westernport) Pty Ltd v Shire of Hastings*. This has been approved and applied in numerous decisions in this Court. The Privy Council specified five conditions which, whilst they might overlap, must be satisfied before a court may imply a term in a contract which the parties had not thought fit to express. First, the term must be 'reasonable and equitable'; secondly, it must be necessary to give 'business efficacy to the contract' so that no term will be implied if the contract is effective without it; thirdly, the term must be so obvious that 'it goes without saying'; fourthly, it must be 'capable of clear expression'; and, finally, it must not contradict any express term.

In *BP* itself and in other cases such as *Secured Income Real Estate (Australia) Ltd v St Martins Investments Pty Ltd* (1979) 144 CLR 596, *Codelfa* [442] *Construction Pty Ltd v State Rail Authority (NSW)* (1982) 149 CLR 337 and *Adelaide City Corporation v Jennings Industries Ltd* (1985) 156 CLR 274, the question was whether a term should be implied in a formal written contract which was complete upon its face.

That is not the present case. We have referred to the exiguous nature of the evidence as to the form taken by, and the express terms of, the contract of employment between the respondent and the appellants. There are two consequences.

First, this species of implication is concerned with the circumstances of the particular case. The primary judge and Black CJ and Gray J in the Full Court referred to the need to prove facts leading to the implication of a term of this nature. Gray J said (128):

> [T]his Full Court does not know what all of the express terms of the contracts were. It does not know whether they were adequate to make the contracts of employment efficacious or whether any of them would contradict the proposed implied term. An examination of the facts surrounding the creation of each contract of employment might lead to a different result for one appellant from the other.

Secondly, where the contract is not in writing and is oral or partly oral or it appears that the parties themselves did not reduce their agreement to a complete written form, caution is required against an automatic or rigid application of the cumulative criteria identified in *BP*. We should proceed on the footing that the present case is to be approached in this way.

In such situations, the first task is to consider the evidence and find the relevant express terms. Some terms may be inferred from the evidence of a course of dealing between the parties. It may be apparent that the parties have not spelled out all the terms of their contract, but have left some or most of them to be inferred or implied. Some terms may be implied by established custom or usage, as described above. Other terms may satisfy the criterion of being so obvious that they go without saying, in the sense that if the subject had been raised the parties to the contract would have replied 'of course'. If the contract has not been reduced to complete written form, the question is whether the implication of the particular term is necessary for the reasonable or effective operation of the contract in the circumstances of the case; only where this can be seen to be true will the term be implied.

The contractual term propounded by the appellants would operate in a partisan fashion. It would favour the interests of the employee at the [443] expense of those of the employer. Further, in the operation sought to be given the term by the appellants, so as to require procedural regularity or fairness, the term also would qualify what otherwise has been understood to be the general law of the employment contract. . . .

[445] Before answering the question whether cl 11(a) is to be implied in the contracts of employment between the respondent and the appellants as being so obvious that it goes without saying, it is first necessary to consider the part played by cl 11(a) in the scheme established by the Award.

Clause 11(f) provides that, subject to s 5 of the 1904 Act (creating certain offences in relation to dismissal and threatened dismissal and related matters) and ss 119, 122 and 123 (dealing with the enforcement of awards) any dispute or claim arising under cl II shall be dealt with in accordance with cl 41. Clause 41 is headed 'SETTLEMENT OF DISPUTES OR CLAIMS'. It requires any dispute or claim to be discussed first by the aggrieved employee with his or her supervisor, then between the accredited union representative and an appropriate officer of the employer, then by the Branch Secretary or other appropriate official of the union and the appropriate representative of the employer, and then between a representative of the employer and the federal body of the union. If the matter is still not settled, it is submitted to a member of the Australian Conciliation and Arbitration Commission whose decision shall, subject to any appeal in accordance with the 1904 Act, be final and be accepted by the parties. Clause 41 further provides that, until the matter is determined, work shall continue as instructed by the employer.

Upon their face, cll 11 and 41 of the Award do not require a new term to be implied in every relevant contract of employment . . .

Clause 11(a) is not a free-standing provision in the Award. It is an integral part of a regime which, at the same time, establishes a norm by which an unfair dismissal is to be assessed, and provides for the resolution of disputes as to such dismissals and for the enforcement of the Award by the recovery of penalties. Why should cl 11(a) be severed from that context and given a further and distinct operation as a contractual term?

Further, there is force in the following remarks of Jenkinson J in *Gregory v Philip Morris Ltd:*

> It could not in my opinion be predicated in respect of the implication proposed that, if the parties had been asked at the time the contract was made whether the provisions of the award as they should from time to time exist were to be terms of their contract, each would have unhesitatingly responded in the affirmative. The [446] evidence, no

less than what one may be permitted judicially to know, is consistent with each party's believing that some of the matters with respect to which the award made provision, or might in the future make provision, could be regulated by agreement between employer and union representatives of the employer's workers to the greater advantage of that party than that party might expect to gain from the contractual adoption of whatever provision an award applying indifferently to many kinds of industrial enterprises might from time to time contain. Since the provisions of the award as from time to time varied would bind the parties without their agreement, and since the parties would remain free to agree that the appellant should have more than the award prescribed, why should it be thought likely that the appellant would have responded affirmatively, when he entered into the contract of employment, to a question whether his freedom should be fettered by a term of the kind suggested?

In the present case, Beaumont and Heerey JJ dealt with this particular question of implication by saying that, whilst the employee might have agreed that the terms of cl 11(a) be expressly included in the contract of employment, the employer in all probability would be of the contrary view. There is much to be said for their Honours' hypothesis that the employer would indicate that, whilst bound by the terms of the Award and so subject to the penalties prescribed by the legislation for breach, it would not accept cl II (a) as a term of the contract. In the event of breach, the employer would be liable not only to the penalty but also to pay damages in contract.

In contracts of this nature, apparently lacking written formality and detailed specificity, it still is necessary to show that the term in question would have been accepted by the contracting parties as a matter so obvious that it would go without saying. That cannot be postulated here.

Nor could it be said that the implication into the contract of employment of a term to the effect of cl 11(a) of the Award would be necessary for their reasonable or effective operation. In the absence of such a contractual provision, there would remain unaffected the entitlement of the employer at general law to terminate at will on giving reasonable notice and to dismiss summarily for misconduct. That this would be the case was accepted in the submissions of both sides to this Court. Thus, there would be no 'gap' which it was necessary to fill by a provision such as cl 11(a).

Accordingly, we accept the submissions for the respondent that the term for which the appellants contend is not to be implied as a matter of business efficacy in its contracts of employment with the appellants.

The case also involved a cross-appeal by Australian Airlines on the matter of failures in the Full Court's reversal of some findings of fact by the trial judge; this cross-appeal was upheld and resulted in the case returning to the Full Court of the Federal Court on that issue.

9.4.2 Establishing necessity

In practice, the requirement to show necessity is a particularly burdensome one for parties arguing for an implied term in fact. The reality that parties may address contractual issues in any number of competing ways, that negotiation may result in a plethora of possible outcomes, and the difficult evidential basis for any such claim all militate against such implications. Necessity arguments failed in *Byrne* (above) and *Codelfa* (below).

Codelfa Construction Pty Ltd v State Rail Authority of New South Wales (1982) 149 CLR 337

Facts and issues

A contract was formed between the State Rail Authority (NSW) and an Italian company, Codelfa Construction, to build in a fixed period of time the (mostly underground) Eastern Suburbs train line in Sydney. As a result of an injunction successfully sought by residents who lived above the proposed train line, the work hours and building methods stated in the contract were significantly curtailed, which increased the cost of construction.

Following completion of the project, Codelfa sued the State Rail Authority on a *quantum meruit* basis ('as much as is deserved'; to claim a reasonable sum for the work completed) arguing, amongst other things, that the original contract had been brought to an end and that a higher sum than stated in the contract should be paid by the State Rail Authority. The dispute was initially referred to an Arbitrator, as required by the contract, who made certain findings of fact, although several legal issues had not been determined. After the report of the Arbitrator, Lush J of the New South Wales Supreme Court found for Codelfa on the basis of an implied term that covered the additional costs. A subsequent appeal to the Court of Appeal was largely dismissed (the implied term was maintained although slightly varied). Codelfa appealed to the High Court.

Several issues were examined on appeal. One issue was whether the contract included an implied term that, in the case of certain intervening events, additional costs could be claimed by Codelfa (this issue is the focus of the extracts below). Another issue was whether the contract had been frustrated by the injunction and related changes (see **15.2.4** for extracts in relation to the frustration argument). A further issue was whether Codelfa was estopped from arguing frustration ('issue estoppel'), on the basis that the Arbitrator's decision (which arose out of a power commonly called a '*Scott v Avery* clause') had already determined the question of frustration. The estoppel argument was rejected by the majority, who found that a decision earlier in the litigation by Yeldham J of the New South Wales Supreme Court had excluded the issue of frustration from the Arbitrator's jurisdiction, which meant the issue was still open for later courts to determine.

Decision

Appeal allowed: the implied terms argument was rejected; however, frustration had occurred. The matter could be returned to the Arbitrator to determine Codelfa's entitlement to claim on a *quantum meruit* basis rather than on the fee stated in the contract.

Per Mason J at 345:

> **(1) Implied Term.**
>
> In this ocean of litigious controversy there is one large island of agreement between the parties. It is common ground that their contract consists of the agreement dated 21 March 1972 and the various documents which it incorporates. The appellant does not suggest that dehors [trans. 'outside of'] the agreement and the incorporated documents there is to be found a term actually agreed upon by the parties which together with the contract documents stands as the true contract or which stands in its own right as a collateral contract. Nor does the appellant suggest that there is a case for rectification arising from the existence of such a term on the

footing that it was inadvertently omitted from the contract documents. The appellant's case is that a term has to be implied in the contract to give it business efficacy, to make it workable. Consequently, there is no contest as to what constitutes the contract; rather the contest is as to its meaning and effect.

When we say that the implication of a term raises an issue as to the meaning and effect of the contract we do not intend by that statement to convey that the court is embarking upon an orthodox exercise in the interpretation of the language of a contract, that is, assigning a meaning to a particular provision. Nonetheless, the implication of a term is an exercise in interpretation, though not an orthodox instance.

Of course, I am speaking of an implied term necessary to give business efficacy to a particular contract, not of the implied term which is a legal incident of a particular class of contract, of which *Liverpool City Council v Irwin* ([1977] A.C. 239) is an example. The difference between the two categories of implied term was mentioned by Viscount Simonds in *Lister v Romford Ice and Cold Storage Co. Ltd* ([1957] A.C. 555, at p. 516) where he referred to the search for the second category of [346] implied term as being based 'upon more general considerations', a comment endorsed by Lord Wilberforce in *Irwin*.

The implication of a term is to be compared, and at the same time contrasted, with rectification of the contract. In each case the problem is caused by a deficiency in the expression of the consensual agreement. A term which should have been included has been omitted. The difference is that with rectification the term which has been omitted and should have been included was actually agreed upon; with implication the term is one which it is presumed that the parties would have agreed upon had they turned their minds to it — it is not a term that they have actually agreed upon. Thus, in the case of the implied term the deficiency in the expression of the consensual agreement is caused by the failure of the parties to direct their minds to a particular eventuality and to make explicit provision for it. Rectification ensures that the contract gives effect to the parties' actual intention; the implication of a term is designed to give effect to the parties' presumed intention.

For obvious reasons the courts are slow to imply a term. In many cases, what the parties have actually agreed upon represents the totality of their willingness to agree; each may be prepared to take his chance in relation to an eventuality for which no provision is made. The more detailed and comprehensive the contract the less ground there is for supposing that the parties have failed to address their minds to the question at issue. And then there is the difficulty of identifying with any degree of certainty the term which the parties would have settled upon had they considered the question.

Accordingly, the courts have been at pains to emphasize that it is not enough that it is reasonable to imply a term; it must be necessary to do so to give business efficacy to the contract. So in *Heimann v The Commonwealth* ((1938) 38 S.R. (N.S.W.) 691, at p. 695) Jordan C.J., citing *Bell v Lever Brothers Ltd* ([1932) A.C. 161, at p. 226), stressed that in order to justify the importation of an implied term it is 'not sufficient that it would be reasonable to imply the term. ... It must be clearly necessary'. ...

The basis on which the courts act in implying a term was expressed by MacKinnon L.J. in *Shirlaw v Southern Foundries* [347] *(1926) Ltd* (1939) 2 K.B. 206, at p. 227) in terms that have been universally accepted: 'Prima facie that which in any contract is left to be implied and need not be expressed is something so obvious that it goes without saying ...'

The conditions necessary to ground the implication of a term were summarized by the majority in *B.P. Refinery (Westernport) Pty. Ltd v Hastings Shire Council*:

> (1) it must be reasonable and equitable; (2) it must be necessary to give business efficacy to the contract, so that no term will be implied if the contract is effective without

> it; (3) it must be so obvious that 'it goes without saying'; (4) it must be capable of clear expression; (5) it must not contradict any express term of the contract.

Mason J then engaged in an extensive discussion of the role of the parol evidence rule in circumscribing the evidence that could be considered in this form of argument.

> [353] The implication of the term found by the Court of Appeal rests on findings made by the Arbitrator based on circumstances surrounding the making of the contract, including evidence of the discussions between the parties which preceded entry into the contract. Thus the Arbitrator found that there was a common understanding [354] (described as a 'belief' by the Court of Appeal) that the works would be carried out on a three shift continuous basis six days per week and without restriction as to Sundays. He also found that the Authority had represented to Codelfa, and that it had accepted, that no injunction would be granted in relation to noise or other nuisance. He further found that the works could not be carried out in accordance with methods and programmes agreed between the parties unless Codelfa worked three shifts a day for six days a week.
>
> The first question is whether, in the light of the principles as I have explained them, it was legitimate to look to this material on the issue of implication of a term. I think it was. The discussions which generated these findings were not negotiations about the terms of the contract. The terms of the contract documents had been determined in advance by the Authority. By lodging its tender Codelfa accepted the Authority's contract documents. The relevant discussions were therefore directed to the question of price. Their object was to enable Codelfa to inform itself of what was involved in the work and to cost it so as to arrive at a price for inclusion in its tender. The consequence is that the discussions did not have the character of negotiations in the course of which the parties gradually evolved the terms of a bargain ultimately embodied in written form. Had the discussions been of that kind then, as we have seen, recourse to them would have been prohibited for the purpose of interpreting the contract by reference to the parties' actual intentions as expressed before entry into the contract. As it was, the relevant discussions reflect neither the preliminary consensus that merged into the written contract, nor statements made during the course of negotiations indicative of the unilateral intentions of each party. Instead the evidence revealed a matter which was in the common contemplation of the parties yet was not a contractual provision actually agreed upon for the simple reason that it was a matter of common assumption.
>
> To say that the maintenance of three eight hour shifts a day for six days a week was a matter of common contemplation between the parties is not enough in itself to justify the implication of a term. Lord Atkin's example of the sale of a painting believed by both seller and buyer to be the work of an old master (*Bell*) ((1932) A.C., at p. 226) is a striking illustration. It must appear that the matter of common contemplation was necessary to give the contract business efficacy and that the term sought to be implied is so obvious that it goes without saying.
>
> [355] In this case the problem, as I see it, lies not so much in saying that the implication of a term is necessary to give business efficacy to the contract, as in concluding that the particular term to be implied is so obvious that 'it goes without saying'. . . .
>
> . . . there remains an insurmountable problem in saying that 'it goes without saying' that had the parties contemplated the possibility that their legal advice was incorrect and that an injunction might be granted to restrain noise or other nuisance, they would have settled upon the term implied by the Court of Appeal or that implied by the Arbitrator and by Ash J. at first instance. I doubt whether the fiction of treating the parties as reasonable and fair makes the problem any the less difficult. This is not a case in which [356] an obvious provision was overlooked by the parties and omitted from the contract. Rather it was a case in which the

parties made a common assumption which masked the need to explore what provision should be made to cover the event which occurred. In ordinary circumstances negotiation about that matter might have yielded any one of a number of alternative provisions, each being regarded as a reasonable solution.

... My reluctance to imply a term is the stronger because the contract in this case was not a negotiated contract. The terms were determined by the Authority in advance and there is some force in the argument that the Authority looked to Codelfa to shoulder the responsibility for all risks not expressly provided for in the contract. It is a factor which in my view makes it very difficult to conclude that either of the terms sought to be implied is so obvious that it goes without saying.

Per Brennan J at 404:

(1) Implied Term.

Looking at the contract in the present case, in the matrix of the facts in which it was made, I see no necessity for the implication of a term, nor can I find that the criteria set out in *B.P. Refinery* are satisfied by any of the terms proposed respectively by the Court of Appeal, Ash J. and the Arbitrator.

The contract required Codelfa to perform the works described in the specification, taking all reasonable measures possible to avoid noise and nuisance, and providing whatever labour, materials, plant, tools and equipment were necessary for the proper completion of the contract, for a price calculated at the unit prices set out in the tendered schedule of rates adjusted in accordance with the rise and fall clause. Codelfa had promised to complete the works within 130 weeks of the date of the notice to proceed or such extended time as the engineer might allow on account of causes beyond the control of Codelfa and to perform those works regardless of their difficulty. The simple fact was that Codelfa was unable lawfully to perform the works within the promised time. It was entitled to seek an extension of time from the engineer and it did so. The reason given for seeking the extension is that Codelfa could not complete [405] the contract works within the promised time unless it worked three shifts a day and that had been found to cause an actionable nuisance.

The contract reveals no lacuna which must be filled to make it work. It works perfectly well. It is a case of a contractor who promised to complete work within a time which was too short having regard to the hours during which it was lawful to work and the speed at which the construction team was capable of working. It was not an express term of the contract that Codelfa would work three shifts a day and, having regard to the environment in which the works were to be performed, Codelfa could not lawfully have promised that it would do so. Codelfa's promise to complete the works was a promise to do so lawfully. It was not an express term of the contract that Codelfa would not be restrained by injunction if it committed an actionable nuisance. The Commissioner could not have promised that the courts would not intervene if Codelfa committed an actionable nuisance. No doubt the Commissioner and Codelfa shared a mistaken belief that Codelfa would be able to work three shifts a day lawfully, or at least without liability to restraint by injunction, because they mistakenly believed that s. 11 of the City and Suburban Electric Railways Act conferred an immunity upon Codelfa. That mistake could not give rise to an implied term. If, at the time when the parties were signing the contract, the officious bystander had asked what did they intend in the event of the issue of an injunction restraining work during the night shift, they would have replied: 'We have thought of that. It cannot happen.' They cannot be presumed to have agreed upon a term inconsistent with their common belief.

Each of the terms which the Court of Appeal, Ash J. and the Arbitrator respectively held to be implied would entitle Codelfa to additional reward for doing what the contract required to be done at the prices therein specified, or would relieve Codelfa of a liability for failing to complete the contract works within the time therein specified. The only provision for extending time is that contained in G.44(7), but Codelfa sought the implication of a term which would work an extension of time apart from G.44(7) or would affect the financial consequences of its failure in timely performance. Perhaps the divergence of opinion as to the form which an implied term should take points to error in the attempt to imply a term. At least it suggests that the term is not so obvious that 'it goes without saying'. . . .

[406] The refusal by the courts to go outside the four corners of a contract to find a term implied therein may be productive of hardship in particular cases. But the remedy is not to apply some general and inevitably imprecise notion of what is fair or reasonable [407] in order to alter what the parties have agreed. The court simply gives effect to their agreement, and leaves in their hands the arrangements which must be made for their respective protection. The parties in the present case made no provision to alter the consequences of their agreement if their common understanding as to the immunity of Codelfa from injunction should prove to be, as it was, erroneous. Whether they would have reached agreement if they had so negotiated is both impossible and irrelevant to say. It is not for the court to alter the consequences of applying the terms of the contract to the events to which those terms clearly refer. No implied term can be found.

The findings of the Arbitrator upon which Codelfa relied to establish an implied term suggest that its real complaint is that the Commissioner represented and promised that it would be immune from injunction and the representation was false and the promise was broken. Those were not the bases on which Codelfa pursued its claims, though I do not suggest that either basis would have been more fruitful than the bases of the proceedings now under consideration.

Aickin J found there was no implied term as there were too many possible variations of a clause that could be implied without any one version being compelling. Stephen J concurred with Mason J on the implied term argument. Wilson J concurred with Mason and Aickin JJ on the implied term argument.

QUESTIONS

(1) Can *Byrne* be removed from its employment and industrial relations context or is a case limited by the specific characteristics of contracts of employment?

(2) The power to imply a term in fact gives judges a great deal of authority over the terms of a contract; how do Mason and Brennan JJ justify the court's role and what are the risks with this approach?

9.5 Terms implied by custom and practice

Concepts	Short explanation	Relevant authorities	*Principles* text*
Terms implied by custom and practice	Terms may be implied into a contract if the terms are part of a notorious custom or practice in an industry	*Con-Stan Industries of Australia Pty Ltd v Norwich Winterthur Insurance (Australia) Ltd* (1986) 160 CLR 226	Chapter 9: 9.24

* Consult the corresponding section(s) of the *Principles* text for more detail.

9.5.1 Establishing custom and practice

Traditionally, many common terms in commercial contracts arose through implication based on custom and practice in an industry; however, with the rise of greater and greater documentation of contracts, this basis for implied terms is successful less often than it may have been. The relevant test is set out in the case of *Con-Stan* (extracted below).

Con-Stan Industries of Australia Pty Ltd v Norwich Winterthur Insurance (Australia) Ltd (1986) 160 CLR 226

Facts and issues

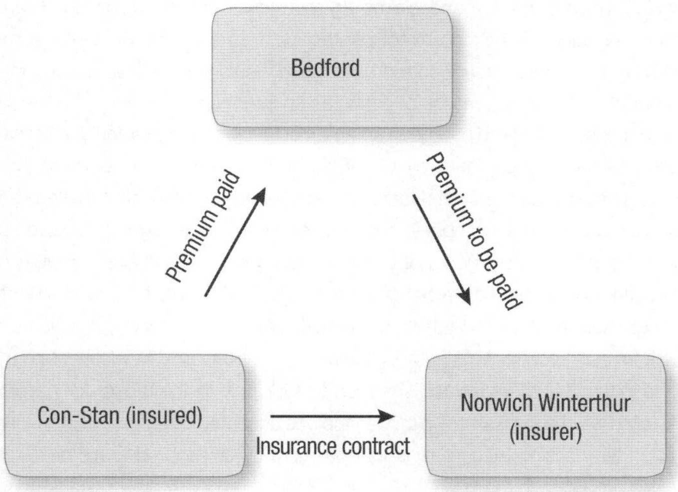

Con-Stan, a commercial business, worked with Bedford Insurance, an insurance broker, to find Con-Stan's commercial insurance. Bedford selected Norwich Winterthur, an insurer (or 'insurance underwriter'), for Con-Stan. Con-Stan, as the insured (or 'assured'), paid the insurance premium for Norwich Winterthur to Bedford to then pass on to Norwich Winterthur. However, Bedford did not pass on the premium. Subsequently, Bedford was wound up (on application by Norwich Winterthur), although the debt to Norwich Winterthur was not covered. Norwich Winterthur then sued Con-Stan for the unpaid premium.

Con-Stan argued that there was an implied term based on custom and usage in the insurance industry that an insurance underwriter could only look to the insurance broker for payment and not the insured party. At trial, Rogers J found for Con-Stan on the basis of such an implied term. The New South Wales Court of Appeal reversed the decision on appeal. Con-Stan then appealed to the High Court.

The issue was whether there was an implied term based on custom and usage that denied Norwich Winterthur's claim against Con-Stan.

Decision

Appeal dismissed: there was an insufficient basis in evidence of custom and usage to imply such a term.

Per Gibbs CJ, Mason, Wilson, Brennan and Dawson JJ at 233:

> The principal issue arising for consideration is whether an insurer may recover outstanding premiums from an assured who has already paid them to his insurance broker, but which the broker has failed to pass on to the insurer. In contracts of marine insurance the matter is governed by s. 59 of the *Marine Insurance Act 1909* (Cth) which provides, in terms which are declaratory of the common law governing such contracts, that unless otherwise agreed, where a marine policy is effected on behalf of the assured by a broker, the broker is directly responsible to the insurer for the premium. The necessary corollary is that an insurer has no recourse against the assured if the broker defaults on payment of the premium. The question that must be decided in this appeal is whether a similar principle applies to general non-maritime insurance . . .
>
> [234] It is clear from these facts [found by Rogers J] that, subject to the cases mentioned below in which insurers have made claims against policy-holders following default by the broker, an insurer generally had no direct contact with an assured. All dealings were done through the broker, but this is really no more than one would expect in a situation in which an agent is engaged for the very purpose of acting as an intermediary.
>
> In the present case, if Bedford had been an agent of Norwich with authority to receive money on the latter's behalf, the payment by Con-Stan of its premiums to Bedford would have constituted payment to the principal. Norwich's sole recourse would then have been against Bedford for failure to account for moneys received in its capacity as agent. However, under the general principles of the law of agency, a broker is the agent of the assured, not the insurer . . .
>
> [235] The principal submission advanced on behalf of the appellant, and the one which assumed the greatest importance both in argument before this Court and at the trial, is that there is an implied term in the contract of insurance between Con-Stan and Norwich, arising by virtue of custom in the industry, that an insurer is entitled to look only to the broker for payment of the premium. An alternative submission, which was the one accepted by Rogers J. at first instance, is that the implied term arising by custom is that payment by an assured to his broker is a good discharge of his obligation to the insurer. The two submissions clearly differ because in the former the existence of an obligation in the assured to pay the premiums to [236] the insurer is denied, whereas in the latter it is accepted but regarded as discharged by payment to the broker. Thus, an assured who made no payment of premiums to his broker would not be liable to the insurer under the primary submission, but would be if the alternative submission were accepted.
>
> The circumstances in which trade custom or usage may form the basis for the implication of terms into a contract have been considered in many cases. The cases have established the following propositions:
>
> (1) The existence of a custom or usage that will justify the implication of a term into a contract is a question of fact: *Nelson v. Dahl* ((1879) 12 Ch. D. 568, at p. 575). The critical dependence of a finding of custom on the facts of the particular case means there is little to be gained by referring (as counsel for the appellant urged us to do) to the practices of the London marine market in the last century, notwithstanding that those practices formed the basis for the implication, in contracts of marine insurance, of a term similar to the first of the terms alternatively contended for in this case . . .
>
> (2) There must be evidence that the custom relied on is so well known and acquiesced in that everyone making a contract in that situation can reasonably be presumed to have imported that term into the contract: *Young v. Tockassie* ((1905) 2 CLR 470, at p. 478); *Summers v. The Commonwealth* ((1918) 25 CLR 144, at p. 148); *Majeau Carrying Co. Pty. Ltd. v. Coastal Rutile Ltd.* ((1973) 129 CLR 48, at pp. 60–61). In the words of Jessel M.R. in

Nelson v. Dahl ((1879) 12 Ch. D. 568, at p. 575), approved by Knox C.J. in *Thornley v. Tilley* ((1925) 36 CLR I, at p. 8):

> [The custom] must be so notorious that everybody in the trade enters into a contract with that usage as an implied term. It must be uniform as well as reasonable, and it must have quite as much certainty as the written contract itself.

However, it is not necessary that the custom be universally accepted, for such a requirement would always be defeated by the denial by one litigant of the very matter that the other party seeks to prove in the proceedings.

(3) A term will not be implied into a contract on the basis of [237] custom where it is contrary to the express terms of the agreement: *Summers v. The Commonwealth* ((1918) 25 CLR, at p. 148); *Rosenhain v. Commonwealth Bank of Australia* ((1922) 31 CLR 46, at p. 53). One explanation of this principle is that, in so far as it relates to written contracts, it is simply an application of the parol evidence rule, by which extrinsic evidence is generally inadmissible to add to, vary or contradict the express terms of a contract which has been reduced to writing: *Bacchus Marsh Concentrated Milk Co. Ltd. (In liq.) v. Joseph Nathan & Co. Ltd.* ((1919) 26 CLR 410, at p. 427); *Hoyt's Proprietary Ltd. v. Spencer* ((1919) 27 CLR 133, at pp. 143–144). A more fundamental explanation is that the presumed intention of the parties, on which the importation of the custom rests *(Produce Brokers Co. Ltd. v. Olympia Oil and Cake Co. Ltd.* ([1916] 1 AC 314, at p. 324; cf. Treitel, *Law of Contract,* 6th ed. (1983), p. 164), must yield to their actual intention as embodied in the express terms of the contract, regardless of whether the contract is written or oral.

It has sometimes been said that the implication of a term into a contract does not depend on the parties' intention, actual or presumed, but on broader considerations: *Shell U.K. Ltd. v. Lostock Garage Ltd.* ([1976] 1 WLR 1187, at p. 1196; [1977] 1 All ER 481, at p. 487); *Lister v. Roniford Ice and Cold Storage Co. Ltd.* ((1957) AC 555, at pp. 576, 579); *Liverpool City Council v. Irwin* ([1977] AC 239, at pp. 257, 258). But these statements are directed to situations in which the courts have been asked to imply terms amounting to rules of law applicable to all contracts of a particular class. The present case is of a different kind in which it may be necessary to speak of presumed intention. In matters of this kind, that phrase means no more than that the general notoriety of the custom makes it reasonable to assume that the parties contracted on the basis of the custom, and that it is therefore reasonable to import such a term into the contract.

(4) A person may be bound by a custom notwithstanding the fact that he had no knowledge of it. Historically the courts approached this question in a rather different way. It was said that, as a general rule, a person who was ignorant of the existence of a custom or usage was not bound by it. To this rule there was a qualification that a person would be presumed to know of the usage if it was of such notoriety that all persons dealing in that sphere could easily ascertain the nature and content of the custom. It would then be reasonable to impute that knowledge to a person, notwithstanding [238] his ignorance of it: see *Halsbury's Laws of England,* 4th ed. vol. 12, pars 467–468; *Jones v. Canavan* ([1972] 2 NSWLR 236 at 243). In this way, the issue of notoriety discussed in (2) above came to be co-extensive with the question of imputed knowledge. The achievement of sufficient notoriety was both a necessary and sufficient condition for knowledge of a custom to be attributed to a person who was in fact unaware of it. The result is that in modern times nothing turns on the presence or absence of actual knowledge of the custom; that matter will stand or fall with the resolution of the issue of the degree of notoriety which the custom has achieved. The respondent's contention that industry practices unknown to the assured are incapable of forming the basis of an implied term of the contract cannot be sustained.

In order to establish a custom to the effect that a broker is alone liable to an insurer for payment of a premium on a policy of insurance, it is not sufficient to show that in the ordinary course of events the premium is paid to the insurer by the broker, nor is it sufficient to show that where a broker has failed to pay a premium the insurer makes its first demand for payment from the broker. Both circumstances are consistent with the continued liability of the assured. It is necessary to establish a clear course of conduct under which insurers do not look to the assured for payment of the premium. This may be established by proving either an absence of claims by insurers against assured, or the existence of claims directed exclusively to brokers as a practice rarely if ever departed from. Having examined the evidence of custom that was led in the present case, we do not think this requirement is satisfied. The evidence to which we shall refer shortly revealed a number of instances of insurers seeking a second payment from the assured notwithstanding that they had already paid their brokers …

[239] At first instance, Mr. Hoffman, a man of considerable experience in the insurance industry both as insurer and broker, was called to give evidence as to his knowledge of other cases in which an insurer sought to recover a second payment from an assured following a broker's default. He stated that prior to 1973 this was virtually unheard of but that since that date it had become 'relatively common practice'. Mr. Wade, who had had some twenty-nine years experience in the insurance industry in Australia, gave evidence of about a dozen cases since 1973 in which the insurance company of which he was manager sought a second payment in similar circumstances. Some of these were said to have occurred before [240] 1977–1978. The same picture is painted by the witness Greenwood, who also said there was a number of such cases prior to 1977. It should be said that there was other evidence of second payments being sought from assured following a broker's default, but these related to instances after 1977 and thus can be of no assistance in determining whether the custom alleged could properly form the basis for the implication of a term in the contract at the time it was concluded. No adverse finding was made as to the veracity or reliability of any of these witnesses. In some of these cases the insurer received full satisfaction of its claim for a second payment of the premium, in some a compromise was reached, while in others the assured refused to make any additional payment – a response which so far as the evidence showed was only once followed up by the institution of legal proceedings. In the Court of Appeal Hutley J.A. did not regard this evidence as destroying the custom alleged. He said ((1983) 1 NSWLR 461, at p. 466):

> The fact that there are occasional departures from a uniform course of business does not prove the non-existence of a custom – otherwise no custom would ever be proved because those denying its existence in the instant case could, by their own eccentric conduct, destroy it as a legal custom. The fact that one soldier is out of step does not show that it is not customary for troops to march in step on parade.

The existence of a custom sufficiently settled in its observance to found the implication of a term into a contract is very much a matter of fact and degree, but, with respect to his Honour, we do not share his view of the effect of the evidence just cited. This evidence supports the inference that at least since 1973, it was a not uncommon view of those involved in the industry that insurers were entitled to look past the broker for payment of the premium. The fact that several assured were prepared to pay the premiums again, in whole or part, may indicate that that was a view with which they did not entirely disagree. Mr. Hoffman agreed that the legal obligations of an assured have been a matter of great uncertainty for a number of years. The learned trial judge was prepared to rely on Mr. Hoffman's conclusion as to accepted practice in the industry, while acknowledging that the parties involved had not addressed their minds to the legal consequences that were to be accepted as accompanying that practice. But, as Glass J.A. observed in the Court of Appeal (67), a custom that falls short of involving a recognition of rights and liabilities fails to provide a firm foundation for the implication of terms in a contract.

In our opinion, in the light of this evidence, it is not possible to [241] say that the custom alleged has been proved to the high standard which the law requires. It has not been shown that the custom relied on is so well known and acquiesced in that everyone making a contract in that situation can reasonably be presumed to have imported that term into the contract. This conclusion accords with the view of Sutton, *Insurance Law in Australia and New Zealand* (1980), pp. 181–182.

QUESTIONS

(1) The outcome of this case turns in large measure on the judges' differing interpretation of the significance of expert testimony; in what ways is this a satisfactory or unsatisfactory basis for achieving consistency on the creation of implied terms?

(2) Given the changing historical context to this form of implied term and the development of an extensive array of statutory remedies for unfair terms, is 'custom and usage' still an appropriate basis for implying a term into a contract?

9.6 Terms implied by law

Concepts	Short explanation	Relevant authorities	*Principles* text*
Terms implied by law	Courts will imply certain terms into particular classes of contract	*Byrne v Australian Airlines Ltd* (1995) 185 CLR 410 (see **9.4.1** for extract)	Chapter 9: 9.25–9.26

* Consult the corresponding section(s) of the *Principles* text for more detail.

9.6.1 Implied terms as default rules

Terms implied by law, as opposed to those implied in fact or by custom, effectively operate as 'default' rules in that they are all implied into all contracts of a particular type. A common example of the types of terms implied by law is from Williams[1], which was cited in *Byrne* at 448:

> Examples of such terms 'implied' into contracts by rules of law are the implied conditions of reasonable fitness and merchantable quality on a contract of sale of goods, the rule that payment and delivery of goods are concurrent conditions, the implied warranty of seaworthiness [for ships], the implied condition on the letting of a furnished house that it is reasonably fit for habitation, the implied promise by one who agrees to build a house that the house will be reasonably fit for habitation, the implied promise by a servant not to disclose secret processes, not to hand over to a rival written work completed for the master, and not, while still in his master's employment, to solicit the master's customers to transfer their custom to himself, the implied promise by an employer (in some cases) to

1 G Williams, 'Language and the Law' (1945) 61 *Law Quarterly Review* 71, 403.

furnish work, the implied duty of care in the carriage of passengers and in looking after bailed goods, and the implied promise by a banker not to disclose the state of his customer's account.

9.7 Statutory obligations for the supply of goods and services

Concepts	Short explanation	Relevant authorities	*Principles* text*
Statutory obligations	Statutes may impose rights and obligations on parties to contracts	*Sale of Goods Act 1923* (NSW) ss 17–20 Australian Consumer Law ss 2–3, 51–64A, 259–273	Chapter 9: 9.27

* Consult the corresponding section(s) of the *Principles* text for more detail.

9.7.1 Terms implied by statute

One method of installing protections for purchasers is by implying conditions directly into contracts by statute. A long-standing example of this approach is the Sale of Goods legislation, originally established in the United Kingdom via the *Sale of Goods Act 1893* then subsequently adopted in Australia. The New South Wales version is extracted below but equivalent provisions exist in all other states and territories: *Goods Act 1958* (Vic) ss 17–20; *Sale of Goods Act 1896* (Qld) ss 15–18; *Sale of Goods Act 1895* (WA) ss 12–15; *Sale of Goods Act 1895* (SA) ss 12–15; *Sale of Goods Act 1896* (Tas) ss 17–20; *Sale of Goods Act 1954* (ACT) ss 17–20; *Sale of Goods Act 1972* (NT) ss 17–20.

Sale of Goods Act 1923 (NSW) ss 17–20

17 Implied undertaking as to title etc

In a contract of sale, unless the circumstances of the contract are such as to show a different intention, there is:

(1) an implied condition on the part of the seller that in the case of a sale the seller has a right to sell the goods, and that in the case of an agreement to sell the seller will have a right to sell the goods at the time when the property is to pass,

(2) an implied warranty that the buyer shall have and enjoy quiet possession of the goods,

(3) an implied warranty that the goods shall be free from any charge or encumbrance in favour of any third party not declared or known to the buyer before or at the time when the contract is made.

18 Sale by description

Where there is a contract for the sale of goods by description, there is an implied condition that the goods shall correspond with the description; and if the sale be by sample as well as by description, it is not sufficient that the bulk of the goods corresponds with the sample if the goods do not also correspond with the description.

19 Implied condition as to quality or fitness

Subject to the provisions of this Act, and of any statute in that behalf, there is no implied warranty or condition as to the quality or fitness for any particular purpose of goods supplied under a contract of sale, except as follows:

(1) Where the buyer expressly or by implication makes known to the seller the particular purpose for which the goods are required so as to show that the buyer relies on the seller's skill or judgment, and the goods are of a description which it is in the course of the seller's business to supply (whether the seller be the manufacturer or not), there is an implied condition that the goods shall be reasonably fit for such purpose:

Provided that in the case of a contract for the sale of a specified article under its patent or other trade name there is no implied condition as to its fitness for any particular purpose.

(2) Where goods are bought by description from a seller who deals in goods of that description (whether the seller be the manufacturer or not), there is an implied condition that the goods shall be of merchantable quality:

Provided that if the buyer has examined the goods there shall be no implied condition as regards defects which such examination ought to have revealed.

(3) An implied warranty or condition as to quality or fitness for a particular purpose may be annexed by the usage of trade.

(4) An express warranty or condition does not negative a warranty or condition implied by this Act unless inconsistent therewith.

20 Sale by sample

(1) A contract of sale is a contract for sale by sample where there is a term in the contract express or implied to that effect.

(2) In the case of a contract for sale by sample:

- **(a)** there is an implied condition that the bulk shall correspond with the sample in quality,
- **(b)** there is an implied condition that the buyer shall have a reasonable opportunity of comparing the bulk with the sample,
- **(c)** there is an implied condition that the goods shall be free from any defect rendering them unmerchantable which would not be apparent on reasonable examination of the sample.

9.7.2 A different approach: consumer guarantees

A more expansive approach to consumer rights was enacted through the *Trade Practices Act 1974* (Cth), which created a broader range of consumer rights for good or services. However, this Act still proceeded on the basis that such rights were to be enforced as implied contract terms. The passing of the *Competition and Consumer Act 2010* (Cth) enacted a much more wide-ranging reform through the creation of the Australian Consumer Law, which replicated aspects of the earlier regime but now established them as statutory rights. The relevant parts on consumer guarantees (Part 3-2) and their enforcement (Part 5-4) are extracted below. Given the extensive nature of these rights, detailed examination of the provisions is found in the *Principles* text at 9.28–9.44.

Australian Consumer Law ss 2–3, 51–64A, 259–273

Chapter 1 – Introduction

2 Definitions

(1) In this Schedule: . . .

goods includes:

(a) ships, aircraft and other vehicles; and

(b) animals, including fish; and

(c) minerals, trees and crops, whether on, under or attached to land or not; and

(d) gas and electricity; and

(e) computer software; and

(f) second-hand goods; and

(g) any component part of, or accessory to, goods.

[. . .]

services includes:

(a) any rights (including rights in relation to, and interests in, real or personal property), benefits, privileges or facilities that are, or are to be, provided, granted or conferred in trade or commerce; and

(b) without limiting paragraph (a), the rights, benefits, privileges or facilities that are, or are to be, provided, granted or conferred under:

(i) a contract for or in relation to the performance of work (including work of a professional nature), whether with or without the supply of goods; or

(ii) a contract for or in relation to the provision of, or the use or enjoyment of facilities for, amusement, entertainment, recreation or instruction; or

(iii) a contract for or in relation to the conferring of rights, benefits or privileges for which remuneration is payable in the form of a royalty, tribute, levy or similar exaction; or

(iv) a contract of insurance; or

(v) a contract between a banker and a customer of the banker entered into in the course of the carrying on by the banker of the business of banking; or

(vi) any contract for or in relation to the lending of money;

but does not include rights or benefits being the supply of goods or the performance of work under a contract of service.

3 Meaning of consumer

Acquiring goods as a consumer

(1) A person is taken to have acquired particular goods as a ***consumer*** if, and only if:

(a) the amount paid or payable for the goods, as worked out under subsections (4) to (9), did not exceed:

(i) $40,000; or

(ii) if a greater amount is prescribed for the purposes of this paragraph—that greater amount; or

(b) the goods were of a kind ordinarily acquired for personal, domestic or household use or consumption; or

(c) the goods consisted of a vehicle or trailer acquired for use principally in the transport of goods on public roads.

(2) However, subsection (1) does not apply if the person acquired the goods, or held himself or herself out as acquiring the goods:

(a) for the purpose of re-supply; or

(b) for the purpose of using them up or transforming them, in trade or commerce:

(i) in the course of a process of production or manufacture; or

(ii) in the course of repairing or treating other goods or fixtures on land.

Acquiring services as a consumer

(3) A person is taken to have acquired particular services as a ***consumer*** if, and only if:

(a) the amount paid or payable for the services, as worked out under subsections (4) to (9), did not exceed:

(i) $40,000; or

(ii) if a greater amount is prescribed for the purposes of subsection (1)(a)—that greater amount; or

(b) the services were of a kind ordinarily acquired for personal, domestic or household use or consumption.

Part 3-2 – Consumer transactions
Division 1 – Consumer guarantees
Subdivision A – Guarantees relating to the supply of goods
51 Guarantee as to title

(1) If a person (the ***supplier***) supplies goods to a consumer, there is a guarantee that the supplier will have a right to dispose of the property in the goods when that property is to pass to the consumer.

(2) Subsection (1) does not apply to a supply (a ***supply of limited title***) if an intention that the supplier of the goods should transfer only such title as the supplier, or another person, may have:

(a) appears from the contract for the supply; or

(b) is to be inferred from the circumstances of that contract.

(3) This section does not apply if the supply is a supply by way of hire or lease.

52 Guarantee as to undisturbed possession

(1) If:

(a) a person (the ***supplier***) supplies goods to a consumer; and

(b) the supply is not a supply of limited title;

there is a guarantee that the consumer has the right to undisturbed possession of the goods.

(2) Subsection (1) does not apply to the extent that the consumer's undisturbed possession of the goods may be lawfully disturbed by a person who is entitled to the benefit of any security, charge or encumbrance disclosed to the consumer before the consumer agreed to the supply.

(3) If:

(a) a person (the ***supplier***) supplies goods to a consumer; and

(b) the supply is a supply of limited title;

there is a guarantee that the following persons will not disturb the consumer's possession of the goods:

(c) the supplier;

(d) if the parties to the contract for the supply intend that the supplier should transfer only such title as another person may have—that other person;

(e) anyone claiming through or under the supplier or that other person (otherwise than under a security, charge or encumbrance disclosed to the consumer before the consumer agreed to the supply).

(4) This section applies to a supply by way of hire or lease only for the period of the hire or lease.

53 Guarantee as to undisclosed securities etc.

(1) If:

(a) a person (the ***supplier***) supplies goods to a consumer; and

(b) the supply is not a supply of limited title;

there is a guarantee that:

(c) the goods are free from any security, charge or encumbrance:

(i) that was not disclosed to the consumer, in writing, before the consumer agreed to the supply; or

(ii) that was not created by or with the express consent of the consumer; and

(d) the goods will remain free from such a security, charge or encumbrance until the time when the property in the goods passes to the consumer.

(2) A supplier does not fail to comply with the guarantee only because of the existence of a floating charge over the supplier's assets unless and until the charge becomes fixed and enforceable by the person to whom the charge is given.

Note: Section 339 of the *Personal Property Securities Act 2009* affects the meaning of the references in this subsection to a floating charge and a fixed charge.

(3) If:

(a) a person (the ***supplier***) supplies goods to a consumer; and

(b) the supply is a supply of limited title;

there is a guarantee that all securities, charges or encumbrances known to the supplier, and not known to the consumer, were disclosed to the consumer before the consumer agreed to the supply.

(4) This section does not apply if the supply is a supply by way of hire or lease.

54 Guarantee as to acceptable quality

(1) If:

(a) a person supplies, in trade or commerce, goods to a consumer; and

(b) the supply does not occur by way of sale by auction;

there is a guarantee that the goods are of acceptable quality.

(2) Goods are of ***acceptable quality*** if they are as:

(a) fit for all the purposes for which goods of that kind are commonly supplied; and

(b) acceptable in appearance and finish; and

(c) free from defects; and

(d) safe; and

(e) durable;

as a reasonable consumer fully acquainted with the state and condition of the goods (including any hidden defects of the goods), would regard as acceptable having regard to the matters in subsection (3).

(3) The matters for the purposes of subsection (2) are:

(a) the nature of the goods; and

(b) the price of the goods (if relevant); and

(c) any statements made about the goods on any packaging or label on the goods; and

(d) any representation made about the goods by the supplier or manufacturer of the goods; and

(e) any other relevant circumstances relating to the supply of the goods.

(4) If:

(a) goods supplied to a consumer are not of acceptable quality; and

(b) the only reason or reasons why they are not of acceptable quality were specifically drawn to the consumer's attention before the consumer agreed to the supply;

the goods are taken to be of acceptable quality.

(5) If:

(a) goods are displayed for sale or hire; and

(b) the goods would not be of acceptable quality if they were supplied to a consumer;

the reason or reasons why they are not of acceptable quality are taken, for the purposes of subsection (4), to have been specifically drawn to a consumer's attention if those reasons were disclosed on a written notice that was displayed with the goods and that was transparent.

(6) Goods do not fail to be of acceptable quality if:

(a) the consumer to whom they are supplied causes them to become of unacceptable quality, or fails to take reasonable steps to prevent them from becoming of unacceptable quality; and

(b) they are damaged by abnormal use.

(7) Goods do not fail to be of acceptable quality if:

(a) the consumer acquiring the goods examines them before the consumer agrees to the supply of the goods; and

(b) the examination ought reasonably to have revealed that the goods were not of acceptable quality.

55 Guarantee as to fitness for any disclosed purpose etc.

(1) If:

(a) a person (the ***supplier***) supplies, in trade or commerce, goods to a consumer; and

(b) the supply does not occur by way of sale by auction;

there is a guarantee that the goods are reasonably fit for any disclosed purpose, and for any purpose for which the supplier represents that they are reasonably fit.

(2) A ***disclosed purpose*** is a particular purpose (whether or not that purpose is a purpose for which the goods are commonly supplied) for which the goods are being acquired by the consumer and that:

(a) the consumer makes known, expressly or by implication, to:

(i) the supplier; or

(ii) a person by whom any prior negotiations or arrangements in relation to the acquisition of the goods were conducted or made; or

(b) the consumer makes known to the manufacturer of the goods either directly or through the supplier or the person referred to in paragraph (a)(ii).

(3) This section does not apply if the circumstances show that the consumer did not rely on, or that it was unreasonable for the consumer to rely on, the skill or judgment of the supplier, the person referred to in subsection (2)(a)(ii) or the manufacturer, as the case may be.

56 Guarantee relating to the supply of goods by description

(1) If:

(a) a person supplies, in trade or commerce, goods by description to a consumer; and

(b) the supply does not occur by way of sale by auction;

there is a guarantee that the goods correspond with the description.

(2) A supply of goods is not prevented from being a supply by description only because, having been exposed for sale or hire, they are selected by the consumer.

(3) If goods are supplied by description as well as by reference to a sample or demonstration model, the guarantees in this section and in section 57 both apply.

57 Guarantees relating to the supply of goods by sample or demonstration model

(1) If:

(a) a person supplies, in trade or commerce, goods to a consumer by reference to a sample or demonstration model; and

(b) the supply does not occur by way of sale by auction;

there is a guarantee that:

(c) the goods correspond with the sample or demonstration model in quality, state or condition; and

(d) if the goods are supplied by reference to a sample—the consumer will have a reasonable opportunity to compare the goods with the sample; and

(e) the goods are free from any defect that:

(i) would not be apparent on reasonable examination of the sample or demonstration model; and

(ii) would cause the goods not to be of acceptable quality.

(2) If goods are supplied by reference to a sample or demonstration model as well as by description, the guarantees in section 56 and in this section both apply.

58 Guarantee as to repairs and spare parts

(1) If:

(a) a person supplies, in trade or commerce, goods to a consumer; and

(b) the supply does not occur by way of sale by auction;

there is a guarantee that the manufacturer of the goods will take reasonable action to ensure that facilities for the repair of the goods, and parts for the goods, are reasonably available for a reasonable period after the goods are supplied.

(2) This section does not apply if the manufacturer took reasonable action to ensure that the consumer would be given written notice, at or before the time when the consumer agrees to the supply of the goods, that:

(a) facilities for the repair of the goods would not be available or would not be available after a specified period; or

(b) parts for the goods would not be available or would not be available after a specified period.

59 Guarantee as to express warranties

(1) If:

(a) a person supplies, in trade or commerce, goods to a consumer; and

(b) the supply does not occur by way of sale by auction;

there is a guarantee that the manufacturer of the goods will comply with any express warranty given or made by the manufacturer in relation to the goods.

(2) If:

(a) a person supplies, in trade or commerce, goods to a consumer; and

(b) the supply does not occur by way of sale by auction;

there is a guarantee that the supplier will comply with any express warranty given or made by the supplier in relation to the goods.

Subdivision B – Guarantees relating to the supply of services

60 Guarantee as to due care and skill

If a person supplies, in trade or commerce, services to a consumer, there is a guarantee that the services will be rendered with due care and skill.

61 Guarantees as to fitness for a particular purpose etc.

(1) If:

(a) a person (the ***supplier***) supplies, in trade or commerce, services to a consumer; and

(b) the consumer, expressly or by implication, makes known to the supplier any particular purpose for which the services are being acquired by the consumer;

there is a guarantee that the services, and any product resulting from the services, will be reasonably fit for that purpose.

(2) If:

(a) a person (the ***supplier***) supplies, in trade or commerce, services to a consumer; and

(b) the consumer makes known, expressly or by implication, to:

(i) the supplier; or

(ii) a person by whom any prior negotiations or arrangements in relation to the acquisition of the services were conducted or made;

the result that the consumer wishes the services to achieve;

there is a guarantee that the services, and any product resulting from the services, will be of such a nature, and quality, state or condition, that they might reasonably be expected to achieve that result.

(3) This section does not apply if the circumstances show that the consumer did not rely on, or that it was unreasonable for the consumer to rely on, the skill or judgment of the supplier.

(4) This section does not apply to a supply of services of a professional nature by a qualified architect or engineer.

62 Guarantee as to reasonable time for supply

If:

(a) a person (the ***supplier***) supplies, in trade or commerce, services to a consumer; and

(b) the time within which the services are to be supplied:

(i) is not fixed by the contract for the supply of the services; or

(ii) is not to be determined in a manner agreed to by the consumer and supplier;

there is a guarantee that the services will be supplied within a reasonable time.

63 Services to which this Subdivision does not apply

(1) This Subdivision does not apply to services that are, or are to be, supplied under:

(a) a contract for or in relation to the transportation or storage of goods for the purposes of a business, trade, profession or occupation carried on or engaged in by the person for whom the goods are transported or stored; or

(b) a contract of insurance.

(2) To avoid doubt, subsection (1)(a) does not apply if the consignee of the goods is not carrying on or engaged in a business, trade, profession or occupation in relation to the goods.

Note: This subsection was inserted as a response to the decision of the High Court of Australia in *Wallis v Downard-Pickford (North Queensland) Pty Ltd* [1994] HCA 17.

Subdivision C – Guarantees not to be excluded etc. by contract

64 Guarantees not to be excluded etc. by contract

(1) A term of a contract (including a term that is not set out in the contract but is incorporated in the contract by another term of the contract) is void to the extent that the term purports to exclude, restrict or modify, or has the effect of excluding, restricting or modifying:

- **(a)** the application of all or any of the provisions of this Division; or
- **(b)** the exercise of a right conferred by such a provision; or
- **(c)** any liability of a person for a failure to comply with a guarantee that applies under this Division to a supply of goods or services.

(2) A term of a contract is not taken, for the purposes of this section, to exclude, restrict or modify the application of a provision of this Division unless the term does so expressly or is inconsistent with the provision.

64A Limitation of liability for failures to comply with guarantees

(1) A term of a contract for the supply by a person of goods other than goods of a kind ordinarily acquired for personal, domestic or household use or consumption is not void under section 64 merely because the term limits the person's liability for failure to comply with a guarantee (other than a guarantee under section 51, 52 or 53) to one or more of the following:

- **(a)** the replacement of the goods or the supply of equivalent goods;
- **(b)** the repair of the goods;
- **(c)** the payment of the cost of replacing the goods or of acquiring equivalent goods;
- **(d)** the payment of the cost of having the goods repaired.

(2) A term of a contract for the supply by a person of services other than services of a kind ordinarily acquired for personal, domestic or household use or consumption is not void under section 64 merely because the term limits the person's liability for failure to comply with a guarantee to:

- **(a)** the supplying of the services again; or
- **(b)** the payment of the cost of having the services supplied again.

(3) This section does not apply in relation to a term of a contract if the person to whom the goods or services were supplied establishes that it is not fair or reasonable for the person who supplied the goods or services to rely on that term of the contract.

(4) In determining for the purposes of subsection (3) whether or not reliance on a term of a contract is fair or reasonable, a court is to have regard to all the circumstances of the case, and in particular to the following matters:

- **(a)** the strength of the bargaining positions of the person who supplied the goods or services and the person to whom the goods or services were supplied (the ***buyer***) relative to each other, taking into account, among other things, the availability of equivalent goods or services and suitable alternative sources of supply;
- **(b)** whether the buyer received an inducement to agree to the term or, in agreeing to the term, had an opportunity of acquiring the goods or services or equivalent goods or services from any source of supply under a contract that did not include that term;

(c) whether the buyer knew or ought reasonably to have known of the existence and extent of the term (having regard, among other things, to any custom of the trade and any previous course of dealing between the parties);

(d) in the case of the supply of goods, whether the goods were manufactured, processed or adapted to the special order of the buyer.

Part 5-4 — Remedies relating to guarantees
Division 1 — Action against suppliers
Subdivision A —Action against suppliers of goods
259 Action against suppliers of goods

(1) A consumer may take action under this section if:
  (a) a person (the ***supplier***) supplies, in trade or commerce, goods to the consumer; and
  (b) a guarantee that applies to the supply under Subdivision A of Division 1 of Part 3-2 (other than sections 58 and 59(1)) is not complied with.

(2) If the failure to comply with the guarantee can be remedied and is not a major failure:
  (a) the consumer may require the supplier to remedy the failure within a reasonable time; or
  (b) if such a requirement is made of the supplier but the supplier refuses or fails to comply with the requirement, or fails to comply with the requirement within a reasonable time—the consumer may:
    (i) otherwise have the failure remedied and, by action against the supplier, recover all reasonable costs incurred by the consumer in having the failure so remedied; or
    (ii) subject to section 262, notify the supplier that the consumer rejects the goods and of the ground or grounds for the rejection.

(3) If the failure to comply with the guarantee cannot be remedied or is a major failure, the consumer may:
  (a) subject to section 262, notify the supplier that the consumer rejects the goods and of the ground or grounds for the rejection; or
  (b) by action against the supplier, recover compensation for any reduction in the value of the goods below the price paid or payable by the consumer for the goods.

(4) The consumer may, by action against the supplier, recover damages for any loss or damage suffered by the consumer because of the failure to comply with the guarantee if it was reasonably foreseeable that the consumer would suffer such loss or damage as a result of such a failure.

(5) Subsection (4) does not apply if the failure to comply with the guarantee occurred only because of a cause independent of human control that occurred after the goods left the control of the supplier.

(6) To avoid doubt, subsection (4) applies in addition to subsections (2) and (3).

(7) The consumer may take action under this section whether or not the goods are in their original packaging.

260 When a failure to comply with a guarantee is a major failure

A failure to comply with a guarantee referred to in section 259(1)(b) that applies to a supply of goods is a ***major failure*** if:

(a) the goods would not have been acquired by a reasonable consumer fully acquainted with the nature and extent of the failure; or

(b) the goods depart in one or more significant respects:
  (i) if they were supplied by description—from that description; or
  (ii) if they were supplied by reference to a sample or demonstration model—from that sample or demonstration model; or

(c) the goods are substantially unfit for a purpose for which goods of the same kind are commonly supplied and they cannot, easily and within a reasonable time, be remedied to make them fit for such a purpose; or

(d) the goods are unfit for a disclosed purpose that was made known to:

(i) the supplier of the goods; or

(ii) a person by whom any prior negotiations or arrangements in relation to the acquisition of the goods were conducted or made;

and they cannot, easily and within a reasonable time, be remedied to make them fit for such a purpose; or

(e) the goods are not of acceptable quality because they are unsafe.

261 How suppliers may remedy a failure to comply with a guarantee

If, under section 259(2)(a), a consumer requires a supplier of goods to remedy a failure to comply with a guarantee referred to in section 259(1)(b), the supplier may comply with the requirement:

(a) if the failure relates to title—by curing any defect in title; or

(b) if the failure does not relate to title—by repairing the goods; or

(c) by replacing the goods with goods of an identical type; or

(d) by refunding:

(i) any money paid by the consumer for the goods; and

(ii) an amount that is equal to the value of any other consideration provided by the consumer for the goods.

262 When consumers are not entitled to reject goods

(1) A consumer is not entitled, under section 259, to notify a supplier of goods that the consumer rejects the goods if:

(a) the rejection period for the goods has ended; or

(b) the goods have been lost, destroyed or disposed of by the consumer; or

(c) the goods were damaged after being delivered to the consumer for reasons not related to their state or condition at the time of supply; or

(d) the goods have been attached to, or incorporated in, any real or personal property and they cannot be detached or isolated without damaging them.

(2) The ***rejection period*** for goods is the period from the time of the supply of the goods to the consumer within which it would be reasonable to expect the relevant failure to comply with a guarantee referred to in section 259(1)(b) to become apparent having regard to:

(a) the type of goods; and

(b) the use to which a consumer is likely to put them; and

(c) the length of time for which it is reasonable for them to be used; and

(d) the amount of use to which it is reasonable for them to be put before such a failure becomes apparent.

263 Consequences of rejecting goods

(1) This section applies if, under section 259, a consumer notifies a supplier of goods that the consumer rejects the goods.

(2) The consumer must return the goods to the supplier unless:

(a) the goods have already been returned to, or retrieved by, the supplier; or

(b) the goods cannot be returned, removed or transported without significant cost to the consumer because of:

(i) the nature of the failure to comply with the guarantee to which the rejection relates; or

(ii) the size or height, or method of attachment, of the goods.

(3) If subsection (2)(b) applies, the supplier must, within a reasonable time, collect the goods at the supplier's expense.

(4) The supplier must, in accordance with an election made by the consumer:

(a) refund:

(i) any money paid by the consumer for the goods; and

(ii) an amount that is equal to the value of any other consideration provided by the consumer for the goods; or

(b) replace the rejected goods with goods of the same type, and of similar value, if such goods are reasonably available to the supplier.

(5) The supplier cannot satisfy subsection (4)(a) by permitting the consumer to acquire goods from the supplier.

(6) If the property in the rejected goods had passed to the consumer before the rejection was notified, the property in those goods revests in the supplier on the notification of the rejection.

264 Replaced goods

If the goods are replaced under section 261(c) or 263(4)(b):

(a) the replacement goods are taken, for the purposes of Division 1 of Part 3-2 and this Part, to be supplied by the supplier; and

(b) the provisions of Division 1 of Part 3-2 and this Part apply in relation to the replacement goods.

265 Termination of contracts for the supply of services that are connected with rejected goods

(1) If:

(a) under section 259, a consumer notifies a supplier of goods that the consumer rejects the goods; and

(b) the supplier is required under section 263(4)(a) to give the consumer a refund; and

(c) a person supplies, in trade or commerce, services to the consumer that are connected with the rejected goods;

the consumer may terminate the contract for the supply of the services.

(2) The termination takes effect:

(a) at the time the termination is made known to the supplier of the services (whether by words or by conduct indicating the consumer's intention to terminate the contract); or

(b) if it is not reasonably practicable to communicate with the supplier of the services—at the time the consumer indicates, by means which are reasonable in the circumstances, his or her intention to terminate the contract.

(3) The consumer is entitled to recover, by action against the supplier of the services, a refund of:

(a) any money paid by the consumer for the services; and

(b) an amount that is equal to the value of any other consideration provided by the consumer for the services;

to the extent that the consumer has not already consumed the services at the time the termination takes effect.

266 Rights of gift recipients

If a consumer acquires goods from a supplier and gives them to another person as a gift, the other person may, subject to any defence which would be available to the supplier against the consumer:

(a) exercise any rights or remedies under this Subdivision which would be available to the other person if he or she had acquired the goods from the supplier; and
(b) any reference in this Subdivision to a consumer includes a reference to the other person accordingly.

Subdivision B – Action against suppliers of services

267 Action against suppliers of services

(1) A consumer may take action under this section if:
  (a) a person (the ***supplier***) supplies, in trade or commerce, services to the consumer; and
  (b) a guarantee that applies to the supply under Subdivision B of Division 1 of Part 3-2 is not complied with; and
  (c) unless the guarantee is the guarantee under section 60—the failure to comply with the guarantee did not occur only because of:
    (i) an act, default or omission of, or a representation made by, any person other than the supplier, or an agent or employee of the supplier; or
    (ii) a cause independent of human control that occurred after the services were supplied.
(2) If the failure to comply with the guarantee can be remedied and is not a major failure:
  (a) the consumer may require the supplier to remedy the failure within a reasonable time; or
  (b) if such a requirement is made of the supplier but the supplier refuses or fails to comply with the requirement, or fails to comply with the requirement within a reasonable time—the consumer may:
    (i) otherwise have the failure remedied and, by action against the supplier, recover all reasonable costs incurred by the consumer in having the failure so remedied; or
    (ii) terminate the contract for the supply of the services.
(3) If the failure to comply with the guarantee cannot be remedied or is a major failure, the consumer may:
  (a) terminate the contract for the supply of the services; or
  (b) by action against the supplier, recover compensation for any reduction in the value of the services below the price paid or payable by the consumer for the services.
(4) The consumer may, by action against the supplier, recover damages for any loss or damage suffered by the consumer because of the failure to comply with the guarantee if it was reasonably foreseeable that the consumer would suffer such loss or damage as a result of such a failure.
(5) To avoid doubt, subsection (4) applies in addition to subsections (2) and (3).

268 When a failure to comply with a guarantee is a major failure

A failure to comply with a guarantee referred to in section 267(1)(b) that applies to a supply of services is a ***major failure*** if:

(a) the services would not have been acquired by a reasonable consumer fully acquainted with the nature and extent of the failure; or
(b) the services are substantially unfit for a purpose for which services of the same kind are commonly supplied and they cannot, easily and within a reasonable time, be remedied to make them fit for such a purpose; or
(c) both of the following apply:
  (i) the services, and any product resulting from the services, are unfit for a particular purpose for which the services were acquired by the consumer that was made known to the supplier of the services;

(ii) the services, and any of those products, cannot, easily and within a reasonable time, be remedied to make them fit for such a purpose; or

(d) both of the following apply:

(i) the services, and any product resulting from the services, are not of such a nature, or quality, state or condition, that they might reasonably be expected to achieve a result desired by the consumer that was made known to the supplier;

(ii) the services, and any of those products, cannot, easily and within a reasonable time, be remedied to achieve such a result; or

(e) the supply of the services creates an unsafe situation.

269 Termination of contracts for the supply of services

(1) This section applies if, under section 267, a consumer terminates a contract for the supply of services.

(2) The termination takes effect:

(a) at the time the termination is made known to the supplier of the services (whether by words or by conduct indicating the consumer's intention to terminate the contract); or

(b) if it is not reasonably practicable to communicate with the supplier of the services—at the time the consumer indicates, by means which are reasonable in the circumstances, his or her intention to terminate the contract.

(3) The consumer is entitled to recover, by action against the supplier of the services, a refund of:

(a) any money paid by the consumer for the services; and

(b) an amount that is equal to the value of any other consideration provided by the consumer for the services;

to the extent that the consumer has not already consumed the services at the time the termination takes effect.

270 Termination of contracts for the supply of goods that are connected with terminated services

(1) If:

(a) under section 267, a consumer terminates a contract for the supply of services; and

(b) a person (the ***supplier***) has supplied, in trade or commerce, goods to the consumer that are connected with the services;

then:

(c) the consumer is taken to have rejected the goods at the time the termination of the contract takes effect; and

(d) the consumer must return the goods to the supplier of the goods unless:

(i) the goods have already been returned to, or retrieved by, the supplier; or

(ii) the goods cannot be returned, removed or transported without significant cost to the consumer because of the nature of the failure to comply with the guarantee to which the rejection relates, or because of the size or height, or method of attachment, of the goods; and

(e) the supplier must refund:

(i) any money paid by the consumer for the goods; and

(ii) an amount that is equal to the value of any other consideration provided by the consumer for the goods.

(2) If subsection (1)(d)(ii) applies, the supplier must collect the goods at the supplier's expense.

Division 2 – Action for damages against manufacturers of goods

271 Action for damages against manufacturers of goods

(1) If:

(a) the guarantee under section 54 applies to a supply of goods to a consumer; and

(b) the guarantee is not complied with;

an affected person in relation to the goods may, by action against the manufacturer of the goods, recover damages from the manufacturer.

(2) Subsection (1) does not apply if the guarantee under section 54 is not complied with only because of:

(a) an act, default or omission of, or any representation made by, any person other than the manufacturer or an employee or agent of the manufacturer; or

(b) a cause independent of human control that occurred after the goods left the control of the manufacturer; or

(c) the fact that the price charged by the supplier was higher than the manufacturer's recommended retail price, or the average retail price, for the goods.

(3) If:

(a) a person supplies, in trade or commerce, goods by description to a consumer; and

(b) the description was applied to the goods by or on behalf of the manufacturer of the goods, or with express or implied consent of the manufacturer; and

(c) the guarantee under section 56 applies to the supply and it is not complied with;

an affected person in relation to the goods may, by action against the manufacturer of the goods, recover damages from the manufacturer.

(4) Subsection (3) does not apply if the guarantee under section 56 is not complied with only because of:

(a) an act, default or omission of any person other than the manufacturer or an employee or agent of the manufacturer; or

(b) a cause independent of human control that occurred after the goods left the control of the manufacturer.

(5) If:

(a) the guarantee under section 58 or 59(1) applies to a supply of goods to a consumer; and

(b) the guarantee is not complied with;

an affected person in relation to the goods may, by action against the manufacturer of the goods, recover damages from the manufacturer.

(6) If an affected person in relation to goods has, in accordance with an express warranty given or made by the manufacturer of the goods, required the manufacturer to remedy a failure to comply with a guarantee referred to in subsection (1), (3) or (5):

(a) by repairing the goods; or

(b) by replacing the goods with goods of an identical type;

then, despite that subsection, the affected person is not entitled to commence an action under that subsection to recover damages of a kind referred to in section 272(1)(a) unless the manufacturer has refused or failed to remedy the failure, or has failed to remedy the failure within a reasonable time.

(7) The affected person in relation to the goods may commence an action under this section whether or not the goods are in their original packaging.

272 Damages that may be recovered by action against manufacturers of goods

(1) In an action for damages under this Division, an affected person in relation to goods is entitled to recover damages for:

(a) any reduction in the value of the goods, resulting from the failure to comply with the guarantee to which the action relates, below whichever of the following prices is lower:
(i) the price paid or payable by the consumer for the goods;
(ii) the average retail price of the goods at the time of supply; and
(b) any loss or damage suffered by the affected person because of the failure to comply with the guarantee to which the action relates if it was reasonably foreseeable that the affected person would suffer such loss or damage as a result of such a failure.
(2) Without limiting subsection (1)(b), the cost of inspecting and returning the goods to the manufacturer is taken to be a reasonably foreseeable loss suffered by the affected person as a result of the failure to comply with the guarantee.
(3) Subsection (1)(b) does not apply to loss or damage suffered through a reduction in the value of the goods.

273 Time limit for actions against manufacturers of goods

An affected person may commence an action for damages under this Division at any time within 3 years after the day on which the affected person first became aware, or ought reasonably to have become aware, that the guarantee to which the action relates has not been complied with.

9.8 International perspectives

9.8.1 Incorporation of terms: *CISG* and UNIDROIT Principles

Incorporation of terms as part of the formation of international commercial contracts governed by the *CISG* or UNIDROIT Principles (see **25.4.1** and **25.4.3** on applicability) takes place in accordance with rules discussed at **25.7.1–25.7.9**. Notably, 'unusual' (see **9.2.5** above) or 'surprising' terms may encounter difficulties in being incorporated into the contract: see art 2.1.20 UNIDROIT Principles, **25.7.3** and **25.7.9**. Whether standard terms have been sufficiently brought to the attention of the other party to be incorporated into the contract is discussed at **25.7.3**. Past practices between the parties and trade usages may be incorporated as terms of the contract. Usages within the *CISG* (**25.7.6**) and UNIDROIT Principles (**25.7.12**) may constitute terms of the contract more readily than under Australian contract law (see **9.4** above).

9.8.2 Statutorily implied terms and the *CISG*

The terms implied by *Sales of Goods Acts* described above (**9.7.1**) will not apply to *CISG* contracts: eg *Goods Act 1958* (Vic) ss 86 and 87. The same is true of guarantees imposed by the ACL (see s 68 ACL), although other ACL provisions (eg s 18 ACL on misleading conduct) may still apply. Note that consumer contracts are not caught by the *CISG*: art 2(a). However, the *CISG* imposes obligations within art 35(1), which oblige sellers to 'deliver goods which are of the quantity, quality and description required by the contract and which are contained or packaged in the manner required by the contract'. Article 35(2) of the *CISG* creates obligations that goods that are fit for purposes for which goods of the same description are ordinarily used (art 35(2)(a)); fit for particular purposes made known to the seller, unless it was unreasonable to (or the buyer did not) rely on the seller's skill (art 35(2)(b)). Goods must conform to samples or models held out (art 35(2)(c)); be adequately packaged (art 35(2)(d)) and/or free from intellectual property or ownership claims by third parties: arts 41 and 42 *CISG*.

9.9 Review

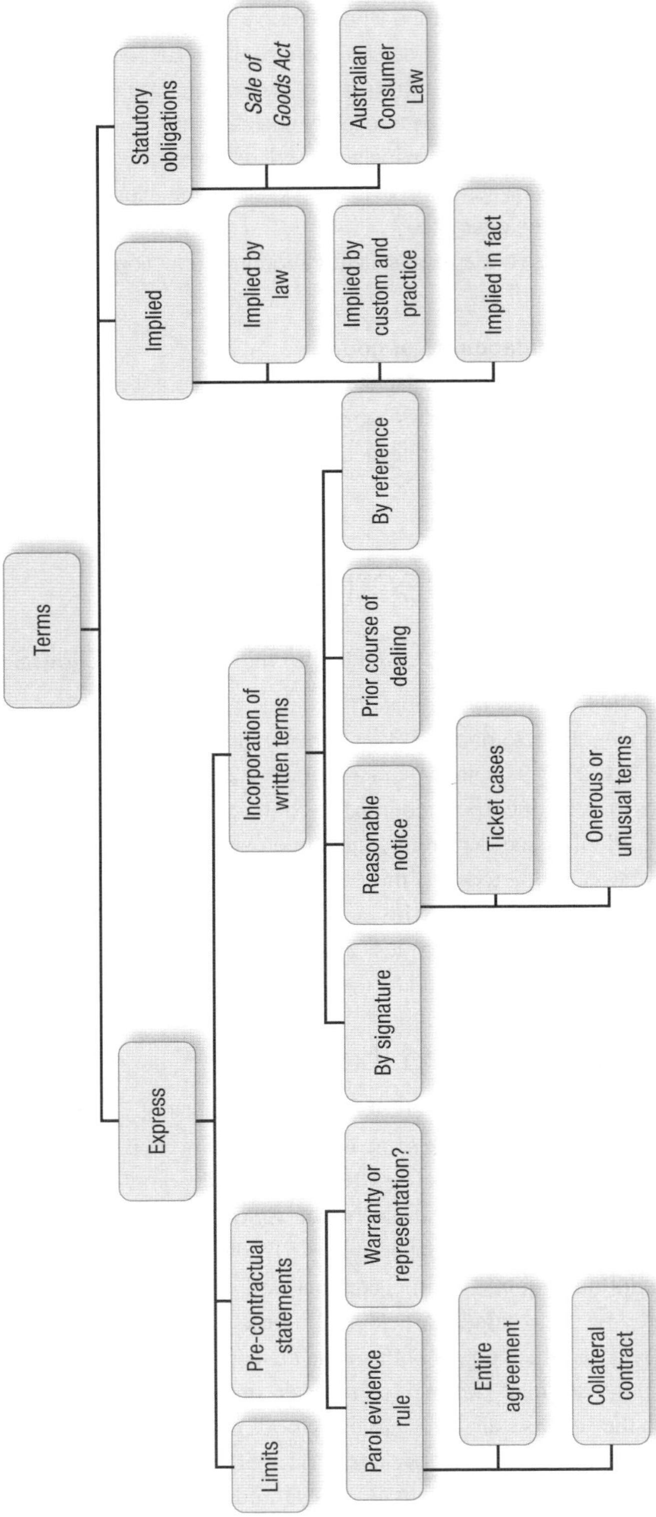
Terms
Statutory obligations
Sale of Goods Act
Australian Consumer Law
Implied
Implied by law
Implied by custom and practice
Implied in fact
Express
Incorporation of written terms
By reference
Prior course of dealing
Reasonable notice
Ticket cases
Onerous or unusual terms
By signature
Pre-contractual statements
Warranty or representation?
Parol evidence rule
Entire agreement
Collateral contract
Limits

TIPS FOR APPLYING THE LAW IN PRACTICE

- There are many separate sets of questions covered in this chapter; do not try to synthesise all of these ideas into one flowchart, other than at a high level (see Diagram 1, p 252).
- Incorporation of terms should be examined on a signature-first approach: is there a signature? If yes, then consider the consequences of a signature and how to circumvent the impact of a signature. If no, then consider the other forms of incorporation.
- Incorporation by notice is an incredibly wide and varied topic—it is important to consider the reality of the experience of the parties and to focus as much as possible on the specific details of their interaction.
- Determining whether a pre-contractual statement is a term of the contract is its own issue. It is important to remember that, if there is a pre-contractual statement and a written document, then there is always a need to consider the operation of the parol evidence rule, although the stringency of that 'rule' has been lessening over time.
- Implied terms are an important but often subsidiary aspect to arguments about enforceable promises; implied terms are sought out when the express terms do not achieve the ends sought by the client. Care must be exercised when adopting the different methods for implying terms—the nuances in the forms of implication are important to recognise, especially in relation to necessity.
- The consumer guarantees are an extensive source of obligation and rights; careful statutory construction is required of each guarantee.

PROBLEM QUESTIONS

(1) Donald, a property developer, and Bill, a builder, wished to enter into an agreement to construct a multi-million dollar wall around a rural property. Donald provided Bill with a printed document that had extensive text printed on it. Bill asked, 'Does any of "this" [pointing to the document] restrict my ability to sue you if this goes wrong?' Donald replied, 'No, not all. Believe me.' Bill also asked, 'Who is painting the wall—you?' Donald replied, 'Don't you worry; it will be looked after.' With those assurances, Bill signed the document without reading it. In fact, the document included a clause that stated, 'All claims under this contract are restricted to a sum of no more than $500'. The contract was silent on the issue of painting, although industry custom and practice was that painting was usually completed by the builder. In due course, Bill built the wall and asked Donald to pay but Donald refused to pay more than $500, relying on the clause in the clause in the signed agreement and claiming that Bill breached the agreement by not painting the wall.

   (a) Has the written document been incorporated into the agreement? Is there any way for Bill to avoid the term of the contract referencing the $500 limit?

   (b) Is Donald's pre-contractual statement about painting a term of the agreement? Does the parol evidence rule restrict the court's consideration of this statement? Might Donald be able to argue that there was an implied term in relation to painting?

(2) Alyssa, a web designer, and Andromeda, an online e-bike retailer, hoped to enter into an agreement whereby Alyssa would design and implement a new and heavily customised retail site through which Andromeda could sell her cutting-edge e-bikes. Alyssa and Andromeda never met in person but they communicated via online video and social media messaging. After some

negotiation on services and prices, Alyssa sent Andromeda a link to an online page and form that had the title, 'Agreement between the parties'. On the page, there included further links with the labels 'Terms', 'Policies' and 'Other Notes'. The links were readable on the page but were not prominently placed nor given any other distinguishing features.

If Andromeda followed the links to 'Terms', she would have read a clause that stated, 'Alyssa can terminate this contract at any time with 24 hours' notice via private message and no damages will be payable.' If Andromeda followed the links to 'Policies', she would have read another clause that stated, 'Parties contracting with Alyssa consent to all personal information being provided to third parties for Alyssa's commercial benefit.' However, Andromeda did not follow the links; instead, she filled out the form with her personal details, clicked a box on the form next to the statement 'I agree to these terms and conditions' and then clicked a button that read 'OK'. The agreed price was $5,000.

Alyssa starts designing the site and Andromeda starts advertising the launch of the new site. With 72 hours to go, Alyssa shows Andromeda a beta version of the site—it looks terrible and the retail/online store function hardly works at all. Then, 48 hours before the advertised new launch date, Alyssa messages Andromeda, 'Sorry—this is too hard; have to terminate; apologies!' Andromeda is devasted. Andromeda then discovers a flood of emails, posts and messages—spam—to her personal online accounts; she realises Alyssa had sold her personal details to others.

(a) Have the clauses on the 'Terms' and 'Policies' pages been successfully incorporated into the contract between Alyssa and Andromeda?

(b) Can Andromeda claim an implied term in fact or by law relating to the standard of work provided by Alyssa that establishes standards for Alyssa's work?

(c) Is Andromeda able to seek relief via any statutory remedies?

RESEARCH QUESTIONS

(1) Why is incorporation of terms via electronic or online contracting still so problematic? Could this issue be resolved by changes to the *Electronic Transaction Acts*? To what extent is there an international response to this issue?

(2) Consumer rights legislation has eroded in many ways the finality of a contract accepted by signature; to what extent is the signature still a relevant expression of acceptance and intention? What alternatives might be considered?

(3) Does 'smart contracting' (in which the formation and execution of the contract may be performed by the interaction of coded algorithms and without direct human involvement at the time of formation) present issues for incorporation? What scope is there for implied terms to be applied to 'smart contracts'? Do the traditional principles apply or is a new paradigm required?

(4) To what extent does the adoption of a statutory rights regime for consumer rights represent a shift away from the contract-based rights seen in earlier legislation, such as the *Sale of Goods Acts*? What are the benefits and problems with a regime of statutory rather than common law or equitable rights?

10

INTERPRETING CONTRACTS

10.1 Overview

The process of ascertaining meaning of the terms of the contractual agreement is known as *interpretation* or *construction*. The meaning of contractual terms is ascertained by reference to the objective standard of interpretation.

A thorny issue in Australian contract law is the type of evidence admissible for the purpose of interpreting the meaning of contractual terms. Evidence of preliminary negotiations and subsequent conduct is generally not permissible for this purpose. Evidence of surrounding circumstances may be permitted where words are ambiguous. Where a written document appears to be intended to encapsulate the whole contract, the parol evidence rule precludes recourse to oral or written evidence beyond the written contract. This rule is subject to a number of exceptions, some of which are contentious.

International commercial contracts governed by the *CISG* and UNIDROIT Principles are also generally interpreted under an objective test of intention. Unlike Australian contract law, both the *CISG* and UNIDROIT Principles reject the parol evidence rule, and allow admission of evidence of preliminary negotiations, post-contractual conduct and surrounding circumstances for the purpose of ascertaining the meaning of contractual terms.

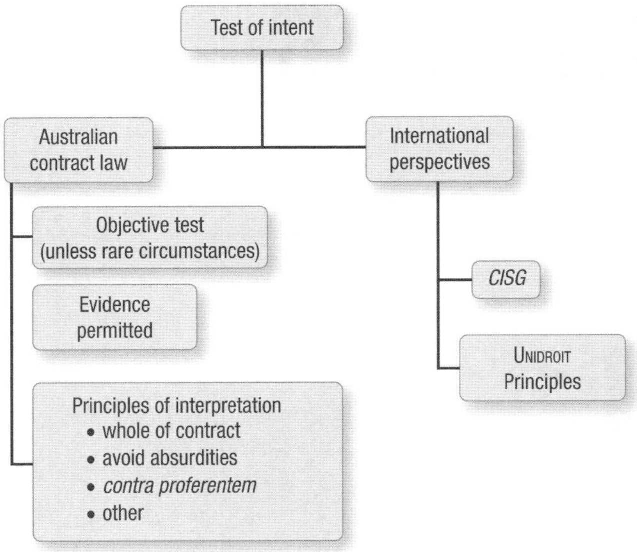

10.2 How courts ascertain meaning

Factor	Short explanation	Relevant authorities	*Principles* text*
Objective approach	Terms are interpreted according to the parties' objective intent, rather than their subjective beliefs	*Toll (FGCT) Pty Ltd v Alphapharm Pty Ltd* (2004) 219 CLR 165	Chapter 10: 10.02

* Consult the corresponding section(s) of the *Principles* text for more detail.

10.2.1 The objective approach

The approach to ascertaining meaning outlined by the High Court involves an objective assessment of the intention manifested by the parties. Where a clear intent is expressly manifested in written contractual terms, this prevails over any subjective intention. The court will assess the meaning of terms to be that which an objective outsider would attribute to the them. Indeed, evidence of the subjective intent of either party is usually not admissible.

Toll (FGCT) Pty Ltd v Alphapharm Pty Ltd (2004) 219 CLR 165

Facts and issues

Finemores (later acquired by Toll) entered a contract with Alphapharm to collect, transport and store flu vaccines imported from the UK. Alphapharm argued that it suffered loss due to Finemores' breach in freezing the vaccines, thereby rendering them worthless, but Finemores relied upon an exclusion of liability clause in standard terms on the reverse of the contract signed by Alphapharm's agent (Thomson). Thompson had not read the terms before signing.

Decision

The High Court heard an appeal by Finemores from a decision of the New South Wales Court of Appeal. In a joint judgment, the High Court held that the fact that Thomson had not read the written contract was irrelevant, as he had signed it. Acceptance of the terms was to be determined according to what a reasonable party in the position of the other party would believe was intended by the words or conduct. Contractual obligations were governed by reasonable understanding of such expressions, not the subjective beliefs each party might have had as to the nature of their obligations.

Per Gleeson CJ, Gummow, Hayne, Callinan and Heydon JJ at 178:

> In their consideration in *Ermogenous v Greek Orthodox Community of SA Inc* of the requisite intention to create contractual relations, Gaudron, McHugh, Hayne and Callinan JJ said:
>
> > Although the word 'intention' is used in this context, it is used in the same sense as it is used in other contractual contexts. It describes what it is that would objectively be conveyed by what was said or done, having regard to the circumstances in which those statements and actions happened. It is not a search for the uncommunicated subjective motives or intentions of the parties.
>
> [179] The point at issue on this appeal concerns not the creation of legal relations but the nature of the legal relations created. . . .
>
> This Court, in *Pacific Carriers Ltd v BNP Paribas*, has recently reaffirmed the principle of objectivity by which the rights and liabilities of the parties to a contract are determined. It is not the subjective beliefs or understandings of the parties about their rights and liabilities that govern their contractual relations. What matters is what each party by words and conduct would have led a reasonable person in the position of the other party to believe. References to the common intention of the parties to a contract are to be understood as referring to what a reasonable person would understand by the language in which the parties have expressed their agreement. The meaning of the terms of a contractual document is to be determined by what a reasonable person would have understood them to mean. That, normally, requires

> consideration not only of the text, but also of the surrounding circumstances known to the parties, and the purpose and object of the transaction.
>
> [180] ... Consistent with this objective approach to the determination of the rights and liabilities of contracting parties is the significance which the law attaches to the signature (or execution) of a contractual document. ...
>
> It should not be overlooked that to sign a document known and intended to affect legal relations is an act which itself ordinarily conveys a representation to a reasonable reader of the document. The [181] representation is that the person who signs either has read and approved the contents of the document or is willing to take the chance of being bound by those contents, as Latham CJ put it, whatever they might be. That representation is even stronger where the signature appears below a perfectly legible written request to read the document before signing it.
>
> The statements ... accord with the well-known principle stated by Scrutton LJ in *L'Estrange v F Graucob Ltd* ...

The appeal was allowed.

QUESTIONS

(1) In *Toll*, the Court took the view that, under an objective approach to interpretation, someone signing a contract is taken to have accepted they are bound by its terms irrespective of whether they have read the terms (the rule in *L'Estrange*: see **9.2.2**; *Principles* text at 9.04.). What would happen in everyday situations of delivery of goods if the Court had not upheld the rule in *L'Estrange*?

(2) What policy reason might explain the Court's preference for the objective approach to interpretation of contractual terms? Would a subjective approach be fairer?

10.3 Admissible evidence in interpretation disputes

Factor	Short explanation	Relevant authorities	*Principles* text*
Parol evidence rule	Extrinsic evidence should not be used in interpretation where a written instrument is complete	*Codelfa Construction Pty Ltd v State Rail Authority of New South Wales* (1982) 149 CLR 337	Chapter 10: 10.05
Exceptions to the parol evidence rule	To prove: the contract was validly concluded; the contract was not wholly in writing; identity of parties or subject matter of contract; an action for rectification; rejection of a proposed term; collateral	*Giliberto v Kenny* (1983) 57 ALJR 283 *Bacchus Marsh Concentrated Milk Co Ltd (in liq) v Joseph Nathan and Co Ltd* (1919) 26 CLR 410	Chapter 10: 10.06

Factor	Short explanation	Relevant authorities	*Principles* text*
	contract; meaning if terms are ambiguous; specialised meaning in custom or trade	*State Rail Authority of New South Wales v Heath Outdoor Pty Ltd* (1986) 7 NSWLR 170	
The rise of 'commercial construction'	Avoidance of interpretations that lead to a commercial nonsense, contextual business understanding taking into account market conditions	*Electricity Generation Corporation v Woodside Energy Ltd* (2014) 251 CLR 640	Chapter 10: 10.07
Royal Botanic and the High Court's puzzle	The admissibility of surrounding circumstance evidence and the 'ambiguity gateway' remains uncertain	*Royal Botanic Gardens and Domain Trust v South Sydney City Council* (2002) 240 CLR 45	Chapter 10: 10.10
A 'gateway' requirement for surrounding circumstances evidence?	High Court confirms 'ambiguity gateway' in *Codelfa*	*Jireh International Pty Ltd v Western Exports Services Inc* [2011] NSWCA 137; and, on appeal, *Western Export Services Inc v Jireh International Pty Ltd* (2011) 86 ALJR 1	Chapter 10: 10.11
Post-contractual conduct	Generally, post-contractual conduct is inadmissible for purposes of contractual interpretation, however exceptions apply	*Agricultural and Rural Finance Pty Ltd v Gardiner* (2008) 238 CLR 570	Chapter 10: 10.13

* Consult the corresponding section(s) of the *Principles* text for more detail.

10.3.1 The parol evidence rule and its effect on interpretation

The *parol evidence rule* is a substantive rule which precludes all evidence for the purpose of interpretation of a written contract which appears complete on its face, other than the written contract itself. Such evidence is often referred to as 'extrinsic evidence', and includes oral and written statements which do not form part of the written instrument.

The operation of the parol evidence rule in the identification of terms was discussed at **9.3.4**. However, in this chapter, the discussion concerns the operation of the parol evidence rule in relation to *interpretation of the meaning* of the written instrument. According to the parol evidence rule, courts must determine meaning from the words of the written contract itself, without reference to extrinsic evidence, unless an exception applies such as where the words are ambiguous.[1] Thus, the parol evidence rule precludes consideration of oral or written

1 However, this arguably conflates the parol evidence rule with the plain meaning rule: see John Carter, *The Contstruction of Commercial Contracts* (Hart, 2013) 262, para. 8.23; Lisa Spagnolo, 'Contract

communications or conduct from either pre- or post-contractual stages.[2] The controversies surrounding this rule are discussed below.

Codelfa Construction Pty Ltd v State Rail Authority of New South Wales (1982) 149 CLR 337

Facts and issues

Codelfa was contracted by the State Rail Authority to perform excavation work involving rock blasting with explosives to create tunnels. The written contract provided work was to be completed within 130 weeks, and exempted Codelfa from liability for delays caused by events beyond its control. Both parties assumed that the *City and Suburban Electric Railways (Amendment) Act 1967* (NSW) s 11 protected Codelfa from injunctions due to nuisance, and thus Codelfa could roster three shifts a day for seven days per week, allowing timely completion. However, residents concerned about vibrations in fact obtained an injunction, and Codelfa had to reduce shifts to two per day on only six days per week, which led to extra costs and delays. Codelfa claimed costs and lost profits from the State Rail Authority on the basis of an implied term concerning hours during which works could proceed and, in the alternative, claimed a *quantum meruit* for the value of the works on the basis that the contract had been frustrated. The case turned on the issues of parol evidence rule, implied terms, and frustration.

Decision

Arbitral proceedings were appealed to the New South Wales Supreme Court, Court of Appeal and High Court. In relation to the parol evidence rule, Mason J held that extrinsic evidence may only be admitted to resolve ambiguity in contractual terms. There was no term concerning the hours during which works could be conducted; thus, there was no ambiguous term to interpret in light of extrinsic evidence. The High Court also unanimously rejected an argument that there was an implied term to this effect.

Per Mason J at 352:

> The true rule is that evidence of surrounding circumstances is admissible to assist in the interpretation of the contract if the language is ambiguous or susceptible of more than one meaning. But it is not admissible to contradict the language of the contract when it has a plain meaning. Generally speaking facts existing when the contract was made will not be receivable as part of the surrounding circumstances as an aid to construction, unless they were known to both parties, although, as we have seen, if the facts are notorious knowledge of them will be presumed.

Interpretation' in LA DiMatteo, A Janssen, U Magnus & R Schulze (eds), *International Sales Law: Contract, Principles & Practice* (Beck/Hart/Nomos, 2016) 713, 753–754, paras 101–109.

2 John Carter, *Contract Law in Australia* (Lexis, 6th ed, 2013) 270–271. See also *Principles* text 10.13. However, see Yihan Goh, 'A Wrong Turn in History: Re-understanding the Exclusionary Rule against Prior Negotiations in Contractual Interpretation' (2014) 5 *Journal of Business Law* 360 (arguing a historical view of the exclusionary rule in relation to prior negotiations is less strict or significant than is usually thought).

It is here that a difficulty arises with respect to the evidence of prior negotiations. Obviously the prior negotiations will tend to establish objective background facts which were known to both parties and the subject matter of the contract. To the extent to which they have this tendency they are admissible. But in so far as they consist of statements and actions of the parties which are reflective of their actual intentions and expectations they are not receivable. The point is that such statements and actions reveal the terms of the contract which the parties intended or hoped to make. They are superseded by, and merged in, the contract itself. The object of the parol evidence rule is to exclude them, the prior oral agreement of the parties being inadmissible in aid of construction, though admissible in an action for rectification.

Consequently when the issue is which of two or more possible meanings is to be given to a contractual provision we look, not to the actual intentions, aspirations or expectations of the parties before or at the time of the contract, except in so far as they are expressed in the contract, but to the objective framework of facts within which the contract came into existence, and to the parties' presumed intention in this setting. We do not take into account the actual intentions of the parties and for the very good reason that an investigation of those matters would not only be time consuming but it would also be unrewarding as it would tend to give too much weight to these factors at the expense of the actual language of the written contract.

There may perhaps be one situation in which evidence of the actual intention of the parties should be allowed to prevail over their presumed intention. If it transpires that the parties have refused to include in the contract a provision which would give effect to the presumed intention of persons in their position it may be proper to receive evidence of that refusal. After all, the court is interpreting [353] the contract which the parties have made and in that exercise the court takes into account what reasonable men in that situation would have intended to convey by the words chosen. But is it right to carry that exercise to the point of placing on the words of the contract a meaning which the parties have united in rejecting? It is possible that evidence of mutual intention, if amounting to concurrence, is receivable so as to negative an inference sought to be drawn from surrounding circumstances. . . .

The importance of this evolution of the law as it affects the construction of contracts is that it centres upon the presumed, rather than the actual, intention of the parties. Once it is accepted that in the construction of the contract account is taken of the presumed intention of the parties . . .

[354] The first question is whether, in the light of the principles as I have explained them, it was legitimate to look to this material on the issue of implication of a term. I think it was. The discussions which generated these findings were not negotiations about the terms of the contract. The terms of the contract documents had been determined in advance by the Authority. By lodging its tender Codelfa accepted the Authority's contract documents. The relevant discussions were therefore directed to the question of price. Their object was to enable Codelfa to inform itself of what was involved in the work and to cost it so as to arrive at a price for inclusion in its tender. The consequence is that the discussions did not have the character of negotiations in the course of which the parties gradually evolved the terms of a bargain ultimately embodied in written form. Had the discussions been of that kind then . . . recourse to them would have been prohibited for the purpose of interpreting the contract by reference to the parties' actual intentions as expressed before entry into the contract. . . . Instead the evidence revealed a matter which was in the common contemplation of the parties yet was not a contractual provision actually agreed upon for the simple reason that it was a matter of common assumption.

To say that the maintenance of three eight hour shifts a day for six days a week was a matter of common contemplation between the parties is not enough in itself to justify the

> implication of a term. ... It must appear that the matter of common contemplation was necessary to give the contract business efficacy and that the term sought to be implied is so obvious that it goes without saying.

Per Brennan J at 402:

> ... where the term propounded is said to be implied in a contract, that term must inhere in its express terms, and reference to extrinsic circumstances is permissible only to construe the contract and to understand its operation. The principle is stated in the judgment of Isaacs, Gavan Duffy and Rich JJ. in *Purcell v. Bacon* ... (1914) 19 CLR 241, at p 265:
>
> > Any words or expressions if unequivocal speak for themselves; if they are words of doubtful or double signification, that may be settled, where necessary, by first ascertaining the circumstances in reference to which they are used ... When, however, the true meaning of the words themselves is ascertained, and the subject matter settled in reference to which they are used, the intention of the parties must be gathered by construing their own words as they stand, applying them to the given subject matter. ... the Court places itself in the position of the parties. But it cannot place itself in their position for the purpose of finding what words they intended to use and have not used. That would be making a contract for them, and surrounding circumstances are not admissible for any such purpose ...

The appeal was allowed in part and remitted to arbitration on the question of frustration.

10.3.2 Exceptions to the parol evidence rule

Exceptions to the parol evidence rule include the following:

- To prove the contract was validly concluded: *Air Great Lakes Pty Ltd v K S Easter (Holdings) Pty Ltd* (1985) 2 NSWLR 309;
- To show the written contract is incomplete, eg the contract was not wholly in writing, but partly oral. Therefore, the prerequisite basis of the parol evidence rule—that the contract is wholly integrated within the written agreement—is not met: *State Rail Authority v Heath Outdoor* (1986) 7 NSWLR 170 per McHugh JA (below);
- To identify parties to the contract or its subject matter: *Giliberto v Kenny* (1983) (below);
- Action for rectification, where the written contract contains an error: see *Codelfa,* at 352, above. The parol evidence rule does not apply to such actions, therefore extrinsic evidence of intent is admissible: *Bacchus Marsh Concentrated Milk Co Ltd v Joseph Nathan & Co Ltd* (1919) at 427 (below);
- To evidence a refusal to include a particular term: see Mason J in *Codelfa*, at 352, above;
- To prove a collateral contract, provided the collateral promise does not contradict the main agreement;[3]

3 *Hoyt's Pty Ltd v Spencer* (1919) 27 CLR 133. See Spagnolo (n 1) 749–750, para. 91.

- For clarification of meaning, where written terms are ambiguous: see Mason and Brennan JJ in *Codelfa*, at 352 and 402, above; *Giliberto v Kenny* (1983) (below); *Bacchus Marsh v Nathan* (1919) at 427 (below) but even so, external evidence cannot contradict the written term; and
- To demonstrate a term has a specialised meaning in custom or trade, even if words have a plain meaning: *RW Cameron & Co v L Slutzkin Pty Ltd* (1923) 32 CLR 81.

Giliberto v Kenny (1983) 57 ALJR 283

Facts and issues

Mr and Mrs Kenny sought specific performance of a sale of land, which was resisted by Mr Giliberto. Unfortunately, Mr Kenny died before the hearing. Although only signed by 'Mrs Kenny', the contract described the purchaser at one point as 'Mr Kenny' but at another as 'Mrs Kenny'. The issue was whether extrinsic evidence was admissible in the form of oral evidence by Mrs Kenny to clarify the identity of the parties.

Decision

The High Court concluded that this was a case of ambiguity within the written contract. It held that oral evidence was admissible for the purpose of proving Mrs Kenny had acted as agent for her husband, and that the purchasers were both her husband and herself.

Per Gibbs CJ at 284 (Wilson, Brennan, Deane and Dawson JJ agreeing):

> On those facts, one question that arises is whether the circumstances that the first part of Exhibit D described Mrs Kenny as the purchaser and the second part refers to Mr Kenny meant that there was no valid and binding agreement. The document was on one sheet of paper. . . . The judge found that the appellant knew that Mr and Mrs Kenny at all times intended that both should purchase the property, and that the appellant intended to sell to them. Extrinsic evidence was admissible to show, as it did, that Mrs Kenny, in agreeing to buy, was acting as agent for her husband as well as herself. As authority for that proposition it is sufficient to refer to *Phipson on Evidence*, 12th ed par 1907, where it is said:
>
>> Where, however, it is doubtful whether A signs a document as agent for B, or as charging himself as well, extrinsic evidence . . . may be given, such evidence going really to the factum of the instrument.
>
> . . . it has long been established that in construing a contract general evidence of surrounding circumstances is admissible to identify the persons or things referred to: see, for example, the discussion of the principle by Lord Wilberforce in *Prenn v Simmonds* [1971] 1 WLR 1381 at 1383–4. Such evidence does not justify a departure from the ordinary meaning of words where no ambiguity exists, but in the present case the reference in the document to Mrs Kenny in one part and Mr Kenny in the other created a patent ambiguity. The evidence of the mutually-known facts shows that the reference to Mr Kenny was intended to be a reference to him and Mrs Kenny.

The appeal was dismissed.

Bacchus Marsh Concentrated Milk Co Ltd (in liq) v Joseph Nathan and Co Ltd (1919) 26 CLR 410

Facts and issues

Nathan held patents for various manufactured products, including Glaxo. Nathan entered a written contract to sell the patents to Bacchus Marsh, but the patents were not specified adequately. Bacchus Marsh argued that the patents sold included the patent for Glaxo.

Decision

On appeal from the Victorian Supreme Court, the High Court majority (2:1) considered the extrinsic evidence. Isaacs J held that extrinsic evidence was admissible for actions of rectification, in order to show intention of the parties, since equity's task in this regard was to reform instruments so that they accorded with the parties' actual agreement.

Per Isaacs J at 427:

> It is not legitimate to refer to such evidence either for the purpose of adding a term to the written agreement or of altering its ordinary legal construction, and therefore it is not legitimate to show that it was intended to use words bearing a different sense from that which the words used express when applied to the circumstances. But it is legitimate to adduce extrinsic evidence of the surrounding circumstances in order to prove that words susceptible of more than one meaning are applicable to one only of those meanings—that is, not to alter the contract but to identify its subject. Further, for the purpose of identifying the subject of the contract, prior negotiations are available just as any other circumstance would be. But the prior negotiations cannot be used for the purpose of importing additional or different terms—that is, terms other than the words actually used express when the subject matter is fully identified. ... For the purpose of rectification, the position is quite different. The jurisdiction of equity to re-form instruments so as to make them accord with what the parties actually agreed to, or with what one party intended and the other party knew the first intended, is for the very purpose of overcoming in a proper case, by the ordinary rules of evidence, the obstacle presented, since equity construes contracts just as law does. And, further, for the purpose of determining whether or not the contract, or any particular provision in it, [428] material extrinsic fact may be proved ...

Gavan Duffy J also relied upon the extrinsic evidence to allow rectification of the contract. Higgins J dissented on this point, requiring ambiguity before extrinsic evidence was admissible.The decision of Supreme Court of Victoria varied.

State Rail Authority of New South Wales v Heath Outdoor Pty Ltd (1986) 7 NSWLR 170

Facts and issues

Heath contracted with the State Rail Authority (SRA) regarding placement of advertising on hoardings located on railways land. Clause 6 gave the SRA the right to terminate upon one month's notice and provided 'such action shall not give rise to any claim for compensation whatsoever'. Heath objected to this clause during negotiations. SRA's representative, Mr Giles, said that he was not authorised to change the terms, but assured Heath that 'the only time that the clause is ever invoked is for non-payment of rent or if somebody wants to advertise objectionable advertising content'. Heath entered the contract. Heath then contracted with a cigarette company to place advertisements on the hoardings. When the State government banned cigarette advertising, SRA purported to terminate the contract. Heath argued that its contract with SRA was partly written and partly oral, and that Mr Giles' oral assurance formed a contractual term. Among the issues which arose was whether evidence of the oral assurance was admissible.

Decision

The majority of the Court held the evidence was admissible in relation to the question as to whether or not the contract was partly oral and partly written, since a prerequisite to the application of the parol evidence rule was that the written agreement was intended to encapsulate the complete contract. Thus, the parol evidence rule did not apply to the preliminary question as to whether the contract was wholly in writing. Ultimately, however, it was held that the written instrument did contain the entire contract.

Per McHugh JA at 191:

> A preliminary question which arises is whether the so called parol evidence rule prevents reliance on the oral assurances of Mr Giles. Under that rule parol evidence is not admissible to contradict or vary the terms of a written agreement. But it is a rule whose scope and rationale is often misunderstood. It has no operation until it is first determined that the terms of the agreement are wholly contained in writing. The tendering of oral evidence to prove a contractual term, therefore, cannot be excluded until it is determined that any terms in writing record the whole of the parties' agreement: *Corbin on Contracts* (1960) vol 3 at 385; *Air Great Lakes Pty Ltd v K S Easter (Holdings) Pty Ltd* (1985) 2 NSWLR 309 at 337.
>
> When a person alleges that an agreement was partly oral and partly written, it is not always easy to determine whether the writing is the exclusive repository of the bargain. Williston claims that, when a document appears on its face to be a complete record of the parties' contract, it is conclusively presumed to be the contract: *Williston on Contracts*, 3rd ed (1961), s 633. However, Corbin takes a different view and says that the issue is whether the parties assented to a particular writing as the complete and accurate 'integration' of the contract: *Corbin on Contracts* (1960) vol 3 at 358–359. . . . But in my opinion the correct rule is that the existence of writing which appears to represent a written contract between the parties is no more than an evidentiary foundation for a conclusion that their agreement is wholly in writing: *Gillespie Brothers & Co* [192] *v Cheney, Eggar & Co* [1896] 2 QB 59 at 62; *Turner v Forwood* [1951] 1 All ER 746 at 749; *J Evans & Son (Portsmouth) Ltd v Andrea Merzario Ltd* at 1083; 935. In my opinion the English Law Commission correctly stated the law when it said:
>
> > . . . the mere production of a contractual document, however complete it may look, cannot as a matter of law exclude evidence of oral terms if the other party asserts that such terms were agreed. If that assertion is proved, evidence of the oral terms cannot be excluded because the court will, by definition, have found that the contractual terms are partly to be found in what was agreed orally as well as the document in question. No parol evidence rule could apply. On the other hand, if that assertion is not proved, there can be no place for a parol evidence rule because the court will have found that all the terms of the contract were set out in the document in question and, by implication, will thereby have excluded evidence of terms being found elsewhere.

(The Law Commission, Law of Contract, The Parol Evidence Rule (January 1986) Cmnd 9700, par 2.12 at 11.)

While I think that the plaintiff was entitled to rely on the oral assurances of Mr Giles in support of its claim that the advertising contract and/or letter of 12 October 1981 did not contain the whole terms of the parties' agreement, I am of opinion that on the evidence the submission that the contract was partly oral should be rejected. The proper conclusion to be drawn from the discussion between the parties is that, as a matter of contract, condition 6 was one of the contractual terms and that its literal effect was to give the defendant an unfettered right to terminate the contract. Mr Giles made it plain that he had no authority to change any condition of the contract.

Mr Low accepted this. He said that it became apparent to him that Mr Giles was going to have difficulty getting the clauses changed if he had to take them away. Mr Giles also informed Mr Low that the document was a standard authority document which could not be changed. Whatever effect the discussion between Mr Low and Mr Giles had, it did not add to the terms of the contract.

Glass JA agreed on this point and the appeal was allowed by the majority.

10.3.3 The rise of 'commercial construction'

In modern times, a contextual approach has been favoured, especially in relation to commercial contracts. Whilst the problem of the extent to which surrounding circumstances may be used in interpretation remains, the High Court has emphasised the need to avoid interpretations that result in 'commercial nonsense' in favour of constructions which accord with 'what a reasonable businessperson would have understood' terms to mean. Contracts may therefore contain their own standards of reasonableness in relation to the balancing of the parties' respective interests, having regard to commercial market conditions.

Electricity Generation Corporation v Woodside Energy Ltd (2014) 251 CLR 640

Facts and issues

Electricity Generation (Verve) and Woodside (the sellers) entered into a long-term Gas Sale Agreement ('GSA'). Clause 3.3 of the GSA required that Woodside use 'reasonable endeavours' to supply gas. An explosion and fire at a major competitor plant (the Apache incident) severely reduced gas supplies in Western Australia, and prices soared. Woodside refused to supply gas to Verve under the long-term GSA, and genuinely believed its refusal was not in breach of GSA Clause 3.3. Under protest, Verve entered a short-term GSA at a higher price. In addition to duress concerning the short-term contract (discussed at **19.2.3**), the issue of interpretation of Clause 3.3 GSA arose, especially the meaning of 'reasonable endeavours'.

Decision

The High Court majority of French CJ, Hayne, Crennan and Kiefel JJ held that Woodside's obligation under the lower priced long-term GSA to use 'reasonable endeavours' to supply was not absolute, but 'necessarily conditioned by what is reasonable in the circumstances'. It held that contracts may have internal standards of reasonableness, and the GSA expressly entitled Woodside to consider 'relevant commercial, economic and operational matters' in determining whether to supply supplemental gas under its obligation to use 'reasonable endeavours' to supply under Clause 3.3. Given the gas crisis, Woodside was not in breach when it refused to supply Verve at the lower GSA price. Gageler J, in dissent, considered Woodside's desire to maximise profits was irrelevant in construing whether it was 'able' to supply under Clause 3.3.

Per French CJ, Hayne, Crennan and Kiefel JJ at 656:

> ... this Court has reaffirmed the objective approach to be adopted in determining the rights and liabilities of parties to a contract. The meaning of the terms of a commercial contract is to be determined by what a reasonable businessperson would have understood those terms to mean. That approach ... will require consideration of the language used by the parties, the surrounding [657] circumstances known to them and the commercial purpose or objects to be secured by the contract. Appreciation of the commercial purpose or objects is facilitated by an understanding 'of the genesis of the transaction, the background, the context [and] the market in which the parties are operating': [citing *Codelfa Construction Pty Ltd v State Rail Authority of NSW*]. As Arden LJ observed in *Re Golden Key Ltd*, ... a court is entitled to approach the task of giving a commercial contract a businesslike interpretation on the assumption 'that the parties ... intended to produce a commercial result'. A commercial contract is to be construed so as to avoid it 'making commercial nonsense or working commercial inconvenience' [citing *Zhu v Treasurer of New South Wales* [2004] HCA 56; (2004) 218 CLR 530 at 559]. ...
>
> The Sellers urged that, read as a whole, cl 3.3 imposed an obligation to use reasonable endeavours to supply SMDQ, which was qualified or conditioned by the Sellers' entitlement to take into account their own commercial, economic and operational interests in relation to that [658] supply of gas. Applying this construction, the Sellers contended that the Apache incident, and the consequential business conditions in the market, were matters which the Sellers were entitled to take into account under cl 3.3(b) in determining whether they were 'able' ... to supply SMDQ nominated by Verve. ...
>
> ... Verve urged, as it had in the courts below, that the word 'able', as it occurs in cl 3.3(b), should be construed as a reference to the Sellers' *capacity* to deliver SMDQ and not as a reference to their *willingness* to do so.
>
> ... Verve contended that cl 3.3 ... obliged the Sellers to supply nominated SMDQ to Verve, notwithstanding the circumstance that the prevailing market price of gas was significantly higher than the tranche 3 price in the GSA. [Thus Verve argued Woodside had breached its] obligation to use reasonable endeavours to supply SMDQ. ...
>
> [659] Three general observations can be made about obligations to use reasonable endeavours ... First, an obligation expressed thus is not an absolute or unconditional obligation. Second, ... [such] an obligation ... is necessarily conditioned by what is reasonable in the circumstances, which can include circumstances that may affect an obligor's business. This was explained by Mason J in *Hospital Products Ltd v United States Surgical Corporation*, ... His Honour said:
>
>> The qualification [of reasonableness] itself is aimed at situations in which there would be a conflict between the obligation to use best efforts and the independent business interests of the distributor and has the object of resolving those conflicts by the standard of reasonableness ... It therefore involves a recognition that the interests of [the manufacturer] could not be paramount in every case and that in some cases the interests of the distributor would prevail. ...

[660] Third, some contracts containing [such] an obligation . . . contain their own internal standard of what is reasonable, by some express reference relevant to the business interests of an obligor. . . .

The GSA, pre-eminently a commercial contract between parties at arm's length with their own independent business interests, should be given a businesslike interpretation . . .

. . . [T]he chief commercial purpose and objects of the GSA are twofold. First, Verve obtains a secure supply of gas . . . up to the specified MDQ, and secondly, the Sellers have an assured price in respect of the specified AMQ, . . . in respect of the quantities of gas which *must be delivered* by the Sellers and which *must be paid for* by Verve, whether taken or not . . . Those provisions have the effect of insulating the parties from respective risks of fluctuations in demand and price in the context of a large domestic and commercial electricity market . . .

[661] . . . The obligation to use reasonable endeavours to supply SMDQ, provided for in cl 3.3, can be readily contrasted with the unconditional obligation to supply MDQ specified in cl 3.2. . . . and cl 3.3(b) provides an internal standard of reasonableness by which the obligation to use reasonable endeavours to supply SMDQ can be measured.

Taken as a whole, cl 3.3 provides for a balancing of interests if the business interests of the parties . . . do not entirely coincide, or if they conflict. What is a 'reasonable' standard of endeavours obliged by cl 3.3(a) is conditioned both by the Sellers' responsibilities to Verve . . . and by the Sellers' express entitlement to take into account 'relevant commercial, economic and operational matters' when determining whether they are 'able' to supply SMDQ. Compendiously, the expression 'commercial, economic and operational matters' refers to matters affecting the Sellers' business interests. . . . The non-exhaustive examples of circumstances . . . found in cl 3.3(b)(i), (ii) and (iii), are not confined to 'capacity' (or capacity constraints). The effect of cl 3.3(b) is that the Sellers are not obliged to forgo or sacrifice their business interests when using reasonable endeavours . . .

The construction which has been accepted is consistent with surrounding circumstances known to both parties at the time of entering the GSA, which include the circumstances that the Sellers sell and supply gas to customers and buyers in the market other than Verve, some essential services depend on gas supply, and the prevailing market price of gas at any particular time may be greater (or less) than the tranche 3 price in the GSA.

Understood as explained above, cl 3.3 did not oblige . . . the Sellers [662] to supply SMDQ to Verve when the Apache incident occasioned business conditions leading to conflict between the Sellers' business interests and Verve's interest . . .

The appeal was dismissed and the cross-appeal allowed.

10.3.4 The relevance of surrounding circumstances

English courts have at times gone further than Australian courts in emphasising the importance of the 'factual matrix' or surrounding circumstances in interpretation. The high point came in *Investors Compensation Scheme v West Bromwich Building Society* [1998] AC 896. Lord Hoffmann at 912–3 took a contextual, commercial approach, and stated reference might be had to anything which would have been reasonably understood and 'reasonably available to the parties'. Although US decisions have not been consistent, ambiguity is not a precondition to admission of surrounding circumstances evidence to demonstrate an alternative meaning within the US Uniform Commercial Code (UCC).[4]

4 UCC §2-202; Spagnolo, above n 11, 754, para. 109.

10.3.5 *Codelfa* and the 'true rule'

As discussed above in *Codelfa Construction v State Rail Authority* (1982), Mason J at 352 accepted that evidence of surrounding circumstances could help in ascertainment of the parties' presumed intention. However, his Honour insisted that the 'true rule' was that this was only permissible when there were 'two or more possible meanings' available for a contractual term. In other words, the general understanding of Mason J's approach is that the plain meaning of terms prevails, and surrounding evidence is only admissible via an 'ambiguity gateway' to illuminate meaning where ambiguity exists.[5]

10.3.6 *Royal Botanic* and the High Court's puzzle

After *Codelfa*, the High Court took a more liberal approach, utilising evidence of surrounding circumstances without holding first that an ambiguity existed in a number of cases: *Maggbury Pty Ltd v Hafele Australia Pty Ltd* (2001) 210 CLR 181 at [11]; *Toll v Alphapharm* (above). In *Royal Botanic*, their Honours found ambiguity existed, and referred to *Codelfa* and a purported difference in Australian and English positions on this point.

Royal Botanic Gardens and Domain Trust v South Sydney City Council (2002) 240 CLR 45

Facts and issues

The trustees of the Royal Botanic Gardens ('Trustees') leased a car park and footpath to the Sydney City Council for 50 years. Rent was fixed for the first three years, and thereafter rent was to be fixed by the Trustees which, according to clause 4(b), in deciding upon rent, could 'have regard to additional costs and expenses' of the car park. The Council claimed that, in determining the rent, the Trustees had impermissibly considered costs outside clause 4(b), and unsuccessfully sought a declaration in the New South Wales Supreme Court. It then successfully appealed to the New South Wales Court of Appeal, and the Trustees appealed to the High Court.

Decision

In interpreting the lease, the High Court found there was ambiguity, and referred to surrounding circumstances, including the fact that parties were public authorities, the non-commercial character of the lease, the intention to financially protect the lessor, and historical background.

Per Gleeson CJ, Gaudron, McHugh, Gummow and Hayne JJ at [39]:

> It is unnecessary to determine whether [the House of Lords has taken] a broader view of the admissible 'background' than was taken in *Codelfa* or, if so, whether those views should be preferred to those of this Court. Until that determination is made by this Court, other Australian courts, . . . should continue to follow *Codelfa*.
>
> [52] In the present case, the difficulty concerns the phrase in para (iv) of cl 4(b) 'the Trustees may have regard to additional costs and expenses'. Does this mean that the Trustees, in making a determination, cannot have regard to matters other than those additional costs and

5 However, see n 11.

> expenses? ... [T]o specify a particular matter to which a party may have regard without expressly stating ... that it is the only such matter ... to which regard may be had is likely to result in ambiguity. It does so in the present case.

The appeal was dismissed.

10.3.7 A 'gateway' requirement for surrounding circumstances evidence?

Nonetheless, following *Royal Botanic*, High Court decisions continued to consider evidence of surrounding circumstances without first finding ambiguity existed: see eg *Pacific Carriers Ltd v BNP Paribas* (2004) 218 CLR 451, 461–462; *Wilkie v Gordian Runoff Ltd* (2005) 221 CLR 522, 528–529; *International Air Transport Association v Ansett Australia Holdings Ltd* (2008) 234 CLR 151, 160, 174; *Toll v Alphapharm*, 179 (above). This led to a widespread view within Federal and State courts that the High Court had indeed relaxed the 'true rule' of the strict precondition of ambiguity in *Codelfa*: see eg *Lion Nathan Australia Pty Ltd v Coopers Brewery Ltd* (2006) 156 FCR 1; *Franklins Pty Ltd v Metcash Trading Ltd* (2009) 76 NSWLR 603; *MBF Investments Pty Ltd v Nolan* [2011] 37 VR 116, [195]–[204].

However, the High Court took the unusual step in *Western Export v Jireh* (2011) (below) of publishing reasons for refusal of an application for special leave, taking the opportunity to scold lower courts for ignoring the ambiguity requirement in *Codelfa*, and flatly denying the High Court itself had not followed the 'true rule'. Whilst a special leave decision has no binding precedential value, it is nonetheless influential.

Since then, the High Court has continued to refer to evidence of surrounding circumstances, including market conditions and commercial circumstances, without any preliminary finding of ambiguity: see eg *Woodside* (above). Whilst admittedly ambiguity may be readily found in almost any words, this means that the status of the 'gateway requirement' of ambiguity and the 'true rule' remains uncertain. The New South Wales Court of Appeal has ruled that there is no 'ambiguity gateway' requirement in *Mainteck v Stein Heurtey* (2014) 89 NSWLR 633.

However, the High Court has not referred to *Mainteck*. Its approach has been mixed, variously stating on the one hand that contextual interpretation is 'sometimes' required, but on the other hand maintaining commercial contracts 'require' consideration of context and purpose. In *Mount Bruce Mining Pty Ltd v Wright Prospecting Pty Ltd* (2015) 256 CLR 104, French CJ, Nettle and Gordon JJ stated it was '*necessary*' to ask what a 'reasonable businessperson would have understood those terms to mean', entailing consideration of circumstances and contractual purpose: [47] (emphasis added). Yet, if contractual terms are not ambiguous, surrounding circumstances evidence 'cannot be adduced to contradict its plain meaning': [48]. Their Honours stated recourse to surrounding circumstances was necessary only 'sometimes', such as where 'constructional choice' existed, but where this was so, it was admissible only in relation to market history, background and context; whereas statements and actions reflecting actual expectations and intentions remained inadmissible: [50]. Thus, whether or not an 'ambiguity gateway' still exists is, ironically, less than clear.[6]

6 Intriguingly, see comments that an ambiguity requirement may not in fact arise from *Codelfa*: Kiefel and Keane JJ [110]–[113]. Their Honours also emphasised that *Western Exports v Jireh* was not binding.

Jireh International Pty Ltd v Western Exports Services Inc [2011] NSWCA 137; and, on appeal, *Western Export Services Inc v Jireh International Pty Ltd* (2011) 86 ALJR 1

Facts and issues

In a contract for a Gloria Jean's franchise between Colorado-based WES and Jireh, a dispute arose concerning whether commission was payable to WES not only on sales by Jireh to certain stores, but also on sales by two companies associated with Jireh to those stores, by reason of Clause 3. Clause 3 stated: 'For sales by Jireh International Pty Ltd to GJGC Stores in Australia and to other countries, WES shall receive a commission of 5% of the ex-factory price of the coffees, teas and other products.' The question arose as to whether it was permissible to read 'by Jireh' to mean 'by Jireh or an associated entity'.

Decision

The New South Wales Court of Appeal overturned the trial decision[7] to expand the words of Clause 3 to give them a 'commercial and business-like interpretation'. Special leave to appeal was refused by the High Court.

Per Macfarlan JA in the NSW Court of Appeal at [55]:

> . . . courts must of course give commercial agreements a commercial and business-like interpretation. However, their ability to do so is constrained by the language used by the parties . . . [If] a court concludes that the language of a contract is unambiguous, the court must give effect to that language unless to do so would give the contract an absurd operation . . . In the case of absurdity, a court is able to conclude that the parties must have made a mistake in the language that they used and to correct that mistake. A court is not justified in disregarding unambiguous language simply because the contract would have a more commercial and businesslike operation if an interpretation different to that dictated by the language were adopted.

In the High Court[8] per Gummow, Heydon and Bell JJ at 2:

> Acceptance of the applicant's submission, clearly would require reconsideration by this Court of what was said in *Codelfa Construction Pty Ltd v State Rail Authority of NSW* by Mason J, with the concurrence of Stephen J and Wilson J, to be the 'true rule' as to the admission of evidence of surrounding circumstances. Until this Court embarks upon that exercise and disapproves or revises what was said in *Codelfa*, intermediate appellate courts are [3] bound to follow that precedent. The same is true of primary judges, notwithstanding what may appear to have been said by intermediate appellate courts.
>
> The position of *Codelfa*, as a binding authority, was made clear in the joint reasons of five Justices in *Royal Botanic Gardens and Domain Trust v South Sydney City Council* and it should not have been necessary to reiterate the point here.
>
> We do not read anything said in this Court in *Pacific Carriers Ltd v BNP Paribas*; *Toll (FGCT) Pty Ltd v Alphapharm Pty Ltd*; *Wilkie v Gordian Runoff Ltd* and *International Air Transport Association v Ansett Australia Holdings Ltd* as operating inconsistently with what was said by Mason J in the passage in *Codelfa* to which we have referred.

Special leave was refused by the High Court.

7 *Jireh International Pty Ltd v Western Exports Services Inc* [2010] NSWSC 632.
8 *Western Export Services Inc v Jireh International Pty Ltd* (2011) 86 ALJR 1.

10.3.8 Post-contractual conduct

The law in relation to evidence of a party's conduct after the conclusion of the contract for the purpose of establishing intention regarding meaning of terms at the time of conclusion was settled in *Agricultural and Rural Finance v Gardiner* (2008) at 582 (below), where its inadmissibility was confirmed: see also *Franklins v Metcash* (2009) 76 NSWLR 603 [324].

Primarily this is due to the notion that evidence of post-contractual (or subsequent) conduct is inconsistent with an objective approach, since it cannot have informed party intentions when the contract was concluded, or prove background knowledge that a reasonable person should be imbued with in determining the parties' presumed intent. Arguably, it proves only what parties 'meant' to say with the benefit of hindsight, rather than what they actually said or intended,[9] and may simply be self-serving conduct by a disgruntled party. Consequently, it is viewed with distrust by Australian courts,[10] and is generally inadmissible to prove the meaning of terms, despite its potential utility as evidence of a shared reflection of what words were commonly intended to mean when they entered the contract.[11]

However, there are purposes for which evidence of subsequent conduct may be used:

- Admissions of truth about background facts: *Franklins Pty Ltd v Metcash Trading Ltd* (2009) 76 NSWLR 603 [324];
- Proof of intention to enter legal relations: *Australian Broadcasting Corporation v XIVth Commonwealth Games Ltd* (1988) 18 NSWLR 540;
- Proof of identity of parties: *Nurisvan Investment Ltd v Anyoption Holdings Ltd* [2017] VSCA 141;
- Proof the contract is partly oral and partly written: *Lym International Pty Ltd v Marcolongo* (2011) BPR 29,465;
- To establish estoppel: (see **Chapter 7**);
- Characterisation of contract for purposes of legislative or regulatory classification;
- For interpretation of international contracts under *CISG* art 8(3) or UNIDROIT Principles art 4.3 (below **10.5.1–10.5.2**).

9 David McLauchlan, 'Contract Formation, Contract Interpretation and Subsequent Conduct' (2006) 25(1) *University of Queensland Law Journal* 77, 93.

10 *L Schuler AG v Wickman Machine Tool Sales Ltd* [1974] AC 235, 268. Contra, Tipping J in *Gibbons Holdings Ltd v Wholesale Distributors Ltd* [2008] 1 NZLR 277.

11 See calling for courts to revisit the exclusion of evidence of subsequent conduct for the purpose of determining the meaning of terms: McLauchlan, above n 9, 84, 103; Sir Roy Goode, *Goode on Commercial Law* (Penguin, 4th ed, 2010) 101–102; Sir Johan Steyn, 'Written Contracts: To What Extent May Evidence Control Language' (1986) *Current Legal Problems* 23; Lord Nicholls of Birkehead, 'My Kingdom for a Horse: The Meaning of Words' (2005) 121 *Law Quarterly Review* 577; David McLauchlan, 'Subsequent Conduct as an Aid to Interpretation' (1996) 2 *New Zealand Business Law Quarterly* 237; David McLauchlan, 'Subsequent Conduct and Contract Interpretation – An Update' (1997) 3 *New Zealand Business Law Quarterly* 147. By contrast, see the approach in international contract law: *CISG* art 8(3) and UNIDROIT Principles art 4.3 (below).

Agricultural and Rural Finance Pty Ltd v Gardiner (2008) 238 CLR 570

Facts and issues

Mr Gardiner was an investor in a plantation scheme set up by Oceania Agriculture ('OAL'). Under the scheme, Agriculture and Rural Finance ('ARF') (the lender) made loans to Mr Gardiner, each requiring periodic repayments. At the time of each loan, an indemnity agreement was entered into between ARF, Mr Gardiner, and OAL, pursuant to which OAL agreed in exchange for a flat fee to indemnify Mr Gardiner against any demand for repayment by ARF if he ceased business due to certain events. This indemnity was only enforceable if Mr Gardiner 'punctually paid' the amounts due under the related loan agreement. On two of the loans, Mr Gardiner made late payments which were accepted by ARF, then later ceased business due to an event specified in the indemnity. The case turned on the meaning of 'punctually', and whether acceptance of late payments constituted a waiver by ARF of the condition for indemnity. Thus, in relation to the meaning of this term, evidence of the conduct of ARF in accepting late payments was said to prove the meaning of 'punctual'. As this was conduct subsequent to conclusion of the contract, the question of evidence of post-contractual conduct in contractual interpretation arose.

Decision

The New South Wales Court of Appeal had been divided on the issue of whether payments had been made 'punctually'. In holding for ARF, the High Court found that payments had not been punctual. It elaborated primarily upon waiver, estoppel and release, but also mentioned that evidence of post-contractual conduct was not generally admissible in contractual interpretation.

> [582] . . . 'What is meant by treating a payment as punctual?' . . . On its face it is an expression that seeks to attach legal consequences to the fact of receipt. . . . In particular, if more is meant than that the payment was received *without* the Lender exercising the choice it had under the loan agreements of accelerating payment of the balance, the content of that additional element is not explained. In addition, to approach issues of construction in this way would be at odds with the general principle that 'it is not legitimate to use as an aid in the construction of [a] contract anything which the parties said or did after it was made'.

The appeal was allowed.

10.3.9 Admissible evidence: the position summarised

Evidence of subjective intentions and post-contractual conduct are not permitted in contractual interpretation in Australian contract law. Evidence of surrounding circumstances can help establish background facts known to both parties for other purposes (see **Chapter 9**), but cannot be admitted for purposes of interpretation of the meaning of terms, unless the terms of the contract are ambiguous. The status of the 'ambiguity gateway' is somewhat controversial, but unless the High Court expressly rules otherwise, it is prudent to establish ambiguity. Moreover, ambiguity can usually be easily found. Aside from the prevalence of the objective test, Australian contract law is in direct contrast to the position taken in international contract law (below **10.5.1–10.5.2**).

QUESTIONS

(1) What is the purpose of the parol evidence rule?

(2) In the *Codelfa* case, the works program was considered relevant to understanding the meaning of the terms. Why didn't the parol evidence rule operate to preclude recourse to this evidence?

10.4 Principles of interpretation

Factor	Short explanation	Relevant authorities	*Principles* text*
Considering the whole of the contract	The need to read contracts as a whole. Additional principle to interpret terms that do not render them ineffective	*Metropolitan Gas Co v Federated Gas Employees' Industrial Union* (1925) 35 CLR 449	Chapter 10: 10.16
Absurdity and unlikelihood	Where two meanings are possible, the meaning that does not result in an absurdity should be preferred	*Australian Broadcasting Commission v Australasian Performing Right Association* (1973) 129 CLR 99	Chapter 10: 10.12
Contra proferentem	In certain circumstances, ambiguous words should be interpreted against the party which drafted the term	–	Chapter 10: 10.17
Other maxims	Further maxims may aid interpretation such as *expressio unius est exclusio alterius, ejusdem generis* (and its variant *noscitur a sociis),* and preference for an interpretation that results in validity/legality rather than one leading to invalidity/illegality	*SCN Pty Ltd v Smith* [2006] QCA 360 *Goldsbrough, Mort & Co Ltd v Tolson* (1909) 10 CLR 470	Chapter 10: 10.18

* Consult the corresponding section(s) of the *Principles* text for more detail.

10.4.1 The canons of construction

Canons of construction are maxims of ancient origin, with relevance in interpretation beyond contract. It is important to recognise they are mere aids to interpretation, not binding rules.

10.4.2 Considering the whole of the contract

A principle frequently relied upon is the need to read the contract (or any document) as a whole, rather than read specific words or a particular term in isolation. This principle is also recognised in the international context: **25.5.8.3**. Another principle concerns preference for the interpretation of contractual terms in a manner that does not render them nugatory or ineffective, but rather so as to give them effect.[12] Both principles are also recognised in international contract laws (**25.5.8.4**).

Metropolitan Gas Co v Federated Gas Employees' Industrial Union (1925) 35 CLR 449

Facts and issues

The Federated Gas Employees' Industrial Union ('the Union') had unsuccessfully demanded that firms pay minimum award wages. The Metropolitan Gas Company ('the Gas Company') sought an injunction to restrain a strike by employees of contractors. The case turned upon interpretation of s 6a of the *Conciliation and Arbitration Act 1904-21* (Cth), which prohibited strikes by those under an award. The question was whether s 6a (which dealt with strikes after an award) must be read together with s 6 (which dealt with strikes before awards were rendered).

Decision

Reading the legislation as a whole, the High Court held that s 6a was a counterpart to s 6, and thus its scope was limited to prohibition of strike action only by those bound by an award. While the Gas Company was a party to the award, the striking men were not, since they were not employees of the Gas Company. Thus the High Court refused the injunction.

Per Isaacs and Rich JJ at 454:

> . . . The only two possibly relevant provisions of the Act are secs. 6 and 6a. The argument for the Company did not suggest that the case fell under sec. 6, but it did press the view that the case fell within the literal terms of sec. 6a. That section is as follows '6a. No person or organization bound by an award of the Court, or entitled to the benefit of an award of the Court, shall do anything in the nature of a lock-out or strike, or continue any lock-out or strike. Penalty: one thousand pounds.' It is said that sec. 6a is satisfied because (1) the Union is a 'person entitled to the benefit of an award of the Court' and (2) the men and Union are doing something 'in the nature of a strike.' 'Strike,' it is said, being unqualified is not confined to the award or the industrial dispute in respect of which the award was made . . . but includes any strike anywhere in Australia, in any person's employment . . . [455] . . . The first thing that impresses the mind when faced with that contention is the utter one-sidedness of the position. It would punish the men in the present case for striking in the employ of the 'outsider,' as he may be termed, but it would leave the 'outsider' entirely free to lock them out. This is so because, as he is neither 'bound by an award of the Court' nor 'entitled to the benefit of an award of the Court,' he is altogether outside the prohibition of sec. 6a. To impute to the Legislature an intention so obviously unfair would require language of the most intractable character. But there are further reasons opposed to the contention and based on ordinary rules of legal construction. It is a received canon of interpretation that every passage in a document must be read, not as if it were entirely divorced from its context, but as part of the whole instrument: *Ex antecedentibus et consequentibus fit optima interpretatio.* In construing an instrument 'every part of it should be

12 See eg *Chapmans Ltd v Australian Stock Exchange Ltd* (1996) 67 FCR 402.

> brought into action, in order to collect from the whole one uniform and consistent sense, if that may be done; or, in other words, the construction must be made upon the entire instrument, and not merely upon disjointed parts of it; the whole context must be considered, in endeavouring to collect the intention of the parties, although the immediate object of inquiry be the meaning of an isolated clause' ... If, when so read, the meaning of the section is literally clear and unambiguous, nothing remains but to give effect to the unqualified words. ...

The application was dismissed.

10.4.3 Absurdity and unlikelihood

Courts must walk the fine line between giving effect to unambiguous words of a contract, and the need to avoid absurd meanings that might arise from a literal reading. The test, stated in *ABC v APRA* (1973) (below), is echoed in many cases including by Macfarlan JA in *Jireh v Western Exports* (2011) at [55] (above).

Australian Broadcasting Commission v Australasian Performing Right Association (1973) 129 CLR 99

Facts and issues

Australasian Performing Right Association ('APRA') was an agent for owners of recorded music works, and contracted on behalf of owners in 1966 with the ABC for public broadcast of music. Clause 2 of the contract provided for 11 monthly payments per year, plus a 12th monthly payment calculated according to a formula which included indexation to adjust for inflation. The dispute concerned whether the formula should be interpreted literally, which would lead to an uncommercial outcome.

Decision

By majority decision, the clause was held to be unambiguous and given its literal meaning.

Per Gibbs J at 109:

> If the words used are unambiguous the court must give effect to them, notwithstanding that the result may appear capricious or unreasonable, and notwithstanding that it may be guessed or suspected that the parties intended something different. The court has no power to remake or amend a contract for the purpose of avoiding a result which is considered to be inconvenient or unjust. On the other hand, if the language is open to two constructions, that will be preferred which will avoid consequences which appear to be capricious, unreasonable, inconvenient or unjust ...

The appeal was allowed.

10.4.4 Resolving ambiguities

Another canon of interpretation is the *contra proferentem* principle, whereby ambiguities in a written contract are resolved against the party who proposed the terms. There is some controversy over its exact manner of operation, and it has been referred to as a principle of 'last resort' (*McCann v Switzerland Insurance* (2000) 203 CLR 579). Nonetheless, it is utilised as a general principle of interpretation, and also as justification for the strict interpretation of guarantees (see **11.5**), and standard form exclusion and limitation clauses.[13] The principle is also recognised in international contexts: **25.5.8.7**. See **11.3** for further discussion of the *contra proferentem* principle.

10.4.5 Other maxims

The principle of *expressio unius est exclusio alterius,* encapsulates the notion that if only one option or thing is expressed, other options or things are excluded, and is a well-known canon of broad application. This is also true of *ejusdem generis*, whereby in a list of items ending with 'others', the latter will include only items of the same type: see, referring to a variant of *ejusdem generis, noscitur a sociis, Goldsbrough, Mort & Co Ltd v Tolson* (1909) 10 CLR 470 (below). There are also principles to the effect that an interpretation giving a contract validity or legality should be favoured over one which renders it invalid or illegal: *Hillas & Co Ltd v Arcos* (1932) 43 LJ L Rep 359; *Langley v Foster* (1906) 4 CLR 167. Similarly, another principle concerns preference for interpretation of contractual terms in a manner that does not render them nugatory or ineffective, but rather so as to give them effect.[14] The latter principles are also recognised in international contract laws (**25.5.8.4**).

SCN Pty Ltd v Smith [2006] QCA 360

Facts and issues

Smith contracted to sell land to SCN. The contract was subject to special conditions. SCN failed to apply for operational works approval within 60 days as required by the special conditions. SCN's request for extension was ignored by Smith, and SCN purported to exercise a power granted to it under Clause 9, which would have rendered the contract unconditional and binding. However, Smith purported to terminate the contract, and subsequently contracted to sell to a different purchaser. Smith's purported termination was pursuant to Clause 1 which stated:

> This contract is subject to and conditional upon the Purchaser lodging an application for material change of use application, development application and operational works (herein after called the 'application') in respect of the property with the Local Authority on or before 60 days from the date hereof and approval of such application being received by the Purchaser on or before 15 months from the date hereof. If the Purchaser fails to lodge the material change of use application with the local authority within 60 days of the date hereof then the Vendor may by notice in writing terminate the contract.

The question on appeal involved interpretation of Clause 1, particularly whether the second sentence reference to failure to lodge an application for approval of 'material change of use' gave Smith the right to terminate for a failure to lodge an application for approval of 'operational works' as mentioned in the first sentence.

13 See eg *Darlington Futures Ltd v Delco Australia Pty Ltd* (1986) 161 CLR 500. See further **11.3**.
14 See eg *Chapmans Ltd v Australian Stock Exchange Ltd* (1996) 67 FCR 402.

Decision

The Court of Appeal upheld the trial decision, referring to the maxim *expressio unius est exclusio alterius* to hold that, as the second sentence (conferring the right of termination upon Smith) only referred to failures to lodge 'material change of use' applications, failure to lodge 'operational works' applications did not confer the right to terminate.

Per McPherson JA at [6]:

> . . . The critical question is, however, who may exercise the power conferred by special conditions 1 and 3 to terminate the contract and in what circumstances. As to this, special condition 1 is, I think, clear in its terms. The Vendor may terminate the contract, but he may do so only 'if the Purchaser fails to lodge the material change of use application within 60 days' of the contract date of 29 July 2004. It is true that the first sentence of the clause is not elegantly drafted. There is, in the use of the words 'material change of use application' and 'development application', an element of unnecessary repetition or perhaps tautology; but neither that, nor the specific reference in the first sentence to 'operational works', justifies the conclusion that it or the second sentence is designed to arm the Vendor with power to terminate the contract if the Purchaser fails to lodge an 'operational works' application within 60 days of the contract date. The second sentence is quite specific about the event on the happening of which the Vendor may give notice of termination. It operates on the Purchaser's failure to lodge 'the material change of use application', and nothing else.
>
> [7] I agree with what Keane JA has written on this point in his reasons on this appeal. *Expressio unius est exclusio alterius*: see *North Stafford Steel Co v Ward* (1868) LR 3 Ex 172, 177, per Willes J. But it is hardly necessary to clothe the thought in authority or in Latin garb. If one alternative is expressly and specifically mentioned, it rationally tends to exclude the implication of another or of any other. . . .

The appeal was dismissed.

Goldsbrough, Mort & Co Ltd v Tolson (1909) 10 CLR 470

Facts and issues

A dispute arose concerning a clause within mortgage deeds assigning rural properties to Goldsbrough Mort. Tolson had paid certain taxes, and then assigned the property to Goldsbrough Mort under mortgage deeds. Tolson argued that he was entitled to a refund of the taxes paid as evidenced by certain certificates, but Goldsbrough Mort claimed that it was entitled to the refund pursuant to the clause, by which Tolson had assigned to it 'all and singular the sheep cattle horses stock chattels and effects which are now or may at any time during the continuance of this security be upon or belonging to the said stations'.

Decision

The case turned upon the meaning of 'chattels and effects'. The High Court held that, while the right to a refund of the taxes was a personal right in the nature of a chose in action, and thus could be included within the category of 'chattels', the list of items preceding 'chattels' indicated that the class of items intended to be included was merely physical choses in possession rather than incorporeal choses in action, such as the certificates which entitled the holder to tax refunds. Thus, by reference to the maxim *noscitur a sociis*, a variant of the principle of *ejusdem generis,* the High Court held the certificates were not assigned to Goldsborough Mort.

Per O'Connor J at 478:

> ... This is not a case in which what is generally understood as the *ejusdem generis* rule is applicable. A maxim more appropriate to the matter in hand is *noscitur a sociis,* but the rule and the [479] maxim rest upon the same principle, which I take to be this— *prima facie* you must take general words as used in their most extensive meaning, unless you find something in the context in which they stand or in the rest of the deed to indicate that the parties have intended them to have a more restricted meaning. Applying the rule to the present case, I have no doubt that the expression 'chattels and effects' is capable of including in its meaning a certificate such as that in question ... But after careful consideration of the language of the whole deed and of the context in which the general words stand, I am satisfied that such an interpretation would not carry out the intention of the parties. The deed mentions with much particularity the various objects assigned. In the long string of them there is not one which is not a material object capable of physical acquisition. Nothing incorporeal is dealt with in that part of the deed except the right to compensation for improvements ... which follows immediately after the words which effect an assignment of the improvements themselves. Full effect can be given to the expression 'chattels and effects' by construing it as operating on the innumerable things not mentioned in the deed, but of the same substance and tangibility as those mentioned, and which go to make up the working equipment of stations taken over ... To extend the meaning of the expression beyond that would be ... to read into the words used by the parties a meaning which, judging by the context, could not have been present to their minds at the time they used them. ... It follows that the certificates remained the property of the respondent ...

The appeal was dismissed.

QUESTIONS

(1) Can you think of any circumstances in which one of the above maxims would directly contradict the outcome of another of the maxims?

(2) What is the policy behind the *contra proferentem* rule?

10.5 International perspectives

Factor	Short explanation	Relevant authorities	*Principles* text*
CISG	An objective test of intent at the time the contract was concluded is the usual standard, but the parol evidence rule does not apply. Courts must consider evidence of preliminary negotiations, surrounding circumstances and post-contractual conduct	*CISG* arts 8–9, 11	–

(cont.)

Factor	Short explanation	Relevant authorities	*Principles* text*
	without any ambiguity precondition. International trade usages and past practices may aid interpretation		
UNIDROIT Principles (Opt In)	As per *CISG*, but also: • expressly lists principles including *contra proferentem*, preference for negotiated versus general terms; whole of contract interpretation; and • directly imposes a duty of good faith which may have an impact upon interpretation	UNIDROIT Principles arts 4.1–4.3	–

* Consult the corresponding section(s) of the *Principles* text for more detail.

10.5.1 *CISG*—contractual interpretation

For details on when the 1980 *UN Convention on Contracts for the International Sale of Goods* (the *CISG*) applies to international contracts, see **25.4.1**. As discussed in **Chapter 25**, the *CISG* contains its own interpretive method. Article 8 of the *CISG* outlines the test for intention. Like Australian contract law (above **10.2.1**), the *CISG* uses an objective test. Words and conduct of parties must be interpreted in accordance with the understanding of a reasonable person in the position of the addressee: art 8(2) *CISG*. Subjective intent is only relevant in rare cases when an addressee 'knew or could not have been unaware' of the other's intent: art 8(1) *CISG*. Thus, the objective standard applies in the overwhelming majority of cases.

However, the *CISG* differs significantly from the Australian position in regard to evidence that is admissible to establish the understanding of a reasonable person in the addressee's position, and the clarity of such rules. Australian contract law restricts the type of evidence that may be adduced to determine intent (above **10.3.4–10.3.8**), and there are unanswered questions as to the role of the ambiguity gateway: **10.3.7**. By contrast, the *CISG* directs courts and tribunals to consider a far broader range of evidence to determine intent, including preliminary negotiations, surrounding circumstances and post-contractual conduct: art 8(3) *CISG*. Such evidence is admissible where the contract is governed by the *CISG* in order to prove the intent of parties at the time the contract was concluded, and there is no precondition of ambiguity before recourse to such evidence: **25.5.5.1**. The plain meaning rule, which would exclude other evidence if written words are unambiguous, does not apply where the *CISG* governs the contract: **25.5.5.1**.[15] In other words, it is always permissible and indeed necessary to consider such evidence, unless parties have agreed to the contrary.[16]

15 CISG Advisory Council, *Opinion No 3*, Comment para 3.2; Spagnolo (n 1) 740, paras 60–61. See **25.5.5.1**.
16 Such as by means of a merger clause: **25.5.6**.

Thus, the position under the *CISG*, which is now the international standard, is far simpler than under Australian law. Arguably, such evidence may be highly valuable in determining what a reasonable party in the position of an addressee understood by the contractual terms at the time the contract was concluded.[17] Any one-sided or self-serving post-contractual conduct, or preliminary negotiations which fail to clearly demonstrate intent may be dealt with by an appropriate adjustment in the weight accorded to such evidence.[18] The operation of this rule has not been met with difficulty in practice.

The much vexed parol evidence rule has no place in the interpretation of contracts governed by the *CISG*: arts 8(3) and 11 *CISG* (**25.5.5.1**). Thus, the court will not be confined to the written contractual terms, but should consider other oral or written evidence as to both identification and meaning of terms (see **25.5.5.1**), unless parties have agreed otherwise; for example, by merger clause: **25.5.6**.[19]

Past practices between parties (arts 8(3), 9(1) *CISG*), and widely recognised international usages of trade can aid interpretation or supply additional terms: **25.5.7** and **25.7.6**. Certain interpretive principles described above, such as *contra proferentem*, may also be used within the *CISG*, although it does not contain express provisions to that effect: **25.5.8**.

CISG arts 8–9, 11

Article 8

(1) For the purposes of this Convention statements made by and other conduct of a party are to be interpreted according to his intent where the other party knew or could not have been unaware what that intent was.

(2) If the preceding paragraph is not applicable, statements made by and other conduct of a party are to be interpreted according to the understanding that a reasonable person of the same kind as the other party would have had in the same circumstances.

(3) In determining the intent of a party or the understanding a reasonable person would have had, due consideration is to be given to all relevant circumstances of the case including the negotiations, any practices which the parties have established between themselves, usages and any subsequent conduct of the parties.

Article 9

(1) The parties are bound by any usage to which they have agreed and by any practices which they have established between themselves.

(2) The parties are considered, unless otherwise agreed, to have impliedly made applicable to their contract or its formation a usage of which the parties knew or ought to have known and which in international trade is widely known to, and regularly observed by, parties to contracts of the type involved in the particular trade concerned.

Article 11

A contract of sale need not be concluded in or evidenced by writing and is not subject to any other requirement as to form. It may be proved by any means, including witnesses.

17 McLauchlan (n 7) 83, 101, 109–110.
18 McLauchlan (n 7) 84, 103.
19 Or in the case of amendments, a no oral modification clause.

10.5.2 UNIDROIT Principles: contractual interpretation

For details on when UNIDROIT Principles of International Commercial Contracts (UNIDROIT Principles) apply, see **25.4.3**. The interpretive provisions within the UNIDROIT Principles are very similar to those of the *CISG*. The test for intent is primarily objective, although rarely subjective: arts 4.1 and 4.2 UNIDROIT Principles: see **25.5.5.2**. Permissible evidence also includes preliminary negotiations, post-contractual conduct and surrounding circumstances, and trade usages and past practices may aid interpretation and supply terms: art 4.3 and see **25.7.12**. Likewise, the parol evidence rule does not apply: art 1.2 UNIDROIT Principles.[20]

Where the UNIDROIT Principles differ to the *CISG* is that they impose a direct obligation of good faith at all contracting stages, including during the pre-contractual period: art 1.7.1 UNIDROIT Principles; see **25.5.4**. This significantly affects interpretation of obligations.

The UNIDROIT Principles expressly set out general principles to aid interpretation. Contrary to the approach in Australian law, the plain meaning rule is rejected in favour of a purposive and commercially reasonable approach (art 4.3(d)). Negotiated terms prevail over standard terms (arts 2.1.19 and 2.1.21), and original contracts are preferred to translated versions in cases of inconsistency: art 4.7 UNIDROIT Principles. Similarly to interpretive maxims in Australian law (see above **10.4.1–10.4.5**), the UNIDROIT Principles expressly state: the whole of the contract must be considered (art 4.4); an interpretation which gives effect is preferred to one which renders terms redundant (art 4.5); specific terms prevail over general terms (art 4.4, Comment para 2); and *contra proferentem* applies (art 4.6). Arguably, many of these also apply under the *CISG*: see **25.5.8**.

UNIDROIT Principles arts 4.1–4.3

Article 4.1 (Intention of the Parties)

(1) A contract shall be interpreted according to the common intention of the parties.

(2) If such an intention cannot be established, the contract shall be interpreted according to the meaning that reasonable persons of the same kind as the parties would give to it in the same circumstances.

Article 4.2 (Interpretation of Statements and other Conduct)

(1) The statements and other conduct of a party shall be interpreted according to that party's intention if the other party knew or could not have been unaware of that intention.

(2) If the preceding paragraph is not applicable, such statements and other conduct shall be interpreted according to the meaning that a reasonable person of the same kind as the other party would give to it in the same circumstances.

Article 4.3 (Relevant Circumstances)

In applying Articles 4.1 and 4.2, regard shall be had to all the circumstances, including

20 UNIDROIT Principles, art 1.2, Comment para 1. See **25.5.5.2**.

(a) preliminary negotiations between the parties;
(b) practices which the parties have established between themselves;
(c) the conduct of the parties subsequent to the conclusion of the contract;
(d) the nature and purpose of the contract;
(e) the meaning commonly given to terms and expressions in the trade concerned;
(f) usages.

10.6 Review

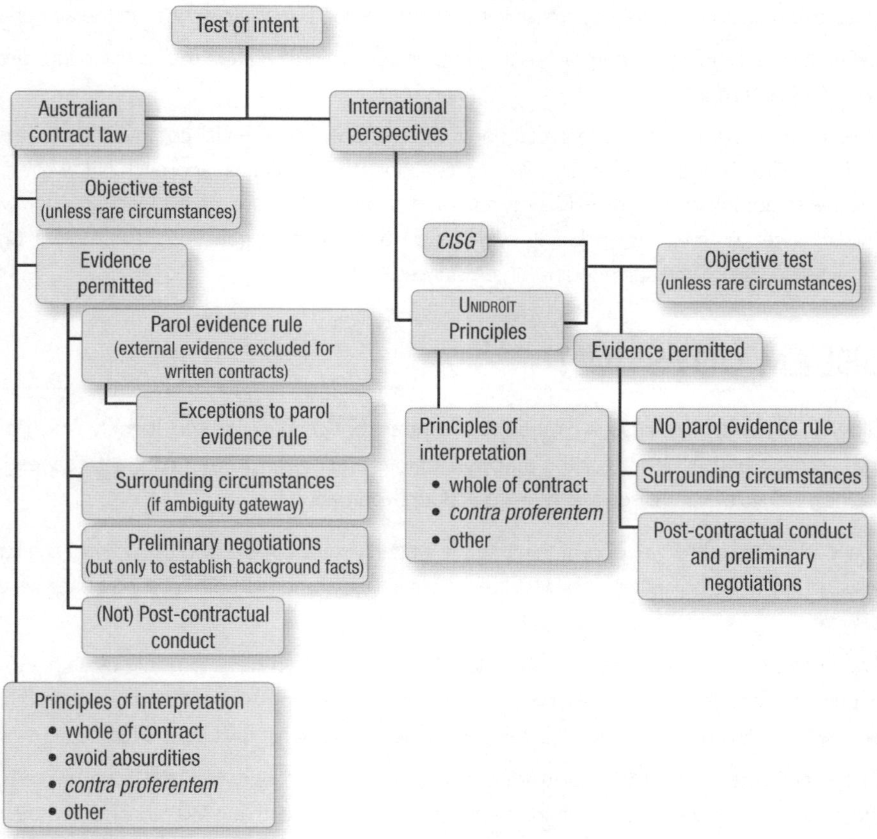

TIPS FOR APPLYING THE LAW IN PRACTICE

- Interpretation (or construction) is the process whereby the meaning of contractual terms is determined.
- The objective standard of interpretation is used to ascertain the meaning of contractual terms.
- The extent to which courts may refer to extrinsic evidence to ascertain the meaning of written terms is a complex and contentious issue in Australia.

- Generally, recourse to evidence of preliminary negotiations and subsequent conduct is not permissible for the purposes of interpreting contractual terms.
- Evidence of surrounding circumstances may be permitted for the purpose of interpreting contractual terms where words are ambiguous.
- The parol evidence rule precludes recourse to oral or written evidence beyond a written contract which appears to be intended to encapsulate the whole contract.
- Exceptions to the parol evidence rule allow the use of extrinsic evidence for specific purposes, including: identification of parties/subject matter, actions for rectification, collateral contract, or to demonstrate the written contract is incomplete, or that a term carried a specialised meaning in trade.
- Another exception to the parol evidence rule is where written words are ambiguous. If the exception applies, extrinsic evidence will be admissible to clarify meaning, but not to contradict the written words.
- Maxims such as reading the contract as a whole, and *contra proferentem* may assist in interpretation of contractual terms.
- In the international context, interpretation of international commercial contracts under the *CISG* and UNIDROIT Principles generally also relies upon the objective approach. However, these instruments abolish the parol evidence rule, and mandate the use of evidence beyond written terms to ascertain meaning, including evidence of preliminary negotiations, subsequent or post-contractual conduct and surrounding circumstances.

PROBLEM QUESTION

The following circumstances arise in relation to a contract between Jo and Mo. Identify which of them would be admissible as evidence for the purposes of interpreting the written contract between them, and why/not, citing relevant cases and rules to support your view.

(1) Jo and Mo were drinking alcohol at the time the written contract was drawn up by them at a bar. As a result, Jo wrote '16 boxes' were to be delivered, but in fact, Jo and Mo both meant 6 boxes were to be delivered.

(2) The price of $100 was agreed because delivery was envisaged to be possible by ship. However, unbeknownst to Jo or Mo, no ship would take cargo of the type contained in the boxes. Thus, the only legal means of delivery for this cargo is by helicopter, which will cost $10,000.

(3) By the time they came to the bottom of the paper serviette on which the terms were written, they had run out of space. Jo said, 'Don't worry, we agree that I will accompany the boxes personally, to look after them', and Mo answered 'OK, that can be part of the agreement'. They both signed the serviette, but Mo did not read the terms written on it. One of them stated 'Nobody is to accompany the boxes on delivery'. (Ignore issues relating to frustration or validity.)

RESEARCH QUESTION

If you were to design a system of interpretation, would you adopt different rules regarding admissibility of evidence in ascertaining meaning of terms? If so, what rules would you adopt, and why? How would these differ from existing rules?

11

LIMITING OR EXTENDING LIABILITY

11.1 Overview

It is quite common for a contract to contain a clause which seeks to exclude completely or limit the potential liability of a particular party or parties in certain circumstances. This chapter will examine the use and nature of exemption clauses, the interpretation and application of such clauses, as well as statutory control of the use of these types of clauses. A brief look at the use of guarantees and indemnities as another way of altering the allocation of liability is also included.

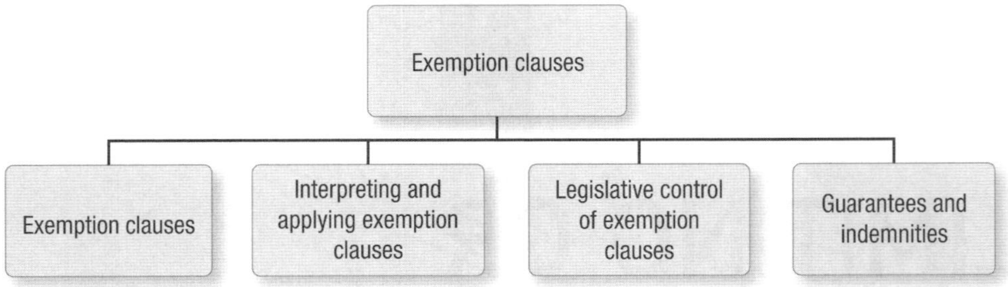

11.2 Exemption clauses

Concept	Short explanation	Relevant authorities	*Principles* text*
Exemption clauses are used to manage and allocate risk	These types of clauses seek to limit or remove completely the liability of a party for breach of contract or other wrong and can be utilised in relation to even fundamental breaches	*Photo Production Ltd v Securicor Transport Ltd* [1980] AC 827	Chapter 11: 11.02–11.03

* Consult the corresponding section(s) of the *Principles* text for more detail.

Frequently a contract will contain an exemption clause. Such clauses are used to exclude (sometimes referred to as 'exclusion clauses') or limit (sometimes referred to as 'limitation clauses') the liability of parties for breach of contract or otherwise wrongful conduct.[1] An exemption clause may act to exclude the liability of a party completely by appearing in the form of a defence, or to reduce or eliminate liability on the basis that that party's obligation is reduced or eliminated. Parties are free to enter into contracts containing exemption clauses,[2] although often the reality is that this type of clause is imposed by one party on the other (weaker) party.

1 For example, liability arising under the tort of negligence (discussed at **11.3.1**).
2 Subject, of course, to applicable legislative controls (discussed at **11.4**).

The below case of *Photo Production Ltd v Securicor Transport Ltd*[3] demonstrates the use of an exemption clause to exclude liability. There was substantial discussion in this case of the doctrine of fundamental breach—the idea that certain breaches were too fundamental for any exemption clause to operate to exclude liability in relation to such breaches. The following extracts illustrate that the Court ultimately moved away from this rule and concluded that the focus should rather be on the construction of the particular exemption clause. The result being that, *as a matter of construction*, an exemption clause can extend to exclude liability for fundamental breaches. It is important to note at this point that the High Court declined to adopt the doctrine of fundamental breach in Australia[4]—the paramount consideration being the construction of the particular exemption clause (rather than whether or not there was a 'fundamental breach' of the contract).

Photo Production Ltd v Securicor Transport Ltd [1980] AC 827

Facts and issues

Photo Production Ltd ('PP') entered into a contract with Securicor Transport Ltd ('ST') for the provision of security services by ST. Specifically, ST was engaged to provide regular night patrols of PP's factory to protect against, mainly, fire and theft. An employee of ST, while on one such patrol, purposely started a fire which burned down PP's factory. There was a clause in the contract ('Condition 1') which relevantly provided:

> (1) Under no circumstances shall [ST] be responsible for any injurious act or default by any employee of the company unless such act or default could have been foreseen and avoided by the exercise of due diligence on the part of [ST] as his employer; nor, in any event, shall the company be held responsible for:
>
> (a) Any loss suffered by the customer through . . . fire or any other cause, except insofar as such loss is attributable to the negligence of [ST's] employees acting within the course of their employment.

The second part of the clause ('Condition 2') limited ST's potential liability both under the contract and 'at common law'. PP, understandably, sought damages on the basis of breach of contract and/or negligence. The issue for determination by the court was whether the exemption clause described above excluded ST's liability for the conduct of its employee and subsequent losses suffered by PP. At first instance, the claim was denied on the basis that Condition 1 acted to exclude liability. PP appealed this decision and succeeded. The current case constituted an appeal by ST from the decision of the Court of Appeal.

Decision

Per Lord Wilberforce at 840:

> It is first necessary to decide upon the correct approach to a case such as this where it is sought to invoke an exception or limitation clause in the contract. The approach of [Lord

3 [1980] AC 827.
4 See *Council of the City of Sydney v West* (1965) 114 CLR 481, extracted in section **11.3** below.

> Denning M.R.] in the Court of Appeal was to consider first whether the breach was 'fundamental'. If so, he said, the court itself deprives the party of the benefit of an exemption or limitation clause ([1978] 1 WLR 856, 863) . . .
>
> [842] I have no second thoughts as to the main proposition that the question whether, and to what extent, an exclusion clause is to be applied to a fundamental breach, or a breach [843] of a fundamental term, or indeed to any breach of contract, is a matter of construction of the contract. Many difficult questions arise and will continue to arise in the infinitely varied situations in which contracts come to be breached . . . But there are ample resources in the normal rules of contract law for dealing with these without the superimposition of a judicially invented rule of law . . .
>
> [846] As a preliminary, . . . does condition 1 apply? It is drafted in strong terms, 'Under no circumstances' . . . 'any injurious act or default by any employee'. These words have to be approached with the aid of the cardinal rules of construction that they must be read *contra proferentem* and that in order to escape from the consequences of one's own wrongdoing, or that of one's servant, clear words are necessary. I think that these words are clear. The respondents in fact relied upon them for an argument that since they exempted from negligence they must be taken as not exempting from the consequence of deliberate acts. But this is a perversion of the rule that if a clause can cover something other than negligence, it will not be applied to negligence. Whether, in addition to negligence, it covers other, e.g., deliberate, acts, remains a matter of constructions requiring, of course, clear words. I am of opinion that it does, and being free to construe and apply the clause, I must hold that liability is excluded. On this part of the case I agree with the judge and adopt his reasons for judgment. I would allow the appeal.

Per Lord Diplock at 846:

> It is not disputed that the act of Securicor's servant, Musgrove, in starting a fire in the factory which they had undertaken to protect was a breach of contract by Securicor; and since it [847] was the cause of an event, the destruction of the factory, that rendered further performance of the contract impossible it is not an unnatural use of ordinary language to describe it as a 'fundamental breach' . . .
>
> A basic principle of the common law of contract, to which there are no exceptions that are relevant in the instant case, is that parties to a contract are free to determine for themselves what primary obligations they will accept . . . if the parties wish to reject or modify primary obligations which would otherwise be so incorporated, they are fully at liberty to do so by express words . . .
>
> [850] My Lords, an exclusion clause is one which excludes or modifies an obligation, whether primary, general secondary or anticipatory secondary, that would otherwise arise under the contract by implication of law. Parties are free to agree to whatever exclusion or modification of all types of obligations as they please within the limits that the agreement must retain the legal characteristics of a contract . . .
>
> [851] In commercial contracts negotiated between business-men capable of looking after their own interests and of deciding how risks inherent in the performance of various kinds of contract can be most economically borne (generally by insurance), it is, in my view, wrong to place a strained construction upon words in an exclusion clause which are clear and fairly susceptible of one meaning only even after due allowance has been made for the presumption in favour of the implied primary and secondary obligations . . . [I]t seems to me that this apportionment of the risk of the factory being damaged or destroyed by the injurious act of an employee of Securicor while carrying out a visit to the factory is one which reasonable businessmen in the position of Securicor and the factory owners might well think was the most economical.

The appeal was allowed.

11.3 Interpreting and applying exemption clauses

Concept	Short explanation	Relevant authorities	*Principles* text*
General approach to construction	An exemption clause is to be interpreted according to its natural and ordinary meaning, read in light of the contract as a whole	*Darlington Futures Ltd v Delco Australia Pty Ltd* (1986) 161 CLR 500	Chapter 11: 11.04, 11.06
Contra proferentem rule	In the case of ambiguity, an exemption clause is interpreted against the party who drafted it	*Wallis, Son & Wells v Pratt & Haynes* [1911] AC 394 *Insight Vacations Pty Ltd v Young* (2011) 243 CLR 149	Chapter 11: 11.04–11.06
Four corners rule	An exemption clause will only apply to conduct occurring in performance of the contract	*Council of the City of Sydney v West* (1965) 114 CLR 481	Chapter 11: 11.04–11.05
Deviation rule	In contracts involving the carriage of goods, an exemption clause will not be effective if the route of carriage is deviated from	*Thomas National Transport (Melbourne) Pty Ltd* v *May & Baker (Australia)* Pty Ltd (1966) 115 CLR 353	Chapter 11: 11.04–11.05
Exemption clauses can exclude liability for negligence	In order to succeed in excluding liability for negligence, an exemption clause must clearly refer to negligence	*White v John Warrick & Co Ltd* [1953] 2 All ER 1021 *Davis v Pearce Parking Station Pty Ltd* (1954) 91 CLR 642	Chapter 11: 11.07–11.08

* Consult the corresponding section(s) of the *Principles* text for more detail.

Construction of an exemption clause is a very significant exercise. Exemption clauses will only operate to exclude or reduce liability in the particular circumstances if it can be said that the clause as drafted is wide enough to capture those circumstances. Essentially, the task of the court when an exemption clause is present is to determine whether the particular wrongful conduct of a party is covered by the relevant clause so as to limit or exclude liability in relation to that conduct. Subject to any relevant legislative restrictions (discussed at **11.4**), a clearly and appropriately drafted exemption clause will operate effectively to exclude or limit the relevant liability.

A number of rules of construction are utilised by the courts when interpreting and applying exemption clauses to ensure such clauses only protect a party where they unmistakeably cover the particular conduct. The approach taken by the courts to the interpretation of exemption clauses was usefully outlined by the High Court in the below case.

Darlington Futures Ltd v Delco Australia Pty Ltd (1986) 161 CLR 500

Facts and issues

Delco Australia Pty Ltd ('Delco') entered into a contract with Darlington Futures Ltd ('Darlington') for Darlington to deal on the commodities futures market on its behalf. The contract contained the following exemption clauses:

> (6) ... The Client ... acknowledges that the Agent will not be responsible for any loss should the Client follow any of the Agent's trading recommendations or suggestions, nor for any loss, in the case of Discretionary Accounts, arising from trading by the Agent on behalf of the Client. The Client finally acknowledges that the Agent will not be responsible for any loss arising in any way out of any trading activity undertaken on behalf of the Client whether pursuant to this Agreement or not ...
>
> (7) ...
>
> (c) Any liability on the Agent's part or on the part of its servants or agents for damages for or in respect of any claim arising out of or in connection with the relationship established by this agreement or any conduct under it or any orders or instructions given to the Agent by the Client, other than any liability which is totally excluded by paragraphs (a) and (h) hereof, shall not in any event (and whether or not such liability results from or involves negligence) exceed one hundred dollars.

Darlington engaged in a number of dealings without Delco's authorisation which resulted in significant losses for Delco. Delco brought proceedings to recover these losses but failed at first instance, with Darlington successfully relying on the exemption clauses. Subsequently, Delco was successful on appeal to the Supreme Court of South Australia. Darlington then appealed to the High Court. The issue for determination by the High Court was whether Darlington's conduct in entering into transactions without Delco's authorisation was covered by the exemption clauses, thereby protecting Darlington from liability for the losses suffered by Delco.

Decision

Per the Court (Mason, Wilson, Brennan, Deane and Dawson JJ) at 510:

> ... the interpretation of an exclusion clause is to be determined by construing the clause according to its natural and ordinary meaning, read in the light of the contract as a whole, thereby giving due weight to the context in which the clause appears including the nature and object of the contract, and, where appropriate, construing the clause contra proferentem in case of ambiguity. Notwithstanding the comments of Lord Fraser in *Ailsa Craig* [[1983] 1 WLR at p. 970], the same principle applies to the construction of limitation clauses. As King C.J. noted in his judgment in the Supreme Court, a limitation clause may be so severe in its operation as to make its effect virtually indistinguishable from that of an exclusion clause. And the principle, in the form in which we have expressed it, does no more than express the general approach to the interpretation of contracts and it is of sufficient generality to accommodate the different considerations that may arise in the interpretation of a wide variety of exclusion and [511] limitation clauses in formal commercial contracts between business people where no question of the reasonableness or fairness of the clause arises.
>
> Turning now to cl. 6 of the contract between the appellant and the respondent, the question is whether the relevant losses arose 'in any way out of any trading activity undertaken on behalf of the Client whether pursuant to this agreement or not'. Read in context these words plainly refer to

trading activity undertaken by the appellant for the respondent with the respondent's authority, whether pursuant to the agreement or not. It can scarcely be supposed that the parties intended to exclude liability on the part of the appellant for losses arising from trading activity in which it presumed to engage on behalf of the respondent when the appellant had no authority so to do.

The final question is whether the appellant is protected by cl. 7(c) of the contract. This provision limits the liability of the appellant to $100 in relation to claims of three kinds: (1) claims arising out of or in connexion with the relationship established by the agreement; (2) claims arising out of or in connexion with any conduct under the agreement; and (3) claims arising out of or in connexion with any orders or instructions given by the client to the broker. The Full Court of the Supreme Court considered that cl. 7(c) by its terms had no application to claims arising out of conduct which is outside the scope of the agreement and the relationship between the parties established by it. This, in our opinion, is to place a more restrictive interpretation on the clause than its language will naturally bear. In particular, it is expressed to comprehend claims arising out of or *in connexion with* the relationship established by the agreement. A claim in respect of an unauthorized transaction may nonetheless have a connexion, indeed a substantial connexion, with the relationship of broker and client established by the agreement. We are unable to discern any basis on which cl. 7(c) can be construed so as not to apply to such a claim. The present case is one in which the respondent's claim arises in connexion with the relationship of broker and client established by the contract between the parties, notwithstanding the finding that the relevant transactions were not authorized.

In the result cl. 7(c) operates to limit the appellant's liability to $100 in respect of each of the unauthorized coffee and silver contracts.

We would allow the appeal.

An important rule of construction is that exemption clauses are to be interpreted *contra proferentem*. That is, where there is ambiguity surrounding such a clause, it will be construed in favour of the party who did not draft it (who is ordinarily also the party who does *not* benefit from the insertion of such a clause). This is illustrated in the below cases.

Wallis, Son & Wells v Pratt & Haynes [1911] AC 394

Facts and issues

Wallis, Son & Wells ('Wallis') purchased seed from Pratt & Haynes ('Pratt'). A condition of the contract was that the 'sellers give no warranty expressed or implied as to growth, description or any other matters' ('exemption clause'). Unbeknown to Wallis, the seed delivered was not that ordered (in breach of an implied condition under the *Sale of Goods Act 1893* (UK)) and Wallis subsequently resold this seed to other parties. As a result of this mistake, Wallis was obliged to pay damages to these other parties. Consequently, Wallis brought an action for breach of contract against Pratt. Pratt sought to rely on the exemption clause. On appeal to the House of Lords, the issue for determination was whether Pratt's conduct was covered by the exemption clause so that it was protected from liability in relation to the supply of the wrong seed.

Decision

Per Lord Loreburn LC at 396:

> There is no doubt that when you are dealing in a commodity the inspection of which does not enable you to distinguish its exact nature, there are risks both on the buyer and on the seller if they think fit to sell by description. But if it is desired by a seller to throw the risk of any honest mistake on to the buyer, then he must use apt language, and I should have thought the clearer he tries to make the language the better. I do not think he has done so ...

On the question of distinction between 'warranty' (as used in the exemption clause) and 'condition' (as used in s 13 of the *Sale of Goods Act 1893* (UK)), Lord Alverstone CJ stated:

> [396] I think every section [of the *Sale of Goods Act 1893* (UK)] shows that the distinction between 'condition' and 'warranty' is clearly understood and recognized, and that different remedies are intended to be given in the one [397] case and in the other. For that reason I submit it is impossible for the respondents to contend that when the sellers said they gave no warranty they meant to say they would not be responsible for any breaches of condition ...
>
> [398] I turn for a moment to s. 13; and we find again there that that which might have been described as a 'warranty', if it was so intended, is described as a 'condition' ...
>
> ... I think it is quite impossible to suggest that in the year 1906, when these parties made a contract whereby they required that the goods should be common English sainfoin, and the sellers put in a stipulation that they would not give any warranty, express or implied, it was intended that it was always to be understood that they were not making themselves liable in regard to any condition as to the goods or for the consequences of a breach of the condition.

The appeal was allowed.

Insight Vacations Pty Ltd v Young (2011) 243 CLR 149

Facts and issues

Mrs Young purchased a tour package from Insight Vacations Pty Ltd ('Insight'). While in Europe travelling on a coach, Mrs Young was injured when she stood up to retrieve something from her luggage and the coach braked suddenly. She brought a breach of contract claim against Insight for personal injuries on the basis that it had breached s 74(1) of the *Trade Practices Act 1974* (Cth) which provided for an implied warranty that services would be rendered by Insight with due care and skill. Insight sought to rely on an exemption clause in the contract which stated:

> Where the passenger occupies a motorcoach seat fitted with a safety belt, neither the Operators [Insight] nor their agents or co-operating organisations will be liable for any injury, illness or death or for any damages or claims whatsoever arising from any accident or incident, if the safety belt is not being worn at the time of such accident or incident.

Mrs Young was successful at first instance and on appeal by Insight to the New South Wales Supreme Court, Court of Appeal. Special leave to appeal to the High Court was then granted to Insight. One of the issues before the High Court was whether the exemption clause operated to preclude liability on the part of Insight.

Decision

Per the Court (French CJ, Gummow, Hayne, Kiefel and Bell JJ) at 154:

> ... on its true construction, the exemption clause did not apply to the events that happened. The exemption clause should be construed as engaged only when a passenger was seated, and as having no application when the passenger was standing or moving about the coach ...
>
> [162] ... It will be recalled that the first part of the clause read: 'Where the passenger *occupies* a motorcoach *seat* fitted with a safety belt' (emphasis added). That element of the clause should be given its ordinary meaning. It limits the times to which the clause applies to the times when the passenger occupies a seat. That is, it should be read as referring only to times when the passenger is seated, not to times when the passenger stands up to move around the coach or to retrieve some item from an overhead shelf or for some other reason. The contract of carriage did not require passengers to remain seated at all times while the coach was in motion. The provision of a lavatory at the rear of the coach shows that the operator accepted that a passenger could, and sometimes would, get out of his or her seat.
>
> [163] If the introductory words of the exemption clause had omitted the word 'seat', it might have been possible to say that the exemption clause applied to any occasion when the passenger was aboard (or 'occupie[d]') a motorcoach fitted with seat belts, regardless of whether and why the passenger got out of the seat. But that is not how the clause was cast. The words 'occupies a motorcoach seat' should be understood as meaning sitting in the seat and able to wear the safety belt. Mrs Young was not sitting in her seat when she fell. The exemption clause did not apply.
>
> The appeal should be dismissed with costs.

The following case illustrates what has been referred to as the 'four corners' rule; that is, the principle that an exemption clause will only operate in relation to conduct which constitutes performance of the contract and is thus within its 'four corners'.

Council of the City of Sydney v West (1965) 114 CLR 481

Facts and issues

The Sydney City Council ('Council') operated a parking station. Upon parking his car in this station, West received a parking ticket which included the following under the heading 'Parking Conditions':

> (1) The Council does not accept any responsibility for the loss or damage to any vehicle or for loss of or damage to any article or thing in or upon any vehicle or for any injury to any person however such loss, damage or injury may arise or be caused.

Also included on the ticket was a clause headed 'Important' which provided: 'This ticket must be presented for time stamping and payment before taking delivery of the vehicle'.

West's car was stolen from the parking station by an individual who had obtained a duplicate parking ticket by fraudulently claiming to have lost his ticket with respect to a different car. When the thief went to exit the parking station with West's car and the duplicate ticket, the attendant failed to check that the registration number shown on the ticket matched the car being driven (which it did not). West brought action against the Council for damages relating to the loss of his car. The Council relied on the exemption clause contained on the parking ticket and was originally successful. On appeal to the Full Court of the Supreme Court of New South Wales, however, West succeeded and a new trial was ordered. The Council appealed this decision to the High Court. One of the issues for determination by the High Court was whether or not the exemption clause absolved the Council of liability arising from the theft of West's car.

Decision

Per Barwick CJ and Taylor J at 488:

> ... There is no doubt, of course, that in the case where a contract of bailment contains an exempting clause much as we have to consider the protection afforded by the clause will be lost if the goods the subject of the bailment are stored in a place or in a manner other than that authorized by the contract or if the bailee consumes or destroys them instead of storing them or if he sells them. But we would deny the application of such a clause in those circumstances simply upon the interpretation of the clause itself. Such a clause contemplates that loss or damage may occur by reason of negligence on the part of the warehouseman or his servants in carrying out the obligations created by the contract. But in our view it has no application to negligence in relation to acts done with respect to a bailor's goods which are neither authorized nor permitted by the contract. For instance, if, in the present case, one of the attendants at the parking station had been allowed by the management to use the respondent's car for his own purposes and, in the course of driving it, had caused damage to it by his negligent driving, the clause would afford no protection. Negligence in these circumstances would be right outside the purview of the clause. The same result would follow if an attendant had proceeded, without authority, to make adjustments or repairs to the respondent's vehicle while it was in the parking station and had carried out such work negligently and thereby caused damage. To our minds the clause clearly appears as one which contemplates that, in the performance of the Council's obligations under the contract of bailment, some loss or damage may be caused by reason of its servants' negligence but it does not contemplate or provide an excuse for negligence on the part of [489] the Council's servants in doing something which it is neither authorized nor permitted to do by the terms of the contract.
>
> How then is the question of liability to be resolved in the present case? The appellant has sought to explain the loss of the car by evidence which, upon a trial, would probably be accepted. Of course, if it were not, the loss would remain unexplained and the respondent would be entitled to recover. It is, therefore, necessary to consider the question whether the loss, in the circumstances deposed to, was a loss resulting merely from the failure on the part of the appellant to use reasonable care to keep the car safely whilst it was in its possession as a bailee or whether by some positive act the appellant can be said to have delivered possession of the car to 'Robinson'. If it did then, in our view, this constituted an unauthorized act performed by the appellant in relation to the respondent's car and he is entitled to recover. But in order to solve this problem some addition should be made to the evidence already mentioned. In order to drive out of the parking station 'Robinson' had to pass through a designated exit where an attendant was stationed and it was this official's function to permit vehicles to proceed only upon the surrender by the driver of an appropriate parking ticket. It was such a ticket which, as was said by the superintendent of the parking station, entitled 'a person to go into the parking station and drive a car out of the parking station after handing that ticket in to the attendant at the exit'. The parking ticket was his 'entrance card into and out of the parking station'. Possession of any car leaving the station, it seems to us, was, therefore,

retained by the appellant until presentation and surrender of such a ticket by the driver of the car. To our minds, therefore, the act of the attendant in permitting 'Robinson' to proceed after handing over the duplicate ticket which he had obtained constituted an unauthorized delivery of possession by him to 'Robinson' and not a mere act of negligence in relation to some act authorized by the contract of bailment . . .

The fact that the attendant at the exit through which the car was driven was negligent is of no consequence in the case; the act of delivery was one which was neither authorized nor permitted [490] by the contract and in our view the appellant was not entitled to be exonerated by the exempting clause . . .

For these reasons the appeal should, in our opinion, be dismissed . . .

In the course of finding that the appeal should be dismissed (although on the basis of the 'narrower route' that the car was to be delivered only on the presentation of a valid ticket), Windeyer J emphasised the importance of focusing on the interpretation of the exemption clause in each individual case:

[500] . . . The doctrine of fundamental terms and fundamental breaches as it has recently been expounded, which the Supreme Court to a large extent adopted, has many difficulties. It does not I think provide the solution of the question [501] in this case . . . Whatever may be the position in other cases, it seems to me that here we have simply to interpret the contract made between the parties . . .

[502] The principle that *Scrutton* L.J. enunciated in *Gibaud v. Great Eastern Railway Co.* [1921] 2 KB 426, referred to in the House [503] of Lords in *London and North Western Railway Co.* v. *Neilson* [1922] 2 AC 263, is in point. His Lordship said that ' . . . if you undertake to do a thing in a certain way, or to keep a thing in a certain place, with certain conditions protecting it, and have broken the contract by not doing the thing contracted for in the way contracted for, or not keeping the article in the place in which you have contracted to keep it, you cannot rely on the conditions which were only intended to protect you if you carried out the contract in the way in which you had contracted to do it' [1921] 2 KB at p. 435. In this case the contract was broken because the appellant did not do the thing it had contracted to do in the way in which it had contracted to do it . . .

I am therefore of opinion that this appeal should be disposed of in the way that the Chief Justice and *Taylor* J. propose in their judgment which I have had the advantage of reading. I reach the same conclusion as do their Honours, but by a somewhat different, and perhaps narrower route. That does not mean, however, that I might not in another case be ready to follow their path. Much depends in every case upon the precise meaning of the words that the parties used read in their context and circumstances; for the question, as I see it, is one of interpretation. It is not for a court to say that persons may not contract out of the obligations that the law of bailment imposes, or put new limits on their power to do so. The question for a court is only whether they have done so. The answer to that question, in a case such as this, depends upon the ascertainment of two matters: whether the writing on the ticket in fact formed part of the contract: if so, what is its meaning.

Menzies and Kitto JJ dissented.

The 'deviation rule' applies to carriage of goods contracts and provides that if a party deviates from the agreed, usual or customary route of carriage, then an exemption clause will not be effective. An example of a deviation case is set out below, where an exemption clause could not be relied on as goods were damaged due to a deviation from the agreed route of carriage.

Thomas National Transport (Melbourne) Pty Ltd v May & Baker (Australia) Pty Ltd (1966) 115 CLR 353

Facts and issues

May & Baker (Australia) Pty Ltd ('MB') engaged Thomas National Transport (Melbourne) Pty Ltd ('TNT') to carry its goods interstate. TNT often sent a subcontractor to collect MB's goods and take the goods to TNT's Melbourne depot, with the goods then being transferred to Sydney for delivery. The contracts between MB and TNT did not specify the route the goods were to be taken or state that goods collected should be taken to the depot. On one occasion, when the subcontractor arrived at the depot with MB's goods at the end of a collection round and found it to be closed, he took the goods home with him in his truck, which he parked in his garage. The goods were damaged in the early morning of the next day when fire engulfed the garage. MB brought action against both TNT and the subcontractor for damages. TNT relied on an exemption clause in the contracts which provided that it and its agent were exempted from responsibility for loss, damage or misdelivery of the goods 'in transit or in storage' for any reason whatsoever. Nevertheless, MB succeeded against both parties at first instance. TNT and the subcontractor subsequently appealed to the High Court. One of the issues for determination was whether the exemption clause operated to protect TNT (and its subcontractor) from liability in relation to the damage of the goods via fire while stored in the subcontractor's garage.

Decision

Per McTiernan, Taylor and Owen JJ at 364:

> ... [I]t is necessary to consider what was involved in T.N.T.'s undertaking to carry the goods from the respondent's premises in Melbourne to the various consignees in the other States. This it proceeded to do, as a first step in the carriage, by providing a 'pick-up' service in Melbourne. It is not contended that this was not a permissible way of performing part of its obligations under the contract whether the 'pick-up' service was conducted by its own servants or by an independent contractor. But however the service was conducted it would be necessary that the first stage of the journey should be from the respondent's premises to T.N.T.'s depot. Obviously the goods would be transported by the 'pick-up' service to T.N.T.'s depot in Melbourne in order that they might be sorted and assembled with other goods accepted for carriage upon appropriate trucks for carriage to the other States ...
>
> [365] But it is not suggested that the respondent knew of or assented to its goods being taken on any occasion to Pay's home and kept there during the night. Nor is there any suggestion that it was aware that T.N.T.'s depot closed at any particular time and, therefore, that it was not, after that time, available for the receipt of goods which had been picked up. Further there is no evidence that the course adopted on this occasion was justified by some particular custom or usage in the trade ...
>
> It seems to us that it must have been taken to have been implicit in the contract which T.N.T. made with the respondent that its goods would be taken to T.N.T.'s depot and that the depot would be available for their reception at the conclusion of the pick-up round. It is, to our minds, unthinkable that it was within the contemplation of the parties that an extremely valuable consignment of goods was to be kept overnight by T.N.T.'s servant or sub-contractor in the yard of a suburban cottage. On the contrary, the only conclusion consistent with its primary obligation was that they would be taken to and received in the depot at the conclusion of the

'pick-up' round. This conclusion is [366] unaffected by consideration of the clause incorporated in a number of the contracts that the carrier 'is hereby expressly authorized by the Consignor to carry all goods or to have them carried by any *method* as he in his absolute discretion deems fit and notwithstanding any instruction verbal or otherwise of the Consignor that the goods are to be carried by another method'. The italics are ours and it seems to us that the expression 'method', which must mean method of carriage, is quite inappropriate to cover the circumstances of this case. What the respondent complains of is not the method which was employed to carry the goods but, rather, that the goods were carried, not to T.N.T.'s depot but to Pay's home and kept there overnight.

A variety of cases may be cited to illustrate how and in what circumstances a carrier so far departs from his contract of carriage as to preclude him from relying upon exempting provisions designed to relieve him from liability for loss or damage occurring during the performance of his contract. But it is sufficient to refer to *Bontex Knitting Works, Ltd.* v. *St. Johns Garage* the decision in which case was approved by the Court of Appeal and referred to with evident approval by the Judicial Committee in *Sze Hai Tong Bank Ltd. v. Rambler Cycle Co. Ltd*. The facts of that case are dissimilar but the present case is, if anything, stronger from the point of view of the respondent.

The effect of this conclusion is, of course, that T.NT. cannot protect itself by seeking to rely upon the exemption clauses and there is the clearest authority for the proposition that, in such circumstances as the present, it must be held liable for the damage which occurred whether or not it can be said to have resulted from lack of care or to have been directly caused by T.N.T.'s unauthorized departure from the terms of the contract.

Barwick CJ agreeing, TNT's appeal was dismissed, although noting that the Court did uphold the subcontractor's appeal, considering that he was not negligent. During the course of Windeyer J's dissent, his Honour outlined the rationale behind the development of the deviation rule:

[375] ... It may be that the law is defective in allowing persons to contract out of liabilities which from the nature of their callings or undertakings they would otherwise incur. Lengthy conditions in small type are printed on the back of tickets and similar documents. Customers often have little time to read them, yet in a practical sense they must accept them, having no opportunity of rejection or counter-offer. This has been often remarked upon, recently and forcefully by Lord Reid, as a regrettable result of the freedom of contract that the law, as it stands, allows ... [376] But the task for a court is to ascertain what was the bargain that the parties made, not to modify it ...

[379] Cases concerning the effect of deviations in a voyage upon contracts of affreightment by sea are merely an example of these general principles of the law of contract. Their peculiar character is only in the strictness of the established rule that any deviation from the contract voyage – that is the one expressly stipulated for in the contract, or stipulated by implication as the usual and customary route of the vessel – is a breach that goes to the root of the contract of affreightment, a breach that entitles the cargo owner to treat the whole contract as at an end, unless with knowledge of the breach he has affirmed the contract. As Fletcher Moulton L.J. put it:

> The cases show that, for a long series of years, the courts have held that a deviation is such a serious matter, and changes the character of the contemplated voyage so essentially, that a shipowner who has been guilty of a deviation cannot be considered as having performed his part of the bill of lading contract, but something fundamentally different, and therefore he cannot claim the benefit of stipulations in his favour contained in the bill of lading: *Joseph Thorley Ltd.* v. *Orchis Steamship Company Ltd* ...

[380] . . . The strictness of the rule as to deviation in sea voyages appears to be based upon the assumption that deviation alters the risks of the voyage, and to be related to, perhaps a by-product of, the law of marine insurance. A deviation alters the risks of the contemplated voyage by adding or substituting the hazards of further time and a different place. In some cases, especially in war-time, a deviation may actually reduce the perils of a voyage. Nevertheless the general principle is that a deviation, except for a purpose recognized and permitted by the contract, discharges the underwriter simply because it substitutes a risk that is different, whether it be in fact greater or less than before: *Company of African Merchants* v. *British and Foreign Marine Insurance Co.* That rule, now in the *Marine Insurance Act,* goes back for hundreds of years: *Elliot* v. *Wilson*; *Goram* v. *Sweeting* . . .

[381] . . . A common carrier by land is deemed to contract to carry by his customary route if no route be expressly stipulated. And the strictness of the rule about deviations in contracts of carriage by sea has been imported by analogy into the contracts of carriage by land. And now the term 'deviation' has come to be used some-times to describe not only departures from a carrier's geographical route, but also other radical breaches of his contract. But, except in the case of deviations from the contract route, it inverts the question to ask of a departure in method, Is it a deviation? – and say that if it is a breach of a term that lies at the root of the contract. The correct question is, Is this departure a radical breach of the contract? If it is, it may sometimes be conveniently called a deviation simply because it has the consequences which by law geographical deviations have long had in contracts of carriage . . .

[382] . . . A further aspect of deviations is of some importance. It is that a deviation does not mean only that an exception clause will not avail a carrier against liability for loss occurring during the deviation. It also prevents him relying upon the exception clause in the event of a loss occurring afterwards, unless it be shown that the same loss would have occurred if there had not been a deviation: *James Morrison & Co. Ltd.* v. *Shaw, Savill and Albion Co. Ltd.*; *Hain Steamship Company Ltd.* v. *Tate & Lyle Ltd.*; *A/S Rendal* v. *Arcos Ltd.* This tends to be lost sight of when, as in the present case, the loss occurs during the alleged deviation. But if, as the respondent May & Baker contends, T.N.T. cannot rely upon the conditions endorsed on the freight note because the goods were in Pay's garage for the night – that being, it is claimed, a deviation then it could not rely upon them if they had been delivered safely to the depot next morning but had thereafter been lost or damaged by the negligence of some servant of T.N.T. at the depot or had been later lost or damaged at some stage on their inter-State journey to their destination. This merely brings into sharp relief that a deviation means a departure from a fundamental obligation of the contract . . .

11.3.1 Excluding liability for negligence

Exemption clauses will sometimes seek to exclude liability for negligence arising under breach of contract or tort law. In order for an exemption clause to successfully exclude liability for negligence, it must make specific reference to negligence or incorporate language which could only be interpreted as referring to negligence. Otherwise, an exemption clause will not operate to protect a party from liability arising from negligence. This was outlined by Windeyer J in *Thomas National Transport (Melbourne) Pty Ltd v May & Baker (Australia) Pty Ltd*[5] (extracted above in **11.3**) at 376:

5 (1966) 115 CLR 353.

> [An exemption clause] is not construed as relieving [a party] against liability for negligence of himself or his servants, unless it expressly or by implication covers such liability. It will by implication do so if there can be no ground of liability other than negligence to which it could refer...

This is demonstrated in the below case extract.

White v John Warrick & Co Ltd [1953] 2 All ER 1021

Facts and issues

White hired a tricycle from John Warrick & Co Ltd ('JW'), which he used for the delivery of goods. As part of the agreement, JW agreed to maintain and repair the tricycle as required and provide a spare tricycle while such work was being undertaken. When White's tricycle needed repairing, JW duly left a spare tricycle for White to use in the meantime. However, upon riding the spare tricycle, the seat, which was loose, caused White to be thrown off and injured. White subsequently brought an action for damages for personal injury. JW sought to rely on a clause ('cl. 11') in the hire contract which provided:

> Nothing in this agreement shall render [JW] liable for any personal injuries to the riders of the machines hired nor for any third-party claims, nor loss of any goods, belonging to the hirer [White], in the machines.

JW was successful at first instance, with Parker J finding that liability for negligence was excluded under this exemption clause. White then appealed to the English Court of Appeal. The Court was required to determine whether the exemption clause operated to exclude liability for negligence and, if so, whether this included liability arising under both contract and in tort.

Decision

Per Singleton LJ at 1024:

> ... It is clear ... that an action for damages for breach of contract and an action for a tort may arise from the same set of facts. It is said that that position arises in this case, and that, though an action for damages for breach of contract may be said to be barred by cl. 11 of the contract, it cannot be said that the words of that clause shut out the hirer from what he would normally have, an action for damages for the tort of negligence ...
>
> [1025] In the circumstances of the present case the primary object of the clause, one would think, is to relieve the owners from liability for breach of contract or for breach of warranty. Unless, then, there be clear words which would also exempt from liability for negligence, the clause ought not to be construed as giving absolution to the owners if negligence is proved against them. The result is that cl. 11 ought not, I think, to be read as absolving the owners from liability for negligence if it is proved that the injury which the plaintiff sustained was due to lack of that care which one in the owners' position ought to take when supplying a tricycle for the use of a hirer. If that is proved, then the owners do not escape liability by reason of cl. 11.
>
> The difficulty in this case arises from the fact that there is no finding on negligence ... In those circumstances, we are not in a position to deal with this case finally, and it appears to be necessary that there should be a new trial on the subject of negligence, with the expression of opinion of this court that, if negligence is proved against the owners, they do not escape liability

by reason of the terms of cl. 11. In that sense, I think this appeal ought to be allowed, and there ought to be a direction for a new trial between the parties.

Per Denning LJ at 1025:

> ... In this type of case, two principles are well settled. The first is that, if a person desires to exempt himself from a liability which the common law imposes on him, he can only do so by a contract freely and deliberately entered into by the injured party in words that are clear beyond the possibility of misunderstanding. The second is that, if there are two possible heads of liability on the defendant, one for negligence, and the other a strict liability, an exemption clause will be construed, so far as possible, as exempting the defendant only from his strict liability and not as relieving him from his liability for negligence.
>
> In the present case, there are two possible heads of liability on the owners, one for negligence, the other for breach of contract. The liability for breach of contract is more strict than the liability for negligence. The owners may be liable in contract for supplying a defective machine, even though they were not negligent ... In these circumstances, the exemption clause must, I think, be construed as exempting the owners only from their liability in contract, and not from their liability for negligence ...
>
> ... In my opinion, the claim for negligence in this case is founded in tort and not on contract ...
>
> [1026] ... In my judgment, [cl. 11] exempts the owners from liability in contract, but not from liability in tort. If the plaintiff can make out his cause of action in negligence, he is, in my opinion, entitled to do so, although the same facts also give a cause of action in contract from which the owners are exempt. I agree, therefore, with my Lord that this appeal should be allowed, but, as there is no definite finding of negligence or no negligence, and we have no transcript of the evidence with which to decide it ourselves, there must be a new trial to decide that point.

Morris LJ concurring with Singleton and Denning LJJ, the appeal was allowed.

The below case discusses, among other things, the approach to interpretation of an exemption clause where the only basis for liability is negligence (sometimes called the 'negligence only' rule).

Davis v Pearce Parking Station Pty Ltd (1954) 91 CLR 642

Facts and issues

When Davis parked her car at a parking station owned by Pearce Parking Station Pty Ltd ('Pearce'), she received a document which consisted of a 'delivery ticket' and a 'parking check'. On the back of the parking check was the following:

> Conditions —The motor vehicle mentioned on the other side hereof is garaged at the owner's risk, and Gough's Auto Parking Station will not be responsible for loss or damage of any description. This check must be exchanged for a delivery ticket at office to obtain re-delivery of vehicle. No servant or agent has any authority to waive or modify any of these conditions.

As a result of Pearce's negligence, Davis' car was stolen from the parking station and badly damaged. She consequently brought action for damages on the basis of breach of contract against Pearce. Pearce relied on the exemption clause (contained on the back of the parking check) and successfully defended the claim at first instance. Davis subsequently appealed to the High Court. One of the issues for determination was whether the exemption clause should be interpreted as excluding liability for negligence. If it did, then no liability could arise on the part of Pearce.

Decision

Per Dixon CJ, McTiernan, Webb, Fullagar and Kitto JJ at 649:

> ... It has never been doubted that a bailee may exempt himself by express contract from the consequences of negligence on the part of himself or his servants. But it has been repeatedly said that an exempting clause must be construed strictly, and that clear words are necessary to exclude liability for negligence. In *Price & Co. v. Union Lighterage Co. Walton* J. said:– 'The law of England ... does not forbid the carrier to exempt himself by contract from liability for the negligence of himself and his servants; but, if the carrier desires so to exempt himself, it requires that he shall do so in express, plain, and unambiguous terms' ...
>
> [650] ... In some cases a distinction has been drawn between cases, such as that of a common carrier, in which the responsibility of the bailee, apart from special contract, is that of an insurer, and cases, such as that of a warehouseman, in which, apart from special contract, there is no liability in the absence of negligence. It has [651] been said that in the former class of case general words may be apt to exclude the liability of an insurer but not liability for negligence, whereas in the latter class of case similar words may be held to exclude liability for negligence on the ground that on any other view they would be entirely without effect. The distinction is logical, and has high authority to support it ...
>
> The present case is a case in which general words are used, and there is no special reference to any manner in which loss or damage may be caused. On the other hand, the case is clearly one in which the bailee would not, apart from special contract, be liable for loss or damage occurring without negligence. And there is, in our opinion, ample authority to justify construing the exemption clause as excluding liability for negligence ... [Their Honours then proceeded to discuss a number of cases where a question had arisen as to whether the relevant exemption clause excluded liability for negligence.]
>
> [652] The point is made that in these cases (as in the present case) the bailee is making a very small charge for taking the custody of goods which are or may be of great value. He is likely to intend, and the bailor would reasonably expect him to intend, to protect himself against (inter alia) a possibly very heavy liability arising from the negligence of a servant. Either party can insure, and such a clause may reasonably be taken by the bailor to mean that, if he wishes to be protected against loss or damage at all, he must insure. Malicious damage is, of course, outside the contemplation of either party ...
>
> [653] ... We are of opinion that the judgment of the learned trial judge was entirely correct, and this appeal must be dismissed.

QUESTIONS

(1) Can an exemption clause exclude or reduce liability for fundamental breaches of a contract? Provide case authorities in your answer.

(2) What is the rationale behind the *contra proferentem* rule?

(3) Why have the courts developed specific rules in relation to excluding liability for negligence?

11.4 Statutory controls on exemption clauses

Concept	Short explanation	Relevant authorities	*Principles* text*
The operation of exemption clauses may be limited by statute	A number of statutes place controls over when and to what extent exemption clauses will be effective	Australian Consumer Law ss 64, 64A *Competition and Consumer Act 2010* (Cth) s 139A	Chapter 11: 11.09–11.10

* Consult the corresponding section(s) of the *Principles* text for more detail.

As has been seen through the above cases, freedom of contract means that liability for even fundamental breaches can be successfully excluded by an exemption clause. However, the effectiveness of such exemption clauses has been limited to some extent by various statutes. A prime example is the Australian Consumer Law (contained in Schedule 2 of the *Competition and Consumer Act 2010* (Cth) ('Act'))[6] which contains a number of provisions preventing exemption clauses from excluding liability for obligations imposed on a party under this Act. These sections, as well as s 139A of the Act, are extracted below.

Australian Consumer Law ss 64, 64A

Section 64: Guarantees not to be excluded etc. by contract

(1) A term of a contract (including a term that is not set out in the contract but is incorporated in the contract by another term of the contract) is void to the extent that the term purports to exclude, restrict or modify, or has the effect of excluding, restricting or modifying:
  - **(a)** the application of all or any of the provisions of this Division; or
  - **(b)** the exercise of a right conferred by such a provision; or
  - **(c)** any liability of a person for a failure to comply with a guarantee that applies under this Division to a supply of goods or services.

(2) A term of a contract is not taken, for the purposes of this section, to exclude, restrict or modify the application of a provision of this Division unless the term does so expressly or is inconsistent with the provision.

Section 64A: Limitation of liability for failures to comply with guarantees

(1) A term of a contract for the supply by a person of goods other than goods of a kind ordinarily acquired for personal, domestic or household use or consumption is not void under section

6 See also s 52 of the *Insurance Contracts Act 1984* and s 191 of the *National Credit Code* as further examples of legislative control of exemption clauses.

64 merely because the term limits the person's liability for failure to comply with a guarantee (other than a guarantee under section 51, 52 or 53) to one or more of the following:

(a) the replacement of the goods or the supply of equivalent goods;

(b) the repair of the goods;

(c) the payment of the cost of replacing the goods or of acquiring equivalent goods;

(d) the payment of the cost of having the goods repaired.

(2) A term of a contract for the supply by a person of services other than services of a kind ordinarily acquired for personal, domestic or household use or consumption is not void under section 64 merely because the term limits the person's liability for failure to comply with a guarantee to:

(a) the supplying of the services again; or

(b) the payment of the cost of having the services supplied again.

(3) This section does not apply in relation to a term of a contract if the person to whom the goods or services were supplied establishes that it is not fair or reasonable for the person who supplied the goods or services to rely on that term of the contract.

(4) In determining for the purposes of subsection (3) whether or not reliance on a term of a contract is fair or reasonable, a court is to have regard to all the circumstances of the case, and in particular to the following matters:

(a) the strength of the bargaining positions of the person who supplied the goods or services and the person to whom the goods or services were supplied (the ***buyer***) relative to each other, taking into account, among other things, the availability of equivalent goods or services and suitable alternative sources of supply;

(b) whether the buyer received an inducement to agree to the term or, in agreeing to the term, had an opportunity of acquiring the goods or services or equivalent goods or services from any source of supply under a contract that did not include that term;

(c) whether the buyer knew or ought reasonably to have known of the existence and extent of the term (having regard, among other things, to any custom of the trade and any previous course of dealing between the parties);

(d) in the case of the supply of goods, whether the goods were manufactured, processed or adapted to the special order of the buyer.

Competition and Consumer Act 2010 (Cth) s 139A

Section 139A: Terms excluding consumer guarantees from supplies of recreational services

(1) A term of a contract for the supply of recreational services to a consumer by a person is not void under section 64 of the Australian Consumer Law only because the term excludes, restricts or modifies, or has the effect of excluding, restricting or modifying:

(a) the application of all or any of the provisions of Subdivision B of Division 1 of Part 3-2 of the Australian Consumer Law; or

(b) the exercise of a right conferred by such a provision; or

(c) any liability of the person for a failure to comply with a guarantee that applies under that Subdivision to the supply.

(2) ***Recreational services*** are services that consist of participation in:
 (a) a sporting activity or a similar leisure time pursuit; or
 (b) any other activity that:
  (i) involves a significant degree of physical exertion or physical risk; and
  (ii) is undertaken for the purposes of recreation, enjoyment or leisure.

(3) This section does not apply unless the exclusion, restriction or modification is limited to liability for:
 (a) death; or
 (b) a physical or mental injury of an individual (including the aggravation, acceleration or recurrence of such an injury of the individual); or
 (c) the contraction, aggravation or acceleration of a disease of an individual; or
 (d) the coming into existence, the aggravation, acceleration or recurrence of any other condition, circumstance, occurrence, activity, form of behaviour, course of conduct or state of affairs in relation to an individual:
  (i) that is or may be harmful or disadvantageous to the individual or community; or
  (ii) that may result in harm or disadvantage to the individual or community.

(4) This section does not apply if the exclusion, restriction or modification would apply to significant personal injury suffered by a person that is caused by the reckless conduct of the supplier of the recreational services.

(5) The supplier's conduct is ***reckless conduct*** if the supplier:
 (a) is aware, or should reasonably have been aware, of a significant risk that the conduct could result in personal injury to another person; and
 (b) engages in the conduct despite the risk and without adequate justification.

QUESTIONS

(1) What is the rationale behind legislative control of exemption clauses?

(2) In what circumstances will ss 64, 64A and 139A of the *Competition and Consumer Act 2010* apply?

(3) What consequences arise if an exemption clause is in breach of s 64?

11.5 Guarantees

Concept	Short explanation	Relevant authorities	*Principles* text*
Guarantees can be used to adjust the burden of liability	Under a guarantee, liability for failure to perform contractual obligations is placed on a third party	*Ankar Pty Ltd v National Westminster Finance (Australia) Ltd* (1987) 162 CLR 549	Chapter 11: 11.11–11.18

* Consult the corresponding section(s) of the *Principles* text for more detail.

Guarantees can also be used to impact the allocation of liability for breach of contract. These can be used essentially to move liability from one person to another—in other words, a third party (the guarantor) agrees to be responsible when a party to the agreement fails to perform their obligations under it. Special rules of construction apply in relation to the interpretation of guarantees and there are numerous grounds upon which a guarantor may be able to avoid liability.[7] In the case extracted below, the High Court discusses the approach to interpretation of guarantees and discharge of liability where a guarantor's rights are altered without their consent.

Ankar Pty Ltd v National Westminster Finance (Australia) Ltd (1987) 162 CLR 549

Facts and issues

Ankar Pty Ltd ('Ankar') entered into a Security Deposit Agreement with National Westminster Finance (Australia) Ltd (previously known as Lombard Australia Ltd) ('Lombard') to guarantee the performance of General Energy (Manufacturing) Pty Ltd ('Manufacturing') under a machinery leasing agreement between Manufacturing and Lombard. Under the Security Deposit Agreement, Lombard agreed to notify Ankar if Manufacturing intended to sell or assign its interest in the machinery (by clause 8). Lombard also agreed to notify Ankar if Manufacturing had defaulted under the lease and to consult with Ankar about what steps Lombard would take after such a default (by clause 9). Manufacturing subsequently defaulted and assigned its interest in the machinery to its parent company. Lombard assented to this assignment but did not notify Ankar as required under the Security Deposit Agreement or consult Ankar about what action Lombard would take in relation to the default by Machinery. Ankar sought a declaration from the Supreme Court of New South Wales that it was no longer subject to its obligations under the Security Deposit Agreement. Ankar succeeded in obtaining this declaration at first instance but an appeal to the Court of Appeal was allowed. Subsequently, Ankar appealed to the High Court.

The issue for determination by the High Court was whether Lombard's breaches of the Security Deposit Agreement discharged Ankar from its liability under the contract of guarantee.

Decision

Per Mason ACJ, Wilson, Brennan and Dawson JJ at 559, in relation to the 'special principle' applicable to contracts of guarantee; namely, that 'the surety is discharged from its obligations by the creditor's breach of that contract, so long at any rate as the breach materially prejudices the interests of the surety' (at 557):

> . . . [T]he principle is the by-product, not so much of the general law of contract, as of the special relationship between creditor and surety arising out of the suretyship contract upon which equity fastened to protect the surety when the creditor's conduct affected the surety's liability . . . According to the English cases, the principle applies so as to discharge the surety when conduct on the part of the creditor has the effect of altering the surety's rights, unless the alteration is unsubstantial and not prejudicial to the surety. The rule does not permit the courts

7 See **Part VI** for a discussion of vitiating factors such as mistake, misrepresentation, fraud, duress, undue influence and unconscionable conduct.

> to inquire into the effect of the alteration. The consequence is that, to hold the surety to its bargain, the creditor must show that the nature of the alteration can be beneficial to the surety only or that by its nature it cannot in any circumstances increase the surety's risk, e.g., a reduction in the [560] debtor's debt or in the interest payable by the surety. The mere possibility of detriment is enough to bring about the discharge of the surety.
>
> The foundation of the rule is that the creditor, by varying the principal contract or extending time, has altered the surety's rights without consulting it though the surety has an interest in the principal contract, and that the creditor cannot be permitted to do ... Thus the liability of the surety was seen to be strictissimi juris and the suretyship contract was construed strictly in his favour ...

In the course of finding that Ankar was discharged from liability, Mason ACJ, Wilson, Brennan and Dawson JJ outlined the position with respect to the interpretation of guarantees:

> [561] ... At law, as in equity, the traditional view is that the liability of the surety is strictissimi juris and that ambiguous contractual provisions should be construed in favour of the surety. The doctrine of strictissimi juris provides a counterpoise to the law's preference for a construction that reads a provision otherwise than as a condition. A doubt as to the status of a provision in a guarantee should therefore be resolved in favour of the surety and so the provision should be interpreted as a condition, or perhaps as an innominate term, instead of a mere warranty ... Of course, in construing the contract the court is entitled to look to the general setting in which the contract has come into existence ...
>
> [562] ... [R]eturning to the earlier discussion of the two provisions in the context of conditions, the special characteristics of the suretyship relationship and the fact that it creates a liability strictissimi juris on the part of the surety are enough, when added to the factors mentioned earlier in this judgment, to justify treating the relevant obligations in the two provisions as conditions, breach of which, at Ankar's option, discharged it from performance of its obligations under the Security Deposit Agreement to the extent to which they related to the sum of $125,000.
>
> In the result we would allow the appeals.

11.6 Indemnities

Concept	Short explanation	Relevant authorities	*Principles* text*
Contractual indemnities operate to either extend or limit liability	By a contractual indemnity, one party agrees to indemnify another for loss suffered	*Ankar Pty Ltd v National Westminster Finance (Australia) Ltd* (1987) 162 CLR 549 (see **11.5** for extract) *Andar Transport Pty Ltd v Brambles Ltd* (2004) 217 CLR 424	Chapter 11: 11.19–11.25

* Consult the corresponding section(s) of the *Principles* text for more detail.

Pursuant to an indemnity, one party promises to indemnify another for any loss suffered. Consequently, such clauses can be used to either extend or limit the liability of a party. When construing indemnity clauses, Australian courts follow the same strict rules of construction as apply in relation to guarantees (outlined in *Ankar Pty Ltd v National Westminster Finance (Australia) Ltd*[8] at **11.5** above). This is demonstrated in the following decision, in which the High Court also discusses the nature of guarantees and indemnities.

Andar Transport Pty Ltd v Brambles Ltd (2004) 217 CLR 424

Facts and issues

Brambles Ltd ('Brambles') engaged Andar Transport Pty Ltd ('Andar') as a subcontractor to assist with its laundry delivery business. The director of Andar ('Mr Wail') was injured while completing this work and obtained damages in negligence from Brambles. Brambles brought a claim against Andar on the basis of a contractual indemnity provided by Andar (in particular, through cl 8 of the contract) or, alternatively, contribution pursuant to s 23B of the *Wrongs Act 1958* (Vic). At first instance, Brambles' claims were dismissed. However, Brambles succeeded on appeal and Andar then appealed to the High Court. One of the issues to be determined was whether the contractual indemnity provided in cl 8 of the contract obliged Andar to indemnify Brambles in relation to Mr Wail's injury.

Decision

The following extracts focus primarily on the contractual indemnity aspect of Brambles' claim against Andar.

Per Gleeson CJ, McHugh, Gummow, Hayne and Heydon JJ at 433:

> The proper construction of cll 8.2.2 and 8.2.3 cannot be undertaken without reference to the principles of construction applicable to contractual indemnities. The starting-point is the decision of this Court in *Ankar Pty Ltd v National Westminster Finance (Australia) Ltd*. In that case, the Court considered whether two clauses of a guarantee operated as conditions the breach of which would discharge the surety from liability. In answering that question in the affirmative, Mason ACJ, Wilson, Brennan and Dawson JJ said:
>
> > At law, as in equity, the traditional view is that the liability of the surety is strictissimi juris and that ambiguous contractual provisions should be construed in favour of the surety. The doctrine of strictissimi juris provides a counterpoise to the law's preference for a construction that reads a provision otherwise than as a condition. A doubt as to the status of a provision in a guarantee should therefore be resolved in favour of the surety.
> >
> > [...]
>
> [436] ... This case concerns not a guarantee but an indemnity: guarantee provisions such as those considered in *Ankar* and indemnity clauses such as those at issue in the present case differ in form and effect. In *Sunbird Plaza Pty Ltd v Maloney*, Mason CJ said:
>
> > Discussion of the question must begin with the proposition, established by the cases on s 4 of the *Statute of Frauds* 1677 (UK) that a contract of guarantee is, subject to any qualifications made by the particular instrument, a collateral contract to answer for the debt, default or miscarriage of another who is or is contemplated to be or [437] to become liable to the person to whom the guarantee is given. Such a promise was

8 (1987) 162 CLR 549.

> required by s 4 of the *Statute of Frauds* to be evidenced in writing, unlike a contract of indemnity, which stands outside the statutory requirement. An indemnity is a promise by the promisor that he will keep the promisee harmless against loss as a result of entering into a transaction with a third party.

However, notwithstanding the differences in the operation of guarantees and indemnities, both are designed to satisfy a liability owed by someone other than the guarantor or indemnifier to a third person. The principles adopted in *Ankar*, and applied in *Chan*, are therefore relevant to the construction of indemnity clauses.

Before this Court, Andar submits that cll 8.2.2 and 8.2.3 are limited to the indemnification of Brambles against any vicarious liability which Brambles might incur against third parties. Such a construction would, if adopted, prevent recourse to the clauses in respect of injuries suffered by employees of Andar such as Mr Wail.

On their face, neither cl 8.2.2 nor cl 8.2.3 expressly provides that liability arising on the part of Brambles as a result of injuries suffered to employees of Andar falls within the terms of the indemnity. That omission is not surprising. As noted earlier in these reasons, one of the primary concerns of the Agreement is to ensure that, to *outside observers*, Brambles appears to be the sole entity involved in the provision of the relevant laundry services. In this way, the Agreement may be seen as an attempt to minimise, as far as is possible, the practical effects of the change in business practice embarked upon by Brambles when it required employees such as Mr Wail to be employed by independent corporations. The obligation upon Andar to paint the vehicle used by Mr Wail with the Brambles livery and name is a practical example of this desire to present to the public at large a seamless delivery operation. The possibility of a suit against Brambles premised upon vicarious liability was, in these circumstances, a distinct possibility.

There are additional reasons for adopting Andar's proposed construction of the indemnity. With respect to cl 8.2.2, the indemnity is limited to liability arising in connection with the 'conduct of the Delivery Round by [Andar]'. As noted earlier in these reasons, the effect of cl 2.1 of the Agreement was that the Delivery Round could only be 'conducted' by Andar through a nominated driver. In the [438] absence of an express provision to the contrary, it is unlikely that the indemnity contained in cl 8 extends to liability arising in respect of injuries suffered by that nominated driver as a result of the conduct of the Delivery Round by that person.

With respect to cl 8.2.3, the phrase 'injury ... from any cause to property or person occasioned or contributed to by any act, omission, neglect or breach or default of [Andar]' is critical. That expression contains two elements: first, an injury suffered by a 'person' and, secondly, a requirement that the injury be occasioned, or contributed to, by the conduct of Andar. In the context of the Agreement as a whole, the latter element required the involvement of Mr Wail as driver. The structure of the clause therefore suggests that the person mentioned in the first element is a person other than the person necessarily encompassed within the second.

This construction of cll 8.2.2 and 8.2.3 has the advantage of operating consistently with cl 4.6. That clause provides for an indemnity granted by Andar in favour of Brambles which does not extend to liabilities arising from the operation of the truck which are attributable to the negligent acts or omissions of Brambles. The liability for which Brambles now seeks an indemnity clearly falls within that limitation.

Finally, to the extent that cll 8.2.2 and 8.2.3 remain ambiguous, the principles of construction outlined earlier in these reasons require the provisions to be construed in favour of Andar. Accordingly, cll 8.2.2 and 8.2.3 do not oblige Andar to indemnify Brambles in respect of liability arising as a result of Mr Wail's injury. That conclusion makes it unnecessary to consider the extent to which the terms of the Agreement continued in force after their formal expiry on 4 April 1993 ...

Per Kirby J at 452:

> ... Indemnity clauses are provisions that purport to exempt one party from civil liability which the law would otherwise impose upon it. They are provisions that shift to another party the civil liability otherwise attached by law to the first party. Self-evidently this is a serious thing to do or to attempt to do. Where such indemnities are said to arise out of contracts which are ambiguous or unclear, it is not unreasonable that their provisions should be construed so that any uncertainty is resolved favourably to the party thereby burdened by legal obligations that would not otherwise attach to it. In every case judges must struggle with the language of the contract. They must not use mechanical formulae. Nor do rules of interpretation provide [453] easy answers to the judicial task. However, it is sometimes useful to remember, and apply, time honoured approaches. A feature that makes doing so specially appropriate is that the propounded interpretation would shift legal liability from that which the law would otherwise normally provide.
>
> This is also a principle of construction more readily applied where, as here, the contractual indemnity appears in a standard form of contract designed to impose upon a party in a weaker bargaining position the obligations demanded by a party in a stronger economic position, which party drafts and presents the written contract for execution. It has special significance in a case like the present where there are features of the factual relationship between the parties that are designed to give an appearance to outsiders of a different relationship from that purportedly established in law by the written agreement. Here the object of the Agreement was to maintain the appearance of Brambles' control (the use of Brambles' signs and livery on the delivery truck and Brambles' supervision and power over the use of particular truck drivers). The Agreement was designed to establish a different regime of legal liability from that which therefore appeared to be the case and that which had formerly been the case. That was an employment relationship between Brambles and the truck driver engaged in driving and using the truck with Brambles' marking according to a delivery round substantially, or exclusively, designed to meet Brambles' requirements, standards and conditions.
>
> It is on this footing that I agree with the reasoning of the joint reasons that a strict construction should be adopted with respect to the terms of the contractual indemnity contained in the Agreement upon the basis of which Brambles sued Andar seeking indemnity ...

Callinan J in dissent.

QUESTIONS

(1) What is the main difference between a guarantee and an indemnity?

(2) In what way are guarantees and indemnities the same? Consider the aim of such clauses.

(3) Do you agree that guarantees and indemnities should be strictly interpreted as against the person receiving the benefit?

11.7 International perspectives

For international commercial sale of goods contracts governed by the *CISG* (see **25.4.1** on applicability), interpretation of exemption and limitation of liability clauses is no different to that of other clauses.[9] As discussed in **Chapter 10**, interpretive principles such as *contra proferentem* may be considered in a *CISG* context **25.5.8.7**, but additionally, many more evidentiary tools are available: see **10.5.1** and **25.5.5**. It should be recalled, however, that the *CISG* does not usually deal with issues of validity, thus domestic rules invalidating clauses for unfairness still apply.[10] The UNIDROIT Principles, however, contain a special provision dealing with clauses excluding liability, which precludes reliance upon such clauses in some situations:

UNIDROIT Principles art 7.1.6 (Exemption clauses)

A clause which limits or excludes one party's liability for non-performance or which permits one party to render performance substantially different from what the other party reasonably expected may not be invoked if it would be grossly unfair to do so, having regard to the purpose of the contract.

11.8 Review

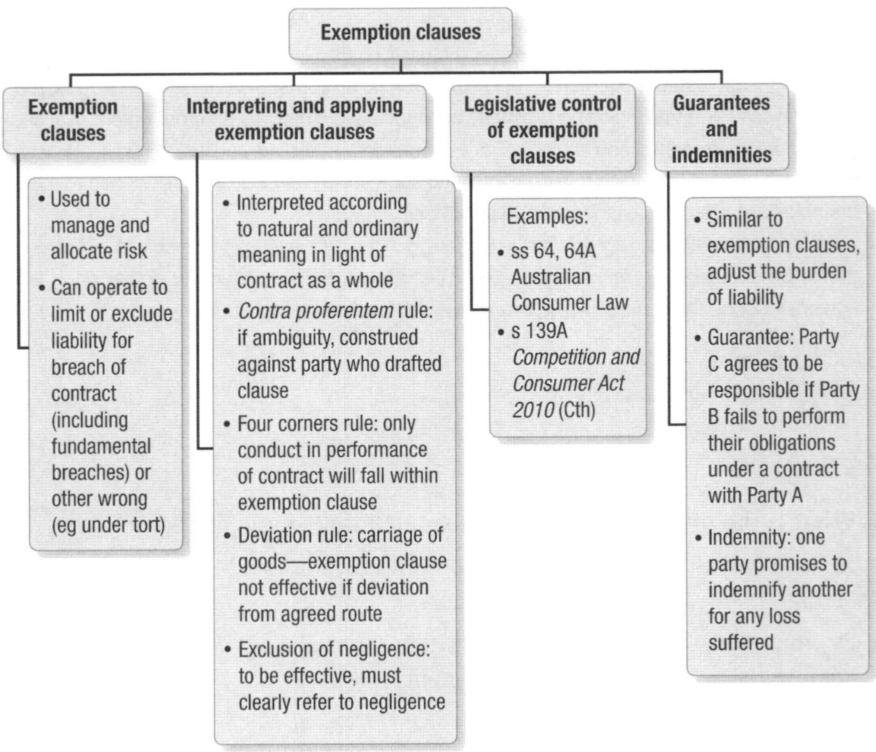

9 Note that discussion of fundamental breach in *Photo Securicor* at **11.2** bears no relationship to the *CISG* concept of fundamental breach in art 25 *CISG*.

10 CISG Advisory Council, Opinion No. 17, 'Limitation and Exclusion Clauses in CISG Contracts', Rapporteur: Prof. Lauro Gama Jr.

TIPS FOR APPLYING THE LAW IN PRACTICE

- It is extremely important when analysing a contract to look further than the rights and obligations specified and pay close attention to any exemption clauses which might alter the nature or extent of those rights and obligations. Be aware also of any guarantees or indemnities.
- Do not assume that the exemption clause will operate to reduce or exclude liability—consider whether the clause is wide enough to cover the particular breach or wrongful conduct.
- When drafting an exemption clause, and when reviewing exemption clauses in contracts, ensure you turn your mind to the question of whether any legislative provisions may apply to preclude or limit the effectiveness of such a clause.

PROBLEM QUESTION

Your client, Supplies Galore Pty Ltd ('Supplies'), has engaged you to draft a contract to be entered into with Cleaning Services Ltd ('Cleaning') by which Supplies is providing large volumes of disinfectant soap to Cleaning. Being a prudent lawyer, you want to include an exemption clause which prevents Supplies from being liable for: (a) any injuries caused by any defects in the disinfectant soap; and (b) a failure of the soap to adequately disinfect surfaces.

Draft an appropriate exemption clause.

RESEARCH QUESTION

Can you think of a situation in which it might be beneficial for a party to agree to act as guarantor or to provide an indemnity? Why?

12

PERFORMANCE OF CONTRACTUAL OBLIGATIONS

12.1 Overview

This chapter discusses the concept of 'performance' of a contract, and a number of issues which arise in this regard. Specifically, the question of time of performance, as well as the order and completeness of performance (including the doctrine of substantial performance) are considered. The question of to what extent parties are subject to a duty to co-operate and to act in good faith when performing contractual obligations is also explored.

Potential consequences flowing from non-performance of a contract are discussed in **Part V**.

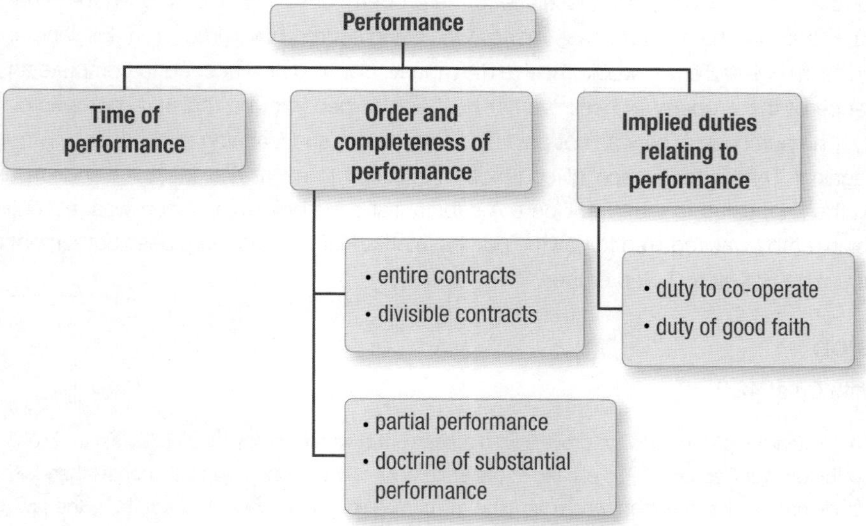

12.2 Time of performance

Concept	Short explanation	Relevant authorities	*Principles* text*
Where no time for performance is specified, performance is to occur within a 'reasonable time'	What amounts to a 'reasonable time' for performance of a contract will depend on the particular circumstances of each case	*Canning v Temby* (1905) 3 CLR 419	Chapter 12: 12.05

* Consult the corresponding section(s) of the *Principles* text for more detail.

When evaluating a contract, a key question is: when must performance of the obligations under that contract occur? The matter is relatively straightforward when a time for performance is expressly specified in the agreement. However, where no time for performance is stated in the contract, performance must occur within a 'reasonable time'.[1] What constitutes a 'reasonable time' will depend on the relevant circumstances, with the conduct of the parties being a key consideration. This issue is discussed in the following case extract.

Canning v Temby (1905) 3 CLR 419

Facts and issues

Temby agreed to purchase property from Canning. No definite time was specified in the contract for payment of the purchase price. Temby was aware that if the purchase price was not paid by 1 September, then Canning might lose title to the property due to foreclosure. On the other hand, Canning was aware that the purchase money was being sourced by Temby from England and that it was uncertain when Temby would receive the money. Canning also needed to complete an earlier conveyance of the property to her from her husband to become the registered proprietor of the property. The purchase price was not paid by 1 September and Canning subsequently brought an action against Temby for breach of contract. The action failed at first instance and on appeal. Canning then appealed to the High Court. A substantial issue before the Court was, essentially, at what point Temby was required to pay the purchase price; that is, had there been agreement to pay this amount on or before 1 September?

Decision

Per Griffith CJ at 424:

> At the trial the plaintiff failed to prove a valid agreement in writing to pay the purchase money on or before 1st September, as alleged in the statement of claim, and plaintiff's counsel then fell back on the doctrine that, where no time for completion is specified in a contract, the law implies that it is to be performed within a reasonable time. That is, no doubt, a sound proposition, and if the first of September was It reasonable time for completion by the purchaser, having regard to all the circumstances of the case, and having regard also to the true meaning of the term, then the plaintiff's cause of action was complete, and it was only a matter of assessment of damages. ...
>
> [426] In my opinion the only question in this case is whether the plaintiff has made out a case at law. The learned Judges were, as I have already said, of opinion that, under the circumstances, it could not be said that the 1st of September was a reasonable time for completion in the sense that the defendants by mere non-payment upon that date committed a breach of contract. What is a 'reasonable time' must depend upon circumstances. In the case of a contract for the sale of mining shares of [427] uncertain value, where no time for completion is specified, it would clearly be necessary that the purchaser should be ready and willing to complete and pay within a tolerably short time, and that the vendor should be ready and willing to transfer within a similar time. So, in the case of the purchase of an option, if both parties knew that the option would only last for a few days, and no time was specified, it must be taken that it was in the contemplation of the parties that a reasonable time was a period not later than the

1 This requirement also appears in legislation: see eg s 62 of the Australian Consumer Law (which is contained in Schedule 2 of the *Competition and Consumer Act 2010* (Cth)).

> expiration of the option ... Can it then be said in this case that the first of September was a reasonable time in the sense that either party failing to complete by that date would commit a breach of contract? It is very difficult to say that it was. The money, as both parties knew, was to come from London, and might or might not be here at the time appointed for redemption of the mortgage. Again, the title of the plaintiff was incomplete; she was not the registered proprietor of the land, and it was necessary before she could transfer to register a conveyance from her husband to her, which had been made some time before. It appears also that there was a second mortgage upon the property, of which she at that time was ignorant. Under these circumstances I agree with the learned Judges in the Supreme Court that it cannot be said that there was an absolute breach of contract by the mere failure to pay upon the 1st of September ...

Per O'Connor J at 433:

> The plaintiff has failed, in my opinion, to establish that, under all the circumstances of the case, a reasonable time for completion means on or before the 1st September. Both parties no doubt were aware of the vital importance of completing the matter by the 1st September, but both parties also knew that the money had to be arranged for in England, and that the payment was to come from England, and they must have been aware that the time of the remittance of that money was uncertain, and the evidence taken altogether would appear to show that, although it was of the utmost importance that this purchase should if possible be completed on the 1st September, both parties were aware of circumstances which might, without default on either side, make the completion on the exact date impossible. Then again, look at the conduct of the parties – and we may look at their conduct after the making of the contract as well as before in order to determine what was in their minds as to date of completion when the contract was made, and what was their view at that time of completion by the 1st September being essential to a reasonable compliance with the contract. We find, all through from the time of the making of the contract, Temby indicating by correspondence and conduct that he was doing his best to get the money by the 1st September, and that he would complete by that date if possible, whilst on the part of the plaintiff there was no expression of surprise or protest as to delay in completion, nor did she at any time in the correspondence after that date take up the position that the contract had been broken by failure to complete on the 1st September. She seemed rather to hope and expect that the money would arrive, although after that date, in time to save the property from the threatened foreclosure ...
>
> [434] ... The whole correspondence and actions of the parties prove conclusively to my mind that there was no understanding that the 1st September was to be the date of completion, or that it was ever within their contemplation that completion by that date was the only reasonable compliance with the contract. *McMillan* J. who had the advantage of hearing the evidence has given strong reasons, in which I entirely agree, for his decision upon the facts. With regard to the second point mentioned by my learned brother the Chief Justice, that under the terms of this contract the plaintiff could not succeed, whether completion by the 1st September was reasonable or not, without notifying that she was ready and willing upon that date to carry out her part of the contract, I entirely concur with his reasons and his conclusions. I agree that the appeal must be dismissed.

Barton J concurred with Griffith CJ and O'Connor J. The action also failed on the basis that there were defects in the statement of claim relating to what the Court viewed as a condition precedent; namely, that Canning be in a position to transfer the property to Temby. The appeal was dismissed.

QUESTIONS

(1) Do you agree with the decision in *Canning v Temby*? Why/why not?

(2) Outline 2–3 factors which may influence a determination of what constitutes a 'reasonable time' for performance.

12.3 Order and completeness of performance

Concept	Short explanation	Relevant authorities	*Principles* text*
The order of performance depends on the type of promises	Obligations may be dependent (an entire contract) or independent (a divisible contract)	Entire contracts: *Automatic Fire Sprinklers Pty Ltd v Watson* (1946) 72 CLR 435 *Cutter v Powell* [1775–1802] All ER Rep 159 Divisible contracts: *Mersey Steel & Iron Co (Ltd) v Naylor, Benzon & Co* (1884) 9 App Cas 434	Chapter 12: 12.07 – 12.09 and 12.14
Apportionment legislation	Legislation may result in an entire contract being rendered divisible	*Supreme Court Act 1986* (Vic) s 54	Chapter 12: 12.10
Partial performance	Partial performance and performance which does not comply strictly with a party's contractual obligations will generally not suffice	*Luna Park (NSW) Ltd v Tramways Advertising Pty Ltd* (1938) 61 CLR 286	Chapter 12: 12.11
The doctrine of substantial performance	If a party has substantially (but not completely) performed their obligations, the other party should perform their obligations but is entitled to seek damages for breach by the first party	*Hoenig v Isaacs* [1952] 2 All ER 176 *Bolton v Mahadeva* [1972] 1 WLR 1009	Chapter 12: 12.12–12.14

* Consult the corresponding section(s) of the *Principles* text for more detail.

The promises made by each party under a contract may be dependent on one another, or independent of one another. The determination of how the relationship between the promises should be categorised will impact on the order and completeness of performance.

12.3.1 Entire contracts

Where performance by one party ('Party X') is *dependent* on performance by the other party ('Party Y') first occurring, the contract is known as an entire contract. In such circumstances, performance by Party X is conditional on Party Y completing their contractual obligations; that is, performance by Party Y is a condition precedent. A common example is a contract of employment where the work must first be performed by the employee before the employer is obliged to pay their salary. Whether or not performance is conditional in this way (and the agreement therefore an 'entire contract') is a question of the intention of the parties. The following cases discuss performance under entire contracts.

Automatic Fire Sprinklers Pty Ltd v Watson (1946) 72 CLR 435

Facts and issues

Watson was appointed as general manager of Automatic Fire Sprinklers Pty Ltd ('AFS') and Independent Industrial Investments Pty Ltd for a period of six years beginning in October 1937. The agreement provided that the board of directors could terminate the agreement if they were of the opinion that Watson was unfit to act as general manager. Watson continued in his position after the expiration of the six-year period. Subsequently, the board of directors passed a resolution indicating that they believed Watson was unfit to continue in the position and he was then dismissed by letter dated 29 September 1944. Watson did not accept his dismissal and continued to attend work, ready and willing to perform his duties. This continued for almost a year, until 19 September 1945, at which point Watson was excluded from the premises. During arbitration, it was decided as a matter of fact that the board of directors were not actually of the view that Watson had become or was unfit to act as general manager. One of the issues to be determined by the Court (which is the focus of the below extract) was whether Watson was entitled to payment for the period commencing after the dismissal letter and ending when he was excluded from the premises.

Decision

Per Dixon J at 463:

> In certain forms of executory contract where the promise of one party is to pay the other money in consideration of his transferring property, of his doing work, of his serving the former as his master, and, perhaps, of his providing other tangible things or definite services, the money to be paid is regarded as the price of or reward for the property or service when and so often as the transfer of the one or the performance of the other affords an executed consideration. In these contracts the promise to pay the price or reward is not construed as a simple obligation to pay a sum or sums at a future date supported solely by a consideration consisting in the corresponding promise to transfer the property, do the work, serve, or provide the things or services by the other party, so that a mere readiness and willingness on the one side of the latter to perform his [464] part is enough to entitle him to the payments, notwithstanding that, whether owing to the fault of the former, or without fault on either side, the property is not transferred, the work is not done, the relation of master and servant ceases, or the things or services are not provided. The most familiar example is that of the sale of goods.

> There the common understanding of an agreement to sell is that it is the goods and not the promises to deliver that are to be paid for. The result is that, if the seller tenders goods in accordance with his contract but the buyer rejects them in breach of his contract, the seller cannot sue for the price; his remedy is for unliquidated damages for non-acceptance ...
>
> ... [465] A contract for the establishment of the relation of master and servant falls into the ... general category of agreements to pay in respect of the consideration when and so often as it is executed, and is, therefore, commonly understood as involving no liability for wages or salary unless earned by service, even though the failure to serve is a consequence of the master's wrongful act.
>
> It is, of course, possible for the parties to make a contract for the payment of periodical sums by the master to the servant independently of his service ... But, to say the least, it is not usual. The common understanding of a contract of employment at wages or salary periodically payable is that it is the service that earns the remuneration and even a wrongful discharge from the service means that wages or salary cannot be earned however ready and willing the employee may be to serve and however much he stand by his contract and decline to treat it as discharged by breach ...
>
> His only remedy is in unliquidated damages for wrongful dismissal ...
>
> ... [466] In the present case the question for decision is, in substance, whether the general manager of two companies which, without justification, purported to dismiss him from that position can recover wages for a period in which he continued to proffer his service, or must be content with unliquidated damages. The contract of employment consists in a document under the seals of the companies and possibly that of the employee, containing special terms. But, in my opinion, the terms include no provision which could take the employment out of the category I have discussed. That is to say, there is nothing in the agreement which makes the [467] payment of salary independent of actual service, or which would operate to give the employee a title to salary, notwithstanding that he had been discharged from the service of the companies, however wrongfully...

While the Court was of the view that Watson could not, at common law, recover his salary for the relevant period, legislation meant that he was so entitled. Consequently, the appeal was dismissed.

Cutter v Powell [1775–1802] All ER Rep 159

Facts and issues

Cutter, a sailor, entered into an agreement with Powell to work on a voyage from Jamaica to Liverpool. The contract provided as follows:

> Ten days after the ship Governor Parry, myself master, arrives at Liverpool, promise to pay to T Cutter the sum of 30 guineas, provided he proceeds, continues, and does his duty as second mate in the said ship from hence to the port of Liverpool.

Although Cutter duly performed his duties as a second mate, he died shortly before the ship reached Liverpool. The administratrix of his estate brought an action for payment for the work he had undertaken on the voyage, up to the point of his death. At issue was whether the contract was divisible so that Powell was obligated to provide partial payment even though Cutter had not completed his promised performance; that is, serving as second mate until the ship reached Liverpool.

Decision

Per Lord Kenyon at 161:

> ... Here the defendant expressly promised to pay the intestate 30 guineas provided he proceeded, continued and did his duty as second mate in the ship from Jamaica to Liverpool, and the accompanying circumstances disclosed in the case are that the common rate of wages is 4 pounds per month when the party is paid in proportion to the time he serves, and that this voyage is generally performed in two months. Therefore, if there had been no contract between these parties, all that the intestate could have recovered on a quantum meruit for the voyage would have been 8 pounds, whereas here the defendant contracted to pay 30 guineas provided the mate continued to do his duty as mate during the whole voyage, in which case the latter would have received nearly four times as much as if he were paid for the number of months he served. He stipulated to receive the larger sum if the whole duty were performed, and nothing unless the whole of that duty were performed. It was a kind of insurance. On this particular contract, my opinion is formed at present.

Per Ashhurst J at 161:

> ... This is a written contract, and it speaks for itself. As it is entire and, as the defendant's promise depends on a condition precedent to be performed by the other party, the condition must be performed before the other party is entitled to receive anything under it. It has been argued, however, that the plaintiff may now recover on a *quantum meruit*, but she has no right to desert the agreement for wherever there is an express contract the parties must be guided by it, and one party cannot relinquish or abide by it as it may suit his advantage. Here the intestate was by the terms of his contract to perform a given duty before he could call on the defendant to pay him anything; it was a condition precedent, without performing which the defendant is not liable. That seems to me to conclude the question. The intestate did not perform the contract on his part; he was not indeed to blame for not doing it; but still as this was a condition precedent, and as he did not perform it, his representative is not entitled to recover.

Per Grose J at 161:

> ... in this case the agreement is conclusive. The defendant only engaged to pay the intestate on condition of his continuing to do his duty on board during the whole voyage, and the latter was to be entitled either to 30 guineas or to nothing, for such was the contract between the parties.
>
> When we recollect how large a price was to be given in the event of the mate continuing on board during the whole voyage instead of the small sum which is usually given per [162] month, it may fairly be considered that the parties themselves understood that, if the whole duty were performed, the mate was to receive the whole sum and that he was not to receive anything unless he did continue on board during the whole voyage. That seems to me to be the situation in which the mate chose to put himself; and, as the condition was not complied with, his representative cannot now recover anything ...

Lawrence J agreed.

12.3.2 Divisible contracts

In contrast to entire contracts, a divisible (or severable) contract is one in which performance by a party must occur even if performance by the other party is not complete. A prime example of a divisible contract is a contract involving instalments; that is, one party becomes entitled to payment once work has progressed to a certain stage although its performance of *all* contractual obligations is not complete.

Mersey Steel & Iron Co (Ltd) v Naylor, Benzon & Co (1884) 9 App Cas 434

Facts and issues

Naylor, Benzon & Co ('Naylor') bought 5000 tons of steel from The Mersey Steel and Iron Co (Ltd) ('Mersey'). The agreement specified that 1000 tons were to be delivered monthly with payment to be made within three days of receiving the relevant shipping documents. In the first month (January 1881), Mersey delivered part of the agreed shipment, making another delivery in February. Just before Naylor was required to make payment, a petition to wind up Mersey was made. Naylor, on the basis of legal advice, refused to make payment unless and until Mersey obtained leave of the court. Mersey advised Naylor that it considered this a breach of the contract. The company was subsequently wound up. No further deliveries of steel were made and the liquidator brought an action to recover the amounts owing in relation to the two deliveries that were made. A counterclaim was made by Naylor on the basis that Mersey had failed to deliver in accordance with the agreement. A key issue to be decided by the House of Lords was whether payment for a delivery of steel was a condition precedent to the next delivery occurring (so that performance was dependent, as is the case under an entire contract).

Decision

Per Earl of Shelborne LC at 439:

> . . . I must say one or two words in order to shew why I cannot adopt [the] argument, as far as it represented the payment by the respondents for the iron delivered as in this case a condition precedent, and coming within the rules of law applicable to conditions precedent. If it were so, of course there would be an end of the case; but to me it is plain beyond the possibility of controversy, that upon the proper construction of this contract it is not and cannot be a condition precedent. The contract is for the purchase of 5000 tons of steel blooms of the company's manufacture; therefore it is one contract for the purchase of that quantity of steel blooms. No doubt there are subsidiary terms in the contract, as to the time of delivery, 'Delivery 1000 tons monthly commencing January next;' and as to the time of payment, 'Payment nett cash within three days after receipt of shipping documents;' but that does not split up the contract into as many contracts as there shall be deliveries for the purpose, of so many distinct quantities of iron. It is quite consistent with the natural meaning of the contract, that it is to be one contract for the purchase of that quantity of iron, to be delivered at those times and in that manner, and for which payment is so to be made. It is perfectly clear that no particular payment can be a condition precedent of the entire contract, because the delivery under the contract was most certainly to precede payment; and that being so, I do not see how, without express words, it can possibly be made a condition precedent to the subsequent fulfilment of the unfulfilled part of the contract, by the delivery of the undelivered steel . . .

12.3.3 Apportionment legislation

Legislative provisions may apply which change the nature of a contract from entire to divisible. This is achieved by specifying that, in particular circumstances, payments accrue from day to day, rendering the agreement divisible. Extracted below is an example of such apportionment legislation.[2]

Supreme Court Act 1986 (Vic) s 54

Section 54: Rents etc. to accrue from day to day and be apportionable

All rents, annuities, dividends and other periodical payments in the nature of income (whether reserved or made payable under an instrument in writing or otherwise) are to be considered as accruing from day to day and are apportionable in respect of time accordingly.

[Note that, pursuant to s 53(4), the parties can exclude this apportionment by providing so expressly.]

12.3.4 Partial performance

Generally speaking, common law requires parties to perform their obligations under the contract exactly as set out therein. Performance, as well as being exact, must also be complete. However, the parties themselves can agree, either expressly or by implication, that exact and complete performance is not required; for example, approximate attainment of a requirement may suffice. This is discussed in the below case.

Luna Park (NSW) Ltd v Tramways Advertising Pty Ltd (1938) 61 CLR 286

Facts and issues

Luna Park (NSW) Ltd ('Luna Park'), which operated an amusement park in Sydney, entered into an agreement with Tramways Advertising Pty Ltd ('Tramways') for Tramways to supply advertising for a fee. Under the agreement, Tramways was to display 53 roof boards advertising Luna Park on trams running on certain routes for a period of 52 weeks in total across three seasons. The agreement also included the following promise by Tramways: 'We guarantee that these boards will be on the tracks at least eight hours per day throughout your season.' Tramways brought an action to recover money owing under the contract in relation to the advertising. Luna Park defended the action, claiming damages for breach of contract on the basis that Tramways had not met its obligations under the contract. Specifically, Luna Park claimed that Tramways had not completely performed

2 See also: *Conveyancing Act 1919* (NSW) ss 144(1), 144(5); *Property Law Act 1974* (Qld) ss 232, 233(2); *Property Law Act 1969* (WA) ss 131, 134(2); *Law of Property Act 1936* (SA) ss 64, 68; *Apportionment Act 1871* (Tas) ss 2, 7; *Civil Law (Property) Act 2006* (ACT) ss 250, 253(2); *Law of Property Act 2000* (NT) ss 212(1), 213(2).

the contract in terms of displaying the boards for at least eight hours a day during the relevant period. At first instance, Luna Park succeeded in its cross-claim, but Tramways was subsequently successful on appeal. Luna Park then appealed to the High Court.

Decision

Per Latham CJ at 296:

> . . . After the second season the Luna Park Co. objected that the display contracted for was not being provided. The company contended that the provision quoted meant that each of the fiftythree boards would be on the tracks for at least eight hours on every day during three seasons. It is admitted that this service was not given. The advertising company, on the other hand, contended that the obligation imposed by the clause was performed if during each season each board was displayed for an average time of at least eight hours per day. According to this view of the meaning of the provision there would be no breach if no boards at all or only a small number of boards were shown on some days, provided that the display on other days was such as to bring the average for each board over a season to at least eight hours per day. It is admitted that if the provision bears this meaning the advertising company has performed its contract.
>
> . . . [299] . . . [Tramways Advertising] contends that the reference to the average time for which the cars of the tramway service are on the tracks affects the construction of the 'guarantee,' which should accordingly be regarded as providing only for an average time of display. In my opinion this contention is opposed to the natural meaning of the words. What is called the guarantee is a guarantee as to each and every board. It is an undertaking that each board will be on the tracks for at least eight hours on every day all through each season. The statement in the body of the letter is a statement which indicates the nature of the service which the normal running of the cars would be expected to provide. It is clear, however, that the Luna Park company was not satisfied with a mere statement that the average time that each car was on the track was eight hours per day. It required something more definite. The guarantee is an undertaking which is not in any way inconsistent with the statement of fact contained in the letter. The effect of the undertaking, read with the statement in the letter, is that, whatever might be the average time that cars were on the track, the roof boards were to be displayed for at least eight hours on every day. The guarantee contains no reference to averages, and it is apparent that there may be business reasons why the defendant required regular and continuous publicity . . .
>
> It follows that in my opinion the plaintiff must fail upon the claim because the plaintiff sues upon the special contract and has not [300] performed the contract in accordance with its terms . . .
>
> In the cross-action, the defendant claimed damages for breach of contract by the plaintiff in not displaying the fifty-three roof boards daily throughout the whole contract period of fifty-two weeks . . .
>
> It is admitted by the plaintiff that if the defendant's construction of the clause is adopted the contract has been broken by the plaintiff . . .
>
> [302] . . . The essential character of the clause in question appears both from its own terms and from the circumstances in which the contract was made. In the first place the words 'we guarantee' are particularly suited, in a contract drawn by laymen, to emphasize [303] the importance of the clause which they introduce. In the next place, the payment of £20 per week was not to begin until the complete number of roof boards, namely, fifty-three, were all displayed at the same time. The money is made payable 'from date of first appearance of complete number of boards 53 in all.' Thus, if the advertising company displayed even as many as fifty-two

boards on every day throughout a whole season, it would never become entitled to recover any payment. This provision in the contract therefore supports the view that the parties regarded the completeness of the display contracted for as an essential element in the contract ...

[304] ... But it is still necessary to consider what default will amount to a breach of the clause. The clause used the words 'at least eight hours,' but, in my opinion, such a phrase should not be interpreted with absolute mathematical exactitude in a commercials contract of this class. In some contracts it may be proper to construe references to time with absolute and precise accuracy down to minutes and seconds, but in a contract dealing with the display of roof boards on trams for at least eight hours per day the words 'eight hours per day' should be understood as meaning substantially eight hours per day. The clause would not, in my opinion, be broken by small occasional deficiencies ... I take the admission that each board was not exhibited for at least eight hours a day as an admission that it was not the case that each board was exhibited for substantially eight hours each day. I am accordingly of opinion that the defendant was entitled to determine the contract by reason of the past breaches of the plaintiff ...

[305] ... I think that the appeal should be allowed, the judgment of the Supreme Court set aside, and the claim of the plaintiff dismissed ...

In individual judgments, Rich and McTiernan JJ agreed that Tramways had not complied with its obligation to display the boards for eight hours every day. Dixon J, however, dissented, holding that an average of eight hours of display per day per tram was sufficient performance by Tramways. The appeal was allowed.

12.3.5 The doctrine of substantial performance

Despite the general rule that performance must be complete, under the doctrine of substantial performance, if one party ('Party X') has substantially performed its obligations, the other party ('Party Y') may still be required to perform as agreed; for example, by paying the agreed price which relates to the part performance by Party X—otherwise, Party X can bring action to recover the debt. That said, in such a situation, Party Y remains able to recover damages for breach in relation to Party X not fully performing the contract.

This doctrine, including what constitutes 'substantial' performance, was discussed in the following cases.

Hoenig v Isaacs [1952] 2 All ER 176

Facts and issues

Hoenig engaged Isaacs to decorate and furnish his apartment. The agreed sum of £750 for this work was to be paid 'net cash, as the work proceeds, and balance on completion'. A total of £400 was paid by Hoenig in instalments. Although he subsequently lived in the apartment and used the furniture, Hoenig made no further payments to Isaacs, claiming that part of the work and certain items of furniture supplied by Isaacs were defective. Isaacs brought an action to recover the balance of the money owing. He succeeded at first instance before an official referee and Hoenig appealed. At issue was whether Isaacs was entitled to recover the remaining money given the existence of defects, which Hoenig argued meant the work was not in accordance with the contract and therefore that the contract had not been performed.

Decision

Per Denning LJ at 180:

> ... This case raises the familiar question: Was entire performance a condition precedent to payment? That depends on the true construction of the contract ...
>
> In determining this issue the first question is whether, on the true construction of the contract, entire performance was a condition precedent to payment. It was a lump sum contract, but that does not mean that entire performance was a condition precedent to payment.
>
> When a contract provides for a specific sum to be paid on completion of specified work, the courts lean against a construction of the contract which would deprive the contractor of any payment at all simply because there are some defects or omissions. The promise to complete the work is, therefore, construed as a term of the contract, but not [181] as a condition. It is not every breach of that term which absolves the employer from his promise to pay the price, but only a breach which goes to the root of the contract, such as an abandonment of the work when it is only half done. Unless the breach does go to the root of the matter, the employer cannot resist payment of the price. He must pay it and bring a cross-claim for the defects and omissions, or, alternatively, set them up in diminution of the price. The measure is the amount which the work is worth less by reason of the defects and omissions, and is usually calculated by the cost of making them good ...
>
> It is, of course, always open to the parties by express words to make entire performance a condition precedent. A familiar instance is when the contract provides for progress payments to be made as the work proceeds, but for retention money to be held until completion. Then entire performance is usually a condition precedent to payment of the retention money, but not, of course, to the progress payments. The contractor is entitled to payment pro rata as the work proceeds, less a deduction for retention money. But he is not entitled to the retention money until the work is entirely finished, without defects or omissions.
>
> In the present case the contract provided for 'net cash, as the work proceeds; and balance on completion.' If the balance could be regarded as retention money, then it might well be that the contractor ought to have done all the work correctly, without defects or omissions, in order to be entitled to the balance. But I do not think the balance should be regarded as retention money. Retention money is usually only ten per cent., or fifteen per cent., whereas this balance was more than fifty per cent. I think this contract should be regarded as an ordinary lump sum contract. It was substantially performed. The contractor is entitled, therefore, to the contract price, less a deduction for the defects ...
>
> [182] ... In my opinion, the Official Referee was right and this appeal should be dismissed.

Per Romer LJ at 182:

> I agree that this appeal fails. ... The defendant, by instalments, paid £400 of the agreed price and kept the furniture, but, when sued for the balance, refused to pay any more and said, indeed, and argued before us that he was not in law liable to pay anything under the contract at all because of certain defects in the furniture. The ground on which he based this claim was that the contract was an entire contract, that the plaintiff could not sue for any part of the purchase price unless and until he had wholly performed his obligations thereunder, and that this was a condition precedent which had never been fulfilled. Inasmuch as the learned official referee who tried the case found that, notwithstanding the most searching investigation by the defendant into every possible source of complaint, a sum of £55.18s.2d. only was required to put right such defects in the work as he (the referee) found to have been established, the defendant's contention would appear on the face of it to be somewhat harsh, and it is to be observed that

the contention could have been similarly used had the remedial expenditure amounted to no more than a £5 note . . .

In certain cases it is right that the rigid rule for which the defendant contends should be applied, for example, if a man tells a contractor to build a 10 ft. wall for him in his garden and agrees to pay £X for it, it would not be right that he should be held liable for any part of the contract price if the contractor builds the wall to 2 ft. and then renounces further performance of the contract, or builds the wall of a totally different material from that which was ordered, or builds it at the wrong end of the garden. The work contracted for has not been done and the corresponding obligation to pay consequently never arises. But when a man fully performs his contract in the sense that he supplies all that he agreed to supply but what he supplies is subject to defects of so minor a character that he can be said to have substantially performed his promise, it is, in my judgment, far more equitable to apply the [doctrine of substantial performance] than to deprive him wholly of his contractual rights and relegate him to such remedy (if any) as he may have on a quantum meruit . . .

[183] . . . I am, accordingly, of the opinion, as already indicated, that the learned official refer fell into no error of law and that this appeal fails . . .

The appeal was dismissed.

Bolton v Mahadeva [1972] 1 WLR 1009

Facts and issues

Mahadeva engaged Bolton to conduct work in his home, including the installation of a central heating system. The agreed price for the central heating work was a lump sum of £560. The work was carried out by Bolton but Mahadeva refused to pay, claiming that the work was defective. Bolton brought an action to recover the contract price for the work. At first instance, Bolton succeeded, with a deduction being made for the amount required to remedy the defects (being £174.50). Mahadeva appealed. The issue for determination was whether Bolton was entitled to the agreed payment for the work. Given the defects, what needed to be determined was whether substantial performance by Bolton had occurred, thereby providing a basis for this recovery.

Decision

Per Cairns LJ at 1011:

The main question in the case is whether the defects in workmanship found by the judge to be such as to cost £174 to repair — that is, between one third and one quarter of the contract price — were of such a character and amount that the plaintiff could not be said to have substantially performed his contract. That is, in my view, clearly the legal principle which has to be applied to cases of this kind . . .

[1013] . . . In considering whether there was substantial performance I am of opinion that it is relevant to take into account both the nature of the defects and the proportion between the cost of rectifying them and the contract price. It would be wrong to say that the contractor is only entitled to payment if the defects are so trifling as to be covered by the de minimis rule.

The main matters that were complained of in this case were that when the heating system was put on, fumes were given out which made some of the living rooms (to put it at the lowest) extremely uncomfortable and inconvenient to use; secondly, that by reason of there being

> insufficient radiators and insufficient insulation, the heating obtained by the central heating system was far below what it should have been . . .
>
> [1014] . . . For my part, I find it impossible to say that the judge was right in reaching the conclusion that in those circumstances the contract had been substantially performed. The contract was a contract to install a central heating system. If a central heating system when installed is such that it does not heat the house adequately and is such, further, that fumes are given out, so as to make living rooms uncomfortable, and if the putting right of those defects is not something which can be done by some slight amendment of the system, then I think that the contract is not substantially performed . . . I have reached the conclusion that the judge was wrong in saying that this contract had been substantially completed; and, on my view of the law, it follows that the plaintiff was not entitled to recover under that contract . . .
>
> [1015] . . . It appears to me that the result should be this, that the appeal should be allowed and the judgment in favour of the plaintiff should be set aside . . .

Per Sachs LJ at 1015:

> When, however, one looks at the aggregate of the number of defects that [the judge] held to have been established, at the importance of some of those defects, and at the way in which some of them prevented the installation being one that did what was intended, I find myself, like Cairns L.J., quite unable to agree that there was a substantial performance by the plaintiff of this lump sum contract. It is not merely that so very much of the work was shoddy, but it is the general ineffectiveness of it for its primary purpose that leads me to that conclusion . . .

Buckley LJ agreed with Cairns and Sachs LJJ and the appeal was allowed.

QUESTIONS

(1) How does an entire contract differ from a divisible contract?

(2) What is the rationale behind apportionment legislation?

(3) In what circumstances will a party be able to recover under a contract which has only been partially performed?

12.4 Co-operation and good faith

Concept	Short explanation	Relevant authorities	*Principles* text*
The duty of co-operation	The parties must co-operate with each other in the performance of the contract	*Commonwealth Bank of Australia v Barker* (2014) 253 CLR 169	Chapter 12: 12.15
The requirement of 'good faith'	At common law, certain contracts are viewed as those 'of utmost good faith'. A prime example is contracts of insurance	*CGU Insurance Ltd v AMP Financial Planning Pty Ltd* (2007) 235 CLR 1	Chapter 12: 12.17–12.22

Concept	Short explanation	Relevant authorities	*Principles* text*
	Whether there is a more general implied duty of good faith is unsettled	*Burger King Corporation v Hungry Jack's Pty Ltd* (2001) 69 NSWLR 558 *Vodafone Pacific Ltd v Mobile Innovations Ltd* [2004] NSWCA 15 *Virk Pty Ltd (in liq) v YUM! Restaurants Australia Pty Ltd* [2017] FCAFC 190	

* Consult the corresponding section(s) of the *Principles* text for more detail.

12.4.1 The duty of co-operation

A duty of co-operation exists whereby the parties to a contract are required to co-operate in order to ensure that performance occurs. The source and nature of this duty was discussed by the High Court in the following case:

Commonwealth Bank of Australia v Barker (2014) 253 CLR 169

Facts and issues

Barker was made redundant by the Commonwealth Bank of Australia ('CBA'). CBA had advised Barker that this redundancy would come into effect if he could not be redeployed within four weeks. During this period, an alternative position arose but Barker was not contacted by the relevant recruitment consultant, although he was informed about the position in the last week of the four-week period. Having been made redundant, Barker brought an action against CBA arguing, in part, that CBA had breached the duty of co-operation in relation to his potential redeployment within the bank. Barker succeeded at first instance and on appeal. CBA then appealed to the High Court.

The below extract is focused only on the issue of whether or not CBA had breached the duty of co-operation, noting that Barker also raised an argument based on an implied term of mutual trust and confidence.

Decision

Per French CJ, Bell and Keane JJ at 187:

> . . . It has been accepted in this Court that some rules treated as implications of terms in law in particular classes of contract, or contracts generally, can also be characterised as rules of construction. Mason J, in *Secured Income Real Estate (Aust) Ltd v St Martins Investments Pty Ltd*, so characterised the principle enunciated by Lord Blackburn in *Mackay v Dick*:

> [W]here in a written contract it appears that both parties have agreed that something shall be done, which cannot effectually be done unless both concur in doing it, the construction of the contract is that each agrees to do all that is necessary to be done on his part for the carrying out of that thing, though there may be no express [188] words to that effect. What is the part of each must depend on circumstances.

The language of Lord Blackburn was indicative of a rule of construction rather than of implication. Nevertheless, Mason J also referred to the rule as defining an implied 'duty to co-operate'.

The majority in the Full Court of the Federal Court referred to the implied duty of co-operation as providing an 'alternative approach' to the application of the implied duty of mutual trust and confidence. Their Honours relied upon its formulation in *Secured Income* as one which 'requires a party to a contract to do all things necessary to enable the other party to have the benefit of the contract'. That obligation of co-operation required the Bank to take the positive steps necessary to enable Mr Barker to have the benefit of cl 8, which contemplated the possibility of redeployment within the Bank as an alternative to termination ...

As to the direct application of the implied duty of co-operation, the Bank submitted in this Court, as Jessup J had reasoned in his dissent, that there was no relevant contractual benefit with which the implied term could engage. Clause 8 conferred a benefit by way of a termination payment but did not confer a contractual entitlement to the benefit of the Redeployment Policy. The submission made on behalf of Mr Barker that 'the prospect of ... redeployment was a benefit in the relevant sense' should not be accepted ...

Their Honours then discussed the implied term of mutual trust and confidence, before continuing at 201:

> ... The courts will also imply an obligation on the part of each party to a contract to co-operate in the doing of acts necessary to performance, or to enable the other party to secure a benefit provided by the contract. Such an obligation may be traced to *Mackay v Dick* ...
>
> [209] ... as the majority in the Full Court correctly observed, the duty of co-operation 'is anchored upon the need for one party to take a positive step without which the other party is unable to enjoy a right or benefit conferred upon it by the contract'.

12.4.2 The requirement of good faith

In relation to certain contracts, courts have in the past held that a requirement to act in 'good faith' exists. The meaning of 'good faith' was discussed by the High Court in *CGU Insurance Ltd v AMP Financial Planning Pty Ltd*,[3] per Gleeson CJ and Crennan J at 15:

> We accept the wider view of the requirement of utmost good faith ... in preference to the view that absence of good faith is limited to dishonesty. In particular, we accept that utmost good faith may require an insurer to act with due regard to the legitimate interests of an insured, as well as to its own interests. The classic example of an insured's obligation of utmost good faith is a requirement of full disclosure to an insurer, that is to say, a requirement to pay regard to the legitimate interests of the insurer. Conversely, an insurer's statutory obligation to act with utmost good faith may require an insurer to act,

3 (2007) 235 CLR 1.

> consistently with commercial standards of decency and fairness, with due regard to the interests of the insured. Such an obligation may well affect the conduct of an insurer in making a timely response to a claim for indemnity . . .

A requirement to act in good faith certainly exists in relation to contracts of insurance—a position statutorily embodied in the *Insurance Contracts Act 1984* (Cth) which requires parties to act 'with the utmost good faith'.[4] However, the question of whether there is more generally an implied duty of good faith in Australia is less settled.[5]

Nevertheless, courts have in the past been prepared to recognise and imply such a duty, as illustrated in the following cases.

Burger King Corporation v Hungry Jack's Pty Ltd (2001) 69 NSWLR 558

Facts and issues

Burger King Corporation ('Burger King') (the franchisor) terminated its agreement with Hungry Jack's Pty Ltd ('Hungry Jack's') (the franchisee) on the basis that Hungry Jack's had not developed and opened the required number of businesses per year in West Australia, South Australia and Queensland. Hungry Jack's brought an action against Burger King alleging, among other things, that it had failed to act in good faith by impeding the performance of Hungry Jack's development obligations under the contract. Hungry Jack's succeeded at first instance and Burger King appealed. One of the issues to be determined by the court was whether Burger King had acted in bad faith and therefore could not rely on subsequent breaches by Hungry Jack's as grounds for terminating the agreement.

Decision

Per Sheller, Beazley and Stein JJA at 565:

> Hungry Jack's Pty Ltd claimed that there were implied into the Development Agreement terms: that Burger King Corporation would do all that was reasonably necessary to enable Hungry Jack's Pty Ltd to enjoy the benefits of, inter alia, the Development Agreement (the implied term of co-operation); that Burger King Corporation must act reasonably in exercising its powers under the Development Agreement; and that there was an implied obligation on Burger King Corporation to act in good faith in the exercise of its contractual powers . . .
>
> The implication of the implied term of co-operation was not controversial nor a matter in dispute between the parties . . .
>
> [566] . . . Until *Renard Constructions*, there had only been tentative acceptance in Australian jurisprudence of an implied term of good faith. However, in *Renard Constructions* Priestley JA said (at 268):
>
>> . . . that people generally, including judges and other lawyers, from all strands of the community, have grown used to the courts applying standards of fairness to contract which are wholly consistent with the existence in all contracts of a duty upon the parties

4 See the discussion of the *Insurance Contracts Act 1984* (Cth) in this regard in **Chapter 4**.
5 See *Principles* text at 12.18–12.22 for a detailed discussion in this regard.

> of good faith and fair dealing in its performance. In my view this is in these days the expected standard, and anything less is contrary to prevailing community expectations . . .

[568] . . . A review of cases . . . indicates that courts in various Australian jurisdictions have, for the most part, proceeded upon an assumption that there may be implied, as a legal incident of a commercial contract, terms of good faith and reasonableness . . .

[569] . . . There also appears to be increasing acceptance. . . that if terms of good faith and reasonableness are to be implied, they are to be implied as a matter of law. We consider that to be correct. . .

[570] . . . it is worth noting that the Australian cases make no distinction of substance between the implied term of reasonableness and that of good faith. . .

[571] . . . the granting of operational, financial and legal approval is within 'the sole discretion' of Burger King Corporation. If full force is given to that concept, it would allow Burger King Corporation to give or to withhold relevant approval 'at its whim' including capriciously, or with the sole intent of engineering a default of the Development Agreement, giving rise to a right to terminate.

[573] . . . There is such an extraordinary range of detailed considerations, particularly in relation to whether operational requirements have been satisfied, contained within cl 4.1(a), that unless there was an implied requirement of reasonableness and good faith, Burger King Corporation could, for the slightest of breaches, bring to an end the very valuable rights which Hungry Jack's Pty Ltd had under the Development Agreement . . .

. . . Burger King Corporation's contractual powers . . . are to be exercised in good faith and reasonably. That does not mean that Burger King Corporation is not entitled to have regard only to its own legitimate interests in exercising its discretion. However, it must not do so for a purpose extraneous to the contract — for example, by withholding financial or operational approval where there is no basis to do so, so as to thwart Hungry Jack's Pty Ltd's rights under the contract.

In conclusion, therefore, we are of the opinion that the Development Agreement is subject to implied terms of reasonableness and good faith and his Honour was correct to so find.

Vodafone Pacific Ltd v Mobile Innovations Ltd [2004] NSWCA 15

Facts and issues

Mobile Innovations Ltd ('Mobile') acted as an agent for Vodafone Pacific Ltd ('Vodafone'). Pursuant to a series of agreements, Mobile was responsible for acquiring new subscribers to the Vodafone network and providing certain customer management services. Under the agreements, Vodafone had a large degree of discretion when it came to setting targets for Mobile. Eventually Vodafone set the customer acquisition target to nil—meaning, effectively, that Mobile could no longer acquire new customers. Mobile subsequently brought action against Vodafone for breaches of the agreements. Mobile succeeded at first instance and Vodafone appealed. One of the issues to be determined was whether Vodafone had breached an implied duty to act in good faith by setting the acquisition target to nil and thereby effectively stalling the arrangement with Mobile. The following extract is focused on this issue.

Decision

Per Giles JA at [123]:

> . . . So far as Vodafone failed to determine target levels, it was in breach of contract and there was no need or room for any breach of an obligation to co-operate or an obligation of good faith

and reasonableness. So far as Vodafone determined a target level of nil, if on the proper construction of the agreement it was not entitled to do so again there was no need or room for the overlay of an implied term. It was necessary first to ascertain what Vodafone had power to do on the proper construction of the agreement. If it was entitled to determine a target level of nil, an implied term might control the exercise of the power. The construction of the agreement would itself bear upon whether an implied term required that it exercise its discretion by determining a target level other than nil.

[124] As to the implied terms, this was not a case of the *Mackay v Dick* (1881) 6 App Cas 251 kind, with the question whether each party was obliged to do all that was necessary to be done on its part for the doing of what the contract said should be done. Vodafone had a contractual power, the question was what it could do in the exercise of its discretion . . .

[125] An obligation of good faith and reasonableness in the performance of a contractual obligation or the exercise of a contractual power may be implied as a matter of law as a legal incident of a commercial contract . . . The focus in the present case should have been on the pleaded term that Vodafone would act in good faith and reasonably in exercising its powers under the ASP [Agency] Agreement . . . so that even if on the construction of the agreement Vodafone was entitled to determine a target level of nil, the exercise of its discretion in good faith and reasonably called for determination of a target level of some particular number of connections of New Subscribers . . .

[188] In the present case the implied terms were separated, but effectively an implied term that Vodafone would act in good faith and reasonably in exercising its powers under the ASP Agreement was said to be implied by law. Thus it is necessary to ask whether the ASP Agreement is one of a class of contracts as a legal incident of which such a term is implied, including whether it is to be given that status for the first time, and if so whether the implication by law is precluded by expression of contrary intent. The inquiry, however, can not be made in the abstract. Because there may be exclusion by express provision or inconsistency with the terms of the contract on their proper construction . . ., it is necessary to address the relevant power, that conferred by. . . the agreement.

[189] As I have said. . . an obligation of good faith and reasonableness in the performance of a contractual obligation or the exercise of a contractual power may be implied as a matter of law as a legal incident of a commercial contract. In *Burger King Corporation v Hungry Jack's Pty Ltd*, however, the Court said only that courts had 'for the most part proceeded on the assumption' that there may be such an implication in a commercial contract (at [159]). It said that the contract there in question 'does not fall into any of the traditional class of cases where terms have been implied as an incident of the contract' (at [166]), and went on to consider by the test of what was reasonable and necessary whether the term should be implied at law as a new class of case (at [167–186]). This fell short of, indeed rejected, treating commercial contracts as a class of contracts carrying the implied term as a legal incident . . .

[191] The ASP Agreement was no doubt a commercial contract. It was not suggested that it fell within some other class of contract already carrying the implied term as a legal incident or which it should now be found to have that status. I do not think the law has yet gone so far as to say that commercial contracts are a class of contracts carrying the implied terms as a legal incident, and the width and indeterminancy of the class of contracts would make it a large step. However, I am content to assume, expressly without deciding, that unless excluded by express provision or because inconsistent with the terms of the contract, Vodafone was under an implied obligation to act in good faith and reasonably in exercising its powers under the ASP Agreement, specifically the power of determining target levels . . . Whether the assumption might be justified by commercial contracts already carrying the implied term or now being found

to have that status does not matter. I consider that the present case can be decided by addressing whether the implication of the term as a matter of law, as to the power conferred by ... the ASP Agreement, is precluded by expression of a contrary intent.

[192] In addressing contrary intent, it is necessary to have in mind a content for the obligation of good faith and reasonableness. Only then can one sensibly enquire whether there is inconsistency with the terms of the contract. There is regrettable lack of uniformity in the cases. Reasonableness can be seen as part of good faith, and acting in bad faith is hardly reasonable. The difficulty in arriving at the content of an obligation of good faith, in particular, has often been noted ...

[195] The power in cl 18.4 was emphatically described as a sole discretion. Since there was only one Vodafone (whichever of the entities it was), the point of 'sole' lay in the exclusion of any constraint upon Vodafone. Its exercise was excluded from the dispute resolution procedure, with the further emphasis that 'Vodafone's decision will be conclusive and binding on the parties' (cl 32.6) and the emphasis again that it could be exercised in any manner Vodafone saw fit (cl 41). These words in the ASP Agreement can not be passed over, and they weigh against the implied obligation of good faith and reasonableness in the exercise of the power ...

[198] Without more, in my opinion, the implication of the obligation to act in good faith and reasonably in exercising the power of determining target levels in cl 18.4 was excluded ...

[206] The obligation to exercise the power in cl 18.4 in good faith and reasonably, if found, is an obligation imposed by law by adding to the express words 'will have the sole discretion' the further words 'to be exercised in good faith and reasonably'. It seems to me an accurate use of language to give it the description of an implied term, when from the premise of a contractual intent attributed in law to the parties they did not in fact use the express words with the added meaning. It is also a preferable use of language, since it recognizes that the obligation is imposed by law — because the term is implied in law — and does not proceed on a fiction that an intention of the parties is being found by a process of construction ...

[208] In my opinion ... Vodafone was not obliged by an implied term to act in good faith and reasonably, in the respects found by the judge, in determining target levels ...

[215] ... the content of the obligation of good faith and reasonableness for which Mobile contended in the appeal was rather enlarged. The bad faith did not lie just in Vodafone so exercising the discretion that as a matter of fact Mobile would be brought to stagnation. It extended to Vodafone exercising the discretion for the extraneous purpose of bringing the ASP Agreement to an end.

[216] Apart from any implied obligations to co-operate and of good faith and reasonableness ... the law has long provided remedies for the exercise of a power otherwise than for the purpose for which it was conferred. Equity will intervene to restrain the exercise of the power or to set aside the result of its exercise ...

Both Sheller and Ipp JJA agreed with the judgment of Giles JA.

Virk Pty Ltd (in liq) v YUM! Restaurants Australia Pty Ltd [2017] FCAFC 190

Facts and issues

YUM! Restaurants Australia Pty Ltd ('YUM!') was the franchisor of Pizza Hut restaurants in Australia. Virk Pty Ltd (in liq) ('Virk') was a franchisee of a Pizza Hut restaurant. In 2014, YUM! implemented a 'value strategy' whereby it reduced the price of pizzas pursuant to its right under the contracts with franchisees to set maximum prices. There was objection to this among the franchisees, based on a concern that they would be unable to operate profitably under the value strategy. Accordingly, the franchisees, via a representative (at first instance, Diab Pty Ltd and on appeal, Virk), brought an action against YUM! alleging, among other things, that YUM! had breached its duty of good faith by implementing the value strategy. At first instance, the franchisees did not succeed, subsequently appealing to the Full Federal Court. There were a number of issues to be decided in this case, one being whether YUM! had breached a duty of good faith when setting the price of pizzas pursuant to the value strategy. The following extract is focused on this issue.

Decision

Per the Court (Gilmour, Nicholas and Moshinsky JJ) at [149]:

> [Good faith and reasonableness] These grounds raise legal and factual challenges arising from the primary judge's finding that Yum's discretionary power to fix maximum prices was subject to an (implied) obligation that it be exercised honestly and reasonably and with reasonable cause . . . This we take to be referring to what is more usually described as a duty or obligation of good faith and reasonableness. Synonymous phrases such as 'good faith and fidelity to the bargain' and 'good faith and fair dealing' are also employed . . .
>
> [164] . . . The obligation, expressed as one of good faith and reasonableness, is to be considered in a composite and interrelated sense. To the extent that consideration is given to whether a party's conduct is reasonable or not, it is directed to the primary component of the obligation, namely of good faith. Reasonableness is not to be approached in a case such as this as akin to a tortious duty to exercise due care and skill or to produce a reasonable outcome. Rather it goes to the quality of the conduct, here in exercising the price setting power, to discern whether it was capricious, dishonest, unconscionable, arbitrary or the product of a motive which was antithetical to the object of the contractual power. Conduct attended by any of those qualities could never be said to be in good faith. Consideration of the relevant conduct within these confines informs the question whether or not the power has been exercised in good faith.
>
> [165] The converse, in our opinion, also follows. Where, as in this case, there is a finding of good faith (or, specifically, a finding that there was an absence of bad faith: in effect, not having demonstrated that there was a lack of good faith) attaching to the exercise of the contractual power, then that exercise must necessarily also have been reasonable . . .
>
> [167] We do not propose to embark upon any general discussion as to when, and by what legal method, the law will imply an obligation of good faith and reasonableness in a contract. Nor do we propose to discuss whether such an obligation is to be implied or arises as a matter of construction of a given contract. It is sufficient that in this case it was common ground that under the International Franchise Agreement such an obligation arose . . . However, it is necessary to consider what such an obligation involves.
>
> [174] It may generally be noted, as Allsop CJ observed in *Paciocco* at [287], that good faith in the performance of contracts is a good example of the presence of values in the common law. As to the nature of those values, it is again useful to have recourse to Allsop CJ in *Paciocco*, where, at [292], his Honour observed that good faith is rooted in honest and reasonable fair dealing . . . Kiefel J . . . in *Commonwealth Bank of Australia v Barker* (2014) 253 CLR 169 at [104] similarly observed that fairness in dealings as between contracting parties may be understood as an aspect of a duty of good faith. Sir Anthony Mason in his Cambridge Lecture stated that he used 'good faith' mainly in the sense of loyalty to the promise itself and as excluding 'bad faith behaviour'.
>
> [175] Thus viewed, reasonableness is referable to the standard of a party's conduct or behaviour in relation to the performance of a contractual obligation or exercise of a contractual

> power. It may, for example, include consideration of a party's real intention or purpose in exercising a contractual power. It calls into consideration, for example, whether that conduct is or is not honest, capricious, arbitrary or for an extraneous purpose . . . Such characterisations of conduct are ascertained upon the evidence in a particular case and in the context of the particular contract, having regard to acceptable norms of commercial conduct . . .
>
> [178] Importantly, and contrary to the appellant's alternative submission, it may also be seen that 'reasonableness' as an adjunct to an obligation of good faith has never been regarded as a duty to exercise due care and skill or to produce a reasonable outcome.
>
> [179] Thus, the expressions within the composite phrase are necessarily and closely related. Consideration of the reasonableness of a party's conduct will inform the question of whether good faith or its absence has been brought to the performance of the contractual obligation or exercise of the power . . .
>
> [192] . . . the primary judge resolved the composite and related concepts of good faith and reasonableness upon a consideration of the evidence of the conduct of Yum and of the relevant terms of the International Franchise Agreement as a whole and having regard to the agreement in which the implied obligation of good faith and reasonableness arose. These obligations her Honour assessed holistically, accepting the interrelated nature of the two concepts of good faith and reasonableness . . . neither her Honour's conclusions, nor the test she applied in making findings of fact, demonstrate error. Accordingly, the appeal, to the extent it depends on these questions, must fail.

The appeal was dismissed.

QUESTIONS

(1) Explain the duty of co-operation with reference to case law (as appropriate).

(2) Can the duty of good faith be excluded from a contract?

(3) What does 'reasonableness' mean in the context of a duty to act in good faith?

12.5 International perspectives

12.5.1 Concurrency of obligations, time for performance, cure and *Nachfrist*

For cross-border commercial contracts, questions of performance will be determined differently if the *CISG* or UNIDROIT Principles govern the contract: on applicability see **25.4.1** or **25.4.3**. The order of performance is determined in accordance with the contractual terms, thus notions of completeness of performance or 'entire contract' (**12.3**) are not concepts within the *CISG* or UNIDROIT Principles.[6] If time for performance is not specified, delivery of goods is due within a 'reasonable time' of conclusion of the contract (art 33(c) *CISG*) and payment of the

6 See, on order of performance, art 6.1.4 UNIDROIT Principles, which essentially looks to the intent of the parties.

price is due upon delivery of the goods: art 58 *CISG*; art 6.1.1 UNIDROIT Principles (compare **12.2**). Interestingly, unlike Australian common law, the *CISG* allows the defaulting party an opportunity to cure defects if it will not cause unreasonable inconvenience or costs to the other party: art 48 *CISG*; art 7.1.4 UNIDROIT Principles (see **25.9.1**). Another feature is that an aggrieved party who is unsure whether a 'reasonable time' has passed for delivery may set an additional reasonable period for delivery (a *Nachfrist*), by notice to the seller: arts 47 and 63 *CISG*; art 7.1.5 UNIDROIT Principles. If the seller still fails to perform, the aggrieved party has an unequivocal right to avoid (terminate) the contract by notice: arts 49(1)(b) and 64(1)(b) *CISG*; **25.9.2**. This reduces uncertainty about rights to end the contract.

12.5.2 Obligation to perform with remedies of damages and price reduction

Unless parties have agreed to the contrary, or there is a fundamental breach or non-delivery (arts 49(1) and 64(1) *CISG*), then contractual obligations must still be performed by the other party (eg it must pay the price, subject to right to suspend below), but may rely upon the self-help remedy of proportional price reduction for partial or non-conforming delivery of goods (arts 50–52 *CISG*; **25.9.6**), or claim damages with interest (arts 74 and 78 *CISG*; arts 7.4.1 and 7.4.9 UNIDROIT Principles; see **23.4.1–23.4.2** and **25.9.6–25.9.7**).

12.5.3 The right to suspend performance

If an anticipatory substantial non-performance becomes 'apparent', the aggrieved party has the right to suspend their own performance and seek assurances from the other party: art 71(1) *CISG*. The UNIDROIT Principles include the higher hurdle of reasonable belief of anticipatory fundamental non-performance: art 7.3.3 UNIDROIT Principles. In both cases, if an adequate assurance is provided, performance must continue, but if not, notice of avoidance (termination) can be given. See further **25.9.5**.

12.5.4 Good faith in performance

Duties of co-operation are inherent in general principles underlying the *CISG* (see also art 5.1.3 UNIDROIT Principles). Moreover, an express provision disallows an aggrieved party from relying upon a breach of the other to the extent it caused the breach itself: art 80 *CISG*; art 7.1.2 UNIDROIT Principles. The vexed approach of Australian contract law on good faith in the exercise of contractual discretion (see **12.4**) is in contrast to the international approach. The *CISG* does not impose direct duties of good faith, but requires its provisions to be interpreted to promote good faith in trade (art 7(1)). Unless agreed otherwise, parties would be required to exercise discretionary powers in good faith. The UNIDROIT Principles go further, imposing direct duties of good faith upon all parties in performance of their contract (art 1.7 UNIDROIT Principles, see also arts 5.1.4–5 and 5.3.4). Moreover, parties purportedly cannot contract out of good faith within the UNIDROIT Principles. See **25.5.4** for further discussion.

12.6 Review

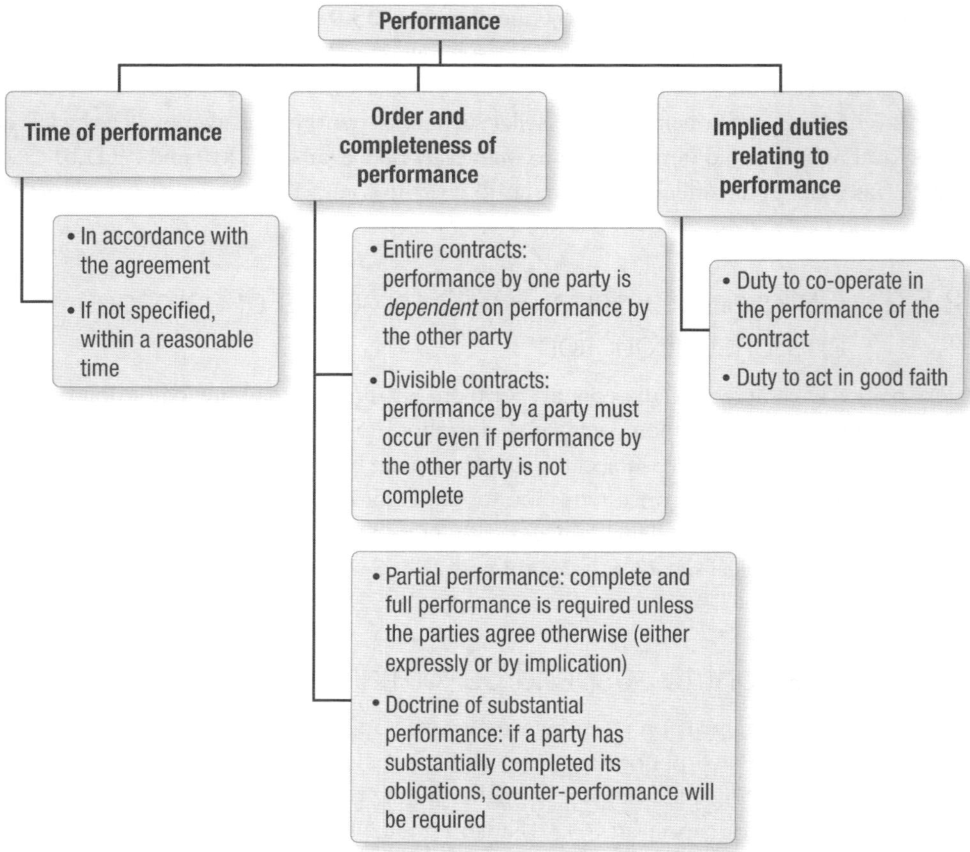

TIPS FOR APPLYING THE LAW IN PRACTICE

- As a point of practice, it is preferable to clearly specify in every contract a time for performance to avoid disputes on the question of what constitutes a 'reasonable time'.
- Be very careful when drafting a contract: do the parties intend that their obligations will be *dependent* or *independent* of one another? Clear drafting is required otherwise unintended and adverse consequences may flow for your client (meaning potential liability for you).
- If you are analysing a problem question involving the termination of a contract by one party on the basis of breach, consider whether a question of compliance with the duty to act in good faith also arises and should therefore be discussed.

PROBLEM QUESTION

Troy is a landscape gardener. Jones engages Troy to landscape his front garden. The work is to include the installation by Troy of a drainage system that ensures water runs away from Jones' weatherboard house. The agreement provides that payment of $800 is to be made upon completion of this landscaping work. Unfortunately, as soon as Troy completed the work it became apparent that the drainage he laid was causing water to pool up against the side of Jones' house. Jones is therefore refusing to pay Troy anything, claiming that he has not performed the contract as agreed (namely, by ensuring water from the front garden runs away from Jones' house) and therefore is not entitled to any payment. Advise Troy whether he can recover any money under the contract.

RESEARCH QUESTION

Do you agree with the operation of the doctrine of substantial performance?

PART IV

ADJUSTING A CONTRACT

13

VARYING TERMS

13.1 Overview

There are clear but limited grounds upon which the terms of a contract can be varied after the contract is validly formed. The important issue to determine is whether either the original contract has been terminated and a new contract formed or the original contract continues but with a variation to the original terms.

If the contract is varied, the main issue is whether additional consideration has been provided by one party to make binding any additional promises by the other party. (If a new contract is formed, the renewed exchange of promises is usually the consideration that makes the new contract binding.) Arguably, one ground for showing additional consideration to make a variation binding is if the other party receives a 'practical benefit' from the variation, although the precise requirements for this ground are still the subject of judicial development.

There are 'limiting mechanisms' to protect both parties from 'unwanted' variations, including economic duress and formalities, and there are alternative mechanisms to enforce additional promises, including estoppel, waiver, rectification and statutory rights.

13.2 How a contract can be varied

Concepts	Short explanation	Relevant authorities	*Principles* text*
New or modified contract?	Have the parties varied the contract in such a way that the original contract continues to operate or has a new contract been formed? The test focuses on the intention of the parties	*Commissioner of Taxation (Cth) v Sara Lee Household & Body Care (Australia) Pty Ltd* (2000) 201 CLR 520 *Quinn v Jack Chia (Australia) Ltd* [1992] 1 VR 567	Chapter 13: 13.01–13.03

* Consult the corresponding section(s) of the *Principles* text for more detail.

As with many areas of contract law, the underlying issue for variations is a question of intention. The following three cases provide examples of the judicial techniques involved in determining whether there was an intention for a contract to be modified or a new contract formed. Notice the ways each case describes the role of intention and the evidence relied on to identify that intention.

It is important to note that these cases arise in circumstances where an express contractual right to vary the contract, either unilaterally or with consent, did not exist in the original contract and so the common law techniques in relation to variation needed to be considered.

13.2.1 Methods of variation

Commissioner of Taxation (Cth) v Sara Lee Household & Body Care (Australia) Pty Ltd (2000) 201 CLR 520

Facts and issues

In a complicated cross-border purchase and sale transaction, which was structured to limit possible tax liabilities, the parties to the original purchase and sale agreement ('PSA', dated 31 May 1991) purported to vary the PSA in terms of price and ongoing obligations ('amendment agreement', dated 30 August). The issue, which has significance for when a tax liability may arise, was whether the variation of the PSA was a modification or a replacement of the original agreement.

Decision

Appeal allowed: the amendment agreement was a variation, not a replacement, of the PSA.

Per Gleeson CJ, Gaudron, McHugh and Hayne JJ at 533:

> . . . [T]here is an issue as to the effect of the amendment agreement of 30 August 1991 upon the purchase and sale agreement of 31 May 1991. The variations to the rights and obligations of the contracting parties made by the amendment agreement were not insubstantial. The purchase price was altered by US$1,000,000. The obligations of Roche in relation to employees of the respondent were significantly modified. Nicholas Products Pty Ltd was identified as the company which was to acquire the Australian assets, although it was not itself a party to the amendment agreement.
>
> When the parties to an existing contract enter into a further contract by which they vary the original contract, then, by hypothesis, they have made two contracts. For one reason or another, it may be material to determine whether the effect of the second contract is to bring an end to the first contract and replace it with the second, or whether the effect is to leave the first contract standing, subject to the alteration. For example, something may turn upon the place, or the time, or the form, of the contract, and it may therefore be necessary to decide whether the original contract subsists. In the present case, if the effect of what occurred on 30 August 1991 had been to rescind the agreement of 31 May 1991, then that would go a long way towards [534] providing an answer to the appellant's argument that the assignment which occurred on 30 August was pursuant to the agreement of 31 May, with whatever that entails for the application of Pt IIIA of the Act.
>
> In *Tallerman & Co Pty Ltd v Nathan's Merchandise (Victoria) Pty Ltd* [(1957) 98 CLR 93 at 144], Taylor J said:
>
> > It is firmly established by a long line of cases . . . that the parties to an agreement may vary some of its terms by a subsequent agreement. They may, of course, rescind the earlier agreement altogether, and this may be done either expressly or by implication, but the determining factor must always be the intention of the parties as disclosed by the later agreement.
>
> That passage was cited with approval by Wilson and Dawson JJ in *Dan v Barclays Australia Ltd* [(1983) 57 ALJR 442 at 448-449; 46 ALR 437 at 448]. It accords with principle and with authority [eg *Morris v Baron and Company* [1918] AC 1; *British and Beningtons, Ld v N W Cachar Tea Co & Ors* [1923] AC 48; *United Dominions Corporation (Jamaica) Ltd v Shoucair* [1969] 1 AC 340].

> It is clear that the parties to the agreements of 31 May and 30 August 1991 did not intend that the agreement of 31 May should be wholly rescinded. That is apparent from a number of the provisions of the 30 August agreement. In particular, it was made clear by s 11 of the 30 August agreement, which has been quoted above. This is hardly surprising. The agreement of 31 May had worldwide operation, and covered many dispositions and acquisitions that were unaffected by the alterations proposed in relation to Australia. It is also to be observed that the deed of assignment executed by the respondent and Nicholas Products Pty Ltd on 30 August 1991 recited that it was entered into pursuant to the agreement of 31 May 1991, as amended. The manifest intention of the parties was not that the agreement of 31 May 1991 should be wholly rescinded and replaced by a new agreement, but that the rights and liabilities under, and the mode of performance of, the agreement, should be varied in certain respects.

Quinn v Jack Chia (Australia) Ltd [1992] 1 VR 567

Facts and issues

Quinn was originally employed in January 1985 as an assistant manager by Jack Chia (Australia) Ltd on a contract that allowed termination with one month's notice. Quinn was subsequently promoted in August 1985 to construction manager, then general manager and was also appointed a board member of related construction companies. Two years after commencing employment, Jack Chia (Australia) Ltd purported to terminate Quinn with one month's notice, which Quinn argued was too short for a person in his position and that two years' notice was required. An issue was whether a new contract arose as Quinn's position changed.

Decision

The Court ruled in favour of Quinn: a new contract was formed, which included an implied term requiring a longer notice period than one month.

Per Ashley J at 575:

> It was common ground between the parties that the facts of a particular case may show that a contract of employment between employer and employee has been supplanted by a new contract between them. Alternatively, the facts may disclose a continuing contract within which variation of circumstances may occur without there being any need for variation of contracted terms, or a contract which has been subject to specific variation.
>
> [. . .]
>
> It has been implied, see *Marriott* at 191 (QB); 988 (WLR), per Lord Denning MR, that agreed variation of a contract of employment and agreement to rescind such a contract and replace it with another should each be regarded as involving a consensual termination. To much the same effect, Macken, McCarry and Sappideen's, *The Law of Employment,* 3rd ed 188, propounds the following: 'Unless the initial contract allows it we suggest that an agreed change of job or a regrading will almost always amount to a termination of the existing contract and the commencement of a new one by consent. In the absence of a contract allowing it, the employer cannot force changes on an employee. An attempt to do so will involve the employer in a breach of contract if the employer presses her or his requirements in the manner exemplified in *Molesworth*.'
>
> Arguably, in my opinion, those propositions are too wide. Clearly enough, if the parties advert to the potential distinction between rescission and variation, and make use of a word suggesting the former, for example 'rescinded', 'abrogated', 'abandoned', 'discharged', there should

be no difficulty in concluding that the prior agreement was terminated and replaced by another. Otherwise, somewhat unhelpfully, text writers have suggested that the problem is difficult: see Lindgren, Carter and Harland, *Contract Law in Australia* 156.

In *Adrema Ltd v Jenkinson* [1945] KB 446, to which Mr Houghton referred me, Humphreys J concluded, upon the facts, that an agreed change of duties but without pay alteration did not constitute a termination of a worker. In the context of a case stated arising out of a criminal prosecution brought against the employer for breach of a wartime employment order this was, no doubt, a sensible outcome.

... [576] There are a series of Australian authorities that provide instances of courts concluding that, on the facts, new contracts replaced the old ... In *Federated Mutual Insurance* [1920] SALR 284, a man who was elevated in his employment from assistant State manager of an insurance company was dismissed on a month's notice. That had been the period of notice fixed when he entered the employment as an insurance salesman (this position was later re-described as assistant State manager). The learned Chief Justice said, at 292:

> If [the defendant's] argument were sound, a man who had been originally employed by a company as an office boy at weekly wages, subject to the express condition that he might leave or be discharged on a week's notice, would be entitled to retire, or be liable to be dismissed, on the same notice when he had been promoted to the position of manager of the Company, in case no new arrangement had been made with regard to the length of notice to be given for terminating his appointment. I cannot believe that the law requires us to so hold. The true view, I think, is that unless the original agreement gave the employer the right to the services of the employee in any capacity he chose to direct from time to time there would be a new employment whenever a change was made in the duties to be performed, and it would be a question of fact in each case what the terms of the new employment were.

Whether his Honour went too far in that proposition is open to question. But the passage highlights what seems to me to be a valid point — that where employer and employee agree to an alteration in the employee's duties and responsibilities which is profound, a court should be more ready to hold (unless the original contract of employment provided for the [577] contingency) that a new contract has replaced the old; or at least that the old contract, as varied, contained terms objectively appropriate to the new relationship created.

In *O'Connor*, O'Bryan J appears to have implicitly accepted, at 386, the proposition that the decision in *Adrema* could be attributed to the phrase in the relevant English order, viz 'employment in the undertaking'.

[...]

Ultimately, in the present case, if I am satisfied that the contract of employment did not authorise the changes in the plaintiff's position and responsibilities which were effected in April 1985 and/or August 1985, the question becomes what term, if any, as to termination was incorporated into:

- a new contract, if that there was;
- the original contract as varied, if that were the situation.

It does not necessarily follow that the term would be different depending upon which of the two alternative analyses were regarded as correct.

... I have come to the conclusion that the change to the plaintiff's situation in August 1985 was exceptional, far reaching, not within the original [578] contemplation of the parties and not comprehended by the contract initially made between them; and that it did give rise to the institution of a fresh contract of service between the plaintiff and the defendant rather than merely a variation of that earlier agreement. In these circumstances I do not deal with the respective submissions relating to the April 1985 situation.

... I have concluded that the original contract between plaintiff and defendant was replaced rather than varied not simply by taking the position that any change in position and salary not contemplated by the original agreement necessarily requires the conclusion that a new contract has been set up, but rather by focussing on the circumstance that a change of great magnitude in the relationship between the parties was effected as at August 1985. In my opinion, a new and very different employment relationship then arose; and it is inapposite to describe it as involving no more than a variation of the earlier agreement between the parties. No reason in law was suggested why the parties could not by a parol agreement discharge the original contract (which was partly written and partly oral) and replace it with another.

QUESTIONS

(1) What are the underlying policy concerns that may motivate when the courts will find a varied contract or a replaced contract?

(2) What reasons might exist for distinguishing employment cases from other types of contracts?

13.3 The requirement for fresh consideration

Concepts	Short explanation	Relevant authorities	*Principles* text*
Fresh consideration: practical benefit?	Since an existing legal duty cannot be good consideration for a further promise, does the promissor receive a practical benefit in return for making the further promise?	*Stilk v Myrick* (1809) 2 Camp 317; 6 Esp 129 *Hartley v Ponsonby* (1857) 119 ER 1471 *Williams v Roffey Bros & Nicholls (Contractors) Ltd* [1991] 1 QB 1 *Musumeci v Winadell Pty Ltd* (1994) 34 NSWLR 723	Chapter 13: 13.07–13.08
Fresh consideration: part payment of a debt?	The payment of less than the full amount of a debt on or after the date for payment cannot be consideration to make the creditor's promise not to sue binding	*Foakes v Beer* (1884) 9 App Cas 605	Chapter 13: 13.09–13.10

* Consult the corresponding section(s) of the *Principles* text for more detail.

When a court determines the intention of the parties was to modify the contract, then parties must identify fresh consideration to make the additional promises binding. This requirement is made very problematic in the context of contract variations because of the common law's view that the performance of an existing legal duty (such as the terms of the original contract) cannot be viewed as fresh consideration. The cases below examine both the common law's reluctance to recognise existing legal duties as fresh consideration and some techniques for circumventing that reluctance.

13.3.1 Performance of an existing legal duty: a history

The case of *Stilk v Myrick* is traditionally viewed as the basis for the rule that existing legal duties cannot be fresh consideration; however, the case is very problematic as a key authority in a number of ways. One limitation with the case is the absence of an authoritative report of the decision. Another limitation is whether there were strong contemporary policy reasons for the decision that may no longer be relevant. As the *Principles* text discusses the significance of there being two different reports of the case, both versions are extracted here in their original format. The significance of the case is also questioned by the subsequent decision in *Hartley v Ponsonby*, which was similar in some ways but in which a different conclusion was reached. Both cases are extracted below.

Stilk v Myrick (1809) 2 Camp 317; 6 Esp 129

Facts and issue

After several seamen abandoned a ship on its journey to London, the captain promised the remaining seamen could share the foregone wages if the ship successfully got to London. The ship duly arrived in London and the captain refused to pay the seamen more than their original wages. The issue was whether there was fresh consideration provided by the seamen to make the captain's additional promise binding.

Decision

Action dismissed: the seamen failed to enforce the additional promise and could only claim their original wages as the sailors did not provide fresh consideration for the additional promise.

Version 1: 2 Camp 317, 170 ER 1168

[317] (In the course of a voyage some of the seamen desert, and the captain not being able to find others to supply their place, promises to divide the wages which would have become due to them among the remainder of the crew. This promise is void for want of consideration.)

[S.C. 6 Esp. 129.]

This was an action for seaman's wages, on a voyage from London to the Baltic and back.

By the ship's articles, executed before the commencement [318] of the voyage, the plaintiff was to be paid at the rate of £5 a month; and the principal question in the cause was, whether he was entitled to a higher rate of wages? In the course of the voyage two of the seamen deserted; and the captain having in vain attempted to supply their places at Cronstadt, there entered into an agreement with the rest of the crew, that they should have the wages of the two who had deserted equally divided among them, if he could not procure two other hands at Gottenburgh. This was found impossible; and the ship was worked back to London by the plaintiff and eight more of the original crew, with whom the agreement had been made at Cronstadt.

Garrow for the defendant insisted, that this agreement was contrary to public policy, and utterly void. In West India voyages, crews are often thinned greatly by death and desertion; and if a promise of advanced wages were valid, exorbitant claims would be set up on all such occasions. This ground was strongly taken by Lord Kenyon in *Harris v. Watson*, Peak. Cas. 72, where that learned Judge held, that no action would lie at the suit of a sailor on a promise of a captain to pay him extra wages, in consideration of his doing more than the ordinary share of duty in navigating the ship; and his Lordship said, that if such a promise could be enforced, sailors would in many cases suffer a ship to sink unless the captain would accede to any extravagant demand they might think proper to make.

[319] The Attorney-General, *contra*, distinguished this case from *Harris v. Watson*, as the agreement here was made on shore, when there was no danger or pressing emergency, and when the captain could not be supposed to be under any constraint or apprehension. The mariners were not to be permitted on any sudden danger to force concessions from the captain; but why should they be deprived of the compensation he voluntarily offers them in perfect security for their extra labour during the remainder of the voyage?

Lord Ellenborough: I think *Harris v. Watson* was rightly decided; but I doubt whether the ground of public policy, upon which Lord Kenyon is stated to have proceeded, be the true principle on which the decision is to be supported. Here, I say, the agreement is void for want of consideration. There was no consideration for the ulterior pay promised to the mariners who remained with the ship. Before they sailed from London they had undertaken to do all that they could under all the emergencies of the voyage. They had sold all their services till the voyage should be completed. If they had been at liberty to quit the vessel at Cronstadt, the case would have been quite different; or if the captain had capriciously discharged the two men who were wanting, the others might not have been compellable to take the whole duty upon themselves, and their agreeing to do so might have been a sufficient consideration for the promise of an advance of wages. But the desertion of a part of the crew is to be [320] considered an emergency of the voyage as much as their death; and those who remain are bound by the terms of their original contract to exert themselves to the utmost to bring the ship in safety to her destined port. Therefore, without looking to the policy of this agreement, I think it is void for want of consideration, and that the plaintiff can only recover at the rate of £5 a month. Verdict accordingly.*

The Attorney-General and Espinasse for the plaintiff. Garrow and Reader for the defendant.

Footnote in original text follows.

* But where a seaman performs some service beyond the scope of his original contract, the case is otherwise. Thus before the ransoming of ships was prohibited, a promise by the captain of a captured ship to pay monthly wages to one of the sailors, in order to induce him to become a hostage, was held binding on the owners, although they abandoned the ship and cargo. *Yates v. Hall*, 1 T.R. 73. A seaman at monthly wages, who is impressed or enters from a merchant ship into the royal navy during a voyage is not entitled to wages to the time of his quitting the ship, unless the voyage be completed.

Anon. coram Lord Ellenborough, at Guildhall, December 11th, 1806.

Action for seaman's wages: The plaintiff entered on board the defendant's ship at Shields, and was to have the monthly wages of £6, 3s. The ship was bound to Gibraltar with a cargo of coals, and she arrived there in safety. She then sailed for Zante, where she was to take in a cargo, with which she was to return to England. In the course of this voyage, the plaintiff was impressed; and before it was completed the ship was captured. The defend-[321]-ant had paid into Court the amount of the plaintiff's wages to Gibraltar; and the question was, whether anything more was due? On the part of the plaintiff, it was contended that by virtue of stat.

2 Geo. II. c. 36, s. 13, he was entitled to recover his wages from his leaving Gibraltar to the period of his being impressed. It is thereby enacted 'that nothing in that Act contained shall extend, or be construed to extend, to debar any seaman or mariner belonging to any merchant ship or vessel, from entering or being entered into the service of his Majesty, his heirs, &c. on board of any of his or their ships or vessels; nor shall such seaman or mariner for such entry forfeit the wages due to him during the term of his service in such merchant ship or vessel.' And even before the passing of that statute, it was held by Holt, C. J. (*Wiggins v. Ingleton*, 2 Ld. Raym. 1211) that an impressed seaman is entitled to his wages *pro tanto*. It followed, that the plaintiff was entitled to payment at the time when he left the ship, and therefore that he could not be affected by the subsequent casualties of the voyage. But Lord Ellenborough held, that the plaintiff was not placed in a better situation than the other seamen; and was not entitled to any apportionment of wages for his service during a voyage which had not been completed.

Version 2: 6 Espinasse 129[1]

This was an action brought by the Plaintiff private sailor to recover the amount of his wages on a voyage from *London* to the *Baltick* [sic] and back. The sum claimed was partly for monthly wages, according to articles which he had signed, and further sum claimed under these circumstances. Two sailors, part of the crew, had deserted ship, and the master (the Defendant), not able to supply their places at *Cronstadt* promised to divide among the crew, in addition to their wages, the wages due to the two men who deserted.

[130] Upon this being claimed, it was objected, That any engagement by the master for a larger sum than was stipulated for by the articles was void and the case of *Harris v Watson* Peake NP Cases p 72 cited.

It was answered, That this case was very different from the case cited: That this engagement was made before the ship sailed on her voyage home; it was made under no coercion, from the apprehension of danger, nor extorted from the Captain; but a voluntary offer on his part for extraordinary service.

Lord Ellenborough ruled, That the Plaintiff could not recover this part of his demand. His Lordship said, That he recognized the principle of the case of *Harris v Watson* as founded on just and proper policy. When the Defendant entered on board the ship, he stipulated to do all the work his situation called upon him to do. Here the voyage was to the *Baltick* and back, not to *Cronstadt* only; if the voyage had then terminated, the sailors might have made what terms they pleased. If any part of the crew had died, would not the remainder have been forced to work the ship home? If that accident would have left them liable to do the whole work without any extraordinary remuneration, why should not desertion or casualty equally demand it?

Verdict for the monthly wages only.

Hartley v Ponsonby (1857) 119 ER 1471

Facts and issues

Seventeen seamen refused to re-board a ship (*The Mobile*) at Port Philip, Victoria that they had contracted to sail over a period of three years from Liverpool, United Kingdom to Port Philip then to various destinations in Asia before returning to Liverpool. With 17 seamen gone, the captain,

1 Isaac Espinasse, *Reports and Cases Ruled and Argued at Nisi Prius* (vol 6) (via Google Books), Preface, p v.

Ponsonby, promised to pay the remaining 19 seamen, including Hartley, a substantial sum of money if they completed the journey to Bombay, where additional mariners could be hired. The trip to Bombay was particularly treacherous; however, the ship successfully docked in Bombay, where more seamen were hired and the ship continued to Liverpool. Upon arrival at Liverpool, the seamen, including Hartley sued the captain for the promised sum.

The issue was whether there was fresh consideration provided by the seamen to make the captain's additional promise binding. At trial, a jury found in favour of the seamen. Ponsonby sought to challenge the outcome.

Decision

Jury decision affirmed: the seamen did provide additional consideration to make the captain's promise binding.

Lord Campbell CJ at 1473:

> I think that this verdict should stand. The answer given by the jury ... imports to my mind that for the ship to go to sea with so few hands was dangerous to life. If so, it was not incumbent on the plaintiff to perform the work; and he was in the condition of a free man. There was therefore a consideration for the contract; and the captain made it without coercion. This is therefore a voluntary agreement upon sufficient consideration. This decision will not conflict with any former decisions. In *The Araminta (Feran)* (1 Spinks' Ece. & Adm. Rep. 229) Dr. Lushington says: 'I do not wish it to be inferred from anything I now say, that mariners, having completed the voyage outwards, are compellable to make the return voyage when the number of the crew is so small that risk of life may be incurred.' In *Harris v. Carter* (3 E. & B. 559) there was no such risk. As to the weight of evidence, the evidence was conflicting: but my brother Erle is not dissatisfied with the verdict.

Per Coleridge J at 1473:

> I am of the same opinion, and for the same reasons. I understand the finding of the jury to be, that the ship was unseaworthy; and that, owing to the excessive labour which would be imposed, it was not reasonable to require the mariners to go to sea. If they were not bound to go, they were free to make a new contract: and the master was justified in hiring them on the best terms he could make. It may be that the plaintiff took advantage of his position to make a hard bargain; but there was no duress.

Per Erle J at 1473:

> I am of the same opinion. I was deeply impressed with the consequence of not holding the plaintiff liable to perform his original engagement. But there is a point of danger at which it becomes unreasonable for mariners to be required to go on. That is a question for a jury. The mariners, not being bound to go on, were to all intents and purposes free, and might make the best contract they could.

Per Crompton J at 1473:

> The jury have found that this was a free bargain. As regards public policy, it would be very dangerous to lay down that, under all circumstances and at any risk of life, seamen are bound to proceed on a voyage. The jury have found in this case (and, I think, upon the evidence, correctly) that it was not reasonable to require the seamen to go on. Where, from a ship being

> short-handed, it would be [1474] unsafe for the seamen to go to sea, they become free to make any new contract that they like.

The rule was discharged.

13.3.2 Contractual modification and the concept of practical benefit

Given the difficulties in identifying fresh consideration to support a modification to an existing contract, some judges have developed the concept of a 'practical benefit' as a form of fresh consideration. The following cases explore the (limited) development of the concept in England and Australia.

Williams v Roffey Bros & Nicholls (Contractors) Ltd [1991] 1 QB 1

Facts and issues

Williams, a carpenter, entered into a contract with Roffey Bros Ltd for Williams to carry out carpentry work for £20,000 to refurbish 27 apartments that Roffey Bros had agreed to perform by way of another contract with the Shepherds Bush Housing Association Ltd. The contract between Roffey Bros and Shepherds Bush contained a 'penalty clause' that meant delays in the delivery of refurbished apartments would require Roffey Bros to pay Shepherds Bush. When it was clear that Williams would not deliver all of the apartments on time, Roffey Bros agreed to a further payment of £10,300 to ensure on-time delivery. Williams failed to complete all of the apartments but sued for the value of those that had been completed. The issue was whether there was 'fresh' consideration provided by Williams for the promise by Roffey Bros of an additional £10,300. At trial, Williams succeeded.

Decision

Appeal dismissed: yes, there was 'fresh' consideration provided by Williams.

Per Glidewell LJ at 10:

> ... The judge quoted and accepted the evidence of Mr. Cottrell to the effect that a main contractor who agrees too low a price with a subcontractor is acting contrary to his own interests. He will never get the job finished without paying more money. The judge therefore concluded:
>
> > In my view where the original subcontract price is too low, and the parties subsequently agree that additional moneys shall be paid to the subcontractor, this agreement is in the interests of both parties. This is what happened in the present case, and in my opinion the agreement of 9 April 1986 does not fail for lack of consideration.
>
> [15] ... the present state of the law on this subject can be expressed in the following proposition:
>
> (i) if A has entered into a contract with B to do work for, or to supply goods or services to, B in return for payment by B; and

(ii) at some stage before A has completely performed his obligations under the contract B has reason to doubt whether A will, or will be able to, complete his side of the bargain; and
(iii) B thereupon promises A an additional payment in return for A's promise to perform [16] his contractual obligations on time; and
(iv) as a result of giving his promise, B obtains in practice a benefit, or obviates a disbenefit; and
(v) B's promise is not given as a result of economic duress or fraud on the part of A; then
(vi) the benefit to B is capable of being consideration for B's promise, so that the promise will be legally binding.

As I have said, Mr. Evans accepts that in the present case by promising to pay the extra £10,300 his client secured benefits. There is no finding, and no suggestion, that in this case the promise was given as a result of fraud or duress.

If it be objected that the propositions above contravene the principle in *Stilk v. Myrick*, 2 Camp. 317, I answer that in my view they do not; they refine, and limit the application of that principle, but they leave the principle unscathed e.g. where B secures no benefit by his promise. It is not in my view surprising that a principle enunciated in relation to the rigours of seafaring life during the Napoleonic wars should be subjected during the succeeding 180 years to a process of refinement and limitation in its application in the present day.

It is therefore my opinion that on his findings of fact in the present case, the judge was entitled to hold, as he did, that the defendants' promise to pay the extra £10,300 was supported by valuable consideration, and thus constituted an enforceable agreement.

Per Russell LJ at 19:

... True it was that the plaintiff did not undertake to do any work additional to that which he had originally undertaken to do but the terms upon which he was to carry out the work were varied and, in my judgment, that variation was supported by consideration which a pragmatic approach to the true relationship between the parties readily demonstrates.

For my part I wish to make it plain that I do not base my judgment upon any reservation as to the correctness of the law long ago enunciated in *Stilk v. Myrick*. A gratuitous promise, pure and simple, remains unenforceable unless given under seal. But where, as in this case, a party undertakes to make a payment because by so doing it will gain an advantage arising out of the continuing relationship with the promisee the new bargain will not fail for want of consideration.

Per Purchas LJ at 21:

... In my judgment, therefore, the rule in *Stilk v. Myrick*, 2 Camp 317 remains valid as a matter of principle, namely that a contract not under seal must be supported by consideration. Thus, where the agreement upon which reliance is placed provides that an extra payment is to be made for work to be done by the payee which he is already obliged to perform then unless some other consideration is detected to support the agreement to pay the extra sum that agreement will not be enforceable. The two cases, *Harris v. Watson*, Peake 102 and *Stilk v. Myrick*, 2 Camp 317 involved circumstances of a very special nature, namely the extraordinary conditions existing at the turn of the 18th century under which seamen had to serve their contracts of employment on the high seas. There were strong public policy grounds at that time to protect the master and owners of a ship from being held to ransom by disaffected crews. Thus, the decision that the promise to pay extra wages even in the circumstances established in those cases, was not supported by consideration is readily understandable. Of course, conditions today on the high seas have changed dramatically and it is at least questionable, as Mr. Makey submitted, whether these cases might not well have been decided differently if they were tried today. The modern cases tend to depend more upon the defence of duress in a commercial context rather than lack of consideration for the second agreement. In the present case the question of duress does not arise. ... Nevertheless, the court is more ready in the presence of this defence being available in the commercial context to look for mutual advantages which would amount to sufficient consideration to support the second agreement under which the extra money is paid.

[...]

[23] ... I consider that the modern approach to the question of consideration would be that where there were benefits derived by each party to a contract of variation even though one party did not suffer a detriment this would not be fatal to the establishing of sufficient consideration to support the agreement. If both parties benefit from an agreement it is not necessary that each also suffers a detriment.

13.3.3 Practical benefit in Australia

The following case is a classic example of the expansion of the common law through persuasive precedent. Although the case's authority is limited by it being a single-judge decision of a superior court, the structure and method of argument provides a basis for further judicial development in the Australian context.

Musumeci v Winadell Pty Ltd (1994) 34 NSWLR 723

Facts and issues

The Musumeci family (wife and husband) operated a fruit and vegetable shop in space rented within a shopping centre owned by Winadell Pty Ltd. When Winadell allowed a competing (and larger) fruit and vegetable shop to open in the shopping centre, the Musumecis asked for a rent reduction and new lease to cover the loss of customers. Winadell refused a new lease but did offer a rent reduction (of one-third). Despite ongoing disputes about the rent (including about whether there even was a rent reduction), the Musumecis paid and Winadell accepted a lower rental payment for around 18 months. At this stage, Winadell purported to terminate the lease, remove the Musumecis from the premises and demanded the Musumecis pay the outstanding rent payments. The Musumecis refused. An issue was whether the Musumecis provided additional consideration that would make Winadell's promised rent reduction binding.

Decision

Judgment for the plaintiff: yes, the Musumecis did provide additional consideration.

Per Santow J at 738:

Practical benefit or detriment as consideration?

... [T]he plaintiffs' contention that consideration was in fact provided for the rent concession ... relies upon the decision of the Court of Appeal in *Williams v Roffey Bros & Nicholls (Contractors) Ltd* [1991] 1 QB 1. That case held that A's promise to B to perform an existing duty owed to B may be consideration, notwithstanding the rule that a promise to perform an existing duty is not consideration. This rule is avoided only where the promisor in fact obtains in practice a benefit or obviates a 'disbenefit', from the promise or its performance, so enabling the promisee's reciprocal promise to be enforced. This is despite such benefit (or avoidance of disbenefit) not being expressly promised.

In that case, the principal contractor B agreed to pay a subcontractor A an additional sum over and above what was payable under the subcontract in D order to secure the benefit of more assured performance from A. Thus the benefits which the defendant B was said to have obtained by so securing the plaintiff A's performance were twofold. First, there was a measure of protection against the risk that, as a result of the main contract to refurbish, B would be liable to pay liquidated damages if A failed to perform when that was a real risk and, secondly, avoidance of trouble and expense in finding a replacement for A.

Essentially the plaintiffs in the present case have to overcome the difficulty that, if a formal binding forbearance to sue were not the consideration, then the plaintiffs might be said to be merely promising, as consideration, to perform a contractual duty already owed to the lessor and nothing more. If so, this could not be good consideration: *Stilk v Myrick* (1809) 2 Camp 317; 170 ER 1168. This decision has not been over-ruled, though is possibly explicable today as denying enforcement to a promise exacted by duress. The duress was by threatening desertion and thus a breach of contract, so as to secure more advantageous terms to perform an existing contractual duty. There was, after all, a similar practical benefit to the shipowner (or the Captain) from performance by the sailors of their duty to complete the voyage (despite desertion by two of them) of the sort that would have satisfied the *Williams v Roffey* test. Thus, in *Wigan v Edwards* (at 594; 512) Mason J said:

> The general rule is that a promise to perform an existing duty is no consideration, at least when the promise is made by a party to a pre-existing contract, when it is made to the promisee under that contract, and it is to do no more than the promisor is bound to do under that contract. The rule expresses the concept that the new promise, indistinguishable from the old, is an illusory consideration. And it gives no comfort to a party who by merely threatening a breach of contract seeks to secure an additional contractual benefit from the other party on the footing that the first party's new promise of performance will provide sufficient consideration for that benefit.

[740] . . . In truth, there has been a continuing trend to side-step the artificial results of a strict doctrine of consideration. Consideration did not need to be adequate. The fact that the promisor is under an existing duty to A is no matter if the promise be repeated to B; *Pao On v Lau Yiu Long* [1980] AC 614 at 632. A deed dispenses with consideration altogether. And promissory and related equitable estoppels may be called in aid, when consideration is lacking but it would be unconscionable for a voluntary promisor to escape altogether. Though affording lesser protection than a contract for consideration, by reason of the likely inherent temporality of the suspension of the promisor's rights, equity nonetheless provided a flexible remedy, moulded to the circumstances, under the general notion of unconscionability: see Carter and Harland, *Contract Law in Australia*, 2nd ed (1991) at 119-138. This has evoked the comment that the situations which give rise to estoppel should, at least in Australia, be dealt with under its more flexible doctrines and remedies than by an artificial extension of the doctrine of consideration: see Halyk 'Consideration, Practical Benefits and Promissory Estoppel: Enforcement of Contract Modification in light of *Williams v Roffey Brothers*' (1991) 55 Sask L Rev 393. I discuss this issue later in this judgment.

Glidewell LJ in *Williams v Roffey* (at 15–16) departed from this traditional approach, when allowing consequential practical benefits to suffice that were never explicitly the subject of the parties' promised bargain. He did so in reasoning encapsulated in the following five elements leading to the conclusion in (vi) [see **13.3.2** above for the direct quote].

[741] . . . So far as element (iii) is concerned, conceptually it can make no difference whether B promises A an additional payment for A's promise of performance or grants A the equivalent

concession of promising a reduction in A's payment obligations, where these pre-exist. To reflect this, it is suggested element (iii) should have added the words 'or other concession (such as reducing A's original obligation)' immediately after 'payment'. (In the discussion which follows I refer to A and B in the context of Glidewell LJ's proposition.)

In either case the question is whether such a payment is nonetheless made for an illusory consideration in that it buys merely a promise by the same party to perform its existing contractual obligation. But should Australian courts follow the English Court of Appeal, in taking a more pragmatic approach to the true relationship between the parties in accepting practical benefits as consideration? And, if so, subject to what qualifications? I deal with that basic issue below.

Williams v Roffey – should it be followed in Australia?

There are three reasons which might be put as to why a contract to perform an existing obligation should not be enforced.

First, to protect the promisor from extortion, such as may result from threatening to breach a contract in order to exact a concession. Thus, for example, the two dollar unguaranteed corporate tenant in a falling market, whose directors threaten to walk away from a lease, unless rent concessions are conceded . . .

[742] [D]oes it follow that, because there is not as yet a fully developed doctrine for the avoidance of contracts on the grounds of economic duress . . ., that therefore strict consideration should remain the discrimen for enforceability of contractual modifications? There are a number of reasons why not. If it be assumed that the underlying concern is to prevent coercive modifications, the traditional notion of consideration does not perform that role very well. Its very certainty is bought at the price of inflexibility. This produces a real disincentive to re-negotiate a contract which changed circumstances have made unduly onerous. This is especially if the outcome is likely to be unenforceable by reason of lack of consideration. Even the presence of consideration does not preclude there having been economic duress inducing the contract. Consideration expressed in formalistic terms of one dollar can indeed actually cloak duress rather than expose it.

. . . Indeed the very fact that a concession is extended by B, without extortion, supports an inference, though by no means conclusively, that consideration from A, in a real and practical sense, has moved that concession. The law is increasingly tending away from the artificial towards the substantive. Such a practical notion of consideration reflects that trend. It is a notorious fact, that concessions are made to avoid the necessity for enforcing a contract whose performance is in jeopardy. It would indeed be far more artificial to treat such concessional modification to the contract as moved by a consideration consisting of cancellation of the old contract in return for the [745] new, an approach which the Court of Appeal in *Williams v Roffey* expressly and correctly disclaimed.

. . . What then is a sufficient practical benefit to B, so as to take the situation beyond a wholly gratuitous promise by B? . . . It is indeed inherent in the situation posed by *Williams v Roffey* itself (and indeed in *Stilk's* case itself, despite the decision). There the subcontractor A's performance was worth more to B (the principal contractor) than likely damages, even taking into account the cost of any concession to obtain greater assurance of the performance. [. . .]

To all this it might be said that such a relaxation of the doctrine of [746] consideration, if adopted, will discourage concessions, since they would then too readily become legally binding throughout the term of the contract. But the answer to that is simply [sic] enough. The courts should be alert to distinguish promises intended by their terms to be no more than temporary, or truly ex gratia, concessions, for example fi [sic] expressly limited to a period of difficult circumstances for performance by the other party, which may not be permanent. And 'care must also be taken not to inefr [sic] anterior promises from conduct which represents no more than an adjustment of their relationship in the light of changing circumstances': per McHugh JA in *Integrated Computer Services Pty Ltd v Digital Equipment Corporation (Aust) Pty Ltd* (1988) 5 BPR 11,110 at 11,117.

... Accordingly, I [a]m satisfied to conclude that, subject to the earlier re-casting of the five elements of Glidewell LJ, *Williams v Roffey* should be [747] followed in allowing a practical benefit or detriment to suffice as consideration. For convenience, I set out below the re-cast elements, changes indicated by italics. I recognise that they will be further refined in light of experience. One particular issue is the extent to which a benefit or detriment, said to be 'practical', as distinct from explicitly bargained for, must nonetheless be consistent with, and not extraneous to, the bargaining process, as at least its intended result if not necessarily its moving force:

The present state of the law on this subject can be expressed in the following proposition:

(i) If A has entered into a contract with B to do work for, or to supply goods or services to, B in return for the payment by B, and

(ii) At some stage before A has completely performed his obligations under the contract B has reason to doubt whether A will, or be able to, complete his side of the bargain, and

(iii) B thereupon promises A an additional payment *or other concession (such as reducing A's original obligation)* in return for A's promise to perform this contractual obligation at the time, and

(iv) (a) As a result of giving his promise B obtains in practice a benefit, or obviates a disbenefit *provided that A's performance, having regard to what has been so obtained, is capable of being viewed by B as worth more to B than any likely remedy against A (allowing for any defences or cross-claims), taking into account the cost to B of any such payment or concession to obtain greater assurance of A's performance*, or

(b) *as a result of giving his promise, A suffers a detriment (or obviates a benefit) provided that A is thereby foregoing the opportunity of not performing the original contract, in circumstances where such non-performance, taking into account B's likely remedy against A (and allowing for any defences or cross-claims) is capable of being viewed by A as worth more to A than performing that contract, in the absence of B's promised payment or concession to A.*

(v) B's promise is not given as a result of economic duress or fraud *or undue influence or unconscionable conduct* on the part of A *nor is it induced as a result of unfair pressure on the part of A, having regard to the circumstances*, then,

(vi) The benefit to B *or the detriment to A* is capable of being consideration for B's promise, so that the promise will be legally binding.

Application of William v Roffey to present circumstances:

Applying that reasoning to the present circumstances, the practical benefit that the lessor gained from the concession of lower future rental, was argued to be the enhanced capacity of the plaintiffs to stay in occupation, able to carry out their future reduced lease obligations, notwithstanding substantial newly introduced competition from the other tenant. What this practical benefit consists of therefore is enhanced capacity for the lessor to maintain a [748] full shopping centre with another competing tenant, when the original tenant is no longer at so great a risk of defaulting and more likely to stay. That is a practical benefit, even though legally there be no inhibition on the lessor to introduce new competition.

... Thus I find that the particular practical benefit here, was that the lessor had greater assurance of the lessees staying in occupation and maintaining viability and capacity to perform by reason of their reduction in their rent, notwithstanding the introduction of a major, much larger competing tenant.

[749] The practical detriment to the lessees lay in risking their capacity to survive against a much stronger competitor, by staying in occupancy under their lease, rather than walking away at the cost of damages, if the lessees' defences, including under the *Contracts Review Act* 1980, were unsuccessful. From the lessees' actions, it is evident that without the rent concession, the latter course was viewed as more likely to be in the lessees' interests than staying in occupation.

... I do accept that practical removal of the threat of litigation can and should be treated as a part of the more general context earlier described, and relevant for the purpose of testing fulfilment of the proviso to element (iv) of the earlier formulation. Thus it is true that the lessees' litigation, like industrial unrest in the cases referred to earlier, was, in the events that happened, effectively removed as a risk, even if the actual bargaining process in theory preserved this weapon for the lessees.

I am satisfied in the circumstances that the remaining elements set out earlier are made out, including element (v), (or more precisely, absence of any element of extortion in the sense there set out). The lessees' reaction to the original introduction of a competing, powerful tenant, with the perceived capacity to wipe them out, was to threaten redress to legal remedies. In the circumstances that was not coercive, but a simply defensive, if fairly aggressive, reaction designed to elicit a constructive response.

As to element (iv) which, in its proviso, is designed to eliminate 'wholly' gratuitous promises, there is evidence before me that the plaintiffs' goodwill was at risk of destruction by the introduction of the much stronger competitor on a concessional basis, unless the rent reduction were forthcoming. That makes it a proper inference for me to draw that there was indeed a *sufficient* practical benefit, procured by maintaining the plaintiffs as viable tenants on the promise of reduced rental. This is compared to the evidently less attractive alternative of finding another tenant and suing for any rent shortfall, particularly where the lessees might plead a number of foreshadowed defences and cross-claims.

13.3.4 Part-payment of debts: the rule in *Foakes v Beer*

Similar to *Stilk v Myrick*, the case of *Foakes v Beer* has an outsize influence on the challenge to find fresh consideration to support the modification of an existing contract. The case is extracted extensively below in order to highlight the tension between, on the one hand, the importance of precedent and, on the other hand, the need to recognise commercial reality, which is a challenge the courts continue to face today.

Foakes v Beer (1884) 9 App Cas 605

Facts and issues

Beer successfully sued Foakes and obtained a judgment debt, on which she can claim interest under legislation. In return for a promise by Beer not to sue, Foakes promised to pay £500 immediately and the remainder of the debt by way of instalments. When Foakes paid back the equivalent of the judgment debt, Beer sued for the additional interest. The issue was whether there was 'fresh' consideration by Foakes to make Beer's additional promise binding.

Decision

Appeal dismissed: there was no 'fresh' consideration.

Per Lord Blackburn at 615:

> It would have been easy to have expressed, in unmistakeable words, that on payment down of £500, and punctual payment at the rate of £300 a year till £2090 19s. was paid, the judgment should not be enforced either for principal or interest; or language might have been used which should equally clearly have expressed that, though time was to be given, interest was to be paid in addition to the instalments. The words actually used are such that I think it is quite possible that the two parties put a different construction on the words at the time; but I think the words 'till the said sum of £2090 19s. shall have been fully paid and satisfied' cannot be construed as meaning 'till that sum, with interest from the day judgment was signed, shall have been fully paid and satisfied,' nor can the promise 'not to take any proceedings whatever on the judgment' be cut down to meaning any proceedings except those necessary to enforce payment of interest.
>
> I think, therefore, that it is necessary to consider the ground on which the Court of Appeal did base their judgment, and to say whether the agreement can be enforced. I construe it as accepting and taking £500 in satisfaction of the whole £2090 19s., subject to the condition that unless the balance of the principal debt was paid by the instalments, the whole might be enforced with interest. If, instead of £500 in money, it had been a horse valued at £500, or a promissory note for £500, the authorities are that it would have been a good satisfaction, but it is said to be otherwise as it was money.
>
> This is a question, I think, of difficulty.
>
> In Coke, Littleton 212 b, Lord Coke says: 'where the condition is for payment of £20, the obligor or feoffor cannot at the time appointed pay a lesser sum in satisfaction of the whole, because *it is apparent* that a lesser sum of money *cannot* be a satisfaction of a greater . . . If the obligor or feoffor pay a lesser sum either before the day or at another place than is limited by the condition, and the obligee or feoffee receiveth it, this is a good satisfaction.' For this he cites *Pinnel's Case*. That was an action on a bond for £16, conditioned for the payment of £8 10*s.* on the 11th of November 1600. Plea that [616] defendant, at plaintiff's request, before the said day, to wit, on the 1st of October, paid to the plaintiff £5 2*s.* 2*d.*, which the plaintiff accepted in full satisfaction of the £8 10*s.* The plaintiff had judgment for the insufficient pleading. But though this was so, Lord Coke reports that it was resolved by the whole Court of Common Pleas
>
>> that payment of a lesser sum on the day in satisfaction of a greater cannot be any satisfaction for the whole, because it appears to the judges that by no possibility a lesser sum can be a satisfaction to the plaintiff for a greater sum: but the gift of a horse, hawk, or robe, &c., in satisfaction is good, for it shall be intended that a horse, hawk, or robe, &c., might be more beneficial to the plaintiff than the money, in respect of some circumstance, or otherwise the plaintiff would not have accepted of it in satisfaction. But when the whole sum is due, by no intendment the acceptance of parcel can be a satisfaction to the plaintiff; but in the case at bar it was resolved that the payment and acceptance of parcel before the day in satisfaction of the whole would be a good satisfaction in regard of circumstance of time; for peradventure parcel of it before the day would be more beneficial to him than the whole at the day, and the value of the satisfaction is not material; so if I am bound in £20 to pay you £10 at Westminster, and

> you request me to pay you £5 at the day at York, and you will accept it in full satisfaction for the whole £10, it is a good satisfaction for the whole, for the expenses to pay it at York is sufficient satisfaction.

There are two things here resolved. First, that where a matter paid and accepted in satisfaction of a debt certain might by any possibility be more beneficial to the creditor than his debt, the Court will not inquire into the adequacy of the consideration. If the creditor, without any fraud, accepted it in satisfaction when it was not a sufficient satisfaction it was his own fault. And that payment before the day might be more beneficial, and consequently that the plea was in substance good, and this must have been decided in the case.

There is a second point stated to have been resolved, viz.: 'That payment of a lesser sum on the day cannot be any satisfaction of the whole, because it appears to the judges that by no possibility a lesser sum can be a satisfaction to the plaintiff for a [617] greater sum.' This was certainly not necessary for the decision of the case; but though the resolution of the Court of Common Pleas was only a dictum, it seems to me clear that Lord Coke deliberately adopted the dictum, and the great weight of his authority makes it necessary to be cautious before saying that what he deliberately adopted as law was a mistake. . . . [N]otwithstanding the very high authority of Lord [618] Coke, I think it is not the fact that to accept prompt payment of a part only of a liquidated demand, can never be more beneficial than to insist on payment of the whole. And if it be not the fact, it cannot be apparent to the judges.

I will first examine the authorities. . . . Strangely enough it seems long to have been thought that if the defendant kept within reasonable bounds neither he nor his lawyers were to blame in getting time in this way by a sham plea — that a chattel was given and accepted in satisfaction of the debt. The recognised forms were giving and accepting in satisfaction a beaver hat: *Young v. Rudd* 5 Mod. 86, 87 ER 135, or a pipe of wine (3 Chit. Plead. 7th (Ed.) 92). All this is now antiquated. But whilst it continued to be the practice, the pleas founded on the first part of the resolution in *Pinnel's Case* were very common, and that law was perfectly trite. No one for a moment supposed that a beaver hat was really given and accepted; but every one knew that the law was that if it was really given and accepted it was a good satisfaction. But special pleas founded on the other resolution in *Pinnel's Case*, on what I have ventured to call the dictum, were certainly not common. I doubt if a real defence of this sort was ever specially pleaded. When there really was a question as to whether a debt was satisfied by a payment of a smaller sum the defendant pleaded the general issue, and if it was proved to the satisfaction of the jury that a smaller sum had been paid and accepted in satisfaction of a greater, if objection was raised the jury might perhaps . . . find that the circumstances were such that the legal effect was to be as if the whole was paid down and a portion thrown back as a god's-penny. This, however, seems to me to be an unsatisfactory and [619] artificial way of avoiding the effect of the dictum, and it could not be applied to such an agreement as that now before this House.

For whatever reason it was, I know of no case in which the question was raised whether a payment of a lesser sum could be satisfaction of a liquidated demand from *Pinnel's Case* down to *Cumber v. Wane*, 5 Geo. 1, a period of 115 years.

[622] . . . What principally weighs with me in thinking that Lord Coke made a mistake of fact is my conviction that all men [sic] of business, whether merchants or tradesmen, do every day recognise and act on the ground that prompt payment of a part of their demand may be more beneficial to them than it would be to insist on their rights and enforce payment of the whole. Even where the debtor is perfectly solvent, and sure to pay at last, this often is so. Where the credit of the debtor is doubtful it must be more so. I had persuaded myself that there was no such long-continued action on this dictum as to render it improper in this House to reconsider

the question. I had written my reasons for [623] so thinking; but as they were not satisfactory to the other noble and learned Lords who heard the case, I do not now repeat them nor persist in them.

I assent to the judgment proposed, though it is not that which I had originally thought proper.

The Earl of Selborne and Lord Fitzgerald substantially agreed with Lord Blackburn. Lord Watson did not agree with their Lordships' construction of the agreement, but did concur with the conclusion that the agreement was 'nudum pactum' and thus the appeal should be dismissed.

QUESTIONS

(1) On what basis is a distinction drawn between *Stilk* and *Hartley*? What are the factual differences between the cases? Are these 'significant'?

(2) Is the 'practical benefit' test an objective or subjective test? Should it be?

(3) What are the limitations with relying on duress (even in its modern conception) as the bulwark against unethical demands placed by one contracting party on another contracting party after the contract has been formed?

(4) What is the appropriate authority to be placed on 'old' cases? Does a strict conception of *stare decisis* provide stability and certainty to the law or does the adherence to outdated rules undermine the authority of law more broadly?

(5) What role should courts have in determining the 'views' of business people when determining legal rules? Is this consistent with an 'objective' approach to contracts or a perversion of the 'objectivity' of judges?

13.4 Statutory powers of variation

Concepts	Short explanation	Relevant authorities	*Principles* text*
Statutory powers of variation	Statutory alternatives to enforcing variations	National Credit Code, *National Consumer Credit Protection Act 2009* (Cth) Sch 1 ss 72, 74 *Independent Contractors Act 2006* (Cth) ss 3–5, 12–17 *Independent Contractors Regulation 2016* (Cth) reg 7	Chapter 13: 13.20

* Consult the corresponding section(s) of the *Principles* text for more detail.

Given the challenges faced by parties in attempting to enforce variations to contracts, legislatures developed some statutory alternatives. Relevant reforms include the Australian Consumer Law (see **Chapters 9**, **18** and **20** for extracts from relevant legislation) and the *Contracts Review Act 1980* (NSW) (see **Chapter 9** for extracts from relevant legislation).

Two novel statutory powers in relation to consumer credit and independent contractors are extracted below.

13.4.1 Key examples of statutory variation powers

National Credit Code, *National Consumer Credit Protection Act 2009* (Cth) Sch 1, ss 72, 74

72 Changes on grounds of hardship

Hardship notice

(1) If a debtor considers that he or she is or will be unable to meet his or her obligations under a credit contract, the debtor may give the credit provider notice (a hardship notice), orally or in writing, of the debtor's inability to meet the obligations.

[. . .]

Further information

(2) Within 21 days after the day of receiving the debtor's hardship notice, the credit provider may give the debtor notice, orally or in writing, requiring the debtor to give the credit provider specified information within 21 days of the date of the notice stated in the notice. The information specified must be relevant to deciding:

- **(a)** whether the debtor is or will be unable to meet the debtor's obligations under the contract; or
- **(b)** how to change the contract if the debtor is or will be unable to meet those obligations.

(3) The debtor must comply with the requirement.

Note: The credit provider need not agree to change the credit contract, especially if the credit provider:

- **(a)** does not believe there is a reasonable cause (such as illness or unemployment) for the debtor's inability to meet his or her obligations; or
- **(b)** reasonably believes the debtor would not be able to meet his or her obligations under the contract even if it were changed.

Notice of decision on changing credit contract

(4) The credit provider must, before the end of the period identified under subsection (5), give the debtor a notice:

- **(a)** that is in the form (if any) prescribed by the regulations and records the fact that the credit provider and the debtor have agreed to change the credit contract; or
- **(b)** that is in the form (if any) prescribed by the regulations and states:
  - **(i)** the credit provider and the debtor have not agreed to change the credit contract; and
  - **(ii)** the reasons why they have not agreed; and
  - **(iii)** the name and contact details of the approved external dispute resolution scheme of which the credit provider is a member; and
  - **(iv)** the debtor's rights under that scheme.

Civil penalty: 2,000 penalty units.

(5) The credit provider must give the notice before the end of the period identified using the table.

	Period for giving notice	
	If:	**The period is:**
1	The credit provider does not require information under subsection (2)	21 days after the day of receiving the hardship notice
2	The credit provider requires information under subsection (2) but does not receive any information in compliance with the requirement	28 days after the stated date of the notice under subsection (2)
3	The credit provider requires information under subsection (2) and receives information in compliance with the requirement	21 days after the day of receiving the information

[...]

74 Changes by court

(1) If the credit provider does not change the credit contract as a result of a hardship notice by the debtor, the debtor may apply to the court to change the terms of the credit contract.

(2) The court may, after allowing the applicant, the credit provider and any guarantor a reasonable opportunity to be heard:

(a) by order change the credit contract (but not so as to reduce the amount ultimately payable by the debtor to the credit provider under the contract), and make such other orders as it thinks fit; or

(b) refuse to change the credit contract.

(3) The court may, if it thinks it appropriate in the circumstances, stay any enforcement proceedings under the credit contract, and make such other orders as it thinks fit, until the application has been determined.

Independent Contractors Act 2006 (Cth) ss 3–5, 12–17

3 Objects of this Act

(1) The principal objects of this Act are:

(a) to protect the freedom of independent contractors to enter into services contracts; and

(b) to recognise independent contracting as a legitimate form of work arrangement that is primarily commercial; and

(c) to prevent interference with the terms of genuine independent contracting arrangements.

(2) The Act achieves these objects, principally, by providing for the rights, entitlements, obligations and liabilities of parties to services contracts to be governed by the terms of those contracts, subject to:

(a) the rules of common law and equity as applying in relation to those contracts; and

(b) the laws of the Commonwealth as applying in relation to those contracts; and

(c) the laws of the States and Territories as applying in relation to those contracts, other (in general) than any such laws that confer or impose rights, entitlements, obligations or liabilities of a kind more commonly associated with employment relationships.

4 Definitions

In this Act:

Commonwealth authority means:

(a) a body corporate established for a public purpose by or under a law of the Commonwealth; or

(b) a body corporate:

(i) incorporated under a law of the Commonwealth or a State or Territory; and

(ii) in which the Commonwealth has a controlling interest.

constitutional corporation means a corporation to which paragraph 51(xx) of the Constitution applies.

Court means the Federal Court of Australia or the Federal Circuit Court of Australia.

exclusion provisions means subsections 7(1) and 10(1).

independent contractor is not limited to a natural person.

organisation means an organisation that is registered or an association that is recognised under the *Fair Work (Registered Organisations) Act 2009*.

services contract has the meaning given by section 5.

5 Services contract

General meaning

(1) A ***services contract*** is a contract for services:

(a) to which an independent contractor is a party; and

(b) that relates to the performance of work by the independent contractor; and

(c) that has the requisite constitutional connection specified in subsection (2).

Note: Conditions or collateral arrangements relating to a services contract may be taken to be part of the services contract: see subsection (4).

The requisite constitutional connection

(2) A contract for services has the ***requisite constitutional connection*** if:

(a) at least one party to the contract is:

(i) a constitutional corporation; or

(ii) the Commonwealth or a Commonwealth authority; or

(iii) a body corporate incorporated in a Territory in Australia; or

(b) one or more of the following subparagraphs is satisfied:

(i) the work concerned is wholly or principally to be performed in a Territory in Australia;

(ii) the contract was entered into in a Territory in Australia;

(iii) at least one party to the contract is a natural person who is resident in, or a body corporate that has its principal place of business in, a Territory in Australia.

(3) Without limiting its effect apart from this subsection, subparagraph (2)(a)(i) also has the effect it would have if the reference to a constitutional corporation were, by express provision, confined to a constitutional corporation that has entered into the contract for the purposes of the business of the corporation.

Conditions and collateral arrangements

(4) A condition or collateral arrangement that relates to a services contract is taken to be part of that services contract if, were the condition or arrangement itself a contract for services, it would have the requisite constitutional connection.

Part 3 —Unfair contracts

12 Court may review services contract

(1) An application may be made to the Court to review a services contract on either or both of the following grounds:

(a) the contract is unfair;

(b) the contract is harsh.

Note: A proceeding pending in the Federal Circuit Court of Australia may be transferred to the Federal Court of Australia: see Part 5 of the *Federal Circuit Court of Australia Act 1999*.

(2) An application under subsection (1) may be made only by a party to the services contract.

(3) In reviewing a services contract, the Court must only have regard to:

(a) the terms of the contract when it was made; and

(b) to the extent that this Part allows the Court to consider other matters—other matters as existing at the time when the contract was made.

(4) For the purposes of this Part, ***services contract*** includes a contract to vary a services contract.

Note: The effect of subsection (4) is that a contract to vary a services contract can be reviewed under this Part, as the contract to vary will itself be a services contract.

13 Limitation on applications for review of services contracts—prescribed circumstances

An application to review a services contract must not be made under subsection 12(1) in the circumstances prescribed by the regulations.

14 Limitation on applications for review of services contracts—other proceedings in progress

(1) An application to review a services contract must not be made under subsection 12(1) if other review proceedings have been commenced in relation to the services contract, unless the other review proceedings:

(a) have been discontinued by the person who commenced them; or

(b) have failed for want of jurisdiction.

(2) A person must not commence other review proceedings in relation to a services contract if an application to review the contract has been made under subsection 12(1), unless:

(a) the application has been discontinued by the person who made it; or

(b) the proceedings in relation to the application have failed for want of jurisdiction.

(3) In this section:

other review proceedings means proceedings in relation to a services contract:

(a) under a provision of a law of a State or Territory that makes provision as mentioned in paragraph 7(1)(c) and is not affected by the exclusion provisions; or

(b) under a provision of a law of the Commonwealth, or of a State or Territory, that is specified in regulations made for the purposes of this paragraph.

Note: Paragraph 7(1)(c) relates to laws that provide for contracts to be void etc. on an unfairness ground.

15 Powers of Court

(1) In reviewing a services contract in relation to which an application has been made under subsection 12(1), the Court may have regard to:

- **(a)** the relative strengths of the bargaining positions of the parties to the contract and, if applicable, any persons acting on behalf of the parties; and
- **(b)** whether any undue influence or pressure was exerted on, or any unfair tactics were used against, a party to the contract; and
- **(c)** whether the contract provides total remuneration that is, or is likely to be, less than that of an employee performing similar work; and
- **(d)** any other matter that the Court thinks is relevant.

(3) If the Court forms the opinion that a ground referred to in subsection 12(1) is established in relation to the whole or a part of the services contract, the Court must record its opinion, stating whether the opinion relates to the whole or a specified part of the contract.

(4) The Court may form the opinion that a ground referred to in subsection 12(1) is established in relation to the whole or a part of the services contract even if the ground was not canvassed in the application.

Note: An alternative dispute resolution process (for example, mediation) may be used to deal with some or all of the matters in dispute in a proceeding under this Part: see Part 4 of the *Federal Circuit Court of Australia Act 1999* and section 53A of the *Federal Court of Australia Act 1976*.

16 Orders that Court may make

(1) If the Court records an opinion under section 15 in relation to a services contract, the Court may make one or more of the following orders in relation to the opinion:

- **(a)** an order setting aside the whole or a part of the contract;
- **(b)** an order varying the contract.

(2) An order may only be made for the purpose of placing the parties to the services contract as nearly as practicable on such a footing that the ground on which the opinion is based no longer applies.

(3) If an application under this Part is pending, the Court may make an interim order if it considers it is desirable to do so to preserve the position of a party to the services contract.

(4) An order takes effect on the date of the order or a later date specified in the order.

(5) A party to the services contract may apply to the Court to enforce an order by injunction or otherwise as the Court considers appropriate.

(6) Subject to section 14, this section does not limit any other rights of a party to the services contract.

Note 1: The rights of a party to a services contract may be affected by the exclusion provisions.

Note 2: An appeal may be brought to the Federal Court of Australia from a judgment of the Federal Circuit Court of Australia: see section 24 of the *Federal Court of Australia Act 1976*.

17 Costs only where proceeding instituted vexatiously

(1) A party (the ***first party***) to a proceeding (including an appeal) in a matter arising under this Part must not be ordered to pay costs incurred by any other party to the proceeding unless the first party instituted the proceeding vexatiously or without reasonable cause.

(2) Despite subsection (1), if a court hearing a proceeding (including an appeal) in a matter arising under this Part is satisfied that a party (the ***first party***) to the proceeding has, by unreasonable act or omission, caused another party to the proceeding to incur costs in connection with the proceeding, the court may order the first party to pay some or all of those costs.

(3) In this section:

costs includes all legal and professional costs and disbursements, and expenses of witnesses.

Independent Contractors Regulation 2016 (Cth) reg 7

7 Circumstances in which application must not be made to review services contract as harsh or unfair

For the purposes of section 13 of the Act (which prohibits an application to the Court in prescribed circumstances to review a services contract), this section prescribes the circumstances that both of the following apply:

(a) 12 months have passed since the services contract ended;

(b) the Court has not allowed the making of the application after being satisfied that there are exceptional circumstances justifying the making of the application.

13.5 International perspectives

Variation in cross-border commercial sales contracts governed by the *CISG* (see **25.4.1** on *CISG* applicability) is a far less complex matter than under Australian domestic contract law. This is because the *CISG* does not require consideration for contractual formation. Instead, the normal requirements for formation apply to variation agreements (eg offer and acceptance). Thus a 'mere agreement' to modify the contract will be binding upon the parties: art 29 *CISG*. The issues discussed above regarding past consideration and existing legal duty (**13.3.1**) and practical benefit (**13.3.2**) do not arise within the *CISG*. Whether or not there is an objective intent to modify the terms of a contract is not to be inferred lightly.[2] Parties may vary their contract orally or in writing: arts 8(3) and 11 *CISG*. Parties can include a clause to require variation agreements to be in writing. Often referred to as 'no oral modification' (NOM) clauses, these will be effective with two qualifications: the first is that oral evidence will be considered at least to determine the intended effect of the clause to preclude oral evidence; and second, a party may by their conduct be prevented from relying on the NOM clause, if the other party has relied on their conduct, to ensure NOM clauses are not abused. This position is also reflected in art 2.1.18 UNIDROIT Principles.

2 CISG Advisory Council, Opinion No 16: 'Exclusion of the CISG under Art. 6', Rapporteur: Dr L Spagnolo, Comment [2.5].

CISG art 29

Article 29

(1) A contract may be modified or terminated by the mere agreement of the parties.

(2) A contract in writing which contains a provision requiring any modification or termination by agreement to be in writing may not be otherwise modified or terminated by agreement. However, a party may be precluded by his conduct from asserting such a provision to the extent that the other party has relied on that conduct.

13.6 Review

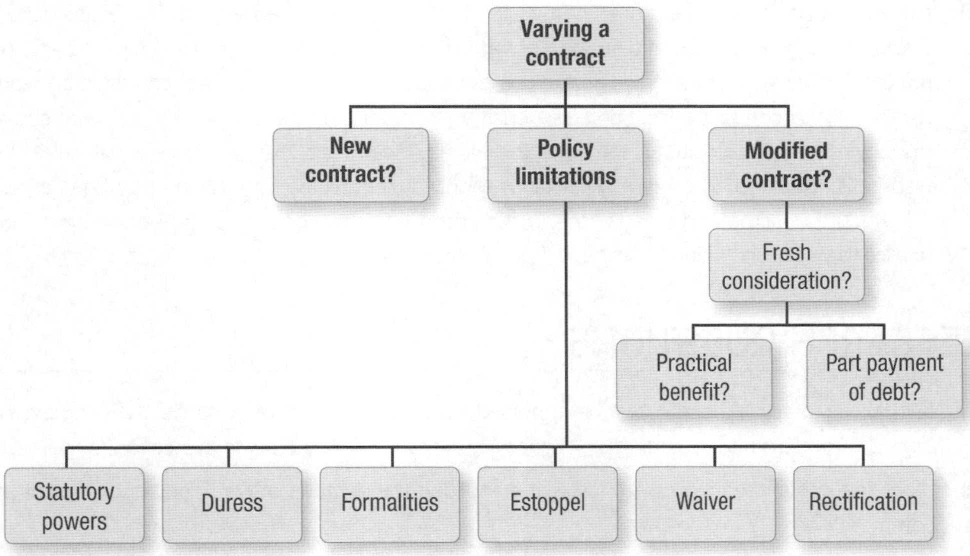

TIPS FOR APPLYING THE LAW IN PRACTICE

- It is always important to identify what the varied—or second —promise will be in these situations. Often the 'second promise' is the promise not to enforce the first promise and, thus, the issue is what makes the second promise enforceable.
- Remember, the issue of 'further' consideration, such as via a 'practical benefit' test, only arises in the context of a variation to an existing contract, not a new contract. If there is a new contract formed for future conduct, then the exchange of promises underlying the new contract will be the consideration.
- The scope of the 'practical benefit' test is still being determined so be prepared to argue by analogy with *Musumeci* and *Williams* in an answer to a problem question.

- Remember that, from a client's perspective, it is the outcome that is important—the enforcement of the promise—not necessarily the mechanism, so always be open to the use of waiver, estoppel or statutory powers to achieve the preferred outcome.

PROBLEM QUESTIONS

(1) Cara and Ding are parties to a building contract in which Cara is the owner of a house and Ding is a builder. Ding promised Cara to renovate a house for $150,000 and to complete it in 12 weeks. After Ding purchases the materials but before building commences, Cara tells Ding that she does not want to renovate the house but wants the house knocked down and a completely new house built and Cara promises that she will now pay Ding $180,000. Ding quickly agrees. After construction of the new house commences, Ding realises that 12 weeks is not enough time to complete the work. Can Ding claim that a new contract was formed with a longer (perhaps more reasonable) time period to complete the work?

(2) Adnan and Ben are parties to a contract in which Ben, a website designer, is creating a new website for Adnan, a motivational speaker who relies on his public profile to generate work. As the date for delivery of the new website comes closer, Ben realises he cannot complete his work for the original contract price. Ben tells Adnan that Adnan must pay an extra 50 per cent above the original price in order to complete the work. Adnan fears that his business will fail if the website is not launched on time. Reluctantly, Adnan agrees to the increase in price. Ben delivers the website on time and asks for the increased price. Adnan only pays the original price and refuses to pay more. Can Ben enforce Adnan's promise to pay the increased price?

RESEARCH QUESTIONS

(1) Should the 'practical benefit' test be endorsed by the High Court of Australia? To what extent does the modern understanding of (economic) duress provide adequate protection for parties?

(2) Does the 'modification' problem justify the abolition the doctrine of consideration in Australian common law?

(3) To what extent does *Foakes v Beer* represent a conflation of adequacy and sufficiency of consideration, at least to the extent that adequacy has always been left to the parties?

14

TRANSFERRING RIGHTS AND OBLIGATIONS

14.1 Overview

In general, parties to a contract can change who can benefit from or enforce the contract, usually by the consent of all current parties but sometimes without such consent. The rules in relation to transferring rights and obligations—assignment and novation—require an examination of the nature of the benefits and obligations being transferred, as well as any relevant statutory modifications to the underlying practices of the common law and equity. An overriding concern of the courts is whether the performance under the contract was meant to be 'personal', in the sense that it was the intention of the parties that the actual party to the contract was to perform the contract, and not others.

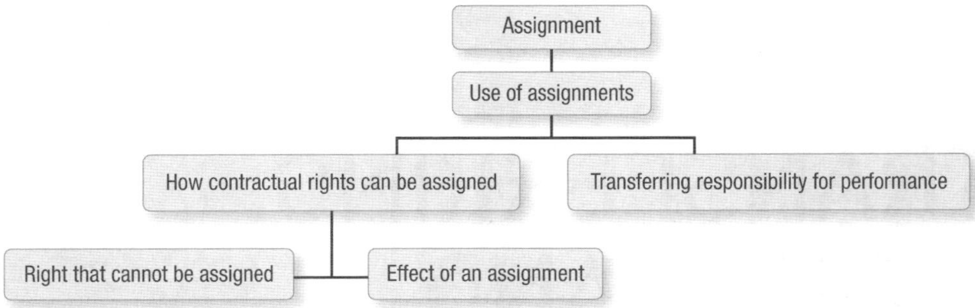

14.2 Assignment of contractual rights

Concepts	Short explanation	Relevant authorities	*Principles* text*
Limited right to assignment without consent	The common law has had an evolving view on assignment of contract rights, which originally could not be assigned but now can be, if a benefit	*Pacific Brands Sport & Leisure Pty Ltd v Underworks Pty Ltd* (2006) 149 FCR 395 *Conveyancing Act 1919* (NSW) s 12	Chapter 14: 14.02–14.03
'Personal' contract	A benefit that was intended to be 'personal' cannot be assigned without consent	*Linden Gardens Trust Ltd v Lenesta Sludge Disposals Ltd* [1994] 1 AC 85 *Devefi Pty Ltd v Mateffy Perl Nagy Pty Ltd* (1993) 113 ALR 225 *Equuscorp Pty Ltd v Haxton* (2012) 246 CLR 498	Chapter 14: 14.04
Obligations cannot be assigned without consent	Despite allowing assignment in some circumstances, obligations cannot be assigned without the consent of all parties. Often, a novation would be executed to achieve this outcome	*Tolhurst v Associated Portland Cement Manufacturers (1900) Ltd* [1902] 2 KB 660	Chapter 14: 14.06

* Consult the corresponding section(s) of the *Principles* text for more detail.

The simplest assignment situation is where one party can assign or transfer their rights or benefits of an agreement to someone else without the consent of the other party to the contract, usually as a result of an express right to do so in the contract. However, more commonly, the consent of the other party is required for the assignment to be effective. Reported cases often arise in situations where that consent is not forthcoming and the first party looks to proceed with the assignment. This is particularly the case when the assignment is part of a larger commercial transaction, such as a sale of business, where the transfer of existing contractual rights is an important, if not fundamental, part of the transaction.

14.2.1 The use of assignments

Assignments are a necessary part of many commercial transactions, especially the buying and selling of businesses. These arrangements can become quite complex when there are large corporate structures involved, as seen in the case of *Pacific Brands* (extracted below).

Pacific Brands Sport & Leisure Pty Ltd v Underworks Pty Ltd (2006) 149 FCR 395

Facts and issues

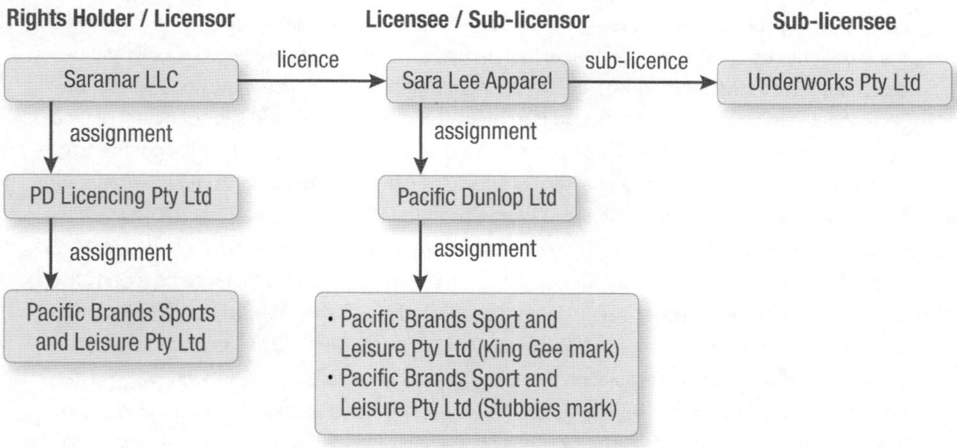

The holder of the intellectual property rights for Australian clothing brands 'King Gee' and 'Stubbies', a company called Saramar LLC, licenced those rights to a related company, Sara Lee Apparel (Australasia) to exploit those rights by making clothes under those brand names. Sara Lee then sub-licenced those rights in relation to clothes not currently being made under the licence (such as underwear and children's socks) to another company, Underworks. Some time later, Sara Lee sold its Australian clothing interests to the Pacific Dunlop group. The intellectual property rights were assigned to PD Licencing Pty Ltd and the licence was assigned to Pacific Dunlop. PD Licencing then assigned the rights to Pacific Brands Sports and Leisure, and Pacific Dunlop assigned the licence to two Pacific Brands companies, which were direct competitors of Underworks. After negotiation to have Underworks consent to the assignments failed, Pacific Brands Sports and Leisure purported to terminate the sub-licence of Underworks due to breaches of the sub-licence.

Decision

Appeal dismissed: the licence could possibly have been assigned but there was only a limited ability to assign the rights that were the basis of the purported breach and termination.

Per Finn and Sundberg JJ at 404:

> By way of background, it is appropriate to begin with a number of relatively non-contentious propositions. *First*, it is well accepted that assignable contractual rights are choses in action; are a species of personal proprietary right; and can be transferred to a third party at law or in equity in accordance with the formal rules governing the transfer of such rights: see *Norman v Federal Commissioner of Taxation* (1963) 109 CLR 9 at 26; *Loxton v Moir* (1914) 18 CLR 360 at 379. *Secondly*, while it is not legally possible to assign the burden of a contract (i.e. the obligation to render performance), it may be possible to assign (a) the entire benefit of a contract (i.e. the right to receive performance): *Don King Productions Inc v Warren* [2000] Ch 291 at 318 ('*Don King*'); (b) if a right under a contract is separate and severable, such a separate and severable right: cf *Federal Commissioner of Taxation v Everett* (1980) 143 CLR 440 at 449–450; or (c) if some only of the rights under a contract are assignable, those rights. '[A]ssignability is not a matter of all obligations arising under a contract or none at all': *Don King*, above, at 319. *Thirdly*, a contract may expressly or impliedly authorise assignment of rights in a contract which would not otherwise be assignable: *Devefi Pty Ltd v Mateffy Perl Nagy Pty Ltd* (1993) 113 ALR 225 at 235 ('*Devefi v Mateffy*'); or, conversely, may expressly or impliedly prohibit assignment of rights otherwise prima facie assignable: *Don King*, above, at 319. 'Such contractual provisions are legally effective' as between the contracting parties: *Don King*, ibid; *Linden Gardens Trust Ltd v Lenesta Sludge Disposals Ltd* [1994] 1 AC 85 at 103 ff ('*Linden Gardens Trust*'). *Fourthly*, while the product to be derived from a contractual performance (the 'fruits of performance') may be assigned; *Devefi v Mateffy*, above, at 234; the right to that performance may, nonetheless, be unassignable because, having regard to the nature of the contract and the subject matter of the contractual right in question, that right is personal in the sense that the identity of the contractual obligee is material to the contractual relationship itself (i.e. it is a 'personal contract': *Peters v General Accident Fire & Life Assurance Corporation Ltd* [1938] 2 All ER 267 at 270; *Moore v Collins* [1937] SASR 195; or to the contractual performance to be rendered: *Linden Gardens Trust Ltd v Lenesta Sludge Disposals Ltd* (1992) 57 BLR 57 at 77 (contract requiring a party to act on the other's instructions); see generally Seddon and Ellinghaus, *Cheshire and Fifoot's Law of Contract* (8th Aust ed, 2002), [8-6]; Furmston (ed), above, 6.299 ff; *Chitty on Contracts*, Vol 1 19-053 ff (29th ed, 2004); Farnsworth, above, §11.4. A contractual right, though, will not be personal if, construed in its setting, 'it can make no difference to the person on whom the [corresponding] obligation lies to which of two persons [i.e. assignor or assignee] he is to discharge it': *Tolhurst v Associated Portland Cement Manufacturers (1900) Ltd* [1902] 2 KB 660 at 668. *Fifthly*, seemingly, a contractual right may itself be of such a personal character that it cannot properly be characterised as property: cf *Jack v Smail* (1905) 2 CLR 684 at 704–705; but it is not clear whether this proposition has salience only in contexts other than assignment of such a right, e.g. insolvency, because of the proposition immediately preceding this which relates expressly to assignments of 'personal' contractual rights. *Sixthly,* the assignee of a contractual right under a legal assignment is entitled, as owner of that right, to take action in respect of it: e.g. *Conveyancing Act 1919* (NSW), s 12. *Seventhly*, a third party may become a 'substituted contracting party' by novation of the original contract. Novation will, ordinarily, require the agreement of the original and the substituted party although the original contract itself may, on its proper construction, authorise a party to substitute a contracting party in its place without need for a further tri-partite agreement: see *Harry v Fidelity Nominees Pty Ltd*

(1985) 41 SASR 458 at 460. On novation, though, there is no assignment of rights and obligations, but rather the creation of new rights and obligations in a new contract: *Olsson v Dyson* (1969) 120 CLR 365 at 388; *Cheshire & Fifoot's Law of Contract*, above, [8.45] ff. *Eighthly*, a contractual obligation cannot be assigned without the consent of the other contracting party: *Tolhurst v Associated Portland Cement Manufacturers (1900) Ltd* [1902] 2 KB 660 at 668. This, for practical purposes, requires novation of the original contract; Furmston, *'The Assignment of Contractual Burdens'* (1998) 13 Jo Contract Law 42; see also *Vickery v Woods* (1952) 85 CLR 336 at 345; *Fightvision Pty Ltd v Onisforou* (1999) 47 NSWLR 473 at 491–493. *Ninthly*, the delegation of performance of contractual obligations is permissible where the obligations assumed do not require personal performance but only the producing of a result: *Bruce v Tyley* (1916) 21 CLR 277; *British Wagon Co v Lea & Co* (1880) 5 QBD 149. In such cases perfect performance by the delegate will discharge the delegating contractor's obligation, although that contractor will remain liable unless and until such performance is rendered. 'Whether or not in any given contract performance can properly be carried out by the employment of a sub-contractor must depend on the proper inference to be drawn from the contract itself, the subject matter of it, and other material surrounding circumstances': *Davies v Collins* [1945] 1 All ER 247 at 250 . . .

406 As a matter of convenience the various assignment issues raised on the appeal will be dealt with compositely under the following headings: (i) What rights under the Sublicence were prima facie assignable? (ii) Was the cl 18.2 power to terminate prima facie assignable? (iii) Was Sara Lee's identity material to the contract or its performance? (iv) Was Underworks' consent required for the assignment? (v) Was Underworks' consent given to the assignment? We have used the description 'prima facie assignable' for this reason. A right may be 'proprietary' in character but may, in a given setting, not be assignable either because such is prohibited by the contract itself, or because it nonetheless is a 'personal right' in that the obligee's identity was material to the obligor . . .

(i) What rights were prima facie assignable?

The parties' disagreement in the appeal over this conclusion is in substance a disagreement as to how one determines whether contractual rights are prima facie assignable at all . . .

[408] In consequence we consider that the proper approach to be taken is that (i) all of a party's contractual rights, being parts of a chose in action, have a proprietary character for assignment purposes and are prima facie assignable but (ii) whether in a given case they or some of them are unassignable will depend upon whether there is a reason which nonetheless precludes assignment. Apart from prohibitions created by statute or public policy, the most common such reasons will be a contractual prohibition on assignment, the materiality of the identity of the obligee to the contractual relationship or to the obligor's performance, or, less commonly, in the case of an assignment of a part of a composite chose, the various rights are not separable in the manner attempted. We would add that we consider that this approach not only is more likely to engender greater certainty in routine commercial dealings where assignments are the common place than that adopted by the primary judge, but also it avoids what we consider to be a process of characterisation fraught with uncertainty.

Accordingly, and putting to one side the cl 18.2 power to terminate, we consider his Honour erred insofar as he concluded that various rights and powers under this contract were not assignable because they were not proprietary in character.

[409] (ii) Was the cl 18.2 power to terminate prime facie assignable? Was the common law power to rescind available to the appellants?

It is appropriate to deal with these particular matters separately notwithstanding that our conclusion is encompassed in what we have said above . . .

[410] If it were the case that all of Sara Lee's substantive rights were assigned – i.e. the entire chose was assigned – the consequence of that would be that not only did the assignee acquire the legal right to the chose but also 'all legal and other remedies for the same': *Conveyancing Act 1919* (NSW) s 12. The effect of the assignment would have been to put the assignees in the same position in relation to repudiatory conduct as Sara Lee would have been had it retained the chose. Accordingly, we consider the assignees would have had available to them by way of remedy (inter alia) the right to claim damages for non-performance of Underworks' primary obligation and the power to elect to put an end to all primary obligations of both parties that remained unperformed. It would be anomalous to insist that, while Sara Lee had disposed of its interest in the contract, it nonetheless was the only party entitled to accept a repudiation. We can see no reason for being driven to such a conclusion.

We again consider his Honour to have been incorrect in the view he took of the power to terminate at common law. We should again add, though, that we reserve our view as to whether this power would be available to an assignee in the case of a partial assignment of rights.

(iii) Was Sara Lee's identity material to the contract or its performance?

This is the pivotal issue in this appeal . . .

[411] It characteristically is said that it is a question of construction whether a contract itself or particular rights or obligations, involve personal considerations such as to render the contract or those rights unassignable, or the obligations not delegable: see e.g. *Tolhurst v Associated Portland Cement Manufacturers (1900) Ltd* [1903] AC 414 at 416–417; *National Carbonising Co Ltd v British Coal Distillation Ltd* (1936) 54 RPC 41 at 54; *Australis Media Holdings Pty Ltd v Telstra Corporation Ltd* (1998) 43 NSWLR 104 at 118–120; see also Furmston (ed), above, 6.299, 6.301–6.324; *Chitty on Contracts*, above, par 19-053; cf *Cheshire & Fifoot's Law of Contract*, above, [8.6]. However, given the particular purpose for which the contract and its terms are being construed, implicit in the question of construction are, ordinarily, issues of characterisation and of inference in which the significance to be attributed, variously, to identity, to the qualities or attributes one or both parties are expected to exhibit and to the character of the parties' relationship, can loom large.

It is fair to say at the outset that the drafting of the Sublicence betrays oversight, a lack of prescience and mistakes in the identification of the proper party in particular clauses (as to the last see cl 3.1, 8.5).

The Sublicence imposed no express prohibition on assignment of rights by Sara Lee. This contrasts with the cl 14.1 prohibition binding Underworks. But neither did the Sublicence define Sara Lee for the purposes of the contract as 'Sara Lee and its assigns'. Save in exceptional circumstances, such a definition would signify a contractual intent that Sara Lee's benefit of the contract would [412] be assignable: *Peacocke Land Co Ltd v Hamilton Milk Producers Co Ltd* [1963] NZLR 576; *Devefi v Mateffy*, above, at 235, 238–239. Clause 1.2 of the Sublicence merely stated in general terms that a reference to a party to the Sublicence or to 'any other agreement or document includes the party's successors and permitted substitutes or assigns'. As we will indicate in the next part of these reasons, that clause in the context of this Sublicence did not reveal an intent that Sara Lee could assign its rights without Underworks' consent.

One, in consequence, is left to discern whether and to what extent Sara Lee's rights were assignable from what the Sublicence objectively construed conveyed to a reasonable person. This exercise 'requires consideration not only of the text of the [Sublicence], but also the surrounding circumstances known to [the parties], and the purpose and object of the transaction': *Pacific Carrier's Ltd v BNP Paribas* (2004) 218 CLR 451 at [22].

It is not unimportant to notice that the Sublicence related to the use of a trademark. Some number of its provisions, and particularly those relating to Sara Lee's powers to control the use of the marks and to maintain its own reputation in its products and brands, reflected what was reasonably predictable given the 'control' requirements of s 8 of the *Trade Marks Act 1995* (Cth) defining an 'authorised user' of a mark: see generally Davison, Johnston and Kennedy, *Shanahan's Australian Law of Trade Marks and Passing Off*, [17.25] ff (3rd ed, 2003). While Sara Lee's licence with Saramar is not in evidence, it is probable that some of the provisions of the Sublicence have their provenance, if not necessarily their language, in the requirements of that licence. Be that as it may, it is fair to say in general terms that some number of the terms and conditions of the Sublicence have characters one would reasonably expect of a Sublicence for a trade mark.

What is important for present purposes, though, is the manner in which these provisions appeared to tie Sara Lee to Underworks. Clause 4.3 required the sublicensee 'to exploit the Products . . . to the best advantage of the parties'. Clause 6.1 required the sublicensor to furnish to the sublicensee such assistance and advice as the sublicensor deemed helpful in the sublicensee's promotion and sale of the products. If both of these provisions reveal some level of reciprocal responsibility of one party for the other, standing alone they do not suggest that what was intended was some form of cooperative endeavour or 'quasi-partnership': cf *National Carbonising Co Ltd v British Coal Distillation Ltd*, above; in which Sara Lee as such had tutelary responsibilities: (cl 6).

There are, though, significant indications in some number of the provisions of the Sublicence which suggest that the Sara Lee/Underworks relationship was contemplated to be a personal and an enduring one for the life of the Sublicence. Some number of sub-clauses impose obligations or create rights, which are related specifically and expressly to Sara Lee or to the Sara Lee Corporation. We refer, for example, to cl 8.7 (authorising Underworks to indicate its corporate name as manufacturer on products etc with the notation that it does so under Sublicence from Sara Lee); to cll 11 and 12 (in relation to Sara Lee Corporation's Guidelines and the part they are to play in the Sublicence). Unless and until these provisions were varied as part of a novation, both Sara Lee and Underworks were bound by them. When these provisions are considered in the context of some other of the clauses giving the 'Sub-Licensor' judgmental power over the 'Sub-Licensee', they in turn suggest an intent that that power so given was personal to Sara Lee. In other words, the [413] standards to be adhered to, and the judgments to be made about protecting the mark through quality control (cl 8.5) and mark use (cll 8.4 and 8.1 to 8.3) and in approving manufacturing facilities (cl 10), were to be set, or made, by Sara Lee.

When one turns to the context of the Sublicence, the evidence is particularly sparse. It was the case that, at the time of its execution, Sara Lee was not using the Stubbies mark to produce socks and underwear nor was it so using the King Gee mark (save for work socks). Though the Sublicence did not prohibit Sara Lee from competing with Underworks on socks and underwear, and it could do so under other brands, the licence itself was an exclusive licence though within customer and geographic limits. While the Sublicence permitted Sara Lee to use the marks outside those limits, it envisaged the possibility of its obtaining product from Underworks. Beyond this and what we have already said about the significance of the subject matter of the Sublicence (i.e. it related to trade marks), there is little else that throws light on the construction issue although we would also note that the agreement not only imposed a general confidentiality obligation on the parties (cl 9), it also positively protected the more sensitive parts of the sublicensee's business information from disclosure to the sublicensor notwithstanding the independent audit requirement imposed in association with verifying royalties payable (cl 5.5). The reasons for both such obligations are understandable. The former reflected a predictable appreciation that some level of personal trust and confidence necessarily underlay the business relations of the contracting parties. The latter, while respecting that confidence, nonetheless imposed an accountability requirement through the independent audit requirement.

Considered in its totality, we are satisfied that the Sublicence in its setting, while not of a type that was necessarily inherently personal in character: cf Furmston (ed), above, 6.308–6.309; was nonetheless intended to create an enduring relationship in which the identity of Sara Lee as the sublicensor was material and was made so by Sara Lee in particular.

> While acknowledging the legitimate interest the sublicensor had in exercising control over the use of the mark and hence having contractual powers to that end, we consider that there are sufficient indications in the text of the Sublicence itself that the particular will to which the Sublicence was asked to subject itself was Sara Lee's, and that that was a state of affairs that Underworks agreed to (especially having regard to the terms in which certain control and veto powers were cast, e.g. cll 8.4, 10 and 12) because it could not be changed without its consent: cf *L/M International Construction Inc v The Circle Ltd Partnership* (1995) 49 Con LR 12 at 25. As indicated above, those clauses in the agreement which referred specifically and expressly to Sara Lee or to the Sara Lee Corporation are of particular significance in this.
>
> Accordingly we agree with his Honour's conclusion in this particular matter …
>
> [415] The appellants' case is an untenable one. We agree that the primary judge's characterisation of Underworks' conduct vis-à-vis Pacific Brands for the purposes of the novation claim apply, equally, to the consent claim. It would, in our view, be quite incongruous in this setting to find that Underworks consented to Pacific Brands acquiring some of the very rights which it (Underworks) strenuously objected to its acquiring under the proposed deed of novation. The parties' conduct must be evaluated under the shadow of the novation negotiations and, importantly, in light of the fact that Underworks was conducting a going concern at the time. So considered, we consider its dealings with Pacific Brands did not constitute a consent to the assignment, but rather was in the nature of a holding measure at a time at which it was in a position of unexpected vulnerability to a competitor, pending a satisfactory resolution of the matter.
>
> The appeal must be dismissed as the substantive obligations of the Sublicence the appellants allege Underworks breached were not assigned to them. They remained with Sara Lee with the consequence that, if they were breached, it was for Sara Lee to complain of this.

Emmett J came to the same conclusion as Finn and Sunnberg JJ, and also found that the notice of termination was not effective such that, even if the rights were assigned, they were not exercised in a legally effective manner.

14.2.2 How contractual rights can be assigned

Although most contract law rights are products of the agreements that give rise to them, the right to sue for the breach of those rights is a chose in action, which is a property right. There is a statutory restriction on the assignments of those rights, of which s 12 of the *Conveyancing Act 1919* (NSW) is one example.[1]

Conveyancing Act 1919 (NSW) s 12

Section 12 Assignments of debts and choses in action

Any absolute assignment by writing under the hand of the assignor (not purporting to be by way of charge only) of any debt or other legal chose in action, of which express notice in writing has been given to the debtor, trustee, or other person from whom the assignor would have been entitled to receive or claim such debt or chose in action, shall be, and be deemed to have been effectual in law

1 See also *Property Law Act 1958* (Vic) s 134; *Property Law Act 1974* (Qld) s 199; *Property Law Act 1969* (WA) s 20; *Law of Property Act 1936* (SA) s 15; *Conveyancing and Law of Property Act 1884* (Tas) s 86; *Civil Law (Property) Act 2006* (ACT) s 205; *Law of Property Act 2000* (NT) s 182.

(subject to all equities which would have been entitled to priority over the right of the assignee if this Act had not passed) to pass and transfer the legal right to such debt or chose in action from the date of such notice, and all legal and other remedies for the same, and the power to give a good discharge for the same without the concurrence of the assignor:

> Provided always that if the debtor, trustee, or other person liable in respect of such debt or chose in action has had notice that such assignment is disputed by the assignor or anyone claiming under the assignor, or of any other opposing or conflicting claims to such debt or chose in action, the debtor, trustee or other person liable shall be entitled, if he or she thinks fit, to call upon the several persons making claim thereto to interplead concerning the same, or he or she may, if he or she thinks fit, pay the same into court under and in conformity with the provisions of the Acts for the relief of trustees.

14.2.3 Rights that cannot be assigned

Despite the broader notion that parties are free to contract on whatever terms they wish, the law has long imposed restrictions on when those rights can be assigned. The following three cases highlight the factors that courts tend to take into account, including matters of public policy.

Linden Gardens Trust Ltd v Lenesta Sludge Disposals Ltd [1994] 1 AC 85

Facts and issues

Case 1

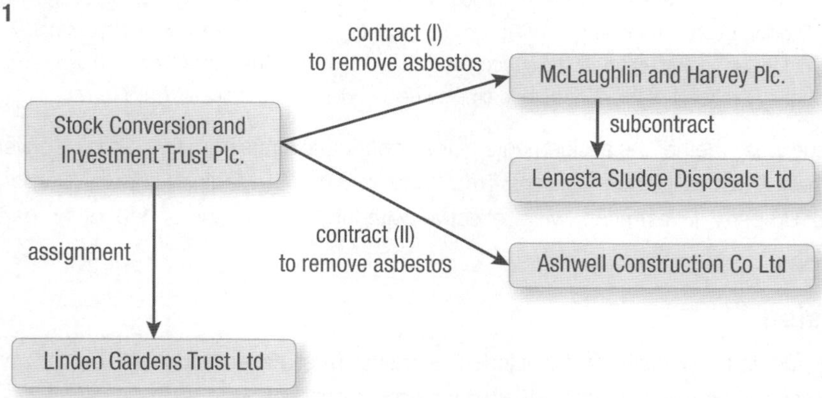

Case 2

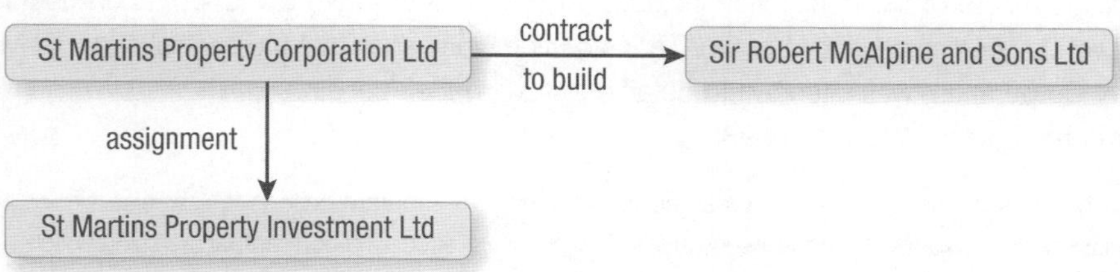

This case is actually the hearing of two separate cases that are related to the extent they raise the same legal issues in relation to a standard form industry contract. In the Linden Gardens case, the lessees of a property, Stock Conversion and Investment Trust, entered into two agreements with companies, McLaughlin and Harvey (who then subcontracted the work to Lenesta Sludge Disposals) and Ashwell Construction, to remove asbestos from its property. Disputes arose in relation to the work of both companies at different times. Subsequent to the work being undertaken, Stock Conversion and Investment Trust transferred the lease to Linden Gardens Trust and the transfer included a purported assignment of contractual rights held by Stock Conversion and Investment Trust to Linden Gardens Trust. Linden Gardens Trust then purported to sue McLaughlin, Lenesta and Ashwell in relation to the asbestos works. At first instance, the assignment was found not to be effective; however, on appeal the Court of Appeal found it was effective.

In the second case, St Martins Property Construction Corporation entered into a building contract with Sir Robert McAlpine and Sons for the construction of an extensive residential and commercial building complex. Shortly thereafter, St Martins Property Construction Corporation assigned the rights under that contract to a related company, St Martins Property Investment. Some time later, defects were found in the building complex and extensive remedial work was required. St Martins Property Investment sued Sir Robert McAlpine and Sons for the cost of that remedial work. At first instance and on appeal, the assignment was found not to be effective; however, the party to the original contract could still sue and recover damages.

Both cases involved the use of a standard form industry contract, which included a clause that limited assignment or subcontracting:

> Clause 17 (1) The employer shall not without the written consent of the contractor assign this contract. (2) The contractor shall not without the written consent of the employer assign this contract, and shall not without the written consent of the architect (which consent shall not be unreasonably withheld to the prejudice of the contractor) sublet any portion of the works. Provided that it shall be a condition in any subletting which may occur that the employment of the subcontractor under the subcontract shall determine immediately upon the determination (for any reason) of the contractor's employment under this contract.

The issue was whether the assignments of the contractual rights from first, Stock Conversation and Investment Trust to Linden Gardens Trust, and second, St Martins Property Corporation to St Martins Property Investment, were effective without the consent of the other parties to the contracts.

Decision

Appeal allowed in relation to the Linden Gardens Trust case: clause 17 did not allow for an assignment of the relevant contractual rights without consent.

Appeal dismissed in relation to the St Martins Property Investment case: although clause 17 applied, the nature of the transaction included the notion that future owners of apartments (third parties) would need protection from faulty construction work, such that the original party, St Martins Property Corporation, was intended to be able to sue on their behalf.

Per Lord Browne-Wilkinson at 98:

> My Lords, these appeals and cross-appeal arise in two separate actions which raise similar issues. In broad terms, those issues are, first, what is the effect of a contractual provision which prohibits a party from assigning the benefit of a contract and, second, can a building owner recover substantial damages for breach of [99] a building contract if he has parted with the

property. The appeals relate to preliminary issues directed to be tried in both actions. As the cases have proceeded, certain of those issues have become irrelevant. I propose therefore to state shortly the facts of each case, then deal with the matters which fall for decision by this House and, at the end, indicate the answers which should in my view be given to the questions posed by the preliminary issues which have been directed . . .

[102] (1) Does clause 17 prohibit the assignment of the benefit of building contracts?

Staughton L.J. (dissenting on this point) held that on its true construction clause 17 did not prohibit the assignment by the employer of the benefit [103] of the building contract. It was urged before your Lordships on behalf of Linden Gardens and Investments that his views were correct.

The argument runs as follows. On any basis, clause 17 is unhappily drafted in that it refers to an assignment of 'the contract.' It is trite law that it is, in any event, impossible to assign 'the contract' as a whole, i.e. including both burden and benefit. The burden of a contract can never be assigned without the consent of the other party to the contract in which event such consent will give rise to a novation. Therefore one has to discover what the parties meant by this inelegant phrase. It is said that the intention of the parties in using the words 'assign this contract' is demonstrated by clause 17(2) which prohibits both the assignment of the contract by the contractor without the employer's consent and the sub-letting of any portion of the works without the consent of the architect. In clause 17(2), the contractor is only expressly prevented from sub-letting 'any *portion* of the works.' Yet it must have been the party's intention to limit the contractor's rights to sublet the *whole* of the works. Accordingly, the words in clause 17(2) 'assign this contract' have to be read as meaning 'sublet the whole of the works.' If that is the meaning of the words 'assign this contract' in clause 17(2) they must bear the same meaning in clause 17(1), which accordingly only prohibits the employer from giving substitute performance and does not prohibit the assignment of the benefit of the contract.

Like the majority of the Court of Appeal, I am unable to accept this argument. Although it is true that the phrase 'assign this contract' is not strictly accurate, lawyers frequently use those words inaccurately to describe an assignment of the benefit of a contract since every lawyer knows that the burden of a contract cannot be assigned: see, for example, *Nokes v. Doncaster Amalgamated Collieries Ltd.* [1940] A.C. 1014, 1019–1020. The prohibition in clause 17(2) against subletting 'any portion of the works' necessarily produces a prohibition against the subletting of the whole of the works: any subletting of the whole will necessarily include a subletting of a portion and is therefore prohibited. Therefore there is no ground for reading the words 'assign this contract' in clause 17(1) as referring only to subletting the whole. Decisively, both clause 17(1) and (2) clearly distinguish between 'assignment' and 'subletting:' it is therefore impossible to read the word 'assign' as meaning 'sublet.' Finally, I find it difficult to comprehend the concept of an employer 'subletting' the performance of his contractual duties which consist primarily of providing access to the site and paying for the works.

Accordingly, in my view clause 17(1) of the contract prohibited the assignment by the employer of the benefit of the contract. This, by itself, is fatal to the claim by Investments (as assignee) in the St. Martins case.

(2) Does clause 17(1) prohibit the assignment of accrued rights of action?

The majority in the Court of Appeal drew a distinction between an assignment of the right to require future performance of a contract by [104] the other party on the one hand and an assignment of the benefits arising *under* the contract (e.g. to receive payment due under it or to enforce accrued rights of action) on the other hand. They held that clause 17 only prohibited the assignment of the right to future performance and did not prohibit the assignment of the benefits arising under the contract, in particular accrued causes of action. Therefore, in the

Linden Gardens case, where all the relevant breaches of contract by the contractors pre-dated the assignment, an assignment to Linden Gardens of the accrued rights of action for breach was not prohibited. In contrast, in the St. Martins case, where all the breaches of contract occurred after the date of the assignment, the majority of the Court of Appeal held that it was a breach of clause 17 to seek to transfer the right to future performance . . .

[105] The question is to what extent does clause 17 on its true construction restrict rights of assignment which would otherwise exist? In the context of a complicated building contract, I find it impossible to construe clause 17 as prohibiting only the assignment of rights to future performance, leaving each party free to assign the fruits of the contract. The reason for including the contractual prohibition viewed from the contractor's point of view must be that the contractor wishes to ensure that he deals, and deals only, with the particular employer with whom he has chosen to enter into a contract. Building contracts are pregnant with disputes: some employers are much more reasonable than others in dealing with such disputes. The disputes frequently arise in the context of the contractor suing for the price and being met by a claim for abatement of the price or cross-claims founded on an allegation that the performance of the contract has been defective. Say that, before the final instalment of the price has been paid, the employer has assigned the benefits under the contract to a third party, there being at the time existing rights of action for defective work. On the Court of Appeal's view, those rights of action would have vested in the assignee. Would the original employer be entitled to an abatement of the price, even though the cross-claims would be vested in the assignee? If so, would the assignee be a necessary party to any settlement or litigation of the claims for defective work, thereby requiring the contractor to deal with two parties (one not of his choice) in order to recover the price for the works from the employer? I cannot believe that the parties ever intended to permit such a confused position to arise. . . .

[106] (3) Is a prohibition on assignment void as being contrary to public policy? It was submitted that it is normally unlawful as being contrary to public policy to seek to render property inalienable. Since contractual rights are a species of property, it is said that a prohibition against assigning such rights is void as being illegal.

This submission faces formidable difficulties both on authority and in principle. As to the authorities, in *In re Turcan*, 40 Ch.D. 5, a man effected an insurance policy which contained a term that it should not be assignable in any case whatever. He had previously covenanted with trustees to settle after-acquired property. The Court of Appeal held that although he could not assign the benefit of the policy so as to give the trustees the power to recover the money from the insurance company, he could validly make a declaration of trust of the proceeds which required him to hand over such proceeds to the trustees. This case proceeded, therefore, on the footing that the contractual restriction on assignment was valid. In *Helstan Securities* [1978] 3 All E.R. 262 Croom-Johnson J. enforced such a prohibition. In *Reed Publishing Holdings Ltd. v. Kings Reach Investments Ltd.* (unreported), 25 May 1983; Court of Appeal (Civil Division) Transcript No. 231 of 1983, the Court of Appeal had to consider an application to join as a party to an action an assignee of the benefit of a contract which contained a prohibition on such assignment. One of their grounds for refusing the application was that by reason of the prohibition the assignment was of no effect.

In none of these cases was the public policy argument advanced. But they indicate a long-term acceptance of the validity of such a prohibition which is accepted as part of the law in *Chitty on Contracts*, 26th ed. (1989), vol. 1, p. 883, para. 1413. We were referred to a decision of the [107] Supreme Court of South Africa, *Paiges v. Van Ryn Gold Mines Estates Ltd.*, 1920 A.D. 600 in which it was expressly decided that a term prohibiting a workman from assigning his wages was not contrary to public policy. In Scotland a covenant against assigning a lease of minerals (which was treated simply as a contract) was held not to infringe public policy: *Duke of Portland v. Baird and Co.* (1865) 4 Macph. 10. We were referred to certain cases in the United States, but they give no unequivocal guidance.

In the face of this authority, the House is being invited to change the law by holding that such a prohibition is void as contrary to public policy. For myself I can see no good reason for so doing. Nothing was urged in argument as showing that such a prohibition was contrary to the public interest beyond the fact that such prohibition renders the chose in action inalienable. Certainly in the context of rights over land the law does not favour restrictions on alienability. But even in relation to land law a prohibition against the assignment of a lease is valid. We were not referred to any English case in which the courts have had to consider restrictions on the alienation of tangible personal property, probably because there are few cases in which there would be any desire to restrict such alienation. In the case of real property there is a defined and limited supply of the commodity, and it has been held contrary to public policy to restrict the free market. But no such reason can apply to contractual rights: there is no public need for a market in choses in action. A party to a building contract, as I have sought to explain, can have a genuine commercial interest in seeking to ensure that he is in contractual relations only with a person whom he has selected as the other party to the contract. In the circumstances, I can see no policy reason why a contractual prohibition on assignment of contractual rights should be held contrary to public policy . . .

(4) Are the assignments (although prohibited) effective to transfer the causes of action to the assignees?

It was submitted that, even though the assignments were in breach of clause 17, they were effective to vest the causes of action in the assignees, . . . This argument was founded on two bases: first, the decision in *Tom Shaw and Co. v. Moss Empires Ltd.* (1908) 25 T.L.R. 190; second, the fact that an assignment of a leasehold term in breach of a covenant against assignment is effective to vest the term in the assignee . . .

[108] In the *Helstan Securities case* [1978] 3 All E.R. 262 Croom-Johnson J. did not follow the *Tom Shaw* case and held that the purported assignment in breach of the contractual provision was ineffective to vest the cause of action in the assignee. That decision was followed and applied by the Court of Appeal in the *Reed Publishing Holdings case*, 25 May 1983: see also *In re Turcan*, 40 Ch.D. 5.

Therefore the existing authorities establish that an attempted assignment of contractual rights in breach of a contractual prohibition is ineffective to transfer such contractual rights. I regard the law as being satisfactorily settled in that sense. If the law were otherwise, it would defeat the legitimate commercial reason for inserting the contractual prohibition, viz., to ensure that the original parties to the contract are not brought into direct contractual relations with third parties . . .

As to the analogy with leases, I was originally impressed by the fact that an assignment of the term in breach of covenant is effective to vest the term in the assignee . . . The law became settled that an assignment in breach of covenant gave rise to a forfeiture, but pending forfeiture the term was vested in the assignee. In contrast, the development of the law affecting the assignment of contractual rights was wholly different. It started from exactly the opposite position, viz., contractual rights were personal and not assignable. Only gradually did the law permitting assignment develop . . . It is therefore not surprising if the law applicable to assignment of contractual rights differs from that applicable to the assignment of leases.

Therefore in my judgment an assignment of contractual rights in breach of a prohibition against such assignment is ineffective to vest the contractual rights in the assignee. It follows that the claim by Linden Gardens fails and the Linden Garden action must be dismissed.

Lord Keith of Kinkel, Lord Bridge of Harwich and Lord Ackner concurred with Lord Browne-Wilson. Lord Griffiths also concurred with Lord Browne-Wilson, although he differed on the issue of what damages could be claimed.

Devefi Pty Ltd v Mateffy Perl Nagy Pty Ltd (1993) 113 ALR 225

Facts and issues

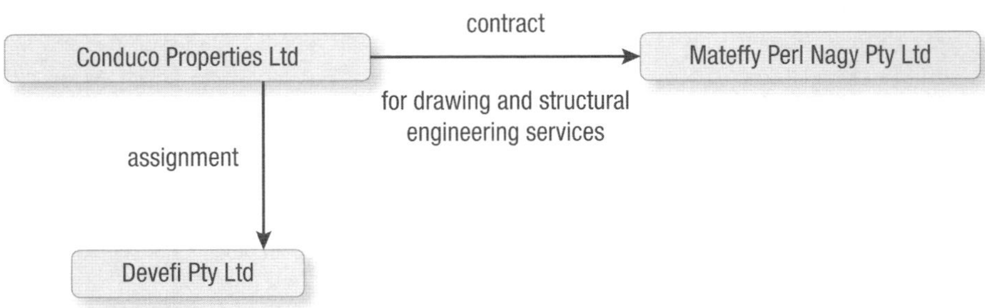

Conduco Properties, a property developer and owner of some land, contracted with Mateffy Perl Nagy, a firm of engineering consultants, for Mateffy Perl Nagy to provide drawings and structural engineering services in relation to a building Conduco Properties hoped to construct. Some time after the diagrams were provided, but while the engineering services were still to be provided, Conduco sold the land to Devefi and purported to also assign their contractual rights to Devefi. Devefi then contracted with another builder, Southern Cross, to construct the building but Devefi provided Mateffy Perl Nagy's diagrams to Southern Cross to be used in the construction. After some initial confusion and negotiation, Mateffy Perl Nagy assisted Southern Cross in the construction for a separate fee but sued Devefi for breach of the copyright in the drawings. The contract between Conduco Properties and Mateffy Perl Nagy included specific clauses on copyright and assignment:

> **5.1 Copyright**
> Copyright in all drawings, reports, specifications, bills of quantities, calculations and other documents provided by the Consulting Engineer in connection with the Project shall remain vested in the Consulting Engineer.
>
> **5.2 Client's Right to Use Documents**
> The Client shall have a licence to use the documents referred to in Clause 5.1 for the purpose of completing the Project; however, the Client shall not use nor make copies of such documents in connection with any work other than work comprised in the Project unless express approval is given in advance by the Consulting Engineer.
>
> **5.3 Publication of Articles**
> The Consulting Engineer may with the consent of the Client publish, either alone or in conjunction with others, articles, photographs and other illustrations relating to the project [sic].
>
> **Part 8.1 Transfer and Assignment**
> (1) The Consulting Engineer and the Client each binds himself and his partners, successors, executors, administrators, assigns and legal representatives to the other party to this

Agreement and to the partners, successors, executors, administrators, assigns and legal representatives of the other party in respect to all convenants [sic] and obligations of this Agreement.

(2) Neither the Consulting Engineer nor the Client shall assign, sublet or transfer any right or obligation under the Agreement without the written consent of the other party. Unless specifically stated to the contrary in any written consent to an assignment, no assignment shall release or discharge the assignor from any obligation under the Agreement.

(3) The Consulting Engineer may at any time change the structure of his practice to or from that of an incorporated company in accordance with the rules of the ACEA. In such case the present Agreement shall be deemed to have been replaced by an identical agreement between the Client and the Consulting Engineer's practice in its new form.

(4) Except in the case of death or incapacity the consulting engineer [sic] shall give the client at least 60 days' notice of intention of a Partner or Partners to leave the partnership. On receipt of such notice the client may terminate the agreement in accordance with Clause 7.1(2) when clause 3.8 will apply. In this case the consulting engineer [sic] or his Successors shall surrender all available documents necessary for continuation of the work.

(5) Nothing contained in this Clause shall prevent the Consulting Engineer from employing within this fee such persons or companies as he may deem appropriate to assist him in the performance of the Agreement.

The issue in the case was whether Conduco Properties had any ability to assign any rights to use the drawings to Devefi without consent from Mateffy Perl Nagy. At trial, the claim by Mateffy Perl Nagy was upheld.

Decision

Appeal dismissed: the contract did not give Conduco Properties a right to assign the use of the drawings.

Per Northrop, Gummow and Hill JJ at 228:

As consulting structural engineers for the project, Mateffy was to do more than prepare the drawings, the copyright in which was to be vested in it. It was to provide 'consultative advisory assistance to the Architect and [Conduco] at design stage' and to visit the site to review and approve the correctness of reinforcement for concreting after this had been checked by the builder, and to advise on other structural matters. Thus, although this appeal is concerned with questions of copyright infringement, and so with the use to which the drawings were put, it would be incorrect to construe provisions in the Mateffy agreement without regard to the circumstance that the preparation and supply of the drawings was but part of a larger 'package' of professional services to be provided to the client by its consulting engineers.

For example, Pt 8.1 must be read with this wider picture in mind . . .

[234] Assignment of the benefit of contractual licences

The nature and contractual effect of the purported assignment by Conduco to Devefi of its rights to use the drawings for the project is to be assessed in the light of propositions of some complexity. They are as follows:

(1) As a general proposition, the benefit of the performance of a contract involving personal skill and confidence cannot be assigned, any more than such a contract may be made the subject of an order for specific performance: *Bruce v Tyley* (1916) 21 CLR 277 (a contract to remove kitchen refuse from a military camp in war-time); Jones and Goodhart, *Specific*

Performance, 1986, p 136; cf *Posner v Scott-Lewis* [1987] Ch 25 . However, what may be called the 'fruits of performance' stand in a different situation. They may be assignable. Thus, copyright in a literary or artistic work itself may be licensed or assigned, and the right of an author to royalties may be dealt with by the author. However, contracts between authors and publishers have been held to be of a personal nature on both sides, so that the benefit of performance is not assignable by either party without the consent of the other: *Stevens v Benning* (1855) 6 De GM & G 223; 43 ER 1218; *Griffith v Tower Publishing Co Ltd* [1897] 1 Ch 21; Laddie, Prescott & Vitoria, *The Modern Law of Copyright*, 1980, para 10.99.

On the present appeal, the respondent submitted that a licence by an engineer or architect of artistic copyright in plans for use by a developer or builder was insusceptible of assignment. It will be necessary to return to this [235] submission, which is of prime importance for the proper construction to be given to Parts 5 and 8 of the Mateffy agreement and the characterisation of that contract as a whole.

(2) The benefits provided under a contract of personal services, which would otherwise not be assignable, may be assigned if (and to the extent to which) upon its proper construction the contract expressly or impliedly contemplates such an assignment. The authorities are discussed by the New Zealand Court of Appeal in *Peacocke Land Co Ltd v Hamilton Milk Producers Co Ltd* [1963] NZLR 576 at 582–3. That case concerned a contract for the supply of milk for consumption in a particular town and the parties were defined as including their respective 'assigns'. In the present case, there is an issue whether cl 8.1 of the Mateffy contract was to like effect.

(3) The subject matter of a contractual licence may be intangible rights which are not of a description which, under the general law or by reason of statute, is treated as unassignable. Nevertheless, the licence may contain an express provision which is said to bar assignment of the licence of those rights. The nature and operation of such a provision will vary according to its terms and from case to case. The possibilities include the following:

(a) The obligation of the licensor may, on its proper construction, be limited to an obligation in favour of the licensee, so that 'the limitation is not so much imposed on the obligee's right of alienation as upon the obligor's duty to perform'; 'neither public policy nor consistency requires that [the chose in action] be enforceable against the promisor except in accordance with the terms on which his promise was made': *Sacks v Neptune Meter Co* (1932) 258 NYS 254 at 262, discussed in Allcock, 'Restrictions on the Assignment of Contractual Rights' [1983] 42 *CLJ* 328 at 338–9. To similar effect is the observation by Croom-Johnson J in *Helstan Securities Ltd v Hertfordshire County Council* [1978] 3 All ER 262 at 265–6:

> There are certain kinds of choses in action which, for one reason or another, are not assignable, and there is no reason why the parties to an agreement may not contract to give its subject matter the quality of unassignability. In these circumstances, one has to look at the clause itself.

Speaking of that decision (and with particular reference to assignments of debts) Professor Goode, "Inalienable Rights?" (1979) 42 MLR 553, has said:

> Now in so far as the case decided that the assignment was ineffective as between the plaintiffs and the defendant it is unexceptionable. If A, when contracting to pay money to B, makes it clear that his undertaking to B is of a personal character and that payment will be made to B alone, there is no reason why he should be compelled to accept a variation of the contract by being required to pay B's assignee, C. Though the payment of money to one party rather than another may not seem a particular hardship, the debtor may have

> perfectly good commercial reasons for stipulating that he will not recognise the title of an assignee of the debt. In the first place, a debtor who overlooks receipt of a notice of assignment (a not uncommon event in a busy office) and pays the assignor does not get a good discharge and can be compelled to pay a second time, to the assignee. So it is understandable that the debtor may wish to safeguard himself against the consequences of a slip of this kind. Secondly, an assignment to some extent restricts the efficacy of mutual dealings between the debtor and the assignor in that the debtor cannot set up against the assignee equities arising after receipt by him of notice of assignment. Again, it is natural that the debtor should want to avoid being fettered in his ability to set up defences against the assignee.

[236] See also, Goode, *Legal Problems of Credit and Security*, 2nd ed, 1988, pp 123–4.

So, for example, the terms of an option agreement may show that it was intended to be open to acceptance only by the offeree personally: *Carter v Hyde* (1923) 33 CLR 115 at 120–1, 125, 130–2; *Wilson v Commissioner of Probate Duties (Vic)* 78 ATC 4278 at 4282 (affd 79 ATC 4580). The current state of English authority as to the effectiveness of express prohibitions against assignment is discussed by Wallace QC, 'Assignment of Rights to Sue for Breach of Construction Contracts' (1993) 109 *LQR* 82 at 85–8. Even if ineffective between the obligor or promisor and assignor, an assignment may have effect between the assignor and the assignee in various ways: Allcock, supra, at 330–1, 335–6. If the obligor or promisor, after the purported assignment, performs the contract in favour of the assignor, the assignor may hold the fruits of such performance upon trust for the assignee, by analogy to the treatment in equity of contracts to assign after-acquired property. Where the assignment was for value received by the assignor from the assignee, the contract may be taken to contain an implied warranty as to title by the assignor, sounding in damages. It is unnecessary in this litigation to consider the effect of such principles upon the relations between Conduco and Devefi pursuant to cl 40 of their contract for the sale of the site.

(Covenants against assignment of leases of land gave rise to a distinct body of authority. Such a covenant ran with the land and an assignment in breach of it was not void and was effectual to vest the term in the assignee notwithstanding the fact that the lessor might treat the assignment as a cause of forfeiture: *Halsbury's Laws of England*, 1st ed, 1911, vol 18, pp 575–6; *Old Grovebury Manor Farm Ltd v W Seymour Plant Sales and Hire Ltd* [1979] 1 WLR 1397 at 1400. Another distinct body of principle deals with restraints upon alienation of land; see *Hall v Busst* (1960) 104 CLR 206 at 217–18, 224–5, 245–6.)

(b) Upon their proper construction, the terms of the prohibition may operate not to circumscribe the nature of the obligation, but as a promise by the assignor to the obligor or promisor not to assign the benefit of the contract, or to assign it only if certain procedures are followed, such as the giving of consent by the promisor. A purported assignment will be a breach of such a promise. It will be a question of construction whether the prohibition is contravened not only by an assignment but also by a declaration of trust by the licensee; a declaration of trust by the licensee in favour of X differs in character from an assignment to X: *Re Turcan* (1888) 40 Ch D 5 at 10–11 *Williams v Commissioner of Inland Revenue* [1965] NZLR 395 at 401.

In each particular case of breach, it will be necessary to determine whether (i) the promisor has merely an action in damages against the assignor, or (ii) the promisor has the election between claiming damages and terminating the contract with the assignor, thereby severing at the root the source of the rights otherwise acquired by the assignee, or (iii) the term is neither a warranty nor a condition corresponding with the above formulation in (i) and (ii), but a term which stands somewhere between a condition and a warranty so that it is capable of operating, according to the gravity of the breach, as either a condition or a warranty: see [237] *Ankar Pty Ltd v National Westminster Finance (Australia) Ltd* (1987) 162 CLR 549 at 561–2; 70 ALR 641. Where there is an exercise by the promisor of a right of termination, then the circumstances of the case may be such as to attract equitable intervention to relieve against forfeiture, a point made by Professor Goode (42 *MLR* at 557).

In *Hodder & Tolley Ltd v Cornes* [1923] NZLR 876, Salmond J considered a mail contract which prohibited the contractor from assigning any moneys due thereunder without the consent of the Postmaster-General, and made forfeiture of moneys due under the contract the penalty for breach of the prohibition. His Honour held that a purported assignment was a good equitable assignment, and that the Crown had not chosen to exercise its right of forfeiture of moneys due under the contract. Salmond J (at 879) referred by way of analogy to the position with covenants against assignments of leases. His Honour held that the true result of the assignment in breach of the contract was not that the assignment was inoperative, but that the moneys assigned became forfeitable to the Crown in accordance with the express provisions of the contract: see also *Annin v Anning* (1907) 4 CLR 1049 at 1067.

What then is the appropriate characterisation of para (2) of Pt 8.1 of the Mateffy contract as it applies to the licence to use the drawings, the copyright in which was vested in Mateffy?

Express licence

The appellant submitted that upon its proper construction, cl 5.2 of the Mateffy agreement, in conferring on 'the client' the right to use the documents for the purpose of completing 'the project', conferred the right on Conduco to assign the licence to a successor in title for that purpose. Then it was submitted that cl 8.1 was ineffective to prevent Conduco from assigning the benefit of the licence because nothing in cl 8.1 cut down the provisions of the 'code' found in cl 5.

In our view, these submissions should not be accepted.

The Mateffy agreement, taken as a whole, provides for the rendering of complex professional services in which, as in many such relationships, personal trust and confidence in the exercise of specialised skills ordinarily would be of great importance to the client; the identity of the client, whose retainer is accepted, would be of considerable importance to the provider of the services. In general, a court of equity would be most reluctant to grant injunctive relief which might have the effect indirectly of specifically enforcing a contract between builder and owner: *Graham H Roberts Pty Ltd v Maurbeth Investments Pty Ltd* [1974] 1 NSWLR 93 at 108. It is then hardly to be supposed that such relief would be given to enforce the supply of services by a consulting engineer to such a project.

If that be so, the contract between Mateffy and Conduco, taken as a whole, was for the provision by Mateffy of services which were of a personal nature and as such the benefit of it, in whole or part, would not ordinarily be treated as assignable by the party to whom the services were to be provided.

It may well be that these personal elements are not present in transactions which are but the bare bones of a licence to use, for reward, an artistic work in which the licensor owns the copyright. But, as we have indicated, more is involved here, in the same way as more than a dealing in copyright is involved in a contract between an author and a publisher.

[238] In our view, Parts 5 and 8 of the Mateffy agreement are to be construed, prima facie, from the position that assignment of the benefit of the agreement is to be permitted only to the extent to which express provision is made see *CB Peacocke Land Co Ltd v Hamilton Milk Producers Co Ltd,* supra. Thus, the present is not a case where the court is dealing with no

more than a contractual licence of intangible rights which ordinarily are treated as freely assignable. Certainly the Act, as we have indicated, contemplates the free assignment and licensing of copyrights. But the licence of the drawings given by Mateffy to Conduco was, in our view, an inseverable part of a broader transaction to which there applied the inhibition against the assignment of benefits of contracts involving personal skill or confidence.

We turn then further to consider Pts 5 and 8 of the Mateffy agreement. [The relevant text is set out earlier in these reasons.]

Part 5 does not deal at all with the question of assignment by 'the client'. The first half of cl 5.2 confers the licence 'to use' the documents 'for the purpose of completing the project'. The phrase 'to use' in our view would embrace the giving of authorisation by the client to the builder working on the project under a contract with the client, to use the plans for that purpose. As we have said, this right of authorisation is a constituent element in the artistic copyright; by cl 5.2 it has been licensed to Conduco as the client.

The second half of cl 5.2 is introduced by the word 'however'. The affirmative grant in the opening passage of cl 5.2 ordinarily would carry with it an implied negative forbidding the client from otherwise using the documents or making copies of them. The second half of the clause contains a conditional relaxation upon what otherwise would be this general restraint. If express approval is given in advance by the consulting engineer [i.e. Mateffy], the client may use and make copies of the documents in connection with work other than that comprised in the project. But in all its operations and qualifications, cl 5.2 must be read subject to the primary provision in cl 5.1. This states that the copyright shall remain vested in the consulting engineer.

We turn then to Part 8. The terms used in cl 8.1 are apt to deal with subcontracting and novation. The reference to obligations as well as rights indicates this. Of course, any novation would require joinder of all three parties and in that sense the provision is strictly unnecessary. The width of the language used is such as also to include assignments of the benefit of contractual rights. Paragraph (2) thereof is directed to the whole range of activities with which the contract is concerned, not merely the copyright licence. It requires the written consent of the other party to either party assigning, subletting or transferring any right or obligation under the agreement.

It was suggested that the term 'sublet' was apt to describe what was involved in the use of the plans by a builder under an arrangement with the client, so that there was some clash between cl 5.2 and cl 8.1. However, the reference to 'subletting' in standard English construction contracts is accepted as a reference to the subcontracting of obligations under the contract: *Hudson on Building and Engineering Contracts*, 10th ed, p 734; *Wallace on Building and Civil Engineering Standard Forms*, p 309. These passages have recently been collected and approved by Staughton LJ in *St* [239] *Martin Property Corp Ltd v Sir Robert McAlpine and Sons Ltd; Linden Gardens Trust Ltd v Lenesta Sludge Disposals Ltd* (13 February 1992, pp 22–23 of the print; the case is unreported, save for the brief account (1992) 57 BLR 57, but is discussed by Wallace QC in his article, supra).

In any event, it follows, in our view, that given the nature of the bundle of rights licensed to the client by cl 5.2, the engagement of the builder by the client is directly and immediately encompassed by the primary grant of the right to use the documents, and that it is not appropriate to describe the operation of cl 5.2 as involving a sub-licence to the builder. Rather, there is a licence of the 'authorisation right' which is an integral part of the consulting engineer's copyright. On the other hand, what cl 5.2 does not do is to license this bundle of rights not only to the client but to any successor in title or assignee of the client.

Returning to cl 8.1, it is true that in para (1) there is an express reference to 'assigns'. But this should be read as identifying those assigns who take pursuant to a transaction of the kind permitted under para (2) or by other operation of law. It should not be read as including those whose title rests upon a transaction effected by a party in breach of para (2).

When the nature of the contract for provision of professional services is appreciated and para (2) of cl 8.1 is read with cl 5.2, the result is that the licence thereby conferred upon the client may be assigned by the client only with the written consent of the consulting engineer. There was no subject matter to which the purported assignment to Devefi of the copyright licence could attach. This is not a case of the kind considered above, in which the assignment, albeit in breach of contract, is effective to pass an interest to the assignee which binds the obligor.

It follows that the case for the existence of an express grant now enjoyed by Devefi fails. We turn to holding (b).

In relation to the other issues raised by Devefi, the Court found that there was no licence to Conduco Properties implied by law because this issue was expressly covered in Parts 5 and 8, and no licence implied by conduct because Mateffy explicitly reserved its rights in all correspondence during negotiations and subsequent work with Southern Cross. An estoppel claim by Devefi was also rejected.

Equuscorp Pty Ltd v Haxton (2012) 246 CLR 498

Facts and issues

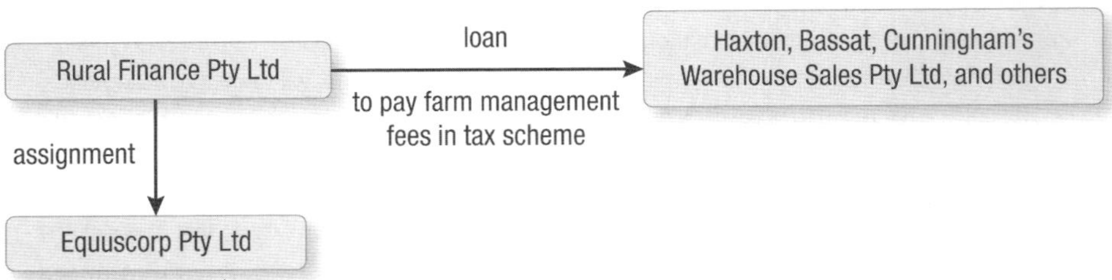

As part of a complex, and ultimately unsuccessful, tax minimisation scheme, Rural Finance provided a loan to investors in a blueberry farm, including Mr Haxton, for the purpose of paying the up-front management fees to the party who was to operate the blueberry farm on behalf of the investor (which allowed the investor to claim the management fees as a tax deduction). At some later point, Rural Finance purported to assign the rights to those loans to Equuscorp. The documentation for the assignment included the following text:

(1) Pursuant to clause 5.2(a) of the Asset Sale Agreement, Rural, as legal and beneficial owner, hereby sells, assigns, transfers and sets over the debts, its interests under the loan contracts, its interests under the guarantees and its interests under the securities, free from all encumbrances to Equus and all interest due and becoming due on the debts for Equus to hold absolutely ('the assignment').
(2) The assignment is an absolute assignment intended to take effect immediately as a legal assignment of, inter alia,
    (a) the legal right to such debts, interests under the guarantors [sic] and its interests under the securities and all interest due and becoming due on the debts.
    (b) all legal and other remedies for these matters in the preceding sub-paragraph (a).
    (c) the power to give good discharge for those matters referred to in sub-paragraph (a) without the concurrence of Rural.

The scheme was unsuccessful; in part, because the aspect of the scheme requiring investment in the blueberry farm did not fulfil the disclosure and prospectus requirements of the Corporations Law (then known as the 'Company Code'), which made the underlying contract to the tax minimisation scheme illegal and unenforceable.

The issue was whether the rights held by Rural, including a possible right of restitution, could be assigned to Equuscorp such that Equuscorp could recover the loan amounts from the borrowers as money 'had and received'. At trial and on appeal, Equuscorp was not able to recover the funds.

Decision

Appeal dismissed (by majority, 5:1, Heydon J in dissent): the assignment was not effective, although the assignment of restitutionary rights may be successful in other circumstances.

Per French CJ, Crennan and Kiefel JJ at 523:

> **Whether Rural's claims for restitution were assignable**
>
> The primary judge found that Rural's rights to claim for restitutionary relief were assigned by the Deed. His Honour did so on the unexamined premise that the rights were assignable. In the Court of Appeal, Dodds-Streeton JA, after a careful review of the authorities, correctly concluded that they offered no clear guidance on the question. Her Honour held that the better view was that the rights were assignable. In so holding, she recognised that the nature of the restitutionary right, informed by equitable considerations and subject to defences such as change of position, could pose difficulties for an assignee. These, however, were problems which would affect the availability and nature of the remedy, rather than constituting an absolute barrier to assignment.
>
> Gummow and Bell JJ point out in their joint reasons that it might be said that Rural's claims against the respondents for money had and received only accrued when the respondents pleaded the unenforceability of the loan agreements in their defences. As their Honours observe, however, the provision of value by Equuscorp under the asset sale agreement would have overcome the difficulty that the claims were mere expectancies at the time the Deed was executed. The questions which remain are whether such claims are assignable and whether they were the subject of assignment.
>
> The respondents submitted that a claim for money had and received is not a 'chose in action' but a 'bare right of action' and therefore not assignable. The concept of the chose in action has a tangled historical background, linked closely to questions of assignability which, in turn, reflected logical concerns about the personal nature of contractual and delictual rights and policy concerns about maintenance. O R Marshall, writing in 1950, observed that historically the question [524] whether something was a chose in action was independent of the question whether it was assignable. Then confusion arose:
>
>> A thing in action is not assignable; that which is not assignable is a thing in action. This is a vicious circle. There is no test for determining a chose in action or assignability apart from their interrelation.
>
> Marshall argued that the assignability of choses in action depended upon a positive common law prohibition which has gradually been relaxed. That the relaxation did not extend to tortious actions was, he suggested, a survival of the objection that the subject matter of a grant must be certain.
>
> In *Campbells Cash and Carry Pty Ltd v Fostif Pty Ltd*, Gummow, Hayne and Crennan JJ observed that:
>
>> The distinction between the assignment of an item of property and the assignment of a bare right to litigate was regarded as fundamental to the application of the law of maintenance and champerty. But drawing that distinction was not always easy. And it

> was a distinction whose policy roots were not readily discernible, the undesirability of maintenance and champerty being treated as self-evident.

In *Ellis v Torrington*, Scrutton LJ referred to the common position of Courts of Law and Equity in opposition to the assignment of 'a bare right of action, a bare power to bring an action'. Such an assignment was seen 'as offending against the law of maintenance or champerty or both.' That opposition was qualified however:

> [E]arly in the development of the law the Courts of equity and perhaps the Courts of common law also took the view that where the right of action was not a bare right, but was incident or subsidiary to a right in property, an assignment of the right of action was permissible, and did not savour of champerty or maintenance.

The attenuated role of maintenance and champerty in relation to assignability was acknowledged by Lord Mustill in *Giles v Thompson* who spoke of them as maintaining a living presence in only two respects, first as the source of the rule against contingency fees and, secondly, as the ground for denying recognition to the [525] assignment of a 'bare right of action'. Of the latter, Lord Mustill said it was, in his opinion, 'best treated as having achieved an independent life of its own.'

The criteria for assignability of causes of action were widened by the decision of the House of Lords in *Trendtex Trading Corporation v Credit Suisse*. The non-assignability of a bare right to litigate was still treated as a fundamental principle. Nevertheless, Lord Roskill said:

> But it is today true to say that in English law an assignee who can show that he has a genuine commercial interest in the enforcement of the claim of another and to that extent takes an assignment of that claim to himself is entitled to enforce that assignment unless by the terms of that assignment he falls foul of our law of champerty, which, as has often been said, is a branch of our law of maintenance.

The application of criteria of assignability to restitutionary claims has remained uncertain. However, as is pointed out in Smith, *The Law of Assignment*:

> [a]s with tortious causes of action, restitutionary claims can arise independently of any prior relationship between the parties. That said, a restitutionary claim can be so intertwined with a contract, that a legitimate interest may be easy to establish.

The author points out that the question has received very little consideration either in the case law or in text books.

Australian authority on the assignability of restitutionary rights is sparse. In *Mutual Pools & Staff Pty Ltd v The Commonwealth*, Mason CJ observed, without elaboration, that a claim for restitution of taxes mistakenly paid was not based on a contractual right and was not assignable. On the other hand, Brennan J referred to a debt owed by the Commonwealth under an agreement or in restitution as 'a common law chose in action vested in the plaintiff and assignable by it.'

A restitutionary claim for money had and received under an unenforceable loan agreement is inescapably linked to the performance of that agreement. If assigned along with contractual rights, albeit their existence is contestable, it is not assigned as a bare cause of action. Neither policy nor logic stands against its assignability in such a case. The assignment of the purported contractual rights for value indicates a legitimate commercial interest on the part of the assignee in acquiring [526] the restitutionary rights should the contract be found to be unenforceable. Equuscorp fell into the category of a party with a genuine commercial interest in the restitutionary rights. Notwithstanding the difficulties that may attend the claims having regard to particular circumstances and defences which might affect their vindication, the better view is that adopted by the Court of Appeal, namely, that the restitutionary claims were assignable. The question that next arises is whether they were assigned.

Whether the Deed assigned restitutionary claims

[528] The primary judge held that Rural's rights to claim for money had and received were assigned to Equuscorp by operation of cl 2(b) of the Deed. His Honour did not refer to s 199 of the *Property Law Act*. He accepted the submission by Equuscorp that the assignment was expressed in broad terms with the evident intention of giving Equuscorp the right to recover, by whatever remedy was available, the loan debts. He accepted that there would be little purpose in the receivers and managers of Rural selling off the contractual rights and reserving to Rural the common law rights so closely associated with the contractual rights.

The Court of Appeal held that the language of the Deed, construed according to its ordinary meaning and in its total context, including the asset sales agreement, indicated that the assignment was limited to the loan contracts, debts, guarantees and securities. No basis for the implication of a term extending the assignment to alternative restitutionary rights or remedies was identified. The Court held that the reference in cl 2(b) of the Deed to 'all legal and other remedies' was, 'in context, merely an element of a composite phrase which expressly related back to the loan contracts and associated securities'.

Equuscorp submitted that by virtue of s 199(1)(b) the Deed was effectual in law to transfer to Equuscorp 'all legal and other remedies for' the debts and interests under the loans. That term, it submitted, encompassed the causes of action for money had and received in respect of irrecoverable debts or unenforceable loans. Equuscorp submitted that the Court of Appeal's construction of cl 2(b) of the Deed defied commercial sense and well known principles for [529] construing contracts and interpreting legislation which seek to avoid commercial inconvenience. The submissions should be rejected.

The scope of the term 'legal and other remedies' in s 25(6) of the *Judicature Act 1873*, from which s 199(1) is descended, was described by Lord Esher MR in *Read v Brown*:

> the words mean what they say; they transfer the legal right to the debt as well as the legal remedies for its recovery.

At the heart of that observation, supported by the words 'for the same', was the proposition that the relevant legal and other remedies were those which could be invoked to enforce the debt or chose in action assigned. Consistently with that proposition the assignment of a judgment debt has been held to attract the right to invoke garnishee procedures. The assignment of a debt owing by a company enables the assignee to petition for the winding up of the company for, by s 25(6):

> new rights [were] given to the assignees of debts, and all legal and other remedies for the assertion of those rights.

Because of the illegality which infected the schemes, the loan agreements were unenforceable and any debts owing pursuant to them irrecoverable. Actions for recovery of money had and received under the agreements were not actions to enforce the agreements. So much is obvious. It also appears from the decision of this Court in *Pavey & Matthews*. In that case, the Court accepted the principle that an action in quantum meruit, brought as a restitutionary claim for services rendered under an unenforceable contract, did not involve enforcement of the contract. That principle extended to other restitutionary claims in respect of benefits received under contracts which, for one reason or another, are unenforceable. As Deane J said:

> The quasi-contractual obligation to pay fair and just compensation for a benefit which has been accepted will only arise in a case where there is no applicable genuine agreement or where such an agreement is frustrated, avoided or unenforceable. In such a case, it is the very fact that there is no genuine agreement or that the genuine agreement is frustrated, avoided or unenforceable that provides the occasion for (and

> part of the circumstances giving rise to) the imposition by the law of the obligation to make restitution.

Clause 2(b) adopted the language of s 199(1)(b) with its inherent limitations and should be construed accordingly. Rural's rights to claim for money had and received, if they existed, would not have been transferred to Equuscorp by operation of cl 2(b) as a legal remedy within the meaning of s 199(1)(b).

[530] Clause 1 of the Deed relevantly assigned Rural's debts and 'its interests under the loan contracts'. Equuscorp did not rely upon it. In any event, neither of those terms was apt to encompass non-contractual claims for restitutionary relief. The Deed was not expressed in terms of restitutionary rights.

The question whether the asset sale agreement and the Deed made pursuant to it may be said to amount to an assignment, for value, of restitutionary rights which may arise in the future in connection with the monies advanced under the loan agreements, and thus amount to an agreement to assign them, which equity would recognise, was not considered in the court below and was not raised in argument on these appeals.

Conclusion

For the preceding reasons the appeals should be dismissed with costs ...

Per Gummow and Bell JJ at 531:

The Court of Appeal, differing from Byrne J, held that while 'a robust construction' was applicable to 'commercial documents', the subject matter of the Assignment did not extend to alternative rights and remedies which were predicated upon the unenforceability of the loan agreements.

The reasoning of Byrne J is to be preferred and should be accepted. Clause 1 of the Assignment assigned the debts of Rural and its interests under the loan agreements. This did not catch the claims Rural might have to recover from the borrowers upon an action for money had and received. But the effect of cl 2 was that the instrument was to take effect as an immediate and absolute legal assignment not only of the subject matter of cl 1 but also of all 'other remedies for these matters'. Any action for money had and received was a remedy 'for these matters' in the sense that it arose out of or by reason of the failure of the loan agreements. There would have been little sense for the [532] receivers and managers to retain these restitutionary actions and for Equuscorp to pay for some but not all of the rights of Rural against the borrowers.

It may be said that the actions by Rural against the respondents for money had and received only accrued after the Assignment, when in the course of the subsequent litigation the respondents, by their defences, pleaded that the loan agreements were unenforceable at their option. However, even if the actions for money had and received were to be regarded as no more than expectancies at the date of the Assignment, the presence of the value given by Equuscorp to the receivers and managers of Rural in equity would have immediately transferred the equitable title to the choses in action to Equuscorp when the actions accrued.

A further analysis, which may avoid any issues arising from the absence of Rural as a party to the enforcement of an equitable assignment of a legal chose in action, was offered by Equuscorp and is as follows. Section 420(2)(g) of the Corporations Law empowered the receivers and managers of Rural to convert its 'property ... into money'. 'Property' was so defined in s 9 as to include any legal or equitable estate or interest, whether present or future, vested or contingent. The legislative end in view is the turning to account of all property of the company, including expectancies, in the course of the conduct of the receivership so as to remove the company from any further involvement as a necessary party in any subsequent litigation brought by the purchaser against an obligor – here, the respondent investors.

However that may be, an action by an equitable assignee without joining the assignor is not a nullity; the action may be liable to be stayed pending joinder, but no such application for a stay has been made in the present litigation. The authorities considered by Lord Collins of Mapesbury in *Roberts v Gill & Co* indicate that any outstanding assignor must be joined before final judgment can be obtained by the assignee, but that has been held not to be necessary where the assignee is seeking interlocutory relief. As noted above, if Equuscorp were to obtain the relief it seeks in these appeals, this would not be final in nature.

Finally, the Assignment was not open to the objection that it dealt with no more than 'bare' rights of action and so attracted the statements of principle in *Poulton v The Commonwealth*. It has [533] long been held that an exception exists where the assignee has an interest in the suit, and a genuine and substantial commercial interest is now regarded as sufficient. In the present litigation this was satisfied by the charge which Equuscorp held over the assets of Rural to secure the indebtedness of Rural; the recovery on the restitutionary claim would, as counsel put it, 'fill the gap created by the debts imploding under illegality'.

14.2.4 Transferring responsibility for performance

In general, this chapter examines the assignment of benefits—who can sue to be paid for a breach of contract? However, transfer of responsibility under a contract is more fraught. Although there can be arrangements where subcontractors are hired by party to a (head) contract to perform certain tasks on their behalf, the subcontractor does not become liable to the other party in the head contract for performance. If the original party to the contract wishes to transfer responsibility for performance, then a novation must be established—not merely an assignment. The issue of transferring responsibilities is discussed in the case of *Tolhurst*, extracted below.

Tolhurst v Associated Portland Cement Manufacturers (1900) Ltd [1902] 2 KB 660

Facts and issues

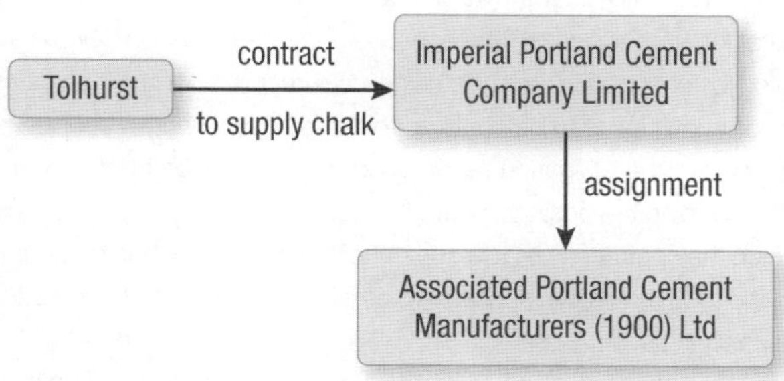

Tolhurst entered into a contract with Imperial Portland Cement to supply chalk to a new cement facility constructed by Imperial. The contract included a set price of 1 shilling and 3 pence per ton of chalk. Nearly two years later, Imperial voluntarily liquidated its business and purported to assign all its rights and assets to Associated Portland Cement Manufacturers (1900) Ltd, which was a much larger entity. Tolhurst agreed to continue chalk deliveries but demanded a higher price: 2 shillings per ton (which was a significant increase; there were 12 pence to a shilling). Associated Portland refused. Tolhurst sued Associated Portland for deliveries completed and Associated Portland cross-claimed, alleging it could enforce the original agreement.

The issue was whether the assignment from Imperial Portland to Associated Portland was effective.

At trial, Tolhurst was successful.

Decision

Appeal allowed: the assignment to Associated Portland was ineffective; however, Imperial Portland still could enforce the contract.

Per Collins MR at 665:

> The question raised in these appeals is whether a contract made between one Tolhurst and the Imperial Portland Cement Company, Limited, for the supply of chalk by Tolhurst to the company for their manufacture of Portland cement upon a certain piece of land can be enforced against Tolhurst, the company having assigned to another company called the Associated Portland Cement Manufacturers (1900), Limited, its property and undertaking, including the contract in question, without the consent of Tolhurst.
>
> [668] It is, I think, quite clear that neither at law nor in equity could the burden of a contract be shifted off the shoulders of a contractor on to those of another without the consent of the contractee. A debtor cannot relieve himself of his liability to his creditor by assigning the burden of the obligation to some one else; this can only be brought about by the consent of all three, and involves the release of the original debtor: see *Liversidge v. Broadbent*, and cases collected in the notes to *Lampleigh v. Brathwait.* On the other hand, it is equally clear that the benefit of a contract can be assigned, and wherever the consideration has been executed and nothing more remains but to enforce the obligation against the party who has received the consideration, the right to enforce it can be assigned, and can be put in suit by the assignee in his own name after notice. Whether the right so created involves privity between the debtor and the assignee is, I think, doubtful; and the rule of the common law that the action must be brought in the name of the assignor shews that it did not regard such a transaction as equivalent to a novatio. The right seems rather to be based on the equitable principle that it would be against conscience on the part of the person on whom the obligation lay to discharge it to the original contractee after he had notice that the latter had assigned the benefit of it to another person. The special right of ignoring altogether the consent of the person upon whom the obligation lies to the substitution of one person for another as the recipient of the benefit would seem in principle and in common justice to be confined to those cases where it can make no difference to the person on whom the obligation lies to which of two persons he is to discharge it, and I think the right of dropping the original contractee out of the discussion must be limited to those cases only in which the contract — that is, the benefit of all that remains to be done under it has been assigned; and [669] it is in this sense only, as it seems to me, that contracts can be said in strictness to be assignable.
>
> There is, however, another class of contracts, where there are mutual obligations still to be enforced and where it is impossible to say that the whole consideration has been executed. Contracts of this class cannot be assigned at all in the sense of discharging the original

contractee and creating privity or quasi privity with a substituted person. 'You have a right,' says Lord Denman C.J., in a passage cited by Gray J. in delivering the judgment of the Supreme Court of the United States in the case of *Arkansas Smelting Co. v. Belden Co.*, 'to the benefit you contemplate from the character, credit, and substance of the party with whom you contract': *Humble v. Hunter.* To suits on these contracts, therefore, the original contractee must be a party, whatever his rights as between him and his assignee. He cannot enforce the contract without shewing ability on his part to perform the conditions performable by him under the contract. This is the reason why contracts involving special personal qualifications in the contractor are said, perhaps somewhat loosely, not to be assignable. What is meant is, not that contracts involving obligations not special and personal can be assigned in the full sense of shifting the burden of the obligation on to a substituted contractor any more than where it is special and personal, but that in the first case the assignor may rely upon the act of another as performance by himself, whereas in the second case he cannot. He cannot vouch the capacity of another to perform that which the other party to the contract might, however unreasonably, insist was what alone he undertook to pay for — namely, work to be executed by the party himself. If, for instance, he had ordered a painting from some unknown artist of his own choice, he could not be compelled to accept instead of it the work of another artist, however eminent.

These considerations seem to me to establish beyond all question that the present case is not one where it would be possible to assert that on any rule of law or equity the new [670] company could be deemed to be substituted into the place of the old one at the mere will of the assignor without the consent of Mr. Tolhurst. The latter may be wrong, but he is entitled, it seems to me, to have a choice in the matter of the person or company to whom he is asked to give credit, and he may prefer, and I think he is entitled to prefer, to deal with a particular company doing business in one place on a comparatively small scale, rather than with one which is about to embark upon a large combination of competing businesses requiring a very large capital and involving commensurate risks. No instance of such a contract being sued on in the name of the assignee has been adduced, and the judgment of the Supreme Court of the United States in the case cited is clear against it; while for the reasons I have above given it seems to me to fall outside that limited class of cases in which privity or quasi privity can be said to be established without novation.

Collins MR then examined whether the liquidation brought the original contract to an end and he concluded that it did not bring the contract to an end.

[674] I have attempted to consider the question of the change of position brought about by the consignment on purely legal principles; but it seems to me on the facts, so far as we know them from the correspondence, that these considerations had really nothing to do with Mr. Tolhurst's attitude. He seems to have seized a convenient opportunity of getting rid of a burdensome contract, not because of any real or supposed change of position by reason of the assignment, but because the market price of chalk had risen considerably above the contract price, and he was very willing if he could to reap the advantage of the rise. He must have been cognisant of all that had taken place in the antecedent negotiations involving assignments of the benefit of his contract to nominees, and ultimately to the new company, before final and formal execution, and he continued to deliver throughout this period and for a week after formal notice without objection. His objection when made is put on technical grounds only. Having regard also to the length of time contemplated by the contract for the [675] continuance of the arrangement, he must, I think, have contemplated possible changes by devolution or assignment on both sides. For the reasons I have given, therefore, I feel compelled to differ from the conclusion arrived at

by Mathew J. But, as far as I can see, we differ only upon an inference of fact as to what under all the circumstances was the real meaning of the bargain. Was it intended to exclude performance by any person other than the old company itself of their part of the obligation? I have come to the conclusion that it was not. I think, therefore, that the appeals must be allowed.

The President of the Probate Division agrees with this judgment.

Per Cozens-Hardy LJ at 676:

Under these circumstances the plaintiffs contend (1) that the Associated Company, as the assignees of the contract, can sue the defendant for breach thereof, or alternatively (2) that the Imperial Company can sue the defendant, there having been no breach on their part, and no abandonment of the contract.

As to the first point, it is clear that at common law no action could be maintained by an assignee for breach of a contract of this nature. There is no privity between the Associated Company and the defendant. But it is said that all this has been altered by s. 25, sub-s. 6, of the *Judicature Act, 1873* — that there is here an 'absolute assignment' of a 'legal chose in action' which is effectual to transfer the legal right to such chose in action.

Now, this section relates to procedure only. It does not enlarge the class of choses in action, the assignability of which was previously recognised either at law or in equity. It is designed to avoid the necessity of going first to a Court of [677] equity and then to a Court of law. Some limit must be put upon the words used. It is plain that there are many contracts of such a personal nature that they do not admit of being assigned, e.g., a contract to paint a picture. And even where the personal element did not come in, the old Court of Chancery did not, any more than the Courts of Common Law, regard the burthen of a contract as assignable. There was an exception in the case of contracts of which specific performance could be granted. But the contract of January 5, 1898, is not in its nature capable of specific performance. In old days the Associated Company could not have maintained a bill in Chancery to enforce it, and I think the Judicature Act in no way alters the position ...

[680] I agree with the Master of the Rolls in holding that the plaintiffs are entitled to a declaration that the agreement of January 5, 1898, is a subsisting and valid and binding agreement [681] between the Imperial Company and the defendant, and to consequential relief on that footing.

QUESTIONS

(1) Why are the trademarks held by a separate company from the company actually using or exploiting the trademark, even though both companies are part of the same corporate group? What is the commercial benefit of such an arrangement?

(2) Were all of the assignments completely ineffective in these cases or was it the assignment of only certain rights that failed? What differences are the courts examining in coming to their decisions?

(3) To what extent are these cases a basis of an argument that large commercial transactions are doomed to fail, as an assignment of certain rights may never be possible without the consent of a potentially large number of other parties?

(4) To what extent is it appropriate that the notion of 'assignment' applies to both contractual and non-contractual rights? Should different tests apply?

(5) What economic interest is protected or undermined by narrowly defining when rights can be assigned?

(6) What are the practical problems with relying on the original parties to the agreement to enforce promises under the agreement on behalf of others?

14.3 International perspectives

The matter of assignment of rights is not dealt with by the *CISG*. Thus, for a contract governed by the CISG (see **25.4.1** on applicability), any questions relating to the assignment of a contract will fall for determination in accordance with the relevant domestic law, determined by the law deemed applicable under the conflict of laws rules of the court or tribunal. Where UNIDROIT Principles apply (see **25.4.3**); its rules on assignment of rights may be relevant: see **Chapter 9**, UNIDROIT Principles. However, any mandatory rules of relevant domestic law in relation to assignment will prevail over these rules: art 1.4 UNIDROIT Principles.

14.4 Review

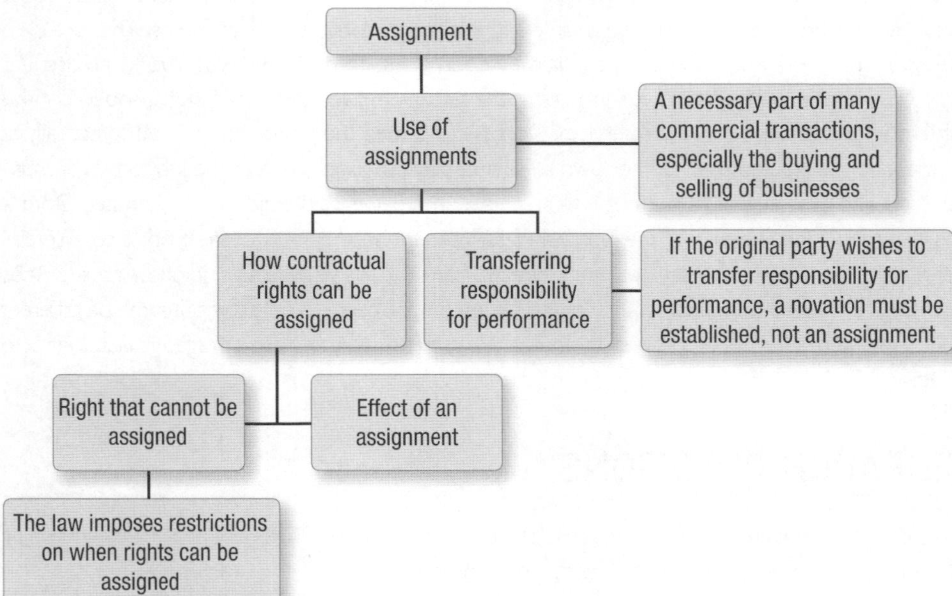

TIPS FOR APPLYING THE LAW IN PRACTICE

- It is not usually the original parties to the contract who are in dispute in an assignment problem; it may be that there have been several assignments on both sides of a contract, and that the dispute arises between two subsequent assignees. In these circumstances, it can be helpful to draw a case diagram to clearly identify who is claiming from which original party to the contract.

- The distinction between assignment and novation is an important one when advising clients prospectively—should they go down the assignment path or the novation path? In many circumstances, the novation path is the more prudent approach. However, when answering problem questions in an exam, there is usually no scope to 'advise' in relation to novation—usually the dispute is about whether a purported assignment was effective or not.
- The courts adopt a nuanced and layered approach to issues of assignment. Judges are often having to examine both broad and narrow issues; such as, what kind of contract exists and which specific rights are being assigned. Make sure an exam answer does not present an overly simplistic approach to the analysis.
- Remember that this is one area in which the possibility of statutory intervention into the underlying common law and equitable principles is high, so always be alert to whether specific acts may operate to limit or facilitate assignment in relation to the specific rights and contract under examination.

PROBLEM QUESTION

Dora is a carpenter, who specialises in repairing the woodwork in old buildings. Robert is a property developer and he recently purchased a large old factory to convert to apartments. The factory has extensive woodwork but it is in poor condition. Robert wants to repair the woodwork and use it as a feature in the new apartments. Given the size of the factory, this will be a lot of work. Robert contracts with Dora for the carpentry repair services. Dora is concerned the job is too big, both practically and financially, for her to complete on her own so she purports to assign parts of the job to two friends, Jo and Anh, who are carpenters but not with expertise in repairing old buildings. Jo, Anh and Dora are each responsible for one-third of the job. Dora falls ill and the vast majority of the work is completed by Jo and Anh. Jo and Anh now seek payment directly from Robert, who refuses. Jo and Anh sue Robert for 85 per cent of the total value of the contract. Can they succeed? Would this outcome be different if Jo and Anh were hired as employees by Dora? What if Jo and Anh were engaged as subcontractors by Dora?

RESEARCH QUESTIONS

(1) To what extent are the principles applied by courts to issues of assignment evolving over time or is there a common thread to the court's decisions in this area?

(2) Disputes over assignment require the courts to balance, on the one hand, the rights of parties to act with freedom of contract and, on the other hand, the protection of parties who are providing something 'personal' in nature; is this a balance the courts can legitimately enforce? What assumptions and values are built into what the courts may identify as 'personal'?

15

IMPOSSIBILITY AND CHANGE IN CIRCUMSTANCES

15.1 Overview

The common law is attempting to balance the need for legal certainty with the reality of a changing world. This presents a challenge for the doctrine of frustration. Although the language in which the test for frustration is expressed has varied over time, the underlying principle is relatively clear: that performance of the contract is so fundamentally different from what was originally agreed to that the contract should no longer be enforced. This chapter examines the common law development of the doctrine, in particular its refinement in the Australian context, and presents the sporadic statutory attempts at reform in some jurisdictions.

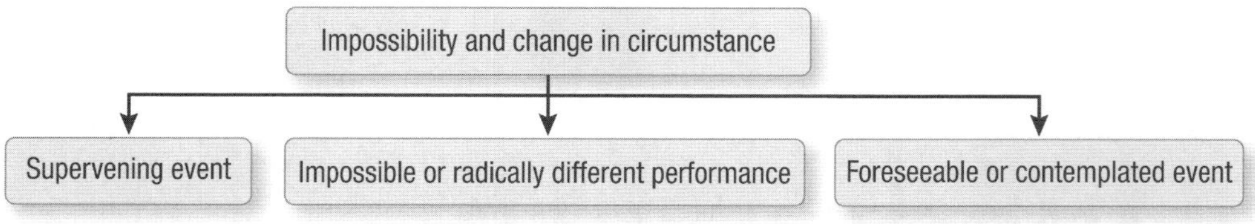

15.2 Frustration

Concepts	Short explanation	Relevant authorities	*Principles* text*
When has the supervening event occurred?	The supervening event has to have occurred after the contract was formed; compare this with 'mistake' in which the event occurred before the contract was formed (often with neither party being aware of the event)	*Taylor v Caldwell* (1863) 3 B & S 826 *Sale of Goods Act 1923* (NSW) s 12 *Codelfa Construction Pty Ltd v State Rail of Authority of New South Wales* (1982) 149 CLR 337	Chapter 15: 15.01–15.02
Is performance of the contract now impossible or radically different?	The impact of the supervening event on the contract is that it is impossible to perform the obligations under the contract or performance is now radically different from what was originally contemplated by the parties. This argument may also apply if a 'common purpose' was frustrated	*Codelfa Construction Pty Ltd v State Rail of Authority of New South Wales* (1982) 149 CLR 337 (including *Davis Contractors Ltd v Fareham Urban District Council* [1956] AC 69) *Tsakiroglou & Co Ltd v Noblee Thorl GmbH* [1962] AC 93 *oOh! Media Roadside Pty Ltd v Diamond Wheels Pty Ltd* (2011) 32 VR 255 *Brisbane City Council v Group Projects Pty Ltd* (1979) 145 CLR 143	Chapter 15: 15.05–15.09

Concepts	Short explanation	Relevant authorities	*Principles* text*
Was the supervening event foreseeable or averred to in the contract?	If the supervening event was forseeable or averred to, then frustration cannot be found	*Codelfa Construction Pty Ltd v State Rail of Authority of New South Wales* (1982) 149 CLR 337 *oOh! Media Roadside Pty Ltd v Diamond Wheels Pty Ltd* (2011) 32 VR 255	Chapter 15: 15.09

* Consult the corresponding section(s) of the *Principles* text for more detail.

15.2.1 The impact of post-contractual changes

The conceptual difficulty underlying the doctrine of frustration is the attempt to find a principled basis to balancing the need for certainty with the desire for flexibility. Too rigid a maintenance of the original contract will undermine the utility of the law. Too loose an approach and the necessary certainty created by contracts is eroded. The issues examined in this chapter highlight the court's attempts to assess the impact of post-contractual changes to the performance of the contract in a principled manner.

15.2.2 Absolute obligations and the doctrine of frustration

At common law, the chance that supervening events may impact on the performance of the contract, such as via the destruction of the subject of the contract, was a matter left to the parties to determine in the negotiation of the contract. 'After the fact' intervention by courts was not possible. Gradually that view changed. The total destruction of goods subject to contract (in other words, when the destruction occurs after the contract is formed) was the subject of the classic English case of *Taylor v Caldwell* (1863), which recognised some role for the common law to come to the assistance of the parties; however, the basis for that assistance has evolved in Australia and the specific situation of destroyed goods is now covered by the *Sale of Goods* statutes. The case and the statute are extracted below.

Taylor v Caldwell (1863) 3 B & S 826

Facts and issues

Caldwell, the owner of The Surrey Gardens and Music Hall, agreed to allow Taylor to occupy the Gardens and Music Hall for four days over several months to conduct a concert series. However, before the first concert, the Music Hall burned down and could not be used by Taylor. Taylor sued Caldwell claiming Caldwell was in breach of the agreement.

The issue was whether the destruction of the Music Hall removed Caldwell's obligation to fulfil the contract.

Decision

Claim dismissed: the continued existence of the Music Hall was an implied term in the agreement such that the destruction of the Music Hall excused performance by Caldwell.

Per Blackburn J at 832:

> In this case the plaintiffs and defendants had, on the 27th May, 1861, entered into a contract by which the defendants agreed to let the plaintiffs have the use of The Surrey Gardens and Music Hall on four days then to come, viz., the 17th June, 15th July, 5th August and 19th August, for the purpose of giving a series of four grand concerts, and day and night fetes at the Gardens and Hall on those days respectively; . . . The agreement then proceeds to set out various stipulations between the parties as to what each was to supply for these concerts and entertainments, and as to the manner in which they should be carried on. The effect of the whole is to shew that the existence of the Music Hall in the Surrey Gardens in a state fit for a concert was essential for the fulfilment of the contract – such entertainments as the parties contemplated in their agreement could not be given without it.
>
> After the making of the agreement, and before the first day on which a concert was to be given, the Hall was destroyed by fire. This destruction, we must take it on the evidence, was without the fault of either party, and was so complete that in consequence the concerts [833] could not be given as intended. And the question we have to decide is whether, under these circumstances, the loss which the plaintiffs have sustained is to fall upon the defendants. The parties when framing their agreement evidently had not present to their minds the possibility of such a disaster, and have made no express stipulation with reference to it, so that the answer to the question must depend upon the general rules of law applicable to such a contract.
>
> There seems no doubt that where there is a positive contract to do a thing, not in itself unlawful, the contractor must perform it or pay damages for not doing it, although in consequence of unforeseen accidents, the performance of his contract has become unexpectedly burthensome or even impossible. . . . But this rule is only applicable when the contract is positive and absolute, and not subject to any condition either express or implied: and there are authorities which, as we think, establish the principle that where, from the nature of the contract, it appears that the parties must from the beginning have known that it could not be fulfilled unless when the time for the fulfilment of the contract arrived some particular specified thing continued to exist, so that, when entering into the contract, they must have contemplated such continuing existence as the foundation of what was to be done; there, in the absence of any express or implied warranty that the thing shall exist, the contract is not to be construed as a positive contract, but as subject to an implied con-[834]-dition that the parties shall be excused in case, before breach, performance becomes impossible from the perishing of the thing without default of the contractor.
>
> There seems little doubt that this implication tends to further the great object of making the legal construction such as to fulfil the intention of those who entered into the contract. For in the course of affairs men in making such contracts in general would, if it were brought to their minds, say that there should be such a condition. . . .
>
> [839] In the present case, looking at the whole contract, we find that the parties contracted or the basis of the continued existence of the Music Hall at the time when the concerts were to be given; that being essential to their performance.

[840] We think, therefore, that the Music Hall having ceased to exist, without fault of either party, both parties are excused, the plaintiffs from taking the gardens and paying the money, the defendants from performing their promise to give the use of the Hall and Gardens and other things. Consequently the rule must be absolute to enter the verdict for the defendants.

Sale of Goods Act 1923 (NSW) s 12[1]

Section 12 Goods perishing before sale but after agreement to sell
Where there is an agreement to sell specific goods, and subsequently the goods without any fault on the part of the seller or buyer perish before the risk passes to the buyer, the agreement is thereby avoided.

The precedent set by *Taylor v Caldwell* expanded beyond the specific circumstances and came to apply in many different settings. This development resulted in the 'modern' approach that adopts the 'radically different' test, which was first stated, in the English context, in the case of *Davis Contractors Ltd v Fareham Urban District Council* [1956] AC 69, and which was then adopted in the Australian context in *Codelfa* (1952). The case of *Davis Contractors* is discussed extensively in the extracts in *Codelfa*, below. Although this idea was initially seen as having an 'implied term' basis, the current approach eschews the 'implied term' analysis and instead purports to identify the 'true construction' of the contract.

15.2.3 The consequences of frustration

The consequences of frustration at common law are severe—the contract is avoided and losses fall where they fall. Money paid under the contract is very rarely recoverable. Recent statutory inroads have attempted to ameliorate this aspect of the law, although with limited success (see below at **15.3**).

15.2.4 The role of contract planning

In accordance with the common law's traditional approach to post-contract changes to performance, there is a role of parties to plan for eventualities during contract negotiation. Flexibility in obligations can be drafted, including the 'rise and fall' clauses often seen in construction contracts, in which the final 'price' may increase or decrease depending on changes in the price of materials; for example, during the period of construction. Another example is a 'force majeure' clause, which specifically allows the contract to be brought to an end if certain named events occur, such as armed conflict or environmental disasters.

The modern Australian statement of the doctrine of frustration is found in the case of *Codelfa v SRA*, although the decision includes a strong dissent from Brennan J, some of which is extracted below.

1 See also *Goods Act 1958* (Vic) s 12; *Sale of Goods Act 1896* (Qld) s 10; *Sale of Goods Act 1895* (WA) s 7; *Sale of Goods Act 1895* (SA) s 7; *Sale of Goods Act 1896* (Tas) s 12; *Sale of Goods Act 1954* (ACT) s 12; *Sale of Goods Act 1972* (NT) s 12.

Codelfa Construction Pty Ltd v State Rail Authority of New South Wales (1982) 149 CLR 337

Facts and issues

See **9.4.2** for the facts and issues of this case.

Decision

Appeal allowed: frustration had occurred; the matter could be returned to the Arbitrator to determine Codelfa's entitlement to claim on a *quantum meruit* basis rather than on the fee stated in the contract.

Per Mason J at 356:

> In *Brisbane City Council v Group Projects Pty Ltd*, Stephen J. discussed the authorities [See extracts below at **15.2.6**, p 490.] . . . [357] I agree with Stephen J.'s acceptance of the approach adopted by Lord Reid and Lord Radcliffe in *Davis Contractors*. Lord Reid said that the task of the court is to determine 'on the true construction of the terms which are in the contract read in light of the nature of the contract and of the relevant surrounding circumstances', 'whether the contract which they did make is . . . wide enough to apply to the new situation: if it is not, then it is at an end'. Later he described frustration as 'the termination of the contract by operation of law on the emergence of a fundamentally different situation'.
>
> Lord Radcliffe said:
>
> > . . . frustration occurs whenever the law recognizes that without default of either party a contractual obligation has become incapable of being performed because the circumstances in which performance is called for would render it a thing radically different from that which was undertaken by the contract. . . . It was not this that I promised to do.
>
> His Lordship, noting that special importance attaches to an unexpected event, observed 'There must be as well such a change in the significance of the obligation that the thing undertaken would, if performed, be a different thing from that contracted for'.
>
> It is implicit, if not explicit, in the judgment of Stephen J., as in the speeches of Lord Reid and Lord Radcliffe in *Davis Contractors*, that to express a preference for this view of frustration as against the theory of the implied condition and other suggested bases is not to cast doubt on the authority of earlier decisions. This is of critical importance because the earlier cases provide many illustrations of the proposition that a contract will be frustrated when the parties enter into it on the common assumption that some particular thing or state of affairs essential to its performance will continue to exist or be available, neither party undertaking responsibility in that regard, and that common assumption proves to be mistaken . . . Two objections may be urged to the width of the proposition I have stated.

The first objection related to whether a common assumption had to be found in the contract itself, which Mason J rejected and found the assumption could be found in extrinsic materials.

> [. . .]
>
> [359] The second objection is that the proposition does not sufficiently acknowledge the fact that the event which generally, if not universally, works a frustration, is an event which supervenes after the making of the contract, viz. a change in the law which makes it impossible for the parties to execute the contract. It is not surprising that the cases commonly throw up situations

of supervening impossibility caused by a change in the law — they are the more common instances of the unforeseen or unexpected occurrence. But in principle there is no reason why a mutual assumption arising from a mistaken view that an activity is immune from injunctive relief should not attract the principle of frustration. No doubt it is more difficult in such a case to show that the grant of injunctive relief was not foreseen or could not reasonably have been foreseen, but if that can be shown then the doctrine of frustration should apply. The injunction is a supervening event though it does not stem from any alteration in the law.

An unusual element in the present case is that the parties appear to have received, accepted and acted on erroneous legal advice that the contract work could not be impeded by the grant of an injunction to restrain noise or other nuisance, advice which was based on an erroneous interpretation of s. 11 of the *City and Suburban Electric Railways Act 1915* (NSW). One might have expected the parties and their advisers to have had reservations about the correctness of the advice and to have given consideration to the possibility that, despite the advice, an injunction might be granted. However, the findings do not reflect the existence of any reservations; indeed, they record Codelfa's acceptance of the representations made by the Authority. Codelfa is a wholly owned subsidiary of an Italian company and this may explain Codelfa's willingness to accept and act on the representation made by the Authority.

[360] The doctrine of frustration is closely related to the concept of mutual mistake. However, in general, relief on the ground of mutual mistake is confined to mistakes of fact, not of law. If the common contractual assumption is of present fact it is a case of mutual mistake; if the assumption is of future fact it is a case of frustration . . . , the distinction being that in one case the contract is void ab initio and in the other it is binding until the assumption is falsified. Here the mistake is not one of present fact; it is either a mistake as to future fact or a mistake of law. Even if it be a mistake of law, this is not, I think, fatal to the application of the doctrine of frustration. The unsatisfactory distinction between a mistake of fact and one of law has not so far been carried over into frustration and I see no reason to further complicate the doctrine by invoking this distinction.

The critical issue then is whether the situation resulting from the grant of the injunction is fundamentally different from the situation contemplated by the contract on its true construction in the light of the surrounding circumstances. The contract itself did not require that the work be carried out on a three shift continuous basis six days a week without restriction as to Sundays. But it required completion of the works within 130 weeks. And Codelfa with its tender had submitted a construction programme which involved a three shift continuous basis six days a week. By cl. S.6 of the specifications Codelfa was required to submit a revised programme of work to the Engineer for his determination within thirty calendar days of the issue of a notice to proceed under the contract. This Codelfa did. Again it made provision for the method of operation already mentioned. It was accepted by the Engineer.

Mason J then quoted from the Arbitrator's award, paragraphs 14–19, noting that both parties contemplated three continuous shifts on a six-day basis, no restrictions on possible Sunday work and no injunction, and that the injunction resulted in the original program not being possible, which led to additional costs for Codelfa.

[. . .]

[361] The submission of the proposed programme of work with the tender, its supersession by the revised programme pursuant to cl. S.6 of the specifications, together with the very provisions of cl. S.6 itself dealing with the construction programme, provide a link between the contract and the antecedent discussions so as to enable us, subject to a consideration of specific provisions in the specifications, to say that the contract contemplated that completion

would be achieved within the time stipulated by the method of work already mentioned, it being assumed that it could not be disturbed by the grant of an injunction.

I reject the Authority's argument that cl. S.6 is inconsistent with the notion that the contract looked to this method of work as the mode by which the work was to be completed. Certainly cl. S.6(5) envisaged that a major change to the work diagram as determined by the Engineer might be required by 'revisions to the programme'. It seems that the responsibility for initiating such a change lay with Codelfa. But I do not think that this is necessarily inconsistent with Codelfa's case on frustration nor do I think that cl. G.44(7) of the contract, which provides for the grant of an extension of time in case of delays 'owing to causes beyond the control or without the fault or negligence of the Contractor', covers the position. Delay due to the grant of an injunction on the ground of nuisance committed by [362] Codelfa scarcely answers this description, even though it results from performance of the work in the only manner which will enable completion to take place within the time stipulated.

Clause S.8(2)(c) however, poses a greater obstacle. It provides:

> The operation of all plant and construction equipment shall be such that it does not cause undue noise, pollution or nuisance. This may require the use of sound insulated compressors and air tools, silencers on ventilating fans and restrictions on the working hours of plant or such other measures as approved by the Engineer. The Contractor shall not be entitled to additional payment if the Engineer requires that measures be taken to reduce noise and pollution.

Once the injunctions were granted the Engineer gave notices reflecting the provisions of the injunctions, restricting the hours of work so as to prohibit work at night and thereby inhibited Codelfa from continuing with its three shift operation under the contract.

The first paragraph of cl. S.8(2)(c) contains a promise by Codelfa that it will not operate plant and equipment so as to cause a nuisance. The second specifically looks to the possibility of a restriction on working hours of plant. And the third denies additional remuneration if the Engineer requires measures to be taken to reduce noise and pollution.

Do these provisions support the view that Codelfa was undertaking in any event to perform the contract work, even though the method contemplated by the parties might prove to be unlawful or impossible by reason of its amounting to a nuisance and its being restrained by injunction? I do not think that cl. S.8(2)(c) has such a wide-ranging effect. It involves no subtraction from the language of the provisions to say that it is quite consistent with the contemplated method of work being an essential element of the contract. Indeed, there would be no inconsistency between these provisions and an explicit provision for termination of the contract in the event that the method of work was restrained by injunction. There was plenty of scope for an exercise of the Engineer's power under the second paragraph so long as it did not displace the continuation of that method of work.

I come back then to the question whether the performance of the contract in the new situation was fundamentally different from performance in the situation contemplated by the contract. The answer must, I think, be in the affirmative. Paragraphs 14, 15, 16, 18 and 19 of the Arbitrator's award go a long way towards establishing this answer. The finding contained in par. 16 proceeds on the footing that the contract work could not be carried out as contemplated by the contract once injunctions were granted, the effect of which was to prohibit the continuous three shift a day [363] operation six days a week. Performance by means of a two shift operation, necessitated by the grant of the injunctions, was fundamentally different from that contemplated by the contract.

There is, of course, no inconsistency between the conclusion that a term cannot be implied and the conclusion that events have occurred which have brought about a frustration of the contract. I find it impossible to imply a term because I am not satisfied that in the circumstances of this case the term sought to be implied was one which parties in that situation would necessarily have agreed upon as an appropriate provision to cover the eventuality which has arisen. On the other hand I find it much easier to come to the conclusion that the performance of the contract in the events which have occurred is radically different from performance of the contract in the circumstances which it, construed in the light of surrounding circumstances, contemplated.

[. . .]

Per Brennan J (dissenting) at 409:

The injunction was not a supervening alteration of the law which made illegal the further performance of the contract in the manner stipulated therein. The circumstances in which Codelfa was bound to perform the contract works did not change on 28 June 1972. Prior to that time — though the parties may not have known it to be so — Codelfa was required to avoid the commission of an actionable nuisance in performing the contract, and the injunction required it to avoid the commission of an actionable nuisance in performing its contract after that time. The circumstances in which performance was called for were no different from those which affected the performance of the contract from the time when it was made. The injunction limiting working hours did no more than enforce judicially a limitation by which Codelfa was already legally bound.

[. . .]

Whichever juridical basis is selected as appropriate to the present contract, Codelfa cannot establish that the granting of the injunction was a frustrating event. The case falls within what Latham C.J. in *Scanlan's New Neon Ltd v Tooheys Ltd* (1943) called 'the general rule':

> . . . a man who makes a promise is bound to perform it or to pay damages if he fails to do so, and that he cannot excuse himself by relying upon circumstances dehors the contract for the purpose of showing that he did not mean what he clearly said, or that he should be excused from performance because the contract did not work out in the manner expected by one or even by both of the parties.

After 28 June 1972 Codelfa's work was done in performance of the contract and it was entitled to remuneration in accordance with its terms. The appeal in the frustration action was rightly dismissed.

Aickin, Stephen and Wilson JJ concurred with Mason J in relation to frustration and allowed the appeal.

15.2.5 Contracts which are impossible to perform

Although the language of 'impossibility' seems clear, the courts have often found quite torturous means for distinguishing cases such as *Taylor v Caldwell* and finding no impossibility. The Suez Canal cases are infamous on this point. One of those cases, *Tsakiroglou v Noblee* (1962), is extracted extensively below.

Tsakiroglou & Co Ltd v Noblee Thorl GmbH [1962] AC 93

Facts and issues

Tsakiroglou sold a shipment of groundnuts to Noblee. Tsakiroglou, under a C.I.F. contract ('Cargo. Insurance. Freight.', which means the shipper is responsible for the shipped goods from origin until they are delivered to the destination port) was meant to ship the goods from Port Sudan, Sudan to Hamburg, Germany. The expected path of the trip was via the Suez Canal; however, the Canal was closed to shipping for about six months due to actions by the Egyptian Government and subsequent military action by the Israeli, British and French Governments. The alternate path was the much longer route around the Cape of Good Hope. In the end, the goods were never shipped.

The issue was whether the closure of the Suez Canal was a frustrating event such that the contract was terminated.

Decision

Appeal dismissed: the contract was not frustrated by the closure of the Suez Canal, even though the alternate path was longer and more expensive for the shipper.

Per Viscount Simonds at 110:

> All groundnuts exported from the Sudan to Europe are shipped from Port Sudan, which is the only suitable port. At the date of the contract (October 4, 1956), the usual and normal route for the shipment of Sudanese groundnuts from Port Sudan to Hamburg was via the Suez Canal. Both parties then contemplated that shipment would be made by that route. It would have been unusual and rare for any substantial parcel of Sudanese groundnuts from Port Sudan to Europe to be shipped via the Cape of Good Hope. ... The Suez Canal was blocked on November 2 and remained closed for effective purposes until at least April 9, 1957. But the appellants could have transported the goods from Port Sudan to Hamburg via the Cape of Good Hope during November and December, 1956.
>
> The distance from Port Sudan to Hamburg via the Suez Canal is about 4,386 miles, and via the Cape about 11,137 miles. [111] The freight ruling at the time of the contract for the shipment of groundnuts from Port Sudan to Hamburg via the Canal was about £7 10s. per ton. After the closure of the Canal the Port Sudan United Kingdom Conference imposed the following surcharges for goods supplied on vessels proceeding via the Cape, namely, as from November 10, 1956, 25 per cent., and as from December 13, 1956, 100 per cent. The market price of Sudanese nuts in shell shipped from Port Sudan c.i.f. Hamburg was £68 15*s.* per ton between January 1 and 13, 1957. As has been already said the appellants did not ship any nuts. They claimed that they were entitled to consider the contract as cancelled, and to this view they adhered.
>
> The contract provided by clause 6 that 'In case of prohibition of import or export, blockade or war, epidemic or strike, and in all cases of force majeure preventing the shipment within the time fixed, or the delivery, the period allowed for shipment or delivery shall be extended by not exceeding two months. After that, if the case of force majeure be still operating, the contract shall be cancelled.'
>
> The award was in these terms:
>
> So far as it is a question of fact we find and as far as it is a question of law we hold:
>
> (i) There were hostilities but not war in Egypt at the material time:
>
> (ii) Neither war nor force majeure prevented shipment of the contract goods during the contract period if the word 'shipment' means placing the goods on board a vessel destined for the Port of Hamburg:

(iii) If the word 'shipment' includes not only the placing of the contract goods on board a vessel but also their transportation to the contract destination then shipment via the Suez Canal was prevented during the contract period of shipment by reason of force majeure but shipment via the Cape was not so prevented:
(iv) It was not an implied term of the contract that shipment or transportation should be made via the Suez Canal:
(v) The contract was not frustrated by the closure of the Suez Canal:
(vi) The performance of the contract by shipping the goods on a vessel routed via the Cape of Good Hope was not commercially or fundamentally different from its being performed by shipping the goods on a vessel routed via the Suez Canal. . . .

[112] I come then to the main issue and, as usual, I find two questions interlocked: (1) What does the contract mean? In other words, is there an implied term that the goods shall be carried by a particular route? (2) Is the contract frustrated?

It is convenient to examine the first question first, though the answer may be inconclusive. For it appears to me that it does not automatically follow that, because one term of a contract, for example, that the goods shall be carried by a particular route, becomes impossible of performance, the whole contract is thereby abrogated. Nor does it follow, because as a matter of construction a term cannot be implied, that the contract may not be frustrated by events. In the instant case, for example, the impossibility of the route via Suez, if that were assumed to be the implied contractual obligation, would not necessarily spell the frustration of the contract.

It is put in the forefront of the appellants' case that the contract was a contract for the shipment of goods via Suez. This contention can only prevail if a term is implied, for the contract does not say so. To say that that is nevertheless its meaning is to say in other words that the term must be implied. For this I see no ground. It has been rejected by the learned trial judge and each of the members of the Court of Appeal . . .

[114] I turn now to what was the main argument for the appellants: that the contract was frustrated by the closure of the Canal from November 2, 1956, till April 1957. Were it not for the decision of McNair J. in *Green's case* [1959] 1 QB 131 I should not have thought this contention arguable and I must say with the greatest respect to that learned judge that I cannot think he has given full weight to the decisions old and new of this House upon the doctrine of frustration. He correctly held upon the authority of *Reardon Smith Line Ltd v. Black Sea and Baltic General Insurance Co Ltd* [1939] AC 562 that 'where a contract, expressly or by necessary implication, provides that performance, or a particular part of the performance, is to be carried out in a customary manner, the performance must be carried out in a manner which is customary at the time when the performance is called for.' But he concluded that the continued availability of the Suez route was a fundamental assumption at the time when the contract was made and that to impose upon the sellers the obligation to ship by an emergency route via the Cape would be to impose upon them a fundamentally different obligation which neither party could at the time when the contract was performed have dreamed that the sellers would be required to perform. Your Lordships will observe how similar this line of argument is to that which supports the implication of a term that the route should be via Suez and no other. I can see no justification for it. We are concerned with a c.i.f. contract for the sale of goods, not a contract of affreightment, though part of the sellers' obligation will be to procure a contract of affreightment. There is no evidence that the buyers attached [115] any importance to the route. They were content that the nuts should be shipped at any date in November or December. There was no evidence, and I suppose could not be, that the nuts would deteriorate as the result of a longer voyage and a double crossing of the Equator, nor any evidence that the market was seasonable. In a word, there was no evidence that the buyers cared by what route or, within reasonable limits, when

the nuts arrived. What, then, of the sellers? ... Clearly the contract of affreightment will be different and so may be the terms of insurance. In both these respects the sellers may be put to greater cost: their profit may be reduced or even disappear. But it hardly needs reasserting that an increase of expense is not a ground of frustration ...

Nothing else remains to justify the view that the nature of the contract was 'fundamentally' altered. That is the word used by Viscount Simon in *British Movietonews Ltd. v. London and District Cinemas Ltd.* and by my noble and learned friend Lord Reid in *Davis Contractors Ltd. v. Fareham Urban District Council* In the latter case my noble and learned friend Lord Radcliffe used the expression 'radically different' and I think that the two expressions mean the same thing, as perhaps do other adverbs which have been used in this context. Whatever expression is used, I venture to say what I have said myself before and others more authoritatively have said before me: that the doctrine of frustration must be applied within very narrow limits. In my opinion this case falls far short of satisfying the necessary conditions. Reluctant as I am to differ from a judge so experienced in commercial law as McNair J., I am glad to find that my view is shared by Ashworth J. and all the members of the Court of Appeal ...

[116] In my opinion the appeal should be dismissed with costs.

In separate judgments, Lord Reid, Lord Radcliffe, Lord Hodson and Lord Guest concurred with Viscount Simmonds on similar grounds.

15.2.6 Frustration of common purpose

A possible ground of frustration is if a common purpose for the contract is frustrated by a supervening event. A traditional example is the coronation case of *Krell v Henry* (1903) (discussed in *oOh! Media* (2011) below); however, as explained by the Court in *oOh! Media* (2011), the application of *Krell v Henry* has been significantly curtailed because of the concern that the certainty of contracts could be undermined with an overly broad application of this ground.

oOh! Media Roadside Pty Ltd v Diamond Wheels Pty Ltd (2011) 32 VR 255

Facts and issues

oOh! Media had a licence to display advertising billboards and related materials on the side of a building owned by Diamond Wheels on the southern end of the Melbourne Central Business District. The billboard position had been prominently visible from a busy road when the licence was originally issued in 1967 but the construction of a large office tower on the adjoining land in 2007 significantly reduced the visibility of the location and the associated revenue. Although there was a right to terminate the agreement if the site ever become 'unsuitable', the reduction in visibility was not so great as to make the site 'unsuitable' for advertising.

The issues were whether the construction of the adjoining office tower was not foreseeable such that frustration could be claimed and whether that made performance radically different, such that the construction could frustrate the contract.

Decision

Appeal dismissed: the impact on visibility of future construction did not make performance radically different and it was foreseeable, such that it could have been dealt with by oOh! Media in the contract; however, they had not done so and therefore had accepted the risk of a future impact.

Per Nettle JA at 271:

> **(i) Test for frustration ...**
>
> [273] ... Consistently with *Codelfa*, I take the law to be that a contract is not frustrated unless a supervening event:
>
> (a) confounds a mistaken common assumption that some particular thing or state of affairs essential to the performance of the contract will continue to exist or be available, neither party undertaking responsibility in that regard; and
> (b) in so doing has the effect that, without default of either party, a contractual obligation becomes incapable of being performed because the circumstances in which performance is called for would render it a thing radically different from that which was undertaken by the contract.
>
> In this case, there is no question that the construction of the Northbank Office Tower supervened after the licence agreement was entered into in 2005. The issue is whether the original licensor and licensee are to be taken as having entered into the licence agreement in 2005 on the basis of a common contractual assumption that the line of the sight from the north bound carriageway of Kings Way between the Casino tunnel and the railway viaduct could not be blocked out or obstructed during the term of the agreement.
>
> **(ii) Foreseeability of obstruction**
>
> A number of the single instance decisions to which Stephen J referred in *Brisbane City Council* were concerned with application of the doctrine of frustration in circumstances where a supervening event was foreseeable or foreseen at the time of entry into the contract. As Lord Wright said in *Maritime National Fish Ltd v Ocean Trawlers Ltd* [1935] AC 524, where a supervening event is not only foreseeable but actually foreseen at the time of entry into a contract, it is more difficult to conceive of the parties as having entered into the contract on the basis of a common understanding that the event could not occur during the life of the contract. Where, however, a supervening event, although foreseeable, was not foreseen at the time of entry into the contract, the fact that it was foreseeable may not be of much significance unless the degree of foreseeability is particularly high.
>
> Consequently, as later cases demonstrate, it is important to be precise about the nature and degree of foresight. So far as foreseen events are concerned, the parties to a contract may have foreseen an event but not foreseen the nature or extent of it. In *The Sea Angel* [2007] 2 All ER (Comm) 634, Rix LJ gave as an example, based on *The Nema* [1982] AC 724, a case where the possibility of an industrial strike was foreseen, and actually provided for in the contract, but lasted so long as to go beyond the risk assumed under the contract. It was held to have frustrated the contract. *Cheshire and Fifoot's Law of Contract* suggests that in some cases it may also appear that, 'Failure to provide expressly for an event that was foreseen [is] due to ... a deliberate decision to leave matters to be sorted out by the parties, or by the law'.
>
> [274] In the case of foreseeable but unforeseen events, the nature and extent of foreseeability is critical. Since most events are foreseeable in one sense or another, the parties to a contract will not ordinarily be taken to have assumed the risk of an event occurring during the life of the contract unless the degree of foreseeability of that event is very substantial. Hence, as the position is summarised in *Chitty on Contracts*:

> Much turns on the extent to which the event was foreseeable. The issue which the court must consider is whether or not one or other party has assumed the risk of the occurrence of the event. The degree of foreseeability required to exclude the doctrine of frustration is ... a high one: 'foreseeability' will support the inference of risk-assumption only where the supervening event is one which any person of ordinary intelligence would regard as likely to occur or ... 'one which the parties could reasonably be thought to have foreseen as a real possibility'.

It is not suggested that the parties in this case foresaw that the line of sight from the northbound carriageway of Kings Way to the Sign would be blocked or obscured to the extent that it has been. But there was a dispute before the judge as to whether the fact of blockage or obstruction was foreseeable. The appellant conceded below that it was foreseeable 'that sites can be built out in the Central Business District'. But counsel for the appellant argued that partial or complete obstruction of the line of sight was not foreseeable, because it was not foreseeable that a building would be constructed on the Northbank land.

In my view, the judge was correct to reject that argument. In reality, there were and are any number of ways in which the line of sight from the north bound carriageway of Kings Way to the Site could be blocked or obstructed. The relevant question was whether it was foreseeable that the line of sight could be blocked or obstructed in any of those ways, and the evidence was clear. As the judge recorded, it revealed that the whole area, including Docklands, had changed significantly in the last 14 years. Southbank had been developed. The Casino had been constructed. Apartment towers had gone up and the Aquarium had been erected. It was obvious from the CBD location of the Site that the skyline was constantly changing and that, as a result, the line of sight could be blocked in any number of ways by the construction of buildings or other structures either on the Northbank land or on any of the three buildings fronting Kings Way between Flinders Lane and the building on which the Sign is erected, or in other ways.

In addition to the photographs which were in evidence, Mr Luke Brett, the development and asset manager for the appellant, frankly conceded in answer to questions put to him in cross-examination that it was 'foreseeable ... that things could impede upon that visibility'; that 'it may well be the case that you could have a build-out situation whereby the Waterside Hotel is developed' and 'turn into an office tower one day'; that 'it's foreseeable that that land could have been [275] developed and caused an obstruction to the visibility of the signboard'; and that 'landscapes change'. Mr Dollisson added in the course of his cross-examination that the possibility of a site being built out in a CBD location was well understood in the advertising industry and something against which members of the Outdoor Advertising Association of Australia (of which the appellant was one) were advised to guard by means of appropriate contractual provisions.

[...]

The clause which Mr Dollisson recommended was as follows:

> If at any time during the term, visibility or profile of advertising material displayed on the structure, for the time being erected on the premises, is materially reduced in any way whatsoever '[there was a right to terminate]'.

And '[t]he reason he was giving this sort of advice to the industry, [was] because it's a foreseeable thing'.

In face of that evidence, it seems to me that it was plainly foreseeable at the time of entry into the licence agreement in 2005 that the line of sight from the Kings Street Bridge north bound carriageways to the Sign was at risk of being partially or completely obstructed during the course of the licence agreement. At least, it presents as something which a person of ordinary intelligence would regard as likely to occur or something 'which the parties could reasonably be thought to have foreseen as a real possibility'. That being so, the fact that the appellant did not seek the inclusion of a reduction-in-visibility clause (of the kind to which Mr Dollisson referred in his evidence) tends to support an inference that the appellant assumed the risk of line of sight obstruction.

(iii) Performance not rendered radically different

[277] I turn to the judge's conclusion that . . . the construction of the Northbank tower (even if not foreseeable) did not render performance of the licence agreement 'a thing radically different from that which was undertaken by the contract', or as the judge put it, did not constitute 'a radical and/or fundamental change in circumstances and a wholesale destruction of the value of the Site'.

Counsel for the applicant submitted that the individual case which provided the greatest support for the appellant's claim of frustration was the decision of the English Court of Appeal in *Krell v Henry* [1903] 2 KB 740. It involved a contract for the hire of a flat for two days which, it was said, was entered into on the basis of an unexpressed common assumption that the flat was being hired to view the coronation procession of King Edward VII. The Court of Appeal held that the procession taking place was the foundation of the contract so that, when the procession was cancelled due to the King's illness, the contract was dissolved and the rent was not recoverable. Counsel for the appellant contended that, in the same way here, the unexpressed common assumption on the basis of which the original parties entered into the licence agreement was that motor traffic travelling north over King Street bridge would have an uninterrupted view of the Sign. Thus, once the view was impeded by the construction of the Northbank Office Tower, the agreement was dissolved and rent for the Site ceased to be payable . . .

[278] I do not consider that . . . case supports the appellant's claim. In *Krell v Henry* there was substantial evidence of surrounding circumstances that the parties entered into the agreement on the basis of a common assumption that the hiring of the flat was for the purpose of viewing the coronation procession. It included that the owner of the premises advertised the premises as windows to view the procession and that, when the hirer responded to the advertisement, he was told that the owner was willing to let the rooms for the purpose of seeing the Royal procession for both days, but not nights, of 26 and 27 June 1902. In substance, the agreement was a licence to use the flat for limited periods of time for the particular purpose of watching the procession and for no other purpose. In those circumstances, Vaughan Williams LJ concluded that:

> . . . it cannot reasonably be supposed to have been in the contemplation of the contracting parties, when the contract was made, that the coronation would not be held on the proclaimed days, or the processions not take place on those days along the proclaimed route; and I think that the words imposing on the defendant the obligation to accept and pay for the use of the rooms for the named days, although general and unconditional, were not used with reference to the possibility of the particular contingency which afterwards occurred.

[279] . . . Contrastingly, in this case, there was nothing in the evidence of surrounding circumstances which suggested that the parties shared an understanding at the time of entering into the licence agreement in 2005 that the Site was being let for the sole purpose of displaying advertising and promotional materials to motor traffic travelling north over King's

Street Bridge. Nor was there anything to suggest that the owner of the Site believed or represented to the licensee that the view from parts of the northbound carriageway might not one day be blocked or obscured by the construction of one or more buildings in the line of sight . . .

[282] Although the admissible evidence in this case may not have gone far enough to sustain the judge's conclusion that the possibility of development of the Northbank land was a 'fair business risk', it was plainly foreseeable that something might be developed somewhere along in the line of sight between the north bound carriageway and the Sign and, if it were developed, that it might so obstruct the line of sight as to lessen the number of advertisers who would be interested in the Site and the amount which they would be prepared to pay for its use. In my view, that was a 'fair business risk'.

Looked at objectively, therefore, it can hardly be supposed that an honest and reasonable licensor entering into a long term licence of a valuable advertising site would have been prepared to accept the risk of the agreement coming to an [283] end whenever and if the line of sight from the northbound carriageway of Kings Way was in some way be obstructed. To adopt and adapt the words of Williams J in *Scanlon's New Neon Ltd v Tooheys Ltd*, it would not be reasonable for the licensee as a 'fair dealer' to expect the licensor to make such a contract.

Possibly if not probably, the construction of the Northbank Office Tower was productive of financial hardship; and, doubtless, there may come a point at which hardship turns to frustration. It is a question of fact and degree dependent on the facts and circumstances of each case. But, given the facts and circumstances as they existed in this case at the time of entry into the licence agreement, I do not accept that such economic hardship as may have resulted from the construction of the tower on the Northbank land amounted to frustration.

In my view, the judge was right to reject the claim that construction of the Northbank Office Tower rendered performance of the licence agreement radically different. . . .

Conclusion

I would dismiss the appeal.

Weinberg and Redlich JJA, in separate judgments, concurred with Nettle JA.

Brisbane City Council v Group Projects Pty Ltd (1979) 145 CLR 143

Facts and issues

Group Projects and Brisbane City Council entered into an agreement in which Group Projects agreed to provide extensive urban works, including sewerage, water, footpaths and other amenities, on land not owned by Group Projects conditional on a rezoning occurring that would allow Group Projects to construct residential buildings on adjacent land owned by Group Projects. After the agreement was entered into, but before any rezoning occurred, the land owned by Group Projects was resumed by the Queensland Government to build a school. Group Projects sought to terminate the agreement with Brisbane City Council on the basis that the underlying purpose of the agreement had now been frustrated.

The issue was whether resumption by the Queensland Government and delay in rezoning had frustrated the contract.

Decision

Appeal dismissed: the agreement could not be enforced by Brisbane City Council; although the decision was unanimous, the judgments differed on the ground relied on. Stephen J based his decision on frustration (extracted below). Wilson J based his decision on the legal conclusion that the zoning could never occur once the land had been resumed by the Crown, and therefore the obligations of Group Projects never arose; a conclusion which is supported by Gibbs and Mason JJ but rejected by Stephen J. Murphy J concurred, in part, with Stephen J.

Per Stephen J at 160:

> In *Port Line Ltd. v. Ben Line Steamers Ltd* [1958] 2 QB 146 Diplock J. said:
>
> > It would appear to be the fate of frustration cases when they reach the highest tribunals that either there should be agreement as to the principle but differences as to its application, or differences as to the principle but agreement as to its application.
>
> This was said despite, or perhaps in the light of, what is the leading modern authority in the field, the decision of their Lordships in the *Davis Contractors Case*, pronounced in 1956. Such divergency of principle as commentators have extracted from their Lordships' speeches do not, I think, affect the present case. In the *Davis Contractors Case* Viscount Simonds and Lord Morton offer no guide to principle, although they do reflect the general disinclination to allow much scope to the operation of frustration. Lord Somervell agrees with Lord Reid's conclusion upon 'the proper basis of frustration'. It is in the speeches of Lord Reid and Lord Radcliffe that extensive discussion of principle occurs.
>
> Lord Reid rejected the notion of the implied term as the basis of the doctrine. He says that the task for a court, confronted with the parties' contract, is to determine, on the true construction of the terms of the contract, read in the light of the nature of the contract and of the relevant surrounding circumstances when the parties made it, 'whether the contract which they did make is, on its true construction, wide enough to apply to the new situation: if it is not, then it is at an end.' Frustration he describes as 'the termination of the contract by operation of law on the emergence of a fundamentally different situation'. What I understand his Lordship's approach to involve is, then, a comparison between the contemplated situation, as revealed by the terms of the contract on its true construction, and the situation in fact resulting from the frustrating event. If they be 'fundamentally different' the contract is frustrated subject, of course, to the frustrating event not being the fault of the party seeking to rely upon the doctrine.
>
> Lord Radcliffe considers those cases which treat frustration as involving an implied term, cases which involved diverse approaches, sometimes subjective and sometimes objective, in [161] ascertaining the content of the term to be implied. His Lordship suggests that 'frustration occurs whenever the law recognizes that without default of either party a contractual obligation has become incapable of being performed because the circumstances in which performance is called for would render it a thing radically different from that which was undertaken by the contract. Non haec in foedera veni. It was not this that I promised to do.' This is close to the views of Lord Reid and together they represent the approach which I would apply in the present case. It should, however, be noted that Lord Radcliffe tends rather to concentrate on a change in obligation. Thus he says: 'it is not hardship or inconvenience or material loss itself which calls the principle of frustration into play. There must be as well such a change in the significance of the obligation that the thing undertaken would, if performed, be a different thing from that contracted for.' Lord Radcliffe also introduces the limitation that the frustrating event must not be one which the parties could 'reasonably be thought to have foreseen'. As already mentioned, the 'change in obligation' test proposed by Lord Radcliffe, no doubt apt enough in most frustration situations, seems to be inapplicable here, as it was in the so-called Coronation

cases, of which *Krell v. Henry* [1903] 2 KB 740 is the leading example. But I do not understand his Lordship to say that without change in obligation there can be no frustration: it is 'the occurrence of any unexpected event that, as it were, changes the face of things', that give rise to frustration. His Lordship's emphasis upon change in obligation is, I think, to be understood in the context of the factual situation under discussion in the *Davis Contractors Case*.

Later cases in which frustration was discussed, many of them arising following the sudden closure of the Suez Canal, appear to me to throw little further light upon the principle of the doctrine so far as relevant to the present case. In *Albert D. Gaon & Co. v. Société Interprofessionelle des Oléagineux Fluides Alimentaires* [1960] 2 QB 318 Ashworth J. referred to the need for a 'fundamental commercial difference' between contemplated and actual performance, a view echoed on appeal by Sellers L.J.. In *Tsakiroglou & Co. Ltd. v. Noblee Thorl* [1962] AC 63 (which at first instance and in the Court of Appeal is reported with *Gaon's Case*), Viscount Simonds, referred to the criterion of whether [162] 'the nature of the contract ... "fundamentally" altered', as did Lord Reid. Lord Guest, referred to the 'juridical basis' of the doctrine of frustration as discussed by Lord Reid and Lord Radcliffe in *Davis Contractors*. In *The Eugenia* [1964] 2 QB 226 Lord Denning spoke of 'a fundamentally different situation' arising for which the parties made no provision, 'so much so that it would not be just in the new situation to hold them bound to its terms'. He appears to reject the relevance of foreseeability, to which Lord Radcliffe had attached importance in the *Davis Contractors Case*. In *Roberts v. Independent Publishers Ltd* [1974] 1 NZLR 459 in the New Zealand Court of Appeal the leading judgment of Beattie J. follows the recent English authorities, from the *Davis Contractors Case* onwards, accompanied by detailed reference to earlier authorities.

Whether Lord Loreburn's theory of the implied term – *F. A. Tamplin Steamship Co. Ltd. v. Anglo-Mexican Petroleum Products Co. Ltd* [1916] 2 AC 397 or that of the disappearance of the basis of the contract – *Tatem Ltd. v. Gamboa* [1939] 1 KB 132 per Goddard J., or Lord Wright's just and reasonable solution for reconciling the sanctity of contract with the special exceptions which justice demands – *Denny Mott & Dickson Ltd. v. Fraser & Co. Ltd* [1944] AC 265 or, again, the approaches manifest in the speeches in the *Davis Contractors Case*, are to be preferred, the result in the present case appears to me to be the same. In saying this I echo the words of Diplock J. in the *Port Line Case*, who said: 'I think, however, that whichever of the many suggested tests are applied, the result in this case is the same.' I prefer to express the matter in terms of Lord Reid's approach in the *Davis Contractors Case*, but, however expressed the conclusion should, I think, be that this contract has been frustrated. There has arisen, as a result of the compulsory acquisition of the land by the Crown for a school site, such a fundamentally different situation from that contemplated when the contract was entered into that it is properly to be regarded as having come to an end at the date of acquisition by the Crown.

It is no doubt true, as critics complain, that the various expositions of the true basis of the doctrine of frustration leave imprecise its actual operation when applied to the facts of particular cases. How dramatic must be the impact of an allegedly frustrating event? To what degree or extent must such [163] an event overturn expectations, or affect the foundation upon which the parties have contracted, or, again, how unjust and unreasonable a result must flow or how radically different from that originally undertaken must a contract become (to use the language of some of the various expositions), before it is to be regarded as frustrated? The cases provide little more than single instances of solutions to these questions. These difficulties of application of the doctrine of frustration were keenly appreciated both by Latham C.J. and by Williams J. in their consideration of the doctrine in *Scanlan's New Neon Ltd. v. Tooheys Ltd* (1943) 67 CLR 169. They are, perhaps, inevitable in questions of degree arising when a broad principle must be applied to infinitely variable factual situations.

On this question of the application of the doctrine to the present facts I can, I think, do no more than re-state those factors which have led me to conclude that this contract should be treated as having been frustrated. Looking at the position of the parties, I take that of Group Projects first. It is straightforward enough: everything points to frustration of the contract. The Crown's acquisition of the land caused, for Group Projects, a complete overturning of its entire project for subdivisional development. The position of the Council is not that of a party to a commercial venture, concerned exclusively with the promotion of its own financial interests. If the contract be declared to be frustrated the Council will not be deprived of some commercial advantage which it sought to attain when it entered into the contract, as is usually the case of a contracting party who seeks to resist the application to his contract of the doctrine of frustration. The relevant primary concern of the Council was in the proper development of this proposed residential sub-division. Once this proposal aborts, the Council's particular concern comes to an end; whatever the needs may be for the proper development of a school site, they will certainly not be identical with those embodied in the deed. In this sense the destructive impact of the compulsory acquisition is not confined to the interests of Group Projects; it extends in a degree to those of the Council. The interests of the parties apart, to consider the nature of the actual works specified in the schedules to the deed is to appreciate the radical effect which the acquisition has had upon them: some of them have become altogether impossible of execution; many of them must surely now be impractical or unnecessary.

[164] The combination of these considerations satisfy me that this is a proper case for the application of the doctrine of frustration. If the deed was frustrated by the acquisition, so too will be the Bond and the mortgage security associated with it, as was held by Dunn J.

I would accordingly dismiss this appeal.

QUESTIONS

(1) The agreement in *Taylor v Caldwell* was negotiated between the parties as were many aspects of performance—in those circumstances, why should a court intervene into the agreement between the parties rather than allow the loss to fall where it falls?

(2) Has the Court, in *Taylor v Caldwell*, adopted an unnecessarily low bar to excusing performance by parties? To what extent do the *Sale of Goods Acts* establish a higher or lower bar to excusing performance?

(3) How clear is the 'test' for frustration drawn by Stephen J in *Brisbane City Council*? Is it easily applicable in other circumstances? To what extent does Stephen J re-cast the test of frustration? Is this decision more of a review of the existing authorities or a re-statement of those authorities?

(4) To what extent are the cases in this section examples of the importance of contract planning in dealing with post-contract changes? Noting how the parties did not in fact foresee the specific developments occurring, how does the notion of foreseeability in these decisions differ from the notion of foreseeability applied in *Codelfa*?

(5) To what extent do the cases in this section develop or extend the notion of what is 'radically different performance'?

15.3 The effects of frustration

Concepts	Short explanation	Relevant authorities	*Principles* text*
If frustration is found, the contract is terminated immediately, but are losses recoverable or must they remain where they fall?	At common law, the losses fall where they fall and there is limited opportunity to shift losses; whereas under the statutory reforms, some ability exists to share losses between parties to the contract	*Frustrated Contracts Act 1978* (NSW) ss 5–15 *Frustrated Contracts Act 1988* (SA) ss 4, 6–8 *Australian Consumer Law and Fair Trading Act 2012* (Vic) ss 35–38, 41	Chapter 15: 15.14–15.17 Chapter 24: 24.04–24.05

* Consult the corresponding section(s) of the *Principles* text for more detail.

15.3.1 The common law rules

At common law, the effect of a finding of frustration was that the contract ended and future obligations were terminated. Losses fell where they were at that point in time. If money had been paid before the date for the corresponding service or good to be delivered, then the money could not be reclaimed, unless there was a total failure of consideration (see **Chapter 24**). If the good was delivered before the date for payment, then the future payment could not be claimed and the good could not be recovered. However, obligations that had arisen before the supervening event usually would still need to be performed.

This result was viewed as unsatisfactory and several states modified the effect of frustration at common law by statute, largely with the intention to share losses between the parties in cases of frustration. The three statutory reforms in Australia—Victoria, New South Wales and South Australia—are extracted below.

Frustrated Contracts Act 1978 (NSW) ss 5–15

5 Interpretation

(1) In this Act, except to the extent that the context or subject-matter otherwise indicates or requires:

agreed return, in relation to performance of a contract by a party, means such performance of the contract by another party as is contemplated by the contract as consideration for the first-mentioned performance.

court, in relation to any matter, means the court or arbitrator before whom the matter falls to be determined.

frustration includes avoidance of an agreement under section 12 of the *Sale of Goods Act 1923*.

party includes the assigns of a party.

performance, in relation to a contract, means:

(a) performance, wholly or in part, of a promise in the contract, or
(b) fulfilment, wholly or in part, of a condition of or in the contract.

(2) Where performance of a contract is referred to in a provision of this Act:
(a) a reference in the provision to the performing party is a reference to the party to the contract by whom the performance was, or was intended to be, given, and
(b) a reference in the provision to the other party to the contract is a reference to the party by whom performance of the contract is contemplated by the contract as consideration for the performance referred to in the provision.

(3) For the purposes of this Act, performance of a contract is given and received if received as contemplated by the contract, whether received by a party to the contract or not.

(4) For the purposes of this Act, where a contract has been frustrated and a thing is done or suffered under the contract after the time of frustration but before the party who does or suffers that thing knows or ought to know of the circumstances (whether matters of fact or law) giving rise to the frustration, that thing has effect as if done or suffered before the time of frustration.

(5) It is the intention of Parliament that, except to the extent that the parties to a contract otherwise agree, a court other than a court of New South Wales may exercise the powers given to a court by Part 3 in relation to the contract.

6 Act does not apply to certain contracts

(1) This Act:
(a) does not apply to a contract made before the commencement of this Act,
(b) does not apply to a charter-party, except a time charter-party and except a charter-party by way of demise,
(c) does not apply to a contract (other than a charter-party) for the carriage of goods by sea,
(d) does not apply to a contract of insurance, and
(e) does not apply to any other contract in so far as the parties thereto have agreed that this Act does not apply to the contract.

(2) This Act does not apply to a contract embodied in or constituted by the memorandum or articles of association or rules or other instrument or agreement constituting, or regulating the affairs of, any of the following bodies:
(a) a company within the meaning of the *Corporations Act 2001* of the Commonwealth,
(b) a registrable body within the meaning of the *Corporations Act 2001* of the Commonwealth,
(b1) a co-operative registered under the *Co-operatives National Law (NSW)*,
(c) a society registered under the *Friendly Societies Act 1989*, the *Financial Institutions (NSW) Code* or the *Co-operative Housing and Starr-Bowkett Societies Act 1998*,
(d) an association registered under the *Associations Incorporation Act 2009*,
(e) an industrial organisation within the meaning of the *Industrial Relations Act 1996* that is a State organisation incorporated under that Act,
(f) a partnership within the meaning of the *Partnership Act 1892*, or
(g) any association which, on a proper case arising, is liable to be wound up or dissolved by order of the Supreme Court of New South Wales,

in any case in which the circumstances alleged to give rise to frustration of the contract furnish a case for the winding up or dissolution of the body.

(3) Where a contract is severable into parts and one or more but not all parts are frustrated, this Act does not apply to the part or parts not frustrated.

Part 2 Effect of frustration of contract

7 Promise not performed

(1) Where a promise under a frustrated contract was due to be, but was not, performed before the time of frustration, the promise is discharged except to the extent necessary to support a claim for damages for breach of the promise before the time of frustration.

(2) Subsection (1) does not affect a promise due for performance before frustration which would not have been discharged by the frustration if it had been due for performance after the time of frustration.

8 Damages assessed after frustration

Where a contract is frustrated and a liability for damages for breach of the contract has accrued before the time of frustration, regard shall be had, in assessing those damages after that time, to the fact that the contract has been frustrated.

Part 3 Adjustment on frustration of contract

Division 1 Adjustment where performance (excluding payment of money) received

9 Definitions

In this Division ***performance*** in relation to a contract does not include:

(a) performance, wholly or in part, of a promise in the contract to pay money, or

(b) fulfilment, wholly or in part, of a condition of or in the contract that money be paid.

10 Adjustment where whole performance received

Where a contract is frustrated and the whole of the performance to be given by a party under the contract has been received before the time of frustration, the performing party shall be paid by the other party to the contract an amount equal to the value of the agreed return for the performance.

11 Adjustment where part performance only received

(1) In this section:

attributable cost, in relation to performance received under a frustrated contract, means:

(a) where there is no incidental gain to the performing party, and except as provided by paragraph (c)—an amount equal to the reasonable cost of the performance,

(b) where there is an incidental gain to the performing party, and except as provided by paragraph (c)—such part of the reasonable cost of the performance as is equal to an amount calculated by deducting from the reasonable cost of the performance the value of that incidental gain, or

(c) where the amount referred to in paragraph (a) or (b) exceeds the proportionate allowance for the performance—such part of the reasonable cost of the performance as is equal in amount to that proportionate allowance.

attributable value, in relation to performance received under a frustrated contract, means an amount equal to the value of the proportionate allowance for that performance reduced by the lost value of that performance.

incidental gain, in relation to a party to a contract who suffers a detriment referred to in the definition of 'reasonable cost', means any property or improvement to property acquired or derived by that party as a consequence of doing or suffering the acts or things that caused that party to suffer the detriment, except to the extent that the property or improvement so acquired or derived is comprised in any performance given by that party under the contract or is expended or disposed of in giving any such performance.

lost value, in relation to performance received under a frustrated contract, is a reference to the amount (if any) by which the value of that performance was reduced by reason of the frustration of the contract, that value being assessed as at the time immediately before the frustration of the contract and on the basis that the contract would not be frustrated.

proportionate allowance, in relation to performance received under a frustrated contract, means such part of the value of the agreed return for complete performance of the contract by the performing party as is appropriate to be charged to the other party for the performance received, having regard to the extent to which the performance received is less than the whole of the performance contracted to be given by the performing party.

reasonable cost, in relation to performance received under a frustrated contract, is an amount that would be fair compensation to the performing party for any detriment suffered by that party in reasonably paying money, doing work or doing or suffering any other act or thing to the extent to which the detriment was suffered for the purpose of giving the performance so received.

(2) Where a contract is frustrated and part, but not the whole, of the performance to be given by a party under the contract has been received before the time of frustration, the performing party shall be paid by the other party to the contract:

(a) an amount equal to the attributable value of the performance, except where the attributable cost of the performance exceeds its attributable value, or

(b) where the attributable cost of the performance exceeds its attributable value—an amount equal to the sum of:

(i) the attributable value of the performance, and

(ii) one-half of the amount by which the attributable cost of the performance exceeds its attributable value.

Division 2 Other adjustments

12 Return of money paid

Where a contract is frustrated and a party to the contract has paid money to another person (whether or not a party to the contract) as, or as part of, an agreed return for performance of the contract by another party (whether or not that other party is the person to whom the payment was made and whether or not there has been any such performance) that other party shall pay the same amount of money to the party who made the payment.

13 Adjustment of certain losses and gains

(1) Where a contract is frustrated and, by reasonably paying money, doing work or doing or suffering any other act or thing for the purpose of giving performance under the contract (not being performance which has been received) the performing party has suffered a detriment, the performing party shall be paid by the other party to the contract an amount equal to one-half of the amount that would be fair compensation for the detriment suffered.

(2) Where a performing party referred to in subsection (1) has, as a consequence of doing or suffering the acts or things that caused that party to suffer the detriment so referred to, acquired or derived any property or improvement to property, the performing party shall pay to the other party so referred to one-half of the value of the property or improvement so acquired or derived.

Division 3 Recovery of money payable

14 Recovery of money as a debt

A person entitled under Division 1 or 2 to be paid an amount of money by another person may recover the amount from that other person as a debt in a court of competent jurisdiction.

Division 4 Adjustment by the court

15 Adjustment by court

(1) Where the court is satisfied that the terms of a frustrated contract or the events which have occurred are such that, in respect of the contract:

(a) Divisions 1 and 2 are manifestly inadequate or inappropriate,

(b) application of Divisions 1 and 2 would cause manifest injustice, or

(c) application of Divisions 1 and 2 would be excessively difficult or expensive,

the court may, by order, exclude the contract from the operation of Divisions 1 and 2 and, subject to subsection (8), may, by order, substitute such adjustments in money or otherwise as it considers proper.

(2) Orders which the court may make under subsection (1) include:

(a) orders for the payment of interest, and

(b) orders as to the time when money shall be paid.

(3) In addition to its jurisdiction under subsections (1) and (2), the Supreme Court or the District Court may, for the purposes of this section, make orders for:

(a) the making of any disposition of property,

(b) the sale or other realisation of property,

(c) the disposal of the proceeds of sale or other realisation of property,

(d) the creation of a charge on property in favour of any person,

(e) the enforcement of a charge so created,

(f) the appointment and regulation of the proceedings of a receiver of property, and

(g) the vesting of property in any person.

(4) Sections 78 and 79 of the *Trustee Act 1925* apply to a vesting order, and to the power to make a vesting order, under subsection (3).

(5) Section 78 (2) of the *Trustee Act 1925* applies to a vesting order under subsection (3) as if subsection (3) were included in the provisions of Part 3 of that Act.

(6) In relation to a vesting order of the District Court, sections 78 and 79 of the *Trustee Act 1925* shall be read as if 'Court' in those sections meant the District Court.

(7) Subsections (2) to (6) do not limit the generality of subsection (1).

(8) This section does not authorise the Local Court to give a judgment otherwise than for the payment of money.

Frustrated Contracts Act 1988 (SA) ss 4, 6–8

4 Application of this Act

(1) Subject to subsection (2), this Act applies to a frustrated contract—

(a) irrespective of whether there is, in consequence of the frustration, a total failure of consideration under the contract; but

(b) subject to any provision made in the contract itself as to the consequences of frustration.

(2) This Act does not apply to—

(a) a contract made before the commencement of this Act;

(b) a charter-party (not being a time charter-party or a charter-party by way of demise);

(c) a contract (other than a charter-party) for the carriage of goods by sea;
(d) a contract of insurance;
(e) a contract under which an association is constituted or rules governing the administration of, or rights of membership in, an association are laid down; or
(f) a partnership agreement.

(3) This Act binds the Crown.

[...]

6 Effect of frustration on contractual obligations

(1) Subject to subsection (2), the frustration of a contract discharges the parties from all contractual obligations (including obligations that should have been, but were not, performed before the date of frustration).

(2) The frustration of a contract does not affect—
(a) an obligation that is, according to the proper construction of the contract, to survive frustration; or
(b) a right of action, that arose before frustration, for damages for breach of contract (but, in the assessment of any such damages, the fact that the contract has been frustrated and any consequential adjustment, or right to an adjustment, under this Act will be taken into account).

7 Adjustment of losses on frustration of contract

(1) Where a contract is frustrated, there will be an adjustment between the parties so that no party is unfairly advantaged or disadvantaged in consequence of the frustration.

(2) Subject to this section, for the purposes of the adjustment referred to in subsection (1)—
(a) the value of contractual benefits received up to the date of frustration by each party to
(b) the contract will be assessed as at the date of frustration and those values aggregated;
(c) the value of the contractual performance, up to the date of frustration, of each party to
(d) the contract will be calculated and those values aggregated;
(e) the aggregate amount arrived at under paragraph (b) will be subtracted from the aggregate amount arrived at under paragraph (a), and the remainder notionally divided between the parties in equal shares;
(f) an adjustment will be made between the parties so that there is an equalization of the contractual return of each at the figure attributed under paragraph (c).

(3) Where the contractual performance of a party to a contract is referable to a number of separate contracts, the value of that contractual performance will, for the purposes of this section, be apportioned between the various contracts in such proportions as may be just.

(4) Where, in the opinion of a court, there is, in the circumstances of a particular case, a more equitable basis for making the adjustment referred to in subsection (1) than the one set out in subsection (2), the court may make an adjustment on that basis rather than on the basis of subsection (2).

(5) For the purpose of giving effect to an adjustment under this section, a court may make orders for—
(a) the payment of money (including interest);
(b) the disposition, sale or realization of property;

(c) the creation of a charge on property;
(d) the appointment and powers of a receiver;
(e) any incidental or ancillary matter.

(6) Where—
(a) a party to a contract purportedly performs a contractual obligation, or an act preparatory to the performance of a contractual obligation, after frustration of the contract; but
(b) the party did not know, and could not reasonably be expected to have known, that the contract had been frustrated,

the value of the performance (and of any consequent contractual benefits) will be brought into account for the purposes of an adjustment under this section as if it had occurred before frustration of the contract.

(7) Where two or more persons are jointly parties to a contract in the same capacity, those parties will be grouped together and treated as a single party to the contract for the purposes of this section.

8 Action for adjustment assimilated to action on the contract

An action for an adjustment under this Act, and for consequential orders to give effect to such an adjustment, may be commenced before a court as if it were an action under the contract that arose at the time of frustration of the contract.

Australian Consumer Law and Fair Trading Act 2012 (Vic) ss 35–38, 41

[These provisions were originally enacted as the *Frustrated Contracts Act 1959* (Vic).]

Part 3.2 – Frustrated contracts

Division 1 – Introductory

35 Contracts to which this Part applies

(1) This Part applies to a contract if the parties to the contract are discharged from the further performance of the contract because—
(a) performance of the contract becomes impossible; or
(b) the contract is otherwise frustrated; or
(c) the contract is avoided by the operation of section 12 of the *Goods Act 1958*.

(2) This Part applies to contracts made before or after 1 July 2008 if the time of discharge of the contract is after 29 September 1959.

(3) This Part does not apply to—
(a) any charter-party, except a time charter-party or a charter-party by way of demise; or
(b) any contract (other than a charter-party) for the carriage of goods by sea; or
(c) any contract of insurance except as provided for in section 40.

Division 2—Consequences of frustrated contract

36 Adjustment of amounts paid or payable to parties to discharged contracts

(1) All amounts paid to any party under a discharged contract before the time of discharge are recoverable.

(2) All amounts payable to any party under a discharged contract before the time of discharge cease to be payable.

37 Court may allow amounts paid or payable to be recovered or paid

Despite section 36, the court may, if it considers it just to do so having regard to all the circumstances of the case, allow a party to a discharged contract–

(a) to whom amounts were paid or are payable under that contract before the time of discharge; and

(b) who has incurred expenses before the time of discharge in or for the purpose of the performance of that contract–

to retain or recover (as the case may be) the whole or any part of the amounts paid or payable to that party under the contract in an amount not exceeding the expenses incurred.

38 Parties to pay an amount for valuable benefits obtained

(1) This section applies if a party to a discharged contract obtained a valuable benefit (other than a payment of money to which section 36 or 37 applies) before the time of discharge because of anything done by another party in or for the purpose of the performance of the contract.

(2) Despite section 36, the benefited party is liable to pay to that other party any amount (not exceeding the value of the benefit obtained) that the court considers just having regard to all the circumstances of the case.

(3) For the purpose of subsection (2), the court may have regard to—

 (a) the amount of any expenses the benefited party incurred before the time of discharge in or for the purpose of the performance of the contract, including any amount paid or payable by the benefited party to any other party under the contract and retained or recoverable by that party under section 36 or 37; or

 (b) the effect, in relation to the benefit obtained, of the circumstances giving rise to the frustration or avoidance of the contract.

(4) For the purpose of this section, if a party to the contract has assumed obligations under the contract in consideration of the conferral of a benefit by another party to the contract on any other person (whether or not that person is a party to the contract), the court may, if in all the circumstances of the case it considers it just to do so, treat any benefit conferred on that other person as a benefit obtained by the party who has assumed those obligations.

Division 3—General

41 Circumstances in which contract provisions continue to have effect despite frustration

If any contract to which this Part applies contains a provision that on the true construction of the contract–

(a) is intended to continue to have effect in circumstances that operate or would, but for that provision, operate to frustrate or avoid the contract; or

(b) is intended to have effect whether or not circumstances that operate or would, but for that provision, operate to frustrate or avoid the contract arise–

the court must give effect to that provision and must only give effect to Division 2 to the extent that the court is satisfied that it is consistent with the provision of the contract.

QUESTIONS

(1) To what extent do the statutory reforms reflect a strong concern not to 'overcompensate' one party over the other?

(2) To what extent do the statutory reforms resolve the unfairness of the common law by imposing an equally inflexible alternative?

15.4 International perspectives

15.4.1 *CISG*

Where the *CISG* governs cross-border sales (see **25.4.1**), the *CISG* excuses liability for failures to perform in certain circumstances, pursuant to art 79. Where an impediment is beyond the control of the non-performing party, then liability will be excused, but only if the impediment or its consequences could not have been avoided or overcome, and where the impediment could not reasonably have been taken into account at the time of contracting. To rely on art 79, the non-performing party must give notice of the impediment: art 79(4) *CISG*. Notably, the type of impediment upheld under art 79 has traditionally involved situations of impossibility; however, more recently, some cases and scholars have supported inclusion of situations where performance is possible, but would involve significant hardship; eg currency devaluations of 80 per cent.[2] A successful invocation of art 79 merely excuses liability for damages, but other remedies remain available, such as termination (avoidance): art 79(5) *CISG*.

CISG art 79(1)

(1) A party is not liable for a failure to perform any of his obligations if he proves that the failure was due to an impediment beyond his control and that he could not reasonably be expected to have taken the impediment into account at the time of the conclusion of the contract or to have avoided or overcome it, or its consequences. . . .

15.4.2 UNIDROIT Principles

Where applicable (see **25.4.3**), the UNIDROIT Principles provide excuse for non-performance in art 7.1.7 in cases of force majeure (impossibility). Moreover, in arts 6.2.2 and 6.2.3, the UNIDROIT Principles expressly deal with 'hardship', defined as occurring if events 'fundamentally alter the equilibrium' of the contract. In these cases, the right to renegotiate the contract

2 CISG Advisory Council, Opinion No 7: 'Exemption of Liability for Damages under Article 79 of the CISG', Rapporteur: Professor A Garro, Rule 3.1, Comment [33].

arises, and if agreement cannot be reached, the party affected may seek an order adapting the contract in light of the new circumstances, or termination: art 6.2.3(4).

UNIDROIT Principles art 6.2.2 (Definition of hardship)

There is hardship where the occurrence of events fundamentally alters the equilibrium of the contract either because the cost of a party's performance has increased or because the value of the performance a party receives has diminished, and

(a) the events occur or become known to the disadvantaged party after the conclusion of the contract;

(b) the events could not reasonably have been taken into account by the disadvantaged party at the time of the conclusion of the contract;

(c) the events are beyond the control of the disadvantaged party; and

(d) the risk of the events was not assumed by the disadvantaged party.

15.5 Review

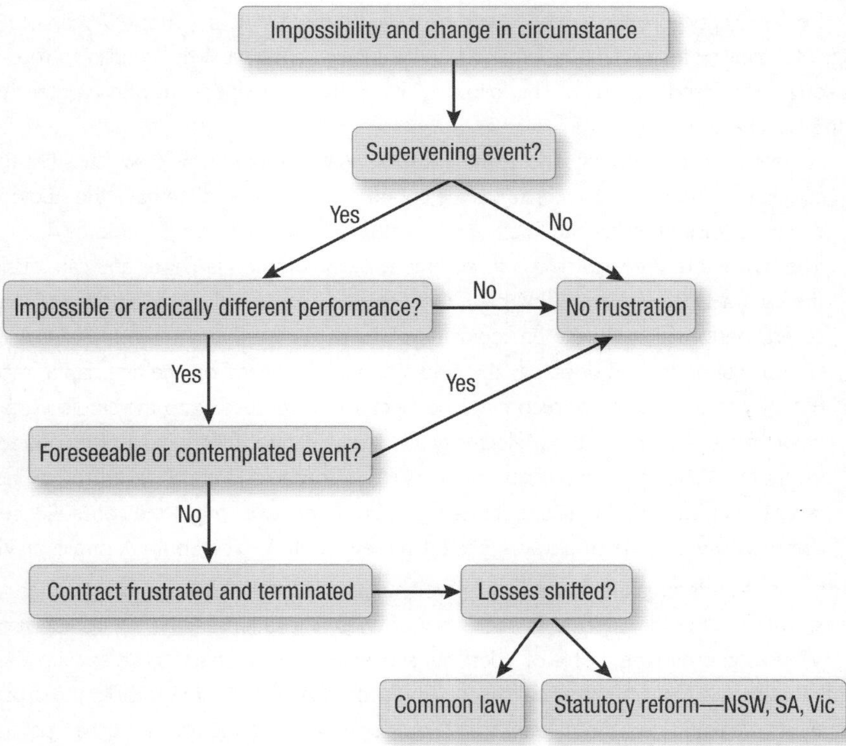

TIPS FOR APPLYING THE LAW IN PRACTICE

- The starting point for any 'frustration' analysis needs to be the careful identification of the 'supervening event'—what is the event? Is it conduct or perhaps a change of law? Has the event arisen after the contract was formed? Was the event foreseeable at the time the contract was formed?
- Remember that, if an item is destroyed (or the 'event' occurs) after the contract is formed, then the doctrine of frustration may apply; if the item was destroyed (or the 'event' occurs) before the contract was formed and neither party knew about it, then the doctrine of mistake may apply.
- The distinction between 'impossibility to perform' in frustration and anticipatory breach is that, 'impossibility to perform' in the context of frustration must arise due to an event that was unforeseeable at the time the contract was formed and for which neither party is responsible. 'Anticipatory breach' often involves situations in which the impossibility was either foreseeable or arose as a result of the failure of one of the parties.
- 'Radically different performance' in an economic context is often difficult to identify in real life; the issue is often not one of degree but rather that certain characteristics of the contract have now changed, although identifying those characteristics can be difficult.

PROBLEM QUESTIONS

(1) Brendan is a music producer who owns his own studio. Uri is a young 19-year old singer-songwriter looking for his first big break. Uri enters into a contract with Brendan to record Uri's first song using Brendan's studio. The following situations are independent of each other but rely on the facts here.

(a) A week before recording is to commence, Brendan's studio burns down in a fire that was caused by a freak lightning storm; has the contract been frustrated? What if the studio burned down because Brendan had lit a fire in the studio to warm it up on a cold day?

(b) The day before the recording is to commence, Uri contracts laryngitis and cannot sing; has the contract been frustrated? What if the laryngitis was caused by Uri singing very loudly at several performances in the preceding days?

(c) Uri is required to, and does, pay the studio hire fee 'up front' on the first day of recording. But, on the second day of recording, the electricity wires leading to the studio are brought down in a storm and, without electricity, the studio cannot function; has the contract been frustrated? What if the electricity supply was 'cut' because Brendan failed to pay his most recent electricity bill? If the contract has been frustrated, what might the consequences be at common law or if the studio was located in New South Wales, South Australia or Victoria?

(2) Emma is an events organiser who usually works with small businesses or rich families to hold parties, dinners and other 'events' in interesting or unusual locations. Abuk is a fashion promotor who wants to improve the profile of a designer she works with and plans to do so with a series of events that should 'go viral' on social media. Abuk contracts with Emma to hold three parties—one every weekend for three weekends—outdoors on a barge on water as part of the promotion. The contract notes that Emma will be paid after all three parties are held. The following situations are independent of each other but rely on the facts stated here.

(a) The first party was a viral success and there was an expectation that many, many people will attempt to attend the second party; however, Emma cannot run the second party without significantly increasing security, which would cost a lot of money; has the contract been frustrated?

(b) On the eve of the first party, a flood affected the area where the barge was to be moored and the party had to be moved onto land, which would cost less but was less likely to 'go viral'; has the contract been frustrated?

(c) Just before the third party, the local police 'ban' the party because of how unsafe the previous parties have been, as there were too many people on the barges and there were insufficient life preservers; has the contract been frustrated?

RESEARCH QUESTIONS

(1) To what extent does the shift from 'impossibility' to 'radically different performance' represent an unjustified widening of the scope of the doctrine of frustration?

(2) Do the statutory attempts at reform provide an adequate solution to the perceived unfairness of the outcome at common law?

(3) To what extent does the steady development of 'unjust enrichment' undermine the need for a separate ground of 'frustration'?

PART V

ENDING A CONTRACT

16

TERMINATION OF CONTRACTS

16.1 Overview

This chapter discusses the ending (ie cessation) of contracts, particularly when and how a party may have the right to terminate (ie end) a contract when things do not go according to expectations. A contract may end for various reasons. First, a contract may end following due performance (ie the parties are *discharged* because they all have performed their obligations in accordance with the terms of the contract). Second, a contract may end upon expiration (of, say, a time fixed by the contract). Third, a contract may end by agreement of the parties, either in accordance with the terms of the contract or by a subsequent, separate, agreement to terminate an existing contract. Fourth, a party may end a contract by termination, because of breach or repudiation.[1]

The focus of this chapter is on termination for breach or repudiation. A breach of contract occurs when a party, without lawful excuse, fails or refuses to perform what is due from them under the contract, or performs their obligation defectively or incapacitates themselves from performing.[2] Repudiation occurs where a party, whether through words or conduct, exhibits an intention no longer to be bound by the contract or to only perform the contract in a manner that is substantially inconsistent with their obligations under the contract.[3]

A series of common law rules allow the other party (the aggrieved party) to terminate the contract for breach in some circumstances, or for repudiation. Not every breach allows termination by the aggrieved party (though every breach gives rise to damages). For the purposes of determining when a breach gives rise to the right to terminate, the common law classifies contract terms into three types, namely: (1) essential terms (or 'conditions'); (2) intermediate terms (or 'innominate terms'); and (3) non-essential terms (or 'warranties').

Any breach of a condition, however trivial the breach, allows the aggrieved party to terminate. Only a serious breach of an intermediate term allows the aggrieved party to terminate. Repudiation gives the aggrieved party the right to terminate. No breach of a warranty (non-essential term) gives the aggrieved party the right to terminate (though gross breaches of warranty may be held to constitute repudiation, which then gives the aggrieved party the right to terminate).

The cases extracted in this chapter focus on these common law rules (including rules of equity) on termination. Thus, they illustrate:

- classification of terms;
- termination for breach of an essential term;
- termination for breach of an intermediate term;
- termination for repudiation;

1 A contract may also end in a number of other ways. An example is *frustration,* which discharges the parties from any contractual obligations falling due for performance because, without the fault of either party to the contract, an event has occurred (the frustrating event) that has made performance radically different from what was contemplated by the parties (see **Chapter 15**). Another example is *rescission,* which allows a party to end a contract because some impropriety (such as misinformation, deceit, duress, undue influence, and unconscionability) was perpetrated by a party in the process of concluding the contract (see **Chapters 18–21**).

2 See Edwin Peel, *Treitel on the Law of Contract* (Thomson Reuters Legal, 12th ed, 2007) [17-049].

3 See *Koompahtoo Local Aboriginal Land Council v Sanpine Pty Ltd* (2007) 233 CLR 115, 135.

- termination for delay (of performance);
- relief against forfeiture (an equitable restriction on the right to terminate).

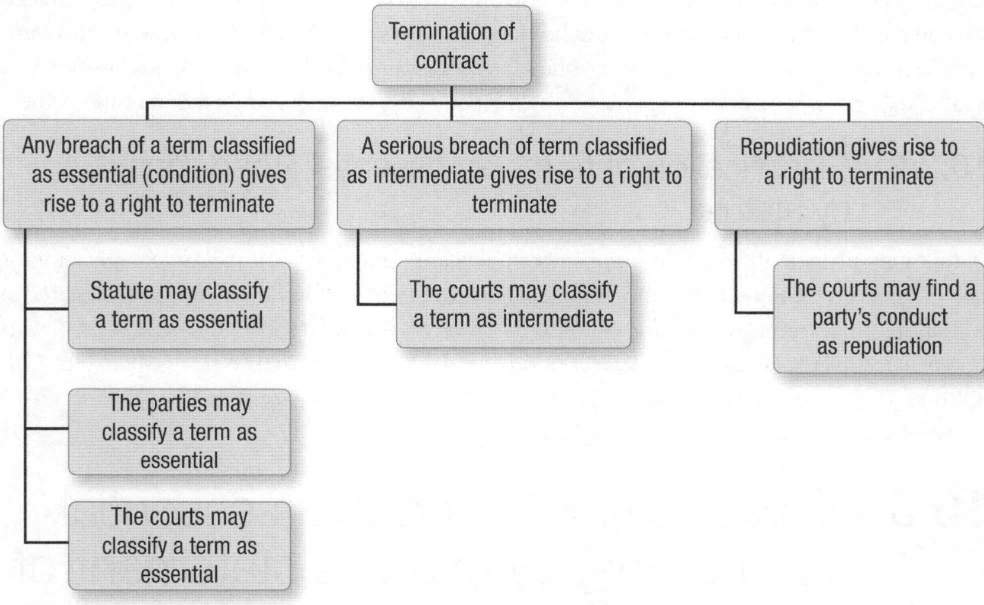

16.2 Essential terms

Concept	Short explanation	Relevant authorities	*Principles* text*
Termination for breach of an essential term	Any breach of a condition, however trivial the breach, allows the aggrieved party to terminate the contract. But, how is a term classified as a condition?	Extracted at **16.3**: *L Schuler AG v Wickman Machine Tool Sales Ltd* [1974] AC 235 *Luna Park (NSW) Ltd v Tramways Advertising Pty Ltd* (1938) 61 CLR 286 *Associated Newspapers Ltd v Bancks* (1951) 83 CLR 322	Chapter 16: 16.03–16.05
Intention to be legally bound and completeness of terms are both key	Statute may provide that certain terms in certain contracts are conditions. For example, legislation on sale of goods typically imply into contracts for the sale of goods various terms designated as conditions	Examples (not extracted here): *Sale of Goods Act 1954* (ACT) ss 17–19 *Sale of Goods Act 1923* (NSW) ss 17–19 *Sale of Goods Act 1972* (NT) ss 17–19 *Sale of Goods Act 1896* (Qld) ss 15–17 *Sale of Goods Act 1895* (WA) ss 12–14	Chapter 16: 16.03–6.05

* Consult the corresponding section(s) of the *Principles* text for more detail.

16.2.1 Termination for breach of an essential term (ie a condition)

At common law, any breach of a condition, however trivial, allows the aggrieved party to terminate the contract. However, first the term must be classified as an essential term (a condition). How, and by what means or sources are terms classified (as conditions or not)? Terms may be classified by a statute, express statement of the parties or by the courts (as the deduced intention of the parties).

16.2.2 Classification of terms as essential (conditions) by statute

Statute may provide that certain terms in contracts are conditions. For example, legislation on sale of goods typically implies into contracts for the sale of goods various terms designated as conditions or warranties. See, for example, *Sale of Goods Act 1954* (ACT) ss 17–19; *Sale of Goods Act 1923* (NSW) ss 17–19; *Sale of Goods Act 1972* (NT) ss 17–19; *Sale of Goods Act 1896* (Qld) ss 15–17; *Sale of Goods Act 1895* (SA) ss 12–14; *Sale of Goods Act 1896* (Tas) ss 17–19; *Goods Act 1958* (Vic) ss 17–19; *Sale of Goods Act 1895* (WA) ss 12–14.[4]

16.3 Classification of terms as essential (conditions) by express statement of the parties and by the courts

Concept	Short explanation	Relevant authorities	*Principles* text*
Classification of terms as conditions by agreement of the parties to the contract	Parties to a contract can classify terms in their contract as conditions. Contract law allows parties to decide the terms of their agreement, and the importance they place on those terms However, the terminology used by parties is not conclusive	*L Schuler AG v Wickman Machine Tool Sales Ltd* [1974] AC 235	Chapter 16: 6.03–6.05
Classification of terms as essential (ie conditions) by the courts	Where there is no statutory classification of a term as condition or express classification by the parties, the courts may deduce from the facts of the case that the parties intended the term to be essential (ie condition)	*Luna Park (NSW) Ltd v Tramways Advertising Pty Ltd* (1938) 61 CLR 286 *Associated Newspapers Ltd v Bancks* (1951) 83 CLR 322	Chapter 16: 16.03–6.05

* Consult the corresponding section(s) of the *Principles* text for more detail.

4 Note, however, that in New South Wales the concept of an intermediate term is also now recognised: *Sale of Goods Act 1923* (NSW) s 4(5).

16.3.1 Classification of terms as essential (conditions) by express statement of the parties

Parties to a contract can classify terms in their contract as conditions. However, the terminology used by parties is not conclusive. The case of *L Schuler v Wickman Machine Tool Sales*[5] illustrates the approach of the courts.

L Schuler AG v Wickman Machine Tool Sales Ltd [1974] AC 235

Facts and issues

Schuler, a German manufacturer, granted to Wickman, an English company, the sole selling rights of Schuler's products in the UK for four and a half years. Clause 7(b) of the contract made it a condition that: '(i) [Wickman] shall send representatives to visit the six largest motor manufacturers in the UK at least once a week for the purpose of soliciting orders for Schuler's products'. None of the other 20 clauses was described as a condition.

In the first eight months of the contract, Wickman failed in the visiting obligations on a scale found to be a 'material breach', but remediable under Clause 11 of the contract. The breaches were subsequently waived by Schuler. In the following six months, Wickman committed 'immaterial breaches' of its visiting obligations, some for good reasons. Schuler claimed it had the right to terminate—and terminated—the contract on the basis of these 'immaterial breaches'.

The issue was whether Schuler had the right to terminate the contract. This depended on whether the visitation obligation in Clause 7(b) was a condition in the technical sense, so that any breach, however trivial, gave the aggrieved party (in this case, Schuler) the right to terminate.

Decision

The trial judge (Mocatta J) held in favour of Schuler. By a majority, the Court of Appeal reversed the decision. Schuler's appealed to the House of Lords was unsuccessful, by a majority of 4:1.

Per Lord Reid at 251:

> Schuler maintains that the use of the word 'condition' is in itself enough to establish this intention [to make any breach, however small, to entitle Schuler to terminate the contract]. No doubt some words used by lawyers do have a rigid inflexible meaning. But we must remember that we are seeking to discover intention as disclosed by the contract as a whole. Use of the word 'condition' is an indication—even a strong indication—of such an intention but it is by no means conclusive.
>
> The fact that a particular construction leads to a very unreasonable result must be a relevant consideration. The more unreasonable the result the more unlikely it is that the parties can have intended it, and if they do intend it, the more necessary it is that they shall make that intention abundantly clear.
>
> Clause 7(b) requires that over a long period, each of the six firms shall be visited every week by one or other of two named representatives. It makes no provision for Wickman being entitled to substitute others even on the death or retirement of one of the named representatives. Even if one could imply some right to do this, it makes no provision for both representatives being ill

5 [1974] AC 235.

> during a particular week. And it makes no provision for the possibility that one or other of the firms may tell Wickman that they cannot receive Wickman's representative during a particular week. So if the parties gave any thought to the matter at all they must have realised the probability that in a few cases out of the 1,400 required visits, a visit as stipulated would be impossible. But if Schuler's contention is right failure to make even one visit entitles them to terminate the contract however blameless Wickman might be.
>
> This is so unreasonable that it must make me search for some other possible meaning of the contract. If none can be found then Wickman must suffer the consequences. But only if that is the only possible interpretation.
>
> If I have to construe clause 7 standing by itself then I do find difficulty in reaching any other interpretation. But if clause 7 must be read with clause 11 the difficulty disappears. The word 'condition' would make [252] any breach of clause 7(b), however excusable, a material breach. That would then entitle Schuler to give notice under clause 11(a)(i) requiring the breach to be remedied ... If they did not [remedy] within the period of the notice then Schuler would be entitled to rescind.
>
> In my view, that is a possible and reasonable construction of the contract and I would therefore adopt it ... So I would dismiss the appeal.

Lords Morris, Simon and Kilbradon delivered separate judgments in largely similar terms, dismissing the appeal.

Lord Wilberforce (dissenting) held that Schuler should have been able to terminate.

16.3.2 Classification of terms as essential (conditions) by the courts

If there is no statutory classification or express (intended) classification by the parties, the courts will deduce the intention of the parties by construing the contract. This approach is confirmed by statute in some jurisdictions. An example is the *Goods Act 1958* (Vic) s 16(2), which provides that whether 'a stipulation in a contract of sale is a condition or warranty depends in each case on the construction of the contract'. Courts use what is referred to as the 'essentiality test'; the importance of the term to the promisee of the particular promise in question in entering into contract. The following cases illustrates the courts' approach.

Luna Park (NSW) Ltd v Tramways Advertising Pty Ltd (1938) 61 CLR 286

Facts and issues

On 10 December 1935, Luna Park (NSW) Ltd, a company that conducts an amusement enterprise in Sydney, entered into a contract with Tramways Advertising Pty Ltd, a company in the business of advertising, for the advertising of Luna Park's entertainments in Sydney by means of 53 boards to be displayed on the roofs of tram-cars. The contract was to operate for three seasons; a season begins from about October and ends around March. One of the terms of the contract provided: 'We [Tramways Advertising Ltd] guarantee that these boards will be on the tracks at least eight hours per day throughout your [Luna Park's] season.'

After the second season, Luna Park alleged that Tramways was not displaying the boards as agreed. Luna Park contended that the 'guarantee' term meant that each of the 53 boards would be on the tracks for at least eight hours every day during the three seasons. It was not disputed that each of the boards had not been displayed for at least eight hours each day. However, Tramways argued that the obligation imposed by the clause was performed if, during each season, each board was displayed for an average time of at least eight hours per day. On this view, there would be no breach if no boards at all or only a small number of boards were shown on some days, provided the display on other days was such as to bring the average for each board over a season to at least eight hours per day.

Luna Park argued that the 'guarantee' clause was an essential term, which had been breached, and that the breach gave it the right to terminate, and it had terminated, the contract. Tramways purported to continue to perform and, after displaying the boards for a month, sued Luna Park to recover the unpaid invoice. In addition to defending the case on the basis that it had rightfully terminated it, Luna Park claimed damaged for breach of contract by way of cross-action.

The issue was whether the relevant term was a condition, the condition had been breached by Tramways, and Luna Park had the right to terminate.

The trial judge held for Luna Park. Tramways appealed to the Supreme Court of Appeal, which, by a majority (Jordan CJ and Davidson J; Nicholas J dissenting) reversed the trial judge's decision.

In the Supreme Court of Appeal, Jordan CJ, with whom Davidson J concurred, stated the test for determining whether a term is essential (a condition) in the following terms:

> The question whether a term in a contract is a condition or a warranty, that is, an essential or a non-essential promise, depends upon the intention of the parties as appearing in or from the contract. The test of essentiality is whether it appears from the general nature of the contract, or from some particular term or terms, that the promise is of such importance to the promisee that he would not have entered into the contract unless he had been assured of a strict [or a substantial] performance of the promise, as the case may be, and this ought to have been apparent to the promisor ... If the innocent party would not have entered into the contract unless assured of a strict and literal performance of the promise, he may in general treat himself as discharged upon any breach of the promise, however, slight.[6]

He concluded that, on this basis, the term was a condition. However, he held that an average daily running time of eight hours, not an actual running time of that duration on each and every day of a season, fulfilled the undertaken. Accordingly, Tramways had not breached the contract.

Luna Park appealed to the High Court.

Decision

By a majority (Latham CJ, Rich and McTiernan JJ; Dixon J, dissenting) the High Court held that the term was a condition, and required strict adherence; that is, each board must be on the tracks for a minimum of eight hours each day. As Tramways has breached the term, Luna Park had the right to terminate the contract. The Court held further that, by evidencing its intention (notwithstanding Luna Park's challenge) to continue to perform the contract in the future on the basis of an average of eight hours per day, Tramways had repudiated the contract, which, too, gave Luna Park the right to terminate [see **16.5** below for the right to terminate for repudiation].

6 *Tramways Advertising Pty Ltd v Luna Park (NSW) Ltd* (1938) 38 SR (NSW) 632, 641.

Per Latham CJ at 298:

> The determination of the appeal depends upon the interpretation of the clause which has already been quoted. The agreement consists of two documents, a letter and a contract note. The letter, dated 7th December 1935, was written by the advertising company to the Luna Park company. It stated that the advertising company would be prepared to accept a contract for fifty-three roof boards on Sydney trams, the advertising company to supply certain of the boards, to paint, erect and maintain them, the contract 'to operate for the duration of two or three seasons.' No rate of payment was specified, and it is clear that the letter was not an offer the acceptance of which could result in the making of a contract. The letter contained the following statement: 'The average time that each car is on the tracks is eight hours per day, and we would recommend all routes serving the industrial suburbs.' It is upon this statement that the argument of the plaintiff principally depends. The terms of the letter show that a form of contract note was forwarded with the letter.
>
> On 10th December 1935 a contract note, which is the other document constituting the contract, was signed on behalf of the parties.
>
> [...]
>
> At the time when the contract note was signed the parties made two memoranda on the letter of 7th December. The first memorandum [299] signed on behalf of both parties, was: 'This letter is part and parcel of the contract.' The second memorandum, signed on behalf of the advertising company, consisted of the provision already mentioned, namely: 'We guarantee that these boards will be on the tracks at least eight hours per day throughout your season.'
>
> The plaintiff contends that the reference to the average time for which the cars of the tramway service are on the tracks affects the construction of the 'guarantee,' which should accordingly be regarded as providing only for an average time of display. In my opinion this contention is opposed to the natural meaning of the words. What is called the guarantee is a guarantee as to each and every board. It is an undertaking that each board will be on the tracks for at least eight hours on every day all through each season. The statement in the body of the letter is a statement which indicates the nature of the service which the normal running of the cars would be expected to provide. It is clear, however, that the Luna Park company was not satisfied with a mere statement that the average time that each car was on the track was eight hours per day. It required something more definite. The guarantee is an undertaking which is not in any way inconsistent with the statement of fact contained in the letter. The effect of the undertaking, read with the statement in the letter, is that, whatever might be the average time that cars were on the track, the roof boards were to be displayed for at least eight hours on every day. The guarantee contains no reference to averages, and it is apparent that there may be business reasons why the defendant required regular and continuous publicity. I agree with what Nicholas J says in his reasons for judgment — the guarantee 'was an assurance to the advertiser that, whatever might be the ordinary practice of the Tramway Department, the boards advertising Luna Park would be on the track not only for an average period of eight hours but for eight hours on every day, and that by this means a proclamation of the allurements of Luna Park would continuously be thrust upon the attention of residents of the industrial suburbs' ... It follows that the plaintiff must fail ...
>
> [301] In the Supreme Court a great deal of attention was devoted to the consideration of the question whether the particular clause in question was a condition or a warranty.
>
> [...]
>
> [302] I agree with the Full court that the guarantee clause was a condition and not a warranty ... It was a term of the contract which went so directly to the substance of the

> contract or was so 'essential to its very nature that its non-performance may fairly be considered by the other party as a substantial failure to perform the contract at all.' The breach of such a term by one party entitles the other party not only to obtain damages but also to refuse to perform any of the obligations resting upon him.
>
> The essential character of the clause in question appears both from its own terms and from the circumstances in which the contract was made. In the first place the words 'we guarantee' are particularly suited, in a contract drawn by laymen, to emphasize [303] the importance of the clause which they introduce. In the next place, the payment of £20 per week was not to begin until the complete number of roof boards, namely, fifty-three, were all displayed at the same time.
>
> [...]
>
> Further, the preliminary correspondence shows that the advertising company represented continuity of display as an important feature ... For these reasons, in my opinion, [304] the clause was a condition and not a mere warranty. Accordingly, any breach of the clause would entitle the defendant to determine the contract.
>
> But it is still necessary to consider what default will amount to a breach of the clause. The clause used the words 'at least eight hours,' but, in my opinion, such a phrase should not be interpreted with absolute mathematical exactitude in a commercial contract of this class. In some contracts it may be proper to construe references to time with absolute and precise accuracy down to minutes and seconds, but in a contract dealing with the display of roof boards on trams for at least eight hours per day the words 'eight hours per day' should be understood as meaning substantially eight hours per day. The clause would not, in my opinion, be broken by small occasional deficiencies.
>
> [...]
>
> I take the admission that each board was not exhibited for at least eight hours a day as an admission that it was not the case that each board was exhibited for substantially eight hours each day. I am accordingly of opinion that the defendant was entitled to determine the contract by reason of the past breaches of the plaintiff.
>
> I think that the appeal should be allowed, the judgment of the Supreme Court set aside, and the claim of the plaintiff dismissed.

His Honour went on to say that Tramways' insistence on an average of eight hours constituted repudiation, which also gave Luna Park the right to terminate the contract. Rich and McTiernan JJ deliverd separate, short judgments that echoed the judgment of Latham CJ, allowing the appeal].

Per Dixon J (dissenting) 307:

> This litigation depends primarily upon the meaning to be placed upon a contract composed of a letter and a printed form, which is neither well expressed nor altogether appropriate for the particular purpose of the parties... [308] In the Supreme Court Jordan CJ, with whom Davidson J concurred, gave the provision an intermediate meaning. He took it as requiring a daily running time of eight hours upon an average only ... According to his Honour's interpretation, the average of each car bearing a roof board must be taken separately over the season and must work out at an average running time of eight hours a day. In this interpretation I agree. The reasons for it, a statement of which is contained in his Honour's judgment, may be summarized as follows: — (1) The form of expression adopted in the memorandum or note, saying that the boards would be on the tracks eight hours per day throughout the season, appears to me to be capable of meaning that the duration of the appearance of the boards upon the tracks would amount upon an average to eight hours a day ... (3) The respondent which gave the guarantee

or promise is not in control of the tramways, and upon the face of the documents it plainly appears that what it is purporting to do is to warrant the time during which, in the usual course of management of the service upon the routes concerned, the advertisements will be exhibited in the public streets. During a season the withdrawal for a day or so.

[...]

[309] ... If routine examination and repair do not require it, some accident or mishap is almost sure to do so. To make the guarantee absolute in respect of every day for every car appears an unreasonable construction. (4) At the end of the 1935-to-1936 season the respondent made it clear to the appellant that the performance or fulfilment it was giving was according to an average only, and the appellant took no objection to the assumption thus impliedly made as to the meaning of the clause.

[...]

[311] ... I think the appeal should simply be dismissed.

Associated Newspapers Ltd v Bancks (1951) 83 CLR 322

Facts and issues

Bancks, a cartoonist, was contracted by Associated Newspapers, a publisher, for a term of 10 years commencing September 1948, to provide cartoons weekly for publication by Associated Newspaper. Under the contract, Associated undertook 'that each weekly full-page drawing will be presented on the front page of the Comic Section of the "Sunday Sun & Guardian"'. Associated complied with the term for the first year, and then started presenting the cartoons on other pages.

Bancks purported to terminate the contract for breach of condition. Associated sought an injunction to prevent Bancks from terminating the contract and providing cartoons to a rival publisher.

The issue was whether the term was a condition, the breach of which granted Bancks the right to terminate.

Decision

The Supreme Court of New South Wales held in favour of Bancks. On appeal by Associated Newspapers, the High Court held that the term was a condition, the breach of which entitled Bancks to terminate the contract.

Per Dixon, Williams, Webb, Fullagar and Kitto JJ at 336:

> The first question is whether the company's undertaking to present the defendant's drawings on the front page of the comic is a condition or essential term of the contract going to its very root, the breach of which would immediately entitle the defendant at his option to rescind the contract and sue for damages for the loss of the contract, or a mere warranty or non-essential and subsidiary term the breach of which would entitle the defendant to damages. Various tests have been advanced by the courts from time to time to determine what is a condition as opposed to a warranty. In... the absence of any express declaration by the parties, as in the present case, 'we think that we are to look at the whole contract and applying the rule stated by Parke B to be acknowledged in *Graves v Legg* (1854) 9 Ex 709, at p 716... to see whether the particular stipulation goes to the root of the matter, so that a failure to perform it would render the performance of the rest of the contract by the plaintiff a thing different in substance from

what the defendant has stipulated for; or whether it merely partially affects it and may be compensated for in damages'.

[...]

> [337] The test of essentiality is whether it appears from the general nature of the contract considered as a whole, or from some particular term or terms, that the promise is of such importance to the promisee that he would not have entered into the contract unless he had been assured of a strict or a substantial performance of the promise, as the case may be, and that this ought to have been apparent to the promisor... If the innocent party would not have entered into the contract unless assured of a strict and literal performance of the promise, he may in general treat himself as discharged upon any breach of the promise, however slight.

At least it is clear that the obligation of the defendant to supply a weekly full-page drawing of 'Us Fellers' and the plaintiff's undertaking to present the drawing each week on the front page of the comic section are concurrent and correlative promises. And it would not seem open to doubt that the obligation of the defendant is a condition ... It would be strange if his obligation was a condition of the contract while the undertaking of the plaintiff was a subsidiary term the breach of which would only sound in damages ...

[...]

[338] ... Obviously it was of prime importance to the defendant that there should be continuity of publication so that his work should be kept continuously before the public, that his work should be published as a whole and not mutilated, and that it should be published on the most conspicuous page of the comic section.

[...]

[339] In the present case the undertaking of the plaintiff company that each weekly full-page drawing would be presented on the front page of the comic section formed a condition a substantial failure in the performance of which would enable the defendant to treat the contract as at an end. ... He exercised this right by his letter of 26 February.

[...]

[340] The appeal should be dismissed with costs.

QUESTIONS

(1) When can a party terminate a contract for breach at the common law?

(2) What is a condition, and what are the main legal tests to determine whether a term is a condition?

(3) 'The test for essentiality, as expressed by Jordan CJ in *Luna Park (NSW) Ltd v Tramways Advertising Pty Ltd* in the New South Wales Supreme Court of Appeal, is easier stated than applied. This is particularly so when one considers that applying the same test, Jordan CJ and Davidson J (in the Supreme Court of Appeal) and Dixon J (in the High Court) ruled in favour of Tramways, while Latham CJ, Rich and McTiernan JJ (in the High Court) ruled in favour of Luna Park.'

Discuss the above statement, indicating your agreement or disagreement with the statement.

16.4 Termination for breach of an intermediate term

Concept	Short explanation	Relevant authorities	*Principles* text*
A serious breach of an intermediate term gives the aggrieved party the right to terminate the contract	An intermediate term is neither a condition nor a warranty; it is in between the two in its importance. It can be breached in a variety of ways and the consequence of its breach can vary widely, depending of the nature of breach. If the breach is serious, depriving the aggrieved party of substantially the whole of the benefit of the contract, the aggrieved party will have the right to terminate. If the breach is minor, the aggrieved party will not have the right to terminate	*Hong Kong Fir Shipping Co Ltd v Kawasaki Kisen Kaisha Ltd* [1962] 1 All ER 474 *Koompahtoo Local Aboriginal Land Council v Sanpine Pty Ltd* (2007) 233 CLR 115	Chapter 16: 16.03–6.05

* Consult the corresponding section(s) of the *Principles* text for more detail.

At common law, a term that is not classified as a condition would be an intermediate term or a warranty. An intermediate term is neither a condition nor a warranty; that is, it is less than a condition, but more than a warranty; it is in between the two (in its importance). It is sometimes referred to as an 'innominate term'; that is, it is not nominated to either condition or warranty.

Typically, an intermediate term is a kind that can be breached in a variety of ways and the consequence of its breach can vary widely, depending of the nature of breach. An aggrieved party would be conferred the right to terminate if a breach of such an intermediate term goes to the root of the contract or is fundamental, depriving the aggrieved party of substantially the whole of the benefit of the contract.

Hong Kong Fir Shipping Co Ltd v Kawasaki Kisen Kaisha Ltd [1962] 1 All ER 474

Facts and issues

Kawasaki charted a vessel (the *Hong Kong Fir*) from its owners for a period of 24 months. The charter contract provided that the vessel be delivered to the charterers at Liverpool 'she being in every way fitted for ordinary cargo service', and (in Clause 3) that the owners would 'maintain her in a thoroughly efficient state in hull and machinery during service'. The vessel was delivered to Kawasaki on 13 February 1957, and sailed for Newport Mews, USA, to load a cargo of coal to transport to Osaka, Japan. The delivered vessel had undermanned and incompetent engine-room staff. During the voyage to Osaka, the vessel broke down and needed repairs for about five weeks. Upon arrival in Osaka, on 25 May 1957, it was found that the engines were in a bad state and needed a further 15 weeks to repair. On 6 June 1957 (and also on 27 July 1957), Kawasaki wrote to the owners to terminate the charter contract.

In an action by the owners for wrongful termination, the issue was whether the owners had breached the seaworthiness clause and, if yes, whether the breach entitled Kawasaki to terminate the contract. To determine this, the court had to decide on the classification of the seaworthiness clause.

Decision

The trial judge (Salmon J) held that the owners were in breach of the seaworthiness clause, but the breach did not entitle Kawasaki to terminate the charter. On appeal, the Court of Appeal confirmed the trial judge's decision, holding that neither unseaworthiness by itself nor the delay entailed by the owners' breaches of contract was so great as to frustrate the commercial purpose of the contract.

Per Sellers LJ at 479:

> Ships have been held to be unseaworthy in a variety of ways, and those who have been put to loss by reason thereof (in the absence of any protecting clause in favour of a shipowner) have been able to recover damages as for a breach of warranty. It would be unthinkable that all the relatively trivial matters which have been held to be unseaworthiness could be regarded as conditions of the contract... and justify in themselves a cancellation or refusal to perform on the part of the charterer. If, in the present case, the inadequacy and incompetence of the engine-room staff had been known to them, the charterers could have complained of the failure by the owners to deliver the vessel at Liverpool in accordance with cl 1 of the charter-party, and could have refused to take her in that condition.
>
> [...]
>
> If the owners had refused or failed so to do, their conduct, and not the unseaworthiness, would have amounted to a repudiation of the charterparty and entitled the charterers to accept it and treat the contract as at an end.
>
> [...]
>
> The charterer may rightly terminate the engagement if the delay in remedying any breach is so long in fact, or likely to be so long in reasonable anticipation, that the commercial purpose of the contract would be frustrated.
>
> [...]
>
> [482] In my judgment, Salmon J was clearly right in the answers he gave to both the contentions of the charterers relied on in this court, supported as the answers were by established authority and good commercial reason.
>
> I would dismiss the appeal.

Per Upjohn LJ at 482:

> I agree entirely with the judgment which has just been delivered. I shall not recite any of the facts, and propose only to add a few words on the two main submissions ... The charter-party ... contained the seaworthiness clause in these terms: 'she being in every way fitted for ordinary cargo service'. At first sight, that would seem to be a basic term underlying the whole of the charter-party, for how could the vessel perform the tasks which the owners warranted that she was fit to perform unless she is in fact fit to meet the perils of the sea? So basic is this obligation in a charter-party that, unless there is an express clause of exclusion, it will be implied where not expressed. Yet... it seems to me quite clear that the seaworthiness clause is not in general treated as a condition.

[…]

This is established by a number of authorities over a long period of years and I mention them without quoting from them … [483] Why is this apparently basic and underlying condition of seaworthiness not, in fact, treated as a condition? It is for the simple reason that the seaworthiness clause is breached by the slightest failure to be fitted 'in every way' for service. Thus, to take examples from the judgments in some of the cases I have mentioned about, if a nail is missing from one of the timbers of a wooden vessel, or if proper medical supplies or two anchors are not on board at the time of sailing, the owners are in breach of the seaworthiness stipulation. It is contrary to common sense to suppose that, in such circumstances, the parties contemplated that the charterer should at once be entitled to treat the contract as at an end for such trifling breaches.

[…]

It is open to the parties to a contract to make it clear either expressly or by necessary implication that a particular stipulation is to be regarded as a condition which goes to the root of the contract, so that it is clear that the parties contemplate that *any* breach of it entitles the other party at once to treat the contract as at an end … Bramwell … has warned against the dangers of too ready an implication of such a condition.

[…]

[484] In my judgment, the remedies open to the innocent party for breach of a stipulation which is not a condition strictly so called, depend entirely on the nature of the breach and its foreseeable consequence … The … question to be answered is, does the breach of the stipulation go so much to the root of the contract that it makes further commercial performance of the contract impossible, or, in other words, is the whole contract frustrated? If yea, the innocent party may treat the contract as at an end. If nay, his claim sounds in damages only …

Accordingly, I agree that this appeal must be dismissed.

Per Diplock LJ at 485:

With his analysis of the cases, as with the clear and careful judgment of Salmon J, I am in agreement, and I desire to add only some general observations on the legal questions which this case involves … The contract may itself expressly define some of these events, as in the cancellation clause in a charterparty, but, human prescience being limited, it seldom does so exhaustively and often fails to do so at all. In some classes of contracts… where an event occurs the occurrence of which neither the parties nor Parliament have expressly stated will discharge one of the parties from further performance of his undertakings, it is for the court to determine whether the event has this effect or not. The test whether an event has this effect or not has been stated in a number of metaphors all of which I think amount to the same thing: does the occurrence of the event deprive the party who has further undertakings still to perform of substantially the whole benefit which it was the intention of the parties as expressed in the contract that he should obtain as the consideration for performing those undertakings?

[…]

[488] As my brethren have already pointed out, the shipowner's undertaking to tender a seaworthy ship has, as a result of numerous decisions as to what can amount to 'unseaworthiness', become one of the most complex of contractual undertakings. It embraces obligations with respect to every part of the hull and machinery, stores and equipment and the crew itself. It can be broken by the presence of trivial defects easily and rapidly remediable as well as by defects which must inevitably result in a total loss of the vessel.

[…]

It is ... by no means surprising that, among the many hundreds of previous cases about the shipowner's undertaking to deliver a seaworthy ship, there is none where it was found profitable to discuss in the judgments the question whether that undertaking is a 'condition' or a 'warranty'; for the true answer, as I have already indicated, is that it is neither, but one of that large class of contractual undertakings, one breach of which may have the same effect as that ascribed to a breach of 'condition' ... and a different breach of which may have only the same effect as that ascribed to a breach of 'warranty' ...

What the learned judge had to do in the present case as in any other case where one party to a contract relies on a breach by the other party as giving him a right to elect to rescind the contract, was to look at the events which had occurred as a result of the breach at the time at which the charterers purported [489] to rescind the charterparty, and to decide whether the occurrence of those events deprived the charterers of substantially the whole benefit which it was the intention of the parties as expressed in the charter-party that the charterers should obtain from the further performance of their own contractual undertakings ...

The question which the learned judge had to ask himself was, as he rightly decided, whether or not, at the date when the charterers purported to rescind the contract, namely 6 June 1957, or when the owners purported to accept such rescission, namely 8 August 1957, the delay which had already occurred as a result of the incompetence of the engine-room staff, and the delay which was likely to occur in repairing the engines of the vessel and the conduct of the owners by that date in taking steps to remedy these two matters, were, when taken together, such as to deprive the charterers of substantially the whole benefit which it was the intention of the parties they should obtain from further use of the vessel under the charter-party.

In my view, in his judgment — on which I would not seek to improve — the learned judge took into account and gave due weight to all the relevant considerations and arrived at the right answer for the right reasons.

Appeal dismissed. Leave to appeal to the House of Lords refused.

Koompahtoo Local Aboriginal Land Council v Sanpine Pty Ltd (2007) 233 CLR 115

Facts and issues

In a joint venture agreement between Koompahtoo and Sanpine in which each had 50 per cent interest, Koompahtoo provided land and Sanpine was to manage the project. Sanpine was required to maintain proper books of accounts 'so as to permit the affairs of the Joint Venture to be duly assessed ... and in such a manner as enables the Venturers to extract from the Books any information in relation to the affairs of the Joint Venture as that Venturer may reasonably require from time to time.'

Sanpine breached its obligation regarding dealings with funds and record of accounts-keeping. The venture failed and an administrator was appointed. Following several unsuccessful attempts to extract financial records information from Sanpine, Koompahtoo terminated the contract on the basis that Sanpine's breaches of its record-keeping obligations gave it (Koompahtoo) the right to terminate.

The issue was whether Koompahtoo had the right to terminate—determination of which depended on the classification of the relevant terms breached.

Decision

The High Court held, referring to the judgment of Diplock LJ in *Hong Kong Fir Shipping* (referred to above), that the relevant terms were intermediate terms, which had been seriously breached, and that gave Koompahtoo the right to terminate the agreement.

Per Gleeson CJ, Gummow, Heydon and Crennan JJ at 122:

> This litigation arises from the termination, or purported termination, of a joint venture agreement for the commercial development of land.
>
> On 14 July 1997, the first appellant, Koompahtoo Local Aboriginal Land Council ('Koompahtoo'), and the first respondent, Sanpine Pty Ltd ('Sanpine'), entered into a joint venture agreement ('the Agreement') for the development and sale of a large area of land near Morisset, north of Sydney... Koompahtoo contributed the land. Sanpine, which had no other business, was the manager of the project. Each party had a 50% interest in the joint venture. Sanpine was also entitled to receive a management fee equal to 25% of the total project costs.
>
> [...]
>
> Although ... [123] liabilities in excess of $2 million were incurred on the security of mortgages over the land, the project ... never proceeded even to the initial stage of obtaining rezoning of the land. In April 2002, a caveat was placed on the title to the land, which had the practical effect of impeding the prospects of further funding. In June 2002, the New South Wales Aboriginal Land Council ('NSWALC') appointed an investigator of Koompahtoo ... On 10 April 2003, a mortgagee went into possession of the land. From February 2003 until December 2003, the administrator made attempts to obtain from Sanpine information as to the financial position of the joint venture. Proper books of account and financial records of the joint venture had never been kept by Sanpine. On 12 December 2003, the administrator, on behalf of Koompahtoo, terminated the Agreement. Sanpine commenced proceedings in the Supreme Court of New South Wales, seeking a declaration that the termination was invalid and that the Agreement was still on foot ...
>
> Campbell J, at first instance, ... [held] that having regard to the nature of the Agreement and the consequences of the breaches, the breaches were 'sufficiently serious' to give Koompahtoo a right to terminate. For the reasons that follow, the conclusion of Campbell J was correct.
>
> [...]
>
> [131] Not long after the administrator was appointed, Lot 556 (which included part of, but was not limited to, the land Koompahtoo had agreed to contribute to the joint venture) was in the possession of a mortgagee who claimed to be owed $2.3 million. When the administrator set out to find where the money had gone to, there were no meaningful joint venture accounts, and the records of Sanpine did not explain or justify significant amounts claimed by Sanpine to be expenses chargeable to the joint venture.
>
> [...]
>
> [132] As to the breaches in category 3, cl 16 required the opening of a joint venture bank account and the depositing to the credit of that account of funds received concerning the development. An example of such funds received was the money borrowed on the security of Lot 556. Such funds were not dealt with in that way. They were deposited to the credit of a bank account of Sanpine. A joint venture account was opened, with authorised signatures from both sides of the joint venture, but it was operated as what was described as a 'sweep account'. Whenever a debit was to be made to that account, enough money to cover the debit would be transferred to it, on the day the debit was due to be made, from the Sanpine account. The balance at the close of any day was nil. The amounts which were paid into, and debited to,

that [133] account were insignificant. The account was closed on 13 December 2000. Substantial payments went through the Sanpine account only. There were, therefore, regular, and indeed systematic, breaches of cl 16 ...

Campbell J described as 'particularly problematic' a payment of $183,314.48 to the wife of one of the controllers of Sanpine. The payment was never satisfactorily explained, there were no records to support it, and Campbell J considered that it was likely that the amount involved was not an expense of the joint venture.

[...]

There were no separate sets of accounts relating to the joint venture; no ledger, journal or cashbook. ... There were no [134] accounts or financial statements of the joint venture which recorded or reflected the expenditure, over the years, of more than $2.3 million ... requests for financial information were met by Sanpine with what Campbell J described as 'evasion and prevarication'. Campbell J described the 'total failure to keep books of original entry for the Joint Venture, on the basis of which annual accounts could be drawn up and audited each year', as 'a gross departure from the terms of [the Agreement]'.

This was not a finding of some technical breach as, for instance, keeping accounts in the wrong place.

[...]

[136] For present purposes, there are two relevant circumstances in which a breach of contract by one party may entitle the other to terminate. The first is where the obligation with which there has been failure to comply has been agreed by the contracting parties to be essential. Such an obligation is sometimes described as a condition.

[...]

[138] The second relevant circumstance is where there has been a sufficiently serious breach of a non-essential term ...

[139] It may be true that this Court has yet to accept *Hongkong Fir* as an essential element in the grounds for decision in any particular case. However, in *Ankar Pty Ltd v National Westminster Finance (Australia) Ltd*, Mason A-CJ, Wilson, Brennan and Dawson JJ referred to *Hongkong Fir* with evident approval and said that the concept of the intermediate and innominate term brings a greater flexibility to the law of contract. With that in mind, it was entirely appropriate for Campbell J to proceed with an analysis of the facts in which *Hongkong Fir* was applied.

The practical utility of a classification which includes intermediate terms, and the consequent greater flexibility of which the Court spoke in *Ankar*, appears from several consequences. First, the interests of justice are promoted by limiting rights to rescind to instances of serious and substantial breaches of contract. Secondly, a just outcome is facilitated in cases where the breach is of a term which is inessential.

[...]

[140] ... we rest our decision in the appeal not upon the ground of breach of an essential obligation, but upon application of the doctrine respecting intermediate terms ... [147] the breaches of Sanpine were in a number of respects gross, and their consequences were serious ... Such breaches justified termination. On that ground, we would uphold the decision of the primary judge.

[...]

[148] The appeal should be allowed with costs.

Kirby J delivered a separate judgment in which, while holding in favour of Koompahtoo, he rejected the majority's endorsement of the intermediate term formulation. Instead, he preferred an approach proposed by Dr Seddon and Associate Professor Ellinghaus in the Australia edition of *Cheshire & Fifoot*.[7] Their opinion is that a third, intermediate term, classification is unnecessary. There are essential terms (conditions) and non-essential terms. A right to terminate arises in respect of: (1) breach of an essential term; or (2) breach of a non-essential term causing substantial loss of benefit. And, of course, a right to terminate arises in respect of repudiation (in the sense of 'renunciation').

QUESTIONS

(1) What is the legal test to determine whether there is a sufficiently serious breach of an intermediate term that would enable termination of a contract?

(2) Why was 'seaworthiness' held to be an intermediate term (rather than a condition) in *Hong Kong Fir Shipping Co Ltd v Kawasaki Kisen Kaisha Ltd* [1962] 1 All ER 474; considering dangers associated with sea voyages, is seaworthiness not essential?

(3) Accepting seaworthiness as an intermediate term, as held in *Hong Kong Fir Shipping Co Ltd v Kawasaki Kisen Kaisha Ltd* [1962] 1 All ER 474, why was inadequate crew and incompetent engine-room staff, coupled with repeated breakdown (loss of five weeks between March and May, and need for further 15 weeks to repair) not sufficiently serious breach of the intermediate term affording Kawasaki the right to terminate?

16.5 Termination for repudiation

Concept	Short explanation	Relevant authorities	*Principles* text*
Where a party renounces a contract, or otherwise manifests an unwillingness to perform their obligation under the contract, that party is said to have repudiated the contract	Repudiation confers on the other (innocent or aggrieved) party the right to terminate	*Carr v J A Berriman Pty Ltd* (1953) 89 CLR 327 *Progressive Mailing House Pty Ltd v Tabali Pty Ltd* (1985) 157 CLR 17	Chapter 6: 6.03–6.05

* Consult the corresponding section(s) of the *Principles* text for more detail.

Where one party manifests an unwillingness or inability to perform his or her obligation under the contract, that party is said to have repudiated the contract. Repudiation confers on the other (innocent) party the right to terminate.

7 Nicholas Seddon and Manfred Ellinghaus, *Cheshire & Fifoot Law of Contract* (LexisNexis, 9th Australian ed, 2008) 1032 [21.22].

'Repudiation is a drastic conclusion which should only be held to arise in clear cases of a refusal, in a matter going to the root of the contract, to perform contractual obligations.'[8] To be a repudiation, the absence of willingness or ability to perform must relate to the whole contract, a condition of the contract, or otherwise be 'fundamental' (deprive the innocent party of substantially the whole benefit of the contract). Repudiation may be evinced through the repudiating party's words, conduct or factual inability to perform.

Carr v J A Berriman Pty Ltd (1953) 89 CLR 327

Facts and issues

Carr contracted Berriman, a builder, to construct a factory for him (Carr) on land owned by Carr. The contract provided for the appointment of Carr's architect to supervise the works. Carr was required, among other things, to: (1) undertake and complete excavation of the site to a specified level and deliver the site to Berriman on or before 29 May 1950; and (2) provide the steel to be used for the construction of the building to Berriman (or Berriman's contractor) for fabrication for the building.

Carr did not excavate the site as required. He also engaged a steel fabricator directly to undertake the manufacture of the steel, instead of providing the steel to the Berriman, thereby depriving Berriman a significant portion of the works (and profit) under the contract.

By letter dated 31 July 1950, Berriman's solicitors wrote to Carr's architect advising that as a result of Carr's failure to complete the excavations (first breach) and also his failure to provide the steel (second breach), Berriman was terminating the contract.

The issue was whether Carr repudiated the contract by his conduct, entitling Berriman to terminate the contract as it had purported to do by the 31 July 1950 letter.

Decision

In holding that Carr's conduct was repudiatory, the Court (Fullagar J, with whom Williams, Webb and Kitto JJ and Dixon CJ agreed) concluded that a reasonable person could hardly draw any other inference than that Carr did not intend to take the contract seriously; and that he was prepared to carry out his part of the contract only if and when it suited him.

Per Fullagar at 343:

> The letter of 31st July alleges two breaches of contract by the building owner as entitling the builder to rescind. The first is a 'failure to prepare the site', and the second is the 'making of an arrangement' with a company named Arcos Products Pty Ltd [for the steelworks] . . .
>
> The . . . [344] proprietor was required by the contract (1) to excavate the site to the prescribed level and (2) to give possession of it duly excavated to the builder on or before 29 May . . . It appears that Berriman and Oser and Morthen and Carr's foreman went to the site about 15th or 18th May. There was then 'heavy machinery all over it'. From this and other evidence I gather that the site was practically covered by heavy material . . . Both Berriman and Morthen visited the site again both before and after 29th May . . . and both say that nothing whatever appeared to have been done.
>
> [...]

8 *Woodar Investment Development Ltd v Wimpey Constructions* [1980] 1 WLR 277, 283.

From the time of the inspection about 18th May up to [345] the middle of July, Berriman telephoned Oser 'at least once a week' complaining that nothing was being done. Oser said that he would 'get in touch with Carr to see if he could not get the thing hurried up', and later that he (Oser) was 'doing all he could'. During August, Oser and Carr were insisting that the contract had not been effectively determined but was still subsisting, but on 21 September 1950 Carr entered into a new contract with another builder. This contract did not fix a date for excavation and delivery of site. Berriman said that in the middle of September the land was still covered with heavy material. It was not until about Christmas that the land was in fact cleared of material and excavated to the required level.

With regard to the other breach of contract alleged . . . the structural steel is to be supplied by the proprietor, but is to be fabricated by the contractor or by a sub-contractor to him. Before the making of the contract Mr Berriman had obtained a tender from a company named Hurll & Douglas Pty Ltd for the fabricating of this steel. The price quoted was £3948. On 7th June 1950 the company wrote to Hurll & Douglas, advising that this quotation was accepted. It was a term of the rise and fall clause of the contract that the builder should enter into all necessary sub-contracts within eight weeks of the signing of the contract. That period expired on 28th June. Oser was informed of the acceptance of the tender of Hurll & Douglas shortly after 7th June. On 19th July Oser wrote a letter to the company in the following terms:

> I have been instructed to inform you that my clients, Messrs T Carr & Co, have made arrangements with Arcos Products Pty Ltd of Parramatta Road, Lidcombe, to supply and fabricate the structural steel work for the above job, and that the respective order has been placed with this firm. In explanation I would like to add that this arrangement was made necessary by the peculiar steel supply position of to-day. I shall be glad if you would kindly inform me at the earliest of your allowance for the fabrication of the steel, which thus becomes a deduction post (sic) from your contract

. . . [348] It is impossible, to my mind, to regard this letter as either more or less than a communication by architect to builder of a repudiation of part of the contract by the building owner.

For these reasons I am of opinion that the company's solicitor was fully justified in asserting, as he did in his letter of 31st July, that two breaches of contract had been committed by Carr. He had not given possession of the building site, duly excavated or at all, on the date required by the contract or thereafter. And he had repudiated his obligation to deliver the structural steel for fabrication. As soon as this position is realized, the case becomes, in my opinion, a reasonably clear one.

[...]

[351] One would be disposed to think that this second breach alone amounted to such repudiation as justified rescission. It is to be remembered that Carr's action in placing the fabrication of the steel in other hands was deliberate . . . [W]hen this second breach is viewed alongside the existing position with regard to the site, the case does not seem to admit of doubt. An election not to rescind for failure to deliver the excavated site on the due date could not deprive that failure of all significance. When a second breach occurs, the two combined may have a significance which it might not be legitimate to attach to the first alone. The position when Mr Oser's letter was received was this. . . . The intention 'evinced' here is an intention not to be bound by [352] the contract. When such an intention is shown, the other party is entitled to rescind the contract. Mr Berriman thought that such an intention had been shown, and he acted accordingly. In my opinion, he was justified in the view which he took, and acted as he was legally entitled to act . . .

Both appeals should be dismissed with costs.

Progressive Mailing House Pty Ltd v Tabali Pty Ltd (1985) 157 CLR 17

Facts and issues

Progressive was a lessee of Tabali's property. Progressive committed a series of breaches of the lease, including failing to pay rent, misuse of the property, causing damage to the property and omitting to remedy the damage, and subletting in breach of the terms of the lease.

Tabali sued to terminate the lease, re-enter (ie reposess) the property, and to recover damages.

The issue was whether, by its conduct, Progressive had repudiated the contract, giving Tabali the right to terminate the lease, re-enter and to recover damages.

Decision

The Court held that the various breaches by Progressive, put together, constituted a repudiation of the lease.

Per Mason J at 21:

> Clause 3.1 required the lessee during the whole of the term to pay to the lessor the rent ... [of] $7750 per month payable monthly. [T]he lessee covenanted, inter alia, not to do or permit to be done anything which might render any increased premium payable for the insurance of the premises ... [T]he lessee was prohibited from assigning or subletting the premises without the consent of the lessor. Part 5 imposed on the lessee a number of requirements with regard to the maintenance and repair of the premises and alterations, the principal obligations with regard to alterations being imposed by cl 5.1 and with regard to maintenance and repair being imposed by cl 5.2. Clause 5.3 dealt specifically with the lessee's obligation to repair and replace broken glass as well as heating, lighting and electrical equipment.
>
> [...]
>
> [32] [T]he appellant points out, correctly, that repudiation of a contract is a serious matter and is not to be lightly inferred and that neither a breach of a covenant to pay rent nor a breach of a covenant to repair, without more, [33] constitutes a breach of a fundamental term, nor amounts to a repudiation of a lease.
>
> [...]
>
> What needs to be established in order to constitute a repudiation is that the party evinces an intention no longer to be bound by the contract or that he intends to fulfil the contract only in a manner substantially inconsistent with his obligations and not in any other way (*Shevill,* at pp 625–7).
>
> [...]
>
> [34] It is evident that the appellant was responsible for physical damage to the premises which it failed to rectify in accordance with the requirements of the respondent's notice dated 16 August 1979. ... [35] By May 1979 damage was done by the appellant to the electrical system on the premises. This included smashed light fittings, illegal joints in cables, exposed wiring, smashed power outlets and damaged wiring. In that month the respondent rectified earlier breaches, but it then caused further damage so that in August 1979 ... Damage was also done to down pipes leading to leaks, but it seems that no effort was made to repair down pipes until June 1981 ... The appellant sublet part of the premises, being approximately one tenth of the area, without having sought consent to do so.
>
> [...]
>
> The appellant was also in breach of cl 5.8 of the lease. This clause required the lessee to comply with all laws governing the use of the premises ... The appellant [in breach of local government law] caused the vehicular drive-through area to be obstructed by steel shelving

used for storage of commodities and caused the parking and loading area to be blocked and obstructed by crates and rubbish.

[...]

It is not suggested that the breaches so far discussed, viewed in isolation, amounted to a repudiation or fundamental breach of the [36] lease. It is the breach of the covenant to pay rent, in association with the other breaches, which is the central feature of the respondent's case on this issue.

[...]

[37] In the result the evidence supports the conclusion that the appellant's conduct amounted to a repudiation of the lease or a fundamental breach of its obligations under the lease . . .

I would dismiss the appeal.

Wilson, Brennan, Deane and Dawson JJ all delivered similar judgments, in which they broadly agreed with Mason J.

QUESTIONS

(1) What is the legal test to determine whether a party has repudiated a contract?

(2) In *Carr v J A Berriman Pty Ltd* (1953) 89 CLR 327, Carr commenced legal action to stop Berriman from terminating the contract, and to keep the contract afoot. This is contrary to the notion of renunciation of the contract, which repudiation entails. Why did the Court hold that Carr had repudiated the contract?

(3) What reasons did the High Court give for holding that Progressive (the lessee) had repudiated the lease in *Progressive Mailing House Pty Ltd v Tabali Pty Ltd* (1985) 157 CLR 17?

16.6 Termination for delay

Concept	Short explanation	Relevant authorities	*Principles* text*
Delay in performing a contractual obligation constitutes breach, and that breach may give the aggrieved party the right to terminate the contract	Failure to perform contractual obligations in time constitutes a delay and a breach of contract. Breach by delay, like other forms of breaches, would give the innocent party the right to terminate if the delay constitutes: (1) breach of a condition; (2) a serious breach of an intermediate term; or (3) a repudiation	*Laurinda Pty Ltd v Capalaba Park Shopping Centre Pty Ltd* (1989) 166 CLR 623	Chapter 16: 16.03–16.05

* Consult the corresponding section(s) of the *Principles* text for more detail.

Failure to perform contractual obligations by the time specified for performance without lawful excuse or, where no time is stated, failure to perform within a reasonable time, constitutes a delay and a breach of contract. Breach by delay, like other forms of breaches, would give the innocent party the right to terminate if the delay constitutes: (1) breach of a condition; (2) a serious breach of an intermediate term; or (3) a repudiation. *Laurinda Pty Ltd v Capalaba Park Shopping Centre Pty Ltd* (1989) 166 CLR 623 helps illustrate the law regarding breach by delay in performance.

Laurinda Pty Ltd v Capalaba Park Shopping Centre Pty Ltd (1989) 166 CLR 623

Facts and issues

By a lease dated 31 October 1985, Capalaba ('the Lessor') agreed to lease to Laurinda ('the Lessee') and the second appellants ('the Guarantor') a shop in Capalaba's shopping centre for a term of six years. The Lessee was to pay to the Lessor, upon demand, all legal costs and other costs and expenses incidental to the preparation, execution and stamping of the lease. Laurinda entered into possession of the shop on or before 3 December 1985, paid the rental, and $2,317.00 to Capalaba's solicitors for registration and stamping of the lease, and for other related costs. Laurinda remained in occupation until 5 September 1986, when it vacated the premises and purported to terminate the lease agreement on the ground that Capalaba had repudiated the agreement or was in breach of essential conditions of the agreement as a result of Capalaba's failure to register the lease or to deliver to Laurinda a lease in registrable form. Capalaba treated Laurinda's termination as a wrongful repudiation of the agreement.

On 31 October 1986, Laurinda commenced an action for a declaration that they had validly terminated the lease, and an order for the return of the sum of $2,317.00, plus damages and interest.

The issue was whether Capalaba's delay in delivering to Laurinda the lease in registerable form constituted repudiation (or breach of an essential term).

Decision

The trial judge held in favour of Laurinda. The Court of Appeal reversed the decision. On further appeal, the High Court held in favour of Laurinda, on the ground that Capalaba's actions constituted repudiation.

Per Mason CJ at 633:

> Mere delay on the part of Capalaba in performing a non-essential contractual obligation cannot justify a refusal by Laurinda to perform its obligations. Something more — whether it be conduct amounting to a clear repudiation by Capalaba of the requirement to complete or failure to comply with a valid notice given by Laurinda fixing a time for completion and making time of the essence in that respect — would be required.
>
> [...]

[634] There is a difference between evincing an intention to carry out a contract only if and when it suits the party to do so and evincing an intention to carry out a contract as and when it suits the party to do so. In the first case the party intends not to carry out the contract at all in the event that it does not suit him. In the second case the party intends to carry out the contract, but only to carry it out as and when it suits him. It is much easier to say of the first than of the second case that the party has evinced an intention no longer to be bound by the contract or to fulfil it only in a manner substantially inconsistent with his obligations and not in any other way. But the outcome in the second case will depend upon its particular circumstances, including the terms of the contract. In some situations the intention to carry out the contract as and when it suits the party may be taken to such lengths that it amounts to an intention to fulfil the contract only in a manner substantially inconsistent with the party's obligations and not in any other way.

It is necessary to review the correspondence. On 28 November 1985 Capalaba's solicitors informed Laurinda's solicitors that the Deed and the lease had been executed and would be sent shortly by Capalaba to its solicitors. On 14 March 1986 a firm of accountants who appear to have been acting for all the appellants requested Capalaba's solicitors 'to forward a copy of the above lease at your earliest opportunity'. The letter continued:

> They consider that four months is a reasonable time for you to have complied with their request particularly as they were under pressure by you to execute the lease without adequate time to study the provisions of such lease.

The terms of the letter suggest that a request of a like nature to that made on 14 March 1986 had been [635] made four months earlier.

[…]

Capalaba's solicitors replied on 25 March 1986 in these terms:

> The lease documents were forwarded to Melbourne for execution by the Lessor in October last year. They have not been returned. However, we have been advised that they have been executed by the Lessor. We expect that they will be returned in the not too distant future. We will provide your client with its stamped parts of the documents as soon as we are able to.

[…]

Subsequently on 21 August 1986 the appellants' solicitors wrote to Capalaba's solicitors. After stating that the appellants were concerned that the lease had not been registered despite the fact that the documentation had been executed and should have been completed over ten months before, the letter continued:

> It is clearly of critical importance to our clients that the Lease be registered immediately to safeguard their rights of tenure. To that end our clients have already paid to your firm on 6th January this year sufficient funds to allow registration of the Lease to be effected by your client. In such circumstances, and in view of the unexplained and lengthy delay, it appears reasonable that our clients require your client to complete registration within fourteen days from the date hereof. If the registration is not completed within that time then our clients naturally reserve their rights in respect of your client's default.

Capalaba's solicitors responded by letter dated 3 September 1986 stating merely that they had referred the letter of 21 August to Capalaba for its instructions which would be communicated as soon [636] as they were received.

[...]

The correspondence culminated in the letter dated 5 September 1986 from the appellants' solicitors to Capalaba's solicitors which asserted [repudiation on the part of Capalaba, went on to advise that Laurinda terminated the lease].

If for the moment we put to one side the question whether the letter of 21 August 1986 validly fixed a time for registration of the lease, this correspondence demonstrates an attitude on the part of Capalaba which was not only dilatory but also cavalier and recalcitrant. Capalaba was remiss in failing to respond in a more positive way to the appellants' requests, especially after the letter of 21 August. More than that, Capalaba's solicitors had on two occasions made incorrect statements about the progress of the matter. There was the incorrect statement in the letter of 28 November 1985 that the lease had been executed and would be sent 'shortly'. Then there was the statement in the letter of 25 March 1986 that the lease documents would be returned by Capalaba to its solicitors 'in the not too distant future' and that the stamped parts of its documents would be provided to Laurinda 'as soon as we are able to'. Moreover, in the face of the letter of 21 August 1986, Capalaba's solicitors only say on 3 September that they have referred the letter for instructions... Although the matter is finely balanced, the unjustified delay on the part of Capalaba between March and 3 September 1986, accompanied by incorrect statements and unfulfilled assurances sustained the inference of repudiation drawn by Connolly J. Based on Capalaba's unwillingness to deliver a registrable lease to Laurinda, it seems to me that Capalaba's intention was only to perform the contract in a manner substantially inconsistent with its [637] obligations, such as would allow Laurinda to treat Capalaba as having repudiated the contract.

[...]

[640] The finding of repudiation by Capalaba necessitates the allowing of the appeal.

Per Brennan J 641:

The time to be implied for performance of the intending lessor's obligation is a reasonable time ... Time was not of the essence of Capalaba's implied promise to procure registration of an appropriate instrument of a six-year lease from Capalaba to Laurinda.

[...]

[642] The implied promise by Capalaba to procure registration of an appropriate instrument was thus at the heart of the agreement. It was a promise of such importance to the promisee that it would not have entered into the contract unless it had been assured of substantial performance and this ought to have been apparent to the promisor. It answered the criterion of an essential promise in the sense that an outright repudiation of the promise would have entitled Laurinda to rescind. The criterion of an essential promise which I have stated in terms relevant to the present case is derived from the criterion expressed by Jordan CJ in *Tramways Advertising Pty Ltd v Luna Park (NSW) Ltd* (1938) 38 SR (NSW) 632 at 641–642) and frequently adopted in this Court, most recently in *Ankar Pty Ltd v National Westminster Finance (Australia) Ltd* [1987] HCA 15; (1987) 162 CLR 549 at 556, but I have modified it by using the term 'substantial performance' rather than the usual formula of 'a strict or a substantial performance'. The modification is necessary when, no day for performance being stipulated and the subject matter of the promise not being such as to require strictly timeous performance, time is not of the essence of the promise either in law or in equity... When time is not of the essence, the promisee must have been willing to enter into the contract without an assurance that the promise would be performed strictly, albeit with an assurance that the promise would be performed substantially.

[...]

Where an essential term — in the sense defined — is to be performed within a reasonable time, there being no stipulated day for performance, and that time passes without performance, the innocent party does not acquire a right to rescind unless the defaulting party repudiates or has repudiated his obligation to [643] perform ... More than a mere failure in timeous performance is necessary to warrant an inference of repudiation, but delay may be so serious as to amount to a refusal to perform and in such a case an innocent party has a right to rescind.

[...]

The difference between a contract which contains a stipulated day for performance of an essential term and a contract which, expressly or impliedly, requires performance within a reasonable time is important when the question is whether, on failure to perform within the time limited by the contract, the innocent party is entitled to rescind. In the former case, a right to rescind arises at law when the stipulated day passes; in the latter, that right does not necessarily arise when the reasonable time expires but only when repudiation is clearly to be inferred from the circumstances in which the delay occurs. Delay will amount to repudiation if the defaulting party 'evinces an intention no longer to be bound by the contract ... or shows that he intends to fulfil the contract only in a manner substantially inconsistent with his obligations and not in any other way'.

[...]

If the inference to be drawn from the circumstances is that the defaulting party intends to perform an essential promise after some minor delay, repudiation cannot be inferred; but if the inference is that the defaulting party intends so to delay performance that the promisee will be substantially deprived of the benefit of the promise, repudiation can be inferred ...

[644] As I attempted to explain in *Louinder v Leis* (at pp 532–536), a notice to complete does not make time of the essence of the contract when the contract itself does not do so, but it is a step towards lifting an equitable restraint on the exercise of a right to rescind which arises aliunde ...

When a reasonable time is prescribed for performance of an essential term of a contract, a notice to complete requiring performance of that term by a specified day can be given only if the party to whom it is given is already in breach of his contractual obligation: *Neeta (Epping) Pty Ltd v Phillips*, at p 299 ...

His Honour went on to hold that the 14 days' notice given by Laurinda was too short, and therefore ineffective. However, Capalaba's actions, taken as a whole, amounted to repudiation, which entitled Laurinda to terminate the contract.

Deane and Dawson JJ delivered a joint judgment in favour of Laurinda, allowing the appeal; as did Gaudron J, in a separate judgment.

QUESTIONS

(1) When does delay give rise to the right to terminate?

(2) When is delay a breach of a condition?

(3) Can time for performance be an intermediate term?

16.7 Relief against forfeiture

Concept	Short explanation	Relevant authorities	*Principles* text*
Where termination of contract results in forfeiture of proprietary interest of the breaching (or repudiating) party, a court may grant that party relief against the forfeiture	Sometimes rightful termination of a contract may result in forfeiture of proprietary interest of the breaching (or repudiating) party, for instance instalments paid up to the date of termination. In extreme cases, a court may, in exercising its equitable jurisdiction, grant the breaching party relief against forfeiture. The aim is to protect against the unconscientious exercise of legal rights	*Tanwar Enterprises Pty Ltd v Cauchi* (2003) 217 CLR 315	Chapter 16: 16.03–6.05

* Consult the corresponding section(s) of the *Principles* text for more detail.

Sometimes rightful termination of a contract for breach or repudiation may result in forfeiture of proprietary interest of the breaching (or repudiating) party. For instance, where a purchaser of property has made some payments, but then defaults in a manner that gives the vendor the right to terminate the contract of sale, the vendor may be able to keep both the payments and the property.

In extreme cases, a court may, in exercising its equitable jurisdiction, grant the breaching party relief against forfeiture. The aim is to protect against the unconscientious exercise of legal rights. The principles regarding relief against forfeiture are discussed in detail in *Tanwar Enterprises Pty Ltd v Cauchi* (2003) 217 CLR 315.

Tanwar Enterprises Pty Ltd v Cauchi (2003) 217 CLR 315

Facts and issues

Members of the Cauchi family and Mr Dalley ('the vendors'), owned three adjoining parcels of land near Sydney. In October 1999, they entered into separate contracts to sell the land to Tanwar Enterprises Pty Ltd ('the purchaser') for a combined price of approximately $4.5 million. The original date for completion of the contracts was 28 February 2000. This was later extended to August 2000. That date was not adhered to. On 20 August 2000, the vendors issued notices of termination of each contract. However, the parties eventually negotiated deeds dated 5 June 2001, each containing a new completion date of Monday 25 June 2001. Tanwar paid 10 per cent deposit, totalling $450,252.64—an additional $397,473.40 of the purchase price—and also $80,000 in consideration of the extension of time to complete.

Tanwar was unable to settle on 25 June. It informed the vendors that it was waiting for funds from overseas, which would be available for settlement the next day (26 June). However, the vendors terminated the contract on 26 June when they were told the funds were now available and settlement could proceed.

Tanwar commenced action asking for, among other things, relief against forfeiture.

Decision

The trial judge denied Tanwar's request, holding in favour of the vendors. Tanwar's appeals to the Court of Appeal and the High Court were dismissed.

Per Gleeson CJ, McHugh, Gummow, Hayne and Heydon JJ at 324:

> In the present case ... the question [is] why the vendors ought not to be heard to assert the exercise of their legal right to terminate in answer to the claim by Tanwar for specific performance. The conscience of the vendors which equity seeks to relieve is, as Gleeson CJ put it in *Australian Broadcasting Corp v Lenah Game Meats Pty Ltd*, a 'properly formed and instructed conscience'.
>
> [326] In *Legione*, Mason and Deane JJ instanced 'fraud, mistake, accident, [and] surprise' as elements which may make it inequitable to insist on termination of a contract for failure to observe its strict terms. Subsequently, in *Stern*, Mason CJ ... stated that equity intervenes only where the vendor has, by the vendor's conduct, caused or contributed to a circumstance rendering it unconscionable for the vendor to insist upon its legal rights. That helps explain why mere supervening events and changes in the relevant circumstances are insufficient. But it should be noted that cases falling within the heads of mistake or accident will not necessarily be the result of activity by the vendor. In addition, his Honour spoke in *Stern* of the circumstances being 'exceptional' to attract equitable intervention.
>
> [...]
>
> What Lord Wilberforce in *Shiloh Spinners* called 'the special heads of fraud, accident, mistake or surprise' identify in a broad sense the circumstances making it inequitable for the vendors to rely upon their termination of Tanwar's contracts as an answer to its claim for specific performance. No doubt the decided cases in which the operation of these 'special heads' is considered do not disclose exhaustively the circumstances which merit this equitable intervention. But, at least where accident and mistake are not involved, it will be necessary to point to the conduct of the vendor as having in some significant respect caused or contributed to the breach of the essential time stipulation. Tanwar's situation falls beyond that pale. The statement by Mason CJ *in Stern* respecting the insignificance of subsequent events for which the vendors were in no way responsible is fatal to the main thrust of Tanwar's case.
>
> Thus, it remains for Tanwar to show that it is against conscience for the vendors to set up the termination of the contracts. In the present appeal, as already has been indicated, there was no representation by the vendors which could found any estoppel. Nor has Tanwar asserted that there was any mistake in any relevant sense.
>
> [...]
>
> [336] In its extremity, Tanwar then founds upon the jurisdiction to relieve against the consequences of 'accident'...
>
> [337] It is here that the circumstances leading up to, and the terms of, the 2001 Deeds are of critical importance. The vendors withdrew the earlier notices of termination in return for the assumption by Tanwar of obligations to complete couched in unqualified terms. ... The failure by Tanwar to avail itself of the advantages it obtained by negotiating the 2001 Deeds and by keeping the contracts on foot had the effect of exposing Tanwar again to the exercise by the vendors of their rights to terminate the contracts. Equity does not intervene to prevent the

effective exercise of those rights. The claim by Tanwar for relief against the consequences of the failure in the timely provision of the second mortgage does not succeed.

Kirby and Callinan JJ delivered separate judgments dismissing the appeal.

QUESTIONS

(1) When may a court grant relief against forfeiture?

(2) Why did the High Court decline to grant Tanwar Enterprises relief against forfeiture in *Tanwar Enterprises Pty Ltd v Cauchi* (2003) 217 CLR 315?

(3) Do you agree with the outcome of the High Court's decision in *Tanwar Enterprises Pty Ltd v Cauchi* (2003) 217 CLR 315? Give reasons for your position.

16.8 International perspectives

For international commercial sales contracts governed by the *CISG* (see **25.4.1** on applicability), or commercial contracts subject to UNIDROIT Principles (see **25.4.3** on applicability), rights of termination are not dependent on a three-level classification of conditions, intermediate terms and warranties (contrast **16.1** above). Instead, a threshold must be met before the right to terminate arises (although parties can tailor this to their own circumstances by agreement: art 6 *CISG*). The primary threshold for avoidance (termination) is fundamental breach: art 49(1)(a) *CISG*, 'fundamental non-performance': art 7.3.1(1) UNIDROIT Principles. Alternatively, non-delivery after an additional reasonable time can also provide grounds for avoidance: art 49(1)(b) *CISG*, art 7.3.1(3) UNIDROIT Principles, see further **12.5.1** and **25.9.2**. Fundamental breach is defined in art 25 *CISG* (below), as involving 'substantial deprivation' of benefits a party is 'entitled to expect', unless this was not reasonably foreseeable: see also art 7.3.1(2) UNIDROIT Principles. This is consistent with the *CISG*'s aim of keeping the contract on foot, and providing other remedies (such as damages) than the costly unwinding of an international contract, except in serious cases.

However, whether a breach is fundamental is determined by interpretation of the parties' intent. The terms, circumstances or other evidence may demonstrate that a particular performance was highly important or essential, thus failure would foreseeably result in substantial deprivation; ie that breach of it would be 'fundamental'. Moreover, practices between the parties and international usages may shed further light on this: see **25.5.7**. The right to avoid, however, will be lost if the aggrieved party fails to give notice of fundamental breach (or non-delivery) and avoidance within a reasonable time: arts 26, 49(2) *CISG*, art. 7.3.2 UNIDROIT Principles. Multiple breaches may amount to fundamental breach.[9] On anticipated fundamental breach, see **25.9.5**. Note that classification of terms pursuant to the Australian *Sale of Goods Acts* (see **16.2.2**) will not apply to contracts governed by the *CISG*: eg *Goods Act 1958* (Vic) ss 86–87.

9 *Wire Rod Case II* (Judgment) (Bundesgericht, Switzerland, Case No 4A_614/2014, 2 April 2015).

CISG art 25

A breach of contract committed by one of the parties is fundamental if it results in such detriment to the other party as substantially to deprive him of what he is entitled to expect under the contract, unless the party in breach did not foresee and a reasonable person of the same kind in the same circumstances would not have foreseen such a result.

16.9 Review

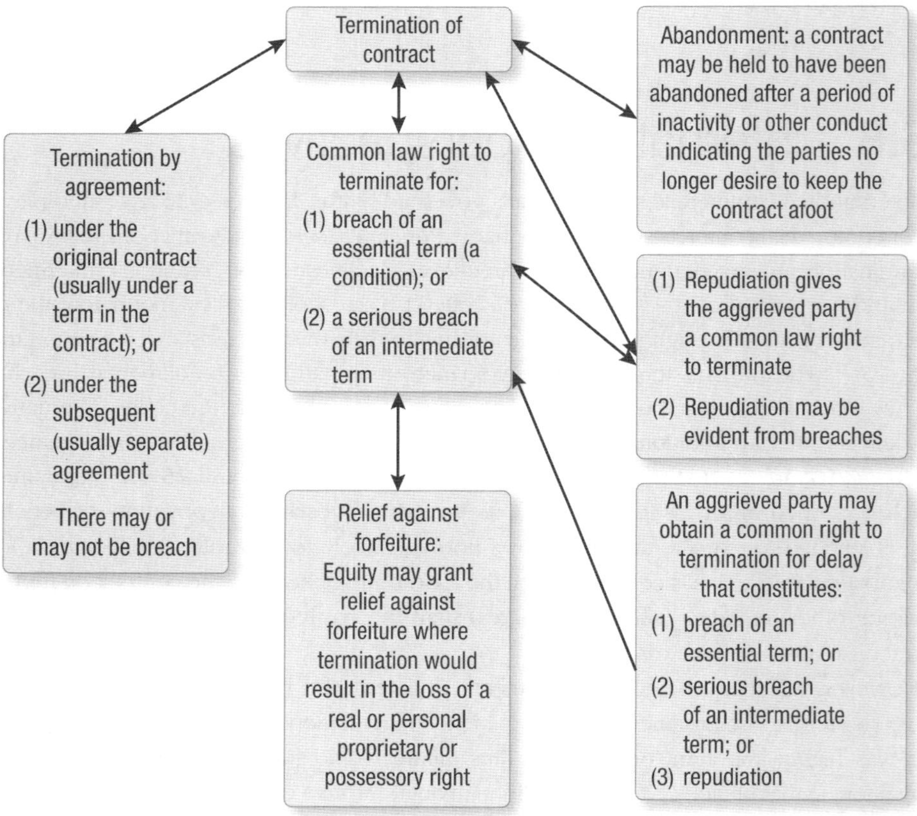

- A party may end a contract by termination, because of breach or repudiation.
- A breach of contract occurs when a party, without lawful excuse, fails or refuses to perform what is due from them under the contract, or performs their obligation defectively or incapacitates themselves from performing.
- Repudiation occurs where a party, whether through words or conduct, exhibits an intention to no longer be bound by the contract or to only perform the contract in a manner that is substantially inconsistent with their obligations under the contract.

- At common law, any breach of a condition, however trivial the breach, allows the aggrieved party to terminate.
- Only a serious breach of an intermediate term allows the aggrieved party to terminate.
- Repudiation gives the aggrieved party the right to terminate.
- No breach of a warranty (non-essential term) gives the aggrieved party the right to terminate (though gross breaches of warranty may be held to constitute repudiation, which then gives the aggrieved party the right to terminate).

TIPS FOR APPLYING THE LAW IN PRACTICE

- Remember the classes of terms and sources of classification (statute, statement of the parties, and the courts).
- Note when an aggrieved party gains the right to terminate for breach or repudiation.
- Familiarise yourself with what constitutes repudiation.
- Remember relief against forfeiture.

PROBLEM QUESTIONS

Consider the common facts below, and the further facts given under each of Questions 1 and 2. Advise Caroline in respect of the scenarios below. Each scenario is independent of the other, and no scenario follows on from any other.

Common facts

Dr Caroline Smith decides to start her own General Practice to provide medical services. She buys a property for this purpose, and engages some tradespeople to carry out various renovations and fittings. Caroline wants a light-box sign installed at the front of her practice featuring her name, logo and other information.

David, owner of Best Signs Pty Ltd, agrees to install the light-box for $9000. The contract with Best Signs does not include cost of connecting electricity to the light-box.

Caroline contracts with Joseph, the electrician who was doing all the electrical work during the renovation, to connect the electricity to the light-box. Joseph lays some electrical cables to the spot where the light-box is to be installed.

(1) The contract between Best Signs provided that Caroline is to pay the contract price by three equal instalments (each payment being $3000) on the first day of each of the next three months. It also provides that time is of the essence, and that should Caroline breach the contract, Best Signs shall have the right to terminate the contract and Caroline will forfeit all payments made.

Caroline pays the first instalment of $3000 as required. The cheque for the second instalment was incorrectly addressed, and so was not delivered. Best Signs terminates the contract on the day after it was due to receive the second instalment. Caroline stresses that she posted a cheque in time and threatens to take legal action. On day 5 of the month, three days after Best Sign's termination, Caroline receives the cheque she posted, with the notation 'undeliverable'.

Caroline seeks your advice as to whether she can claim return of the $3000.

(2) Assume that the scenario in Question 1 above did not occur. Caroline pays for the light-box and Best Signs duly installs the light-box on 2 November. On the same day, Caroline calls Joseph, who has quoted $500 for the light-box connection, to do the connection. Joseph says he is working on a job at Phillip Island and will not be back till 4 November. He promises to do the connection first thing on 5 November. Joseph then fails to show up on this date. On 6 November, Caroline calls to query Joseph, who says he forgot and promises to do the connection the next day. Again, Joseph fails to turn up as promised. In the following days, Caroline is unable to reach Joseph, as he does not answer his phone or return Caroline's calls.

Caroline is anxious for all work to be completed ahead of the scheduled opening on 14 December. She wishes to know if she has the right to terminate the contract with Joseph and to get another electrician to do the connection.

(3) A hospital enters into a 12-month agreement with a caterer for the supply of catering services to the hospital. Under the agreement, the caterer will prepare meals for patients and staff on the hospital's premises. The meals will be distributed by hospital staff. Advise the hospital if it has a right to terminate in each of the following scenarios.

(a) The contract requires that the caterer 'strictly' comply with any specific dietary requirements of patients with anaphylactic allergy issues. Patient X has a peanut allergy. This was notified to the caterer. However, the caterer supplied a meal containing peanuts to Patient X.

(b) The contract requires that the caterer maintain appropriate food safety practices. The caterer makes some dim sims using ingredients that were past their use-by date. While no health issues associated with the ingredients were reported, hospital management became aware of the breach. The hospital wishes to terminate the contract with the caterer.

RESEARCH QUESTIONS

(1) Read Kirby J's judgment in *Koompahtoo Local Aboriginal Land Council v Sanpine Pty Ltd* (2007) 233 CLR 115 (not extracted in this casebook), and examine whether Australian law should retain the intermediate term classification.

(2) Have the circumstances for granting relief against forfeiture become too narrow following the High Court's decision in *Tanwar Enterprises Pty Ltd v Cauchi* (2003) 217 CLR 315?

17

CONSEQUENCES OF TERMINATION

17.1 Overview

This chapter discusses the consequences of termination of contract following breach. When a contract is terminated, the contract ends and future performance of primary obligations undertaken under the contract cease; that is, both parties are relieved from further performance of the obligations they undertook in the contract that had not fallen due at the time of the termination. However, accrued rights and obligations survive; if a party was entitled to receive a performance of an obligation by the other party (for instance, payment of money) prior to the time of termination, but had not yet received the performance at the time of the termination, the right and obligation remain and must be performed, subject to exceptions. Exceptions include claims for total failure of consideration in relation to money paid or due, other than deposit. Deposit paid or due at the time of the termination are treated differently from other payments (paid or due). While termination will relieve the party in breach of future performance of their *primary* obligation (ie the obligation undertaken under the contract), the aggrieved party can claim damages for loss of the breaching party's further performance (of the primary obligation); that is, the party in breach comes under a *secondary* (remedial) obligation to pay compensation by way of 'loss of bargain' damages to the aggrieved party: see **17.4**.

The cases extracted in this chapter illustrate the common law rules (including rules of equity) regarding consequences of termination. Topics illustrated are:

- accrued rights
- total failure of consideration
- deposits
- restitutionary claims for work done.

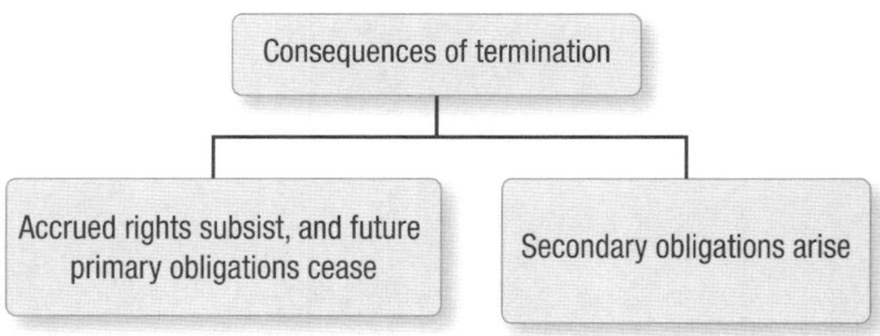

17.2 Accrued rights

Concept	Short explanation	Relevant authorities	*Principles* text*
Rights that have accrued to one party at the time of the termination remain and must be performed, subject to exceptions	The party who has not yet performed their obligation that has fallen due owes that performance. The party to whom that obligation is owed has a right to the performance	*McDonald v Dennys Lascelles Ltd* (1933) 48 CLR 457	Chapter 17: 17.04–17.05

Concept	Short explanation	Relevant authorities	*Principles* text*
While obligations that have fallen due, but not yet performed at the time of the termination remain and must be performed, the party who owes that obligation will be excused if they will receive no consideration in return for their performance	The party who has not yet performed their obligation that has fallen due owes that performance. But that obligation must be supported by consideration from the party to whom that obligation is owed. If there is no such consideration, the breaching party will be excused	*McDonald v Dennys Lascelles Ltd* (1933) 48 CLR 457	Chapter 17: 17.04–17.05

* Consult the corresponding section(s) of the *Principles* text for more detail.

It is not uncommon for a party to breach their obligation under a contract by failing to perform according to the terms of the contract; for example, failing to pay an amount when payment was due. As discussed in **Chapter 16**, a breach may, in appropriate circumstances, give the other party the right to terminate the contract. In the example given, if failure to pay results in a right to terminate, and that right is exercised by the aggrieved party, although the termination would discharge all parties from their future obligations, the aggrieved party will be entitled to unpaid amounts, subject to a few exceptions.

McDonald v Dennys Lascelles Ltd (1933) 48 CLR 457

Facts and issues

Besley and others ('the vendors'), themselves purchasers of certain lands under another contract, sold the lands to Dunkley and Rye Grazing Company for £23,462. The deposit on the sale in the second contract was £6,000, and the balance was to be met by payments of £1,000 on 24 January in each of the years 1928, 1929 and 1930, and the balance of £14,462 on 24 January 1931. The conditions of sale provided for termination of the contract and forfeiture of payments if the purchasers defaulted in paying any of the instalments or part of it. Time was of the essence. The vendors assigned their interest to Dennys Lascelles Ltd. The purchasers defaulted in the instalment of £1,000 falling due on 24 January 1930. Arrangement was made, extending the time to 24 January 1931, upon the execution of the guarantee by McDonald, a director of Rye Grazing Company. The purchasers did not pay the instalment on 24 January 1931 as agreed or the balance of the purchase money, £14,462, due under the contract on that date.

On 5 June 1931, Dennys Lascelles Ltd brought an action on the guarantee to recover from McDonald the amounts owing.

On 19 June 1931, the purchasers, though in default, became aware that the vendors were in breach of the contract of sale under which they were buying the lands that they had sold to the purchasers in this contract, and that that contract had been terminated, meaning they would not be able to convey title to the purchasers under this contract. The purchasers intimated that they treated their contract as terminated, because their vendors, and the assignee, Dennys Lascelles Ltd, were no longer able, ready or willing to complete the contract.

The issue was whether the collapse of the contract between vendor/assignor and the purchasers relieved the purchasers of paying the instalment of £1,000 and, if yes, whether thereupon the defendants ceased to be liable under their guarantee.

Decision

By a majority of 4:1 (Rich, Starke, Dixon, and McTiernan JJ; Evatt dissenting), the High Court held that a party in default remains liable for damages for their breach. However, instalments of purchase money, other than the deposit payable, upon a sale of land cannot be retained or recovered by the vendor after the contract has been terminated. Under a contract for the sale of land, the vendor's right to keep or seek purchase price instalments (paid or payable in advance) is not absolute, but is conditional upon the transfer of the land to the purchaser. The vendor 'cannot have its land and its value too', on the basis of total failure of consideration. The unpaid instalment was not payable.

Per Starke J at 470:

> It is of no little importance in the present case to ascertain the consequences of the rescission. The precise terms of the contract often determine those consequences. But, apart from any special stipulations of the contract, I apprehend that a purchaser who is not himself in default is discharged from further performance of the contract and is entitled to recover any money paid or property transferred by him thereunder; he is entitled to take proceedings in equity to assert his right and secure restitution, or to sue at law (*Palmer v. Temple*; *Mayson v. Clouet*; *Williams* on *Vendor and Purchaser*, 3rd ed. (1923), vol. 2, pp. 1012, 1013). On the other hand, a vendor who is not himself in default is discharged from further performance of the contract, and is entitled to the return of his land the subject matter of the contract, or his interest therein, but is bound to restore any moneys paid or property transferred to him thereunder: the vendor cannot have the land and its value too (*Laird v. Pim*; *Williams* on *Vendor and Purchaser*, 3rd ed., vol. 2, p. 1013). A deposit paid as security for the completion of the contract stands perhaps in an exceptional position, because the intent of the parties is that, if the contract goes off by default of the purchaser, the vendor shall retain it (*Howe v. Smith*). On the other hand, stipulations providing for forfeiture of instalments of purchase money in case of default have been treated as in the nature of a penalty and relief given against them (*In re Dagenham (Thames) Dock Co.; Ex parte Hulse*; *Kilmer v. British Columbia Orchard Lands Ltd.*; and cf. *Palmer v. Moore*). Relief against forfeiture is no doubt an equitable remedy. But, in the case of a rescission of a contract of sale of land by a vendor, moneys paid under the contract by a purchaser in default that are not forfeited can be recovered at law. That is recognized, I think, in *Palmer v. Temple* and in *Ockenden v. Henly*; and, if it be not a legal remedy, still the equitable remedy is clear and well established. Consequently, after the rescission of the contract, about June 1931 [471] an action or proceeding for the recovery of the instalment of £1,000, the payment of which had been extended to 24th January 1931, and of the balance of purchase money, could not have succeeded, for the vendors were not entitled to both the land (or their interest therein) and the purchase money. The assignee of the vendors stands in no better position
>
> [...]
>
> I now turn to the guarantee ... A surety, however, is not liable on his guarantee where the principal debt cannot be enforced, because the essence of the obligation is that there is an enforceable obligation of a principal debtor.
>
> The appeal should be allowed.

Per Dixon J at 475:

> It must be borne in mind that the instalment in dispute was overdue when the contract came to an end ... Was it then recoverable as a sum certain in money? Convincing reasons for an affirmative answer have been given in Victoria and in New Zealand. Sir *John Salmond* has stated the principles determining this conclusion:—'As a general rule, on the failure or refusal of a purchaser to complete an executory contract for the purchase of land the vendor is not entitled to sue for the purchase money as a debt. He is entitled merely to sue for specific performance or for damages for the loss of his bargain. It is only when the contract has been completed by the execution and acceptance of a conveyance that unpaid purchase money may become a debt and can be recovered accordingly. This general rule is sufficiently illustrated and established by the case of *Laird v. Pim* [1841] EngR 237; 151 E.R. 852. The sale of land is in this respect similar to the sale of goods. In the case of goods sold and delivered, and [476] of goods bargained and sold, the property in each case having passed to the buyer, the seller's remedy is to sue for the price. But if under any executory contract the buyer wrongfully refuses to accept the goods the seller's only remedy is an action for damages. The general rule, however, that in an executory contract for the sale of land the vendor cannot sue for the price is excluded whenever a contrary intention is shown by the express terms of the contract. And it seems established by authority that a contrary intention is sufficiently shown in all cases in which by the express terms of the contract the purchase money or any part thereof is made payable on a fixed day, not being the agreed day for the completion of the contract by conveyance. In all such cases the purchase money or such part thereof becomes, on the day so fixed for its payment, a debt immediately recoverable by the vendor irrespective of the question whether a conveyance has been executed and notwithstanding the fact that the purchaser may have repudiated his contract. Notwithstanding such repudiation the vendor is not bound to sue for damages or specific performance, but may recover the agreed purchase money' (*Ruddenklau v. Charlesworth*). In *Reynolds v. Fury*, the Full Court of Victoria, after a very full examination of the authorities, decided that instalments of purchase money, which, by the conditions of a contract of sale of land are payable at fixed times before conveyance, become immediately recoverable as debts or liquidated demands, notwithstanding that the sale has not yet been completed by conveyance.
>
> From this it follows that after 24th January 1930, subject to the vendors' agreement to forbear between a date about 18th March 1930, when the conditions stipulated for their forbearance were complied with, and 24th January 1931, the instalment might have been recovered from the sub-purchasers as a liquidated demand. Did the subsequent discharge of the second contract relieve the sub-purchasers of this liability? When a party to a simple contract, upon a breach by the other contracting party of a condition of the contract, elects to treat the contract as no longer binding upon him, the contract is not rescinded as from the beginning. Both parties [477] are discharged from the further performance of the contract, but rights are not divested or discharged which have already been unconditionally acquired. Rights and obligations which arise from the partial execution of the contract and causes of action which have accrued from its breach alike continue unaffected.
>
> [...]
>
> It does not, however, necessarily follow from these principles that when, under an executory contract for the sale of property, the price or part of it is paid or payable in advance, the seller may both retain what he has received, or recover overdue instalments, and at the same time treat himself as relieved from the obligation of transferring the property to the buyer. When a contract stipulates for payment of part of the purchase money in advance, the purchaser relying only on the vendor's promise to give him a conveyance, the vendor is entitled to enforce

payment before the time has arrived for conveying the land; yet his title to retain the money has been considered not to be absolute but conditional upon the subsequent completion of the contract. 'The very idea of payment falls to the ground when both have treated the bargain as at an end; and from that moment the vendor holds the money advanced to the use of the purchaser' (*Palmer v. Temple*). In *Laird v. Pim*, *Parke* B. says: 'It is clear he cannot [478] have the land and its value too' ... It is now beyond question that instalments already paid may be recovered by a defaulting purchaser when the vendor elects to discharge the contract (*Mayson v. Clouet*). Although the parties might by express agreement give the vendor an absolute right at law to retain the instalments in the event of the contract going off, yet in equity such a contract is considered to involve a forfeiture from which the purchaser is entitled to be relieved (see the judgment of Long Innes J. in *Pitt v. Curotta*). The view adopted in *In re Dagenham (Thames) Dock Co.; Ex parte Hulse* seems to have been that relief should be granted, not against the forfeiture of the instalments, but against the forfeiture of the estate under a contract which involved the retention of the purchase money: and this may have been the ground upon which Lord Moulton proceeded in *Kilmer v. British Columbia Orchard Lands Ltd.*, notwithstanding the explanation of that case given in *Steedman v. Drinkle* and *Brickles v. Snell*. However, these cases establish the purchaser's right to recover the instalments, other than the deposit, although the contract is not carried into execution.

[...]

[479] ... If, therefore, the instalment originally due on 24th January 1930 had been paid by the purchasers to the vendors, they would, in my opinion, have been entitled to recover it from the vendors. The right so to recover it is legal and not equitable. It arises out of the nature of the contract itself. This would be so even if the second contract was rescinded by the vendors upon the purchasers' default. If in the present case the purchasers' claim to rescind this contract were justified, an instalment already paid would have been recoverable as on an ordinary failure of consideration. But, if the difference be material, I am disposed to think that the purchasers' claim to rescind was not, in the circumstances, well founded and that the second contract should be treated as discharged by the vendors' acceptance of the repudiation by the purchasers involved in their attempt to rescind. It appears to me inevitably to follow from the principles upon which instalments paid are recoverable that an unpaid overdue instalment ceases to be payable by the purchasers when the contract is discharged. The fact that the contract was assigned does not increase or vary the purchasers' liabilities under it, and, accordingly, I think that the purchasers upon the sub-sale ceased to be liable for the instalment guaranteed.

The second question remains, namely, whether the cesser of the sub-purchasers' liability for the instalment of £1,000 operates to discharge the sureties. Their liability had, like that of the sub-purchasers, become immediately enforceable, and it is said that it could not be discharged by a subsequent failure of the obligation guaranteed. The consequences of the dissolution of the principal obligation are 'that the extinction of the principal obligation necessarily induces [480] that of the surety; it being of the nature of an accessory obligation, that it cannot exist without its principal; therefore, wherever the principal is discharged, in whatever manner it may be, not only by actual payment or a compensation, but also by a release, the surety is discharged likewise; for the essence of the obligation being, that the surety is only obliged on behalf of a principal debtor, he therefore is no longer obliged, when there is no longer any principal debtor for whom he is obliged.'

[...]

[482] ... For these reasons I am of opinion that the appeal should be allowed.

Rich and McTienan JJ concurred with Starke and Dixon JJ; Evatt dissented.

17.2.1 Total failure of consideration

In *McDonald v Dennys Lascelles Ltd* (above), after the purchasers defaulted in the instalment of £1,000 falling due on 24 January 1930, they were given extension of time to 24 January 1931, upon McDonald executing a guarantee, but again defaulted. Thus, the instalment had accrued at the time of termination of the contract in June 1931. But the High Court held that the purchasers, and for that matter the guarantor (McDonald), were not liable to pay because the instalments of purchase money were in return for the (ultimate) transfer of the land to the purchaser. As the contract was terminated, and the vendor was no longer going to transfer the land to the purchasers, the vendor cannot have the land and the value (payments) too. If not, the purchasers will pay the price of the land and get nothing in return (ie fail to realise the consideration for their payment).

QUESTIONS

(1) What are accrued rights, and why do those survive termination?

(2) List two of the exceptions to enforcement of accrued rights, and explain the principles underpinning those exceptions.

(3) Refer to *McDonald v Dennys Lascelles Ltd* (1933) 48 CLR 457. Would the vendors have been entitled to payment of the outstanding instalment if their purchase contract under the first contract had not been terminated?

17.3 Deposits

Concept	Short explanation	Relevant authorities	*Principles* text*
A guarantee, an amount in earnest to bind a bargain	Deposits are treated differently from instalments. The consideration for the deposit is not the actual delivery, but the vendor's (or service provider's) entry into the contract	*Bot v Ristevski* [1981] VR 120	Chapter 17: 17.06

* Consult the corresponding section(s) of the *Principles* text for more detail.

Deposits are treated differently from instalments. The consideration for the deposit is not the actual delivery, but the vendor's or service provider's entry into the contract. A deposit is seen as a guarantee that the purchaser or service acquirer means business, and is committed to the contract.[1] If the contract is performed, the deposit becomes part of the purchase price (the purchaser pays the difference between the deposit paid and the contract price). If the purchaser breaches or repudiates the contract, and the breach enables the vendor to terminate the contract at common law, the vendor can retain the deposit (if it has been paid

1 *Yardley v Saunders* [1982] WAR 231, 236.

by the purchaser) or recover the deposit (if the deposit has become due but not yet paid), notwithstanding that the purchaser will not receive the subject matter of the contract; there is no total failure of consideration. If the vendor breaches or repudiates that contract and the purchaser terminates the contract, the purchaser can recover the deposit (for total failure of consideration) as well as damages for other losses incurred that the purchaser may have suffered.

In some jurisdictions, such as Victoria and New South Wales, legislation gives the courts discretion to vary the classical approach of the common law, such as order repayment of deposit to a purchaser in breach (see eg *Property Law Act* 1958 (Vic) s 49; *Conveyancing Act 1919* (NSW) s 55(2A)). The law regarding deposits is aptly illustrated by the case of *Bot v Ristevski* [1981] VR 120.

Bot v Ristevski [1981] VR 120

Facts and issues

Vendors sold house and land to purchasers for a price payable by part-deposit on signing, balance of the deposit payable within seven days of signing, and the balance of the purchase price at a later date

After payment of the initial part-deposit, but before the rest of the deposit was paid, the purchasers repudiated the contract and the vendors terminated the contract. The vendors sued the purchasers for the unpaid portion of the deposit.

The issue was whether the vendors can recover the unpaid deposit.

Decision

The Supreme Court of Victoria held that a vendor who terminates a contract of sale of land by accepting the purchaser's repudiation is entitled to recover from the purchaser a deposit that should have been paid before the contract was terminated.

Per Brooking J at 120:

> 'Everybody', said Lord Macnaghten in *Soper v Arnold* (1889) 14 AC 429, at p. 435, 'knows what a deposit is'; but unhappily the law is not clear on the simple question whether a vendor who puts an end to the contract by accepting the purchaser's repudiation of it may recover a deposit that has been promised but not paid.
>
> [...]
>
> [121] ... By the sale note, the balance of the deposit was payable within [122] seven days of 28 January 1976. Once this seven day period had expired, the plaintiffs were entitled to sue the defendants for the unpaid balance, $1800, as a debt. The question is whether the plaintiffs have lost this right by electing to discharge the contract in reliance upon the defendants' repudiation. It is clear that the determination of a contract by the acceptance of a repudiation does not in general affect rights which have already been acquired by reason of the contract ...
>
> [123] Where the vendor discharges a contract for breach, the contract may expressly empower him to forfeit instalments of purchase money payable in advance of conveyance or transfer, so as to make it necessary for the purchaser to invoke equitable relief against forfeiture.

If the contract gives no express power of forfeiture, the purchaser may recover by action at law instalments of purchase money paid in advance of conveyance or transfer and will have a good defence at law to an action by the vendor claiming payment of instalments of purchase money which were overdue by the time when the contract was discharged. The vendor's title to retain or recover the purchase money is conditional upon the subsequent completion of the contract by conveyance or transfer: if the contract is not completed, the consideration wholly fails: *McDonald v Dennys Lascelles Ltd.*, supra, at pp. 477–9; *Berry v Mahony* [1933] VLR 314, at p. 320; *Real Estate Securities Ltd. v Kew Golf Links Estate Pty. Ltd.* [1935] VLR 114, at pp. 119–20; *Automatic Fire Sprinklers Pty. Ltd. v Watson* (1946) 72 CLR 435 at pp. 464–5; *Cowan v Stanhill Estates Pty. Ltd.* (No. 2) [1967] VR 641, at p. 650.

The vendor's title to retain or recover a deposit is not conditional in this sense, and accordingly it will not be defeated or divested by the subsequent discharge of the contract: *Ettridge v Vermin Board of the District of Murat Bay* [1928] SASR 124, at p. 128. True it is that a deposit wears two aspects: if the purchase is carried out, it goes against the purchase money, but its primary purpose is that it is a guarantee that the purchaser means business (*Depree v Bedborough* [1863] 66 ER 795; *Howe v Smith* (1884) 27 Ch D 89, at p. 101, per Fry, LJ; *Soper v Arnold* (1889) 14 AC 429, at p. 435, per Lord Macnaghten). There is no failure of consideration if the land is not conveyed or transferred, for the purchaser has had the benefit of the entry into the contract of sale by the vendor. 'Here the purchaser made an unconditional promise to pay a deposit immediately and, although if the contract was completed the moneys would according to ordinary principles be credited towards the purchase price and until then would constitute an earnest for performance, the agreement to pay was not in consideration of conveyance but was in consideration of the contract. It was the price or part of the price of the vendor's promise to sell. . .': *Farrant v Leburn*, [1970] WAR 179, at p. 184 . . .

[129] Some additional support for the view that a vendor who accepts a repudiation can recover an unpaid deposit can, I think, be drawn from cases in which the deposit has been paid, not to the vendor, but to a stakeholder. One such case is *Hall v Burnell*, [1911] 2 Ch 551, where the purchaser had made default in completing the purchase. The deposit of 50 pounds had been paid to the vendor's solicitors as stakeholders and it was an implied term of the contract of sale (see pp. 554–5) that the deposit so paid should be forfeited to the vendor if the contract went off on the default of the purchaser. The vendor brought an action against the purchaser and sought an order rescinding the contract and a declaration that he was entitled to the 50 pounds in the hands of his solicitors, and Eve J made the order and declaration sought. So the vendor succeeded in obtaining declaratory relief based on the implied terms of the contract concerning the deposit; Eve, J held that the vendor was entitled to forfeit the deposit and that it made no difference that the deposit had not been paid to the vendor but was in the hands of stakeholders. Similarly, in *Collins v Stimson* (1883) 11 QBD 142 it was laid down that a deposit paid to an auctioneer as stakeholder is forfeited to the vendor where the contract goes off by default of a purchaser.

Principle and authority have combined to lead me to the conclusion that Horridge, J. was right after all in ruling that a vendor who discharges the contract in consequence of the purchaser's repudiation of it can recover a deposit that should have been paid before the contract was discharged and that I should not follow *Lyon v Magnet Nominees Pty. Ltd.*, [1978] VR 673. . . .

[130] The claim by the present plaintiffs for payment of the balance of the deposit succeeds. Judgment and orders accordingly.

QUESTIONS

(1) Why is it that, in contrast to *McDonald v Dennys Lascelles Ltd*, in *Bot v Ristevski* the vendors were able to claim and retain the deposit although they did not have to convey title to the purchasers? In other words, why was there no total failure of consideration in respect of the deposit?

(2) If the vendors had been the parties who repudiated the contract, would the purchasers have been entitled to a return of their deposit?

(3) Why did the Court not use its discretion under s 49 of the *Property Law Act 1958* (Vic) to relieve the purchasers of the loss of their deposit?

17.4 Restitutionary claims for work done

Concept	Short explanation	Relevant authorities	*Principles* text*
Restitution may be available to a party to recover (money paid or other asset transferred) an amount for services rendered or goods delivered under a 'failed' or terminated contract	Restitution is a form of remedy given in various situations, including in the contractual context. It is separate to contract law, but important to contracts. It helps in situations where contract law may not. It is underpinned by the notion of unjust enrichment	*Steele v Tardiani* (1946) 72 CLR 386 *Pavey & Matthews Pty Ltd v Paul* (1987) 162 CLR 221 (see **24.3** for extract)	Chapter 17: 17.06, 17.10 Chapter 24: 24.65

* Consult the corresponding section(s) of the *Principles* text for more detail.

Restitution is a form of remedy given in various situations, including in the contractual context. It is separate to contract law, but important to contracts. Restitution may be available to a party to recover money paid or other asset transferred (say, by mistake), or an amount for work done or goods delivered under a contract that has 'failed'—for instance, due to the contract being declared to be void or unenforceable, or being terminated by a party, or being frustrated. Restitution is underpinned by a principle aimed at avoiding unjust enrichment. A restitutionary claim may be upheld against a party who has benefited under the failed contract at the expense of another party, but in circumstances such that there is no claim in contract against the benefiting party. An example is where a party, in performing a contract, breached their obligation by performing the contract defectively in circumstances that allows the aggrieved party to terminate the contract. The breaching party's defective performance may have conferred a benefit on the aggrieved party, yet they (the breaching party) may not be able to claim in contract because they are the party in breach. The case of *Steele v Tardiani* (1946) 72 CLR 386 illustrates this point.

Steele v Tardiani (1946) 72 CLR 386

Facts and issues

Tardiani and two others alleged a contract with Steele, under which they were to cut Steele's firewood to six feet long and six inches in diameter. The plaintiffs further alleged that they were to be paid per ton of firewood cut. They cut about 1500 tons of firewood but most of it was not of the required width. Steele did not object, did not tell them to re-cut, and agreed to pay for the work once the firewood was sold to other buyers, but he later objected and refused to pay them. The plaintiffs commenced legal action.

The issues were whether the plaintiffs were entitled to be paid for: (1) the firewood that had been cut to the proper dimensions; and (2) the firewood that had been cut in breach of the dimensions.

Decision

The trial judge (Douglas J) held that Steele was liable to accept and pay for the firewood that was cut to the proper dimensions, and that he was also liable to pay a fair price for the other wood because he, in fact, accepted the benefit of the plaintiff's work by taking possession of the firewood and selling it. On appeal by Steele, a majority of the Full Court (Philp and Mansfield JJ) upheld the decision of the trial judge, and varied the awarded amount upward (from £367 17s. 10d to £400). Steele appealed, further, to the High Court. The High Court restored the decision of the trail judge, while increasing the awarded amount to £447 4s. 6d.

Per Dixon J at 396:

> The plaintiffs, who are the respondents upon this appeal, are three Italians who, in 1942, were interned in Queensland. The appellant, who is the defendant in the action, described himself as [397] 'a solicitor and registered firewood producer.' ...
>
> About 30th January 1943, the defendant ... employed the three plaintiffs to cut firewood at a price per ton... According to the defendant they were employed at the award rate, which was six shillings and one penny per ton, and were required to cut wood in lengths of six feet and split it into sections six inches wide, or six inches 'in diameter' and to stack it, and, if necessary, to load it ... For the most part the plaintiffs did not split the wood into pieces of six-inch section or diameter and they did not stack it.
>
> [398] The defendant's version is that he refused to pay them until the wood could be removed and that he told them that a lot was over twenty feet in length and that it would all have to be cut to six feet and that a lot was a foot and over in diameter and it would all have to be split six inches wide. The plaintiffs' case was that no such complaint was made, but that the defendant said he would pay them as and when the wood was delivered to buyers ...
>
> [401] Taking, therefore, the defendant's contract to have been to pay so much per ton for firewood cut to a length of about six feet and to a width or diameter of about six inches, it is clear that, for the greater part of the wood they cut, the plaintiffs failed to split the wood to the required width. Upon what basis then can they recover remuneration in respect of work incompletely performed? It is true that they were not employed to do a single piece of work under one entire contract so that, until the whole had been substantially performed, they would obtain no right to any payment. In that sense, it is not like the contract to build two houses for a single lump sum made by the unsuccessful plaintiff in *Sumpter v Hedges.* The contract made by the three released Italians in the present case is infinitely divisible. For I assume that the amount per ton fixed, whether six shillings or eight shillings, is but a rate of remuneration to be applied to the actual firewood cut

according to the requirements of the contract, even to hundredweights and quarters . . . But it can hardly be denied that the consideration which the employees were to give for the remuneration is firewood cut according to contract and, so to speak, only those billets or sticks can be counted which qualify by substantial or reasonable compliance with the specifications . . .

[402] It is impossible, therefore, for the plaintiffs in respect of timber not split to about six inches in width to recover upon the special contract while it remains thus open and unperformed; unless, that is, there are grounds in the facts of the case for treating them as dispensed from the necessity of splitting the wood to such a width as a condition of payment. To recover under a quantum meruit for wood split to substantially different widths from that required, the plaintiffs must show circumstances removing their right to remuneration from the exact conditions of the special contract. For, if no more appears, the fact of such a contract, open and, to that extent, unperformed, excludes any implied obligation on the part of the defendant to pay a fair and reasonable remuneration for the work done by the plaintiffs in cutting his timber to dimensions outside those allowed by the contract. It is not enough that the work has been beneficial to him by turning his standing timber into the more valuable form of firewood. 'It is a commonplace of the law that there can be no implied contract as to matters covered by an express contract until the express contract is displaced. . . . But where work is done outside the contract, and the benefit of the work is taken, a contract may be implied to pay for the work so done at the current rate of remuneration, and the terms of the express contract may remain binding in so far as they are not inconsistent with the implied contract': per Scrutton LJ, *Steven v Bromley & Son*. But, 'taking the benefit of the work' means that the defendant has done so in the exercise of some choice that was actually open to him . . .

[403] The defendant says that his trees were cut upon his land and the firewood left lying there was his. What was he to do? By what step could he actively 'reject' the [404] advantage which the transmutation of his standing trees into firewood necessarily gave him, however unsuitable to his purpose might be the actual lengths and widths? Was he to allow the wood to rot on the ground? What practical choice had he except to make it clear to the plaintiffs that, to obtain payment, they must split the wood to the contract width, and, when they refused or failed to do so, to employ other labour for the purpose of reducing its width or 'diameter' so far as otherwise he was unable to dispose of the firewood. Why should he be precluded from selling his wood in the shape the plaintiffs wrongfully left it? It was his wood and why should his dealing with it imply a new contract with the plaintiffs?

If it were true that he made it clear to the plaintiffs before they departed that they must complete their contract by splitting the wood to the specified width, these considerations would indeed place him in a strong position. If his evidence were accepted, the plaintiffs would occupy the situation of a party who abandons a special contract to perform work on the property of another before completing the work and leaves that other party no effective choice in accepting or rejecting the benefit. But the defendant's evidence was not accepted by the judge at the trial, who, on the contrary, held that, as the timber cut, whether over six feet or not in length and whether over six inches or not in width, was sold by the defendant, he must pay a reasonable sum for that which he took and sold, even though it did not strictly comply with the terms of the original contract. What detailed facts the learned judge found on which to base this conclusion there is no express statement to show. But the rejection of the defendant's testimony generally is involved in other findings and I think that we must take it that the defendant did not base his refusal or failure to pay the plaintiffs on their failure to split the wood to the specified width, or, at all events, did not express to the plaintiffs his insistence or desire that they should so cut it. Indeed, even in his pleading, the defendant did not take the point as to diameter or width and it was only during cross-examination that it was developed as part of the defence . . .

> [405] In assessing the rate to be paid by the defendant for the work actually done, his Honour proceeded in accordance with the judgment of Parke B in *Mondel v Steel* and I do not think that any valid complaint can be made of the value placed upon the work done. ...
>
> For the foregoing reasons, I think that the appeal should be allowed in part and the judgment of E A Douglas J restored. I would allow this appeal, making no order as to the costs of the appeal, and vary the order of the Full court by discharging so much thereof as ordered that the judgment pronounced by E A Douglas J on 8th November 1944 be varied by striking out the words and figures £367 17s 10d wherever such appear in the said judgment and by inserting in lieu thereof the words and figures £447 4s 6d.

Per McTiernan J at 408:

> I agree that the appeal should be allowed in part, and the judgment of the learned trial judge restored.
>
> I have had the advantage of reading the judgment of my brother Dixon and agree with the reasons there stated, and have nothing to add.

Latham CJ delivered a separate judgment in similar terms as Dixon J.

17.5 International perspectives

For international commercial contracts, where the *CISG* applies (see **25.4.1**), termination must be effected by notice, which must be given within a reasonable time: art 49(2) *CISG*. Where delivery has occurred, or the price has been paid, the right to avoid will only arise in certain circumstances: arts 51(2) and 64. Nonetheless, if partial delivery has occurred, a buyer could exercise the self-help remedy of price reduction (art 50), or seek damages. By contrast, in an 'instalment contract', a party can declare the contract avoided in relation to a particular instalment if breaches concerning it amount to fundamental breach, but leave the remainder of the contract on foot: art 73(1) *CISG*. In other situations, avoidance (termination) of the contract leads to the following consequences:

- Parties are released from obligations, subject to damages: art 81(1) *CISG*;
- Damages are available if a breach caused loss: arts 74–76 *CISG*;
- Each party (as mentioned at **24.5.2**) must make concurrent restitution of goods or moneys paid: arts 81(2)–88 *CISG*. Indeed, inability to do this is a barrier to avoidance (termination), leaving parties to damages claims: art 82(1). Restitution pursuant to the *CISG* requires:
  - return of the goods in kind, in substantially the same condition, except in certain circumstances where inability is not the party's fault or goods were used before the breach could be discovered: art 82(2);
  - buyers to account for any benefits derived from goods: art 84(2) (compare **17.4** above);
  - sellers to return the price with interest: art 84(1).
- The *CISG* goes further in relation to secondary obligations of restitution than Australian common law. The party in possession must take steps to preserve goods pending restitution: arts 85–87 *CISG*. If return is refused or not feasible goods can be sold and proceeds returned: art 88 *CISG*. See further **24.5.2**.

17.5.1 UNIDROIT Principles

As mentioned at **24.5.3**, the UNIDROIT Principles are more flexible. Although they also require restitution following termination (art 7.3.6 UNIDROIT Principles), where this is not possible in kind, they provide for a monetary allowance in lieu. Secondary obligations of restitution might also arise pursuant to art 3.2.15 UNIDROIT Principles if a contract is avoided on the basis of undue pressure or gross disparity: see further **19.4.2–19.4.3**.

17.6 Review

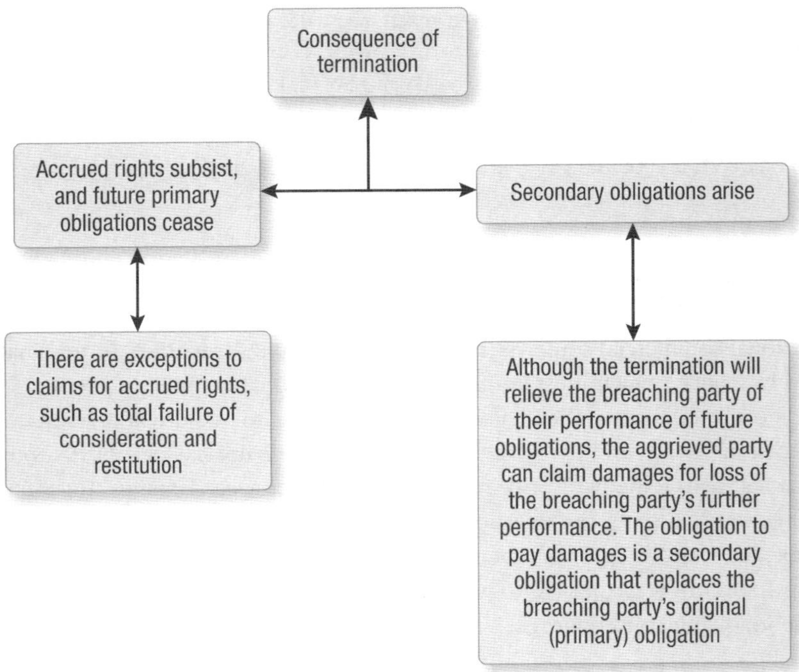

- When a contract is terminated, the contract ends and future performance of primary obligations undertaken under the contract cease.
- Accrued rights and obligations survive termination.
- Entitlement to accrued rights is, where applicable, subject to claims for total failure of consideration in relation to money paid or due, other than deposit.
- Deposits paid or due at the time of the termination are treated differently from other payments (paid or due); a deposit is seen as a guarantee that the purchaser means business, and so it may be retained if the purchaser's breach led to the termination of the contract (subject to legislative provisions in some jurisdictions that give the courts discretion to order return of all or part of the deposit).
- While termination will relieve the party in breach of future performance of their *primary* obligation, they will come under a *secondary* (remedial) obligation to pay compensation by way of 'loss of bargain' damages to the aggrieved party.

- A party in breach, in circumstances that allow the aggrieved party to terminate the contract, may be allowed restitutionary claim where that party has conferred benefit on the aggrieved party at their expense, yet they (the breaching party) are unable to claim in contract because of their breach.

TIPS FOR APPLYING THE LAW IN PRACTICE

- Remember the general rule: accrued rights survive termination. That said, claims of, or enforcement of, accrued rights are subject to exceptions, such as total failure of consideration and restitution.
- Keep in mind that deposits are treated differently from other payments, such as instalments, at common law. Thus, deposits are generally not affected by the total failure of consideration exception. However, in some jurisdictions, legislation gives the courts a discretion to vary the classical approach of the common law, such as to order repayment of deposit to a purchaser in breach.

PROBLEM QUESTIONS

Consider the common facts below, and the further facts given under each of the questions. Advise the specified party as required.

Common facts

James Jones wishes to sell his large farming property in Gippsland (Victoria). Sam Smith wishes to buy the property. James and Sam enter into a contract of sale. Sam is to pay the purchase price of $2,000,000 as follows:

(a) The purchaser is to pay a deposit of $200,000 within seven days of signing the contract.

(b) The purchaser must pay the remaining $1,800,000 by six half-yearly quarterly instalments of $300,000 over the next three years on 30 June and 31 December of each year.

(c) In regard to the payment of the purchase price, time is of the essence.

James and Sam signed the contract on 2 January.

(1) Assume that Sam had a change of mind on 4 January, and decides he no longer wants to go ahead with the contract. Sam, who is yet to pay the deposit of $200,000, informs James of his decision not to continue with the contract on the same day (4 January).

Advise James as to whether he is entitled to claim the $200,000 from Sam. Would your answer be different if Sam had paid the deposit on 3 January, before informing James on 4 January of his decision not to continue with the?

(2) Assume that Sam did not have a change of mind as stated in question 1. Rather, Sam pays the deposit of $200,000 on 7 January. He also pays the first instalment of $300,000 on 30 June. He pays the second instalment one week late. When he tendered the third instalment three days late, James informs him that he has terminated the contract for Sam's breach of payment obligations. James remained in possession of the property at all times, as Sam was to enter possession upon payment of the final instalment.

Sam seeks your advice as to whether he can claim a return of the payments he has made to James under the contract.

(3) Assume that Sam did not have a change of mind as stated in question 1. Rather, Sam pays the deposit of $200,000 on 7 January, and the first instalment of $300,000 on 30 June. Sam takes possession of the land immediately after paying the first instalment, but James retains title to the land. Sam constructs two new farm buildings and a large stable on the land. He also improves the land in other ways. Sam pays the second to fourth instalments on time. He also pays interest on the outstanding balance as agreed in the contract. Sam begins to have some financial difficulties and informs James that he will not be able to pay the fifth instalment on time. James warns that he will terminate the contract if Sam does not pay the fifth instalment on time. Two days after the fifth instalment falls due, James terminates the contract and orders Sam off the property.

Sam seeks your advice as to any rights, and remedy, he may have.

RESEARCH QUESTIONS

(1) It can be argued that the concept of 'total failure of consideration' is a myth, because a party to a valid contract receives some form of consideration. Should the concept be abandoned in Australian law?

(2) Should the courts refrain from ordering (partial or full) return of deposit, where legislation permits, to the breaching party who repudiates a contract?

PART VI

VITIATING FACTORS AND UNFAIR CONDUCT

18

MISINFORMATION

18.1 Overview

This chapter presents 'misinformation' as a holistic genre in contract law, recognising that the concept in truth straddles numerous discrete doctrines. To avoid repetition, wherever the topic is more explicitly addressed elsewhere here or in the *Principles* text, the content will be extensively cross-referenced.

The first and second modules cover *misrepresentation* at common law and damages for misrepresentation. Misrepresentation attracts significant attention, because, almost axiomatically, it *is* 'misinformation'. The third module addresses statutory prohibition on *misleading or deceptive conduct*. This is a crucially important development in the law of 'misinformation'. The treatment of this topic includes not only the fundamental ingredients of the cause of action, but also the fault line between common law misrepresentation and the statutory cause of action for misleading or deceptive conduct. Common law misrepresentation, for example, invokes a consideration of the need for the statement to be of *fact* or of an opinion that was not in fact held; whereas with the statutory cause of action, the primary concern is that the conduct be objectively misleading.

'Mistake' too, is a common law doctrine that arises from the consequences of misinformation, but it is rather more nuanced and complicated than a simplistic instance of misrepresentation because of the widely varying views of the application and limitations of the respective doctrines in common law and equity.

The final module here is *rectification* which is the idea that a contract that has been induced by a mistake as to its content can be amended to conform to the intention of the parties.

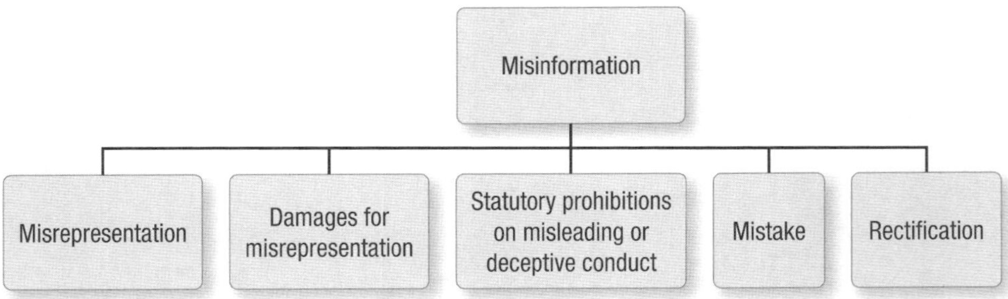

18.2 Misrepresentation

Concept	Short explanation	Relevant authorities	*Principles* text*
Rescission for misrepresentation	Broadly, rescission has the effect of undoing a contract, with the parties restored to their pre-contractual position	–	Chapter 17: 17.01 Chapter 18: 18.16
Puffs	Exaggerated statements made before a contract which do not amount to representation	*Mitchell v Valherie* (2005) 93 SASR 76	Chapter 18: 18.07
Statements of intention or opinion	Statements of opinion do not ordinarily amount to misrepresentation, but the knowledge of the parties might	*Edgington v Fitzmaurice* (1885) 29 Ch D 459 *Bisset v Wilkinson* [1927] AC 177	Chapter 18: 18.08

Concept	Short explanation	Relevant authorities	*Principles* text*
	affect this	*Smith v Land and House Property Corporation* (1884) 28 Ch D 7	
Statements of law	A statement of law is traditionally not regarded as one of fact but the knowledge of the parties might affect this position	*Public Trustee v Taylor* [1978] VR 289 *David Securities Pty Ltd v Commonwealth Bank of Australia* (1992) 175 CLR 353 (see **24.2** for extract)	Chapter 18: 18.09
Conduct and silence	Remaining silent does not generally amount to misrepresentation but there are many exceptions to this general rule	*With v O'Flanagan* [1936] 1 Ch 575 *Jones v Dumbrell* [1981] VR 199	Chapter 18: 18.10
The element of inducement	The misrepresentation must have induced the making of the contract	*Gould v Vaggelas* (1984) 157 CLR 215 *Holmes v Jones* (1907) 4 CLR 1692 *Redgrave v Hurd* (1881) 20 Ch D 1 *Byers v Dorotea Pty Ltd* (1986) 69 ALR 715	Chapter 18: 18.11
The remedy of rescission	Exploring the criteria which govern the right to rescission	*Ivanof v Phillip M Levy Pty Ltd [1971] VR 167*	Chapter 18: 18.12
Bars to rescission	Rescission might be barred when *restitutio in integrum* is not possible Affirmation is potentially a bar to rescission	*Alati v Kruger* (1955) 94 CLR 216 *Brown v Smitt* (1924) 34 CLR 160 *Coastal Estates Pty Ltd v Melevende* [1965] VR 433 *Car and Universal Finance Co Ltd v Caldwell* [1965] 1 QB 525 *Seddon v North Eastern Salt Co Ltd* [1905] 1 Ch 326 ('the rule in Seddon's case')	Chapter 18: 18.13

* Consult the corresponding section(s) of the *Principles* text for more detail.

The overarching concept in the study of misrepresentation as a contractual, as opposed to tortious, remedy, is that it allows the innocent party to rescind the contract, to restore it to its pre-contractual position. 'Rescission for misrepresentation' is addressed below. This module will address the various considerations that affect the availability of rescission.

18.2.1 Puffs

'Puffs' are exaggerated statements made before a contract, often 'sales talk', and not regarded as misrepresentation, not being a statement of fact. The distinction between a statement of fact and puffery can in truth be difficult to identify.

Mitchell v Valherie (2005) 93 SASR 76

Facts and issues

The dispute concerned the characterisation of the following words in an advertisement for the sale of a house, 'nothing to spend—perfect presentation ... immaculate style'. The evidence was that there were defects in the house. The issue was whether these words amounted to misrepresentations.

Decision

Per White J at 90:

> It was contended that the trial judge had erred in finding that the words 'Nothing to Spend' constituted a representation of fact. In particular, it was submitted that the expression was of a kind commonly used in real estate advertising material and that it could not reasonably be understood as indicating literally that no expenditure would be required of a purchaser, or that the house was free of structural defects. It was submitted that these words were merely a form of general promotion of the house, that is, intended to attract the attention of prospective purchasers. In short, they were a form of puffery.
>
> [...]
>
> It is clear enough that it is not every statement made in contractual [91] negotiations, or as a prelude to contractual negotiations, which will be regarded as conveying a representation. To constitute a representation, the statement must be a representation of fact:
>
> > The essence of misrepresentation is that it led the representee into error. This must be tested objectively — would a reasonable person in the position of the representee have been led into error by the statement?
>
> [...]
>
> The second consideration is that the words, 'Nothing to Spend — Perfect Presentation', have to be read as a whole. The words 'Perfect Presentation' are clearly enough words of promotional puffery. A reasonable prospective purchaser of real estate would not understand those words as conveying a representation of fact. The words 'Nothing to Spend' which immediately precede them take their colour, to some extent, from those words.
>
> The third consideration is that the words were used in a context in which some hyperbole is commonplace. Exaggerated descriptions of houses are a common, even expected, feature of real estate advertising. Reasonable persons would not, in my opinion, understand words of this kind to be conveying a representation about the structural integrity of the property.

18.2.2 Statements of intention or opinion

Statements of intention or opinion are an integral ingredient of the study of common law misrepresentation. Statements of opinion or intention, not being of fact, do not amount to misrepresentation though they might be when the representor misrepresents his state of mind. The corollary is that a statement of opinion honestly held might not amount to a misrepresentation and a relevant factor in assessing whether a statement is considered to be of fact is the relative knowledge of the parties. This area has spawned several seminal cases, amongst them *Edgington v Fitzmaurice*[1] and *Bisset v Wilkinson,*[2] which will be explored below.

Edgington v Fitzmaurice (1885) 29 Ch D 459

Facts and issues

A prospectus inviting subscriptions for debentures stated that the objects of the issue of debentures were to complete alterations in the buildings of the company and develop the trade of the company. This turned out to be untrue, as the moneys were always intended to be used instead to pay debts of the company. The issue was whether the statements were of fact or mere statements of future intention, in which case they would not be misrepresentations.

Decision

Per Cotton LJ at 479:

> It was argued that this was only the statement of an intention, and that the mere fact that an intention was not carried into effect could not make the Defendants liable to the Plaintiff. I agree that it was a statement of intention, But it is nevertheless a [480] statement of fact, and if it could not be fairly said that the objects of the issue of the debentures were those which were stated in the prospectus the defendants were stating a fact, which was not true; and if they knew that it was not true, or made it recklessly, not caring whether it was true or not, they would be liable . . .

Per Bowen LJ at 483:

> There must be a misstatement of an existing fact: but the state of a man's mind is as much a fact as the state of his digestion. It is true that it is very difficult to prove what the state of a man's mind at a particular time is, but if it can be ascertained it is as much a fact as anything else. A misrepresentation as to the state of a man's mind is, therefore, a misstatement of fact.

Bisset v Wilkinson [1927] AC 177

Facts and issues

The vendor of land, never having used to run sheep, represented that in his judgment the land could accommodate 2000 sheep if worked with a good six-horse team. The short question was whether that statement was merely a statement of opinion or of fact.

1 (1885) 29 Ch D 459.
2 [1927] AC 177.

Decision

Per Lord Merrivale, on behalf of their Lordships in the Privy Council, at 182:

> In a case where the facts are equally well known to both parties, what one of them says to the other is frequently nothing but an expression of opinion. The statement of such opinion is in a sense a statement of fact, about the condition of the man's own mind, but only of an irrelevant fact, for it is of no consequence what the opinion is. But if the facts are not equally well known to both sides, then a statement of opinion by one who knows the facts best involves very often a statement of a material [183] fact, for he impliedly states that he knows facts which justify his opinion.'
>
> [. . .]
>
> The decisive inquiries came to be: what meaning was actually conveyed to the party complaining; was he deceived, and, as the action was based on a charge of fraud, was the statement in question made fraudulently?
>
> In the present case, as in those cited, the material facts of the transaction, the knowledge of the parties respectively, and their relative positions, the words of representation used, and the actual condition of the subject-matter spoken of, are relevant to the two inquiries necessary to be made: What was the meaning of the representation? Was it true?
>
> [. . .]
>
> As was said by Sim J.: 'In ordinary [184] circumstances, any statement made by an owner who has been occupying his own farm as to its carrying capacity would be regarded as a statement of fact. ... This, however, is not such a case. The defendants knew all about Hogan's block and knew also what sheep the farm was carrying when they inspected it. In these circumstances ... the defendants were not justified in regarding anything said by the plaintiff as to the carrying capacity as being anything more than an expression of his opinion on the subject.'

18.2.3 Statements of law

Statements of law fall within more or less the same doctrinal pigeonhole as statements of intention or opinion, not being regarded of fact in the absence of fraud; the corollary is that a deliberately false statement of law may be a misrepresentation. English judges have sometimes held that a misrepresentation of law, even in the absence of fraud, gives rise to the right to rescind—a position not yet adopted in Australia. Australian courts, however, suggest a movement towards the extinction of the law–fact distinction for the purposes of misrepresentation as most significantly underlined in the High Court's preparedness to treat a mistake of law no differently from a mistake of fact in the seminal case of restitution of *David Securities Pty Ltd v Commonwealth Bank of Australia*.[3]

Smith v Land and House Property Corporation (1884) 28 Ch D 7

Facts and issues

Smith, a landowner, sold a hotel with the existing tenant to Land et al. Smith stated that the tenant was a 'most desirable tenant' but, in fact, the tenant could hardly pay the rent and prior to the

3 (1992) 175 CLR 353: see **24.2**.

completion of the sale went into liquidation. The question was whether the statement as to the tenant was an opinion or fact.

Decision

Per Bowen LJ at 14:

> The action is by vendors for specific performance, and the purchasers allege that there is in the particulars a misrepresentation which disentitles the Plaintiffs to specific performance. To sustain this defence the Defendants must prove that there was a material misrepresentation, and that they entered into the contract on the faith of the representation.
>
> [. . .]
>
> [15] It . . . is often fallaciously assumed that a statement of opinion cannot involve the statement of a fact. . . . if the facts are not equally known to both sides, then a statement of opinion by the one who knows the facts best involves very often a statement of a material fact, for he impliedly states that he knows facts which justify his opinion. Now a landlord knows the relations between himself and his tenant, other persons either do not know them at all or do not know them equally well, and if the landlord says that he considers that the relations between himself and his tenant are satisfactory, he really avers that the facts peculiarly within his knowledge are such as to render that opinion reasonable.
>
> [. . .]
>
> The vendors state that the property is let to a most desirable tenant, what does that mean? . . . it . . . amounts at least to an assertion that nothing has occurred in the relations between the landlords and the tenant which can be considered to make the tenant an unsatisfactory one. That is an assertion of a specific fact. Was it a true assertion? Having regard to what took place between [16] Lady Day and Midsummer, I think that it was not . . .

Public Trustee v Taylor [1978] VR 289

Facts and issues

Advertisements published before the sale of certain property described the property as 'Zoned: Special Use 10. Subject to road widening', although in fact the land was reserved for the purpose of a proposed main road. Having been found that the representation as to the zoning of the property was false to the knowledge of the plaintiff's agent, the relevant question here was whether the representation was of fact or law.

Decision

Per Kaye J at 296:

> My opinion . . . is that the representation by which the defendant was induced to enter into the contract was one of law.
>
> [. . .]
>
> [297] There are, on the other hand, a number of cases where relief was granted to a party who had been induced to enter into an agreement by a misrepresentation of law made fraudulently and there are cases where the right to relief in such circumstances has been recognized [Here, his Honour cites numerous decision to this effect, including inter alia *British*

Workman's and General Insurance Co Ltd v Cunliffe (1902) 18 TLR 502; *Kettlewell v Refuge Assurance Co* [1908] 1 KB 545; *Tofts v Pearl Life Assurance Co Ltd* [1915] 1 KB 189; and *Oudaille v Lawson* [1922] NZLR 259 at p. 261] ... The learned authors of Spencer Bower and Turner, *Actionable Misrepresentation*, 3rd ed. (1974), p. 61, para. 42, after stating that it has been held or recognized in several authorities that if the law is fraudulently misstated, the representor would be held liable for misrepresentation, offer as an explanation for this principle that a statement of law implies a representation that the person professing to expound it believes it to be as stated by him. For my part, I agree with the explanation offered by the learned authors.

[...]

[299] Thus, I conclude it would be unconscionable to permit the plaintiff to gain from a fraudulent misrepresentation of law whether made by himself or by his agent.

[...]

It follows that the plaintiff's claim for specific performance ought to be denied and that the defendant is entitled to a declaration that he has validly rescinded the contract.

18.2.4 Conduct and silence

There is no general duty of disclosure on contracting parties, and remaining silent does not generally amount to misrepresentation. One needs to search for circumstances under which a failure to speak amounts to misrepresentation. These include the propositions that the fact stated may be true but incomplete or that circumstances have changed.

With v O'Flanagan [1936] 1 Ch 575

Facts and issues

In the course of negotiations for the sale of a medical practice, the vendor, a doctor, represented that takings were a certain amount and his patients were a certain number. Those statements were true at the time but, due to a change of circumstances, takings and patients both dropped. The question was whether the failure to disclose the change of circumstances amounted to a misrepresentation.

Decision

In relation to whether there existed a general duty to disclose facts which the representor knows will bear upon the mind of the representee, per Lord Wright MR at 581:

As to the law, which has been challenged, I want to say this. I take the law to be as it was stated by Fry J. in *Davies v London and Provincial Marine Insurance Co.* where it is perhaps most fully expressed ...

[...]

I need not read the whole of the passage in the judgment, but I need only refer to one or two points. The learned judge points out: 'Where parties are contracting with one another, each may, unless there be a duty to disclose, observe silence even in regard to facts which he believes would be operative upon the mind of the other; and it rests upon those who say that there was a duty to disclose, to shew that the duty existed.' [His Lordship went on to discuss instances where such a duty might exist, contracts *uberrimae fidei*].

On the question of whether the changed circumstances gave rise to an obligation of disclosure, his Lordship continued at 582:

> Then he [Fry J] goes on: 'Again, in ordinary contracts the duty may arise from circumstances which occur during the negotiation. Thus, for instance, if one of the negotiating parties has made a statement which is false in fact, but which he believes to be true and which is material to the contract, and during the course of the negotiation he discovers the falsity of that statement, he is under an obligation to correct his erroneous statement; although if he had said nothing he very likely might have been entitled to hold his tongue throughout.' Then he adds what was material in that case and what is material in this case: 'So, again, if a statement has been made which is true at the time, but which during the course of the negotiations becomes untrue, then the person who knows that it has become untrue is under an obligation to disclose to the other the change of circumstances.'
>
> [. . .]
>
> . . . In these cases — I need not refer to others on this point — the position is based upon the duty to communicate the change of circumstances.
>
> [584] The matter, however, may be put in another way though with the same effect, and that is on the ground that a representation made as a matter of inducement to enter into a contract is to be treated as a continuing representation. That view of the position was put in *Smith v. Kay* by Lord Cranworth. He says of a representation made in negotiation some time before the date of a contract: 'It is a continuing representation. The representation does not end for ever when the representation is once made; it continues on. . .'

Jones v Dumbrell [1981] VR 199

Facts and issues

The defendant for himself and on behalf of G Pty Ltd had represented to the plaintiffs that he desired and intended to purchase the plaintiffs' shares in F Pty Ltd in order to continue the business for the benefit of his family. G Pty Ltd had, for a long period, been a shareholder in F Pty Ltd. The plaintiffs preferred the business to be sold to persons associated with D, rather than outsiders and, on the basis of the representation, transferred to G Pty Ltd at an undervalue all their shares in F Pty Ltd and P Pty Ltd. From November 1963 until the completion of the sale, D intended to purchase the shares in order to resell all or part of them at a profit, but he concealed this intention from the plaintiffs. The question was whether it amounted to a misrepresentation to have done so.

Decision

Per Smith J at 202:

> It has been clear law, since the decision of the English Court of Appeal nearly a century ago in *Edgington v Fitzmaurice* (1885) 29 Ch D 459, that a representation by a man as to his state of mind is a representation of fact sufficient to found an action for damages for deceit: see, for example, *Bisset v Wilkinson,* [1927] AC 177, at p. 182; [1926] All ER Rep 343; Winfield, Tort, 1st ed., p. 403; Street. The Law of Torts, 3rd ed., pp. 386–7; Fleming, The Law of Torts, 3rd ed., p. 601.
>
> [. . .]

[203] ... There is, however, an entirely different basis upon which liability in deceit for such representations may be rested; one which does not have to call in aid any equitable doctrines or to introduce into the law of deceit any notions of constructive or technical fraud; and that basis is the continuing nature of most representations: see *With v O'Flanagan*, [1936] Ch D 575, per Lord Wright, MR, at pp. 583–4; *Smith v Kay* (1859) 7 HLC 750, at p. 769.

When a man makes a representation with the object of inducing another to enter into a contract with him, that other will ordinarily understand the representor, by his conduct in continuing the negotiations and concluding the contract, to be asserting, throughout, that the facts remain as they were initially represented to be. And the representor will ordinarily be well aware that his representation is still operating in this way, or at least will continue to desire that it shall do so. Commonly, therefore, an inducing representation is a 'continuing' representation, in reality and not merely by construction of law.

18.2.5 The element of inducement

To be an actionable misrepresentation, the relevant statement must have *induced* the making of the contract. Axiomatically, a misrepresentation that is ignored cannot found a cause of action in misrepresentation. The truth of a representation does not have to be investigated even if there is an opportunity to do so; an appropriate exemption clause might exclude the right to rescission for misrepresentation—but the situation might differ under the statutory action for misleading or deceptive conduct.

Gould v Vaggelas (1984) 157 CLR 215

Facts and issues

A husband and wife, the Goulds, claimed to be induced by misrepresentations by Vaggelas to buy a resort, on behalf of a company to be formed and run by them, on terms including the transfer of valuable property to the vendors and the transfer of a mortgage back to the vendors, in order to secure the balance of the price. They then formed the company and completed the purchase. Close to two years later, the company defaulted due to unprofitable trading. The vendors exercised their power of sale as mortgagees to recover a deficiency and sued the Goulds as guarantors. Suspecting fraud, the Goulds counterclaimed for damages for deceit. The question here was the extent to which the Court addressed the treatment of inducement on the part of the Goulds by Vaggelas.

Decision

On the question of inducement per Wilson J at 236:

Having made those findings, the trial judge proceeded to deal with the submission strongly advanced at the trial by Mr. Pincus and maintained both before the Full Court and this Court that a misrepresentation is no ground for relief unless it induces the representee to enter into the contract and that on the evidence the Goulds had failed to establish the fact of inducement. His Honour correctly elucidated the law in this regard. He referred, inter alia, to *Smith v. Chadwick*, *Arnison v. Smith*; *Holmes v. Jones* and *Cheshire and Fifoot on the Law of Contract*, 4th Aust.

ed., pars. 1028, 1029 and from them drew the applicable principles, which can be re-stated as follows:

(1) Notwithstanding that a representation is both false and fraudulent, if the representee does not rely upon it he has no case.
(2) If a material representation is made which is calculated to induce the representee to enter into a contract and that person in fact enters into the contract there arises a fair inference of fact that he was induced to do so by the representation.
(3) The inference may be rebutted, for example, by showing that the representee, before he entered into the contract, either was possessed of actual knowledge of the true facts and knew them to be true or alternatively made it plain that whether he knew the true facts or not he did not rely on the representation.
(4) The representation need not be the sole inducement. It is sufficient so long as it plays some part even if only a minor part in contributing to the formation of the contract.

Holmes v Jones (1907) 4 CLR 1692

Facts and issues

The owner of a cattle farm made false statements about the number of cattle grazing on it to a man who made enquiries about buying the farm. The man making enquiries was later informed of the inaccuracy of these statements, and then negotiated a sale on different grounds than the number of cattle. He inspected the property and stock, and as a result of the inspection, decided to purchase. The question was whether the representation made initially could form the basis of a cause of action for misrepresentation.

Decision

On the question of inducement per Isaacs J at 1710:

> The plaintiffs have the onus of proving that the representations they complain of were material, and that they were induced to act upon them . . .
>
> [1711] . . . the main question we have to consider is whether, assuming that there was a misrepresentation in the first instance, the plaintiffs are shown not to have relied upon that misrepresentation. I think the documentary evidence and the uncontradicted oral testimony are absolutely conclusive that the plaintiffs did not rely upon that misrepresentation.

Redgrave v Hurd (1881) 20 Ch D 1

Facts and issues

The prospective purchaser of a solicitor's practice queried the accuracy of various statements made about the turnover of the practice. He declined to verify the accuracy of these figures, despite an opportunity to do so. Relevant issues were whether a representee can claim relief in misrepresentation if he had the opportunity to check on the truth of the alleged misrepresentation.

Decision

Per Jessel MR at 14:

> One of the most familiar instances in modern times is where men issue a prospectus in which they make false statements of the contracts made before the formation of a company, and then say that the contracts themselves may be inspected at the offices of the solicitors. It has always been held that those who accepted those false statements as true were not deprived of their remedy merely because they neglected to go and look at the contracts.
>
> [. . .]
>
> [21] . . . for when a person makes a material representation to another to induce him to enter into a contract, and the other enters into that contract, it is not sufficient to say that the party to whom the representation is made does not prove that he entered into the contract, relying upon the representation. If it is a material representation calculated to induce him to enter into the contract, it is an inference of law that he was induced by the representation to enter into it, and in order to take away his title to be relieved from the contract on the ground that the representation was untrue, it must be shewn either that he had knowledge of the facts contrary to the representation, or that he stated in terms, or shewed clearly by his conduct, that he did not rely on the representation.

Byers v Dorotea Pty Ltd (1986) 69 ALR 715

Facts and issues

A contract for the purchase of units contained an exclusion clause by which the purchaser acknowledged, in effect, that he had not relied on any representations by the vendor or its agents in entering it. The purchasers purported to rescind the contracts on the grounds of misrepresentation, which were found to be innocent. The question was whether the exclusion clause was effective to negate the inference of inducement.

Decision

Per Pincus J at 723:

> An answer made to the applicants' claim, so far as it relied upon misrepresentation, is cl 8(c)(i) of each contract: "The purchaser acknowledges that he has not relied on any representations by the vendor, the vendor's agent or any other person or persons or corporation in and about entering into this contract other than as set out herein, and that the conditions and stipulations hereof constitute the only agreement between the purchaser and the vendor."
>
> Although my mind has fluctuated, I have come, in the end, to the opinion that I should apply the views of the Queensland Supreme Court. It seems to me probable that the matter is regarded as practically settled in this State, and it would be inconvenient to act on a different opinion. Thus, while by no means convinced that it is in accordance with the principles laid down by Dixon J and referred to above so to hold, I act on the basis that the clause is effective to defeat a claim based upon innocent misrepresentation.

On the question of whether the clause was effective against a claim for misleading or deceptive conduct, per Pincus J at 723:

> It should be added that it is clear enough that the clause is ineffective against a claim under the *Trade Practices Act*. For reasons akin to those discussed in *Beckford Nominees Pty Ltd v Shell Co of Australia Ltd* (unreported, 1 October 1986) the applicants cannot, in my view, be prevented by estoppel by convention from asserting that there was a breach of s 52 of the *Trade Practices Act* [this being the statutory cause of action for misleading and deceptive conduct in the form that existed then].

18.2.6 The remedy of rescission

The focus is next directed to rescission as a *remedy*. For this, the innocent party must communicate the election to rescind; the right to rescission, to set aside a contract, is flexible in equity when compared to common law and might be ordered even where strictly *restitutio in integrum* is no longer possible because, consistent with equity's flexibility, it is open to make an order for partial rescission.

Ivanof v Phillip M Levy Pty Ltd [1971] VR 167

Facts and issues

Purchasers sought to rescind a contract of sale of land by the purchasers upon discovery by them of the falsity of representations made by the vendors' agents. An issue concerned the requirement of communication of the election to rescind.

Decision

Per McInerney J at 169:

> There was no evidence that the decision of the complainants to disaffirm the contract was communicated to the first-named defendant personally, but it would seem that the case before the magistrate was conducted on the footing that the communication of the decision to the vendor's agent — presumably to the second-named defendant — was a sufficient communication of the disaffirmance of the contract. No doubt, if the first-named defendant had absconded, or had disappeared, leaving no address to which communications intended for him could be forwarded, the complainants could have exercised their intention to disaffirm the contract by some overt means falling short of communication to the vendor: see *Car and Universal Finance Co Ltd v Caldwell*, [1964] 2 WLR 600, at p. 613, per Upjohn, LJ; [1963] 2 All ER 547.
>
> [...]
>
> As was pointed out by Dixon, CJ, Webb, Fullagar, Kitto and Taylor, JJ, in their joint judgment in *Alati v Kruger* (1955) 94 CLR 216, at p. 224; [1955] ALR 1047, at p. 1051: 'Rescission for misrepresentation is always the act of the party himself ... The function of a Court in which proceedings for rescission are taken is to adjudicate upon the validity of the purported disaffirmance as an act avoiding the transaction ab initio, and, if it is valid, to give effect to it and make appropriate consequential orders.' See also the passage in the judgment of Sholl, J, in *Coastal Estates v Melevende*, [1965] VR 433, at p. 439.

18.2.7 Bars to rescission

Rescission might be barred when *restitutio in integrum* is not possible, although the court has significant equitable power to make adjustments to achieve justice; affirmation is a bar to rescission but does not invariably act as a bar to rescission and typically needs to be viewed together with *restitutio in integrum;* affirmation in light of knowledge of the right to rescind (as opposed to the facts giving rise to that right) is *generally* required to lose the right to rescind but this again is not an invariable principle.

When it is not practicable to communicate with a misrepresentor, the requirements of notice to rescind might be satisfied if all necessary and reasonable steps were taken to communicate with the misrepresentor. Where a misrepresentation is not fraudulent, rescission will not ordinarily be ordered where a contract has been fully performed.

Alati v Kruger (1955) 94 CLR 216

Facts and issues

This is a seminal case on the doctrine.

A business selling fruit was conducted on leased premises. The respondent, Kruger, bought the business from the appellant, Alati, alleging it did so on the basis of fraudulent misrepresentations by Alati. Kruger claimed rescission but before trial Kruger entered into a contract under which the landlord agreed to reassign the lease to Alati if the court ordered rescission. In the interim, the business had deteriorated further. Accepting that Alati had engaged in misrepresentation as alleged, it was argued that rescission should not be allowed as *restitutio in integrum* was no longer possible.

Decision

Per Dixon CJ, Webb, Kitto and Taylor JJ at 223:

> If the case had to be decided according to the principles of the common law, it might have been argued that at the date when the respondent issued his writ he was not entitled to rescind the purchase, because he was not then in a position to return to the appellant *in specie* that which he had received under the contract, in the same plight as that in which he had received it: *Clarke v. Dickson*. But it is necessary here to apply the doctrines of equity, and equity has always regarded as valid the disaffirmance of a contract induced by fraud even though precise *restitutio in integrum* is not possible, if the situation is such that, by the exercise of its powers, including the power to take accounts of profits and to direct inquiries as to allowances proper to be made for deterioration, it can do what is practically just between the parties, and by so [224] doing restore them substantially to the *status quo*: . . .
>
> [. . .]
>
> The difference between the legal and the equitable rules on the subject simply was that equity, having means which the common law lacked to ascertain and provide for the adjustments necessary to be made between the parties in cases where a simple handing back of property or repayment of money would not put them in as good a position as before they entered into their transaction, was able to see the possibility of *restitutio in integrum*, and therefore to concede the right of a defrauded party to rescind, in a much wider variety of cases than those which the common law could recognize as admitting of rescission.

In the present case, what changes affecting the possibility of restitution had occurred in the short period between 16th June when the respondent took possession of the business and 29th June when he issued the writ?

[. . .]

The business itself had deteriorated but this would not matter, for, as the trial judge has found, it was not due to any fault on the respondent's part, and even at common law the necessity to return property in its original condition was qualified so as to allow for incidents for which the buyer was not responsible, such as those to which the property was liable either from its inherent nature (cf. *Newbigging v. Adam*; *Adam v. Newbigging*) or in the course of the exercise by the buyer of those rights over it which the contract gave: *Head v. Tattersall*. No other change had occurred. The case was therefore typical of the class of cases in which a defrauded purchaser is regarded by a court exercising equitable jurisdiction as entitled to rescind the purchase and obtain a decree, on proper terms, declaring and giving effect to the rescission as an avoidance of the transaction from the beginning.

There remains, however, the question whether the respondent lost his right to such a decree by his conduct in discontinuing the business and leaving the premises before judgment was given in the action. The remedy is discretionary (*Story on Equity*, 3rd English ed. (1920), pp. 293, 294, 295), and if the respondent had acted unconscientiously during the pendency of the action, as by causing the loss of a valuable leasehold and goodwill by discontinuing the business and abandoning the premises without giving the appellant a reasonable opportunity to take them back, no doubt the court might refuse relief. But nothing of that kind happened. The term was, of course, still vested at law in the respondent, and it is not impossible that, despite low takings and actual losses, the business had some residual goodwill. But it is impossible to convict the respondent of any unfairness in the circumstances. The service of the writ had given the appellant clear notice that if the case alleged against him were made out at the trial the business and the lease would be held to have been his all along. He knew from the judge's announcement of his findings that in fact the issues of fact in the case had gone against him . . . He took his chance, contenting himself with such maintenance of the business as the respondent's continuing conduct of it might afford. But the respondent was under no duty to go on indefinitely, working for nothing and incurring losses, especially after the judge had announced findings of fact in his favour

[. . .]

For these reasons the appeal must fail.

Brown v Smitt (1924) 34 CLR 160

Facts and issues

The case involved an action by a purchaser against a vendor for rescission of a contract for the sale of land where the purchaser had entered into possession of the land, and where the issue was whether he had affirmed the contract and thereby lost the right to rescind.

Decision

Per Knox CJ, Gavan Duffy and Starke JJ at 163:

The learned trial Judge (Mann J.) accepted the evidence of the respondent and his witnesses, and held that the contract was induced by three false and fraudulent representations on the part of the defendant (the vendor) or his agent, namely, (a) that the farm was a first class dairying property; (b) that the soil was of good quality and was volcanic soil, and (c) that 120 acres of the land had been cleared. After rejecting certain defences based on allegations of acquiescence, laches on the part of the plaintiff, and an election to affirm the contract, the learned Judge decreed the rescission of the contract. So far, we think the Judge below was clearly right, substantially for the reasons assigned by him.

Per Isaacs and Rich JJ (who dissented on the question of the extent of relief ordered but whose treatment of rescission was more compendious than the majority) at 167:

The first point of substance raised by the appellant as above stated was based on the contention that on the admitted facts the respondent, assuming an original right of rescission, had disentitled himself to that remedy either by delay or election. With respect to delay, there having been no alteration of the appellant's position caused by the delay and no intervening circumstances affecting third persons such as would make rescission unconscientious on the respondent's part, this objection cannot hold.

[. . .]

The law as to election in such a case is perfectly clear. For its essentials it is unnecessary to refer to prior authorities since the case of *Abram Steamship Co. v. Westville Shipping Co*. The test, as there put, is stated in the judgment of Lord *Dunedin* (which was assented to by the Earl of Birkenhead [168] and Viscount Finlay)—whether what the respondent has said and done should be 'taken as a considered affirmation of the contract.' The same view is expressed by Lord Atkinson, whose judgment was also adopted by the Earl of Birkenhead. At pp. 786–789 various authorities are reviewed. The decisive principle is contained in a passage cited by the learned Lord from *Clough v. London and North-Western Railway Co*., namely, Did the party defrauded at any time after knowledge of the fraud either by express words or by unequivocal acts affirm the contract? An example of an unequivocal act is found in a passage in the judgment of Lord *Parker* (then *Parker* J.) in *Matthews v. Smallwood*. But, referring to that passage, if the landlord merely stated his intention to distrain or receive the rent, and yet did not distrain, and refused to receive the rent, could that be treated as in law a waiver? It is apprehended not. Neither in the circumstances can the acts and letter of the respondent be so regarded. When the whole of the circumstances are considered . . . the proper conclusion is that the respondent did not either expressly or by an unequivocal act affirm the contract. Rescission was neither lost by delay nor surrendered by confirmation. That remedy was therefore appropriate, provided proper conditions are complied with . . .

Coastal Estates Pty Ltd v Melevende [1965] VR 433

Facts and issues

Melevende was induced by fraud to enter into an instalment contract to buy property. Melevende became aware of the fraud in early 1961 but only knew of the right to rescind in September 1962 upon getting legal advice. In the meanwhile, he continued to make instalment payments and even tried to sell the property. The issue was whether this amounted to an affirmation of the contract and that the right to rescind was thereby lost.

Decision

Per Adam J at 453:

> The conclusion I have reached after considering the foregoing and other authorities which were cited to us – particularly the leading case of *Clough v London and North Western Railway* Co – is that the ultimate question to be answered in cases where affirmation is relied upon as a defence to a rescission is whether the representee has after discovery of the falsity of the relevant misrepresentations, in truth elected to affirm the contract and thereby elected not to avoid it. Because the making of an election necessarily presupposes a knowledge that a choice between alternative courses is open, in general, no question of affirmation can arise in the absence of such knowledge.

Car and Universal Finance Co Ltd v Caldwell [1965] 1 QB 525

Facts and issues

The defendant sold his car to a rogue whose cheque bounced. The rogue could not be located. The question was whether by notifying the police and the Automobile Association before the rogue sold the car to an innocent third party, the defendant had rescinded the contract with the rogue so that title in the car would revest in him.

Decision

Per Sellers LJ at 551:

> The position has to be viewed, as I see it, between the two contracting parties involved in the particular contract in question. That another innocent party or parties may suffer does not in my view of the matter justify imposing on a defrauded seller an impossible task. He has to establish, clearly and unequivocally, that he terminates the contract and is no longer to be bound by it. If he cannot communicate his decision he may still satisfy a judge or jury that he had made a final and irrevocable decision and ended the contract. I am in agreement with Lord Denning M.R. who asked 'How is a man in the position of Caldwell. ever to be able to rescind the contract when a fraudulent person absconds as Norris did here?' and answered that he can do so '. . . if he at once, on discovering the fraud, takes all possible steps to regain the goods even though he cannot find the rogue nor communicate with him.'
>
> [. . .]

Ultimately, the claim of the innocent third party, G & C Finance, was defeated and property in the car was revested in the original seller.

Seddon v North Eastern Salt Co Ltd [1905] 1 Ch 326 ('the rule in Seddon's case')

Facts and issues

Seddon bought shares in the London Salt Company in reliance on representations that were found to be false in that the trading losses were grossly understated. Settlement on the purchase had taken place. The question concerned the extent to which rescission would be ordered on the grounds of a non-fraudulent representation where the conveyance had been completely executed.

Decision

Per Joyce J at 332:

> . . . as to the claim founded on alleged misrepresentation, it appears to me, as it has done all through, that the plaintiff's way to succeeding in his claim is beset with difficulties. Now, in the first place, there is no allegation of fraud, and, in point of fact, the imputation of fraud upon the defendants has been expressly disclaimed, and properly so.
>
> [. . .]
>
> Lord Selborne in *Brownlie v. Campbell*, to which I have been referred, says, after explaining the circumstances of that particular case: 'The contract is ultimately entered into upon those terms. Passing from the stage of correspondence and negotiation to the stags of written agreement, the purchaser takes upon himself the risk of errors. I assumed them to be errors unconnected with fraud in the particulars, and when the [333] conveyance takes place it is not, as far as I know, in either country' — that means in Scotland or England — 'the principle of equity that relief should afterwards be given against that conveyance, unless there be a case of fraud.' Now I do not entertain the slightest doubt about that being a correct statement of the law.

The proposition that one could not get rescission of a fully executed contract on the grounds of representation that was not fraudulent is known as 'the rule in Seddon's case'. Its scope, as set out at 18.13 of the *Principles* text, has been significantly eroded.

QUESTIONS

(1) A seminal principle discussed above is that a statement of law is not a statement of fact for the purposes of the tort of misrepresentation. Under what circumstances will a statement of law be regarded as being as one of fact?

(2) What is the *practical* difficulty in implementing the idea that statements of law and opinion should not be regarded as statements of fact, and that they therefore do not amount to misrepresentations?

(3) If: a representation is made that is false; a contract is subsequently made and the falsity of the representation becomes evident following the execution of the contract, does it necessarily follow that the plaintiff (representee) is entitled to relief? What, if anything, does the plaintiff need to establish in order to get relief?

18.3 Damages for misrepresentation

Concept	Short explanation	Relevant authorities	*Principles* text*
Damages in the law of tort	Damages in tort put the innocent party in the position they would be in had the tort not been committed	*Livingstone v Rawyards Coal Ltd* (1880) 5 App Cas 25	Chapter 18: 18.15

Concept	Short explanation	Relevant authorities	*Principles* text*
The tort of deceit	Defining 'deceit' Consequential losses can be recovered for deceit	*Derry v Peek* (1889) 14 App Cas 337 *Palmer Bruyn & Parker Pty Ltd v Parsons* (2001) 208 CLR 388	Chapter 18: 18.16
The tort of negligence	Damages for negligent misrepresentation is for economic loss	*L Shaddock & Associates Pty Ltd v Parramatta City Council (No 1)* (1981) 150 CLR 225 *Esanda Finance Corporation Ltd v Peat Marwick Hungerfords* (1997) 188 CLR 241	Chapter 18: 18.17

* Consult the corresponding section(s) of the *Principles* text for more detail.

Misrepresentation is a tort, of which deceit and negligence will attract liability for damages.

The traditional test for damages in tort is to put the innocent party in the position they would be in had the tort not been committed.

The elements of deceit were set out in *Derry v Peek*:[4] that deceit was a false statement made knowingly or indifferent as to its truth or falsity. Deceit, once established, would enable the innocent party to recover all consequential losses, even if they were not foreseeable.

Damages for negligent misrepresentation is for economic loss which arises as a result of a breach of the defendant's duty of care, which normally would arise when the advice was sought and given in respect of a serious matter where the giver ought to realise that he is being relied on.

The duty could be owed even if no special skill was professed, where the person giving the advice knew it would be relied on. The finding of a duty can be complex, requiring the balancing of numerous factors including reliance, proximity and assumption of responsibility.

Livingstone v Rawyards Coal Ltd (1880) 5 App Cas 25

Facts and issues

Damages were awarded for the unauthorised removal of coal from beneath the appellant's land, even though the site was too small for the appellant to have mined the coal himself. The question was the manner of assessment of those damages. The following is regarded as the classic statement concerning the assessment of damages for tort.

Decision

Per Lord Blackburn at 39:

4 (1889) 14 App Cas 337.

> I do not think there is any difference of opinion as to its being a general rule that, where any injury is to be compensated by damages, in settling the sum of money to be given for reparation of damages you should as nearly as possible get that sum of money which will put the party who has been injured, or who has suffered, in the same position as he would have been in if he had not sustained the wrong for which he is now getting his compensation or reparation. That must be qualified by a great many things which may arise – such, for instance, as by the consideration whether the damage has been maliciously done, or whether it has been done with full knowledge that the person doing it was doing wrong . . .

Derry v Peek (1889) 14 App Cas 337

Facts and issues

A special Act about a tramway company provided that the carriages may be moved by animal power and by steam power with the consent of the Board of Trade. Directors of the tramway company issued a prospectus stating that, by their special Act, the company had the right to use steam power instead of horsepower. The plaintiff took shares on the faith of this statement. The question was whether the defendant's conduct amounted to the tort of deceit. Lord Herschell's following decision is regarded as the classic statement defining elements of the cause of action for deceit.

Decision

Per Lord Herschell at 374:

> First, in order to sustain an action of deceit, there must be proof of fraud, and nothing short of that will suffice. Secondly, fraud is proved when it is shewn that a false representation has been made (1) knowingly, or (2) without belief in its truth, or (3) recklessly, careless whether it be true or false. Although I have treated the second and third as distinct cases, I think the third is but an instance of the second, for one who makes a statement under such circumstances can have no real belief in the truth of what he states. To prevent a false statement being fraudulent, there must, I think, always be an honest belief in its truth. And this probably covers the whole ground, for one who knowingly alleges that which is false, has obviously no such honest belief. Thirdly, if fraud be proved, the motive of the person guilty of it is immaterial. It matters not that there was no intention to cheat or injure the person to whom the statement was made.
>
> [. . .]
>
> In my opinion making a false statement through want of care falls far short of, and is a very different thing from, fraud, and the same may be said of a false representation honestly believed though on insufficient grounds.

Palmer Bruyn & Parker Pty Ltd v Parsons (2001) 208 CLR 388

Facts and issues

The plaintiff claimed damages for injurious falsehood based on false and malicious statements contained in a letter purportedly written by the plaintiff, but was written by the defendant (which was a forgery). Consequential losses claimed included the loss of the consultancy with which the plaintiff was involved by a party who did not doubt the plaintiff's integrity but was concerned about the perception that it was dealing with someone whose integrity was not straightforward. The relevant issue was whether the losses sought were recoverable if they were not foreseeable.

Decision

Per Gummow J at 408:

> In *Doyle v Olby (Ironmongers) Ltd*, Lord Denning MR said:
>
>> In contract, the damages are limited to what may reasonably be supposed to have been in the contemplation of the parties. In fraud, they are not so limited. The defendant is bound to make reparation for all the actual damages directly flowing from the fraudulent inducement ...
>>
>> [I]t does not lie in the mouth of the fraudulent person to say that [the damage] could not reasonably have been foreseen.
>
> This passage was approved by the House of Lords in *Smith New Court Securities Ltd v Scrimgeour Vickers*.
>
> ... the question [of whether reasonable foreseeability is a means of limiting liability]... should now be answered, in line with *Doyle* and *Smith*, so as to deny the applicability of reasonable foreseeability as a means of limiting liability in the tort of injurious falsehood.

L Shaddock & Associates Pty Ltd v Parramatta City Council (No 1) (1981) 150 CLR 225

Facts and issues

Developers sought, and obtained, advice from the local council whether any road-widening proposal affected certain land, and was told there were not. It was the practice of the council to answer such enquiries. The question was whether the council owed a duty of care to developers when they were not in the business of giving such advice.

Decision

Per Gibbs CJ at 232:

> ... the duty in my opinion can exist in relation to the giving of information as well as advice. This was the view of Barwick C.J. in *Mutual Life & Citizens' Assurance Co. Ltd. v. Evatt*, [233] who pointed out, that in many instances the distinction between the two is very slight and that on occasion information becomes inextricable from advice...
>
> I respectfully agree with the opinion of Barwick C.J. that there is no valid ground on which to distinguish between information and advice for the purposes of the rule in *Hedley Byrne* (liability for negligent misrepresentation). Although the giving of advice must always necessarily require an exercise of skill or judgment, and the giving of information may not necessarily do so, a person giving information may be so placed that others can reasonably rely on his ability carefully to ascertain and impart the information. Other authorities support this view. A prospective tenant of a site for a filling station may reasonably rely on a statement made by an employee of an oil company, the owner of the site, as to the potential through-put of the

filling station; the oil company has a duty to use reasonable care to see that the information is correct: *Esso Petroleum Co. Ltd. v. Mardon*.

[. . .]

With all respect I find it difficult to see why in principle the duty should be limited to persons whose business or profession includes giving the sort of advice or information sought and to persons claiming to have the same skill and competence as those carrying on such a business or profession, and why it should not extend to persons who, on a serious occasion, give considered advice or information concerning a business or professional transaction.

Esanda Finance Corporation Ltd v Peat Marwick Hungerfords (1997) 188 CLR 241

Facts and issues

A financier lent money in reliance on audited accounts and auditors' reports. Assuming that auditors might foresee that the financier might rely on the audited accounts in its dealings with the subject company, the question was whether auditors owed a duty of care in negligence in the preparation of the audited accounts.

Decision

Per McHugh J at 282:

> At least six other factors arise for consideration . . .
>
> First, whether or not imposing a duty in favour of third parties will deter auditors from being careless, extending liability will probably reduce the supply of their services . . .
>
> . . .
>
> [283] Thus, the result of widening the circumstances in which auditors will owe a duty of care to third parties may be: (i) a significant increase in the cost of auditing services; (ii) a decrease in the competition for or the provision of such services; and (iii) a reduction in the standard of those services . . .
>
> [. . .]
>
> This would be detrimental to the interests of creditors, investors and business generally.
>
> [. . .]
>
> Second, no examination of the public interest should overlook the effect of an extension of auditor's liability on the administration of the court system. Experience of claims against auditors by public company liquidators over the last thirty years in this country indicates that almost any claim is likely to take many months to hear, not to mention the time taken in interlocutory matters and appeals. This is not surprising.
>
> [. . .]
>
> [286] Third, creditors and shareholders already have an indirect remedy against the auditors in many cases
>
> [. . .]
>
> Fourth, the client's conduct is the primary cause of the plaintiff's loss; the auditor's role is secondary.
>
> [. . .]
>
> [287] Fifth, the need for a plaintiff to prove that he or she relied on the audit report means that the auditor's liability is often problematical even when the auditor has been guilty of gross carelessness.

> [...]
>
> [288] Sixth, the factual issues that arise in auditor's liability cases — was the auditor's opinion negligent, did the plaintiff rely on the audit? — make it almost impossible for an auditor to avoid a trial or settlement even when the auditor is not liable to the plaintiff.

After exploring the above six factors, McHugh J set out what he regarded to be the pivotal considerations at 289:

> Although considered individually none of the six factors to which I have referred points decisively against imposing a duty of care to cover a case such as the present, collectively they support the conclusion that the demands of corrective justice do not require the imposition of such a duty.
>
> In the end, the most powerful point for holding that auditors owe a duty of care in cases like the present is that investors and creditors suffer their losses because they have relied, as the auditor knew or ought reasonably to have known they would, on his or her report, and the auditor has made that report carelessly. As against that, however, is the fact that the auditor did not invite or intend them to rely on it and they have paid nothing to the auditor for the preparation of the work. They require the auditor to compensate them for the loss that arose from their self-induced reliance, but they were not prepared to pay for the auditor's work.

QUESTIONS

(1) State the difference in the principles, respectively, for the calculation of damages for breach of contract, and tort.

(2) Although the local council in *L Shaddock & Associates Pty Ltd v Parramatta City Council (No 1)*[5] was not in the business of giving advice, only information, what was the pivotal finding in the High Court's determination that it owed a duty of care in respect of enquiries made of it concerning the road-widening proposal in question?

(3) Is there a single determinant of the existence of a duty of care in a contractual context? If not, describe the High Court's approach to finding a duty of care.

18.4 Statutory prohibitions on misleading or deceptive conduct

Concept	Short explanation	Relevant authorities	*Principles text**
The requirement of conduct 'in trade or commerce'	The conduct has to be *'in'* trade or commerce	*Shahid v Australian College of Dermatologists* (2008) 168 FCR 46 *Concrete Constructions (NSW) Pty Ltd v Nelson* (1990) 169 CLR 594 *Williams v Pisano* (2015) 90 NSWLR 342 *Houghton v Arms* (2006) 225 CLR 553	Chapter 18: 18.20

5 (1981) 150 CLR 225.

(cont.)

Concept	Short explanation	Relevant authorities	*Principles text**
'Misleading or deceptive'	Conduct needs be misleading or deceptive or *likely* to mislead or deceive	*Parkdale Custom Built Furniture Pty Ltd v Puxu Pty Ltd* (1982) 149 CLR 191 *Hornsby Building Information Centre Pty Ltd v Sydney Building Information Centre Ltd* (1978) 140 CLR 216	Chapter 18: 18.21
The victim(s) of the deception	Exploring the relevance of the nature of the persons alleged to have been deceived	*Butcher v Lachlan Elder Realty Pty Ltd* (2004) 218 CLR 592 *Campomar Sociedad Limitada v Nike International Ltd* (2000) 202 CLR 45	Chapter 18: 18.22
Silence	There is no general duty of disclosure, but circumstances might give rise to a reasonable expectation of disclosure	*Demagogue Pty Ltd v Ramensky* (1992) 39 FCR 31 *Miller & Associates Insurance Broking Pty Ltd v BMW Australia Finance Ltd* (2010) 241 CLR 357	Chapter 18: 18.25
Must silence be deliberate?	Likely 'no'	*CCP Australian Airships Ltd v Primus Telecommunications Pty Ltd* (2005) ATPR ¶42-042	Chapter 18: 18.26
Representations as to the future	A representation as to the future is deemed to be misleading unless the representor had reasonable grounds for its making	Australian Consumer Law s 4 *Digi-Tech (Australia) Ltd v Brand* (2004) Aust Contract R 90-196	Chapter 18: 18.28
Opinions	A representation expressed as an opinion needs to imply a false representation of fact	*Johnson & Johnson Pacific Pty Ltd v Unilever Australia (No 2)* (2007) ATPR ¶42-136	Chapter 18: 18.28
Promises	A contractual promise may be 'conduct'	*Accounting Systems 2000 (Developments) Pty Ltd v CCH Australia Ltd* (1993) 42 FCR 470 *Futuretronics International Pty Ltd v Gadzhis* [1992] 2 VR 217	Chapter 18: 18.29
Relaying information	Whether relaying information is misleading or deceptive conduct	*Yorke v Lucas* (1985) 158 CLR 661 *Google Inc v Australian Competition and Consumer Commission* (2013) 249 CLR 435	Chapter 18: 18.30
Damages	Tortious damages are commonly regarded the best analogy for damages for misleading or deceptive conduct	*Gates v City Mutual Life Assurance Society Ltd* (1986) 160 CLR 1 *Murphy v Overton Investments Pty Ltd* (2004) 216 CLR 388 *Sellars v Adelaide Petroleum NL* (1994) 179 CLR 332	Chapter 18: 18.15, 18.32

Concept	Short explanation	Relevant authorities	*Principles* text*
Causation	Damage must have been caused 'by' the conduct	*Wardley Australia Ltd. v Western Australia* (1992) 175 CLR 514 *Marks v GIO Australia Holdings Pty Ltd* (1998) 196 CLR 494	Chapter 18: 18.34
Exclusion of liability	Generally loss for misleading or deceptive conduct cannot be excluded	*Bowler v Hilda Pty Ltd* (1998) 80 FCR 191 *Butcher v Lachlan Elder Realty Pty Ltd* (2004) 218 CLR 592	Chapter 18: 18.35

* Consult the corresponding section(s) of the *Principles* text for more detail.

Many of disputes previously covered by the common law of misrepresentation can now be brought under the statutory cause of action for misleading or deceptive conduct.

18.4.1 The requirement of conduct 'in trade or commerce'

A prerequisite of conduct being deemed misleading or deceptive, is that the conduct must be '*in trade or commerce*'. The activity must include the carrying on of a profession but not purely instrumental or mundane activities; rather, the conduct has to be *'in'* trade or commerce. The parameters of this requirement are not clear cut; so, for example, conduct in connection with the sale of a residential property is not caught. In a contractual setting the court nowadays favours a broad approach to the requirement 'in trade or commerce'.

Shahid v Australian College of Dermatologists (2008) 168 FCR 46

Facts and issues

The College's handbook contained information relating to the selection process, its record-keeping, and the appeals process. The question was whether the publication of the handbooks was 'in trade or commerce'.

Decision

Per Branson and Stone JJ at 53:

> In our view, in reaching a judgment on whether the College published its Handbooks 'in trade or commerce', it is important to consider the cumulative significance of the above evidence rather than to consider each aspect of the evidence as though it stood alone. Additionally, it must be borne in mind that the words 'trade' and 'commerce' in s 52, and other relevant provisions of the *Trade Practices Act*, carry their ordinary meanings. In *Concrete Constructions* 169 CLR at 602 the majority described them as 'terms of common knowledge of the widest import'. In *Re Ku-ring-gai Co-operative Building Society (No 12) Ltd.* Deane J said of these terms:
>
> > They are not restricted to dealings or communications which can properly be described as being at arm's length in the sense that they are within open markets or

> between strangers or have a dominant objective of profit-making. They are apt to include commercial or business dealings in finance between a company and its members which are not within the mainstream of ordinary commercial activities and which, while being commercial in character, are marked by a degree of altruism which is not compatible with a dominant objective of profit-making.

[. . .]

The publication of the Handbooks was conduct of the College specifically directed to practitioners who intended to apply for positions as trainee registrars and also those who obtained such positions; that is, to practitioners with whom [54] it had a commercial relationship. The Handbooks, by reason of their content, were an important element of that relationship. Their publication was therefore, as it seems to us, conduct 'in the central conception' of the College's commercial activities.

Concrete Constructions (NSW) Pty Ltd v Nelson (1990) 169 CLR 594

Facts and issues

The case concerned statements made by one employee, a foreman, to another about work conditions and safety. The question was whether the statements by the foreman was 'in trade or commerce'. The case is regarded as the seminal case on point.

Decision

Per Mason CJ, Deane, Dawson and Gaudron JJ at 602:

> The real problem involved in the construction of s. 52 of the Act does not, however, spring from the use of the words 'trade or commerce'. It arises from the requirement that the conduct to which the section refers be '*in*' trade or commerce . . .
>
> The phrase 'in trade or commerce' in s. 52 has a restrictive operation. It qualifies the prohibition against engaging in conduct of the specified kind. As a matter of language, a prohibition against engaging in conduct 'in trade or commerce' can be construed as encompassing conduct in the course of the myriad of activities which are not, of their nature, of a trading or commercial character but which are undertaken in the course of, or as incidental to, the [603] carrying on of an overall trading or commercial business. If the words 'in trade or commerce' in s. 52 are construed in that sense, the provisions of the section would extend, for example, to a case where the misleading or deceptive conduct was a failure by a driver to give the correct handsignal when driving a truck in the course of a corporation's haulage business. It would also extend to a case, such as the present, where the alleged misleading or deceptive conduct consisted of the giving of inaccurate information by one employee to another in the course of carrying on the building activities of a commercial builder. Alternatively, the reference to conduct 'in trade or commerce' in s. 52 can be construed as referring only to conduct which is itself an aspect or element of activities or transactions which, of their nature, bear a trading or commercial character
>
> [. . .]
>
> . . . it is plain that s. 52 was not intended to extend to all conduct, regardless of its nature, in which a corporation might engage in the course of, or for the purposes of, its overall trading or commercial business. . . .
>
> [. . .]

[604] What the section is concerned with is the conduct of a corporation towards persons, be they consumers or not, with whom it (or those whose interests it represents or is seeking to promote) has or may have dealings in the course of those activities or transactions which, of their nature, bear a trading or commercial character.

[. . .]

The alleged misleading or deceptive conduct of the Company's foreman in the present case consisted of an internal communication [605] by one employee to another employee in the course of their ordinary activities in and about the construction of a building. It follows from what has been said above that that conduct was not, for relevant purposes, conduct 'in trade or commerce' and would not, if established, constitute a contravention of s 52 of the Act.

Williams v Pisano (2015) 90 NSWLR 342

Facts and issues

Vendors of a property retained a real estate agent to market the property, which had been renovated. The advertising brochure prepared by the agent contained false representations. The question was whether the representations were conduct in trade and commerce on the part of the vendors. This case is illustrative of the difficulties that can arise from trying to identify the fault line between conduct that is caught by the legislation and that which is not.

Decision

Per Emmett JA at 349:

> The terms 'trade' and 'commerce' are ordinary terms that describe the mutual communications, negotiations, verbal and written, bargains and performance that constitute commercial arrangements.
>
> [. . .]
>
> The phrase 'in trade or commerce' operates to qualify the prohibitions in s 18 and s 30 against engaging in conduct of the specified kind. Those provisions were not intended to extend to all conduct, regardless of its nature, in which a person might engage in the course of, or for the purpose of, the overall trading or commercial business of that person.
>
> [. . .]
>
> In ordinary circumstances, a person who sells his home, whether by private treaty or by auction and whether he conducts the negotiations personally or through a real estate agent, would not be said to be undertaking those activities in the course of a trade or business or in a business context. Whether or not an estate agent is used and whether or not that agent advertises the house, by preparing brochures or other advertisements, and whether or not the agent sells by auction or merely negotiates a private treaty, the sale will normally remain a sale by the vendor of his house and not an act done in a business context.
>
> [. . .]
>
> The mere use of an estate agent does not bring about the result that the sale of a capital asset by a householder is a transaction occurring in trade or commerce.
>
> [. . .]

[350] The fact that the Vendors retained the Agent in connection with the sale does not, of itself, make the conduct of the Agent, for which the Vendors were vicariously liable, conduct in trade or commerce, even though the conduct of the Agent may have been conduct in the trade or commerce of the Agent.

[. . .]

The business character of the acts done by an agent cannot be imputed to the acts of the principals.

Houghton v Arms (2006) 225 CLR 553

Facts and issues

Arms entered into a contract with a company WSA Online, which subsequently went into liquidation. Arms had also sued two employees, Student and Houghton, under s 75B of the *Trade Practices Act* as accessories for breaches of that Act by WSA. The provisions relating to accessories required that they were 'knowingly' involved in any such contravention. The question on appeal was whether they could be directly liable for misleading or deceptive conduct, rather than merely as accessories. The case is significant for demonstrating the utility of pursuing natural persons directly where accessorial liability could be problematic due to the fact they may not have been 'knowingly' involved in any such contravention.

Decision

Per Gleeson CJ, Gummow, Hayne, Heydon and Crennan JJ at 565:

> In *Concrete Constructions*, Mason CJ, Deane, Dawson and Gaudron JJ construed the expression 'in trade or commerce' as referring only to conduct with the character of an aspect or element of trading or commercial activities or transactions . The representations to the effect that in order for Mr Arms effectively to operate the auscellardoor web site, he would not be required to obtain from the wineries any documentation other than a form with provision for banking details, undoubtedly were of this nature.
>
> Moreover, in his judgment in *Concrete Constructions*, Toohey J emphasised that, while in most cases, the focus would be on the nature of the business of the party making the representation, s 52 was not so limited; in particular, the section did not, in terms, refer to the trade or commerce of any particular corporation, Accordingly, statements made by a person not himself or herself engaged in trade or commerce may answer the statutory expression if, for example, they are designed to encourage others to invest, or to continue investments, in a particular trading entity.
>
> Mr Arms was engaging in trade and commerce under the name 'Australian Cellar Door' and by means of the auscellardoor web site. He enlisted WSA to provide services and advice for the purposes of his business. It was the business of WSA to provide such advice and services. It is not to the point that Mr Houghton and Mr Student themselves were not business proprietors or that their activities were an aspect or element of the trade or commerce of WSA (and of Australian Cellar Door) but not of 'their' trade or commerce. Mr Houghton and Mr Student nevertheless engaged in conduct in the course of trade or commerce and were thus within the ambit of the FT Act.

18.4.2 'Misleading or deceptive'

The conduct needs to be *misleading or deceptive or likely to mislead or deceive.* The test under the section is objective, without proof of intention to mislead, and thus is very different from the common law of misrepresentation.

Parkdale Custom Built Furniture Pty Ltd v Puxu Pty Ltd (1982) 149 CLR 191

Facts and issues

The parties were furniture manufacturers. The respondent Parkdale supplied a line of furniture which was claimed to closely resemble the furniture of the applicant Puxu. The Parkdale label was tucked under the upholstery of the chair and not easily visible. The question was whether Parkdale's conduct was misleading or deceptive conduct where an ordinary person who read the labels could not possibly be misled, even if the resemblance was so close that a person looking at the chairs without finding the label would likely be misled into thinking the Parkdale chairs were the Puxu chairs.

Decision

Per Gibbs CJ at 196:

> ... the respondent's claim that the conduct of the appellant was misleading or deceptive, or likely to mislead or deceive, rests solely on the fact that the appellant sold goods which were virtually identical in appearance to those sold by the respondent. There is no suggestion of false labelling or false description. Evidence was given of particular instances in which persons were actually misled by the resemblance in appearance of the chairs. I may deal with this evidence very briefly, since it does no more than reinforce the view that an ordinary observer, not seeing the label, might mistake one chair for the other. Two persons, Mrs. Hogg and Mr. Klug, bought 'Rawhide' chairs believing them to be 'Post and Rail' chairs. In each case, however, the labels had been removed from the chairs, and there is no suggestion that the appellant had been in any way responsible for their removal.
>
> [...]
>
> [199] Section 52 does not expressly state what persons or class of persons should be considered as the possible victims for the purpose of deciding whether conduct is misleading or deceptive or likely to mislead or deceive. It seems clear enough that consideration must be given to the class of consumers likely to be affected by the conduct. Although it is true, as has often been said, that ordinarily a class of consumers may include the inexperienced as well as the experienced, and the gullible as well as the astute, the section must in my opinion by regarded as contemplating the effect of the conduct on reasonable members of the class.
>
> [...]
>
> The conduct of a defendant must be viewed as a whole.
>
> [...]
>
> In the present case the conduct of the appellant was not simply to manufacture and sell furniture that resembled that of the respondent. The appellant sold only furniture that had been labelled, in the ordinary way, so as to show the name of the manufacturer. If the appellant's conduct was likely to mislead possible purchasers, it is difficult to see why the respondent's

> conduct in selling its furniture would not also be likely to mislead. However that may be, in my opinion, the conduct of the appellant did not contravene s. 52. Speaking generally, the sale by one manufacturer of goods which closely resemble those of another manufacturer is not a breach of s. 52 if the goods are properly [200] labelled. There are hundreds of ordinary articles of consumption which, although made by different manufacturers and of different quality, closely resemble one another.

Hornsby Building Information Centre Pty Ltd v Sydney Building Information Centre Ltd (1978) 140 CLR 216

Facts and issues

The Sydney Building Information Centre Ltd established a business of displaying building products and techniques and disseminating building information. In 1975, Hornsby Building Information Centre Pty Ltd established a similar business in the Sydney suburb of that name. Its affairs were managed by a former employee of the Sydney Centre. The question was whether the use of the name 'Hornsby Building Information Centre' without any disclaimer of connection with the Sydney Centre was misleading or deceptive. For the purposes of this chapter, the relevant parts of the judgment focus on the question of the effect on the audience to whom the conduct is directed and the relevance of intent. The case is regarded as a seminal case on this point.

Decision

Per Stephen J at 227:

> No doubt the meaning of the statutory prohibition which s. 52 (1) enunciates must be gained from the terms of the sub-section itself; but nothing in those terms suggests that a statement made which is literally true, i.e., that the centre at Hornsby is conducted by Hornsby Building Information Centre Pty. Ltd. may not at the same time be misleading and deceptive. It clearly may be. To announce an opera as one in which a named and famous prima donna will appear and then to produce an unknown young lady bearing by chance that name will clearly be to mislead and deceive. The announcement would be literally true but none the less deceptive, and this because it conveyed to others something more than the literal meaning which the words spelled out. Thus, in passing off, a newly incorporated defendant company may not use, in its newly established business, its true corporate name if it be deceptively similar to that of a plaintiff with an established reputation . . . What has been said of passing off actions applies equally in the present case; as Buckley L.J. remarked in *John Brinsmead & Sons Ltd. v. Brinsmead*, a statement which is literally true and accurate may nevertheless carry with it a false representation.
>
> [228] . . . nothing turns, I think, upon the intent of the Hornsby Centre.
>
> [. . .]
>
> If the consequence is deception, that suffices to make the conduct deceptive. Section 52 (1) creates no offence, it only prescribes a course of conduct deviation from which may result in an order of the Court, made under s. 80 of the Act, forbidding further deviation in the future. The section should be understood as meaning precisely what it says and as involving no questions of intent upon the part of the corporation whose conduct is in question.

18.4.3 The victim(s) of the deception

Next explored is the effect of the conduct on *victim(s) of the deception*; namely, that the outcome of an action may depend on the nature of the persons alleged to have been deceived. Relevantly also, where the conduct is directed not to an identifiable individual but a class of people, it is necessary to isolate their characteristics.

Butcher v Lachlan Elder Realty Pty Ltd (2004) 218 CLR 592

Facts and issues

The applicant Butcher purchased property on the faith of a brochure provided to him by a representative of Lachlan, which misdescribed the property. The information was provided by the previous owner of the property, Harkins, and was included in the brochure by Lachlan. The issue was whether, in those circumstances, Lachlan had engaged in misleading or deceptive conduct. The extract focuses on the relevance of the nature of the alleged victim, a company director engaged in a carpet cleaning business, wanting to buy property for investment.

Decision

Per Gleeson CJ, Hayne and Heydon JJ at 604:

> Questions of allegedly misleading conduct, including questions as to what the conduct was, can be analysed from two points of view. One is employed in relation to 'members of a class to which the conduct in question [is] directed in a general sense'. The other, urged by the purchasers here, is employed where the objects of the conduct are 'identified individuals to whom a particular misrepresentation has been made or from whom a relevant fact, circumstance or proposal was withheld'; they are considered quite apart from any class into which they fall.
>
> [. . .]
>
> The former approach is common when remedies other than those conferred by s 82 (or s 87) of the Act are under consideration. But the former approach is inappropriate, and the latter is inevitable, in cases like the present, where monetary relief is sought by a plaintiff who alleges that a particular misrepresentation was made to identified persons, of whom the plaintiff was one. The plaintiff must establish a causal link between the impugned conduct and the loss that is claimed. That depends on analysing the conduct of the defendant in relation to that plaintiff alone. So here, it is necessary to consider the character of the particular conduct of the particular agent in relation to the particular purchasers, bearing in mind what matters of fact each knew about the other as a result of the nature of their dealings . . .

It was relevant to the ultimate finding that Lachlan did not engage in misleading or deceptive conduct that, on one side, the applicant was a sophisticated company director and his de facto wife, and on the other a suburban real estate agency.

Campomar Sociedad Limitada v Nike International Ltd (2000) 202 CLR 45

Facts and issues

The defendant, a Spanish company, sold a sport fragrance labelled 'Nike Sport Fragrance'. Nike alleged that the defendant had engaged in misleading or deceptive conduct by leading consumers to think that the product was connected with them. Questions, inter alia, were whether consumers would be misled into thinking that this was a Nike product, despite the label indicating that the product was made by 'Campomar'.

Decision

Per Gleeson CJ, Gaudron, McHugh, Gummow, Kirby, Hayne and Callinan JJ at 84:

> The other classes of case which their Honours had in mind include those of actual or threatened conduct involving representations to the public at large or to a section thereof, such as prospective retail purchasers of a product the respondent markets or proposes to market.
>
> [. . .]
>
> [85] It is in these cases of representations to the public, of which the first appeal is one, that there enter the 'ordinary' or 'reasonable' members of the class of prospective purchasers. Although a class of consumers may be expected to include a wide range of persons, in isolating the 'ordinary' or 'reasonable' members of that class, there is an objective attribution of certain characteristics.
>
> [. . .]
>
> Where the persons in question are not identified individuals to whom a particular misrepresentation has been made or from whom a relevant fact, circumstance or proposal was withheld, but are members of a class to which the conduct in question was directed in a general sense, it is necessary to isolate by some criterion a representative member of that class. The inquiry thus is to be made with respect to this hypothetical individual why the misconception complained has arisen or is likely to arise. . .
>
> [88] . . . looking at the matter objectively, there was nothing capricious or unreasonable or unpredictable in Sheppard J's conclusion that the placing of the 'NIKE SPORT FRAGRANCE' product in the same area of pharmacies with other sports fragrances was likely to mislead or deceive members of the public into thinking that the 'NIKE SPORT FRAGRANCE' product was in some way promoted or distributed by Nike International itself or with its consent and approval.

18.4.4 Silence

The treatment of *silence* as misleading or deceptive conduct is not materially different from that in common law misrepresentation. In particular, as with the common law, whilst there is no general duty of disclosure, circumstances might give rise to a reasonable expectation of such. However, an expectation of disclosure does not *necessarily* arise when one party knows that a particular matter is likely to be important to the other.

An associated point is *whether silence must be deliberate*. The authorities suggest the answer is likely 'no'.

Demagogue Pty Ltd v Ramensky (1992) 39 FCR 31

Facts and issues

The plaintiff wished to purchase land. The defendant's agent said there would be access via a driveway to the road. The plan attached to the contract referred to a driveway. The portion of the plan referred to as a driveway was in fact a public road. The issue was whether the defendant's and their agent's silence concerning the character of the road was misleading or deceptive conduct.

Decision

Per Black J at 32:

> Silence is to be assessed as a circumstance like any other. To say this is certainly not to impose any general duty of disclosure; the question is simply whether, having regard to all the relevant circumstances, there has been conduct that is misleading or deceptive or that is likely to mislead or deceive. To speak of 'mere silence' or of a duty of disclosure can divert attention from that primary question. Although 'mere silence' is a convenient way of describing some fact situations, there is in truth no such thing as 'mere silence' because the significance of silence always falls to be considered in the context in which it occurs. That context may or may not include facts giving rise to a reasonable expectation, in the circumstances of the case, that if particular matters exist they will be disclosed [the circumstances of the case gave rise to a duty to disclose the nature of the road, and the silence of the defendant was considered to be misleading or deceptive conduct].

Miller & Associates Insurance Broking Pty Ltd v BMW Australia Finance Ltd (2010) 241 CLR 357

Facts and issues

An insurance broker had negotiated a premium funding loan. The policy for which the loan was sought was a cost of production policy, which was not cancellable, in connection with a plantation investment scheme. The borrower defaulted on the loan. The lender alleged that the broker had engaged in misleading or deceptive conduct. The conduct complained of was that, in response to the lender's request for further details, the broker had provided an insurance certificate which referred to property—property policies being commonly cancellable; alternatively, that the broker's conduct had been misleading by its failure to disclose that the policy was not cancellable.

Decision

Per French CJ and Kiefel J at 371:

> ... as a general proposition, s 52 does not require a party to commercial negotiations to volunteer information which will be of assistance to the decision-making of the other party. A fortiori it does not impose on a party an obligation to volunteer information in order to avoid the consequences of the careless disregard, for its own interests, of another party of equal bargaining power and competence. Yet that appears to have been, in practical effect, the character of the obligation said to have rested upon Miller in this case.
>
> Reasonable expectation analysis is unnecessary in the case of a false representation where the undisclosed fact is the falsity of the representation. A party to precontractual negotiations who provides to another party a document containing a false representation which is not disclaimed will, in all probability, have engaged in misleading or deceptive conduct. When a document contains a statement that is true, non-disclosure of an important qualifying fact will

> be misleading or deceptive if the recipient would be misled, absent such disclosure, into believing that the statement was complete. In some cases it might not be necessary to invoke non-disclosure at all where a statement which is literally true, but incomplete in some material respect, conveys a false representation that it is complete. [This was not such a case and a finding of misleading or deceptive conduct could not be sustained].

CCP Australian Airships Ltd v Primus Telecommunications Pty Ltd (2005) ATPR ¶42-042

Facts and issues

Primus' claim was for relief in respect of an Exclusive Licence agreement. Relevant to the claim for misleading or deceptive conduct was the allegation that CCP deliberately refrained during the period between 16 February 2000 and 7 March 2000 from telling Primus that CCP did not have available funds to pay the deposit for, or otherwise to pay for, the purchase price of the airship and that CCP had no commitments in place or resources for any such funding. The relevant question here was whether silence had to be deliberate.

Decision

Per Nettle JA at [34]:

> As to the law, the misleading and deceptive quality of remaining silent inheres in the non-disclosure of information; not in any refusal to provide it. Consequently, it does not follow from the fact that a failure to act must be intentional in order to be actionable, that silence must be intentional in order to be actionable. It is plain in principle and authority that it is not necessary that silence be intentional in order that it may constitute misleading and deceptive conduct for the purposes of s 52.

18.4.5 Representations as to the future

Representations as to the future, if they do not materialise, are deemed to be misleading unless the representor had reasonable grounds for its making. This is the effect of s 4 of the Australian Consumer Law, a very important provision.

Australian Consumer Law s 4

(1) If:

(a) a person makes a representation with respect to any future matter (including the doing of, or the refusing to do, any act); and

(b) the person does not have reasonable grounds for making the representation;

the representation is taken, for the purposes of this Schedule, to be misleading.

(2) For the purposes of applying subsection (1) in relation to a proceeding concerning a representation made with respect to a future matter by:

(a) a party to the proceeding; or

(b) any other person;

the party or other person is taken not to have had reasonable grounds for making the representation, unless evidence is adduced to the contrary.

(3) To avoid doubt, subsection (2) does not:

(a) have the effect that, merely because such evidence to the contrary is adduced, the person who made the representation is taken to have had reasonable grounds for making the representation; or

(b) have the effect of placing on any person an onus of proving that the person who made the representation had reasonable grounds for making the representation.

(4) Subsection (1) does not limit by implication the meaning of a reference in this Schedule to:

(a) a misleading representation; or

(b) a representation that is misleading in a material particular; or

(c) conduct that is misleading or is likely or liable to mislead;

and, in particular, does not imply that a representation that a person makes with respect to any future matter is not misleading merely because the person has reasonable grounds for making the representation.

Digi-Tech (Australia) Ltd v Brand (2004) Aust Contract R 90-196

Facts and issues

A forecast of sales was expressed as a belief. The question here was whether this would preclude it from being a representation of a future matter.

Decision

Per Sheller, Ipp and McColl JJA at [99]:

> The expression of a belief involves the expression of a state of mind. There is no reason why a person's state of mind should not relate to future matters. Thus, in determining whether an expressed belief relates to future matters, regard must be had to the words used and the context: *Sydney Harbour Casino Properties Pty Limited v Coluzzi & Anor* [2002] NSWCA 74 at [24] per Mason P.
>
> [...]
>
> [102] Accordingly, the mere fact that revenue and profit potential was dealt with explicitly as a matter of DTAL's belief casts a very dim light indeed on the question whether, in expressing that belief, Digi-Tech was making a representation as to a future matter. It certainly does not resolve that question: as we have said, it all depends on the words used and the general context.
>
> [...]
>
> [114] In our opinion the Profit Potential Representation was a representation with respect to a future matter.

18.4.6 Opinions

To be actionable as misleading or deceptive conduct, a representation that is expressed as an *opinion* needs to imply a false representation of fact.

Johnson & Johnson Pacific Pty Ltd v Unilever Australia (No 2) (2007) ATPR ¶42-136

Facts and issues

The applicant was a manufacturer of cosmetics. The respondent launched a competing product. Television and print advertisements claimed that 7 out of 10 users of the applicant's product preferred the respondent's and that the statistic was supported by research.

Decision

Per Bennett J at [117]:

> The advertisements were not a mere reporting of the study ... By presenting the preference claim including the elucidator in this manner, Unilever conveyed the impression that the study provided a basis for the representations (*Global Sportsman Pty Ltd v Mirror Newspapers Pty Ltd* (1984) 2 FCR 82 at 88). A statement of opinion cannot be regarded as false or misleading or as misleading and deceptive simply because it is incorrect (*Global Sportsman* at 88; *Bateman v Slatyer* (1987) 71 ALR 553 at 559). However, in this case, as in *RAIA* at 175, it is implicit in the statement of the comparison that Unilever had ascertained that the facts justified the opinion it presented.
>
> [118] Unilever is liable for these representations that were misleading or deceptive or likely to mislead or deceive in contravention of s 52 of the Act.

18.4.7 Promises

A contractual promise including one as to a future matter may be misleading and caught by the Act.

Accounting Systems 2000 (Developments) Pty Ltd v CCH Australia Ltd (1993) 42 FCR 470

Facts and issues

Accounting Systems gave a warranty to Castle Douglas ('CD') that they owned certain copyright interests in software. CD assigned the licence to use the software to CCH. Accounting Systems were not in fact the owners of the copyright. An issue was whether a corporation, by making a contract containing warranties given by the corporation which are false, thereby engages in misleading or deceptive conduct. CCH was not party to any warranty by Accounting Systems.

Decision

Per Gummow J at 505:

> . . . s 4(2)(a) provides significant support for the conclusion reached in this case by the primary judge, and for the general proposition that the making of a statement as to a presently existing state of affairs, if false, may be the engaging in misleading or deceptive conduct, where the statement is embodied as a provision of a contract. In many cases, there will have been pre-contractual conduct which itself contravenes s 52. The present case is a striking one because it was presented on a narrower basis, and concerned the giving of the warranties in the contract itself.
>
> [. . .]
>
> [506] It is no objection to relief under these provisions that the misleading conduct is found in the making of a contractual provision, and the complainant does not have contractual privity with the defendant.

Futuretronics International Pty Ltd v Gadzhis [1992] 2 VR 217

Facts and issues

The defendant had a bid at auction accepted but refused to sign the contract. The contract was unenforceable for failure to comply with statute of frauds legislation. The plaintiff alleged the defendant, by bidding, represented that the bid was genuine and he intended to be bound, and that his conduct was thereby misleading or deceptive conduct.

Decision

Per Ormiston J at 239:

> In my opinion the mere acceptance of the promise by a promisee cannot ordinarily be characterised as being led into error. In the usual case the consequence would be that the promisee has enforceable rights. It is hard to believe that normally any promisee with ordinary contractual rights would then describe himself as having been deceived or misled. It is only when it becomes apparent that the promise cannot be enforced, because, for example, it is either unenforceable or the promisee's rights are valueless or diminished, that one may return to the original promise to inquire whether that promise was of so little substance that it can be concluded that the promisee was indeed misled or deceived in the first place, at the time of his acceptance of the promise. Thus it may then be seen that the promisor originally had no intention to perform his promise or that he originally had no capacity or ability to perform it. Now, however, by reason of s10A (and s51A) the inquiry is apparently broader for one must also inquire whether at the relevant time the promisor had reasonable grounds for making any implicit representation (where relevant) that he intended in the future to perform his contractual promise, and for this purpose the onus of proof is reversed.
>
> [. . .]
>
> [240] It would seem on the authorities that, at the least, a contractual promise would amount to an implied representation that the promisor then had an intention to carry out that promise. If it can be shown that he had no such intention he would be guilty of misleading or deceptive conduct. Likewise it would seem that such a representation connotes a present ability to fulfil

that promise which, if shown to be untrue at the time of making, would likewise characterise the implied representation as misleading or deceptive.

18.4.8 Relaying information

Relaying information might amount to proscribed conduct; a central question to determine if this would be so is whether the alleged perpetrator endorsed or adopted the contents of the alleged misleading or deceptive statements.

Yorke v Lucas (1985) 158 CLR 661

Facts and issues

It was claimed that a company had engaged in misleading or deceptive conduct by furnishing false information about the turnover of a business. The company's agent had taken pains to confirm the accuracy of the figures before passing them on. The question was whether the company had engaged in misleading or deceptive conduct.

Decision

Per Mason ACJ, Wilson, Deane and Dawson JJ at 666:

> It is, of course, established that contravention of that section does not require an intent to mislead or deceive and even though a corporation acts honestly and reasonably, it may nonetheless engage in conduct that is misleading or deceptive or is likely to mislead or deceive: *Hornsby Building Information Centre Pty. Ltd. v. Sydney Building Information Centre Ltd.*; *Parkdale Custom Built Furniture Pty. Ltd. v. Puxu Pty. Ltd.* That does not, however, mean that a corporation which purports to do no more than pass on information supplied by another must nevertheless be engaging in misleading or deceptive conduct if the information turns out to be false. If the circumstances are such as to make it apparent that the corporation is not the source of the information and that it expressly or impliedly disclaims any belief in its truth or falsity, merely passing it on for what it is worth, we very much doubt that the corporation can properly be said to be itself engaging in conduct that is misleading or deceptive.

Google Inc v Australian Competition and Consumer Commission (2013) 249 CLR 435

Facts and issues

Advertisers on Google, using 'AdWords', were able to enter a competitor's name as a keyword with the result that a sponsored link (in the form of an advertisement linked to the advertiser's website) would appear. Google had no control over the advertiser's choice of search terms. The sponsored links were found to be misleading or deceptive. The issue was whether Google had done more than merely pass on the sponsored links.

Decision

Per French CJ, Crennan and Kiefel JJ at 459:

> The ACCC contended that Google, rather than the advertisers, 'produced' (in the sense of making or creating) the sponsored links which are the subject of this appeal. That submission must be rejected. It is critical to appreciate that, even with the facility of keyword insertion, the advertiser is the author of the sponsored link.
>
> [...]
>
> Google does not create, in any authorial sense, the sponsored links that it publishes or displays.
>
> ... The technology which lies behind the display of a sponsored link merely assembles information provided by others for the purpose of displaying advertisements directed to users of the Google search engine in their capacity as consumers of products and services. In this sense, Google is not relevantly different from other intermediaries, such as newspaper publishers (whether in print or online) or broadcasters (whether radio, television or online), who publish, display or broadcast the advertisements of others. The fact that the provision of information via the internet will — because of the nature of the internet — necessarily involve a response to a request made by an internet user does not, without more, disturb the analogy between Google and other intermediaries. To the extent that it displays sponsored links, the Google search engine is only a means of communication between advertisers and consumers.
>
> The primary judge's findings about the way in which ordinary and reasonable users of the Google search engine would understand the sponsored links were not disturbed in the Full Court. These findings — [460] that ordinary and reasonable users would have understood the sponsored links to be statements made by advertisers which Google had not endorsed, and was merely passing on for what they were worth — were plainly correct.
>
> [...]
>
> Ordinary and reasonable users of the Google search engine would have understood that the sponsored links were created by advertisers. Such users would also have understood that representations made by the sponsored links were those of the advertisers, and were not adopted or endorsed by Google.

18.4.9 Damages

Tortious damages are commonly regarded the best analogy for damages for misleading or deceptive conduct; although, in appropriate cases, the court might assess loss other than in accordance with the tortious measure. The loss of a commercial opportunity might be compensable.

Gates v City Mutual Life Assurance Society Ltd (1986) 160 CLR 1

Facts and issues

The applicant had applied for a total disability insurance on the basis of assurances given by the company's agent concerning the policy benefits. When the benefits were denied, the applicant claimed damages for misleading or deceptive conduct. The question concerned the basis of the assessment of damages.

Decision

Per Mason, Wilson and Dawson JJ at 11:

> Two established measures of damages, those applicable in contract and tort respectively, compete for acceptance. In contract, damages are awarded with the object of placing the plaintiff in the position in which he would have been had the contract been performed — he is entitled to damages for loss of bargain (expectation loss) and damage suffered, including expenditure incurred, in reliance on the contract (reliance loss). In tort, on the other hand, damages are awarded with the object of placing the plaintiff in the position in which he would have been had the tort not been committed (similar to reliance loss).
>
> [. . .]
>
> [12] As his Honour then pointed out, it is a question of determining how much worse off the plaintiff is as a result of entering into the transaction which the representation induced him to enter than he would have been had the transaction not taken place. This entitles the plaintiff to all the consequential loss directly flowing from his reliance on the representation [this being the measure of loss that the court considered appropriate ultimately, not the measure in contract (expectation loss)].

Murphy v Overton Investments Pty Ltd (2004) 216 CLR 388

Facts and issues

The applicants had bought leasehold interests in a retirement village operated by the respondent on the basis inter alia of estimates of outgoings. The estimate was found to be misleading and understated the outgoings, which the respondent then sought to charge. The applicants sought relief. There was no evidence of any difference between the price they paid and the value of the property and no evidence that they were not receiving value for the fees they were paying and thus no reliance loss. The question was whether they could now recover damages for misleading or deceptive conduct. In allowing the appeal, the following is the pivotal part of the High Court's reasoning:

Decision

Per Gleeson CJ, McHugh, Gummow, Kirby, Hayne, Callinan and Heydon JJ at 413:

> The appellants had been induced by the respondent's conduct to undertake an obligation which may, but need not, have been more onerous than the respondent's representation led them to believe. When the respondent started to charge all the outgoings it was entitled to charge, the appellants suffered a loss. The amount of that loss was not to be determined, as the majority of the Full Court held, only by comparing the financial position of the appellants according to whether they entered this lease or took some other accommodation. The appellants did not contend that they had suffered loss in that way. The appellants suffered loss because the continuing financial obligations they undertook when they took the lease proved to be larger than they had been led to believe. The question then became: how much larger was that burden?
>
> [. . .]
>
> [415] The reasoning employed by the Full Court in reaching the conclusion that the appellants proved no loss or damage was erroneous. The appellants did establish that they had undertaken an [416] obligation which, in the events that happened, proved to be larger than the respondent's misleading conduct led them to believe.

Sellars v Adelaide Petroleum NL (1994) 179 CLR 332

Facts and issues

It was alleged that, as a result of acting upon misleading representations, loss and damage were suffered in that, but for the representations, the representee would have entered into an alternative contract ('the Pagini Agreement') but having now lost the benefit of that agreement, they suffered compensable loss and damage for misleading or deceptive conduct.

Decision

Per Mason CJ, Dawson, Toohey and Gaudron JJ at 348:

> In the context of contraventions of s. 52(1) in the form of misleading conduct constituted by misrepresentations, acts done by the representee in reliance upon the misrepresentations amount to a sufficient connexion to satisfy the concept of causation. And, if those acts result in economic or financial loss, it will ordinarily be recoverable under s. 82(1). So, in a case such as the present, the applicant is entitled to recover 'a sum representing the prejudice or disadvantage [the applicant] has suffered in consequence of his altering his position under the inducement.'
>
> [...]
>
> [356] The prejudice or disadvantage which the respondents suffered in the present case was the loss of the opportunity or chance of securing commercial benefits which entry into the Pagini agreement and completion of it would have brought. The lost opportunity or chance, assuming it to have value, is a form of economic loss. The question, therefore, is: how is the value of that lost opportunity or chance to be measured?
>
> [...]
>
> On the findings made by the trial judge, the Pagini contract would have been entered into but for the contraventions of s. 52(1). Although, on the probabilities, it would not have been completed, there was a significant chance that it would be completed. It follows that the Full Court of the Federal Court were not in error in dismissing the appeals.

18.4.10 Causation and contribution

The question of *causation* invokes the simplistic sounding proposition that damage must have been caused 'by' the conduct, although the misleading or deceptive conduct need not be the sole cause of loss.

Wardley Australia Ltd v Western Australia (1992) 175 CLR 514

Facts and issues

As a result of misleading or deceptive conduct, the State of Western Australia granted an indemnity under which it was obliged to make a payment when the loss of the party to be indemnified was ascertained and quantified. The material question was when the indemnifier suffered loss for the purposes of damages for misleading or deceptive conduct.

Decision

Per Mason CJ, Dawson, Gaudron and McHugh JJ at 525:

> As loss or damage is the gist of the statutory cause of action for which s 82(1) provides, the cause of action does not accrue until actual loss or damage is sustained. The statutory cause of action arises when the plaintiff suffers loss or damage 'by' contravening conduct of another person. 'By' is a curious word to use. One might have expected 'by means of', 'by reason of', 'in consequence of' or 'as a result of'. But the word clearly expresses the notion of causation without defining or elucidating it. In this situation, s 82(1) should be understood as taking up the common law practical or common-sense concept of causation . . .
>
> [. . .]
>
> [532] If, contrary to the view which we have just expressed, the English decisions properly understood support the proposition that where, as a result of the defendant's negligent misrepresentation, the plaintiff enters into a contract which exposes him or her to a contingent loss or liability, the plaintiff first suffers loss or damage on entry into the contract, we do not agree with them. In our opinion, in such a case, the plaintiff sustains no actual damage until the contingency is fulfilled and the loss becomes actual; until that happens the loss is prospective and may never be incurred.

Marks v GIO Australia Holdings Pty Ltd (1998) 196 CLR 494

Facts and issues

Borrowers had entered into various loan agreements with GIO. GIO had represented to borrowers that interest was to be charged at a certain rate but the contracts proved otherwise. The question as far as the issue of causation was concerned was whether the misleading or deceptive conduct had to be the exclusive cause of loss for relief.

Decision

Per McHugh, Hayne and Callinan JJ at 512:

> It follows, then, that a comparison must be made between the position in which the party that allegedly has suffered loss or damage is and the position in which that party would have been but for the contravening conduct. And even this inquiry may not conclude the question. Analysing the question of causation only by reference to what is, in essence, a 'but for' test has been found wanting in other contexts and it may well be that it is not an exclusive test of [513] causation in this area either. But that is not a question which we need to consider in this case. For the moment it is enough to say that s 82 requires identification of a causal link between loss or damage and conduct done in contravention of the Act.

18.4.11 Exclusion of liability

Generally, loss for misleading or deceptive conduct cannot be excluded.

Bowler v Hilda Pty Ltd (1998) 80 FCR 191

Facts and issues

A clause of the relevant contract stipulated that the carrying out of the refurbishment and renovation was '. . . subject to the Seller's obtaining all necessary approvals under the Planning Acts'. The first respondent argued that the clause was effective to exclude liability for the misleading or deceptive conduct of its agent 'Leader' inasmuch as the appellants must be taken to have understood that there was always a possibility that the appropriate and necessary approvals would not be obtained.

Decision

Per Heerey J at 207:

> The Leader argument however runs counter to what is now a substantial body of authority in this Court which holds that exclusionary and disclaimer clauses cannot override the statutory prohibition against misleading and deceptive conduct or prevent the grant of appropriate statutory relief where loss or damage is, as a matter of fact, caused by contravention of the statute: see the review by Burchett J in *Lezam Pty Ltd v Seabridge Australia Pty Ltd* (1992) 35 FCR 535 at 556–558.

Butcher v Lachlan Elder Realty Pty Ltd (2004) 218 CLR 592

Facts and issues

The primary facts are set out above. Relevant to the present discussion, the brochure contained a disclaimer in the following terms: 'all information contained herein is gathered from sources we believe to be reliable. However we cannot guarantee its accuracy and interested persons should rely on their own enquiries'. The relevant question concerned the effect of the disclaimer on liability for misleading or deceptive conduct.

Decision

Per Gleeson CJ, Hayne and Heydon JJ at 608:

> The Court of Appeal declined to 'accord [the disclaimers] decisive significance' but they do have some significance . . .
>
> [. . .]
>
> [609] Hence, in the circumstances, the brochure, read as a whole, simply meant:
>
>> The diagram records what a particular surveyor found on a survey in 1980. We are not surveyors. We did not do the survey. We did not engage any surveyor to do the survey. We believe the vendor and the surveyor are reliable, but we cannot guarantee the accuracy of the information they have provided. Whatever you rely on, you must rely on your own enquiries.
>
> Hence it would have been plain to a reasonable purchaser that the agent was not the source of the information which was said to be misleading.

QUESTIONS

(1) A requirement to attract the prohibition of misleading or deceptive conduct is that the conduct in question has to be 'in trade or commerce'. Explain, by reference to the authorities, what this means.

(2) In relation to the state of mind of the perpetrator, identify the primary differences between the common law of misrepresentation and the statutory cause of action for misleading or deceptive conduct.

(3) Comment on the way in which s 4 of the Australian Consumer Law affects the burden of proving a representation about any future matter. Include in your discussion the position under misrepresentation at common law.

18.5 Mistake

Concept	Short explanation	Relevant authorities	*Principles* text*
Mutual mistake	Each party believes they are contracting about something else	*Raffles v Wichelhaus* (1864) 2 H & C 906 (discussion only)	Chapter 18: 18.37
Unilateral mistake as to the terms of a contract	When one party makes a serious mistake about the contents of a contract and the other takes advantage of the mistake, the contract can be set aside	*Taylor v Johnson* (1983) 151 CLR 422 (discussion only)	Chapter 18: 18.39
Unilateral mistakes of identity	Where one party contracts with another believing them to be someone else	*Lewis v Averay* [1972] 1 QB 198 *Papas v Bianca Investments Pty Ltd* (2002) 82 SASR 581	Chapter 18: 18.40
Common mistake	When both parties make the same mistake	*McRae v Commonwealth Disposals Commission* (1951) 84 CLR 377 *Australia Estates Pty Ltd v Cairns City Council* [2005] QCA 328	Chapter 18: 18.41
Non est factum	A rare defence where a party to a written contract asserts that 'it is not my deed'	*Petelin v Cullen* (1975) 132 CLR 355 *Saunders v Anglia Building Society* [1971] AC 1004	Chapter 18: 18.42

* Consult the corresponding section(s) of the *Principles* text for more detail.

Mistake is another concept at common law by which a contract is vitiated.

18.5.1 Mutual mistake

The concept of *mutual mistake,* which arises when each party believes they are contracting about something else and can render the contract void, is a highly unusual situation[6] and, frankly, one which is unlikely to be encountered in practice. The classic case on mutual mistake is the 19th century case *Raffles v Wichelhaus* (1864) 2 H & C 906.

18.5.2 Unilateral mistake

A unilateral mistake as to the terms of a contract arises where one party makes a serious mistake about the contents of a contract and the other takes advantage of the mistake. In such a situation, the contract can be set aside. The leading Australian case on this point is *Taylor v Johnson.*[7]

Unilateral mistakes of identity are the type of mistake where one party contracts with another believing them to be someone else. There are fairly fine distinctions between the 'face-to-face' cases, explored at 18.40 of the *Principles* text. In face-to-face cases, the presumption is that the innocent contracting party intends to contract with the other and the contract is voidable but not void.

Lewis v Averay [1972] 1 QB 198

Facts and issues

Lewis wished to sell his car and showed it to a person claiming to be a well-known actor Richard Greene, but was a rogue. Lewis asked for proof that he was Richard Greene, whereupon the rogue produced an official Pinewood Studios pass with the name on it. Lewis was satisfied and handed over the logbooks and the car. The rogue's cheque bounced. In the meanwhile, the rogue had sold the car to Averay, an innocent purchaser. The question was whether Lewis could recover the car, and this depended on whether the contract between Lewis and the rogue was void.

Decision

Per Lord Denning MR at 207:

> As I listened to the argument in this case, I felt it wrong that an innocent purchaser (who knew nothing of what passed between the seller and the rogue) should have his title depend on such refinements. After all, he has acted with complete circumspection and in entire good faith: whereas it was the seller who let the rogue have the goods and thus enabled him to commit the fraud. I do not, therefore, accept the theory that a mistake as to identity renders a contract void. I think the true principle is that which underlies the decision of this court in *King's Norton Metal Co. Ltd. v. Edridge Merrett & Co. Ltd*. and of Horridge J. in *Phillips v. Brooks*, which has stood for these last 50 years. It is this: When two parties have come to a contract — or rather what appears, on the face of it, to be a contract — the fact that one party is mistaken as to the identity of the other does not mean that there is no contract, or that the contract is a nullity and

6 See *Principles* text at 18.37.
7 (1983) 151 CLR 422—see *Principles* text at 5.02.

void from the beginning. It only means that the contract is voidable, that is, liable to be set aside at the instance of the mistaken person, so long as he does so before third parties have in good faith acquired rights under it.

[...]

When a dealing is had between a seller like Mr. Lewis and a person who is actually there present before him, then the presumption in law is that there is a contract, even though there is a fraudulent impersonation by the buyer representing himself as a different man than he is. There is a contract made with the very person there, who is present in person. It is liable no doubt to be avoided for fraud, but it is still a good contract under which title will pass unless and until it is avoided.

Papas v Bianca Investments Pty Ltd (2002) 82 SASR 581

Facts and issues

The plaintiff's husband traded in used cars. The car was inspected by two men who agreed to purchase the car. One of the men identified himself as a Mr Cherrington, and produced a temporary driver's licence (without a photograph). The man paid for the car with a bank cheque which subsequently was discovered had been tampered with and was dishonoured. The man who identified himself as Mr Cherrington (a false identity) approached a second-hand dealer for a loan and offered as security the car obtained from the plaintiff. He again produced the temporary licence, but this was not sufficient for the second-hand dealer. The man returned with a statutory declaration and the registration papers to the car. Following completion of registration checks to ensure the car was not stolen, the second-hand dealer loaned the man $5,500 with the car as security. The plaintiff claimed that good title to the car had not passed and the defendant had acquired no interest in the car.

Decision

Per Doyle CJ at 583:

... it suffices to refer only to the decision in *Lewis* [*v Averay*]. The facts are similar ...

[...]

[584] Lord Denning rejected the view that a mistake as to identity always meant that a contract was void. ...

[...]

He [Lord Denning] stated the relevant principle as follows (at 207):

> When two parties have come to a contract — or rather what appears, on the face of it, to be a contract — the fact that one party is mistaken as to the identity of the other does not mean that there is no contract, or that the contract is a nullity and void from the beginning. It only means that the contract is voidable, that is, liable to be set aside at the instance of the mistaken person, so long as he does so before third parties have in good faith acquired rights under it.

[...]

To the extent that there is a difference between these approaches, I prefer that of Lord Denning. However, that is not to say that the relevant principle is as unqualified as his statement would suggest.

In the present case the identity of the purchaser was immaterial to Mr Papas and to his son. They were willing to sell the motor car to any person who provided cash or a good bank cheque. The inquiry as to the identity of the purchaser was probably made with a view to keeping an appropriate record of the transaction, with a view to complying with requirements of the Registrar of Motor Vehicles, and as some kind of protection against fraud. But there is no reason to think that it mattered to the plaintiff who the purchaser was. All that mattered was that the plaintiff would receive cash or, what the plaintiff thought was equally good, a bank cheque. In the present case there was the appearance of a contract. The purchaser misrepresented his identity and knowingly tendered a bad cheque. The plaintiff was certainly entitled to rescind the contract on the basis of these misrepresentations, and possibly on the basis of the former alone. But, in my opinion, there is no reason to treat the plaintiff's mistake as to the identity and creditworthiness of the purchaser as preventing any contract at all coming into existence. This was not a case in which the plaintiff was willing to sell only to Mr Cherrington.

18.5.3 Common mistake

A *common mistake*, on the other hand, occurs when both parties make the same mistake. There are great difficulties in avoiding a contract on the grounds of common mistake. A stringent position has been adopted in Australia, rejecting the more flexible approach to common mistake in equity. It is suggested that unconscionable behaviour is required to set aside a contract for common mistake.

McRae v Commonwealth Disposals Commission (1951) 84 CLR 377

Facts and issues

The defendant, the Commonwealth Disposals Commission, advertised for tenders to purchase a submerged oil tanker. The plaintiff's tender was accepted. After incurring expense in fitting out a salvage operation, it was discovered that the tanker was non-existent. The defendant argued there was a common mistake, as a result of which the contract was void and the defendant would not be liable for damages.

Decision

Per Dixon and Fullagar JJ at 409:

> The buyers relied upon, and acted upon, the assertion of the seller that there was a tanker in existence. It is not a case in which the parties can be seen to have proceeded on the basis of a common assumption of fact so as to justify the conclusion that the correctness of the assumption was intended by both parties to be a condition precedent to the creation of contractual obligations. The officers of the Commission made an assumption, but the plaintiffs did not make an assumption in the same sense.
>
> [. . .]
>
> [410] If, on the other hand, the case of Couturier v. Hastie and this case ought to be treated as cases raising a question of 'mistake', then the Commission cannot in this case rely on any mistake as avoiding the contract, because any mistake was induced by the serious fault of their

> own servants, who asserted the existence of a tanker recklessly and without any reasonable ground. There *was* a contract, and the Commission contracted that a tanker existed in the position specified. Since there was no such tanker, there has been a breach of contract, and the plaintiffs are entitled to damages for that breach.

Australia Estates Pty Ltd v Cairns City Council [2005] QCA 328

Facts and issues

A contract between the parties was subject to development approval. The central question concerned the effect of the parties' common mistake as to whether the development approval had been obtained. The case is significant for the position taken on whether there exists in Australia a doctrine of common mistake in equity.

Decision

Per Atkinson J at [48]:

> In *Great Peace Shipping Ltd v Tsavliris Salvage (International) Ltd*, the Court of Appeal, in a judgment of conspicuous clarity, examined the common law of mistake and the equitable doctrine of rescission for mistake. The court held that the following elements must be present if common mistake is to avoid a contract at common law:
>
> (i) there must be a common assumption as to the existence of a state of affairs;
> (ii) there must be no warranty by either party that that state of affairs exists;
> (iii) the non-existence of the state of affairs must not be attributable to the fault of either party;
> (iv) the non-existence of the state of affairs must render performance of the contract impossible;
> (v) the state of affairs may be the existence, or a vital attribute, of the consideration to be provided or circumstances which must subsist if performance of the contractual adventure is to be possible.
>
> [. . .]
>
> [64] In my view, the correct question to be posed on this appeal is whether the agreement is void at common law for common mistake. The test that should be applied is that found in the five elements set out in *Great Peace Shipping v Tsavliris*. It is abundantly clear in applying those elements to this case that the common law of mistake could not be used to declare the agreement void. For the reasons discussed below, there was no mistake. Even if there had been, the mistake (or non-existence of a state of affairs) alleged by the appellant did not render the performance of the agreement impossible. There is no equitable jurisdiction to set aside, on the ground of common mistake, an agreement, which is valid and enforceable at common law.
>
> [65] If, contrary to my view, the test to be posed is that found in *Taylor v Johnson*, the appellant must show that when it entered into the agreement to vary the completion date of the contract, the Council was aware that circumstances existed which showed that Australia Estates entered into that agreement under a serious mistake or misapprehension about the content or subject matter of a fundamental term and that the Council deliberately set out to ensure that Australia Estates did not become aware of the existence of its mistake or misapprehension.

18.5.4 Non est factum

Non est factum literally means 'it is not my deed' and is a rare defence—one particular difficulty being that the document executed had to be *radically* different to that thought to have been signed.

Petelin v Cullen (1975) 132 CLR 355

Facts and issues

Petelin, who could speak only a little English and could not read at all, signed an extension of an option to purchase land, thinking it was a receipt. The question is whether he could rely on the defence of non est factum to resist the exercise of the option.

Decision

Per Barwick CJ, McTiernan, Gibbs, Stephen and Mason JJ at 359:

> The class of persons who can avail themselves of the defence is limited. It is available to those who are unable to read owing to blindness or illiteracy and who must rely on others for advice as to what they are signing; it is also available to those who through no fault of their own are unable to have any understanding of the [360] purport of a particular document. To make out the defence a defendant must show that he signed the document in the belief that it was radically different from what it was in fact and that, at least as against innocent persons, his failure to read and understand it was not due to carelessness on his part. Finally, it is accepted that there is a heavy onus on a defendant who seeks to establish the defence. All this is made clear by the recent decision of the House of Lords in *Saunders v Anglia Building Society (Gallie v Lee)*.

Saunders v Anglia Building Society [1971] AC 1004

Facts and issues

Mrs Gallie was 78-years old and very shortsighted and was the proprietor of a house. She wanted to transfer her house to her nephew so he could raise money on it, but on condition she remain in occupation until her death. Her nephew and a friend presented her with a document to sign, represented to be a document that assigned the house as a gift but was in fact a transfer to Lee. Mrs Gallie did not have her glasses and could not see. Lee mortgaged it to a building society. The question was whether the transfer to Lee was void by reason of non est factum.

Decision

Per Lord Hodson at 1018:

> I agree ... that the identity of the transferee (namely Lee instead of Parkin) does not make the deed of a totally different character from that which she intended to sign. On this ground the plea of non est factum must fail.

[. . .]

[1019] Donovan L.J. said, delivering the judgment of the Court of Appeal in *Muskham Finance Ltd. v. Howard* [1963] 1 Q.B. 904, 912: 'The plea of non est factum is a plea which must necessarily be kept within narrow limits.' To take an example, the man who in the course of his business signs a pile of documents without checking them takes the responsibility for them by appending his signature. It would be surprising if he was allowed to repudiate one of those documents on eke ground of non est factum.

I agree with the robust conclusion reached by the Master of the Rolls on the facts of this case that the appellant having signed the questioned document, obviously a legal document, upon which the building society advanced money on the faith of its being her document, cannot now be allowed to disavow her signature.

QUESTIONS

(1) Would you regard the doctrine of common mistake as being of wide application in Australia?

(2) Comment briefly on the scope of the likely application of the remedy of non est factum.

(3) What principles govern relief for the consequences of a unilateral mistake as to the terms of a contract in Australia?

18.6 Rectification

Concept	Short explanation	Relevant authorities	*Principles* text*
Rectification for common mistake	The parties must have a common intention as to what the document would express	*Simic v New South Wales Land and Housing Corporation* (2016) 260 CLR 85	Chapter 18: 18.43
Rectification of unilateral mistakes	Where only one party is mistaken	*Leibler v Air New Zealand Ltd (No 2)* [1999] 1 VR 1	Chapter 18: 18.44

* Consult the corresponding section(s) of the *Principles* text for more detail.

The idea of rectification is to make a written document conform to the true agreement of the parties where it does not do so. There are two fundamental areas for consideration:

(1) Rectification for common mistake where the parties must have a common intention as to what the document would express but the document does not do so. The relevant test is to ascertain what was in truth the common intention of the parties.

(2) Rectification of unilateral mistakes refers to a situation where only one party is mistaken, and may be ordered where it would be unconscionable for the non-mistaken party to enforce the unrectified contract.

Simic v New South Wales Land and Housing Corporation (2016) 260 CLR 85

Facts and issues

[The headnote, which is succinct, is substantially reproduced here]: A statutory corporation entered into a construction contract with a builder. A term of the contract required the builder to provide the corporation with instruments issued by a bank in the form of an unconditional promise to pay the corporation, as security for the purpose of ensuring the due and proper performance of the contract. The builder obtained two such instruments from a bank and provided them to the corporation. Both the builder and the bank had misstated the corporation's name and other information such that the amount in each instrument was expressed to be payable in favour of a named 'Principal' that did not exist. The corporation made a demand for payment under each instrument. The bank refused to pay on the basis that the corporation was not the Principal named as payee in each instrument.

Decision

Per Gageler, Nettle and Gordon JJ at 117:

> Rectification is an equitable remedy, the purpose of which is to make a written instrument 'conform to the true agreement of the parties where the writing by common mistake fails to express that agreement accurately'. For relief by rectification, it must be demonstrated that, at the time of the execution of the written instrument sought to be rectified, there was an 'agreement' between the parties in the sense that the parties had a 'common intention', and that the written instrument was to conform to that agreement. Critically, it must also be demonstrated that the written instrument does not reflect the 'agreement' because of a common mistake. Unless those elements are established, the 'hypothesis arising from execution of the written instrument, namely, that it is the true agreement of the parties' cannot be displaced.
>
> The issue may be approached by asking — what was the actual or true common intention of the parties? There is no requirement for communication of that common intention by express statement , but it must at least be the parties' actual intentions, viewed objectively from their words or actions, and must be correspondingly held by each party.

Leibler v Air New Zealand Ltd (No 2) [1999] 1 VR 1

Facts and issues

The purchasers' solicitors under a sale agreement mistakenly notified the vendors' solicitors to delete a clause, which the vendors' solicitors did knowing that a mistake had been made. The sale agreement was executed, with the vendors knowing that the purchasers were labouring under the misapprehension that the clause had been amended as agreed. The question was whether rectification of the sale agreement should be ordered by reinstating the clause.

Decision

Per Kenny J at 14:

> The principles which govern an application for rectification of a contract on the ground of unilateral mistake can be briefly stated. If (1) one party, A, makes an agreement under a misapprehension that the agreement contains a particular provision which the agreement does not in fact contain; and (2) the other party, B, knows of the omission and that it is due to a mistake on A's part; and (3) lets A remain under the misapprehension and concludes the agreement on the mistaken basis in circumstances where equity would require B to take some step or steps, depending on those circumstances, to bring the mistake to A's attention; then (4) B will be precluded from relying upon A's execution of the agreement to resist A's claim for rectification to give effect to A's intention.
>
> [...]
>
> Whether or not the mistake must be one which operates in favour of B or merely to the detriment of A is not entirely clear: cf. *Maralinga Pty. Ltd. v Major Enterprises Pty. Ltd.* at 351 and *Thomas Bates & Son Ltd. v Wyndham's (Lingerie) Ltd.* at 1086 per Buckley L.J., 1090 per Eveleigh L.J. (Brightman L.J. agreeing). Accordingly, the respondents' claim for rectification required them to prove that on 12 December 1985 when the shareholders' agreement was executed:
>
> (1) they were under a misapprehension that the shareholders' agreement included a form of cl. 10.9 as it stood on 28 October 1985, modified so as to take account of the matters agreed upon by Isi Leibler and Geary on that date;
> (2) Isi Leibler and N.A.P.L. knew that the respondents were acting under that misapprehension in executing the shareholders' agreement; and
> (3) the appellants let the respondents remain under the misapprehension and concluded the shareholders' agreement on the mistaken basis in circumstances in which equity required the appellants to take some step (which they did not take) to bring the mistake to the respondents' attention.

QUESTIONS

(1) It was held in *Simic* that the intention of the parties is a reference to the parties' *actual* intentions. How is this to be ascertained?

(2) The various criteria for rectification set out in *Leibler v Air New Zealand* above are reminiscent of the treatment of rescission for unilateral mistake in *Taylor v Johnson*. What are the similarities?

18.7 International perspectives

18.7.1 *CISG*

The *CISG*, where applicable to international commercial sales (see **25.4.1**), does not provide remedies for situations where a contract has never been formed. Moreover, it does not overtly provide remedies for situations involving common or unilateral mistake per se. Domestic remedies for torts of deceit (fraud) and mistake continue to apply. This may be the Australian law as described above, if the conflict of laws rules deem Australian law applicable. However, other than for fraud, if the mistake or tort relates to the quality of the goods or contractual obligations, the *CISG* may exclusively govern the situation, since it deals with obligations concerning quality of goods or formation and interpretation of contractual terms. Also of relevance is a general principle of the *CISG*, *venire contra factum proprium* (see **25.5.3**), which precludes inconsistent conduct by parties, especially where the mistaken party has relied upon their earlier conduct. Note that the ACL prohibition on misleading conduct in s 18 may apply to *CISG* situations.

18.7.2 UNIDROIT Principles

Unlike the *CISG*, the UNIDROIT Principles (where applicable **25.4.3**) contain rules relating to mistake, and provide remedies of avoidance. Thus a party affected by mistake may avoid the contract in certain circumstances: arts 3.2.1–3.2.2 UNIDROIT Principles. The prohibition on misleading conduct under ACL s 18 may still apply.

UNIDROIT Principles arts 3.2.1–3.2.2

Art 3.2.1 (Definition of mistake)
Mistake is an erroneous assumption relating to facts or to law existing when the contract was concluded.

Art 3.2.2 (Relevant mistake)

(1) A party may only avoid the contract for mistake if, when the contract was concluded, the mistake was of such importance that a reasonable person in the same situation as the party in error would only have concluded the contract on materially different terms or would not have concluded it at all if the true state of affairs had been known, and
- **(a)** the other party made the same mistake, or caused the mistake, or knew or ought to have known of the mistake and it was contrary to reasonable commercial standards of fair dealing to leave the mistaken party in error; or
- **(b)** the other party had not at the time of avoidance reasonably acted in reliance on the contract.

(2) However, a party may not avoid the contract if
- **(a)** it was grossly negligent in committing the mistake; or
- **(b)** the mistake relates to a matter in regard to which the risk of mistake was assumed or, having regard to the circumstances, should be borne by the mistaken party.

18.8 Review

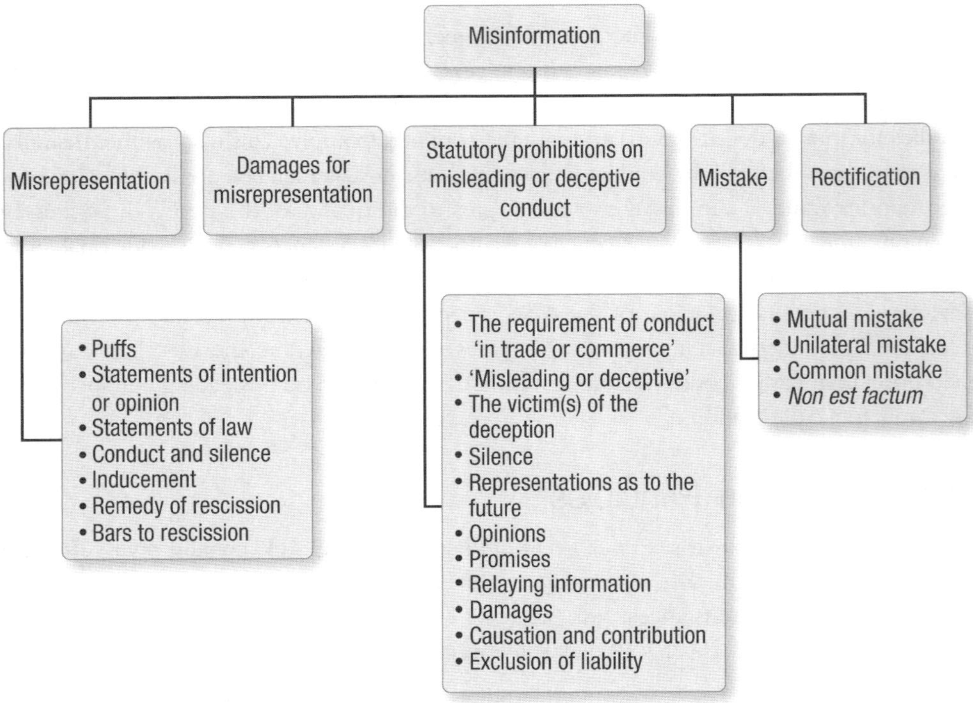

TIPS FOR APPLYING THE LAW IN PRACTICE

- A temptation exists, because of the relative simplicity of the statement of the doctrine, to conclude too readily that a particular situation attracts the operation of non est factum. In truth, non est factum is of narrow application, confined, for practical purposes, to situations in which the person seeking relief has some particularly acute disability such as blindness or illiteracy.[8] Additionally, the nature of the document thought to have been executed must be of a 'totally different' character from that thought to have been signed.[9] The stringency of the latter point is well illustrated by the fact that the difference in identity of the transferee did not make the deed of a totally different character from that intended to be signed.
- Caution should also be exercised in analysing common mistake. It is arguable that the appropriate approach is that at common law, with no room for the more flexible equitable doctrine. Whilst, due to the lack of uniformity of approach in *Australia Estates v Cairns City Council*[10] it cannot be confidently said that the common law approach is to be applied to the absolute exclusion of the equitable approach, the balance of opinion, reflected on that bench, suggests that this is the case. The stringency of the common law approach leaves limited room for the operation of the doctrine.

8 *Petelin v Cullen* (1975) 132 CLR 355.
9 *Saunders v Anglia Building Society* [1971] AC 1004.
10 Page 361 *Principles* text refers to the division of opinion.

- Whilst misrepresentation remains a significant area of doctrinal study, provided the requirement of the conduct's being 'in trade and commerce' is satisfied, the statutory cause of action for misleading or deceptive conduct is far simpler to establish than common law misrepresentation. Focus should therefore be on the statutory cause of action once those prerequisites are satisfied.
- In trying to provide advice whether to pursue a cause of action based on tort, breach of contract, or both, it is prudent to weigh up the likelihood of success, and the cost and expense of each against the measure of damages. For breach of contract, in a typical case of a simple breach, such as for the failure to deliver goods of a particular description, the measure of damages is to put the injured party in the position he would be in had the contract not been breached. This follows from a basic application of the principles in *Robinson v Harman* (1848) 154 ER 363, discussed at **23.2**. In such cases, the measure of damages is likely to be far greater if based on breach of contract rather than negligent misrepresentation but against that must be weighed the likely additional difficulty of establishing that the misrepresentation in question was a term of the contract rather than merely a misrepresentation.
- Do not mix and match concepts of tort and contract for the purposes of damages. In particular, you will be confused if you conflated the idea of damages for misrepresentation in contract and in tort. The relief for a misrepresentation in a contractual sense is damages for breach of contract but only if the misrepresentation became a term of the contract. For present purposes, it would serve your learning outcomes if you maintained a strict separation of the two concepts.

PROBLEM QUESTIONS

(1) This question is designed to test your broad understanding of common law misrepresentation and is somewhat lengthy for that reason:

Peter asks John, who conducts the business of the sale of car accessories, the following question in the course of his negotiations for the purchase of John's business: 'Can I import car accessories from Japan?'

John replies: 'No problem, there is nothing in the law that stops you. I reckon it can be done easily.'

The fact is, John himself has previously tried to import those components and was told that there was a (mythical) statute that renders the private import of such components prohibitively expensive.

Peter, acting on the faith of what John said, agrees to buy John's business.

Discuss whether Peter has a cause of action in misrepresentation against John.

(2) Assuming the same facts as in the above scenario, discuss Peter's prospects of succeeding in an action under the Australian Consumer Law for misleading or deceptive conduct on the part of John.

RESEARCH QUESTIONS

(1) In *MLC v Evatt*, the Privy Council considered that it was necessary that the representor had to have a 'special skill' in order for there to be liability in misrepresentation. In what way was the approach of our High Court in *L Shaddock & Associates v Council of Parramatta* at variance?

(2) In *McRae v Commonwealth Disposals Commission* despite the non-existence of the subject tanker, the Court did not consider that there was a common mistake that rendered the contract void. What was the rationalisation for that conclusion?

19

UNDUE PRESSURE

19.1 Overview

Undue pressure is found in various forms: common law duress; equitable undue influence; statutory duress; and equitable unconscionability (see **Chapter 20**). This chapter covers duress, statutory duress and undue influence, as well as international perspectives.

Duress involves a contract arising from illegitimate pressure being applied to a weaker party. Statutory duress comprises either undue harassment or coercion. Exertion of undue influence often involves an antecedent relationship of influence, from which a contract arises due to actual or presumed exercise of influence by a stronger party over a weaker party. In international contracts, voidability for improper conduct falls outside the scope of the *CISG*, but, where applicable, is dealt with in the UNIDROIT Principles.

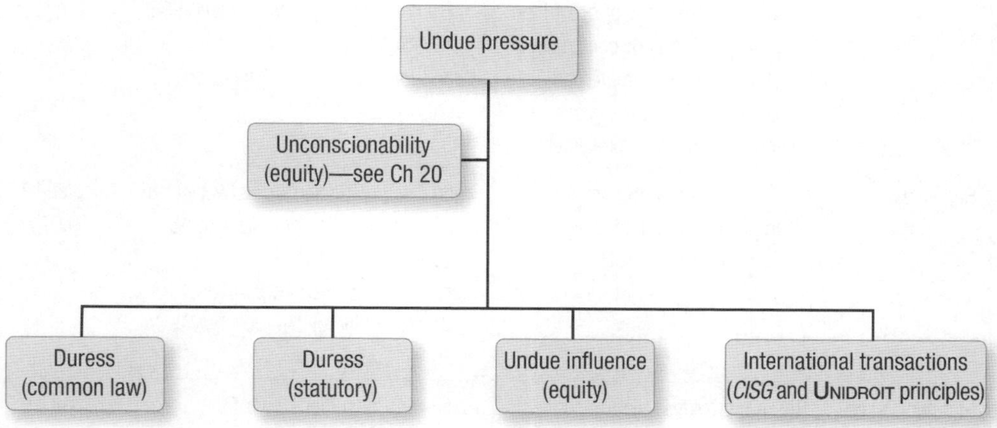

19.2 Duress

Factor	Short explanation	Relevant authorities	Principles text*
Types of duress	Causes of action in relation to duress to the person, or to goods, or economic duress	–	Chapter 19: 19.02
Rationale	Whilst the rationale was once the overbearing of the victim's will, this is no longer required. Instead, the fact that consent is affected by illegitimate pressure is now sufficient	*Occidental Worldwide Investment Corporation v Skibs A/S Avanti (The Siboen & The Sibotre)* [1976] 1 Lloyd's Rep 293 *Crescendo Management Pty Ltd v Westpac Banking Corporation* (1988) 19 NSWLR 40	Chapter 19: 19.03
Illegitimate pressure	Relevant factors include context, and the unlawfulness of an action or threatened action	*Electricity Generation Corporation v Woodside Energy Ltd* [2013] WASCA 36 *Beerens v Bluescope Distribution Pty Ltd* (2012) 39 VR 1	Chapter 19: 19.04

(cont.)

Factor	Short explanation	Relevant authorities	*Principles* text*
Scope of economic duress	Economic duress has an uncertain definition, and courts have shown reluctance to develop it, noting that it overlaps with undue influence, unconscionability and statutory duress	*Australia and New Zealand Banking Group v Karam* (2004) 64 NSWLR 149	Chapter 19: 19.05
Causation	Illegitimate pressure must be one of the reasons for entry into contract. The onus of proof then switches. Actual or constructive knowledge by a counterparty is required, where a third party applies illegitimate pressure	*Barton v Armstrong* [1976] AC 104 *Crescendo Management Pty Ltd v Westpac Banking Corporation* (1988) 19 NSWLR 40 *Dunwoodie v Teachers Mutual Bank Ltd* [2014] NSWCA 24	Chapter 19: 19.06
Remedies	Contracts concluded under duress are voidable, and can be rescinded by the victim	*North Ocean Shipping Co Ltd v Hyundai Construction Co Ltd ('The Atlantic Baron')* [1979] QB 705 *Electricity Generation Corporation v Woodside Energy Ltd* [2013] WASCA 36	Chapter 19: 19.07
Statutory Duress	The ACL provides relief for contracts brought about by 'physical force, or undue harassment or coercion'. Damages are available under the ACL	Australian Consumer Law s 50 *Australian Competition and Consumer Commission v McCaskey* (2000) 104 FCR 8	Chapter 19: 19.08

* Consult the corresponding section(s) of the *Principles* text for more detail.

Duress is a doctrine that protects parties who have entered into a contract while being subjected to illegitimate pressure. Contract law is founded upon the concept of voluntary consent. The voluntary quality of consent is negatively affected when a person (often referred to as the 'victim') is subject to illegitimate or unacceptable pressure. In older cases, it was said that the victim's free will was 'overborne' by the pressure: but see **19.2.2**. Where the victim's choice to contract under such circumstances has been affected, the contract may be voidable for duress. Establishment of duress requires proof of:

- illegitimate pressure—in relation to persons, goods or economic duress;
- causation—that the illegitimate pressure was one of the causes of the transaction.

19.2.1 Types of duress

The subject matter of duress has shifted over time. Duress at common law began with physical duress to the person. Since then, it has developed slowly to include duress to goods, and finally, economic duress. Although the claim for economic duress was not upheld on the facts, Kerr J in *The Siboen and the Sibotre* first recognised economic duress at common law: see **19.2.2**.

19.2.2 Rationale of duress at common law

The rationale of duress has also changed over time. While duress originally embraced the theory of overbearing the victim's will, in more recent cases, a more realistic view has been favoured. It is now acknowledged that, despite illegitimate pressure, the victim's consent to a contract is nonetheless real. The consent is affected, but not destroyed by the illegitimate pressure, and therefore contractual consent is revocable, rendering the contract voidable.

Occidental Worldwide Investment Corporation v Skibs A/S Avanti (The Siboen & The Sibotre) [1976] 1 Lloyd's Rep 293

Facts and issues

One year into a three-year charter hire agreement for two ships, the hirers requested a reduction in hire rates, stating that it would otherwise go into liquidation. This was completely untrue. The owner's representative agreed and signed an amendment to the contract reducing the hire rate, and then subsequently reduced it further, but later discovered the hirers were making substantial profits. The hirers refused to revert to the original hire rate, and the owner withdrew the vessels. The hirers claimed damages for wrongful termination. The owner claimed it was entitled to rescind the contract for duress.

Decision

The first case, to recognise economic duress as a cause of action, did so in obiter, for it was ultimately held that pressure to sign the addenda was merely commercial pressure which was insufficient to vitiate consent. However, the hirers were held liable for fraudulent and innocent misrepresentation.

Per Kerr J at 336:

> [T]he Court must in every case at least be satisfied that the consent of the other party was overborne by compulsion so as to deprive him of any animus contrahendi. This would depend on the facts of each case. One relevant factor would be whether the party relying on duress made any protest at the time or shortly thereafter... [In this case,] ... Captain Tschudi made no protest about having to conclude the addenda ... He was acting under great pressure, but only commercial pressure, and not under anything which would in law be regarded as coercion of his will so as to vitiate his consent. I therefore hold that the plea of duress fails.

Crescendo Management Pty Ltd v Westpac Banking Corporation (1988) 19 NSWLR 40

Facts and issues

Andrew Hilbrink was the director of the Upward Group of companies, which was indebted to Westpac and in financial difficulty. When the Hilbrinks sold their family home, Westpac received the proceeds of sale, and was authorised by the Hilbrinks to use the funds to discharge their home loan and personal overdraft, and to pay surplus into an account held by Mrs Hilbrink at another bank. However, Westpac refused to release the surplus until the Hilbrinks signed a mortgage securing the Upward Group's debts. They signed, and Westpac used the surplus to pay down debts owed by Upward Group to Westpac. Subsequently, the Hilbrinks claimed they only signed the mortgage due to Westpac's duress and undue influence.

Decision

Per McHugh JA at 45:

> ... The rationale of the doctrine of economic duress is that the law will not give effect to an apparent consent which was induced by pressure exercised upon one party by another party when the law regards that pressure as illegitimate: *Universe Tankships Inc of Monrovia v International Transport Workers Federation* [1983] 1 AC 366 at 384 per Lord Diplock. As his Lordship pointed out, the consequence is that the 'consent is treated in law as revocable unless approbated either expressly or by implication after the illegitimate pressure has ceased to operate on his mind' (at 384). In the same case Lord Scarman declared (at 400) that the authorities show that there are two elements in the realm of duress: (a) pressure amounting to compulsion of the will of the victim and (b) the illegitimacy of the pressure exerted. 'There must be pressure', said Lord Scarman 'the practical effect of which is compulsion or the absence of choice'.
>
> The reference in *Universe Tankships* ... and other cases to compulsion 'of the will' of the victim is unfortunate. They appear to have overlooked that in *Director of Public Prosecutions for Northern Ireland v Lynch* [1975] AC 653, a case concerned with duress as a defence to a criminal proceeding, the House of Lords rejected the notion that duress is concerned with overbearing the will of the accused. The Law Lords were unanimous in coming to the conclusion, perhaps best expressed (at 695) in the speech of Lord Simon of Glaisdale 'that duress is not inconsistent with act and will, the will being deflected, not destroyed'. Indeed, if the true basis of duress is that the will is overborne, a contract entered into under duress should be void. Yet the accepted doctrine is that the contract is merely voidable.
>
> In my opinion the overbearing of the will theory of duress should be rejected. A person who is the subject of duress usually knows only too well [46] what he is doing. But he chooses to submit to the demand or pressure rather than take an alternative course of action. The proper approach in my opinion is to ask whether any applied pressure induced the victim to enter into the contract and then ask whether that pressure went beyond what the law is prepared to countenance as legitimate? Pressure will be illegitimate if it consists of unlawful threats or amounts to unconscionable conduct. But the categories are not closed. Even overwhelming pressure, not amounting to unconscionable or unlawful conduct, however, will not necessarily constitute economic duress.

McHugh JA dismissed the appeal for absence of 'operative duress': see **19.2.5** below. Samuels and Mahoney JJA agreed that the appeal should be dismissed.

19.2.3 Illegitimate pressure

Not every type of pressure can support a conclusion of duress. Pressure must be illegitimate. Illegitimacy turns on factors which must be weighed to determine if pressure is improper or unacceptable. Relevant to the question of illegitimate pressure is any context which suggests opportunism, exploitation, or alternatively, proper and commercially prudent behaviour: *Beerens v Bluescope Distribution Pty Ltd* (2012) 39 VR 1. Predictably, unlawful acts or threats to take unlawful action are generally considered improper. Breaches of contract are unlawful and illegitimate.

However, the contrary is not necessarily true. Lawful acts, or threats to undertake lawful acts, are not necessarily proper or legitimate. Indeed, opportunism or extortion may render threats to take lawful steps improper. Moreover, good faith does not always preclude duress, as the case of *Woodside* (below) demonstrates.

Electricity Generation Corporation v Woodside Energy Ltd [2013] WASCA 36

Facts and issues

Electricity Generation (Verve) and Woodside ('the sellers') entered into a long-term Gas Sale Agreement ('GSA'). An explosion and fire at a major competitor plant ('the Apache incident') severely reduced gas supplies in Western Australia, and prices soared. Woodside refused to supply gas to Verve under the long-term GSA, and genuinely believed it was not in breach. Under protest, Verve entered a short-term GSA at a higher price. In addition to claiming breach of the GSA which raised issues of interpretation (discussed at **10.3.3**), it claimed the short-term GSA was void for duress, and sought repayment of the difference in price paid pursuant to it.

Decision

The Western Australian Court of Appeal found duress was established, and held Woodside had knowingly applied illegitimate pressure upon Verve. It found the actual or threatened breach of contract was unlawful, and constituted illegitimate pressure for the purposes of duress. Furthermore, for illegitimacy, bad faith by the breaching party was not required. An appeal by Verve to the High Court on interpretation of Clause 3.3 was dismissed.[1]

McLure P (Newnes JA agreeing) at [24]:

> There are two material facts of the cause of action in economic duress being (1) that illegitimate pressure was applied which (2) induced the victim to enter into the contract (or make a non-contractual payment); the illegitimate pressure does not have to be the sole reason for the victim entering into the contract, it is sufficient if it is one of the reasons: *Crescendo Management Pty Ltd v Westpac Banking Corporation* (1988) 19 NSWLR 40 at 46 (McHugh JA).
>
> [25] If the pressure involves an actual or threatened unlawful act, it is prima facie illegitimate. If the pressure is lawful, it may be illegitimate if there is no reasonable or justifiable connection between the pressure being applied and the demand which that pressure supports: *Universe Tankships Inc of Monrovia v International Transport Workers Federation* [1983] 1 AC 366 at 401 (Lord Scarman) . . .
>
> [26] An actual or threatened breach of contract is unlawful conduct for the purposes of the economic duress doctrine: *Furphy v Nixon* (1925) 37 CLR 161; *Smith v William Charlick Ltd* [1924] HCA 13; (1924) 34 CLR 38.

1 (2014) 251 CLR 640.

> [. . .]
>
> [28] There is no finding below that the Sellers acted for an improper purpose. The Sellers advised Verve that they would not supply [pursuant to the GSA]. The evidence does not support an inference that this was done for the purpose of compelling Verve to enter into the short term gas supply agreements. To the contrary, the evidence was that the Sellers were unable to satisfy all of the demand for gas in the relevant period. Moreover, . . . the Sellers acted in the genuine belief that they were not in breach . . . under the GSA.
>
> [29] . . . the Sellers knew that their refusal to supply [pursuant to the GSA] placed enormous pressure on Verve which left it with no option but to accept the Sellers' offer . . . The live question is whether the Sellers 'applied' pressure on Verve, not whether they made threats or demands (express or implied) . . . In my view they did. The known consequences of their conduct [were] . . . so dramatic that threats . . . were superfluous.
>
> [30] . . . the Sellers' genuine belief that they were not acting in breach of the GSA does not preclude a finding of economic duress. A knowing breach . . . is not a material fact on which the cause of action depends.
>
> [31] The Sellers' refusal to supply [pursuant to the GSA] . . . constituted the application of illegitimate pressure on Verve which was a cause of it entering into the short term gas supply agreements. Accordingly, the short term gas supply agreements are voidable . . .

Murphy JA also agreed duress was established. The appeal was allowed in part.

Beerens v Bluescope Distribution Pty Ltd (2012) 39 VR 1

Facts and issues

G&B agreed to buy steel under a credit arrangement with BlueScope, including Clause 6.6 which permitted BlueScope to withdraw credit if G&B was presumed insolvent. Later, liquidation proceedings were filed against G&B by one of its customers, Proline, allegedly for improper purposes. Pursuant to Clause 6.6, BlueScope withdrew credit, demanded cash on delivery for future orders, a personal guarantee and indemnity securing G&B's debts from its director, Mr Beerens, and threatened to support the winding-up application if these demands were not met. Mr Beerens executed the personal guarantee. G&B was wound up, but the liquidation proceedings were ultimately held to be an abuse of process. BlueScope sought to enforce its guarantee against Mr Beerens, who argued it was obtained under economic duress.

Decision

The Victorian Court of Appeal held threats to commence proceedings, including bankruptcy and liquidation proceedings, would not generally constitute improper pressure, unless groundless or motivated by improper purpose. Moreover, not every improper pressure can vitiate the contract; a contract might be agreed merely to avoid a dispute; whereas for duress, the pressure must have an overbearing effect on the debtor's mind. It found BlueScope's actions were not improper, and thus the guarantee and indemnity were not voidable for duress.

Nettle JA (with Redlich JA agreeing) at 7:

> Mr Persaud . . . told Mr Beerens that, if he wanted to get off [cash on delivery] terms, he would have to sign a guarantee and that, if he did not sign it, BlueScope would 'get on the back of the

winding up proceeding'. Mr Beerens' evidence was that he was horrified that he was being threatened with a winding-up application ...

[9] ... Mr Beerens ... clarified that ... he was concerned that, if the company were wound up, the moneys which his family had lent to the company would be lost; and, hence, he felt compelled to sign. ...

[10] ... BlueScope was entitled to demand payment of all amounts outstanding, and to refuse to supply on credit, unless and until a guarantee was provided; and there was nothing improper about BlueScope demanding that on this occasion.

Generally speaking, it is not improper pressure to threaten recovery proceedings, including bankruptcy and winding-up proceedings, in good faith ... to persuade a debtor to pay what is due. ...

... [A]s is now known, Proline's application to wind up the company was an abuse of process and, therefore, improper. The thrust of the appellant's argument ... was that, because Proline's application was improper, it followed that BlueScope's threat to support it was also improper ...

[11] If a creditor makes a threat to bring a proceeding which the creditor knows to be groundless or for an improper purpose, the threat is improper and may impose improper pressure sufficient to vitiate a transaction ... Similarly, if a creditor makes a threat to do something unlawful, even though the creditor believes he is lawfully entitled to do it ... the law will regard the threat as amounting to improper pressure ... But in a commercial context, [this is] likely to be rare. It is ... not unlawful to support an application to wind up a company and [it would not be] ... improper pressure to do so where all that is known of the validity of the application is that it is disputed ...

... there is no reason to infer that BlueScope knew that the Proline application was improper. Although ... ultimately determined to be an abuse of process, there is no evidence that, at relevant times, BlueScope knew any more ... than that [G&B] disputed its validity ...

... BlueScope's threat to support the Proline application was not shown to be other than ...[made] in good faith in order to recover amounts which were due ... [12] ... In turn, ... Mr Beerens' decision to execute the guarantee was ... a decision to compromise BlueScope's claim, rather than run the risk of the winding-up application succeeding ...

Per Tate JA at 34:

... the threat made by BlueScope to exercise its contractual rights under the credit agreement, bona fide, and join as a supporting creditor in Proline's winding-up application, can scarcely be different from a bona fide threat to sue.

... In my view, the status of the company as presumptively insolvent under the Corporations Act, together with the risk that it would not be able to prove its solvency ... justified BlueScope protecting its own commercial position by obtaining the guarantee and indemnity ... The threat by BlueScope to exercise its rights under the credit agreement in the face of those circumstances did not amount to illegitimate pressure. ...

The appeal was dismissed.

19.2.4 The scope of economic duress

Courts have demonstrated a reluctance to find economic duress. Particular difficulty is created by the level of uncertainty in defining economic duress, and the overlaps between duress, undue influence, unconscionability and statutory relief. This creates a degree of confusion, as the following case demonstrates.

Australia and New Zealand Banking Group v Karam (2004) 64 NSWLR 149

Facts and issues

The Karam brothers ran a company which was in financial difficulty. To obtain further loans from ANZ, the brothers and their wives signed guarantees and a cross-deed of covenant and acknowledgement that ANZ's mortgages over properties, including their family homes, secured not only their personal debts, but also the company's debts to ANZ.

Decision

The trial judge found ANZ had engaged in economic duress and unconscionable conduct, given the extreme financial pressure on the company at the time they were signed, and lack of independent legal advice. However, the New South Wales Court of Appeal held there had not been duress. It found ANZ had not acted unlawfully, but simply provided an indulgence in return for improved security. Furthermore, ANZ did not cause the financial difficulty.

Per Beazley, Ipp and Basten JJA at 166:

> How the doctrine of economic duress fits with the equitable doctrines is unclear. The reference to 'unlawful' conduct, read in context of the earlier authorities, was originally a reference to unlawful detention of goods. Concepts of 'illegitimate pressure' and 'unconscionable conduct', if they do not refer to equitable principles, lack clear meaning, outside, possibly, concepts of illegitimate pressure in the field of industrial relations.
>
> [...]
>
> **[167]** The vagueness inherent in the terms 'economic duress' and 'illegitimate pressure' can be avoided by treating the concept of 'duress' as limited to threatened or actual unlawful conduct. The threat or conduct in question need not be directed to the person or property of the victim . . . but can be to the legitimate commercial and financial interests of the party. Secondly, if the conduct or threat is not unlawful, the resulting agreement may nevertheless be set aside where the weaker party establishes undue influence (actual or presumptive) or unconscionable conduct based on an unconscientious taking advantage of his or her special disability or special disadvantage, in the sense identified in *Commercial Bank of Australia Ltd v Amadio*. Thirdly, ... [p]ursuant to both provisions of the *Trade Practices Act* (Cth) and the *Contracts Review Act*, the relative strengths of the bargaining positions of the parties, and their ability to negotiate terms, will be relevant.

The appeal was allowed.

19.2.5 Causation

The causal link between illegitimate pressure and the decision to enter the contract forms an important element of duress. To establish causation, the illegitimate pressure exerted upon the victim must be at least one of the reasons for choosing to enter the contract: *Barton v Armstrong* [1976] AC 104. The timing of the pressure is also important: *Crescendo Management Pty Ltd v Westpac Banking Corporation* (1989) 19 NSWLR 40.

Where illegitimate pressure does not originate with the other contracting party, but is instead exerted by a third party, it will be important to establish that the contracting party had actual or constructive knowledge of the pressure (see *Dunwoodie v Teachers Mutual Bank Ltd* [2014] NSWCA 24), and also of its illegitimacy: see *Beerens v Bluescope* at **19.2.3**.

Barton v Armstrong [1976] AC 104

Facts and issues

Armstrong was chairman of Landmark Corporation Ltd, and Barton was its managing director. Both held significant shareholdings in the Landmark group. Armstrong and other directors sought to remove Barton from the group. Ultimately, the agreement in return for his resignation was highly advantageous to Barton, providing not only for repayment of a large loan previously made to Landmark by an entity associated with Barton, along with interest, but an upfront payment of $140,000 and purchase of his shares at an inflated price. During negotiations, Armstrong hired a surveillance team to watch Barton, made menacing calls in early hours of the morning, and made many threats to kill Barton. Barton claimed he had been coerced into the agreement by unlawful pressure.

Decision

The Privy Council (3:2) held that threats or pressure exerted need only be 'a' reason for entering the agreement. The majority held that although Barton might have executed the agreements even in the absence of threats, the unlawful pressure contributed to his decision. Accordingly, the appeal was allowed and the deeds of agreement were declared void.

Per Lord Cross of Chelsea (with Lord Kilbrandon and Sir Garfield Barwick) at 118:

> . . . If it were established that Barton did not allow the representation to affect his judgment then he could not make [duress] a ground for relief even though the representation was designed and known by Barton to be designed to affect his judgment. If on the other hand Barton relied on the misrepresentation Armstrong could not have defeated his claim to relief by showing that there were other more weighty causes which contributed to his decision to execute the deed, for in this field the Court does not allow an examination into the relative importance of contributory causes: 'Once make out that there has been anything like deception and no contract resting in any degree on that [119] foundation can stand' (per Lord Cranworth LJ in *Reynell v Sprye* . . . Their Lordships think that the same rule should apply in cases of duress and that if Armstrong's threats were 'a' reason for Barton's executing the deed he is entitled to relief, even though he might well have entered into the contract if Armstrong had uttered no threats to induce him to do so. . . .
>
> [120] If Barton had to establish that he would not have made the agreement but for Armstrong's threats then . . . he [would not have] made out his case. But no such onus lay on him. On the contrary it was for Armstrong to establish . . . that . . . the unlawful pressure which he was exerting . . . in fact contributed nothing to Barton's decision to sign. The judge has found that during the ten days or so before the documents were executed Barton was in genuine fear that Armstrong was planning to have him killed if the agreement was not signed. . . . The proper inference to be drawn . . . [is] that though it may be that Barton would have executed the documents even if Armstrong had made no threats . . . the threats and unlawful pressure in fact contributed to his decision to sign the documents . . . [T]he appeal should be allowed and a declaration made that the deeds . . . were executed by Barton under duress and are void . . .

Lord Wilberforce and Lord Simon of Glaisdale dissented on other grounds. The appeal was allowed.

Crescendo Management Pty Ltd v Westpac Banking Corporation (1988) 19 NSWLR 40

Facts and issues

The facts and issues are detailed above at **19.2.2**.

Decision

Per McHugh JA at 46:

> . . . It is unnecessary . . . for the victim to prove that the illegitimate pressure was the sole reason for him entering into the contract. It is sufficient that the illegitimate pressure was one of the reasons for the person entering into the agreement. Once the evidence establishes that the pressure exerted on the victim was illegitimate, the onus lies on the person applying the pressure to show that it made no contribution to the victim entering into the agreement . . .
>
> **No operative duress:**
>
> . . . [T]he assertion by Westpac that it would detain the whole of the sum of $27,000 until various documents were executed was improper and constituted an unlawful detention of Mrs Hilbrink's half interest in the proceeds . . .
>
> [47] . . . Although the pressure applied by Westpac . . . was unlawful, I am of opinion that it played no part in the execution of the mortgage which had occurred before the pressure was applied. . . . [T]he pressure had no causal connection with the execution of the mortgage. . . . the execution of the mortgage was not associated with any threat by Westpac. . . . If the letter of Mr Hilbrink dated 27 July 1977 is accurate, Westpac did not apply pressure until 14 July 1977. . . . The overall impression of this letter is that the directors and their wives were aware of the need to . . . enter into an arrangement with Westpac so as to enable the companies to carry on operations. They seem to have been quite happy to give the guarantees and mortgages. . . . Indeed they were simply bowing to the inevitable. Refusal . . . would have probably brought immediate problems for the companies.

The appeal was dismissed.

Dunwoodie v Teachers Mutual Bank Ltd [2014] NSWCA 24

Facts and issues

Dunwoodie held an account with Teachers Credit Union ('TMB'). He was coerced by the Hell's Angels bikie gang through threats of violence to cash a worthless cheque and pay the gang the proceeds. TMB allowed him to cash the cheque without waiting for funds to be cleared, but once the cheque proved worthless, sought to recover from Dunwoodie.

Decision

The New South Wales Court of Appeal held that a third party's duress could not be relied upon since TMB had no actual or constructive knowledge of it. However, it held a contractual term to be unjust pursuant to the *Contracts Review Act 1980* (NSW).

Per McColl JA at [2]:

> The applicant's case . . . is that he was acting under duress from members of the Hells Angels bikie gang when he withdrew . . . $59,950 from his account . . .
>
> [51] Avoidance of a contract for duress is a common law remedy. It operates in circumstances where illegitimate pressure imposed on the victim renders his apparent consent revocable . . . Knowledge of the facts, actual or constructive, constituting alleged duress by both parties to the contract is an essential element
>
> [. . .]
>
> [53] *Chitty on Contracts* . . . states:
>
>> Where it is sought to avoid a contract on the ground of duress exercised, not by the party seeking to enforce the agreement, but by [18] some third person, the party seeking to avoid the contract must prove that the other party knew of the duress, or had constructive notice of it or had procured the making of the contract through the agency of the party who exercised the duress. . . .
>
> [60] Finally, I would refer to *Smith v William Charlick Ltd* . . . (1924) 34 CLR 38 where Isaacs J, . . . described as 'ancient principle' (at 56) the statement in 1 *Rolle's Abridgment* (at 688) . . . that . . . '[i]t is clear that duress created by persons or circumstances unconnected with a party to a contract is no cause for impeaching the bargain with him'.
>
> [. . .]
>
> . . . duress [62] . . .[is] not fairly arguable in law, there being no suggestion that the respondent was in any way a participant in, or cognisant of . . . the duress . . .

Basten and Ward JJA agreed with McColl JA. The matter was remitted to the District Court for determination pursuant to the *Contracts Review Act*.

19.2.6 Remedies

Contracts concluded under duress are voidable. The victim has a choice to proceed with the contract, or to rescind it. If the victim wishes to proceed, they may affirm the contract. Failure to take action to rescind may be upheld as affirmation of the contract: *North Ocean Shipping Co Ltd v Hyundai Construction Co Ltd ('The Atlantic Baron')* [1979] QB 705. Thus, if they wish to avoid the contract, the victim must take active steps to exercise their right of election to rescind: *Electricity Generation Corporation v Woodside Energy Ltd* [2013] WASCA 36. Obstacles to rescission can arise, including equitable bars such as laches and unclean hands. If a contract is rescinded, money paid pursuant to its terms may be recovered in restitution upon avoidance: see *Electricity Generation v Woodside*.

Even if not rescinded, the party guilty of duress may still face difficulties in enforcing the contract; for example, orders for specific performance may be refused for 'unclean hands'.

North Ocean Shipping Co Ltd v Hyundai Construction Co Ltd ('The Atlantic Baron') [1979] QB 705

Facts and issues

Hyundai contracted to build a tanker for North Ocean for US$30.95 million, payable in five instalments. After the first instalment, the US dollar fell by 10 per cent. Hyundai claimed a 10 per cent increase for remaining instalments, and threatened to terminate the contract if North Ocean refused. Anxious to fulfil a profitable charter contract, North Ocean agreed to the price increase, paid the last four instalments, and took delivery on 27 November 1974, all without protest. Eight months later, it sought to recover the additional 10 per cent price.

Decision

The Court held the agreement voidable for economic duress. However, since it had treated the agreement as binding, and had failed to protest even after the illegitimate pressure ceased, North Ocean had effectively affirmed the agreement, and was bound by it.

Per Mocatta J at 720:

> [Thus] what is said in *Chitty on Contracts* ... is relevant, namely that a contract entered into under duress is voidable and not void:
>
> > that a person who has entered into the contract may either affirm or avoid such contract after the duress has ceased; and if he has so voluntarily acted under it with a full knowledge of all the circumstances he may be held bound on the ground of ratification, or if, after escaping from the duress, he takes no steps to set aside the transaction, he may be found to have affirmed it ...
>
> The owners were ... free from the duress on 27 November 1974 and took no action by way of protest or otherwise ... [until] their formal claim ... [T]he owners did not believe that if they made any protest [during] ... delivery ... the yard would have refused to deliver the vessel ... [721] ... [T]he important points here are that (i) since there was no danger at this time in registering a protest, (ii) the final payments were made without any qualification, and (iii) were followed by a delay until 31 July 1975 before the owners put forward their claim, the correct inference to draw ... is that the action and inaction of the owners can only be regarded as an affirmation of the variation ... to pay the additional ten per cent. ... I do not think that an intention on the part of the owners not to affirm ... can avail them in view of their overt acts. As was said in *Deacon v Transport Regulation Board* ([1958] VR 458 at 460) in considering whether a payment was made voluntarily or not: 'No secret mental reservation of the doer is material. The question is—what would his conduct indicate to a reasonable man as his mental state.' ...

The Court found for Hyundai on the Special Case formulated by the Arbitral Tribunal.

Electricity Generation Corporation v Woodside Energy Ltd [2013] WASCA 36

Facts and issues

The facts and issues are detailed above at **19.2.3**.

Decision

Although the Court of Appeal found duress had been established, it nonetheless held that Verve had no cause of action in unjust enrichment for the price difference extracted by duress, since Verve had not elected to rescind the short-term GSA.

Per McLure P (Newnes JA agreeing) at [31]:

> The Sellers refusal to supply [pursuant to the GSA], resulting from a breach of their reasonable endeavours obligation under the GSA, [which] constituted the application of illegitimate pressure on Verve which was a cause of it entering into the short term gas supply agreements. Accordingly, the short term gas supply agreements are voidable . . .
>
> However, there was no plea . . . seeking a finding that Verve had elected to avoid (rescind) the short term gas supply agreements. This is rescission at the election of the contractual party not a court ordered remedy. . . .
>
> . . . Verve can have no cause of action in unjust enrichment for economic duress . . . unless and until the short term gas supply contracts are rescinded. . . . Accordingly, any unjust enrichment economic duress claim must fail. Verve of course would also be entitled to the excess paid under the short term gas supply contracts as damages flowing from the breach of the GSA but for the damages cap in cl 22 of the GSA. The economic duress claim was relied on in an attempt to avoid the effect of cl 22.7(c) and cl 22.9 of the GSA. . . .

The appeal was allowed in part.

19.2.7 Statutory duress

The Australian Consumer Law (ACL) provides statutory remedies in relation to certain contracts which were entered due to the use of 'physical force, or undue harassment or coercion': s 50 ACL. However, to date there is little case law to flesh out the meaning of provisions.

In relation to statutory duress, definitions of 'coercion' and 'harassment' are not yet fully developed. Harassment must be 'undue'; however, coercion need not be 'undue': *Australian Competition and Consumer Commission v Maritime Union of Australia* (2001) 114 FCR 472. Notably, lawful conduct may be caught by s 50 ACL, and remedies are wider than general law, and damages: s 236.

Australian Consumer Law s 50

Section 50 – Harassment and coercion

(1) A person must not use physical force, or undue harassment or coercion, in connection with:

- **(a)** the supply or possible supply of goods or services; or
- **(b)** the payment for goods or services; or
- **(c)** the sale or grant, or the possible sale or grant, of an interest in land; or
- **(d)** the payment for an interest in land. . . .

Australian Competition and Consumer Commission v McCaskey (2000) 104 FCR 8

Facts and issues

Pursuant to the predecessor of s 50 ACL, s 60 of the *Trade Practices Act 1974* (Cth) (*TPA*), the ACCC sought declarations and injunctions against a debt collection agency, Cash Return

Mercantile Pty Ltd (Cash Return), and its employee, McCaskey. McCaskey had made aggressive and intimidating phone calls to the complainants and their families.

Decision

The Federal Court held that the legislation did not require threats of illegal acts, but that harassment must be undue. The nature and content of communications and their purpose were key. Relevant matters included abusive, obscene or intimidatory language, time and place of demands, the person to whom demands were directed, and situations designed to embarrass or humiliate in front of family or third parties. It held the respondents had contravened s 60 *TPA*.

Per French J at 27:

> ... The word 'undue' adds an extra layer of evaluation which is more relevant to the case of debt recovery than to the sale of goods or services. Repeated unwelcome approaches to a potential acquirer of goods or services could qualify as harassment and, so qualified, require very little additional evidence, if any, to attract the characterisation of 'undue harassment'. ... If legitimate demands are reasonably made, on more than one occasion, for the purpose of reminding the debtor of his or her obligation and drawing the debtor's attention to the likelihood of legal proceedings if payment is not made, then that conduct, if it be harassment, is not undue harassment. If, however, the frequency, nature or content of the approaches and communications associated with them is such that they are calculated to intimidate or demoralise, tire out or exhaust a debtor rather than convey the demand and an associated legitimate threat of proceedings, the harassment will be undue.
>
> [28] ... Where the demand includes content which does not serve legitimate purposes of reminding the debtor of the obligation and threatening legal proceedings for recovery but is calculated otherwise to intimidate or threaten the debtor, then the coercion may be undue. ... Quite apart from content the manner or circumstances of a demand or communication, including the language used, the time and place at which it is made and the person to whom it is communicated, may go beyond the legitimate purposes of drawing attention to the existence of the obligation and the consequences for non-compliance. ... Obvious examples include the use of personally abusive or obscene language, conveying the demand to uninvolved family members, particularly children, or conveying the demand through a third party in order to embarrass the debtor when the debtor could reasonably have been the subject of a direct communication. ...
>
> A supplier ... [or] debt collector, in deciding upon the approach to be taken ... should ask the question: 'Are the content, the timing, the location and other circumstances of my demand for payment reasonably calculated to remind the debtor of his or her obligation, specify a time within which it must be satisfied and indicate that civil proceedings for recovery will be instituted if payment is not made?'

The Court granted declarations, injunctions and other orders by consent.

QUESTIONS

(1) Why was the overbearing of will theory ultimately rejected by the Court in *Crescendo Management v Westpac*? Can you think of any circumstances in which the former test would be satisfied?

(2) Do you think that, had BlueScope known of the improper purpose of the third party who instituted liquidation proceedings against G&B, the Court would have come to a different conclusion in *Beerens v Bluescope*? If so, why should this make a difference?

(3) In your opinion, can the existence of circumstances which make the contract 'inevitable' such as the financial difficulties in *ANZ v Karam* (or *Crescendo v Westpac*) be equated to illegitimate pressure unknown to the contracting counterparty, such as the pressure by the Hell's Angels in *Dunwoodie*? Why were neither of these pressures ultimately sufficient to found duress?

(4) If threats of both lawful and unlawful acts can ground a claim of duress at common law, what determines whether or not pressure is 'illegitimate'?

19.3 Undue influence

Factor	Short explanation	Relevant authorities	*Principles* text*
Actual undue influence	Affirmatively proven exercise of undue pressure	–	Chapter 19: 19.11
Presumed undue influence: special classes of relationship	Exercise of influence is presumed, for certain classes of special relationship eg lawyer–client, doctor–patient, parent–child	*Westmelton (Vic) Pty Ltd (rec and mgr apptd) v Archer & Shulman* [1982] VR 305 *Hartigan v International Society for Krishna Consciousness Inc* [2002] NSWSC 810	Chapter 19: 19.12
Presumed undue influence: relationship of influence	Exercise of influence is presumed where evidence establishes a relationship of influence	*Johnson v Buttress* (1936) 56 CLR 113 *Thorne v Kennedy* (2017) 263 CLR 85	Chapter 19: 19.13
Rebutting the presumption of undue influence	Once a presumption of undue influence arises, the onus to rebut falls upon the stronger party	*Johnson v Buttress* (1936) 56 CLR 113 *Badman v Drake* [2008] NSWSC 1366 *Westmelton (Vic) Pty Ltd (rec and mgr apptd) v Archer & Shulman* [1982] VR 305	Chapter 19: 19.14

* Consult the corresponding section(s) of the *Principles* text for more detail.

Undue influence describes situations whereby a stronger party who stands in a position of dominance vis-à-vis a weaker party exerts influence to extract a transaction or gift. Traditionally, there are two categories of undue influence: actual and presumed. These categories describe the types of onuses required to establish undue influence.

- Actual undue influence: Where no antecedent relationship of influence exists, exertion of influence may be established by evidence: see **19.3.1**.
- Presumed undue influence: Where a relevant antecedent relationship exists, exertion of influence will be presumed. There are two types of antecedent relationship:

- Special classes of relationships, which are, by their nature, presumed relationships of influence: see **19.3.2**; or
- Relationship of influence established by evidence, where evidence establishes that the weaker party reposed high levels of trust and confidence in the stronger party, or was dependent upon them: see **19.3.3**.

More recently, the High Court has arguably blurred these previously clear categories: *Thorne v Kennedy* (2017) 263 CLR 85 (see **19.3.3)**.

19.3.1 Actual undue influence

Actual undue influence is the most difficult category to establish, as there is no reliance on any kind of antecedent relationship. Instead, evidence is led of a situation which demonstrates the exertion of undue influence over a weaker party. Dixon J describes in *Johnson v Buttress* (1936) 56 CLR 113 (see **19.3.3**) (at 134) that:

> [t]he source of power . . . may [sometimes] be found . . . [not in] antecedent relation, but in a particular situation, or . . . deliberate contrivance . . . If this be so, facts must be proved showing that the transaction was the outcome of . . . actual influence over the mind of the . . . [victim, such] that it cannot be considered his free act.

Such situations are rare, and often overlap with duress.

19.3.2 Presumed undue influence: special classes of relationship

A presumption will arise that undue influence has been exerted whenever the relationship falls within a 'special class' of relationship. Equity thus protects the weaker party, in special circumstances commonly recognised as ones which involve trust and confidence (and thus opportunity for influence), by shifting the onus of proof onto the stronger party to show the transaction resulted from free will. Notably, the direction of influence recognised is 'one way' only. Special classes include, but are not limited to:

- solicitor and client;
- doctor and patient;
- religious advisor and advisee;
- trustee and beneficiary;
- guardian and ward;
- parent and child.

Westmelton (Vic) Pty Ltd (rec and mgr apptd) v Archer & Shulman [1982] VR 305

Facts and issues

Westmelton, a property development company, engaged Archer as its solicitor. He was also appointed director and chairman of Westmelton's board of directors. Westmelton entered an agreement with Archer & Shulman, entitling it to 7.5 per cent of its future profits in consideration of a $10,000 reduction of its outstanding invoice for legal services. The decision was taken by the board of directors in Archer's absence.

Decision

The Full Court of the Supreme Court of Victoria held that where special relationships of confidence exist, including solicitor and client, the court applies a rebuttable presumption of undue influence to any transactions between them. Thus, the burden always falls upon the solicitor to prove that the dealing was at arm's length. However, the weight of the burden will vary depending on the circumstances. Proof of (independent) advice is not the sole way to rebut the presumption. It found the transaction was at arm's length, and Westmelton was not disadvantaged, despite absence of advice.

Per Starke, Kaye, and Fullagar JJ at 312:

> In some cases of confidential relationship, and the relationship of solicitor and client is one of them, where the person ... has dealings with that other person, the court views the transactions with suspicion, and applies a presumption that the other's will was unduly overborne ... and the court imposes a burden on the confidant to prove that ... the dealings were at arm's length and that the other's will was in no way overborne by the relationship of confidence. ... The extent and weight of the burden cast ... and the matters ... of which the court will require to be satisfied before it will regard the presumption as having been negatived, must vary enormously with all the circumstances ... [313] In *Re Coomber; Coomber v Coomber*, [1911] 1 Ch 723, at p. 726, Cozens-Hardy, MR [stated]: '... A solicitor cannot, in ordinary circumstances, take a gift from his client in a matter in which he is the solicitor because there is from that relationship in itself a presumption of undue influence; a presumption which, of course, may be rebutted. It may be rebutted in various ways; most frequently, by proving that the solicitor told his client, "I cannot take this unless you have independent advice; consult an independent solicitor, put the matter before him, and he must explain the matter fully to you" ...'

The appeal was dismissed.

Hartigan v International Society for Krishna Consciousness Inc [2002] NSWSC 810

Facts and issues

The Hartigans lived on farm owned by Mrs Hartigan, near a Krishna religious order, of which they were devotees. Mrs Hartigan gifted her farm to the Krishna order. After the couple divorced, Mrs Hartigan sought damages on the basis the gift was procured by undue influence.

Decision

The New South Wales Supreme Court awarded damages. It found the Krishna order failed to rebut the presumption of influence, given the size of the gift, and lack of independent advice.

Per Bryson J at [28]:

> The court's approach, in cases of gifts influenced by religious advisers or religious beliefs, is more exacting than ordinary community standards and goes well beyond overcoming deliberate exploitation. It may be unconscionable to accept ... a gift ... where the intention to make the gift was produced by religious belief. ...

[36] . . . The enormity of the gift is particularly great in the plaintiff's circumstances where she had small children whose housing she was giving up, and she had no other resources . . .

[37] . . . [T]here was . . . [no] deliberate attempt by . . . anyone in the Krishna [order] to get the better of the plaintiff, to overbear her or deceive her. . . [but] . . . the extreme improvidence of the gift would have been obvious to any reasonable [person] . . .

[89] Mrs Hartigan made the donation without . . . any independent advice . . .

[91] . . . [T]he defendant bears the burden of showing that the gift was not affected by undue influence. . . .

[92] On Mr Evans' and Mr Barrow's own accounts of what took place . . . clearly show that they were persons in whom she reposed trust and confidence. . . She was proposing to take herself and her family into a religious community and trust to it for . . . basic needs. Her dependency and reliance upon the community . . . were obvious to Mr Evans and to Mr Barrow. [Mrs Hartigan's] . . . intention was produced by her misunderstanding of religious instruction . . . which emphasised . . . avoidance of materialism . . . [and thus she] came to a conclusion which . . . was entirely contrary to her interest, needs and responsibilities for herself and her family, and in every way profoundly improvident. . . . [S]he was susceptible to be influenced even by the . . . most subtle indications . . . [favouring] the donation.

[93] Mr Barrow had a clear understanding of . . . the need for caution and management by a legal adviser, but he did not give Mrs Hartigan the benefit of this insight. . . . [T]he [Krishna order] has not discharged the burden of proof . . . of showing the absence of undue influence. . .

[94] Making the gift was an enormity, quite outside the range of benefactions which a person could be expected to make . . . according to ordinary community standards . . . This should have been obvious to anyone who knew the circumstances, and indeed it appears to me that it was obvious to Mr Barrow. . . . [I]t would be altogether unconscionable for the [Krishna order] to rely on the validity of the donation, and [it should be set aside].

The Court awarded damages.

19.3.3 Presumed undue influence: relationships of influence established by evidence

Outside recognised special categories, a relationship of influence may still be established on the basis of evidence of trust and dependence within an antecedent relationship. Evidence may provide 'proof that the history of the particular relationship involved one party occupying a similar position of ascendency or influence, and the other a corresponding position of dependency or trust': *Thorne v Kennedy* (2017) 263 CLR 85. Equity then steps in to protect the weaker party by altering the burden of proof, by raising a presumption that the influence has been exerted over the weaker party, unless rebutted.

Johnson v Buttress (1936) 56 CLR 113

Facts and issues

Buttress was an elderly, unintelligent and illiterate man. After the death of his wife, upon whom he had been heavily dependent, Buttress latched onto one family member after another for support, but fell out with each soon after. He changed his will frequently to reflect this. Johnson was a family friend who was kind to Buttress and his wife. Buttress visited Johnson often, relied upon her to deal with a difficult tenant, and lived at the Johnsons' home for a short time. Buttress transferred his cottage to Johnson. Thereafter, he lived for years on a bush block owned by Johnson, first in a tent and then a shed. Johnson visited him, took him supplies, and organised his mail. Years later, Buttress changed his will to benefit his niece. After Buttress died, the executor of his will sought to set aside the transfer of the cottage to Johnson for undue influence.

Decision

The High Court dismissed Johnson's appeal. Although not within a special class, evidence established their relationship was nonetheless a relationship of actual influence (dominion), leading to a presumption of exertion of influence, which Johnson failed to rebut.

Per Dixon J (Evatt J agreeing) at 134:

> [T]he parties may antecedently stand in a relation that gives to one an . . . influence over the other from the abuse of which it is proper that he should be protected. When they stand in such a relation, the party in the position of influence cannot maintain his beneficial title to property of substantial value made over to him by the other as a gift, unless he satisfies the court that he took no advantage of the donor, but that the gift was the independent and well understood act of a man in a position to exercise a free judgment based on information as full as that of the donee. This burden is imposed upon one of the parties to certain well-known relations as soon as it appears that the relation existed, and that he has obtained a substantial benefit from the other. A solicitor must thus justify the receipt of such a benefit from his client, a physician from his patient, a parent from his child, a guardian from his ward . . . [However] the doctrine which throws upon the recipient the burden of justifying the transaction is confined to no fixed category. It rests upon a principle. It applies whenever one party occupies or assumes [135] towards another a position naturally involving an ascendancy or influence over that other, or a dependence or trust on his part. One occupying such a position falls under a duty in which fiduciary characteristics may be seen. It is his duty to use his position of influence in the interest of no one but the man who . . . entrusts him with his welfare. When he takes from that man a substantial gift of property, it is incumbent upon him to show that it cannot be ascribed to the inequality between . . .
>
> [136] The decision . . . depends . . . on the question whether, before the transfer, Mrs Johnson . . . stood in a special relation of influence to Buttress. . . .
>
> The first and most important consideration affecting the question is the standard of intelligence, the equipment and character of Buttress . . . [137] . . . [I]n this peculiar case it is the man's illiteracy, his ignorance of affairs, and his strangeness in disposition and manner that provide the foundation for the suggested relation. For many years he had leant upon his wife, and . . . after her death, he was at a loss for guidance and support. He turned first to one and then to another for a prop. His affairs of business were in reality few and simple. But to him they seem to have loomed large. . . .
>
> . . . he began to place increasing reliance upon Mrs Johnson . . . Then the difficulties with his tenants developed. . . . [I]t is clear that . . . he could not cope. He relied on the Johnsons to manage it for him. . . . his connection with them must have steadily grown. His will in favour of Mrs Johnson marks its progress. From 13th April, 1931, although he did not live at Rose Bay, he must have spent the greater part of his time there. Little doubt can be felt that ultimately he came so to depend upon Mrs Johnson that a full relation of influence over him subsisted. . . .
>
> [138] I think that when the circumstances of the case are considered with the character and capacity of Buttress, they lead to the conclusion that an antecedent relation of influence existed which throws upon Mrs Johnson the burden of justifying the transfer by showing that it was the result of the free exercise of the donor's independent will. This . . . she has quite failed to do.

Latham CJ, Starke, and McTiernan JJ delivered separate judgments agreeing to dismiss the appeal. The appeal was dismissed.

Thorne v Kennedy (2017) 263 CLR 85

Facts and issues

Kennedy was a wealthy 67-year old man who, in 2006, met Thorne online. Thorne was a 36-year old woman living in the Middle East, with no substantial assets and who spoke little English. From the outset, he said if they were to be married, she would need to sign papers preserving his money for his children. In 2007, they moved to Australia, intending to marry on 30 September 2007. Seven weeks before the wedding, Kennedy had a solicitor draft a prenuptial agreement. Eleven days before the wedding, Kennedy told Thorne that for the wedding to proceed, she must sign the agreement, and the next day, took her to see Harrison, an independent solicitor. Harrison strongly advised Thorne not to sign, as it was the worst agreement she had ever seen, and protected only Kennedy's interests. Despite this, four days before the wedding, Thorne signed the agreement. After the wedding, Kennedy required Thorne to sign another almost identical agreement within 30 days. Despite Harrison's strong advice, Thorne signed the second agreement five days after the wedding. The couple separated almost four years later. Thorne sought to have both agreements set aside under the *Family Law Act 1975* (Cth) for duress, undue influence or unconscionable conduct. Kennedy died during trial.

Decision

Per Kiefel CJ, Bell, Gageler, Keane and Edelman JJ at 101:

> There are different ways to prove ... undue influence. One method ... is by direct evidence of the circumstances of the particular transaction. That was the approach relied upon by the primary judge in this case. Another way ... undue influence ... is by presumption. This presumption was relied upon by Ms Thorne in this Court as an alternative. ... [the judgment describes presumption of undue influence in special classes of relationship, see **19.3.2**]. Outside recognised categories, the presumption can also be raised by proof that the history of the particular relationship involved one party occupying a similar position of ascendency or influence, and the other a corresponding position of dependency or trust. In either case, the presumption is rebuttable by the other party proving ... [the] transaction ... was nevertheless the result of the weaker party's free will. ...
>
> [109] ... the agreements could not have operated more adversely to Ms Thorne. ...
>
> ... it can be an indicium of undue influence if a pre-nuptial or post-nuptial agreement is signed despite being known to be grossly unreasonable ... In other words, ...[the] gap between ... Ms Harrison's strong advice not to sign ... and Ms Thorne's actions in signing ... [was] relevant to whether an inference should be drawn of undue influence.
>
> ...
>
> ... Each of the ... [110] [factors considered by the trial judge were relevant] in the overall evaluation of whether Ms Thorne had been the subject of undue influence ... [and] it was open to the primary judge to conclude that Ms Thorne ... was powerless other than to enter the agreements. In other words, the extent to which she was unable to make 'clear, calm or rational decisions' was so significant that she could not aptly be described as a free agent. ...
>
> ... some of the factors which may have prominence include ... (i) whether the agreement was offered on a basis that it was not subject to negotiation; (ii) the emotional circumstances ... including any explicit or implicit threat to end a marriage or ... engagement; (iii) whether there was any time for careful reflection; (iv) the nature of the parties' relationship; (v) the [111] relative financial positions of the parties; and (vi) ... independent advice ... and whether there was time to reflect on that advice. ...

In the joint judgment, their Honours held the agreements were vitiated for undue influence and unconscionable conduct. Nettle and Gordon JJ agreed on the ground of unconscionable conduct. Gordon J rejected arguments of undue influence.

Unfortunately, the joint judgment conflates two questions: (1) whether the relationship was one of influence, ie whether Thorne reposed trust and confidence in, or was dependent on Kennedy, or was dependent upon him; with (2) whether Kennedy exercised influence in obtaining the agreements, ie the 'evaluation' of whether Thorne was the 'subject of undue influence': see the above case at 110. However, traditionally, the establishment of a relation of influence would lead to a presumption that influence was exerted. This presumption would prevail, unless rebutted by Kennedy.

Yet this is not how the joint judgment approached the matter. It held that the nature of the couple's relationship was just one of many factors which demonstrated that Thorne did not enter the contract as a result of her free will, and that the evidence supported a conclusion that undue influence was exerted by Kennedy. It has been argued that this means the majority implicitly altered the traditional test to require all who allege undue influence (other than special classes) to prove exertion of influence, in accordance with the English approach.[2] If so, this would effectively abolish the presumption of exertion of influence where evidence establishes a relationship of influence, thereby merging this category with the category of actual undue influence (see **19.3.1**), and raising the evidentiary burden for weaker parties.

However, it is far from clear that the joint judgment actually sought to alter the traditional test in *Johnson*. Indeed, the conflation may merely be due to the way the case was argued: see the above case at 101. Moreover, their Honours outlined the categories of the test from *Johnson*, and did not expressly overturn or vary them: see the above case at 101.

19.3.4 Rebutting the presumption of undue influence

Once a relationship of influence is established whether by evidence (see **19.3.3**) or by presumption (see **19.3.2**), then a further presumption arises that influence has been exercised, and the stronger party bears the onus of proving the transaction resulted from a free and voluntary exercise of will. However, as the following cases show, the weight of the burden of proof will vary depending on the facts. Furthermore, the existence of independent advice is important, but not determinative.

Badman v Drake [2008] NSWSC 1366

Facts and issues

Mrs Badman was an 87-year old, who feared being left on her own without support. She befriended the Drakes, who visited regularly, took her shopping and to medical appointments. The Drakes were threatened with eviction by their mortgagee. Mrs Badman suggested she gift them $343,000 to

2 Arguing the High Court has departed from *Johnson v Buttress* and embraced the English approach, see Rick Bigwood, 'The Undue Influence of 'Non-Australian' Undue Influence Law on Australian Undue Influence Law: Farewell *Johnson v Buttress?* Part I' (2018) 35 *Journal of Contract Law* 56.

purchase their home from the mortgagee, and that all three live together. Lawyers advised they would need approval of a Public Trustee, but approval was unlikely for such a gift. The Drakes felt the lawyers were too expensive and overcomplicating matters. All three signed a self-styled contract, attaching references from a doctor and religious ministers, and including a 'special clause' obliging them to support one another.

Decision

The Court set aside the gift, and ordered equitable compensation. It emphasised that in such circumstances, ensuring legal capacity and independent advice were important.

Per Young CJ at [55]:

> The [mortgagee's solicitor] was asked: 'Did it not occur to you that Mrs Badman was in a position where she might be taken advantage of?'...
>
> [56] ... Where a professional solicitor sees an old lady of 87 who may be in a vulnerable situation, it is impermissible for any solicitor to take the view that because monies are going to flow ... to the advantage of his or her client, that they can just close their eyes to the fraud that may be being perpetrated on the vulnerable person. ...
>
> [67] The plaintiff was elderly and lonely; she relied on the ... defendants to keep her out of a nursing home; ... the solicitor could see that the situation was fraught with difficulties; the ... defendants had a solicitor who also indicated that the transaction needed to be handled with care. Mr Mattick advised that, at least without ... independent assessment of the plaintiff's capacity to understand the transaction, it was at risk ...
>
> [75] It is not at all unusual in undue influence cases for the persons receiving the benefit to have been generous to the person whose property they have taken. Sometimes this is out of the goodness of their hearts ... Other times it is just the bait ...
>
> [76] ... as most lawyers know and as Ms Flanagan and Mr Mattick appreciated ... where there is doubt about a person's capacity, the transaction is always in some danger ...
>
> [80] Had the transaction been properly explained and had there been independent advice, it may well be that there would have been sufficient material together with Dr Lowe's advice to show that the plaintiff had capacity ...
>
> [82] The ... defendants say that they cared for the plaintiff ... They were good to her, she had capacity and she wanted to benefit them. They say that it is only now that her son has realised that there are hundreds of thousands of dollars awaiting him if he looks after his mother, that the position has changed.
>
> [83] There is something to be said for the ... defendants' position. However, ... when one is dealing with an elderly person who is lonely and friendless, a person who befriends her must, if they are to gain a personal benefit, be extremely careful to ensure that there is no unworthy conduct.
>
> [84] ... it is necessary for the community to be sure that there has not been undue influence over an elderly vulnerable person, for that person to have had independent advice, usually independent legal advice, and their capacity to understand is established and they freely and voluntarily wished to ... [make the gift]. Where the transaction involves a large amount of money for which the elderly person receives very little ... benefit, it is even harder ...
>
> [85] In the instant case, two experienced solicitors were finding their way through the situation. ... had they been left to finish [this work] ... defendants [might have been able to] retained their house.
>
> [87] ... The plaintiff got virtually nothing from the transaction, though she doubtless thought that she was getting a friendly roof over her head for an indefinite period. The transaction should be set aside.

The Court ordered equitable compensation.

Westmelton (Vic) Pty Ltd (rec and mgr apptd) v Archer & Shulman [1982] VR 305

Facts and issue

The facts and issues are detailed above at **19.3.2**.

Decision

Per Starke, Kaye, and Fullagar JJ at 315:

> . . . It is a presumption which 'may be rebutted in various ways' as Lord Cozens-Hardy said, and indeed it is impossible to limit the ways in which it may be rebutted.
>
> [318] . . . in substance the most [findings of fact] are as follows: —(1) . . . that . . . Archer was an honest and reliable witness. (2) . . . the plaintiffs had given . . . full disclosure and had dealt with . . . [Westmelton] openly and fairly. . . (3) The directors . . . were able and experienced businessmen who were well informed on the details of the West Melton project. (4) The directors did not in fact depend on the solicitors in any way to tell them anything as to the monetary potential (and thus value) of the profit-sharing rights they were passing to Mr Archer. (5) The directors had discussed [the matter] . . . in the absence of Mr Archer . . . and they had concluded that the benefit passing to the company by the agreement well justified the passing to the solicitors of the profit-sharing rights, whatever they might in the future amount to in money terms. (6) Although . . . Mr Archer was the person who first mentioned the possibility in general terms . . . the director representing Cambridge Credit Corporation, . . .was the person who proposed the actual agreement . . . (7) . . . nothing in the terms of the offer itself . . . suggested that the plaintiffs . . . were in any way taking advantage of the sophisticated and well-informed defendant company. . . . [319] . . . the plaintiffs concealed nothing. . . .
>
> The evidence leads us to the conclusion that the appellant company had more expertise in commerce and finance than most solicitors would have, and we do not think that there was any obligation . . . [to] advise the obtaining, of independent legal advice. . . .

The appeal was dismissed with costs.

QUESTIONS

(1) Comparing the situations in *Badman v Drake* and *Westmelton v Archer*, what factors do you think account for the difference in outcome?

(2) In *Thorne v Kennedy*, the High Court arguably moved directly to consideration of exertion of undue influence, rather than determining whether an antecedent relationship of undue influence existed. Some have argued that this means any victim who cannot point to a 'special class' of relationship must prove that influence was exerted. Would Mrs Johnson retain the gift of the cottage if the facts of *Johnson v Buttress* were again before the Court under such a test?

19.4 International perspectives

19.4.1 *CISG*

For details on when the 1980 *UN Convention on Contracts for the International Sale of Goods* ('*CISG*') applies to international contracts, see **25.4.1**. Although it may be the applicable law governing an international commercial sales contract, the *CISG* does not cover within its scope most matters relating to validity of contract: see art 4(a) below. Instead, voidability for improper conduct is determined according to the domestic law applicable in accordance with the court's choice of law rules.

CISG art 4(a)

This Convention governs only the formation of the contract of sale and the rights and obligations of the seller and the buyer arising from such a contract. In particular, except as otherwise expressly provided in this Convention, it is not concerned with:

(a) the validity of the contract or of any of its provisions or of any usage; . . .

19.4.2 UNIDROIT Principles: Threat

For details on when UNIDROIT Principles of International Commercial Contracts (UNIDROIT Principles) apply, see **25.4.3**. Under the UNIDROIT Principles, threats may give rise to a right to avoid the contract: art 3.2.6. The threat must be 'imminent and serious' such that it leaves the victim with 'no reasonable alternative' but to enter the contract;[3] and 'unjustified' in the sense that threats are wrongful, or made for wrongful purposes: art 3.2.6, Comment [2]. Threats may be against persons, goods, reputation, or economic interests, and tests are objective in nature: art. 3.2.6, Comment [2], Illustration 2, UNIDROIT Principles.

UNIDROIT Principles art 3.2.6 (Threat)

A party may avoid the contract when it has been led to conclude the contract by the other party's unjustified threat which, having regard to the circumstances, is so imminent and serious as to leave the first party no reasonable alternative. In particular, a threat is unjustified if the act or omission with which a party has been threatened is wrongful in itself, or it is wrongful to use it as a means to obtain the conclusion of the contract.

Confirmation of the contract by the person entitled to avoid, whether expressly or impliedly, may preclude them from avoidance of the contract: art 3.2.9 UNIDROIT Principles. Threats by third parties may give rise to the right to avoid if the contracting party is responsible for the third party[4], or knew or ought to have known of the threats: art 3.2.8, Comment [2], UNIDROIT Principles.

3 UNIDROIT Principles, art 3.2.6, Comment [1].

4 UNIDROIT Principles, art 3.2.8 (Third Parties):

(1) Where fraud, threat, gross disparity or a party's mistake is imputable to, or is known or ought to be known by, a third person for whose acts the other party is responsible, the contract may be avoided under the same conditions as if the behaviour or knowledge had been that of the party itself.

The right to avoid must be exercised by notice to the other party: art 3.2.11 UNIDROIT Principles. Notice must be given within a reasonable time: art 3.2.12. Avoidance, once effected, has a retroactive effect: art 3.2.14 UNIDROIT Principles.

19.4.3 UNIDROIT Principles: Gross disparity

Whilst the UNIDROIT Principles contain no directly comparable equivalent to undue influence, art 3.2.7 on gross disparity may capture similar situations, since it seeks to protect weaker parties whose special disadvantage has been exploited by a stronger party, resulting in unfairly imbalanced contractual terms.

Contracts may be avoided if terms are excessively advantageous to one party, once a range of matters are taken into consideration; in other words, when a serious imbalance exists between respective obligations of the parties: art 3.2.7, Comment [1], UNIDROIT Principles.

Whereas the equitable concept of undue influence focuses on the unfair behaviour during contractual negotiations, while looking to the improvidence of the transaction as evidence that influence (see eg *Thorne v Kennedy* (2017) 263 CLR 85 (at **19.3.3**)), by contrast, the civil law concept of gross disparity directly focuses upon the substantive unfairness of the bargain, encouraging the adjudicator to evaluate the content of the contract whilst looking to unfair conduct as evidence the advantage is 'unjustified'.

Under UNIDROIT Principles art 3.2.7, the first requirement for gross disparity is that there is an 'excessive advantage' whereby, upon comparison of the respective obligations of the parties, one party is comparatively excessively advantaged: art 3.2.7, Comment [1]. It is not enough that there is 'considerable disparity' in value, price, or other obligations: art 3.2.7, Comment [1]. Instead, the disequilibrium must be 'so great as to shock the conscience of a reasonable person': art 3.2.7, Comment [1].

Moreover, the advantage must be 'unjustified' in the circumstances. This may be indicated by: the taking of unfair advantage of dependence, economic distress, inexperience; lack of bargaining skill; ignorance or improvidence;[5] or unequal bargaining power.[6] The prevailing ethics of the trading sector will also be relevant.[7] However, dependence brought about simply by market conditions alone will be insufficient: art 3.2.7, Comment [2a].

In determining gross disparity, only imbalance at the time of conclusion is relevant. Change of circumstance leading to disparity after conclusion may trigger hardship provisions, but not gross disparity: arts 6.2.1–3.

A party affected by gross disparity may request the court order an adaption of the contractual terms to correct the imbalance: art 3.2.7(2). The principles discussed above concerning confirmation of the contract (art 3.2.9), and acts of third parties (art 3.2.8) also apply to gross disparity.

(2) Where fraud, threat or gross disparity is imputable to a third person for whose acts the other party is not responsible, the contract may be avoided if that party knew or ought to have known of the fraud, threat or disparity, or has not at the time of avoidance reasonably acted in reliance on the contract.

5 UNIDROIT Principles, art 3.2.7(1)(a).

6 UNIDROIT Principles, art 3.2.7, Comment [1].

7 UNIDROIT Principles, art 3.2.7, Comment [2c].

UNIDROIT Principles art 3.2.7 (Gross disparity)

(1) A party may avoid the contract or an individual term of it if, at the time of the conclusion of the contract, the contract or term unjustifiably gave the other party an excessive advantage. Regard is to be had, among other factors, to

(a) the fact that the other party has taken unfair advantage of the first party's dependence, economic distress or urgent needs, or of its improvidence, ignorance, inexperience or lack of bargaining skill; and

(b) the nature and purpose of the contract.

(2) Upon the request of the party entitled to avoidance, a court may adapt the contract or term in order to make it accord with reasonable commercial standards of fair dealing.

(3) A court may also adapt the contract or term upon the request of the party receiving notice of avoidance, provided that that party informs the other party of its request promptly after receiving such notice and before the other party has reasonably acted in reliance on it. Article 3.2.10(2) applies accordingly.

19.5 Review

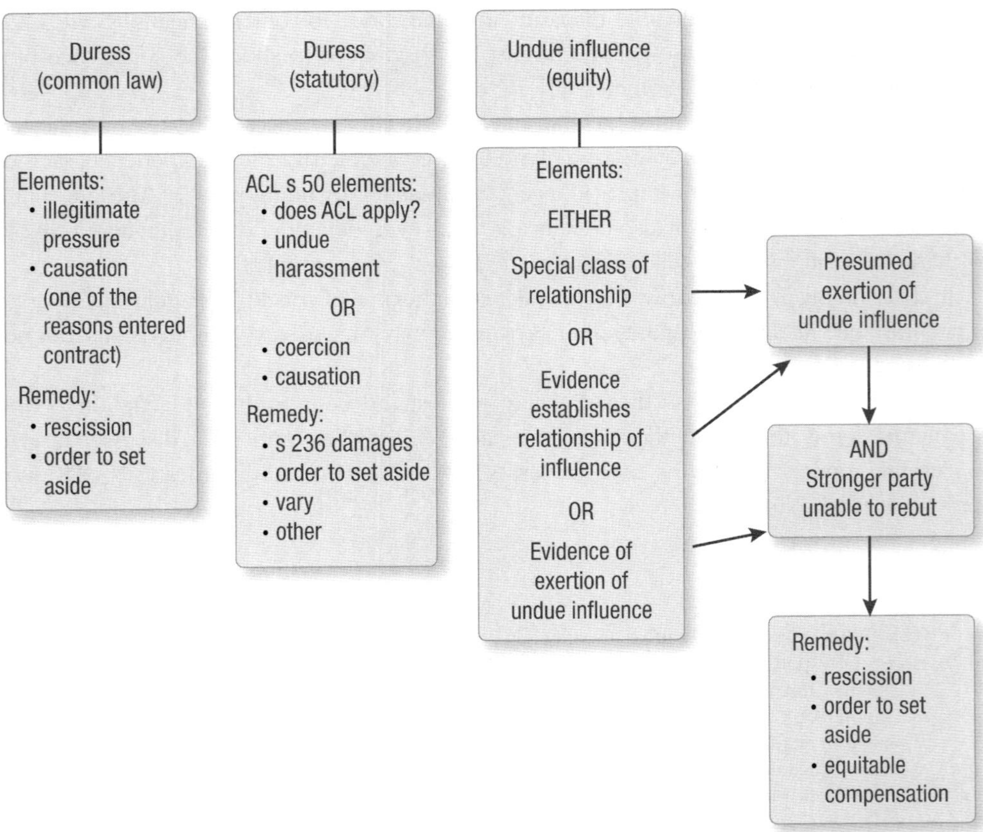

TIPS FOR APPLYING THE LAW IN PRACTICE

- Duress may be to the person, to goods, or be in the form of economic duress.
- Duress requires illegitimate pressure to be one of the causes of entry into the contract.
- If the person applying pressure is not party to the contract, then duress will not render the contract voidable, unless the other contracting party had actual or constructive knowledge of the duress.
- The remedy for duress is usually rescission or an order to set aside the contract.
- Statutory duress comprises either undue harassment or coercion.
- Exertion of undue influence may be proven by evidence, but more commonly is presumed due to an antecedent relationship of influence.
- An antecedent relationship of influence is presumed in special classes of relationship.
- In other circumstances, an antecedent relationship of influence may be proven by evidence.
- Alternatively, and more rarely, exertion of undue influence may be proven by evidence in the absence of an antecedent relationship.
- Once presumed, the stronger party must rebut the presumption that undue influence has been exerted.
- International perspectives: Voidability of contracts due to issues relating to coercion or improper conduct is outside the scope of the *CISG*, but rights to avoid contracts for unjustifiable threats and gross disparity are dealt with in UNIDROIT Principles.

PROBLEM QUESTION

Emma is a doctor. Over the past year, she has spent many hours treating a child, Ben, who is terminally ill. Ben's parents are very grateful for the special care Emma has provided to Ben. Shortly after Ben dies, Emma is approached by Ben's parents. They are naturally distraught, but feel that Ben would have wanted them to provide Emma with a substantial gift to say thank you for looking after him in his last year. They want to give Emma $100,000, and they tell Emma that they would be very hurt if she refuses their gift, as they know it would mean so much to Ben. Emma comes to you seeking advice. She wants to know whether she can accept the gift, and if so, what would be the best way to proceed.

RESEARCH QUESTIONS

(1) Consider the similarities and differences between UNIDROIT Principles art 3.2.6 and the common law of duress, noting what the consequences of those differences might mean for parties who have contracted due to threats.

(2) Within undue influence, can you think of any types of relationships in which the law might in future presume to be relationships of influence? What might be the pros and cons of deeming such relationships as ones of presumed influence?

20

UNCONSCIONABILITY AND UNFAIRNESS

20.1 Overview

The starting points for an understanding of the twin concepts of unconscionability and unfairness is that they do not operate on a simplistic application of basic notions of decency and morality. As noted in *Cheshire & Fifoot*, the concept of unconscionable conduct raises the fundamental dilemma of: 'How should the courts strike the balance between the rough and tumble of the marketplace and the protection of those too weak to participate fully or meaningfully in the marketplace?'[1]

The difficulty in articulating a coherent theory of unconscionability finds expression in *Cheshire & Fifoot*'s observation that unconscionability is an 'all pervasive, yet persistently elusive undercurrent in Australian contract law'.[2]

Chapter 20 of the *Principles* text and this chapter are an attempt, in common with many other authors who have tried to do so, to rationalise the law of unconscionability as a coherent whole. Our treatment thus reflects the nuance and tension of the topic, commencing with the role of 'conscience' followed by the idea that unconscionability does not without more operate as a cause of action and that the exercise of the court's power must be brought within some identifiable categories.

The 'special equity' for married women, which has its genesis in the seminal decision of *Yerkey v Jones*[3], is a particularly nuanced expression of just such an 'identifiable' category—the category of married women.

The final module in this chapter addresses statutory prohibitions on unconscionable conduct.

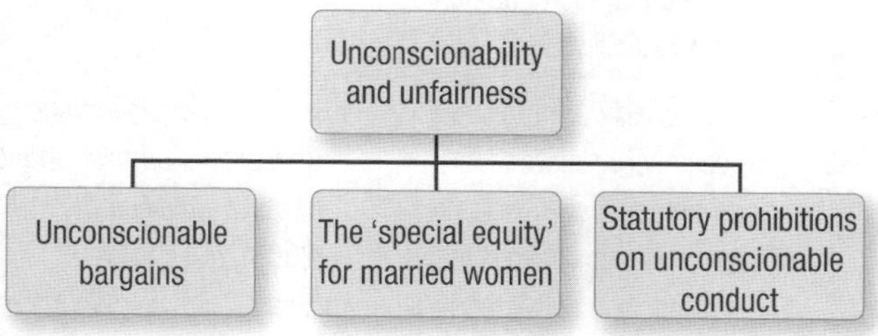

20.2 Unconscionable bargains

Concept	Short explanation	Relevant authorities	*Principles* text*
The role of conscience in modern contract law	'Unconscionability' without more does not operate as a cause of action but must be brought within some established doctrine The exercise of the court's power must be by reference to identifiable categories	*Australian Broadcasting Corporation v Lenah Game Meats Pty Ltd* (2001) 208 CLR 199 *Tanwar Enterprises Pty Ltd v Cauchi* (2003) 217 CLR 315	Chapter 20: 20.02

1 Nick Seddon and Rick Bigwood, *Cheshire & Fifoot Law of Contract* (LexisNexis Butterworths, 11th Australian ed, 2017) 825.
2 Ibid 823.
3 (1939) 63 CLR 649.

(cont.)

Concept	Short explanation	Relevant authorities	*Principles text**
Relief against unconscionable bargains	The circumstances that would qualify as an unconscionable dealing are broad	*Blomley v Ryan* (1956) 99 CLR 362	Chapter 20: 20.03
The elements of the unconscionable bargain doctrine	Establishing the criteria whereby a transaction can be set aside on the grounds of unconscionable dealing	*Commercial Bank of Australia Ltd v Amadio* (1983) 151 CLR 447	Chapter 20: 20.04
Extending the doctrine	The doctrine can be extended beyond merely a situation of some inherent disdvantage, such as where the donee has manipulated the emotions of the donor Even the fact of a relationship absent emotional manipulation might, without more, amount to unconscionability	*Louth v Diprose* (1992) 175 CLR 621 *Bridgewater v Leahy* (1998) 194 CLR 457	Chapter 20: 20.05
Restricting the scope of the doctrine	A mere inequality of bargaining power is not a relevant disadvantage Voluntary conduct, where the perpetrator has not acted in a predatory or surreptitious way, is unlikely to attract the operation of the doctrine On the other hand, unconscionability is broader in scope than undue influence; when undue influence was used that, however, inevitably would show a special disadvantage	*Australian Competition and Consumer Commission v C G Berbatis Holdings Pty Ltd* (2003) 214 CLR 51 *Kakavas v Crown Melbourne Ltd* (2013) 250 CLR 392 *Thorne v Kennedy* (2017) 263 CLR 85	Chapter 20: 20.06
Defences to a claim of unconscionability	In showing that the transaction was fair, having full knowledge of the implications of the transaction, following the provision of independent legal advice, is a signficant factor, though much depends on the quality of the advice	*Thorne v Kennedy* (2017) 263 CLR 85 *Micarone v Perpetual Trustees Australia Ltd* (1999) 75 SASR 1	Chapter 20: 20.07

Concept	Short explanation	Relevant authorities	*Principles* text*
	The decision to obtain legal advice might sometimes actually underscore the fact of the disadvantage		

* Consult the corresponding section(s) of the *Principles* text for more detail.

This part commences with a discussion of the role of 'conscience' in the development of doctrine, followed by the important proposition that unconscionability does not without more operate as a cause of action and that the exercise of the court's power must be brought within some identifiable categories. The most significant case here is *Commercial Bank of Australia Ltd v Amadio,*[4] which incorporates, among other things, a retrospective examination of the rationalisation for the doctrine. The underpinnings of the High Court's reasoning then found expression in almost every subsequent case in which the doctrine has been invoked. Underlining the significance of the case, this continues to hold true today.

This analysis naturally dovetails into the next modules, which deal with attempts to categorise and rationalise 'unconscionability', including a discussion of the elements of the unconscionable bargain doctrine, followed by extending and restricting the scope of the doctrine, and the 'defences' to claims of unconscionability. Whilst the idea of the 'elements' of the unconscionable bargain finds expression in slightly different ways,[5] the formulation in *Amadio* has been selected for its impact on the jurisprudence of the subject.

The concept of 'extending the doctrine' is that unconscionability can be construed in extreme terms by characterising the imbalance of power in a way that a finding of unconscionability is open. *Bridgewater v Leahy*[6] is our selected exemplar of such.

The converse, *restricting* the scope of the doctrine, is a timely reminder that despite having some form of disadvantage, such as a pathological urge to gamble,[7] the doctrine is, after all, limited in its scope to those to who can show a *special* disability and that this was exploited. The greater width of the unconscionable bargain, when compared to the concept of undue influence, was also explained in *Thorne v Kennedy* (2017) 263 CLR 85.

The concept of 'defences to a claim of unconscionability' is based on the idea that once the elements of unconscionability are made out there are means by which the donee/defendant might then show that the transaction was fair, one of the most significant of these being legal advice. The overarching notion, even then, relates to the negation of the disadvantage, and where the disadvantage cannot be overcome despite obtaining legal advice, then the transaction still cannot be saved from the effects of unconscionability. Such was the case in *Thorne v Kennedy.*[8]

4 (1983) 151 CLR 447.
5 *Principles* text p 382.
6 (1998) 194 CLR 457.
7 *Kakavas v Crown Melbourne Ltd* (2013) 250 CLR 392.
8 (2017) 263 CLR 85.

Australian Broadcasting Corporation v Lenah Game Meats Pty Ltd (2001) 208 CLR 199

Facts and issues

The respondent sought injunctions to restrain the broadcasting of a film of the respondent's operations at a 'brush tail possum processing facility'. The film was made surreptitiously and unlawfully with the use of hidden cameras, and was given to the appellant with the evident purpose that the appellant would broadcast it. There was evidence that the broadcasting would cause financial harm to the respondent. A question was whether there was a power to grant relief based on a general notion of unconscientious conduct. The answer to this question was in the negative, but note that in the circumstances of the case the Court found that there was entitlement to relief based on the notion of confidential information.

Decision

Per Gleeson CJ at 227:

> No doubt it is correct to say that, if equity will intervene to restrain publication of the film by the appellant, the ultimate ground upon which it will act will be that, in all the circumstances, it would be unconscientious of the appellant to publish. But that leaves for decision the question of the principles according to which equity will reach that conclusion. The conscience of the appellant, which equity will seek to relieve, is a properly formed and instructed conscience. The real task is to decide what a properly formed and instructed conscience has to say about publication in a case such as the present . . .
>
> [. . .]
>
> [230] For reasons already given, I regard the law of breach of confidence as providing a remedy, in a case such as the present, if the nature of [231] the information obtained by the trespasser is such as to permit the information to be regarded as confidential.

Tanwar Enterprises Pty Ltd v Cauchi (2003) 217 CLR 315

Facts and issues

Various contracts for the sale of land stipulated the same completion date. After the completion date was extended several times, a new date was fixed and time was made of the essence. The purchaser was unable to complete the contracts on the new date because of a delay in obtaining finance. Finance became available the following day. The vendors were aware that the purchaser wished to complete the contracts but issued notices of termination. The purchaser sought specific performance on the basis that the contracts had not been validly terminated, and relief against forfeiture of the contracts.

Decision

In relation to the question of whether a general power existed to intervene on the ground of the unconscionable use of legal rights generally, see Gleeson CJ, McHugh, Gummow, Hayne and Heydon JJ at 324:

> The terms 'unconscientious' and 'unconscionable' are, as was emphasised in *Australian Competition and Consumer Commission v C G Berbatis Holdings Pty Ltd* used across a broad range of the equity jurisdiction. They describe in their various applications the formation and instruction of conscience by reference to well developed principles. Thus, it may be said that breaches of trust and abuses of fiduciary position manifest unconscientious conduct; but whether a particular case amounts to a breach of trust or abuse of fiduciary duty is determined by reference to well developed principles, both specific and flexible in character. It is to those principles that the court has first regard rather than entering into the case at that higher level of abstraction involved in notions of unconscientious conduct in some loose sense where all principles are at large.
>
> [...]
>
> In the present case, that more accurate term directs attention to the question why the vendors ought not to be heard to assert the exercise of their legal right to terminate in answer to the claim by Tanwar for [325] specific performance. The conscience of the vendors which equity seeks to relieve is, as Gleeson CJ put it in *Australian Broadcasting Corporation v Lenah Game Meats Pty Ltd*, a 'properly formed and instructed conscience'.

Blomley v Ryan (1956) 99 CLR 362

Facts and issues

Ryan, an alcoholic, owned a grazing property. Blomley and his agent tried to convince him to sell and drafted a contract which contained a sale price well under the market value, and on terms otherwise very favourable to Blomley. Ryan refused to complete. The question was the extent to which Ryan's various infirmities (which included lacking in education, suffering from intoxication, and being mentally and physically unfit) could be relied on in resisting specific performance. The case is regarded as a leading case in the development of the unconscionability doctrine; in particular, in its discussion of the requirement that the party to a transaction seeking relief must suffer from a characteristic that amounts to a position of disadvantage.

Decision

Per Fullagar J at 405:

> So we find it said again and again that *mere* drunkenness affords no ground for resisting a suit to enforce a contract. Where, however, there is real ground for thinking that the judgment of one party was, to the knowledge of the other, seriously affected by drink, equity will generally refuse specific performance at the suit of that other, leaving him to pursue a remedy at law if he so desires. And, where the court is satisfied that a contract disadvantageous to the party affected has been obtained by 'drawing him in to drink', or that there has been real unfairness in taking advantage of his condition, the contract may be set aside.
>
> One other general observation may be made before proceeding to the facts of the present case. The circumstances adversely affecting a party, which may induce a court of equity either to refuse its aid or to set a transaction aside, are of great variety and can hardly be satisfactorily classified. Among them are poverty or need of any kind, sickness, age, sex, infirmity of body or mind, drunkenness, illiteracy or lack of education, lack of assistance or explanation where assistance or explanation is necessary. The common characteristic seems to be that they have the effect of

placing one party at a serious disadvantage *vis-à-vis* the other. It does not appear to be essential in all cases that the party at a disadvantage should suffer loss or detriment by the bargain.

Commercial Bank of Australia Ltd v Amadio (1983) 151 CLR 447

Facts and issues

The Amadios were elderly with limited English. Their son, Vincenzo, asked them to provide a mortgage over commercial premises. He told them that the duration of the mortgage was six months and their liability was limited to $50,000. The bank was aware that Vincenzo's business was in financial difficulties. The mortgage they signed in fact included a guarantee to secure the existing debts of Vincenzo's business and any future indebtedness without any restrictions. The question was whether the Amadios were entitled to set aside the mortgage on the grounds of unconscionability. This decision is regarded as the definitive common law case on unconscionability and to contain the framework for the application of the doctrine. Central features of the decision were the explicit disavowal of the notion that mere inequality of bargaining power could amount to a special disadvantage, and the discussion of the need for some qualifying 'special disadvantage'.

Decision

Per Mason J at 461:

> It goes almost without saying that it is impossible to describe definitively all the situations in which relief will be granted on the ground of unconscionable conduct. As Fullagar J. said in *Blomley v. Ryan*:
>
>> [462] The circumstances adversely affecting a party, which may induce a court of equity either to refuse its aid or to set a transaction aside, are of great variety and can hardly be satisfactorily classified. Among them are poverty or need of any kind, sickness, age, sex, infirmity of body or mind, drunkenness, illiteracy or lack of education, lack of assistance or explanation where assistance or explanation is necessary. The common characteristic seems to be that they have the effect of placing one party at a serious disadvantage vis-à-vis the other.
>
> [...]
>
> It is not to be thought that relief will be granted only in the particular situations mentioned by their Honours. It is made plain enough, especially by Fullagar J., that the situations mentioned are no more than particular exemplifications of an underlying general principle which may be invoked whenever one party by reason of some condition or circumstance is placed at a special disadvantage vis-à-vis another and unfair or unconscientious advantage is then taken of the opportunity thereby created. I qualify the word 'disadvantage' by the adjective 'special' in order to disavow any suggestion that the principle applies whenever there is some difference in the bargaining power of the parties and in order to emphasize that the disabling condition or circumstance is one which seriously affects the ability of the innocent party to make a judgment as to his own best interests, when the other party knows or ought to know of the existence of that condition or circumstance and of its effect on the innocent party.
>
> [...]
>
> [467] As we have seen, if A having actual knowledge that B occupies a situation of special disadvantage in relation to an intended transaction, so that B cannot make a judgment as to

what is in his own interests, takes unfair advantage of his (A's) superior bargaining power or position by entering into that transaction, his conduct in so doing is unconscionable. And if, instead of having actual knowledge of that situation, A is aware of the possibility that that situation may exist or is aware of facts that would raise that possibility in the mind of any reasonable person, the result will be the same.

Per Deane J at 474:

The jurisdiction of courts of equity to relieve against unconscionable dealing developed from the jurisdiction which the Court of Chancery assumed, at a very early period, to set aside transactions in which expectant heirs had dealt with their expectations without being adequately protected against the pressure put upon them by their poverty (see *O'Rorke v. Bolingbroke*). The jurisdiction is long established as extending generally to circumstances in which (i) a party to a transaction was under a special disability in dealing with the other party with the consequence that there was an absence of any reasonable degree of equality between them and (ii) that disability was sufficiently evident to the stronger party to make it prima facie unfair or 'unconscientious' that he procure, or accept, the weaker party's assent to the impugned transaction in the circumstances in which he procured or accepted it. Where such circumstances are shown to have existed, an onus is cast upon the stronger party to show that the transaction was fair, just and reasonable: 'the burthen of shewing the fairness of the transaction is thrown on the person who seeks to obtain the benefit of the contract' (see per Lord Hatherley, *O'Rorke v. Bolingbroke*; *Fry v. Lane; Blomley v. Ryan*).

[...]

[476] The bank, for its part, was a major national financial institution. It was privy to the business affairs and financial instability of Amadio Builders. It was aware that that company had, for some time, been unable to meet its debts as they fell due. It was aware of the state of Amadio Builders' two overdrawn accounts with it and of past failures to observe agreed borrowing limits. It had actually suggested, through Mr. Statton, that Mr. and Mrs. Amadio enter into the mortgage transaction to secure Amadio Builders' indebtedness to it. It was aware of the contents of its own document which Mr. Virgo presented to Mr. and Mrs. Amadio for their signature.

In contrast was the position of Mr. and Mrs. Amadio. Their personal circumstances have already been mentioned. They were advanced in years. Their grasp of written English was limited. They relied on Vincenzo for the management of their business affairs and believed that he and Amadio Builders were prosperous and successful. They were approached in their kitchen by the bank, acting through Mr. Virgo, at a time when Mr. Amadio was reading the newspaper after lunch and Mrs. Amadio was washing dishes. They were presented with a complicated and lengthy document for their immediate signature. They had received no independent advice in relation to the transaction which that document embodied and about which they had learned only hours earlier from Vincenzo who, it is common ground in the present appeal, had misled them as regards the extent and duration of their potential liability under it. Apart from indicating that the guarantee/mortgage was unlimited in point of time, Mr. Virgo made no personal attempt to explain it to them. Foolishly, but — in view of their limited grasp of written English and their knowledge that Mr. Virgo came to them with the approval of their son — perhaps understandably, they did not attempt to read the document for themselves. They signed it in the mistaken belief that their potential liability was limited to a maximum of $50,000.

[...]

[477] That weakness constituted a special disability of Mr. and Mrs. Amadio in their dealing with the bank of the type necessary to enliven the equitable principles relating to relief against

> unconscionable dealing. Put more precisely, the result of the combination of their age, their limited grasp of written English, the circumstances in which the bank presented the document to them for their signature and, most importantly, their lack of knowledge and understanding of the contents of the document was that, to adapt the words of Fullagar J. quoted above, they lacked assistance and advice where assistance and advice were plainly necessary if there were to be any reasonable degree of equality between themselves and the bank.

Louth v Diprose (1992) 175 CLR 621

Facts and issues

The plaintiff was infatuated with the defendant. The defendant manipulated his feelings by making suicide threats connected with her desire to acquire a house. He gave her a significant sum of money to buy a house. The issue was whether his gift to her could be avoided on the grounds of unconscionability. The case is significant for the recognition that the donor was not typically 'disadvantaged' but that his infatuation and the donee's manipulation of it led to that finding.

Decision

Per Deane J at 636:

> The relationship between the respondent and the appellant went back to an initial relationship between them ... There was an extreme contrast between their respective attitudes to one another. For his part, the respondent was 'utterly infatuated' by the appellant. He was 'completely in love' with her. In contrast, the appellant had become 'quite indifferent to' the respondent. The motives for her continued association with him 'were of a material nature'. His infatuation placed the respondent 'in a position of emotional dependence upon the appellant and gave her a position of great influence on his actions and decisions'.
>
> [...]
>
> The appellant set out on a planned course of conduct aimed at [637] persuading the respondent to provide the money necessary to enable her to purchase the house from her brother-in-law. She 'deliberately manufactured' a false 'atmosphere of crisis in order to influence the [respondent] to provide the money [to purchase] the house'. She falsely told the respondent that she was required to leave the house. She said that, if forced to vacate the house, she would commit suicide.
>
> [...]
>
> It has long been established that the jurisdiction of courts of equity to relieve against unconscionable dealing extends generally to circumstances in which (i) a party to a transaction was under a special disability in dealing with the other party to the transaction with the consequence that there was an absence of any reasonable degree of equality between them and (ii) that special disability was sufficiently evident to the other party to make it prima facie unfair or 'unconscionable' that that other party procure, accept or retain the benefit of, the disadvantaged party's assent to the impugned transaction in the circumstances in which he or she procured or accepted it. Where such circumstances are shown to have existed, an onus is cast upon the stronger party to show that the transaction was fair, just and reasonable: 'the burthen of shewing the fairness of the transaction is thrown on the person who seeks to obtain' or retain the benefit of it.

> [...]
>
> [638] On the findings of the learned trial judge in the present case, the relationship between the respondent and the appellant at the time of the impugned gift was plainly such that the respondent was under a special disability in dealing with the appellant. That special disability arose not merely from the respondent's infatuation. It extended to the extraordinary vulnerability of the respondent in the false 'atmosphere of crisis' in which he believed that the woman with whom he was 'completely in love' and upon whom he was emotionally dependent was facing eviction from her home and suicide unless he provided the money for the purchase of the house. The appellant was aware of that special disability. Indeed, to a significant extent, she had deliberately created it. She manipulated it to her advantage to influence the respondent to make the gift of the money to purchase the house. When asked for restitution she refused. From the respondent's point of view, the whole transaction was plainly a most improvident one.
>
> In these circumstances, the learned trial judge's conclusion that the appellant had been guilty of unconscionable conduct in procuring and retaining the gift of $59,206.55 was not only open to him. In the context of his Honour's findings of fact, it was inevitable and plainly correct. On those findings, the case was not simply one in which the respondent had, under the influence of his love for, or infatuation with, the appellant, made an imprudent gift in her favour. The case was one in which the appellant deliberately used that love or infatuation and her own deceit to create a situation in which she could unconscientiously manipulate the respondent to part with a large proportion of his property. The intervention of equity is not merely to relieve the plaintiff from the consequences of his own foolishness. It is to prevent his victimisation.

Bridgewater v Leahy (1998) 194 CLR 457

Facts and issues

An elderly man, devoted to his nephew, but found to be competent and to have understood what he was doing, transferred his properties to his nephew at a significant undervalue. It had been found by the Queensland Court of Appeal below that the transaction was neither tainted by undue influence nor did the *Amadio* principles apply. The question was whether the transaction should be set aside as being tainted by unconscionability. By taking emotional dependence to a level whereby, in the absence of manipulation, it could amount to unconscionability, the case can fairly be considered the benchmark[9] of the doctrine.

Decision

Per Gaudron, Gummow and Kirby JJ 490:

> The position of disadvantage which renders one party subject to exploitation by another such that the benefit of an improvident disposition by the disadvantaged party may not in good conscience be retained may stem from a strong emotional dependence or attachment. *Louth v Diprose* was such a case. In his judgment in the South Australian Full Court, a decision which was upheld in this Court, Jacobs ACJ said:

9 *Principles* text p 384.

> It is an oversimplification to say that because the respondent acted as he did with his eyes open, and with a full understanding of what he was doing, he was not in a position of disadvantage, and therefore not the victim of unconscionable conduct.

There are passages in the reasons of the primary judge which appear to suggest that the existence of such a position of disadvantage necessarily involves physical frailty and enfeeblement with diminished knowledge by the party in question of that party's property and affairs generally. That will not necessarily be the case.

[. . .]

[491] We have referred to the primary judge's conclusion that Bill had 'the capacity then to know what he was doing and to make informed decisions about the disposition of his property'. That however is not an answer to the question whether, on the primary facts, the conclusion should have been reached that advantage was taken of Bill's disadvantaged position.

[. . .]

[493] Bill's goal to preserve his rural interests intact and his perception that Neil was the candidate to provide reliable and experienced management thereof were significant elements in his emotional attachment to and dependency upon Neil. The initiative to utilise the circumstance of the sale of the Injune Land (to the retention of which Bill had been opposed) for the irreversible implementation of Bill's wishes during his lifetime came from Neil.

[. . .]

Relief

The relationship between Bill and Neil meant that, when Neil raised the question of using the proceeds of sale of the Injune Land, they were meeting on unequal terms. Neil took advantage of this position to obtain a benefit through a grossly improvident transaction on the part of his uncle.

[. . .]

In some cases, the equity that arises by reason of an unconscientious or unconscionable dealing of the nature with which this appeal is concerned may be satisfied only by setting aside that dealing in its entirety. The dealing may be embodied in the one instrument which contains several provisions or in several instruments. In other circumstances, of which this case is an example, the equity may be satisfied by orders setting aside some but not all of these instruments or some but not all of the provisions thereof.

It is unconscionable for Neil and his wife to retain the benefit of the improvident transaction. . .

Australian Competition and Consumer Commission v C G Berbatis Holdings Pty Ltd (2003) 214 CLR 51

Facts and issues

Tenants of a shopping centre wished to negotiate a new term for their lease. There was some urgency as their lease was due to expire. Centre owners agreed to a new term on the basis the lessees agreed by a proposed deed of assignment to discharge owners from several claims, and to discontinue proceedings against the owners. The ACCC brought proceedings against the lessors alleging unconscionable conduct under s 51AA of the *Trade Practices Act* (as it was then), which provided for a remedy for unconscionable conduct 'within the meaning of the written law' ie the common law. It was stressed that those sections did not affect the position at common law

(*Amadio*): namely, that an inequality of bargaining power did not give rise to an inference of unconscionability.

Decision

Per Gleeson CJ at 64:

> One thing is clear, and is illustrated by the decision in *Samton Holdings* itself. A person is not in a position of relevant disadvantage, constitutional, situational, or otherwise, simply because of inequality of bargaining power. Many, perhaps even most, contracts are made between parties of unequal bargaining power, and good conscience does not require parties to contractual negotiations to forfeit their advantages, or neglect their own interests.
>
> In *Amadio*, Mason J said that the point of using the qualifying word 'special' before 'disadvantage' in this context is 'to disavow any suggestion that the principle applies whenever there is some difference in the bargaining power of the parties and in order to emphasise that the disabling condition or circumstance is one which seriously affects the ability of the innocent party to make a judgment as to his own best interests'. It was the inability of a party to judge his or her own best interests that was said by McTiernan J in *Blomley v Ryan*, and again by Deane J in *Amadio*, to be the essence of the relevant weakness.
>
> The adjective 'special' was also used by Kitto J in *Blomley v Ryan* when he referred to the 'well-known head of equity' invoked in that case. He said:
>
>> It applies whenever one party to a transaction is at a special disadvantage in dealing with the other party because illness, ignorance, inexperience, impaired faculties, financial need or other circumstances affect his ability to conserve his own interests, and the other party unconscientiously takes advantage of the opportunity thus placed in his hands.
>
> Unconscientious exploitation of another's inability, or diminished ability, to conserve his or her own interests is not to be confused with taking advantage of a superior bargaining position. There may be cases where both elements are involved, but, in such cases, it is the first, not the second, element that is of legal consequence. It is neither the purpose nor the effect of s 51AA to treat people generally, when they deal with others in a stronger position, as though they were all expectant heirs in the nineteenth century, dealing with a usurer.
>
> In the present case, there was neither a special disadvantage on the part of the lessees, nor unconscientious conduct on the part of the lessors. All the people involved in the transaction were business people, concerned to advance or protect their own financial interests. The critical disadvantage from which the lessees suffered was that they had no legal entitlement to a renewal or extension of their lease; and they depended upon the lessors' willingness to grant such an extension or renewal for their capacity to sell the goodwill of their business for a substantial price. They were thus compelled to approach the lessors, seeking their agreement to such an extension or renewal, against a background of current claims and litigation in which they were involved. They were at a distinct disadvantage, but there was nothing 'special' about it.

Kakavas v Crown Melbourne Ltd (2013) 250 CLR 392

Facts and issues

Kakavas was a high stakes gambler. Following serious losses, he brought a claim against the casino to recover his net losses, alleging that they had engaged in unconscionable conduct contrary to s 51AA of the *Trade Practices Act 1974* (Cth) and the general law. He alleged that the casino had lured him, a known problem gambler, to gamble at the casino by providing incentives, such as rebates on losses and the use of its private facilities. The case represents a somewhat limited view on the doctrine by its finding that a pathological gambler could not avail himself of the doctrine as his gambling was nonetheless considered to be voluntary.

Decision

Per French CJ, Hayne, Crennan, Kiefel, Bell, Gageler and Keane JJ at 402:

> To focus, as the appellant's case now does, on his state of excitement while he was actually at the gaming table is to lose sight of the reality that he was present at the gaming table on each of these occasions because of decisions voluntarily made by him when he was not in the grip of his abnormal enthusiasm. Importantly in this regard, the appellant does not have the benefit of a finding of fact that he suffered from a continuously operating compulsion which disabled him from choosing to stay away from the gaming tables. It was the appellant's choice — exercised many times over a period of many weeks when he was indisputably not at the tables in the casino in the grip of any gambling frenzy — to put himself in the position in which he might lose money at Crown's tables.
>
> [. . .]
>
> [426] In *Jenyns v Public Curator (Qld)* Dixon CJ, McTiernan and Kitto JJ explained that the invocation of equitable doctrines, such as those concerned with the conscience of a party to a transaction, in order to impugn that transaction . . .:
>
>> calls for a precise examination of the particular facts, a scrutiny of the exact relations established between the parties and a consideration of the mental capacities, processes and idiosyncrasies of the [other party].
>
> [. . .]
>
> It does not accord with that approach to consider the appellant's 'special disadvantage' separately, in isolation from the other circumstances of the impugned transactions which bear upon the principle invoked by the appellant. The issue as to special disadvantage must be considered as part of the broader question, which is whether the impugned transactions were procured by Crown's taking advantage of an inability on the appellant's part to make worthwhile decisions in his own interests, which inability was sufficiently evident to Crown's employees to render their conduct exploitative.
>
> [. . .]
>
> [432] . . . we do not accept that the appellant's pathological interest in gambling was a special disadvantage which made him susceptible to exploitation by Crown. He was able to make rational decisions to refrain from gambling altogether had he chosen to do so. He was certainly able to choose to refrain from gambling with Crown.
>
> [. . .]
>
> [439] Equitable intervention to deprive a party of the benefit of its bargain on the basis that it was procured by unfair exploitation of the weakness of the other party requires proof of a predatory state of mind. Heedlessness of, or indifference to, the best interests of the other party is not sufficient for this purpose. The principle is not engaged by mere inadvertence, or even indifference, to the circumstances of the other party to an arm's length commercial transaction. Inadvertence, or indifference, falls short of the victimisation or exploitation with which the principle is concerned.

Thorne v Kennedy (2017) 263 CLR 85

Facts and issues

The appellant, an Eastern European woman, and the respondent, a wealthy Australian property developer, having met online, entered into a pre-nuptial and a post-nuptial agreement. The appellant was induced to come to Australia with minimal possessions. The appellant obtained legal advice not to sign the documents; however, the respondent told the appellant the wedding would not go ahead otherwise. The documents were subsequently signed. The parties separated and the appellant began proceedings to set aside the agreements. The primary issue was whether the respondent's conduct was unconscionable. The fact that she obtained legal advice did not deprive her of her right to set aside the pre-nuptial agreements on the grounds of unconscionability because, in the light of the six factors set out on p 106 of the High Court's judgment below, the appellant's plight was such that the inference that the respondent had exploited her plight unconscionably was not displaced.

Decision

Per Kiefel CJ, Bell, Gageler, Keane and Edelman JJ at 103:

> A conclusion of unconscionable conduct requires the innocent party to be subject to a special disadvantage 'which seriously affects the ability of the innocent party to make a judgment as to [the innocent party's] own best interests'. The other party must also unconscientiously take advantage of that special disadvantage. This has been variously described as requiring 'victimisation', 'unconscientious conduct', or 'exploitation'. Before there can be a finding of unconscientious taking of advantage, it is also generally necessary that the other party knew or ought to have known of the existence and effect of the special disadvantage.
>
> In *Commercial Bank of Australia Ltd v Amadio*, Deane J said that the equitable principles concerning relief against unconscionable conduct are closely related to those concerned with undue influence. The same circumstances can result in the conclusion that the person seeking relief (i) has been subject to undue influence, and (ii) is in a position of special disadvantage for the purposes of the doctrine concerned with unconscionable conduct. For instance, in *Diprose v Louth (No 1)*, the trial judge, King CJ, observed that both doctrines were satisfied where the defendant 'was in a position of emotional dominance which gave her an influence over the [plaintiff] which she exercised unconscientiously to procure the gift of the house'. Before the High Court in that case, Mr Diprose relied only upon the ground of unconscionable conduct.
>
> Although undue influence and unconscionable conduct will overlap, they have distinct spheres of operation. One difference is that although one way in which the element of special disadvantage for a finding of unconscionable conduct can be established is by a finding of undue influence, there are many other circumstances that can amount to a special disadvantage which would not establish undue influence. A further difference between the doctrines is that although undue influence cases will often arise from the assertion of pressure by the other party which might amount to victimisation or exploitation, this is not always required. In *Commercial Bank of Australia Ltd v Amadio*, Mason J emphasised the difference between unconscionable conduct and undue influence as follows:
>
>> In the latter the will of the innocent party is not independent and voluntary because it is overborne. In the former the will of the innocent party, even if independent and

> voluntary, is the result of the disadvantageous position in which he is placed and of the other party unconscientiously taking advantage of that position.

[. . .]

[106] The primary judge set out six matters which, in combination, led her to the conclusion that Ms Thorne had 'no choice' or was powerless: (i) her lack of financial equality with Mr Kennedy; (ii) her lack of permanent status in Australia at the time; (iii) her reliance on Mr Kennedy for all things; (iv) her emotional connectedness to their relationship and the prospect of motherhood; (v) her emotional preparation for marriage; and (vi) the 'publicness' of her upcoming marriage. These six matters were the basis for the vivid description by the primary judge of Ms Thorne's circumstances:

> She was in Australia only in furtherance of their relationship. She had left behind her life and minimal possessions . . . She brought no assets of substance to the relationship. If the relationship ended, she would have nothing. No job, no visa, no home, no place, no community. The consequences of the relationship being at an end would have significant and serious consequences to Ms Thorne. She would not be entitled to remain in Australia and she had nothing to return to anywhere else in the world.
>
> Every bargaining chip and every power was in Mr Kennedy's hands. Either the document, as it was, was signed, or the relationship was at an end. The husband made that clear.

[. . .]

[112] The Full Court recognised that Ms Thorne was labouring under a disadvantage, although the Court did not add the adjective 'special', which, as Mason J in *Commercial Bank of Australia Ltd v Amadio* explained, is used to emphasise that the disadvantage is not a mere difference in the bargaining power but requires an inability for a person to make a judgment as to his or her own best interests. The findings by the primary judge that Ms Thorne was subject to undue influence – powerless, with what she saw as no choice but to enter the agreements – point inevitably to the conclusion that she was subject to a special disadvantage in her entry into the agreements.

Ms Thorne's special disadvantage was known to Mr Kennedy. Her special disadvantage had been, in part, created by him. He created the urgency with which the pre-nuptial agreement was required to be signed and the haste surrounding the post-nuptial agreement and the advice upon it. While Ms Thorne knew Mr Kennedy required her acknowledgment that his death would not result in her receiving a windfall inheritance at the expense of his children, she had no reason to anticipate an intention on his part to insist upon terms of marriage that were as unreasonable as those contained in the agreements. Further, Ms Thorne and her family members had been brought to Australia for the wedding by Mr Kennedy and his ultimatum was not accompanied by any offer to assist them to return home. These matters increased the pressure which contributed to the substantial subordination of Ms Thorne's free will in relation to the agreements. Mr Kennedy took advantage of Ms Thorne's vulnerability to obtain agreements which, on Ms Harrison's uncontested assessment, were entirely inappropriate and wholly inadequate. Even within that class of agreement, the agreements which Ms Thorne signed involved 'gross inequality'.

Further, in relation to the specific point concerning the effect of legal advice, per Gordon J at 128:

It is not a sufficient response to the conclusion of unconscionable conduct to point to the fact that Ms Thorne received independent legal advice about the two agreements and chose to reject her solicitor's recommendation on each occasion. The fact that Ms Thorne was willing to sign both agreements *despite* being advised that they were 'terrible' serves to underscore the extent of the special disadvantage under which Ms Thorne laboured, and to reinforce the conclusion that in these circumstances, which Mr Kennedy had substantially created, it was unconscientious for Mr Kennedy to procure or accept her assent.

Micarone v Perpetual Trustees Australia Ltd (1999) 75 SASR 1

Facts and issues

The action concerned the enforceability of certain mortgages executed by the plaintiffs, none of whom was a natural born Australian citizen. Allegations of unconscionability were made in relation to an action brought by it for possession under the relevant mortgages. The discussion of the decision below is restricted to the question of whether the obtaining of legal advice would impact the allegations of unconscionability.

Decision

Per Olsson J at 43:

> [Counsel] sought to dismiss such a line of reasoning by saying that, even given the entrustment scenario, it was well established on the authorities that the intervention of a solicitor such as *Belperio* to give independent legal advice was a complete answer. He argued that this negated operation of the principle adverted to in *Pandya*.
>
> He relied for that proposition on the reasoning of the Court of Appeal in *Bank of Baroda v Shah* [1988] 3 All ER 24 (Baroda), *Coldunell* and *Massey v Midland Bank plc* [1995] 1 All ER 929 (Massey), as authorities for such a proposition.
>
> Those cases establish that, generally speaking, a financier is entitled to act upon an understanding, reasonably arrived at, that independent legal advice has been given to a proposed mortgagee. It is not required to inquire into the precise nature of the advice, or the circumstances in which it is given. If, on the facts, the financier has *required* the giving of independent advice; the relevant security document is transmitted by it, or its solicitors, to a solicitor who is reasonably understood to be acting for the proposed mortgagee as an independent adviser; and it is thereafter returned by that solicitor apparently regularly executed and witnessed, then it cannot be said (within *Pandya*) that it has been left to the principal debtor to procure the relevant execution.
>
> The above authorities focus on the commercial unreality and unreasonableness of requiring a financier to go behind a situation in which it has taken positive, reasonable steps to require independent advice and, prima facie, it has no reason to doubt that such advice has been obtained.
>
> [...]
>
> [44] But those situations were a far cry from the instant case.
>
> [...]
>
> Even when those certificates came to hand it must have been patently obvious that all seven executing parties had allegedly been the subject of earlier independent advice from a single solicitor, despite what were prima facie conflict of interest situations.
>
> In other words, at time of execution, PUMA had no reason to believe that true independent advice had been given to each plaintiff; and, when the ex post facto certificates were sought

and obtained, the very circumstances (including Tony's involvement in what occurred) begged obvious questions. Furthermore, neither PUMA nor IF&I took any steps to ensure that such knowledge that they possessed was made available to *Belperio* for the purpose of any advice which he may have given.

[. . .]

[46] In this case *Perpetual* sought to derive comfort from what was said by Perry J in *Nicholson* to the effect that, far from the lender seeking to take advantage of any perceived position of advantage, it had been at pains to ensure that independent advice was given to the guarantors in that case. In so doing they followed best banking practice; and no more could reasonably be expected of them than that. Indeed, it went further. It contended that the relevant solicitor's certificates '*provide an absolute shield to the allegations of unconscionable conduct*'.

[. . .]

These contentions were, of course, also advanced before the learned trial judge. He took the view that the certificates were not an absolute shield. They merely constituted a matter to be taken into account when considering the issue of unconscionability [His Honour held, as a result of his earlier analysis, that this was not such a case].

QUESTIONS

(1) Identify the common thread, or the common elements, which must be satisfied for the finding of an unconscionable bargain.

(2) Identify the difference between the idea of a 'special' disadvantage with some other form of disadvantage and with some inequality of bargaining power.

(3) In what sense is it considered that *Louth* and *Bridgewater* (more so the latter) extended the operation of the doctrine?

20.3 The 'special equity' for married women

Concept	Short explanation	Relevant authorities	*Principles* text*
Background	A guarantee may be set A wife, because she is the wife, might have the right to have a guarantee set aside when the creditor knows of the relationship of marriage	*Yerkey v Jones* (1939) 63 CLR 649	Chapter 20: 20.08
The modern position	The rule in *Yerkey v Jones* has been confirmed, and now subsumed into the doctrine of unconscionable bargain	*Garcia v National Australia Bank Ltd* (1998) 194 CLR 395	Chapter 20: 20.09

Concept	Short explanation	Relevant authorities	*Principles* text*
The rationale and scope of the rule in *Yerkey v Jones*	The principle is based not on the subservience of the wife, but on a lack of information, a product of the trust and confidence married people have in each other The rule does not apply other than to guarantees	*Garcia v National Australia Bank Ltd* (1998) 194 CLR 395 *Narain v Euroasia (Pacific) Pty Ltd* (2009) 26 VR 387	Chapter 20: 20.10

* Consult the corresponding section(s) of the *Principles* text for more detail.

The 'special equity for married women' is an especially nuanced aspect of the principles of unconscionability; the High Court in *Yerkey v Jones*[10], despite recognising that the category of man and wife did not carry a presumption of undue influence by the man over his wife, nonetheless considered that the guarantee of a wife would be liable to be set aside on the basis of the creditor's knowledge of the marriage relationship. Not without controversy[11], the reception of this principle into contemporary Australian jurisprudence was facilitated via its treatment in *Garcia v National Australia Bank Ltd*.[12]

Yerkey v Jones (1939) 63 CLR 649

Facts and issues

Jones was interested in buying a property from the Yerkeys and as security for instalment payments provided a mortgage executed over property in his wife's name. At all times, Jones negotiated directly with the Yerkeys. The issue concerned whether the mortgage was enforceable against Mrs Jones. Ultimately, the mortgage was found to be enforceable, but more importantly, the Court considered more broadly the enforceability of a guarantee provided by a wife for a debt of the husband.

Decision

Per Dixon J at 678:

> Although the relation of husband to wife is not one of influence, yet the opportunities it gives are such that if the husband procures his wife to become surety for his debt a creditor who accepts her suretyship obtained through her husband has been treated as taking it subject to any invalidating conduct on the part of her husband even if the creditor be not actually privy to such conduct. It is evident, however, that in many cases, though it is the husband who obtains his

10 (1939) 63 CLR 649.

11 See eg Nick Seddon and Rick Bigwood, *Cheshire & Fifoot Law of Contract* (LexisNexis Butterworths, 11th Australian ed, 2017).

12 (1998) 194 CLR 395.

> wife's consent to act as guarantor or surety, yet the creditor or his agents will deal directly with the wife personally. It must then be a question how far an apparent or real comprehension on the part of the wife or advice or explanation received by her will prevent any earlier improper conduct on the part of the husband from operating to make the transaction voidable.
>
> [. . .]
>
> [683] Although the relation of husband to wife is not one of influence, yet the opportunities it gives are such that if the husband procures his wife to become surety for his debt a creditor who accepts her suretyship obtained through her husband has been treated as taking it subject to any invalidating conduct on the part of her husband even if the creditor be not actually privy to such conduct. It is evident, however, that in many cases, though it is the husband who obtains his wife's consent to act as guarantor or surety, yet the creditor or his agents will deal directly with the wife personally. It must then be a question how far an apparent or real comprehension on the part of the wife or advice or explanation received by her will prevent any earlier improper conduct on the part of the husband from operating to make the transaction voidable.

Garcia v National Australia Bank Ltd (1998) 194 CLR 395

Facts and issues

Mrs Garcia was a capable, professional woman who executed a mortgage over properties over the matrimonial property, which was in her name, to secure loans made to businesses conducted by her husband. She obtained no personal benefit from the loans. The Garcias subsequently divorced. The question was whether she was entitled to have the mortgage set aside.

Decision

Rationalising the *Yerkey v Jones* principle, see Gaudron, McHugh, Gummow and Hayne JJ at 404:

> In his reasons for decision in *Yerkey v Jones,* Dixon J dealt with at least two kinds of circumstances: the first in which there is actual undue influence by a husband over a wife and the second, that dealt with in *Mueller*, in which there is no undue influence but there is a failure to explain adequately and accurately the suretyship transaction which the husband seeks to have the wife enter for the immediate economic benefit not of the wife but of the husband, or the [405] circumstances in which her liability may arise. The former kind of case is one concerning what today is seen as an imbalance of power. In point of legal principle, however, it is actual undue influence in that the wife, lacking economic or other power, is overborne by her husband and goes surety for her husband's debts when she does not bring a free mind and will to that decision. The latter case is not so much concerned with imbalances of power as with lack of proper information about the purport and effect of the transaction. The present appeal concerns circumstances of the latter kind rather than the former.

The following passage contains the High Court's seminal treatment of the requirements to be satisfied for relief in favour of the wife:

> [408] The principles applied in *Yerkey v Jones* do not depend upon the creditor having, at the time the guarantee is taken, notice of some unconscionable dealing between the husband as borrower and the wife as surety. *Yerkey v Jones* begins with the recognition that the surety is a

volunteer: a person who obtained no financial benefit from the transaction, performance of the obligations of which she agreed to guarantee. It holds, in what we have called the first kind of case, that to enforce that voluntary transaction against her when in fact she did not bring a free will to its execution would be unconscionable. It holds further, in the second kind of case, that to enforce it against her if it later emerges that she did not understand the purport and effect of the transaction of suretyship would be unconscionable (even though she is a willing party to it) if the lender took no steps itself to explain its purport and effect to her or did not reasonably believe that its purport and effect had been explained to her by a competent, independent and disinterested stranger. And what makes it unconscionable to enforce it in the second kind of case is the combination of circumstances that: (a) in fact the surety did not understand the purport and effect of the transaction; (b) the transaction was voluntary (in the sense that the surety obtained no gain from the contract the performance of which was guaranteed); (c) the lender is to be taken to have understood that, as a wife, the surety may repose trust and confidence in her husband in matters of business and therefore to have understood that the husband may not fully and accurately explain the purport and effect of the transaction to his wife; and yet (d) the lender did not itself take steps to explain the transaction to the wife or find out that a stranger had explained it to her [the 'second kind of case' above is regarded as the definitive *Yerkey v Jones* rule].

Narain v Euroasia (Pacific) Pty Ltd (2009) 26 VR 387

Facts and issues

The question in brief was whether the *Yerkey* rule was confined to a suretyship which operates to a wife's husband's advantage.

Decision

Per Nettle JA at 396:

> … I reject the contention that *Yerkey* is capable of application to instruments apart from suretyship which operate to a wife's husband's advantage or confer a voluntary benefit on him. In my judgment, therefore, Hollingworth J was right to hold that *Yerkey* does not apply to instruments other than instruments of suretyship.

QUESTION

As explained in the *Principles* text and the cases referred to there[13], the fact that the potentially vulnerable party has obtained legal advice is often relied on as a 'defence' to an allegation of unconscionability. When will the fact of legal advice *not* save a transaction from an allegation of unconscionability?

13 See *Principles* text at 20.07.

20.4 Statutory prohibitions on unconscionable conduct

Concept	Short explanation	Relevant authorities	*Principles* text*
The relationship between ss 20 and 21 of the Australian Consumer Law	The relevant provisions will be set out	Australian Consumer Law ss 20–21	Chapter 20: 20.12
The relationship between s 20 and unconscionable conduct in equity	The scope of the proscribed conduct might change from time to time, with s 20 itself sometimes being the driver of the change	*Australian Competition and Consumer Commission v Samton Holdings Pty Ltd* (2002) 117 FCR 301	Chapter 20: 20.13
'Unconscionable conduct within the meaning of the unwritten law'	The statutory sanction is broader than the equitable concept of unconscionability	*Australian Competition and Consumer Commission v Samton Holdings Pty Ltd* (2002) 117 FCR 301 *Australian Competition and Consumer Commission v Radio Rentals Ltd* (2005) 146 FCR 292	Chapter 20: 20.13
The unconscionability standard under s 21	'Unconscionability' lacks precision and has been described as open-ended and value-laden One oft-repeated standard is that the proscribed conduct must involve a high degree of 'moral obliquy' The Federal Court has warned against the use of synonyms; rather, one must perform an evaluation of the conduct by reference to normative values prescribed by parliament	*Australian Competition and Consumer Commission v Seal-A-Fridge Pty Ltd* [2010] FCA 525 *Attorney-General (NSW) v World Best Holdings Ltd* (2005) 63 NSWLR 557 *Paciocco v Australia and New Zealand Banking Group Ltd* (2015) 236 FCR 199	Chapter 20: 20.16
Relevant factors	Here, relevant statutory provisions will be set out The High Court has stated that a finding of unconscionable conduct can only be drawn having regard to all the circumstances of the case	*Paciocco v Australia and New Zealand Banking Group Ltd* (2016) 258 CLR 525	Chapter 20: 20.17

Concept	Short explanation	Relevant authorities	*Principles* text*
Examples of conduct breaching s 21: consumer transactions	Conduct in relation to contracts providing for periodical payments by women in Indigenous communities was held to be unconscionable The absence of predatory conduct is significant in finding the conduct is not unconscionable Coercion on the part of the creditor to make payments by the creation of fake complaints was held to be unconscionable	Australian Consumer Law s 22(1), (2) *Australian Competition and Consumer Commission v Keshow* [2005] FCA 558 *Kobelt v Australian Securities and Investments Commission* (2018) 325 ALR 689 *Australian Competition and Consumer Commission v Excite Mobile Pty Ltd* [2013] FCA 350	Chapter 20: 20.18
Examples of conduct breaching ss 20 and 21: business transactions	Whilst taking advantage of superior bargaining power was not unconscionable, it would be to do so in conjunction with falsehoods Exercising a contractual right to terminate a contract without more is not unconscionable	*Australian Competition and Consumer Commission v Seal-A-Fridge Pty Ltd* [2010] FCA 525 *Robert McGill Freier v Australian Postal Corporation (No 2)* [2012] NSWSC 61	Chapter 20: 20.19

* Consult the corresponding section(s) of the *Principles* text for more detail.

The statutory prohibitions on unconscionable conduct, sections 20 and 21 of the Australian Consumer Law, are adjacent to the unconscionable bargains doctrine at common law.

Section 20 proscribes unconscionable conduct within the meaning of the unwritten law; ie the law distinct from *statutory* principles. It presently is uncertain if the section is intended to 'catch' conduct, other than the equitable concept of the exploitation of special disadvantage or some wider range of areas and doctrines.[14] Section 21, on the one hand, is restricted to conduct that occurs in connection with the supply or acquisition (or potential supply or acquisition) of goods or services but, on the other hand, is wider than the unwritten law when it does apply.[15]

The discussion below explores ss 20 and 21, and after setting out the underpinnings and scope of both sections, focuses on the standards to be applied in s 21, including the factors that may be considered under that section.

The chapter ends with a discussion of examples of conduct which were considered to breach s 21.

14 See *Australian Competition and Consumer Commission v C G Berbatis Holdings Pty Ltd* (2003) 214 CLR 51, and the discussion at 20.14 of the *Principles* text.

15 Section 21(4) ACL is to that specific effect.

Australian Consumer Law ss 20–21

20 Unconscionable conduct within the meaning of the unwritten law

(1) A person must not, in trade or commerce, engage in conduct that is unconscionable, within the meaning of the unwritten law from time to time.

Note: A pecuniary penalty may be imposed for a contravention of this subsection.

(2) This section does not apply to conduct that is prohibited by section 21.

21 Unconscionable conduct in connection with goods or services

(1) A person must not, in trade or commerce, in connection with:

(a) the supply or possible supply of goods or services to a person; or

(b) the acquisition or possible acquisition of goods or services from a person;

engage in conduct that is, in all the circumstances, unconscionable.

(2) This section does not apply to conduct that is engaged in only because the person engaging in the conduct:

(a) institutes legal proceedings in relation to the supply or possible supply, or in relation to the acquisition or possible acquisition; or

(b) refers to arbitration a dispute or claim in relation to the supply or possible supply, or in relation to the acquisition or possible acquisition.

(3) For the purpose of determining whether a person has contravened subsection (1):

(a) the court must not have regard to any circumstances that were not reasonably foreseeable at the time of the alleged contravention; and

(b) the court may have regard to conduct engaged in, or circumstances existing, before the commencement of this section.

(4) It is the intention of the Parliament that:

(a) this section is not limited by the unwritten law relating to unconscionable conduct; and

(b) this section is capable of applying to a system of conduct or pattern of behaviour, whether or not a particular individual is identified as having been disadvantaged by the conduct or behaviour; and

(c) in considering whether conduct to which a contract relates is unconscionable, a court's consideration of the contract may include consideration of:

(i) the terms of the contract; and

(ii) the manner in which and the extent to which the contract is carried out;

and is not limited to consideration of the circumstances relating to formation of the contract.

Australian Competition and Consumer Commission v Samton Holdings Pty Ltd (2002) 117 FCR 301

Facts and issues

The case involved negotiations over the option to renew a lease of commercial premises. The tenant failed to renew on time. Combined with other business factors, the tenant was in a vulnerable position in relation to those negotiations. The question was whether this amounted to unconscionable conduct, and relatedly, the interrelationship between the s 20 and common law principles.

This decision addresses the discrete concept of what is meant by the expression 'unconscionable conduct within the meaning of the unwritten law'.

Decision

Per Gray, French and Stone JJ at 316:

> The prohibition created by the section therefore relates to a sub-class of the class of conduct which answers the description 'unconscionable within the meaning of the unwritten law'. It is the sub-class defined by the requirements that it be conduct within the meaning of that term as defined in s 4(2) of the Act, engaged in, in the sense used in that same definition and in 'trade or commerce'. These criteria do not extend the principles by which the unwritten law identifies unconscionable conduct. The unwritten law may, as the section recognises, change from time to time but that change is effected through a process of judicial decision-making. The section itself does not operate to extend the application of the principles of unconscionable conduct. In so saying, it must be recognised that, the section now being in force, the development of the judge-made or 'unwritten' law may be affected in part by decisions in proceedings in which the section is invoked.

In relation to the discrete question concerning the broad categories of unconscionable conduct envisaged by s 51AA of the *Trade Practices Act* (the predecessor to s 20 of the Australian Consumer Law) per Gray, French and Stone JJ at 318:

> Under the rubric of unconscionable conduct, equity will:
>
> (i) Set aside a contract or disposition resulting from the knowing exploitation by one party of the special disadvantage of another. The special disadvantage may be constitutional, deriving from age, illness, poverty, inexperience or lack of education — *Commercial Bank of Australia Ltd v Amadio*. Or it may be situational, deriving from particular features of a relationship between actors in the transaction such as the emotional dependence of one on the other — *Louth v Diprose*; *Bridgewater v Leahy* (1998) 194 CLR 457.
>
> (ii) Set aside as against third parties a transaction entered into as the result of the defective comprehension by a party to the transaction, the influence of another and the want of any independent explanation to the complaining party — *Garcia v National Australia Bank Ltd* (1988) 194 CLR 395.
>
> (iii) Prevent a party from exercising a legal right in a way that involves unconscionable departure from a representation relied upon by another to his or her detriment — *Waltons Stores (Interstate) Ltd v Maher*; *Commonwealth v Verwayen*.
>
> (iv) Relieve against forfeiture and penalty — *Legione v Hateley*; *Stern v McArthur*.
>
> (v) Rescind contracts entered into under the influence of unilateral mistake — *Taylor v Johnson*.

Each of these categories of case (the list may not be exhaustive) involves the identification of unconscionable conduct, albeit its content and degree will vary according to the category. It is a term which has various shades of meaning according to its context. There are different thresholds of conduct in various categories, all of which may be described as unconscionable.[16]

16 G Dal Pont, 'The Varying Shades of "Unconscionable" Conduct — Same Term, Different Meaning' (2000) 19 *Australian Bar Review* 135, 165.

Australian Competition and Consumer Commission v Radio Rentals Ltd (2005) 146 FCR 292

Facts and issues

The case concerned allegations of unconscionable conduct against a disabled customer. The customer had acquired different items and dealt with various employees of the companies. The question was whether it was open for the court to apply the aggregate knowledge of the employees of the company in order for the company to infer that the customer was disabled.

Decision

Per Finn J at 325:

> The various communications made by Mr Groth to the call centre which were entered in Mr Groth's credit and service histories were made by individual Radio Rentals' employees. The submission does not suggest that any individual operator had or ought to have had the knowledge that the ACCC ascribes to Radio Rentals, although that operator did have at least the knowledge of what was entered at the time of its entry. Rather it seems to be based on an aggregation of what was so known by each individual call centre operator, with Radio Rentals being ascribed such knowledge about Mr Groth as that aggregated information might reveal.
>
> [. . .]
>
> In my view the situation is no different where the aggregated knowledge to be attributed to a company is a prerequisite to a finding that it engaged in unconscionable conduct (or an equitable fraud). The present submission cannot properly be characterised as one in which the individual operators who recorded entries etc were involved in 'different aspects of one transaction'. The records embody unrelated events, transactions and communications. There has not been — and on the state of the pleading could not be — any suggestion that the records sought to be aggregated have been contrivedly or artificially kept in a disaggregated form. There is, I would add, no evidence either that it was the duty of any Radio Rentals' employee to monitor customer records to discern suspicious or out of the ordinary occurrences in those records or that any employee actually interrogated records in circumstances that would have alerted a reasonable person to suspicious or out of the ordinary occurrences in the records interrogated. In such circumstances, the state of mind to be attributed to Radio Rentals can be no different from, and no less innocent than that of, the personnel who made the entries in its records.

Australian Competition and Consumer Commission v Seal-A-Fridge Pty Ltd [2010] FCA 525

Facts and issues

It was alleged that Seal-A-Fridge had, contrary to s 51AC of the *Trade Practices Act 1974* (the predecessor to s 21 Australian Consumer Law) engaged in unconscionable conduct by demanding and obtaining from its franchisees payment of increased weekly franchise fees. For present purposes, the relevant issue concerned the criteria of 'unconscionability' and that the range of matters that can be taken into account would include, but are not limited to, those listed in s 51AC(3) and (4) of the *Trade Practices* Act (the content of these sub-sections now find expression as s 22(1) and (2) of the Australian Consumer Law).

Decision

Per Logan J at [12]:

> 'Unconscionable conduct' for the purposes of s 51AC is ultimately an open-ended concept. It is plain from the way the sub-section is cast that the considerations listed in s 51AC(3) (and s 51AC(4) for that matter) are neither intended to be exhaustive nor to limit the meaning of 'unconscionable conduct'.

Attorney-General (NSW) v World Best Holdings Ltd (2005) 63 NSWLR 557

Facts and issues

So far as relevant to the present, it suffices to note that World Best Holdings Pty Ltd was party to an unconscionable conduct claim in the Retail Leases Division of the Administrative Decisions Tribunal. The relevant aspect of the court's decision concerned, again, the criteria of unconscionability. Spigelman CJ's formulation below has been much repeated, demanding a high degree of 'moral obloquy' to satisfy the requirement, rather than it simply being a matter of not conforming to an idea of what was fair or just.

Decision

Per Spigelman CJ at 583:

> The Ministerial Second Reading speech, quoted above, indicates a similar concern to distinguish what is unconscionable from what is merely unfair or unjust. Even if the concept of unconscionability in s62B of the *Retail Leases Act* is not confined by equitable doctrine, as the decisions under s51AC of the *Trade Practices Act* suggest, restraint in decision-making remains appropriate. Even if the concept of unconscionability in s62B of the *Retail Leases Act* is not confined by equitable doctrine, as the decisions under s51AC of the *Trade Practices Act* suggest, restraint in decision-making remains appropriate. Unconscionability is a concept which requires a high level of moral obloquy. If it were to be applied as if it were equivalent to what was 'fair' or 'just', it could transform commercial relationships in a manner which the Minister expressly stated was not the intention of the legislation. The principle of 'unconscionability' would not be a doctrine of occasional application, when the circumstances are highly unethical, it would be transformed into the first and easiest port of call when any dispute about a retail lease arises.

Paciocco v Australia and New Zealand Banking Group Ltd (2015) 236 FCR 199; and, on appeal, *Paciocco v Australia and New Zealand Banking Group Ltd* (2016) 258 CLR 525

Facts and issues

The case is arguably the seminal case concerning the penalty doctrine, where the question that was considered was whether the penalty doctrine could apply to provisions that entitled the bank to their payment where there was no breach. A more complete summary of the relevant facts is set out at **1.5**, p 21. The present discussion focuses more on whether the conduct of the bank amounted to 'moral obloquy'. Note the court's discussion that the reference point of the concept was not some disembodied value laden concept, but the values and norms considered by parliament.

Decision

Per Allsop CJ, in the Full Federal Court, in *Paciocco v Australia and New Zealand Banking Group Ltd* (2015) 236 FCR 199 at 266:

> That a degree of morality lies within the word 'unconscionable' is clear. 'Unconscionability' is a value-laden concept. 'Obloquy' is 'the condition of being spoken against; bad repute; reproach; disgrace; a cause of detraction or reproach,'; 'obliquity' is 'a deviation from moral rectitude, sound thinking or right practice; a delinquency; a fault or error': *The Shorter Oxford English Dictionary on Historical Principles* (3rd ed, Oxford, 1969) Vol 2 p 1428. That unconscionability contains an element of deviation from rectitude or right practice or of delinquency can be readily accepted, as long as the phrase 'moral obloquy' is not taken to import into unconscionability a necessary conception of dishonesty. The statutory language is 'unconscionable': that is, against conscience. A sense of moral obloquy or moral obliquity can be accommodated within the meaning or conception of unconscientious or unconscionable conduct. That said, an understanding of the meaning conveyed by the word 'unconscionable' in the statute is not simply restated by substituting other words for those chosen by Parliament; danger easily lurks in the use of other words to capture the meaning of the statutory language. The task involved is not the choice of synonyms; rather, it is to identify and apply the values and norms that Parliament must be taken to have considered relevant to the assessment of unconscionability: being the values and norms from the text and structure of the Act, and from the context of the provision. Parliament has given some guidance to its proper application (and to its meaning) by identifying in s 12CC certain non-exhaustive factors that may be taken into account by a court in deciding whether conduct was unconscionable. Given the value-laden character of the word, it is necessary to ascertain and organise the relevant values and norms by reference to which the meaning of the word is to be ascertained, and by reference to which the application of the section is to be undertaken (the two tasks being distinct). It must, however, be emphasised at the outset that the values and norms that are relevant are those that Parliament has considered, or must be taken to have considered, as relevant. The following discussion should be understood as dealing with those matters, and not with any values or norms disembodied from, or unconnected with, the choice made by Parliament.

On appeal to the High Court[17], on the question of whether the imposition of a late payment in credit card agreements was unconscionable was limited to a consideration of the recovery of legally recoverable damages or was wider, per Gageler J at 588:

17 *Paciocco v Australia and New Zealand Banking Group Ltd* (2016) 258 CLR 52.

Section 76(2) of the *National Credit Code* provided that, in determining whether a term of a particular credit contract was unjust in the circumstances relating to it at the time it was entered into, a court was 'to have regard to the public interest and to all the circumstances of the case'. Section 76(2) added that the court 'may' have regard to a long list of specifically enumerated factors, the last of which was expressed to be 'any other relevant factor'. One of those factors, enumerated as s 76(2)(e), was 'whether or not any of the provisions of the contract ... impose[d] conditions that [were] ... not reasonably necessary for the protection of the legitimate interests of a party to the contract'... Section 76(4) was similar to s 12CB(4)(a) of the ASIC Act in [589] prohibiting a court from considering 'injustice arising from circumstances that were not reasonably foreseeable when the contract ... was entered into'.

Having regard to the evidence of Mr Inglis quantifying the average costs incurred by ANZ in connection with the occurrence of an event giving rise to an entitlement to charge the late payment fee as having been in excess of $35 or $50, it could not be concluded that the conditions of Mr Paciocco's credit card contracts which imposed the late payment fee of either $35 or $20 were not reasonably necessary for the protection of the legitimate interests of ANZ.

[...]

But, again, even if it were to be accepted that charging Mr Paciocco the late payment fee resulted in windfall gains to ANZ (which on the evidence of Mr Inglis it did not), that would not be enough to justify the conclusion that the credit card contracts were unjust. Section 76(2) made clear that a conclusion about whether a contract was unjust could only be drawn having regard to all of the circumstances of the case.

Australian Consumer Law s 22(1), (2)

22 Matters the court may have regard to for the purposes of section 21

(1) Without limiting the matters to which the court may have regard for the purpose of determining whether a person (the ***supplier***) has contravened section 21 in connection with the supply or possible supply of goods or services to a person (the ***customer***), the court may have regard to:

(a) the relative strengths of the bargaining positions of the supplier and the customer; and

(b) whether, as a result of conduct engaged in by the supplier, the customer was required to comply with conditions that were not reasonably necessary for the protection of the legitimate interests of the supplier; and

(c) whether the customer was able to understand any documents relating to the supply or possible supply of the goods or services; and

(d) whether any undue influence or pressure was exerted on, or any unfair tactics were used against, the customer or a person acting on behalf of the customer by the supplier or a person acting on behalf of the supplier in relation to the supply or possible supply of the goods or services; and

(e) the amount for which, and the circumstances under which, the customer could have acquired identical or equivalent goods or services from a person other than the supplier; and

(f) the extent to which the supplier's conduct towards the customer was consistent with the supplier's conduct in similar transactions between the supplier and other like customers; and
(g) the requirements of any applicable industry code; and
(h) the requirements of any other industry code, if the customer acted on the reasonable belief that the supplier would comply with that code; and
(i) the extent to which the supplier unreasonably failed to disclose to the customer:
 (i) any intended conduct of the supplier that might affect the interests of the customer; and
 (ii) any risks to the customer arising from the supplier's intended conduct (being risks that the supplier should have foreseen would not be apparent to the customer); and
(j) if there is a contract between the supplier and the customer for the supply of the goods or services:
 (i) the extent to which the supplier was willing to negotiate the terms and conditions of the contract with the customer; and
 (ii) the terms and conditions of the contract; and
 (iii) the conduct of the supplier and the customer in complying with the terms and conditions of the contract; and
 (iv) any conduct that the supplier or the customer engaged in, in connection with their commercial relationship, after they entered into the contract; and
(k) without limiting paragraph (j), whether the supplier has a contractual right to vary unilaterally a term or condition of a contract between the supplier and the customer for the supply of the goods or services; and
(l) the extent to which the supplier and the customer acted in good faith.

(2) Without limiting the matters to which the court may have regard for the purpose of determining whether a person (the ***acquirer***) has contravened section 21 in connection with the acquisition or possible acquisition of goods or services from a person (the ***supplier***), the court may have regard to:
(a) the relative strengths of the bargaining positions of the acquirer and the supplier; and
(b) whether, as a result of conduct engaged in by the acquirer, the supplier was required to comply with conditions that were not reasonably necessary for the protection of the legitimate interests of the acquirer; and
(c) whether the supplier was able to understand any documents relating to the acquisition or possible acquisition of the goods or services; and
(d) whether any undue influence or pressure was exerted on, or any unfair tactics were used against, the supplier or a person acting on behalf of the supplier by the acquirer or a person acting on behalf of the acquirer in relation to the acquisition or possible acquisition of the goods or services; and
(e) the amount for which, and the circumstances in which, the supplier could have supplied identical or equivalent goods or services to a person other than the acquirer; and
(f) the extent to which the acquirer's conduct towards the supplier was consistent with the acquirer's conduct in similar transactions between the acquirer and other like suppliers; and
(g) the requirements of any applicable industry code; and
(h) the requirements of any other industry code, if the supplier acted on the reasonable belief that the acquirer would comply with that code; and

(i) the extent to which the acquirer unreasonably failed to disclose to the supplier:
  (i) any intended conduct of the acquirer that might affect the interests of the supplier; and
  (ii) any risks to the supplier arising from the acquirer's intended conduct (being risks that the acquirer should have foreseen would not be apparent to the supplier); and

(j) if there is a contract between the acquirer and the supplier for the acquisition of the goods or services:
  (i) the extent to which the acquirer was willing to negotiate the terms and conditions of the contract with the supplier; and
  (ii) the terms and conditions of the contract; and
  (iii) the conduct of the acquirer and the supplier in complying with the terms and conditions of the contract; and
  (iv) any conduct that the acquirer or the supplier engaged in, in connection with their commercial relationship, after they entered into the contract; and

(k) without limiting paragraph (j), whether the acquirer has a contractual right to vary unilaterally a term or condition of a contract between the acquirer and the supplier for the acquisition of the goods or services; and

(l) the extent to which the acquirer and the supplier acted in good faith.

Australian Competition and Consumer Commission v Keshow [2005] FCA 558

Facts and issues

Women in Indigenous communities entered into periodical payment agreements for the supply of children's educational material. The women had limited commercial experience and did not fully understand the transaction. The question was whether the respondent had acted unconscionably having regard to the factors set out in s 51AB *Trade Practices Act*, the predecessor to s 22 Australian Consumer Law.

Decision

Per Mansfield J at [100]:

> There is nothing inherently unconscionable about procuring the sale of goods by unsolicited approaches to consumers. In this matter, however, the respondent's conduct had the features which satisfy me that it was unconscionable in the sense referred to in the authorities discussed above.
>
> [101] ... Imbalance between a retailer and consumer in educational or commercial literacy generally will not of itself be enough to make a transaction unconscionable. In this matter, the respondent's dealings had additional features. He was a mature person clearly well able to understand the nature of the transactions into which he entered, and to appreciate those things which a consumer with normal commercial acumen might inquire about, or expect. Clearly, as I have found, none of the complainants made such inquiries or pursued such expectations. In particular, the respondent did not proffer, and none of the complainants sought, any written

record of the contract into which they had entered. The respondent must have realized that. The respondent did not proffer, and none of the complainants sought.

[...]

The periodical payment forms used by the respondent imposed conditions upon the complainants, and the respondent's customers, which were not reasonably necessary for the protection of the legitimate interests of the respondent: see s 51AB(2)(b).

[...]

[After setting out evidence relating to whether the complainants understood the nature of the transactions] Those matters illustrate firstly that the respondent's customers, including the complainants, did not fully understand the nature of the transactions they entered into.

[...]

And I am satisfied that each of the respondent's customers including the complainants did not fully understand the nature of the transactions into which they entered.

[102] The quality of the respondent's record keeping indicates that his commitment to supply goods agreed to be sold by him was, at best, half-hearted and somewhat random.

[...]

More importantly, in my view, it illustrates that his purpose in entering into the agreements was not simply to secure the sale of particular goods of a particular value or at a particular price, and to provide those goods in a timely manner to the purchaser. His preparedness to take advantage of the complainants and of the respondent's customers by securing open-ended periodical payment forms in those circumstances, in my judgment, illustrates more than the relevant strengths of the bargaining positions of the respondent on the one hand and of the complainants and of the respondent's customers on the other. It also indicates the imposition of conditions by the respondent that were not reasonably required for the protection of the legitimate interests of the respondent.

[103] I have found that the complainants...did not understand the full implications of the periodical payment form which they executed.

[...]

[104] The particular considerations referred to in s 51AB(2)(a), (b) and (c) in particular, together with the more general considerations to which I have referred, all point very firmly to the conclusion of unconscionable conduct.

Kobelt v Australian Securities and Investments Commission (2018) 352 ALR 689

Facts and issues

The case concerned conduct in relation to the sale of second-hand vehicles to Indigenous residents by means of 'book up' (informal credit). The focal point of the following extract concerns whether the vendor had acted in a predatory fashion.

Decision

Per Besanko and Gilmour JJ at 736:

... the primary judge found that the Nobbys' customers voluntarily entered into the book-up arrangements. In our opinion, the fact that the Nobbys' customers understood the basic elements of the book-up arrangements and voluntarily entered into them is a powerful consideration against a finding of unconscionable conduct, particularly (as we will explain in the next point) in the absence of predatory conduct or exploitation.

Finally, we are not satisfied that the appellant's conduct was predatory in the relevant sense.

[...]

As to exploitation, in what in many respects is a critical passage in terms of his Honour's conclusions (at [620]), he said the advantages to the appellant of the tying effect of the conduct constituted a 'form of exploitation' of his customers. With respect, we think that is an error and the conduct is neither predatory nor does it involve exploitation in the relevant sense.

[...]

We uphold the appellant's challenge to the primary judge's conclusion that he engaged in unconscionable conduct contrary to s 12CB(1) of the ASIC Act.

Australian Competition and Consumer Commission v Excite Mobile Pty Ltd [2013] FCA 350

Facts and issues

In the course of attempting to collect debts, the respondent threatened proceedings and also foreshadowed the prospect that, unless paid, the alleged debtor might suffer having its personal belongings repossessed, among other things. The issue was whether such conduct was unconscionable.

Decision

Per Mansfield J at [215]:

> It is clear that debt collection processes, including the threat of proceedings, are not of themselves unconscionable. Nor are such processes unconscionable when carried out by a debt collector. I am not therefore minded to conclude that the 'impersonation' by Excite Mobile as an independent debt collector is itself unconscionable. It may be that such conduct presents to the customer/debtor that the creditor has a serious intention to take court action to recover the debt.
>
> [...]
>
> [217] In my view, two elements of that content lead to the conclusion that the conduct was unconscionable. That content is first, the false assertion that a Court would make an order imposing, in essence, an extra charge of 20% of the outstanding debt for late payment, and secondly, that a Court would make a repossession order of all assets of the debtor, including personal assets such as children's toys. Those matters are not correct. Although a Court may award interest on an unpaid debt according to the terms of the contract, it would not impose a 20% extra charge or payment absent such a contractual term and it would not routinely order repossession of all assets of a debtor including personal assets. In the context of a commercial enterprise such as Excite Mobile dealing with small, and no doubt in many instances uninformed, customers who might know no better, I regard those two threats as clearly unfair and unreasonable. They fall within the range of conduct which attracts a pejorative moral judgment.

Australian Competition and Consumer Commission v Seal-A-Fridge Pty Ltd [2010] FCA 525

Facts and issues

The facts of the case are set out above at p 666. The conduct said to be unconscionable was of seeking price increases on the basis inter alia of falsehoods, detailed in the extract below.

Decision

Per Logan J at [142]:

> In its circular letter to franchisees of 15 January 2001 in respect of the increase of the weekly fee from $50 to $75 Seal-A-Fridge put forward that Telstra's charges to it had recently increased. This was false. There was no such recent increase. The promotion to the franchisees that there existed this basis for the increased demanded evidenced an absence of good faith on the part of Seal-A-Fridge.
>
> [...]
>
> [145] In the context of the present case, and having regard to the central role played by the 13 number in the promotion by various advertising means of the generic 'Seal-A-Fridge' business name, there can be no doubt that continued access to calls directed to a franchisee following a call to that 13 number was essential to the continued conduct of that franchisee's business. Essentiality of access to the 13 number by franchisees gave Seal-A-Fridge a position of strength in relation to them in the event of non-payment. Yet that essentiality does not *per se* make the highlighting of the withdrawal of access to that service in the event of non-payment unconscionable. So much was, as I understood it, accepted by the ACCC. Rather, so the ACCC submitted, it was the *abuse* of that position of strength that was relevant to the characterisation of the conduct of Seal-A-Fridge as unconscionable, in all of the circumstances. I agree.
>
> [146] What emerges is that the 2001 weekly fee increase was demanded and obtained by Seal-A-Fridge, without contractual authority but supported by falsehood and abuse of a position of strength for the purpose of gaining additional profit. These means also led eventually to the securing of the agreement of the franchisees concerned to the variation of their respective franchise agreements. Viewed as a whole and having regard to the general statements in the authorities mentioned above as to the meaning of s 51AC, the adoption of these means by Seal-A-Fridge in respect of the 2001 increase constituted unconscionable conduct on the part of Seal-Fridge.

Robert McGill Freier v Australian Postal Corporation (No 2) [2012] NSWSC 61

Facts and issues

The licensee sought an interlocutory injunction to restrain Australia Post from terminating a licensing agreement. It was argued that it was unconscionable for it to do so.

Decision

Per Ball J at [24]:

> ... Australia Post was entitled to terminate the agreement for any reason; and, for the reasons I have given, I do not think that it is arguable that the exercise of that right was unconscionable.
>
> [...]
>
> However, where the agreement is for an indefinite term and permits termination for any reason and provides for the payment of compensation in the event of termination, I doubt that the mere failure to give an accurate reason for termination is unconscionable.

QUESTIONS

(1) What is the present state of law concerning the parameters of 'unconscionable conduct within the meaning of the unwritten law' in s 20 of the Australian Consumer Law?

(2) Section 22 of the Australian Consumer Law sets out a fairly detailed catalogue of 'factors' that the court 'may have regard to' in determining whether a supplier has contravened s 21 of the Australian Consumer Law. In particular, consider whether in 'having regard' to those factors, a court is at liberty to implement notions of fairness or justness.

(3) What is the judicial treatment of s 22 of the Australian Consumer Law? Is it a complete code of conduct or can the court take into account other considerations in its assessment of unconscionability which otherwise falls within s 21 of the Australian Consumer Law?

20.5 International perspectives

The *CISG* does not generally deal with matters of validity: art 4(a) *CISG*. Thus, for international sales contracts governed by the *CISG* (see **25.4.1** on applicability), questions of validity will be determined in accordance with the domestic law deemed applicable to that matter by the conflicts rules of the court or tribunal. If this is Australian law, then the concepts of unconscionability, special equity for married women, and statutory unconscionability discussed in this chapter will be relevant, since these are rules impacting upon enforceability on the basis of fairness in order to protect weaker parties.

Where applicable, the UNIDROIT Principles do contain rules related to validity, and rules designed to counter unfairness where there is fraud, threats, or contractual imbalance (gross disparity): see the discussion at **19.4.2–19.4.3**. The UNIDROIT Principles also impose broad duties to act in good faith upon each party: see eg art 1.7 UNIDROIT Principles (see **25.8.7**). Nonetheless, mandatory domestic rules concerning questions of fairness and protection of weaker parties will still apply.

20.6 Review

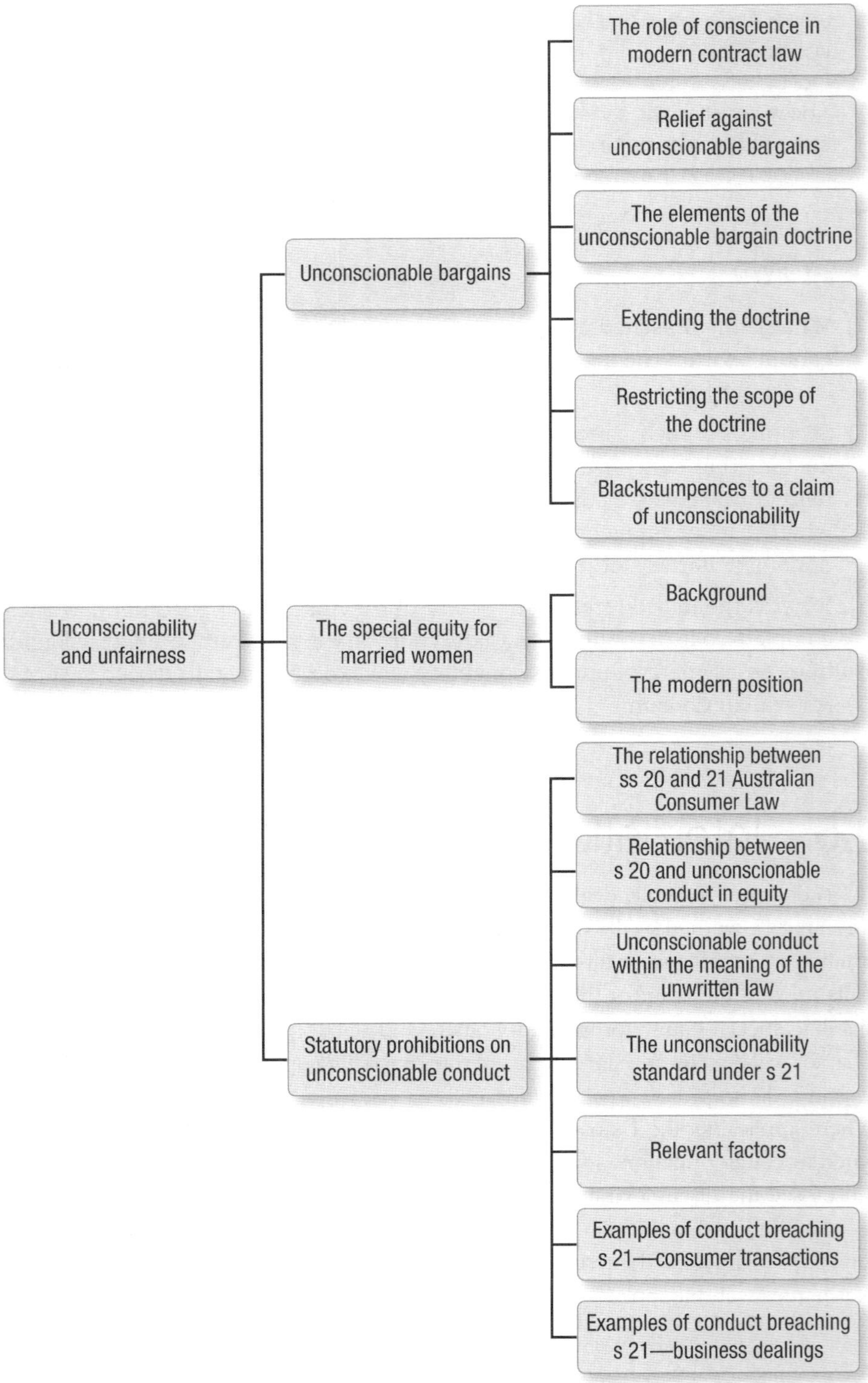
Unconscionability and unfairness
Unconscionable bargains
The role of conscience in modern contract law
Relief against unconscionable bargains
The elements of the unconscionable bargain doctrine
Extending the doctrine
Restricting the scope of the doctrine
Blackstumpences to a claim of unconscionability
The special equity for married women
Background
The modern position
Statutory prohibitions on unconscionable conduct
The relationship between ss 20 and 21 Australian Consumer Law
Relationship between s 20 and unconscionable conduct in equity
Unconscionable conduct within the meaning of the unwritten law
The unconscionability standard under s 21
Relevant factors
Examples of conduct breaching s 21—consumer transactions
Examples of conduct breaching s 21—business dealings

TIPS FOR APPLYING THE LAW IN PRACTICE

- It is unhelpful to adopt a value judgment in determining if a particular transaction is tainted by unconscionability. Whenever the question arises, it is crucial not merely to 'ground' the principle by reference to definitions in the abstract, whichever the cause of action might be. An obvious example is 'special disadvantage'; the cornerstone of the unconscionable bargain doctrine per *Amadio* itself. Rather than argue in the abstract what 'special disadvantage' might be, you should always search for the emphasised factors in the cases by which the court inferred that there was or was not a relevant special disadvantage. The language difficulty in *Amadio*[18] was such a case; whilst the finding in *Kakavas*[19] above, that a pathological gambler was not deprived of his freedom of choice, was central to the conclusion that he did not suffer from any relevant special disadvantage.
- Whilst in rationalising the *Yerkey v Jones* principle the High Court majority in *Garcia* referred to 'actual undue influence', it is important to read the case carefully to understand that ultimately the setting aside a guarantee provided by a wife did not depend on a finding of the knowledge of any unconscionable conduct on the part of the husband. It was the fact of the marriage rather than of any unconscionable conduct which attracted the operation of the seminal requirements of the doctrine—see *Garcia* at 407.
- In determining, broadly, the scope of the application of each of the statutory provisions vis-à-vis the common law, it should be noted that: s 21 Australian Consumer Law has far broader scope than the common law doctrine of unconscionable conduct when it does apply; eg s 21(4)(b) is not restricted to conduct that can be shown to result in disadvantage to a particular individual but can apply to a pattern of behaviour;[20] s 20 is the residual provision, which applies to conduct not already caught by s 21.[21] But we arguably go back full circle when we consider the scope of s 20, because on the state of the present law, following the decision in *Berbatis*,[22] it is uncertain if its scope goes beyond the common law concept of unconscionability.[23]

PROBLEM QUESTION

Paul and Julie were husband and wife, and are directors of the fictional ABC Pty Ltd. Paul is the only shareholder. All the assets of the marriage, including the matrimonial home, are in Julie's name.

One day, Paul and Julie approach the bank to obtain a loan of $1,500,000 for ABC Pty Ltd, which is in dire financial straits. Although Julie is a director, she has nothing to do with the company.

The bank is aware of the dire financial situation of ABC, so requires a guarantee before considering granting a loan. With both of them present, they explain to Julie that they require a guarantee from her.

The bank then prepares a guarantee, supported by a registrable mortgage over the family home in blank form (to be executed by Julie), and presents it to Paul (in Julie's presence) and asks the two of them to think about it and then 'get back' to the bank.

18 n 4 above.
19 n 7 above.
20 See the discussion at *Principles* text 20.16.
21 See 20.12 of the *Principles* text.
22 *Australian Competition and Consumer Commission v C G Berbatis Holdings Pty Ltd* (2003) 214 CLR 51.
23 See the discussion at 20.14 of the *Principles* text.

The bank, having been in business for some time, knows of the implications of the *Garcia* decision, but in the light of the fact that Paul, Julie and ABC are long-time customers, the bank officer in question makes an executive decision and does not insist on a certificate of independent legal advice.

Paul discloses nothing of the circumstances of the terms of the loan, how much is to be repaid, what his earning capacity is, what other assets are owned by the company, and generally whether ABC is capable of servicing the loan. Julie is unaware of all these things.

Julie is an intelligent person. She does understand what a guarantee and a mortgage are in general terms (that she will be liable if ABC defaults and/or that 'we may lose the house') but, at Paul's request, executes each document.

ABC defaults, and the bank then seeks to enforce the guarantee against Julie, and to enforce the mortgage by taking possession of the family home.

Upon learning of ABC's and Paul's dire financial situation, Julie separates from Paul and immediately seeks to set aside the guarantee and mortgage relying on principles in *Garcia*. Discuss her prospects of success.

RESEARCH QUESTION

The following question is designed to test your basic understanding of the overlapping parameters of the causes of action for unconscionable conduct at common law, and under the Australian Consumer Law.

Eleanor is an 80-year old grandmother. She knows little about computers and can fairly be described as 'computer illiterate'.

She has a grandson named Reggie, who is 8-years old. Just before Christmas, Reggie expresses a desire to get the latest computer gadget, a Super Duper Widget Gizmo which 'all my friends have'.

Eleanor has no idea what this is but, anxious to please Reggie, she takes him to the shops to look for the Gizmo on the afternoon of 22 December. They trudge around three shops without success.

Around 3.00 pm, they chance upon a shop in the suburbs run and owned by BLACKSTUMP Pty Ltd. Sunny is a director of BLACKSTUMP Pty Ltd, and runs the shop. Sunny advises them that he does have a Gizmo. He notices that Eleanor has utterly no idea what a Gizmo does or how it works and that she looks to Reggie for guidance. Reggie is only interested in getting the toy and has no interest nor knowledge as to how much it costs.

Sunny sees a chance to make a killing. He advises Eleanor that its price is $1,200.

The facts are that: the normal retail price is $100; it is about to be superseded by a new model which will be released the very next day (for maximum impact before Christmas); the shops will be flooded with Gizmo Mark 2; and the retail price of the Gizmo Mark 2 will be $220.

None of this is known to Eleanor nor Reggie.

Keen to please Reggie, Eleanor pays the asking price of $1,200.

Eleanor is anxious to seek relief against BLACKSTUMP Pty Ltd. Discuss her right to relief under the common law unconscionable bargain doctrine and under ss 20 and 21 of the Australian Consumer Law.

21

ILLEGALITY AND PUBLIC POLICY

21.1 Overview

This chapter considers both types of illegality, under a statute and at common law. They share the common feature of involving conduct that is prohibited, either by the common law or under legislation. Both varieties invoke, broadly, the idea that the consequences of illegality depend on what is regarded as 'public policy'.

Illustrating this, the common law position is that a contract in restraint of trade is illegal because it is contrary to public policy to restrict a man's liberty to trade—this being the central proposition in the seminal case of *Nordenfelt v Maxim Nordenfelt Guns & Ammunition Co Ltd*.[1] The proposition is reprised in cases involving statutory illegality, such as *Equuscorp v Haxton*[2], where the High Court emphasised that, where a statute was involved, there should be a flexible approach taken, ie 'there is no one-size-fits-all answer to the question of recoverability'.[3]

Thus, the identification of these 'policy' considerations is at the core of this chapter.

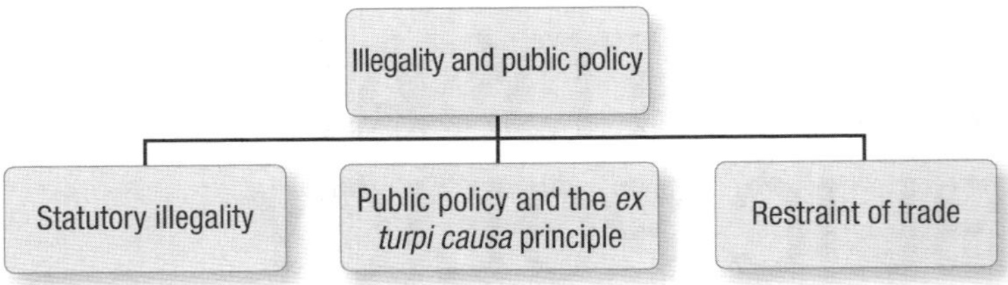

21.2 Introduction

Concept	Short explanation	Relevant authorities	*Principles* text*
The changing impact of illegality	Concepts of public policy have given rise to inconsistent views of when a contract might be set aside on grounds of illegality, often with compelling arguments on both sides. The contemporary test is to emphasise consistency with the purpose of the relevant statute	*Equuscorp Pty Ltd v Haxton* (2012) 246 CLR 498	Chapter 21: 21.01
'Illegal and void'	Whether a contract is 'illegal' or 'void' depends largely on the case for invalidity in the light of public policy considerations	*Brooks v Burns Philp Trustee Co Ltd* (1969) 121 CLR 432	Chapter 21: 21.02
Raising the question of illegality	The party relying on illegality must establish the factual basis for the contention	*Venus Adult Shops Pty Ltd v Fraserside Holdings Ltd* (2006) 157 FCR 442	Chapter 21: 21.03

* Consult the corresponding section(s) of the *Principles* text for more detail.

1 [1894] AC 535, 565 (Lord Macnaghten).
2 (2012) 246 CLR 498.
3 Ibid 518.

This short introduction serves to remind the reader that the concept of 'illegality' itself gives little if no guidance as to the consequences of that illegality, and that it is up to the party relying on the illegality to raise it for if not, a court will not necessarily assume that any particular contract is illegal, or, if it is illegal, what the consequences are. It particularly introduces the reader to the idea that, consistent with the contemporary approach to illegality, a flexible approach will be taken, with the courts being guided by extant policy considerations both as to the concept of illegality and the consequences of illegality, if found.

Equuscorp Pty Ltd v Haxton (2012) 246 CLR 498

Facts and issues

The facts were complex: Rural Finance Pty Ltd loaned money to enable investors to invest in a scheme designed to take advantage of tax laws that permitted investors to deduct farming expenses from non-farming income. Rural assigned its interest in the loan agreements, entered into with the respondent Haxton (and other investors) to the appellant Equuscorp. The scheme was illegal, and the loan agreements were unenforceable, being an agricultural investment scheme without a registered prospectus. Having held that the statutory obligation to register a prospectus was intended for the benefit of potential investors, the relevant question was whether the appellant could recover the money from the investors by way of restitution.

Decision

In relation to the central question, of the effect of legislation on the restitution of benefits having regard to the illegality of the scheme, per French CJ, Crennan and Kiefel JJ at 518:

> . . . under a contract which is unenforceable for illegality, will depend upon whether it would be unjust for the recipient of a benefit under the contract to retain that benefit. There is no one-size-fits-all answer to the question of recoverability. As with the question of recoverability under a contract affected by illegality the outcome of the claim will depend upon the scope and purpose of the relevant statute. The central policy consideration at stake, as this Court said in *Miller*, is the coherence of the law. In that context it will be relevant that the statutory purpose is protective of a class of persons from whom the claimant seeks recovery. Also relevant will be the position of the claimant and whether it is an innocent party or involved in the illegality.
>
> [. . .]
>
> [519] The importance of policy in determining the effect of illegality upon a restitutionary claim was central to Lord Mansfield's observation in *Holman v Johnson*:
>
> > It is not for [the defendant's] sake, however, that the objection is ever allowed; but it is founded in general principles of policy, which the defendant has the advantage of, contrary to the real justice, as between him and the plaintiff, by accident, if I may so say.
>
> [. . .]
>
> There were often compelling policy arguments on both sides. In listing reasons for and against the grant of relief in relation to illegal transactions, Professor John Wade, writing in the *Texas Law Review* in 1946, said that:
>
> > The balancing process . . . leaves on one side the view that a court should not help a man who has engaged in an illegal transaction out of the predicament in which he has

> placed himself, and on the other the view that a court should not permit unjust enrichment of one person at the expense of another. Of these two arguments, each of which seems most nearly determinative upon its side of the question, neither takes precedence upon logical analysis.

The search then is for a principled basis for determining whether or not relief is to be allowed.

[...]

[540] The determinative issue, as Equuscorp accepted, is whether the policy of the statute law represented by Pt IV Div 6 of the Code denies any scope for an action for money had and received.

[...]

[541] The *Restatement of the Law Third, Restitution and Unjust Enrichment*, adopted and promulgated in 2010, deals separately with 'Unenforceability' (§31) and 'Illegality' (§32), but to relevantly similar effect. A person who renders performance under an agreement that cannot be enforced against the recipient by reason of the failure to satisfy an extrinsic requirement of enforceability, such as the *Statute of Frauds* 1677 ... does not have a restitutionary claim against the recipient if the allowance of that claim 'would defeat the policy of the law that makes the agreement unenforceable' (§31(2)). A person who renders performance under an 'illegal' agreement may not obtain restitution if the allowance of restitution will 'defeat or frustrate the policy of the underlying prohibition' (§32(2)).

[...]

[543] The respondents correctly submit that this principle applies here but to the opposite effect. This is because the prospectus provisions were not enacted for the protection of Rural and the other Johnson interests, but for the protection of the respondents as investors in the prescribed interests. [It was ultimately held that the loan monies were not recoverable under principles of restitution.]

Brooks v Burns Philp Trustee Co Ltd (1969) 121 CLR 432

Facts and issues

The executor of a deceased estate sought a determination whether the estate was liable to make payments to the deceased's widow under a deed executed by the couple, in which the widow agreed to give up all claims for maintenance in return for specified weekly payments. The agreement was considered to be an exclusion of the jurisdiction of the court. The question was whether such a clause was void.

Decision

Per Kitto J at 437:

> But cl. 2 was obviously intended to operate immediately and unconditionally, and according to its plain meaning it bound the wife not to ask the Court for more than the terms of the deed provided and not to take more by virtue of any order that the Court might see fit to make. Thus its operation, if it was valid, was to nullify as between the parties the Court's discretion as to alimony and maintenance by substituting the agreement of the parties for the opinion of the judge as the determinant of the amount the wife should be entitled to receive ...
>
> [...]
>
> Clause 2 was therefore devoid of legal effect ...

Per Windeyer J at 458:

> I have in this judgment used the words 'invalid', 'unenforceable' or 'ineffectual', as, in similar cases, other judges have done. Other words and phrases can be used. For example, in the judgment under appeal the appellant's covenant is called 'illegal and void'. A similar promise was called by Asquith L.J. 'void and unenforceable': *Gaisberg v. Storr*. The words used do not matter if the actual legal result they are used to express be not in doubt or debate. But it has always seemed to me likely to lead to error, in matters such as this, to adopt first one of the familiar legal adjectives—'illegal', 'void', 'unenforceable', 'ineffectual', 'nugatory'—and then having given an act a label, to deduce from that its results in law. That is to invert the order of inquiry, and by so doing to beg the question, and allow linguistics to determine legal rights [though in the end result, his Honour dissented].

Per Taylor J at 440:

> The problem in the case arises because of the presence in the deed of the appellant's covenant (2) 'that she will accept the terms provided by this Deed in full settlement of all claims against the husband for alimony and maintenance of any description'. Prima facie, at least, such a covenant purported to oust the jurisdiction of the Court to make an order or orders with respect to alimony in the cause then pending and is, therefore, unenforceable; it is against public policy to permit such a covenant to operate ... [His Honour went on to discuss whether the offensive provision could be severed.]

Venus Adult Shops Pty Ltd v Fraserside Holdings Ltd (2006) 157 FCR 442

Facts and issues

The respondents (Fraserside) commenced proceedings against the appellants (Venus) for breach of copyright in pornographic films. Fraserside alleged that Venus had sold and offered for sale counterfeit copies of films without a licence. Two principal issues arose: (a) whether copyright in pornographic films could be denied on public interest grounds; and (b) to what extent the illegality of the sale of goods in which copyright subsists should be taken into account when calculating conversion damages. These facts are provided primarily for background to the question being addressed: who needs to raise the question of illegality.

Decision

Per French and Kiefel JJ at 471:

> There may be cases in which the illegality of a transaction or conduct relied upon to support a cause of action is patent and the court obliged to have regard to that illegality whether or not it is raised by a party. It is not for the Court, however, to search out illegality whether in contract cases or otherwise. As a general rule the party who affirms illegality much [sic] establish the necessary factual basis for that contention. The burden of proof does not apply to the establishment of a proposition of law based upon facts found, but the party advancing the proposition will ordinarily be expected to make it good in argument.

In the case of a claim for damages for conversion of goods where the owner of the goods has shown that there is a market for their sale and the illegality of their sale is not patent, it is not for the owner to demonstrate that their sale in that market is lawful. It is for the respondent to show the facts upon which it could be concluded that their lawful sale is not possible or that it is so conditioned by statutory restrictions as to affect their value.

QUESTIONS

(1) Whilst the courts have stressed that policy considerations are at the forefront of determining if a particular contract is illegal and of the consequences of illegality, what are the complications in adopting 'policy' as a determinant of enforceability?

(2) What is the common theme which underpins the resolution to the question of the rights of parties to a contract said to be illegal, both at common law, and under a statute?

(3) Contracts in restraint of trade are a very important area, given their prevalence in business. What is the basis for the fundamental proposition that contracts in restraint of trade are, prima facie, void and unenforceable?

21.3 Statutory illegality

Concept	Short explanation	Relevant authorities	*Principles* text*
The different forms of statutory illegality	The process of statutory construction will always be adopted to determine the consequences of illegality in any given claim	*Gnych v Polish Club Ltd* (2015) 255 CLR 414	Chapter 21: 21.04
Express prohibition	Where a contract is prohibited, the traditional approach, not the sole one, is to regard the statute as precluding either party from enforcing the contract The fact that a party is innocent or uninvolved in any contravention may be a factor permitting enforcement where that could be consistent with the scope and purpose of the legislation	*Gnych v Polish Club Ltd* (2015) 255 CLR 414 *Yango Pastoral Co Pty Ltd v First Chicago Australia Ltd* (1978) 139 CLR 410	Chapter 21: 21.05
Contracts or provisions declared to be void	Declaring certain contracts 'void' without directly prohibiting anyone making it does not necessarily make the contract illegal	*Unlawful Gaming Act 1998* (NSW) s 56 *Zurich Australia Insurance Ltd v Metals & Minerals*	Chapter 21: 21.06

Concept	Short explanation	Relevant authorities	*Principles* text*
	Unless the statute is interpreted as prohibiting the whole contract, its effect is only to annul the term or prevent it operating with the proscribed effect leaving the rest of the contract intact	*Insurance Pty Ltd* (2009) 240 CLR 391	
Implied prohibition	Even without an express statement prohibiting the making of a contract, a statute might have that effect; but whether this is so would still depend on an analysis of the relevant legislative scheme	*Yango Pastoral Co Pty Ltd v First Chicago Australia Ltd* (1978) 139 CLR 410	Chapter 21: 21.07
Statutory declarations of validity	Provisions that expressly declare a contract not to be invalidated because of a breach of statute	*Life Insurance Act 1995* (Cth) s 230	Chapter 21: 21.08

* Consult the corresponding section(s) of the *Principles* text for more detail.

Statutes that affect conduct which might be the subject matter of a contract (using language which is deliberately loose) can do so in a number of different ways: ranging from explicitly making a contract unenforceable, to rendering certain forms of conduct illegal but not specifically addressing the question of whether a contract to perform those things is illegal and unenforceable. The overarching question thus is whether or not the statute in question ultimately renders illegal and void and unenforceable a contract, or if it merely penalises the conduct in question, without necessarily rendering a contract made in contravention of the section itself void.

Gnych v Polish Club Ltd (2015) 255 CLR 414

Facts and issues

The New South Wales *Liquor Act 2007* prohibits a licensee under that Act from leasing or subleasing any part of licensed premises on which liquor is ordinarily sold or supplied for consumption on the premises or on which approved gaming machines are ordinarily kept, used or operated. The Act also prohibits a licensee from leasing or subleasing any other part of licensed premises except with the approval of the Independent Liquor and Gaming Authority.

A licensee leased part of its premises without approval from the Authority. Liquor was not sold or supplied on that part of the premises and gaming machines were not kept, used or operated there. The lessees entered into possession. The licensee subsequently claimed that the lease was void and unenforceable for contravention of the Act, whilst the lessees sought a declaration that they had a leasehold interest, and the licensees claimed that the lease was void and unenforceable.

Decision

Per French CJ, Kiefel, Keane and Nettle JJ at 426:

> As a matter of legislative construction, the likelihood of adverse consequences for the 'innocent party' to a bargain has been recognised as a consideration which tends against the attribution of an intention to avoid the bargain to the legislature. That consideration is consistent with the general disinclination on the part of the courts to allow a party to a contract to take advantage of its own [427] wrongdoing. There may be cases where the legislation which creates the illegality is sufficiently clear as to overcome that disinclination; but it is hardly surprising that the courts are not astute to ascribe such an intention to the legislature where it is not made manifest by the statutory language. And in the present case, this unattractive aspect of the Club's argument is compounded by the circumstance that, as its counsel acknowledged, the Club was obliged to take steps to seek the approval of the Authority for the grant of the lease and did not do so.

Per Gageler J at 431:

> Making an agreement in breach of an express or implied statutory prohibition can have either of two differently sourced consequences for the legal enforcement of the agreement which has come to exist in fact. One is a statutory consequence, the nature and extent of which turns entirely on the construction of the statute imposing the prohibition or of some other statute. The other is a common law (or equitable) consequence, limited to withholding (or imposing conditions on) the grant of a remedy to enforce the agreement at the suit of one or more parties, the application of which turns on considerations of public policy. The distinction between those differently sourced consequences, although fundamental, has not always been recognised in the case law.
>
> The nature and extent of any statutory consequence of breach of a statutory prohibition on making, or on some step in making, an agreement is a question of statutory construction which is distinct from the question of statutory construction which determines the scope of that prohibition (if the prohibition is express) or the existence and scope of that prohibition (if the prohibition is implied). A statutory consequence of making an agreement in breach of an express statutory prohibition is sometimes set out in exhaustive terms in the statutory text. Almost inevitably in the case of an implied prohibition, and sometimes in the case of an express prohibition, the statutory consequence is left in whole or in part to statutory implication. and sometimes in the case of an express prohibition, the statutory consequence is left in whole or in part to statutory implication.

The outcome was that the contravention by the licensee of the *Liquor Act* did not have the consequence of avoiding the lease.

Yango Pastoral Co Pty Ltd v First Chicago Australia Ltd (1978) 139 CLR 410

Facts and issues

A lender sued a borrower for money payable under a loan contract secured by a mortgage and guarantee. The borrower claimed the contract was illegal because the lender carried on the business of banking without Commonwealth authority, as required under the *Banking Act*. The section made no reference to contracts as such, but the borrower argued that by implication the making of contracts was forbidden. The question was as to whether the contract for the lending of money was void. What the *Principles* text describes as the 'traditional approach' is dealt with in the judgment of Jacobs J. Gibbs ACJ also addressed the question of an *implied* prohibition.

Decision

Per Jacobs J at 430:

> When a statute expressly prohibits the making of a particular contract, a contract made in breach of the prohibition will be illegal, void and unenforceable, unless the statute otherwise provides either expressly or by implication from its language. The reported cases which support this principle are numerous. I need refer only to one cited in the course of the argument, *In re Mahmoud and Ispahani*. An example of a case where the statute was held on its true construction to provide otherwise is *Batu Pahat Bank Ltd. v. Official Assignee.*
>
> Where a statute makes it an offence to make a particular contract or to make it in defined circumstances, that will be construed as an implied prohibition of the making of the contract unless the statutory provision is merely in aid of the revenue: *Cope v. Rowlands*, where at p. 157 Parke B. stated:
>
> > It is perfectly settled, that where the contract which the plaintiff seeks to enforce, be it express or implied, is expressly or by implication forbidden by the common or statute law, no court will lend its assistance to give it effect. It is equally clear that a contract is void if prohibited by a statute, though the statute inflicts a penalty only, because such a penalty implies a prohibition: Lord Holt, Bartlett v. Vinor. And it may be safely laid down, notwithstanding some dicta apparently to the contrary, that if the contract be rendered illegal, it can make no difference, in point of law, whether the statute which makes it so has in view the protection of the revenue, or any other object. The sole question is, whether the statute means to prohibit the contract?

In relation to the question of whether the statute impliedly (as opposed to expressly) prohibited the making of the contract, per Gibbs ACJ at 413:

> Where a statute imposes a penalty upon the making or performance of a contract, it is a question of construction whether the statute intends to prohibit the contract in this sense, that is, to render it void and unenforceable, or whether it intends only that the penalty for which it provides shall be inflicted if the contract is made or performed.
>
> The question whether a statute, on its proper construction, intends to vitiate a contract made in breach of its provisions, is one which must be determined in accordance with the ordinary principles that govern the construction of statutes. 'The determining factor is the true effect and meaning of the statute' (*St. John Shipping Corporation v. Joseph Rank Ltd.*). 'One must have regard to the language used and to the scope and purpose of the statute' (*Archbolds (Freightage) Ltd. v. S. Spanglett Ltd.*). One consideration that has been regarded as important in a great many cases, of which *Cope v. Rowlands* is a notable example, is whether the object of the statute—or one of its objects—is the protection of the public. An antithesis is commonly suggested between an intention to protect the public and an intention simply to secure the revenue, and it is said that when the former intention appears the contract must be taken to be prohibited, whereas if the intention is only to protect the revenue the statute will not be

construed as imposing a prohibition on contracts. The question whether the statute was passed for the protection of the public is one test of whether it was intended to vitiate a contract made in breach of its provisions, but I am with respect in full agreement with the views expressed in *St. John Shipping Corporation v. Joseph Rank Ltd.* and *Shaw v. Groom* that it is not the only test. It would be contrary to reason and principle to allow one circumstance to override all other considerations in the interpretation of a statute. As Devlin J. said in *St. John Shipping Corporation v. Joseph Rank Ltd.*: 'The fundamental question is whether the statute means to prohibit the contract. The statute is to be construed in the ordinary way: one must have regard to all relevant considerations and no single consideration, however important, is conclusive.'

[. . .]

[415] Another relevant consideration is the fact that the penalty which s. 8 imposes is a pecuniary sum for each day during which the contravention continues. It is immaterial whether, on any day, the body corporate makes one contract, or one hundred; the penalty is the same. This is an indication that the Parliament did not intend to prohibit each contract made in the course of the business, but only to penalize the carrying on of the business without authority—see *Smith v. Mawhood* and *Victorian Daylesford Syndicate Ltd. v. Dott.*

Per Mason J at 423:

The principle that a contract the making of which is expressly or impliedly prohibited by statute is illegal and void is one of long standing but it has always been recognized that the principle is necessarily subject to any contrary intention manifested by the statute. It is perhaps more accurate to say that the question whether a contract prohibited by statute is void is, like the associated question whether the statute prohibits the contract, a question of statutory construction and that the principle to which I have referred does no more than enunciate the ordinary rule which will be applied when the statute itself is silent upon the question. Primarily, then, it is a matter of construing the statute and in construing the statute the court will have regard not only to its language, which may or may not touch upon the question, but also to the scope and purpose of the statute from which inferences may be drawn as to the legislative intention regarding the extent and the effect of the prohibition which the statute contains.

[. . .]

[426] In this context there is little to be said for the view that the statute intends to prohibit contracts made by unauthorized banks in the course of carrying on banking business. To do so would be to prejudice depositors, not to protect them. The implication of such a prohibition would deny to innocent depositors the right to recover moneys deposited unlawfully with persons carrying on banking business because ex hypothesi the prohibited contract would be illegal and void. To place the defendants' interpretation upon the statute would confer an extraordinary advantage on the wrongdoer in enabling it to resist repayment of moneys deposited with it. In this respect the advantage given to the wrongdoer might conceivably go some distance towards outweighing the punishment imposed upon it by way of penalty under s. 8.

[427] It is not rational to suppose that the Parliament intended to inflict such dire consequences on innocent depositors. Nor is it rational to suppose that the Parliament intended to advantage innocent borrowers whilst penalizing innocent depositors. Even less is it to be supposed that the Parliament intended to invalidate the wide range of commercial and other securities which are brought into existence in the course of carrying on a banking business and thereby to inflict loss on the many persons acquiring such securities. I therefore conclude that the purpose of the Act is adequately served by the imposition of the very heavy penalty which is prescribed for a contravention of s. 8 and that it does not prohibit and thereby invalidate

> contracts and transactions entered into in the course of carrying on banking business in breach of the section.

Per Jacobs J at 434:

> Therefore the contract is only unenforceable if the courts should decline to enforce it because it is associated with the illegal purpose or activity of carrying on the banking business. This is where it is necessary to consider public policy. What public policy of the law would be served? In this connexion it is proper, as was done in *Archbolds (Freightage) Ltd. v. S. Spanglett Ltd.*, to have regard primarily to the scope and purpose of the statutory provision, to consider whether the legislative purpose will be fulfilled without the courts regarding the contract as void and unenforceable. I cannot see that any legislative purpose of s. 8 of the *Banking Act* would be served by preventing a corporation in breach of its provisions from recovering moneys lent on mortgage. A primary purpose of the *Banking Act* is to protect against loss depositors of money with a corporation which by accepting that money and safeguarding it and lending it out again thereby carries on the business of banking. That purpose is defeated if the depositors' money, lent out by the corporation, is thereby irrevocably lost to the corporation and consequently to the depositors. The avoidance of the contract would cause grave injury to depositors, particularly those who had deposited their money without the knowledge that the corporation had no authority to carry on the banking business. Their right to recovery of their money would be of no avail to such depositors if the corporation could not recover the money which it had in turn lent. I find this a sufficient reason of public policy, based as it is on the scope and purpose of s. 8 itself, to decline to apply any rule of public policy that a contract made in association with an illegal purpose cannot be sued on.

In the end result, the contract for the loan of moneys was found not to be void.

Unlawful Gambling Act 1998 (NSW) s 56

Agreements relating to unlawful gambling unenforceable

(1) Any agreement, whether oral or in writing, that relates to any form of gambling that is prohibited under this Act has no effect, and no action may be brought or maintained in any court to recover any money alleged to have been won from, or any money paid in connection with, any such form of gambling.

[...]

Zurich Australia Insurance Ltd v Metals & Minerals Insurance Pty Ltd (2009) 240 CLR 391

Facts and issues

Section 45(1) of the *Insurance Contracts Act* renders void a provision in a contract of insurance that limits or excludes liability by reason that the insured has entered into some other contract of insurance covering the same risk. The question was whether such a clause would make void the entire clause because part of it would be caught by the statute.

Decision

Per French CJ, Gummow and Crennan JJ at 405:

> This question requires attention to be given to the meaning of 'provision' in s 45(1). The word 'provision' has been described rightly as 'a word of diverse meanings which slide easily into each other.' As Lord Simonds, who made that comment, observed:
>
> > It may mean a clause or proviso, a defined part of a written instrument. Or it may mean the result ensuing from, that which is provided by, a written instrument or part of it.
>
> It is clear enough that 'provision' in s 45(1) is used in the former sense. The relevant definition in the *Oxford English Dictionary* is:
>
> > Each of the clauses or divisions of a legal or formal statement, or such a statement itself, providing for some particular matter; also, a clause in such a statement which makes an express stipulation or condition; a proviso.
>
> The important element of that definition is that a provision provides 'for some particular matter'. The fact that there may be more than one provision for a particular matter in one numbered clause of a contract is an accident of drafting. The inclusion in one clause of two statements of rights or liabilities in the form 'if X, then Z' and 'if Y, then Z' has the same effect as the inclusion of those statements in two separate numbered clauses. Each statement is a provision of the contract. There is no requirement to construe s 45(1) so that its operation depends upon accidents of paragraphing or numbering in contracts of insurance. The Underlying Insurance clause contains two statements each specifying a circumstance in which the Hamersley Policy will be reduced to an Excess Insurance policy. Each is properly regarded as a 'provision' of that insurance contract. The question whether a clause of an insurance contract may contain a 'provision', within the meaning of s 45(1), with different elements so intertwined that neither can be regarded as a distinct 'provision', does not arise in this case. In the result, s 45(1) operates only to render void that part of the Underlying Insurance clause in the Hamersley Policy which relates to double insurance to which the insured is a party.

Life Insurance Act 1995 (Cth) s 230

230 Policies not invalidated by contraventions of the Act

A life company's failure to comply with this Act does not invalidate any policy issued by the company.

QUESTIONS

(1) *Equuscorp* is a significant case, as it contains the contemporary iteration of the law relating to the effect of legislation on restitutionary claims: broadly that the question be determined with a view to the need for consistency with the purpose of the relevant statute. What, in your view, was the dilemma faced by the Court in *Equuscorp* in trying to determine the entitlement to restitution that arose in that case?

(2) The Court noted in *Equuscorp* that there was no 'one-size-fits-all' test that was determinative, in relation to the question of recoverability of restitution. What was the strongest factor that militated against an order for restitution?

(3) A contract is made which is the subject of an express statutory prohibition on the making of such a contract. Based on these somewhat incomplete facts, would it be *necessarily* the case that the contract would be void?

21.4 Public policy and the *ex turpi causa* principle

Concept	Short explanation	Relevant authorities	*Principles* text*
The principle denying relief for illegal or immoral conduct	The fundamental notion that the court will not lend its aid to a person who founds a cause of action on an immoral or illegal act Whether the court will lend its aid to the enforcement of a contract depends on the offender's state of knowledge and the likelihood that enforcement would promote the commission of similar wrongs, among other things	*Holman v Johnson* (1775) 1 Cowp 341 *FAI General Insurance Co Ltd (in liq) v Sherry* [2002] SASC 431	Chapter 21: 21.09
'Public policy'	That there may be consequences for the enforcement of a contract even where no positive law transgressed Standards of 'immorality' and policy change from time to time with no fixed standards	*Wilkinson v Osborne* (1915) 21 CLR 89 *Maxcon Constructions Pty Ltd v Vadasz (No 2)* (2017) 127 SASR 193	Chapter 21: 21.10
Other agreements contrary to public policy	The old cases relating to maintenance and champerty as being contrary to public policy must now be treated with caution The contemporary attitude towards contracts tending to promote sexual immorality is generally more relaxed than previously	*Campbell's Cash and Carry Pty Ltd v Fostif Pty Ltd* (2006) 229 CLR 386 *Barac v Farnell* (1994) 53 FCR 193	Chapter 21: 21.12
Ousting the jurisdiction of the courts	Prima facie, a contract which seeks to oust the jurisdiction of the courts is void—or which tends to have that effect	*Materials Fabrication Pty Ltd v Baulderstone Pty Ltd* [2009] VSC 405 *Hooper Bailie Associated Ltd v Natcon Group Pty Ltd* (1992) 28 NSWLR 194	Chapter 21: 21.13

(cont.)

Concept	Short explanation	Relevant authorities	*Principles* text*
Surrender of statutory rights	There is a distinction between purely private rights and rights which have been created for the benefit of the public; the surrender of the latter is likely to be regarded as contrary to public policy A clause surrendering a right to invoke a limitation period is valid, as the right is a private statutory entitlement capable of being surrendered A clause limiting a spouse's right to claim maintenance would essentially seek to oust the discretion of the court and is invalid	*Brown v The Queen* (1986) 160 CLR 171 *Commonwealth v Verwayen (1990)* 170 CLR 394 *Brooks v Burns Philp Trustee Co Ltd* (1969) 121 CLR 432 (see **21.2** for extract)	Chapter 21: 21.14
The enforceability of a contract that is contrary to public policy	Despite older decisions to the contrary, the contemporary approach is to treat the question of enforcement of a contract made contrary to statute flexibly, with the High Court observing that 'no single consideration, however important, is conclusive' The courts will, prima facie, refuse the enforcement of a contract which furthered a purpose contrary to public policy Even where a contract was to perform an act that was prohibited, such as where a licence was required but was not obtained, the court, taking a flexible approach, might refuse to permit illegality to be used as a defence	*Yango Pastoral Co Pty Ltd v First Chicago Australia Ltd* (1978) 139 CLR 410 (see **21.3** for extract) *A v Hayden (No 2)* (1984) 156 CLR 532 *Fitzgerald v Leonhardt Pty Ltd* (1997) 189 CLR 215	Chapter 21: 21.16
Severance of objectionable terms	A provision or set of provisions tainted by illegality *might* be severed leaving the remainder intact. In so doing, the court will enquire whether the illegal promise substantially affects the extent but not the nature of the contract The nature and severity of the illegality is a consideration	*Carney v Herbert* [1985] AC 301 *McFarlane v Daniell* (1938) 38 SR (NSW) 337	Chapter 21: 21.17
Effect of legislation on restitutionary claims	Leaving aside the effect of express provisions affecting such claims, restitution may still be awarded if consistent with the statutory scheme	*Equuscorp Pty Ltd v Haxton* (2012) 246 CLR 498 (see **21.2** for extract)	Chapter 21: 21.19

Concept	Short explanation	Relevant authorities	*Principles* text*
Claims under collateral or related agreements	A claim under an agreement that is collateral to a contract tainted by illegality may be allowed	*Strongman (1945) v Sincock* [1955] 2 QB 525	Chapter 21: 21.20
Tort claims	The parameters of the *ex turpi causa* principle in its application to tort claims, focusing on the question of whether there is a need for there to be a relationship with the illegal conduct	*Miller v Miller* (2011) 242 CLR 446	Chapter 21: 21.21
Restitutionary claims	One approach is that recovery might be possible where the claimant does not found a claim on the illegal transaction The contemporary approach, rather, is to enquire if such a claim is congruent with the purposes of any relevant statute	*Bowmakers Ltd v Barnet Instruments Ltd* [1946] 1 KB 65 *Nelson v Nelson* (1995) 184 CLR 538	Chapter 21: 21.22
What constitutes a 'restraint'?	The question of the type of restraint that needs to be justified and those that do not	*Peters (WA) Ltd v Petersville Ltd* (2001) 205 CLR 126 (see **21.5** for extract)	Chapter 21: 21.24

* Consult the corresponding section(s) of the *Principles* text for more detail.

The principle *ex turpi causa* literally means 'from a base cause' and applies to a situation where someone founds a cause of action on some transgression of the law, and the court consequently will not lend its assistance to that person.

The earlier discussion concerned the consequences of illegality, such as if illegality can be used to resist a claim. *Yango* was an example of a case where such an argument came up. The earlier discussion also explores the broad policy considerations that might affect the question of which party might enforce a contract that was made contrary to the provisions of a statute; the position of the innocent party, for example, was considered in *Gnych,* whereas the court in *Yango* explored the broad policy considerations of whether a contract that had been entered into in contravention of a statute should be void. The discussion of the *ex turpi causa* principle cannot realistically be separated from those considerations.

Holman v Johnson (1775) 1 Cowp 341

Facts and issues

The claimant sold tea to the defendant. The claimant knew it was intended to be smuggled into England, but was not involved with the process. The claimant brought an action for non-payment, and the defendant contended that it could not be enforced because the contract was unlawful. Lord

Mansfield's judgment in the case is commonly regarded as the *locus classicus* of the approach to the denial of relief on public policy grounds.

Decision

Per Lord Mansfield CJ at 342:

> The objection, that a contract is immoral or illegal as between plaintiff and defendant, sounds at all times very ill in the mouth of the defendant. It is not for his sake, however, that the objection is ever allowed; but it is founded in general principles of policy, which the defendant has the advantage of, contrary to the real justice, as between him and the plaintiff, by accident, if I may say so. The principle of public policy is this; *ex dolo malo non oritur actio*.
>
> [343] No court will lend its aid to a man who founds his cause of action upon an immoral or an illegal act. If, from the plaintiff's own standing or otherwise, the cause of action appears to arise *ex turpi causa*, or the transgression of a positive law of this country, there the court says he has no right to be assisted. It is upon that ground the court goes; not for the sake of the defendant, but because they will not lend their aid to such a plaintiff. So if the plaintiff and defendant were to change sides, and the defendant was to bring his action against the plaintiff, the latter would then have the advantage of it; for where both were equally in fault, *potior est conditio defendentis*.

FAI General Insurance Co Ltd (in liq) v Sherry [2002] SASC 431

Facts and issues

A company director, Davies, signed an insurance proposal without disclosing any wrongdoing, whereby the loss claimed from him was attributable to the intended consequence of a deliberate act on his part. An issue was whether the company of which Davies was director was unable to claim indemnity because of the dishonest completion of the proposal and because the circumstances in which the claim arose were a result of the conduct of Mr Davies as a director of the company.

Decision

Per Doyle CJ at [80]:

> . . . it becomes necessary to consider the submission that to allow Mr Davies to claim protection under the policy is contrary to public policy. For this purpose I am content to adopt the principles stated by the Full Court of the Supreme Court of Victoria in *Fire and All Risks Insurance Co Ltd v Powell* [1966] VR 513. The position is conveniently summarised by O'Bryan and Pape JJ at 521–522, in a passage which came after their consideration of the case law dealing with the maxim *ex turpi causa non oritur actio*:
>
>> So much for the special application of the maxim *ex turpi causa non oritur actio* to contracts of insurance against third-party liability. The principles upon which this maxim operates in general are more difficult to state with precision. In what cases does public policy demand that a person shall not be allowed to recover damages or an indemnity or contribution, as the case may be, from another, when the event upon which such claim is based has happened while the claimant is engaged in doing an unlawful or maybe a criminal act? When does public policy demand that the claim shall

> not be entertained in the courts of justice? It may be that each case is to be decided on its own particular facts. The gravity of the illegal or criminal act in question, the possible tendency to encourage the doing of such acts if civil claims are entertained in respect of them, the necessity for the courts to uphold a deterrence to the doing of such acts, all spring to the mind as relevant considerations. The cases seem to support the view that they are all relevant.

This is a notoriously difficult area of the law ...

[133] A question of public policy may arise where the claim involves the commission of a crime by the insured. However, it is not an inflexible rule that liability will be denied in every case which involves commission of a crime. In *Fire & All Risks Insurance Co Ltd v Powell* (supra) Smith J said, at 527:

> It is to be noted that in *Beresford v Royal Insurance Co Ltd* [1938] AC 586, the authorities relied upon were cases of murder, of intentional killing constituting manslaughter, and of death by execution for a capital offence. And it may be that in relation to crimes of the gravest sort the rule, in its application, is inflexible, taking no account of the particular circumstances: cf. *Cleaver v Mutual Reserve Fund Life Association*, [1892] 1 QB 147 at p 152; [1891–4] All ER Rep 335. Outside that field, however, it would seem that the basis on which the rule rests requires that its application should depend upon a weighing, with reference to the public interest, of all the relevant circumstances. And these, I consider, must include the gravity of the class of crime; the offender's knowledge of facts or law making his conduct a crime; the degree of likelihood that if enforcement were allowed the commission of similar crimes would be promoted; the degree of likelihood that enforceability would promote the interests of the victims; and the public interest in the observance of contracts. . .

[176] I have concluded that Mr Davies was not entitled to indemnity and that Amjex may be. In my opinion there are insufficient facts available on which to give a proper answer to this question. I would set aside the answer of the trial Judge and to both parts (a) and (b) I would answer: 'Not appropriate to answer'.

Wilkinson v Osborne (1915) 21 CLR 89

Facts and issues

The question concerned the enforceability of a contract for the payment of commission to a real estate agent who was a member of parliament.

Decision

Per Isaacs J at 97:

> In my opinion the 'public policy' which a Court is entitled to apply as a test of validity to a contract is in relation to some definite and governing principle which the community as a whole has already adopted either formally by law or tacitly by its general course of corporate life, and which the Courts of the country can therefore recognize and enforce. The Court is not a legislator: it cannot initiate the principle; it can only state or formulate it if it already exists.
>
> The rule of law as to contracts against public policy is constant—namely, that every bargain contrary to such a social governing principle is regarded as prejudicial to the State, or, in other

> words, contrary to 'public policy' or, as it is sometimes called, 'policy of the law,' and the State by its tribunals refuses to enforce it.
>
> But, as was said by the Judicial Committee in *Evanturel v. Evanturel*, 'the determination of what is contrary to the so-called "policy of the law" necessarily varies from time to time. Many transactions are upheld now by our own Courts which a former generation would have avoided as contrary to the supposed policy of the law. The rule remains, but its application varies with the principles which for the time being guide public opinion.'

Maxcon Constructions Pty Ltd v Vadasz (No 2) (2017) 127 SASR 193

Facts and issues

The primary relevant issue was whether a contract, having been entered into by Vadasz in the course of carrying on a business under a firm name without disclosure of his bankruptcy in breach of a relevant statute, was void at common law as being contrary to public policy.

Decision

Per Blue J at 214:

> A contract, or a covenant within a contract, is void and unenforceable if the performance of the contract or covenant necessarily entails (or sometimes if the purpose of the contract or covenant is) the commission of:
>
> (1) a crime or tort;
> (2) immoral conduct of a recognised type; or
> (3) conduct prejudicial to a recognised category of public policy.
>
> If a covenant, as opposed to the whole contract, is impugned, the covenant itself will be void but the balance of the contract will survive if that is the contractual intention of the parties under the doctrine of severance.
>
> Although the categories are not fixed and new categories can be recognised, considerable caution must be exercised before doing so.
>
> Recognised categories of immoral conduct falling within the second broad group historically involved sexual immorality. This category originated in a different era of attitudes to the social contract and before the advent of extensive statutory and regulatory control. It has waned in modern times and new categories within this group of immoral conduct are unlikely to be recognised in future . . .

Campbell's Cash and Carry Pty Ltd v Fostif Pty Ltd (2006) 229 CLR 386

Facts and issues

The case involved a litigation funding scheme. The material facts were that 'Firmstone' had sought authority to commence legal proceedings on terms inter alia that they would bear costs if the action was unsuccessful but would be entitled to a 'success fee' if the action was successful. The issue was whether such agreements were contrary to public policy.

Decision

Per Gummow, Hayne and Crennan JJ at 432:

> The appellants sought to encapsulate their submissions on this aspect of the appeals by describing Firmstones' conduct as 'trafficking' in the litigation. Expressed in that way, the appellants' submission may be understood as conflating two separate propositions: first, that the funding arrangements constituted maintenance or champerty and, secondly, that for the maintainer to institute and continue proceedings, in the name of or on behalf of plaintiffs who were thus maintained, was an abuse of process which could be avoided only by ordering a stay of the proceedings. The second of these propositions, about abuse of process, assumed that maintenance and champerty give rise to public policy questions beyond those that would be relevant when considering the enforceability of the agreement for maintenance of the proceedings as between the parties to the agreement.
>
> In jurisdictions where legislation has been enacted to the same effect as the Abolition Act, the premise for the second proposition identified is not valid; there are several reasons to reject it. It is neither necessary nor appropriate to decide what would be the position in those jurisdictions where maintenance and champerty may remain as torts, perhaps even crimes.
>
> . . .

Per Kirby J at 451:

> The importance of access to justice, as a fundamental human right which ought to be readily available to all, is clearly a new consideration that stimulates fresh thinking about representative or 'grouped' proceedings. It is this consideration that has informed the decisions of other Australian appellate courts on such questions and also a decision of the Supreme Court of Appeal of South Africa.
>
> *No abuse of process*: When the foregoing considerations are taken into account, I agree with the conclusion reached on this issue in the reasons of Gummow, Hayne and Crennan JJ. In these appeals the appellants failed to demonstrate an abuse of process to warrant the primary judge's conclusion that they were entitled to a permanent stay on that basis.

Barac v Farnell (1994) 53 FCR 193

Facts and issues

The primary issue arose out of a claim for workers compensation; the relevant question was whether a contract of employment as a receptionist in a brothel was void as being contrary to public policy.

Decision

Per Beaumont J at 207:

> In the present case, as has been noted, there was no suggestion of solicitation so far as the respondent was concerned.
>
> In *Pearce v Brooks* (1866) LR 1 Exch 213, a prostitute was sued by a coach-builder for the hire of a brougham. The hiring was made in the knowledge that she was a prostitute and that

the brougham would be used by her, as it was, as part of her display to attract men. It was held that the plaintiffs could not recover.

Pollock CB said (at 217–218):

> I have always considered it as settled law, that any person who contributes to the performance of an illegal act by supplying a thing with the knowledge that it is going to be used for that purpose, cannot recover the price of the thing so supplied. If, to create that incapacity, it was ever considered necessary that the price should be bargained or expected to be paid out of the fruits of the illegal act (which I do not stop to examine), that proposition has been overruled by the cases I have referred to, and has now ceased to be law. Nor can any distinction be made between an illegal and an immoral purpose; the rule which is applicable to the matter is, *Ex turpi causa non oritur actio*, and whether it is an immoral or an illegal purpose *in which the plaintiff has participated*, it comes equally within the terms of that maxim, and the effect is the same; no cause of action can arise out of either the one or the other. (Emphasis added)

In my opinion, having regard to the routine character of the respondent's duties, this decision may be distinguished here. If there is any illegal or immoral conduct, it would be wrong to characterise the respondent as a participant in it. The participants, in the above sense, were those who organised and controlled the business and not persons merely employed to perform routine functions.

Materials Fabrication Pty Ltd v Baulderstone Pty Ltd [2009] VSC 405

Facts and issues

The question concerned the validity of a clause in a contract, in effect requiring one party to pay money into trust as security for the other's costs before commencing proceedings under the contract.

Decision

Per Vickery J at [36]:

> Although Mr Fairweather attacked sub-clause 20.3 on the basis that it was analogous to a penalty and therefore should be declared void on that ground, it is more appropriate, in my opinion, to consider whether the sub-clause is contrary to public policy because of its tendency to oust jurisdiction of the Court.
>
> It is a well recognised principle that no provision purporting to exclude a right to sue in Court will be recognised: *Doleman & Sons v Ossett Corporation*.
>
> [38] However, the general rule yields to countervailing interests of public policy in the appropriate case.
>
> [...]
>
> [46] As far as sub-clause 20.3 is concerned there is no balancing consideration of public policy such as the interest in pursuing alternative dispute resolution or achieving finality in a dispute by an agreed and binding settlement which effectively releases them from further action. In my opinion sub-clause 20.3 of the subcontracts offends public policy. It is void and is of no effect on that ground.

Hooper Bailie Associated Ltd v Natcon Group Pty Ltd (1992) 28 NSWLR 194

Facts and issues

The applicant sought a stay of arbitration proceedings on the grounds, inter alia, that it had been agreed between them that arbitration would not continue until a process of conciliation had concluded. At issue was the validity of the reference to conciliation.

Decision

Per Giles J at 210:

> But there may be a stay of proceedings having the consequence that a party to the proceedings must give effect to an arbitration agreement, even against its will (see s 53 of the *Commercial Arbitration Act 1984*), and that illustrates that there is nothing offensive in indirectly requiring participation in a process of dispute resolution provided there is sufficient certainty in the conduct required by way of participation.

Brown v The Queen (1986) 160 CLR 171

Facts and issues

An accused person argued that trial by jury, required under the Constitution, was a privilege and could be waived, 'surrendered'. The question concerned whether that right was one that could, in fact, be waived.

Decision

Per Dawson J at 208:

> There can be no real doubt that the words of s 80, given their literal meaning, required the appellant to be tried by jury. He was charged, it was agreed, by indictment and he was charged with an offence against a law of the Commonwealth. But the argument is put — and I hope I do it no injustice by stating it shortly — that s 80 affords no more than a personal guarantee of trial by jury which, because it is for the benefit of the appellant, may be waived by him. The strength of that argument, if not its origin, is to be found in decisions upon comparable provisions in the Constitution of the United States of America: *Patton v United States* (1930) 281 US 276; 74 Law Ed 854; *Adams v US Ex rel McCann* (1942) 317 US 269; 87 Law Ed 268; *Singer v United States* (1965) 380 US 24; 13 Law Ed 2d 630. Those provisions, when read together as they must be, are by no means identical and are comparable in a broad sense only.
>
> [216] ... there is, in my view, no warrant for departure from the plain terms of s 80 merely because waiver of trial by jury is seen by some as a convenient device in modern times. It is an erroneous view that changing circumstances are of themselves a sufficient justification for the adaptation of constitutional provisions, whether or not the result is in disregard of the original intent. The interpretation of the Constitution still involves, as it always has, ascertaining and giving effect to the intention which is to be gathered from its words. It is not a process which

allows those words to be given any meaning which they can bear merely because it is thought that changed circumstances require a different response.

[. . .]

[217] The result is that when an offence against a law of the Commonwealth is tried on indictment, there can be no waiver of trial by jury. That is a result which is required by s 80, but the precise way in which the requirement is met under the current legislation calls for further examination.

Commonwealth v Verwayen (1990) 170 CLR 394

Facts and issues

This was a well-known estoppel case; relevant to the present discussion is the question of whether an agreement not to invoke a limitation period could be enforced.

Decision

Per Mason CJ at 404:

> Putting estoppel to one side for the moment, it is desirable to consider, as Mr. Thomson invited, the existence of a doctrine of 'waiver of the benefit of a statutory right'. Undoubtedly, some statutory rights are capable of being extinguished by the person for whose benefit they have been conferred: *Sandringham Corporation v. Rayment; Wilson v. McIntosh.* However, some statutory rights may also operate as a condition precedent to a court's jurisdiction: Park Gate Iron Co. v. Coates; *Kammins Ballrooms Co. Ltd. v. Zenith Investments (Torquay) Ltd.* More importantly, some rights may be conferred for reasons of public policy so as to preclude contracting out or abandonment by the individual concerned: see *Lieberman v. Morris*. It is therefore necessary to examine the relevant statutory provision in this case in order to ascertain whether it is susceptible to extinguishment in this way.
>
> [. . .]
>
> [405] On the footing that the right to plead the statute as a defence is a right conferred by statute, the respondent's contention that the right is capable of waiver hinges on the scope and policy of the particular statute: *Admiralty Commissioners v. Valverda (Owners)*. The issue is not whether the relevant provisions are beneficial to the public, but whether they are 'dictated by public policy' and enacted 'not for the benefit of any individuals or body of individuals, but for considerations of State'. Although, in one sense, all statutes give effect to some public policy (see *Lieberman v. Morris*), the critical question is whether the benefit is personal or private or whether it rests upon public policy or expediency: *Brown v. The Queen*.
>
> In this case there is the public policy that there should be finality in civil litigation. However, the Parliament has seen fit to implement this policy, not by imposing a jurisdictional restriction, but by conferring on defendants a right to plead as a defence the expiry of the relevant time period. In these circumstances and having regard to the nature of the statutory defence, I conclude that the purpose of the statute is to confer a benefit upon persons as individuals rather than to meet some public need which must be satisfied to the exclusion of the right of access of individuals to the courts. On that basis, it is possible to 'contract out' of the statutory provisions, and it is equally possible to deprive them of effect by other means such as waiver. Put differently, the provisions are procedural rather than substantive in nature, which suggests that they are capable of waiver: *Admiralty Commissioners v. Valverda.*

A v Hayden (No 2) (1984) 156 CLR 532

Facts and issues

Commonwealth officers sought to enforce a term in their contracts of employment obliging the Commonwealth not to disclose their identity to third parties. The question was whether the term was unenforceable on the grounds of public policy. The factual background is sufficiently clear from the following extract.

Decision

Per Gibbs CJ at 544:

> The contracts were entered into by the Commonwealth with persons who, we were told, were actuated by high motives and who were joining a service whose functions are important to society and which could not properly operate unless the identity of its agents was kept secret. An agreement to keep the identity of such persons secret is not contrary to public policy, unless, of course, its actual purpose was to shield one of the parties from liability for a breach of the law. Where a contract is not unlawful on its face and is capable of performance without any violation of the law, it will be enforceable unless it is proved that one or both of the parties intended to perform it in an illegal manner or to effect an illegal purpose: *Waugh v. Morris*; *Hutchinson v. Scott*; *Patterson v. Lowe*. The mere possibility that the contract in the present case might, if performed, obstruct the course of justice was not enough to render it invalid. There is no proof that the parties intended the contract to have any effect on the administration of justice. The contractual term was a valid one.
>
> [. . .]
>
> The fact that the contractual term is not in itself invalid is not however the end of the matter. The Court will refuse to exercise its discretion in favour of granting equitable relief, such as an [545] injunction, to enforce an obligation of confidentiality when the consequence would be to prevent the disclosure of criminality which in all the circumstances it would be in the public interest to reveal. In *Gartside v. Outram* it was held that it would be an answer to a bill for an injunction to restrain the defendant, a former servant, from disclosing materials obtained in the course of his employment, that the materials showed that the business had been fraudulently conducted.

Fitzgerald v Leonhardt Pty Ltd (1997) 189 CLR 215

Facts and issues

A landowner had engaged a driller to drill water, which required statutory permits. The landowner then tried to resist the payment to the driller on the grounds that the contract was illegal. The following judgment is significant also for its endorsement of the approach in *Nelson v Nelson* (1995) 184 CLR 538.

Decision

Per McHugh and Gummow JJ at 226:

> The action by the driller to recover moneys owing to it by the owner [227] was not an action by a party to a contract who had chosen to perform it illegally. The penalty imposed by s 56(1) was

directed at a party in the position of the owner rather than the driller. Further, it has not been suggested that the driller acted otherwise than in good faith or that the driller had aided and abetted the owner in any offence committed by him . . .

The question then becomes whether, as a matter of public policy, the court should decline to enforce the contract because of its association with the illegal activity of the owner in, if not causing, then at least suffering or permitting the construction and drilling of bores, within the meaning of s 56(1), without the grant to the owner of permits pursuant to s 57. The refusal of the courts in such a case to regard the contract as enforceable stems not from express or implied legislative prohibition but from the policy of the law, commonly called public policy. Regard is to be had primarily to the scope and purpose of the statute to consider whether the legislative purpose will be fulfilled without regarding the contract as void and unenforceable.

Section 56 prescribes a penalty. In such a case, the role of the common law in determining the legal consequences of commission of the offence may thereby be diminished because the purpose of the statute is sufficiently served by the penalty. Here, the imposition of an additional sanction, namely inability of the driller to recover moneys otherwise owing by the owner, would be an inappropriate adjunct to the scheme for which the Act provides. The contrary decision would cause prejudice to an innocent party without furthering the objects of the legislation.

[. . .]

[228] The imposition of such a sanction upon the driller by failing to keep the owner to his bargain would be disproportionate to the seriousness of the breaches of s 56 and would be unnecessary to protect the objects or policies of the Act.

In *Nelson v Nelson*, McHugh J referred to the dictum of Lord Mansfield in *Holman v Johnson* that no court would lend its aid to a plaintiff founding the cause of action upon an immoral or illegal act.

[. . .]

[229] This is said to be that, notwithstanding the illegality, relief may still be available to the plaintiff if the plaintiff not be in equal fault with the defendant, that is to say not in pari delicto. However, in the light of the approach taken in *Nelson v Nelson* to comparable questions arising with respect to trusts, the issues of contract law in this case should not be approached by considering any general in pari delicto doctrine.

The preferable course, in cases of contract alike to those involving trusts, is as follows. A case may come within one of the accepted exceptions or qualifications to *Holman v Johnson*. As indicated above, these are set forth, with examples from authority, in the following passage from the judgment of McHugh J in *Nelson v Nelson*:

> First, the courts will not refuse relief where the claimant was ignorant or mistaken as to the factual circumstances which render an agreement or arrangement illegal. Second, the courts will not refuse relief where the statutory scheme rendering a contract or arrangement illegal was enacted for the benefit of a class of which the claimant is a member. Third, the courts will not refuse relief where an illegal agreement was induced by the defendant's fraud, oppression or undue influence. Fourth, the courts will not refuse relief where the illegal purpose has not been carried into effect.

Even if the case does not come within one of those exceptions, the courts should not refuse to enforce contractual rights arising under a contract, merely because the contract is associated with or in furtherance of an illegal purpose, where the contract was not made in breach of a statutory prohibition upon its formation or upon the doing of a particular act essential to the performance of the contract or otherwise making unlawful the manner in which the contract is performed. Rather, the policy of the law should accord with the principles set out by McHugh J in *Nelson v Nelson*. His Honour said:

> Accordingly, in my opinion, even if a case does not come within one of the four exceptions to the *Holman* dictum to which I have referred, courts should not refuse to enforce legal or equitable rights simply because they arose out of or were associated with an unlawful purpose unless: (a) the statute discloses an intention that those rights should be unenforceable in all circumstances; or (b)(i) the sanction of refusing to enforce those rights is not disproportionate to the seriousness of the unlawful conduct; (ii) the imposition of the sanction is necessary, having regard to the terms of the statute, to protect its objects or policies; and (iii) the statute does not disclose an intention that the sanctions and remedies contained in the statute are to be the only legal consequences of a breach of the statute or the frustration of its policies.

Carney v Herbert [1985] AC 301

Facts and issues

A provision that provided that the payment of the purchase price for shares in a company would be secured by mortgages to be provided by a subsidiary company of the company whose shares were the subject of sale was illegal. The mortgages themselves were void. The question was whether the buyers could be compelled to pay the purchase price.

Decision

Per Lord Brightman at 310:

> . . . [I]t may be helpful to quote from the judgment of Lopes LJ [in *Kearney v Whitehaven Colliery Co* [1893] 1 QB 700] at p. 713:
>
> > The law is clear that where the consideration for a promise or promises contained in the contract is unlawful, the whole agreement is void. The reason is that it is impossible to discriminate between the weight to be given to different parts of the consideration, and therefore you cannot sever the legal from the illegal part. But where there is no illegality in the consideration, and some of the provisions are legal and others illegal, the illegality of those which are bad does not communicate itself to, or contaminate, those which are good, unless they are inseparable from and dependent upon one another. Here the consideration moving from the master to the men is the employment and the payment of wages. The consideration moving from the men to the master is the services rendered by them. Both are good and lawful considerations. Then we come to the stipulation with respect to deductions. I am of opinion that that stipulation is altogether separable from and independent of the consideration.

Per Lord Brightman at 311:

> There are . . . two matters to be considered where a contract contains an illegal term, first, whether as a matter of construction the lawful part of the contract can be severed from the unlawful part, thus enabling the plaintiff to sue on a promise unaffected by any illegality; secondly, whether, despite severability, there is a bar to enforceability arising out of the nature of the illegality.

Per Lord Brightman at 316:

> The contract in the present case was basically one for the sale by the plaintiffs to the defendant or his nominated company of shares in Airfoil. The mortgages, like the guarantee, were ancillary to that contract for the sole purpose of ensuring the due performance of the contract by the purchaser. The defendant wanted only the shares in Airfoil. The plaintiffs wanted only the purchase money. It made no difference to the plaintiffs, or to the nature of the transaction, what security was provided so long as it was satisfactory security. The mortgage did not go to the heart of the transaction, and its elimination would leave unchanged the subject matter of the contract and the primary obligations of the vendors and the purchaser. The debenture is therefore capable of being severed from the remainder of the transaction, and its illegality does not taint the whole contract. There is no public policy objection to the enforcement of the contract from which the debenture has been divorced.

In the end result, it was determined that the mortgages were ancillary to the overall transaction and could be severed and the plaintiffs accordingly were not precluded from enforcing the relevant sale agreement.

McFarlane v Daniell (1938) 38 SR (NSW) 337

Facts and issues

The plaintiff claimed moneys under a contract of employment as an actor in the production of films. The contract contained clauses which were held to be in unreasonable restraint of trade. The relevant question was the extent to which his claim was severable from those relating to the unreasonable restraint of trade.

Decision:

Per Jordan CJ at 345:

> When valid promises supported by legal consideration are associated with, but separate in form from, invalid promises, the test of whether they are severable is whether they are in substance so connected with the others as to form an indivisible whole which cannot be taken to pieces without altering its nature.
>
> [. . .]
>
> [346] The exact scope and limits of the doctrine that a legal promise associated with, but severable from, an illegal promise is capable of enforcement, are not clear. It can hardly be imagined that a Court would enforce a promise, however inherently valid and however severable, if contained in a contract one of the terms of which provided for assassination. In some of the authorities relied on for the proposition the invalid promises were not illegal but merely void. However this may be, it is at least well established that, as a general rule, a promise (not itself capable of further subdivision) is unenforceable if it is to do an act or acts all or any of which is illegal, and that a promise to do a lawful act is unenforceable if all or any part of the consideration for the promise is illegal. Thus, as a general rule, if a group of promises is supported by an inseverable consideration all or part of which is illegal, none of the promises is enforceable: *Lake View and Star Ltd. v Cominelli*, [1937] AC 653, at p. 664. If, according to the terms of a contract, a party cannot be called upon to pay money except upon the performance by the other party of the whole consideration, then if any part of the consideration is illegal the money cannot be recovered . . .
>
> [. . .]

Strongman (1945) v Sincock [1955] 2 QB 525

Facts and issues

The defendant undertook to obtain licences for certain work. The plaintiff performed the work in question but could not recover under the building contract because they were unlicensed. They then sought to recover on the basis that the promise to obtain the licences was a collateral contract to the main contract to do the work.

Decision

Per Lord Denning MR at 534:

> Applying the test which Lord Moulton laid down in *Heilbut, Symons & Co. v. Buckleton*, the assurance given by the architect [535] amounted to a collateral contract by which the architect promised that he would get any necessary supplementary licences or, if he could not get them, that he would stop the work.
>
> ...
>
> The second question is whether the builders can recover in law on this collateral promise. The promise itself was not illegal, but it is said that damages cannot be recovered for the breach of it. It is said that, if damages could be recovered, it would be an easy way of getting round the law about illegality. This does not alarm me at all. It is, of course, a settled principle that a man cannot recover for the consequences of his own unlawful act, but this has always been confined to cases where the doer of the act knows it to be unlawful or is himself in some way morally culpable. It does not apply when he is an entirely innocent party.

Miller v Miller (2011) 242 CLR 446

Facts and issues

Ms Danelle Evelyn Miller, the appellant, a passenger in a motor car which she had stolen, was seriously injured when the driver, Maurin Miller, lost control of the car. Before the accident occurred, Ms Miller had essentially taken all reasonable steps to prevent the commission of the offence, including asking to be let out. Ms Miller sued the driver (Maurin Miller) for damages for negligence. The issue was whether he owed her a duty of care.

Decision

Per French CJ, Gummow, Hayne, Crennan, Kiefel and Bell JJ at 454:

> One point that emerges with complete clarity from the cases and the commentary is that the relevant principles are not identified by stopping the inquiry at the point of observing that a plaintiff has contravened the criminal law in the course of the events that the plaintiff alleges render the defendant liable to the plaintiff in tort. Nor are the principles identified by asserting, without further explanation, that public policy 'requires' that such a plaintiff have no claim. Likewise the principles are not identified by simply intoning the Latin maxim *ex turpi causa non oritur actio*. As Windeyer J demonstrated, in *Smith v Jenkins*, it is greatly to be doubted that the maxim, properly understood, has any application in tort. Its intrusion into the debate 'has

caused a confusion which would not have occurred if the writers had condescended to translation and had not taken the maxim into territory where it does not belong. In any event, reference to the maxim does not reveal the reasoning that leads to the conclusion that liability is denied. The maxim 'notwithstanding the dignity of a learned language, is, like most maxims, lacking in precise definition'.

None of these observations denies that questions of public policy are presented when a plaintiff sues another for damages sustained by the plaintiff in the course of, or as a result of, some illegal conduct of the plaintiff. They are. But it is important to identify not only what are the policy considerations that are engaged, and how they are said to be engaged in the particular case, but also, and more fundamentally, *why* policy considerations are engaged.

These reasons will show that the central policy consideration at stake is the coherence of the law. The importance of that consideration has been remarked on in decisions of this Court . . .

Bowmakers Ltd v Barnet Instruments Ltd [1946] 1 KB 65

Facts and issues

The owner of certain machine tools delivered them to the defendant under a contract that was illegal under certain regulations. The question was whether he was entitled to recover them.

Decision:

Per du Parq LJ (delivering the judgment of the Court) at 70:

> They simply say that the machines were their property, and this, we think, cannot be denied. We understood Mr. Gallop to concede that the property had passed from Smith to the plaintiffs, and still remained in the plaintiffs at the date of the conversion. At any rate, we have no doubt that this is the legal result of the transaction.
>
> [. . .]
>
> Why then should not the plaintiffs have what is their own? No question of the defendants' rights arises. They do not, and cannot, pretend to have had any legal right to possession of the goods at the date of the conversion.
>
> [. . .]
>
> [71] In our opinion, a man's right to possess his own chattels will as a general rule be enforced against one who, without any claim of right, is detaining them, or has converted them to his own use, even though it may appear either from the pleadings, or in the course of the trial, that the chattels in question came into the defendant's possession by reason of an illegal contract between himself and the plaintiff, provided that the plaintiff does not seek, and is not forced, either to found his claim on the illegal contract or to plead its illegality in order to support his claim.

Nelson v Nelson (1995) 184 CLR 538

Facts and issues

A house was acquired with Bettie June Nelson's ('Bettie') money but transferred into the names of her children in order to allow her to claim a statutory benefit by falsely claiming she did not have a financial interest in the house. Bettie sought to argue that the proceeds of the house were subject to a trust in her favour. The question was whether she could maintain her interest in the house in the light of the illegal purpose of the transaction.

Decision

Per McHugh J at 616:

> In this case, we are concerned with an agreement or transaction that was not, per se, illegal but which was entered into for an illegal purpose.
>
> [. . .]
>
> As the examination of the Act has disclosed, it contains internal mechanisms for dealing with false declarations and applications by persons who are not entitled to subsidised advances. The Act recognises that ineligible persons may apply for subsidised advances and provides for recovery of the subsidy paid in relation to such persons. These provisions lend weight to the submission of the appellant that the policy of the Act will not be defeated if the Court enforces her equitable rights. They also suggest that the policy of the Act is not frustrated so long as there is recovery of the benefit given. This view is strengthened by the vesting of a discretionary power of waiver in the Secretary.
>
> . . . it is hard to see how the policy of the Act is defeated if a court exercising equitable jurisdiction enforced a resulting trust in favour of Mrs Nelson on terms that the benefit obtained under the Act must be repaid. The existence of criminal sanctions strengthens this analysis because the existence of a range of sanctions together with the omission of a provision that makes unenforceable any agreement made in breach of or to evade the Act is a powerful indication that no other sanctions are needed.
>
> [. . .]
>
> [617] Of course, equity cannot condone Mrs Nelson's unlawful purpose or encourage it. So far as is possible, rights associated with or arising out of unlawful conduct should only be enforced on condition that the wrongdoer takes all lawful steps to overcome the consequences of that conduct.

QUESTIONS

(1) In the cases above, the word 'policy' is referred to frequently. It therefore is important to understand what judges mean by 'policy'. Provide a convenient discussion of 'policy'.

(2) At its most fundamental, what is the rationalisation of the *ex turpi causa* principle?

(3) The Court in *FAI General Insurance Co Ltd v Sherry* stated that, under a policy of insurance (this being a relevant 'contract'), indemnity would not invariably be denied where the claim involved the commission of a crime by the insured. In what way did the reasoning of the Court reflect broader policy considerations under the *ex turpi causa* principle?

21.5 Restraint of trade

Concept	Short explanation	Relevant authorities	*Principles* text*
The common law doctrine	A restraint of trade is presumed to be invalid in principle This presumption can be rebutted, generally by reference to the circumstances at the time of the making of the contract Issues concerning public interest tend to be subsumed in the question of what is a reasonable restraint	*Nordenfelt v Maxim Nordenfelt Guns & Ammunition Co Ltd* [1894] AC 535 *Lindner v Murdock's Garage* (1950) 83 CLR 628 *Amoco Australia Pty Ltd v Rocca Brothers Motor Engineering Co Pty Ltd* (1973) 133 CLR 288	Chapter 21: 21.24
What is a 'restraint'?	Certain types of contracts do not attract the operation of the doctrine and are not regarded as 'restraints' The 'trading society test' has been accepted as one such test which appears to have found acceptance in Australia, although as outlined in *Peters*, no definitive statement exists concerning whether any particular restraint should be immune from the doctrine of restraint of trade	*Peters (WA) Ltd v Petersville Ltd* (2001) 205 CLR 126 *Australian Capital Territory v Munday* (2000) 99 FCR 72	Chapter 21: 21.24
Legitimate interests for a restraint	Goodwill is a legitimate interest and, in this respect, the courts take a stricter view of a restraint as between employer and employee than between seller and buyer Generally the two grounds to justify a post-employment restraint are trade secrets or other confidential information, or personal connections with the employer's customers	*Geraghty v Minter* (1979) 142 CLR 177 *Herbert Morris Ltd v Saxelby* [1916] AC 688	Chapter 21: 21.25
The scope of a restraint	A restraint is only enforceable if it is reasonable; the scope must be commensurate with the interest sought to be protected Where the covenantee's interest involves guarding against customers being lured away, a consideration could be how long it would take reasonably to break the connection between covenantor and those persons they used to deal with With key personnel, a lengthier restraint might be justified	*Lindner v Murdock's Garage* (1950) 83 CLR 628 *NE Perry Pty Ltd v Judge* (2002) 84 SASR 86 *Pearson v HRX Holdings Pty Ltd* (2010) 205 FCR 187	Chapter 21: 21.26

* Consult the corresponding section(s) of the *Principles* text for more detail.

The concept was introduced in the overview to this chapter that a contract in restraint of trade is prima facie illegal and contrary to public policy because it restricts a person's liberty to trade; this being so, it must be 'justified' by the special circumstances of a particular case—*Nordenfelt*.

The cases below focus, in order, on the following propositions: what a 'restraint' is in the first place; what are legitimate interests for a restraint; and the scope of a legitimate restraint.

Nordenfelt v Maxim Nordenfelt Guns & Ammunition Co Ltd [1894] AC 535

Facts and issues

A gun manufacturer covenanted with the transferee of its business that it would not, for 25 years, engage in the business of a manufacturer of guns or ammunition. The issue was as to the validity of the restraint. The following judgment is regarded as the seminal judgment concerning the validity of restraints of trade.

Decision

Per Lord Macnaghten at 565:

> The true view at the present time I think, is this: The public have an interest in every person's carrying on his trade freely: so has the individual. All interference with individual liberty of action in trading, and all restraints of trade of themselves, if there is nothing more, are contrary to public policy, and therefore void. That is the general rule. But there are exceptions: restraints of trade and interference with individual liberty of action may be justified by the special circumstances of a particular case. It is a sufficient justification, and indeed it is the only justification, if the restriction is reasonable — reasonable, that is, in reference to the interests of the parties concerned and reasonable in reference to the interests of the public, so framed and so guarded as to afford adequate protection to the party in whose favour it is imposed, while at the same time it is in no way injurious to the public. That, I think, is the fair result of all the authorities.

Lindner v Murdock's Garage (1950) 83 CLR 628

Facts and issues

A contract of employment provided that the employee would not 'during his employment or within one year from the determination ... be engaged concerned or interested in the business of garage proprietors ... or in any other similar business now carried on by the employers within the same area'. A schedule to the agreement provided for the geographic operation of the restraint, relevantly being two areas: 'This agreement shall apply to the sales territory for motor cars, trucks and tractors etc. of M.—Crystal Brook and Wirrabara'. Upon the termination of his employment, the issue concerned the enforceability of the restraint.

Decision

Per Latham CJ at 638:

> It was argued that the area within which the covenant applied, namely Wirrabara as well as Crystal Brook, was too wide because the defendant in fact was employed only at the garage at Crystal Brook and not at the garage at Wirrabara. But this fact in my opinion cannot affect the validity of the covenant. The validity of the covenant must be determinable at the time when the contract is made. The defendant might consistently with the terms of the contract have been employed in work either at Crystal Brook or Wirrabara. I can see no reason for holding that the area of the restraint is too wide. A covenant in restraint of trade is not invalid by reason of the area to which it applies unless the area exceeds that 'fairly covered by the business of the covenantee at the date of the agreement or which might at that date reasonably be expected to be covered by such business on the expiration of the agreement' (*Brightman v. Lamson Paragon Ltd.*).

Per McTiernan J at 642:

> The modern rule was stated by Lord Macnaghten in the *Nordenfelt Case*. His Lordship there said
>
>> The true view at the present time I think, is this: The public have an interest in every person's carrying on his trade freely: so has the individual. All interference with individual liberty of action in trading, and all restraints of trade of themselves, if there is nothing more, are contrary to public policy, and therefore void. That is the general rule. But there are exceptions: restraints of trade and interference with individual liberty of action may be justified by the special circumstances of a particular case. It is a sufficient justification, and indeed it is the only justification, if the restriction is reasonable—reasonable, that is, in reference to the interests of the parties concerned and reasonable in reference to the interests of the public, so framed and so guarded as to afford adequate protection to the party in whose favour it is imposed, while at the same time it is in no way injurious to the public.

The Court then dealt with the question of whether the restraints in question were reasonable. The following extract of the reasoning of Kitto J is particularly relevant to this question.

> [655] But in order that a restraint may be made reasonable in reference to the interests of the parties by means of a geographical limitation, the limitation must, I think, be such as will fairly approximate to a limitation expressed by reference to the employer's customers of whom the employee is likely to acquire special knowledge or with whom the employee is likely to be brought into a personal relation while in the employment.
>
> [...]
>
> [658] In the present case the evidence did not establish that the appellant if working at Crystal Brook or at Wirrabara would not be brought into touch with customers from the area surrounding the other of those towns; but the onus lay upon the respondents to prove facts in the light of which it was reasonable for the parties, when framing the restrictive clause of the agreement, to expect that the appellant, if working in one area, would be likely to come into contact with customers of the respondents' business in the other area, and no such evidence was given.
>
> [...]
>
> [659] In order to be valid it should, I think, have been so limited in respect of each area as not to operate therein unless the appellant should be employed by the respondents in their business in that area within some specified reasonable period preceding the termination of his service. Not being so limited, the clause, even if free from objection in any other respect, appears to me to exceed what was reasonably required in order to obviate the danger from which the respondents were entitled to obtain protection. Accordingly I am of opinion that the restrictive clause should be held invalid as being in unlawful restraint of trade.

Amoco Australia Pty Ltd v Rocca Brothers Motor Engineering Co Pty Ltd (1973) 133 CLR 288

Facts and issues

A sublease between a petroleum supplier, Amoco, and a service station operator, Rocca, contained inter alia covenants that Rocca would buy a minimum amount of petrol each month and not buy petrol from anyone else. The dispute concerned whether Rocca was at liberty to buy from anyone else, contrary to that covenant. The extract below is confined to the discussion of the intersection of the need for the restraints to be reasonable as between the parties, and reasonable in the public interest.

Decision

Per Walsh J at 307:

> It is public policy which lies at the root of the rule that agreements in restraint of trade are, prima facie, unenforceable. A decision whether the circumstances of a particular case call for the application of that rule or justify a departure from it is a decision on a matter concerning public policy. Therefore, if a restraint is imposed which is more than that which is required (in the judgment of the court) to protect the interests of the parties, that is a matter which is relevant to the considerations of public policy which underlie the whole doctrine, since to that extent the deprivation of a person of his liberty of action is regarded as detrimental to the public interest: see *McEllistrim v. Ballymacelligott Co-operative Agricultural and Dairy Society Ltd.* I acknowledge that the consequence of what I have just stated is that there is to some extent a merging of the second branch of the *Nordenfelt* formulation of the applicable principle with its first branch. But this does not mean that the distinction between them is wholly obliterated. In order to justify a restraint of trade both tests must be satisfied. The restraint must be reasonable in the interests of the parties in that it affords no more than adequate protection to the covenantee 'while at the same time it is in no way injurious to the public' (see the *Nordenfelt Case*). It may be that although a restraint satisfies the first requirement it is injurious to the public for some reason other than being in excess of what is reasonable in the interests of the parties. Perhaps this will [308] rarely be so.

Peters (WA) Ltd v Petersville Ltd (2001) 205 CLR 126

Facts and issues

The following text is adapted from the headnote to the case: Two companies manufactured and sold ice cream in partnership throughout Australia under one brand name and throughout Australia (except in Western Australia) under another brand name. A third company manufactured and sold ice cream under that other brand name only in Western Australia. The first two companies sold their Western Australian land, plant, equipment, goodwill and stock to the third company and, for a royalty, granted it an exclusive licence for a stipulated period to use, on products sold by it in Western Australia, the brand name which at the time they used throughout Australia and certain associated trademarks. They agreed to make available to the third company for the period of the licence information concerning product development, manufacturing know-how, and marketing.

For that period, they also covenanted not to sell, supply or distribute to any person in Western Australia ice cream or frozen confections manufactured or distributed by them; not to sell, supply or distribute such items to any person anywhere which to their knowledge were ultimately intended for sale, supply or distribution in Western Australia; and not to carry on, or permit any subsidiary or related company to carry on, in Western Australia, the business of manufacturer or distributor of ice cream or frozen confections.

The issue concerned whether the restraint was of a type that needed to be justified at law.

Decision

Per Gleeson CJ, Gummow, Kirby and Hayne JJ at 135:

> That there are some species of restraint of trade which do not attract the operation of the common law doctrine is well established. The question is whether the present case falls within any of them or, at least, is the first of a newly discerned immune species and, if so, what criteria are applicable to isolate that species.
>
> [...]
>
> [138] In *Esso*, Lord Wilberforce, after his consideration of the established instances where the doctrine was understood to have no application, said that the treatment of the transactions involved in this way could only truly be explained: 'by saying that they have become part of the accepted machinery of a type of transaction which is generally found acceptable and necessary, so that instead of being regarded as restrictive they are accepted as part of the structure of a trading society.' That rationale has been adopted by the Full Federal Court in *Australian Capital Territory v Munday* after a full review of the authorities since *Esso* in a number of jurisdictions. However, it is inappropriate to express here any concluded view on the matter.
>
> [141] The expression 'sterilisation of capacity' has been used to describe the purport of the remarks by Lord Pearce in *Esso* upon which Peters WA relies. In general terms, the effect of those remarks is that the restraint of trade doctrine does not apply to contracts which absorb the capacity of a covenantor rather than sterilise it. The relevant passages in his Lordship's speech have been criticised in the following terms:
>
>> [F]irst, [Lord Pearce's] application of the test is inconsistent, for he says covenants taken on the conveyance or lease of land are outside the doctrine, though they may sterilise a covenantor. Secondly, the test depends on exploded doctrines — that restraint of [142] trade does not apply during the continuance of contracts, and that it does not apply where trade is promoted rather than restrained. Thirdly, the test relies on cases in which the restraint of trade doctrine was not applied but which on analysis appear to sterilise the capacities of the covenantors.
>
> There are other objections of a more fundamental kind.
>
> [...]
>
> The deprivation by restraint, even if originally imposed consensually, upon the liberty of action of a trader has been regarded as detrimental to the public interest. What matter of public interest requires the removal of what otherwise is the requirement of justification for the upholding of a restraint such as that in Art 7.1? ...

Per Callinan J at 147:

> There are, I think, uncertainties involved in the application of any of the tests propounded from time to time by the courts, and, in particular, the three tests formulated in *Esso Petroleum Co*

Ltd v Harper's Garage (Stourport) Ltd. The appellant here sought to have this Court adopt the sterilisation of capacity test proffered by Lord Pearce, who said this:

> The doctrine does not apply to ordinary commercial contracts for the regulation and promotion of trade during the existence of the contract, provided that any prevention of work outside the contract, viewed as a whole, is directed towards the absorption of the parties' services and not their sterilisation.
>
> [...]

[148] His Lordship's test involves, in my respectful opinion, the same sorts of difficulties as do the other tests. Lord Pearce refers to 'ordinary commercial contracts' and to negative ties which are 'incidental and normal to the positive commercial arrangements at which the contract aims'. There is great scope for difference of opinion on these matters; indeed, despite what his Lordship says, that no question of reasonableness will arise in the case of ordinary commercial contracts and normal and incidental ties, the question of what is an ordinary commercial contract, or what is incidental and normal will rarely be able to be divorced from a question of what is reasonable between the parties. So too, the question of what is an ordinary commercial contract and what is 'normal' when complex commercial arrangements are under consideration will not always admit of one clear answer.

The Court determined that the restraints in question were covenants of the type to which the doctrine of restraints would apply and would be prima facie void at common law, and that they did attract the operation of the common law doctrine of restraints.

Australian Capital Territory v Munday (2000) 99 FCR 72

Facts and issues

The issue was whether the doctrine of the restraint of trade applied to conditions of entry to a rubbish tip that prohibited tenants from trading within the tip.

Decision

Per Heerey J at 78:

> ... before the reasonableness of a restraint is considered there is the anterior question as to whether the doctrine applies at all to a transaction of the kind in question. This issue has important practical consequences. If the doctrine does not apply, no question of reasonableness arises and the party seeking to justify the restraint does not have the burden of going into evidence.
>
> [...]
>
> [92] ... it [the trading society test] accords more satisfactorily with common law methodology and with the need for the law to adapt to methods of doing business which are constantly changing.
>
> [...]
>
> [93] If one treats the appellant's occupation of the land as relevant but not conclusive it is possible to apply the trading society test in a way which would satisfy the reasonable expectation of the community as well as the requirements of public policy.

> A common, and important, way of deriving economic benefit from land is the grant of exclusive licences for the conduct of business thereon. Such licences are only of value because of the expectation that other persons will enter upon the land and be customers, but not competitors. So persons gaining admission to the Melbourne Cricket Ground who happen to be caterers would not expect to be able to set up a pie stall in competition with those who have been granted exclusive catering rights by the MCG.
>
> [. . .]
>
> Thus in the context of the appellant's contract with Revolve, I would hold that the doctrine of restraint of trade has no application to the contractual terms of licences under which the respondent and others are permitted to enter the Tip.

Geraghty v Minter (1979) 142 CLR 177

Facts and issues

A deed of partnership provided that, upon its determination, the appellants were restrained from exercising or being concerned or engaging in a trade or business of a similar nature within 20 miles by road of the office of the partnership business. The issue concerned the validity of that restraint.

Per Gibbs J at 185:

> The fact that the appellants were admitted as partners, rather than merely employed, cannot in itself mean that the respondents have any less right to protect their interest in the business. The courts in general take a stricter and less favourable view of covenants in restraint of trade entered into between employer and employee than of similar covenants between vendor and purchaser:
>
> [. . .]
>
> In my opinion, when the appellants became partners, with a forty per cent share in the business, the respondents did not cease to have an interest in the business which they were entitled to protect by a covenant framed in appropriate terms. The respondents retained a substantial interest in the goodwill, and they were entitled to protect that interest. Viewing the matter more broadly, the respondents retained an interest in the business which they had built up, and when they took in partners they were entitled to protect themselves against the possibility that the newcomers might use to their own advantage the trade connexions which were vital to the success of that business.
>
> [. . .]
>
> [186] The question that then arises is whether the covenant imposed by cl. 21 provided more than adequate protection for the interest of the respondents.
>
> [. . .]
>
> In my opinion, the deed, on its proper construction, did no more than prevent the appellants from carrying on a business of the same character as that carried on by the partnership. In this regard, therefore, it is impossible to hold that the provisions of cl. 21 are too wide.
>
> [. . .]
>
> [188] The restraint imposed by cl. 21 was, in my opinion, reasonable and valid. I would accordingly dismiss the appeal.

Herbert Morris Ltd v Saxelby [1916] AC 688

Facts and issues

The plaintiff company were manufacturers of hoisting machinery. The defendant was engaged by the company as engineer under an agreement which contained a covenant by the defendant with the company that he would not be concerned in the sale or manufacture of pulley blocks and other items and other specific terms. This is a seminal case setting out the type of interest that an employer needs to have to justify a restraint, hence the somewhat detailed treatment.

Decision

Per Lord Atkinson at 700:

> In the case of *Leather Cloth Co. v. Lorsont* a case, no doubt, of the sale of the goodwill of a business, I find James V.-C. also used the phrase 'not unreasonable for the protection of the parties,' meaning both covenantor and covenantee. Dealing with the contention that a general restraint of trade throughout the United Kingdom is bad on the face of it, he says:
>
>> I do not read [701] the cases as having laid down that unrebuttable presumption. . . . All the cases, when they come to be examined, seem to establish this principle, that all restraints upon trade are bad as being in violation of public policy, unless they are natural, and not unreasonable for the protection of the parties in dealing legally with some subject matter of contract. The principle is this: Public policy requires that every man shall be at liberty to work for himself, and shall not be at liberty to deprive himself or the State of his labour, skill, or talent, by any contract that he enters into. On the other hand, public policy requires that when a man has by skill or by any other means obtained something which he wants to sell, he should be at liberty to sell it in the most advantageous way in the market; and in order to enable him to sell it advantageously in the market it is necessary that he should be able to preclude himself from entering into competition with the purchaser. In such a case the same public policy that enables him to do that does not restrain him from alienating that which he wants to alienate, and, therefore, enables him to enter into any stipulation however restrictive it is, provided that restriction in the judgment of the Court is not unreasonable, having regard to the subject matter of the contract.
>
> These considerations in themselves differentiate, in my opinion, the case of the sale of goodwill from the case of master and servant or employer and employee. The vendor in the former case would in the absence of some restrictive covenant be entitled to set up in the same line of business as he sold in competition with the purchaser, though he could not solicit his own old customers. The possibility of such competition would necessarily depreciate the value of the goodwill. The covenant excluding it necessarily enhances that value, and presumably the price demanded and paid, and, therefore, all those restrictions on trading are permissible which are necessary at once to secure that the vendor shall get the highest price for what he has to sell and that the purchaser shall get all he has paid for. Restrictions on freedom of trading are in both classes of case imposed, no doubt, with the common object of protecting property. But the resemblance between them, I think, ends there.
>
> In all cases such as this, one has to ask oneself what are the interests of the employer that are to be protected, and against what is he entitled to have them protected.

> [702] He is undoubtedly entitled to have his interest in his trade secrets protected, such as secret processes of manufacture which may be of vast value. And that protection may be secured by restraining the employee from divulging these secrets or putting them to his own use. He is also entitled not to have his old customers by solicitation or such other means enticed away from him. But freedom from all competition per se apart from both these things, however lucrative it might be to him, he is not entitled to be protected against. He must be prepared to encounter that even at the hands of a former employee.
>
> [. . .]

Per Lord Parker of Waddington at 709:

> It is quite different in the case of an employer taking such a covenant from his employee or apprentice. The goodwill of his business is, under the conditions in which we live, necessarily subject to the competition of all persons (including the servant or apprentice) who choose to engage in a similar trade. The employer in such a case is not endeavouring to protect what he has, but to gain a special advantage which he could not otherwise secure. I cannot find any case in which a covenant against competition by a servant or apprentice has, as such, ever been upheld by the Court. Wherever such covenants have been upheld it has been on the ground, not that the servant or apprentice would, by reason of his employment or training, obtain the skill and knowledge necessary to equip him as a possible competitor in the trade, but that he might obtain such persona. l knowledge of and influence over the customers of his employer, or such an acquaintance with his employer's trade secrets as would enable him, if competition were allowed, to take advantage of his employer's trade connection or utilize information confidentially obtained.
>
> [. . .]
>
> [711] An attempt was, however, made in argument to justify the restraint on the ground that it was no more than adequate for the protection of the plaintiffs' trade connection and trade secrets. I am of opinion that this attempt completely failed. With regard to the plaintiffs' connection, there is little or no evidence that the defendant ever came into personal contact with the plaintiffs' customers.
>
> [. . .]
>
> With regard to trade secrets, I am not satisfied that the defendant was entrusted with any trade secret in the proper sense. . . . Mr. Walter boldly argued that the expression trade secrets ought to be extended so as to include everything which Mr. Morris claimed to be peculiar to the plaintiffs' method of carrying on their business.
>
> [. . .]
>
> [712] All that he could carry away was the general method and character of the scheme of organization practised by the plaintiff company. Such scheme and method can hardly be regarded as a trade secret.

NE Perry Pty Ltd v Judge (2002) 84 SASR 86

Facts and issues

The parties were companies owned by chiropractors and doing business as such. The 'Judge' company through its director, Judge, was engaged by the plaintiff to provide chiropractic services. The relevant restraint of trade clause precluded the Judge company from practising in Whyalla for two years following termination of the engagement.

Decision

Per Doyle CJ, Bleby and Besanko JJ at 91:

> The fundamental issue is whether the restriction is reasonable in the interests of the parties, or whether it affords no more than adequate protection to NEP. On the assumption that NEP would replace AMJ with another chiropractor, and continue its practice, the period of time within which a replacement chiropractor would have an opportunity to demonstrate his or her effectiveness to patients at the Clinic may well be much the same as the period of time required to sever the connection between Dr Judge and patients of the Clinic. However, I agree that it is safer to focus on the period of time reasonably required to break the connection with AMJ and Dr Judge, rather than the period of time within which there would be an opportunity for NEP to establish a new connection.
>
> [. . .]
>
> [93] Like the judge, I have no difficulty accepting that a 12-month restraint is reasonable. The subjective nature of the assessment involved makes me cautious about concluding that two years is unreasonable and provides more than adequate protection. But in this respect it is relevant to take into account the fact that, from a practical point of view, the restraint would make it difficult, and perhaps impossible, for Dr Judge, at least while employed by and a director of AMJ, to continue to live in Whyalla. For the period of the restraint it may well be necessary for him to live elsewhere. I remind myself that the courts have taken a stricter approach to restraints found in employment contracts. That approach applies to a contract of the type in question here. Having reflected on the matter, I am not persuaded that a two-year restraint is reasonable in the interests of the parties, and affords no more than adequate protection to NEP. In the end, the onus was on NEP to prove that it was reasonable.

Pearson v HRX Holdings Pty Ltd (2010) 205 FCR 187

Facts and issues

The plaintiff carried on a human resources business and the defendant was its chief operating officer whose role was essentially to represent the plaintiff in meetings. The relevant restraint precluded him from being concerned in a business in competition to the plaintiff for two years. This restraint was found to be valid and the central point, discussed below, concerned the fact that the employee was in a position of influence.

Decision

Per Keane CJ, Foster and Griffiths JJ at 200:

> It is apparent from the factual findings of the primary judge that Mr Pearson's position of influence over HRX's customers is no less strong than that evidently enjoyed by Mr Elsley.
>
> [. . .]
>
> In our respectful opinion, HRX's interest in protecting its customer connections was sufficient to justify HRX's bargaining for protection against the risk that the personal contacts made by Mr Pearson in the course of HRX's business would follow him unbidden to a new employer. That interest went beyond HRX's interest in confidential information and would not sufficiently be

protected by the confidentiality provision of the service agreement. And the non-solicitation provision would not have protected HRX from the risk that its customers, knowing of Mr Pearson's move to Talent2, would choose to move their business to Talent2 unbidden by Mr Pearson and without even discussing the move with him.

[...]

QUESTIONS

(1) What are the overarching themes that underpin the idea of the invalidity—and validity—of covenants in restraint of trade?

(2) In light of the reasoning in *Nordenfelt* concerning the need for a restraint of trade clause to be justified by the 'special circumstances' of a case, identify broadly what interests the law has seen fit to protect by an appropriate restraint of trade clause.

(3) Assuming that the employee did have dealings with the ex-employer's clients, such that the employer had an interest worth protecting by way of a restrictive covenant restraining the ex-employee from trading or doing business in a particular way or in a particular locality, what general guidelines will the court apply in determining the time and geographical scope of the restraint?

21.6 International perspectives

The *CISG* does not generally deal with matters of validity, and leaves such questions for the domestic law: art 4(a) *CISG*. Issues of illegality and public policy will normally be considered matters of validity for this purpose. By contrast, the UNIDROIT Principles contain some rules concerning the consequences of illegality, but do not specify the content of what constitutes illegality, which is a matter for domestic law. Thus, under the UNIDROIT Principles, the domestic law rendering the contract illegal also determines the effects of this upon the contract (art 3.3.1(1)); however, where the domestic law does not specify consequences for the contract, the parties may exercise any remedies reasonable in the circumstances (art 3.3.1(2)), where reasonability is determined according to criteria in art 3.3.1(3). Restitution is provided as a default remedy: art 3.3.2 UNIDROIT Principles.

Where a particular country's regulations require certain standards to be met, or require public permissions to be acquired (such as licences, certification etc), a slightly different issue is introduced. Failure to comply with requirements for registration of a design, safety standards etc may mean that goods cannot be sold in a particular country; or that the contract cannot be performed because import is banned; or, in some cases, the contract might be statutorily rendered unenforceable. In such cases, the question as to which party was obliged to comply with the public regulation or standard might arise. This will have implications for remedies. See further **25.8.3** (*CISG*) and **25.8.6** (UNIDROIT Principles).

21.7 Review

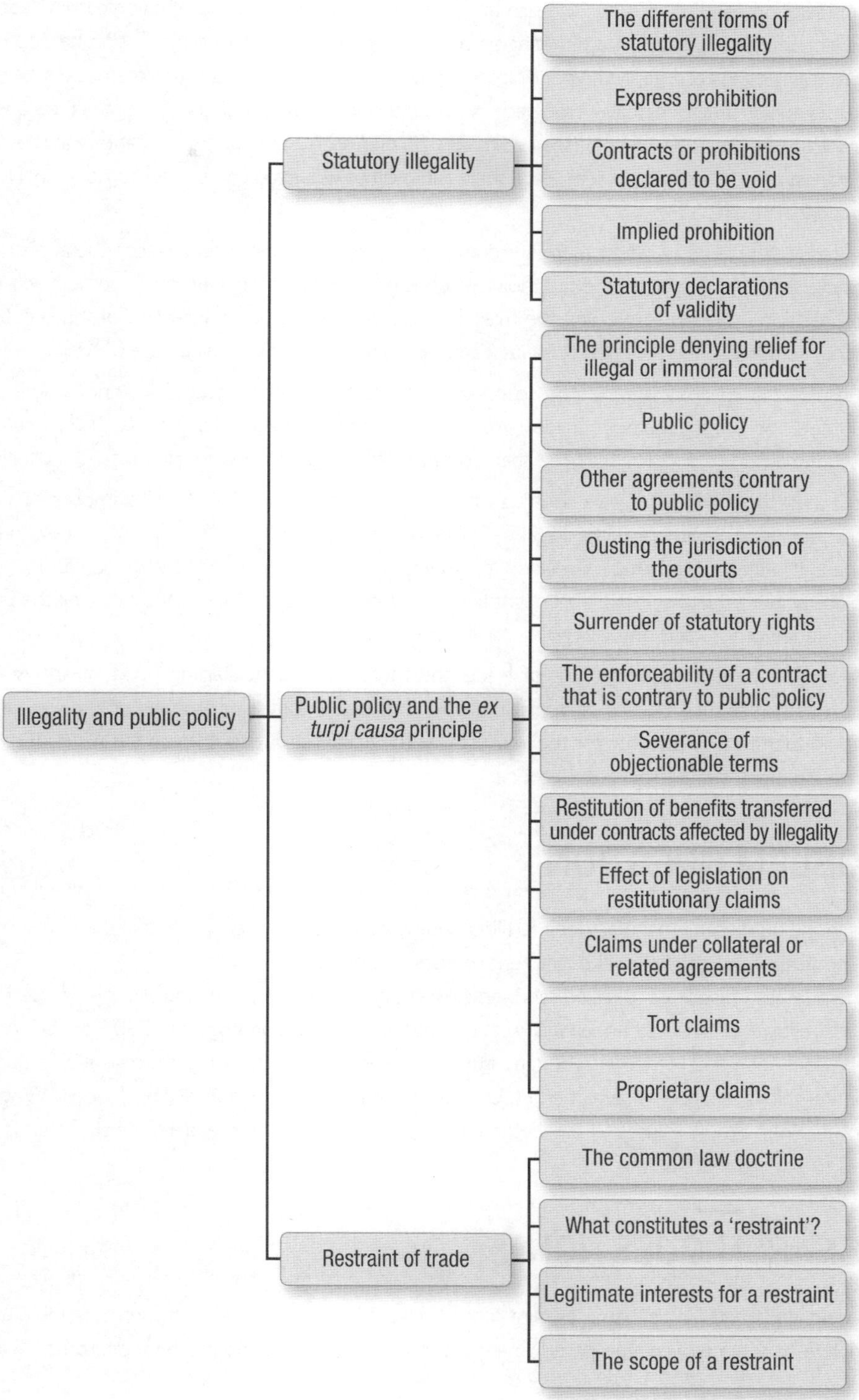
Illegality and public policy
Statutory illegality
The different forms of statutory illegality
Express prohibition
Contracts or prohibitions declared to be void
Implied prohibition
Statutory declarations of validity
Public policy and the *ex turpi causa* principle
The principle denying relief for illegal or immoral conduct
Public policy
Other agreements contrary to public policy
Ousting the jurisdiction of the courts
Surrender of statutory rights
The enforceability of a contract that is contrary to public policy
Severance of objectionable terms
Restitution of benefits transferred under contracts affected by illegality
Effect of legislation on restitutionary claims
Claims under collateral or related agreements
Tort claims
Proprietary claims
Restraint of trade
The common law doctrine
What constitutes a 'restraint'?
Legitimate interests for a restraint
The scope of a restraint

TIPS FOR APPLYING THE LAW IN PRACTICE

- Because the enforcement of a contract tainted (loosely speaking) by illegality is dependent upon 'policy' considerations, and there is no 'one-size-fits-all' resolution to the question of enforceability (adopting the language in *Equuscorp*), it is tempting simply to rely on intuition and instinct. It is prudent to refrain from doing so; instead, apply the principles that have been applied by the courts themselves. Over the years, general categories have emerged—such as the ideas, variously, that a contract to oust the jurisdiction of the courts is void (see eg *Brooks v Burns Philp Trustee Co Ltd*) or that offering someone a financial inducement not to seek election to public office would be contrary to public policy (*Taylor v Taylor* [2019] VSC 533).
- With statutory illegality, whilst there are numerous refinements and subsidiary considerations, at the highest level of abstraction, the first point of enquiry is whether the statute in question was on its construction intended to prohibit the making of the contract, or if the intention of the statute was merely to penalise the conduct. This was a central point made in the seminal case of *Yango*.
- The next tier of analysis would be to consider the factors that the courts, at various times, have adopted, again noting the point made in *Yango*, adopting the reasoning in *St John Shipping Corporation v Joseph Rank Ltd* [1957] 1 QB 267— that 'no single consideration, however important, is conclusive'.
- Illustrating the point, not even a contract for the commission of an act that might amount to a crime is necessarily and without more illegal. *FAI General Insurance Co Ltd (in liq) v Sherry* is a case in point, where it was stressed that in relation to gravest offences, it was unlikely there would be any flexibility, but otherwise the Court might take into account a variety of factors, including the parties' knowledge of the facts and law giving rise to the crime.
- Turning to covenants in restraint of trade, the most convenient starting point of analysis is to appreciate that such clauses prima facie are void as being contrary to public policy. The analysis should then turn to a search for the interest that the party seeking to enforce the restraint has that might support the validity of the covenant.

PROBLEM QUESTION

John is in the business of manufacturing fertiliser, which is a product which falls within the definition of a 'specified fertiliser' in the fictional enactment reproduced below.

The purchase or sale of specified fertiliser is expressly prohibited, unless the seller is licensed to do so under regulations enacted under this Act. The penalty for non-compliance is $300 per offence.

John does not have a licence and you can assume that he is thereby in breach of the regulation in question.

John employs an apprentice named Peter to assist him with the manufacturing process. When pay day comes, John simply refuses to pay Peter, pleading the illegality of the work done by Peter. Is Peter entitled to payment of his wages?

RESEARCH QUESTION

It was held in *Herbert Morris* that a restraint of trade clause is viewed more strictly when made between an employer and employee, compared to a vendor and purchaser. Explain the rationalisation for this.

PART VII

REMEDIES

22

ENFORCING A CONTRACT

22.1 Overview

'Enforcing' a contract encompasses specific performance, injunctions, debt, and the recovery of liquidated damage, each being remedies the innocent party seeks *under* the contract by way of its enforcement. The idea of enforcing a contract is thus to be distinguished from damages for breach of contract, which is compensation for the consequences of non-performance.

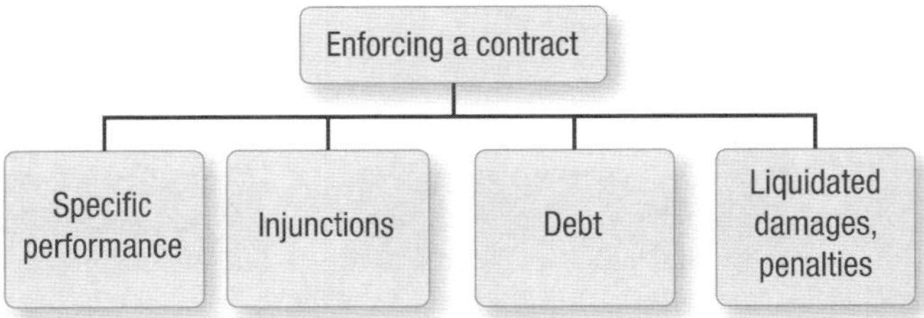

22.2 Specific performance

Concept	Short explanation	Relevant authorities	*Principles* text*
Inadequacy of damages	Specific performance will not normally be ordered if damages are an adequate remedy. Because of the unique qualities of land, the purchase of land is usually regarded as appropriate for specific performance. On the other hand, the purchase of chattels is not generally regarded as appropriate for specific performance, because damages would ordinarily compensate the innocent party for their loss, unless those chattels were unique	*Wight v Haberdan Pty Ltd* [1984] 2 NSWLR 280 *Adderley v Dixon* (1824) 1 Sim & St 607; 57 ER 239 *Pianta v National Finance & Trustees Ltd* (1964) 180 CLR 146 *Loan Investment Corporation of Australasia v Bonner* [1970] NZLR 724 *Semelhago v Paramadevan* [1996] 2 SCR 415 *Dougan v Ley* (1945) 71 CLR 142	Chapter 22: 22.02–22.03
Impossibility and futility	Specific performance will not be ordered when it is impossible or futile	*Wenham v Ella* (1972) 127 CLR 454 *Verrall v Great Yarmouth Borough Council* [1981] QB 202	Chapter 22: 22.04
The problem of constant supervision	Specific performance will not normally be ordered where constant supervision is required—noting the qualifications in *Patrick Stevedores*	*J C Williamson Ltd v Lukey* (1931) 45 CLR 282 *Patrick Stevedores Operations No 2 Pty Ltd v Maritime Union of Australia* (1998) 195 CLR 1	Chapter 22: 22.05

Concept	Short explanation	Relevant authorities	*Principles* text*
Mutuality	Mutuality is a concept whereby the law seeks to protect both parties. So, the court will not generally enforce the obligations of the defendant by specific performance unless it can also enforce the obligations of the plaintiff The concept of mutuality has been rationalised on the grounds of hardship; namely, whether granting specific performance to the plaintiff would produce hardship to the defendant The relevant date for assessing mutuality is the date of the hearing	*Cannavo v FCD (Holdings) Pty Ltd* [2000] NSWSC 304 *Price v Strange* [1977] 3 All ER 371	Chapter 22: 22.06
Personal services or relationships	Contracts for the provision of ongoing personal services are generally not susceptible to specific performance, subject to the qualifications in *Patrick Stevedores* where specific performance might be granted where the obligation was to carry out a business activity	*J C Williamson Ltd v Lukey* (1931) 45 CLR 282 *Byrne v Australian Airlines Ltd* (1995) 185 CLR 410	Chapter 22: 22.07
Breach, unreadiness, unwillingness, and inability to perform	Applying broadly the 'clean hands' doctrine, a party may be precluded from specific performance if it is not ready, willing and able to perform Breach of contract is regarded as the type of conduct which would be caught by the doctrine and which might disentitle an applicant from specific performance	*Green v Sommerville* (1979) 141 CLR 594 *Mehmet v Benson* (1965) 113 CLR 295	Chapter 22: 22.08
Hardship or unfairness in the making of the contract	Specific performance could be refused if it imposed undue hardship on the defendant but it must be highly unreasonable to order specific performance; also, the hardship must be weighed against the hardship to the plaintiff as a result of the refusal of specific performance	*Wedgwood v Adams* (1843) 6 Beav 600; 49 ER 958 *Fitzgerald v Masters* (1956) 95 CLR 420 *Coles Supermarkets Australia Pty Ltd v Australian Retail Freeholds Pty Ltd* (1996) 16 WAR 282	Chapter 22: 22.09

(cont.)

Concept	Short explanation	Relevant authorities	*Principles* text*
Mistake or misrepresentation	Even if there is no right of rescission on the ground of mistake, specific performance may be refused—but not (generally) where the plaintiff has not induced or contributed to the mistake	*Slee v Warke* (1949) 86 CLR 271	Chapter 22: 22.10
Laches, delay and acquiescence	Laches and acquiescence are related but separate doctrines. Laches is delay associated with acquiescence in bringing or prosecuting a claim	*Lamshed v Lamshed* (1963) 109 CLR 440 *Lindsay Petroleum Co v Hurd, Farewell & Kemp* (1874) LR 5 PC 221	Chapter 22: 22.11

* Consult the corresponding section(s) of the *Principles* text for more detail.

'Specific performance' is the most axiomatic instance of the enforcement of a contract, since, literally, it invokes the idea of the enforcement of a contract by demanding performance of it!

Once the fact of a contract is established, damages at common law are recoverable for a breached contract as of right and are thus the primary remedy for a breached contract.[1] Recognising this, the first category selected for consideration below is whether damages are adequate to compensate the injured party for, if so, specific performance generally will not be granted. The cases suggest that a holistic view is taken, with the whole question of the availability of specific performance being one for the court's overall discretion.[2]

The proposition that specific performance is ultimately discretionary is both explicitly and implicitly expressed below. Understanding this is essential to appreciating the parameters of the doctrine. One example only of the former is the proposition in *Price v Strange* [1977] 3 All ER 371 that the availability of the defence of the want of mutuality dealt with a question of whether 'the discretionary remedy of specific performance should be granted'.[3] This proposition highlights the court's assumption that the availability of the remedy was discretionary.

Thus, whilst various discrete factors are said to affect the availability of specific performance, each nonetheless attracts the discretion of the court. This theme underpins each of the various heads considered below.

Thus, for example, 'impossibility and futility', although sounding categorical, in truth invoke subsidiary questions of just what the court regards as 'futile' or 'impossible'.

The 'problem of constant supervision' too is nuanced, with varying views being articulated as to the type of contract regarded as not being amenable to constant supervision.

'Mutuality' is a particularly nuanced topic. The court in the recent case of *Cannavo v FCD (Holdings) Pty Ltd* [2000] NSWSC 304 attempted to rationalise the concept on the basis of hardship, the assessment of which axiomatically would attract discretionary considerations.

1 See *Principles* text at 23.10.
2 See *Principles* text at 23.02.
3 *Price v Strange* [1977] 3 All ER 371, 383.

'Personal services' invokes the idea of 'the problem of constant supervision' in a particular context, with the cases providing guidance as to the circumstances in which the court might, in some cases, view a particular contract which might be regarded as being for personal services nonetheless amenable to an order for specific performance.

On the same note, 'breach, unreadiness and inability to perform' overtly attract a judicial discretion, since the question of whether a plaintiff had soiled their hands to the extent to disentitle them to specific performance, is an assessment which by its nature is somewhat imprecise. The discretionary nature of these considerations is neatly indicated by the broad treatment in *Green v Sommerville*, where the Court essentially had to make an assessment of whether the plaintiff had *in substance* performed or was ready and willing to perform the contract.

Similarly, overtly attracting discretionary considerations is the assessment of hardship of unfairness in the making of the contract. A study of the cases collected below suggests that specific performance could be refused if it imposed undue hardship and it must be highly unreasonable to order specific performance. The concepts of 'undue' hardship and of a high degree of unreasonableness by their nature can only be assessed by a process attracting a measure of discretion.

'Mistake or misrepresentation' is a relatively insignificant consideration but nevertheless, in common with the modules above, attracts a discretion, including a consideration of the question of whether the plaintiff did or did not induce, or contribute to, the mistake.

A far more significant area, attracting much judicial comment over time, is acquiescence and laches. The discretionary nature of each as a disentitling factor of specific performance is readily apparent from a comparison of the outcomes as evidenced in Kitto J's observation in the seminal case of *Lamshed v Lamshed* (1963) 109 CLR 440 that there was little point in citing cases for comparing periods of delay; rather, the Court examined whether, under all the circumstances, it would not allow the remedy to hang 'unfairly' over the head of a party who denies the existence of a contract.

Wight v Haberdan Pty Ltd [1984] 2 NSWLR 280

Facts and issues

The plaintiff, a land developer, contracted to buy land from the first defendant and sought, from the second defendant, mortgage finance to complete his purchase. The first defendant had given a notice to complete the contract of purchase. The plaintiff, while challenging the validity of such notice to complete, also sought to compel the second defendant to provide finance to complete his purchase.

The relevant issue was whether the plaintiff was entitled to specific performance of the agreement with the second defendant, even though it was for the loan of money, which ordinarily would not have been amenable to specific performance. En route to its decision, the Court needed to confront the proposition that the plaintiff would have been entitled to damages for a thwarted contract for the loan of money, as a breach of a contract relating to a 'loan of money' axiomatically, it would have seemed, would have been compensable by damages. The case is useful for the Court's observations that the question of the entitlement of specific performance, even in such a case, attracts the discretion of the court and, in the circumstances, the Court awarded specific performance, recognising that the circumstances were an 'exception to the general rule' (that specific performance would not be ordered where damages were adequate to compensate the plaintiff).

Decision

Per Kearney J at 281:

> [The plaintiff] looks to the second defendant (Beneficial) for mortgage finance to complete his purchase.
>
> [289] . . . there is no doubt that the general rule is that a contract to lend money cannot be specifically enforced either by the proposed borrower or the proposed lender, and that it is immaterial whether the loan is to be with or without security . . .
>
> The rule is generally accepted to be founded upon the proposition that in the case of such an agreement damages are an adequate remedy, that is, that the complaining party's proper remedy lies at law.
>
> [290] . . . In relation to the question of whether damages are an adequate remedy the true rule requires in my view consideration of the circumstances of the particular case in hand. The test is, in my view, whether by leaving a plaintiff to a remedy in damages justice is done. In other words, the question to be determined is whether such a remedy in damages is adequate to satisfy the demands of justice. In the present instance it is obvious that if the plaintiff is left to pursue common law claims for damages the most complex questions will arise. There will be necessarily difficult questions as to the measure of damages and the remoteness of damages. There will be obviously great delay and expense and at the end of the day the question of what damages could be awarded would, in my view, be extremely difficult, if not virtually impossible, to assess with reasonable accuracy. After all, the rule under which a plaintiff is left to his remedy in damages is founded on an assumption of fact, as was pointed out by Barwick C J in *Bonner's* case where his Honour says (at 742):
>
>> No doubt the general assumption is that damages for breach of a mere promise to lend money adequately compensates the would be borrower. But, in my opinion, that assumption of fact is not necessarily of universal validity and, again in my opinion, must yield in any case when in fact in the particular circumstances damages would not do justice between the parties. So it seems to me that equity in the more complicated situations of the modern world may well yet find an occasion when justice can only be done in relation to a contract merely to lend money by ordering its specific performance.
>
> Following his Honour's train of thought, the complications involved in the plaintiff being left to pursue a claim for damages in this instance are so monumental and the prospects of an adequate recovery are so remote as to render such a course an unjust imposition upon the plaintiff.
>
> [291] . . . In short, the circumstances create an exception to the general rule, and warrant the conclusion that specific performance ought to be ordered.

Adderley v Dixon (1824) 1 Sim & St 607; 57 ER 239

Facts and issues

This is an ancient and oft-quoted case which gave consideration to whether specific performance should be granted for a thwarted contract to transfer land. Note particularly the weight the Court placed on the idea that land may have a 'peculiar and special' value.

Decision

Per Sir John Leach VC at 240:

> The Defendant . . . submitted that the matter of the agreement was not the proper subject of a bill in equity for a specific performance . . .

Per Sir John Leach VC at 240:

> Courts of Equity decree the specific performance of contracts, not upon any distinction between realty and personalty, but because damages at law may not, in the particular case, afford a complete remedy. Thus a Court of Equity decrees performance of a contract for land, not because of the real nature of the land, but because damages at law, which must be calculated upon the general money value of land, may not be a complete remedy to the purchaser, to whom the land may have a peculiar and special value. So a Court of Equity will not, [241] generally, decree performance of a contract for the sale of stock or goods, not because of their personal nature, but because damages at law, calculated upon the market price of the stock or goods, are as complete a remedy to the purchaser as the delivery of the stock or goods contracted for; inasmuch as, with the damages, he may purchase the same quantity of the like stock or goods.

Pianta v National Finance & Trustees Ltd (1964) 180 CLR 146

Facts and issues

The relevant issue here was whether a developer of land was entitled to specific performance for its purchase. The case is often regarded as the seminal case for the proposition that, since the purchaser was a developer of land buying it entirely for commercial purposes, specific performance would invariably be granted for a thwarted contract for the sale of land at the instance of the purchaser. In truth, only Barwick CJ of the High Court bench confronted this issue and then only somewhat obliquely, as appears in the judgment below.

Decision

Per Barwick CJ at 151:

> It will be convenient if I say at once that I can discover no reason why a decree for specific performance should not have been made, if there was a binding agreement between the appellants and the respondent. If his Honour was right to conclude that an agreement for sale had been made between the parties to this appeal on 26 July, on no view of the facts was the agreement to sell to Chamberlain made on or before 26 July. Nor was there any material before his Honour on which the plaintiff's equity could be found to have lost its priority derived from the time of its creation. There was a faint endeavour made on behalf of the appellants to support the refusal of a decree for specific performance on the ground that, because the respondent was a land developer, damages would be an adequate remedy. But in my opinion this proposition is without foundation in law, even if the respondent had had no other business than that of subdividing and selling land and had made a decision to subdivide and sell the subject land.

Loan Investment Corporation of Australasia v Bonner [1970] NZLR 724

Facts and issues

Bonner sold land to Loan Investment who wanted to develop it, and also agreed to lend a portion of the purchase price. It was thus a composite contract, involving the transfer of land as well as the loan of money. Bonner repudiated, and Loan Investment sought specific performance of the whole of the contract. The more 'enduring'[4] view, reproduced, was the dissenting judgment of Barwick CJ, whose views were adopted in *Wight v Haberdan* (extracted above). The case is useful as it provides an insight into Barwick CJ's views on the availability of specific performance to the purchaser of commercial land. Whilst Barwick CJ in his much shorter decision in the earlier case of *Pianta* (extracted above) considered that specific performance would be available to a purchaser of commercial land, he did not then go into any detail to explain the rationale for his decision. *Loan Investment* is therefore particularly useful for providing a detailed insight into Barwick CJ's views concerning the question whether specific performance should be available to the purchaser of commercial land.

Decision

Per Barwick CJ at 741:

> Vice-Chancellor Kindersley in *Falcke v. Gray* (1859) 4 Drew 651; 62 E.R. 250 a case in which he granted specific performance in relation to a contract to purchase chattels, said this:
>
>> What is the difference in the view of the Court between realty and personalty in respect to the question whether the Court will interfere or not? Upon what principle does the Court decree specific performance of any contract whatever? Lord Redesdale in Harnett v. Yeilding (2 Sch. & Lef. 549) says: 'Whether Courts of Equity in their determinations on this subject have always considered what was the original foundation for decrees of this nature I very much doubt. I believe that from something of habit, decrees of this kind have been carried to an extent which has tended to injustice. Unquestionably the original foundation of these decrees was simply this, that damages at law would not give the party the compensation to which he was entitled; that is, would not put him in a situation as beneficial to him as if the agreement were specifically performed'. So that the principle on which a Court of Equity proceeds is this. A Court of law gives damages for the non-performance, but a Court of Equity will decree specific performance, because a mere compensation in damages is not a sufficient remedy and satisfaction for the loss of the performance of the contract.
>
> In my respectful opinion, Lord Redesdale's explanation of the expression 'damages is not an adequate remedy' which is quoted by the Vice-Chancellor is appropriate to the present case

4 As described in Wayne Covell, Keith Lupton and Jay Forder, *Covell & Lupton Principles of Remedies* (LexisNexis Butterworths, 3rd ed, 2015) 274.

> when he says that it means that an award of damages would not put the plaintiff 'in a situation as beneficial to him as if the agreement were specifically performed.' It is because in general an award of damages for the non-performance of an agreement to lend money whether on security or not does place the intended borrower in as beneficial position as he would have been in had the promise to lend the money been performed, that specific performance is in general refused of a contract to lend money. It is not refused, in my opinion, because the Court cannot supervise the re-payment of the money lent or because of any supposed inequality between the position of the lender and the borrower in the case of an unsecured loan or of any difficulty in ordering the payment of money. It is solely, in my opinion, because, in general, damages will place the plaintiff seeking to enforce the promise to lend in as beneficial position as he would have been had the money been lent to him on the agreed terms. However, though generally this is the position, in my opinion, it is erroneous therefore to conclude that a contract to lend money can never in any circumstances be ordered to be specifically performed. In this connection see *Rogers v. Challis* (1859) 27 Beav. 175; 54 E.R. 68; *Larios v. Bonany y Gurety* (1873) L.R. 5 P.C. 346 and *South African Territories v. Wallington* [1898] A.C. 309. None of the reasons [742] offered for refusing specific performance in these cases lend colour, in my opinion, to the proposition that equity will never in any circumstances order specific performance of an agreement to lend money; nor, and perhaps this is more significant in this case, to the proposition that equity will not grant specific performance of a contract otherwise specifically enforceable merely because one of its terms calls for a loan of money by one of the parties to the other. The Courts of Equity last century found that whilst an agreement to sell consols would not be specifically performed because of their ready availability in the market, specific performance would be granted of a promise to sell shares in a company which were not so readily available. They did so because a mere difference in price reflected in an award of damages did not do justice in the circumstances. The possession of the particular shares was an advantage which a money verdict did not necessarily replace; see *Duncuft v. Albrecht* (1841) 12 Sim. 189; 59 E.R. 1104.

On whether the plaintiff should be denied specific performance because it wanted the land as an asset to be sold, per Barwick CJ at 744:

> In this connection, it is said that because the appellant wanted the land as an asset to be sold or to be used as security for the raising of money it had no such peculiar or special value to him as justified specific performance. In my respectful submission this statement misconceives what was said by Sir John Leach in *Adderley v. Dixon* (supra) and the basis upon which specific performance of contracts for the sale and purchase of land apart from equitable defences is granted almost as of right. Lord Hardwicke in *Buxton v. Lister* (1746) 3 Atk. 383; 26 E.R. 1020 said:
>
>> As to the cases of contracts for purchase of lands, or things that relate to realties, those are of a permanent nature, and if a person [745] agrees to purchase them, it is on a particular liking to the land, and is quite a different thing from matters in the way of trade.
>
> This to my mind gives the key to what Sir John Leach said in *Adderley v. Dixon* (supra). The plaintiff by selecting any piece of land for purchase thereby and without more manifests what Lord Hardwicke calls his 'liking to the land' or as Sir John Leach said his 'peculiar and special value' in it.

Semelhago v Paramadevan [1996] 2 SCR 415

Facts and issues

The plaintiff had agreed to purchase a house. The plaintiff had already elected to take damages so specific performance did not arise on the facts on the case. *Semelhago* is noted for its treatment, obiter, of the question of whether specific performance would be granted for the purchase of a piece of generic land. This case long post-dated *Pianta* and is often cited as authority for the proposition that, in this day and age, when land is treated analogously to chattels, the court might in an appropriate case refuse an order for specific performance for a thwarted contract for the sale of land.

Decision

Per Sopinka CJ at 428:

> It is no longer appropriate, therefore, to maintain a distinction in the approach to specific performance as between realty and personalty. It cannot be assumed that damages for breach of contract for the purchase and sale of real estate will be an inadequate remedy in all cases. The common law recognized that the distinction might not be valid when the land had no peculiar or special value. In *Adderley v. Dixon* (1824), 1 Sim. & St. 607, 57 E.R. 239, Sir John Leach, V.C., stated (at p. 240) [This passage is reproduced above.]
>
> [429] Courts have tended, however, to simply treat all real estate as being unique and to decree specific performance unless there was some other reason for refusing equitable relief. See *Roberto v. Bumb*, [1943] O.R. 299 (C.A.), at p. 311; *Roy v. Kloepfer Wholesale Hardware and Automotive Co.,* [1952] 2 S.C.R. 465; *Nepean Carleton Developments Ltd. v. Hope* (1976), [1978] 1 S.C.R. 427, at p. 438. Some courts, however, have begun to question the assumption that damages will afford an inadequate remedy for breach of contract for the purchase of land. In *Chaulk v. Fairview Construction Ltd.* (1977), 14 Nfld. & P.E.I.R. 13, the Newfoundland Court of Appeal (per Gushue J.A.), after quoting the above passage from *Adderley v. Dixon*, stated, at p. 21:
>
>> The question here is whether damages would have afforded Chaulk an adequate remedy, and I have no doubt that they could, and would, have. There was nothing whatever unique or irreplaceable about the houses and lots bargained for. They were merely subdivision lots with houses, all of the same general design, built on them, which the respondent was purchasing for investment or re-sale purposes only. He had sold the first two almost immediately at a profit, and intended to do the same with the remainder. It would be quite different if we were dealing with a house or houses which were of a particular architectural design, or were situated in a particularly desirable location, but this was certainly not the case.
>
> Specific performance should, therefore, not be granted as a matter of course absent evidence that the property is unique to the extent that its substitute would not be readily available. . .

Dougan v Ley (1945) 71 CLR 142

Facts and issues

The issue in the question was whether a contract for the sale of a taxi licence should be the subject of an order for specific performance. This case, as a useful counterpoint to the cases involving real property, explores the proposition that in an appropriate case the court might order specific performance of a contract for the sale of a chattel.

Decision

Per Dixon J at 149:

> The subject matter, it is said, is the sale of a chattel and, in general, a suit for the specific performance of an agreement to sell and deliver chattels will not be entertained. But, when the substance of the matter is considered, the agreement is not of this simple character. ... The contract is in fact for the transfer of a valuable privilege annexed to a chattel.
>
> [150] Though in earlier times the absence of an adequate theory of simple contract had led to the interposition of chancery on wider grounds, by the seventeenth century, if not before, it had come to be 'taken for a good cause of dismission' of a bill 'in most causes, to say that he' the plaintiff 'hath remedy at the common law'. So it became the received doctrine that the foundation of decrees for specific performance was 'that damages at law would not give the party the compensation to which he was entitled; that is, would not put him in a situation as beneficial to him as if the agreement were specifically performed' (per Lord Redesdale, *Harnett v Yeilding*).
>
> 'The Court gives specific performance instead of damages, only when it can by that means do more perfect and complete justice' (per Lord Selborne, *Wilson v Northampton and Banbury Junction Railway Co.*).
>
> In the case of goods or securities obtainable upon the market, damages at law place the disappointed buyer or seller in as good a position as delivery of the articles or receipt of the price because it enables him to go upon the market. But damages at law for the refusal of a vendor of land to go on with the contract might not be a complete remedy to the purchaser, to whom the land might have a special value (*Adderley v Dixon*), and the vendor's failure to complete through defect of title left the purchaser without any adequate remedy at law ...
>
> But apart from land, a contract for which has always been considered a proper subject of specific performance, the question raised for the court of Chancery was to say in what circumstances equity [151] considered the purchaser entitled to the specific thing contracted to be sold or the vendor to divest himself of it and receive the price, rather than in either case being bound to accept damages as the price of the loss of the contract ...
>
> It was not difficult to say that a purchaser of 'articles of unusual beauty rarity and distinction' was entitled to obtain them in specie (*Falcke v Gray*). Though a less obvious case, it was settled that 'a certain number of railway shares of a particular description, which railway shares are limited in number' and are not to be obtained by going on the share market, are a subject in respect of which a contract of sale will be enforced specifically (*Duncuft v Albrecht*) ...
>
> In the present case I think that we should have no difficulty in concluding that, because of the limited number of vehicles registered and licensed as taxi-cabs, because of the extent to which the price represents the value of the licence, and because of the essentiality to the purchasers' calling of the chattel and the licence annexed thereto, we should treat the contract as within the scope of the remedy of specific performance.

Wenham v Ella (1972) 127 CLR 454

Facts and issues

The appellants agreed to procure the transfer to the respondent of an interest in land. The respondent performed his part of the contract but the appellants failed to procure the transfer of the interest.

The contract was not capable of being specifically performed. The relevant issue was whether specific performance of the transfer could be ordered.

Decision

Per Barwick CJ at 460:

> Before discussing the matter further, I should observe that the claim in this case was a claim for specific performance of a contract for the transfer of an interest in land. That is to say, it was a claim which the Court of Chancery would clearly have had jurisdiction to entertain. It was not a contract for the sale of goods, or of shares in an incorporated company available in the market. The land was income-producing and the interest in it the subject of this agreement was in the nature of an income-producing investment.
>
> However, by the date of hearing of the action, specific performance could not have been ordered. The remedy of the respondent then was damages for breach of the promise to cause delivery of the transfer of the described interest in land at the agreed time . . .
>
> Accordingly, I shall treat the present case, so far as concerns the points raised by the amended grounds of appeal, as involving no more than a claim for damages for breach of a contract to procure the transfer of an income-producing interest in land . . .

Verrall v Great Yarmouth Borough Council [1981] QB 202

Facts and issues

The defendant council agreed to a two-day hiring of a hall by the National Front, a political party. The council, following a change in its political control, repudiated the contract of hire. An action was brought on behalf of the National Front for specific performance of the contract. The question on appeal was, given the duration of the hire, two days, it was open for specific performance to be ordered.

Decision

Per Lord Denning MR at 215:

> . . . Mr. Lightman referred us to a footnote in *Halsbury's Laws of England,* 3rd ed., vol. 23 (1958), p. 464: 'A letting for a single day to view a procession cannot be specifically enforced,' citing *Glasse* v *Woolgar* & *Roberts (No.* 2) (1897) 41 S.J. 573. That case is quite out of date. Mr. Lightman cited other cases too saying that a lease for a year could not be specifically enforced. But I do not think we need go through them now. Suffice it to quote *Gilbey* v. *Cossey* (1912) 106 L.T.R. 607 when Darling J. said, at p. 608:
>
>> At one time it was said in the Courts of Chancery that there could not be a decree for the specific performance of an agreement from year to year, upon the ground that it was inconceivable that a case could be heard within a twelvemonth. That idea, however, has now been given up, and the court would make such an order before a tenancy of this kind would have expired.
>
> So that point fails.

Per Roskill LJ at 220:

> . . . it is the duty of the court to protect, where it is appropriate to do so, any interest whether it be an estate in land or a licence by injunction or specific performance as the case may be.
>
> [. . .]
>
> Another perhaps equally good example is of the Earls Court Motor Show – supposing the licensee at Earls Court found his licence repudiated at the last moment. I find it difficult to believe that a court in those circumstances could not — let alone would not — grant equitable relief by way of specific performance or a mandatory injunction to require the licensor to fulfil his obligations. How much more is that so, in my judgment, whereas here there has been a long standing contract entered into by the licensee for which that licensee has given full consideration. We were referred to a 19th century decision of Kay J. in *Hart* v. *Hart* (1881) 18 Ch.D. 670, where the judge referred, at p. 685, to the judgment of Turner L.J. in *Wilson* v. *West Hartlepool Railway* G *Co.* (1865) 2 De G.J. & Sm. 475:
>
>> . . . that when an agreement for valuable consideration between two parties has been partially performed, the court ought to do its utmost to carry out that agreement by a decree for specific performance. I think, if I do not misquote the words, Turner L.J. went as far as this: it is the duty of the court, as far as it is possible to do so, to ascertain the terms of the agreement, and to give effect to it . . .

J C Williamson Ltd v Lukey (1931) 45 CLR 282

Facts and issues

The plaintiff, a confectioner, was granted an exclusive right to sell confectionary, ice cream and non-alcoholic drinks in the defendant's theatre and a licence to enter the theatre. After the defendant repudiated the agreement and revoked the licence, the plaintiff sought specific performance. Concurrent with the defendant's obligation to allow the plaintiff and employees access to the theatre, were conditions governing inter alia the goods to be sold by the plaintiff, and the time, place and manner of their supply, and other matters associated with their supply.

Decision

Per Dixon J at 297:

> . . . the remedy (of specific performance) is not available unless complete relief can be given, and the contract carried into full and final execution, so that the parties are put in the relation contemplated by their agreement. Specific performance is inapplicable when the [298] continued supervision of the Court is necessary in order to ensure the fulfilment of the contract. It is not a form of relief which can be granted if the contract involves the performance by one party of services to the other, or requires their continual cooperation. The doctrine of the Court of Chancery was against decreeing one party to perform specifically obligations which the contract imposed upon him, if it was unable to secure to him the performance by the other contracting party of the conditions upon which those obligations depended, and could only leave him to his action of damages at law in the event of the conditions being unperformed.

> In the present case the condition of the contract which entitles the plaintiffs and their servants to admission for the purpose of selling confectionery in the theatre is concurrent with the conditions governing the time, place and manner of supply, the character of the goods supplied, and the appearance, dress and behaviour of their servants. It would be contrary to principle to bind the Company by a decree to perform its obligations, leaving it only a remedy sounding in damages in the event of a breach by the plaintiffs of the conditions to be observed by them. It would be equally contrary to principle for the Court to undertake the supervision of the specific fulfilment of these conditions. . . .
>
> It would be contrary to principle to bind the Company by a decree to perform its obligations, leaving it only a remedy sounding in damages in the event of a breach by the plaintiffs of the conditions to be observed by them. It would be equally contrary to principle for the Court to undertake the supervision of the specific fulfilment of these conditions.

Patrick Stevedores Operations No 2 Pty Ltd v Maritime Union of Australia (1998) 195 CLR 1

Facts and issues

The proceedings essentially concerned an appeal from the judgment of the Full Federal Court granting interlocutory orders restraining certain employers from terminating the contracts of employment of various employees who were members of the Maritime Union of Australia ('MUA'). The following passages are relevant to the question of whether the Court could order specific performance of a contract for personal services or employment which conventionally, due to their personal nature, are considered inappropriate for specific performance.

Decision

Per Brennan CJ, McHugh, Gummow, Kirby and Hayne JJ at 46:

> We see in the orders no defect which sometimes is expressed as the involvement of the court in 'constant supervision' of continued conduct. Reservations of that nature have been expressed in decisions of this Court. However, questions of degree rather than absolute restrictions upon the scope of curial relief are involved. Reference was made in the Federal Court judgments and in submissions to this Court to the speech of Lord Hoffmann in *Co-operative Insurance Society Ltd v Argyll Stores (Holdings) Ltd*. His Lordship affirmed the refusal by the judge at first instance of an order for specific performance of a lease for a term of 35 years containing a covenant to keep premises open for retail trade during usual hours of business in the locality. His Lordship's statement that the usual practice was not to grant specific performance to carry on an activity over a period of time was made in response to a submission by the lessor to the effect that the equitable remedy was no longer to be understood as granted in the auxiliary jurisdiction where damages would be an inadequate remedy. The lessor submitted, without success, that in cases such as *Argyll Stores* the court 'should look at the whole panoply of available remedies and consider the appropriate one rather than the gloss of rules put on them restricting their use'.
>
> The House of Lords discharged the order for specific performance which the Court of Appeal had made. The significance of Lord Hoffmann's speech for present purposes is not the rejection of the lessor's submissions. That rejection, with respect, was virtually inevitable.

What is significant is the acceptance by the House of Lords that the concept of 'constant supervision by the court' by itself is no longer an effective or useful criterion for refusing a decree of specific [47] performance. Rather, Lord Hoffmann placed stress on other propositions. First, a person who is subject to a mandatory order attended by contempt sanction (which 'must realistically be seen as criminal in nature' ought to know with precision what is required; and, second, the possibility of 'repeated applications for rulings on compliance' with orders requiring a party 'to carry on an activity, such as running a business over a more or less extended period of time' should be discouraged.

Reference to constant court applications should not be misunderstood. The courts are well accustomed to the exercise of supervisory jurisdiction upon applications by trustees, receivers, provisional liquidators and others with the responsibility for the conduct of administrations. The reservation of liberty to apply to the Federal Court in respect of certain of the orders to be made is in no way out of ordinary in the exercise of equitable jurisdiction.

Further, those orders do not, in form or in substance, require the administrators to carry on business activities in the sense with which the *Argyll* case was concerned. Nor do the undertakings and orders leave those bound by them not knowing what is expected of them. This is not a case, referred to by Isaacs and Rich JJ in *Pakenham Upper Fruit Co Ltd v Crosby*, where the Court 'could never be sure that it was in a position to enforce its order without injustice'.

Cannavo v FCD (Holdings) Pty Ltd [2000] NSWSC 304

Facts and issues

The proceedings concerned an application by the plaintiff for specific performance in relation to a claim to an interest in a company, and an interlocutory injunction to restrain the first defendant from certain shares in it. So far as it related to mutuality, the following facts were pertinent: that the contract sought to be enforced involved one of personal services where the relationship between the parties had broken down. The decision is particularly useful in providing an accessible, relatively recent, rationalisation of mutuality.

Decision

Per Santow J at [62]:

> Given that specific performance would not be allowed in the case of such a contract of personal services more especially where the relationship between the parties had broken down, clearly enough the Plaintiff could not enforce the effectuation of his appointment as managing director insofar as completion of the corporate formalities to bring that about were concerned. Likewise, were the Defendants to seek to enforce the contract against an unwilling Plaintiff, a situation at odds with reality, the Plaintiff could not be compelled to act as managing director for the same reason. I say at odds with reality, because clearly enough the Defendants would not wish to have the Plaintiff be managing director when their relationship has broken down. In those circumstances it would be quite unfair for there to be one fundamental part of the arrangements that could not be specifically enforced in circumstances where specific enforcement were then applied to the remaining parts of the contract and in particular to the acquisition of the twenty-five per cent equity.

> [63] That is not to invoke Fry's much criticised statement of the rule requiring mutuality as appears in his 'Specific Performance' 6th Ed at 619: 'A contract to be specifically enforced by the Court must, as a general rule be mutual – that is to say, such that it might, at the time it was entered into, have been enforced by either of the parties against the other of them.'
>
> [64] . . . The real basis of any notion of mutuality in this context is that it points to the weighing up process that a court necessarily carries out in order to determine whether granting specific performance at the behest of the plaintiff would, by reason of the plaintiff being unable to be required to carry out his obligations in specie, produce such hardship to the defendant that to compel specific performance would be inequitable.
>
> [65] Here, the obligation with respect to appointment of the Plaintiff as managing director is not severable. It then becomes a question of whether enforcement of the contract would be such as to cause undue hardship upon the Defendants. This is in forcing them to accept the Plaintiff not merely as an investor with a twenty-five per cent equity but as a managing director, when this was unacceptable by reason of the breakdown of their personal relations. That hardship is such that it clearly would be unjust to require specific performance.

Price v Strange [1977] 3 All ER 371

Facts and issues

The plaintiff as sublessee sought specific performance of an oral agreement whereby the defendant landlord agreed to renew his sublease at an increased rent in return for his effecting repairs to the building. The agreement was a disposition of an interest in land and was thus (initially) unenforceable unless supported by part performance. Subsequently, the plaintiff paid and the defendant accepted rent at the increased rate. He performed part of the repairs but was not allowed to complete them as the defendant repudiated the agreement. The defendant continued to accept rent for a few months.

The defendant argued that as at the time of the (unenforceable) oral agreement, the remedy was not mutual and specific performance could not be granted. Whilst the case addressed the specific question of the date upon which mutuality was to be determined, the case is often cited as authority for the more general proposition that mutuality, in common with equitable concepts broadly, attracted considerations that were discretionary.

Decision

Per Goff LJ at 377:

> The plaintiff's main case is that the statement in Fry that mutuality has to be determined at the date of the contract is not good law, and that on the contrary the question of mutuality is simply one of the factors, which like hardship, mistake and delay has to be considered in the exercise of a judicial discretion when the court is considering whether or not to order specific performance, and therefore the relevant time is that of the hearing, and he argues if that be the proper rule, then having regard to all the circumstances this is a proper case for an order, especially as the work has now been finished and complete justice can be done by a monetary adjustment . . .

[380] . . . Spry formulates the rule thus:

> Although, therefore, the authorities on these questions are by no means clear, the view which appears to be most widely supported, and to accord most with equitable principle, is that mutuality, when it is material, need be looked at only as at the time of the making of the proposed order of the court.

[. . .]

[381] In my judgment the vendor and purchaser cases show that want of mutuality raises a question of the court's discretion to be exercised according to everything that has happened up to the decree; see first *Halkett v Earl of Dudley*, where Parker J, after referring to the purchaser's right of rescission, said:

> If this be so, the right of repudiation in question must be distinguished from the common law right of recission, and arises out of that want of mutuality which, unless waived, is generally fatal to relief by way of specific performance.

The significant word there is 'generally' and, quoting from the judgment of the Vice-Chancellor in *Salisbury v Hatcher*, Parker J went on to say:

> In cases of specific performance the want of mutuality is a consideration generally material, but it is contrary to principle and authority to say that perfect mutuality is requisite in order to call a Court of Equity into action. There are cases in which plaintiffs have had a decree for specific performance against defendants, who, when the bill was filed, were not in a condition to enforce specific performance in their own favor. Where no legal invalidity affects the contract, the enforcement of it in this Court is a matter of judicial discretion.
>
> [. . .]

[383] Surely the defence of want of mutuality should be governed by the state of affairs as seen at the hearing, since one is dealing not with a question affecting the initial validity of the contract, but with whether or not the discretionary remedy of specific performance should be granted. I find support for this view in *Eastern Counties Railway Co v Hawkes*, to which I have already referred, where Lord Campbell said:

> But I am of opinion that whereas, in considering the validity of the agreement, the proper time to regard is the time when it was entered into—as to the specific performance, regard is to be had to the state of things when the bill was filed.

In my judgment, therefore, the proposition in Fry is wrong and the true principle is that one judges the defence of want of mutuality on the facts and circumstances as they exist at the hearing . . .

Byrne v Australian Airlines Ltd (1995) 185 CLR 410

Facts and issues

Two airport baggage handlers were dismissed by their employer airline. The primary issue concerned their allegations that, in dismissing them, the airline had failed to observe procedural fairness, and they sought orders for the imposition of a penalty and common law damages. The question of specific performance arose somewhat obliquely, and in the context of whether they had the right to claim remuneration for their services, a situation to be contrasted with the right to damages for wrongful termination.

Decision

Per Brennan CJ, Dawson and Toohey JJ at 428:

> . . . even if an employee who is wrongfully dismissed chooses to keep the contract of employment on foot, he or she cannot claim remuneration in respect of any period after the wrongful dismissal because the right to receive remuneration for services is dependent upon the services having been rendered. The employee is also under a duty to mitigate any damage. Moreover, a court will not save in exceptional circumstances order specific performance of a contract of personal service. The possible continuation of the contract of employment after a wrongful dismissal will, therefore, ordinarily be of no real significance as it will for all practical purposes be at an end.
>
> There is no reason to doubt that in the present case the dismissal of the appellants by the respondent rightly or wrongly put an end to the employment relationship.

Green v Sommerville (1979) 141 CLR 594

Facts and issues

The purchaser of land failed to settle on the purchase price, but was allowed into possession. Tender of the purchase price was refused on the grounds that the purchaser failed to pay interest on the purchase price as required under the contract.

Decision

Per Mason CJ at 610:

> Does the respondent's failure to pay the amount of interest due on settlement, though not a breach of an essential term, disentitle her to specific performance on the ground that she was not ready and willing? In my opinion, it does not. It is well settled that a plaintiff in a suit for specific performance is not required to show that he has strictly complied with all his obligations under the contract; it is enough that he has performed and is ready and willing to perform the substance of the contract (*Fullers' Theatres Ltd v Musgrove* (1923) 31 CLR 524 at 550). In *Mehmet v Benson* the purchaser was in default in payment of instalments of purchase price and interest under a terms contract. Yet he succeeded in a suit for specific performance. Barwick CJ said (1965) 113 CLR 295 at 307:
>
>> The question as to whether or not the plaintiff has been and is ready and willing to perform the contract is one of substance not to be resolved in any technical or narrow sense. It is important to bear in mind what is the substantial thing for which the parties contract and what on the part of the plaintiff in a suit for specific performance are his essential obligations. Here the substantial thing for which the defendant bargained was the payment of the price: and, unless time be and remain of the essence, he obtains what he bargained for if by the decree he obtains his price with such ancillary orders as recompense him for (1979) 27 ALR 351 at 364 the delay in its receipt. To order specific

performance in this case would not involve the court in dispensing with anything for which the vendor essentially contracted.

Of course, the plaintiff must not by his unreadiness or unwillingness to perform have disowned his obligation to do so, or abandoned his rights to the benefit of the contract. But it is the essential terms of the contract which he must be ready and willing to perform. He seeks a transfer of the interest in land, the subject of the contract: the counterpart obligation is the payment of the price.

[...]

[611] In *Mehmet v Benson* the plaintiff offered to pay the full balance of the purchase price before the contracted time. In the present case, the respondent alleged her readiness and willingness to perform the contract but, by insisting that it was agreed that the payment of interest should be waived, she was insisting on a mode of performance of the contract to which she was not entitled. What is more, she did not in her statement of claim offer to perform the contract on its true construction. However, in the circumstances of this case I do not think that these considerations are inconsistent with a finding that the respondent was ready and willing to perform the contract at the commencement of the suit. First, the respondent was, on the view which I take of the contract, ready and willing to perform her essential obligation under the contract, that is, by paying the balance of the purchase price. Secondly, it is a general principle of the law of contract that the court will not readily infer from a party's insistence on a wrong construction of a contract that he is unwilling to perform it according to its true construction. This principle applies to the plaintiff's readiness and willingness in a suit for specific performance (*Sweet & Maxwell Ltd v Universal News Services Ltd* [1964] 2 QB 699 at 734; [1964] 3 All ER 30 at 42–3). Although there is, as far as I am aware, no recorded instance of the application of this or of a similar principle to circumstances in which the plaintiff, as here, has insisted on an oral variation of the contract which is determined against her, I can see no reason why the principle should not apply to a case in which there is a dispute as to the nature and effect of an oral agreement and the view for which the plaintiff contends is bona fide held by her. The fact is, as the primary judge found, that both parties maintained an incorrect view as to the amount of interest payable. In this situation I agree with Burt CJ in the Full Court when, quoting the observations of Stephen, Mason and Jacobs JJ in *DTR Nominees Pty Ltd v Mona Homes Pty Ltd* (1978) 138 CLR 423 at p 432, he said that it was a case in which the respondent 'though asserting a wrong view of a contract because he believes it to be correct, is willing to perform the contract according to its tenor'. It was not a case in which the plaintiff persisted in an untenable view of the contract. Nor was it a case in which it could be said that the respondent came with unclean hands. This is important because the concept of readiness and willingness is an exemplification of the maxim: 'He who comes to equity must come with clean hands'.

Mehmet v Benson (1965) 113 CLR 295

Facts and issues

The plaintiff agreed to pay the purchase price of land in instalments plus interest but, after paying the purchase price, fell into arrears. The question was whether the plaintiff would be entitled to specific performance notwithstanding their breach.

Decision

Barwick CJ's reasons, at 307–308, were cited in *Green v Sommerville* and reproduced in the extract of *Green* above; reading it together with Mason CJ's own judgment in *Green* will best help the reader understand the purport of *Mehmet*.

Wedgwood v Adams (1843) 6 Beav 600; 49 ER 958

Facts and issues

Under an 'ill-drawn contract', three trustees were conveyed certain real estate on trust to sell and apply the produce in satisfaction of encumbrances and it was held that they thereby incurred a personal obligation to do so. The question was whether specific performance would lie to compel the performance of the contract.

Decision

Per Lord Langdale MR at 960:

> On the construction of the contract, I am inclined to think that its effect is to create a personal obligation in the trustees, but I can hardly believe that this effect could have been known to the parties at the time. It is to me extraordinary, that trustees who had no interest whatever in the matter, should knowingly enter into a personal obligation to exonerate the trust estate from every incumbrance that might affect it . . .
>
> I conceive this to be an ill-drawn contract: the effect may however be that contended for by the Plaintiff. Suppose it to be so, the question then arises, whether, under the circumstances, it is a fit contract to be specifically performed .
>
> . . . the question is, whether the contract is of such a nature, as, under the circumstances, the Court will decree a specific performance? . . .
>
> I conceive the doctrine of the Court to be this, that the Court exercises a discretion, in cases of specific performance, and directs specific performance unless it should be what is called highly unreasonable to do so. What is more or less reasonable, is not a thing that you can define, it must depend on the circumstances of each particular case . . . [and the Court opined that this was such a case].

Fitzgerald v Masters (1956) 95 CLR 420

Facts and issues

The defendants were executors of a deceased estate. The plaintiff had made a contract with the deceased to purchase certain land. Over time, the land increased in value. The plaintiff sought specific performance of the contract and a relevant issue was whether the increase in value was a ground on which specific performance could be resisted.

Decision

Per Dixon CJ and Fullagar J at 433:

> ... There appear to be no circumstances, apart from delay as such, which would make it inequitable to decree specific performance. The land is said to have increased greatly in value over the years, but that cannot be a material consideration. Improvements may have been effected, but, if so, these can be provided for in any ultimate decree. There has been no prejudicing alteration in the position of the vendor or his estate: delay may indeed be said to have been to the advantage of the vendor, who enjoyed all the benefit to be derived from sole possession from 1932 to his death. There are no third parties whose interests may be affected. In these circumstances equity does not, we think, refuse specific performance unless it thinks that the plaintiff ought to be regarded as having abandoned any rights he ever had ...

Coles Supermarkets Australia Pty Ltd v Australian Retail Freeholds Pty Ltd (1996) 16 WAR 282

Facts and issues

The plaintiff held the benefit of a lease of commercial premises owned by the first defendant. The second defendant held an option to acquire property in the premises. The lease contained covenants which made it practically impossible for the premises to be redeveloped disadvantageously to the plaintiff. A relevant question was whether enforcement of the covenants would cause undue hardship to the defendants. Whilst the application concerned the grant of injunctions to restrain the enforcement of the covenants, Anderson J explicitly applied principles of specific performance insofar as the orders raised the question of the enforcement of the relevant covenants.

Decision

Per Anderson J at 288:

> As I have observed, it is agreed on all sides that this shopping centre is in need of modernisation. It is not an attractive shopping centre as it presently stands and a number of the specialty shops are vacant. A development such as the one proposed would be generally beneficial to residents within the market catchment area and, of course, to the first defendant. No doubt it would be beneficial to some, if not all, of the specialty tenants whose trade would be enhanced by a larger number of people being attracted to the upgraded and expanded centre.
>
> It is accepted that there is always a discretion to withhold an injunction and it would be a relevant consideration if enforcement of covenants would cause undue hardship to the defendant or to others. As to considerations of hardship I think the following passage in I C F Spry, *Equitable Remedies* (4th ed, 1990) p 195 correctly states the law:
>
>> It must not be forgotten that if damages are inadequate an applicant is prima facie entitled to specific performance of a valid and enforceable contract. Specific performance is not refused merely because inconvenience or even hardship to the defendant would be caused thereby. But if the hardship suffered by the defendant, if specific

> enforcement took place, would be so much greater than the detriment that would be suffered by the plaintiff if he were confined to remedies and damages that it would be unreasonable and oppressive to grant relief, specific enforcement is denied. In these regards there must be a balancing of the interests of the parties; and indeed, the court takes into account other matters as well, such as the manner in which the grant of relief would affect third persons or any advantage that the plaintiff may have taken of the defendant at the time of entry into the material agreement, in order to determine what course is most reasonable in all the circumstances.

It is not difficult to think how that doctrine might be applied by the courts justly to decline specific performance of covenants in a shopping centre lease. If the lessor proposed some minor alteration to the configuration of the car park so as to cure, say, a drainage problem seriously affecting other tenants, and if the alteration could have no practical effect on the plaintiff's tenancy the court would probably not assist the plaintiff to stop the works. But that is a very different case from the case under consideration. Here the hardship pointed to as likely to flow from the grant of an injunction is really the first defendant's inability to take advantage of a particular commercial opportunity, that is, to obtain a price for the centre enhanced by a redevelopment . . .

Slee v Warke (1949) 86 CLR 271

Facts and issues

The defendant, the owner of a hotel, had entered into negotiations for a lease of the hotel to the plaintiff. One of the terms discussed was that the plaintiff would have an option to be exercised to purchase the hotel at a stipulated price. The defendant intended that, although the option was to be exercised during the first year, the sale was not to be completed before the end of that year. He informed his solicitor, but the plaintiff was not informed. When executed, the lease in fact allowed the option to be exercised by the plaintiff at any time after the expiration of one year from the date of possession. The plaintiff thought the defendant had changed his intentions and executed the lease in that belief. The defendant executed the document without having read it.

Decision

Per Rich J, Dixon J and Williams J at 277:

> The decision of Page Wood V.C. in *Wood v. Scarth* must be read in the light of the facts of the case. His Lordship evidently considered that it would be a hardship on the defendant to compel him specifically to perform the contract. The defendant had in terms offered a lease of his public house for twenty-five years at an annual rent of £65, but the Vice-Chancellor was satisfied that by [278] mistake he had omitted to say that there was a premium of £500. His letter stated that he was giving brewers the offer in rotation and it was shown that the offer he had so submitted was expressed in the earlier cases to include the premium of £500. The error was clearly of an essential character. But the decision has not escaped the criticism of Sir Frederick Pollock. In his *Principles of Contract*, 11th ed., p. 399, he says that, although the authorities admit the possibility that a mistake to which the vendor did not contribute and which he could not be expected to perceive may in circumstances of special hardship be a bar to specific

performance, it is certain that such cases are rare. In a note the learned author said: '*Wood v. Scarth* is the only authority which appears to have actually decided so much: *quaere* how far it would now be followed'.

Where there is a unilateral mistake on the part of the defendant not contributed to by the plaintiff, the question whether the Court should in the exercise of its discretion make a decree for specific performance or leave the plaintiff to sue for damages must, we think, depend on the circumstances of the particular case. But the general rule governing the exercise of the discretion is we think, that laid down by James L.J. in *Tamplin v. James*, where he said: 'for the most part the cases where a Defendant has escaped on the ground of a mistake not contributed to by the Plaintiff, have been cases where a hardship amounting to injustice would have been inflicted upon him by holding him to his bargain, and it was unreasonable to hold him to it'.

Lamshed v Lamshed (1963) 109 CLR 440

Facts and issues

The appellant sold land to the respondents but repudiated. An action was commenced but lay dormant for about four years, during which time the appellant sold the land to a third party. This is regarded as a seminal case on acquiescence or delay, particularly Kitto J's famous comment that there was little point in simply citing cases for the purposes of comparison.

Decision

Per Kitto J at 452:

> . . . the doctrine has ever since been maintained that the special remedy of specific performance is available to those only who are prompt to claim it. [453] The degree of promptness required depends on the nature of the case and all its circumstances: *Eads v. Williams*, *Barclay v. Messenger*. Accordingly there is little point in citing cases for the purpose of comparing the period of delay in the present case with the delay which has been considered fatal to claims for specific performance in the circumstances of other cases . . .
>
> [. . .]
>
> Equity will not allow the possibility of its making such a decree to be held unfairly long over the head of the party who denies the existence of the contract and asserts a right to deal with the property as his own. This is a particular application of the general principle of laches as expounded in *Lindsay Petroleum Co. v. Hurd* and *Erlanger v. New Sombrero Phosphate Co.* To repeat words from the latter case, 'a court of equity requires that those who come to it to ask its active interposition to give them relief, should use due diligence, after there has been such notice or knowledge as to make it inequitable to lie by' . . .
>
> [. . .]
>
> [454] Plainly it would have been inequitable for the respondents in the present case, if they wanted specific performance, to lie by until 26th March 1962, continuing to assert the existence of a contract but taking no proceedings and leaving the appellant in the position of not knowing whether any money he might spend on the property would benefit him or the respondents, or whether he was free to sell the property to a third party, or whether his estate, if he should die, would include the property or the purchase money for which the respondents said that he had agreed to sell it.

> [. . .]
> [455] Ultimately, in 1962, the appellant, having waited for more than four years, sold the land to the Hallos. The case is therefore not one of bare delay; it is not even one in which all that can be said against the granting of relief is that the plaintiffs' delay has unfairly placed the appellant in a position of uncertainty over a substantial period; it is a case in which a defendant, not precipitately but at length, in circumstances which made it not altogether unreasonable to do so, has prejudiced his position; and it is a case in which third parties, not shown to be in any way at fault and not being warned by any caveat on the title, have acquired interests which will be defeated if a decree for specific performance should now be made. It seems to me a clear case for refusing relief on the ground of delay unless the law be that delay after action brought cannot afford a defence to a suit for specific performance.

Lindsay Petroleum Co v Hurd, Farewell & Kemp (1874) LR 5 PC 221

Facts and issues

Lindsay Petroleum is another seminal case of laches and delay. Fraud had been established against the respondents. The question related to the circumstances under which such a party who induced another into a contract by their fraud, could raise the defence of laches.

The central point was that the defendant needed to show that they were prejudiced by delay and this was something which could not be assessed merely by a consideration in the abstract by the length of the delay. In this respect, the analysis was consistent with the conventional treatment of delay as a disentitling factor of equitable relief. Indeed, Kitto J in *Lamshed* noted that the case before him was 'a particular application of the general principle of laches as expounded in *Lindsay Petroluem v Hurd*'.

Decision

The judgment of their Lordships (Lord Chancellor, Sir Barnes Peacock, Sir Montague Smith and Sir Robert Collier) were delivered by Sir Barnes Peacock at 239:

> Now the doctrine of laches in courts of equity is not an arbitrary or technical doctrine. Where it would be practically unjust to give a remedy, either because the party has by his conduct [240] done that which might fairly be regarded as equivalent to a waiver of it, or where by his conduct and neglect he has, though perhaps not waiving that remedy, yet put the other party in a situation in which it would not be reasonable to place him if the remedy were afterwards to be asserted in either of these cases, lapse of time and delay are most material. But in every case if an argument against relief which otherwise would be just is founded upon mere delay that delay of course not amounting to a bar by any statute of limitations, the validity of that defence must be tried upon principles substantial equitable. Two circumstances, always important in such case, are the length of the delay and the nature of the acts done during the interval, which might affect either party and cause a balance of justice or injustice in taking the one course or the other, so far as relates to the remedy.

QUESTIONS

(1) What is, broadly, the primary consideration in determining the entitlement to specific performance?

(2) Dixon J stated in *Williamson* in absolute terms that specific performance is not available unless 'complete relief' can be given. What did he mean by this?

(3) Santow J in *Cannavo* said that the question of whether a court might be minded to grant specific performance despite a lack of mutuality was a matter of discretion. What was the pivotal consideration in Santow J's 'weighing up process'?

22.3 Injunctions

Concept	Short explanation	Relevant authorities	*Principles* text*
The use of interlocutory injunctions in contract disputes	Interlocutory injunctions in aid of a contractual right will attract the operation of ordinary principles of interlocutory injunctions There was a commonly held view that there was no discretion to refuse an injunction to enforce a negative covenant but that view is now rejected	*Corporate Transport Services Pty Ltd v Toll* [2005] NSWSC 166 *Australian Broadcasting Corporation v O'Neill* (2006) 227 CLR 57 *Dalgety Wine Estates Pty Ltd v Rizzon* (1979) 141 CLR 552	Chapter 22: 22.14–22.15
Contracts of personal service	An injunction might be refused where to grant one would practically amount to specific performance of a contract of personal service	*Lumley v Wagner* (1852) 1 De GM & G 604; 42 ER 687 *Page One Records Ltd v Britton* [1968] 1 WLR 157 *Curro v Beyond Productions Pty Ltd* (1993) 30 NSWLR 337	Chapter 22: 22.15

* Consult the corresponding section(s) of the *Principles* text for more detail.

Injunctions —whether permanent or interlocutory—may be granted to restrain the breach of contract, so the question might be asked why the topic of injunctions should be included in a module on *enforcing* a contract.

Injunctions are not limited in their scope to restraining breaches of contract, although it is the latter we are solely concerned with in this chapter. Injunctions enforce a contract in the sense that they prevent breaches of contract. Thus, for example, an interlocutory injunction may be sought by one person to restrain the other from terminating a contract or to restrain the breach of negative covenants, which are contractual promises not to do a certain act.[5]

5 See *Principles* text, p 443, footnote 30.

It is important to note that, highlighting the difference between injunctive relief and specific performance, the courts are unprepared to grant an injunction if, by so doing, it will be tantamount to the grant of specific performance of a contract where specific performance would not otherwise lie, thus granting specific performance by the 'back door'.[6] This has led to fine line distinctions.[7]

Corporate Transport Services Pty Ltd v Toll [2005] NSWSC 166

Facts and issues

The plaintiff, CTS, acted as agent for the defendant, Toll, in providing transport services. CTS had, in reliance on the continuance of that engagement, incurred various obligations. Toll purported to give notice terminating that engagement. Then CTS sought an interlocutory injunction to restrain Toll from treating its termination notice as valid, relying, relevantly, on promissory estoppel.

Decision

Per Campbell J at [34]:

> [Counsel] also reminds me of the principle that a court is reluctant to issue an interlocutory order which will in practice require constant supervision, and reluctant to issue an interlocutory order in a circumstances where people will be kept in a relationship which involves personal trust and confidence.
>
> [. . .]
>
> [35] The High Court in *Patrick Stevedores Operations (No 2) v Maritime Union of Australia* (1998) 195 CLR 1 paras [78] — [80] made clear there is no absolute bar to the granting of an injunction which involves supervision by the court, and rather it is a matter of degree.
>
> [37] Here, in any event, the services which are being provided are not personal services in the sense in which the 19th century cases talked about the expression, where one natural person works in close proximity to, and interacts with, another natural person. Rather, they are commercial services, provided by one corporation to another . . .
>
> [42] I turn to the balance of convenience. There was a submission made by the defendant that I ought have regard only to the detriment which the plaintiff would suffer in considering the balance of convenience. I do not accept that submission. Whenever a court is making a judgment about the balance of convenience, it is making a pragmatic judgment about what is the best way of preserving the situation pending a hearing. For that purpose, it can take into account how the granting, or refusing, of the injunction will affect third parties, or the general public.
>
> [. . .]
>
> [44]. . . the plaintiff has offered the usual undertaking as to damages. The evidence suggests that the plaintiff is in a financially precarious situation . . .
>
> I would regard it as necessary, to protect the defendant, for there to be more than the undertaking of the plaintiff to support an undertaking as to damages. If an undertaking as to damages were forthcoming from AIPT — which is the extra undertaking the defendant seeks — as well as from the plaintiff, I would have been prepared to grant an interlocutory injunction . . .

6 See *Principles* text, p 443, footnote 32.

7 See eg *Lumley v Wagner* (1852) 1 De GM & G 604; 42 ER 687. See generally *Principles* text 22.14.

Australian Broadcasting Corporation v O'Neill (2006) 227 CLR 57

Facts and issues

The case concerned the grant of interlocutory injunctions to restrain the publication of material said to be defamatory, but is more celebrated for its treatment of the general principles governing interlocutory injunctions in Australia; in particular, the question of the relationship between the requisite strength of case and the balance of convenience.

Decision

In discussing the requisite strength of case for the grant of an interlocutory injunction, the court approved the following passage from *Beecham Group Ltd v Bristol Laboratories Pty Ltd*, per Gummow and Hayne JJ at 82:[8]

> How strong the probability needs to be depends, no doubt, upon the nature of the rights [the plaintiff] asserts and the practical consequences likely to flow from the order he seeks.

In discussing whether there should be any objection to the use of the expression 'serious question', at 83:

> There is then no objection to the use of the phrase 'serious question' if it is understood as conveying the notion that the seriousness of the question, like the strength of the probability referred to in *Beecham*, depends upon the considerations emphasised in *Beecham* [namely, the passage cited immediately above].

Dalgety Wine Estates Pty Ltd v Rizzon (1979) 141 CLR 552

Facts and issues

The licensee of licensed liquor premises was in breach of a covenant not to do any act or thing to prevent the lessor from obtaining a renewal of the liquor licence by applying to the Licensing Court for its removal. The lessor applied for an injunction to restrain it.

Decision

Per Mason CJ at 573:

> Lord Cairns L.C. in *Doherty v. Allman* said that a court of equity has no discretion to exercise when an injunction is sought to enforce a negative covenant in a contract. . . .
>
> There has been general agreement that Lord Cairns' statement that a court of equity has no discretion to refuse an injunction restraining a breach of a negative covenant is not accurate. . . .
>
> However, there has been general disagreement as to how Lord Cairns' statement should be reformed if it is to accurately express the true principle. The reason for this is that it is quite

8 (1968) 118 CLR 618, 622.

impossible to formulate an illuminating statement of principle which is capable of universal application . . .

[574] . . . Thus, the courts have frequently refused injunctions to restrain a breach of a negative stipulation in a contract for the sale of chattels or goods, in a contract for personal service and in a contract the enforcement of which would require the court to supervise the performance of the contract. Although these instances clearly demonstrate that the courts have a general discretion to refuse relief by way of injunction . . . [His Honour went on to discuss why the qualifications would not apply in the present case.]

Lumley v Wagner (1852) 1 De GM & G 604; 42 ER 687

Facts and issues

Wagner, a renowned singer, was contracted to perform at Her Majesty's Theatre and was bound under a restrictive covenant not to sing at any other theatre or opera house. The question was whether an injunction to restrain her from breaching the covenant had the practical effect of compelling Wagner to perform at Her Majesty's Theatre and thus should not be ordered.

Decision

Per Lord St Leonards LC at 93:

> It was objected that the operation of the injunction in the present case was mischievous, excluding the Defendant J. Wagner from performing at any other theatre while this Court had no power to compel her to perform at Her Majesty's Theatre. It is true that I have not the means of compelling her to sing, but she has no cause of complaint if I compel her to abstain from the commission of an act which she has bound herself not to do, and thus possibly cause her to fulfil her engagement.

Page One Records Ltd v Britton [1968] 1 WLR 157

Facts and issues

The Troggs, musicians, entered into a management contract with Page One Records, which contained a covenant by which they agreed not to engage anyone else to manage them. The Troggs engaged another manager and Page One sought injunctions to restrain the breach of the covenant.

Decision

Per Stamp J at 166:

> . . . the Troggs are simple persons, of no business experience, and could not survive without the services of a manager. As a practical matter on the evidence before me, I entertain no doubt that they would be compelled, if the injunction was granted, on the terms that the plaintiffs seek, to continue to employ the first plaintiff as their manager and agent and it is, I think, on this point that this case diverges from *Lumley v. Wagner* . . .

Curro v Beyond Productions Pty Ltd (1993) 30 NSWLR 337

Facts and issues

Tracey Curro, a media personality, was, pursuant to her contract with the program *Beyond 2000*, bound by a restraint of trade clause which prevented her from taking up a position that would prevent her from rendering her services to *Beyond 2000.* She accepted an offer from another network and declined to give an undertaking that her engagements would not conflict with her duties to *Beyond 2000,* who then sought an injunction to prevent her from breaching her contract. One argument raised was that the injunction would have the same effect as specific performance in that, if granted, and if she could not take up her new position with the other network, she would have no choice but to return to work with *Beyond 2000.* This would then mean (so it was argued) that the injunction was tantamount to specific performance of a contract of employment, something that the court would not order.

Decision

On the question of whether the injunction, in a practical sense, compelled her to either work for *Beyond 2000* or remain idle, Meagher, Handley and Cripps JJA said at 347:

> In some cases an attempt to obtain an injunction based on *Lumley v* [348] *Wagner* has failed.
>
> [...]
>
> In the present case, to grant the injunction sought is not to order specific performance of the service and services contracts. Miss Curro could comply with the injunctions without resuming work for Beyond. She would not be forced to choose between service with Beyond or idleness. Other employments would be open to her.

QUESTIONS

(1) In what way do the considerations of the strength of the case and the balance of convenience affect each other in assessing a case for interlocutory injunctions?

(2) Is the court bound to grant an injunction to restrain the breach of a negative covenant?

(3) What was the fundamental difference between, on the one hand, *Lumley v Wagner* and *Curro* (where injunctions were granted to restrain breaches of negative covenants) and on the other hand, *Page One Records*, where an injunction was refused?

22.4 Recovery of debts

Concept	Short explanation	Relevant authorities	*Principles* text*
The action for debt—advantages and availability	To be contrasted with an action for damages for breach of contract; an action for debt does not require proof of damage, only proof of the debt under the contract	*Young v Queensland Trustees Ltd* (1954) 99 CLR 560 *White and Carter (Councils) Ltd v McGregor* [1962] AC 413	Chapter 22: 22.16–22.17

(cont.)

Concept	Short explanation	Relevant authorities	*Principles* text*
Contractual sums accruing independently of performance	In relation to certain types of contracts, particularly the sale of land, subject to the vendor's not being in breach, the payments of certain types of moneys are considered to be deposits and are debts; the vendor's entitlement to those moneys arises independently of performance	*McDonald v Dennys Lascelles Ltd* (1933) 48 CLR 457 (see **17.2** for commentary and extract) *Bot v Ristevski* [1981] VR 120	Chapter 22: 22.18

* Consult the corresponding section(s) of the *Principles* text for more detail.

An action for recovery of debt is not to be confused with suing for damages for breach of contract; although both involve suing to recover money. The idea behind an action for the recovery of debt, however, is that the innocent party is suing to recover moneys which they say are due under the contract; whereas the idea of suing for damages for breach of contract carries the idea that damages are being sought to compensate the innocent party for the consequences of breach. The relevance of this crucial distinction and its implications are well explained in *Young v Queensland Trustees Ltd*[9] discussed below.

At a more nuanced level of analysis, one needs to recognise the concept of contractual sums that arise independently of performance, like deposits. The consequence of an obligation's being characterised as a 'deposit' is that, even where a contract is terminated and the obligations of the parties are discharged, the vendor's right to recover a deposit, as opposed to instalments of the purchase price, survives termination and can be recovered as a debt where the vendor is not in breach.

Young v Queensland Trustees Ltd (1954) 99 CLR 560

Facts and issues

The plaintiff successfully sued to recover the repayment of certain loans. The questions that the High Court addressed concerned the various onuses of proof that a lender or borrower had to discharge. *Young* is conventionally regarded as the seminal Australian case on point, clarifying this point succinctly by establishing that, in an action for debt, the defendant is the one who must prove payment in defence to a claim in debt.

9 (1954) 99 CLR 560.

Decision

Per Dixon CJ, McTiernan and Taylor JJ at 567:

> The common law does not and never did conceive of indebtedness in a sum certain for an executed consideration as a mere breach of contract: it is rather the detention of a sum of money . . .
>
> [569] The law was and is that, speaking generally, the [570] defendant must allege and prove payment by way of discharge as a defence to an action for indebtedness in respect of an executed consideration.

White and Carter (Councils) Ltd v McGregor [1962] AC 413

Facts and issues

The defendant McGregor had repudiated its contract with White and Carter who did not accept the repudiation and continued to perform their obligations under it, subsequently suing McGregor for the full contract price. Issues that arose were whether White and Carter had a duty to mitigate and if they were obliged to act 'reasonably'. This case explores a very important proposition: an innocent party is not usually bound to terminate a breached contract and be compelled to sue for damages for breach with all the attendant difficulties that such proceedings would entail, including mitigation and proving damages. Rather, the innocent party can generally continue to insist on performance of the contract and sue for the contract price (again—to be distinguished from damages for breach).

Decision

Per Lord Reid at 427:

> The general rule cannot be in doubt. It was settled in Scotland at least as early as 1848 and it has been authoritatively stated time and again in both Scotland and England. If one party to a contract repudiates it in the sense of making it clear to the other party that he refuses or will refuse to carry out his part of the contract, the other party, the innocent party, has an option. He may accept that repudiation and sue for damages for breach of contract, whether or not the time for performance has come; or he may if he chooses disregard or refuse to accept it and then the contract remains in full effect.

Per Lord Hodson at 445:

> The true position is that the contract survives and does so not only where specific implement is available. When the assistance of the court is not required the innocent party can choose whether he will accept repudiation and sue for damages for anticipatory breach or await the date of performance by the guilt party. Then, if there is failure in performance, his rights are preserved.
>
> [. . .]
>
> [446] The only material obligation which the respondent was bound to fulfil was to pay the sum of money claimed and it is difficult to see how damages should be assessed for breach of this obligation.

Bot v Ristevski [1981] VR 120

Facts and issues

The situation that was addressed in the earlier case of *McDonald v Dennys Lascelles Ltd*[10] was whether the vendor's entitlement to an instalment of the purchase price survived the termination of the contract. This is discussed in the passages from that case reproduced at pp 543–44 above. In the present case, *Bot*, the question was whether the vendor's entitlement to a deposit, as opposed to an instalment of the purchase price, survives the termination of the contract. The relevant extract from the decision dealing with that point is reproduced at p 548 above. Pay particular attention to the decision of Brooking J at 123 as stated below.

Decision

Per Brooking J at 123:

> The vendor's title to retain or recover a deposit is not conditional in this sense, and accordingly it will not be defeated or divested by the subsequent discharge of the contract: ... True it is that a deposit wears two aspects: if the purchase is carried out, it goes against the purchase money, but its primary purpose is that it is a guarantee that the purchaser means business ...
>
> There is no failure of consideration if the land is not conveyed or transferred, for the purchaser has had the benefit of the entry into the contract of sale by the vendor. 'Here the purchaser made an unconditional promise to pay a deposit immediately and, although if the contract was completed the moneys would according to ordinary principles be credited towards the purchase price and until then would constitute an earnest for performance, the agreement to pay was not in consideration of conveyance but was in consideration of the contract. It was the price or part of the price of the vendor's promise to sell...'.

QUESTIONS

(1) Why is an action for debt often simpler than suing for damages?

(2) Is the innocent party to a repudiated contract bound to accept the repudiation and sue for damages?

(3) Why is a 'deposit' similar to an 'instalment'? How are they different for the purposes of recovery from the vendor?

10 (1933) 48 CLR 457.

22.5 Liquidated damages and penalty clauses

Concept	Short explanation	Relevant authorities	*Principles* text*
The contemporary Australian approach—when is a provision a penalty	The approach to the penalty doctrine previously was that the assessment of whether the stipulation in question was a penalty involved comparing the stipulated sum with the loss that could be proved following the breach The contemporary Australian approach of whether the party seeking the moneys under the subject clause had an interest in compensation in the limited sense of liquidated damages for breach of contract has yielded to a broader test of a comparison of the stipulated sum with the 'interest in performance'	*Andrews v Australia and New Zealand Banking Group Ltd* (2012) 247 CLR 205 *Paciocco v Australia and New Zealand Banking Group Ltd* (2016) 258 CLR 525	Chapter 22: 22.21–22.22
Consequences of a stipulation being a penalty	At least for provisions that included losses that fall within the (expanded) scope of the principles in *Andrews*, a 'penalty' would be enforceable up to the amount of the actual loss	*Andrews v Australia and New Zealand Banking Group Ltd* (2012) 247 CLR 205 *Arab Bank Australia Ltd v Sayde Developments Pty Ltd* (2016) 93 NSWLR 231	Chapter 22: 22.23–22.24

* Consult the corresponding section(s) of the *Principles* text for more detail.

This part of the module considers the idea that the parties might in advance agree on the consequences of breach. At its most general, if the provision is found to be legitimate then it would be characterised as a liquidated damages clause. The term 'liquidated damages clause' invokes the notion that the parties can sue under the contract for the stipulated sum (or whatever the clause provides) as opposed to the idea that the innocent party must sue for unliquidated damages for breach of contract, which might be uncertain and inconvenient. Distinct from an enforceable liquidated damages clause is a penalty, in which case it would not be enforceable.

This section traces the development of the penalty doctrine via its treatment in recent Australian case law. The traditional view was that the clause had to be a genuine pre-estimate of loss, taking into account all the inherent circumstances of the contract. Without expressly overruling the traditional view, the contemporary Australian view is that loss was not to be read in a narrow sense, but had to take into account the other party's 'interest in performance'.

The recent developments in the penalty doctrine have led to great confusion and uncertainty.

Andrews v Australia and New Zealand Banking Group Ltd (2012) 247 CLR 205

Facts and issues

A preliminary issue was raised as to whether bank fees imposed for default were penalties and, more broadly, whether the doctrine of penalties could apply to provisions in a contract which did not require a breach of contract to be recoverable.

Decision

Per French CJ, Gummow, Crennan, Kiefel and Bell JJ at 216:

> In general terms, a stipulation *prima facie* imposes a penalty on a party ('the first party') if, as a matter of substance, it is collateral (or accessory) to a primary stipulation in favour of a second party and this collateral stipulation, upon the failure of the primary stipulation, imposes upon the first party an additional detriment, the penalty, to the benefit of the second party. In that sense, the collateral or accessory stipulation is described as being in the nature of a security for and *in terrorem* of the satisfaction of the primary stipulation. If compensation can be made to the second party for the prejudice suffered by failure of the primary stipulation, the collateral stipulation and the penalty are enforced only to the extent of that compensation. The first party is relieved to that degree from liability to satisfy the collateral stipulation.
>
> [...]
>
> [221] In reaching her conclusion respecting the scope of the penalty doctrine, the primary judge, with respect quite properly, followed what had been decided by the New South Wales Court of Appeal in *Interstar Wholesale Finance Pty Ltd v Integral Home Loans Pty Ltd*. In that [222] case the Court of Appeal held that the primary judge (Brereton J) had erred in denying that the doctrine had ceased to be one of equity and now was wholly legal in nature and in concluding that the doctrine was not limited to the failure of stipulations which were breaches of contract.
>
> [...]
>
> [227] Thus, while the ANZ maintains that the penalty doctrine has the limited scope, respecting breaches of contract, which in *Interstar* the Court of Appeal identified with *ECGD*, this limitation should not be accepted.

Paciocco v Australia and New Zealand Banking Group Ltd (2016) 258 CLR 525

Facts and issues

The case, like *Andrews*, concerned the recoverability of bank fees. In particular, the case explored whether contractual clauses governing the recoverability of those fees where there was no breach of contract, attracted the application of the penalty doctrine.

Decision

Per Kiefel J at 547:

> The distinction drawn by Lord Dunedin [in *Dunlop Pneumatic Tyre Co Ltd v New Garage and Motor Co Ltd* [1915] AC 79] between liquidated damages and a penalty, whilst useful, should not be understood as a limiting rule. It does not mean that if no pre-estimate is made at the time a contract is entered into, as is the case here, a sum stipulated will be a penalty. Nor does it mean that a sum reflecting, or attempting to reflect, other kinds of loss or damage to a party's interests beyond those directly caused by the breach will be a penalty. Indeed the provision in *Dunlop*, which was held not to be a penalty, was of this kind ...
>
> [555] It is important at this point to identify the ANZ's interests. The ANZ had an interest in receiving timeous repayment of the credit that it extended to its customers, including the appellants. As explained below, late payment impacted the ANZ's interests in three relevant respects: through operational costs, loss provisioning and increases in regulatory capital costs ...
>
> [556] the question is not what the ANZ could recover in an action for breach of contract, but rather whether the costs to it and the effects upon its financial interests by default may be taken into account in assessing whether the Late Payment Fees are penalties ...
>
> [557] The effect of Mr Inglis' evidence was to identify potential costs to the ANZ, from late payments, which reflect injuries to its financial position. They were real because they had to be taken into account by the ANZ. The evidence called for the appellants did not address damage of this kind. It cannot therefore be concluded that the sums of $20.00 and $35.00 were out of all proportion to the interests so identified ... [with the end result that the late payment fees were found not to be penalties].

Per Gageler J at 566:

> In the first of the appeals to this Court, in which the ultimate issue is whether the late payment fee was unenforceable as a penalty at common law, the parties agree that the governing principles are to be found in *Andrews* and in *Dunlop Pneumatic Tyre Co Ltd v New Garage and Motor Company Ltd*.[11] The heart of the dispute between them concerns the nature and content of the propositions of law for which *Dunlop* is to be treated as continuing authority in Australia.

Keifel J considered the *Dunlop* formulation was 'not to be understood as a limiting rule'. She, however, did not suggest that it be overruled; rather, she stated that the *Dunlop* formulation was expressed too narrowly. Indeed, Gageler J had accepted that the principles in it continued to be the law in Australia in respect of the type of dispute it addressed.

It is therefore extremely useful to revisit the *Dunlop* formulation itself. *Dunlop* was an English case, and the High Court's following explicit affirmation of it in *Ringrow Pty Ltd v BP Australia Pty Ltd*[12] is very useful; in particular, their Honours prescience in foreshadowing that those principles

11 [1915] AC 79.
12 (2005) 224 CLR 656.

might need to be reformulated at some appropriate time. Per Gleeson CJ, Gummow, Kirby, Hayne, Callinan and Heydon JJ at 662:

> The starting point for the appellant was the following passage in Lord Dunedin's speech in *Dunlop Pneumatic Tyre Co Ltd v New Garage and Motor Co Ltd*[13]:
>
> (2) The essence of a penalty is a payment of money stipulated as in terrorem of the offending party; the essence of liquidated damages is a genuine covenanted pre-estimate of damage . . .
> (3) The question whether a sum stipulated is penalty or liquidated damages is a question of construction to be decided upon the terms and inherent circumstances of each particular contract, judged of as at the time of the making of the contract, not as at the time of the breach . . .
> (4) To assist this task of construction various tests have been suggested, which if applicable to the case under consideration may prove helpful, or even conclusive. Such are:
>   (a) It will be held to be penalty if the sum stipulated for is extravagant and unconscionable in amount in comparison with the greatest loss that could conceivably be proved to have followed from the breach . . .
>   (b) It will be held to be a penalty if the breach consists only in not paying a sum of money, and the sum stipulated is a sum greater than the sum which ought to have been paid . . .
>   (c) There is a presumption (but no more) that it is penalty when 'a single lump sum is made payable by way of compensation, on the occurrence of one or more or all of several events, some of which may occasion serious and others but trifling damage'.
>
> [663] It is therefore proper to proceed on the basis that *Dunlop Pneumatic Tyre Co Ltd v New Garage and Motor Co Ltd* continues to express the law applicable in this country, leaving any more substantial reconsideration than that advanced, to a future case where reconsideration or reformulation is in issue.

Arab Bank Australia Ltd v Sayde Developments Pty Ltd (2016) 93 NSWLR 231

Facts and issues

The subject banking facility provided for interest to be payable at a default rate, if monthly interest payments were not made on time. The customer commenced proceedings claiming that the total amount of default interest was a penalty.

Decision

Per Sackville J at 233:

> Lord Hodge recognised that although the penalty doctrine is often said to be aimed at preventing oppression of the weaker contracting party, the application of the doctrine does not depend on any disparity of bargaining power between the parties. His Lordship also acknowledged the criticism that the penalty doctrine promotes uncertainty in commercial dealings because the contracting parties may not be able to predict accurately 'the judges' value judgment on whether a particular provision is exorbitant or unconscionable'.

13 [1915] AC 79 at 86-87.

[...]

[234] Expert evidence is nearly always expensive to obtain, especially when it concerns financial practices and transactions. It is likely that the total costs generated in this case will prove to be not much less than the amount in dispute. ...

In Australia, recent decisions of the High Court have both potentially expanded and contracted the scope of the doctrine. Whether the result will be to increase or decrease the extent to which the doctrine is invoked is as yet uncertain. ...

Whether the doctrine should be retained, modified or abolished is a policy issue that in my view courts are ill-equipped to consider.

QUESTIONS

(1) Prior to *Andrews*, what was considered to be the limitation of the application of the doctrine of penalties?

(2) Following *Andrews* and *Paciocco*, what are now the parameters of an 'interest' that an innocent party is seen to have under a liquidated damages clause?

(3) Is the *Dunlop* test—that liquidated damages be a 'genuine covenanted pre-estimate of damages'—a useful practical guide to be applied by analogy to the broader 'interests' test?

22.6 International perspectives

All parties to cross-border sales contracts governed by the *CISG* (see **25.4.1** on applicability) may seek performance of the contract by the other party: arts 46 and 62 *CISG*. An order for performance is not treated within the *CISG* as a special remedy only available in circumstances where damages are inadequate (contrast above **22.2**). However, a domestic court is not bound to order performance if, in similar circumstances under its domestic law, it would decline to do so: art 28 *CISG*. Thus, an Australian court could decline to order performance of a *CISG* contract due to delay: **22.2**. Recovery of debt (above **22.2**) is treated as enforcement of the buyer's obligation to pay the price (art 53 *CISG*) by an order for performance: art 62 *CISG*. As discussed at **25.9.3**, the same right exists within UNIDROIT Principles (see **25.4.3** on applicability). Parties may seek performance of an obligation within a reasonable time after they become aware of non-performance, unless performance is impossible, or unreasonably burdensome (art 7.2.2), and courts may order performance: art 7.2.4 UNIDROIT Principles.

Within the *CISG*, liquidated damages and penalties are generally treated as relating to a question concerning the extent of 'enforceability' and equivalent to matters of validity. As such, this is not a question covered by the *CISG* itself, but instead is external to the scope of the *CISG*: art 4(a). Therefore, the issue of enforceability of a liquidated damages clause within a *CISG* contract is determined under the applicable domestic law,[14] and the rules above (**22.5**) will apply if Australian law is denoted by the choice of law rules of the court or tribunal deciding the dispute.

14 CISG Advisory Council, Opinion No 10: 'Agreed Sums Payable upon Breach of an Obligation in CISG Contracts', Rapporteur: Dr P Hachem, Comment [4.3.8].

22.7 Review

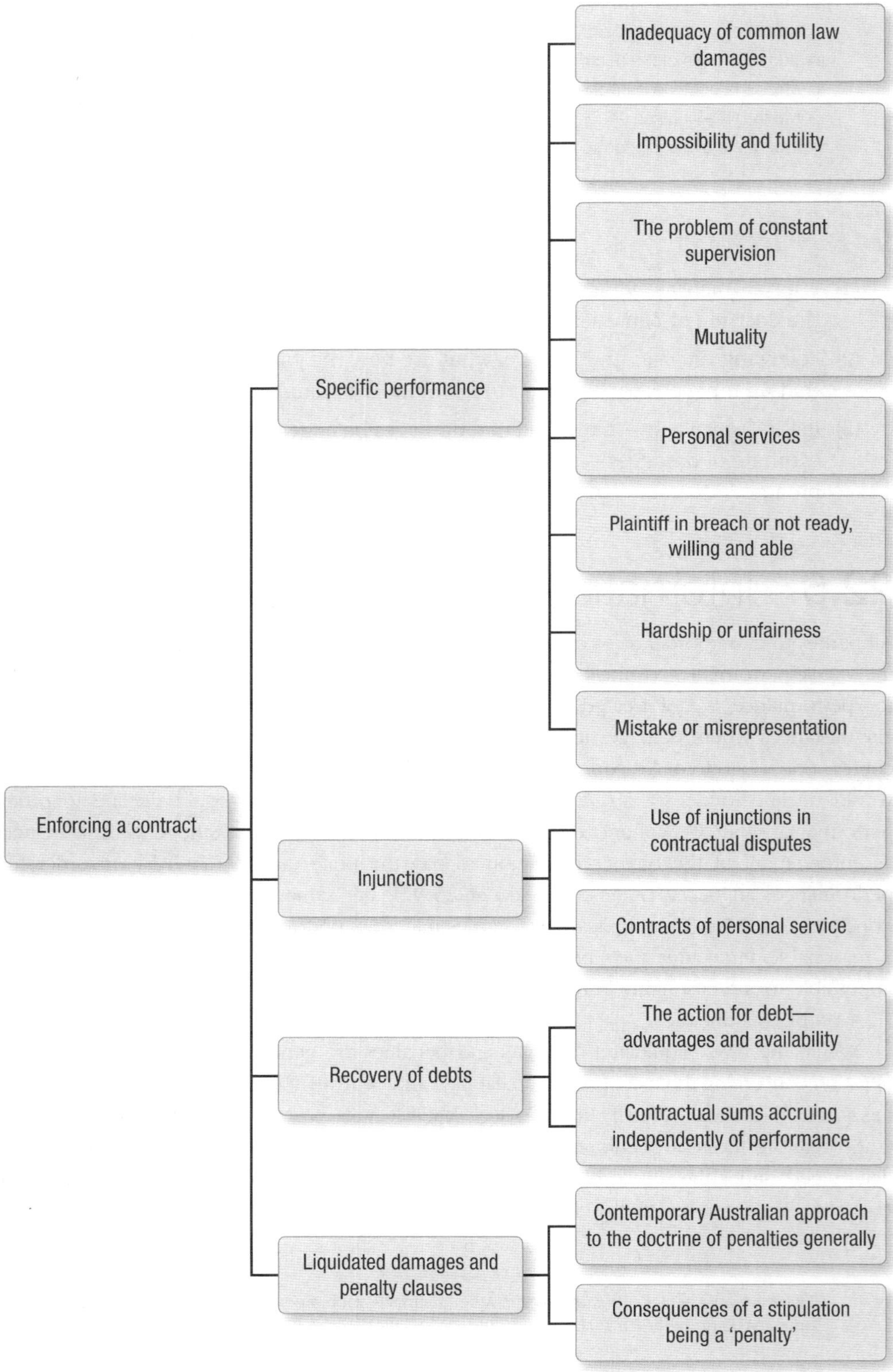
Enforcing a contract
Specific performance
Inadequacy of common law damages
Impossibility and futility
The problem of constant supervision
Mutuality
Personal services
Plaintiff in breach or not ready, willing and able
Hardship or unfairness
Mistake or misrepresentation
Injunctions
Use of injunctions in contractual disputes
Contracts of personal service
Recovery of debts
The action for debt—advantages and availability
Contractual sums accruing independently of performance
Liquidated damages and penalty clauses
Contemporary Australian approach to the doctrine of penalties generally
Consequences of a stipulation being a 'penalty'

TIPS FOR APPLYING THE LAW IN PRACTICE

- Be mindful that the content of this chapter concerns itself with remedies for the enforcement of contracts; do not confuse any of these principles with those that would apply to the recovery of damages for breach of contract (to be addressed in **Chapter 23**).
- One convenient way of illustrating the fault line between the two concepts is via the discussion of liquidated damages. Although the word 'damages' is used, at its core, the idea is of suing under the contract for that remedy, which is established under that contract, rather than damages for breach of contract. This should become clearer after you have studied **Chapter 23**.
- Another useful illustration is in the evolution of the principle that a contract for personal services (subject to the matters explored in *Patrick Stevedores*) cannot be enforced. Why? This is because that type of obligation cannot readily be supervised.
- Laches, acquiescence and delay are related concepts—whilst effluxion of time is obviously significant, the pivotal consideration is the prejudice suffered by the fact of delay.
- An area where particular attention was given in the treatment of both specific performance and injunctions was where an injunction had the effect of compelling someone to do something that could not be specifically performed. The underlying common equitable theme linking these ideas should be noted.

PROBLEM QUESTIONS

(1) John, the vendor, defaults on a contract for the sale of land. Ellen is too preoccupied with other things to take any action. Four years go by. At this point, Ellen finally decides to sue John. On these facts, is Ellen entitled to specific performance of the sale? What if any difference would it make if in the meanwhile John had sold the land to someone else?

(2) Peter is a dentist who enjoys playing football in his spare time. He is bound by a restrictive covenant in his contract with the Blackstump Rovers not to play with any other team. Assume the covenant to be valid. He accepts a contract to play with the Whitegrove Rangers. Will Blackstump Rovers succeed in injuncting him from playing with Whitegrove Rangers? The facts are loosely based on an Australian decision, *Hawthorn Football Club v Harding* [1988] VR 49, whose outcome should be compared to *Buckenara v Hawthorn Football Club* [1988] VR 39.

RESEARCH QUESTION

Specific performance would not ordinarily be ordered for the purchase of a chattel, whereas land is considered to be an appropriate case for specific performance. What is the rationalisation for this? Conversely, could one get specific performance for the purchase of a chattel, but not for a piece of land?

23

DAMAGES FOR BREACH OF CONTRACT

23.1 Overview

Damages is the most significant remedy under the common law. This is because an innocent party to a breached contract is entitled to damages as of right for a breach of contract if a compensable loss occurs which is not too remote and which could not have been avoided by mitigation.[1]

This broad proposition provides a useful overview to the study of damages for breach of contract as it introduces the idea of a compensable loss for breach of contract, followed by the more nuanced application of that general principle, that damages are recoverable as of right.

This chapter generally follows those contours, commencing with the concept of expectation damages being the primary form of compensation (*Robinson v Harman*)[2] followed by more sophisticated layers of analysis such as the various bases for the assessment of loss, then the various restrictions on recovery: causation, remoteness, mitigation, and contributory negligence. Finally, the question of the recovery of interest and the loss of the use of money as damages is discretely addressed as an aspect of remoteness. This is explored in the case of *Hungerford v Walker*.[3]

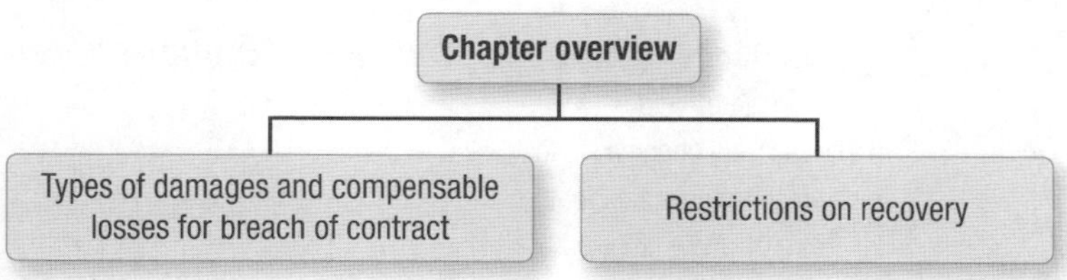

23.2 Types of damages and compensable losses for breach of contract

Concept	Short explanation	Relevant authorities	*Principles* text*
Expectation damages are the primary compensation for breach of contract	Expectation damages are designed to put the innocent party in the position they would have occupied had the contract not been breached or had been performed	*Robinson v Harman* (1848) 154 ER 363 *Commonwealth v Amann Aviation Pty Ltd* (1991) 174 CLR 64	Chapter 23: 23.06, 23.09

1 *Hungerfords v Walker* (1989) 171 CLR 125.
2 (1848) 154 ER 363.
3 (1989) 171 CLR 125.

(cont.)

Concept	Short explanation	Relevant authorities	*Principles* text*
'Reliance damages' compensate the plaintiff for actual expenditure wasted in anticipation of performance of the contract	Reliance damages are more rarely granted; but, subject to the rule against double recovery the plaintiff can claim both expectation and reliance damages	*McRae v Commonwealth Disposals Commission* (1951) 84 CLR 377 *Commonwealth v Amann Aviation Pty Ltd* (1991) 174 CLR 64	Chapter 23: 23.08
Damages in contracts for the sale of good and land	Damages for contracts for sale of goods are affected by specific legislation which essentially codifies the common law Special rules apply to the recovery of damages for breached contracts for the sale of land The recovery of damages for breached contracts for the sale of land is affected by legislation including the abolition of the rule in *Bain v Fothergill* in some jurisdictions	Sale of Goods legislation: *Sale of Goods Act 1923* (NSW) s 53 (example) *Wenham v Ella* (1972) 127 CLR 454 *Bain v Fothergill* (1874) LR 7 HL 158 *Conveyancing Act 1919* (NSW) s 54B	Chapter 23: 23.10
The cost of rectification can be granted as damages for breach of contract	The principle is invoked where damages measured according to the diminution in value of the subject matter may not adequately compensate the plaintiff. The cost of rectification may however be refused where it is unreasonable	*Bellgrove v Eldridge* (1954) 90 CLR 613 *Tabcorp Holdings Ltd v Bowen Investments Pty Ltd* (2009) 236 CLR 272	Chapter 23: 23.11
The loss of a chance is compensable as damages for breach of contract	If an estimate of a chance can be calculated, a loss of a chance can be compensated The loss of a commercial opportunity is likewise compensable, based on these principles	*Chaplin v Hicks* [1911] 2 KB 786 *Sellars v Adelaide Petroleum NL* (1994) 179 CLR 332 *Baltic Shipping Co v Dillon ('Mikhail Lermontov')* (1933) 176 CLR 344 *Addis v Gramophone Co Ltd* [1909] AC 488 *Insight Vacations Pty Ltd v Young* (2010) 78 NSWLR 641	Chapter 23: 23.12

* Consult the corresponding section(s) of the *Principles* text for more detail.

This part commences with an explanation of the fundamental basis for the assessment of damages for breach of contract: that it is designed to compensate a party for a breach of contract by putting them in the position they should be in had the contract not been breached—see *Robinson v Harman*[4] discussed below. The various types of damage explored in this section are more nuanced applications of this general principle, but they essentially still give expression to this broad principle in *Robinson v Harman*. It is thus particularly necessary to keep an eye broadly on the principle in *Robinson v Harman* in navigating this part.

Robinson v Harman (1848) 154 ER 363

Facts and issues

The defendant agreed to grant a lease having knowledge that he had no title. The primary question was the damages that the plaintiff was entitled to recover. The decision of Parke B at 363 is described frequently as the classic statement of contract damages. It is also reproduced in full in the extract of *Amann* below where the principle stated by Parke B was approved; it can be described now as being the definitive statement governing the recovery of damages for breach of contract.

Decision

Per Parke B at 363:

> . . . where a party sustains a loss by reason of a breach of contract, he is, so far as money can do it, to be placed in the same situation, with respect to damages, as if the contract had been performed.

Commonwealth v Amann Aviation Pty Ltd (1991) 174 CLR 64

Facts and issues

The parties entered into a contract for the plaintiff company to conduct aerial coastal surveillance for three years, which the Commonwealth repudiated. Evidence was given of the profit that the company would have made had the contract run the distance and of the prospect that the Commonwealth would have validly terminated the contract. Additionally, evidence was given of the company's wasted expenditure in preparing to perform the contract. The High Court, in a seminal judgment, explored the legal principles underpinning damages for breach of contract generally, including the intersection and movement between reliance and expectation damages. The High Court took the opportunity of exploring the right to recover damages for breach of contract. This case is a leading case and the principles in it arise for consideration in a number of discrete areas, including (within this chapter) the right to recover reliance damages and remoteness.

4 (1848) 154 ER 363.

Decision

Per Mason CJ and Dawson J at 80:

> The general rule at common law, as stated by Parke B. in *Robinson v. Harman*, is 'that where a party sustains a loss by reason of a breach of contract, he is, so far as money can do it, to be placed in the same situation, with respect to damages, as if the contract had been performed'. This statement of principle has been accepted and applied in Australia.
>
> The award of damages for breach of contract protects a plaintiff's expectation of receiving the defendant's performance. That expectation arises out of or is created by the contract. Hence, damages for breach of contract are often described as 'expectation damages'. The onus of proving damages sustained lies on a plaintiff and the amount of damages awarded will be commensurate with the plaintiff's expectation, objectively determined, rather than subjectively ascertained. That is to say, a plaintiff must prove, on the balance of probabilities, that his or her expectation of a certain outcome, as a result of performance of the contract, had a likelihood of attainment rather than being mere expectation.
>
> [81] In the ordinary course of commercial dealings, a party supplying goods or rendering services will enter into a contract with a view to securing a profit, that is to say, that party will expect a certain margin of gain to be achieved in addition to the recouping of any expenses reasonably incurred by it in the discharge of its contractual obligations. It is for this reason that expectation damages are often described as damages for loss of profits. Damages recoverable as lost profits are constituted by the combination of expenses justifiably incurred by a plaintiff in the discharge of contractual obligations and any amount by which gross receipts would have exceeded those expenses. This second amount is the net profit.

McRae v Commonwealth Disposals Commission (1951) 84 CLR 377

Facts and issues

The parties had entered into a contract for the salvage of an oil tanker which did not exist. In rejecting the argument that there was a common mistake as to the existence of the tanker, the Court held that, on a correct construction of the contract, it was an implied term, which the Commission had breached, that the tanker existed. The extract below addresses the question of whether the plaintiff could recover damages based on their wasted expenditure.

Decision

Per Dixon and Fullagar JJ at 414:

> If we regard the case as a simple and normal case of breach by non-delivery, the plaintiffs have no starting-point. The burden of proof is on them, and they cannot establish that they have suffered any damage unless they can show that a tanker delivered in performance of the contract would have had some value, and this they cannot show. But when the contract alleged is a contract that there was a tanker in a particular place, and the breach assigned is that there was no tanker there, and the damages claimed are measured by expenditure incurred on the faith of the promise that there was a tanker in that place, the plaintiffs are in a very different position. They have now a starting-point. They can say: (1) this

expense was incurred; (2) it was incurred because you promised us that there was a tanker; (3) the fact that there was no tanker made it certain that this expense would be wasted. The plaintiffs have in this way a starting-point. They make a prima-facie case. The fact that the expense was wasted flowed prima facie from the fact that there was no tanker; and the first fact is damage, and the second fact is breach of contract. The burden is now thrown on the Commission of establishing that, if there had been a tanker, the expense incurred would equally have been wasted. This, of course, the Commission cannot establish. The fact is that the impossibility of assessing damages on the basis of a comparison between what was promised and what was delivered arises not because what was promised was valueless but because it is impossible to value a non-existent thing. It is the breach of contract itself which makes it impossible even to undertake an assessment on that basis. It is not impossible, however, to undertake an assessment on another basis, and, in so far as the Commission's breach of contract itself reduces the possibility of an accurate assessment, it is not for the Commission to complain.

Commonwealth v Amann Aviation Pty Ltd (1991) 174 CLR 64

Facts and issues

The fundamental facts are as set out above. A question that arose was whether the plaintiff was entitled to recover its reliance damages (that is, the expenditure incurred in reliance on the contract) and, if so, the extent to which it could recover expectation loss (that is, the position that it would be in had the contract been performed). The extract below addresses the recoverability of reliance damages where loss of profits cannot be proven with certainty.

Decision

In relation to the specific point of the entitlement to reliance damages where the recovery of loss of profits might be problematic, per Toohey J at 136:

> I agree with the Chief Justice and Dawson J. that opinions expressed in decisions such as *Anglia Television Ltd. v.* [137] *Reed*, and *CCC Films Ltd. v. Impact Quadrant Films Ltd.*, that a plaintiff may, at his option, claim for loss of profits or wasted expenditure are not appropriate ways of looking at the question. Reliance damages are a means of compensating the plaintiff where there has been no loss of profits or, more likely, where the plaintiff cannot prove loss of profits with any certainty.

Concerning the question of the rationalisation that underpinned the recovery of reliance damages, whilst it was held that *Amann* was entitled to recover them, the most useful rationalisation for present purposes, and not inconsistent with the reasoning of the remainder, was the following reasoning on the part of McHugh J who said at 166:

> I would reject the explanation that the basis of cases such as *McRae* is or ought to be that proof of expenditure gives rise to a prima facie inference that it will be recouped by the carrying out of the contract. The rule in *McRae* is satisfactorily based on the broad principle of justice that, if the breach of the defendant has made it impossible to ascertain whether or not the plaintiff would have made a profit from the performance of the contract, it is only fair that

the defendant should reimburse the plaintiff for expenditure which it has wasted as the result of the breach.

[. . .]

Ex hypothesi, once it is proved that it is impossible to assess the outcome of the contract, no issue can arise as to whether 'the expense incurred would equally have been wasted'. In a case like *McRae*, until the plaintiff proves that the defendant's breach has made it impossible to prove the outcome of the contract or the value of the defendant's promise, expenditure wasted in reliance on the defendant's promise is not recoverable. But once the plaintiff discharges that burden of proof, it is entitled [167] to be compensated for all expenditure wasted in reasonable reliance on the defendant's promise to perform its side of the contract.

Sale of Goods Act 1923 (NSW) s 53

53 Damages for non-delivery

(1) Where the seller wrongfully neglects or refuses to deliver the goods to the buyer, the buyer may maintain an action against the seller for damages for non-delivery.

(2) The measure of damages is the estimated loss directly and naturally resulting in the ordinary course of events from the seller's breach of contract.

(3) Where there is an available market for the goods in question, the measure of damages is prima facie to be ascertained by the difference between the contract price and the market or current price of the goods at the time or times when they ought to have been delivered, or if no time was fixed, then at the time of the refusal to deliver.

Wenham v Ella (1972) 127 CLR 454

Facts and issues

The appellant contracted to procure to the respondent the transfer of an interest in land. The appellant breached the contract, which was not capable of being specifically performed after breach. The question concerned the extent of the respondent's damages for breach of contract.

Decision

Per Barwick CJ at 460:

. . . I shall treat the present case, so far as concerns the points raised by the amended grounds of appeal, as involving no more than a claim for damages for breach of a contract to procure the transfer of an income-producing interest in land. The general rule in such a case is that the party not in default is to be placed in the same position as that in which he would have been had the contract been performed . . .

[461] We are dealing with a purchaser who has given to his vendor the full consideration for the purchase of an interest in land, not procurable in the market. Indeed the reason for the

appellants' failure to perform would appear to have been his inability to procure the delivery to the respondent of the agreed interest in land.

In my opinion, the respondent was entitled at common law, in the circumstances of this case, to recover, in addition to the value of the interest in land of which transfers were promised to be delivered and for which he had paid, damages for the loss of the income which such interest in land would have produced from the date when the transfers ought to have been delivered to the date of judgment, at which time his further rights are to be found in that judgment.

Bain v Fothergill (1874) LR 7 HL 158

Facts and issues

The House of Lords considered here, relevantly, whether upon a contract for the sale of real estate, where the vendor, without his default, is unable to make a good title, the purchaser is by law entitled to recover damages for the loss of his bargain.

Decision

Per Lord Chelmsford at 201:

> . . . the rule established by *Flureau v Thornhill* [(1746) 96 ER 635] is, that upon a contract for the purchase of a real estate, if the vendor, without fraud, is incapable of making a good title, the intended purchaser is not entitled to any compensation for the loss of his bargain.

Addressing the question of whether the case fell within an exception to that rule, his Lordship said at 207:

> If a person enters into a contract for the sale of a real estate knowing that he has no title to it, nor any means of acquiring it, the purchaser cannot recover damages beyond the expenses he has incurred by an action for the breach of the contract; he can only obtain other damages by an action for deceit. [208] It is only necessary to add that, in my opinion, if there were any exceptions from the rule in *Flureau v Thornhill* the present case would not fall within any of them, but is within the rule itself. There is no reason to think that the respondents were not acting throughout under a bona fide belief that the lessor's consent might be obtained at any time upon application. They were prevented from performing their contract, not from any wilful act or fraud on their part, but by an unexpected defect in their title, which it was beyond their power to cure. The case falls precisely within the terms of the rule, as stated in *Flureau v Thornhill* and, therefore, in my opinion, the judgment appealed from is right, and ought to be affirmed.

Legislation has, in some jurisdictions, abolished the rule in *Bain v Fothergill.*

Conveyancing Act 1919 (NSW) s 54B

54B Damages: defective title

(1) The rule of law known as the rule in *Bain v Fothergill* is abolished in relation to contracts for the sale or other disposal of land or any interest in land made after the commencement of this section.

(2) The Court may award damages for loss of bargain against a vendor who cannot perform such a contract because of a defect in the vendor's title.

(3) This section has effect notwithstanding any stipulation to the contrary. . .

Bellgrove v Eldridge (1954) 90 CLR 613

Facts and issues

The defendant, a builder, had breached its contract with the owner by substantially departing from the specifications, and the building works were defective in relation to the concrete foundations and the mortar. The question was the measure of damages to be applied, focusing on the idea that the test was whether the damages were necessary and a reasonable course to adopt.

Decision

Per Dixon CJ, Webb and Taylor JJ at 617:

> In the present case, the respondent was entitled to have a building erected *upon her land* in accordance with the contract and the plans and specifications which formed part of it, and her damage is the loss which she has sustained by the failure of the appellant to perform his obligation to her. This loss cannot be measured by comparing the value of the building which has been erected with the value it would have borne if erected in accordance with the contract; her loss can, prima facie, be measured only by ascertaining the amount required to rectify the defects complained of and so give to her the equivalent of a building on her land which is substantially in accordance with the contract. One or two illustrations are sufficient to show that the prima facie rule for assessing damages for a breach of warranty upon the sale of goods has no application to the present case. Departures from the plans and specifications forming part of a contract for the erection of a building may result in the completion of a building which, whilst differing in some particulars from that contracted for, is no less valuable. For instance, particular rooms in such a building may be finished in one colour instead of quite a different colour as specified. Is the owner in these circumstances without a remedy? In our opinion he is not; he is entitled to the reasonable cost of rectifying the departure or defect so far as that is possible. Subject to a qualification to which we shall refer presently the rule is, we think, correctly stated in *Hudson on Building Contracts*, 7th ed. (1946), p. 343. 'The measure of the damages recoverable by the building owner for the breach of a building contract is, it is submitted, the difference between the contract price of the work or building contracted for and the cost of making the work [618] or building conform to the contract, with the addition, in most cases, of the amount of profits or earnings lost by the breach' . . .
>
> But the work necessary to remedy defects in a building and so produce conformity with the plans and specifications may, and frequently will, require the removal or demolition of some part of the structure. And it is obvious that the necessary remedial work may call for the removal or demolition of a more or less substantial part of the building . . .
>
> The qualification, however, to which this rule is subject is that, not only must the work undertaken be necessary to produce conformity, but that also, it must be a reasonable course to adopt. No one would doubt that where pursuant to a building contract calling for the erection of a house with cement rendered external walls of second-hand bricks, the builder has constructed the walls of new bricks of first quality the owner would not be entitled to the cost of demolishing the walls and re-erecting them in second-hand bricks . . .

[619] As to what remedial work is both 'necessary' and 'reasonable' in any particular case is a question of fact. But the question whether demolition and re-erection is a reasonable method of remedying defects does not arise when defective foundations seriously threaten the stability of a house and when the threat can be removed only by such a course. That work, in such circumstances, is obviously reasonable and in our opinion, may be undertaken at the expense of the builder.

Tabcorp Holdings Ltd v Bowen Investments Pty Ltd (2009) 236 CLR 272

Facts and issues

A tenant, in breach of covenants in the lease, performed work without consent. The work in question did not significantly affect the value of the property but the cost of remediation was significant. The question in the case concerned the measure of damages in the context of an argument that reinstatement or remedial costs were unreasonable and unnecessary. The tenant sought to argue that damages should be assessed on the basis of the reduction in the value of the premises (about $34,000) rather than the cost of reinstatement, $580,000.

Decision

Per French CJ, Gummow, Heydon, Crennan and Kiefel JJ at 286:

> The 'ruling principle', confirmed in this Court on numerous occasions, with respect to damages at common law for breach of contract is that stated by Parke B in *Robinson v Harman*:
>
> > The rule of the common law is, that where a party sustains a loss by reason of a breach of contract, he is, so far as money can do it, to be placed in the same situation, with respect to damages, as if the contract had been performed.
>
> [...]
>
> But as Staughton LJ explained in *Ruxley Electronics Ltd v Forsyth* such a measure of damages seeks only to reflect the financial consequences of a notional transaction whereby the buyer sells the defective goods on the market and purchases the contract goods. The buyer is thus placed in the 'same situation ... as if the contract had been performed', with the loss being the difference in market value. However, in cases where the contract is not for the sale of marketable commodities, selling the defective item and purchasing an item corresponding with the contract is not possible. In such cases, diminution in value damages will not restore the innocent party to the 'same situation ... as if the contract had been performed' ...
>
> [288] The Tenant stressed that in *Bellgrove v Eldridge* this Court pointed out that there was a qualification to the rule it stated in regard to damages recoverable by a building owner for the breach of a building contract. 'The qualification ... is that, not only must the work undertaken be necessary to produce conformity, but that also, it must be a reasonable course to adopt.' The example which the Court gave of unreasonableness was the following:
>
> > No one would doubt that where pursuant to a building contract calling for the erection of a house with cement rendered external walls of second-hand bricks, the builder has constructed the walls of new bricks of first quality the owner would not be entitled to the cost of demolishing the walls and re-erecting them in second-hand bricks.'

That tends to indicate that the test of 'unreasonableness' is only to be satisfied by fairly exceptional circumstances. The example given by the Court aligns closely with what Oliver J said in *Radford v De Froberville*, that is, that the diminution in value measure of damages will only apply where the innocent party is 'merely using a technical breach to secure an uncovenanted profit.' It is also important to note that the 'reasonableness' exception was not found to exist in *Bellgrove v Eldridge*. Nothing in the reasoning in that case suggested that where the reasoning is applied to the present circumstances, the course which the Landlord proposed is unnecessary or unreasonable.

Chaplin v Hicks [1911] 2 KB 786

Facts and issues

The plaintiff was deprived of a chance to win a prize in a beauty contest by the defendant's breach of contract. The plaintiff could not prove with certainty at trial that she would have won. The question was whether she was entitled to damages on the basis of her lost opportunity.

Decision

Per Vaughan Williams LJ at 791:

> Then came the point that was more strenuously argued, that the damages were of such a nature as to be impossible of assessment. It was said that the plaintiff's chance of winning a prize turned on such a number of contingencies that it was impossible for any one, even after arriving at the conclusion that the plaintiff had lost her opportunity by the breach, to say that there was any assessable value of that loss. It is said that in a case which involves so many contingencies it is impossible to say what was the plaintiff's pecuniary loss. I am unable to agree with that contention. I agree that the presence of all the contingencies upon which the gaining of the prize might depend makes the calculation not only difficult but incapable of being carried out with certainty or precision. The proposition is that, whenever the contingencies on which the result depends are numerous and difficult to deal with, it is impossible to recover any damages for the loss of the chance or opportunity of winning the prize. In the present case I understand that there were fifty selected competitors, of whom the plaintiff was one, and twelve prizes, so that the average chance of each competitor was about one in four. Then it is said that the questions which might arise in the minds of the judges are so numerous that it is impossible to say that the case is one in which it [792] is possible to apply the doctrine of averages at all. I do not agree with the contention that, if certainty is impossible of attainment, the damages for a breach of contract are unassessable. I agree, however, that damages might be so unassessable that the doctrine of averages would be inapplicable because the necessary figures for working upon would not be forthcoming; there are several decisions, which I need not deal with, to that effect. I only wish to deny with emphasis that, because precision cannot be arrived at, the jury has no function in the assessment of damages.
>
> In early days when it was necessary to assess damages, no rules were laid down by the Courts to guide juries in the assessment of damages for breach of contract; it was left to the jury absolutely. But in course of time judges began to give advice to juries; as the stress of commerce increased, let us say between the reigns of Queen Elizabeth and Queen Victoria, rule after rule was suggested by way of advice to juries by the judges when damages for breach of contract had to be assessed. But from first to last there were, as there are

> now, many cases in which it was difficult to apply definite rules. In the case of a breach of a contract for the delivery of goods the damages are usually supplied by the fact of there being a market in which similar goods can be immediately bought, and the difference between the contract price and the price given for the substituted goods in the open market is the measure of damages; that rule has been always recognized. Sometimes, however, there is no market for the particular class of goods; but no one has ever suggested that, because there is no market, there are no damages. In such a case the jury must do the best they can, and it may be that the amount of their verdict will really be a matter of guesswork. But the fact that damages cannot be assessed with certainty does not relieve the wrong-doer of the necessity of paying damages for his breach of contract. I do not wish to lay down any such rule as that a judge can in every case leave it to the jury to assess damages for a breach of contract . . .

Sellars v Adelaide Petroleum NL (1994) 179 CLR 332

Facts and issues

The plaintiff, Adelaide Petroleum, was in contractual negotiations with a third party which it broke off as a result of the defendant, Poseidon's, misleading or deceptive conduct. Upon discovering the truth of the matters, those negotiations resumed and led to a contract and the plaintiff argued that there was a chance it would have reached a more favourable agreement with third party had the negotiations not been interrupted. The issue concerned whether the plaintiff could recover damages on the basis of the lost opportunity to make a contract with the third party on those terms.

Decision

Per Mason CJ, Dawson, Toohey and Gaudron JJ at 349:

> In the realm of contract law, the loss of a chance to win a prize in a competition resulting from breach of a contract to provide the chance is compensable, notwithstanding that, on the balance of probabilities, it is more likely than not that the plaintiff would not win the competition. As the contract contained a promise to provide the chance, the breach of the contract resulted in the loss of the chance and that loss was for relevant purposes an actual loss, in the sense in which Dixon and McTiernan JJ. used that expression in *Fink v. Fink*. And, where there has been an actual loss of some sort, the common law does not permit difficulties of estimating the loss in money to defeat an award of damages. The damages will then be ascertained by reference to the degree of probabilities, or possibilities, inherent in the plaintiffs succeeding had the plaintiff been given the chance which the contract promised.
>
> This approach is not confined to contracts relating to games of chance, sporting contests or other competitions. *Fink v. Fink* concerned a contract to provide an opportunity for a reconciliation, breach of which was held to entitle the wife to damages. And there can be no doubt that a contract to provide a commercial advantage or opportunity, if breached, enables the innocent party to bring an action for damages for the loss of that advantage or opportunity. So, in *The Commonwealth v. Amann Aviation Pty. Ltd.*, Mason CJ. and Dawson J. Brennan J. and Deane J. concluded that a lost commercial advantage or opportunity was a compensable loss, even though there was a less than 50 per cent likelihood that the commercial advantage would be realized. Damages for breach of contract were assessed by reference to the probabilities or possibilities of what would have happened.

Baltic Shipping Co v Dillon ('Mikhail Lermontov') (1993) 176 CLR 344

Facts and issues

A passenger on a cruise ship suffered injury when it sank and sued for damages for breach of contract. The High Court's judgment addressed the question of the entitlement to damages for non-pecuniary losses in the following seminal judgment.

Decision

On the question of whether there was any general rule addressing the availability of damages for non-pecuniary losses, the following passages in the case address the treatment: first, of whether there is a general rule addressing that question; second, exceptions to that general rule.

As to the first of these two points, the following passage, at 394 sets out what McHugh J considered to be the 'general rule':

> *The general rule relating to damages for distress and disappointment*
>
> Damages for breach of contract cannot ordinarily be awarded for distress or disappointment arising from that breach. In *Hamlin v Great Northern Railway Co.*[5], Pollock C.B. said at 411:
>
>> In actions for breaches of contract the damages must be such as are capable of being appreciated or estimated ... it may be laid down as a rule, that generally in actions upon contracts no damages can be given which cannot be stated specifically, and that the plaintiff is entitled to recover whatever damages naturally result from the breach of contract, but not damages for the disappointment of mind occasioned by the breach of contract.

Concerning the second question, exceptions to that general rule, per Mason CJ at 363:

> The approach which has been taken in the more recent English decisions, particularly those decisions which vindicate the last three of the exceptions set forth above, is based on the rule in *Hadley v Baxendale.* Thus, in *Cox v Philips Industries Ltd,* Lawson J concluded that there was:
>
>> ... no reason in principle why, if a situation arises which within the contemplation of the parties would have given rise to vexation, distress and general disappointment and frustration, the person who is injured by a contractual breach should not be compensated in damages for that breach ...
>
> [364] Thus, in *Watts v Morrow,* Bingham LJ denied that the general exclusionary rule was founded on the assumption that the plaintiff's feelings are not foreseeable and asserted that it was founded on considerations of policy. He went on carefully and convincingly to delineate the circumstances in which damages could be awarded, observing:
>
>> But the rule is not absolute. Where the very object of a contract is to provide pleasure, relaxation, peace of mind or freedom from molestation, damages will be awarded if the fruit of the contract is not provided or if the contrary result is procured instead. If the law did not cater for this exceptional category of case it would be defective. A contract to survey the condition of a house for a prospective purchaser does not, however, fall within this exceptional category.
>>
>> In cases not falling within this exceptional category, damages are in my view recoverable for physical inconvenience and discomfort caused by the breach and mental suffering directly related to that inconvenience and discomfort.

5 (1856) 1 H&N 408.

Also, on that point, per Deane and Dawson JJ at 381:

> The many cases in which an award of damages for breach of contract has included compensation for mental distress can be grouped (sometimes a little uncomfortably) into a number of different categories, including breach of promise of marriage, breach of contract causing physical injury and breach of contract directly causing physical inconvenience . . .

Addis v Gramophone Co Ltd [1909] AC 488

Facts and issues

The plaintiff sought damages for wrongful dismissal. The relevant question was the extent to which damages for injured feelings, mental distress or damages to reputation could be granted caused by the dismissal.

Decision

Per Lord Loreburn LC at 490:

> In any case there was a breach of contract in not allowing the plaintiff to discharge his duties as manager, and the damages are exactly the same in either view. They are, in my opinion, the [491] salary to which the plaintiff was entitled for the six months between October 1905, and April 1906, together with the commission which the jury think he would have earned had he been allowed to manage the business himself. I cannot agree that the manner of dismissal affects these damages. Such considerations have never been allowed to influence damages in this kind of case. An expression of Lord Coleridge, CJ (*Maw v Jones*) has been quoted as authority to the contrary. I doubt if the learned Lord Chief Justice so intended it. If he did, I cannot agree with him. If there be a dismissal without notice the employer must pay an indemnity; but, that indemnity cannot include compensation either for the injured feelings of the servant or for the loss he may sustain from the fact that his having been dismissed of itself makes it more difficult for him to obtain fresh employment.

Insight Vacations Pty Ltd v Young (2010) 78 NSWLR 641

Facts and issues

The plaintiff was injured on a coach tour and sued the defendant company from whom she had purchased the tour. The defendant was found to have breached contractual warranties to render services with due care and skill. The trial judge awarded damages independently for breach of contract for disappointment and loss of enjoyment. The relevant question was whether a contractual claim for anxiety and disappointment constituted an 'impairment of a person's mental condition' within the meaning of, and limited by, the *Civil Liability Act 2002* (NSW).

Decision

Per Sackville AJA at 654:

... Mason CJ pointed out (at 362) [of *Baltic Shipping*] that 'it is beyond question that a plaintiff can recover damages for pain and suffering, including mental suffering and anxiety, where the defendant's breach of contract causes physical injury to the plaintiff'. It would seem to follow, as a matter of principle, that a plaintiff who suffers physical injury by reason of the defendant's breach of contract may also recover damages for loss of amenities ...

In my view, the damages awarded by the primary Judge in the present case for disappointment constituted 'damages that relate to the ... injury of a person' within the definition of 'personal injury damages' in s 11 of the *Civil Liability Act*. The disappointment, on the primary Judge's findings, resulted from the respondent's inability to enjoy her tour by reason of the injuries sustained in the course of the tour. These injuries were the consequence of the applicant's breach of the implied term of the contract obliging it to render the relevant services with due care and skill. It follows that Part 2 of the *Civil Liability Act* applies to the award.

[...]

[655] It follows that the primary Judge was in error in awarding damages for disappointment independently of the Table in s 16(3) of the *Civil Liability Act* ...[For present purposes, it suffices to note that s 16 of the *Civil Liability Act* provided that damages for non-economic loss were to be determined according to that table.]

QUESTIONS

(1) What is the primary relief for breach of contract?

(2) Why are these described as 'expectation' damages?

(3) When, if at all, would it be feasible, if not desirable, to seek reliance damages rather than expectation damages?

23.3 Restrictions on recovery

Concept	Short explanation	Relevant authorities	*Principles* text*
Causation provides the 'link' between breach and loss	Under the traditional 'but for' test, the question is whether 'but for' the breach, the loss would have occurred Where the plaintiff's act breaks the chain of causation, the defendant is no longer liable for damages for their breach of contract Even if there is a causal connection between the breach and the loss, the breach might be so superseded by supervening events so as not to be at law the cause of the loss	*Reg Glass Pty Ltd v Rivers Locking Systems Pty Ltd* (1968) 120 CLR 516 *Lexmead (Basingstoke) Ltd v Lewis* [1982] AC 225 *Alexander v Cambridge Credit Corporation Ltd* (1987) 9 NSWLR 310	Chapter 23: 23.15
Remoteness	Losses must arise either naturally or as a result of the usual course of things or be within the reasonable contemplation of the parties at the time of entering the contract	*Hadley v Baxendale* (1854) 156 ER 145 *Commonwealth v Amann Aviation Pty Ltd* (1991) 174 CLR 64	Chapter 23: 23.16

Concept	Short explanation	Relevant authorities	*Principles* text*
	The two limbs of remoteness in *Hadley* is the traditional test of remoteness Losses that 'arise naturally' are taken to be in the reasonable contemplation of the parties; losses that do not arise naturally can also be within the reasonable contemplation of the parties only when special circumstances are known It is necessary for loss of a particular type to be in the reasonable contemplation of the parties, but not its precise extent	*Victoria Laundry (Windsor) Ltd v Newman Industries Ltd* [1949] 2 KB 528 *H Parsons (Livestock) Ltd v Uttley Ingham & Co Ltd* [1978] QB 791	
Mitigation	The extent to which the plaintiff has avoided or reduced the loss inflicted by the defendant's breach by mitigating will be taken into account in the calculation of damages The cost of reasonable mitigation can be recovered as damages even if it actually increases the loss The burden of showing the plaintiff has not acted reasonably is placed on the defendant. Whilst the burden is heavy, the courts have on occasion found there to be a failure to mitigate	*British Westinghouse Electric and Manufacturing Co Ltd v Underground Electric Railways Co of London Ltd* [1912] AC 673 *Simonious Vischer & Co v Holt & Thompson* [1979] 2 NSWLR 322 *Burns v MAN Automotive (Australia) Pty Ltd* (1986) 161 CLR 653	
Contributory negligence	Where the defendant breaches a concurrent contractual and tortious duty and the plaintiff is contributorily negligent, apportionment legislation will result in a reduction in damages to the extent the court considers just and equitable Irrespective of whether the case is pleaded in negligence or breach of contract, the question, rather, is whether a concurrent contractual and tortious duty is owed, and if so apportionment legislation will apply	Apportionment legislation: *Law Reform (Miscellaneous Provisions) Act 1965* (NSW) s 9 (example) *Indresco Pty Ltd v Hawker Noyes Equipment Pty Ltd* [1999] WASCA 60 *Hungerfords v Walker* (1989) 171 CLR 125 *Hardie v Shadbolt* [2004] WASCA 175	Chapter 23: 23.19

* Consult the corresponding section(s) of the *Principles* text for more detail.

Whilst damages are awarded to compensate a party for the consequences of breach, numerous considerations operate to restrict the recovery of damages: the first being whether the breach caused the damage at all. This is the first aspect that will be discussed, followed by a logical sequence of treatment: whether the damages were too remote, which concerns itself with whether, even if the damages were caused by the breach, they arose in the usual course of things or were otherwise within the contemplation of the parties. This is followed then by the idea of restrictions on the recovery of damages: whether the damages could have been avoided by appropriate mitigation, and contributory negligence.

Reg Glass Pty Ltd v Rivers Locking Systems Pty Ltd (1968) 120 CLR 516

Facts and issues

The defendant breached a contract to supply a security door by installing a door not fit for its purpose. The plaintiff's premises were burgled. The relevant question was whether the fact of the door's unfitness for purpose caused the plaintiff's loss and if the defendant was thereby liable for that loss.

Decision

Per Barwick CJ, McTiernan and Menzies JJ at 523:

> It is true that it cannot be predicated that a door complying with the warranty would have prevented the thieves from breaking into the shop but once breach of warranty is established, and it appears that the actual entry made was due to the breach of warranty, we think that the loss suffered from the entry is prima facie the measure of damages for breach of warranty. This involves two steps. First that the loss suffered resulted from the breach, and secondly that the loss suffered was, when the contract was made, reasonably foreseeable as likely to result from such a breach. His Honour's affirmative finding as to both these matters cannot, we think, be disturbed.

Lexmead (Basingstoke) Ltd v Lewis [1982] AC 225

Facts and issues

The plaintiff had bought a towing hitch from the defendant which, in breach of contract, had a design defect causing it to break. After it broke, the plaintiff continued to use it. A serious accident occurred. The plaintiff claimed damages for breach of contract.

Decision

Per Lord Diplock at 1192:

> The Court of Appeal reasoned that, since there was no break in the chain of causation between negligence of the manufacturers, which consisted in the defective design of the coupling, and the plaintiff's damage, there could be no such break between the dealers' breach of warranty, which likewise consisted in the defective design of the coupling, and the farmer's loss occasioned by his share of the liability for the plaintiff's damage. With respect, this reasoning was erroneous. The farmer's liability arose not from the defective design of the coupling but from his own negligence in failing, when he knew that the coupling was damaged, to have it repaired or to ascertain if it was still safe to use. The issue of causation, therefore, on which the farmer's claim against the dealers depended was whether *his* negligence resulted directly and naturally, in the ordinary course of events, from the dealers' breach of warranty. Manifestly it did not.

Alexander v Cambridge Credit Corporation Ltd (1987) 9 NSWLR 310

Facts and issues

Cambridge Credit's liquidator sued its auditor in relation to the auditor's failure to qualify the company's balance sheet. Had this breach not occurred, the company would have been placed into receivership. The auditors, during the next three years, repeated the breach. Three years later, the company went into receivership. Then liquidator relied on the original breach, seeking damages for the losses suffered in those three years. It was alleged that, as a result of that failure, the company's debts soared. It was argued that those losses were solely brought about by the federal government's budgetary measures. The following extract addresses the Court's resolution of the question of causation.

Decision

Per McHugh J at 350:

> Since the act or omission of a person will only be one of the set of conditions or relations necessary and sufficient to produce the result to which legal liability attaches, a choice has been forced upon the law. ... Hence in the law of contract, it is sufficient that the breach 'causally contributed' to the loss.
>
> [351] Legal cause was to be determined by asking whether the breach was the dominant or real and efficient cause of the damage. However, I am of the opinion that, leaving aside the question of the intervention of a new act — the *novus actus interveniens*, the issue of causation is to be resolved in general by simply applying the 'but for' test in a practical commonsense way. I say in general because in the case of damage caused by the simultaneous operation of two separate and independent events each of which alone was sufficient to cause the damage, the 'but for' test is plainly inadequate. And there may be other cases where the rationale of the 'but for' rule may require a more elaborate formulation to be applied to the facts of those cases. Rules relating to causation and remoteness are to be liberally construed and not applied so rigidly as to cause injustice:
>
> [352] A material contribution to damage exists when the contribution is not de minimis. Thus a breach materially contributes to the damage although its responsibility for the damage is only 10 per centum: cf *Podrebersek v Australian Iron and Steel Pty. Ltd.* and *Bankstown Foundry Pty Ltd. v Braistina.* Accordingly, there is no conflict between the 'material contribution' requirement and the application of the 'but for' test in a practical, commonsense manner as the exclusive test of causation.
>
> So far as the law of tort is concerned, the 'but for' test must be taken in this Court to be the leading and, in all but exceptional cases, the exclusive test of causation. And I can see no reason why the same test should not be applied in contract.
>
> ... In the law of tort it is well-established that it is sufficient that the wrongful act or omission of the defendant is *a* material cause of the plaintiff's injury or damage. In principle the same rule must apply in the law of contract unless the terms of the contract require the sole or dominant cause to be determined
>
> [358] ... to establish a causal connection between a breach of contract and the damage which the plaintiff has suffered, he needs only to show that the breach was a cause of the loss. This is to be decided by the application of commonsense principles. In general, the application of the 'but for' test will be sufficient to prove the necessary causal connection. But that test is only a guide. The ultimate question is whether, as a matter of commonsense, the relevant act or omission was a cause.

> In my opinion Cambridge failed to prove that the breach of contract by the auditors in 1971 was a cause of the loss of $145,000,000 which it suffered.
>
> ... whatever causal significance the certificates of the auditors in 1971 may have had in keeping the company in trade, their effect was well and truly spent by 1973.
>
> [361] Notwithstanding that a defendant's act or omission has a causal connection with the damage of the person aggrieved, no liability arises if an independent intervening act or event in conjunction with the defendant's act or omission has brought about the plaintiff's damage and the intervening act or event can be treated in a practical sense as the sole cause of the damage. In this case the auditors contended that in a practical sense the credit squeeze was the sole cause of Cambridge's loss.
>
> It is well-established that, in contract as in tort, the intervening act, sufficient to constitute a *novus actus interveniens* and break the chain of causation, can be the act of a third party
>
> If, contrary to my view, the breach of contract by the auditors in 1971 was a cause of the loss of $145,000,000 by Cambridge the collapse of the real estate market, as the result of the policies of the then Australian government constituted a *novus actus interveniens* which in point of law broke the causal connection. Strictly speaking, it may be more correct to regard the *novus actus interveniens* as consisting of a package of the following factors [these being contributed to or caused by the Federal Government's budgetary measures] ...
>
> [362] So if, contrary to my view, there was a causal connection between the breach of contract and the loss of $145,000,000, then, by reason of the *novus actus interveniens*, the auditors are not responsible for that loss. The package of factors, together with the investment and borrowing decisions of the directors of Cambridge after 1971, were, in a practical sense, the sole cause of the loss ...

Hadley v Baxendale (1854) 156 ER 145

Facts and issues

The defendant had contracted to deliver the plaintiff's broken camshaft of its flour mill to Greenwich, to be used as a model to recast a replacement. In breach, the delivery was delayed, and as a result the plaintiff's mill was idle resulting in a loss of profits. The question here concerned the extent to which the plaintiff was entitled to recover its lost profits as damages for breach of contract. The case is the seminal case dealing with remoteness of damage in contract. Whilst Alderson B's decision below is expressed as a single test, its application depends on the degree of relevant knowledge. Under the first limb, damages are recoverable naturally from the breach; and under the second limb, damages are recoverable from special circumstances known to the defendant, as the probable result of the breach of the contract.

Decision

Per Alderson B at 151:

> Now we think the proper rule in such a case as the present is this: — Where two parties have made a contract which one of them bas broken, the damages which the other party ought to receive in respect of such breach of contract should be such as may fairly and reasonably be considered either arising naturally, i.e., according to the usual course of things, from such breach of contract itself, or such as may reasonably be supposed to have been in the

contemplation of both parties, at the time they made the contract, as the probable result of the breach of it. Now, if the special circumstances under winch the contract was actually made were communicated by the plaintiffs to the defendants, and thus known to both parties, the damages resulting from the breach of such a contract, which they would reasonably contemplate, would be the amount of injury which would ordinarily follow from a breach of contract under these special circumstances so known and communicated. But, on the other hand, if these special circumstances were wholly unknown to the party breaking the contract, he, at the most, could only be supposed to have had in his contemplation the amount of injury which would arise generally, and in the great multitude of cases not affected by any special circumstances, from such a breach of contract.

Commonwealth v Amann Aviation Pty Ltd (1991) 174 CLR 64

Facts and issues

The fundamental facts and issues in the case are set out at **23.2**. It was argued that the performance of the contract by Amann would have placed it in an advantageous position to secure a renewal of the contract, a commercial benefit, and that its losses should include compensation for the loss of the prospect of renewing the contract.

Decision

On the question of whether the rule in Hadley was, in truth, a two-limbed rule, per Mason CJ and Dawson J at 91:

> However, the rule that the defendant is not liable in damages for not doing that which he or she has not promised to do is necessarily subject to the rule in Hadley v. Baxendale. According to Alderson B.'s renowned formulation, the plaintiff is entitled to recover such damages as arise naturally, that is, according to the usual course of things, from the breach, or such as may reasonably be supposed to have been in the contemplation of both parties at [92] the time they made the contract as the probable result of the breach. It is now accepted that this is the statement of a single principle and that its application may depend on the degree of relevant knowledge possessed by the defendant in the particular case.
>
> [...]
>
> [In the present case] the application of the rule in *Hadley v. Baxendale* turns not on the degree of knowledge possessed by the defendant but on what may reasonably be supposed to have been in the contemplation of the parties as the probable result of the breach.

Victoria Laundry (Windsor) Ltd v Newman Industries Ltd [1949] 2 KB 528

Facts and issues

By a contract between the plaintiff and defendant, the defendant agreed to supply a boiler for its dyeing and dry cleaning business. Delivery was delayed for a significant period of time. The plaintiff sought damages for the recovery of profits lost as a result of not having the boiler delivered on time; these included not only the profits for its existing business but from a particular, lucrative contract as well.

Decision

Per Asquith J at 533:

> Seeing that the issue is as to the measure of recoverable damages and the application of the rules in *Hadley v Baxendale*, it is important to inquire what information the defendants possessed at the time when the contract was made as to such matters as the time at which, and the purpose for which, the plaintiffs required the boiler. The defendants knew before and at the time of the contract that the plaintiffs were laundrymen and dyers and required the boiler for purposes of their business as such.
>
> [536] He [the trial judge] took the view that the loss of profit claimed was due to special circumstances, and, therefore, recoverable, if at all, only under the second rule in *Hadley v Baxendale*, and not recoverable in the present case because such special circumstances were not at the time of the contract communicated to the defendants...
>
> [539] (3) What was at that time reasonably foreseeable depends on the knowledge then possessed by the parties or, at all events, by the party who later commits the breach.
>
> (4) For this purpose, knowledge 'possessed' is of two kinds; one imputed, the other actual. Everyone, as a reasonable person, is taken to know the 'ordinary course of things' and consequently what loss is liable to result from a breach in that ordinary course. This is the subject-matter of the 'first rule' in in *Hadley v Baxendale,* but to this knowledge, which a contract-breaker is assumed to possess whether he actually possesses it or not, there may have to be added in a particular case knowledge which he actually possesses of special circumstances outside the 'ordinary course of things' of such a kind that a breach in those special circumstances would be liable to cause more loss. Such a case attracts the operation of the 'second rule' so as to make additional loss also recoverable.
>
> [540] (5) In order to make the contract-breaker liable under either rule it is not necessary that he should actually have asked himself what loss is liable to result from a breach.
>
> [...]
>
> [543] Reasonable persons in the shoes of the defendants must be taken to foresee, without any express intimation, that a laundry which, at a time when there was a famine of laundry facilities, was paying £2,000 odd for plant and intended at such a time to put such plant 'into use' immediately, would be likely to suffer in pocket from five months' delay in delivery of the plant in question, whether they intended by means of it to extend their business, or merely to maintain it, or to reduce a loss; *(c)* the 'circumstance' that the plaintiffs had the assured expectation of special contracts, which they could only fulfil by securing punctual delivery of the boiler. Here, no doubt, the learned judge had in mind the particularly lucrative dyeing contracts to which the plaintiffs looked forward and which they mention in para 10 of the statement of claim. We agree that in order that the plaintiffs should recover specifically and as such the profits expected on these contracts, the defendants would have had to know, at the time of their agreement with the plaintiffs, of the prospect and terms of such contracts. We also agree that they did not, in fact, know these things. It does not, however, follow that the plaintiffs are precluded from recovering some general (and perhaps conjectural) sum for loss of business in respect of dyeing contracts to be reasonably expected any more than in respect of laundering contracts to be reasonably expected.

H Parsons (Livestock) Ltd v Uttley Ingham & Co Ltd [1978] QB 791

Facts and issues

The plaintiff, a pig farmer, bought a food storage hopper from the defendant to store pig nuts. In breach of contractual warranties of fitness for purpose, the defendant failed to unseal the ventilator with the result that nuts dispensed were mouldy, causing the outbreak of infection, killing a number of pigs. One issue was the extent of the defendant's knowledge of the foreseeability of damage.

Decision

Per Scarman LJ at 812:

> . . . I think the judge was making the approach which, according to Lord Reid, is the correct one. He was saying, in effect, that the parties to this contract must have appreciated that, if, as happened in the event, the hopper, unventilated, proved not to be suitable for the storage of pig nuts to be fed to the plaintiffs' pigs, it was not unlikely, there was a serious possibility, that the pigs would become ill. The judge put it in this way:
>
>> The *natural* result of feeding toxic food to animals is damage to their health and maybe death, which is what occurred, albeit from a hitherto unknown disease and to particularly susceptible animals. There was therefore no need to invoke the question of *reasonable* contemplation in order to make the defendants liable. [Emphasis added.]
>
> [. . .]
>
> [813] I would agree with *McGregor on Damages*, 13th ed. (1972), pp. 131–132 that
>
>> . . . in contract as in tort, it should suffice that, if physical injury or damage is within the contemplation of the parties, recovery is not to be limited because the degree of physical injury or damage could not have been anticipated.
>
> This is so, in my judgment, not because there is, or ought to be, a specific rule of law governing cases of physical injury but because it would be absurd to regulate damages in such cases on the necessity of supposing the parties had a prophetic foresight as to the exact nature of the injury that does in fact arise. It is enough if on the hypothesis predicated physical injury must have been a serious possibility.
>
> As I read the judgment under appeal, this was how the judge, whose handling of the issues at trial was such that none save one survives for our consideration, reached this decision. In my judgment, he was right, on the facts as found, to apply the first rule in *Hadley v Baxendale* . . .

British Westinghouse Electric and Manufacturing Co Ltd v Underground Electric Railways Co of London Ltd [1912] AC 673

Facts and issues

British Westinghouse ('BW') sold a number of turbines to Underground Electric Railways Company of London ('UERC') which, contrary to contract specifications, did not perform as specified. BW used the turbines for a while then replaced them with more efficient ones. BW claimed damages for breach of contract calculated on the basis of the continued use of the defective turbines for their estimated lifespan.

Decision

Per Viscount Haldane at 689:

> The fundamental basis [for the assessment of damages for breach of contract] is thus compensation for pecuniary loss naturally flowing from the breech; but this first principle is qualified by a second, which imposes on a plaintiff the duty of taking all reasonable steps to mitigate the loss consequent on the breach, and debars hire from claiming in respect of any part of the damage which is due to his neglect to take such steps.
>
> ... As James LJ indicates, this second principle does not, impose on the plaintiff an obligation to take any step which a reasonable and prudent men would not ordinarily take in the course of his business. But when, in the course of his business, he has taken action arising out of the transaction, which action has diminished his loss, the effect in actual diminution of the loss which ice has suffered may be taken into account, even though there was no duty on him to act.
>
> [691] I think that the principle which applies here is that which makes it right for the jury or arbitrator to look at what actually happened, and to balance loss and gain. The transaction was not res inter alios acta, but one in which the person whose contract was broken took a reasonable and prudent course arising quite naturally out of the circumstances in which he was placed by the breach. Apart from the breach of contract, the lapse of time had rendered the appellants' machines obsolete, and men of business would be doing the only thing which they could properly do in replacing them with new and up-to-date machines ...

His Lordship took the view that the increased efficiency of the new turbines brought about a saving of cost which had to be taken into account in assessing damages. The end result was that UERC could not recover anything for the period after the acquisition of the new machines.

Simonious Vischer & Co v Holt & Thompson [1979] 2 NSWLR 322

Facts and issues

The plaintiff, as a result of the defendant's breach of contract, was left with a number of speculative contracts. It could have, but did not, close out the contracts, but held on to them in the hope that things would improve. The hope was in vain, and the question was whether the defendant was liable in damages for the increased loss resulting from the plaintiff's decision.

Decision

Per Samuels JA at 355:

> ... Sheppard J. applied the well-known dictum of Lord Macmillan in *Banco de Portugal v. Waterlow & Sons Ltd.* His Lordship said:
>
> > Where the sufferer from a breach of contract finds himself in consequence of that breach placed in a position of embarrassment the measures which he may be driven to adopt in order to extricate himself ought not to be weighed in nice scales at the instance of the party whose breach of contract has occasioned the difficulty. It is often easy after an emergency has passed to criticize the steps which have been taken to meet it, but such criticism does not come well from those who have themselves created the emergency. The law is satisfied if the party placed in a difficult situation

> by reason of the breach of a duty owed to him has acted reasonably in the adoption of remedial measures, and he will not be held disentitled to recover the cost of such measures merely because the party in breach can suggest that other measures less burdensome to him might have been taken.
>
> I think that that statement has considerable point in this case.
>
> [356] It would seem to follow that, once the plaintiffs' conduct is found to have been reasonable, the defendants are bound to make good the loss thereby sustained.

Upon exhaustively analysing the facts, his Honour did find the plaintiff's conduct to be reasonable, with the result that the defendants were ordered to make good the additional losses.

Burns v MAN Automotive (Australia) Pty Ltd (1986) 161 CLR 653

Facts and issues

The plaintiff, a road haulier, acquired a truck from the defendant by hire purchase. The defendant warranted that its engine had been fully reconditioned. This was not the case, and the engine's faults caused considerable disruption to the buyer's business. A year after the purchase, the plaintiff became aware that the engine had not been fully reconditioned so that it could not be used on interstate routes. He could not afford the $8,000 cost of refurbishing it. The plaintiff was forced to limit his business to the less profitable local haulage business until the end of 1979, when the engine completely broke down, and the vehicle was repossessed by the hire purchase company. The plaintiff claimed loss of profits as damages. Remoteness and mitigation were both in issue as the hire purchase agreement could have been terminated and the plaintiff could have limited his loss of profit to the period before he became aware that the engine had not been reconditioned.

Decision

On the specific question of whether the plaintiff had mitigated his loss, per Gibbs CJ at 658:

> . . . this is a case in which it is necessary to consider whether the appellant did what he could to mitigate the damage caused by the breach of warranty.
>
> [After determining that the losses were not too remote] . . . however, the appellant was bound to take all reasonable steps to mitigate the loss, and one course open to him to mitigate the damage, if he could have afforded to take it, was to have the engine reconditioned or to buy another to replace it. However, his impecuniosity prevented him from taking that course. The question arises whether it should be held that the appellant is [659] debarred from claiming such part of the damages as is attributable to his failure to take the necessary steps in mitigation, when he was unable to take those steps because of his lack of means.
>
> That question must be answered in the negative . . .
>
> . . . a plaintiff's duty to mitigate his damage does not require him to do what is unreasonable and it would seem unjust to prevent a plaintiff from recovering in full damages caused by a breach of contract simply because he lacked the means to avert the consequences of the breach. There are, in the present case, the additional features that the financial difficulties of the appellant were largely brought about by the actions of the respondent in supplying him with a defective engine and refusing properly to rectify the defects, although the respondent should have known that the appellant lacked the financial resources that would have enabled him to pay to

have the engine reconditioned. I respectfully agree with the statement of Megaw LJ in *Dodd Properties v Canterbury City Council*:

> A plaintiff who is under a duty to mitigate is not obliged, in order to reduce the damages, to do that which he cannot afford to do: particularly where, as here, the plaintiffs' 'financial stringency', so far as it was relevant at all, arose, as a matter of common sense, if not as a matter of law, solely as a consequence of the defendants' wrongdoing.

[. . .]

[660] There are other cases that support the view that a defendant cannot rely on the plaintiff's failure to mitigate the consequences of the defendant's wrongful act when that wrongful act itself made it impossible for the plaintiff to take the necessary steps in mitigation: see *Fox* v Wood (1981) 35 ALR 607; 148 CLR 438 at 445–6; *Archer v Brown* [1985] QB 401 at 417–18 and *Freedhoff v Pomalift Industries Ltd* (1970) 13 DLR (3d) 523 at 532–3.

For these reasons it appears to me that the appellant is entitled to recover whatever damage it has been proved that he suffered by way of loss of profits that would otherwise have been earned during the four years of the effective life of the motor.

However, there is another reason why the appellant did not do all that he reasonably could to mitigate his damage. It was not reasonable for him to carry on his business with the defective prime mover, once he knew that he was operating at a loss and should have known that he had no prospect of making a profit. As Connolly J pointed out, this was not a case of a purchaser locked into a business; the appellant was under no compulsion to go on losing money. In the calculation of damages it was not wrong to hold that the respondent should not be charged with actual losses incurred by the appellant after June 1978 . . . [This was when the condition of the engine had been discovered.]

23.3.1 Contributory negligence

The effect of *Astley v Austrust Ltd*[6] was that apportionment legislation would not apply to apportion liability in contract if there was breach of a contractual and tortious duty; the apportionment in tort would thus be irrelevant. The effect of *Astley* was explicitly negated by revised apportionment legislation, such as the *Law Reform (Miscellaneous Provisions) Act 1965* (NSW) s 9.[7]

Law Reform (Miscellaneous Provisions) Act 1965 (NSW) s 9

9 Apportionment of liability in cases of contributory negligence

(1) If a person (the '**claimant**') suffers damage as the result partly of the claimant's failure to take reasonable care ('**contributory negligence**') and partly of the wrong of any other person:

(a) a claim in respect of the damage is not defeated by reason of the contributory negligence of the claimant, and

6 (1999) 197 CLR 1.

7 Legislation to similar effect is in force in all the other States and Territories: *Miscellaneous Provisions Act* (NT) ss 15–16; *Civil Law (Wrongs) Act 2002* (ACT) s 102; *Wrongs Act 1958 (Vic)* s 26; *Law Reform (Contributory Negligence and Tortfeasors' Contribution) Act 1947* (WA) ss 3A–4.

(b) the damages recoverable in respect of the wrong are to be reduced to such extent as the court thinks just and equitable having regard to the claimant's share in the responsibility for the damage.

[. . .]

Indresco Pty Ltd v Hawker Noyes Equipment Pty Ltd [1999] WASCA 60

Facts and issues

The third party claimed against the fourth party to be indemnified against the defendant's claim on the grounds that the fourth party had, in breach of express warranties, supplied machinery that was not of merchantable quality or fit for its purpose. The primary issue was whether, having made a claim only in contract and not in tort, there could be recourse to apportionment legislation.

Decision

Per Kennedy J at [7]:

> The amendments added a claim against the appellant for negligently causing economic loss. There is no plea that, if the respondent is liable to the defendant, then it is entitled to an indemnity or to contribution from the appellant on the footing that, as between them, there exists a common liability in tort. If that were to be established, the fact that the claim against the respondent was based solely in contract would not be a bar to recovery. A claim for an indemnity or for contribution should not fail merely for the reason that a plaintiff (or third party) has elected to sue in contract, notwithstanding that he could just as easily have sued in tort. In my opinion, this conclusion is supported by the more recent authorities . . .
>
> [. . .]
>
> [9] In *Macpherson's case*, [*Macpherson v Prunty and Associates* [1983] VR 573] the plaintiffs, who were not parties to the appeal, had made claims in both contract and tort against two firms of solicitors. The trial Judge found that the appellant solicitors were liable to
>
>> the plaintiffs only in contract and not in tort, and for that reason this could not have recourse to the contributory negligence legislation. The majority of the court, Lush and Beach JJ, held that the appellants were entitled to a contribution order against the other firm of solicitors. It was pointed out by Lush J, however, at 582, that the contractual duty in that case was co-extensive with any duty which the law might have implied independently of contract.
>
> [10] In the *Dairy Containers Ltd* case, the decision of the New Zealand Court of Appeal in *McLaren Maycroft & Co v Fletcher Development Co Ltd* [1973] 2 NZLR 100, having regard to the subsequent decision of the House of Lords in *Henderson v Merrett Syndicates Ltd* [1994] 2 AC 145, was not followed, and Thomas J held that a wrongdoer sued in contract may be also sued in tort. He was prepared to hold that the phrase 'tortfeasor liable in respect of that damage' includes a wrongdoer who is actually liable in tort, although that wrongdoer may have been sued and held liable only in contract. See also *Rap Industries Pty Ltd v Royal Insurance Australia Ltd* (1988) 5 ANZ Insurance Cases 60-876 and *AWA Ltd v Daniels trading as Deloitte Haskins & Sells* (1992) 7 ACSR 759.

Hungerfords v Walker (1989) 171 CLR 125

Facts and issues

As a result of accountants' negligence, their clients overpaid their tax. The clients, who operated their business using borrowed money, sued in negligence and breach of contract. Their claim for compensation included the loss of the use of money.

Decision

Per Mason CJ and Wilson J at 142:

> If a plaintiff sustains loss or damage in relation to money which he has paid out or forgone, why is he not entitled to recover damages for loss of the use of money when the loss or damage sustained was reasonably foreseeable as liable to result from the relevant breach of contract or tort? After all, that is the fundamental rule governing the recovery of damages, according to the first limb in *Hadley v. Baxendale Ltd.* (see *Victoria Laundry (Windsor) Ltd. v. Newman Industries Ltd.*). The object of the second limb in *Hadley v. Baxendale* was to include loss arising from special circumstances of which the defendant had actual knowledge when that loss does not fall within the first limb because it does not arise from 'the ordinary course of things' of which the defendant has imputed knowledge: see *Victoria Laundry.*
>
> If the distinction between the two limbs is to be rigorously applied in claims for damages for loss of the use of money, a plaintiff who actually incurs the expense of interest on borrowed money to replace money paid away or withheld from him will be entitled to recover that cost, so long as the defendant was aware of the special circumstances, but not otherwise. The expense must fall within the second limb of *Hadley v. Baxendale* in order to be compensable. It cannot fall within the first limb because the defendant cannot be fixed with imputed knowledge of the plaintiff's financial situation and of his need to incur expense by borrowing money ...
>
> [143] ... the fundamental principle [is] that a plaintiff is entitled to restitutio in integrum. According to that principle, the plaintiff is entitled to full compensation for the loss which he sustains in consequence of the defendant's wrong, subject to the rules as to remoteness of damage and to the plaintiff's duty to mitigate his loss. In principle he should be awarded the compensation which would restore him to the position he would have been in but for the defendant's breach of contract or negligence.
>
> [...]
>
> The requirement of foreseeability is no obstacle to the award of damages, calculated by reference to the appropriate interest rates, for loss of the use of money. Opportunity cost, more so than incurred expense, is a plainly foreseeable loss because, according to common understanding, it represents the market price of obtaining money. But, even in the case of incurred expense, it is at least strongly arguable that a plaintiff's loss or damage represented by this expense is not too remote on the score of foreseeability. In truth, it is an expense which represents loss or damage flowing [144] naturally and directly from the defendant's wrongful act or omission, particularly when that act or omission results in the withholding of money from a plaintiff or causes the plaintiff to pay away money ...
>
> [...]
>
> Incurred expense and opportunity cost arising from paying money away or the withholding of moneys due to the defendant's wrong ... are pecuniary losses suffered by the plaintiff as a result of the defendant's wrong and therefore constitute an integral element of the loss for which he is entitled to be compensated by an award of damages. ...

> [149] On this footing the Full Court was correct in awarding damages for the added cost of funding the business with borrowed money as a result of the loss of the use of money overpaid in tax. The award of interest was of necessity compound interest. Simple interest would not reflect accurately the extent of the respondents' loss.

Hardie v Shadbolt [2004] WASCA 175

Facts and issues

The defendants breached various contracts of loan. The relevant question here concerned the extent to which the plaintiffs could recover damages, based on the lost opportunity to invest and make greater profits.

Decision

Per Roberts-Smith J at [57]:

> In their statements of claim the respondents claimed in the alternative damages for breach of the Agreement, quantified as the amount due on the termination date (comprising the amount of the principal plus the specific amount of interest to that date), plus loss of opportunity to use the moneys comprising the principal outstanding from time to time to their commercial advantage, being an amount equivalent to interest earned on the outstanding moneys at the rate of 18 per cent per annum compounded at four monthly rests.
>
> [58] If established, such a claim may be allowed under the principle of *Hungerfords v Walker* (1989) 171 CLR 125, per Mason CJ and Wilson J at 144-146 and Brennan and Deane JJ at 152.

Ultimately, due to the vagueness of the evidence concerning how the respondents/plaintiffs had proposed to apply those moneys, the appeal was allowed and the damages awarded below reduced to reflect the statutory rate of interest only.

QUESTIONS

(1) Is the relevant contribution legislation in your view a beneficial development for plaintiffs in the case of a breach of contract or not?

(2) What was the primary difficulty faced by the plaintiff in *Cambridge Credit*?

(3) How do the courts view the 'obligation' to mitigate? Would you regard the duty as a high or stringent one?

23.4 International perspectives

23.4.1 *CISG*

Under the *CISG*, damages are available as a remedy for loss due to breach of contract, and are awarded pursuant to the 'compensation' principle.[8] There is no separate equitable jurisdiction,

8 CISG Advisory Council, 'Opinion No 6, Calculation of Damages under CISG Article 74', Rapporteur: Prof. John Y. Gotanda.

and therefore the question of damages in lieu of specific performance simply does not arise. The main provision on damages is art 74. Where relevant, damages might alternatively be calculated, according to the value of an actual or hypothetical substitute transaction: see arts 75 and 76 *CISG*. The limitation on damages is primarily the foreseeability threshold, which is slightly lower than that of the common law.[9] Foreseeability in art 74 refers to foreseeability of the damage, not the breach, and is an objective standard, assessed at the time of conclusion of the contract. Loss of profits are recoverable. Loss of a chance, although controversial, is considered available under art 74.[10] The aggrieved party is under a duty to mitigate their loss: art 77 *CISG*. See further **25.9.6**.

23.4.2 UNIDROIT Principles

Damages arise pursuant to art 7.4.1 of the UNIDROIT Principles to compensate for harm due to non-performance, including for physical suffering and emotional distress. The test is reasonable foreseeability when the contract was concluded: art 7.4.4 UNIDROIT Principles. A reasonable degree of certainty is required, and loss of chance is recoverable: art 7.4.3 UNIDROIT Principles. Mitigation duties also apply pursuant to art 7.4.8.

23.5 Review

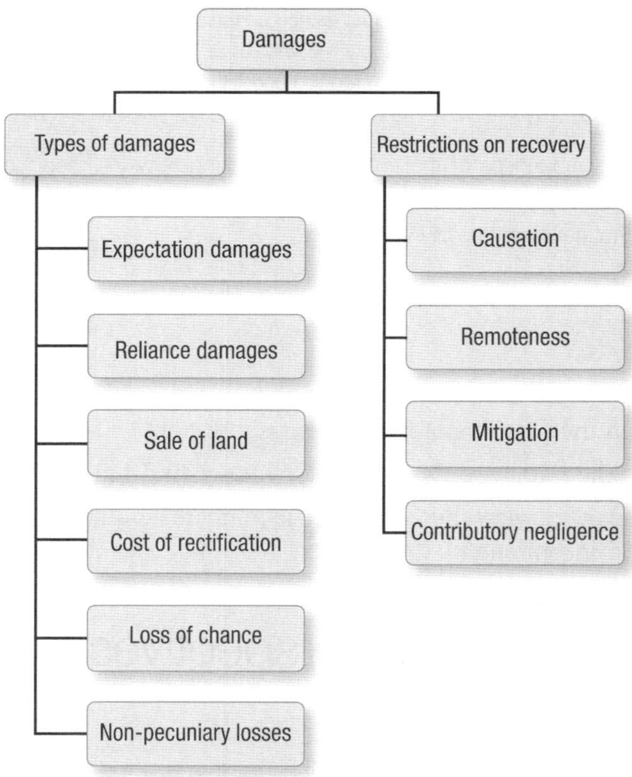

9 Ingeborg Schwenzer, in I. Schwenzer (ed), *Schlechtriem & Schwenzer: Commentary on the Convention on International Sale of Goods (CISG)* (Oxford Univeristy Press, 4th ed, 2016) art 74, para 48.
10 Schwenzer (n 67) art 74, para 39.

TIPS FOR APPLYING THE LAW IN PRACTICE

- One often-stated principle of damages for breach of contract is to put the party in the same position as if the contract had been performed, so far as money can do it: *Robinson v Harman.*
- The governing principle in determining whether damages, in the form of the cost of borrowing money, would be recoverable is whether those losses fell within the scope of remoteness as set out in *Hadley v Baxendale*.

PROBLEM QUESTIONS

(1) Veronica purchases from Janice what she believed to be a genuine branded handbag—let's call this 'the Handbag'—for $150.

It is, in fact, a fake—albeit a very high quality fake. A handbag of the same quality as the (fake) handbag that Veronica had acquired would have cost a purchaser $200 to acquire.

Assume that by selling Veronica the Handbag that was an imitation, Janice is in breach of an express term of the contract by failing to deliver to Veronica a handbag that complied with the description thereunder, namely that of a genuine branded handbag.

Discuss the quantum of damages for breach of contract should Veronica be successful in an action for breach of contract against Janice based on the fundamental principles in *Robinson v Harman.*

(2) Phil is under a contract to deliver barley to John on Tuesday 23 March. The barley is riddled with disease and entirely unsuitable for supply. Phil is in breach of express and implied terms of merchantable quality and fitness for purpose and the goods unsaleable in that condition. There is a sudden and severe storm which strikes on Monday 22 March. There is hail, rain and local flooding, as a result of which the truck is immersed in floodwater and the entire contents are totally destroyed and lost. The barley is never delivered and, as a consequence, John has suffered loss and damage. Discuss Phil's liability in breach of contract. Confine your answer to a discussion of causation only.

RESEARCH QUESTIONS

(1) Having regard to the facts and arguments set out in *Commonwealth v Amann Aviation Pty Ltd* (1991) 174 CLR 64, discuss the difficulties which would have been faced in recovering expectation damages, and why, in such a case, it might have been more beneficial to pursue reliance damages.

(2) In *Alexander v Cambridge Credit*, McHugh J held that even if the breach of contract by the auditors was a cause of the loss suffered by Cambridge, the breach by the auditors was not a cause of the loss of $145,000,000. Demonstrating your understanding of McHugh J's reasoning, explain why this was so.

24

RESTITUTIONARY REMEDIES

24.1 Overview

The overarching concept governing *restitution* is that it allows the innocent party to recover the gains made by the other at their expense.

Broadly, conceptually at least, the idea of restitution invokes the idea of putting the innocent party in the position they were in before their rights were infracted, and thereby differs from breach of contract or tort, which confers a remedy for some wrong committed. The former, the focus of this chapter, is practically axiomatic from the topic descriptions themselves. The idea, say, of 'mistaken payments' thereby invokes the idea that someone who has paid another by mistake might have grounds to recover their payments.

This chapter, save for the last module 'The rise and fall of unjust enrichment in Australia', follows those contours in exploring the various heads of restitution.

'Unjust enrichment', the right to payment for executed consideration under an unenforceable contract, has at times been treated as a significant category of restitution, and sometimes treated as a taxonomic pigeonhole. The extent to which this reflects the present Australian position or whether the entitlement to such moneys in truth is invoked as a result of the operation of other discrete doctrines, is explored in the last module, 'The rise and fall of unjust enrichment in Australia'.

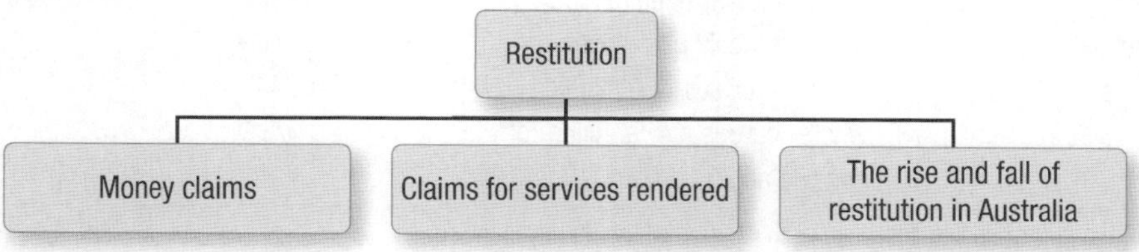

24.2 Money claims

Concept	Short explanation	Relevant authorities	*Principles* text*
Moneys had and received	The recovery of moneys where the law regards it as unjust for it to be retained	*Equuscorp Pty Ltd Haxton* (2012) 246 CLR 498	Chapter 24: 24.02
Mistaken payments	The recovery of mistaken payments does not depend on whether the mistake was of law or fact but simply whether the mistake was fundamental and caused the payment	*David Securities Pty Ltd v Commonwealth Bank of Australia* (1992) 175 CLR 353	Chapter 24: 24.03
Payments under contracts that are	There is no all-embracing theory of restitutionary rights; rather a total	*Roxborough v Rothmans of Pall Mall Australia*	Chapter 24: 24.04

(cont.)

Concept	Short explanation	Relevant authorities	*Principles* text*
void, voidable or unenforceable	failure of consideration is required The law might preclude recovery under principles of unjust enrichment even under a void contract if justice demands Payment under a contract that is unenforceable for lack of formality is recoverable The right to recovery of moneys as moneys had and received paid under an illegal contract depends on the construction and scheme of the statute contravened	*Ltd* (2001) 208 CLR 516 *Ford v Perpetual Trustees Victoria Ltd* (2009) 75 NSWLR 42 *Freedom v A.H.R. Constructions Pty Ltd* [1987] 1 Qd R 59 *Equuscorp Pty Ltd Haxton* (2012) 246 CLR 498	
Payments when a contract is discharged	When a contract is terminated or frustrated, payments already made can only be recovered under principles of restitution where there is a total failure of consideration	*Baltic Shipping Co v Dillon ('Mikhail Lermontov')* (1993) 176 CLR 344	Chapter 24: 24.05

* Consult the corresponding section(s) of the *Principles* text for more detail.

The primary area for the application of restitutionary principles relates, obviously, to the recovery of moneys. The treatment in this section covers the following categories which broadly increase in sophistication and nuance: *moneys had and received,* which is the remedy for the recovery of the value of money paid, rather than the physical currency; *mistaken payments,* eponymously a reference to the recovery of moneys paid by mistake where the mistake *caused* the payment; *payments under contracts that are void, voidable and unenforceable,* which attracts the idea that the availability of relief depends on whether justice is served by the retention of the money; *payments when a contract is discharged*, where a contract has been discharged, whether for breach or by frustration or some other reason, certain payments can be recovered. This module deals with the effect of a total failure of consideration on the recovery of payments, including the factors which govern the question of whether in truth there has been a 'total failure of consideration'.

Equuscorp Pty Ltd v Haxton (2012) 246 CLR 498

Facts and issues

The appellant was the assignee of a lender of moneys, Rural; the respondents were borrowers. The loan agreements were illegal, the illegal purpose being an agricultural investment scheme without a registered prospectus. Note, broadly, the observations concerning the extent to which the purpose of the relevant statutory scheme impacted the recovery of restitution.

Decision

Per French CJ and Crennan and Kiefel JJ at 516:

> In *David Securities Pty Ltd v Commonwealth Bank of Australia*, this Court explained the part played by unjust enrichment in a claim for money had and received (in that case for recovery of a payment made under mistake of law). That explanation may be expressed, at a fairly high level of abstraction, as an approach to determining such claims. In summary:
>
> - recovery depends upon enrichment of the defendant by reason of one or more recognised classes of 'qualifying or vitiating' factors;
> - the category of case must involve a qualifying or vitiating factor such as mistake, duress, illegality or failure of consideration, by reason of which the enrichment of the defendant is treated by the law as unjust;
> - unjust enrichment so identified gives rise to a prima facie obligation to make restitution;
> - the prima facie liability can be displaced by circumstances which the law recognises would make an order for restitution unjust.
>
> Unjust enrichment therefore has a taxonomical function referring to categories of cases in which the law allows recovery by one person of a benefit retained by another. In that aspect, it does not found or reflect any 'all-embracing theory of restitutionary rights and remedies'[1]. It does not, however, exclude the emergence of novel occasions of unjust enrichment supporting claims for restitutionary relief.

On the specific question of whether those moneys were recoverable in the light of the illegality of the contract, per French CJ and Crennan and Kiefel JJ at 522:

> The loan agreements were an integral part of the schemes and in so far as they involved the issue of invitations and offers to investors to take up prescribed interests without the benefit of the protections required by the Code, furthered that illegal purpose. As in the *Hurst* case, while not essential to the investments, the loans made the investments more attractive. Recovery from the investors [523] would have been recovery from persons whose protection was the object of the statutory scheme. The respondents were not in pari delicto with Rural. The failure of consideration invoked by Equuscorp was the product of Rural's own conduct in offering the loan agreements in furtherance of an illegal purpose. This is a clear case in which the coherence of the law, and the avoidance of stultification of the statutory purpose by the common law, lead to the conclusion that Rural did not have a right to claim recovery of money advanced under the loan agreements as money had and received. There was therefore no right to claim such relief available for assignment to Equuscorp.

1 *Roxborough v Rothmans of Pall Mall Australia Ltd* (2001) 208 CLR 516 544 [72] (Gummow J).

David Securities Pty Ltd v Commonwealth Bank of Australia (1992) 175 CLR 353

Facts and issues

The plaintiff had borrowed money from the bank and had repaid moneys to the bank pursuant to a clause that was invalid. It sought to recover those moneys from the bank on the basis of unjust enrichment. The case contains the seminal Australian treatment of the recovery of mistaken payments, and the rejection of the long-held principle that the mistake had to be of fact rather than of law, focusing instead on the question of whether the mistake caused the payment and that it was the fact of the 'mistake' that would make the enrichment unjust.

Decision

Per Mason CJ, Deane, Dawson, Toohey, Gaudron and McHugh JJ at 373:

> An important feature of the relevant judgments in these three cases is the emphasis placed on voluntariness or election by the plaintiff. The payment is voluntary or there is an election if the plaintiff chooses to make the payment even though he or she believes a particular law or contractual provision requiring the payment is, or may be, invalid, or is not concerned to query whether payment is legally required; he or she is prepared to assume the validity of the obligation, or is prepared to make the payment [374] irrespective of the validity or invalidity of the obligation, rather than contest the claim for payment. We use the term 'voluntary' therefore to refer to a payment made in satisfaction of an honest claim, rather than a payment not made under any form of compulsion or undue influence. If such qualifying, factual circumstances are considered relevant, the sweeping principle that money paid under a mistake of law is irrecoverable or even the Federal Court's modification of that principle to the effect that mistake of law does not on its own found an action for the recovery of money paid is broader and more preclusive than is necessary. As the authorities cited earlier in explanation of the term 'mistake of law' make clear, the concept includes cases of sheer ignorance as well as cases of positive but incorrect belief. To define 'mistake' as the supposition that a specific fact is true, as Parke B. did in *Kelly v Solari*, which was a mistake of fact case, leaves out of account many fact situations. A narrower principle, founded firmly on the policy that the law wishes to uphold bargains and enforce compromises freely entered into, would be more accurate and equitable.
>
> [. . .]
>
> The identification and acceptance of such a narrow principle is strongly supported by the difficulty and illogicality of seeking to draw a rigid distinction between cases of mistake of law and mistake of fact. The artificiality of this distinction and the numerous exceptions to it lie behind many of the calls for abolition of the traditional rule [that the recovery of money paid under a mistake of law was irrecoverable].
>
> [. . .]
>
> [378] So, the payer will be entitled prima facie to recover moneys paid under a mistake if it appears that the moneys were paid by the payer in the mistaken belief that he or she was under a legal obligation to pay the moneys or that the payee was legally entitled to payment of the moneys. Such a mistake would be causative of the payment.

Roxborough v Rothmans of Pall Mall Australia Ltd (2001) 208 CLR 516

Facts and issues

The plaintiffs bought cigarettes from the defendant, a wholesaler, and sought recovery of moneys paid to meet licence fees imposed under an Act that was found to be unconstitutional. The following extract is relevant to the finding there was not a total failure of consideration but a partial failure in respect of a severable consideration, namely the part paid for the licence fees, and the consequences of such.

Decision

Per Gummow J at 543:

> ... in *Baltic Shipping*, Mason CJ said that, in cases of money had and received, the retention of the money in question
>
> > is regarded, in the language of Lord Mansfield, as 'against conscience' or, in the modern terminology, as an unjust enrichment of the defendant because the condition upon which it was paid, namely, performance by the defendant may not have occurred.
>
> Nevertheless, reflection will demonstrate that the notion of unjust enrichment cannot be accepted as a modern synonym for a refusal 'against conscience' to pay the money in question.
>
> [544] ... practical experience, suggest[s] caution in judicial acceptance of any all-embracing theory of restitutionary rights and remedies founded upon a notion of 'unjust enrichment'. To the lawyer whose mind has been moulded by civilian influences, the theory may come first, and the source of the theory may be the writing of jurists not the decisions of judges. However, that is not the way in which a system based on case law develops; over time, general principle is derived from judicial decisions upon particular instances, not the other way around.
>
> [557] In the present case, there has been no failure in the performance by Rothmans of any promise it made. No question of repudiation by it of its contractual obligations arises ...
>
> ... Here, 'failure of consideration' identifies the failure to sustain itself of the state of affairs contemplated as a basis for the payments the appellants seek to recover.
>
> At this stage attention is required to the notion that the failure relied upon be 'total'. The general rule, exemplified in *Baltic Shipping*, is that where there has been a partial failure in performance of a contractual promise there is no right to recover back a proportionate part of the money paid on an action for money had and received ...
>
> [558] The parties contracted not only for the supply of the tobacco products but also, in the light of the provisions of s 41 of the Act, with respect to the renewal of the wholesaler's licence and the funding for that to take place. Whilst that is understood, the very form of the transactions indicates that the payments made by the appellants can be 'broken up'.

Ford v Perpetual Trustees Victoria Ltd (2009) 75 NSWLR 42

Facts and issues

The appellant suffered an intellectual disability, and was the borrower of moneys. Having found that the defence of non est factum had been established and that the loan agreement was thereby void, the question then turned to whether the respondent was entitled to the recovery of the loan moneys. Note the manner in which the court paid heed to the fact that the recipient was innocent and how the court rationalised why, under these circumstances, the lender should bear the risk.

Decision

Per Allsop P and Young JA at 64:

> We find no error in the primary judge's conclusion that the plea of non est factum was made out. On the facts found, we conclude that the plea was made out. The loan and mortgage were therefore not signed in law by Mr Ford and were void and of no effect against him . . .
>
> [. . .]
>
> The success of the plea of non est factum means that there was no signature. Thus, there was no relevant contract for the purposes of the *Contracts Review Act* . . .
>
> [66] The question arises whether, in the light of Perpetual's lack of knowledge of Mr Ford's disabilities and of his son's manipulation the Court should draw back from granting relief which would deprive Perpetual of the benefit of the contract and, in effect, of its property . . .
>
> [. . .]
>
> [68] It is plain, however, that Perpetual took no step to investigate the borrower. It propounded documents which contemplated a request (that was made here) that the loan be assessed without regard to documentary evidence of the borrower's income and financial position. Those facts are indisputable. No doubt there were sufficient commercial reasons for Perpetual to deal in this way. No criticism is to be levelled against Perpetual from these facts alone. They can, as indisputable facts, be taken into account, in the exercise of discretion as to whether to grant relief under s 7. They are, however, not necessary for our conclusion that relief would be given under s 7.
>
> Given the helpless position of Mr Ford, the plain injustice of the loan and mortgage contracts from his perspective for the reasons that we have given, we would make an order varying the contract of loan and mortgage to limit his liability to $24,857 plus interest. This conclusion is reinforced by the recognition that Perpetual took no steps whatsoever to ascertain the circumstances of the borrower.

Freedom v A.H.R. Constructions Pty Ltd [1987] 1 Qd R 59

Facts and issues

The plaintiff sought recovery of moneys paid on account of certain units to the defendant, a developer. No enforceable agreement ultimately materialised, among other reasons because the plaintiff herself did not have the wherewithal to complete performance. On the question of whether there was thus a total failure of consideration and she was thereby entitled to the return of her deposit the following brief extract from the judgment provides adequate explanation.

Decision

Per McPherson J at 64:

> It is convenient before considering other factual matters to recall some propositions of law relevant to the recovery of money paid on account of purchase price under a contract for the

sale of land that goes off before completion. For present purposes it is sufficient to repeat what I said on the subject in *Lexane Pty Ltd v. Highfern Pty Ltd*:

> The fundamental principle applicable to a vendor who rescinds for breach after receiving payment, wholly or in part, on account of the price is that 'he cannot have the land and its value too': *Laird v. Pim* (1841) 7 M. & W. 474, 478; 151 E.R. 852, 854, per Parke B. Hence money so paid by the purchaser is recoverable from the vendor. At law it is recoverable as money had and received upon [66] a total failure of consideration where the consideration for which it was paid is the conveyance or transfer that has not taken place: *McDonald v. Dennys Lascelles Ltd.* (1933) 48 CLR 457, 477–478, per Dixon J.; in equity it is recoverable by proceedings for restitution.

[69] Neither of the parties here now seeks directly to enforce the contract specifically. Their rights in this action rest on the common law. I have arrived at the conclusion that the parties did intend, from some time in late February 1983, to be bound by a contract for sale of unit 16C for a price of $140,000. The sums totalling $47,000 were paid in of that contract. The right, if any, of the plaintiff to recover that amount or part of it therefore depends on the principles to which I have referred in connection with deposits and other moneys paid on account of the purchase price under a contract of sale of land. Prima facie the plaintiff is entitled to recover her money unless it was intended to be a deposit liable to forfeiture in event of the contract going off by her default.

His Honour held that these principles applied to the present situation with the ultimate outcome that, upon finding that the payment was not a deposit and that there had been a total failure of consideration, the plaintiff was entitled to its recovery.

Baltic Shipping Co v Dillon ('Mikhail Lermontov') (1993) 176 CLR 344

Facts and issues

A passenger on a cruise vessel suffered injury when the vessel sank 10 days into a 14-day cruise. The question was whether she was entitled to a refund of the whole fare. Whilst the situation in the present day would be almost entirely governed by consumer protection legislation, the case remains as a seminal case for the enunciation of the more fundamental principles relating to restitution where there has not been a total, only partial, failure of consideration.

Decision

Per Mason CJ at 350:

> When, however, an innocent party seeks to recover money paid in advance under a contract in expectation of the entire performance by the contract-breaker of its obligations under the contract and the contract-breaker renders an incomplete performance, in general, the innocent party cannot recover unless there has been a total failure of consideration. If the incomplete performance results in the innocent party receiving and retaining any substantial part of the benefit expected under the contract, there will not be a total failure of consideration.
>
> In the context of the recovery of money paid on the footing that there has been a total failure of consideration, it is the performance of the defendant's promise, not the promise itself, which is the relevant consideration
>
> [...]

[353] I have come to the conclusion in the present case that the respondent is not entitled to recover the cruise fare on either of the grounds just discussed. The consequence of the respondent's enjoyment of the benefits provided under the contract during the first eight full days of the cruise is that the failure of consideration was partial, not total. I do not understand how, viewed from the perspective of failure of consideration, the enjoyment of those benefits was 'entirely negated by the catastrophe which occurred'.

QUESTIONS

(1) Gregory has been receiving weekly payments from his insurer, being a benefit that he became entitled to nine years ago as a result of suffering from a disability. At the start of 2018, the insurer requested that Gregory submit himself for a medical examination. It is assumed that until then, the insurer believed all along that his condition entitled Gregory to payments.

Gregory duly complied, whereupon it was discovered that as of five years ago, Gregory had in fact recovered to the point that he was no longer entitled to weekly payments from that point in time. The insurer, had it known of Gregory's recovery, could legitimately have ceased making weekly payments to Gregory altogether and it would have done so. Can the insurer recover the weekly payments on the ground of mistake?

(2) Why is it said that the payment of the insurer was mistakenly paid, applying the reasoning in *David Securities*? This is essentially a logical extension of the questions raised above.

24.3 Claims for services rendered

Concept	Short explanation	Relevant authorities	*Principles* text*
Determining the right to remuneration, and valuing remuneration in *quantum meruit* claims	A person who has rendered services under an unenforceable contract might be entitled to relief in a claim based on unjust enrichment and in this regard the most significant question is whether there is 'free acceptance' of those benefits. The usual, but not invariably applied, basis of remuneration is the market value of the services Recovery is not limited to amounts recoverable as damages for breach of contract and might exceed contractual damages	*Pavey & Matthews Pty Ltd v Paul* (1987) 162 CLR 221 *Renard Constructions (ME) Pty Ltd v Minister for Public Works* (1992) 26 NSWLR 234	Chapter 24: 24.06–24.07

Concept	Short explanation	Relevant authorities	*Principles* text*
The relevance of, and need for, a request for the services provided	Free acceptance of a benefit is insufficient to ground a claim for restitution and a request for the services might be required —albeit between contracting parties the fact of request can readily be inferred	*Lumbers v W Cook Builders Pty Ltd (in liq)* (2008) 232 CLR 635	Chapter 24: 24.10
Remuneration when the contract is discharged	Where the party in breach has performed services, the defaulting party might have a right to payment based on the other's free acceptance Despite *Lumbers*, the concept of free acceptance as the basis for relief cannot be ruled out Part performance of a contract does not itself confer any entitlement to remuneration	*Sumpter v Hedges* [1898] 1 QB 673 *Lampson (Australia) Pty Ltd v Fortescue Metals Group Ltd (No 3)* [2014] WASC 162 *Appleby v Myers* (1867) LR 2 CP 651	Chapter 24: 24.09.
Services rendered in anticipation of contract	Restitution has been granted for services performed in anticipation of a contract that did not eventuate based on free acceptance Given the decision in *Lumbers*, it is uncertain if free acceptance in the absence of a request for the services can support a claim for restitution	*Sabemo Pty Ltd v North Sydney Municipal Council* [1977] 2 NSWLR 880 *Lumbers v W Cook Builders Pty Ltd (in liq)* (2008) 232 CLR 635	Chapter 24: 24.10

* Consult the corresponding section(s) of the *Principles* text for more detail.

The fundamental theme in this module is there might, under some circumstances, be a right to restitution for services rendered.

The primary authority in this module is *Pavey & Matthews v Paul*,[2] in which the High Court propounded several seminal propositions: first, that where work is performed under a valid contract recovery is based entirely on the terms of the contract and there can be no restitutionary claim outside the terms of the contract (ie the entitlement to consideration); second, that someone who has rendered services under an unenforceable contract might be entitled to

2 *Pavey & Matthews Pty Ltd v Paul* (1987) 162 CLR 221.

relief in a claim based on unjust enrichment where the most significant question was whether there was 'free acceptance' of those benefits.

The cases below, including the older, pre-*Pavey* cases, reflect various, more nuanced, aspects of these central themes.

The module concludes with a discussion of the vexed and complicated questions posed by the judgment in *Lumbers*[3] which raised some uncertainty as to whether the fact of a benefit that was allegedly 'accepted' can give rise to a claim for restitution where the party that did the work did not have a contract with the other.

Pavey & Matthews Pty Ltd v Paul (1987) 162 CLR 221

Facts and issues

Builders agreed to do building work for Mrs Paul under an oral contract at prevailing market rates. The builders could not recover the agreed contract price as the contract was unenforceable, not being in writing as required under the requisite New South Wales Act. The builder argued, however, that they were entitled to a *quantum meruit* for the work performed. The case is a seminal case for the proposition that one might have an entitlement to remuneration for freely accepted benefits; note also the basis on which those benefits were valued.

Decision

Per Deane J at 256:

> . . . if there was a valid and enforceable agreement governing the claimant's right to compensation, there would be neither occasion nor legal justification for the law to superimpose or impute an obligation or promise to pay a reasonable remuneration. The quasi-contractual obligation to pay fair and just compensation for a benefit which has been accepted will only arise in a case where there is no applicable genuine agreement or where such an agreement is frustrated, avoided or unenforceable In such a case, it is the very fact that there is no genuine agreement or that the genuine agreement is frustrated, avoided or unenforceable that provides the occasion for (and part of the circumstances giving rise to) the imposition by the law of the obligation to make restitution.
>
> To identify the basis of such actions as restitution and not genuine agreement is not to assert a judicial discretion to do whatever idiosyncratic notions of what is fair and just might dictate. The circumstances in which the common law imposes an enforceable obligation to pay compensation for a benefit accepted under an unenforceable agreement have been explored in the reported cases and in learned writings and are unlikely to be greatly affected by the perception that the basis of such an obligation, when the common law imposes it, is preferably seen as lying in restitution rather than in the implication of a genuine agreement where in fact the unenforceable agreement left no room for one. That is not to deny the importance of the concept of unjust enrichment in the law of this country. It constitutes a unifying legal concept which explains [257] why the law recognizes, in a variety of distinct categories of case, an obligation on the part of a defendant to make fair and just restitution for a benefit derived at the expense of a plaintiff and which assists in the determination, by the ordinary processes of legal

3 *Lumbers v W Cook Builders Pty Ltd (in liq)* (2008) 232 CLR 635.

> reasoning, of the question whether the law should, in justice, recognize such an obligation in a new or developing category of case: see *Muschinski v. Dodds*; Goff & Jones, op. cit., pp 11ff. In a category of case where the law recognizes an obligation to pay a reasonable remuneration or compensation for a benefit actually or constructively accepted, the general concept of restitution or unjust enrichment is, as is pointed out subsequently in this judgment, also relevant, in a more direct sense, to the identification of the proper basis upon which the quantum of remuneration or compensation should be ascertained in that particular category of case.

On the question of the *valuation* of the remuneration for the *quantum meruit* claim only per Deane J at 263:

> What the concept of monetary restitution involves is the payment of an amount which constitutes, in all the relevant circumstances, fair and just [264] compensation for the benefit or 'enrichment' actually or constructively accepted. Ordinarily, that will correspond to the fair value of the benefit provided (e.g. remuneration calculated at a reasonable rate for work actually done or the fair market value of materials supplied). In some categories of case, however, it would be to affront rather than satisfy the requirements of good conscience and justice which inspire the concept or principle of restitution or unjust enrichment to determine what constitutes fair and just compensation for a benefit accepted by reference only to what would represent a fair remuneration for the work involved or a fair market value of materials supplied. One such category of case is that in which unsolicited but subsequently accepted work is done in improving property in circumstances where remuneration for the unsolicited work calculated at what was a reasonable rate would far exceed the enhanced value of the property. More relevant for present purposes is the special category of case where restitution is sought by one party for work which he has executed under a contract which has become unenforceable by reason of his failure to comply with the requirements of a statutory provision which was enacted to protect the other party. In that category of case, it would be contrary to the general notions of restitution or unjust enrichment if what constituted fair and just compensation for the benefit accepted by the other party were to be ascertained without regard to any identifiable real detriment sustained by that other party by reason of the failure of the first party to ensure that the requirements of the statutory provision were satisfied. Thus, if it is established on the hearing of the present case that Mrs. Paul has sustained an identifiable real detriment by reason of the failure of the builder to ensure that there was a written memorandum of the oral contract which satisfied the requirements of s. 45 of the Act, that would be an important factor in determining what constituted fair and just restitution in the circumstances of the case for the work done and materials supplied of which she has accepted the benefit.

Renard Constructions (ME) Pty Ltd v Minister for Public Works (1992) 26 NSWLR 234

Facts and issues

The plaintiff company agreed to construct certain works for the defendant. Prior to completion, the defendant repudiated and the plaintiff accepted the repudiation. Two issues were: (1) whether the plaintiff had the choice of suing for damages for breach of contract or for restitution; and (2) whether, if they sued for restitution, the contract price represented a ceiling on the restitution claim.

Decision

On the first issue, per Meagher JA at 277:

> The law is clear enough that an innocent party who accepts the defaulting party's repudiation of a contract has the option of either suing for damages for breach of contract or suing on a *quantum meruit* for work done. An election presupposes a choice between different remedies, which presumably may lead to different results. The nature of these different remedies renders it highly likely that the results will be different. If the former remedy is chosen the innocent party is entitled to damages amounting to the loss of profit which he would have made if the contract had been performed rather than repudiated; it has nothing to do with reasonableness. If the latter remedy is chosen, he is entitled to a verdict representing the reasonable cost of the work he has done and the money he has expended; the profit he might have made does not enter into that exercise.

On the second issue, His Honour said, at 277:

> There is nothing anomalous in the notion that two different remedies, proceeding on entirely different principles, might yield different results. Nor is there anything anomalous in the fact that either remedy may yield a higher monetary figure than the other. Nor is there anything anomalous in the prospect that a figure arrived at on a *quantum meruit* might exceed, or even far exceed, the profit which would have been made if the contract had been fully performed. Such a result would only be anomalous if there were some rule of law that the remuneration arrived at [278] contractually as the greatest possible remuneration available, or that it was a reasonable remuneration for all work requiring to be performed. There is no such rule of law . . .
>
> . . . it would be extremely anomalous if the defaulting party when sued on a *quantum meruit* could invoke the contract which he has repudiated in order to impose a ceiling on amounts otherwise recoverable.

Lumbers v W Cook Builders Pty Ltd (in liq) (2008) 232 CLR 635

Facts and issues

The defendant made a contract with W Cook & Sons Pty Ltd ('Cook & Sons') to build a house. Without the knowledge of the defendants, most of the work was performed by the plaintiff, W Cook Builders, which was a related company. Cook & Sons was a licensed builder but the plaintiff was not. There being no enforceable contract with the plaintiff (who had done most of the work), the plaintiff made a claim in restitution for some amounts after completion of the works. Given that the defendant did not request the work done from the party who eventually did perform the work (the plaintiff), the relevant issues were: first, did the defendant freely accept the work? Second, would it be necessary for their *quantum meruit* claim that they must have requested the work even if they did freely accept the work? To put these issues into perspective, it must be recounted that there was an effective contract between Lumbers and Cook & Sons, who did not perform the work. This gave rise to the question of whether there was 'free acceptance' of the benefits of the work, where the work was not performed by the company that was contractually bound to do it, Cook & Sons, but by W Cook Builders, who did not have a contract with Lumbers.

Decision

The answer to the first question, whether the defendant did 'freely accept the work', was 'no', per Gleeson CJ at 656:

> In *Steele v Tardiani* ,which in one sense was a simpler case than the present because there was only one contract involved, Dixon J explained the problems of identifying, for the purpose of a *quantum meruit* claim not based on the contract, a 'benefit' conferred on a building owner by the performance of work otherwise than in accordance with the contract. He accepted that, where building work is done outside the contract, and the benefit of the work is taken, there may arise an obligation to pay for the work. He went on to refer, however, to 'the dilemma in which a building owner is placed'. He quoted Collins LJ, who said, in *Sumpter v Hedges*:
>
> > Where, as in the case of work done on land, the circumstances are such as to give the defendant no option whether he will take the benefit of the work or not, then one must look to other facts than the mere taking the benefit of the work in order to ground the inference of a new contract . . . The mere fact that a defendant is in possession of what he cannot help keeping, or even has done work upon it, affords no ground for such an inference.
>
> [. . .]
>
> The concept of 'free acceptance' invoked by the majority in the Full Court, whatever its exact scope, is commonly related to a defendant who 'did not take a reasonable opportunity open to him to reject the proffered services'. That was not the situation of the *Lumbers* in the present case . . .

Gleeson CJ's view would have sufficed to dispose of the matter but nevertheless the plurality of the High Court considered the question: would it be necessary for the *quantum meruit* claim that there must have been a request to do the work even if the defendant did freely accept the work? In answering 'yes', per Gummow, Hayne, Crennan and Kiefel JJ at 666, they implicitly rejected the sufficiency of 'free acceptance'.

> Adapting what was said by Doyle CJ in *Angelopoulos* to the facts of this case, the nine factors identified by Builders as supporting its claim were: (a) the plaintiff (here, Builders) did not do the work gratuitously; (b) Builders did not act 'entirely at [its] own initiative' but at the implied request of the Lumbers; . . .
>
> It will be noted that the second of the matters identified was the making of an 'implied request' by the Lumbers to Builders to do the work and to pay money. At once it should be pointed out that, if Builders did whatever work it did and paid whatever money it paid at the Lumbers' request, Builders' claim for a reasonable price for the work and for the money it paid would fall neatly within long-established principles. It would matter not at all whether the request was made expressly, or its making was to be implied from the actions of the parties in the circumstances of the case. Builders would have an action for work and labour done or money paid for and at the request of the Lumbers.
>
> And if Builders did work or paid money at the Lumbers' request, it would also follow that it would be neither necessary nor appropriate to consider any of the other eight factors identified in *Angelopoulos* in deciding whether Builders could recover a fair price for the work it had done and the amount it had paid for and at the request of the Lumbers . . .
>
> [667] But in the end Builders did not submit that it could be found that the Lumbers had made any request directed to Builders. Rather, Builders' arguments proceeded from the premise that,

> in the present case, the Lumbers' request (or requests) for work to be done and money paid was (or were) directed to Sons and not to Builders.
>
> [674] Because Builders had no dealings with the Lumbers, Builders has no claim against the Lumbers for the price of any work and labour Builders performed or for any money that Builders may have paid in relation to the construction. Builders has no such claim because it can point to no request by the Lumbers directed to Builders that Builders do any work it did or pay any money it did. Reference to whether the Lumbers 'accepted' any work that Builders did or 'accepted' the benefit of any money it paid is irrelevant. It is irrelevant because it distracts attention from the legal relationships between the three parties: the Lumbers, Sons and Builders. To now impose on the Lumbers an obligation to pay Builders would constitute a radical alteration of the bargains the parties struck and of the rights and obligations which each party thus assumed.

The claim for a *quantum meruit* in the end result failed because the work had not been carried out at the request of the defendants; the plurality of the High Court thereby implicitly rejected the sufficiency of 'free acceptance' as the basis for a claim in *quantum meruit*.

Sumpter v Hedges [1898] 1 QB 673

Facts and issues

Sumpter, who had contracted to build two houses, repudiated the contract by abandoning those works. The unused building material was used by the owner. Sumpter made two claims in restitution, for the unused building materials (*quantum valebat*) and for the incomplete building work (*quantum meruit*). The judge gave judgment for the value of the materials but allowed nothing in respect of the work done. The builder appealed.

Decision

In respect of the recovery of a *quantum valebat* (for the value of the materials) per Chitty LJ at 675:

> . . . Bramwell B. [in *Pattinson v Luckley* (1875) LR 10 Ex 330] there pointed out with his usual clearness that in the case of a building erected upon land the mere fact that the defendant [676] remains in possession of his land is no evidence upon which an inference of a new contract can be founded ... He says: 'In the case of goods sold and delivered, it is easy to shew a contract from the retention of the goods; but that is not so where work is done on real property.' I think the learned judge was quite right in holding that in this case there was no evidence from which a fresh contract to pay for the work done could be inferred.

In respect of the recovery of the recovery of a *quantum meruit* (for the incomplete building work) per Collins LJ at 676:

> There are cases in which, though the plaintiff has abandoned the performance of a contract, it is possible for him to raise the inference of a new contract to pay for the work done on a *quantum meruit* from the defendant's having taken the benefit of that work, but, in order that that may be done, the circumstances must be such as to give an option to the defendant to take or not to take the benefit of the work done. It is only where the circumstances are such as to give that

option that there is any evidence on which to ground the inference of a new contract. Where, as in the case of work done on land, the circumstances are such as to give the defendant no option whether he will take the benefit of the work or not, then one must look to other facts than the mere taking the benefit of the work in order to ground the inference of a new contract. In this case I see no other facts on which such an inference can be founded. The mere fact that a defendant is in possession of what he cannot help keeping, or even has done work upon it, affords no ground for such an inference. He is not bound to keep unfinished a building which in an incomplete state would be a nuisance on his land. I am [677] therefore of opinion that the plaintiff was not entitled to recover for the work which he had done.

Lampson (Australia) Pty Ltd v Fortescue Metals Group Ltd (No 3) [2014] WASC 162

Facts and issues

Noting that the claim had been distilled by counsel, Edelman J said that 'the claim was not complex', namely at [6]:

> The claim now brought by Lampson Australia is only for restitution of $2,228,179, with interest, for work done in anticipation of a contract that did not materialise.

Argument primarily was focused on the proposition that following *Lumbers,* free acceptance was no longer to be used as the basis for a restitutionary claim. Essentially, Edelman J propounded that absent a definitive ruling, free acceptance could not be ruled out as a basis for relief.

It is fair to say that the complications that arose in *Lumbers* were arguably somewhat unusual (the work was done not by the contracting party but by a party related to the contracting party). One might argue that the fact of a request in a more commonplace instance would be readily satisfied as arising from the parties being in some form of arrangement, such as was the case in the well-known circumstances in *Pavey* itself (the ultimately unenforceable contract).

Decision

Per Edelman J at [51]:

> Provided that unjust enrichment is not applied as a direct source of liability, in Australia the taxonomic category of unjust enrichment has served a useful function and *might* continue to do so [emphasis added].

Edelman J then noted at [76] the following facts in *Lumbers*:

> The claim in *Lumbers* is conceptually distinct from the claim in this case in at least one significant respect: the existence of a contract between the Lumbers and Builders in relation to work the value of which the Lumbers sought restitution from Sons.

In relation to the question whether, under the circumstances, as a result of the decision in *Lumbers* the concept of free acceptance as a basis for the recovery of restitution was extinguished, his Honour said at [77]:

The question for the application in this case is whether the High Court of Australia in *Lumbers* so clearly rejected the concept of free acceptance that, despite some possible support for free acceptance in earlier authorities, *Lampson* Australia's claim based on free acceptance should be struck out and *Lampson* Australia should be precluded from making the claim.

[78] I reiterate that the context in which this question is asked is the need for a trial judge to take care not to risk stifling the development of the law by summarily rejecting a claim where there is a reasonable possibility that, as the law develops, it will be found that a cause of action will lie. For this reason, I have not embarked in a comprehensive examination of the decision in *Lumbers*. No doubt, this analysis will take place at trial if the facts emerge in a manner in which liability depends upon proof of free acceptance.

[79] For five reasons, the free acceptance plea should not be struck out [Note: only two of the reasons explored by Edelman J, those being relevant to the present discussion, will be explored here].

[80] *First*, the relevant discussion in *Lumbers*, by Gummow, Hayne, Crennan and Kiefel JJ, did not expressly reject the possibility that liability could be based on an unjust factor arising from acceptance of a benefit, with knowledge that it was not provided gratuitously, and without taking a reasonable opportunity open to reject the benefit.

[81] The defendants in this application rely on the rejection in the joint judgment in *Lumbers* of a particular submission by Builders. That rejected submission was that acceptance of a benefit, without a request, suffices to found an action for work and labour done or money paid. Although this submission was rejected, it is difficult to see how the mere references to 'acceptance' in the joint judgment High Court can be read as also rejecting the more specific doctrine of 'free acceptance', including the three elements described above.

[82] In one paragraph to which counsel for the defendants pointed, the joint judgment said that 'the *bare fact* of conferral of the benefit or provision of the service does not suffice to establish an entitlement to recovery' (emphasis added). This is not a reference to the three matters comprising the doctrine of free acceptance. And even in relation to the bare fact of conferral of a benefit, the joint judgment spoke of the *general* principle that work done to benefit the property of another does not create any obligation to repay the expenditure. Their Honours said that this principle 'is not unqualified' and that 'it is not necessary to examine in this case how extensive are those further qualifications or what is their content'.

[83] In another paragraph relied upon by the defendants, the joint judgment rejected the proposition that acceptance of a benefit, without a request, would be sufficient, *at least in this case*, to found an action by Builders for work and labour done or money paid' (emphasis added).

[84] In *Friend v Booker*, French CJ, Gummow, Hayne and Bell JJ also later explained the decision on this point in Lumbers in even narrower terms: 'the *bare fact* of the conferral of some benefit upon another does not suffice to establish an obligation to repay the expenditure in providing that benefit' (emphasis added).

[85] *Secondly,* in the separate judgment of Gleeson CJ, his Honour emphasised that '[t]here was no acquiescence by the Lumbers in the provision of services by Builders'. The Chief Justice, in a passage cited with approval in this Court, later explained that:

> The concept of 'free acceptance' invoked by the majority in the Full Court, whatever its exact scope, is commonly related to a defendant who 'did not take a reasonable opportunity open to him to reject the proffered services'. That was not the situation of the Lumbers in the present case.

Although a decision of a State Supreme Court, and not the High Court, *Lampson* assumes significance as Edelman J was subsequently appointed to the High Court.

Appleby v Myers (1867) LR 2 CP 651

Facts and issues

The plaintiffs agreed to erect machinery at the defendant's premises. It was a term of the contract that the plaintiff would only be paid at the completion of the work. Prior to completion, the works were destroyed by fire. Having held that the fire was a frustrating event, the question was whether the plaintiff could recover the value of the work done.

Decision

Per Blackburn J at 659:

> ... we do not think that, under such a contract as this, the plaintiffs could recover anything unless the whole work was completed.
>
> [660] It is not material whether in such a case the non-completion is because the shipwright did not choose to go on with the work, as was the case in *Roberts v. Havelock,* or because in consequence of a fire he could not go on with it, as in *Menetone v. Atliawes*.

Sabemo Pty Ltd v North Sydney Municipal Council [1977] 2 NSWLR 880

Facts and issues

Sabemo, a builder, performed work intended to have been the subject of a contract with the defendant, a council. The project for which the works were intended was abandoned by the defendant without a contract being formed. Sabemo sought recovery of the reasonable value of those works.

Decision

Per Sheppard J at 899:

> The question I must ask myself is whether, at this stage [900] of the development of the law in this country, it is right to say that, in some circumstances, in a case of this kind, there will be occasions when the law, irrespective of the common intention of the parties, will impose on one an obligation to pay the other for work done. After due reflection I have reached the conclusion, notwithstanding the weighty authority which the early Australian decisions have, that there is such a principle in existence.
>
> [...]
>
> In a judgment of this kind it would be most unwise, and in any event impossible, to fix the limitations which should circumscribe the extent of the right to recover. It is enough for me to say that I think that there is one circumstance here which leads to the conclusion that the plaintiff is entitled to succeed. That circumstance is the fact that the defendant deliberately decided to drop the proposal. It may have had good reasons for doing so, but they had nothing to do with the plaintiff, which, in good faith over a period exceeding three years, had worked assiduously towards the day when it would take a building lease of the land and erect thereon the Civic Centre which the defendant, during that long period, has so earnestly desired.

QUESTIONS

(1) Neil shows Manfred plans and specifications for modifications to his home. The plans and specifications simply do not 'work'. Nevertheless, Manfred agrees to build a house 'as described in the specification'. The end result is that, at significant additional cost to Manfred, the modifications are complete. What, if anything, can Manfred recover in respect of the additional, significant work and materials that he expended in order to effect the modifications as a result of the fact that the original plans and specifications provided by Neil were simply unworkable?

(2) John is a carpenter who is contracted to construct some couches for Lisa. John has repudiated the contract and Lisa brings the contract to an end. None of the upholstery has been commenced. Focus on John's entitlement to a *quantum meruit* or *quantum valebat* in respect of the work done. Some of the chairs have had all the framework completed, ready for upholstering. Lisa believes that she can get someone else to complete the upholstery and wishes to do so. Discuss John's remedies.

24.4 Explaining restitution and its rise and fall

Concept	Short explanation	Relevant authorities	*Principles* text*
Rationalising restitution, and its rise and fall	*The rise*: the obligation to make payment for executed consideration under an unenforceable contract lies in restitution or unjust enrichment *The fall*: free acceptance, hitherto treated as the cornerstone of a restitutionary claim, should no longer be regarded as the basis for such a claim *Rationalising the current Australian jurisprudence*—provided that unjust enrichment is not applied as a direct source of liability, in Australia the taxonomic category of unjust enrichment has served a useful function and *might* continue to do so	*Pavey & Matthews Pty Ltd v Paul* (1987) 162 CLR 221 (see **24.3** for extract) *Lumbers v W Cook Builders Pty Ltd (in liq)* (2008) 232 CLR 635 (see **24.3** for extract) *Lampson (Australia) Pty Ltd v Fortescue Metals Group Ltd (No 3)* [2014] WASC 162 (see **24.3** for extract)	Chapter 24: 24.11–24.12

* Consult the corresponding section(s) of the *Principles* text for more detail.

This module traces the evolution and *arguable* decline of the concept of unjust enrichment as a basis for liability. The cases relevant to the discussion have been already introduced elsewhere, so this discussion simply adds a fresh nuance to the aspects already explored.

Pavey & Matthews Pty Ltd v Paul (1987) 162 CLR 221, the seminal decision of our High Court discussed at length earlier, can fairly be considered the prelude to the reception of unjust enrichment as the basis for the recovery of payment for work performed under an unenforceable contract; and by focusing on the aspect of 'free acceptance' might fairly be regarded as the zenith of the proposition that the obligation to make payment for executed consideration under an unenforceable contract lies in restitution.

Since then, following the adoption of the notion of unjust enrichment in cases like *David Securities Pty Ltd v Commonwealth Bank of Australia* (1992) 175 CLR 353 (see the extract in **24.2** above) Australian courts have tended to eschew the idea of unjust enrichment; a selection of relevant cases is contained in 24.12 of the *Principles* text. The apparent high water mark, at least to date, of the *rejection* of unjust enrichment, is the judgment of Gummow, Hayne Crennan and Kiefel JJ in *Lumbers,* relevant portions of which, from pages 665 and 674, are set out in **24.3**. Rather, the right to recovery was conditioned upon the need for a request for the services.

The present Australian jurisprudence on whether in all cases the entitlement to recovery is conditioned on the need for a request for the services, is in a state of flux. This is illustrated by Edelman J's judgment in *Lampson*, which culminates in the pivotal (if somewhat equivocal) observation at [51] (reproduced above at p 807).

QUESTIONS

(1) In a practical sense, would the insistence on the requirement of *request* in *Lumbers* make much of a difference in a claim between contracting parties?

(2) Edelman J in *Lampson*, in ultimately suggesting that the High Court in *Lumbers* arguably at least did not lay down an overarching requirement that there needed to be a request for performance, drew particular attention to the fact, at p 76 that:

> The claim in *Lumbers* is conceptually distinct from the claim in this case in at least one significant respect: the existence of a contract between the Lumbers and Builders in relation to work the value of which the Lumbers sought restitution from Sons.

What in your view is the corollary of the argument that the requirement for a request is directed particularly to a case where the party that actually did the work (relevantly *Cook Builders*) was not the contracting party (relevantly *Cook & Sons*)?

24.5 International perspectives

24.5.1 General

For cross-border commercial contracts, depending on the context, issues of restitution might be governed by international rules or by domestic law. In a cross-border relationship where no contract has ever been formed, but goods and/or money have been exchanged, the first question arising is which country's laws are to determine the issue of restitution. This turns on the choice of law (conflict of laws) rules of the forum deciding the issue: see **25.2.1–25.2.2**. If those rules indicate the application of Australian law to the question of restitution, then the position described above will determine the matter **24.2–24.3**. If another country's laws are indicated by the choice of law rules, then the domestic laws of that country will determine the matter. Alternatively, in other situations, remedial restitutionary obligations will arise under the *CISG* (or more rarely, UNIDROIT Principles). These are described below (and also at **25.9.8**).

24.5.2 *CISG*

If an international commercial sales contract governed by the *CISG* was formed (see **25.4.1** on applicability), but has subsequently been terminated pursuant to contractual clauses or under the *CISG*'s termination rules (termination is called 'avoidance' within the *CISG*), then the *CISG* will impose obligations of restitution concerning the goods and any moneys paid: arts 81(2)–88 *CISG*. In essence, where a contract has been terminated (avoided), concurrent obligations arise to make restitution of goods and payments received: art 81(2) *CISG*. Sellers must return the price with interest: art 84(1). Buyers must account for any benefits derived from the goods: art 84(2). Parties in possession of goods in such circumstances are obliged to take steps to preserve them: arts 85–87 *CISG*. However, if a seller refuses return of the goods, or if return is not feasible (eg, because goods are highly perishable), then the party in possession of them may sell the goods, and refund the proceeds of sale, less reasonable costs incurred: art 88 *CISG*. These rules are designed to provide cost-effective and practical solutions for long-distance cross-border trade.

24.5.3 UNIDROIT Principles

As briefly discussed at **25.9.8**, the UNIDROIT Principles where applicable (see **25.4.3** on applicability) contain similar obligations of restitution following termination in art 7.3.6 UNIDROIT Principles. Thus, each party can claim back that which was supplied to the other or, if this is not possible in kind, a monetary allowance. If the parties, perhaps under a preliminary agreement, have selected UNIDROIT Principles, then secondary obligations of restitution might arise pursuant to art 3.2.15, where the contract is avoided on the basis of validity issues such as undue pressure or gross disparity: see discussion at **19.4.2–19.4.3**.

24.6 Review

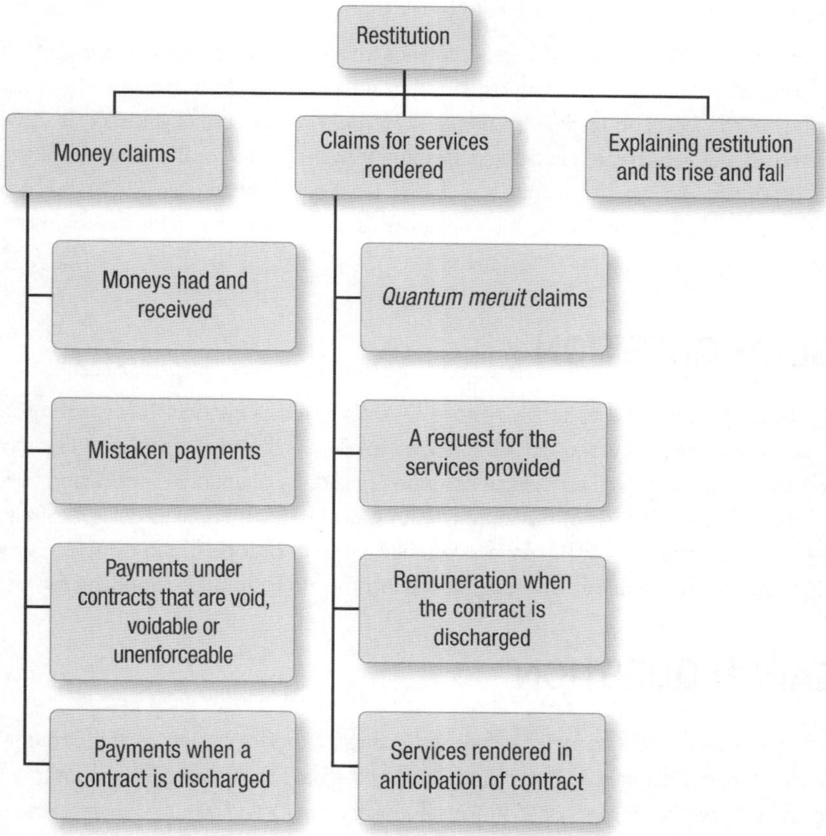

TIPS FOR APPLYING THE LAW IN PRACTICE

- A mistake often made is for students to conflate the ideas of substantial performance (addressed at 12.12 and 12.13 of the *Principles* text) and restitution. Although the same set of facts may give rise to remedies under both doctrines, they attract very different precepts. In brief, when considering *substantial performance*, you are concerned with the question of whether the level of performance is sufficient to permit the promisee to recover their consideration or any part of it. When considering *restitution*, the entitlement to relief depends not on the level of performance, but on whether one party has made a gain at the expense of the other, which is a different concept from the level of performance required to satisfy substantial performance.
- Whilst jurisprudentially *Lumbers* has a significant effect, it might not be necessary to overanalyse its impact from a practical viewpoint. There are two reasons for this: the first is that, to the extent that

the principle in *Lumbers* renders it necessary that the work or services be performed pursuant to a request, then the fact of an agreement between the parties would satisfy the requirement of request. The second is that Edelman J (then a judge of the Supreme Court of Western Australia) expressed the view in *Lampson* that the High Court did not so clearly reject the concept of free acceptance that the claim in the case before him should be struck out.

- To the extent that the concept of 'free acceptance' remains applicable (and, it is suggested, that for the reasons set out in the above dot point, for practical purposes this might well be the case) then a brief study of the facts and findings in *Sumpter v Hedges* provides useful guidance as to whether in any given case this requirement is satisfied. Restitution was allowed for the unused building material as the defendant did have the option of taking the benefit of the same. On the other hand, restitution was not allowed for the incomplete building work as the defendant did not have any option whether to take the benefit of the work.

PROBLEM QUESTION

Mike is a mechanic contracted to totally restore Quentin's vintage car, which is worth around $2M. Mike did not complete the work, as the job was totally beyond his capability. He simply totally abandoned the work with significant portions unperformed. By abandoning the work, Mike can be assumed to have been in breach of his contract with Quentin. Quentin takes delivery of his car in its incomplete state of restoration. Mike has inadvertently left a set of tools in the car which Quentin has kept. Is Mike entitled to restitution in respect of the incomplete restoration work and for his tools?

RESEARCH QUESTION

The effect of *Lumbers* is said to be that free acceptance, hitherto treated as the cornerstone of a restitutionary claim, has declined in importance. Identify the basis for the original proposition (that free acceptance should be the cornerstone of a restitutionary claim) and whether in practical terms the imposition of the superadded requirement in *Lumbers* of an 'implied request' would make any significant difference to your analysis in a case where the party which had benefited from the work was a party to an unenforceable contract with the person who performed the work.

PART VIII

INTERNATIONAL ASPECTS OF CONTRACT LAW

25

CONTRACT IN THE INTERNATIONAL CONTEXT

25.1 Overview

Contracts may be considered to be 'international' where they are concluded between two parties located in different countries. In the international context, issues relating to contract become more complex and varied. A number of matters should be considered, with the first considerations being to identify the relevant applicable law, and any choice of forum.

These matters are crucial. A contract will be of little use if it cannot be enforced. Its enforceability will be determined by the law applicable to the relevant issue in question, a matter which itself is determined, in turn, by choice of law (conflicts rules) of the forum seized of the matter. Whether a particular forum has or chooses to exercise jurisdiction may itself be affected by any choice of forum which has been agreed between the parties.

This chapter provides an overview of choices of law in international contracting and *CISG* and UNIDROIT Principles.

25.2 Choices of law in international contracting

Naturally, where a contract is concluded between parties from different countries, there are a number of potential laws which could apply to any one legal issue arising from that contract.

Choice of law rules (also known as 'conflict of laws rules') are the rules applied within each forum to determine which law applies in relation to a particular issue.

For example, an Australian court may, where a case comes before them involving a matter of tort where multiple countries are involved, apply a choice of law rule that the law of the place where the conduct constituting the wrong occurred shall be the applicable law. This could result in an Australian court applying, for example, French law of delict, if an action is brought in Australia concerning an injury sustained in France.[1] This will be on the basis that the primary choice of law rule prevailing in Australia, in relation to torts, is that the applicable law will be that of the place where the wrong occurred.[2] Courts can decline to exercise jurisdiction on the basis of *forum non conveniens*, especially if most of the witnesses and evidence are located in another country.[3]

When faced with a contract with international elements, the court will need to determine the applicable law. The general choice of law rule in Australia concerning contracts is presently the law of the place having the 'closest and most real connection' with the contract.[4] Thus, the place of performance may be important.[5] However, if the issue concerns ownership or property, the place where the relevant items are physically located, or *lex situs*, will be the main conflict of laws rule applicable in Australian courts.[6] If there are a range of issues, multiple laws may apply.

However, this is an overly simplified picture of choice of law issues. Although a particular choice of law rule may predominate in a forum, alternative choice of law rules may also exist. Thus, a particular forum might normally apply 'the law of the place most closely connected' test, but may sometimes resort to the law of 'the place of the seller' or take into account other factors, such as currency, or where the contract was concluded. Additionally, irrespective of applicable law, courts may still apply overriding mandatory domestic rules from their own jurisdiction. This reduces certainty of outcomes for international contracts.

Moreover, there are numerous forums around the world, each with its own conflict of laws rules, and those rules differ from one country to another, and change over time. Whilst there are admirable efforts to harmonise choice of law rules, they are yet to become widespread.[7] The present multitude of rules, combined with uncertainty in their application, makes conflict of laws notoriously unpredictable.

---

1 See *Regie Nationale des Usines Renault SA v Zhang* (2002) 210 CLR 491; *Palmer v Turnbull* [2019] 1 Qd R 286.

2 The *lex loci delicti*: *Regie Nationale des Usines Renault SA v Zhang* (2002) 210 CLR 491 [66], [75].

3 *Voth v Manildra Flour Mills Pty Ltd* (1990) 171 CLR 538 (the test being the clearly inappropriate forum). The test is now embodied within various rules of procedure. See eg *Supreme Court (General Civil Procedure) Rules 2005* (Vic), r 7.05; *Regie Nationale des Usines Renault SA v Zhang* (2002) 210 CLR 491 [23].

4 *Bonython v Commonwealth* (1950) 81 CLR 486, 498; *Akai Pty Ltd v People's Insurance Co Ltd* (1996) 188 CLR 418.

5 For further discussion, see Brooke Adele Marshall, 'Reconsidering the Proper Law of the Contract' (2012) 13 *Melbourne Journal of International Law* 1, 23.

6 *Lex situs:* Lawrence Collins, *Dicey and Morris on the Conflict of Laws*, Volume 1 (Sweet & Maxwell, 15th ed, 2000) 74; *Haque v Haque (No 2)* (1965) 114 CLR 98.

7 See Hague Conference on Private International Law, *Principles on Choice of Law in International Commercial Contracts* (adopted 19 March 2015). However, see harmonisation within Europe's Rome Regulation I: *Regulation (EC) No 593/2008 of the European Parliament and of the Council of 17 June 2008 on the law applicable to contractual obligations* (Rome I) OJ L 177 (Rome Regulation I).

25.2.1 Choice of law in courts

Parties may attempt to overcome these problems by inserting a choice of law clause, signifying agreement on the issue. Courts will usually respect the parties' choice of law.[8] Thus, an express choice of law increases the predictability of outcomes concerning applicable law, but it does not provide a guarantee. In some instances, the manner in which the clause is construed by the court will not match what parties had anticipated.

The same is true of choice of forum clauses. In a clause providing for exclusive jurisdiction in courts in Florence, Italy, the following was held insufficient to embrace a claim for breach:

> For any disputes, none excluded, arising from the interpretation, execution or application of this contract, the competent court of law shall be the Florence court, section of Empoli, even in the case the payment has been agreed against a draft and this, with express exclusion of any other conventional court of law or court mentioned by the law.[9]

The word 'executed' was narrowly construed by the Australian court to refer only to the signing and exchange of contracts; whereas, within Italian legal practice, 'execution' commonly refers to contractual performance. Thus, the Australian court exercised jurisdiction, an eventuality probably not anticipated by parties when the contract was concluded.

Moreover, an agreed choice of law will not be effective if it is deemed invalid pursuant to the law of the forum (*lex fori*). Some jurisdictions prohibit certain choices of law. For example, Brazilian courts generally apply the law of the place where the contract was entered, irrespective of contrary agreement by the parties.[10] Thus, a choice of law clause will not always be effective, although in most instances it will achieve the desired end.

25.2.2 Choice of law in arbitration

International arbitral tribunals must also determine the law applicable to the contract. In relation to international commercial arbitration, the *Model Law on International Commercial Arbitration*,[11] now adopted by 80 countries, helps to clarify this, at least to some extent. It binds arbitral tribunals to uphold choices of law agreed by the parties.[12] Thus Brazilian parties can overcome the restriction within their own courts on freedom in choice of law by selecting

8 See eg, English *Arbitration Act 1996*, s 46(1); *French Code of Civil Procedure*, art 1511; *Swiss Law on Private International Law*, art 187; Marc Blessing, 'Choice of Substantive Law in International Arbitration' (1997) 14(2) *Journal of International Arbitration* 39; Gary B Born, *International Commercial Arbitration* (Wolters Kluwer, 2nd ed, 2014) §19.01.

9 *Vetreria Etrusca Srl v Kingston Estate Wines Pty Ltd* [2008] SASC 75. See also R Garnett, 'Jurisdiction Clauses since Akai' (2013) 87 *Australian Law Journal* 134, fn 40.

10 Until the new *Code of Civil Procedure* ('*NCPC*') came into force in March 2016, parties were neither free to select the exclusive jurisdiction of another country, nor the law of the contract. Article 25 of the *NCPC* now allows parties to agree to the exclusive jurisdiction of foreign courts, but it remains the case that the law of the place where the contract was entered is the governing contract law regardless of party agreement: art 9, II, *Law of Introduction to Brazilian Legal Norms, Brazilian Introductory Law (LINDB)* (Decree No 4,657/1942) to the Code of Civil Procedure 1973.

11 *UNCITRAL Model Law on International Commercial Arbitration 1985*, as amended in 2006, GA Res A/40/72, UN Doc A/40/17 annex I (11 December 1985) and GA Res A/RES/61/33, UN Doc A/61/17 annex I (4 December 2006) ('Model Law on ICA').

12 Model Law on ICA art 28(1).

arbitration. Where no choice of law has been agreed, the tribunal is directed by the Model Law to determine the 'law ... by the conflict of laws rules it considers applicable'.[13]

25.2.3 Party negotiation for choice of law and neutral laws

Subject to their choice being valid pursuant to the *lex fori,* parties to an international contract have autonomy to agree upon selection of any law they wish. Normally, irrespective of how advantageous or disadvantageous the substantive rules are, parties attempt to negotiate for the selection of the law of their home state. In international contracting, this creates an obvious issue. Where one party has greater bargaining power, it may well succeed in pressing for their home state choice of law. However, if bargaining power is held evenly, parties often resolve the impasse by a 'neutral' choice; that is, a law which is the law of neither party. Inter alia, common choices are the laws of England, or Switzerland.[14]

Notably, the *Convention on Contracts for the International Sale of Goods 1980* (*CISG*)[15] is available as a neutral choice of law, as it exists autonomously despite being part of the domestic law of every member state. Thus, where bargaining power is relatively even, selection of the law of a country that has adopted the *CISG* is another solution to negotiation impasse on choice of law.[16]

To some extent, harmonisation of choice of law rules for commercial sales contracts has occurred within the *CISG*. The *CISG* contains rules relating to its own applicability, which in part amount to uniform conflict of law rules,[17] and which in part defer to choice of law rules of the forum.[18] Thus, if parties have failed to agree on choice of law, and have places of business in different countries, both being *CISG* member states, then the *CISG* will be the applicable law by default.[19] The latter constitutes a conflicts rule that replaces the uncertainty discussed above. Since there are now 89 member states (known as 'Contracting States'), this significantly reduces unpredictability.

Additionally, the *CISG* could be applicable law by virtue of art 1(1)(b), even if only one or neither party is from a *CISG* member state, provided forum conflicts rules lead to the application of the law of a member state.[20] If parties to an international commercial contract agree to

13 Model Law on ICA art 28(2).

14 If one of the parties is from a civil law background, choice of English law may not appear neutral. Moreover, Swiss law, while perceived as politically neutral, is far from legally neutral in balancing rights of sellers and buyers, and can be highly unpredictable.

15 *Vienna Convention on Contracts for the International Sale of Goods*, adopted 10 April 1980, UN Doc A/CONF.97/18, opened for signature 11 April 1980, 1489 UNTS 3 (entered into force 1 January 1988).

16 Indeed, some large international entities use this approach as a strategy to harmonise choice of law amongst the many contracts they enter globally. For further discussion, see Lisa Spagnolo, 'Unification, Disintegration or Optimization: Purposes of Modern Sales Law' in D Saidov (ed.), *Unity and Diversity in the Law of Sale of Goods* (Elgar, 2019) §III.

17 *CISG* art 1(1)(a) discussed below at **25.4.1**.

18 *CISG* art 1(1)(b) discussed below at **25.4.1**.

19 *CISG* art 1(1)(a) discussed below at **25.4.1**.

20 This will not always follow. A few countries, when signing the *CISG*, made a reservation pursuant to art 95 *CISG* which precluded application of art 1(1)(b)—notably including the USA and China. The effect of this is controversial, but its importance is limited, and its impact on the decline as the trend for reservation countries to withdraw their reservation continues. See CISG Advisory Council, 'CISG-AC Opinion No. 15, Reservations under Articles 95 and 96 CISG', Rapporteur: Prof Dr Ulrich G Schroeter.

select the national law of a member state to the *CISG*, then the *CISG* may apply, unless the parties exclude its application.

25.2.4 Choice of soft laws/rules

Parties may select by agreement any law they wish, provided their choice is considered a valid choice of law by the forum seized of the matter. Parties may, however, wish to apply a non-national or a-national law. This can best be characterised as a choice of 'soft law' as opposed to national 'hard law'.

The selection of soft rules can take a number of forms. Parties in international commerce frequently refer to the UCP600,[21] INCOTERMS,[22] and may, although far less frequently, select as their choice of law the UNIDROIT Principles of International Commercial Contracts ('UNIDROIT Principles').[23]

INCOTERMS and UCP600 are standardised rules defining specific contractual matters. INCOTERMS are promulgated by the ICC, and deal with issues of the passing of risk, insurance, obligations to arrange carriage and delivery. Parties often use INCOTERMS within their contracts by referring to terms such as, inter alia, 'CIF', 'FOB' or 'EXW'. By doing so, it is likely that they will be held to have impliedly incorporated within their contract the corresponding INCOTERM definitions of the term used. Likewise, parties referring to the ICC's UCP600 will probably be held to have imported its limited rules in regard to letters of credit, a method of payment commonly used in international trade.

The UNIDROIT Principles are less frequently selected as a choice of law. Selection of them as the law of the contract raises issues regarding validity of choice of soft law.[24] However, they do offer comprehensive rules regarding a broad range of topics. An overview of the *CISG* and UNIDROIT Principles is provided in the following section, which deals with their application and effect, interpretation, formality requirements, formation, rights and obligations, and remedies arising pursuant to them.

25.3 *CISG* and UNIDROIT Principles

The *CISG* has been applicable law in all States, Territories and federally in Australia from 1988.[25] As mentioned above, the UNIDROIT Principles are soft law, and therefore not implemented within Australian law.

21 International Chamber Commerce, *Uniform Customs and Practice for Documentary Credits (UCP) 600* (Paris: ICC, 2007).

22 International Chamber of Commerce, *Incoterms 2010* (Paris: ICC, 2010) ('Incoterms®').

23 International Institute for the Unification of Private Law (UNIDROIT), *Principles of International Commercial Contracts (2016)* ('UNIDROIT Principles'), available at https://www.unidroit.org/instruments/commercial-contracts/unidroit-principles-2016.

24 Discussed at **25.4.3**.

25 *Competition and Consumer Act 2010* (Cth) sch 2 s 68; *Sale of Goods (Vienna Convention) Act 1986* (WA) sch 1; *Sale of Goods (Vienna Convention) Act 1987* (Tas) sch 1; *Sale of Goods (Vienna Convention) Act 1986* (NSW) sch 1; *Sale of Goods (Vienna Convention) Act 1987* (ACT) sch 1; *Sale of Goods (Vienna Convention) Act 1986* (SA) sch pt 1; *Sale of Goods (Vienna Convention) Act 1986* (Qld) sch pt 1; *Sale of Goods (Vienna Convention) Act 1987* (NT) sch 1 pt 1; *Goods Act 1958* (Vic) sch pt 1.

The UNIDROIT Principles offer a comprehensive range of rules governing commercial contractual relations, including contractual formation, contractual rights and obligations, contractual remedies, as well as validity, effects of agency on contractual obligations with third parties, set-off and assignment, third-party beneficiaries and multi-party contracts.[26]

The *CISG*, by comparison, covers a narrower set of topics. It deals only with sales of goods (or mixed goods and services).[27] It does not deal with questions of validity (other than form), agency, or assignment. However, it covers issues that give rise to the bulk of questions which arise in international commercial contracts, including formation, rights and obligations, and remedies. Moreover, whereas the UNIDROIT Principles impose a positive duty of good faith upon parties, the *CISG* does not.

25.4 Application and effect

Where it applies, the *CISG* governs most aspects of contract and sales law in regard to international sales. Essentially, its application displaces non-mandatory domestic law covering subjects within its scope.

25.4.1 Applicability of the *CISG*

The *CISG* applies automatically by default in certain circumstances. The *CISG* outlines the test for applicability in art 1. It then describes subject matters and issues that do not fall within its scope in arts 2-5 in terms of: (A) geographic applicability, and scope in terms of (B) types of contracts and (C) legal issues, and (D) the ability of parties to exclude its application in art 6 *CISG*.

25.4.1.1 Geographical applicability and application by choice

A variety of situations lead to the *CISG*'s application:

- when both parties are from member states (art 1(1)(a));
- when the rules of private international law lead to application of the law of a member state (art 1(1)(b));[28]
- where the parties 'opt into' the *CISG* by their choice of law, if this choice is valid under the rules of the forum.[29] Usually such a choice will be by selection of the law of a *CISG* member state, as discussed below ('indirect choice');
- where the parties 'opt into' the *CISG* by their choice of the *CISG* as a soft law, where this choice is valid under rules of the forum, rather than through the national law of a member state ('direct choice');

26 UNIDROIT Principles ch 1 (General); ch 2 (Formation & Agency); ch 3 (Validity); ch 4 (Interpretation); ch 5 (Third Party Rights); ch 6 (Performance); ch 7 (Non-Performance); ch 8 (Set-Off); ch 9 (Assignment); ch 10 (Limitation Periods); ch 11 (Plurality of Parties).

27 *CISG* art 3(2), discussed below.

28 A proviso exists in relation to art 95 reservations: see above n 20.

29 Discussed above at **25.2.1**.

- and further, the *CISG* can and often does apply as an embodiment of the *lex mercatoria*, where arbitral tribunals or courts wish to resort to general principles of trade in interpretation.

25.4.1.2 Types of contracts

The *CISG* applies to commercial sales transactions; that is, sales between businesses (B2B). It will not generally apply to consumer sales (B2C): art 2(a). Certain specific types of transactions are excluded: auctions, sales of ships, gas, electricity etc: art 2. For reasons perhaps lost to time, hovercraft are also excluded.

Pure service contracts are not covered, at least by default application of the *CISG*; however, the *CISG* can apply to contracts involving both goods and services if the preponderant part of the contract is for goods: art 3(2). Exactly how this is to be tested has been the subject of cases and commentary. It can be based on economic value, but if the goods are the 'essential' part of the contract and services, although more valuable, are incidental, then economic value might not be an appropriate indicator.[30] Most academic commentators consider software to be a good for this purpose, although whether the *CISG* can apply to short-term software licences is debated.[31]

25.4.1.3 Scope of legal issues

As mentioned earlier, there are legal questions which fall beyond the scope of the *CISG*. Notably, except in specific instances, the *CISG* does not generally deal with questions of validity (art 4(a)), but it does regulate the issue of form by specifying that contracts need not be in writing.[32] The *CISG* does not determine the passing of proprietary interests (art 4(b)), nor personal injury claims: art 5. These matters are left to the applicable residual domestic law.

25.4.1.4 Exclusion by agreement

Parties can agree to opt out of the *CISG*. The application of the *CISG* can be excluded by agreement of the parties under art 6. However, the *CISG* applies prima facie if the other prerequisites are met. In order for an agreement to opt out to be effective, the exclusion will need to comply with the requirements under the *CISG*.[33] The following illustrates this in practice.

The choice of law of a member state, without more, will not operate as an exclusion of the *CISG*. For example, 'The law of France governs this contract' will not operate as an exclusion of the *CISG*'s application. As France is a member state, the *CISG* forms part of the domestic laws of France, and thus this choice of law leads to the application of the *CISG* (assuming the choice is valid under forum law). This general rule is established from the majority of cases decided on

30 Bradley J Richards, 'Contracts for the International Sale of Goods: Applicability of the United Nations Convention' (1983) 69 *Iowa Law Review* 209, 240.

31 Peter Schlechtriem and Petra Butler, *UN Law on International Sales* (Springer, 2009), para 32b; Trevor Cox, 'Chaos versus Uniformity: The Divergent Views of Software in the International Community' (2000) 4 *Vindobona Journal of International Commercial Law & Arbitration* 3.

32 *CISG* art 11. Thus, contracts can be concluded orally, in writing or through conduct, unless a member state has made a reservation pursuant to art 96 *CISG*: See further discussion below at **25.6.1**.

33 CISG Advisory Council, 'CISG-AC Opinion No. 16, Exclusion of the CISG under Article 6', Rapporteur: Dr Lisa Spagnolo, Rules 1-3, Comments para 2.3.

the *CISG* from around the world.[34] Moreover, 'the law of Victoria' will have the same effect, as the *CISG* forms part of the law of the State of Victoria, and all other States in Australia.

However, choice of a particular code or Act may exclude the *CISG*. For example, 'The UCC applies to this contract' may oust the *CISG* as an implicit exclusion.[35] An express exclusion will be far more effective; for example: 'This contract is governed by the law of China, excluding the *CISG*'. In this case, the domestic rules of Chinese law would apply. However, it should be noted that, in pragmatic terms, this would not produce any vastly different result for the parties, since Chinese law is based on the *CISG* and UNIDROIT Principles.[36]

25.4.2 Effect of the *CISG*

The effect of its application means that the law of the contract is the *CISG*, with residual domestic law filling in for those issues not dealt with by the *CISG*. For example, the *CISG* will deal with formation, breach and remedy, but validity will be determined by domestic law. Choice of law rules will determine which is the applicable residual domestic law (discussed above).

For most issues governed by the *CISG*, its rules exclusively determine matters falling within its scope, as it generally displaces domestic law for those issues.

25.4.3 UNIDROIT Principles: application and effect

The UNIDROIT Principles can only become applicable by choice of the parties. Unlike the *CISG*, there is no default application. The manner in which they apply may ultimately be either as:

(1) 'rules of law' where a choice of a-national rules of law (soft law) is permitted, or

(2) as terms incorporated into the contract by reference, depending on the relevant conflict of laws rules.

The latter is the approach currently taken within Australia since,[37] like many other jurisdictions, only choice of a national or State law is permitted.[38] In international commercial arbitration, the

34 See eg *Sté Ceramique Culinaire de France v Sté Musgrave Ltd*, Cour de Cassation, France, 17 December 1996, http://cisgw3.law.pace.edu/cases/961217f1.html; Oberster Gerichtshof [Supreme Court], Austria, 26 January 2005, http://cisgw3.law.pace.edu/cases/050126a3.html; International Chamber of Commerce (ICC) Award No. 7565 of 1994, http://cisgw3.law.pace.edu/cases/947565i1.html; Bundesgerichtshof [Federal Supreme Court] (BGH), Germany, 25 November 1998, http://cisgw3.law.pace.edu/cases/981125g1.html; *St Paul Guardian Insurance Company and Travelers Insurance Company v Neuromed Medical Systems & Support*, GmbH, 2002 U.S. Dist. LEXIS 5096 (S.D.N.Y.), 26 March 2002, http://cisgw3.law.pace.edu/cases/020326u1.html; *BP International, Ltd v Empresa Estatal Petroleos de Ecuador*, 332 F.3d 333, US Court of Appeals (5th Cir.), 11 June 2003, http://cisgw3.law.pace.edu/cases/030611u1.html.

35 CISG-AC Opinion No. 16, above n 33, Rule 4(a)(iii).

36 See «中华人民共和国合同法» Contract Law of the People's Republic of China National People's Congress, 15 March 1999.

37 *Engel v Adelaide Hebrew Congregation Inc* (2007) 98 SASR 402; *Re South Head & District Synagogue (Sydney) (admin apptd)* [2017] NSWSC 823, [29]. These cases follow the UK position: see *Halpern v Halpern (Nos 1 and 2)* [2008] QB 195; *Shamil Bank of Bahrain EC v Beximco Pharmaceuticals Ltd* [2004] 1 WLR 1784, [51]; Michael Douglas and Nicholas Loadsman, 'The Impact of The Hague Principles on Choice of Law' (2018) 19(1) *Melbourne Journal of International Law* 1, 9.

38 See eg Rome Regulation I, Recital 13, art 3; *Beximco Pharmaceuticals Ltd v Shamil Bank of Bahrain* [2004] 1 WLR 1784; Petra Butler, 'Choices of Law' in LA DiMatteo, A Janssen, U Magnus and R Schulze (eds), *International Sales Law: Contract, Principles & Practice* (Hart Publishing, 2016) 1025, para 23.

2006 update to the Model Law on International Commercial Arbitration now explicitly allows the application of soft 'rules of law', as opposed to allowing only national or hard law: art 28 Model Law on ICA. Obviously, as the UNIDROIT Principles are selected as 'soft law', they cannot apply as part of national domestic law.

Importantly, contrary to the *CISG*, which applies unless parties opt out, UNIDROIT Principles only apply if and when parties opt in.

The subject matter of UNIDROIT Principles is broader than that of the *CISG*, therefore they may apply to pure service contracts. The UNIDROIT Principles will, in most cases, provide the contractual rules unless mandatory domestic rules override them.[39] In matters not dealt with by the UNIDROIT Principles, the domestic national law applicable pursuant to the conflict of laws rules of the forum will apply.

25.5 Interpretation

Echoes of the *CISG* interpretive model are found within the UNIDROIT Principles, albeit in a modified form with additional guidelines. The following briefly outlines the *CISG* and UNIDROIT approaches, and the main differences between them.

25.5.1 Implementing legislation

One of the most common misconceptions about the *CISG* in Australia is about how and when it should be applied. The wording of the legislation implementing the *CISG* in Australia has been interpreted by some courts, beginning with the Victorian Supreme Court in *Playcorp Pty Ltd v Taiyo Kogyo Ltd*,[40] to mean that the *CISG* need only be applied if it leads to a different result than domestic law.

Playcorp Pty Ltd v Taiyo Kogyo Ltd [2003] VSC 108

Facts and issues

An Australian buyer and Japanese seller entered into a sales contract for radio-controlled toys. Defects arose, supply was refused, and litigation ensued. Although the *CISG* was pleaded, counsel for both parties at hearing argued on the basis of the domestic *Goods Act 1958* (Vic).

Decision

Per Hansen J at [245]:

39 UNIDROIT Principles art 1.4.

40 *Playcorp Pty Ltd v Taiyo Kogyo Ltd* [2003] VSC 108 http://cisgw3.law.pace.edu/cases/030424a2.html [235] and [245] (holding it 'unnecessary to consider ... the proper law of the contract. ... [T]he Convention has the benefit of paramountcy over the Goods Act in the event of any inconsistency between the two. As I have said, no such inconsistency was suggested, and having regard also to the way in which the case was conducted, it is appropriate to proceed on the basis that there is none.'); *Attorney-General of Botswana v Aussie Diamond Products Pty Ltd* [2010] WASC 141 http://cisgw3.law.pace.edu/cases/100623a2.html [210].

> [The Court held it was] unnecessary to consider ... the proper law of the contract. ... [T]he Convention has the benefit of paramountcy over the *Goods Act* in the event of any inconsistency between the two. As I have said, no such inconsistency was suggested, and having regard also to the way in which the case was conducted, it is appropriate to proceed on the basis that there is none.

This decision is indeed unfortunate, and does not reflect the intention of the legislatures, which implemented the *CISG* to give effect to Australia's international obligations as a signatory to the Convention.[41] The following legislative provisions implementing the *CISG* are identical throughout Australia, and mirror provisions in many other countries.

Goods Act 1958 (Vic) ss 86–87

86 Convention to have the force of law
The provisions of the Convention have the force of law in Victoria.

87 Convention to prevail in event of inconsistency
The provisions of the Convention prevail over any other law in force in Victoria to the extent of any inconsistency.

It is submitted that the first provision giving the *CISG* the force of law is intended to have primacy.[42] Thus the *CISG* should be applied in accordance with its own terms where it is the applicable law. The second provision stating the *CISG* shall prevail over domestic law where inconsistent[43] should be viewed only as a secondary clarification of the *CISG*'s effect in displacing domestic law dealing with topics that fall within its scope; not as a mandate for the application of domestic law despite applicability of the *CISG* on the basis that the outcome is the same. The latter view would undermine development of the *CISG* in Australia and would lead to a failure to properly implement the uniform global sales law, as intended by signatories to the Convention.[44] More recent cases have ignored this line of authority, but this aspect of *Playcorp* is yet to be expressly overruled.

41 Lisa Spagnolo, 'The Last Outpost: Automatic CISG Opt Outs, Misapplications and the Costs of Ignoring the Vienna Sales Convention for Australian Lawyers' (2009) 10(1) Melbourne Journal of International Law 141, 190–191.

42 Bruno Zeller, 'Editorial Remarks' in Pace Law School, *CISG Case Presentation: Playcorp Pty Ltd v Taiyo Kogyo Limited* (2003) http://cisgw3.law.pace.edu/cases/030424a2.html#ce; Spagnolo, 'Last Outpost' above n 41. See *Goods Act 1958* (Vic) s 86; *Sale of Goods (Vienna Convention) Act 1986* (WA) s 5; *Sale of Goods (Vienna Convention) Act 1987* (Tas) s 5; *Sale of Goods (Vienna Convention) Act 1986* (NSW) s 5; *Sale of Goods (Vienna Convention) Act 1987* (ACT) s 5; *Sale of Goods (Vienna Convention) Act 1986* (SA) s 4; *Sale of Goods (Vienna Convention) Act 1986* (Qld) s 5; *Sale of Goods (Vienna Convention) Act 1987* (NT) s 5.

43 See *Goods Act 1958* (Vic) s 87; *Sale of Goods (Vienna Convention) Act 1986* (WA) s 6; *Sale of Goods (Vienna Convention) Act 1987* (Tas) s 6; *Sale of Goods (Vienna Convention) Act 1986* (NSW) s 6; *Sale of Goods (Vienna Convention) Act 1987* (ACT) s 6; *Sale of Goods (Vienna Convention) Act 1986* (SA) s 5; *Sale of Goods (Vienna Convention) Act 1986* (Qld) s 6; *Sale of Goods (Vienna Convention) Act 1987* (NT) s 6.

44 As to whether failure to present arguments based on the *CISG* in court amounts to agreement to exclude the *CISG*, or waiver, see: CISG-AC Opinion No. 16, above n 33, rr 5, 6, Comments para 5.14.

As the UNIDROIT Principles can only apply as soft rules of law chosen by parties opting in, the question of implementing legislation naturally does not arise.

25.5.2 Autonomous interpretation

25.5.2.1 *CISG*

The *CISG* has its own interpretive rules and method. Thus, it is not to be applied as one would apply a domestic statute, and rules of statutory interpretation relevant to domestic legislation are not relevant to the *CISG*. It should not be viewed through 'domestic lenses' but in a way that preserves its uniformity.

Article 7(1) is paramount. It states that the *CISG* is to be interpreted having regard to its uniform and international nature. This means it must be interpreted and applied autonomously, ie independently of domestic law influences. Courts and tribunals interpreting the *CISG* should not refer to domestic legislation or domestic case law. The *CISG* has its own body of cases, which are freely available online, and may be referred to by courts all around the world. There are now thousands of cases from many jurisdictions, and many are either translated into English, or an English abstract is available.[45] There are official digests collecting case law published by UNCITRAL, also freely available online, with hyperlinks to cases.[46] These conveniently organise and present the cases in a way that makes the principles and decisions easy to access.

Obviously, court decisions from other jurisdictions are not binding on Australian courts, but they have persuasive value, especially given the mandate in art 7(1) to have regard to the international character of the *CISG*. It is important, if the aim of uniformity is to be realised, that courts and tribunals remember this direction.

The legislative history of the *CISG* is available online and can be referred to for additional clarification.[47] Autonomous interpretation is generally also taken to mean that it is widely acceptable to refer to scholarship on the *CISG* in its application. Ample material is available, with highly organised and well-respected commentaries such as those edited by Schwenzer (soon to be Schroeter), and another edited by Kröll, Mistelis and Viscasillas, as well as many others.[48] There are numerous papers, and editorial remarks on decided cases.

45 Pace Kritzer Database http://www.cisg.law.pace.edu/ (journal articles, most cases, bibliography). Users will need to create an account to use this website, but can do so for free; CISG-online http://www.cisg-online.ch/index.cfm?pageID=29; UNCITRAL http://www.uncitral.org/uncitral/en/uncitral_texts/sale_goods.html (CLOUT case abstracts).

46 Annotated UN Digest of Cases: http://cisgw3.law.pace.edu/cisg/text/digest-2012-toc.html (organised by article number). See also Pace Law School, *Recently added cases, case translations and commentaries* (2016) http://cisgw3.law.pace.edu/cisg/new-cases.html.

47 Legislative history can be found at Pace Kritzer https://www.cisg.law.pace.edu/cisg/conference.html; or UNCITRAL Website Yearbooks http://www.uncitral.org/uncitral/publications/yearbook.html.

48 Ingerborg Schwenzer (ed), *Schlechtriem & Schwenzer: Commentary on the Convention on International Sale of Goods (CISG)* (Oxford University Press, 4th ed, 2016); Stefan Kröll, Loukas A Mistelis and Maria del Pilar Perales Viscasillas (eds), *UN Convention on Contracts for the International Sale of Goods*, (CH Beck, 2nd ed, 2018). See also John Honnold (Harry M Flechtner (ed)), *Uniform Law for International Sales under the 1980 United Nations Convention* (Kluwer, 4th ed, 2009); Peter Huber and Alastair Mullis, *The CISG: A new textbook for Students and Practitioners* (Sellier, 2007) and older texts such as Cesare Massimo Bianca and Michael Joachim Bonell, *Commentary on the International Sales Law: The 1980 Vienna Sales Convention* (Giuffrè, 1987).

One further resource should be noted. As there is no appellate court for appeals from national court decisions on the *CISG*, a body of respected *CISG* scholars established a private body, the CISG Advisory Council, which issues Opinions to resolve divergence in court decisions on important aspects. There are now 17 such Opinions, again available online.[49] These are considerable works of scholarship, which analyse comparative law, *CISG* cases, and divergent views, before providing reasoned conclusions which restate the law in black letter form with further elaborative comments. The CISG Advisory Council Opinions are now cited by courts and tribunals as valuable interpretive aids, and assist in developing and maintaining the *CISG*'s internationally uniform application.

25.5.2.2 UNIDROIT Principles

The UNIDROIT Principles have their own interpretive method. Like the *CISG*, they should not be viewed through 'domestic lenses'. Article 1.6.1 of the UNIDROIT Principles adopts similar wording as the *CISG*, thereby requiring they be interpreted with regard to their international character and the need to promote uniformity in their application.

There are some cases decided on the basis of UNIDROIT Principles, although the numbers of cases are far lower than under the *CISG*. The cases may be located online, with abstracts in English.[50] While non-Australian cases are not binding on Australian courts, they still have persuasive value in the interpretation of the UNIDROIT Principles.

Additionally, the UNIDROIT Principles contain extensive official comments which expand and explain the rules, and provide helpful examples illustrating how they should be applied. There are also a number of scholarly commentaries which may provide additional guidance, principally the Vogenauer commentary.[51]

25.5.3 Approaches to internal and external gaps

In every piece of legislation, issues exist for which no clear answer is apparent on the face of the express provisions. In the *CISG*, art 7(2) contains an interpretive hierarchy and deals with internal gaps; that is, 'gaps' within the scope of issues governed by the *CISG*. It requires matters governed by the *CISG* but not expressly settled by it to be resolved by application of 'general principles' of the *CISG*. Only where this is not possible should domestic law resolve the issue. Thus courts and tribunals should aim to resolve 'internal gaps' by reference to general principles. There is no explicit list of these, but many have been identified by scholars through a process of deduction. One such principle is *favor contractus*—the principle that the contract should be kept on foot where possible. Others include duties of communication, and the principle against inconsistent behaviour (*venire contra factum proprium*).[52]

49 CISG Advisory Council, http://www.cisgac.com/opinions/.

50 Unilex, *Unilex on CISG & Unidroit Principles: International Case Law & Bibliography* http://www.unilex.info/.

51 Stefan Vogenauer and Jan Vogenauer (eds), *Commentary on the PICC of International Commercial Contracts* (Oxford University Press, 2nd ed, 2015).

52 See eg Ingeborg Schwenzer and Pascal Hachem, 'Article 7' in I Schwenzer (ed), *Schlechtriem & Schwenzer: Commentary on the Convention on International Sale of Goods (CISG)* (Oxford University Press, 4th ed, 2016), art 7 paras 32 and 35.

For issues external to the *CISG*, known as 'external gaps'—such as validity issues, or property in goods—the *CISG* has nothing to say on the matter, as they fall outside its scope. Thus the residual domestic law applicable pursuant to the conflict of laws rules of the forum must resolve such issues.

Article 1.6.2 of the UNIDROIT Principles adopts the same structure as the *CISG* art 7(2).

25.5.4 Good faith

Article 7(1) refers to 'good faith'. The role of good faith within the *CISG* is still debated; however, the majority view is that this is a directive to courts in member states to interpret and apply the *CISG* in a manner which promotes good faith, rather than a positive duty of good faith imposed directly upon the parties.[53] Thus the better view is that it influences interpretation of the provisions of the *CISG*, and only has an indirect impact on the shape of the duties of parties. Certainly it is not a general clause in the nature of a German *Treu und Glauben*, which creates a general duty of good faith imposed on the parties directly.

The orientation of good faith is very different within the UNIDROIT Principles. The role of good faith in UNIDROIT is much broader, reflecting stronger civil law influences. Article 1.7.1 of the UNIDROIT Principles directly imposes a duty of good faith on parties, and states that this cannot be excluded if parties have selected the UNIDROIT Principles to govern their contract: art 1.7.2.[54]

25.5.5 Interpretation of party intent, extrinsic evidence and the parol evidence rule

25.5.5.1 *CISG*

The *CISG* sets out a subjective/objective test for party intent. Subjective intent is only relevant where the other party either knew of the intent, or could not have been unaware: art 8(1) *CISG*. This is of course also true in Australian law. Where the addressee knows that the speaker is joking then, difficult issues of proof aside, the speaker's subjective intent prevails.[55] Naturally, it will be a very rare case where the subjective intent test prevails. The threshold for knowledge under art 8(1) *CISG* is so high that it is rarely applied in determining intent. In the vast bulk of cases, the only relevant intent is that which a reasonable addressee would attribute to the speaker: art 8(2) *CISG*. Thus, in practice, the predominant test of intent is the objective standard of intent found in art 8(2).

---

53 On the range of views, see eg (interpretive or gap filling only): Schwenzer and Hachem, above n 52, art 7 para 18; Michael Bridge, *The International Sale of Goods* (Oxford University Press, 3rd ed, 2013) 509. But see (good faith as a positive duty): Fritz Enderlein and Dietrich Maskow, *International Sales Law* (Oceana, 1992) art 7 para 2.1; Ulrich Magnus, 'Remarks on Good Faith' (1998) 10 *Pace International Law Review* 89. See also Lisa Spagnolo, 'Opening Pandora's Box: Good Faith & Precontractual Liability in the CISG' (2007) 21(2) *Temple International & Comparative Law Journal* 261.

54 However, see discussion below at n 114.

55 See *R v Clarke* (1927) 40 CLR 227; *Air Great Lakes Pty Ltd v K S Easter (Holdings) Pty Ltd* (1985) 2 NSWLR 309, 337–39. But see, in the USA, *Lucy v Zehmer*, 196 Ca. 493, 84 SE 2d 516 (1954) (the fact that sellers considered the sale of land a joke did not prevent an order for specific performance).

Yet an important difference between the *CISG* and Australian domestic law lies in how intent may be proven. Notably, the *CISG* rejects the parol evidence rule and plain meaning rule: arts 8(3) and 11 *CISG*.[56] Article 8(3) makes it plain that 'all relevant circumstances' should be considered, including surrounding circumstances and negotiations. Moreover, unlike the position in Australian law, art 8(3) allows subsequent conduct of parties to be considered to determine their intent at the time of concluding the contract, although of course the weight attributed to such evidence is a matter for the adjudicator. Thus permitted evidence of intent is far less restrictive than would be the case under Australian law (contrast the position set out at **10.3**.

Such evidence is relevant under the *CISG* to both identify the terms and to ascertain their meaning. The *CISG* does not distinguish between these purposes, contrary to Australian law. Moreover, unlike the Australian position, there is no precondition of 'ambiguity' for resort to these forms of evidence under the *CISG*,[57] as this 'would impede one of the basic goals of contract interpretation under the *CISG*, which is to focus on the parties' actual intent'.[58]

25.5.5.2 UNIDROIT Principles

The UNIDROIT Principles adopt the same subjective/objective structure for intent as the *CISG*, but restates the test twice: once for interpretation of the contract as a whole (art 4.1), and again for interpretation of the words and conduct of the parties: art 4.2 UNIDROIT Principles. Ultimately, the tests are very similar,[59] and achieve the same effect as the *CISG* art 8(1) and (2). The main objective test is found in arts 4.1.2 and 4.2.2 UNIDROIT Principles. Similarly, the Official Comments elaborate that the reasonable person stands in the shoes of the addressee, and is attributed with the addressee's knowledge and background. The reasonable person thus has an understanding which 'could reasonably be expected of persons with ... the same linguistic knowledge, technical skill, or business experience as the parties' rather than some 'general and abstract criterion of reasonableness'.[60]

56 While there were early suggestions the parol evidence rule involved a matter of validity outside the *CISG*'s scope, the overwhelming view within both scholarship and cases has been that domestic parol evidence rules are overridden by the *CISG*: see eg CISG Advisory Council, 'CISG-AC Opinion No 3 Parol Evidence Rule, Plain Meaning Rule, Contractual Merger Clause and the CISG', Rapporteur: Prof. Richard Hyland, Rule 1, Comments paras 2.1–2.8; *MCC-Marble Ceramic Center, Inc v Ceramica Nuova D'Agostino, SpA*, 114 F 3d 1384, 1392–93 (11th Cir 1998), USA, 29 June 1998 http://cisgw3.law.pace.edu/cases/980629u1.html (*CISG* precludes application of the parol evidence rule); *Claudia v Olivieri Footwear Ltd*, 1998 WL 164824, 5-6 (SDNY), USA, 6 April 1998, http://cisgw3.law.pace.edu/cases/980406u1.html; *Filanto SpA v Chilewich International Corporation*, 789 F Supp. 1229, 1238 n 7 (SDNY 1992), app. dismissed, 984 F 2d 58 (2nd Cir 1993), USA, 14 April 1992, http://cisgw3.law.pace.edu/cases/920414u1.html.

57 Thus the *CISG* and the UNIDROIT Principles both reject the 'plain meaning rule' whereby, in ascertaining the meaning of words, one must look to the plain meaning of the words, and not have recourse to extrinsic evidence unless ambiguity exists. See CISG Advisory Council, CISG-AC Opinion No 3, above n 56, Rule 2, Comments para. 3.3; Lisa Spagnolo, 'Contractual Interpretation', in LA DiMatteo, A Janssen, U Magnus and R Schulze (eds), *International Sales Law: Contract, Principles & Practice* (Beck/Hart/Nomos, 2016) paras 60–61.

58 CISG-AC Opinion No 3, above n 56, Comment para 3.2.

59 Stefan Vogenauer, 'Introduction to Article 4', in Stefan Vogenauer (ed), *Commentary on the PICC of International Commercial Contracts* (Oxford University Press, 2nd ed, 2015) Introduction to art 4 para 5.

60 UNIDROIT Principles art 4.1, Comments para 2.

The UNIDROIT Principles add an additional subjective layer of intent within art 4.1.1, by requiring contracts be interpreted according to the parties' 'common intention'. However, as the Official Comments concede, this test will rarely be useful.[61]

In the same manner as the *CISG*, art 4.3(a) UNIDROIT Principles includes 'preliminary negotiations' as a relevant factor in determining intent, while the nature of the contract, and any conduct of parties subsequent to conclusion of the contract is also relevant: art 4.3(c) UNIDROIT Principles.[62] Evidence of preliminary negotiations could include catalogues, web-pages, minutes of meetings and letters of intent.[63]

25.5.6 Merger/entire agreement clauses to limit extrinsic evidence

Parties are free to agree on restriction of extrinsic evidence regarding the contractual terms by the inclusion of 'merger' clauses or 'entire agreement' clauses, as the *CISG*'s rules can be tailored by the parties: art 6 *CISG*. An example of a merger clause is as follows:[64]

> This contract with exhibits attached, constitutes the entire agreement of the parties and supersedes all other written or oral agreements between the parties concerning its subject matter.

These clauses indicate agreement that the written contractual terms within the document comprise their entire agreement. In such clauses, parties may acknowledge that any prior oral or written statements do not form part of the contractual terms (and, depending on the wording, that they waive reliance upon such prior statements). They seek to ensure that earlier promises, statements or conduct are disregarded in construing the contract, so that the adjudicator looks only to the written agreement to identify contractual terms.[65]

Merger clauses will be effective in modifying art 8(3) *CISG*, although extrinsic evidence may still be used to determine the preliminary question as to the meaning of the merger clause, and in particular, whether such an exclusionary effect was intended by parties.[66] Merger clauses are expressly covered in art 2.1.17 UNIDROIT Principles,[67] which also supports their enforceability and consequent exclusion of extrinsic evidence in interpretation of contracts containing such clauses, provided the adjudicator finds parties indeed intended the clause to have such effect. Article 2.1.17 ensures the adjudicator may use extrinsic evidence to interpret the meaning of such a clause.

61 UNIDROIT Principles art 4.2, Comments para 1.

62 See Vogenauer, above n 59, art 4.3, para 19.

63 Ibid, art 4.3 para 5.

64 Larry DiMatteo, 'Merger Clauses', in LA DiMatteo, A Janssen, U Magnus and R Schulze (eds), *International Sales Law: Contract, Principles & Practice* (Beck/Hart/Nomos, 2016) para 184.

65 Within domestic law, doctrines relating to estoppel may circumvent the effectiveness of such clauses in precluding earlier statements from being upheld as contractual terms. Furthermore, an entire agreement clause might be ineffective to prevent a claim being made on non-contractual grounds, such as negligent misrepresentation, or statutory breaches, such as misleading or deceptive conduct. See eg, s 18 Australian Consumer Law; sch 2 *Competition and Consumer Act 2010* (Cth).

66 CISG-AC Opinion No 3, above n 56, Rule 3. It may be 'prudent that a preliminary agreement be entered to derogate from CISG article 11's "no writing" requirement': DiMatteo, above n 64, para 174.

67 UNIDROIT Principles art 2.1.17. Merger clauses are also mentioned in art 4.3, Comment 4 in passing, since they affect the relevance of preliminary negotiations which are otherwise an interpretive aid.

25.5.7 Relevance of usages and practices

Usages may be considered if they are international in nature and regularly observed, as long as parties have not agreed to the contrary: art 9(2) *CISG*. The requirement that usages be 'widely known to' or 'regularly observed by' parties engaged in 'international trade' may result in regionally specific usages being insufficient. Any past practices established between parties are also relevant: arts 8(3) and 9(1) *CISG*. For something to amount to a past practice, a significant pattern of usage will need to be established.[68]

UNIDROIT Principles art 4.3 also recognises past practices and trade usage as relevant to contractual interpretation. Practices which the parties have established between themselves, meanings commonly attributed to terms and expressions in the trade, and usages in a general sense are to be taken into account.[69] The UNIDROIT Principles separate trade specific from general usages, and, contrary to the *CISG*, do not require usages to be international.

25.5.8 General interpretive principles

The *CISG* lacks a list of interpretive guidelines, although some have gradually developed over time through scholarship and cases. By contrast, the UNIDROIT Principles contain a number of general interpretive rules. In this section, the *CISG* and UNIDROIT Principles are discussed together.

25.5.8.1 Plain meaning vs purposive

The *CISG* and UNIDROIT Principles both focus on the parties' actual intent, and thus reject the plain meaning rule which confines adjudicators to the contractual wording unless ambiguity exists.[70] Instead, irrespective of ambiguity, they expressly direct attention of courts and tribunals to extrinsic evidence in determining the meaning of terms:[71] art 8(3) *CISG*; UNIDROIT Principles arts 4.1–4.3. The UNIDROIT Principles include 'the nature and purpose of the contract' amongst relevant circumstances to be considered.[72] Furthermore, the test of the 'reasonableness' in the understanding of the addressee promotes a test of commercial reasonableness in contract interpretation: art 8(2) *CISG*.

68 Two past instances have been held to be too low: Civil Court Basel, Switzerland 3 December 1997 (*White urea case*), http://cisgw3.law.pace.edu/cases/971203s2.html; Lower Court Duisburg, Germany 13 April 2000 (*Pizza cartons case*), http://cisgw3.law.pace.edu/cases/000413g1.html; whilst 12 instances have been considered sufficient to amount to established past practices: Guangdong High People's Court [Appellate Court], PR China 2005 (*Possehl (HK) Ltd v China Metals & Minerals Import & Export (Shenshen) Corporation*), http://cisgw3.law.pace.edu/cases/050000c2.html. However, each case turns on its individual circumstances. See further, UNCITRAL, *CISG Case Digest* (2012), http://www.cisg.law.pace.edu/cisg/text/digest-2012-09.html, at para 7.

69 UNIDROIT Principles arts 4.3(b), (e), (f).

70 CISG Advisory Council Opinion No 3, above n 56, Comments para 3.2.

71 *CISG* art 8(3). See M Schmidt-Kessel, 'Article 8' in P Schlechtriem and I Schwenzer (eds), *Commentary on the UN Convention on the International Sale of Goods (CISG)* (Oxford University Press, 3rd ed, 2010) art 8 para 18.

72 UNIDROIT Principles art 4.3(d).

25.5.8.2 Negotiated vs standard terms

Article 2.1.21 of the UNIDROIT Principles state that negotiated terms prevail over standard terms. The Official Comments to UNIDROIT Principles art 2.1.21 explains that: 'standard terms are by definition prepared in advance . . . without their content being discussed by the parties [thus it] is therefore logical that [specifically negotiated] provisions will prevail over conflicting standard terms since they are more likely to reflect the intention of the parties in the given case'. Within the UNIDROIT Principles, as in the *CISG*, the prevalence of negotiated over standard terms is treated as a question of formation.[73]

25.5.8.3 Whole contract

UNIDROIT Principles art 4.4 provides that 'terms and expressions shall be interpreted in the light of the whole contract or statement in which they appear'. While the *CISG* does not explicitly mention this rule, in practice it is applied within *CISG* cases.

25.5.8.4 Contractual effect

The UNIDROIT Principles art 4.5 Comments state 'it is to be expected that when drafting their contract parties do not use words to no purpose'. Article 4.5 of the UNIDROIT Principles thus provides that 'contract terms shall be interpreted so as to give effect to all the terms rather than to deprive some of them of effect'. The *CISG* is silent on this issue. However, this *effet utile* approach is consistent with an objectively reasonable understanding: art 8(2) *CISG*.

25.5.8.5 Linguistic discrepancies

A recurrent problem in international contracts is conclusion of contracts in multiple languages. The *CISG* does not expressly mention this issue. However, standard terms written in a language that the other party could not be expected to understand should not be considered to have been incorporated into the contract under the *CISG*.[74] This accords with the objective understanding of a reasonable person in the addressee's position: art 8(2) *CISG*. The UNIDROIT Principles explain that parties may nominate which language version of a contract is the authoritative version: art 4.7 UNIDROIT Principles.[75]

25.5.8.6 Specific vs general

The UNIDROIT Principles suggest that more specific clauses prevail over clauses of a general nature: UNIDROIT Principles art 4.4 Comment 2. This can be seen as a sub-rule of the notion that contracts should be read as a whole, because it requires the characterisation of clauses as relatively general or specific in relation to one another.

73 Ingeborg Schwenzer, Pascal Hachem and Christopher Kee, *Global Sales and Contract Law* (Oxford University Press, 2011) 296 para 26.17.

74 CISG Advisory Council, 'CISG-AC Opinion No 13 Inclusion of Standard Terms under the CISG', Rapporteur: Prof. Sieg Eiselen, Rule 5, Comments para 5.2.

75 See also UNIDROIT Principles art 4.7, Comment.

25.5.8.7 *Contra proferentem* rule

This rule of interpretation which resolves any ambiguity against the party which drafted the clause may be applied within the *CISG* in regard to standard terms.[76] UNIDROIT Principles art 4.6 broadens the *contra proferentem* rule beyond standard terms, and provides that whenever terms are unclear, interpretation against the party supplying them is preferred. The Comments to UNIDROIT Principles art 4.6 clarifies that the party supplying the term 'bears the risk of possible lack of clarity'.[77]

25.6 Formalities

25.6.1 Freedom of form

CISG contracts may be concluded orally, or in writing, or by a combination of both. This is confirmed by art 11 *CISG* which states that contracts need not be in writing, and art 8(3) *CISG* which allows 'all relevant circumstances', including extrinsic evidence, to be taken into account in determination of the parties' intent. As mentioned at **25.5.5.1**, in stark contrast to domestic Australian contract law (see **10.3.1**), the *CISG* abolishes the parol evidence rule, and instead adopts a freedom of form for contracts governed by it.[78]

There are only two exceptions to this position. The first is where a member state has made a reservation under art 96, thus preserving domestic 'in writing' requirements, although the number of reservation countries has dwindled to just eight in any event.[79] The second is where parties wish to restrict the form which contracts may take through a merger clause, discussed at **25.5.6** above.

The UNIDROIT Principles likewise uphold the notion of freedom of form, although they may be overridden by mandatory domestic law containing form requirement, as UNIDROIT Principles are soft law: art 1.2 UNIDROIT Principles.

25.6.2 Party agreement on form and no oral modification clauses

Parties also frequently include 'no oral modification' (NOM) clauses within their contracts. NOM clauses attempt to preclude oral post-formation promises from being effective in amending or modifying the written contractual terms. By inclusion of a NOM clause, parties signal their agreement to modify art 29 *CISG*, which would otherwise allow contracts to be amended by oral agreement. Although not expressly mentioned in the *CISG*, NOM clauses will also be respected under the *CISG*, except for the purposes of interpretation of the NOM clause

76 CISG-AC Opinion No 13, above n 74, Rule 9, Comments para 9.2.

77 UNIDROIT Principles art 4.6, Comment.

78 Articles 8(3), 11 *CISG*. See also CISG-AC Opinion No 3, above n 56, Rule 1, Comments paras 2.1–2.8, and above n 56.

79 *CISG* art 96 allows countries to make a reservation to effectively preserve domestic writing requirements, although its effect is problematic. With the fall of the Soviet bloc, most such domestic requirements no longer exist, and a number of former reservation countries have withdrawn their reservation: CISG-AC Opinion No 15, above n 20, Rule 5, Comments paras 4.2–4.3.

itself. In other words, in determining the meaning of a NOM clause, the court or tribunal may have regard to extrinsic evidence.[80] However, a party conducting themselves in an inconsistent manner, in circumstances where the other party has relied upon that conduct, will be precluded from reliance upon a NOM clause: art 29(2).

The following is an example of a NOM clause:

> No variation, modification or amendment to this agreement shall be effective unless it is in writing, signed by each of the parties.

UNIDROIT Principles art 2.1.18 expressly enables parties to use NOM clauses to render ineffective any modification or termination other than in the agreed form, but like the *CISG*, creates an exception precluding parties from relying upon a NOM clause where they have conducted themselves in a contrary manner and the other party has relied on that conduct. In relation to domestic law, see the operation of domestic estoppel in similar circumstances: **7.2**.

25.7 Formation

25.7.1 *CISG*—offers, withdrawal and revocation

Under the *CISG* art 14, offers must be:

(1) sufficiently definite; and
(2) manifest an intention to be bound if accepted.

In order to be sufficiently definite, usually the goods, quantity, parties and price must be included in the offer, or at least a means to determine those elements. However, if no price is agreed, art 55 *CISG* may supply a default 'price generally charged' at the time of conclusion for goods sold in 'comparable circumstances'. Offers made to the public rather than to specific addressees are normally considered mere invitations to make an offer: art 14(2) *CISG*. Offers become effective once they 'reach' the offeree: art 15(1) *CISG*.

Standard terms may be incorporated within an offer, or indeed an acceptance, provided two tests are satisfied. There must be:

(1) a reference to the standard terms, manifesting an intention to incorporate them, as would be understood by a reasonable person in the addressee's position; and,
(2) the standard terms must be 'made available'.

This test is fair within international trade, where different languages and legal backgrounds may easily cause confusion. Thus, to incorporate standard terms into an offer, the offeror must 'make them available' to the offeree, either by attaching them to the offer, printing them on the reverse of the offer, or including a hyperlink to them within an emailed offer. As explained by the CISG Advisory Council, the main concern is the ease of access to the terms, so as to have a

80 CISG-AC Opinion No 3, above n 56, Comments para 4.6 (extrinsic evidence admissible to first determine whether there was clear intent for the clause to have this effect). See Pilar Perales Viscasillas, 'Modification and Termination of the Contract (art 29 CISG)' (2005-2006) 25 *Journal of Law & Commerce* 167, 179.

'reasonable opportunity' to read and preserve (ie print or save) them. Thus, any link that requires the addressee to 'hunt' further for the correct set of standard terms from amongst many sets of standard terms, or to click through various pages on a website to locate them, may not satisfy the 'making available' test.[81]

Unlike Australian law (see **5.3**), offers may be irrevocable if they are 'firm' offers; that is, they exhibit an intention to be irrevocable: art 16(2)(a) *CISG*; for example, if an offer expressly or impliedly indicates that it will be held open for a period.[82] A rebuttable presumption of irrevocability will arise if the offer sets a fixed period or deadline for acceptance.[83] An offer might also become irrevocable if the offeree reasonably relies upon it. Reasonable reliance could include contract preparations, hiring staff or commencing production. Irrevocability due to reasonable reliance arises in accordance with art 16(2)(b) *CISG*, a provision which embodies one of the general principles of the *CISG*, that parties are prohibited from contradictory behaviour (*venire contra factum proprium*).

Whether revocable or irrevocable, any offer may be withdrawn, provided the withdrawal reaches the offeree before or at the same time as the offer: art 15(2) *CISG*. Where an offer is not irrevocable, it may be revoked after it reaches the offeree, provided an acceptance has not yet been dispatched: art 16(1) *CISG*. An offer will terminate upon any rejection reaching the offeror: art 17 *CISG*.

In formation under the *CISG*, notices generally take effect upon receipt (art 24). In terms of calculation of the time of receipt, some guidance is contained in art 20 *CISG*.

25.7.2 *CISG*—acceptance and modified acceptance

Acceptance must occur either within the time fixed for acceptance, or alternatively, within a reasonable time of the offer (art 18(2) *CISG*), a measure of time which varies depending on the circumstances, such as perishability of the goods. However, oral offers must be accepted immediately: art 18(2) *CISG*.[84]

Acceptance in the form of an indication of assent must normally 'reach' the offeree to become effective: art 18(2) *CISG*. Unlike the traditional common law 'postal rule' (mail box rule), which held that acceptance by paper mail took effect when mailed or dispatched (see **5.4**), by contrast, the *CISG* relies purely upon a 'receipt' rule for acceptances.

Indications of assent must exhibit an intention to be bound, as would be understood by a reasonable person in the offeror's position: art 8(2) *CISG*. Indications of assent can take the form of words or conduct; for example, payment of the price. Like the common law,

81 CISG-AC Opinion No 13, above n 74, Comments paras 3.4 and 6.5; Bundesgerichtshof [Federal Supreme Court] (BGH), Germany, 31 October 2001 (Machinery case), http://cisgw3.law.pace.edu/cases/011031g1.html.

82 Words such as 'firm offer', 'fixed', 'will be held open', 'we stand by our offer until' or 'held open until' may be reasonably understood as indicating such an intent, although not determinative: Henry Mather, 'Firm Offers under the UCC and the CISG' (2000) 105(1) *Dickinson Law Review* 31, 44, 55; Ulrich Schroeter, 'Article 16' in I Schwenzer (ed), *Commentary on the UN Convention on the International Sale of Goods (CISG)* (Oxford University Press, 4th ed, 2016) art 16 para 8. In part, this is because the *CISG* does not require consideration for binding obligations.

83 Honnold, above n 48, art 16 para 143.1; Schroeter, above n 82, art 16 para 9.

84 Late acceptance can be effective under certain circumstances: art 21 *CISG*.

acceptance cannot be effected by mere silence alone: art 18(1) *CISG*. However, silence accompanied by conduct may be sufficient.

Normally, acceptance in the *CISG* involves an indication of assent, whether words or conduct, which becomes effective upon it 'reaching' the offeree. However, in certain limited circumstances, the need to indicate assent is waived by the offer; for example, by asking for a 'rush shipment', or through past practices, usage or a framework agreement.[85] Under this rare exception, acceptance can take effect immediately, not through indication of assent, but by conduct alone: art 18(3) *CISG*.

As to electronic communications, when the *CISG* was created in 1980, nobody had yet heard of email.[86] Electronic communication rules in the *UNCITRAL Model Law on Electronic Commerce 1994*[87] and the *2005 Convention on the Use of Electronic Communications in International Contracts* (e-CC)[88] were designed to work with the *CISG*. While yet to be widely recognised worldwide, the e-CC has been implemented in every Australian jurisdiction, within the *Electronic Transactions Acts*.[89] Irrespective of this, interpretation of the *CISG* has encompassed modern forms of communications.[90]

Unlike the traditional common law approach which required the terms within offers and acceptances to 'mirror' one another in order to successfully form a contract (see **Chapter 5**), on its face, art 19 *CISG* appears to allow acceptances to contain non-material differences to the offer which will form part of the terms unless they are objected to promptly ('without undue delay'). However, the exceptions to this rule listed in art 19(3) are so wide that this leaves little to comprise the category of 'non-material' changes. Article 19(3) *CISG* sets up a presumption that the following are 'material': price, payment, quality, quantity, delivery time and place, dispute resolution and liability. Nonetheless, the presumption may be rebutted if the divergence is to the advantage of the offeror, or where a purported change merely mirrors a *CISG* rule which would have been applicable in any event. Alternatively, usages or practices may help rebut the presumption.

A materially different acceptance will constitute a rejection and counter-offer: art 19(1) *CISG*. This might be accepted by conduct. An immaterially different acceptance will result in the conclusion of a contract with the modified terms, unless an there is an objection.

---

85 Lisa Spagnolo, 'Article 24' in P Mankowski (ed), *Commercial Law* (Nomos, 2018) art 24, paras 24–54.

86 Article 13 *CISG* expressly contemplates electronic communication, but only in the form of telegrams.

87 *UNCITRAL Model Law on Electronic Commerce* (1996), GA Res. 51/162, UN Doc. A/51/162 with additional art 5 bis adopted 1998 (1999).

88 *New York Convention on the Use of Electronic Communications in International* Contracts (2005), UN Doc. A/60/515 (entered into force 2013) ('e-CC').

89 *Electronic Transactions Act 1999* (Cth); *Electronic Transactions (Victoria) Act 2000* (Vic); *Electronic Transactions Act 2000* (NSW); *Electronic Transactions Act 2000* (SA); *Electronic Transactions Act 2000* (Tas); *Electronic Transactions Act 2011* (WA); *Electronic Transactions (Queensland) Act 2001* (Qld); *Electronic Transactions Act 2001* (ACT); *Electronic Transactions Act 2011* (NT). Australia is not yet a signatory at the time of writing, despite having expressed an intention to ratify, and already having implemented e-CC provisions in domestic legislation.

90 See CISG Advisory Council, 'CISG-AC Opinion No 1 Electronic Communications under CISG', Rapporteur: Prof. Christina Ramberg. For detailed discussion regarding different methods of online communications and their treatment within the *CISG* see Spagnolo, above n 85, paras 24–54.

Despite this apparently rigid formulation, the case law has developed to recognise more flexible formation methods, where no clear offer and acceptance arose, but parties went ahead with the contract anyway.[91]

25.7.3 *CISG*—standard terms and battle of the forms

An interesting development within the *CISG* relates to 'battle of the forms' scenarios, where each side proposes different standard terms, but goes ahead and performs without resolving which terms prevail. Notably, although on its face the *CISG* adopts a 'last shot' approach to formation in battle of form situations, the current prevailing opinion is that the 'knock out' rule should be applied. There is no express provision within the *CISG* on this matter. Instead, this development, which is not yet fully settled, appears to be slowly emerging from decided cases and scholarship.[92] The knock out approach essentially takes the view that any terms which clash are 'knocked out', and the contract is comprised of all remaining terms.[93] The Australian domestic law position on battle of the forms is discussed at **5.4**. It has also been suggested that a rule against incorporation of surprising terms contained within standard terms exists under the *CISG*.[94]

25.7.4 *CISG*—consideration

Contrary to Australian domestic law which requires consideration be established for formation (see **5.6**), the *CISG* abandons any requirement of consideration. Instead, agreements comprised of offer and acceptance alone form binding contracts. This is fairly uncontroversial in regard to formation, since the *CISG* deals with sales, and outlines obligations to deliver goods and pay the price. However, the issue gains prominence concerning modification or amendment of contract, which may be agreed without supporting consideration: art 29 *CISG*.

25.7.5 *CISG*—exemption and limitation clauses

CISG formation provisions determine whether or not exemption or limitation clauses have been incorporated within a contract, but unlike UNIDROIT Principles, the *CISG* does not govern their validity, in terms of fairness or excessiveness, as these matters fall outside the *CISG*'s scope, and are therefore dealt with by the relevant domestic law.

25.7.6 *CISG*—usages and practices

Terms may be incorporated by widely known and internationally observed usages: art 9(1) *CISG*. More readily than is the case under Australian law, terms may be incorporated on the basis of practices established between the parties, where a pattern of usage is established:[95] art 9(2) *CISG*. By contrast with Australian domestic law (see **9.4.1**), it need not be shown that a

91 Hof van Beroep [Court of Appeal] Gent, Belgium, 15 May 2002, CISG-online 746.
92 CISG-AC Opinion No 13, above n 74, Rule 10, Comments paras 10.6–10.8.
93 CISG-AC Opinion No 13, above n 74, Comments paras 10.5 and 10.8.
94 Although no express provision exists. See CISG-AC Opinion No 13, above n 74, Rule 7.
95 See above n 68.

term was necessary to give the contract business efficacy, although an established pattern will need to be proven.

25.7.7 UNIDROIT Principles—offers, withdrawal and revocation

Article 2.1.2 UNIDROIT Principles deals with offers, stipulating the offer must be sufficiently definite and indicate an intention to be bound. However, a number of articles provide default positions regarding quality (art 5.1.6), price determination (art 5.1.7), time and place of performance (arts 6.1.1 and 6.1.6), and currency (art 6.6.10). Offers become effective when they reach the offeree and may be withdrawn if the notice of withdrawal reaches the offeree at the same time or before the offer: art 2.1.3(1); art 2.1.3(2) UNIDROIT Principles.

Mirroring the *CISG*, art 2.1.4 UNIDROIT Principles allows offers to be revoked until acceptance is dispatched, unless the offer is irrevocable. An offer will be irrevocable in similar circumstances to the *CISG* discussed above (at **25.7.1**): where the offer indicates an intention to be irrevocable, inter alia, by reason of being expressed as open for a fixed period; or where an offeree has reasonably relied on the irrevocability of the offer (art 2.1.4(2)).

As is the case within the *CISG*, a prohibition against inconsistent conduct also exists within UNIDROIT Principles where there has been reasonable reliance: art 1.8 UNIDROIT Principles.

25.7.8 UNIDROIT Principles—acceptance and modified acceptance

Acceptance in the UNIDROIT Principles operates in a similar manner to the *CISG*. Acceptance is by indication of assent through statements or conduct: art 2.1.6 UNIDROIT Principles. Likewise, silence alone cannot be acceptance (art 2.1.6(1)), as is the case within Australian common law: **Chapter 5**. Acceptance by indication of assent takes effect when it reaches the offeror: art 2.1.6 (2). However, acceptance may also occur by conduct showing agreement due to practices or usages, in which case acceptance becomes effective at the time of the conduct: art 2.1.6(3) UNIDROIT Principles. Further elaboration is found in art 2.1.1 UNIDROIT Principles. Acceptance must be within the time fixed in the offer, or within a reasonable time: art 2.1.7 UNIDROIT Principles.

Like the *CISG*, UNIDROIT Principles provide for modified acceptance and, provided alterations are not material, a contract will be concluded on the basis of terms of the modified acceptance, unless the offeror objects without undue delay: art 2.1.11 UNIDROIT Principles.

Notices become effective upon reaching the addressee: art 1.10 UNIDROIT Principles.

25.7.9 UNIDROIT Principles—standard terms and battle of the forms

UNIDROIT Principles contain express provisions addressing standard terms, which are defined at art 2.1.19. They adopt the 'knock out' approach to the battle of the forms: art 2.1.22 UNIDROIT Principles. Article 2.1.20 UNIDROIT Principles makes surprising terms contained within standard terms ineffective. Standard terms may be surprising due to their content, language or presentation. As noted at **25.7.3**, it has been suggested this rule also exists in *CISG*.

25.7.10 UNIDROIT Principles—consideration, mistake, gross disparity and validity

Like the *CISG*, the UNIDROIT Principles do not require consideration for formation of binding contracts, nor for modification of an existing contract, which may be achieved by mere agreement: art 3.1.2 UNIDROIT Principles.

In contrast to the *CISG* (art 4(a)), the UNIDROIT Principles tackle the issue of validity. Initial impossibility from the outset will not affect validity (art 3.1.3 UNIDROIT Principles), and the Principles do not deal with contractual capacity: art 3.1.1 UNIDROIT Principles.

Mistake is covered by UNIDROIT Principles. Article 3.2.1 defines mistake broadly to include erroneous assumptions of law or fact at the time the contract was concluded. This is broader than Australian law of mistake, discussed at **18.5**, which traditionally eschews mistake of law (see *Principles* text at 18.09). Pursuant to art 3.2.2(1) UNIDROIT Principles, the contract may be avoided if:

- the mistake was of such importance that the party wishing to avoid would not have entered the contract at all, or only on materially different terms; and
- the other party either:
  - made the same mistake;
  - knew of the mistake but did not correct it contrary to fair dealing;
  - knew or ought to have known of the mistake; or
  - had not reasonably relied upon the contract.

However, avoidance is not available if the mistake was caused by the gross negligence of the party wishing to avoid, or that party had assumed or ought to bear the relevant risk: art 3.2.2(2) UNIDROIT Principles.

Other issues of validity covered within UNIDROIT Principles which lead to the remedy of avoidance of the contract include:

- fraud: for fraudulent representation or non-disclosure (art 3.2.5);
- threat: where the contract has resulted from an unjustifiable, serious and imminent threat (art 3.2.6) (see **Chapter 19** for the Australian position); and
- gross disparity: where the contract terms are grossly disproportionate, and give excessive advantage to one party, due to that party taking unfair advantage of the other's economic distress, poverty, ignorance or inexperience at the time of concluding the contract. The aggrieved party also has the right to enter into renegotiations, or to have the contract adapted by the court: art 3.2.7. This concept is broader than the Australian domestic concept of unconscionable conduct (see **Chapter 20**).

A further provision attempts to deal with the thorny issue of illegality: art 3.3.1. The UNIDROIT Principles purportedly deem mandatory all provisions on fraud, threat, gross disparity and illegality: art 3.1.4.[96]

96 As mentioned below, the 'mandatory' nature of these provisions is debatable: see below n 114.

25.7.11 UNIDROIT Principles—exemption and limitation clauses

Unlike the *CISG*,[97] UNIDROIT Principles contain a specific rule on exemption and limitation clauses. Article 7.1.6 precludes parties from invoking exclusion or limitation clauses where these are grossly unfair and allow performance substantially different to what the other party was entitled to expect. For discussion on the Australian domestic treatment of exemption and limitation clauses, see **Chapter 11**.

25.7.12 UNIDROIT Principles—usages, practices and supplemented terms

Parties may be bound by past practices and widely observed usages: art 1.9 UNIDROIT Principles, discussed above at **25.5.7**. Moreover, where parties have omitted to include an important term, the UNIDROIT Principles allow the adjudicator to supply the omitted term, upon consideration as to what is appropriate given the parties' intent, the purpose of the contract, reasonableness and good faith: art 4.8 UNIDROIT Principles. The provision goes beyond that known to the common law in relation to implied terms (see **9.4–9.6**). No equivalent provision exists in the *CISG*.

25.8 Rights and obligations

The following is a brief summary of some of the most important obligations.

25.8.1 *CISG*—seller obligations: conformity, delivery, ownership and third-party rights

Express contractual terms override any obligations within the *CISG* where they are inconsistent with them. This is the effect of party autonomy under art 6. However, art 35(1) deals with express terms, requiring that the 'seller must deliver goods which are of the quantity, quality and description required by the contract and which are contained or packaged in the manner required by the contract'.

Unless parties agree to the contrary, art 35(2) *CISG* creates obligations for the seller to deliver goods:

- fit for purposes for which goods of the same description are ordinarily used (art 35(2)(a));
- fit for particular purposes made known to the seller, unless it was unreasonable to rely on the seller's skill, or the buyer did not rely on that skill (art 35(2)(b));
- which have the qualities of sample or model held out by the seller (art 35(2)(c)); and,
- which are adequately packaged (art 35(2)(d)).

Unless agreed otherwise, the seller must deliver goods free from any third-party claims regarding relevant intellectual property or ownership: arts 41 and 42 *CISG*.

97 See above at **25.7.5**.

Note that any terms that would otherwise be implied into commercial contracts by *Sales of Goods Acts* (see **9.7.1**) will not apply to *CISG* contracts: eg *Goods Act 1958* (Vic) ss 86, 87. The same is true of ACL consumer guarantees (s 68 ACL), although other ACL provisions (eg s 18 ACL on misleading conduct) may still apply.

25.8.2 *CISG*—buyer obligations: inspection, notice of non-conformity, payment of price

The buyer must:

- pay the price as required by the contract or *CISG* (irrespective of demand for payment) (arts 53 and 59);
- comply with laws or regulations to enable payment of the price (art 54);
- take delivery (art 53);
- inspect the goods within a reasonable time (art 38); and
- give notice of non-conformity to the seller within a reasonable time: art 39(1) *CISG*.

The requirement that the buyer must give notice of non-conformity within a reasonable time is very important, but unfortunately has sometimes been overlooked in Australia.[98] Australian domestic law does not contain an equivalent requirement. However, under the *CISG*, failure to give notice of non-conformity within reasonable time will result in the buyer losing its right to remedies, unless the seller knew or could not have been unaware of the non-conformity yet failed to disclose it to the buyer: art 40 *CISG*.

What is a 'reasonable period' depends on the nature of the goods (eg perishables will require very prompt notice, such as a day or two), past practices and usages (arts 8(3) and 9), and of course the express terms. Article 39(2) *CISG* provides an absolute maximum period for notice of two years; however, cases on art 39 *CISG* indicate a much shorter period of notice is required, with scholars suggesting one month (known as 'the Noble Month'), with this rule of thumb period to be adjusted upward or downward, depending on the goods, purpose or character of the contract.[99]

25.8.3 *CISG*—public permissions and standards

CISG jurisprudence has developed around the issue of standards prevailing in the buyer's (or destination) jurisdiction. The question revolves around whether conformity with the fitness requirement within art 35(2)(a) is determined by quality standards prevailing in the jurisdiction for which goods are destined. In one influential case, delivery to the buyer's jurisdiction was held insufficient for standards prevailing in that jurisdiction to constitute the requirement for 'ordinary purposes'. The German Supreme Court indicated breach of health regulations in the

98 See eg *Ginza Pty Ltd v Vista Corporation Pty Ltd* [2003] WASC 11 ('*Ginza*'), http://cisgw3.law.pace.edu/cases/030117a2.html; *Playcorp Pty Ltd v Taiyo Kogyo Ltd* [2003] VSC 108, http://cisgw3.law.pace.edu/cases/030424a2.html; Spagnolo, *Last Outpost*, above n 41, 187 and 192.

99 Ingeborg Schwenzer, 'The "Noble Month": The Story Behind the Scenery' (2005) 7(3-4) *European Journal of Law Reform* 353; Camilla Andersen, 'Article 39 of the CISG and Its Noble Month for Notice-Giving; A (Gracefully) Ageing Doctrine' (2012) 30 *Journal of Law and Commerce* 185.

buyer's country did not necessarily indicate non-conformity under art 35(2)(a) *CISG*. However, it stated standards of the buyer's jurisdiction might apply where:[100]

- the same standards existed in the seller's jurisdiction;
- the buyer had directed the seller's attention to the standards and relied on the seller's expertise (per art 35(2)(b); or
- 'special circumstances' existed, such as where the seller had:[101]
  - a branch in the buyer's country;
  - long-standing business connection with the buyer;[102]
  - often exported into the buyer's country; or
  - promoted its products in that country.

Bundesgerichtshof [Federal Supreme Court] [BGH] Germany 8 March 1995 (*New Zealand Mussels case*)[103]

Facts and issues

A Swiss seller delivered to the German buyer New Zealand mussels containing a cadmium concentration exceeding limits recommended by the German health authority. The question arose as to whether this meant the goods were non-conforming and thus whether the seller was in breach.

Decision[104]

> [I] ... There is no evidence that the parties implicitly agreed to comply with the [German] standards. Even if [seller] knew that [buyer] wanted to market the goods in Germany, one cannot make such an assumption ... [II a)] The mere fact that the mussels should be delivered to the storage facility ... does not necessarily constitute an agreement regarding the resalability of the goods, especially in Germany ... [II b)] Where the parties have not agreed on anything, the goods do not conform with the contract if they are unsuitable for the ordinary use or for a specific purpose expressly or impliedly made known to the seller (*CISG* art 35(2)(a) and (b)). The [alleged] cadmium contamination ... does not allow us to assume that the goods ... do not conform with the contract. [II bb)] ... standards in the buyer's country can only be taken into account if they exist in the seller's country as well ... or if, ... within the scope of *CISG* art 35(2)(b), the buyer has pointed them out to the seller ... and, thereby, relied on and ... the seller's expertise or, maybe, if the relevant provisions in the anticipated export country are known or should be known to the seller due to the particular circumstances of the case ...

100 The celebrated 'New Zealand Mussels case'. See extract below.

101 *Medical Marketing International Inc v Internazionale Medico Scientifica*, Srl, CLOUT case No 418, Federal District Court [Louisiana], USA, 17 May 1999, http://cisgw3.law.pace.edu/cases/990517u1.html.

102 Cour d'appel, Grenoble, France, 13 September 1995, CLOUT case No 202, http://cisgw3.law.pace.edu/cases/950913f1.html.

103 Bundesgerichtshof [Federal Supreme Court] (BGH], Germany, (New Zealand Mussels case), 8 March 1995, CLOUT case No 123, http://cisgw3.law.pace.edu/cases/950308g3.html.

104 English translation by Alston & Bird LLP, http://cisgw3.law.pace.edu/cases/950308g3.html.

[II bbb)] ... even if [the place of delivery or destination] could be viewed as an indication by [buyer] of the anticipated marketing in Germany, neither under ... *CISG* 35(2) [(b) nor (c) is this] sufficient to judge whether the mussels conform with the contract pursuant to [German] cadmium standards ... Decisive is that a foreign seller can simply not be required to know the not easily determinable public law provisions and/or administrative practices of the country to which he exports, and that the purchaser, therefore, cannot rationally rely upon such knowledge of the seller, but rather, the buyer can be expected to have such expert knowledge of the conditions in his own country or in the place of destination, as determined by him, and, therefore, he can be expected to inform the seller accordingly. This applies even more in a case like this, where ... there are no statutes regulating the permissible cadmium contamination ...

[II ccc)] This Court need not decide [because the Buyer did not allege such facts] whether the situation changes if the seller knows the public law provisions in the country of destination or if the purchaser can assume that the seller knows these provisions because, for instance, he has a branch in that country ... because he has already had a business connection with the buyer for some time ..., because he often exports into the buyer's country ... or because he has promoted his products in that country...

25.8.4 UNIDROIT Principles—time for performance

As it covers a broader range of contracts, the UNIDROIT Principles are shaped in more general terms than obligations under the *CISG*. Article 6.1.1 requires performance take place within the time fixed by the contract, or within a reasonable time after the contract's conclusion. However, earlier performance may not be rejected without legitimate reason: art 6.1.5 UNIDROIT Principles. Any additional expenses must be borne by the early performer.

25.8.5 UNIDROIT Principles—currency

Unlike the *CISG*, the UNIDROIT Principles contain rules regarding contract price and payment currency. Where price is expressed in a currency other than that of the place of payment, it can be paid in either contract currency, or currency of place of payment, unless the latter is not a hard currency, or parties have agreed that only the contract currency is acceptable: art 6.1.9 UNIDROIT Principles. Where no currency is expressed in the contract, payment must be in the currency of place of payment: art 6.1.10 UNIDROIT Principles. Importantly, the conversion rate is that prevailing on date of payment: art 6.1.9 UNIDROIT Principles.

25.8.6 UNIDROIT Principles—public permissions

As discussed at **25.8.3**, responsibility for obtaining public permissions is a matter upon which jurisprudence has grown within the *CISG*. UNIDROIT Principles contain at least some specific express rules on the issue. Where the law of a State requires a public permission to be granted as a matter affecting contractual validity, the party which has its place of business in that State is obliged to obtain the permission and bear the costs of doing so: arts 6.1.14 and 6.1.15 UNIDROIT Principles. Where no party has a business in the relevant State, the obligation to obtain permissions and bear associated costs falls upon the party whose performance triggers the requirement: arts 6.1.14 and 6.1.15 UNIDROIT Principles. UNIDROIT Principles do not include rules on any standards other than those which affect validity.

25.8.7 UNIDROIT Principles—good faith obligations: negotiations, performance and enforcement

In addition to the general broad and direct duty of good faith imposed in art 1.7.1 UNIDROIT Principles, many other rules in the Principles elaborate specific obligations of good faith. The Official Comments elaborate that good faith in UNIDROIT Principles includes a prohibition on abuse of rights, including acting in a manner that is malicious or disproportionate in the exercise of rights.[105]

Unlike the *CISG* which does not impose pre-contractual liability,[106] parties that negotiate in bad faith, or without intention to reach agreement, for ulterior purposes, or who suddenly break off negotiations in bad faith without justification may be liable under art 2.1.15 UNIDROIT Principles.

However, the UNIDROIT Principles only become applicable by reason of agreement between parties to opt in, thus these obligations become relevant only if parties negotiate pursuant to a binding preliminary agreement selecting UNIDROIT Principles to govern their negotiations, or ultimately conclude a contract applying them.[107]

25.8.8 UNIDROIT Principles—confidentiality

Article 2.1.16 UNIDROIT Principles creates an obligation not to disclose or improperly use information obtained in negotiation, and provide for damages for breach of duty.

25.9 Remedies

Remedies within the *CISG* and UNIDROIT Principles are discussed together below.

25.9.1 Cure

Under the *CISG*, if the goods are non-conforming, the seller may cure the defect if this causes no unreasonable inconvenience or cost to the buyer: art 48 *CISG*. The requirement of notice of non-conformity provides an opportunity for the seller to cure, and thus facilitates the aim of keeping the contract on foot.

Article 7.1.4 UNIDROIT Principles also provides the non-performing party with a right to cure the non-performance if cure is appropriate, effected promptly, and not precluded by right of termination, provided the non-performing party gives notice of intent to cure. No similar concept exists within Australian domestic contract law, although cure provisions can be found

105 UNIDROIT Principles art 1.7, Comment 2.

106 The majority view is that the *CISG* does not impose a duty to negotiate in good faith: see Spagnolo, above n 53 (comparing views).

107 See below n 114.

in the US Uniform Commercial Code.[108] When interpreting contractual terms containing the right to cure, Australian courts have referred to the *CISG*.[109]

25.9.2 Additional period for performance

The aggrieved party may set an additional reasonable fixed time for performance: arts 47 and 63 *CISG*. This is the so-called *Nachfrist* mechanism, originally inspired by German law.[110] In cases of non-delivery, the aggrieved party can set an additional reasonable period for performance, in which case failure to comply leads to the right to avoid the contract: arts 49(1)(b) and 64(1)(b) *CISG*. This serves two functions. On the one hand, the aggrieved party gains clarity concerning the right to avoid, and on the other, the breaching party is afforded an opportunity to rectify the problem and keep the contract on foot. The same right exists within UNIDROIT Principles: art 7.1.5. Australian law contains no formal mechanism of a similar nature. When interpreting contractual terms containing *Nachfrist* provisions, Australian courts have referred to the *CISG*.[111]

25.9.3 Performance

An aggrieved party has the right to seek performance of the contract: arts 46 and 62 *CISG*. However, a domestic court may decline to order specific performance where it would have declined that remedy in an equivalent domestic setting: art 28 *CISG*. Thus, if the circumstances would lead an Australian court to deny specific performance due to an equitable bar such as unclean hands had the contract been between domestic parties, it may decline specific performance for a *CISG* contract.

The same right exists within UNIDROIT Principles. Pursuant to art 7.2.2, parties may seek performance of an obligation within a reasonable time after they become aware of non-performance, unless performance is impossible, or unreasonably burdensome. Courts may order performance under art 7.2.4 UNIDROIT Principles.

25.9.4 Termination

The *CISG* restricts availability of the right to terminate the contract, known as 'avoidance'. This is one of the *CISG*'s key features. As it is designed to promote efficient international trade, the *CISG* adopts the general principle of *favor contractus*, since it is usually less costly to keep the contract on foot and provide remedies such as damages, rather than to reverse the contract, given that return shipment is usually expensive in an international contract.

Restriction on termination is achieved primarily through the concept of fundamental breach, which sets a high threshold requirement. A fundamental breach exists where a breach causes a detriment which substantially deprives the aggrieved party of what they were entitled

108 Uniform Commercial Code, §2-508(1) (USA).

109 See eg *Olivaylle Pty Ltd v Flottweg GmbH & Co KGAA (No 4)* (2009) 255 ALR 632, http://cisgw3.law.pace.edu/cases/090520a2.html at [203]–[209].

110 See Martin Davies and David V Snyder, *International Transactions in Goods: Global Sales in Comparative Context* (Oxford University Press, 2014) 379.

111 See eg *Olivaylle v Flottweg*, above n 109.

to expect under the contract, unless the detriment was not foreseen by the breaching party, nor reasonably foreseeable by the same kind of party in the same circumstances: art 25 *CISG*. This is the main method of triggering termination, per arts 49(1)(a) and 64(1)(a) *CISG*. The other trigger for termination (per art 49(1)(b)) is non-delivery, where the breaching party has been afforded a further reasonable period to make delivery by notice, but still fails to deliver: art 47 *CISG*. The threshold for avoidance under *CISG* is therefore defined differently to the common law, which traditionally reserved termination for breach of conditions, although development of the intermediate term concept brings the Australian law somewhat closer to the *CISG* international standard. Compare to Australian domestic contract law classification of terms (condition, intermediate, warranty) in **Chapter 16**.

A fundamental breach may be cured by the seller pursuant to art 48 *CISG* if this will not be unreasonably inconvenient or costly for the buyer. Some have contemplated that where cure is forthcoming, a breach may not be fundamental at all, despite the fact that the right to cure is expressed as 'subject to' the right to avoid under art 49.[112]

If either trigger exists, the contract is not avoided automatically. Instead, in accordance with the *CISG* general principle of communication, the party that wishes to terminate must give notice of avoidance under art 26, and must do so within a reasonable time, or the right will be lost: arts 49(2) and 64(2) *CISG*.

Parties can agree to modify default triggers for termination. They might agree that a particular breach will amount to a fundamental breach, perhaps by indicating 'time is of the essence', or simply stipulating that breaches of certain obligations allow the right to terminate. Again, party autonomy is paramount in the *CISG*: art 6. Such agreement might also arise due to past practices or international trade usages (arts 8(3), 9 *CISG*). Thus for a commodities contract, strict compliance in documentary conformity and delivery would be required due to the well-known practice of on-selling commodities obligations through interlinking string contracts.[113]

If the contract is avoided, the buyer must return the goods, and the seller must return the price, in accordance with restitution obligations: arts 84–88 *CISG*. If the buyer cannot do so because non-conformity could not have been discovered until after resale or transformation, it may still avoid the contract: art 82(1) *CISG*. Additionally, damages may be sought pursuant to art 74 *CISG*.

The UNIDROIT Principles contains the similar but more elegantly worded concept of 'fundamental non-performance': art 7.3.1. Fundamental non-performance is defined as a substantial deprivation of what the aggrieved party was entitled to expect under the contract, unless the consequences were not and could not have reasonably been foreseen: art 7.3.1(2). In the context of UNIDROIT Principles, regard is to be had as to whether non-performance is intentional or reckless, and whether termination will result in disproportionate suffering on the part of the non-performing party (art 7.3.1(2)). Fundamental non-performance otherwise gives rise to the right to terminate, upon giving notice, which must be given within reasonable time. The right to terminate is lost upon failure to give such notice: art 7.3.2 UNIDROIT Principles.

112 Markus Müller-Chen, 'Article 48' in I Schwenzer (ed), *Schlechtriem & Schwenzer: Commentary on the Convention on International Sale of Goods (CISG)* (Oxford University Press, 4th ed, 2016) art 48 para 14.

113 Ulrich Schroeter, 'Article 25' in I Schwenzer (ed), *Schlechtriem & Schwenzer: Commentary on the Convention on International Sale of Goods (CISG)* (Oxford University Press, 4th ed, 2016) art 25, para 66.

Naturally, as it is soft law, parties may modify the UNIDROIT Principles.[114] This means that parties can agree on strict compliance, and may stipulate that a particular non-compliance constitutes a fundamental non-performance.

25.9.5 Anticipatory breach and suspension

Article 72 *CISG* allows a party to avoid the contract where it appears clear that a fundamental breach will be committed in future. Reasonable notice of avoidance must be given, unless the other party has declared they will not perform: art 72(2) and (3) *CISG*. Article 71(1) enables a party to suspend their performance for anticipated non-performance if this becomes 'apparent' due to conduct in preparing or performing, deficiency in ability to perform, or creditworthiness, which need not be fundamental, but must be substantial.[115] However, immediate notice must be given, and if an adequate assurance is forthcoming, the suspending party must continue its performance: art 71(3) *CISG*.

If it is clear a fundamental non-performance will arise in future, UNIDROIT Principles art 7.3.3 permits termination for anticipatory non-performance. The aggrieved party may seek adequate assurance if they reasonably believe there will be a fundamental non-performance, and can terminate if this is not forthcoming: art 7.3.4 UNIDROIT Principles.

25.9.6 Damages, price reduction, agreed sums and mitigation

From the outset, it is important to recall that remedies for non-conformity (damages, price reduction etc) are subject to the provision of notice of non-conformity within a reasonable time: art 39 *CISG*. Failure to provide timely notice will result in loss of remedy.

The self-help remedy of proportional price reduction is provided for in arts 50, 51 and 52 *CISG*. This is a novel remedy unknown to Australian domestic law. Thus Australian courts have turned to the *CISG* for guidance when interpreting contractual price reduction clauses.[116]

A general right of damages exists in art 74 *CISG*, and operates on the principle of full compensation.[117] Claims for damages are subject to a foreseeability threshold which is only slightly lower than that of the common law.[118] Foreseeability is measured objectively as at the time the contract was concluded. Loss of profits can be recovered, and although controversial, loss of a chance is now considered available under art 74.[119] Articles 75 and 76 *CISG* allow recovery of the difference in value between the contract and substitute transaction (art 75), or

114 UNIDROIT Principles, arts 1.1 and 1.5. Interestingly, art 1.5 states that parties may not derogate from certain mandatory principles of good faith (art 1.7), validity with certain exceptions (Ch. 3), liquidated damages (art 7.4.13), and limitation periods (art 10.3). However, since this is soft law, these must be taken as attempts to place conditions on the use of UNIDROIT Principles, and it the restriction could be effective to preclude the effectiveness of a clear agreement to exclude these 'mandatory' provisions.

115 Honnold, above n 48, art 71, para 388 (noting differences between arts 71 and 72 were deliberate).

116 See eg *Olivaylle v Flottweg*, above n 109; *Hannaford v Australian Farmlink Pty Ltd* [2008] FCA 1591 http://cisgw3.law.pace.edu/cases/081024a2.html.

117 CISG Advisory Council, 'Opinion No 6, Calculation of Damages under CISG Article 74', Rapporteur: Prof. John Y. Gotanda.

118 Ingeborg Schwenzer, 'Article 74' in I Schwenzer (ed), *Schlechtriem & Schwenzer: Commentary on the Convention on International Sale of Goods (CISG)* (Oxford University Press, 4th ed, 2016) art 74, para 48.

119 Ibid, art 74, para 39.

hypothetical substitute transaction: art 76 *CISG*. Whenever liability for damages arises, the aggrieved party has a duty of mitigation: art 77 *CISG*. See **Chapter 23** for the Australian position.

The incorporation of liquidated damages clauses providing for agreed sums upon breach is a matter controlled by formation provisions of the *CISG*. However, it does not govern their potential invalidity, which is determined under domestic law.[120]

Damages for non-performance may be claimed pursuant to art 7.4.1 UNIDROIT Principles, which also provides damages for breach of confidentiality, fraud, mistake, gross disparity or negotiation in bad faith.[121] Harm must be foreseen or reasonably foreseeable at the time of conclusion of the contract (art 7.4.4), and full compensation is provided for within art 7.4.2, including for physical suffering and emotional distress.[122] For future harm, there must be a reasonable degree of certainty, and loss of chance is recoverable: art 7.4.3 UNIDROIT Principles. Mitigation duties also arise under UNIDROIT Principles pursuant to art 7.4.8.

Agreed sums for liquidated damages are subject to an express rule in UNIDROIT Principles art 7.4.13. This provision entitles parties to rely upon such a provision, unless the amount is grossly excessive in relation to the harm, in which event the amount may be reduced.

25.9.7 Interest

Interest is clearly available under the *CISG* (art 78), although the rate is not specified. This resulted in a divergence of opinion amongst various national courts about the rate of interest which should apply. The matter was considered by the CISG Advisory Council in Opinion No 14 which recommends that 'In the absence of . . . agreement [by the parties], the applicable rate of interest is the rate which the court at the creditor's place of business would grant in a similar contract of sale not governed by the *CISG*'.[123]

The UNIDROIT Principles, by contrast, prescribe an interest at rate of 'average bank short-term lending rate to prime borrowers prevailing for currency of payment at place of payment': art 7.4.9 UNIDROIT Principles.

25.9.8 Restitution

Where the contract is terminated, the party in receipt of goods or money has an obligation to preserve and return the goods (art 84(1)), or if return is not required or feasible, the buyer may resell the goods and return sale proceeds to the seller, after deducting costs of sale and storage:

120 It has been suggested that in applying residual domestic laws concerning fairness and validity of such clauses within contracts governed by the *CISG*, domestic 'reasonableness' or 'proportionality' tests of pre-estimates of loss should consider the reasonableness of the agreed sum within the international setting: CISG Advisory Council, 'CISG-AC Opinion No 10, Agreed Sums Payable upon Breach of an Obligation in CISG Contracts', Rapporteur: Dr Pascal Hachem, Rules 1 and 4, Comments para 4.2.

121 UNIDROIT Principles, arts 2.1.15, 2.1.16, 3.2.16.

122 These are not recoverable under the *CISG*: art 5 *CISG*.

123 CISG Advisory Council, 'CISG-AC Opinion No 14, Interest under Article 78 CISG', Rapporteur: Prof. Dr Yeşim M. Atamer, Rule 9.

art 88 *CISG*. Likewise, a seller that has received the price, must return it with interest after the contract is terminated: art 84(1) *CISG*: see **24.5.2** and **17.5**. On Australian domestic law, see **17.4**.

Under UNIDROIT Principles, following termination, parties may claim restitution, or a monetary allowance if restitution in kind is not possible: art 7.3.6 UNIDROIT Principles. Avoidance of the contract due to validity issues gives rise to specific secondary obligations of restitution (art 3.2.15) and restorative damages: art 3.3.1 UNIDROIT Principles. See further **17.5.1**.

25.9.9 Excuse

Article 79 *CISG* excuses parties from liability for damages in the case of impediments to performance.[124] The impediment must be beyond the control of the parties, and one which they could not reasonably be expected to have taken into account at the time the contract was concluded. Notably, excuse of liability under art 79 does not preclude other forms of relief, such as termination: art 79(5) *CISG*.

Very few cases have upheld excuse under art 79, thus the bar for impediment has been set high, with most costs amounting to 'force majeure' situations of impossibility. Despite this, there is scholarly support for severe cases of hardship to fall within art 79,[125] and severe hardship appears to be a potentially emerging concept under the *CISG*.[126]

The UNIDROIT Principles contain provisions relating to both hardship and force majeure. Article 6.2.2 defines hardship, which extends to 'fundamental alteration of the equilibrium of the contract'. Hardship requires that the circumstances must be beyond the control of parties, and must have only become known only after conclusion of the contract. The risk of the event must not have been assumed by either party, and must be one which could not have been taken into consideration at the conclusion of the contract: art 6.2.2 UNIDROIT Principles.

Under UNIDROIT Principles, hardship includes a cost increase or diminution in value of performance. The Official Comments refer to 'dramatic' price increases.[127] Hardship gives rise to secondary rights to request renegotiation without delay, and courts may adapt the contract or terminate it: art 6.2.3 UNIDROIT Principles.

Non-performance will be excused altogether for impediments beyond the control of the non-performing party, if it could not reasonably be expected to have taken them into account, and could not have avoided their consequences. The party relying upon the impediment must give notice: art 7.1.7 UNIDROIT Principles. Similarly to the *CISG*, excuse by impediment does not preclude termination for fundamental non-performance: art 7.1.7(4) UNIDROIT Principles.

124 On the Australian law of frustration, see **Chapter 15**.

125 The Advisory Council would include cases of hardship, such as serious fluctuations: CISG Advisory Opinion, CISG-AC Opinion No. 7, 'Exemption of Liability for Damages under Article 79 of the CISG', Rapporteur: Prof. Alejandro M. Garro, Rule 3.1, Comments paras 32–39 (Comments para 33 giving an example of 80 per cent currency devaluation due to unpredictable political or economic crisis).

126 CISG-AC Opinion No. 7, ibid. See *Scafom International BV v Lorraine Tubes S.A.S.*, Court of Cassation [Supreme Court] Belgium, 19 June 2009, http://cisgw3.law.pace.edu/cases/090619b1.html.

127 Official comments UNIDROIT Principles, Comment para 2 (giving examples of 'dramatic price increase' and 80 per cent currency devaluation).

25.9.10 Preclusion of reliance on breach and contributory harm

An aggrieved party cannot rely upon the breach of the other party to the extent the first party has themselves caused that breach: art 80 *CISG*. The same rule exists in art 7.1.2 UNIDROIT Principles, which also specifies that in an award of damages, an allowance may be made for that part of the harm to which the aggrieved party has contributed: art 7.4.7 UNIDROIT Principles.

INDEX